The Front Page Story of
WORLD WAR II

This is, at least throughout British Columbia and the West, the war's most famous picture. Taken by C. P. Detloff, **The Vancouver Daily Province** *chief photographer, Oct. 1, 1940, it shows the departure for service of the B.C. Regiment. Copies of it were hung in public schools throughout the province during the war, and it was a prize-winning picture in* Life *magazine.*

The Front Page Story of
WORLD

WAR II

As told through the front pages of Vancouver's daily newspapers from 1939 to 1945

ROBERT R. REID

Foreword by Denny Boyd

DOUGLAS & McINTYRE

VANCOUVER / TORONTO

94 95 96 97 98   5 4 3 2 1

Douglas & McIntyre Ltd.
1615 Venables Street
Vancouver, British Columbia V5L 2H1

The publisher gratefully acknowledges the assistance of the Canada Council, and of the British Columbia Ministry of Tourism, Small Business and Culture for its publishing programs.

Canadian Cataloguing in Publishing Data

Reid, Robert R., 1927–
 The front page story of World War II

 ISBN 1-55054-169-2

 1. WORLD WAR, 1939-1945—Press Coverage—British
Columbia—Vancouver. I. Title
D799.C2R44 1994   940.54'889'71133   C94-910651-8

Editing by Brian Scrivener
Design by Robert R. Reid
Jacket design by Arifin A.Graham
Typeset by Computype, Vancouver
Printed and bound in Canada by D.W. Friesen and Sons Ltd.
Printed on acid-free paper ∞

CONTENTS

FOREWORD

When we asked for more of that which was rationed, our mothers looked at us with patient exasperation and asked, "Don't you know there's a war on?"

We didn't, not at first. We were too young. We were children of the Great Depression, which had been a hard and serious thing for our parents. Now, at the end of the Hungry Thirties, we knew another serious thing was on because our parents and their friends spoke in whispers about what was happening "over there," and what it might mean to our relatives abroad.

We were the lucky ones, too young to be called on to fight, but not so young that we could not revel in the excitement, the spirit, once we figured out what it was all about.

In the summer of 1939, my parents and I had gone by train to visit my father's brother, Uncle Brice, and my Aunt Cherri, on their chicken farm on an island on a tiny lake near Deroche. The sun shone and I fished and the grown-ups talked, again in whispers. At the train station on our way back, my father and Uncle Brice talked about the possibility of "joining up." I thought maybe they meant a club.

The first real indication I had of what was happening occurred when I was nine, playing in the vacant lot between our rooming house, at 1250 West Broadway, and the White Rose Ballroom. I had just assembled a nickel glider, a cheap balsawood toy. I was adjusting the lead weight on the nose to make it do loops when I heard bellowing voices. Boys from the *Vancouver Sun* were trotting up both sides of West Broadway, shouting out headlines about a rescue at a place called Dunkirk. I went inside and asked, and my mother explained to me that we were in a thing called a world war.

That was strange. I first learned about war by hearing about it from the newspaper. But that was all there was then. There was no television. We got our news from the *Sun*, the *Province* and the *News-Herald* (and from CBC and BBC radio and Mr. Kelly on local radio). My father ate the newspaper every night, slowly ingesting and digesting every headline, every story. I wanted him to finish up so I could check out Terry and the Pirates.

It was a serious thing, back then, reporting the war news in the three Vancouver papers, an essential, demanding job and, you will find as you read this book, a job that was done well and proudly by professional journalists.

Veteran reporter-editor-columnist Himie Koshevoy, who worked for all three papers, was at the *Province* when the war broke out. He recalls, "The so-called Phoney War had us fairly ready when the real thing began. We were fortunate that we had Ross Munroe as our war correspondent, and he did wonderful work with his cable reports right from the seat of action. He was always right in the middle of things and told our readers how it was over there. The *Sun* didn't have a correspondent so we were able to stay well ahead of them.

"One of our big things was getting pictures of every local man and woman who joined up. We had them on file when the casualty reports came in. Sometimes we ran entire pages of head-and-shoulder pictures. When they came back from overseas, there was terrific competition between the papers to get the first interviews.

"It was an exciting time, reading the stories that poured in, always waiting to hear the bells that told us an important bulletin was coming. The big one we were always waiting for was news that Japan was attacking the west coast."

When war came in 1939, the Vancouver papers were ready to tell the story, notwithstanding Vancouver's distance from the hostilities. In fact, as early as 1938, the *Province* righteously demanded that Ottawa supply the west coast with an air force and guns capable of warding off attack from the air. "What preparation do we have for such a contingency?", the editorial page asked. "Sending out Khaki uniforms and rifles for the boys . . . will avail nothing. They would be as helpless against a modern bomber as the two six-inch guns in Stanley Park. Where is there an anti-aircraft battery on the Pacific Coast?"

The Vancouver newspapermen (there were few women) of the 1930s and 1940s were a singular lot, as hard-drinking as you may have heard, and a bit raffish, but they were skilled professionals, dedicated to reporting the news. They had to be dedicated because the material rewards of their profession were few: the occasional byline, a free streetcar pass, the satisfaction of beating the opposition to a good story, a slight nod of approval from a hard-bitten senior editor.

They were dreadfully underpaid. A married reporter might be making $16 a week. A great reporter might get $25 or $30. For this they worked six days a week, 16 hours a day if a major story was breaking.

They could be fired on a whim. The editor of the *Province*, the mercurial Bob Elson, who later went on to become managing editor of *Life Magazine*, was famous for firing reporters at 8:05 A.M. and rehiring them by noon. Among those he told to clear out, only to apologize later, were the late Stuart Keate and Pierre Berton. Berton was sacked for reading the funny papers in the newsroom.

But a striking thing about those underpaid reporters was their personal appearance. They sported wonderful wardrobes: three-piece tailored suits with pinched waists, silk ties held in place with stickpins, gleamingly polished shoes (they always had a nickel for a shoeshine) and perfectly blocked fedoras which they never removed. Some copy editors actually still wore green plastic eyeshades and watch fobs.

By today's standards, their newsrooms seemed chaotic—upright typewriters rattling, telephones ringing, editors shouting at reporters, reporters crying out "Copy, copy boy!", the air pungent with cigarette, cigar and pipe-smoke, with an underlying odour of drying pastepots, sweat, brilliantine and printer's ink drifting in from the backshop.

But in this babel they practised superb journalism at all three Vancouver papers. They covered major stories—and a house fire could be a major story on a slow day—bellowed their stories to the rewrite desk by telephone, and were not above ripping out the telephone on the scene to thwart the waiting reporter from the other paper. It was standard procedure to produce up to five editions a day, each with a new front page.

The late Hal Straight, former *Sun* managing editor, explained the competitive nature of the papers: "What we tried to do every day in the old *Sun* was to get something the *Province* didn't have. To do that you had to have lively, energetic people, which is why the second papers made the great reporters. They loved it, they just loved it. Your big problem was to get them not to try too hard and cheat a little bit and not tell the right story."

Peter Stursberg emerged from the Second War as one of the most daring, most admired front-line Canadian war correspondents, reporting history in his rich voice for CBC radio. But before that, he was a newspaperman. He started at the *Victoria Times* and then, thanks to an empire press exchange program, he went to the London *Daily Herald*. "Suddenly, I went from a paper with 10,000 readers to one with two million circulation. What an experience."

Returning to Canada, he joined the *Province* right at the outbreak of war. "It started on September 3; I started at the *Province* September 4. I was a general reporter, $32.50 a week, in the old building at Victory Square, but wanted to go over as a military correspondent. I got nowhere with my requests but they made me their military reporter.

"At the beginning, the Province treated the war as a local story and I provided most of the coverage. I particularly covered the enlistment drive. I did a story on the Seaforth Highlanders that began, 'Yampolsky Quovadis, Costello and Zorn, they are all good Scots in the Seaforth Highlanders of Canada.' "

As the headlines in this book amply prove, the war dominated the front page. The racy local news that had always fueled the street sales was consigned to the inside pages for the duration. One exception was the daily Racing Form, from all the major tracks, which was never pushed off the front page.

The *Sun* used dispatches from Canadian correspondents, the *Province* relied on American wire services, the little *News-Herald* picked up the scraps but showed its spirit by running the Union Jack in its front page logo. (Here's an eye test: See if you can find among the 1944 front pages the bylined story by a young American wire service reporter named Walter Cronkite.)

A Vancouver news editor, facing major decisions in putting out five editions a day, had to have the same daily grasp on troop movements and developing battles as did the Joint Chiefs of Staff in Ottawa, Washington and London.

Veteran reporter Charles Lynch, who died in July of 1994 after half a century of reporting from every part of Canada, was not high in praise of the Vancouver journalism he experienced. In his book, *You Can't Print THAT*, he recalls joining the Vancouver British United Press bureau in 1940. "Those first weeks in Vancouver taught me that everybody in the business there cared only about two things—Vancouver and British Columbia, in that order. The rest of Canada was a far-off place. And to the extent that there was a war, it was Britain's war, though they seemed glad to be in it on her side.

"Everyone who worked at (or owned) the *Sun* was crazy, and the *Sun* itself reflected it. The morning *News-Herald* wasn't much different. The sane people, I was told, all worked at the big paper in town, the *Province*."

Prudently, the Vancouver papers, if they had the knowledge, never fully informed their readers as to how unprepared the west coast was for war.

There was no modernized air force in Vancouver, just a few old training planes and some creaky twin-engine float-planes that did yeoman service patrolling the rugged B.C. coastline, occasionally being sent up to attack hostile U-boats that turned out to be migratory whales.

The navy was miniscule and was immediately bolstered with fishpackers fitted with torpedo tubes and commanded to close with and sink all hostile vessels.

In fear of a German or Japanese fleet suddenly materializing over the horizon, efforts were made to defend Vancouver from the land, with gun emplacements. Mostly small-calibre and often of World War I vintage, howitzers and gun turrets were placed in Stanley Park, Point Grey, Point Atkinson and directly under Lions Gate Bridge, on the north shore side.

This latter emplacement, called Narrows North Fort, had a busy time of it, being required to monitor the arrival of all shipping, to demand proper recognition signals, and to fire warning shots if in doubt.

One day, the owner of a fish packer ignored repeated demands for the proper signal and was first fired on, then duly presented with a bill for $48 to cover the cost of the shell.

Far more memorable was the event of June 1942, when yet another fishpacker chugged into the harbour without identifying itself. After the prescribed number of warnings, Narrows North loosed a shell across the packer's bow. The fish boat stopped abruptly but the shell, instead of sinking, caught a wave and ricocheted across the water like a skipping stone. It was a thoroughly bad luck day for the Narrows gun crew. The rogue shell, still skipping, struck the 9,600 tonne freighter *Fort Rae* directly amidships on the waterline. The *Fort Rae* had just been launched from Burrard Dry Dock and was doing its sea-trials over a measured mile in English Bay. The shell, which did not have an explosive head, punched a neat hole going in, tumbled and created a huge exit hole. The freighter, taking on water and listing, was beached just inside Lions Gate Bridge. Very quickly, it was back at Burrard, undergoing repairs.

The Vancouver papers not only covered both wars, in Europe and the Pacific, thoroughly and accurately, with stories, analysis, maps and cartoons, but they did it with occasionally brilliant flair. One such example is the February 26, 1942 *News-Herald*, which turned out a mock page one, based on the supposition that Germany had invaded and conquered Canada and occupied Vancouver. Under German rule, the *News-Herald's* title became "Neueste Nachrichte" and the front page contained a brutal manifesto of citizen behaviour dictated by the provisional *Gauleiter*. It must have caused Vancouver citizens to gasp over their rationed coffee that morning.

And the front page of the *Vancouver Sun*, August 15, 1945, an extra, is a classic of reporting a massive story with restrained brevity.

The headline says simply "PEACE."

And the first three paragraphs put it all brilliantly:

"The Japanese government has accepted the Allied surrender terms.

"This is official.

"Peace has definitely come to a world at war since 1930."

The war was over. We were older now, my generation, and more able to appreciate the sacrifice in time and life and health that had been made by young men only a year or two older than ourselves. We hadn't been there, but we knew all about it. We'd read about it in the papers.

—Denny Boyd

INTRODUCTION

As a boy of eight or so I first got interested in World War II because my father was retired and had nothing better to do with his time than listen endlessly to the radio and read the newspapers, following the various prewar crises as they developed.

There was Benito Mussolini, the Italian dictator, busy recreating the Roman Empire by trying out his new armies and war equipment on defence-less Ethiopian tribesmen.

There was Ethiopian Emperor Haile Selassie speaking to the League of Nations, trying to warn them that the rest of the world's passivity toward the Italian invasion of his country was setting a bad example to the new breed of fascist dictators that had arisen out of the misery of World War I.

There was Franco waging the Spanish Civil War with the help of German and Italian arms while the democracies were doing their best not to notice.

There was Adolf Hitler, recently elected German Chancellor, on the strength of which he was seizing control of Germany and herding everyone—political opponents, communists, gypsies, Jews—into his infamous concentration camps.

And there was my father, fuming at the lacklustre politicians of the day, who were forever making fatuous statements and doing nothing, while at the same time everyone talked about the coming war.

The political pundits of the time—newspaper columnists Dorothy Thompson and Wesbrook Pegler, and radio commentators H. V. Kaltenborn, Gabriel Heater, Raymond Gram Swing and Lowell Thomas—only inflamed him more. Then came, in quick succession, the German occupation of Austria; the Munich pact, when Neville Chamberlain, the most notorious appeaser of all time, gave away Czechoslovakia to the Nazis; the German attack on Poland, and finally, the declaration of war by France and Britain, which, because of the extent of their empires, effectively included the rest of the world.

Wow! A World War! What a great time for a twelve-year-old to collect headlines. Far more exciting than listening to "The Shadow", "The Green Hornet" or "Jack Armstrong" on the radio after school. Instead, I would hop a street-car to downtown from where I lived on West Tenth, a block from Kitsilano High School. If I got there before 4 o'clock the news vendors would still have copies of the earlier street edition that came out around noon. They had great bold headlines, sometimes in red, to attract attention throughout the day.

The exciting five-star edition hit the newsstands about 4 PM—the FINAL, it was called—and that was always an event. The *Province* and the *Sun* vied in outdoing each other to attract sales. I could never choose; I had to have both papers—the peach-coloured *Sun* always with a touch of red for the word FINAL, or even for a headline later in the war when things heated up, and the *Province*, at first also on peach newsprint but later on white, with a blue streak printed down the side.

They were exciting because there was always news for these editions—real news, hard news, unique news that would never happen again. How many times will the Bismarck be sunk? How many D-Days will there ever be? Big black headlines were functional—they were telling us something important. The bigger the type, the more important the news. It was a unique time when everything meshed—a constant supply of news and the unceasing efforts of the newspapers and their foreign correspondents to bring it to us.

The most memorable day, of course, was Sunday, December 7, 1941. My mother and I were having brunch about noon, without the radio on. We heard sounds in the street—we lived across from Connaught Park and thought something was going on there. It was actually a *News-Herald* newsboy shouting "Extra, extra, Japs bomb Honolulu" and selling newspapers by the dozen as everyone on Tenth Avenue ran out to buy one.

The *News-Herald* was a real early morning paper. If you were out on the town the night before, the first edition would be on the streets about 11 PM, with large black headlines. The home edition was delivered about 5 AM, and at 6 or so a Final edition on green newsprint was distributed in corner boxes throughout the city. Our closest corner box was a short step down the lane, and every morning before breakfast I would run out and get the *News-Herald*.

I'll never forget the morning of December 10, 1941, a few days after Pearl Harbor. The *News-Herald* was still a tabloid—a format I like a lot—and there, printed in huge black type on the green newsprint, almost filling the whole front page, was the stunning news, JAPS SINK 2 BRITISH WARSHIPS. Mighty battleships they were, the *Prince of Wales* and *Repulse*—the pride of the Royal Navy—sunk by aeroplanes off Singapore. From that historical moment everyone knew that battleships were obsolete, that air power was supreme.

To cover the Nazi invasion of Russia I have used two Hearst *Examiners* from Los Angeles, with wonderful headlines. I do not have Vancouver papers on this historic event because I was visiting my older brother in Los Angeles, where he was learning to fly. He eventually spent the war in Bomber Command in Yorkshire with the RCAF.

Some people will notice that there is very little on the Pacific war in this book. Canadians were primarily obsessed with defeating Hitler and the Germans, and that news always commanded the headlines. Essentially, the Pacific war fell on the Americans and was well reported in their press. That is why the best front pages I have on the atomic bomb are from the *Seattle Post-Intelligencer*, available on newsstands in Vancouver. In fact, our Sunday paper was the *P-I*, which we would pick up after church and take home for leisurely reading all Sunday afternoon. The Lord's Day Alliance Act was in full force then, and there really was nothing else to do. Looking back on it, I rather liked Sundays—a very peaceful and relaxing day.

VANCOUVER'S NEWSPAPERS

After school I would occasionally go downtown straight to the corner of Cambie and Pender, where the *Province* pressroom was, behind huge plate glass windows. It was fun to watch the presses running, printing the final edition. Around the Pender Street side the door would be open for ventilation, and I would edge inside so that I could hear the roar of those two matched newspaper presses running at full speed. Magnificent . . . as thrilling as watching a steam locomotive.

After a few minutes I would walk down a block to the *Sun* Tower at the corner of Beatty and Pender. Around the back in the basement was the pressroom, usually with doors wide open, running *their* Final, and that was something. The *Sun* had a huge new state-of-the-art press that ran 60,000 papers an hour, and when it got going the thunderous roar was absolutely stupendous.

The *Vancouver Daily Province* was the best newspaper in Vancouver through the 1930s. Owned by the Southam chain in Toronto, it was, in fact, one of the best newspapers in Canada.

It certainly was the best *produced* paper in the whole country. The printing was always even and black and the layout of the pages and the headlines was meticulously balanced, with the famous Cheltenham type used throughout for headings. The paper was so well done, with so much pride, that rumour has it that one could never find a typographical error.

Founded in Victoria in the late nineteenth century by Walter Nichol, *The Province*, as it was first called, had difficulty competing with the established papers there. So Nichol moved it to Vancouver at the turn of the century and made a great success of it. During the 1930s, Southams, who had bought it for $3,500,000, built the *Province* into the imposing, authoritative newspaper we see in this book, with a circulation of 100,000 all through the depression era. That meant the paper was affluent as well— the jewel in the Southam chain.

The *Vancouver Sun* was always the second paper through the 1930s, with a circulation hovering around 70,000. Although budgets were tight, there were sufficient resources to compete lustily and produce a first-rate newspaper, as can be seen here. During the war, the *Sun's* editors rose to the occasion and produced a very dynamic newspaper. Newsstand sales helped increase circulation—hence the colourful FINAL editions. Over the war years, the two papers ran neck-and-neck, although the *Province* home edition still had its unique front page, the best looking and most readable in Canada.

Things changed in 1946 when the International Typographical Union struck the *Province* and it ceased publication for a time. The *Sun* garnered all its advertising and circulation, and when the *Province* began publishing again it could never regain its number one position. The *Sun* became the rich, powerful newspaper in town, and has been ever since.

The *Sun's* beginning is interesting. Founder Robert Cromie was private secretary to Colonel J. W. Stewart, a powerful political figure who had to leave town over some construction contracts. Cleaning out his effects, Cromie found some worthless stock in the *Vancouver Morning Sun*, a bankrupt Liberal Party newspaper. Rather than throw it out, he used the stock to take over control of the paper, then bought the evening *News-Advertiser* in 1917. Later he bought another evening paper, *The World*, in 1924, and merged the three papers into *The Vancouver Sun*. With *The World* he got its building at the corner of Beatty and Pender that became the famous *Sun* Tower.

A stylish man who entertained lavishly, Robert Cromie died tragically of a stroke in 1936 at the age of forty-nine. Two sons, Don and Sam, took over and published the *Sun* during the war years.

The *Vancouver News-Herald*. In 1932 the *Vancouver Morning Star* was closed down by its owner, Brigadier-General Victor Odlum. The unemployed journalists, spearheaded by managing editor Pat Kelly, got together and started a new morning paper, *The Vancouver News*,

later renamed the *News-Herald* in 1934. Stockbroker Clayton "Slim" Delbridge bought the paper eventually, and was the publisher of the wartime issues.

Never as affluent as the afternoon papers, the *News-Herald* nevertheless had a place in the hearts of Vancouverites as a serious newspaper with excellent columnists: Jack Scott, Evelyn Caldwell, Elmore Philpott and Al Williamson. A great number of Vancouver's journalists started at the *News-Herald*, learned the ropes as cub reporters, and then went on to more remunerative jobs at the *Province* or *Sun*—Pierre Berton, Sandy Ross, Himie Koshevoy, Ray Gardner, to name just a few.

Fifty years ago Vancouver's three major daily newspapers were a vital and dynamic part of the community. Excellently produced and well edited by top-flight journalists, they were among the best newspapers in the country. It seemed natural enough to save them during the war, but carrying them around in cardboard boxes for fifty years required some dedication.

Their front pages today make for exciting reading because one can experience World War II as we did then on the Home Front, boggling at headlines shouting out far-flung events that impinged directly on those of us at home. Everyone had a stake in that war: at school in the army cadets, at work in the war plants, through fathers, sons, brothers, sisters actively serving or through relatives in the warring countries.

For those born during or after the war, who missed the incredible experience of living through the war to end all wars, this book is the closest thing to being there. For those who *were* there, it makes possible a unique trip down memory lane. I have included commentaries to accompany each year in order to provide background information or set the scene for headlines and stories that are not always self explanatory.

Robert R. Reid

1939

The hell on earth that became World War II was at the end of a road paved with the good intentions of the major powers of the day—Britain and France. Because the public of both countries was adamantly opposed to war, or even war-like measures, after the frightful carnage of World War I just a few years before, governments instead took the tragic road of appeasement in coping with the insane demands of Hitler and Mussolini. The road came to a dead end on September 1, 1939, when Germany attacked Poland and further appeasement became impossible. Although the Allies declared war on Germany on September 3, 1939, they were so weak and ill-prepared that they were afraid to move against the aggressor for fear Hitler might retaliate. Thus, the so-called Phoney War closed out 1939.

MAJOR EVENTS

September 1, 1939

BLITZKRIEG IN POLAND

The battle for Poland was over quickly. The Polish army was no match for the Germans. Still mired in a feudal culture, Poland's million-man army sounded more formidable than it was. With only a few hundred tanks and aeroplanes, the army's pride was its dashing cavalry brigades, but pitting them against Nazi tanks was futile. The Polish air force never even got into the air, being knocked out on the ground by Stuka dive bombers. Although Britain and France declared war on Germany and the Royal Navy set up a blockade, by October 6th it was all over for the Poles, who at least fought bravely to defend their country. They exacted enough casualties for the Germans to know they had been in a fight.

What had finally finished off all hope for the Poles was the Red Army's attack from the east on September 17th. This was secretly agreed upon with Germany in the non-aggression pact both had signed only the month before. Dividing Poland between them meant both got back territory that had been included in their empires before World War I, when Poland did not exist as an independent state.

Russia had other, more urgent reasons to seize half of Poland as a buffer. With all of Poland gone Germany would border directly on Russia—a situation Stalin could not tolerate in case of a German attack.

Hitler was genuinely shocked when Britain and France declared war on Germany over the invasion of Poland. In October, after the Poles were subdued, he made peace overtures, only to be rebuffed by the Allies. Even Chamberlain and Eduoard Daladier, the French premier and fellow appeaser at Munich, had had enough of Hitler by then, and were intransigent.

War it was going to be. *[See page 16]*

September 3, 1939

THE U-BOATS STRIKE

Britain's main defense lay in being an island, and it had saved her many times in the past. Not since 1066 had she been invaded successfully. The Royal Navy was her protector—the largest navy in the world—and her vast merchant marine transported the goods to her shores that enabled her to be the "workshop of the world."

The Battle of the Atlantic was crucial, then, with German submarines—the infamous U-boats—preying on British shipping. Only nine hours after war was declared on September 3rd, the first U-boat attack occurred. The British passenger liner *Athenia*, loaded with 1,103 women and children evacuees bound for America, was torpedoed without warning and then shelled by the submarine as passengers attempted to escape in the lifeboats. Because there were Americans on board, Hitler was furious, as it was a similar incident that had brought America into the first world war.

In all, 131 lives were lost, including 28 Americans, but America remained neutral. By the end of September 40 ships had been sunk by the U-boats. Britain still had 3,000 ships to go, but it was a bad beginning that was to get worse before it got better.

September also saw the torpedoing of the aircraft carrier HMS *Courageous* as she was escorting convoys into British ports. She went down in 20 minutes, taking 514 of her crew with her, along with 23 aircraft.

The sinking of a battleship is news at any time, but when one was sunk by a German submarine in Scapa Flow, the tightly guarded impregnable port of the British Home Fleet, it was embarrassing as well.

It happened on the night of October 14, when the submarine U47 made its way into the famous Scottish harbour through a labyrinth of submarine nets. The main fleet had gone on manoeuvres, but there sat unsuspectingly the World War I battleship *Royal Oak*, with 1,257 crew members sleeping below decks.

Of the first salvo of torpedoes, only one hit home, with little effect. The next salvo of three torpedoes smashed full-on into her, and she went to the bottom of Scapa Flow in 17 minutes, taking 833 men with her. U47 escaped safely to Germany and her commander and all his crew received Germany's top medal for bravery, the Iron Cross. *[See page 17]*

November 30, 1939

RUSSIAN STALEMATE IN FINLAND

The Russian invasion of Finland began on November 30, 1939, and by December 23rd had turned into a total disaster for the Red Army. Winter snows, usually their ally, had become an enemy, bogging down tanks and infantry alike, while grounding the air force at the same time.

Four Russian armies, comprising 600,000 men, had attacked Finland's 33,000-man regular army that was backed up by only 100,000 ill-equipped reservists. But the Finns, all expert skiers, revelled in the snow and elected to fight a guerilla war against such an overwhelming force. They would ski out of the forest in surprise hit-and-run raids, skiing alongside a tank rumbling along a snow-covered road and dropping a Molotov cocktail down the hatch, then disappear back into the woods. The Russians dared not leave the roads to chase them, not having skis to support themselves on the snow. Later in the war, the Finns found bundles of skis and *How to Ski* manuals among abandoned equipment as they cut divisions to pieces with their guerilla tactics.

The western press gave the war great coverage. Nothing was happening on the western front during the Phoney War, so correspondents and photographers flocked to Finland to report on the gross incompetence of the Red Army in subduing tiny Finland. The stories were true enough, but no one realized that the Finnish Campaign was a great learning experience for the Russian General Staff, which had been denuded of many of its best and most experienced officers in Stalin's notorious purges of the 1930s. There is no doubt that Hitler got the wrong idea about the mighty Red Army from its pathetic record in Finland. A German General Staff report ended ". . . no match for an army with modern equipment and superior leadership." How lucky for the West that they were later proved wrong.

On March 12, 1940, the Finns made peace and gave in to the Russian demands for the territory they were after to buffer Leningrad in case of a German attack. A short but proud war for the Finns, who were left to their own resources by the rest of the world.

[See page 17]

THE ADMIRAL GRAF SPEE

The first naval engagement of the war ended up as a front page drama that introduced the world to a new German weapon—the pocket battleship.

Limited by the Treaty of Versailles to warships no larger than 10,000 tons with guns no bigger than 11 inches in diameter, the Germans managed, through deft engineering, to pack the wallop of a battleship into a much smaller frame. Thus were born three "pocket battleships" at 12,000 tons each (the Germans cheated a little). Named the *Admiral Graf Spee*, *Deutschland* and *Admiral Scheer*, they roamed the seas as raiders, preying on merchant shipping, and were very dangerous indeed.

In two months, the *Graf Spee* had sunk nine ships in the south Atlantic and Indian oceans. The British and French had eight naval groups searching for it—naval power that should have been guarding convoys from U-boats.

On December 12th Royal Navy Commodore Henry Harwood decided to park his flotilla of three cruisers—HMS *Exeter*, *Achilles* and *Ajax*—off the coast of Uruguay near the shipping lanes emanating from Montevideo. It was an inspired guess because the *Graf Spee* showed up the next morning, and the battle began!

Graf Spee's guns could shoot shells 17 miles compared to *Exeter's* eight-inch guns firing only nine miles. At 11 miles *Graf Spee* opened up with full broadsides on *Exeter*. Eleven hits blew up the torpedo magazine and knocked out the ship's communications system, in addition to killing 50 men.

Exeter withdrew from the action, leaving the smaller *Achilles* and *Ajax* to close on the *Graf Spee* in order to reach it with their smaller six-inch guns. At four miles they managed 17 hits, causing extensive damage—enough to cause the *Graf Spee* to break off the engagement and head for shelter in Montevideo's harbour.

Once in neutral territory, the German warship was allowed only three days for repairs, or risk being interned for the rest of the war. To leave meant facing the waiting British cruisers.

The choice would have been easy except the British had tricked the Germans into believing that now a battleship, the *Rodney*, and an aircraft carrier also awaited them. That meant certain death for the *Graf Spee* and so, with 750,000 Montevideans watching, she weighed anchor and sailed out of the harbour straight onto a mud flat. With all hands abandoning the ship, she proceeded to blow herself apart in a perfect job of scuttling.

The sailors were interned and the ship's captain, who had acted on orders from Berlin, shot himself to save the honour of the German navy. The Germans had scuttled their beautiful ship to keep it from falling into the hands of the British, who ended up buying the wreck from the Uruguayans for whatever secrets they could salvage from it. Commodore Harwood was promoted to Rear Admiral and knighted by King George. [See page 18]

ENIGMA

Poland made a major but secret contribution to victory against Germany that could only be told after the war was over. In 1932 the Poles obtained by good luck one of the Germans' code machines—an incredibly clever device named Enigma. After much effort, they were able to read top-secret coded messages of the German High Command. They even built 15 copies of the machine.

Suddenly in 1938 they drew a blank in deciphering messages because the Germans had switched to a new encoding system. Unable to crack it themselves in the time left before hostilities began, the Poles decided to share their secret with their new-found allies, the British and French.

Imagine the delight of the British in being presented with such a priceless gift—if only they could make it work. From July 1939 until April 1949 the finest minds in Britain were at work on Enigma. And some minds they were, the main one being that of Alan Turing, the mathematical genius credited with the invention of the computer. Finally breaking the code, they were able to use it with devastating results all through the war.

15

The Vancouver Sun EXTRA

Only Evening Newspaper Owned, Controlled and Operated by Vancouver People

FOUNDED 1886 VOL. LIII—No. 279 | OFFICIAL WEATHER FORECAST Cool; Scattered Showers | VANCOUVER, BRITISH COLUMBIA, SUNDAY, SEPTEMBER 3, 1939 | Price 5 Cents | Trinity 4111

BRITAIN AT WAR!

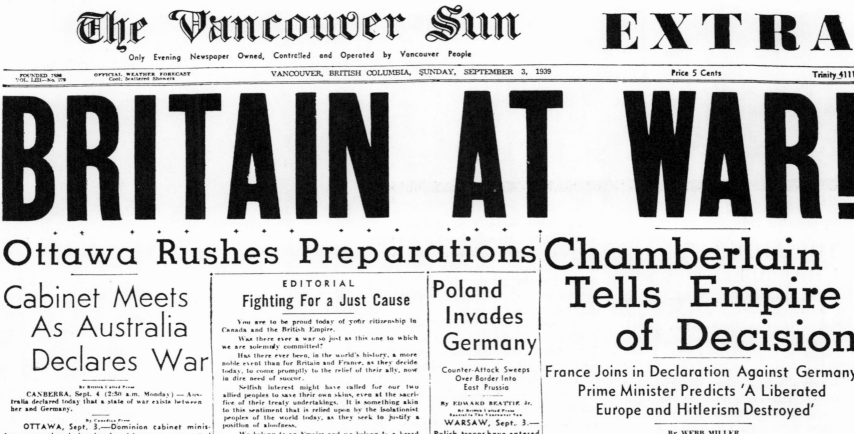

Ottawa Rushes Preparations

Cabinet Meets As Australia Declares War

By British United Press

CANBERRA, Sept. 4 (2:30 a.m. Monday) — Australia declared today that a state of war exists between her and Germany.

By Canadian Press

OTTAWA, Sept. 3.—Dominion cabinet ministers, aroused early by the dread but not unexpected news that Great Britain and the Empire are at war with Germany, hurried through foggy streets today to meet Prime Minister Mackenzie King in the Privy Council chamber at 10 o'clock (6 a.m. Vancouver time).

Mr. King, advised by the Canadian Press a few minutes after the flash was received that Great Britain had declared war, lost no time in communicating with his ministers, who had been warned to be ready for such an emergency.

Hon. Ian Mackenzie, minister of defense, was the first to arrive for the council. He reached the meeting at 9:45 a.m. Shortly afterwards Hon. C. D. Howe, minister of transport; Hon. Ernest Lapointe, minister of justice; Hon. J. G. Gardiner, minister of agriculture; Hon. Norman McLarty, postmaster-general, and Hon. T. A. Crerar, minister of resources, arrived.

Mr. Lapointe who, as acting Secretary of State, will have charge of any press censorship in Canada, said the cabinet has taken power to establish a censorship but could not say whether plans to put in effect have been completed.

So far, however, no censorship applies to the press and the minister declined to comment on reports of the censoring of cables and telegrams at Montreal.

It is understood, it was learned from other sources, that a subcommittee of the cabinet on censorship has been set up under the chairmanship of Mr. McLarty.

The Prime Minister appeared fresh and unworried as he entered the Council chamber after chatting for a few minutes with reporters.

He said he is not sure what procedure will be followed when Parliament meets Thursday. Whether a formal declaration of war will be made by Canada is one of the matters of detail yet to be worked out.

Only a few people watched the minister enter the East Block. A small girl with a dog on a leash played around the door as Mr. King and his colleagues began their deliberations.

As usual, Royal Canadian Mounted Policemen were on duty at the doors, but about the only other spectators were a few newspaper reporters and motion picture photographers.

All is in readiness for speedy action along whatever lines the government proposes to move now that Canada, as a partner in the British Commonwealth of Nations, stands literally if not technically at war with Germany.

It was indicated that necessary Orders-in-Council are ready for merely inking in dates and the formality of adoption to put into effect the various wartime measures which may be needed pending the meeting of Parliament Thursday.

Lord Tweedsmuir, the Governor-General, is at Government House ready to co-operate with the government in speeding orders through. No radical steps will become generally effective.

While it is accepted by all political parties and authorities that when Britain is at war Canada is at war, the actual declaration of

Please Turn to Page Two
See "Canada at War"

Today At a Glance

LONDON: Prime Minister Neville Chamberlain proclaimed by radio to the British Empire and to the world at 2:15 a.m. Vancouver time, that Britain is "at war" with Germany.

BERLIN: Germany rejected Britain's demands for withdrawal of German troops from Poland, blamed Europe's war on the British Cabinet and announced that Fuehrer Adolf Hitler today personally was taking the field of battle with Germany's eastern army. The German Army High Command announced German troops smashing deeper into Polish territory.

PARIS: France demanded a German reply to her ultimatum by 8 a.m. Vancouver-time.

WASHINGTON: White House and state department officials reported that President Roosevelt and Secretary of State Hull were keeping in closest touch with European war developments. President to broadcast at 7 p.m. Vancouver time.

BUDAPEST: Hungary declared her neutrality.

WARSAW: Poland attempting to reinforce the Polish-Rumanian pact of assistance. Lithuanian troops shot down a heavy German airplane. Poland assured Lithuania that her neutrality would be respected.

MOSCOW: Soviet Russia's capital calm. Populace permitted to follow factual accounts of European events in newspapers and radio.

TOKYO. — Japan will remain neutral because of the Soviet-German non-aggression Pact, newspapers reported.

ROME: Italy, so far neutral, in accordance with Mussolini's statement that Italy will take no military initiative.

PARIS: France revealed that she considered herself at war with Germany at the moment that Prime Minister Chamberlain involved Britain in the conflict, although she was not legally at war with the Reich until the expiration of her ultimatum at 5 p.m. (8 a.m. Vancouver time).

CANBERRA, Australia. — The Australian government declares "State of War" between Australia and Germany.

Churchill in Cabinet

LONDON, Sept. 3.—It was officially announced that Rt. Hon. Winston Churchill has been appointed First Lord of the Admiralty in the new war cabinet.

EDITORIAL

Fighting For a Just Cause

You are to be proud today of your citizenship in Canada and the British Empire.

Was there ever a war so just as this one to which we are solemnly committed?

Has there ever been, in the world's history, a more noble event than for Britain and France, as they decide today, to come promptly to the relief of their ally, now in dire need of succor.

Selfish interest might have called for our two allied peoples to save their own skins, even at the sacrifice of their treaty undertakings. It is something akin to this sentiment that is relied upon by the isolationist peoples of the world today, as they seek to justify a position of aloofness.

We belong to an Empire and we belong to a breed which honors its commitments. Poland's fight, and what it stands for, is our fight today.

In Germany, the Allied Front, for what it means, will not be completely understood. The Sun has already noted that the German mistake of 1914 is being repeated 25 years later. And for the second time the lesson must be brought home to the German people. Another generation has been led away—this time by Hitler and a gang of cold-blooded adventurers who already have committed every crime of rapacity and oppression that is listed in the calendar.

In London, this noon, Mr. Chamberlain stood in his place in Britain's Parliament, as chosen head of the free people of this Empire, announced that we are at war with Germany. His was a tragic and difficult task; and we shall all of us face difficult tasks before this conflict is ended. But today we have a great satisfaction. It is that with infinite restraint and patience, we in this Empire, through our chosen leaders, have sought to intervene by every peaceful means that could be summoned to our aid. We have tried to appease and placate and advise; in every way, over a long period, we have thrown our weight and influence on the side where right is not the sole prerogative of might. We have given "last warnings" and have delayed more precious hours to allow those warnings to sink in with full effect. But Herr Hitler, holding to his record of duplicity and grab, has chosen to go unheeding the other way.

Thus, we have arrived, sadly but still firm in resolve, at today's fateful decision. We shall have no fear of the outcome. That is not the British way. It is a part of the propaganda of the Hitler-Stalin ideal that the democratic way of living is to be swept aside for that nameless shambles of ruthlessness and disorder which has reduced the peoples of Germany and Russia to practical serfdom. Don't be fooled by this nonsense! We are facing days of personal worry and national trial, but the calmness and common-sense of mankind will ultimately prevail. There shall be no other end.

Again we say we have a just cause and a clear national conscience. Last Sunday, the clergy of Vancouver and other cities in our land led the people in prayers that we might be delivered from the horror and suffering of another war. Today, we shall devoutly pray again for guidance and for victory over the evil forces which stalk through the world, seeking to ruin the liberty and decent way of life of mankind.

WAR BULLETINS

MOSCOW, Sept. 3. — The appointment of a new Soviet military attache to Berlin was announced today in line with Soviet Russia's swiftly changing foreign policy. The new appointee is M. A. Purkaieff.

BUDAPEST, Sept. 3. — Proclaiming a state of emergency, the Hungarian Government today issued decrees drastically limiting civil rights.

LONDON, Sept. 3.—The air-raid precaution animals committee attempted to call a halt today on the destruction of pet dogs and cats by owners wishing to save them from a more brutal death by bombing. The committee said it had made arrangements for the emergency care of animals.

Please Turn to Page Four
See "Bulletins"

World Radio Broadcast By The King at 9 a.m.

By British United Press

LONDON, Sept. 3.—The British Broadcasting Corporation announced that the King will address his subjects in a world-wide broadcast at 6 p.m., London summer time (9 a.m. Vancouver time).

The King and Queen heard Prime Minister Chamberlain's war declaration over the radio in their private apartments at Buckingham Palace.

NEW YORK, Sept. 3.—The American network broadcasting companies announced that they would rebroadcast a radio address of the King to the Empire at 9 a.m. Vancouver time.

Poland Invades Germany

Counter-Attack Sweeps Over Border Into East Prussia

By EDWARD BEATTIE Jr.
By British United Press
Special to The Vancouver Sun

WARSAW, Sept. 3.—Polish troops have entered Germany.

Polish troops, counter-attacking, crossed into East Prussia in the vicinity of Deutscheylau.

East Prussia is the province of Germany separated from Germany proper by the Polish Corridor.

The Poles are attempting to cut off the German army which has advanced south into the Corridor from East Prussia, has reached the Cze River, about 20 miles south of the southeast corner of East Prussia and is trying to contact the German army driving across the Corridor from West Prussia.

The Polish radio also announced the recapture of Zbaszyn, a town due west of Warsaw on the German frontier in the province of Pznania.

TOWN FALLS

The Polish spokesman confirmed that the army from West Prussia has taken the town of Sepolno, on the west side of the Corridor and that the eastern army has captured Zbaszyn and Myztniec on the southern border of East Prussia. Poles, not expecting an attack, had not been at the border to protect them, he said.

The spokesman said that the town of Wielun had been practically burned out by a "deluge" of incendiary bombs dropped from German planes.

There is heavy fighting along the border of the Polish district of Czestochowa.

(Berlin said German troops had taken that important industrial city).

CITIES BOMBED

An official communique early today said that 12 hours after Poland had accepted a German proposal that both refrain from bombing open cities, German bombers had showered death and destruction on "not less than 24" Polish cities, killing and wounding 1500 persons.

Germany approached Poland through the Netherlands government Friday night, the communique said. Poland accepted at once. Saturday German bombers raided from dawn until dusk, it added.

"The German government Friday night contacted Poland through an intermediary, the Netherlands government, with a proposal not to bomb open cities," the communique said.

"The Polish government declared its agreement. Nevertheless, German fliers, on Sept. 2, bombed not less than 24 cities, including such a holy city as Czestochowa, which is entirely in flames, the textile centre of Lodz, the bath resort of Busco, and many others, causing not less than 1500 deaths and wounding."

HOSPITAL DESTROYED

A spokesman said that incendiary bombs dropped by German planes had destroyed the hospital at Velunje on Friday, and Saturday air raids on Lublin killed 30 persons, including five children, and injured 58. News of new bomb victims was arriving hourly.

The German Embassy staff is

Please Turn to Page Two
See "Fighting"

Chamberlain Tells Empire of Decision

France Joins in Declaration Against Germany; Prime Minister Predicts 'A Liberated Europe and Hitlerism Destroyed'

By WEBB MILLER
Special to The Vancouver Sun
Copyright, 1939, by British United Press

LONDON, Sept. 3.—Great Britain went to war against Germany today—25 years and 30 days from the time she entered the conflict of 1914 against the same enemy.

A brief announcement by Prime Minister Neville Chamberlain that went by radio to all outposts of the Empire sent Britain to war in fulfillment of her pledge to help Poland if that nation was invaded by Adolf Hitler's Nazis.

The French government set its deadline at 5 p.m. (8 a.m. Vancouver time) but announced from Paris that France considered herself automatically at war with Germany the moment Chamberlain made his pronouncement.

"This country is at war with Germany," Chamberlain said in slow, measured tones. "You can imagine what a bitter blow this is to me that all my long struggle to win peace has failed."

A radio hook-up to all places under the Union Jack was made and Chamberlain stepped to the microphone in No. 10 Downing Street to speak the fateful words.

"We have a clear conscience," declared the Prime Minister. "We have done all that any country could do to establish peace, but the situation has become intolerable, and we have resolved to finish it.

"Now may God bless you all and may He defend the right, for it is evil things that we shall be fighting against—force, bad faith, injustice, oppression and persecution. Against them, I am certain, the right will prevail."

"God Save the King" was played on the BBC's Empire hook-up as Chamberlain concluded.

Wounded Polish Airman Battles 12 Nazi Planes

WARSAW, Sept. 3. — Lieutenant Pausiniski of the Polish Air Force was hailed in Warsaw today as an early hero of the war.

Taking off in a combat plane, Pausinski attacked a squadron of 12 German bombers. He shot down one of the attacking planes after a thrilling dogfight, witnessed by thousands of residents of Warsaw.

Several bullets fired by the German planes struck Pasinski's plane, damaging its wings and wounding the Polish flier.

Despite his wounds and the dangerous condition of his plane he made a successful landing from an altitude of about 2500 feet.

'Russia Will Be Neutral'

MOSCOW, Sept. 3. — (5:30 p.m.). Foreign circles today are convinced that Soviet Russia will remain neutral in the new European war, but there was no official comment on Britain's declaration that a state of war exists between the United Kingdom and Germany.

It was unofficially reported, however, that service has been suspended on eight principal domestic airlines.

Throng in Downing Street

The curbstones of Downing Street were thronged as Chamberlain spoke. Cabinet ministers and important members of Parliament hurried to the Prime Minister's residence. Soon the entire south side of Downing Street was crowded with men and women waiting to be told that they were at war.

France, committed to the same stand as Britain in regard to the defense of Polish sovereignty, is expected to go to war, too.

An ultimatum, calling for a reply by Germany to Britain's demand that the Reich withdraw troops from Poland, was the technical step that committed the British to war. A government communique announced that unless such a reply was forthcoming by 11 a.m. (2 a.m. Vancouver time) today a state of war would exist.

The German reply did not arrive before the deadline.

Half an hour before the deadline set in the British ultimatum expired the German embassy here still was waiting word from Berlin.

"There is no news," the German embassy announced as the clock crawled toward war. "We are in constant communication with Berlin."

Apparently there was no slackening in Germany's invasion of Poland. Warsaw said there had been 1500 casualties from German air raiders. The Poles fought back and claimed that their troops had penetrated East Prussia, the isolated piece of Germany that is cut off by the Polish Corridor.

War Machine Moves

Great Britain moved quickly to set her war machine moving. The King convened the Privy Council at 11:45 a.m. (3:45 a.m. Vancouver time) to announce that a State of War exists.

The House of Commons passed the National Service Bill under which the government can conscript all men between the ages of 18 and 41 for military service.

Instructions regarding air raid warnings went out over the British Broadcasting Company system.

The formal notification that Germany must reply by 11 a.m. was delivered in Berlin by Sir Nevile Henderson, British Ambassador. He delivered that notification at 9 a.m.

Please Turn to Page Two See "Britain at War"

MR. CHAMBERLAIN: "Now may God bless you all and may He defend the right, for it is evil things that we shall be fighting against—force, bad faith, injustice, oppression and persecution. Against them, I am certain, the right will prevail."

Sun Barometer Reading
Wednesday, 8 a.m. 29.95
Thursday, 8 a.m. 30.95
Thursday, 1 p.m. 30.00
Indications: Clear.
Official weather report on page 3.

The Vancouver Sun

The Vancouver Evening Newspaper Owned and Operated By Vancouver People

Today's Tides
Vancouver Harbor
High 7:00 p.m., 11.0 feet. Low 2:38 p.m., 8.5 feet.
English Bay
High 6:38 p.m., 11.1 feet. Low 2:20 p.m., 9.0 feet.
First Narrows
High slack 7:22 p.m. Low slack 3:04 p.m.
Tomorrow's Tides Appear on Page 18

FOUNDED 1886
VOL. LIV—No. 52
OFFICIAL WEATHER FORECAST
Cloudy with some rain squalls.
VANCOUVER, BRITISH COLUMBIA, THURSDAY, NOVEMBER 30, 1939 *** Price 3 Cents Trinity 4111

Reds Invade Finland; Bombs Kill Hundreds

Soviet Warplanes, Warships and Mechanized Forces Make Swift Unheralded Assault; Fighting From Gulf to Arctic Circle

By NORMAN B. DEUEL
Special to The Vancouver Sun
Copyright, 1939, by British United Press

HELSINGFORS, Finland, Nov. 30.—Soviet Russia invaded Finland by land, sea and air today, raining death-dealing explosives on Helsingfors, Viborg and half-a-dozen other centres.

Red airplanes roared out of cloudy skies throughout the day and in mid-afternoon unloaded a hail of thermite bombs on the dazed population of Helsingfors, destroying public buildings and apartment houses, starting fires in the centre of the capital and inflicting hundreds of casualties.

Three big fires burned in downtown Helsingfors tonight and at least three suburban homes in Viborg were set afire.

Unofficial estimates of the dead are as high as 200, with many more wounded. Rescue forces are still digging into the wreckage in search of bodies and survivors.

Finland's reply to the undeclared war was given by roaring anti-aircraft guns that brought down one and perhaps two Soviet planes, by stubborn return fire in the frontier areas, especially at Kivena, and an official decree declaring that a state of war exists against the Soviet Union.

The raid on Helsingfors, a city of 268,000 population, caught mid-afternoon crowds in the streets as bombs aimed at the railroad station, the harbor and the airport exploded with terrific force in the centre of the city.

Hotel lobbies and travel bureaus were thronged with foreigners seeking to leave the country quickly.

Darkness descended at 4 p.m. and the city presented an eerie scene, with flashlights winking in the dusk and the flare of burning buildings across the sky. The population, nevertheless, returned quickly to normal business pursuits.

It was established that the Soviet air squadron which attacked Helsingfors today consisted of 11 planes flying in groups of three each, with two planes leading the squadron.

The planes approached at a great height but dived much lower before releasing their bombs.

Invasion From Gulf to Arctic

Government messages showed that the soviet invasion was from all sides.

The Red Army invaded Finnish territory at Suojarvi, on the southeastern frontier, and on Fisherman's Peninsula, in the far northern Arctic Coast, where they moved in on the important port of Petsamo, Finnish advices said.

The Red Fleet, according to unconfirmed reports, passed Hogland Island en route to Helsingfors and Red Army forces landed at the island of Seiskari, in the Gulf of Finland.

Finnish advices said Russian warships had fired on Tammelsuu on the Karelian Isthmus from the Gulf of Finland, that Russian artillery pounded the Finnish sectors of Suojarvi and Kivena, that Red Troops had invaded Finland at Suojarvi and that Soviet planes had raided the Emso valley, Viborg and Imatra.

Un confirmed messages said Hangoe had been bombed and that Russian troops landed there after the bombardment. (Hangoe is a tip of land and an island at the eastern end of the Gulf of Finland, one of the areas which Russia demanded from Finland as a naval base.)

The United States legation announced it was moving immediately to Grankulla, 10 miles from Helsingfors, and Americans employed at the legation were given instructions by the military attache as to how to use their gas masks.

Finland Calls All Reserves

The government of Premier A. K. Cajander—object of bitter attacks by the Soviet—called reserves to the army of 300,000 men and formally put the hero of Finland's fight for independence 22 years ago, Gen. Baron Karl Gustav Emil Mannerheim, in charge of the nation's armed forces.

Finnish messages said the Soviet invading the Suojarvi district, in southeast Finland, had found a "no man's land" there because the Finns withdrew. The area is not important to the military defense of the country.

The Finns' main line of defense now is about 25 miles back of the Suojarvi area, where the terrain provides natural defensive positions.

Some believed the Russians might propose negotiations soon but others thought the Red Army would smash deeply into Finland.

Finns Down 2 Soviet Bombers

Reports indicate the Finns are fighting hard. Anti-aircraft batteries blasted away at the squadron of six Russian planes that raided Helsingfors and accounts of artillery duels indicated the shelling was not entirely one-sided. Two Russian planes were shot down, the Finnish radio reported.

It was announced that at Sveaborg, 12 Russian bombers had appeared over the coast at 10 a.m., and had been driven away by ground batteries before they caused damage.

Bombs dropped on the airport here were small. They exploded harmlessly in the field. The planes also dropped leaflets printed in the Finnish language: "You know we have bread; don't starve."

Fighting is raging at various points along the wild, 600-mile stretch of Soviet-Finnish border extending up to the Arctic. Artillery firing was reported at Rabotchi and Kola, in the far north, a region where the wintry nights now are 19 hours long, and darkness falls at 2 p.m.

Attacks began on all sectors between 9 and 9:30 a.m., (3 and 12:30 a.m., Vancouver time) nine hours after Soviet Premier-Foreign Commissar V. M. Molotov announced in Moscow that diplomatic relations with Finland were severed because the Finns were threatening to "attack" Russia.

Bombs Set Hospital Afire

Other raiding air squadrons bombed the whole Emso valley, trying to destroy cellulose plants. The industrial district of Emso was bombed and a hospital set afire.

Five bombs were dropped on the port of Viborg and three homes in the eastern part of town were set afire.

The town of Imatra was bombed, but the Russians missed their objective there—an electric plant.

The town of Tammelsuu in Karelia was shelled by warships from the Gulf of Finland, and Russian troops crossed the border at Suojarvi, north of Lake Ladoga in southeast Finland and occupied a sector of Finnish ter-

Please Turn to Page Five
See "New War Begins"

Eye-Witness of Red Horror

'I Saw Death Rained Upon Dazed Finns'

Soviet Bombers Hurled Tons of Incendiary Bombs; Three Raids Set Finland Capital Afire

Here is a sensational dramatic eye-witness story of how undeclared Red war descended suddenly upon Helsingfors today. Norman Deuel, British United Press and Vancouver Sun correspondent, now in Helsingfors graphically describes what he saw.—EDITOR.

By NORMAN DEUEL
Special to The Vancouver Sun
Copyright, 1939, by British United Press

HELSINGFORS, Nov. 30.—I saw the Soviet Russian air fury unleashed upon this peaceful city three times today. In morning, afternoon and evening raids, Red bombers hurled down tons of highly incendiary thermite bombs, blasting hundreds of dazed Finnish men, women and children to death, and making the city tonight a red-flamed holocaust.

'Bomb Blast Hurled Me Down'

With Russian bombs falling over the capital I saw several fires started, buildings damaged and windows shattered as I telephoned this despatch.

I was hurled to the floor of my hotel room by the terrific explosion of the bombs.

I saw one automobile bus crushed and bodies thrown out into the street.

At least a dozen bombs were dropped and there were two gigantic blasts among them. Windows for a dozen blocks around were broken.

Anti-aircraft guns are firing continuously as I telephone.

From my hotel window I can see at least three burning buildings. There is smoke and apparently there are other fires in the background.

It would appear that the casualties inflicted by the Soviet planes were high, because the people—recovering from earlier air alarms—had returned to the streets in mid-afternoon when the bombs began falling from a cloudy sky.

The attacking planes were high in the sky. They presumably struck at the railroad station, but if they did their aim was poor and tons of high explosives rained on the centre of this city of 268,000 population.

Observers believed that the raiding planes were dropping "thermite" incendiary bombs, which are designed like aerial torpedoes to penetrate buildings.

As we watched, more bombs fell, and it appeared that 20 or 30 in all were aimed at the city. The continual firing of Finnish guns, however, made it difficult to tell how many had been dropped.

Crowds Dazed by Sudden Fury

The population was dazed by the sudden fury of the aerial attack. There had been air raid warnings during the day, but the people had shaken off their first fear of attack and the streets were crowded in mid-afternoon when the alarm sounded again.

Some shops had reopened and crowds were reading the news on bulletin boards.

The daughter of a member of the British United Press staff, quartered in the Torni Hotel, went out to buy the

Please Turn to Page Five See "Eyewitness' Story"

Russia-Finland Theatre of War

Undeclared war was launched at dawn today (just after midnight Vancouver time) by land, sea and air along the coasts and frontiers of Russia and Finland. Helsingfors, the capital, was bombed twice and 200 persons were reported killed. Viborg (Viipuri), port on the Karelian isthmus, (which separates the Gulf of Finland from Lake Ladoga), is reported in flames, while artillery and infantry attacks were made all along that wild waste of frontier land extending as far north as Rabatchi and Kola. In those sub-Arctic points the night, at this time of the year, is 19 hours long.

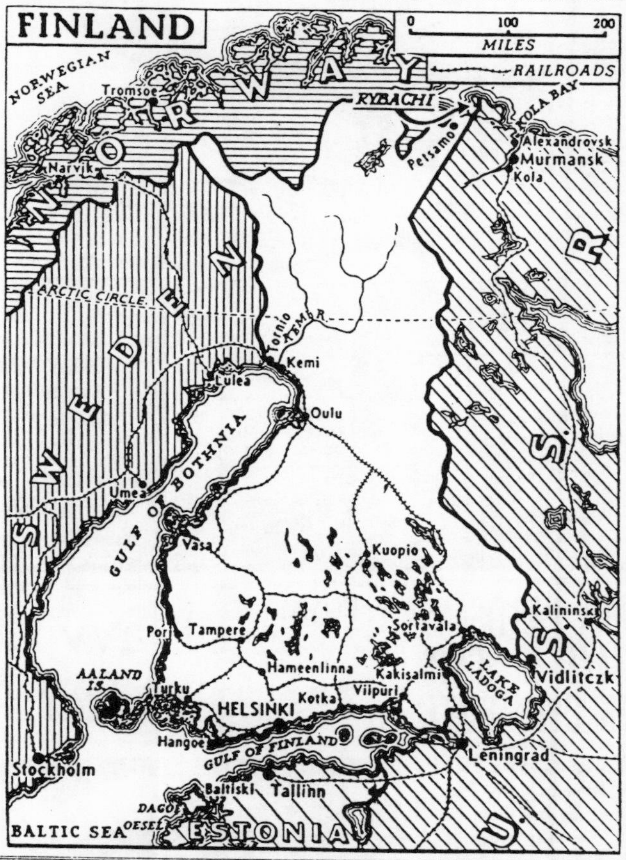

Chamberlain Scores Invasion as 'Act of Unprovoked Aggression'

Helsingfors Note Which Russia Would Not Read 'Most Conciliatory in Character' Premier Informs Parliament

By British United Press

LONDON, Nov. 30.—Soviet Russia's invasion of Finland was characterized today in the House of Commons as apparently "an indefensible act of unprovoked aggression."

Prime Minister Neville Chamberlain, after stating it was difficult for Great Britain to believe that such measures were necessary, was asked by Labor Leader Clement R. Attlee whether the government had received from Moscow "any statement as to the reason for what appears to be an indefensible act of unprovoked aggression."

Chamberlain replied: "No, sir."

"The attitude of the Finnish government was from the outset unprovocative," Chamberlain said.

"It is known that the Finnish note delivered to Moscow immediately before the rupture was most conciliatory in character.

"This government warmly welcomed the offer of mediation made by the United States. The government deeply regrets this fresh attack on a small independent nation which must result in fresh suffering and loss."

He said Finland had proposed to submit the dispute to arbitration and meanwhile to withdraw all troops from the Finnish frontier on the Karelian Isthmus except for ordinary frontier guards and customs officers.

William Gallacher, Communist, was shouted down when he attempted to discuss with Mr. Chamberlain what he described as "Russia's claims."

Cries of "Sit down," "Shut up," "Back to Moscow" came from all sides of the House as the Scots radical attempted to speak.

U.S. Senator Calls for Break With Russia

WASHINGTON, Nov. 30. — President Roosevelt discussed the Finnish-Soviet conflict with Secretary of State Cordell Hull today, and it was indicated that Mr. Roosevelt may summon legislative leaders of both parties to the White House for a conference about U.S. foreign policy.

Officials took a grave view of the new hostilities and the bombing of Helsingfors, but there was no comment forthcoming from Mr. Roosevelt or Hull.

'BLOODY HANDS'

Sen. William H. King, Democrat, Utah, called for the with-

Please Turn to Page Five
See "Reaction"

91st Day of 'The War'

News Digest by G H.S.

Seven years ago Soviet Russia signed a non-aggression treaty with Finland; one clause required six months notice for denunciation of treaty. Day before yesterday Russia denounced the treaty. Today, less than 48 hours afterward, Reds invaded Finland by land, sea and air. Finns, in defense, declared state of war, fought back valiantly.

Moscow had demanded naval bases from Finland, both north and south, also that Finns withdraw troops 12 to 16 miles from their own border. Finland offered some area for bases, not same as Russia demanded; offered to withdraw troops if Russia would do same. Moscow answered by denouncing treaty. Finns replied to this, proposed mutual withdrawal as guarantee of good faith while dispute would be arbitrated, sent their reply to legation in Moscow. Reds refused to receive it. Roosevelt offered good offices of U.S. to help settle peacefully. Finland accepted; Russia refused. Reds invaded at 7 a.m. today.

Thus did Stalin seek to outdo Hitler in undeclared war. In power diplomacy, in radio blasts and threats, finally in armed attack, Stalin's course aped Hitler's of three months ago when he invaded Poland. Stalin told Russians nothing of invasion today, twice denied there had been one.

Red warships attacked coast. Red army bit off Fisherman's Peninsula in north, containing ice-free port of Petsamo which Russia coveted, and where daylight now lasts only five hours. Red bombers attacked Helsingfors and other cities, set large part of capital in flames, killed and wounded hundreds. Mr. Chamberlain in British House said Finns had been conciliatory throughout parleys.

Norway heard Russia wanted three bases on north Norwegian coast. Sweden called extra men to colors and youths rushed to volunteer. All Norse

Please Turn to Page Five
See "War Today"

LATE FLASHES

BUDAPEST, Nov. 30. — Reports from the Ruthenian frontier today said Russian soldiers had opened fire on a number of Hungarian sentries.

It was learned tension had been caused in the frontier region by Hungarian seizures of Russia propaganda pamphlets shipped into Ruthenia.

OSLO, Norway, Nov. 30.— The newspaper Arbeiderbladet today reported some Canadian families who had been staying near the International Nickel Company's mines, in Northern Finland, had arrived in Northern Norway as a result of the Russian invasion.

KIRKENS, Far Northern Norway, Nov. 30. — Finnish towns 200 miles above the Arctic Circle were partly destroyed by Soviet bombing planes today as Russia carried her air operations to the Norwegian border.

COPENHAGEN, Nov. 30.— Sweden, Norway and Denmark, thoroughly alarmed by the Russian invasion of Finland, looked to their own defenses today, but officially maintained a non-committal attitude of neutrality. Many Danes, Norwegians and especially Swedes were expected to go to Finland as volunteers unless their governments prevent it.

At press time an unidentified woman was killed by a Great Northern Railway train near Sunbury, on the Fraser River, about five miles from Ladner.

House Ends Session With Final Flareup

Opposition Accuses Government of 'Throttling' Them; Prorogation This Afternoon

By Sun Staff Reporter

VICTORIA, Nov. 30.—The third session of the nineteenth Legislature of British Columbia ended its brief labors today and is being formally prorogued this afternoon by Lieut.-Governor Eric Hamber.

LENGTHY SITTING

At a lengthy morning sitting the House waded through 14 resolutions on public policy, rejecting about half of them as out of order. The Opposition protested vigorously that the rules were being used to throttle all discussion by private members.

The session's work was finally crystallized in 67 statutes, but none of them is of outstanding importance. The session, lasting just two days over a month, was the shortest on record since party politics were introduced in 1903.

After a big session Wednesday night, the House had nothing left before it today but the resolutions proposed by the opposition and left over to the last moment.

MOTIONS RULED OUT

Mr. Speaker Whittaker ruled out of order C. C. F. motions urging more Liberal old age pensions in Canada on the ground that they affected government expenditures—a matter outside the scope of a private member.

C. C. F. members forced a divi-

Please Turn to Page Five
See "Prorogation"

Soviet Ultimatum: 'Submit or We Will Raze Helsingfors'

By British United Press

COPENHAGEN, Denmark, Nov. 30.—The Berlingskes correspondent at Helsingfors tonight reported that rumors were circulating—apparently with some basis—that Russia had sent an ultimatum to Finland.

The ultimatum was described as demanding capitulation on threat that Helsingfors would be razed from the air "leaving no trace."

The correspondent said that the Russian fleet had occupied Hoagland Island and other islands in the Finnish Gulf.

Six Months in Jail

NORTH VANCOUVER. — Arthur Langton, 25, Vancouver, was sentenced to six months' imprisonment on a charge of theft of boom chains from the Canadian Robert Dollar Co. mill at Dollarton.

French Torpedo Boat Sinks German U-Boat

Allies Score Forty-fourth Victory Over Undersea Raiders; RAF Battles Nazi Bombers

By Canadian Press

PARIS, Nov. 30.—Sinking of a German submarine by a French torpedo boat was reported in tonight's official French war communique.

"One of our torpedo boats successfully attacked an enemy submarine," the communique said.

Earlier this week official sources estimated that the Allied fleets had sunk 45 submarines, with the British fleet "bagging" 33 of the undersea craft.

RAF Battles German Bombers Off Scotland

LONDON, Nov. 30.—Four German reconnaissance planes flew over the east coast of Scotland today and two Heinkel bombers appeared near the First of Forth.

Two German bombers also were sighted north of the Firth of Forth but were driven off by Royal Air Force fighters.

It was reported that a "dog fight" occurred when British fighters went up to engage the Heinkel bombers seen near the Firth of Forth.

A denial of these reports was issued late today and later the denial was withdrawn.

2 Mine-Laying Planes Damaged by British

By JACK BRAYLEY
Canadian Press Staff Writer

LONDON, Nov. 30.—Five German mine-laying seaplanes were strafed with machine-gun fire from Royal Air Force planes when they raided the Nazi air base at Borkum Island, Tuesday.

Pilots who took part in the attack today said two of the mine-laying seaplanes are believed to have been seriously damaged and three machine-gun posts on the air-base's breakwater were put out of action.

The raid was carried out by a dozen long-range aircraft flying so low that one flew through a gap in the breakwater.

The attack was a complete surprise and pilots described a mad scramble on the island airbase to man the guns.

The 500-mile flight was accomplished without a single scratch to the 36 fliers or planes.

Mystery Ship Prowls Off Mexican Coast

SAN DIEGO, Calif., Nov. 30.—The San Diego Union says that reports have been received here of a mysterious 300-foot motorship cruising in Pacific Coast Mexican waters and keeping American fishing craft under surveillance.

The Union said the action on the unknown motorship corroborates reports from Galapagos Island that a German raider is operating on the lower coast.

British Freighter Sinks After Blast

LONDON, Nov. 30.—Sinking of the 3114-ton British vessel "Ionian" off the east coast was disclosed early today when a warship landed her crew of 38 at a British port. The "Ionian" went down after an explosion early Wednesday.

Another British ship, the collier "Sheafcrest," 2830 tons,

Please Turn to Page Five
See "Air, Sea War"

THE VANCOUVER DAILY PROVINCE

45th YEAR—NO. 223 | OFFICIAL FORECAST: MILD WITH RAIN. | VANCOUVER, B. C., THURSDAY, DECEMBER 14, 1939—38 PAGES ★ ★ ★ | PRICE 3 CENTS On Trains, Boats and in the Country, Five Cents

Britain Sends More Warships to Guard Trapped Graf Spee

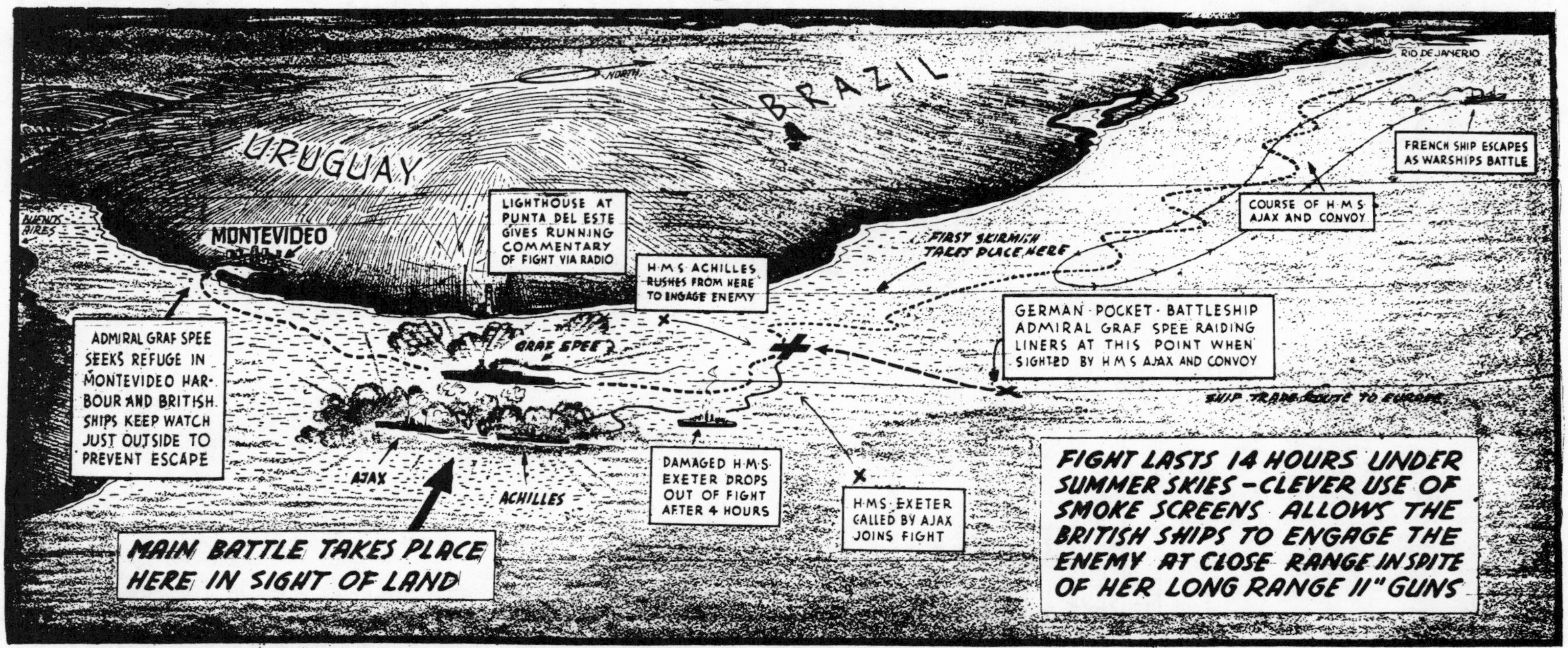

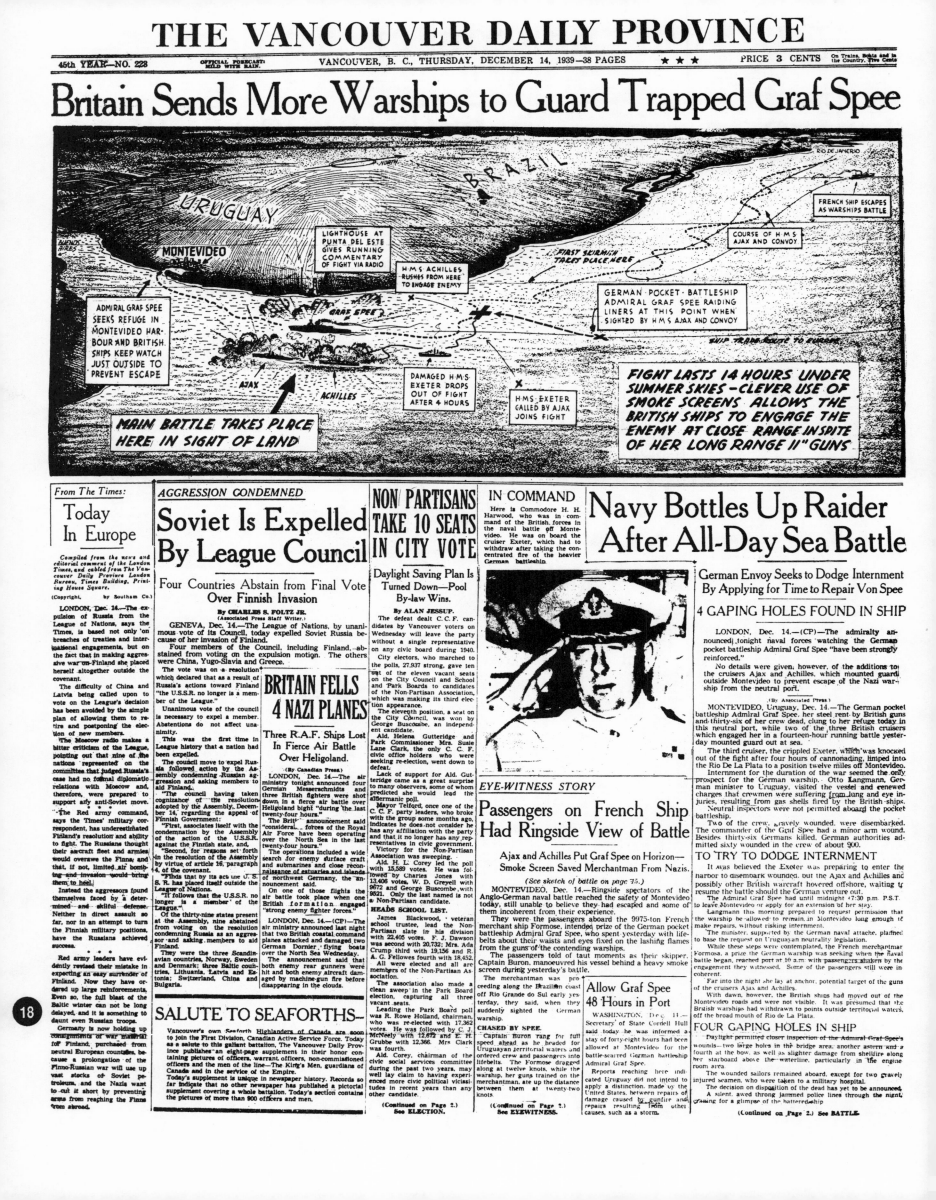

BRAZIL
URUGUAY
NORTH
RIO DE JANERIO
BUENOS AIRES
MONTEVIDEO
FRENCH SHIP ESCAPES AS WARSHIPS BATTLE
COURSE OF H.M.S. AJAX AND CONVOY
LIGHTHOUSE AT PUNTA DEL ESTE GIVES RUNNING COMMENTARY OF FIGHT VIA RADIO
FIRST SKIRMISH TAKES PLACE HERE
H.M.S. ACHILLES RUSHES FROM HERE TO ENGAGE ENEMY
GERMAN POCKET BATTLESHIP ADMIRAL GRAF SPEE RAIDING LINERS AT THIS POINT WHEN SIGHTED BY H.M.S. AJAX AND CONVOY
GRAF SPEE
SHIP TRADE ROUTE TO EUROPE
ADMIRAL GRAF SPEE SEEKS REFUGE IN MONTEVIDEO HARBOUR AND BRITISH SHIPS KEEP WATCH JUST OUTSIDE TO PREVENT ESCAPE
AJAX
ACHILLES
DAMAGED H.M.S. EXETER DROPS OUT OF FIGHT AFTER 4 HOURS
H.M.S. EXETER CALLED BY AJAX JOINS FIGHT
FIGHT LASTS 14 HOURS UNDER SUMMER SKIES—CLEVER USE OF SMOKE SCREENS ALLOWS THE BRITISH SHIPS TO ENGAGE THE ENEMY AT CLOSE RANGE INSPITE OF HER LONG RANGE 11" GUNS
MAIN BATTLE TAKES PLACE HERE IN SIGHT OF LAND

From The Times:

Today In Europe

Compiled from the news and editorial comment of the London Times, and cabled from The Vancouver Daily Province London Bureau, Times Building, Printing House Square.

(Copyright, by Southam Co.)

LONDON, Dec. 14.—The expulsion of Russia from the League of Nations, says the Times, is based not only on breaches of treaties and international engagements, but on the fact that in making aggressive war on Finland she placed herself altogether outside the covenant.

The difficulty of China and Latvia being called upon to vote on the League's decision has been avoided by the simple plan of allowing them to retire and postponing the election of new members.

The Moscow radio makes a bitter criticism of the League, pointing out that nine of the nations represented on the committee that judged Russia's case had no formal diplomatic relations with Moscow and, therefore, were prepared to support any anti-Soviet move.

• • •

The Red army command, says the Times' military correspondent, has underestimated Finland's resolution and ability to fight. The Russians thought their aircraft fleet and armies would overawe the Finns, and that, if not, limited air bombing and invasion would bring them to heel.

Instead the aggressors found themselves faced by a determined and skilful defense. Neither in direct assault so far, nor in an attempt to turn the Finnish military positions, have the Russians achieved success.

• • •

Red army leaders have evidently revised their mistake in expecting an easy surrender of Finland. Now they have ordered up large reinforcements. Even so, the full blast of the Baltic winter can not be long delayed, and it is something to daunt even Russian troops.

Germany is now holding up consignments of war material for Finland, purchased from neutral European countries, because a prolongation of the Finno-Russian war will use up vast stocks of Soviet petroleum, and the Nazis want to cut it short by preventing arms from reaching the Finns from abroad.

AGGRESSION CONDEMNED

Soviet Is Expelled By League Council

Four Countries Abstain from Final Vote Over Finnish Invasion

By CHARLES S. FOLTZ JR.
(Associated Press Staff Writer.)

GENEVA, Dec. 14.—The League of Nations, by unanimous vote of its Council, today expelled Soviet Russia because of her invasion of Finland.

Four members of the Council, including Finland, abstained from voting on the expulsion motion. The others were China, Yugo-Slavia and Greece.

The vote was on a resolution which declared that as a result of Russia's actions toward Finland "the U.S.S.R. no longer is a member of the League."

Unanimous vote of the council is necessary to expel a member. Abstentions do not affect unanimity.

This was the first time in League history that a nation had been expelled.

The council move to expel Russia followed action by the Assembly condemning Russian aggression and asking members to aid Finland.

"The council having taken cognizance of the resolution adopted by the Assembly, December 14, regarding the appeal of Finnish Government:

"First, associates itself with the condemnation by the Assembly of the action of the U.S.S.R. against the Finnish state, and,

"Second, for reasons set forth in the resolution of the Assembly by virtue of article 16, paragraph 4, of the covenant.

"Finds that by its act the U. S. S. R. has placed itself outside the League of Nations.

"It follows that the U.S.S.R. no longer is a member of the League."

Of the thirty-nine states present at the Assembly, nine abstained from voting on the resolution condemning Russia as an aggressor and asking members to aid Finland.

They were the three Scandinavian countries, Norway, Sweden and Denmark; three Baltic countries, Lithuania, Latvia and Estonia; Switzerland, China and Bulgaria.

BRITAIN FELLS 4 NAZI PLANES

Three R.A.F. Ships Lost In Fierce Air Battle Over Heligoland.

(By Canadian Press.)

LONDON, Dec. 14.—The air ministry tonight announced four German Messerschmidts and three British fighters were shot down in a fierce air battle over Heligoland bight "during the last twenty-four hours."

The British announcement said "considerable forces of the Royal Air Force have been operating over the North Sea in the last twenty-four hours."

The operations included a wide search for enemy surface craft and submarines and close reconnaissance of estuaries and islands of northwest Germany, the announcement said.

On one of those flights the air battle took place when one British formation engaged "strong enemy fighter forces."

LONDON, Dec. 14.—(CP)—The air ministry announced last night that two British coastal command planes attacked and damaged two German Dornier flying boats over the North Sea Wednesday.

The announcement said that both enemy rear gunners were hit and both enemy aircraft damaged by machine-gun fire before disappearing in the clouds.

SALUTE TO SEAFORTHS—

Vancouver's own Seaforth Highlanders of Canada are soon to join the First Division, Canadian Active Service Force. Today as a salute to this gallant battalion, The Vancouver Daily Province publishes an eight-page supplement in their honor containing pictures of officers, warrant officers, non-commissioned officers and the men of the line—The King's Men, guardians of Canada and in the service of the Empire.

Today's supplement is unique in newspaper history. Records so far indicate that no other newspaper has published a pictorial supplement covering a whole battalion. Today's section contains the pictures of more than 900 officers and men.

NON PARTISANS TAKE 10 SEATS IN CITY VOTE

Daylight Saving Plan Is Turned Down—Pool By-law Wins.

By ALAN JESSUP.

The defeat dealt C.C.F. candidates by Vancouver voters on Wednesday will leave the party without a single representative on any civic board during 1940.

City electors, who marched to the polls, 27,937 strong, gave ten out of the eleven vacant seats on the City Council and School and Park Boards to candidates of the Non-Partisan Association, which was making its third election appearance.

The eleventh position, a seat on the City Council, was won by George Buscombe, an independent candidate.

Ald. Helena Gutteridge and Park Commissioner Mrs. Susie Lane Clark, the only C. C. F. civic office holders who were seeking re-election, went down to defeat.

Lack of support for Ald. Gutteridge came as a great surprise to many observers, some of whom predicted she would lead the aldermanic poll.

Mayor Telford, once one of the C. C. F. party leaders, who broke with the group some months ago, indicates he does not consider he has any affiliation with the party and that it no longer has any representatives in civic government.

Victory for the Non-Partisan Association was sweeping.

Ald. H. L. Corey led the poll with 15,589 votes. He was followed by Charles Jones with 13,406 votes, W. D. Greyell with 9672 and George Buscombe, with 9521. Only the last named is not a Non-Partisan candidate.

HEADS SCHOOL LIST.

James Blackwood, veteran school trustee, lead the Non-Partisan slate in his division with 22,405 votes. F. J. Dawson was second with 20,732; Mrs. Ada Crump third with 19,156 and R. A. G. Fellowes fourth with 18,452.

All were elected and all are members of the Non-Partisan Association.

The association also made a clean sweep in the Park Board election, capturing all three vacant seats.

Leading the Park Board poll was R. Rowe Holland, chairman, who was re-elected with 17,362 votes. He was followed by C. J. McNeely with 12,672 and E. H. Grubbe with 12,366. Mrs Clark was fourth.

Ald. Corey, chairman of the civic social services committee during the past two years, may well lay claim to having experienced more civic political vicissitudes in recent years than any other candidate.

(Continued on Page 2.)
See ELECTION.

IN COMMAND

Here is Commodore H. H. Harwood, who was in command of the British forces in the naval battle off Montevideo. He was on board the cruiser Exeter, which had to withdraw after taking the concentrated fire of the heavier German battleship.

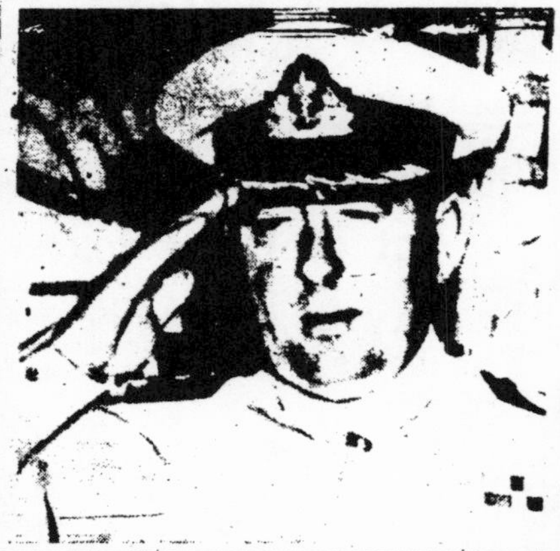

EYE-WITNESS STORY

Passengers on French Ship Had Ringside View of Battle

Ajax and Achilles Put Graf Spee on Horizon—Smoke Screen Saved Merchantman From Nazis.

(See sketch of battle on page 15.)

MONTEVIDEO, Dec. 14.—Ringside spectators of the Anglo-German naval battle reached the safety of Montevideo today, still unable to believe they had escaped and some of them incoherent from their experience.

They were the passengers aboard the 9975-ton French merchant ship Formose, intended prize of the German pocket battleship Admiral Graf Spee, who spent yesterday with lifebelts about their waists and eyes fixed on the lashing flames from the guns of the contending warships.

The passengers told of taut moments as their skipper, Captain Buron, manoeuvred his vessel behind a heavy smoke screen during yesterday's battle.

The merchantman was proceeding along the Brazilian coast off Rio Grande do Sul early yesterday, they said, when they suddenly sighted the German warship.

CHASED BY SPEE.

Captain Buron rang for full speed ahead as he headed for Uruguayan territorial waters and ordered crew and passengers into lifebelts. The Formose dragged along at twelve knots, while the warship, her guns trained on the merchantman, ate up the distance between them at twenty-two knots.

(Continued on Page 2.)
See EYEWITNESS.

Allow Graf Spee 48 Hours in Port

WASHINGTON, Dec. 14.—Secretary of State Cordell Hull said today he was informed a stay of forty-eight hours had been allowed at Montevideo for the battle-scarred German battleship Admiral Graf Spee.

Reports reaching here indicated Uruguay did not intend to apply a distinction, made by the United States, between repairs of damage caused by gunfire and repairs resulting from other causes, such as a storm.

Navy Bottles Up Raider After All-Day Sea Battle

German Envoy Seeks to Dodge Internment By Applying for Time to Repair Von Spee

4 GAPING HOLES FOUND IN SHIP

LONDON, Dec. 14.—(CP)—The admiralty announced tonight naval forces watching the German pocket battleship Admiral Graf Spee "have been strongly reinforced."

No details were given, however, of the additions to the cruisers Ajax and Achilles, which mounted guard outside Montevideo to prevent escape of the Nazi warship from the neutral port.

(By Associated Press.)

MONTEVIDEO, Uruguay, Dec. 14.—The German pocket battleship Admiral Graf Spee, her steel rent by British guns and thirty-six of her crew dead, clung to her refuge today in this neutral port, while two of the three British cruisers which engaged her in a fourteen-hour running battle yesterday mounted guard out at sea.

The third cruiser, the crippled Exeter, which was knocked out of the fight after four hours of cannonading, limped into the Rio De La Plata to a position twelve miles off Montevideo.

Internment for the duration of the war seemed the only prospect for the German warship. Otto Langmann, German minister to Uruguay, visited the vessel and renewed charges that crewmen were suffering from lung and eye injuries, resulting from gas shells fired by the British ships.

Neutral inspectors were not permitted aboard the pocket battleship.

Two of the crew, gravely wounded, were disembarked. The commander of the Graf Spee had a minor arm wound. Besides thirty-six Germans killed, German authorities admitted sixty wounded in the crew of about 900.

TO TRY TO DODGE INTERNMENT

It was believed the Exeter was preparing to enter the harbor to disembark wounded, but the Ajax and Achilles and possibly other British warcraft hovered offshore, waiting to resume the battle should the German venture out.

The Admiral Graf Spee had until midnight (7:30 p.m. P.S.T. to leave Montevideo or apply for an extension of her stay.

Langmann this morning prepared to request permission that the warship be allowed to remain in Montevideo long enough to make repairs, without risking internment.

The minister, supported by the German naval attache, planned to base the request on Uruguayan neutrality legislation.

While these steps were contemplated, the French merchantman Formosa, a prize the German warship was seeking when the naval battle began, reached port at 10 a.m. with passengers shaken by the engagement they witnessed. Some of the passengers still were incoherent.

Far into the night she lay at anchor, potential target of the guns of the cruisers Ajax and Achilles.

With dawn, however, the British ships had moved out of the Montevideo roads and were not visible. It was presumed that the British warships had withdrawn to points outside territorial waters, off the broad mouth of Rio de La Plata.

FOUR GAPING HOLES IN SHIP

Daylight permitted closer inspection of the Admiral Graf Spee's wounds—two large holes in the bridge area, another astern and a fourth at the bow, as well as slighter damage from shellfire along her starboard above the waterline, particularly in the engine room area.

The wounded sailors remained aboard, except for two gravely injured seamen, who were taken to a military hospital.

The decision on disposition of the dead has yet to be announced.

A silent, awed throng jammed police lines through the night, craning for a glimpse of the battered ship

(Continued on Page 2.) See BATTLE.

1940

The Phoney War continued serenely through the spring of 1940 when disaster suddenly struck. *Blitzkrieg!* Hitler launched a lightning war through Holland, Belgium and Northern France that succeeded beyond his wildest dreams. Within weeks the mighty Third Republic of France was consigned to the dustbin of history, while jackbooted Nazis marched through the Arc de Triomphe. The world went into shock while British troops escaped back to Britain through Dunkirk to prepare for the coming German invasion. Instead, the Battle of Britain was fought in the air during the summer and fall of 1940 between German bombers protected by Messerschmitt fighters and British Hurricane and Spitfire fighters. The British claimed they won because the Royal Air Force remained intact, but their cities lay in ruins. Britain now stood alone, armed mainly with the resolute determination of Winston Churchill, one of history's greatest Englishmen. Not completely alone, however, as Canada, Australia, New Zealand and the rest of the Commonwealth provided a strong rear guard.

MAJOR EVENTS

April 9, 1940

THE CONQUEST OF NORWAY

Concurrent with the war in France, there was another war going on in Norway. For tactical reasons Germany decided early in April that it should occupy Denmark and Norway. Denmark was taken in four hours on April 9th to gain control of its air fields and its biggest island, Zeeland, which, in the wrong hands, could have hindered access to the Baltic ports.

Norway was invaded the same day, but a spirited defense delayed its capitulation. Oslo was defended by a battery of guns made in 1892 by Krupp, the German armaments maker. With one shot a brand new German heavy cruiser, the *Blucher*, was hit and its bridge and gunnery control knocked out. Two torpedoes then sent it to the bottom of the fjord with 1,000 men, including a Gestapo unit that was supposed to capture the king.

The German entry into Oslo was delayed long enough for the king, Haakon VII, the royal family, the government, and 20 truckloads of gold to escape to Sweden. From there they were transported to England on a British cruiser for the duration of the war.

The British and French rushed to Norway's aid in a vain attempt to deny the Germans the North Sea ports it was after as bases for the German navy to raid the Atlantic and Murmansk shipping lanes. Because of difficulties and reverses encountered, Allied forces were withdrawn from south and central Norway by May 1st. With the German invasion of France on May 9th, and the subsequent disasters there, the Allies lost interest in saving what was left of Norway, and by June 10th they had evacuated all their men and equipment.

The toll on both sides had been heavy.

May 9, 1940

WINSTON CHURCHILL TAKES THE HELM

Big city taxi drivers are generally recognized as astute observers of human nature. A Parisien driver summed up the French problem succinctly: "Russia has a man. Germany has a man. If only we had a man." Britain was similarly deprived of real leadership until its prime minister, Neville Chamberlain, decided it was time to go. Even after his craven appeasement of Adolf Hitler at Munich and the subsequent military disasters the Allies suffered when the Germans attacked Poland and then Norway. Chamberlain *still* had some support in the House of Commons, but it was fast dwindling.

The logical successor in the mind of the public was the popular Winston Churchill, who had been out of office all through the 1930s because of his outspoken opposition to the build-up of the German army and to the appeasement of Mussolini and Hitler.

A dynamic opponent of fascism was desperately needed to lead a nation soon to have its back to the wall. Churchill was the one man in England who could lead Britain out of the crisis in which its misbegotten policies had landed it.

But despite such critical times, the Conservative party leaders, and even King George, preferred Lord Halifax, a political functionary tainted by the appeasement policies of the Chamberlain cabinet, in which he was Foreign Secretary. Fortunately, Halifax had the good sense to know that he could not lead a war cabinet while sitting in the House of Lords, since members of the Lords were not permitted to set foot in the House of Commons.

Reluctantly, the King asked Churchill to form a government—a coalition war cabinet of people selected from all three parties—Labour, Conservative and Liberal.

In hindsight, one can only say, "Thank God!" Without Churchill's brilliant, fighting speeches—the most powerfully effective use of the English language in this century—the populace in Britain and throughout the empire would have had no rallying cry to respond to.

Britain finally had its man.

[See page 22]

May 10 to June 25, 1940

THE FALL OF FRANCE

The military defeat of France was determined in the first hours of the Germans' dawn attack on the Belgian fort of Eben Emael on May 10, 1940. Manned by 1,200 Belgian soldiers and bristling with cannon designed to pulverize anyone trying to cross the Albert Canal into Belgium, it was thought to be impregnable. But the Germans landed 55 paratroopers in gliders on top of the fort and secured it in 24 hours at the cost of only six lives. It was a stunning victory in itself, but the Allies read far more into it than they should have.

Thinking Belgium and Holland were to bear the main force of the German invasion, Belgium's King Leopold called for British and French help, thus ending his neutrality. The Dutch royal family asked the British navy to evacuate them, the government, their gold bullion, and the crown jewels.

Since the Allies had 3,750,000 troops and 3,600 tanks to Germany's 2,760,000 troops and 2,500 tanks, it seemed reasonable to send them to Belgium and Holland to smash the Nazis as they attempted to overrun the low countries. The Allied high command even had a plan to cover this eventuality—Plan D.

No one realized that the attack on Belgium was just a feint to trick the Allies, and that the main force of the German attack was through the Ardennes Forest near Sedan. This was a narrow strip in southern Belgium just north of the French Maginot Line, the famous fortifications that had been built following World War I to deter a new German invasion. The Ardennes, full of trees and hills, was thought to be impassable to tanks and therefore was neither manned nor fortified.

But here were 2,500 tanks speeding through the forest, followed by three motorized infantry divisions and 37 more divisions on foot. In three days they were 24 hours ahead of schedule, while the Allies were pouring their troops and matériel into Belgium and Holland. They had sent their main force north while Hitler's main force emerged from the Ardennes south of them in an encirclement that became a giant snare. Hitler is quoted as saying, "I could have wept for joy; they'd fallen into the trap."

The Panzer divisions had been noticed racing through the Ardennes by the Allies, but Plan D did not allow for that eventuality, so the ineffectual Allied commander-in-chief, French General Gamelin, ignored the reports. The French prime minister, Paul Reynaud, who knew Gamelin was incompetent, had earlier lost in his bid to have him removed because of Gamelin's powerful political connections.

Hitler's brilliant plan and the Allies' bumbling incompetence conspired to speed the end so quickly that even Hitler could not believe his success. The Allied armies were trapped in the north, the way to Paris open and impeded only by unkempt, ill-trained recruits too raw to send north to participate in Plan D. Paris was entered, undefended, on June 14, 1940.

The French government moved first to Tours, then to Bordeaux while the whole country disintegrated around it. An ignominious peace was signed with the Germans on June 22, and with the Italians on June 24.

[See pages 22–24]

May 29 to June 4, 1940

DUNKIRK EVACUATION

By May 19th, only nine days after hostilities began, the Allies had a million men bottled up in Belgium and northern France near the English Channel port of Dunkirk. Of these, 400,000 consisted of the British Expeditionary Force under the command of Lord Gort, who was now seriously wondering how best to evacuate his army back to England.

In the meantime, advancing from the south and inexorably closing the trap were 45 German divisions commanded by General von Rundstedt. Another 29 divisions commanded by General von Bock were slicing through Belgium and Holland. Even General Erwin Rommel, later famous for his brilliant desert tactics, was in the fight, commanding his own Panzer divisions.

One wonders why a million men couldn't fight off the Germans, but there was little communication or coordination among the Allied armies and confusion reigned—not a winning proposition.

Luckily, Churchill had already ordered the Royal Navy to plan for an evacuation. Boats of every description, from pleasure yachts to fishing boats to destroyers, were gathered in English harbours 20 miles away across the channel.

By May 29th the Dunkirk evacuation was in full swing. It lasted until June 4th, when the attacking Germans could not be held off any longer—338,000 British troops were evacuated, as well as 140,000 French. All of the guns, transport and supplies were left behind, along with extensive casualties and prisoners, but it was a miraculous accomplishment, thanks to the Royal Navy and the Royal Air Force. *[See page 24]*

August to December 1940

THE BATTLE OF BRITAIN

The air war, fought among the fluffy cumulous clouds floating serenely in the blue skies over England in the summer of 1940, was actually a titanic life-and-death battle of good against evil. It would either save civilization as we know it or plunge us into a dark age of bestiality and cruelty such as the modern world had never known.

If Britain lost, she would be overrun by Nazi armies and the whole of Europe would be subject to Hitler's insane will, with no one to say nay to him.

The British won, and it was not an idle statement thought up by speechwriters when Churchill said, with deepest and heartfelt thanks:

> *Never*
> *in the history of warfare*
> *has so much*
> *been owed by so many*
> *to so few.*

How did the British win? At the start of the battle, the Germans had twice as many fighter planes: 1,290 Messerschmitts to Britain's 600 Spitfires and Hurricanes. Reichsmarshall Hermann Goering thought it would be simple to eliminate the fighter squadrons of the Royal Air Force by attrition as they were shot down and by bombing them on their air fields. He had not counted on Lord Beaverbrook's genius at organizing aircraft production, however, and new fighters were in constant supply from the British factories.

Britain also had its secret weapon—radar—which made a big difference in intercepting German planes before they could find their bombing targets.

Shrewd leadership was another factor in Britain's favour. Air Chief Marshal Sir Hugh Dowding commanded the fighter squadrons. He was a brilliant tactician who made the most of what he had to work with. Even then, several times he was close to being beaten. Luckily the

Germans would suddenly change their tactics and give the RAF a breather.

In four months, 1,500 German planes were shot down, including bombers, and the RAF lost some 900. The Spitfire got all the publicity as the glamour plane that won the Battle of Britain. It was a good match for the sensational Messerschmitt, against which it climbed faster, higher and made tighter turns—matters of life and death in aerial warfare of that time.

In the first three weeks of the London blitz, 2,000 were killed and 10,000 injured, and even Buckingham Palace was damaged. The bombing went on sporadically for many more months well into 1941, and exacted a terrible toll on London and other British cities. The British did not crack, the RAF maintained its superiority, and the invasion was permanently postponed, giving Britain time to rebuild its forces and recover the initiative.

[See pages 25, 27–32, 37–38, 43]

November to December 1940

ITALIAN DISASTER IN GREECE

Expecting a walkover, the Italians cavalierly invaded Albania and Greece, which were near-to-hand just across the Adriatic Sea. To Mussolini's consternation, the Greeks made fools of his bumbling generals, whose armies retreated in disarray, abandoning large quantities of valuable equipment. Driven out of Greece and most of Albania, the Italians fought to a stalemate until the Germans, coming to their aid, invaded the whole region the following year. That campaign took up enough of the Wehrmacht's time to delay the invasion of Russia long enough to bog them down in the frigid Russian winter, for which they were ill prepared. Thus, this inept Italian campaign contributed more to the German defeat than many realize. *[See pages 30–31]*

Mr. Chamberlain (in His Broadcast Tonight):

'You and I must stand behind our leader with all our might and all our courage. We must stand fast and fight until this wild beast that has sprung out upon us from his lair be finally crushed and the evil thing stamped out.'

The Weather

A depression centred off Queen Charlotte Islands has caused showers on the British Columbia coast. The weather has been warmer throughout this province.
Temperature at 10 a.m. today: 56
Temperature at 1:30 p.m. today: 60
Yesterday: maximum 67, minimum 57.
Forecast: partly cloudy and cool.
Official weather report on page 14

The Vancouver Sun

Only Evening Newspaper Owned, Controlled and Operated by Vancouver People

Today's Tides

Vancouver Harbor
Low 1:40 p.m.; 0.7 feet High 9:01 p.m.; 12.2 feet
English Bay
Low 1:16 p.m.; 1.5 feet High 8:47 p.m.; 13.1 feet
First Narrows
Low slack 2:11 p.m. High slack 9:31 p.m.
Tomorrow's tides appear on page 26.

FOUNDED 1886
VOL. LIV—No. 188

VANCOUVER, BRITISH COLUMBIA, FRIDAY, MAY 10, 1940

***

Price 3 Cents On Trains, Boats and outside Greater Vancouver, 5c.

MArine 1161

CHURCHILL PRIME MINISTER

'Blitzkrieg Fails,' Allies Shoot Down 102 German Planes

RAF Bombs Nazi Airdromes in Holland; Dutch and Belgian Troops Hurl Back First German Waves

LONDON, May 10.—Adolf Hitler's Blitzkrieg struck Holland, Belgium and Luxembourg today in a mighty effort to win the European war by landing a knockout blow against Great Britain.

But Dutch and Belgian armed forces, given swift Allied support, fought back with fierce and effective resistance against a lightning attack that came through the air, over the sea and on land. A mechanized British army raced through Belgium while French poilus contacted advance patrols of the German thrust on the Luxembourg frontier.

The Dutch High Command tonight broadcast a message to the troops stating that "the strategic surprise attack of the enemy failed."

An estimated 118 German raiding planes were shot to earth by forces of the Allies.

Dutch authorities officially announced 73 Nazi bombers shot down in flames by their anti-aircraft guns. Further heavy losses to the German air force were announced from France where 18 raiders were downed when French key cities were attacked, and from the English south coast where the British coastal defense brought down six more German fliers. The Dutch also blew up an armored train near Venlo.

Fifteen German planes were shot down by Belgian pilots operating Italian-made planes. British fliers shot down 12.

Armada Challenged

Fierce fighting was reported along the Belgian border, especially near Aachen, as the war began in earnest. The Dutch radio said that German troops were being resisted strongly along the line of the Maas and Yssel Rivers and at Delfzijl, opposite Emden, after the flooding of strategic areas by blasting the dykes.

British and French fighting planes challenged the great German aerial armada again and again over the Low Countries, over France, off the Coast of England and over Switzerland, where Nazi craft bombed a railroad during an air battle with the French.

Radio Brussels reported at 4:15 p.m. today (7:15 a.m. Vancouver time) that Belgian Defense Minister Henri Denis had told the chamber of deputies that the German advance had been checked at all points.

RAF Bombs German Troops

Royal Air Force headquarters in France announced that British planes today bombed German troops on the Western Front and British fighters destroyed "numerous" enemy planes in aerial combat.

A communique said that several British airdromes in France had been bombed by German planes but little damage resulted and no lives were lost.

The bombing of German troops was the first reported by R.A.F. headquarters during the war.

French troops for the first time contacted German advance elements on the Luxembourg border, and Allied airplanes (British and French alone) had shot down 30 German aircraft during the day, it was stated at French Army headquarters.

Belgium's Solemn Protest

Text of the note:

"Germany, for the second time, has invaded neutral and loyal Belgium. The present invasion is even worse than that of 1914.

"No ultimatum was given. No official notification. No protests.

"Instead, a direct attack violating the neutrality of the country.

"This attitude deprived Germany of any justification. This violation will hurt the conscience of the entire world abroad.

..."Belgium is resolved to defend herself by all means. She has the right with her and cannot be vanquished."

Please Turn to Page Sixteen See "Blitzkrieg"

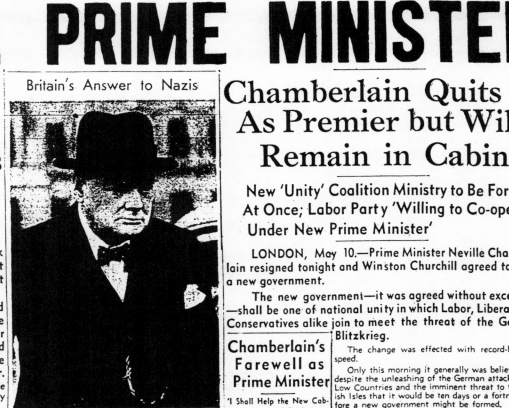

Britain's Answer to Nazis

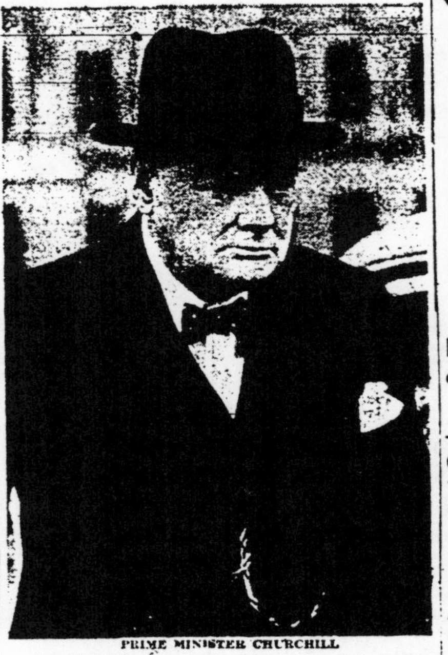

PRIME MINISTER CHURCHILL

Great Britain's most versatile statesman, a prophet who for years warned of Germany's growing might, today became Prime Minister with an overwhelming mandate from the people to crush Nazism.

He is Great Britain's answer to the Nazis, and a symbol of Britain's determination to fight Hitler to the finish. No British leader is more unpopular with demagogues at Berlin.

Vast British Army Rolls Into Belgium

Peasant Girls Pelt Flowers at Tommies On Return to 'Flanders' Fields'

By RICHARD McMILLAN
Special to The Vancouver Sun
Copyright, 1940, by British United Press

WITH THE BRITISH EXPEDITIONARY FORCES IN BELGIUM, May 10.—British Tommies moved into Belgium once again today over roads strewn with flowers by cheering Belgian girls.

As heavy British tanks and artillery caissons rumbled along the roads and across the border, Belgian girls broke branches of lilacs from the wayside and scattered them before the moving column.

Overhead British and German airplanes fought and air raid alarms sounded in the little towns and villages through which the British troops passed.

The air raid alarms did not halt the cheering welcome to the troops.

"BI ENVENU"

Little girls in their red and blue national costums cried "Bien venu les Anglais," and many homes were garlanded with flowers and flags.

Belgian civilians aided customs officials in removing the heavy steel posts that had guarded the Belgian frontier on the French side.

During the early morning hours the frontier was ablaze with acetylene torches burning through feh iron and steel of the barricades.

Even before some of the steel posts were removed British light and heavy tanks crunched across the semi-demolished barricades and toward the fighting front.

Both British and German air forces were raiding points in Belgium throughout the day. The Germans were hitting at airfields which the British might use as bases against them and the British were bombing the fields close to the German frontier where Nazi fighting planes might be based.

Despite the air activity damage in Belgium did not appear to be great.

MODEL BEF ADVANCE

I was told that the BEF advance into Belgium was a model of military tactics.

"It was 100 per cent perfect in precision and rapidity of execution," I was told. "Not a single mechanical breakdown was reported."

Atthe first Belgian village over the border the inhabitants rushed out with mugs of beer for the troops who were thirsty and dusty.

As I write this dispatch I can hear the low rumble and clank of machines as the British columns pour over the frontier and push up toward the fighting. The air raid alarms are sounded again and again as the German air force continues its attacks.

The British soldiers were in high spirits as they moved across the Flanders Fields where many of their fathers and older brothers fought in 1914.

One Belgian who went through the war in 1914-18 and saw the first raw British Territorials rushed into France in the early days of August, said "it is striking to observe the rapidity with which the B.E.F. moved in. The whole army with its ant-tank guns, heavy howitzers and equpment is all mechanized. It moved like one great machine with RAF fighter planes soaring overhead to protect it from German bombers."

French Contact Nazis On Luxembourg Border

By Associated Press

PARIS, May 10.—French military authorities reported tonight that Allied and German advance guards had entered into contact along the French-Luxembourg frontier.

The Germans, preceded by mo-

Please Turn to Page Sixteen See "British"

Nazis' Daring Try to Kidnap Holland Queen

Dutch Smash 10 of 16 Soldier Laden Planes

NEW YORK, May 10. — Two squadrons of Nazi planes, loaded with soldiers, were said today by Edwin Hartrich, Amsterdam correspondent for the Columbia Broadcasting System, to have made a "daring attempt to capture Queen Wilhelmina," which apparently "has met with failure and sudden death for the perpetrators."

In a cable to the broadcasting system he said that 16 large junkers and possibly more landed at the airport of Valkenburg, five miles from the Queen's summer villa at Ruydenhoek and about seven miles from her residence in the outskirts of The Hague.

Other contingents of "aerial kidnappers," the correspondent said, landed at Delet, about four miles south of The Hague.

The strategy was to cut off the city from the rest of the country and take the government by storm.

The correspondent said he came upon a hot pitched battle on the outskirts of Valkenburg.

"Driving behind some military lorries on the Amsterdam-Hague road, our chauffeur was stopped along with the lorries by a sudden burst of machine-gun fire," he stated. "Across the road in the ditches and at the bridge heads, Dutch soldiers were replying with short bursts aimed at a small group of farm houses."

In this battle, 10 of the 16 planes had been set on fire by the Dutch snipers.

Locarno Park Safe

RCAF, authorities have dropped their plan to extend Jericho Air Station by acquiring the remainder of Locarno Park on the west, it was learned at City Hall today. The scheme's abandonment was announced by Hon. Ian Mackenzie in a letter received by Ald. H. L. Corey.

253rd Day of The War

Digest on Pgae 33

Chamberlain Quits As Premier but Will Remain in Cabinet

New 'Unity' Coalition Ministry to Be Formed At Once; Labor Party 'Willing to Co-operate Under New Prime Minister'

LONDON, May 10.—Prime Minister Neville Chamberlain resigned tonight and Winston Churchill agreed to form a new government.

The new government—it was agreed without exception —shall be one of national unity in which Labor, Liberals and Conservatives alike join to meet the threat of the German Blitzkrieg.

The change was effected with record-breaking speed.

Only this morning it generally was believed that despite the unleashing of the German attack on the Low Countries and the imminent threat to the British Isles that it would be ten days or a fortnight before a new government might be formed.

Then sudden conferences were held.

The Labor Party agreed to go into the government if Chamberlain quit and within a few hours the preliminaries which gave Britain a new virile war leader had been accomplished.

ONE IN; ANOTHER OUT

At three minutes before 6 p.m., Chamberlain appeared at Buckingham Palace and at 6:25 p.m., he emerged to be followed immediately by Churchill.

It then was evident that the change had been made—Chamberlain out, Churchill in.

It is the first time in a career devoted to politics—most of it in the spotlight—that Churchill has headed a new government.

LLOYD-GEORGE "IN"

Technically, he is not yet head of a government but none in London tonight doubted that he would be able to enlist the necessary support to achieve a cabinet of national unity.

Had not this been evident, it was regarded as certain that Chamberlain would have deferred his resignation.

What will be the make-up of the new government was not yet known but it was expected to include David Lloyd George, Britain's war Prime Minister and veteran Liberal.

WITHOUT PORTFOLIO

Lloyd George, it was said, doubtless will become a minister without portfolio.

Several Laborites will enter the cabinet, it was agreed, but which members of the Party will be and what their posts will be were not immediately certain.

For the time being—until all formalities are out of the way—the present ministers will remain at their posts.

That is to insure continuity of office and that the country is not without responsible ministers in case of strokes from the German war machine.

ATTLEE, MORRISON, SINCLAIR

The resignation of Chamberlain came at the end of a long, bitter day for the gray, grave-faced Premier. It came after days of bitter criticism such as Chamberlain had never before experienced.

In addition to Lloyd George, the new cabinet members are expected to include Sir Archibald Sinclair, Liberal leader; Major Clement Attlee and Herbert Morrison, Laborite.

Whether Sir John Simon and Sir Samuel Hoare, Chamberlain's closest personal friends and political associates, will remain in office, was not known, but it was believed that they would follow their leader out of office.

The change of government came at a moment as grave as Britain has faced in a generation.

The most dynamic figure in the new cabinet—next to Churchill who was once known as the "boy wonder" and was called by his bitter pre-World War critics "erratic Willie"—is expected to be the 77-year-old Lloyd George.

Lloyd George was believed to have done as much as any man in British politics to bring about the downfall of the Chamberlain government.

Chamberlain had been in office for three years.

The Conservative Party which he led had commanded great power.

The Conservatives came in on Oct. 27, 1931. At that time the party and its allies—the National Liberals and National Laborites—had 546 of the 615 seats in Parliament.

It was the greatest majority in British history.

Since that time the party has lost about 100 seats while Labor has picked up 115.

EMERGENCY SESSION

The Labor party executive, after a meeting at Bournemouth, announced that it was willing to enter a new government under a new Prime Minister who could "command the confidence of the nation."

"In view of the latest series of abominable aggressions by Hitler, and while firmly convinced that drastic reconstruction of the government is vital and urgent in order to win the war, the Labor party reaffirms its determination to do its utmost to achieve victory," the statement added.

Parliament probably will be called back into emergency session Tuesday.

Please Turn to Page Sixteen See "Churchill"

Chamberlain's Farewell as Prime Minister

'I Shall Help the New Cabinet All I Can'

LONDON, May 10.—Authoritative sources said tonight Neville Chamberlain will return to the post of Chancellor of the Exchequer, which he held for five years before he was named Prime Minister. The post is now held by Sir John Simon.

Neville Chamberlain gave a farewell address over the radio after resigning the premiership.

Following is the text of his address, which was heard in Vancouver:

"Early this morning Adolf Hitler entered into another of the many great crimes he has committed against civilization," he said.

"None of those which preceded it have been more horrible than this bombing of unsuspecting Luxembourg.

"Today's action by the Germans proved that we have not miscalculated the mind of this people.

"I am not going to make any comment on the debate in the House of Commons last Wednesday. But when that debate was over I knew that some drastic and immediate action must be taken.

UNITED FRONT

"What was that action to be?"

"It was clear that this was the most critical moment of the war and that it was necessary to form a government that would present a united front.

"It was necessary to ascertain what conditions were necessary to put forward a united government.

"I devoted myself to that question with the assistance of my colleagues yesterday afternoon.

"It was apparent that such government should contain members of the Labor and Liberal

Please Turn to Page Sixteen See "Chamberlain"

Dutch 'Run Arounds' Foil Nazi Bombers

NEW YORK, May 10.—Edwin Hartrich, Columbia Broadcasting System correspondent in Holland, stated today:

"In The Hague area I saw Messerschmitt planes strafing Dutch mobilized columns on the roads. Hundrews of soldiers were sent out as flying squadrons in high-powered cars equipped with machine guns and automatic rifles. They are taking care of German parachutists and receive their orders from couriers in motor cars.

"And from what I saw this new type of aerial blitzkrieg was being effectively handled by the mobile defense of the Dutch, rolling around the countryside on wheels."

LONDON, May 10.—The Air Ministry today issued a call for volunteers.

Bulletins

BUDAPEST, May 10 (By telephone to New York).—The German invasion of Belgium and the Netherlands was taken in Balkan capitals as a reprieve for southeastern Europe. The Germans closed the German-Hungarian and German-Yugoslav frontiers.

LONDON, May 10.—Thirty-seven persons were killed and 61 wounded in a futile German air attack on the Brussels airdrome district, it was said, in authoritative quarters tonight.

WILLEMSTAD, Netherlands West Indies, May 10. — The governor today proclaimed a State of War against Germany in the territory of Curacoa, a possession of the Netherlands.

LONDON, May 10. — Two Heinkel (German) bombing planes were chased away from the southeast coast of England this afternoon by anti-aircraft fire and British fighter planes.

'These Two Great Empires Cannot Die'

Premier Reynaud today: "We have confidence in our great chief, in our soldiers, in our aviators who are covering themselves with glory. I thank the Royal Air Force." (Applause.) . . . "These two great peoples, two great empires, cannot be defeated, cannot die. If I am told: 'A miracle is needed to save France,' then I believe in miracles because I believe in France."

The Vancouver Sun

Only Evening Newspaper Owned, Controlled and Operated by Vancouver People

FOUNDED 1886
VOL. LIV—No. 197

VANCOUVER, BRITISH COLUMBIA, TUESDAY, MAY 21, 1940

***C Price 3 Cents On Trains, Boats and outside Greater Vancouver, 5c.

MArine 1161

The Weather
Pressure remains high over northern British Columbia, and the weather has been fine and warmer throughout this province.
Temperature at 1.30 p.m. today: 68.0.
Temperature during 24 hours ending 4.30 a.m. today: maximum 68, minimum 44.
Forecast: moderate winds, fair and warmer.
Official weather report on page 20.

Today's Tides
Vancouver Harbor
Low 11.39 a.m. 0.3 feet High 6:45 p.m.: 12.8 feet
English Bay
High 6:28 p.m.: 13.5 feet Low 11:45 p.m.: 8.7 feet
Second Narrows
Low slack 12:06 noon High slack 7:12 p.m.
Tomorrow's tides appear on page 20.

(EDITORIAL)

Are We Organized for Victory.

In France today they are facing realities. Quick punishment is threatened for those who betrayed the republic by negligence. German mechanized armies smashed across the Meuse, crashed their way over much of Northern France. Who is responsible? This Empire shall not die, cries the French premier in great earnestness. France faces a crisis. She is fighting for her very life!

And she, by the side of Britain, will win. But it will take every resource we possess. This war is the job of everybody.

In Canada, the people are roused by the pressure of events. But the people fear that the government, bound by set forms, enjoying an implied confidence because of recent victory at the polls, has not been sufficiently roused by action.

It is a healthy sign—this pressure on our leaders from the country at large. Why not enroll the dominion's man-power in a really great national effort? Give us more evidence of speed-up! These are the demands on Ottawa today.

Mr. King is firmly entrenched in office; there was no alternative to his government on March 26. Today, the whole country is behind him, but the country must have action.

It is a patriotic national effort to be spending two million dollars a day—but is the government set-up adequate to obtain maximum results from the spending of this vast amount of money? Is there an executive committee of the cabinet working day and night to design a pattern for victory?

Victory is the only thing that counts. The politics of Canada's internal situation are dwindling in importance. Ottawa holds the key to organized success and the people of Canada are in a mood to insist that the national ability to united action be put at work without any more delay.

Why Does Canada Not Throw Recruiting WIDE OPEN?

M.P.'s Demand More Action Following Premier King's Speech; C. G. Power Becomes New Air Minister

By NORMAN MacLEOD
Special to The Vancouver Sun

OTTAWA, May 21.—The aftermath of yesterday's debate in the House of Commons found both government and opposition parties facing important problems of shuffles in personnel, while a basic situation of unrest continued throughout the rank and file M.P.'s.

Meanwhile Prime Minister Mackenzie King asked members of the House today to remember "in this, probably one of the darkest hours in the history of the Empire," that the outlook was similarly dark in 1918, but that French and British troops rallied nd won.

In government circles, the following is a condensed summary of the situation:

1. Hon. C. G. Power, at present Postmaster-General, becomes the new Minister of Defense for Air. This was announced by Mr. King today.

2. Col. Colin Gibson, M.P. for Hamilton West, is expected to receive Cabinet appointment, probably as Postmaster-General.

3. Hon. C. D. Howe is to be left to devote his full time to his duties as Minister of Munitions and Supplies, and a new Minister of Transport whose identity is not yet revealed, is to be named.

It may be Thomas Vien, M.P., for Montreal-Outremont.

In the Conservative Opposition, the situation that is uppermost is the movement to draft Rt. Hon. Arthur Meighen into the post of official Opposition Leader in the House of Commons.

Reports are persistent in high Tory circles this morning to the effect that this plan has encountered certain snags and that the prospect of it materializing is now remote in the extreme.

Rank and file Conservatives received these rumors with concern which they made no effort to disguise.

264th Day of The War
News Digest by G.H.S.

Blitzkrieg threw in its psychology technique today to support German spearhead mechanized divisions. Motorcycle forces raced at full speed westward, fanning out as they went, parachute troops dropped among French forces and civilian areas along Somme and loosed terrific air offensive against Allied rear lines.

Berlin tonight claimed Nazi troops had reached English Channel at Abbeville, had bottled up million Allied troops north of Somme, had destroyed French Ninth Army and captured General Giraud and

Please Turn to Page Two
See "War Today"

To return, however, to the general parliamentary situation. Among the rank and file of the government's supporters, and to an even greater extent among the Conservatives, yesterday's speech by the Prime Minister has been noteworthy largely for its failure to still current unrest.

That the grave turn taken by events in Europe has aroused a sudden dissatisfaction among the government no less than among opposition M.P.'s with respect to the administration's war effort, is not to be denied.

And every bag of mail that arrives on Parliament Hill fans the flames of unrest.

Parliamentarians notoriously are no stronger than any wind of public sentiment that happens to blow up, and the past week has witnessed a literal hurricane demand from the citizenship generally for a more spectacular war effort.

Please Turn to Page Eleven
See "Recruiting"

Westminsters Getting Ready

The Westminster Regiment (M.G.) is now on the eve of departure but shows no let-up in work.
Top picture—part of "A" Coy. under Lieut. D. L. Watts and Platoon Sgt. Major Fred Shawcross.
Below, left—Sgt. A. G. Head, veteran of the famed Old Contemptibles.
Right, below—Lieut.-Col. J. E. Sager, officer commanding; Major W. J. Williams and Major A. B. Noble.

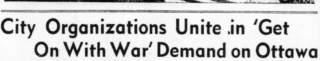

City Organizations Unite in 'Get On With War' Demand on Ottawa

'Can We Finish It Off?'
Bombers Die for Success
By Canadian Press

LONDON, May 21.—This is the story correspondents with the Royal Air Force in France sent back today:

Eight times RAF bombers tried to destroy a German bridge, but failed.

Then the pilots and crews of four bombers went to their commanding officer with the request, "can we finish it off?"

The permission was given.

The four bombers took off.

None returned, but the bridge was destroyed.

$700,000,000 Program Announced by Premier

Canadian Corps in Field; Third Division At Once; Immediate Recruiting; Air Training to Be Speeded
(Detailed report of Mr. King's speech on Page 3.)
By Canadian Press

OTTAWA, May 21.—A $700,000,000 war program involving creation of a Canadian corps in the field, recruitment of a Third Division and early despatch overseas of the Second Division, was outlined in the House of Commons last night by Prime Minister Mackenzie King.

The Prime Minister announced he will ask Parliament for authority to create a new Ministry for Air with supervision over the Commonwealth Air Training Scheme.

'RIGHT OF WAY'

Speaking in the debate on the address in reply to the Speech From the Throne, the Prime Minister urged that government business be given right of way.

He said debate on the address would end Wednesday, so that consideration might be given the war appropriation bill of Hon. J. L. Ralston, Minister of Finance.

War expenditures will now exceed $2,000,000 a day during the current fiscal year, the Prime Minister said, and ordinary expenditures will likewise reach record heights in the current year.

Please Turn to Page Eleven
See "King"

Resolutions Sent to Premier; Plans for Mass Demonstration

Business men, private citizens and veterans, aroused to Canada's need to "Get on With the War," have taken action to let Ottawa know that Vancouver demands a greater and speedier Canadian war effort.

This afternoon the Vancouver Board of Trade called a meeting of business men and heads of returned soldiers' organizations to plan ways and means to speed up Canadian war participation.

"GET INTO WAR PROPERLY"

In Victoria plans are laid for a mass demonstration for a "Get Into the War Properly" movement, to be held at Beacon Hill Park on Sunday.

In Vancouver the Vancouver Zone Council, comprising the five leading veterans' organizations, has been called to hold a special meeting Wednesday night.

A. D. Darlington, secretary of the Zone Council, told The Sun that decision of the council would largely determine veteran participation in any projected mass meeting if one is called for Sunday in some downtown park area.

'FAILING LAMENTABLY'

M. C. Robinson, officer commanding the Fourandex here, told The Sun he believes the telegram crystallizes the growing feeling among Canadians everywhere.

The telegram said:

"This body consists entirely of front-line veterans of the last war, all permanently employed and none looking for benefit from wider war participation, but all imbued with

Please Turn to Page Eleven
See "On With War"

Half-Holiday on Wednesday as Usual

All Vancouver retail stores will be closed on Wednesday afternoon as usual, regardless of the Victoria Day Holiday on Friday. It now takes two statutory full-day holidays to cancel the Wednesday half-holiday.

Sun's Newscast Schedule, CKWX

These are the regular daily news broadcasts by The Vancouver Sun over station CKWX:

CKWX:
7:30 a.m.
12:05 Noon
7:30 p.m.
10:00 p.m.

SOCIAL CREDITER RESIGNS

EDMONTON.—Calculated to provide a seat in the Alberta legislature for Provincial Treasurer Solon Low, the resignation of George Woytkiw, Social Crediter elected in Vegreville in the March 21 election, was received today.

Nazis Turn Full 'Air Fury' Loose On North France

'Red Path of Ruin' in Desperate Drive to Channel; Fierce Fighting at Cambrai

LONDON, May 21.—Alfred Duff Cooper, Minister of Information, told his countrymen tonight that while the present war news is grave, there is "no cause for great alarm."

Acknowledging German success, he declared nevertheless "the armies of Great Britain and France are undefeated.

"As I told you last week, the end of this battle, whatever it may be, cannot entail the defeat of Britain and France," he said.

"These grave events will act, as they have already acted, as a tonic to the nation.

"Through successful employment of a new technique of war, small bodies of the German army have succeeded in penetrating great distances, but they are small bodies only, and the successes that they have achieved, have involved them in fearful danger. Allied armies are in enormously superior numbers."

By RALPH HEINZEN
Special to The Vancouver Sun
(Copyright, 1940, by British United Press)

FRENCH ARMY G.H.Q., May 21.—Germany's vast aerial fleet unleashed all of its fury tonight in a tremendous drive to disorganize the Allied rear lines in Northern France.

French military sources reported that Marshal Hermann Goering's air force, leading German Panzer divisions of tanks and armored cars, had spread a red zone of smoking ruins through Picardy and Flanders.

German parachute soldiers are alleged to have dropped to the ground in considerable numbers with torches to set fire to factories, railroad stations, munitions and fuel dumps in Arras, Amiens and other cities along the path of the German drive toward the English Channel.

Arras and Amiens were occupied by German advance forces today and one small motorcycle unit reached Abbeville, about 16 miles from the English Channel, on the Somme estuary.

'Wild With Destructive Fury'

German bombers are said by the French to be dropping thousands of incendiary bombs on the communications centres and other towns of northern France in addition to their heavy bombing to break a path for motorized units smashing toward the channel.

A French military source said tonight that fighting still is raging furiously in the Cambrai region despite the enemy break-through to Amiens and Arras, and that Generalissimo Maxime Weygand is at the battle front issuing orders designed to correct what Premier Paul Reynaud, before the Senate, described as "incredible faults."

Although the Germans drove through to Amiens and Arras, the military source said, they have not yet been able to consolidate the battle area around Cambrai and heavy engagements are being fought all along the line from Rethel through Lafere to Cambrai.

North of Cambrai a great battle is in progress between the British, whom the Germans had hoped to cut off from the French, and the invaders. The British, the French military source said, are resisting "magnificently."

In the Rethel sector of the "Bulge" front the German offensive failed to dislodge French troops occupying positions on the south bank of the Aisne across from Rethel.

Apparently the Germans have 50,000 to 60,000 troops in their drive to the Channel but huge numbers of Nazi airplanes are leading the way, bombing trains and apparently frustrating any Allied effort to counter-attack.

French dispatches reported that the German air force had "gone wild" with destructive fury and that parachute troops had been dropped to dynamite important communications points and factories.

These dispatches said that a maze of blazing villages dotted the battlefront in the north and that flames are sweeping unchecked in some towns that were once the heart of rich textile, coal and sugar refinery areas.

Hardly a railroad station stands intact tonight in the "Red Zone" area between the Belgian frontier and the French city of Amiens, it was asserted.

The Germans also are reported using 20,000 motorcycle troops to create chaos behind the lines by rushing back and forth on tasks of destruction, co-ordinated with the thrusts of light armored car units.

Germans Using 2500 Tanks

Twenty-five hundred German tanks are now engaged in the valley of the Somme on the drive toward the Channel.

French evacuated Laon, 25 miles south-east of St. Quentin and 80 miles from Paris.

It was from Laon that the Germans in 1918 shelled Paris with their "Big Bertha" gun.

The German advance continues in a north-westerly direction, the army spokesman said, with fighting in the Cambrai-Somme River area and particularly in the Peronne region north-west of St. Quentin.

French troops repulsed three German attacks in the Rethel sector, it was said, and captured small German detachments which crossed the Aisne.

Fresh German assaults in the

Please Turn to Page Eleven
See "Western Front"

Injured by Bomb

'DUKE OF GLOUCESTER'

LONDON, May 21.—The Duke of Gloucester, brother of the King, was reported tonight to be suffering from cuts caused by aerial bomb explosions on the Franco-Belgian front. Both hands also are badly bruised.

For three successive nights the Duke was in areas which were heavily bombed. He has now returned to London.

Last September the Duke, a Major-General, was appointed chief liaison officer to the British field forces in France.

(The Duke, then Prince Henry, was injured in a polo accident at Brighouse Park, Vancouver, June 4, 1929. His pony slipped, throwing him on his right shoulder, breaking the collar bone. The Duke was confined to his hotel until June 15.)

Albania Closes Jugoslav Border

SKOPLJE, Jugoslavia, May 21.—The frontier between Jugoslavia and Italian-held Albania was closed late today by Italian order.

Reports filtering across the frontier to Jugoslavia military quarters here said the Italian army had speeded up transport of large quantities of war materials across the Adriatic to the Albanian port of Durazzo.

It is said that barracks, storehouses and arsenals are being built on 24-hour shifts.

10,000 Navy Planes

WASHINGTON, May 21.—Naval air armada of 10,000 planes and 16,000 pilots was proposed in legislation introduced late today in Congress. Maj.Gen. H. H. Arnold, chief of the army air corps, announced the total 50,000-plan U.S. program would cost $7,000,000,000. He suggested calling on the automobile industry to help production.

Map, Page 24

To enable you to follow the swift war moves over Northern France, The Sun today publishes a map on page 24 giving cities and rivers which are in today's news.

Full Results and Pictures of Sun Marathon on Pages 22-23

The Weather

Pressure remains high over northern British Columbia, and the weather has been fair and warm in all parts of this province.
Temperature at 1:30 p.m. today: 60.
Temperature during 24 hours ending 4:30 a.m. today: maximum 72, minimum 52.
Forecast: cloudy and cool with showers.
Official weather report on page 18.

The Vancouver Sun

Only Evening Newspaper Owned Controlled and Operated by Vancouver People

Today's Tides

Vancouver Harbor
High 1:16 p.m.; 8.0 feet   Low 6:26 p.m.; 6.0 feet
English Bay
High 1:10 p.m.; 8.8 feet   Low 6:10 p.m.; 6.0 feet
First Narrows
High slack 1:51 p.m.   Low slack 6:54 p.m.
Tomorrow's tides appear on page 18.

FOUNDED 1886
VOL. LIV—No. 205

VANCOUVER, BRITISH COLUMBIA, THURSDAY, MAY 30, 1940

***C   Price 3 Cents   On Trains, Boats and outside Greater Vancouver, 5c.   MArine 1161

Allies Escape, Units Reach England

Tory Drive Designed to Oust King

Move to Promote Ralston 'Price of Full War Support' But 'It Will Fail'; Cabinet With Prime Minister

(See Additional Story of Page 2)

By BRUCE HUTCHISON

OTTAWA, May 30.—The Conservative Party has launched a drive for the removal of Premier King and his replacement by Hon. J. L. Ralston, now Minister of Finance.

The Prime Minister's political head apparently is the price of full Conservative support to the present government's war program.

This manoeuvre has broken out into the open in both Houses of Parliament, obviously by arrangement. In Commons, Conservative members demanded Colonel Ralston's elevation.

In the Senate Rt. Hon. Arthur Meighen cut loose with a fierce attack on the government's management of the war and a demand that Mr. King retire in favor of one of his colleagues, obviously the Finance Minister.

WHOLE CABINET SAYS "NO!"

The reply of the Liberal Party through Senator Dandurand, Liberal leader in the Senate, is that if Mr. King goes the government goes.

His Ministers will stand or fall with him.

But at the moment this is all shadowboxing, for Mr. King commands the largest majority in the history of Parliament.

Nevertheless the Canadian people's demand for action has created a tense situation here.

'BOMBARDED' FROM HOME

The pressure on the government is not directly from Parliament but from the people.

The Liberal Party is satisfied that the government is doing now everything humanly possible in the prosecution of the war, but every member is constantly bombarded from home by demands for more action.

He, in turn, demands more action from the government.

In the last few days he has been getting it.

PUBLIC DOESN'T UNDERSTAND

But it is evident now that the people of Canada as a whole have not fully understood, the pattern of the war or the war problem of Canada.

THE PROBLEM TODAY IS NOT THAT OF ENLISTING SOLDIERS BUT OF GETTING MACHINES.

IT IS NOT A MILITARY PROBLEM BUT AN INDUSTRIAL PROBLEM.

IF ANYTHING IS CLEAR FROM THE DISASTER OF BELGIUM, IT IS THAT WHAT THE ALLIES NEED TODAY IS NOT MEN BUT MACHINERY.

Wants Planes, Not Men

It is undoubtedly true that Britain would rather get a few airplanes or tanks from this country than regiments of unequipped infantry.

It is also true in the wholly changed war situation of the last week that Canada must equip its own army from now on and we can not expect Britain to do it.

Thus while the public seems to visualize a real war effort as the enlistment of a large army, the actual job of the government, now fully recognized for the first time, is to get factories established, new processes under way, new war machinery coming off the assembly lines. That is a problem infinitely complex.

JOB REALLY INDUSTRIAL

Thus the question to be faced frankly by the Canadian people today is not whether Mr. King is enlisting enough men but whether he is capable of carrying out the greatest reorganization of industry that the country has ever attempted, something far beyond anything we have dreamed of in the past.

This correspondent has talked to many Liberal members and not one of them believes that Colonel Ralston could do a better job than Mr. King.

HASN'T APPEARED YET

Nor, one can say with absolute certainty, does Colonel Ralston think he could.

It is true, of course, that if there were any man obviously better equipped than Mr. King he would succeed to the Premiership immediately in a situation like this.

No questions of loyalty, party service or seniority would count for a moment.

But if there is in Canada a man better equipped—and there may be—he has not appeared yet.

Must Be Improved

This does not mean that the government cannot be improved.

It will have to be improved.

It will have to be improved not only in the interests of better administration but in the interests of national morale.

Something will have to be done as a symbol of our increasing purpose and determination in this war.

24 Mr. King is too able a statesman not to know that and one may look for some important moves during the next few weeks.

If he had ever thought of taking in some Conservatives like Senator Meighen, that idea evidently has been eliminated by the Conservatives' new attacks on him.

MAY SET UP WAR COUNCIL

There is still the possibility that he will go outside politics altogether and draft a group of leading industrialists to form a kind of war management committee, just as President Roosevelt has done in the management of his rearmament program.

This process in part already is under way.

The government, having revised its conception of the war, is taking much more drastic steps than the public has yet realized.

In the air service, Hon. C. G. Power, the new Minister for Air Defense, today completed a far-reaching shakeup of his administrative organization.

Air Commander L. S. Breadner replaces Air Vice-Marshal Croil as the commander of the Air Force. Air Vice-Marshal Croil becomes Inspector General.

CALLS ON BUSINESS MEN

At the same time Mr. Power today summoned to Ottawa a group of outstanding business men to assist James Duncan, the deputy Minister, who also was

Please Turn to Page Twelve
See "Bruce Hutchison"

'BRIDE OF 1940'—

With this edition is presented a special section of interest to brides. "It's your day!"

It is chock-full of ideas, and a special chart tells "What to Wear."

"Bridal fashions turn back to Victorian days this year. . . ."

Officers Named to High Posts

Two Vancouver officers have been appointed to high positions in the newly organized Second Division, CASF, according to Ottawa announcement today.

On the left is Major H. A. R. Francis, former Brigade Major, Vancouver and Fraser Valley area, who is to be Deputy Assistant Quartermaster-General. He will leave at once to take up his duties.

Lt.-Col. J. P. Mackenzie, D.S.O., V.D. (right), has been named commander, Second Divisional Engineers. Lt.-Col. Mackenzie served with distinction in the first Great War and since the war has taken an active part in local militia affairs. He has been general manager of Hamilton Bridge Company (Western) Limited, here.

Gen. Odlum Appoints Three B.C. Men to Second Division Posts

Lieut.-Col. Mackenzie Commands Engineers; Major Francis Named to Staff

By Canadian Press

OTTAWA, May 30.—Appointments of 20 officers to senior staff and command posts in the Second Division, Canadian Active Service Force, under Major-General Victor W. Odlum of Vancouver, divisional commander, were announced today by Hon. Norman Rogers, Defense Minister.

Mr. Rogers said an effort has been made to give representation to all parts of the Dominion.

ODLUM IN OTTAWA

Both permanent force and the non-permanent active militia were drawn upon and a majority of the officers chosen saw extensive service in the last war. A number, including General Odlum, rose from the ranks.

General Odlum returned to Ottawa from Vancouver by air today and is proceeding at once with the organization and assembly of his staff.

SUMMER CAMPS

The division's units are now moving into summer camps for more advanced training prior to their departure overseas. Recently Prime Minister Mackenzie King announced the division's movement overseas would be expedited.

The appointments follow:

Commander, Second Divisional Engineers, Lt.-Col. J. P. Mackenzie, D.S.O., V.D., Vancouver.

Commander, Sixth Infantry Brigade, Col. D. R. Sargent, Nanaimo.

Deputy Assistant Quartermaster General, Major H. A. Francis, E.D., Vancouver.

Commander Second Divisional Artillery, Brigadier R. A. Fraser, V.D., Montreal.

Please Turn to Page Twelve
See "Appointments"

273rd Day of The War

News Digest by G.H.S.

British and French armies in Flanders fought their way back to the English Channel coast, there to establish delaying line paralleling coast, under screen of blistering barrage from Allied warships, and from air. British still hold their main base depots, while French have strongly fortified lines around Dunkirk.

This front protects withdrawal by sea of British and French forces. Covering establishment of these temporary lines, British long front reaching toward Bruges from Dunkirk, French St. Omer and Cassel, have fought rearguard battle of savagery and intensity that will mark it as one of most valiant in history.

Germans have flung 40 divisions, about 500,000, including major part of 10 mechanized divisions, at them in almost frantic effort to cut them off and break them up, thus to destroy them. In face of this they have by miracle of generalship and epic heroism kept their lines connected, formed steel-walled lane for retreat. Allied navies and air forces form extra shield, not only for land forces, reaching inland 20

Please Turn to Page Twelve
See "War Today"

Shaw Triumphs in 500-Mile Classic

INDIANAPOLIS, Ind., May 30. Little Wilbur Shaw, a home-town boy, won the Indianapolis 500-mile motor marathon for a second successive time today for the only consecutive victories in history, but rain which fell on the great track during the last 125 miles spoiled his chance for a record run.

Rex Mays of Glendale, Calif., was second, 2½ miles behind. The race was stopped then, and the 19 remaining drivers given the positions they held then.

Shaw covered the distance in 4:33:31.16 to verage 114.277 miles an hour.

Three cars crashed during the race, but only one driver, Paul Rignati, was injured.

3 Destroyers Lost in Fight To Save Army

Admiralty Says German Claims Exaggerated

By Canadian Press

LONDON, May 30.—The Admiralty announced tonight that the destroyers Grafton, Grenade and Wakeful had been lost.

One small transport, the Abukir, 689 tons, also was sunk. Certain auxiliary vessels also were said to be lost in actions covering withdrawals of troops from France and Belgium.

The Admiralty statement said:

"The Royal Navy has been and is giving all possible help and support to British and French land forces which are operating in the vicinity of French and Belgian coasts under enemy pressure.

"Warships are giving support and covering fire to the troops impeding the enemy's movements and have inflicted considerable punishment upon the German advanced forces.

"Wounded and a large number of other elements have already been safely withdrawn.

DAY AND NIGHT

"These operations are being conducted ceaselessly by day and night with coolness and determination in face of fierce opposition particularly from the air.

"The German High Command has claimed to have inflicted very

Please Turn to Page Twelve
See "Destroyers"

'Your Turn Next'

RAF Flier Disagrees With Nazi Firing Squad—Escapes

By Canadian Press

LONDON, May 30. — The Air Ministry today issued an account of how a Royal Air Force pilot captured by the Germans, was threatened with death but escaped and returned to the Allied armies. The Ministry said:

"A fighter pilot, who landed his damaged plane in German-held territory, was arrested and taken to a small courtyard crowded with Belgian civilians. At hourly intervals groups of civilians were ordered out, summarily questioned and shot.

"A German officer in charge of the firing squad told the pilot, 'It will be your turn next.'

The pilot protested that he was an officer in uniform who had come down behind the German lines as a result of aerial combat.

"The officer shrugged and replied, 'You are a spy like al these others.'

"Waiting until a new group of civilians, going to face the firing squad afforded the cover of momentary confusion, he did a flying leap straight through a small closed window and, with only a slight cut on the cheek, landed on all fours outside, dashed through the garden and got clear away. Not one shot was fired by the surprised Germans.

"He slept on top of a haystack and the next day mingled with refugees and was given a lift in a Dutch car.

"On the afternoon of the second day he got over the border and reached Lille"

500,000 Germans Fail to Smash Epic Flanders Retreat

War-Worn Troops From Flanders' Battle Reach England

LONDON, May 30.—Thousands of first arrivals from the Flanders battleground reached England tonight in warships, transports and hospital ships — their uniforms torn and their faces grimy, bearded and powder-burned.

The Ministry of Information announced "troops not immediately engaged have been evacuated," and "numbers of troops already have reached this country."

The announcement said that the action was taken in view of increased German pressure and that the battle on the coast is "now raging."

TEXT OF STATEMENT

Text of the announcement follows:

"In view of the increased German pressure on their northern and southern flanks the British Expeditionary Force and French forces in the north have been forced to fall back towards the coast where the battle is now raging.

"This operation has been carried out with great skill and daring. Troops not immediately engaged have been evacuated with the assistance of the royal navy.

"This operation is proceeding with success and numbers of troops have already reached the country.

"The withdrawal and evacuation have been screened by the Royal Air Force who have been constantly engaged with the enemy. Over 70 enemy aircraft were destroyed and many others were damaged yesterday on this front.

Meanwhile the "grim struggle goes on," it was said.

Powder-begrimed and blood-stained veterans of the 20-day campaign told in tired voices tonight of "terrific German losses" as they escaped to this haven in Britain.

WAR-WEARY MEN

Thousands of these war-weary troops came ashore as the Allies withdrew their forces from the country surrounding and protecting certain Channel ports of the continent from German invaders.

They came in warships and transports, and their wounded

Please Turn to Page Twelve
See "BEF"

New Zealand Plans To Mobilize All People, Resources

By Canadian Press

WELLINGTON, May 30. — An "all in" war effort for New Zealand was outlined as Parliament opened today with the introduction of an Emergency Powers Bill and Prime Minister Peter Fraser renewed his efforts to obtain the co-operation of the Opposition in the proposed War Council.

The Emergency Regulations Amendment Bill provides that all persons should place themselves, their property and services at the disposal of the Governor-General.

The Speech from the Throne announced that more than 53,000 men had volunteered for overseas service and that more than 32,000 had been accepted.

It said New Zealand would provide 3000 airplane pilots a year and contribute £2,000,000 ($8,900,000) over a three-year period to the Empire Air Training Scheme.

PARIS, May 30.—French officials said tonight that Gen. Maurice Gamelin, former Commader-in-Chief of the Allied armies in France, is in Paris.

WELLINGTON, May 30. — Prime Minister Fraser announced tonight that immediate provision for compulsory military service is being planned in New Zealand.

Warships Lay 'Curtain of Fire' Between British and French Forces And Onrush of Nazi Invaders

PARIS, May 30.—Two divisions of a trapped French army under Gen. Rene Prioux were reported officially today to have fought their way through powerful German lines and to have occupied defense positions at Dunkirk on the English Channel coast.

The Prioux army, in co-operation with British forces, has been fighting to cut a path through the German trap around Allied armies in the north for several days, and this morning French sources said 40 German divisions—around 500,000 men—had been thrown at the Allied troops pocketed between the coast and the city of Lille.

The official French spokesman late afternoon said the situation is critical but that most of the Allied army had succeeded in escaping a trap which the Germans sought to close between Poperinghe and Cassell, south of Dunkirk.

The British Army, fighting every step of the way, with enemies on three sides, also made progress during the night. Some British units are reported to have reached England after embarking at Dunkirk.

Air Armada Bombs Dunkirk

The number of French forces involved and the number which escaped was not definitely known. The spokesman said they are now approaching the coast, continuing their retreat to defense positions prepared in advance.

This presumably would put them near Dunkirk, which is under constant tremendous bombardment by an estimated 600 to 1000 German airplanes attempting to break up evacuation of Allied forces by sea.

"The situation is still critical and it cannot be said that it has improved," the spokesman said, "but it is not worse despite the enormous German effort."

Fronts along the Somme, Aisne and Rhine rivers were described as calm, but in the north the most terrible conflict of the war had reached its climax.

A spokesman said the fortified Allied camp established at Dunkirk was more strongly attacked today. The Allied positions, however, are being effectively protected by the floods resulting from the opening of Yser River sluice gates, he said.

Yser Floods Help Allies

Fighting gathered momentum during the day. Furiously launced Nazi drives succeeded in making some infiltrations but failed in their primary purpose—to cut the Allied army in two by capturing the "Mountain Line" running from Cassel to Ypres, a French military spokesman said.

Simultaneous German attacks designed to choke off the line of Allied retreat midway between Lille and Dunkirk were launched from the southeast and northwest.

The spokesman here said the Germans were stopped in the northern sector, along the Yser river. The Nazis won a foothold on Mount Cassel, but were turned back when they attempted to drive a deeper wedge into the Allied lines.

Most of the Allied units protecting the flanks of the retreat are British troops. Under their protection, the remainder of the Allied forces, deep in the Flanders pocket, are methodically withdrawing under the plan being carried out by General Rene Prioux.

Fighting vigorous rearguard and flank actions as they move, the British and French forces receive effective aid from their low-flying aircraft.

The gradual compression of the fronts is compensating for the loss of half the Allied effectiveness by the surrender of King Leopold. British troops now heroically stemming the German tide along the Yser river and canal are doing, it was emphasized here, what King Leopold refused to undertake.

The Flanders battleground is described here as a huge funnel, with its axis roughly traced by the line between Lille and Dunkirk. The latter port, although under terrific punishment, is still solidly in Allied hands following defeat of a direct push attempted yesterday by German motorized units from the southwest.

The sides of the funnel are solidly lined by Allied troops, most of them British, forming a double and widening lane through which others were methodically withdrawing northwestward to the coast.

Allies Defend 'Mountain Line'

Northeastward the line is drawn roughly between Nieuport and Ypres, then southwestward between Gravelines and Cassel.

In reality the "Mountain Line" between Cassel and Ypres consists of nothing more than a series of low-lying hills which, however, stand out sharply against the surrounding Flanders plain. They afford excellent positions and their capture by the Germans would tightly bottle up the Allied-divisions still in the southern reaches of the Flanders pocket.

Realizing this, the Nazis attempted a northeastward push from St. Omer toward Cassel. Motorized units meanwhile attempted a secondary diversion movement directly against Dunkirk, but succeeded only in gaining a foothold on Mount Cassel, westernmost of the Flemish hills.

What few infiltrations the Germans succeeded in making were accomplished to the southeast of the "Mountain Line." The gains were not appreciable, however, and the main body of the French force under General Prioux is steadily making its way to the coast.

The military spokesman emphasized that there has been no surrender of any troops. Fighting day and night without respite, they are helped from the air by waves of Allied planes.

R.A.F. PRAISED

Royal Air Force squadrons operating from bases in Eng-

Please Turn to Page Twelve
See "Western Front"

Italy to Keep Pledge

LONDON, May 30. —Great Britain's relations with Italy are believed to have taken a turn for the worse tonight after Fascist Premier Benito Mussolini was reported to have advised President Roosevelt that Italy intends to keep her pledge to Germany.

Informed sources say Mussolini vetoed a proposed agreement alleviating effects of the Allied blockade on Italy. Predictions here are that Italy will enter the war on the side of Germany before the end of next week.

Berlin Says French Armistice Treaty Signed

The Weathe.

A disturbance is approaching Queen Charlotte Islands from westward. The weather has been fair and moderately warm throughout the province.
Temperature at 1:30 p.m. today: 65.8.
Temperature during 24 hours ending 4.30 a.m. today: Maximum 67, minimum 47.
Forecast: Fair and warm.
Official weather report on Page 23.

The Sunday Sun

Only Evening Newspaper Owned, Controlled and Operated by Vancouver People

Today's Tides
Vancouver Harbor
Low 1:21 p.m., 0.5 feet. High 8.38 p.m., 13.4 feet.
English Bay
Low 12.52 p.m., 1.1 feet. High 8.25 p.m., 14.0 feet.
First Narrows
Low slack 1:50 p.m. High slack 9.13 p.m.
Tomorrow's and Monday's tides appear on page 23.

FOUNDED 1886
VOL. LIV—No. 225

VANCOUVER, BRITISH COLUMBIA, SATURDAY, JUNE 22, 1940 *** Price 10 Cents MArine 1161

RAF Bombs Scharnhorst; Raids Berlin

British Fighters and Gunfire Drive Off Nazi Night Fliers; Italian Sub Yields to Minesweeper

Intensified aerial and naval warfare featured on all fronts of the far-flung European battle zone today and culminated in a nine-hour sea and air battle between British fliers and submarines and the Nazi battle cruiser Scharnhorst and her escort in the North Sea. Three heavy bomb hits were registered on the Scharnhorst's deck and she was further damaged by a submarine torpedo.

Other activities included:

1—RAF bombs Berlin, 'marring' Nazi celebration of French defeat, also Krupp works at Essen.

2—Germans driven off in mass raids on England: three killed; Germans adopt 'hit and run' bombing tactics, not stopping to search for objectives.

3—Italians make futile raid on Allied fleet in Alexandria; no warships hit; six civilians killed.

4—A large Italian submarine surrendered to a British minesweeper.

5—British fliers sink 2 German ships in raid on Willemsoord, Dutch naval base, and sink German destroyer and supply ship in North Sea.

Ready for 'Battle of Britain

—A. P. Wirephoto

LONDON.—Prime Minister Churchill, grim and determined, is shown at No. 10 Downing Street after a conference concerning developments in France. Expressing confidence in Britain's ability to defend herself, the Prime Minister declared this week that the "Battle of France" had ended and the "Battle of Britain" had already begun.

Britain Gets Navy Of France

Admirals Join in Ruse Of 'Friendly Kidnap' Arrangement

By Associated Press

WASHINGTON, June 22.—Great Britain has taken over the bulk of the French fleet intact, authoritative sources in the capital heard today. Thus the British navy, most powerful in the world probably has been augmented by the addition of 8 battleships 21 cruisers, 71 destroyers and about 100 submarines.

NAZI CLAIMS DENIED

The New York Herald says today:

"Details are not available as to how the British managed to acquire the French fleet, but presumably it was a 'friendly kidnapping" arranged with the consent of the French admirals.

"German claims that they had captured the new 35-000-ton French battleships Richelieu and Clemenceau at Brest when the Nazis entered that Atlantic seaport were contradicted by the information reaching Washington officials.

"The Germans, it was said, captured only twisted, scorched metal and other debris in the Brest naval yards, as the French, unable to tow away the uncompleted capital ships, had blown them up before retreating from the German invaders."

Reuter's News Agency, in a despatch from Istanbul, said today six French tankers anchored there, have been transferred to British ownership

Pact Ineffective Until France and Italy Also Agree

French Troops Retake Bellegarde in Swiss Frontier Region

By Associated Press

CHANCY, Swiss-French Frontier, June 22.—French sources reported today the French defenders of L'Ecluse fort, near Bellegarde, not only repulsed an attack on the mountain citadel early this afternoon, but drove the Germans out of the town of Bellegarde, five miles away.

DYNAMITE RAILWAY

The guns of the big fort defending the Rhone River gorges and the junction of the Lower Jura with the Alpine foothills below the Italian front were silent in mid-afternoon for the fist time since early morning.

Refugees said the French regained possession of Bellegarde.

The French dynamited the railroad south of Bellegade to prevent an attack north along the Rhone.

Powerful German motorized forces, backed by artillery and supported by bombers, were reported to have captured Bellegarde hours earlier, and were attacking fort L'Ecluse — called the "Gibraltar of the Rhone."

ROCK FORTRESS

L'Ecluse fort is carved out of rock beside the winding highway between the Swiss frontier and the town of Bellegrade.

It dominates the Rhone gorges and rises 1000 feet above sea level. The French call it the Guardian of the Northern entrance of the Alpine frontier with Italy.

Frontier guards on the Swiss side of the Chancy bridge over the Rhone, 10 miles from the town of Bellegrade and five miles from the L'Ecluse fort, heard artillery fire, air bombs and other sounds of battle from Bellegrade.

Refugees later reported the Germans stormed and captured Bellegrade, where the Rhone river vanishes under rock, drops about 30 feet and emerges in a narrow gorge.

Plenipotentiaries Flying to Rome for Conference on Premier Mussolini's Armistice Requirements

LONDON, June 22.—French radio in a broadcast intercepted here, said France had made "some counter proposals" to the German armistice terms.

The same broadcast quoted tonight's French army bulletin as saying that in the Alps region Italians had carried out attacks on several points and were repulsed.

One hundred members of the French Senate met in Bordeaux this evening, the radio added, and voted confidence in Premier Marshal Petain.

NEW YORK, June 22.—A French-German armistice, to become effective six hours after conclusion of a similar agreement between France and Italy, was signed at 6:30 p.m. today (8:50 a.m. Vancouver time), Columbia Broadcasting System and the National Broadcasting Company reported in a joint broadcast from Compiegne Forest. (The report, officially announced in Berlin, was not confirmed at Bordeaux.)

In a special broadcast William A. Shirer, Columbia reporter, said that after signing with Germany the French plenipotentiaries prepared to leave for Rome to negotiate with Italy.

Unconfirmed reports in London said Germany's armistice terms to France included a German-Italian occupation of France until the end of the war with Britain.

Other items, according to these unconfirmed reports: Cession to Germany of the French provinces of Alsace and Lorraine. Surrender of France's war stores, gold, foreign currency reserves, coal and other deliveries in kind over a fixed period.

According to the radio announcers the armistice was signed in the same dining car in which the 1918 armistice was signed and in which Hitler, from the chair occupied by Marshal Ferdinand Foch 22 years ago, handed his terms to the French delegates yesterday.

Col. General Keitel (Chief of the German High Command) signed for Germany, and General Huntziger signed for France.

(DNB Germany news agency carried this official statement: "The High Command announces: June 22, at 6:50 p.m. (German summer time) a German-French armistice was signed in Compiegne Forest.

"The armistice, however, is not effective until six hours after conclusion of the French-Italian armistice.").

Shirer's Eyewitness Story

Shirer said:

"The Armistice has been signed. The Armistice between France and Germany was signed exactly at 6:50 German summer time, that is, one hour and 25 minutes ago on this 22nd day of June, 1940, and it was signed here in the same old railroad coach in the middle of Compiegne Forest where the Armistice of November 11, 1918, was concluded.

"We are standing now about 35 yards from that historic railroad car. We have been keeping watch here since Adolf Hitler opened the Armistice negotiations here at 3:30 yesterday afternoon.

"These negotiations have been going very fast. Faster than in 1918 when it took three days before the Germans could write their names under the terms of the Armistice offered by Marshal Foch.

"Well now, the Armistice, although signed on the dotted line by the French and the Germans, does not go into effect yet. We have just been informed that the French delegation, which has just signed the Armistice with the Germans here, is leaving by special plane for Italy.

"They should arrive there this evening or tomorrow and then Italy will lay down Armistice terms for ceasing its war with France.

"The talks in Italy are expected to take at least as long as those here and then the procedure will be like this:

"As soon as the French and Italians sign their Armistice the news will be flashed to the Germans. They in turn will immediately inform the French government at Bordeaux or wherever it is, by wire or telephone. And then, six hours after this, six hours after the Germans inform the French government at Bordeaux that Italy and France have signed the Armistice, then the fighting stops. The guns cease fire, the airplanes come down, the blood letting of war is at an end.

"Thus will end the war between Germany and Italy on the one hand and France on the other. The war with Britain, of course, goes on."

Nazis Driven From Britain

By Canadian Press

LONDON, June 22.—Waves of German warplanes swooped over Britain early today for the third time in four days, scattered bombs along the East Coast and killed three civilians before they were driven out to sea.

Fierce anti-aircraft fire and quick action of Royal Air Force fighter planes appeared to have scattered the raiders and prevented them from concentrating on any objective. Numerous fires reddened the sky, but the Air Ministry said the damage was not extensive.

One eyewitness said the Germans had resorted to "hit and run" tactics.

COME IN NIGHT

Following the procedure adopted earlier in the week, the Nazi bombers began their attack shortly after midnight, and the thunder of bomb explosions and the boom of anti-aircraft fire echoed along the coast until just before dawn.

Many residents along the southeast, east and northeast shores spent most of the night in air raid shelters.

The three victims were a man, his wife and a servant, who took refuge in the garden of their home in a Suffolk town. The bomb which killed them partly demolished a nearby house. Three others were reported wounded.

One man who saw a blinding flash in the sky said he thought one enemy plane had been shot down, but the report was not immediately confirmed.

One salvo of bombs struck a lumber yard in an east coast town with a series of ear-splitting explosions that shook buildings three miles away.

In one northeastern area the Germans planes attacked in relays for more than two hours. Farther inland explosions occurred intermittently as searchlights stabbed the sky in an effort to locate a high-flying bomber.

Many of the bombs fell into open fields, in one area a series of bombs fell so wide of any mark that it was believed they had been jettisoned by an enemy plane attempting to outrun pursuing British Spitfires.

Residents of one bombed town said the raiders "didn't waste much time in searching for targets of military or industrial importance."

"They were met with terrific anti-aircraft fire," he said, "and left hurriedly after dropping a few bombs. Those that fell in our district merely made craters in fields near a housing estate."

Today's casualties brought to 21 the number of persons killed in Britain this week by German air raiders. Twelve were killed and 30 wounded early Tuesday morning, and six were killed and 60 wounded the following day.

Thursday night and Friday morning there was a respite from the raids.

RAF ON JOB

Reports from the attacked areas said that as soon as the ominous drone of the Nazi craft became audible, their motors were drowned out by speedy British fighters darting into the skies to the attack.

Flares were dropped at intervals for more than an hour in one southeastern section.

Searchlight beams cut patterns into the darkness wherever the drone of motors was heard.

The sound of heavy explosions came repeatedly.

The German planes apparently fanned out before reaching the English coast and spread over an extensive area.

Farther to the north, more waves of German craft swept across the coast and ran into a thunderous fire of machine-gun bullets and anti-aircraft shells.

The British Broadcasting Corporation temporarily shut off its dramatic programs at about 10:45 p.m. "in the interests of national security."

They were resumed with decreased power about 15 minutes later.

Shortwave broadcasts were not interrupted.

Four Italian Planes Shot Down by Warships

Raiders Fail to Damage Allied Fleet in Bombing Attack on Alexandria

By Associated Press

ALEXANDRIA, Egypt, June 22.—The Italian air force renewed its attempt to bomb the Allied war fleet this afternoon. Anti-aircraft guns shot down one of the bombers and drove the others off. The air raid alarm lasted five

BOMB WATERFRONT

The fleet's guns joined coastal batteries in a terrific bombardment of the enemy squadron. Then one Italian bomber fell flaming into the harbor.

Three Italian planes were shot down in the earlier bombing raids. The planes attacked the port but failed to hit warships; then spread bombs over the city' seafront.

No warships were hit in any of the raids and most of the bombs fell harmlessly into the sea.

Anti-aircraft guns of the British and French fleets went into action when the first group of tri-motored bombers appeared at 1:15 a.m. and British fighter planes went up.

(This dispatch indicated that at least part of the French fleet, whose whereabouts have been unreported since France requested an armistice with Germany and Italy, is still co-operating with the British navy and is based beside British warships in Alexandria.)

THREE RAIDER WAVES

The Italians dropped a score of bombs in three appearances. One struck an Arab home near Moharrem Bay and others demolished three homes at Chatby Beach, half-a-mile from the centre of the city.

A British naval communique later said two persons were killed and 23 injured. The injured included two Italians.

LONDON.—The American Red Cross has presented £100,000 (about $445,000) to the British Red Cross and St. John Ambulance organization.

High School Results

Detailed pass lists from the city's high schools are announced today. Names appear on page 9.

PEACE CAR

French and German negotiators, meeting to discuss peace terms, gathered in the same railway car top) in which Marshal Foch dictated the armistice terms of 1918. Adolf Hitler, who insisted on use of the same car, is shown below with Col.-Gen. Wilhelm Keitel (left) and Col.-Gen. Walther von Brauchitsch.

A Don Quixote Over England

Enemy Flier Spends His Valor In Dashing Tilt With Haystack

By D. E. BURRITT
Canadian Press Staff Writer

LONDON, June 22. — One German bomber streaked away from his flight today to "press home the attack" on what he apparently took to be an airport.

He swooped low, dropped a salvo of incendiary and explosive bombs, and zoomed away. A fierce blaze lighted the sky and the invader circled back and dropped a second load. The fire spread.

Apparently he thought, "I'm sure giving them hell." He came still again, firing tracer bullets this time as a blinking farmer and his family watched from an air raid shelter.

Came daylight and the farmer went into the fields to discover the charred remnants of his hay stacks and burned fields. That was the total damage.

At another point on the east coast an incendiary bomb fell through a roof and landed on the bed of an 82-year-old woman who calmly smothered the bomb in blankets and then put in a call for an air raid warden who found her at a table playing patience.

War News On Sun Radio Sunday

The public will be again kept informed of war developments this week-end by The Vancouver Sun's broadcasts over CKWX.

Times for Sunday broadcasts are:

10:45 a.m.
12:30 (noon).
5:00 p.m.
10 p.m.

WINDSORS GO TO MADRID

BARCELONA, Spain. — The Duke anad Duchess of Windsor left here today for Madrid.

French Official Statement

A communique, issued by Minister of Interior Charles Pomaret, indicated that considerable delay was likely before an agreement, if any, to stop fighting can be reached, and that it would be necessary to know and agree on Italy's terms as well as those presented by Adolf Hitler.

Pomaret was asked by reporters to give his personal opinion after reading the communique.

"You need only look at my face," he replied.

He was smiling.

Pomaret gave out the following communique in the name of the French Government:

"The Cabinet deliberated during a large part of the morning and the beginning of the afternoon on texts handed over last night by Gen. Von Keitel to the French plenipotentiaries.

"New Cabinet meetings may be expected before a general arrangement can be reached.

"The negotiations must continue and first of all be brought to a conclusion with the German delegation. Then the French

Please Turn to Page Fifteen
See "France"

296th Day of The War

News Digest and Week's Review on Page 4

This Is a Vancouver-Owned Newspaper

FOR VICTORY!

News-Herald

Largest Morning Circulation West of Toronto

VANCOUVER, B. C., TUESDAY, AUGUST 6, 1940

MAYOR HOUDE IS INTERNED BY RCMP

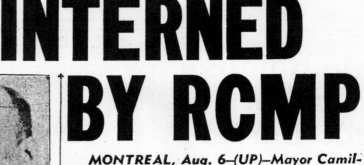

MAYOR HOUDE

First Glance

Perhaps the key to the German offensive against Britain is not to be found in reports from Berlin, Norway or Stockholm but from Rome and Cairo.

This morning despatches from Cairo and from Rome seem to agree that an Axis offensive against Egypt and the Suez Canal zone is imminent. Naturally this arouses speculation as to whether it is timed for the start of the attack on Britain.

The cable from Cairo leaves no doubt but that the British believe that Mussolini is about to embark on a desperate bid to take over control of the Eastern Mediterranean. This is in part confirmed by the Italian command communique which vaguely details the preparations for a possible offensive.

Private advices from neutral quarters for some time have suggested that Hitler has long urged upon Mussolini the need for decisive action in the Mediterranean. Some commentators have suggested that the Germans have been angered and disappointed by the failure of the Italians at sea and the slowness with which they went into action against the British.

Il Duce's Failure

Il Duce so far has not only failed to make any headway against British lines but he has also so far failed to secure control of the Mediterranean that his own supply lines to Libya have been menaced by British air and sea action. Meanwhile at the western gate, Gibraltar still stands.

Strengthening reports of impending action in the Near East was the intimation from reliable sources in Rome that enquiries had been directed to Turkey as to its future attitude in the Balkans. Turkey is the most important Moslem nation in the Near East and might have something to say if Egypt, also predominantly Moslem, were subjected to direct attack.

In Western Europe, the R.A.F. carried the war across the channel to Nazi bases on the French coast and into Germany's great Ruhr valley. There were some sporadic raids on Britain with reports of one large explosion in southeast England but the communiques reported only "negligible damage."

Radios Shut Down

Of the Nazi concentrations in Norway reported from Stockholm there was no more word. The Nazis flew a plane-load of U. S. correspondents to one of their bases on the channel coast but the stories that they permitted the newspapermen to file contained no useful information.

Some quarters attached significance to a German broadcast heard in New York stating that all German radios would go off the air until early this morning. Reasons for the shutdown given Nazi listeners was that "technical adjustments" were necessary.

From Paris via Berlin came reports that the French civil authorities there asked the population for "self-imposed food rationing." This, of course, only confirms what we already know that famine is tightening its grip on Europe.

Thus does the benevolence of German conquest manifest itself to a conquered people.—R.T.E.

1 Dead In Auto Smash

Wanda Stade, 16, Chilliwack, was almost instantly killed at 7 p.m., Monday, when the small car she was driving was in collision with another machine on King Edward Avenue at Windsor Street.

The driver of the light, old model coupe that hit the Stade car was 18-year-old Frank Haworth, Jr., 5885 Fraser Avenue. He was not injured.

It was the third death in three days from traffic accidents in Greater Vancouver, the thirteenth fatality since Jan 1.

Miss Stade died in an ambulance on the way to the General Hospital. She was pronounced dead by an emergency ward doctor, and the body taken to the hospital morgue.

Her sister and mother, who were passengers in the car, were uninjured. Police said the corner of the door of the car apparently pierced her skull as the machine overturned. The death car was travelling eastward on King Edward when hit by Haworth's coupe going south on Windsor Street, crossing King Edward.

Streicher Thought Dead

NEW YORK, Aug. 6. (UP) —Columbia Broadcasting today reported that the British radio expressed satisfaction over an "as yet unconfirmed" report of the death of Julius Streicher, known as Germany's No. 1 Jew-baiter.

The British Broadcast was in German and said that Streicher's "disappearance" from high Nazi circles was supposed to have resulted from a run-in with Marshal Hermann Goering.

Nazi Radios Shut Down

NEW YORK, Aug. 6.—(UP)—The National Broadcasting Company Monday night quoted a broadcast from Berlin at 11:22 p.m., E.D.T., as saying the entire German radio system was going off the air until 5:15 a.m., E.D.T., Tuesday. The broadcast gave "technical alterations" as the reason.

Seek Kidnapper Of City Woman

Police today are seeking a man who kidnapped a 17-year-old girl about 8:30 p.m. Monday in the 4500 block East Pender Street.

She was found unconscious on the road in the 1900 block Cassiar Street, her clothes torn and her nose bleeding. A citizen carried her into his home and called police.

The girl told officers that a car drew alongside her while she was walking on Pender Street, and a man reached out and pulled her into the car, warning her not to scream or he would "fix her."

She escaped from her kidnapper on Broadway at Rupert Street and ran about six blocks to Cassiar Street, where she fell unconscious on the roadway. The assailant was described as wearing a dark coat turned around his face and a dark hat pulled down.

Italians Massing For Suez Drive

CAIRO, Egypt, Aug. 6.—Italian forces were reported massing in great strength today along the Libyan frontier facing Egypt, perhaps for a major drive toward the Suez Canal, after the biggest air battle thus far in the war in Africa.

Six and perhaps nine Italian planes were reported shot down Sunday in two air battles involving at least 100 Italian aircraft over the desert sands of Western Egypt in the Bir El Gobi region, where the heavy Italian troop concentrations were reported.

Fifty Italian planes were said in a Royal Air Force communique here to have attacked a squadron of British reconnaissance planes, escorted by four fighters, in the Bir El Gobi region. Three of the Italian planes were shot down in this battle, the R.A.F. said.

British leaders believed the Italians were throwing all their strength into an effort to take over control of the Eastern Mediterranean, especially the Suez zone, which is vital to the task of supplying Italian Ethiopia and Somililand.

The Italians have been concentrating largely on British merchant shipping, using submarines for the most part and saving their airplanes for land operations. The British said the Italians appeared to believe that attack by undersea craft was cheaper and less hazardous than by air.

Many Sunderland flying boats, the British counterpart of the "Flying Fortress," have been maintaining constant patrol over the British sea lanes and have accounted for 12 Italian planes in the last few weeks and "at least seven submarines."

What's News

Local—

Alderman Wilson to demand council curb Japanese traders here—5*** Motorcycle contingent leaves for training camp—5*** Citizens endorse News-Herald plan to use old Hotel Vancouver —8*** City traffic commission endorses parking meters—8*** War has brought unity to Canada says former Toronto mayor visiting city—9*** Gracie Fields attends civic luncheon, visits military hospital and thrills thousands at Forum—20.

Foreign—

Departments—

Sport—

MONTREAL, Aug. 6—(UP)—Mayor Camillien Houde, of Montreal, was interned early today by order of the Minister of Justice.

He was arrested late last night under Section 21 of the Defense of Canada Regulations. Friday night he created a sensation by announcing he would refuse to comply with the recently-passed Mobilization Bill and asked the public to follow his lead.

Houde was picked up by officers at 11:15 o'clock last night and taken to headquarters of the Royal Canadian Mounted Police where he was questioned for more than 40 minutes.

When he left, Houde, with two officers, was in his own automobile and four automobiles of officers followed. Two motorcycle officers preceded the cars.

The internment order followed a conference between police officials and Minister of Justice Ernest Lapointe. They discussed Houde's Friday night attack on the mobilization bill.

For Duration?

The internment order said that Houde is to be detained "in such a place and under such conditions as the minister of justice may from time to time determine."

Internment could be for duration of the war or it might be for a shorter period.

Houde, as a Canadian citizen, has a right to appeal the order.

He was taken to an internment camp from police headquarters, but the location of the camp was not disclosed.

The Mobilization Act provides for registration of every man and woman in the Dominion, the men to be subject as needed to being called up for military service in the Dominion. They are not subject to overseas service.

Made Statement

Houde, Friday night, issued a written statement to the press setting forth his opposition to the act.

He said he would not register and added, "I ask the population not to conform."

Houde charged that the Dominion government of Prime Minister W. L. Mackenzie King had been returned to office early this year with the idea that there would be no conscription, and that the matter should be one for the voters to decide.

His statement was brought to the attention of King in the House of Commons Saturday and the Prime Minister said he would see to it that the laws of the country were upheld.

Lapointe hurried back to Ottawa today from his summer home where he had been convalescing and immediately went into conference with police authorities.

26

News-Herald

LARGEST MORNING CIRCULATION WEST OF TORONTO

FINAL EDITION

VANCOUVER, B.C., WEDNESDAY, AUGUST 21, 1940 — 3c — Five Cents on boats, trains and in country.

TROTSKY NEAR DEATH; ASSASSIN'S VICTIM

KING DISMISSES PRO-NAZI DUKE

MEXICO CITY, Wednesday, Aug. 21.—(UP)—Critically wounded by a man he considered a friend, Leon Trotsky, exiled former Soviet leader early today was given a slender chance to recover by physicians after an operation at Green Cross emergency hospital.

An attending physician said that Trotsky had a "fighting chance" if he survived beyond 4 a.m. C.S.T.

The 60-year-old former Soviet war commissar received deep head wounds and a fractured skull when attacked Tuesday afternoon in the study of his suburban Coyoacan villa by Jacques Mornard Van Den Dreschd, 36, who struck him with a type of axe used by mountain-climbers.

Struck With Axe

Trotsky also suffered shoulder and knee wounds.

The assailant was described as having been born in Persia.

The operation, which was performed by Dr. Ruben Lenero, chief of the hospital staff, and Dr. Joaquin Baz, took 15 minutes and was intended to relieve pressure on the brain.

Trotsky was placed immediately in an oxygen tent. The surgeons said it was too early to determine the results of the operation. Baz said the most serious wound was the one that pierced the skull and entered the brain, causing a hemorrhage.

Baz said the chances are "90 to 10 that he cannot live."

Guards at Trotsky's home who rushed into the study and overpowered Van Den Dreschd when they heard the famous exile scream, said the assailant probably was a member of the GPU (Russian secret police).

Had Run of House

Considered to be an ardent Trotsky supporter, Van Den Dreschd, who had been admitted to and given the run of the heavily-guarded Coyoacan home for more than eight months.

The guards said a woman, whom they believed to be an American, and who had posed as Van Den Dreschd's wife, also had gained close friendship with Trotsky.

Great patches of blood stained the floor of the study following the attack. Trotsky, according to the police who were called by the guards, apparently struggled desperately with his assailant. The receivers on the telephone in the room had been unhooked which was taken to indicate that he probably had tried to signal for help.

(See Page 2)

SAYS STALIN RESPONSIBLE FOR ATTACK

SAN FRANCISCO, Aug. 21.—(UP)—Diego Rivera, world famed Mexican artist, in an interview Tuesday night, charged the hand of Joseph Stalin, directed by Adolf Hitler, was responsible for the attempted assassination of Leon Trotsky in Mexico City.

Rivera, notified of the attempt on the life of the former Soviet war commissar, appeared emotionally shaken.

"This confirms the affirmation he (Trotsky) always made about the responsibility of Joseph Stalin, totalitarian tyrant of Russia, for the attempt by the painter, David Alfaro Sequieros, and his accomplices, who once before missed Trotsky but succeeded in the assassination of the American citizen, Robert Sheldon Hart, Trotsky's secretary, still unpunished to this day, Rivera said.

What's News

Local

Tourists lured from interior highways when signs are removed—4; Early appointment of Col. Letson's successor here is anticipated—8; Trades and Labor Council snuffs out new Communistic controversy—8; Registrars faced with task of handling half of city population today—8; Mayor confident military authorities will not disrupt police and fire staffs—20.

Foreign

U. S. pushing conscription plans—2; Churchill asks America to send ships, take over base sites—2; Eight more Nazi planes downed in Tuesday's raid—2; King explains Canada's role in U. S. accord—3; Petain advises democracies to profit from French fate—3.

Sport

Capilanos lose second ball game in row to Wenatchee—16; Adanacs primed for boxla playoff opener tonight—17; Hi Briar too good for youngsters in Brighouse racing feature—18.

Departments

Comics 14, 15; Classified 12, 13; Editorial 10; Features 11; Finance 19; Social, Women's 6, 7.

8 Nazi Planes Down Tuesday

LONDON, Aug. 21.—(BUP)—As swarms of German planes Tuesday swept over Britain to resume their raids on a moderate scale, British bombers blasted Nazi bases across the English Channel and swept into Germany, striking as far inland as Berlin's suburbs.

At least eight German planes were shot down Tuesday, the Air Ministry reported, one of them by a Polish squadron of fliers serving with the R.A.F.

The official "bag" of German planes in Sunday's attacks on Great Britain rose to 153 bombers and fighters with an announcement eight additional planes had been brought down in battle. A Nazi flying boat was shot down by anti-aircraft fire off the northeast coast Monday night, it was said.

While Prime Minister Winston Churchill was speaking in the House of Commons two flights numbering from eight to ten German dive bombers each dropped from the clouds and attacked an airdrome in Southeast England.

The Air Ministry said the R. A. F. bombed 30 enemy airdromes in Germany and German-occupied territory, blasted the great Kiel naval base and smashed other military objectives, including oil tanks at Ambes, near Bordeaux, on the French coast.

Numerous hits were reported scored on underground oil stores within the Kiel dockyard. Low level attacks also were made on the Dortmund-Ems and Weser-Elbe canals.

Rail communications over a wide area in Germany were dislocated by the raiders, the ministry said. The Hamm Railway yard, largest assembly point of goods and traffic in Germany, was bombed for the 52nd time and many fires were started, it added.

An airdrome on the outskirts of Paris also was bombed, it was reported. Bombs were seen to burst on the hangars and across the landing ground.

The British bombers pressed home their attacks with new vigor, the Air Ministry said, and came winging back with only two of their number missing to report heavy bombings of an oil refinery at Hanover and a power station at Schornewitz, north of Leipzig, as well as key communication points in the Ruhr Valley.

The Weather

Weather conditions will clear up today, according to the official forecast for Vancouver and vicinity. It reads: "Fresh south shifting to southwest winds, cloudy and cool at first, then clearing and warmer." Temperatures in the city Tuesday ranged between a maximum of 70 and a minimum of 58 degrees.

GERMAN BROADCASTS ARE CUT OFF

BERLIN, Aug. 21—(UP)—Germany's major radio stations went off the air at 11 o'clock Tuesday night presumably to avoid providing direction guides to raiding British planes.

Radio Berlin and Deutschland Sender, which broadcast from Zeesen outside Berlin, signed off at 11 p.m. and the official DNB agency ceased its news transmission at the same hour instead of continuing until 4 a.m. as usual. The DNB said that in future it would sign off at 11 p.m.

Motorcyclist Dead After Hitting Tram

James Herbert Deverill, 1405 East Pender Street, 24-year-old motorcycle driver for the Seaport Crown Fish Company, died at midnight Tuesday of injuries received about 1 p.m. when his motorcycle hit a street car in the 200 block East Hastings.

It was the thirteenth death from traffic accidents on Vancouver streets since Jan. 1, 1940.

Horace Wainwright, 35, 6919 Lanark Street, passenger in the sidecar, was unconscious in the General Hospital today. He was thrown to the pavement. Extent of his injuries is unknown.

LONDON, Aug. 21. — (UP) — King George VI has removed the 46-year-old Duke of Buccleuch, one of Britain's richest landowners, from his post as Lord Steward of the Royal Household in the widespread drive against fifth columnists, it was revealed Tuesday night.

The Scottish duke, a banking associate of Queen Elizabeth's father, was removed because of his alleged Nazi sympathies on May 10 at the time when Prime Minister Churchill shook up his cabinet but news of the development did not leak out until Tuesday.

The duke is related by marriage to the Royal family, his sister having married the Duke of Gloucester, brother of King George.

Rumors that the Duke had been confined to his estates in Scotland as a fifth columnist were denied in high quarters but it was established that he was in London three weeks ago.

At present he is staying in his Drumlanrig castle at Thornhill in Dumfriesshire, Scotland.

Buccleuch left his post as Lord Steward of the Royal Household, which he had held since 1937, at the time Churchill set up his cabinet without exciting comment and was succeeded by the Duke of Hamilton and Brandon.

Some high authorities, it was reported, wanted to go further than merely dropping Buccleuch from his post and make an "example" of him.

Registration Cards Sold In Montreal

MONTREAL, Aug. 21.—(BUP)—Hundreds of registration cards reported stolen or "lost" from registration offices are being sold in Montreal for $1 or $2, according to complaints made to R.C.M.P. officials and provincial police last night.

Quebec provincial police authorities refused to comment on the matter, stating, "This is a federal problem. The information we have received has been passed on to the R.C.M.P."

Mountie headquarters here declined to give any information.

27

7-HOUR LONDON RAID

FOR **VICTORY!**

News-Herald
Largest Morning Circulation West of Toronto

VANCOUVER, B. C. THURSDAY, AUGUST 29, 1940

British bombers roared over the heart of Berlin again last night, carrying the air war to the nerve center of the Reich. Reports from the Nazi Capital said the R.A.F. planes were heard plainly over Unter Den Linden, above, (1), the Bradenburg Gate (2), the Wilhelmstrasse (3), and the French and American embassies (4 and 5).

First Glance
By R. T. ELSON

Millions of British men, women and children are proving themselves as good soldiers as any who ever manned a firing line. They are the people of London who have been under night air attack for six consecutive days and who, last night, endured a raid for seven hours—the longest yet.

So far as is known the damage was not heavy despite the fact that almost 1,000 bombs were dropped and casualties were only a "small number" to quote the official communiques.

This morning the people of London will learn with satisfaction that while they were enduring the cramped air raid shelters their enemy neighbors in Berlin were not having a quiet evening either. The R.A.F. was over Berlin for three hours and even the Nazis, who hate to acknowledge any British raid, were forced to admit that they had visitors.

It is difficult to evaluate the military effect of either raids. Our own communiques speaking of R.A.F. efforts indicate they have achieved a considerable success in demolishing military objectives and demoralizing production within the Reich. So far, British attacks seem to be aimed at military objectives, although the Nazis have tried to claim indiscriminate action in last night's raid. The correspondents' stories by no means confirm this.

'War Nerves'

Meanwhile the despatches from London do confirm the British contention that the Nazi attacks are designed to demoralize the population and create "war nerves." Elsewhere in Britain the Nazis go from time to time at industrial objectives but in London the chain attacks seem definitely aimed principally at disrupting the city's rhythm of life.

In Vienna this morning there opens a conference that may have a far-reaching effect upon the final outcome of the war. German and Italian diplomats are going to try and mediate the Hungarian - Rumanian dispute, which is looking less like a dispute and more like a war every day.

The conference was assembled in some haste. Some commentators have suggested that the haste is prompted by fear that the Russians are about to take another bite at Rumania. One unconfirmed report seems to suggest that the

(Continued on Back Page)

R.A.F. BOMBS NAZI CAPITAL

BERLIN, Thursday, Aug. 29.—(UP) — British planes attacked Berlin for nearly two hours early today, apparently flying over the center of the city, while anti-aircraft guns blazed and booming explosions like bursting bombs rolled in from the outskirts.

The air raid alarm, Berlin's seventh of the war and third in a week lasted from 12:25 until 3:18 a.m.

Planes were heard distinctly over Central Berlin, above the government buildings in the Wilhelmstrasse and Unter Den Linden, but there was no fire from the anti-aircraft batteries atop the ministry buildings an hour and a quarter after the attack began.

Rolling, booming explosions like bursting bombs were heard in the distance.

10 Killed

The red flashes of anti-aircraft fire and groping searchlight beams spread from the northwest to the west of Berlin when the attack had been underway about 15 minutes.

At that time the anti-aircraft fire was heard only faintly, indicating the raiders were attempting to break through beyond the Berlin suburbs.

Ten persons were killed and 28 wounded in Berlin during the raid, the official DNB news agency announced.

REDS THREATEN WAR ON RUMANIA

BUCHAREST, Aug. 29.—(UP)—There were reports here Wednesday, as yet unconfirmed, that Russia has sent a note to already dismembered Rumania threatening to invade Rumania "in self defense" if King Carol's government cedes any territory to Hungary as a result of the Vienna conference.

The Rumanian army tonight ordered its auxiliary services back from the Russian frontier, an official communique said.

At the large Danube port of Galatz, where some reports described "near panic" among the people, the government was reported to have taken precautions to prevent any panicky flight. Galatz probably would be the first objective of any Soviet drive across the Moldavian plain where the Russians operated during the World War.

The Russian note, according to these reports, was being carried to Vienna Wednesday night by Rumanian foreign minister Mihail Manoilescu to be laid before Foreign Ministers Joachim Von Ribbentrop of Germany and Count Galeazzo Ciano of Italy, as well as the Premier and Foreign Minister of Hungary.

According to one version, the Russians said Rumania's cession of territory to either Hungary or Bulgaria—dismemberment of either Transylvania or Southern Dobrudja —might force Russian troops to march westward to the crest of the Carpathians.

The note said Moscow would interpret as an "unfriendly act" the cession of any Rumanian territory and any such submission to Hungary or Bulgaria would "sabotage" Soviet interests in the Balkans and the Danube basin, it was rumored.

What's News

Local

Two hundred husky B. C. woodsmen of Forestry Corps leave for Eastern military camps, 5; B. C. honey producers increasing demand for their product, 5; Vancouverites rush to secure new border cards, 6; Recruiting opens today for World War veterans anxious to serve, 6; "Taxi cab bandit" strikes once more with truck driver as sixth victim, 7; Stream of fair-goers boost attendance past 50,000-mark, 11.

Foreign

Dictators rush Balkan peace talks, 2; Red army reported on Rumanian frontier as Russia opposes rival claims, 2; U. S. Senate passes conscription, 2; London shelters in longest raid. Other attacks accompany bombing of metropolis, 3; British forays hamstring Nazi oil production 3.

Departments

Comics, 14, 15; Classified, 16, 17; Editorial, 12; Features, 13; Finance, Business, 23, 22; Social, Women's, 8, 9; Pictures, 10.

7-HOUR LONDON RAID
By WALLACE CARROLL
(British United Press Correspondent)

LONDON, Thursday, Aug. 29.—(UP)—A seven-hour raid by German warplanes on the London area last night and early today caused "a small number" of fatalities, a communique announced this morning.

Nearly 1,000 incendiary bombs and a number of high explosives were dropped by the raiders which came over singly hour after hour while many of the 8,000,000 inhabitants of Greater London spent a sleepless night huddled in air raid shelters.

Two Fires

The only two large fires started by the bombs—in a shop and a factory — were reported to have been extinguished an hour after the all-clear signal sounded at 4 a.m.

Intensive enemy air attacks were reported from other parts of the British Isles, with some casualties, including deaths, said to have been caused when incendiary and high explosive bombs were dropped on a town in the industrial midlands.

Dan Campbell, United Press Correspondent at Dover, reported heavy German attacks were thrown against Dover and the coast of Kent throughout Wednesday and until early this morning.

Seven Alarms

Campbell reported that one of the most thrilling mass dogfights of the war occurred over the coast and that by midnight there had been seven alarms at Dover, a record for that port.

The attack on London, despite its severity, was regarded by officials as doing small damage in view of the length of the raid and the number of bombs dropped. It was said reliably that no bombs were dropped in London proper or in the fashionable west end.

Scores of small fires were extinguished by air raids precautions wardens, virtually without damage.

An attack on a second town in the midlands shattered two houses and ARP squads were said to be digging in the ruins for victims.

(See Page 3)

The Weather

Don't put off your proposed visit to the Exhibition today because you think the weather doesn't look promising. "Probably a shower" is the optimistic forecast of the weatherman. And surely the probability of a shower wouldn't keep anyone away from that spun-candy counter. Fresh to strong southeasterly winds will blow, and the sky will be partly cloudy, with the temperature moderately warm. Wednesday the mercury hovered between a low of 55 and high of 71.

United Press Correspondent Misses Death By Inches

A member of the United Press London operating staff, G. E. Gregory, missed death by inches Sunday night when a German high explosive bomb struck 20 yards from the front door of his home, almost wrecking the house. Still stunned, he hurried to a telephone and dictated an account of what he called "A Terrific Jolt."

By G. E. GREGORY

LONDON, Sept. 9.—(UP)—Hello, give me dictation, please. This is Gregory. They almost got me a few minutes ago. I'll tell you about it if I can get myself together.

I was sitting in my drawing room playing cards.

Suddenly everything seemed to explode around me. I was covered with dust and my mouth was filled with plaster and rubble.

I rushed upstairs to see if my family was all right. No, none of us was hurt beyond a few scratches. But I'm still stunned and this may not sound just right.

(At this point Gregory, obviously suffering from shock, mumbled incoherently for a few moments).

My house was a shambles. The windows and doors were blown in and the walls were cracked open.

A bomb, a high explosive one, had exploded outside a church at about 20 yards from my front door.

There were a few casualties and they got a gas main. I've been working like a madman helping to smother the fire with sand bags.

There was only a small crater, but it must have been a powerful bomb because windows all along the street were shattered. I believe other bombs fell nearby.

I saw one house just now that was only a skeleton. The occupants, poor devils, must have been killed.

I've gotta get back now. You see we've got 10 people in our house and we're trying to look after them. I hope I'm coherent. It was a terrific jolt."

LONDON WEATHERS WAR'S WORST RAIDS

FOR VICTORY!
News-Herald
Largest Morning Circulation West of Toronto

VANCOUVER, B. C., MONDAY, SEPTEMBER 9, 1940

The Least That We Can Do
AN EDITORIAL

Canada today asks her citizens for a loan of $300,-000,000 to carry on the war.

This morning's headlines, the grim despatches which we print on this front page today, offer the only argument that should be needed to convince Canadians of the urgency of this hour.

Every man and woman living in the safety of Canada, upon reading the news this morning, ought to be glad to give money to our government, let alone lend it at three per cent. Over there the people of London are shielding us without a murmur. All they ask is for more planes with which to smash Hitler.

The least that we can do to help them is to buy a war bond today.

First Glance
By R. T. ELSON

"There is heavy damage in the bombed areas—but damage which is not much more than a bad shaving cut on the face for a city the size of London."

Thus graphically does United Press correspondent Edward Beattie put into proper perspective the results of the German massed raids upon the Empire's capital. These raids started late Saturday and after a brief lull Sunday resumed until a little after dawn this morning. We may expect them to be renewed with twilight today.

But putting these attacks in perspective does not mean to minimize the effect or the damage. It would be better not to do this but to face up to the facts.

All sources admit the damage is severe in the areas hit but not in relation to the nation. The raids have their effect on the civilian population but, as the correspondents report, only to make them defiant and angry, demanding reprisals on Berlin.

Problem of Relief

Chief danger in the situation would seem to be not what damage the Germans can do—for it would take weeks of such raids to "erase London" as Hitler threatened—but how well the British are able to relieve their defenders. R.A.F. fighter units, anti-aircraft batteries, A.R.P. workers, demolition squads, and fire fighters have been fighting without let-up for days now.

Men cannot work without rest and the chief problem will be to see that these vital services are not strained to the point of exhaustion.

Invasion Now

The Press Association — reports of which are always on the conservative side — frankly discusses now the possibility of an attempt at invasion. Partially confirming this is Italian propaganda, which without shame boasts of Italian participation in the London slaughter.

Meanwhile the R.A.F. reports attacks on barge concentrations in the channel area. This is not the first time and is not in itself of special significance because transportation of many vital supplies is accomplished by barges upon the continent.

Evade Question

It is also interesting to mark the German propaganda which evades the question of invasion to remark that the attack on London will continue so long as "the British night attacks on non-military objectives in Germany continue." Meanwhile Goering, in his usual grandiose style, has proclaimed the "historic hour" and announced he has taken personal charge of the attack — from the safety of a hidden base on the channel coast.

HEADS "SUICIDE SQUAD" —Capt. Edward H. Webb, 27, heads the "suicide squad" of Canadian engineers which cleans up Nazi delayed-action bombs after they are dropped by German raiders. Captain Webb was born in Orillia, Ont., and was employed by the Hudson's Bay Co. in Winnipeg.

HERE IT IS:
Easier Reading

Today The News-Herald appears all dressed up in its new Opticon typeface. No need to tell you how much better reading it is than our old type—your eyes will tell you that. If it makes The News-Herald easier for you to read we are happy. This is just one of many improvements we are planning to make this Canada's most interesting morning newspaper.

Thank you.

WHAT'S NEWS

Local:

Veterans Pray For Victory and Peace in Colorful Ceremony, 5; City Factories To Receive New War Orders, Col. W. C. Woodward Says On Arrival, 8.

Foreign:

British Bombard Nazi Bases, 2; Canadian Squadron Bags 11 More Nazi Planes, 2; United Press Correspondent Dodges Death By Inches, 2; Carol Reported On Way To Canada, 3; A. R. P. Crews Work On Despite New Raids, 3; Saturday Raid On London, 4.

By WALLACE CARROLL
British United Press Correspondent

LONDON, Sept. 9.-( )—The destructive might of the German air force was loosed on the bomb and fire scarred capital of the British Empire for more than nine and a half hours last night and early today in continuation of the all-out aerial warfare which took a heavy toll of life in a long Saturday night raid.

The Saturday casualties were at least 400 dead and about 1400 badly injured.

No new estimate of dead and injured in the London area was available immediately after the Sunday night attack had ended, but it was believed that casualties were smaller than for the Saturday night assault because a majority of the people were home Sunday and better situated to get proper air raid protection.

London's skies glowed redly through the night from the light of fires in many districts—some of them fires set in the Saturday night raid.

Bombing in Central London was particularly heavy between 2 and 4 a.m. today and then eased up until the all-clear sounded at 5:35 a.m., nine hours, 37 minutes from the time the alarm began at 7:58 p.m. yesterday.

One bomb dropped outside the office of a big London newspaper whose staff was in air raid shelters at the time. Another struck the embassy of a European power.

Explosive Hits Hospital

High explosive bombs hit a big hospital and two wards were burned out. A porter said he believed there were no casualties; that all patients had been removed to shelters.

"Many hundreds" of buildings had been damaged, some wrecked, after the two relentless weekend raids.

The East End slums were hit badly and heavy loss of life was inflicted there in the Saturday night attack.

Dock areas suffered extensive damage and at some places along the waterfront, gas, electric and water services were not functioning.

The long raid tied up production of morning newspapers and none were available when the alarm ended

Transport at Standstill

Transportation throughout Greater London was at a virtual standstill early today and millions of sleepy-eyed but stoically determined men, women and children drowsed in air raid shelters.

Never had London heard such fierce anti-aircraft fire as the waves of raiders came in, hour after hour, from every side. They came mostly in small groups or even singly, flying 15,000 feet high, criss crossing over the metropolis and dropping bombs in lacework pattern.

The Air Ministry's spokesman said that the mass raids of the past 48 hours had "proved that Germany's fighter strength is not comparable to her bomber strength."

(See Page 2)

29

LEWIS QUITS C.I.O. POST

NEW AIR RECRUITS ARRIVE

★ ★ ★ ★ ★ FINAL

—AP Wirephoto, by Cable

NEVER BEFORE . . . NEVER MORE—No town on earth has known before quite such horrors of total war as Hitler's air legions last week imposed on Coventry, as revealed by the picture above, taken after the English City suffered through an assault which lasted more than ten hours. Glories and ageless beauty, which Coventry counted as part of its everlasting heritage, were reduced to such rubble as is pictured here under Nazi ravaging. No rebuilding can bring back the grandeur of 1000 structures reduced to ruins like these.

—AP Wirephoto, by Cable

CENTURIES . . . AND MINUTES—The beauty that lived at Coventry, in St. Michael's Cathedral—an inspiration through more than five centuries to men whose spirits could be reached through the majesty of gracious architectural lines and in a religion which had given life to a building dating from antiquity—perished in a moment as Nazis last week left the structure and a large part of Coventry looking like this following an air assault which lasted more than ten hours.

THE VANCOUVER DAILY PROVINCE

46th YEAR—NO. 204 VANCOUVER, B. C., MONDAY, NOVEMBER 18, 1940—22 PAGES PRICE 3 CENTS On trains, boats and in the country, Five Cents

Racing

Bowie Race Results

First race—High Nale (Taylor), $19.20, $10.40, $7.10.
Bubble Lil (Pearson), $8.50, $7.60.
High Light (Huff), $9.70.
Time, 1.13 4-5.
Second race—Crack Favor (Kieper), $8.50, $5.80, $3.40.
Dorothy Pomp (Garner), $7.30, $3.70.
Drift Along (Lindberg), $3.10.
Time, 1.14 1-5.
Third race—Stolen Tryst (Mearle), $12.50, $5.30, $3.70.
Machree (Renick), $3.90, $2.80.
Rodia (Kaufman), $5.20.
Time, 1.14.
Fourth race—Maecloud (Sisto), $9.10, $4.70, $3.70.
Acc Call (Packer), $9.40, $4.90.
Madsweep (King), $4.20.
Fifth race—Oasis (Canning), $9.40, $6.10, $3.40.
Jessie Gladys (Garner), $7.70, $4.10.
Early Morn (King), $2.60.
Sixth race—Grede (Dufford), $39.20, $11.00, $8.30.
Maydig (Taylor), $4.20, $3.30.
True Knightness (Lindberg), $5.90.
Seventh race—Black Grouse (Webber), $17.00, $8.10, $5.70.
Repercussion (Canning), $8.50, $4.80.
High Blame (Kieper), $3.30.

(Race Entries on Page 2)

Bay Meadows Selections

By TOM GWYNNE
Daily Province Racing Correspondent

FIRST RACE — Snow Fleet, Ball Baby, Rain Crystal.
SECOND RACE — Taken, Ovid, Archives.
THIRD RACE—Pearl Alma, Hetch Hetch, Sparkling Eyes.
FOURTH RACE—Swinging Doos, King Torch, The Cloud.
FIFTH RACE—Xenora's Fox, Sea-Bread, Routing.
SIXTH RACE—Paper Sun, Fervorita, Ritz Brothers.
SEVENTH RACE—Cayenne, Lady Jacqueline, Siganar.
EIGHTH RACE—Almaha, Fay D., Bagen May.
NINTH RACE—Sky Pirate, Boniluna, Southern Belle.
BEST—Pearl Alma.

Casualty List Includes 909 Prisoners of War

LONDON, Nov. 18.—(AP)—The war office's eighty-fourth casualty list issued on Monday contains 1100 names, made up of 29 killed, 69 wounded, 15 died of wounds, 44 died, 28 previously reported missing now reported prisoners of war, 909 prisoners, one previously reported a prisoner now reported killed, two previously reported wounded now reported not wounded, and three safe.

Among the Canadian troops listed as seriously ill in the same list is Pte. Louis Pete Gamba of the B. C. Regiment, son of Mrs. Erminie Gamba, R.R. 1, Steveston, B. C.

Surplus Water Supply

TORONTO, Nov. 18.—(CP)—Dr. W. O. Gliddon, federal air raid precautions officer for Canada, told members of the Ontario civilian defense committee today that a number of Ontario canals will be kept filled this winter to give firemen an added water surplus.

Air Recruits Arrive Here

(By Vancouver Daily Province Staff Correspondent.)

A WEST COAST CANADIAN PORT, Nov. 18.—Forsaking the sunnier climes of the Straits Settlements, a party of bronzed, husky-looking flyers arrived here today, shivering a little in Canada's crisp cold sunshine, but ready and eager to joint the British Empire's air training plan.

Shouting, singing and laughing they stepped ashore from a Pacific liner to receive a hearty welcome from the Royal Canadian Air Force, Premier Pattullo, Brigadier J. Sutherland-Brown, deputizing for Lieut.-Governor E. W. Hamber, and other provincial dignitaries.

Lined up on the quayside was a guard of honor from Patricia Bay Airport, with bayonetted rifles. The band of the 111th Fighter Squadron played "Roll Out the Barrel," "Tipperary," and other rousing tunes. Crowds of civilians roared in chorus.

ALREADY TRAINED.

Members of British families living in the Straits Settlements the men have already received two months' preliminary training in Singapore, where they gained the rank of leading aircraftmen.

"We are anxious to complete our training as soon as possible and get on with the job," said Acting Corporal J. E. Slade, who is in charge of the detachment.

With him were Leading Aircraftman R. F. Wollaston, who lived in Victoria from 1913 to 1923, attended school at Shawnigan Lake before going to England to continue his education there.

"I returned to Malaya five years ago to work on a rubber plantation," Wollaston said. "Now I'm back in Canada again. I only wish I had time to visit Victoria and Shawnigan Lake to look up old landmarks."

(Continued on Page 2.)
See AIRMEN.

SPANISH TO TAKE PART?

Gibraltar Push Again Hinted As Axis-Spanish Chiefs Meet

(By Associated Press.)

BERCHTESGADEN, Germany, Nov. 18.—Foreign ministers of Germany, Italy and Spain met today in this city near Hitler's Bavarian mountain retreat, where many conferences of far-reaching import in the past have been held.

Informed sources in Berlin said Hitler would have individual talks with the Spanish and Italian visitors and then hold a joint conference, probably later today.

Observers interpreted the visit of the Spaniard, Ramon Serrano Suner, as indicating that Falangist Spain now is in the Axis camp and apparently ready to take a more active part in developments.

(Berne diplomatic circles reported Axis plans for drives on Greece and Gibraltar were to be discussed by German-Italian and Spanish leaders.)

Italian Foreign Minister Ciano's arrival came as no surprise following the visit to Hitler in Berlin last week of Soviet Premier Molotoff.

Axis representatives, it was pointed out, always have conferred immediately after conferences with third parties.

Informed sources said that Ciano, besides learning all about Molotoff's visit at first hand, also can bring first-hand information to German leaders on Mussolini's talks last week with Rumanian Chief of State General Ion Antonescu.

Ribbentrop met both visitors, Serrano Suner in the Berchtesgaden station and Ciano in Salzburg.

Lewis Quits Post as Head Of C. I. O.

(By Associated Press.)

ATLANTIC CITY, Nov. 18.—John L. Lewis, with tears in his eyes, told convention delegates of the C.I.O. at Atlantic City today that he was stepping down as their president.

To a hushed throng which a few minutes earlier had given him a thunderous ovation, Lewis said:

"I won't be with you long. I have done my work and in a few days I'll be out of this office."

It was his keynote speech. It carried an urgent plea to the C.I.O. to remain united or it would "not long endure."

MURRAY TO SUCCEED.

Lewis' term as president expires at the close of the convention. It is expected that Philip Murray will be named his successor. In giving notice that he was about to get out of the C.I.O. leadership, Lewis fulfilled the promise he made to retire if President Roosevelt was re-elected for a third term.

Lewis called on C.I.O. unions for unity among themselves and confidence in their leadership.

On the labor front, he said, C.I.O. had demonstrated its strength and piled up a record of accomplishments.

"It can go forward," he said. "But if you consume your time in criticism and vituperation, you won't have an organization long.

"A leader, no matter how well qualified for the job, is only an individual, because if you don't give him strength, he is nothing."

50 Times Worse

LONDON, Nov. 18.—(AP)—British air blows against Germany are causing the Nazis to suffer 50 times more industrial damage than Britain, Rt. Hon. Arthur Greenwood, minister without portfolio, said today.

"Serious though the attacks have been on this country, particularly in London, Coventry, Birmingham and Liverpool, the punishment we have suffered is nothing to what we are administering to the enemy.

"I am not concerned with killing people in Germany. I am concerned with killing their power to strike at us," he said.

Italian Army Flees Deep Into Albania

(By Associated Press.)

ATHENS, Nov. 18.—The Italians sent wave after wave of infantry crashing against Greek mountain positions today in an effort to prevent the capture of Koritza, Fascist invasion base, but the Greeks reported they repelled all attacks and gained new ground.

In their desperate attempt to thwart the Greek ring of steel being drawn around this most important city in Albania, the Italians were said also to have thrown a large force of dive-bombers into the battle.

The Greek air force, aided by the Royal Air Force, itself bombed Italian positions heavily and pummelled troop-jammed roads leading out of Koritza.

Greeks reported Italian mechanized columns were trapped hopelessly north of Koritza. Foreign sources said one column of 130 Italian tanks had fled into Yugo-Slavia.

(A Reuters News Agency dispatch from the Greek-Yugo-Slav frontier said 600 Italian troops and 130 tanks crossed the border and surrendered to Yugo-Slav authorities last night.)

The hard-pressed Italians were reported falling back from Koritza to a new defense line 25 miles deep in Albania.

(On Sunday it was reported that Italian troops had set fire to Koritza. This was reported by the Greek high command, which added that fleeing Italians had set fire to other places in their retreat.)

All along the border battlefront, Greek military reports indicated, the invasion of Greece—which Italian forces launched three weeks ago today—has turned into a desperate defense of Albania from fierce Greek counter drives.

A government spokesman declared last night that Greek mountain troops who seized new heights commanding Koritza, springboard for the Italian invasion toward Phlorina and Sal-

(Continued on Page 2.)
See GREEK.

Canada to Build New Field Guns

OTTAWA, Nov. 18.—(CP)—Canada is embarked on a program of construction of 25-pounder field guns and it was said today at the munitions and supply department that these guns will be the latest designs.

It was understood these guns are the type referred to by the military correspondent of the London Daily Express who said the weapon makes the famous French 75s look like "pipsqueaks" in comparison.

Actual production of these guns is not expected much before the latter part of 1941 in Canada.

OIL REFINERIES BLASTED

R.A.F. Pours Bombs On Ruhr, Leaves Hamburg Docks Afire

(By Associated Press.)

LONDON, Nov. 18.—Germany's war-vital industries in the rich Ruhr Valley were reported attacked heavily today by the Royal Air Force in a quick follow-up of week-end blows at Axis ports from Hamburg, Germany, to Mogadiscio, Somaliland.

The main force of the British offensive last night was directed at the oil refineries of Gelsenkirchen, near the Netherlands border.

Preceding the night forays, British raiders engaged in Saturday daylight attacks on oil refineries at Cologne and Bremen and the Dortmund-Ems Canal. In this destructive tour, air bases at Rouen, Abbeville, Arras and Cambrai areas in France also were hit hard.

From all these operations, three British planes were reported missing.

In their daylight attack on the Dortmund-Ems Canal, the flyers got in crippling blows against one of the most vital links in the German war machine.

The canal picks up the products of the Ruhr's heavy industries and carries them to Emden, whence they are distributed to Bremen and Hamburg.

Other planes bombed the industrial targets in the Ruhr, rail and river communications in the western part of the Reich, the naval base at Lorient, in Nazi-occupied Brittany, and airdromes in occupied territory.

British planes struck through

(Continued on Page 22.)
See AIR.

SECOND SQUADRON READY

(Canadian Press)

OTTAWA, Nov. 18—Canada will shortly have her second fighter squadron of the Royal Canadian Air Force on active service in Britain, Hon. C. G. Power, minister for air, announced in the House of Commons today.

Major Power said No. 1 Fighter Squadron of the R.C.A.F., has been occupied steadily in the United Kingdom.

No. 1 Squadron has been used with distinction in operation work in connection with the defense of London.

No. 112 Army Co-operation Squadron, in England, had been training in reconnaissance work. Now, because of the flow of trained men from Canada, from the R. C. A. F. and the Commonwealth training scheme, this squadron would shortly become the No. 2 Canadian fighter squadron.

Final Bulletins

Somaliland Bombed

LONDON, Nov. 18.—(CP)—British light naval forces were reported tonight to have bombarded oil tanks and coastal and anti-aircraft batteries at Dante, in Italian Somaliland.

Col. Farr Is Dead

MELBOURNE, Nov. 18.—(AP)—Lieut.-Col. Walter Percy Farr, D.S.O., to whom Mustapha Kemel Pasha surrendered in the first Great War, died today.

Would Bomb Rome

OTTAWA, Nov. 18.—(CP)—Rodney Adamson (Conservative, York West) urged in the House of Commons today the bombing of the capitals of the enemy dictators to drive Hitler and Mussolini from their headquarters.

Coward Down Under

MELBOURNE, Nov. 18.—(AP) Noel Coward, British playright and actor, has arrived here to tour the Commonwealth as a guest of the Australian Government. He will give entertainments at army camps and in aid of the Red Cross.

Raids Net Heavy Fines

TORONTO, Nov. 18.—(CP)—A flood of money expected to total more than $10,000 poured into City and County Courts here today as 489 men arrested in raids on 11 gambling houses Saturday night appeared on various charges.

Ontario Pair Missing

SUDBURY, Ont., Nov. 18.—(CP)—Ontario provincial police said today they had found no clue to the whereabouts of Mr. and Mrs. Earl D. Kirk of North Bay, last seen here on October 4 en route to Winnipeg to visit their parents.

British Plane Crashes

BELGRADE, Yugo-Slavia, Nov. 18.—(AP)—An aircraft which crashed and burned on a mountain near the southern Yugo-Slav town of Danilovgrad, killing its crew of four, was identified officially tonight as a British Blenheim bomber.

Italians Apologize

BELGRADE, Yugo-Slavia, Nov. 18.—(AP)—Yugo-Slavia announced tonight that Italy had expressed regret for an "unintentional mistake" by Italian flyers whose bombs killed nine persons and wounded 21 in the Yugo border town of Bitolj on November 5. It was the first official word on the identity of the planes in that raid.

BATTLE IN S. ATLANTIC

"Bomb Vesuvius!"

LONDON, Dec. 6.—Bomb Mount Vesuvius! That's the war cry echoing in London's crowded air raid shelters.

Londoners think that in one of their raids on Naples, a Royal Air Corps pilot could fly over Vesuvius and drop a 500-pound bomb or two into the crater.

Nobody knows what would happen, but the general opinion of Londoners is that the bombs would "start something" that would make the residents of Naples in the shadow of the great lava erupter, sorry they ever got into the war.

Marshal Badoglio Quits Mussolini

The Weather
Unsettled and mild throughout British Columbia with showers over the interior and heavy rain on the coast.
Temperature at 10 a.m. today: 45.8.
Temperature during 24 hours ending 4:30 a.m. today: maximum 51, minimum 39.
Forecast: cloudy with showers.
Official weather report on page 21.

The Vancouver Sun
Only Evening Newspaper Owned, Controlled and Operated by Vancouver People

Today's Tides
Vancouver Harbor
Low 6:35 p.m.; 6.1 feet High 11:32 p.m.; 8.3 feet
English Bay
Low 6:30 p.m.; 6.8 feet High 11:18 p.m.; 8.6 feet
First Narrows
Low slack 7:10 p.m. High slack 11:56 p.m.
Tomorrow's tides appear on page 36.

FOUNDED 1886
VOL. LV—No. 58
VANCOUVER, BRITISH COLUMBIA, FRIDAY, DECEMBER 6, 1940
Price 3 Cents
On trains, boats, and outside Greater Vancouver, 5c
MArine 1161

Hun Raider Runs Away From Fight

Today In Britain

War events analyzed by Fleet Street writers, cabled from the London Bureau of The Vancouver Sun.

(Copyright, 1940)

LONDON, Dec. 6.—Newspapers confirm the first recorded attempt on the life of Major Vidkun Quisling, Norwegian Nazi leader, which occurred a few days ago when a bomb exploded near him in the streets of Fredrikstad, Southern Norway, failed to harm him.

Major Quisling was visiting Fredrikstad to address his followers. The meeting was held in the public library without incident, although an enormous crowd gathered outside. After the meeting, when the Norwegian "Fuehrer," surrounded by Hirden, the Norwegian storm policemen and members of the troopers, started to tour the town, the bomb exploded. The correspondent does not indicate whether there were any casualties.

* * *

Riots and Arrests

On the same day Major Quisling visited the neighboring town of Sarpsborg and his visit provoked violent street riots. He was attacked by a crowd and only heavy police protection enabled him to escape. The fight began when the Hirden guards attacked persons in the crowd who were wearing anti-Quisling badges and badges of the dissolved political parties. Many Quislingists and demonstrators were admitted to hospitals and four arrests were made.

These continued anti-Quisling demonstrations, to which the Berlin press referred recently as "unrest due to unemployment," are looked upon here as an acute problem for Norway. It is felt that the Germans will not tolerate such opposition much longer, but they are said to be reluctant

Please Turn to Page Twenty-one
See "Britain Today"

News Under The Sun
Where to Find It

HMS. Carnarvon Castle Damaged Slightly in Brief Encounter

By British United Press

LONDON, Dec. 6. — The Admiralty said today that HMS Carnarvon Castle, an auxiliary cruiser, was damaged slightly in an engagement with a German raider in the South Atlantic ocean yesterday.

The German raider, heavily armed and disguised as a merchant ship, had considerable speed and refused to accept battle at close range, the Admiralty said.

There were some casualties aboard the Carnarvon Castle.

There was considerable firing on both sides as the slower, less well-armed Carnarvon Castle pursued the raider, the Admiralty said.

Damage done to the German ship has not been ascertained, the communique said.

FLEEING NORTH

Last reports from the Carnarvon Castle said the German raider was steaming northward at high speed.

Before being taken over by the Admiralty and armed as an auxiliary cruiser, the Carnarvon Castle operated in the service of the Union Castle Mail and Steamship Company. The vessel is of 20,122 tons. It was built in 1926 at Belfast and its home port is London.

It was learned authoritatively that the battle occurred approximately 700 miles northeast of Montevideo, Uruguay, where three British cruisers drove the German Pocket Battleship Admiral Graf Spee to self-destruction last December.

Took 22 Germans Off Brazilian Ship

BUENOS AIRES, Dec. 6.—The 20,122-ton merchant cruiser Carnarvon Castle, which engaged a German raider in the South Atlantic, sailed from Victoria, Brazil, five days ago. She has a cruising speed of 15 knots.

The Carnarvon Castle halted the Brazilian coastal steamship Itape 18 miles off shore, Nov. 30 and removed 22 Germans.

Other British merchant cruisers known to have been in South Atlantic waters recently are the 22,575-ton Queen of Bermuda and the Alcantara, 22,209 tons, which was damaged in a clash with a German raider off the Brazilian coast, July 29.

At Rio de Janeiro, British sources said the Carnarvon Castle was expected here four days ago but, one official explained, she had been "ordered to fulfil another task."

Soviet-Slovak Pact

MOSCOW, Dec. 6.—Soviet Russia signed a trade treaty today with Slovakia, German-protected state which was carved out of the dismembered Czechoslovakia republic.

KOBE, Japan, Dec. 6.—Waterfront rumors circulated today of the arrival and departure from this port of a ship believed by sailors to be a German "prison" vessel.

The Queen Visits Children in Shelter

—A. P. Wirephotos

LONDON.—The Queen, with the King (behind her) chats with children as she inspects the bunks of a deep air raid shelter in South London, Nov. 14. Their Majesties are tireless in their tours of air raid shelters and bombed areas. Their presence does much to cheer the populace.

RAF Defeats Italians in Mass Battle

LONDON, Dec. 6.—Royal Air Force fighters in an air battle with "large numbers" of Italian fighters over Southwestern Albania, destroyed eight planes and severely damaged seven others Wednesday, the Air Ministry announced today. There were no British losses.

Offensive operations of British fliers yesterday also included attacks on an electro-chemical factory at Eindhoven and airports at Rotterdam and Haamstede, all in the Netherlands, and the German submarine base at Lorient, France, the Air Ministry announced.

Two British aircraft were lost in patrols.

Because of bad weather bombing operations last night were cancelled, a communique said.

RAIDERS FOILED

German bombers attempted a "blitz-raid" on a south coast town last night, but bad weather and heavy anti-aircraft fire sent them home by midnight.

London had two air raid alarms, but the attacks were of the "nuisance" type and the city

Please Turn to Page Twenty-one
See "RAF Defeats"

Survivors Rescued

CANBERRA, Australia, Dec. 6.—Thirteen survivors of an unidentified ship were rescued from the wreckage of their vessel off the Australian coast Thursday.

It was reported that six members of the crew of the wrecked vessel were lost. Details of the disaster have not been learned.

Missing Girl Is Found; Police Check Her Story

The 13-year-old Kitsilano Junior High School girl student who disappeared from her home on Tuesday was found unharmed in New Westminster early today.

She is a witness against two East Indians and a white woman charged with statutory offenses and police are checking her story that she disappeared because she was "afraid to go home late from school."

THREATENED SAYS MOTHER

Her mother told The Vancouver Sun on Thursday that the girl had been threatened on the street by a woman and a white man prior to her disappearance, and police are digging into every angle of the case to ascertain if the "youngster was induced to leave home so that she would not appear in court against the charged persons," as one police official phrased it.

Her story that she obtained $2 on Tuesday afternoon from an East Indian "who had helped her out before," is causing authorities much concern.

They are trying to ascertain from the girl the name of the East Indian friend so that they can check her story, but the girl "closed up like a clam" when the officer started to question her.

FAMILY THANKFUL

In the home of the girl there is thankfulness that the child has returned unharmed.

It puts at rest fears of her father and mother that she had been spirited away and harmed because interested persons "wanted her out of the way," as the father phrased it on Thursday night.

Detectives are still working on the theory that the girl might have been "induced to leave home" and they are bending every effort to get to the facts of the case.

The girl told Detective C. A. Mackie of New Westminster police early today that she had been given "$2 by a Hindu who helped me out before" and that she took this mnoey and fled from the city.

'SLEPT IN HAYMOW'

She said that she had slept in a haymow Tuesday night and in a boxcar Wednesday night, but Detective Mackie states that her clothing did not indicate she had slept under such circumstances.

Her story to authorities today was that she had gone to a show after obtaining the money from an East Indian

Please Turn to Page Twenty-one
See "Girl Found"

Greeks Capture 3500 Italians; $9 Million Loot

'Italy's Best Warrior' May Have Been Fired For Reverses

By REYNOLDS PACKARD

Special to The Vancouver Sun
Copyright, 1940, by British United Press

ROME, Dec. 6. — Marshal Pietro Badoglio, Chief of the General Staff, active commander of Italy's land, sea and air forces, resigned today. No reason was given.

LONDON.—Military sources expressed the opinion that Badoglio had been "fired" as a scapegoat for Italian military reverses, or "because he is opposed to the attitude of the party organization."

Badoglio was succeeded by Gen. Ugo Cavallero, a comparatively obscure army veteran who has been commanding troops on the Italian-French frontier.

NEW GREEK EFFORT

It was announced that Gen. Cavallero had taken command iffeidately and that as a result, preparations for a forthcoming Italian offensive against Greece would be speeded up.

Badoglio

Badoglio has an outstanding military record, dating back to the Italian-Turkish campaign in 1910.

Cavallero had some prominence in World War peace negotiations. He headed Italy's military delegation to the Inter-Allied Committee in Versailles after the Armistice, and was president of the Italian military delegation at the peace conference.

He has been a politician as well as a military man, and as Under-Secretary of War in 1925-28 he worked closely wiwth Mussolini in the reorganization of Italian armed forces.

OFFICIAL STATEMENT

The communique announcing the change in chiefs of staff, an office responsible only to King Victor Emmanuel and Mussolini in military matters. read:

"A royal decree announces that Marshal Pietro Badoglio has presented his resignation as Chief of the General Staff of the Italian army, Another royal decree appoints Gen. Ugo Cavallero, who was appointed Army General for his war merits, as Chief of the General Staff of the Italian Army."

Badoglio continues as President of the National Council of h eeR asr hwcchiosrnps gationsi Research, which sponsors investigations into both scientific

Please Turn to Page Twenty-one
See "Badoglio"

Jugoslav Report Claims Argirocastro, Last Fascist Base in South Albania Taken; Hellenes Gain on All Fronts

In addition to smashing victories over the Italians, dispatches from the Albanian front reveal war material gains aggregating $9,000,000 and approximately 3500 prisoners: 1500 reported taken in the fall of Porto Edda, 1000 in the drive on Elbasani in Mid-Albania, and, according to unconfirmed reports, 1000 in the capture of Argirokastro.

ATHENS, Greece, Dec. 6.—Greek troops today occupied the important Fascist coastal base of Porto Edda and were reported striking "unceasingly" toward Italian military headquarters at Elbasan, in mid-Albania.

(Jugoslav dispatches said Greek troops also occupied Argirokastro at noon today and took more than 1000 prisoners.)

Occupation of Porto Edda was announced in a communique recalling that the third largest Albanian port was recently modernized by Italy and named for Countess Edda Ciano, daughter of Premier Benito Mussolini.

While Greek troops and British airplanes are smashing at Italian columns choking the road northward along the coast from Porto Edda, other Greek troops are struggling through snow and winter weather on the central and north fronts in a two-headed drive toward Elbasan, only 20 miles from Tirana.

Guns on 'Breeches Buoys'

The Athens press reported very heavy fighting north of Moskopolis where a general Greek attack was underway in the mountain chain northwest of Koritza.

The Greeks brought up guns to mountain positions by the use of breeches buoys and opened fire on retreating Italians.

The sector was said to be held by a Piedmontese regiment which was virtually out of food. The Piedmontese were said by the Greeks to have fought well in the opening days of the action but finally broke down under fierce Greek bayonet charges.

The Greeks estimated they already have seized more than $8,000,000 worth of equipment abandoned by the retreating Italians, including more than 500 machine-guns.

About 1500 Italians surrendered at Porto Edda, and it is reported that another 1000 have been captured in the drive on Elbasan, Italian base in Mid-Albania.

The Italian army command in South Albania is hopeful of establishing a line based on Port Palermo.

Greek forces are striking without cessation at enemy flank and rear guard units despite heavy bombardment by the Italian Air Force.

Official information from the front lines said that the Italian retreat continues "steadily" from the sea coast to the mountain ranges above Lake Ochrida on the Jugoslav frontier.

One Greek advance force was reported to have taken 500 prisoners and much war material in seizing the Kami heights northwest of Pogradec and about 20 miles from Elbasan.

A second column, sweeping through the hills on a southerly circle of Elbasan, was reported making progress through the Devoli River valley about 35 miles from its objective.

Port Palermo, where the Italians hope to make a stand, is 20 miles north of Porto Edda on the old coast road, which dwindles off to a mule path before it reaches Valona, second largest Albanian port, 70 miles north.

The Greeks had stood before Porto Edda more than 24 hours waiting for the Italians to evacuate before they entered and ocupied the city this morning.

The Italians threw up a rear guard of tanks and armed cars

Please Turn to Page Twenty-one
See "Greeks Advance"

Huns Bomb Windsor Castle

By Canadian Press

LONDON, Dec. 6.—It was disclosed today that three bombs fell in the grounds of Windsor Castle in a recent air raid.

One bomb fell on the golf course, another close to the tennis courts and a third—an oil bomb— fell on the royal household bowling green and quickly burned itself out.

Some damage was done to the Royal Lodge but no casualties were reported. Bombs which also fell on Windsor Town resulted in little damage.

Windows and the roof of a nursing home were badly damaged when a bomb fell in the middle of the street. None of the patients were hurt seriously.

SUN POPULAR PROMENADE CONCERT TONIGHT — AUDITORIUM — 8:30 O'CLOCK —

Markets on Page 21

'DEFEAT NEAR FOR NIGHT BOMBING'

F.D.R. Extends 'Lease-Loan' Plan to Britain's Allies

The Vancouver Sun

Only Evening Newspaper Owned, Controlled and Operated by Vancouver People

FINAL

FOUNDED 1886
VOL. LV—No. 77 VANCOUVER, BRITISH COLUMBIA, MONDAY, DECEMBER 30, 1940 Price 3 Cents

(EDITORIAL)

Butter "Shortage" Just Plain Robbery

Settling a price for butter, the federal government has merely touched on the edge of a disgraceful situation. For years, the price of butter has been manipulated by a group of wholesalers in Montreal. Comparable to their operations is the selfish set-up of the professional traders of the Winnipeg Grain Exchange who have long swung prices and transactions in any direction their sweet will inclined.

Unfortunately for the farmers, the manipulation of the butter market has usually been downward. In Montreal, if you have watched the market through months and years, the emphasis has almost invariably been placed on the huge size of the surplus butterfat products in Canada. In reality, the butter has been sold almost at "dump" prices. Below 30 cents, sales mean practical crucifixion for producers in our own Fraser Valley, for instance.

A few weeks ago, the people who fix the prices in the big eastern market centres evidently saw a chance for a killing, by the creation of a fictitious "shortage." So up the ladder the price was started. The government did quite right to interfere. The net effect was that the consumer was being mulcted in the interests of unjustified profits for the big wholesalers. The compromise gives the farmer a fair price—certainly not too large—and does not allow the product to get out of the reach of the average household.

J. W. Berry, pioneer official of the Fraser Valley Milk Producers' Association, put his finger on the spot—which puts the Montreal manipulators "on the spot"—when he told The Sun on Saturday that the alleged shortage of butter supplies was "just a myth." We had already given our view that there is actually no national shortage of butter and we are glad to be confirmed by an experienced authority like Mr. Berry.

In order that the public may have no doubt about the authenticity of Mr. Berry's views and of our own, it may be well to recall that the last monthly dairy review of Canada, issued at Ottawa on the authority of the Dominion Bureau of Statistics and based on national records, has this to say:

"It seems obvious that a substantial butter surplus still exists. Indications now point to a normal milk production and a diversion of milk from cheese factories to creameries; so that in the course of the next month it is quite possible that the butter output may approximate that of the same month of the preceding year."

Montreal butter manipulators would not, of course, expect the public to be informed of these official conclusions and they hoped to pull off a "shortage" scare. Some newspapers, including one in Vancouver, have published the fiction that so many dairy cattle have been destroyed that the shortage has a substantial basis.

The fact is that the number of cows being milked in Canada dropped just one percent in one year. Nearly ten percent more butter and cheese were produced in all Canada during October, 1940, than in the corresponding month a year ago. For British Columbia the figures were identical.

One may not allow the occasion to pass without calling attention once more to developments in prices of stock feeds. For farmers in the Fraser Valley a JUST PRICE on the grain they are forced to buy from Alberta would give them a decent living now, with the price of butter pegged at what it is. But it is noted (in the same federal official bulletin quoted above) that prices of oats, barley and bran registered an increase in November of 5½ percent above the same month last year. This has occurred in a country where there are today at least 400 million more bushels of grain that is PRACTICALLY UNSALEABLE than existed in storage a year ago. If you can explain this increase in price, against the background of a terrific surplus, by any other reason than that a nefarious manipulation is going on, then you are a lot smarter than we are.

The whole trading position in grain and grain products in Canada is a most fantastic and fictitious build-up against the interests of the people. It cries out for redress. When the government moves to halt the runaway market in butter it is merely touching the fringe of a vast robbery by favored interests who have erected such a buttressed position that they believe themselves immune from attack.

Full Aid For China And Greece

Announcement Made by Morgenthau After Conference With President and Purvis; 'As Fast as Possible'

WASHINGTON, Dec. 30.—Henry Morgenthau, United States treasury secretary, disclosed today that President Roosevelt's "lease-lending" plan for financing war materials "might apply" to Greece, China and other countries.

Morgenthau, who conferred with Mr. Roosevelt and Arthur B. Purvis, chief of the British Purchasing Mission here, told a press conference that the loan-lease plan—providing for American purchase of war materials and their release to Britain—"might apply to anybody."

He added, however, that any application of the policy to Britain or any other country "depends on what Congress does." Legislation to authorize and supply funds for the arms purchases is needed.

Morgenthau declined to comment on the matters which he had discussed with Mr. Roosevelt and Purvis.

He said that his meeting Purvis was "for the purpose of going into his problems," and added that "it didn't begin to cover 10 per cent of the ground."

"He was informing me as to what he has learned concerning Britain's needs," Morgenthau said

"AS FAST AS POSSIBLE"

He denied that any mention of a specific time table for aid to Britain had been made to him, saying that the only time limit he has discussed is "as fast as possible."

Chinese officials also have been discussing with the Treasury the possibility of shipments of warplanes to that country, Morgenthau said, but added that "there just aren't enough planes to go around."

"They may have gotten five or ten planes in the past ten months," Morgenthau said, "but I doubt if it's been more."

Morgenthau flatly refused to comment on reports that the United States might seize or purchase foreign merchant vessels tied up in American ports.

He disclaimed any knowledge of reports that the coast guard had already inspected these ships.

Earlier Purvis said that the loan-lease plan of British aid "opened up a new chapter" in American aid to his homeland.

Axis Reply to Speech—'Roosevelt Puts U.S. in War'

President Roosevelt's address—delivered from the White House to a world-wide audience last night as Nazi bombers started the greatest conflagration London's ancient "City" has seen in 300 years—today caused

*For Editorial Comment See Page 4

Axis spokesmen to charge that United States has entered "an undeclared war" against Germany, Italy and Japan, and brought a forecast that Adolf Hitler may make a personal answer.

In London the speech, jubilantly acclaimed, shared newspaper columns with angry charges that the Nazi Luftwaffe deliberately tried to burn out the heart of London without regard for military objectives.

The Luftwaffe's attack on "The City" furnished a fiery background for President Roosevelt's declaration that Amer-

Please Turn to Page Eleven See "Roosevelt"

'Best Actress'

KATHARINE HEPBURN

NEW YORK, Dec. 30.—Katharine Hepburn has been adjudged "the best actress of the year" by the New York Film Critics' Circle for her work in "The Philadelphia Story" in which she is still appearing.

Late Bulletins

Nova Scotia Protests

HALIFAX, Dec. 30.—Nova Scotia has protested officially against the action of the Wartime Price and Trade Board in pegging the price of butter without parallel action reducing costs of feeds to farmers.

Pacific Ship Making Port

A WEST COAST CANADIAN PORT, Dec. 30.—A schooner which previously had reported herself in difficulty 300 miles off Cape Flattery in the storm-swept Pacific was sighted from this port today.

Brodeur's Stepson Killed

VICTORIA, Dec. 30.—Capt. G. L. Stephens said today he had been advised by Commodore Victor G. Brodeur, Canadian Naval Attache at Washington, that the Commodore's stepson, William Whitfield, 20, has been killed in action in Egypt.

Auto Horn Saves Man's Life

KLAMATH FALLS, Ore., Dec. 30.—Vic Vidall, 40, Klamath Falls carpenter, lost his life when his auto plunged into five feet of water.. A companion, Jacob Sevick, was rescued because he pressed horn button 15 minutes.

GUATEMALA CITY, Guatemala, Dec. 30. — The government announced today 12 persons were executed by firing squads Saturday after having been convicted on charges of sedition and attempted rebellion.

'New Move Will Curb Nazi Raids'

'Won't Be Very Long Before Weight Will Be Taken Out of German Ruthlessness'

OTTAWA, Dec. 30.—A method has been found to defeat the German night raiders who have been showering bombs on British cities for months, Air Marshal Sir Hugh Dowding of the Royal Air Force said in an interview here today.

"I confidentally believe it will not be very long now before all the weight and sting has been taken out of these night bombing attacks," he said.

He would not say exactly when the new defense would be in operation, but expected by spring the worst of the night bombing menace would be over.

When that happened, he said, it was to be expected the Germans would turn their bombing planes loose for more intensive attacks on British sea-borne traffic and preparations were being made to deal with that menace also.

The distinguished British officer, here on his way to Washington to confer with United States authorities on standardization of aircraft equipment, gave no details but said equipment for the new method of air fighting was being rapidly completed.

LONDON, Dec. 30.—Britain now is attacking the problem of night raiders by new night patrols against the continental airports.

Under the new British plan, long-cruising fighter-bombers hop the Channel in the evening and dodge about the Nazi adance airports until the lights are flashed on for takeoffs or landings. Then they attack the field itself or attempt to catch the raiders off base.

Clenched-fist Londoners Amidst Fire Raid Ruins

By H. L. PERCY
British United Press Staff Correspondent

LONDON, Dec. 30.—The ancient "City" area of London lay smoking and blackened today after a German fire raid which Great Britain officially charged was a deliberate Nazi attack on non-military objectives.

Prime Minister Winston Churchill, his shoes muddy with the water from fire hoses and his coat smudged with the soot of charred buildings, walked amid the devastation this afternoon.

He saw angry Britons clench their fists and shout: "We won't crack up! We won't crack up!" And he saw waving from a tottering wall of the devastated Guildhall the Union Jack, planted there last night while flames licked hungrily at the centuries-old timbers.

Tonight the flames which had turned the heavens over London an awesome pink had died to smoking embers, but the anguish of Britain's great loss in history-shrouded structures and business and commercial offices was only beginning to drive home.

THEIR JOBS GONE

There were thousands of persons in London tonight who will draw no pay cheques this week nor for many weeks to come—their offices and enterprises are tangled masses of ruins.

The loss in ancient buildings is the greatest yet wrought by the Luftwaffe—the Guildhall, nine lovely churches built by Sir Christopher Wren, Dr. Samuel Johnson's quarters, a great museum, two hospitals, two theatres, a hotel.

Not all of these are total wrecks, but all were hard hit.

Not all the damage was in the City quarters.

Many other parts of London were hit, particularly in the central section.

There was damage in the City at Cheapside, Ludgate Hill, Bun Hill Row, Queen Victoria Street, Aldermanbury and Basing Hall Street.

Dr. Johnson's famous dictionary was saved, but his quarters were badly gutted.

At the height of the conflagration Sir George Wilkinson, lord

Please Turn to Page Eleven
See "City Raided"

Jobless Girl Dies Alone in Yule Tragedy

By KEN GRANT

Death ended the tragic story early Sunday of beautiful Lillian Chibree, a lonely, unemployed "white collar girl," who spent her last Christmas Eve alone in a West End rooming house.

Miss Chibree died in the Vancouver General Hospital at 4 a.m., 30 hours after she was taken from her room, apparently suffering from disinfectant poisoning.

One of the last persons to see Miss Chibree was a kind-hearted Vancouver woman, Mrs. Daisy Cooper, 3567 Pandora Street, who brought the girl some Christmas presents.

"She was a very lovely girl, and it seemed a shame that she could not enjoy Christmas like the rest of us. I wanted her to

Please Turn to Page Eleven
See "Girl Dies"

AUCKLAND, N. Z. — New Zealand is expediting shipping of refrigerated product to England by a system of fast but smaller ships.

Santa Anita Race Results

CALIFORNIA

FIRST RACE—Six furlongs:
Servant Maid (Corbett) $10.60, $4.60, $3.60.
Milk Bar (Balaski) $4.20, $3.60.
Valdina Knave (Westrope) $3.40.
Time, 1:13.

SECOND RACE—Six furlongs:
Musical Jack (Dew) $11.20, $9.40, $4.00.
Indiantown (Pollard) $4.60, $3.60.
Old Whitey (Craigmyle) $6.40.
Time: 1.13 4-5.

THIRD RACE—One mile:
Queercus (J. Adams) $12.80, $5.40, $3.20.
Gay Mate (A. Bassett) $8.60, $4.00.
Stella Gold (Dew) $2.60.
Time: 1.42 2-5.

FOURTH RACE—Six furlongs:
Transient (Skelly) $14.40, $6.20, $3.80.
Valley Boy (Westrope) $4.00, $3.00.
Brown China (Dew) $2.80.
Time 1.12 3-5.

Tropical Park Race Results

FLORIDA

FIRST RACE—Six furlongs:
Queen Echo (Gonzales) $46.80, $19.20, $11.10.
Blossom Queen (Luce) $16.60, $10.40.
No Ending (Garner) $5.40.
Time, 1:13.

SECOND RACE—Six furlongs:
Locked Out (Taylor) $11, $5.50, $4.20.
Wise Dean (Flinchum) $18, $8.90.
Blue Castle (Anderson) $3.90.
Time, 1:12 4-5.

THIRD RACE—Six furlongs:
Orchard Run (Emery) $58, $21.40, $12.40.
Alseleda (Flinchum) $5.30, $4.30.
Gayova (Howell) $15.20.
Time, 1:12 4-5.

FOURTH RACE—Mile and 70 yds.:
Shaun G (Johnson) $5.70, $4.40, $3.50.
Matchcan (Taylor) $5.60, $4.30.
Bud B (Knisley) $17.60.
Time, 1:45 1-5.

FIFTH RACE—Six furlongs:
Floataway (Knisley) $7.20, $4.20, $3.10.
Throttle Wide (Nash) $13.40, $7.50.
Breathless (Snider) $6.
Time, 1:11 3-5.

SIXTH RACE—Six furlongs:
Arched (Emery) $81.20, $24.10, $11.60.
Weisenheimer (Haskell) $7.70, $5.20.
Bold Turk (Meade) $5.80.
Time, 1:14 4-5.

SEVENTH RACE—Mile and one-sixteenth:
Topee (Atkinson) $17.30, $7.60, $4.90.
Commendador (Mower) $7.60, $5.60.
Paul Pry (Young) $6.60.
Time, 1:44 2-5.

EIGHTH RACE—Mile and seventy yards:
Polina (Luce) $149.40, $44.10, $18.50.
Prince Derek (Knisley) $7.40, $6.00.
Star Bud (Taylor) $5.20.
Time 1:44 3-5.

Race Entries on Page 17

Lennon Can Play—If He Pays Fine

Owen "Lulu" Lennon, Vancouver Lions' hockey player, who was fined a week's pay by Manager Guy Patrick, for "not taking care of himself after being injured" will not be allowed to play in tonight's game against Portland at the Forum unless he pays the fine, Patrick announced this afternoon.

If Lennon doesn't turn up for tonight's tilt he will be suspended for his action. Patrick claims Lennon worked a full eight-hour shift with his leg still in bad shape, which was not in compliance with his doctor's orders.

LONDON.—The rectory of St. James's Piccadilly was destroyed when a bomb fell in the forecourt of the Wren Church.

Roosevelt Speech 'All OK' Declares Al. Smith

By British United Press

NEW YORK, Dec. 30. — Former Gov. Alfred E. Smith, who took a walk from the Democratic Party in 1936 and kept going in 1940, endorsed President Roosevelt's defense broadcast as "all O.K.' today, indicating he favored U.S. participation in the war if such action should be necessary to insure Hitlers defeat, and said he was ready at 67 to "make my share of the sacrifices."

In a birthday interview the 1928 Democratic presidential nominee praised the man whose political foe he has been for nearly eight years for making what he called "a very courageous and straight-hitting speech."

Late Stocks on Page 11

1941

A year of unmitigated disaster for the Allies, which would include both Russia and America by the end of the year. The only redeeming factor was that Britain was no longer alone. First, Germany conquered Yugoslavia, Greece and Crete, thus gaining a measure of control in the eastern Mediterranean. Then HMS *Hood* was sunk in the Atlantic with all hands. Russia was invaded and the German blitzkrieg was at the gates of Moscow. The year ended with the Japanese surprise bombing of Pearl Harbor, the virtual destruction of the American Pacific fleet, and the rapid conquest of the whole of the Far East. Things never looked blacker, but with America now in the war wholeheartedly, optimism prevailed.

MAJOR EVENTS

April 6, 1941

GREECE AND THE BALKANS CAPITULATE

Hitler had already frightened Rumania, Hungary and Bulgaria into signing a Tripartite Pact of Friendship with Germany, and now he tried the same on Prince Paul, regent for young King Peter of Yugoslavia.

Paul acceded to Hitler's demands, but Serb generals in the Yugoslav army exiled him in a coup on March 27th in a moment of defiance. Their plans never went beyond this vain gesture. The Yugoslav army of one million was mired in pre-World War I thinking, their equipment obsolete, their transportation mules and horses, and their air force worthless.

So when German, Italian and Hungarian army groups attacked on April 6, defeat came in less than a month. The Croat part of the army sided with the Germans, and the Serb resistance was so disorganized and feeble that the Germans suffered only 151 dead during the whole campaign.

[See pages 40–41]

Greece was attacked at the same time and the Greek army fared no better, even with the help of a British Expeditionary Force of three divisions. Total chaos reigned when the Greek premier committed suicide on April 18th. With no new leadership emerging, the British saw the writing on the wall and packed up and left, leaving 3,000 dead and 9,000 prisoners. April 27th saw Nazi troops raising the swastika over the Acropolis. *[See pages 42–43]*

To complete the takeover of the region, Hitler felt compelled to add the Island of Crete to his list of conquests. Gliders and parachutists were launched May 20th against the British and New Zealand forces holding the island. By June 1st, the Royal Navy was called upon for another evacuation, this time rescuing 18,000 troops, but leaving behind 12,000 prisoners and 2,000 dead. Another catastrophe for the British! *[See pages 40–45]*

May 23-27, 1941

SINK THE BISMARCK!

The dramatic sea battle between Britain's and Germany's two mightiest warships will always be a major chapter in the annals of naval warfare.

The brand new German battleship *Bismarck* was the most powerful battleship afloat, weighing 42,000 tons—a giant ship

The British battle cruiser HMS *Hood* was the biggest warship in the world. Built in 1921, with eight 15-inch guns and a top speed of 32 knots, its only flaw was a thinly armoured deck, which proved to be disastrous.

Accompanying *Hood* was another new battleship, HMS *Prince of Wales*. They had been searching the North Atlantic near Iceland on learning that the *Bismarck* and the cruiser *Prinz Eugen* had left Norway headed for the Atlantic to raid British shipping lanes.

The U-boats were already sinking 350,000 tons of cargo ships every month, and the *Bismarck* could not be allowed to add to that calamitous total.

The confrontation came on May 23rd when the ships spotted each other just west of Iceland. *Hood* and *Prince of Wales* were exchanging salvoes with the two German ships when one 15-inch shell from the *Bismarck* landed squarely on the deck of the *Hood* and penetrated into the bowels of the ship, where it exploded and set off the *Hood's* magazines. A tremendous explosion rocked the ship, blowing it in half and sinking it in a matter of minutes. There were three survivors out of a crew of 1,420. All of the British Home Fleet was called upon to avenge this disaster the Germans had visited upon the Royal Navy, and the *Bismarck* was hunted to its death over the next few days. The dramatic story is told on pages 46–47.

June 22, 1941

GERMANY INVADES RUSSIA

The greatest blitzkrieg of all time had to be the dawn invasion of Russia by three million German troops, 3,500 tanks and 3,000 aircraft along a thousand-mile front stretching from the Baltic to the Black Sea. Steamrolling over the surprised Russians at the rate of 50 miles a day, three German army groups advanced 600 miles into Russia in five months.

Besides capturing vast amounts of matériel along the way, at Kiev alone they captured 650,000 Russian soldiers. Altogether, 5,700,000 prisoners were taken and sent off to Germany as slave labour—3,300,000 never returned.

Stalin had been warned from several sources of the impending German invasion, but he refused to believe it. His stubbornness left Russia temporarily unprepared for the Nazi onslaught, which had three major objectives. An army group in the north, under Field Marshal von Leeb, was to take Leningrad and join up with the Finns, once again at war with the Russians. An army group in central Russia, under Field Marshal von Bock, was instructed to take Moscow, and another army group in the south, under Field Marshal von Rundstedt, headed for the Caucasus and Russia's oil supplies.

The northern drive resulted in the famous Seige of Leningrad. The city held fast under Marshal Voroshilov, but suffered indescribable privation among its citizens. The Battle of Moscow stopped the Germans dead in their tracks, and the Caucasus drive foundered at Stalingrad the next year, where the most heroic battle of the war was fought and won by the Russians, foretelling the beginning of the end for Nazi Germany.

[See pages 48–51, 53, 55, 57]

August 26, 1941

ALLIED TAKEOVER OF IRAN

At the same time that the Red Army mounted a spirited defense against the Germans' frontal attack in the west, the Allies took measures to make sure Russia's back door remained open.

Indian troops invaded Iran from the east in concert with Russian troops invading from Armenia in the north. British airborne troops also landed in the Anglo-Iranian oil fields to guard against sabotage by German fifth columnists. The major reason for the takeover was to guarantee passage of American lend-lease supplies and equipment overland from the Persian Gulf north to the Russian border.

Once in the country, the Allies found the Iranian roads and railways so primitive that they had to build their supply network almost from scratch. The job got done, however, with most of the tanks, trucks, planes, rice, lead, tires, and a multitude of other matériel getting through to aid the Russian war effort.

[See page 55]

September 30, 1941

THE STRANGE CASE OF RUDOLF HESS

One of the most sensational stories of the war occurred when Rudolf Hess flew secretly to Scotland on May 10th in a Messerschmitt 110 fighter plane to see the Duke of Hamilton on a self-appointed peace mission. He was the deputy fuehrer of Nazi Germany, second only to Hitler.

Hess's navigation was good enough to bring him within 12 miles of the Duke's estate, where he parachuted from the plane. Landing in a field, he asked a farmer to take him to the duke, whom he had met at the 1936 Berlin Olympics. He explained that he was on "a mission of humanity and that the Fuehrer did not want to defeat England and wished to stop the fighting."

Since he was not an official emissary, Churchill refused to see him or to entertain his offer of peace. Hess was very angry over his rejection, and was even more angry when he was treated as a prisoner of war rather than a visiting dignitary.

[See page 56]

November-December 1941

A VICTORY FOR 'GENERAL WINTER' AT MOSCOW

Hitler's assessment of the Red Army's fighting abilities was so coloured by the Finnish debacle that he expected to subdue Russia in two weeks. Any talk of winterized clothing and equipment was considered defeatist. But Russian resistance stiffened several weeks after the initial surprise attack, although the Red Army continued to pursue a "scorched earth" retreat into the depths of Russia until November, when the Germans were only 40 miles from Moscow.

There Stalin's best general, Marshal Georgi Zhukov, dug in to defend the capital, just as the first snow flurries of the coming winter swirled down on the German troops still dressed in their summer uniforms.

With temperatures eventually reaching 73 degrees below zero, over the whole front the Germans would suffer more than a million casualties by the following March, 100,000 of which were from frostbite alone. Soldiers falling asleep on duty would freeze to death. Boiling soup froze in less than a minute. Grease that ammunition was packed in froze solid. Engines would not work because their oil had frozen. Automatic weapons would only fire single shots before jamming. Butter had to be cut with a saw. Suicide was common.

The Russians, on the other hand, were perfectly at home in such weather. All motorized vehicles were equipped with chains, and tanks were on extra-wide treads that functioned in the snow. And all equipment was lubricated with a special machinery oil that didn't freeze.

Some German patrols actually penetrated as far as the suburbs of Moscow, only to be thrown back to their front lines. There they waited out the winter, resisting Russian attacks but going nowhere, until they finally retreated in the face of massive Russian offensives the following year.

[See page 57]

December 7, 1941

DAY OF INFAMY

The "Day that Will Live in Infamy" was President Roosevelt's description of the Japanese attack on the Pearl Harbor naval base in Hawaii on that historic Sunday morning.

The attack took place at 8 AM in Hawaii—10 AM in Vancouver and 1 PM in Washington, D.C. It was about noon in Vancouver when the *News-Herald* hit the street with its EXTRA. There is no one alive at that time who does not remember the details of where they were and what they were doing when they heard the news.

Japan was able to plan the attack in meticulous detail, having done its homework from intelligence gleaned by spies planted in Hawaii months before. They knew that virtually the whole U.S. Pacific Fleet would be neatly lined up in rows—like sitting ducks—at the naval base in Pearl Harbor.

Six Japanese aircraft carriers with 320 torpedo and dive bombers and 40 Zero fighters, along with two battleships, two heavy cruisers, three submarines and assorted destroyers and oilers stealthily made their way in complete secrecy across thousands of miles of the Pacific to within 200 miles of Hawaii. They even managed to launch their first wave of 200 planes before they were discovered by the Army Signal Corps on a radar installation given to them by the British as an early warning device in case of Japanese attack. The new-fangled radar signals were ignored.

One hour later, the Japanese materialized over the naval base and air fields and dealt the Americans their most humiliating military defeat of all time.

The navy lost 13 battleships sunk or damaged and 11 other vessels, plus several thousand lives. The Pacific forces had earlier been put on alert, but were just not *that* alert on such a lovely sunny Sunday morning.

[See pages 50–64, 66]

December 8-25, 1941

HONG KONG FALLS

When the Japanese attacked Hong Kong on December 8th, they encountered two Canadian battalions—the Royal Rifles of Canada and the Winnipeg Grenadiers. They had been hurriedly despatched from Canada at the request of the British in a futile attempt to bolster Hong Kong's defenses.

Overrun in two weeks by the overwhelming force of the Japanese, they suffered the first defeat of Canadian arms in World War II. Although ill-equipped and unprepared, the Canadians nevertheless acquitted themselves with bravery. Their commander, Brigadier J. K. Lawson, died fighting, pistol in hand.

[See pages 61–62, 66]

News FOR VICTORY Herald

LARGEST MORNING CIRCULATION WEST OF TORONTO

FINAL EDITION

VANCOUVER, B.C., SATURDAY, JANUARY 18, 1941

3c Five Cents on boats, trains and in country.

CHURCHILL ASKS FOR AVALANCHE OF U.S. ARMS

Prime Minister Winston Churchill

By W. J. CUMMING
British United Press Correspondent

GLASGOW, Scotland—Prime Minister Winston Churchill said Friday night that Britain must have an avalanche of United States weapons, in far greater quantities "than we are able to pay for," if she is to hold off Adolf Hitler's blows in "the front line of civilization."

Churchill made his dramatic appeal, in a surprise speech here, in the presence of President Roosevelt's personal envoy, Harry L. Hopkins, who sat near him on the speaker's platform. The speech was to an open-air meeting of Air Raid Precaution officials and workers.

Churchill spoke of the stark threat of a German invasion, mentioning the months of February, March and April, because "that bad man (Hitler) never had so great a need as he has now to strike Britain from his path."

But Britain is confident of her ability to beat off any invasion blow, he said, although the dangers ahead "might be fatal" if vigilance were relaxed.

The United States must provide Britain with more weapons, ships, planes and guns, without thought of payment now if the British are to hold the front lines of the United States' own security, the Prime Minister said.

'Weapons, Ships'

Hopkins, recently arrived in England on a mission for Mr. Roosevelt, sat shyly on the platform, his face half-hidden in his hand, as Churchill whirled around to him and said:

"We do not require in 1941 large armies from overseas.

"What we do require is weapons, ships and airplanes.

"All that we can pay for we will pay for but we require far more than we shall be able to pay for."

Britain's armed strength, he said, is fighting the cause of world democracy.

Churchill was glowing in his praise of President Roosevelt's program of all-out aid to Britain.

"I watch with deep emotion," he said, "the stirring processes whereby the democracy of the great American republic is establishing laws and formulating decisions in order to make sure that the British Commonwealth are able to maintain, as they are, the present front line of civilization and progress."

The Prime Minister flatly pledged Britain will fight through to the finish to a victory over Hitlerism, whatever the dangers and hardships.

Turning to Hopkins Churchill said to his audience:

"Mr. Hopkins has come in order to put himself into the closest relations with things here.

"He will return soon to report to his famous chief the impressions he has gathered in our islands."

Churchill then told of Britain's urgent need of ships, planes and guns. He described Britain's powerful army and strong, well-manned defenses against any Nazi invasion.

"Nevertheless, I do not feel it would be right for any of those responsible for the people of this country to generally dismiss from their minds the possibility of invasion," he said.

"Every day this occupation of Austria, Czechoslovakia, Poland, Norway, Denmark, Holland, Belgium and France—and presently perhaps Italy—continues there is built up a volume of hatred for the Nazi creed and for the German name which generations and perhaps centuries will hardly efface."

Stand Four Square

Churchill referred in this statement to a growing British belief that Italy may collapse in the not distant future, and that Adolf Hitler's armies will march into the peninsula.

"Therefore," Churchill continued, "it is for Herr Hitler a matter of supreme consequence to break down the resistance of

(Continued on Back Page)

B.C. Flyer Wins DFC For Heroism Overseas

Pilot Officer John Henry Green of Vancouver was one of three Canadians awarded the Distinguished Flying Cross for heroism in action it was announced in London Friday. The others were Flying Officer Mervyn Mathews Fleming of Ottawa

and Pilot Officer Everett Large Badoux of Stellarton, N.S.

Green joined the Royal Air Force in London in May of 1939 when he was 20 years old, his aunt said last night. His aunt, Mrs. C. J. White, lives at 2869 West Fifth Avenue, Vancouver.

Green's parents, Mr. and Mrs. John L. Green, and his two sisters, live in Port Alberni, Vancouver Island. Green attended public school in Vancouver as a small boy but later moved to Port Alberni where he attended high school.

Report Hun Troops Train For Campaign In Desert

BERLIN, Saturday, (UP)—The possibility of German participation in the African campaign was seen today when Nazi colonial sources disclosed that thousands of German troops are undergoing rigorous training on the sand flats of East Prussia.

Officers of Adolf Hitler's "South troops" were said to have participated as "official observers" in the near East campaign prior to last October. Returning with first hand information regarding fighting under tropical conditions these officers were said to have set about instructing soldiers.

According to these informed sources, the Nazi troops in East Prussia are under command of the Reich's colonial specialist, Col. George Tzschirner, who is said to be thoroughly acquainted

with conditions below the Mediterranean.

The German "South troops" were said to be practicing various maneuvers applicable to desert warfare.

It was stated that uniform factories speeded up production of a special new kind of colonial uniforms shortly before Christmas.

Italian Prisoners Say Ships Sunk

ATHENS — (UP) — Greek troops captured 1800 Italians Friday, some of whom said two Italian liners, the 20,000 ton Lombardia and the 15,345 ton Liguria were torpedoed in the Adriatic when bound for Albania and filled with troops.

INVASION COAST VAST BONFIRE IN RAF RAID

The Sunday Sun

Only Evening Newspaper Owned, Controlled and Operated by Vancouver People

FOUNDED 1886
VOL. LV—No. 118

VANCOUVER, BRITISH COLUMBIA, SATURDAY, FEBRUARY 15, 1941

Price 10 Cents

★ ★ ★ ★ ★ FINAL

'Heartbreak' Dog

Four months ago Edward Scott of Chanute, Kan., went to Camp Ord, Calif., as a volunteer. His Airedale, Laddie, above, missing his master, grew melancholy, finally refused to eat or drink, became too weak to walk.

As Camp Ord officials made arrangements for Private Scott to keep Laddie in camp, doctors gave Laddie intravenous injections and shipped the one-man dog by airplane to California. But it was too late. Laddie reached his master but was unable to recognize him. He died.

Woman's Body On Road; Hint Of Foul Play

Result of investigations by traffic officials today may determine whether Vancouver's traffic has chalked up its ninth street fatality since Jan. 1.

Mrs. Jacqueline Jimes, 33, of 259 Powell Street, was found dead in the roadway in the 700 block Prior Street at 2:30 a.m., and police are trying to discover whether she died in an auto mishap or as a result of other violence.

COULDN'T AVOID BODY

Henry C. Scott, 28, 3370 East Georgia Street, a motorist, told police he saw the body in the centre of the street and could not swerve quickly enough to avoid running over it.

He said he was driving east on Prior Street and was going down a grade east of the Heatley Avenue intersection when he saw the body.

He went to a Union Street taxi stand to call an ambulance.

POLICE SUSPECT FIGHT

Police are checking closely into the possibility that the woman might have been involved in a fight.

Long gashes on her thighs gave rise to suspicions that she might have been left lying in the road following a knifing affray.

Her shoes were found 30 feet away.

The fact that no purse could be found near the woman's body indicated that robbery might have been the motive for an attack.

DEAD BEFORE CAR HIT HER?

Officials will try to determine in their investigation whether Mrs. Jimes was dead before Scott's car passed over her or whether she died after she was struck by the auto.

Scott was not detained by police.

Hair-Raising 'Find' By Two Doctors

SEATTLE, Feb. 15.—News for "bald heads" was given today at the University of Washington. Drs. Earl R. Norris and James Hausechildt have isolated a new vitamain called Inositol which, when given to bald mice has caused their hair to grow. No human experiments have been conducted yet, however.

All French Shore 'Mass Of Flames'

Bombs So Heavy Buildings on British Side of Channel Are Shaken; Constant Roar of Guns and Bombers

LONDON, Feb. 15.—Royal Air Force bombers assaulted the German-controlled Channel Ports shortly after dark tonight and a report reaching London said that the French coastline from Dunkirk to Boulogne "appeared to be a mass of fire."

Observers here said that the "entire French coastline from Dunkirk to Boulogne appeared to be ablaze.

The British attack began soon after dark, it was reported.

An observer at Folkestone said that the French coast looked like a great bonfire.

Skies were clear and the stars were out as the RAF planes went into action.

SHOOK BUILDINGS

British bombers dumped such heavy bomb loads in the first half hour of the attack that the concussion of the explosions shook buildings and windows on the British side of the Channel.

German anti-aircraft guns put up a terrific barrage, but failed to halt the attack.

The Boulogne area appeared to be the hardest hit.

The roar of guns and thunder of bombs rolled across the Channel constantly.

Fires shot up near Boulogne and Calais with smaller ones in between.

German airplanes this afternoon attempted to carry out a mass daylight raid on Great Britain, but were driven off by Spitfire and Hurricane fighter planes.

Strong formations of German planes, flying at great altitude, crossed over the Kent coast not far from Dover.

As the Nazi planes flew inland squadrons of British fighter

Please Turn to Page Ten
See "Ruhr Raids"

Feared Dying

FORMER KING ALFONSO OF SPAIN

ROME, Feb., 15.—Former King Alfonso XIII of Spain recently stricken with a series of heart attacks remained in grave condition today and his physicians expressed the belief his death may not be very far away.

After his first heart attack Thursday he renounced his claims to the throne in favor of his son Prince Juan.

Alfonso has been residing here since he fled Spain in the face of a demand for his abdication and after his Minister of War had declared that the rebellious movement could be put down but that it would mean violence.

Alfonso refused to accept the responsibility for further bloodshed.

Hialeah Park Race Results

FLORIDA

FIRST RACE—Three furlongs:
His Shadow (Young) $4.50, $2.30, $2.30.
Spanish Miss (Meade) $2.40, $2.20.
Bellcoda (Vedder) $3.50.
Time :33 2-5.

SECOND RACE—Mile and one-half (turf):
Merry Son (Eads) $6, $4, $3.30.
Big Brand's Son (Nash) $4.70, $4.10.
Conrad Mann (Hettinger) $5.30.
Time 2:38.

THIRD RACE—Mile and one-quarter:
Gambit (Eads) $5.30, $4.40, $3.20.
Noodles (Smith) $11.80, $6.20.
eWary Flower (Garry) $6.60.
Time 2:04 4-5.

FOURTH RACE—Mile and three-sixteenths:
Comendador II (McCreary) $6.50, $3.60, $2.90.
Phoebus (Eads) $4.70, $3.70.
Consul (Arcaro) $2.90.
Time 1:57 4-5.

FIFTH RACE—Seven furlongs:
The Rhymer (Arcaro) $3, $2.60, $2.40.
Starry Hope (Stout) $5.20, $4.
Hornblende (Robertson) $7.30.
Time 1:24 1-5.

SIXTH RACE.—Mile and one-eighth.
Haltal (McCreary) $12.80, $7.40, $8.60.
Royal Man (Arcaro) $9.10, $7.00.
Dorimar (Linberg) $8.60.
Time 1:49.

SEVENTH RACE—Mile and one-eighth:
Big Pebble (Seabo) $46.90, $16.60, $12.50.
Ringle (Lindberg) $25, $12.20.
Joe Schenk (Vedder) $7.40.
Time: 1:49 4-5.

EIGHTH RACE—Mile and one-half (turf):
Navarin (Eads) $6.10, $4.20, $3.10.
Bettys Bob (McAndrew) $6.80, $4.20
Wodden Indian (Milligan) $4.80.
Time: 2:36 4-5.

NINTH RACE—Mile and one-eighth:
Counterpoise (Arcaro) $9.20, $4.20 $2.90.
Sun Mica (Nash) $5.20, $3.40.
Sandy Boot (Garner) $2.90.
Time: 1:50.

Vernon RCAF Flier Killed

BELLEVILLE, Ont., Feb. 15.—Flying Officer J. F. Mackie, Vernon, B. C., was instantly killed this afternoon when his training plane crashed near Pointe Anne, four miles east of this city. No details of the accident are available at present. Mackie was attached to the Royal Canadian Air Force station at Trenton.

J. F. Mackie

U.S. Consulates at Naples, Palermo Close

ROME. Feb. 15.—It was reported reliably here tonight that United States has decided to close its Consulates at Naples and Palermo at the request of Italian authorities.

Late Bulletins

Gunmen Terrorize Club; Man, Woman Shot to Death

SHANGHAI, Feb. 15.—Seven gunmen late tonight shot up Shanghai's most popular night club and gambling joint—Farren's—and terrorized 600 dancing and wagering members of the foreign community

Bessie Simmons, a British girl, and Albert Lunze, a German employee, were shot and killed.

The gunmean, believed to have been Koreans, opened wild fire around crowded roulette wheels and then dashed to a lower floor where there was dancing.

The bandits fired shots into the ceiling of the ballroom while frightened guests crawled under tables.

Nazi Bombers Over London

LONDON, Feb. 15.—London's second air raid alarm of the night sounded well before midnight tonight.

Italy Closes Frontier

BERNE, Switzerland, Feb. 15.—Italy suspended postal communications with Switzerland today, Berne post office officials disclosed.

'In Possession of Secret Codes'

PENTICTON, B.C., Feb. 15.—An additional charge of having been in possession of secret codes has been laid against Albert James Sutton, Jehovah's Witness.

Relief Worker Shot Dead

BAKERSFIELD, Calif., Feb. 15.—W. P. Fairbanks, a relief client, allegedly enraged when informed his relief check was being reduced, today shot and killed Mrs. Joe Tarbox, 35, state relief worker.

Widow of Capt. Dollar Dies

SAN RAFAEL, Calif., Feb. 15.—Mrs. Margaret Dollar, widow of Captain Robert Dollar, widow of the founder of Dollar Steamship Lines, died today at the family home here.

Greece in War 'to the End'

ATHENS, Feb. 15.—The official Greek News Agency said tonight that "Greece is negotiating with no one" and "the war being fought with Italy will be fought to the end."

Bomber on Way to Australia

HONOLULU, T.H., Feb. 15.—A long range patrol bomber built in San Diego, Calif., for the Australian government, left here today on the second leg of the 8000-mile flight to the Antipodes. It arrived here Wednesday from San Diego.

Quick Thinking Saves Life

RAYMOND, Wash., Feb. 15.—F. C. Quimby, his jugular vein accidentally severed by an axe, was recovering today, thanks to the presence of mind of his father who held the end of the vein together for an hour awaiting the arrival of a doctor.

Church People Must Be Heard

TORONTO, Feb. 15.—Archbishop Derwyn T. Owen, Primate of All Canada, expressed his conviction in a letter today that "it is the duty of our church people . . . especially today, to be more interested in public affairs, and to bring to the consideration of those affairs an instructed Christian conscience."

Japanese Cruiser at Saigon

SAIGON, French Indo-China, Feb. 15. — The Japanese cruiser Nagara arrived at Saigon today and tied up at the dock as 100 Japanese marines ran alongside and shouted a welcome.

It brought equipment and supplies for Japanese troops and airmen who arrived a few days ago without French permission.

Had 'Witness' Pamphlets; Six Months

EDMONTON, Feb. 15.—Charged with failure to notify authorities of a cache of illegal literature, J. F. Barbour of Edmonton, described as "one of the heads" of the Jehovah's Witnesses sect, was sentenced to six months today.

Barbour had thousands of pamphlets printed by the Watchtower Bible and Tract Society.

Five 'Jehovah Witness' Arrests

PRINCETON, B.C., Feb. 15.—Five men from Vernon, B.C., are charged under Defense of Canada regulations. They are Robert Bickert, Michael Charuk, Louis Saporito, Anton Neuman and Donald Goffick.

All were arrested by Constable Earl Nelson of the Provincial Police, ho said they were distributing pamphlets of the outlawed Jehovah's Witnesses sect.

PHILADELPHIA, Pa., Feb. 15.—Robert J. Blotz, missing Philadelphia investment counsellor, accused of swindling clients out of more than $2,500,000, was arrested today.

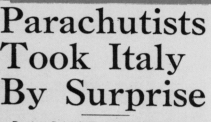

Still Polish and Still a Patriot

IGNACE JAN PADEREWSKI

NEW YORK, Feb. 15.—Musicians begin today a week's celebration of the 50th anniversary of the American debut of Ignace Jan Paderewski, the Polish pianist.

There will be special events in many cities to raise money for Padereswski's Polish Relief Fund.

Messages of congratulations to the National Paderewski testimonial included a letter from President Roosevelt who recalled that "few Americans have known you longer than I, for I have a distinct and vivid memory of attending your concerts as a boy and of meeting you personally for the first time many, many years ago."

'Most Violent Attack RAF Ever Launched'

LONDON, Feb. 15. — In a two-hour attack called by observers the most violent ever launched by the Royal Air Force, British bombers spread fire and explosion over the Nazi-held French coast from Dunkirk to Boulogne tonight and then opened a similar aerial bombardment of the German big gun positions at Cap Griz Nez.

Falling parachute flares signalled the start of this second assault, and Britons standing by thousands upon the English Coast lifted a great cheer when British planes went back to the job.

The German anti-aircraft guns lifted such a mighty barrage that it appeared the Nazis had recently placed many more guns along the invasion coast.

The white beams of the German searchlights were all but obscured now and again by rising columns of black smoke. A bright glow filled the skies.

3 Times Champion

TORONTO, Feb. 15.—Rod Phelan of Toronto Granite Club won his third consecutive Ontario singles title today at the Ontario badminton championships here, whipping Glenn Thompson of Toronto Carlton Club, 15-12, 15-12.

Santa Anita Race Results

CALIFORNIA

FIRST RACE.—Three furlongs.
Doctor Reder (James) $14.80, $7.20, $5.40.
Hubbub (Woolf) $6.6, $5.00.
Radio Joe (Gray) $9.20.
Time :34 2-5.

SECOND RACE—One mile:
Little Long (Pariso) $35.80, $19.40, $8.80.
Recoatna (Longden) $11.40, $6.40.
Palmera T (Nicholson) $4.20.

THIRD RACE—Seven furlongs:
At Play (Pariso) $11, $4.80, $3.60.
Mark (Skelly) $4.40, $3.40.
Pomkee (Gray) $4.20.
Time: 1:26 2-5.

FOURTH RACE—Six furlongs:
Enthrall (Pearson).
Wilton (Skelly).
Lassator (Adams).

Race Entries on Page 10

Parachutists Took Italy By Surprise

Daring British Troops Forced Tieup of Trains; Rome Denies Captured Britons Will Be Executed

By British United Press

ROME, Feb. 15.—Italian officials announced tonight that captured British parachutists will be considered ordinary prisoners of war and will be placed in a concentration camp.

They denied reports that they would consider the parachutists spies and send them before a firing squad.

The International Red Cross has been invited to visit concentration camps and see the prisoners.

By WALLACE CARROLL
Special to The Vancouver Sun
Copyright, 1941, by British United Press

LONDON, Feb. 15.—Britain confirmed today that in its first military raid against the Italian mainland it had dropped parachute troops in Southern Italy, and its confirmation implied that some of them had fulfilled their mission, escaped and returned to base.

An announcement from Rome today, stating "freight traffic along several railway lines in Southern Italy where British parachutists landed has been suspended" gave color to a belief that some of the British adventurers might still be at large in the Fascist homeland.

It was disclosed that the mission was to demolish "certain objectives" connected with ports in southern Italy.

Some May Have Escaped

After 24 hours of complete silence regarding Italian reports of parachutist landings, Britain released its story in a communique from the Ministry of Information which said:

"Soldiers dressed in recognized military uniform were recently dropped by parachute in southern Italy. Their instructions were to demolish certain objectives connected with ports in that area. No statement can be made at present about the results of operations but some men have not returned to their base."

Thus the implication was clear that some of the suicide detachment had escaped and returned to "base."

If the parachutists flew over Italy from ships a rendevous by boat or plane to pick them up was one possible explanation of the reference to their failure to return to base.

The area where the landings took place offers plenty of hiding places in wooded regions.

Giant Aqueduct Target

The Italians said the parachutists made their attack armed with machine guns, hand grenades and dynamite, on the night of Feb. 10-11 and claimed that all of them had been captured "before they could cause the serious damage they intended."

It was presumed in Rome that the principal objective of the British troops was wrecking of the 152-mile-long Apulian aqueduct carrying drinking water to about 2,500,000 Italians.

It was believed the attack was arranged by the Middle East Command with headquarters at Cairo.

Selections at Hialeah

1—Violante ,Star Weista, Remmembering.
2—Royal Ruby II, The Stork, Osisbo.
3—Hunting Home, Gallant Stroke, Hi Kid.
4—Johns Heir, Jelwell, High Scope.
5—Choppy Sea, Ice Water, Inquestion.
6—Ranger II, Close To, Weekly Stipend.
7—Bluesheets, Patsey Begone, Woodwaac.
8—Paul Pry, Shortdistance, Handiboy.

Best—VIOLANTE

LONDON. — Nearly 500 Methodist churches, more than 200 of them in London, have been damaged or destroyed by air raids.

'Chief' Named to Job Insurance Board

OTTAWA, Feb. 15.—V. C. Phelan of Ottawa, acting director of employment in the Labor Department, has been appointed chief employment officer of the Unemployment Insurance Commission. He will supervise some 83 principal and 1500 branch offices of the commission.

Heads Rugby Union

TORONTO, Feb. 15.—E. Floyd Muirhead, sponsor of Toronto Balmy Beach Football Club, was elected president of the Ontario Rugby Football Union at the annual meeting today. He succeeds Rev. M. H. Lynch, appointed a chaplain in the Royal Canadian Air Force.

37

HUNDREDS OF PLANES IN CHANNEL BATTLE

Ex-King Alfonso Dying

The Sunday Sun

Only Evening Newspaper Owned, Controlled and Operated by Vancouver People

FINAL

FOUNDED 1886
VOL. LV—No. 124 VANCOUVER, BRITISH COLUMBIA, SATURDAY, FEBRUARY 22, 1941 Price 10 Cents

'Any Port in a Storm'

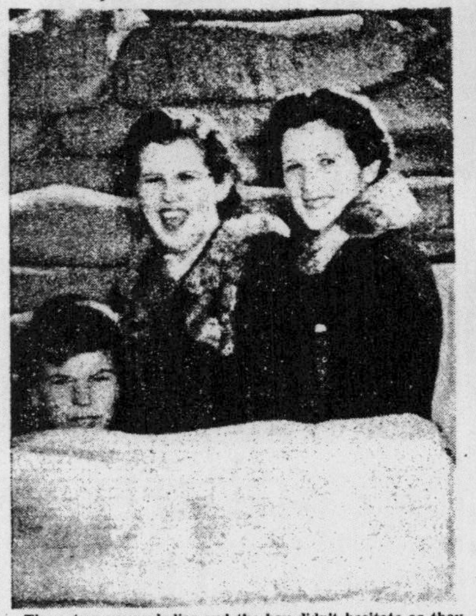

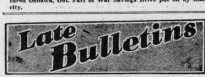

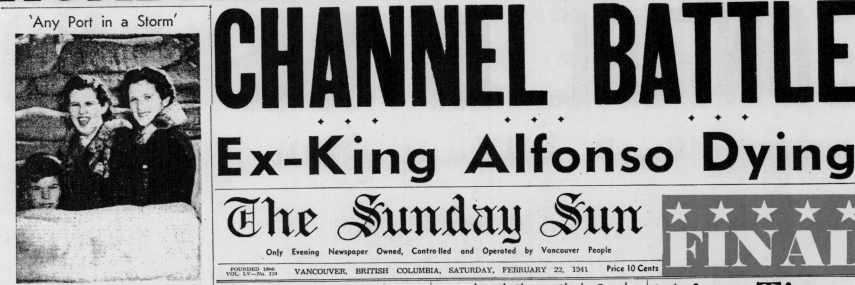

These two young ladies and the boy didn't hesitate as they took shelter in this sandbag dugout when "invading" troops captured Oshawa, Ont. Part of War Savings Drive put on by that city.

Late Bulletins

Concert Artists Defy Union of Musicians

NEW YORK, Feb. 22.—Jascha Heifetz, a member of the American Guild of Musical Artists, said today that the organization of noted concert stars will not submit to the demand of James C. Petrillo, head of the American Federation of Musicians, to join his union or cease giving concerts.

Earthquake Causes Panic

LIMA, Peru, Feb. 22.—A violent earthquake shock occured here today. The city was thrown into a panic for several minutes.

Hurricane Hits Suva

SUVA, Fiji Islands, Feb. 22.—A severe hurricane has struck Suva, causing considerable damage to buildings and gardens.

Jail Rather Than Wife

KANSAS CITY, Mo., Feb. 22.—Roland H. Joost, who says San Quentin prison is preferable to married life demanded today that police send him back to prison as a parole violator.

Street Worker Hit by Car

VICTORIA, Feb. 22.—George Hall was in hospital today with a fractured skull, a broken arm and lacerations to a hand suffered when he was struck by a car while working on a sewer job at Esquimalt late yesterday.

U.S. Goods Going to Enemy

SHANGHAI, Feb. 22.—Britain has made a new request to the United States to prevent its goods from reaching Germany by way of Japan and Russia, after uncovering extensive evidence of such shipments through its censorship at Hong Kong.

'Seal Chewing Up Furniture'

NEWPORT BEACH, Calif., Feb. 22.—A housewife telephoned police that a seal was chewing up her furniture. Officer Walt Dyson found the small seal, its foreflippers folded across its chest, calmly rocking back and forth in a rocking chair.

Students Bolt 'Dictatorship'

SAG HARBOR, N.Y., Feb. 22.—After one day under a dictatorship, 450 students at the Pierson High School voted unanimously today "let's get back to U.S.A." For six hours they were forced to wash dishes, scrub floors, forego free speech and in general kow-tow yesterday to the whims and fancies of "Dictator" E. Raymond Schneible and a squad of "storm troopers."

British Ship Seizure Protested

38

WASHINGTON, Feb. 22.—The United States and a majority of other American governments are supporting a Brazilian proposal for a collective protest to Great Britain for seizing the French steamship Mendoza within the pan-American neutrality zone last month. It was en route to France with food. (Britain declined to recognize the neutrality zone because no postive action was taken to ensure that Nazi raiders would be kept out of it.)

City Hotels All Full; Visitors Turned Away

Vancouver's record February, so far as it affected the hotels, reached its Zenith today when all the leading hotels rejected hundreds of applications for rooms.

Seattle visitors, here during the U. S. holiday, created a peak load. "We lost count after 50," said one hotel clerk when asked how many were turned away.

One large and a few small conventions on the same date complicated the situation.

Outside of a large number of general guests. Hotel Vancouver carried 56 Seattle names on today's register. The hotel was full.

A similar congestion existed at the Devonshire, Georgia, Grosvenor, York and other hostelries.

Royal Navy Rings Italy With Mines

German General Staff Officers Arrive In Bulgarian Capital; Eden Seeking Southeast Bloc to Resist Huns

LONDON, Feb. 22.—The British Navy, in defiance of the Italian fleet and air force, neither of which showed up during the process has mined the entire Central Mediterranean and a wide stretch of Italian coastal waters.

Effect of the operation is to cut off Italy from all practicable sea communication with its North African colonies, prevent the escape by sea of the remnants of the Italian North African army, and bar the sea to any German expedition seeking to attack French North Africa from Italian bases.

The Admiralty announced that waters in the specified areas of the Mediterranean would be "dangerous" to ship-

Please Turn to Page Nine **See "Mediterranean"**

Husband Claims She's Cruel

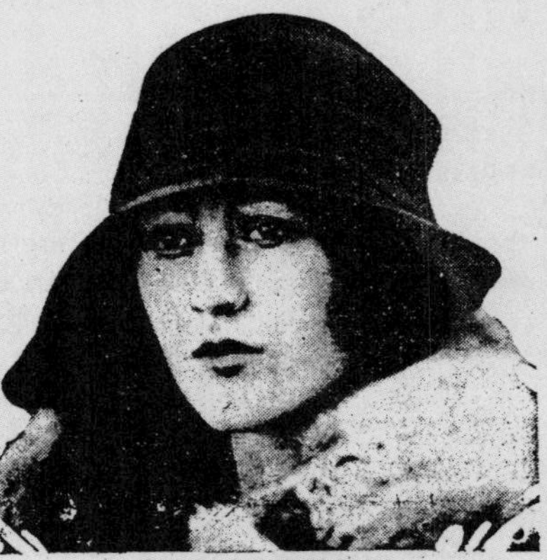

FORMER COUNTESS SALM

NEW YORK, Feb. 22.—Ronald B. Balcom, third husband of the former Mary Millicent Rogers of New York, one time Countess Salm, has filed suit for divorce, alleging extreme cruelty.

The defendant is the daughter of the late Henry Huddleston Rogers, railroad magnate. She previously had married Count Ludwig Salm-Von Hoogstraten of Austria, and Arturo Peralta Ramos, wealthy Argentine merchant. Her marriage to Count Salm was called a "$40,000,000 romance."

'Air at Times Black With Warplanes'

Germans Throw Up Heavy Smoke Screen 'to Hide Something on French Coast'

LONDON, Feb. 22.—The Royal Air Force hurled back the Nazi Luftwaffe today in a great daylight air fight along the southeast coast which the London press called the opening phase of "Battle for the Air Frontier."

Watchers along the British coast said the air battle involved hundreds of planes and was on a scale similar to the great clashes of last August and September.

During it the Germans threw up a heavy smoke screen apparently endeavoring to hide something on the French coast.

The fight apparently climaxed a big day of air action in the English Channel region with German planes making repeated futile attempts to break through British defenses and RAF planes pounding German bases in France.

FIVE MILES UP

Relay after relay of airplane squadrons joined in the combat which broke up into a series of fierce dogfights fought at an altitude of 20,000 to 25,000 feet (five miles up).

The planes could be seen and heard diving and gunning in terrific constant combat.

At times, coastal observers said, the air seemed to be black with aircraft."

A German bomber was shot

Please Turn to Page Nine
See "Air Battle"

Pioneer Engineer Dead in Bathtub

PRINCE GEORGE, Feb. 22.—Lying submerged in a water-filled bathtub, and with a bullet wound in the temple, the pyjama clad body of Ludger Blair, pioneer C. N. R. locomotive engineer was found this morning by Prince George Hotel employees. Death was due to drowning. A sawed-off twenty-two calibre rifle was lying beside the tub.

Mr. Blair, who has suffered from arthritis for several years, returned to Prince George this morning from Kamloops, where he had been receiving treatments.

An inquest will be held by Coroner W. M. Skinner.

He is survived by his wife, one son, Wilfred in Prince George, and a son, Robert with the Canadian army in Calgary.

Whirlaway Scratched

HIALEAH, Fla., Feb. 22.—Whirlaway, leading money-winning juvenile last season, was scratched from the 14th running of the $20,000 Flamingo Stakes at Hialeah Park today, reducing the field to 11 three-year-olds.

Hialeah Park Race Results

FLORIDA

FIRST RACE.—Three furlongs.
Zozo (Meade) $4.70, $2.90, $2.30.
Remembering (Anderson) $3.80, $2.70.
My Myri (Garner) $2.90.
Time :33 3-5.

SECOND RACE.—Six furlongs.
Kansas City (Vedder) $4.10, $3.10, $2.60.
Ponty (Arcaro) $7.80, $4.60.
Tamil (Meade) $3.40.
Time 1:11 3-5.

THIRD RACE—Mile and one-half:
Corydon (Arcaro) $5.90, $3.50, $2.90.
Trimley (McCreary) $5.00, $2.90.
Playhouse (Haskall) $2.60.
Time 2:28 3-5.

FOURTH RACE.—Mile and one-quarter.
Count Natural (Maschek) $37.50, $18.60, $12.20.
Cuckoo (Howell) $21.10, $13.30.
Palco (McAndrews) $10.20.
Time 2:07.

FIFTH RACE.—Mile and one-eighth.
Bimelech (Meade) $2.70, out, out.
Hash (Arcaro) out, out.
Shot Put (Garner) out.
Time 1:49 4-5.

SIXTH RACE.—Mile and one-eighth.
Dispose (Robertson) $4.30, $3.40, $2.80.
Curious Coin (Anderson) $3.80, $3.10.
The Rhymer (Arcaro) $4.20.
Time 1:48 4-5.

SEVENTH RACE—Mile and one-half:
Bettys Bob (McAndrews) $8.00, $4.20, $3.00.
Hand and Glove (McCreary) $7.10, $4.40.
Brown Queen II (Nash) $3.30.
Time, 2:34 3-5.

EIGHTH RACE—Mile and three-sixteenths:
Tony Pandy (Young) $7.20, $4.30, $3.20.
Sun Mica (Haskell) $5.10, $4.10.
Interlace (Lindy) $5.00.
Time: 1:58.

Selections

By BLUE LARKSPUR

HIALEAH

1—Foxworth, Ethel Blume, Jim Lipscombe.
2—Orcus, Spang, All Even.
3—Kind Gesture, Connie Jean, General Jean.
4—Albatross, Small Time, Blossom Lane.
5—Sir Gibson, Rifted Clouds, Williamstown.
6—Dawn Attack, Irish Day, Becomly.
7—Virginia Rose, Patsey Begone, Migal Fay.
8—Shaun G, Etruscan, Handiboy.
Best—Albatross.

OAKLAWN

1—Wise Moss, Misty Queen, High Plume.
2—Little Hig, Office Hour, Axelson.
3—Illinois Tom, Half Time, Essjaytee.
4—Night Editor, Milk Punch, Dusky Duke.
5—Franco Saxon, Bright, Dark Watch.
6—Man Hunt, Brandon Prince, Hijo Radio.
7—Ten Blow, Betrothed, Asoress.
8—The Hare, Geologist, Cannon Blast.
9—Tobacco, Copper Tube, Bull Market.
Best—The Hare.

Former King Sinking

Too Weak to Be Restored To His Bed

ROME, Feb. 22.—Former King Alfonso of Spain sat in a chair in his hotel room tonight awaiting the crisis in his grave illness, too weak to be moved to his bed.

His physicians expected the night to tell whether he would recover from a new series of heart seizures.

The descendant of Bourbon monarchs received Italy's sovereigns, King Vittorio Emanuel and Queen Elena, with a lucid mind and in cheerful spirits before settling down.

They visited him and were the only persons other than relatives and a priest who were permitted to enter the former King's bedroom.

A special medical bulletin issued shortly before 11 p.m. (1 p.m. P.S.T.), said Alfonso's condition had "further worsened."

His physicians said his condition was so grave that his heart might not survive his being moved from the chair to his bed to lie down. He had been seated in the chair to facilitate treatment.

Santa Anita Race Results

CALIFORNIA.

FIRST RACE.—Six furlons.
Tommy Whelan (Martinez) $10.10, $4.20, $3.20.
Clarcarole (Neves) $3.40, $2.80.
Soberano (Nicholson) $3.80.
Time 1:14 1-5.

SECOND RACE—Three furlongs:
Thumbs Up (Rodriguez) $5.00, $3.40 $2.80.
Doctor Reeder (Bierman) $4.20, $3.40.
Hooks (Westrope) $4.40.
Time: :34.

THIRD RACE—One mile:
Guayamas (Bierman) $9.00, $3.80, $3.00.
Torch Lee (Rodriguez) $3.40, $2.80.
Guiding Way (Adams) $4.00.
Time: 1:43 2-5.

Race Entries on Page 26

Bimelech First

MIAMI, Fla., Feb. 22.—E. R. Bradley's Bimelech, last year's champion three-year-old, won his 1941 debut at Hialeah Park today.

Bimelech won the $2500 Eastern Air Lines Purse, an added attraction to the $20,000 added Flamingo Stakes, with Greentree Stable's Hash second, and Mrs. Marie Evans' Shot Put, the 1940 distance champion, third.

John Cowles on Britain

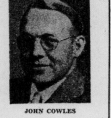

Morale of John Bull Stiffens With Every 'Blitz'

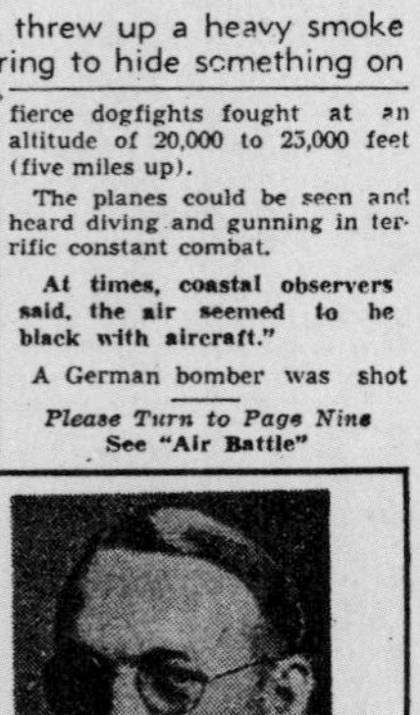

JOHN COWLES

By JOHN COWLES

President of the Minneapolis Star Journal, who accompanied Wendell Willkie on his recent trip to Europe.

The British are suffering frightfully today from the German "blitz" bombing attacks, but anybody who thinks they would consider making a compromise peace is mistaken.

The United Kingdom is a completely unified nation, and the people are single-mindedly determined on two things:

To beat off the German invaders when they come.

Then, regardless of the cost, to destroy utterly the menace of Hitlerism.

The morale of the British people is indescribably high.

Even the millions who, through German bombing, have lost their homes and their pitifully few worldly possessions, SHOW ABSOLUTELY NO SIGN OF WEAKENING.

Eight hundred thousand men, women and children in London alone spend every night in underground public shelter—subway stations, tunnels, cavernous basements.

They are packed in these refuges like cattle in a stock car, wtih inadequate sanitation facilities and with enough narrow, three-tiered bunks for only part of them.

But they are cheerful and uncomplaining, determined that they are going to defeat the Nazis.

Please Turn to Page Twenty-six **See "John Cowles"**

Britain Orders Butter Ration To Be Doubled

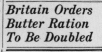

By Canadian Press

LONDON, Feb. 22.—The Food Ministry announced today that the weekly butter ration would be doubled—to four ounces per person — beginning March 10.

This Is a Vancouver-Owned Newspaper

DR. BANTING KILLED

The Vancouver Sun

Only Evening Newspaper Owned, Controlled and Operated by Vancouver People

FOUNDED 1886
VOL. LV—No. 125

VANCOUVER, BRITISH COLUMBIA, MONDAY, FEBRUARY 24, 1941

Price 3 Cents

★★★★★ FINAL

TWO NOTED B.C. MEN ON TORPEDOED SHIP

William Powell Dines Out

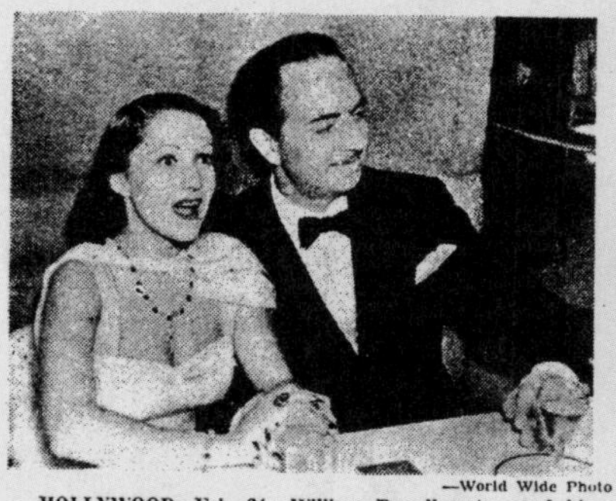

—World Wide Photo

HOLLYWOOD, Feb. 24.—William Powell, actor, and his wife, Diana Lewis, shown dining out recently.

They are watching the tropical birds in the aviary at Mocambo's from their table.

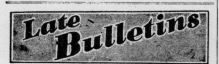

Late Bulletins

British and Nazi Big Guns Stage Duel Over Channel

LONDON, Feb. 24.—British and German long range guns dueled over the English Channel today.

Flashes seen on the Kentish Coast indicated that the Germans were using their biggest batteries in the Cape Gris Nez area.

The German shells landed on this side at intervals of a few minutes but hit mostly in unpeopled areas.

New Storm Sweeps California

LOS ANGELES, Feb. 24.—A new storm swept rain and snow across Southern California today.

20,000 Italian Prisoners in Greece

ATHENS, Feb. 24.—A government spokesman said tonight that there were "no less than 20,000 Italian prisoners in Greece, including 551 officers."

Blackouts Ordered in Bulgaria

SOFIA, Bulgaria, Feb. 24.—Instructions were issued tonight to all citizens of Bulgaria to make the necessary preparations for blackouts expected to start tomorrow or Wednesday night.

'Blackout' Protested

SEATTLE, Feb. 24.—A score of men and women, protesting the Municipal Defense Blackout test scheduled for the night of March 7, picketed the county-city building today.

Canada Must Back Petain'

OTTAWA, Feb. 24.—The Canadian government has a clear duty "to take every necessary action to strengthen the hand of Marshal Petain and his government as presently constituted," Conservative House Leader Hon. R. B. Hanson told Commons today.

Gestapo Action in Germany

BERLIN, Feb. 24.—The Strassburger Zeitung reported today that security police placed 27 persons in concentration camps last week for spreading false reports. Four others were said to have been arrested for making malicious remarks against Germany.

New Vichy Cabinet

VICHY, Feb. 24.—Admiral Jean Francois Darlan completed formation of a new cabinet group tonight. The completed cabinet includes 15 members, five of ministerial rank, eight ranked as secretaries of state and two as general delegates. Darlan holds his posts as vice-premier, minister of foreign affairs, navy and interior.

Both Britain and U.S. Warn Japan

LONDON, Feb. 24.—British and American warnings to Japan against any aggressive move against Singapore, Britain's far Eastern naval stronghold, or the Dutch East Indies was reported in various quarters Monday. (See also page 22.)

Former Regina Pats Player Killed

OTTAWA, Feb. 24. — Royal Canadian Air Force Headquarters today announced the death in a flying accident overseas of Flight Lieut. Joseh Benedict Reynolds, 22, of Lake Lenore, Sask. He was an outstanding athlete and in 1936 played with Regina Rough Riders football team.

Australia Building

SYDNEY, Australia, Feb. 24. — The Ministry of Munitions revealed today naval vessels totalling 40,000 tons are at present under construction in four states. It is expected Australia will be able to supply 95 per cent of materials for building later about 16 10,000-ton merchant vessels.

RAF Bombs Addis Ababa

ADEN, Aden Protectorate, Feb. 24.—A Royal Air Force communique said tonight that British planes had made a heavy attack upon Addis Ababa, capital of Italian - held Ethiopia. Extensive damage was done to hangars at the capital's airport. A transport in the Dessie Alomata area was bombed and machine gunned.

Charlton Golf President

TORONTO, Feb. 24.—The agreement between the Royal Canadian Golf Association and provincial associations will be continued the Associations annual meeting decided today. W. S. Charlton of Vancouver was elected president and the following were included in the executive committee: Hon. John Hart, Victoria, B.C., and A. W. Matthews, Edmonton.

No News of E. G. Hurrell, A. R. Brush

Passengers on Small Freighter Sunk by Enemy Action in Atlantic; Were on Way to Old Country

E. Gwynne Hurrell, sales manager of B. C. Packers Ltd., and Armitage R. Brush, retired resident of Salmon Arm and father-in-law of J. Edward Sears, reeve of West Vancouver, were on a small freighter reported "sunk by enemy action" in the Atlantic recently.

Mr. Hurrell, before joining B. C. Packers, was with the former brokerage and bond firm of R. P. Clark & Co., and later with the Western City Company. He was on his way to the Old Country in connection with salmon marketing in Britain. He is widely known in business circles here.

Mr. Brush was on his way to Edinburgh, Scotland, where a sister has been seriously ill for some time. He had lived in British Columbia for many years and had been in West Vancouver for six weeks with his daughter before leaving for the Atlantic seaboard.

Mr. Hurrell and Mr. Brush, according to letters sent to relatives just before sailing from an Eastern Canadian Port, were to share the same cabin. They were the only Western Canadians in the passenger list of eight.

Nothing has been reported regarding the fate of passengers and crew and it is expected that it may be some time before anything official is heard.

Another Vancouver man, Claude N. Effinger, representative of Seaboard Lumber Sales Co. Ltd., in Britain, just missed being a passenger on the same ship.

Oaklawn Park Race Results

ARKANSAS

FIRST RACE—Six furlongs:
Wise Moss (King) $4.10, $3.70, $3.
Aljack (Cruickshanks) $3.40, $3.
Long Lane (Friedman) $4.
Time 1:15.

SECOND RACE—Six furlongs:
Axelson (Snyder) $10.30, $6.80, $3.
Little Hig (Trombley) $9.80, $4.20.
Office Hour (Cruickshanks) $2.60.
Time 1:15 4-5.

THIRD RACE—Six furlongs:
Future Winning (Cassidy) $10.10, $6.20, $4.30.
Scandalous (Bassett) $9.70, $5.70.
Half Time (Bomar) $3.30.
Time, 1:15.

FOURTH RACE—Six furlongs:
Bill Farnsworth (Calbert) $10.60, $6.30, $4.30.
True Star (King) $29.80, $12.
Blind Eagle (Madden) $4.20.
Time, 1:14 3-5.

FIFTH RACE—Mile and seventy yards:
Fritz (Bemiss) $11.80, $6.00, $4.00.
Sign Up (Kieper) $7.70, $6.20.
Standard Time (Snyder) $9.90.
Time: 1:52.

SIXTH RACE—Mile and seventy yards:
Henry Hatter (Lewis) $30.20, $9.30, $5.60.
American Emblem (Highshoe) $4.20, $3.50.
Bereit (Jedlinski) $3.10.
Time: 1.52.

SEVENTH RACE—Mile one sixteenth:
Adoress (Boyce) $9.10, $5.50, $4.00.
Ten Blow (Bush) $8.00, $6.10.
The Greeter (Wallace) $4.30.
Time: 1.51 2-5.

WASHINGTON, Feb. 24.—Senator Burton K. Wheeler (Dem., Montana) said today that if the Senate approved the British Aid Bill he and other opposition Senators would stump the country "from Boston to California" in an effort "to keep this country out of war."

Late Stocks on Page 8

Selections

By BLUE LARKSPUR

HIALEAH

1—Methodical, Scotland Light, Precision.
2—Conscript, Hunting Home, Mighty Miss.
3—Ingomar, Royal Ruby II, The Stork.
4—Speed To Spare, Bright Trace, Victory Morn.
5—Jayfcee, Sweet Willow, Euistone.
6—Royal Man, Get Off, Sickle T.
7—Silent Witness, Counterpoise, Tony Pandy.
8—Cherry Trifle, Spiteful, Erins Sun.

Best—SILENT WITNESS

OAKLAWN

1—Busy Lutrecia, Light Tack, Mistletoe.
2—Johnnie Dear, Irish Moon, Wise Duke.
3—Routine, Witan, Aureate.
4—Marie Olympia, Lochlea, Grand Court.
5—Lady Thirteen, Little Abner, Vinum.
6—Bold General, Lerno, Khayyam.
7—Billy Van Nuys, Tadpole, Veloz.
8—Fandan, Dustless, Wakita.

Best—ROUTINE

SANTA ANITA

1—Mulligatawney, Praise Worthy, Winsome Beau.
2—Corn Pone, The Raider, Vegas Justice.
3—Aboyne, Enoch Borland, Enchanted.
4—Transmitter, Valdina Joe, Jest Once.
5—Valdina Paul, Sweet Grapes, Caressante.
6—Certainty, Talked About, Straw Hat.
7—At Play, Arjac, Creepymouse.
8—Fay D, Ebony Moon, Danfield.
9—(Sub): Irrelevant, Ocean Bound, Black Highbrow.

BEST — TRANSMITTER.

BERLIN, Feb. 24. — German sources said Saturday Grand Admiral Erich Raeder has ordered the transfer of the German naval medical academy from Kiel to Danzig.

"There can be no mention of any 'evacuation' of Kiel. Numerous naval training centres, etc., remain there."

Dies in Plane Crash

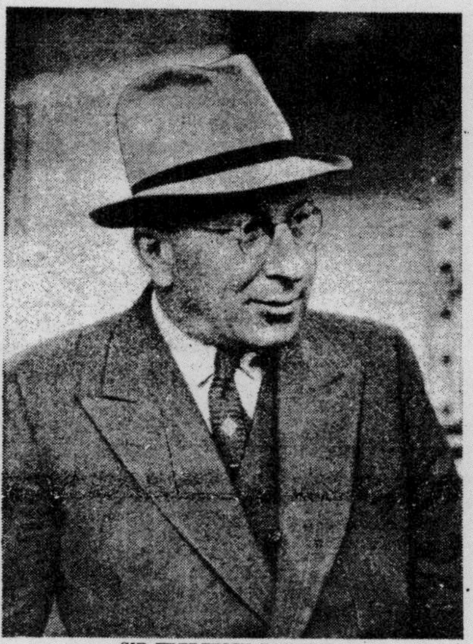

SIR FREDERICK BANTING

(EDITORIAL)

Seek the World Over!

No sentence in Lord Beaverbrook's broadcast Sunday stood out more than this: "Gather together every kind of transport, which will enable us to continue the defense of this Island; seek the whole world over for ships."

That was the climax of his description of "our northwestern approaches." The British navy cannot be beaten; neither can the air force nor the army. But their strength lies in the unfailing convoys. For even in peacetime 90 per cent of Britain's supplies come from overseas. She is a trading nation, and for centuries the ships of John Bull have poked their prows into the seven seas.

The British Isles are a fortress. By force of arms they cannot be stormed. But the whole portent of the Spring offensive is an all-out effort to strangle them by shutting off their supplies, by sinking a greater proportion of their ships than can be replaced.

Again and again The Sun has urged that the whole sum and substance of this ultimate British triumph now lies in ships. More and more ships. Ships turned out to the capacity of every yard in the Empire and the United States.

It is not enough to be told, as Mr. Howe tells us in Parliament, that British Columbia is building more ships than any other province. What does that matter, when this is the second largest province on tidewater? Lord Beaverbrook's call for ships makes us ask again, why are we not building more ships in British Columbia yards? We are building eight, says Howard Green, M.P., when we should be building fifty.

What is the use of comparing us with other provinces? There is only one comparison for British Columbia: The number of ships we are building now compared to the highest possible number we could be building. And that comparison is a sorry one.

"Seek the world over for ships." Yes, and seek in the shipyards of the Empire.

"Geography," says Mr. Howe, explaining why more war contracts are not awarded in British Columbia. But what has that to do with ships? Since the war began we could have built enough wooden ships on this Coast to carry all the lumber and other products this province can send to Britain, and save the steel tonnage for other work in the war's trade routes.

We have not done so, but that is no reason for not starting now.

City Flier Listed as Missing With RAF

LONDON, Feb. 24. — Among eight Canadians listed as missing today by the Royal Air Force is Flying Officer Raymond Grant Lewis of 1657 Barclay Street, Vancouver.

Also missing is Flight-Lieutenant J. R. Fishwick, a native of New Westminster.

Irish Fusiliers Back After Year

First Battalion, Irish Fusiliers (Vancouver Regiment), under Lt. Col. J. N. Burnett, returned to the Vancouver defense area today, after an absence of nearly a year.

Advance guard of the famous regiment arrived in this area over the week-end to prepare for the arrival of the troops.

Discoverer Of Insulin Air Victim

Dies With Three Others in New Foundland Crash of Military Plane; Fourth Occupant of Machine Escapes

OTTAWA, Feb. 24.—Sir Frederick Banting, co-discoverer of insulin, and two companions have been killed in an airplane crash near Trinity Bay, Newfoundland, Col. J. L. Ralston, Minister of National Defense, announced today.

A fourth member of the party, Capt. Joseph Mackey of Kansas City, is alive and is being rescued, Col. Ralston said.

The wreckage of the plane, which has been missing since Friday, was sighted earlier today by a Royal Canadian Air Force plane. Wing Commander Gordon radioed to the Defense Ministry:

"Pilot Mackey is alive. The others are dead. Two trappers have reached the scene and one of our aircrafts has dropped four emergency rations to the rescue party."

Colonel Ralston said two ski-planes would leave Ottawa immediately to bring out the bodies of Dr. Banting, Navigator William Bird of England, and William Snailman of Bedford, N. S.

ANNOUNCED IN HOUSE

First word of the finding of the missing military plane came in an announcement by Hon. C. D. Howe, minister of munitions, in the House of Commons earlier.

The plane was sighted from the air near the north end of Trinity Bay, Newfoundland, Mr. Howe told the House.

Mr. Howe, in his announcement to the Commons, said:

"Just before I came in I had word from the Department of Transport that the plane has been found. It is on a point of a bay on the direct route between Canada and Botwood. There is a message written on the snow which indicated that someone on board the plane is alive at least. A plane has been sent out equipped with skis which will be capable of landing there and it is probable that there will be definite word before the afternoon is over."

A source outside the House said it was believed the plane had de-

Please Turn to Page Eight
See "Banting"

Hialeah Park Race Results

FLORIDA

FIRST RACE—Seven furlongs:
Chorus (Lindberg) $86, $33.30, $10.80.
Bellarmine (Merritt) $6.10, $3.80.
Subura (Borton) $3.60.
Time 1:25 2-5.

SECOND RACE—Six furlongs:
Spang (Meade) $3.20, $4.30, $3.
Treadon (Atkinson) $9.30, $6.70.
Chance Run (Dabson) $5.40.
Time 1:13 3-5.

THIRD RACE—Three furlongs:
(Fade (Arcaro) $6.40, $4, $3.30.
General Jean (Meade) $7.40, 5.50.
Sir War (Howell) $4.50.
Time :33 4-5.

FOURTH RACE—Three furlongs:
Albatross (Anderson) $2.50, $2.50, $2.20.
Curious Roman (Howell) $6.60, $2.60.
Small Time (Caffarella) $2.30.
Time :33 2-5.

FIFTH RACE—Seven furlongs:
Rifted Clouds (Vedder) $9.80, $5.40, $3.50.
Sir Gibson (McCreary) $5.60, $3.60.
Visigoth (Borton) $6.
Time 1:23 4-5.

SIXTH RACE—Six furlongs:
Air Brigade (Arcaro) $6.30, $2.60, $2.40.
Fettacairn (McCreary) $2.50, $2.30.
Dawn Attack (Wright) $3.30.
Time, 1:11 1-5.

SEVENTH RACE—Mile and one-eighth:
Oarboard (Garner) $35.00, $14.30, $6.40.
Patsey Begonne (Meade) $4.80, $3.60.
Noodles (Young) $3.50.
Time: 1.52 3-5.

EIGHTH RACE—Mile an done-sixteenth—
Lady Lyoners (Lindberg) $8.40, $4.50, $3.50.
Bonzar (Roberts) $9.00, $5.60.
Shaun G. (McAndrews) $4.90.
Time: 1.47 3-5.

Race Entries on Page 22

Hitler's 'Ships Sunk' Claims 'Ridiculous'

LONDON, Feb. 24.—Authoritative quarters said tonight there was no truth to Adolf Hitler's assertion that Germany had sunk 215,000 tons of British shipping, including a convoy totalling 125,000 tons.

"The figures contain the same ridiculous exaggeration which characterize German propaganda as a whole," it was said.

(See Also Page 8)

Greek Joke; Italians Hit With Own Planes

WITH THE GREEK ARMY, Albania, Feb. 24.—One of the big jokes Greek aviators get out of this war, is bombing the Italians' front lines with reconditioned planes captured from Il Duce's army and repainted with Greek markings.

Halifax Planning To Visit Canada

WASHINGTON, Feb. 24.—Viscount Halifax, British Ambassador to the United States, hopes to visit Canada this summer, it was learned today.

No date has been set for his trip but it probably will not be until August because he plans returning to London in July for consultations with the British government. He will go to Ottawa and possibly Toronto and Montreal, but may have to forego a desire to see Halifax.

NEW YORK, Feb. 24. — New York Americans of the National Hockey League, in an effort to bolster their injury-riddled, last-place team, today announced the calling up of Bill Benson and Andy Branigan, a couple of youngsters from the American League Farm Club at Springfield.

The recruits will play against Toronto Maple Leafs here tomorrow night.

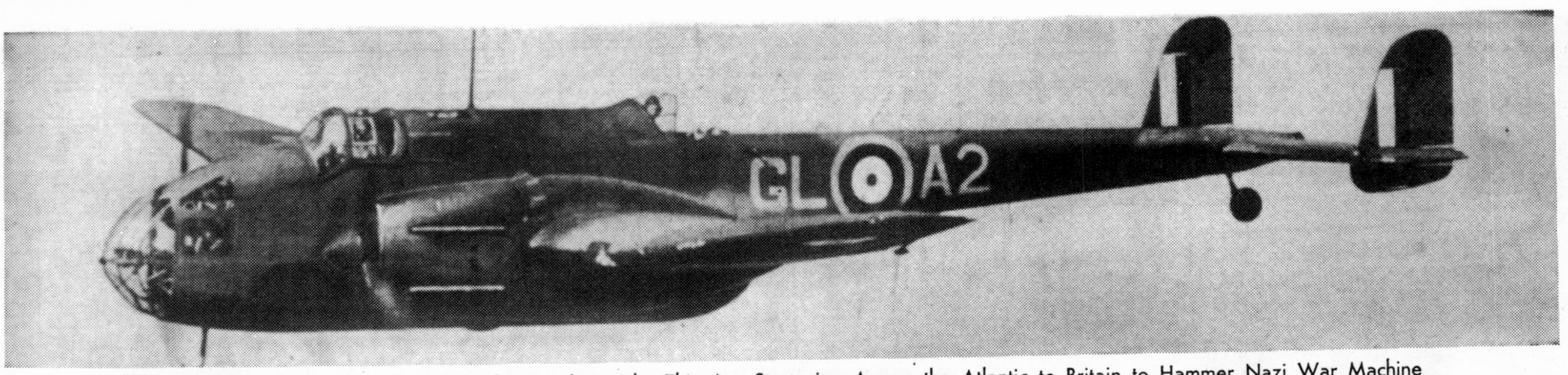

Built in Canada, Handley-Page-Hampden Bombers Like This Are Streaming Across the Atlantic to Britain to Hammer Nazi War Machine

ITALIAN WARSHIP SUNK

The Weather

Partly cloudy and mild over British Columbia. Light to moderate rains and scattered light showers in the interior.
Temperature at 10 a.m. today 47.
Temperature during 24 hours ending 4:30 a.m. today: Maximum 60, minimum 43.
Forecast: Fair and mild.
Official weather report on page 9.

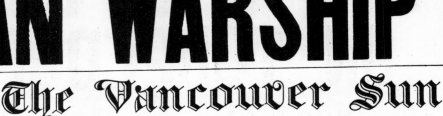

The Vancouver Sun

Only Evening Newspaper Owned, Controlled and Operated by Vancouver People

Today's Tides

Vancouver Harbor
High 12:24 p.m., 10.5 feet. Low 8:14 p.m., 2.8 feet.
English Bay
High 12:19 p.m., 10.8 feet. Low 7:50 p.m., 3.4 feet.
First Narrows
High slack 12:59 p.m. Low slack 8:42 p.m.
Tomorrow's tides appear on page 28.

FOUNDED 1886
VOL. LV—No. 136

VANCOUVER, BRITISH COLUMBIA, SATURDAY, MARCH 8, 1941

Price 10 Cents

MArine 1161

Aid Bill to Pass Today By 2-1 Vote

Opposition to Lend-Lease Law Collapses

By Associated Press

WASHINGTON, March 8.—Democratic Leader Alben Barkley, declaring that Senate opponents of the British aid bill are "co-operating to obtain a final vote today," predicted the momentous legislation would be on President Roosevelt's desk by Monday night.

Saying he is "entirely satisfied" with the administration's consistent victories on the aid legislation Friday, Barkley expressed to reporters belief that the House of Representatives would accept all Senate amendments to the bill.

Thus, if the measure should be approved by the Senate today or tonight, the House could complete Congressional action Monday.

OPPOSITION COLLAPSES

Administration leaders predict the legislation will be approved by the Senate by a vote of 2 to 1.

Opposition to the bill collapsed Friday night, after nearly three weeks of general debate. The opposition rapidly crumpled on a succession of ballots rejecting all the amendments it offered or supported. Most votes ran nearly, or better, than two-to-one for proponents of the bill.

First, the latter snowed under a succession of efforts to restrict the use of the United States armed forces to the Western Hemisphere. This proposal was advanced a full half-dozen times.

Then the administration wrote into the measure its own views on what restrictions should consist of a stipulation that the bill is not to be construed as making any change in existing laws relating to the use of the army and navy, except where new activities connected with the procure-

Please Turn to Page Nine
See "Lease-Lend"

Today In Britain

War events analyzed by Fleet Street writers, cabled from the London Bureau of The Vancouver Sun.
(Copyright, 1941)

LONDON, March 8. — The newspapers of Britain have agreed, at the request of the government, to make a substantial cut in their consumption of newsprint beginning March 16. The step is taken in order to reduce imports of pulp and pulpwood.

The size of the penny newspapers will be reduced from the present six six-page issues weekly to four issues of six pages each and two of four pages each. The two-penny weekly and Sunday newspapers will be reduced from the present maximum of 12 pages to 10. The number of copies each newspaper will be allowed to print will be limited by a weekly tonnage allocation of newsprint. It is expected that other newsprint reductions will be made within the next three months.

* * *

Suppress Italian Talk

A revolution in Italian life has begun with the disappearance of street tables before cafes and restaurants. This time-honored and much-beloved custom has been abolished because the authorities in Rome felt that Italians who sat at these tables and enjoyed sun and air along with plenty of conversation talked too much politics for this particular moment in Italy.

Please Turn to Page Nine
See "Britain Today"

Loyal Dog Saves 4 In Fire

Rouses Children When Flames Sweep Home

The loyalty of a dog for people who had befriended him was largely responsible for saving the lives of four children when their home at 2846 East Fourteenth Avenue, was destroyed by fire at 10:50 p.m., Friday.

The children are Joyce, 11; Beulah, 9; Donna, 5, and Marcella, 3, daughters of Mr. and Mrs. H. Eagleston.

WAKENED CHILD

Joyce was sitting in the front room of the two-room house when the dog, "Spot," dashed in from the kitchen, and started whining and barking to attract Joyce's attention.

She looked up and found the kitchen, in which her three small sisters were sleeping, a mass of flames.

"Spot" raced back thorugh the flames and woke up Beulah by biting her hand and clawing at her head. Joyce followed the dog into the kitchen, managed to bundle up the two younger children and with Beulah made her way out of the house.

The children were alone at the time the fire started, their parents having gone out a few minutes before.

FED BY WIFE

Mr. Eagleston explained the loyalty of "Spot."

"The dog was pretty badly crippled when he came around the house just after we moved in last November," Mr. Eagleston said.

"My wfe doctored and fed him.

"This isn't the first time Spot" has paid us back. He watches Marcella very closely to see that she doesn't fall in the creek that runs right beside our house."

The Eaglesons lost all their possessions in the blaze.

Markets on Page 9

(EDITORIAL)

'....Into the Hand of God'

The King has asked all the churches of the British Empire to observe Sunday, March 23, a day of national prayer.

Look well and solemnly to this, for the testing time is here, and the Royal call to prayer is not only a great religious sacrament, it is a signal to the British race. It is the "alert," timed by the sure guide of the British Military Intelligence Service, whose eyes by an uncanny gift see everywhere.

Again, it is more than that. This dramatic force of our Empire called to prayer under the leadership of the King creates and nourishes that fortitude and tenacity which for time immemorial has at the last stood by the British. In no other way can the common will be invoked and concentrated so powerfully as in the universal act of prayer.

The Empire was called to prayer on May 26, 1940; and there followed the miraculous delivery of Dunkirk.

The Empire was called to prayer last Sept. 8; and the invasion of Britain was forever defeated. For on Sept. 16 came the climactic, deciding fight above the British shores when the Royal Air Force, outnumbered five, even ten to one, drove the German air force out of the skies by sheer, superhuman skill and bewildering courage. On that day came the real turning point in the Battle of Britain.

Go further back into the years, to the summer of 1918 when that historic Empire call to prayer was followed by the August offensive which broke the German line. Never again was it to be re-formed.

Now, in March, another day of prayer signalizes, as surely as the sun rises, a new and decisive phase of this conflict between freedom and slavery.

There is a mystic invincibility about this consecration of the British race in supreme moments; about this cosmic linking of unseen but unbreakable chains of force around the earth against assault. Throughout her long history Britain has stood because of it. She has stood by the superb team-work of her intelligence services abroad, the ingenuity and tenacity of her fighting forces, and the still, deep water of her devoutness. She has fought sometimes on one knee; she has never yielded on both.

The King has called us to prayer. The King, in the fateful days of 1940, sounded the watchword for the Empire: "... PUT YOUR HAND INTO THE HAND OF GOD."

May none of us forget!

Cruiser Victim Of Mine

Mystery Statement At Rome Fails to State Cause

ROME, March 8.—Sinking of an Italian Warship of "medium tonnage" in the Mediterranean from an unknown cause was reported today by the High Command.

(A warship of "medium tonnage" might be assumed to be a cruiser, inasmuch as warships range from tiny coastal boats to battleships of 35,000 tons.)

Most of the crew of the ship were saved, it was said.

Families of men lost have been notified, the High Command said.

The Italian admission that a warship of 'medium tonnage' had been sunk in the Mediterranean, and that the cause was not known, recalled the recent announcement of the British Admiralty that it was mining a great area of the Central Mediterranean in such manner as to block off Italy.

Mussolini Fires General Cavallero

By Associated Press

ATHENS, March 8.—Foreign sources say Gen. Ugo Cavallero, successor of Marshal Pietro Badoglio as Italan General Staff Chief, has been superseded as Commander by Gen. Carolo Gelloso, 11th Army Commander.

(Wether Gen. Gelloso was named just to command the Italians in Albania or was made Chief of Staff of the entire Italian Army was not made clear in the Athens dispatch. The 11th Army has played a prominent role in the Albanian campaign.)

The change in the command, which, if confirmed, would be the third since the start of the Italian-Greek conflict, came as a Greek spokesman and communique told of continued advantages in skirmishes along the central sector of the front.

(Undersecretary of War Gen. Ubaldo Soddu was dispatched by Mussolini to the Albanian front Nov. 10 to speed up the lagging Italian campaign. He superseded

Please Turn to Page Nine
See "Cavallero"

Belgrade to Sign Pact With Axis

Jugoslavs Expect Action to Be Taken At Berlin, Tuesday; Story of U.S. Aid Ridiculed; Turks Ready to Fight

BELGRADE, Jugoslavia, March 8.—Well-informed quarters reported today that Jugoslavia would sign a non-aggression treaty with Germany at Berlin Tuesday

Jugoslav official circles declined today to discuss Hungarian (Nazi) press reports that United States had offered aid to Jugoslavia. They said no denial was necessary "because the whole business is so ridiculous."

Diplomatic quarters, however, said they were prepared for a German attack on Greece at any time.

There were indications that Germany had given Greece a last chance to make peace with Italy and adhere to the German-Italian-Japanese alliance, and that Greece had refused.

Transit Down 'Invasion Valley'

Jugoslavia's acceptance of a "non-aggression" treaty with Germany, and a joint declaration providing for closer political and economic collaboration, apparently was merely a matter of arranging for the diplomatic ceremony.

Similarly, reports from all over the Balkans, while lacking any official substantiation, indicate that Germany might attack Greece at any hour, possibly starting with an airplane bombardment of Salonika.

(Budapest reported that Jugoslavia would agree to permit German forces to pour down the Vardar river "Invasion Valley" toward Salonika and move German war equipment over its railroads.)

Sofia Demands Worry Belgrade

There were reports also that Bulgaria, as a new subordinate partner in the German-Japanese-Italian axis, had lost no time in demanding territory from Jugoslavia and Greece, and that this had hastened the Jugoslav decision to bow to Germany.

Belgrade police, in sudden raids on the headquarters of the Democratic party of the opposition and the home of the party chief, Bilan Girol, seized all copies they could find of an opposition manifesto protesting against the government's foreign policy. A copy of the mani-

Please Turn to Page Nine
See "The Balkans"

New York, Washington Buried by Blizzards

NEW YORK, March 8.—Driving blizzards swept the Atlantic seaboard today, snarling traffic in metropolitan New York where more than 10 inches of snow had fallen. The storm had moved across the nation from California where last week-end it caused widespread damage and torrents of rain.

The heaviest March snowfall in history was recorded at Washington, D.C., where the snow was 10.1 inches deep.

Light snow also fell in Missouri, Kansas and New Mexico.

Tool Order Not Coming

Vancouver machine shops are not to get the expected $2 million order for horizontal boring machines, according to unofficial intimations from Ottawa received in the city today.

Directors of West Coast Industries Ltd., who believed until today that the order was assured, state that while they have not heard anything official they fear the order is being placed in the United States, where, Ottawa claims, it can be filled in much shorter time.

Directors expressed keen disappointment, amounting to disgust, at the handling of the whole affair. Three of them who returned from Ottawa this week, blieved the whole thing was settled.

U.S. Alaska Planes Must Not 'Pick Up' Canadian Business

Canada will give free access to United States airlines to fly their planes across Canada to Alaska, but they are not allowed to do any Canadian business.

Recently, the Northwest Airlines proposed to inaugurate a service, Minneapolis to Winnipeg to Edmonton to White Horse to Dawson and Fairbanks.

Yes, replied the Canadian government, but you must not pick up any Canadian traffic in Winnipeg, Edmonton and White Horse.

This is practically the same arrangement as was applied to Pan-American Airlines which operate from Seattle to Prince George to White Horse and Fairbanks.

Only through Amercan traffic is to be handled over this service.

The inter-Canada business is left for development to Yukon-Southern (affiliated with the C.P.R.) and any other purely Canadian companies.

Canada is planning to spend $7,000,000 in a chain of air-fields in British Columbia and Alberta. Estmates for the Prince George airport run all the way from half to three-quarters of a million dollars.

Prince George will be the key point.

It is located in the exact geographical centre of B.C. New fields are under construction today at Fort St. John and Fort Nelson.

There will be a vast commercial expansion in aviation all through the northwest this year.

News Under The Sun
Where to Find It

'Diabolical' Pseudo-Germans

Britain's Gigantic 'Invasion' Game Gives Invaluable Lessons

By Canadian Press

LONDON, March 8.—Britons reckoned today the results of a mammoth mock invasion, and decided their imitation was better than anything Hitler could offer.

Informed sources said, however, that week-long exercises—held a month ago—had created a high government puzzle as to whether the British officers who acted as Germans had played their part exceptionally well or whether the defending forces were not so brilliant.

Some concern was expressed over civilian reaction. In one locality conditions of France and Belgium were almost duplicated.

People clogged roads and intersections and generally raised havoc with defense plans. The "invaders" took advantage of this to put over some important coups.

That the sham attackers included "some of the most brilliant British staff officers" might have had much to do with the civilian confusion, it was explained.

Any material weakness exposed was declared to have given important lessons in resisting a real invader.

The exercises covered all Britain from Land's End to John o' Groats, and from west Wales to the Wash. The navy, army, civil defense guard, air raid precautions organization and other war auxiliaries collaborated in the vast manoeuvres.

War Secretary David Margesson told the House of Commons that a "German staff housed in special offices" was asked to "think up the most diabolical schemes the German mind could conceive."

They did. But the final summing up of the umpires showed that all in all the "invaders" were checked.

480 Warships

By Canadian Press

GRANTHAM, England, March 8.—Sir Victor Warrender, Financial Secretary to the Admiralty, declared today that when the fiscal year ends March 31 Britain will have completed 480 warsphs, "large and small," in the period.

In a War Weapons Week speech, Sir Victor declared the Navy is "tending old vessels with such skill and daring that they are performing feats of endurance never expected of them by their designers."

Extra Sun Newscast 6:30 p.m. Sunday

Effective this Sunday, The Vancouver Sun newscast may be heard at 6:30 p.m. Sundays as well as 10 p.m.

This broadcast is being given to accommodate many listeners who find the early evening time more convenient on Sunday and means that The Sun will be on CKWB and shortwave station CKFX seven days a week at 6:30 p.m. and 10 p.m.

Although there is no 7:30 a.m. or 12:05 noon newscast on Sundays, bulletins will be flashed on CKWX if the war situation warrants.

SERBS GIRD FOR BATTLE AFTER NEW HUN THREAT

★★★★★ FINAL

THE VANCOUVER DAILY PROVINCE

47th YEAR—NO. 2 VANCOUVER, B.C., THURSDAY, MARCH 27, 1941—34 PAGES PRICE 3 CENTS On trains, boats and in the country, five Cents

Canadian Navy Seizes 2 Ships

Atlantic Battle To Be Won Soon Says Churchill

(By Associated Press.)

LONDON, March 27.—Prime Minister Churchill, predicting victory within a few months in the Battle of the Atlantic and eventual defeat of Hitlerism through the united effort of all English-speaking peoples, today told the central committee of the Conservative party:

"We can not tell how long the road will be. We only know that it will be stony, painful and uphill, and that we shall march along it to the end."

The Prime Minister told the meeting that since the "dark hours" when the German Panzer divisions swept into France, Britain had scored "a series of notable victories."

"First of all there was the frustration of Hitler's invasion

Complete text of the address of Prime Minister Churchill today appears on page 34.

plan by the brilliant exploits of the Royal Air Force.

"Secondly, frustration of his attempt to cow and terrorize the civil population of this country by ruthless air bombing.

"Thirdly, we have the destruction of Italian power and empire in Africa by our armies there. . .

"But there is another supreme event more blessed than victories, namely, the rising of the spirit of the great American nation and

(Continued on Page 6.) See CHURCHILL.

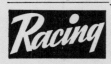

Racing

Tropical Park Results

First race—Bad Cold (Pariso), $8.20, $5.80, $3.20.
Alchemy (Kaufmann), $21.30, $6.50.
Waller (Ryan), $2.40.
Time, 1.11 4-5.
Second race—Indian Penny (Gonzalez), $14.40, $7.40, $4.60.
Come Home (Wilson), $13.40, $7.10.
Foggy Day (Oliver), $36.
Time, 1.12 3-5.
Third race—Remarkable (Arcaro), $4.60, $3.80, $2.70.
My Shadow (Haskell), $7.70, $4.20.
High Plaid (Gonzalez), $3.40.
Time, 1.11 2-5.
Fourth race—Largo Mint (Arcaro), $12.20, $5.40, $4.30.
Milk and Honey (May), $5.20, $3.10.
Meritorious (Cowley), $7.
Time, 1.11 4-5.
Fifth race—Royal Man (Ryan), $6.50, $3.60, $2.60.
Shot Put (May), $5.70, $3.
Corydon (Arcaro), $2.60.
Time, 1.43 1-5.
Sixth race—Big Rover (Vedder), $5.80, $3.40, $2.70.
Brown Bomb (Ryan), $3.90, $3.30.
Manamaid (Delara), $4.60.
Time, 1.44 1-5.
Seventh race—Wee Scot (McCoy), $45.80, $22.80, $12.
Gertrude K. (McAndrews), $18, $8.30.
Red Burr (Caffarella), $5.30.
Eighth race—Radio (Ryan), $22.70, $11.40, $8.40.
Beau Do (Lowe), $11.60, $7.
Consul (Arcaro), $5.

Oaklawn Park Results

First race—Marie Olympia (Calvert), $19.50, $7.30, $3.60.
Ski Patrol (Alberts), $4.20, $2.90.
Dainty Ford (Emery), $4.
Time, 1.15.
Second race—Relief (Brooks), $13.60, $6.50, $3.20.
Norman Sloat (Bomar), $12, $5.30.
Panther Creek (McCombs), $2.50.
Time, 1.16.
Third race—Powder Bluff (Sconza), $8.80, $5, $3.70.
Tomluta (Kieper), $5.60, $4.
Rodes K. (Mozer), $4.60.
Time, .49.
Fourth race—My Crest (Brooks), $43.30, $12.90, $8.20.
*Ronnie (Glidewell), $5.80, $7.20.
*Utica (Emery), $3.20, $4.
Time, 1.51 4-5.
*—Dead heat for place.
Fifth race—Voncell (Brooks), $9, $4.90, $3.70.
Soon (Jedlinski), $3.40, $3.
Light Tack (Scurlock), $3.50.
Time, 1.51 3-5.
Sixth race Emdale (McAddan), $57.20, $20.70, $11.
Kermay (Jedlinski), $4.80, $3.20.
Henry Hatter (Sisto), $4.30.
Time, 1.58 2-5.

Bay Meadows Results

First race—Chief Bud (Rodriguez), $4.20, $3, $2.60.
Copper Toe (Neves), $6, $5.
Laosuna, Robertson), $5.20.
Time, .48 2-5.
Second race—Taj (Neves), $7.60, $5.40, $3.60.
Belisto (Massi), $45.60, $20.
Savings Bank (Pearson), $2.80.
Time, 1.13 1-5.
Third race—High Lark (Balaski)($6, $3.40, $2.80.
Party Spirit (Westrope), $5.40, $3.40
Only Girl (Skelly), $3.60.
Time, 1.11 1-5.

Bay Meadows Selections

By TOM GWYNNE.
(Daily Province Race Correspondent)

FIRST RACE—Seedoe, Spy Ann, Pilatus.

SECOND RACE—Iron Bunker, Tommy Whelan, Rich Star.

THIRD RACE—Swinging Door, Devalue, Middle Cue.

FOURTH RACE—Ilika, Ocean Bound, Man o' Chance.

FIFTH RACE—Mieletta, Miss Lissie, Upsiala.

SIXTH RACE—Palmera T, Lucia's Sun, Gridine.

SEVENTH RACE—Lassator, Anthology, Flying Bonny.

EIGHTH RACE—Taken, Coronado, Carouse.

NINTH (SUB.) RACE—Lt. Greenock, Wise Fox, Ezechias.

BEST BET—Lassator.

(Race Entries on Page 2.)

BRITISH ARMS TO BACK SLAVS

(By Associated Press.)

LONDON, March 27.—Britain will back the new Yugo-Slav Government with her navy, army and air force to lay open the right flank of the German thrust into the Balkans, a reliable source declared today.

This statement followed upon Prime Minister Churchill's prediction that the revolt-torn Balkan kingdom would repudiate her pact with the Axis, and his announcement that, in such an eventuality, Britain would recognize the new Belgrade regime.

The Prime Minister's promise to "make common cause" with the Yugo-Slavs was regarded as a direct move to make them allies.

Britons got their biggest uplift since Gen. Sir Archibald Wavell smashed the Italians in Libya

(Continued on Page 6.) See BRITISH.

Japanese Naval Rendezvous Sighted

ABOARD SS. PRESIDENT JACKSON, March 27.—(AP)—This transpacific liner, en route to San Francisco, today passed the apparent rendezvous of at least 50 Japanese transports and light warships near Senhouse Island in the Parker group, about 90 miles southwest of Shanghai.

Passengers sighted at least 15 destroyers, two cruisers and 33 transports. The transports apparently were lightly loaded and some were entering the harbor as the Jackson passed.

Final BULLETINS

Transports Pass "Rock"

MADRID, March 27.—(AP)—Passage of numerous British troop transports through the Strait of Gibraltar into the Mediterranean in recent weeks was described by Spanish press despatches from La Linea today.

M.P.'s Cheer Revolt

OTTAWA, March 27.—(CP)—Official word of the revolt in Yugo-Slavia, conveyed to the House of Commons today by Prime Minister Mackenzie King, drew applause from members of all parties.

To Meet Tomorrow

WASHINGTON, March 27. — Hon. Charles Stewart and other members of the Alaska Highway Commission arrived in Washington this morning to attend a meeting of the commission, which will be held here tomorrow.

Spies Fly to France

SAIGON, French Indo-China, March 27.—(AP)—French soldiers who have arrived in Saigon from France asserted today British Intelligence Service men are being landed regularly in France by parachute at night.

Survivors Landed

PONTA DELGADA, The Azores, March 27.—(AP)—The Netherlands freighter Venus arrived here yesterday with 20 survivors of a British merchant ship sunk in the north Atlantic. The captain of the British ship, who was among the survivors, declined to disclose its identity.

More Planes for British

WASHINGTON, March 27.—(AP)—Britain has acquired three of the huge four-engine Boeing flying boats ordered for Pan-American Airways, and may get three more of this or a similar type, it was disclosed today in testimony made available by the Senate appropriations committee.

British Airman Missing

PRESCOTT, Ont., March 27.—(CP)—A diver was expected to search the St. Lawrence River here for the body of a man believed to be Wing Cmdr. W. J. B. Elliot, 38, of the Royal Air Force, member of the British Technical Air Mission, who has been missing from Ottawa since last Friday.

Yacht, Trawler Lost

LONDON, March 27.—(AP)—The admiralty issued the following communique Thursday night:

"The board of admiralty regrets to announce that H.M. Yacht Molusc (Temporary Lieut. N. P. Doyle, R.N.R.) and H.M. Trawler Lady Lilian (Temporary Lieut. the Hon. W. K. Rous, R.N.V.R.) have been sunk. There were no casualties in H.M. Yacht Molusc. The next-of-kin of casualties in H.M. Trawler Lady Lilian have been informed."

Two More Italian Counter-attacks Beaten

LONDON, March 27.—The British Broadcasting Corporation tonight quoted the Athens radio as reporting the defeat of two more heavy Italian counter-attacks in Albania. It said Italian dead, numbered in hundreds, littered the ground and lay in ravines before the Greek lines.

The Athens radio was quoted as saying: "The Italian high command continues to remain indifferent to the tremendous loss of life."

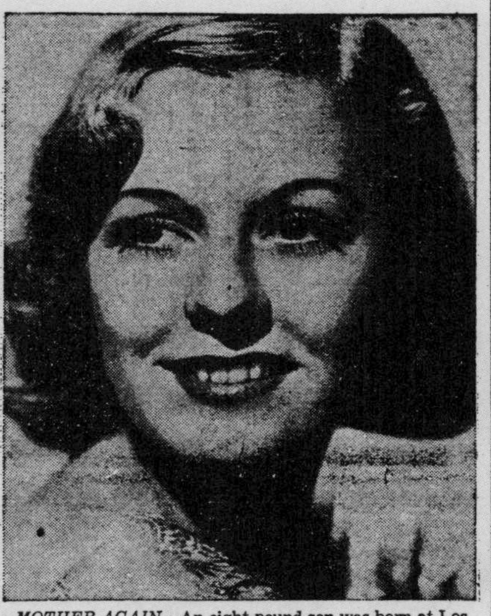

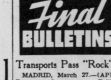

MOTHER AGAIN—An eight-pound son was born at Los Angeles this morning to Margaret Sullavan, film actress. She and her husband, Leland Hayward, theatrical agent, have a 3½-year-old daughter, Brooke.

BIGGEST IN DOMINION'S HISTORY

GREATEST CANADIAN FORCE TAKING SHAPE

By ALLEN BILL.
(Special Correspondent of The Daily Province and Associated Southam Newspapers with the C.A.S.F.)

LONDON, March 27.—With the foundation solidly laid, Canada is now raising the superstructure of its army of future days—a not too distant future—which will exceed in size and striking power any military organization in the Dominion's history.

It will be commanded by a full general—the first time this rank has ever been attained by a Canadian commander.

It will mean promotion all along the line.

At the top will be a full general—presumably the present G. O. C. of the Canadians here, Lt.-General A. G. L. McNaughton—with a lieutenant-general commanding each corps and a major-general at the head of each division, as at present.

The present divisional commanders are Major-Generals Pearkes, First Division; Odlum, Second Division; Price, Third Division, and Sansom, Armored Division.

It is expected this new set-up will result also in the expansion of Canadian military headquarters in London with the senior officer holding lieutenant-general's rank. The senior officer at present holds a rank one grade lower—Major-General Montague. In recent months several officers have been drawn from Canadian military headquarters for important appointments with the fighting units. The most recent appointment, just announced at Ottawa, according to word received here, is that of Lt.-Col. Hugh Young of Calgary, as G. S. O. 1, Armored Division.

Side by side with the army's expansion is the equally striking development of the Royal Canadian Air Force, as The Vancouver Daily Province London correspondence first intimated on January 21.

With this picture of Canada's future military effort unfolding, plus the silent but vital service of the Royal Canadian Navy, the Dominion's fighting role in Hitler's final defeat may be expected to be a formidable one."

One Pair of Pants Grows Where Two Grew Before

VICHY, France, March 27.—(AP)—Frenchmen may now buy new clothes — if they turn in double the quantity of old ones. A new regulation re-opened the sale of clothes, which had been almost completely halted.

Two pairs of old pants turned in by the purchaser of a new pair will be given to the national help organization for distribution free to the needy.

Parley Proceeding At Bethlehem Plant

BETHLEHEM, Pa., March 27.—(AP)—R. A. Lewis, general manager of the Bethlehem Steel Company plant here, announced today that the company hoped that a conference between the company and union officals would lead to an amicable settlement in the very near future. It was Behlehem's first statement on the negotiations started this morning.

Earlier, Thomas Lambert, U.S. labor conciliator, had said the company and C. I. O. steel workers' organizing committee were "not too far apart" in their meeting — the first since the strike began Monday.

The Bethlehem Company has defense orders totalling more than $1,000,000,000.

Adds 18,000 Tons

Big Danish Vessels Seized In West Indies

OTTAWA, March 27.—(CP)—Navy Minister Angus Macdonald disclosed officially today that Royal Canadian Navy units operating in West Indies waters assisted in the recent capture of two Danish ships.

"The addition of these two (Danish) ships adds about 18,000 tons to the mercantile marine service of the Empire," the minister told The Canadian Press.

Names of the naval vessels involved in the capture, which took place "some weeks ago," were not disclosed.

Mr. Macdonald's announcement did not name the Danish ships. However, he made it after he was questioned on an Associated Press despatch from New York, which quoted shipping circles as saying "a Canadian auxiliary cruiser" had intercepted the 8571-ton Scandia and the 9119-ton Christian Holm, two Danish motor tankers.

The AP despatch said the tanker had been released by a British prize court at Trinidad "to be used in defense of the realm."

"Units of the R. C. N. have been serving in West Indies waters for some time," Mr. Macdonald said.

"In this instance two Canadian patrol vessels acted in co-operation and under the direction of a Dutch vessel of war, the master of the Dutch vessel being the senior of the three naval officers.

"The interception was undertaken by the three ships together.

"But the first to arrive and actually board the Danish ships was one of the two Canadian vessels.

"The interception took place some weeks ago, although news of it is only now being given out."

FIVE SEIZURES.

The Danish vessels were the fourth and fifth ships known to have been seized by Canadian naval units or with their aid since the war began.

The auxiliary armed cruiser Prince Robert captured the big German cargo ship Weser off the Pacific Coast of Mexico last year.

Operating with the British units in the Caribbean, the Canadian destroyer Assiniboia assisted British vessels in capture of the German ship Hannover.

Just after Italy entered the war, the Canadian auxiliary mine-sweeper Bras d'Or — subsequently lost at sea with 31 officers and men — overtook and captured the Italian freighter Caio Noli in the St. Lawrence.

Sports Sheet Fights Racing News Fine

EDMONTON, March 27. — (CP) — Hearing of an appeal brought by the Sports Review Ltd. against conviction and $25 fine imposed by Magistrate D. C. Sinclair in Calgary on a charge of publishing information relating to betting on horse racing opened in Alberta Appeal Court today.

It was contended for the appellant company that information contained in the publication, while it could be used for betting purposes, was issued as a guide to race horse breeders. There was no intent the publication should be used to promote betting, counsel contended.

(Weather Report on Page 32.)

New Government Sends 1,200,000 To War Positions

BELGRADE, March 27.—(AP)—Yugo-Slav preparations for war are being pushed with lightning speed tonight.

The nation rushed 1,200,000 fighting men to battle stations tonight in answer to what reports abroad described as a virtual ultimatum from Germany, following overthrow of the Yugo-Slav Government which capitulated to the Axis.

(The foregoing despatch was filed from Belgrade at 10:20 p.m. (12:20 p.m. P.S.T.), the first communication from that city since 2 a.m. (4 p.m. P.S.T. Wednesday),

(The telephone line again was cut to Belgrade after this much of the despatch had been dictated from Belgrade to Berne, Switzerland, for relay to New York.)

(By Associated Press.)

BUDAPEST, Hungary, March 27.—Seventeen-year-old King Peter II. of Yugo-Slavia took the helm in Yugo-Slavia today in a popular surge of disapproval of Tuesday's pact with the Axis, and swore in a government headed by tough Gen. Dusan Simovic to defend the country's independence after a night of rioting and bloody demonstrations.

Regent Prince Paul, who approved the Axis pact, was reported to have fled to Greece with his wife, Princess Olga of Greece, and the government of Premier Dragisa Cvetkovic, who went to Vienna to sign the agreement with Hitler, was overthrown.

Reports from Belgrade said Cvetkovic and Foreign Minister Cincar-Markovic, who also had an important role in the pact signing, and most of the members of the overthrown cabinet were under arrest.

(Axis reaction to the swing in Yugo-Slav policy was swift. From Berlin the German Government sped an "urgent request" to Belgrade to explain the international implications of her changed government, especially as it affects her adherence to the three-power pact. Berlin hoped for a reply tonight.

(Germans said Berlin was not interested in a purely domestic

(Continued on Page 6.) See BALKANS.

Second Canadians

King, Queen Visit Odlum's Division

(By Canadian Press.)

SOMEWHERE IN ENGLAND, March 27.—Bugles blared and a pipe band wailed a military welcome today as the King and Queen paid their first visit to the Canadian 2nd Division.

Everywhere the royal couple went during their six-hour tour thousands of Canadians broke their lines and circled the visitors, cheering them with tin hats hoisted on their rifles and waved wildly in the air.

The King took the cheers at the salute and the Queen smiled her thanks. Calls were made on every unit in the division by Their Majesties, accompanied by Major-General Victor Odlum, general officer commanding the division, several colonels and the divisional general staff.

GREETED BY ODLUM.

When he King arrived at the camp he was greeted by Gen. Odlum on the steps of the mess and then went immediately to the Divisional Signals, where he inspected the unit. He stopped to speak to L.-Cpl. Stan Pearson of Winnipeg and later spent a minute discussing training with Cpl. Lewis Eden of Montreal.

At the Royal Canadian Army Service Corps the King looked over details of equipment and talked with Pte. J. F. Curts of

(Continued on Page 6.) See THE KING.

Viceroy at Jasper

JASPER, Alta., March 27.—(CP)—The Earl of Athlone, Governor-General of Canada, and Princess Alice had their first glimpse of the Canadian Rockies today as they continued their tour of the west. They are due in Vancouver Saturday.

MISSING GIRL SAID TO BE ON WAY HERE

BERKELEY, Cal., March 27.—(AP)—There still was no definite clue today to the disappearance 10 days ago of Violet Ann Lindal, 19, University of California honor student from Winnipeg.

Police had a letter from a Tehama County rancher saying he gave a ride to a girl hitch-hiker who resembled the missing student. They were to send a photograph of Miss Lindal to him for comparison.

The rancher, F. T. Robson, said he picked the girl up near Chico on March 19. She told him she was born in Canada, was on her way to Vancouver, B. C., to visit her grandmother, and intended to enlist as a Canadian nurse.

Rescuers Recover Body Of Trapped Miner

GRINDSTONE, Magdalen Islands, March 27.—(AP)—After four days of frantic efforts, fellow workers on Wednesday night reached the body of Albin Pettipas, 35-year-old miner, trapped at the 45-foot level of a manganese mine here last Saturday.

Pettipas was trapped when a wooden platform on which he was working was shattered by a surface movement of about 30 yards of mine muck. Tons of mud slithered down on the timbering.

They Came In Waves -- To Death
Eyewitness Story Of Greek War

By RICHARD D. McMILLAN (Copyright, 1941, by British (United Press)

ON THE ALLIED FRONT, IN GREECE, April 16, 10 p.m. — Delayed)—(UP)—Germany's crack blitzkrieg troops are being mowed down in a mass slaughter before the British-Greek lines, which they are attempting to smash in great  **News-Herald EXCLUSIVE** sledge-hammer blows.

The battle is raging along the curving Allied front on a scale equalling in fury anything ever seen in last year's German blitzkrieg on the Western front.

Into the gigantic struggle the German high command has thrown at least three "panzer" divisions as well as picked Austrian Alpine mountain troops and brigades of youthful Hitler Stormtroopers known as "Blitzmen."

THE GERMANS ARE BEING THROWN INTO THE BATTLE WITHOUT ANY APPARENT REGARD FOR THE STAGGERING LOSSES INFLICTED UPON THEM BY THE BRITISH AND GREEK ARMIES.

Despite the savagery of the assaults, the Allied line is holding, I was assured.

Fleets of British and German tanks have battled from Monastir Gap at the Jugoslav frontier down to Grevena, 70 miles into Greece, and close to Mount Olympus at Servia Pass.

Australian troops, smashing wave upon wave of German infantry at Servia Pass have left the ground covered with Nazi dead and tanks destroyed by mines and anti-tank guns.

At Grevena, 50 miles west of Olympus, British tanks rushed to the aid of the hard-pressed Greeks and smashed into clanging combat with "lanes of German tanks" in a six-hour, victorious battle.

The crack troops of these German assaults are youths of Hitler's "Blitzmen," many of them mere 19-year-olds.

It is the same German strategy of slashing, knifing attacks which I observed on the Western front in the Battle of France.

Finals of The News-Herald "Search for Talent" Contest, Orpheum Theatre, Tonight, 8:30.

HOME EDITION

News for VICTORY Herald

LARGEST MORNING CIRCULATION WEST OF TORONTO

VANCOUVER, B.C., FRIDAY, APRIL 18, 1941   3c

R.A.F. HITS BACK — BOMBS BERLIN

By NED RUSSELL
(British United Press Staff Correspondent)

LONDON, Friday— (BUP)—The Royal Air Force last night attacked Berlin but clouds over the city made operations difficult and the raid was not "particularly heavy," the Air Ministry reported early today.

In Berlin a communique said the British bombers caused fires in residential districts and again damaged "cultural objects"—the same accusation as that laid against Britain in connection with the previous assault on Berlin.

Was 40th Raid

Last night's attack was the 40th raid on Berlin made by the R.A.F. since the beginning of the war and the first since April 9 when the attackers concentrated on the centre of the city. In that raid the Prussian State Library and the State Opera House on Unter Den Linden were destroyed.

Thursday the R.A.F. raided the French "invasion" coast for the third time in 24 hours. Wednesday night the R.A.F. in widespread operations battered the north German port of Bremen for five hours.

The Weather

Forecast for today: moderate westerly winds, fair and mild. Temperatures Thursday: high 58, low 35.

Greeks Falling Back Under German Blows

By HENRY T. GORRELL
British United Press Correspondent

ATHENS, Friday. — (BUP) —The Greek army has "undergone reverses" under the smashing German blitzkrieg and is falling back under a driving Nazi advance toward the heart of Greece, it was admitted today in an official statement appealing to the Greek people to avoid panic.

Reinforced

The Greek army along the allied line, fighting under "adverse conditions," was said in the official statement to be retiring under the blows of vastly reinforced German blitzkrieg forces.

In Albania at the western end of the allied line the Greek army still is "fighting to its utmost" against an Italian push down upon Argyrocastron, which is about 50 miles north of Janina.

The Greek high command announced the evacuation of Klisura and Erseka above Argyrocastron.

Denied

Rumors that Larissa had fallen were officially denied and the Germans actually are "several miles" north of the city, it was stated.

Today's official communique advised the Greek people to remain calm and avoid panic in the face of the new "reverse" and shopkeepers were ordered to keep their places open. Workers were told to stay at their jobs.

An earlier announcement today by a Greek spokesman had said that the eastern end of the allied line held firm along the 100-mile Greek front and that

Continued on Page 3

At A Glance: Embattled Greece faced a crisis in the Battle of the Balkans today with German forces pushing on Kalabaka in a drive that threatened to cut off British and Greek forces on east and west flanks of the Allied defence lines. The map above shows the approximate positions of the German drives.

Near Mount Olympus British and Greek lines were holding firm in the face of furious assaults by German forces of all types. In the centre the Allies battled to halt the drive on Kalabaka and Larissa. In the west the Greeks slowly fell back from Albania to shorter, more easily defended positions in Greece.

WHAT'S NEWS TODAY
The City

Foreign

Aussies Leap Into Struggle

Battle - hardened British, Australian and New Zealand troops, sun-leathered veterans who shattered the Italian army in North Africa, are leaping into the struggle against the Germans with whooping enthusiasm.

They have inflicted tremendous casualties upon the Germans, holding all mountain passes protecting their section of the Allied line, according to my latest information.

A RECTIFICATION OF THE ALLIED LINE IS ENVISAGED EVENTUALLY, OWING TO THE LIGHTNING GERMAN DRIVE TO SOUTH GREVENA.

(This indicated that McMillan was with the British in or near the Mount Olympus sector on the eastern hinge of the Anglo-Greek line.)

May Form New Lines

(McMillan's dispatch indicated that the British might withdraw southward from Mount Olympus, presumably south to a line running from Larissa—40 miles south of Olympus—across Greece through Trikkala to the Ionian seacoast somewhere opposite Corfu.)

A British major describing to me the furious German assaults on the Allied line, said:

"THEY WERE FOUR ABREAST AND MANY LINES DEEP. WE MOWED THEM DOWN BUT THEY ADVANCED IN SUCH MASSES THAT OUR TROOPS FOUND IT HUMANLY IMPOSSIBLE TO FIRE QUICKLY ENOUGH.

"Then came the tanks, to meet our tanks, which outfought them but were inferior in numbers."

'Been Fighting For Six Days'

"We have been fighting for six days, holding pass after pass to insure the withdrawal southwards from Jugoslavia," a British tank officer told me.

Hard - fighting "Aussies" of the British Imperial infantry met the German tanks near Monastir Gap, blowing them into the air with mine-fields as they charged across onto Greek territory in a blinding snowstorm.

An officer of the British Hus-

Continued on Page 8

Greek Premier Suicide

★ ★

HITLER BIRTHDAY MARKS NEW LONDON RAID

★ ★ ★ ★ ★ FINAL

THE VANCOUVER DAILY PROVINCE

47th YEAR—NO. 21 OFFICIAL FORECAST: TOMORROW: FAIR AND MILD. VANCOUVER, B.C., SATURDAY, APRIL 19, 1941—62 PAGES PRICE 10 CENTS

Raiders Sunk In Far Pacific

New Leader Slays Self

OTHER AXIS SHIPS ARE DISABLED

Parliament Struck In Last Attacks

MECHANICAL MOTHER— These week-old Springer spaniel puppies are alive and thriving thanks to the ingenuity of Fred Barker, jr., of Glen Ellyn, Ill., who devised this mechanical feeder when their mother died at their birth. Made of nursing bottles, boards and an automobile tire tube, the mechanical mother feeds all six at once every three hours. —(A.P. Wirephoto.)

(By Associated Press.)

ATHENS, April 19.—Premier Alexandros Korizis took his own life because of anguish over Greece's unequal struggle with Germany and Italy, it was announced officially tonight.

The 56-year-old premier, less than three months in office, shot himself yesterday at his home.

An announcement said:

"Korizis, having had a nervous breakdown as the result of the strain and emotion of the unequal struggle which Greece is waging against an army of two empires, ended his life."

It was announced officially that King George II., reserving to himself for the time being the presidency of the council of ministers, had entrusted General Alexander Mazarakis with formation of a new cabinet, which will have a military character due to the war circumstances.

(By Associated Press)

ATHENS, April 19. — King George conferred today with a stream of political and military leaders in an effort to form a new government as solid masses of German troops pushed against the Allied Olympus line in a manner reminiscent of the first Great War.

Despite the reshuffling of the government made necessary by the unexpected death yesterday of Premier Alexandros Korizis, the capital was quiet and orderly. Maj.-Gen. Kristou Kavrakos was named military governor of Athens during the crucial period to ensure stability.

The burden of forming a new government was thrust on King

(Continued on Page 6.) See GREECE.

Hint Dominions May Join Cabinet

LONDON, April 19. — (AP) — Great Britain was reported tonight to be arranging direct Dominion collaboration with the cabinet.

Reliable sources said some Empire representatives probably would be invited to sit in with the cabinet to give precise information on what the Dominions might be able to contribute to any particular move

Building Blasted

DENVER, April 19.—(AP)— An explosion and fire wrecked the four-storey Hoeckel building in the lower downtown district today and Fire Chief John F. Healy said saboteurs might have been responsible. No one was injured.

Brooks Blank Bees

BOSTON, April 19 — (AP) — Luke Hamlin blanked the Brooklyn Dodgers took the annual morning Patriots' Day game 8-0. Peewee Reese clubbed out four hits, including a homer. Joe Medwick also hit a homer for Brooklyn.

Missing In Slav War

Mrs. Ruth Mitchell Knowles sister of the late American flyer, General "Billy" Mitchell, has been missing in Yugo-Slavia since it was announced that she had joined the death-defying legion, the Comitaji. She is the first foreign woman in the legion which boasts that no member is ever captured alive. She was made a despatch rider for the legion in the short-lived war the Slavs waged against Germany.

(By Associated Press)

SAN PEDRO, April 19.—Lieut.-Col. Lawrence M. Cosgrave, Canadian trade commissioner to Australia, declared today that four-motored Consolidated bombers had sunk or driven out of action German commerce raiders operating in the far Pacific.

Colonel Cosgrave arrived on the Matson-Oceanic liner Monterey, en route to Ottawa.

He reported great strides in war production in Australia, adding: "We put many German experts, interned at the start of the war, to work designing tools and planes for defense of the Empire."

Also aboard was Reginald B. Jackson, operations manager for a British commercial aviation firm in Thailand (Siam) and an advisor to the Thailand minister of aviation.

He said a Japanese land march through Thailand to Singapore was impracticable for several months because of the rainy season, and declared:

"I have no doubt that Thailand would resist such an aggression. It has a modern air force, a partly mechanized army and a corps of key pilots, all trained at West Point or Kelly Field, Texas. It would be no walkover."

Hepburn to London?

LONDON, April 19. — (CP) — The Associated Press reported tonight that Premier Hepburn of Ontario is expected in London soon. The reference to the Ontario Premier came in a story on reported arrangements for closer collaboration between the British Government and the representatives of the Dominions.

Burns Girl In Furnace

(By Associated Press)

AKRON, O., April 19.—A 58-year-old man told detectives today that he shoved the body of Ruth Zwicker, 24-year-old music teacher, into the firebox of a church heating plant a few hours before Easter morning services, fearing incrimination in her death.

He was held on a charge of being a suspicious person, and Prosecutor Alva Russell said he was considering filing a murder charge.

The man was arrested immediately after human remains, found in the ashes at North Hill Methodist Church, were identified from dental bridgework as those of the missing Miss Zwicker.

The man declared his burning of the young woman's body to keep from being involved in her accidental death.

The young woman had gone to the church last Saturday to practice on the piano. When she had finished, about 11 a.m., the man said he asked her for a kiss and she slapped him. Following a short scuffle, she fell and struck her head against the piano bench, he related.

The suspect then said he believed her dead, and dragged her body to a basement coal bin. He returned about 4 a.m. on Easter morning, he told the officers, and placed her body in the firebox of the church's steam heating plant.

The young woman's father, A. W. Zwicker, told detectives that the man twice had helped him search through the many rooms of the church last Saturday night.

The man is married and the father of three grown children.

LONDON, April 19.—(CP)—German bombers roared on London from two directions tonight, scattering high-explosives and incendiaries in many areas in a Hitler birthday sequel to the ferocious raid of Wednesday night and Thursday morning.

As the anti-aircraft barrage steadily gained in tempo and more planes arrived, Londoners believed the Nazis were intent on a "birthday blitz" for Hitler, who will be 52 years old tomorrow.

Between the boomings of the co-ordinated batteries of anti-aircraft guns, the steady drone of the approaching raiders could be heard. They sounded menacingly near or low.

It was authoritatively stated today that the number of fires started in the raid on London Wednesday night was the largest since the beginning of the war. None of the fires got out of control, however.

LONDON, April 19.—(AP)— Both Houses of Parliament were damaged in recent (probably Wednesday's) air raids, it was announced officially tonight.

All of the windows of the House of Commons library were destroyed, a large water tank was smashed and Nazi bombs ripped a hole in the roof over the members' lobby.

The Parliament Buildings had suffered damage from bomb hits last autumn.

The latest damage included bomb hits on the Speaker's house in the inner quadrangle. The Speaker, Capt. E. A. Fitzroy, was in the residence and no one was injured.

The Commons suffered more than the Lords. In addition to the windows of the library, where members spend much of their time when Parliament is not sitting, being blown out, the contents were damaged.

Along the Terrace by the Thames hundreds of windows were shattered and the apartments of the office-keeper were struck.

Neither House was in session. There were no casualties among the staff of the firewatchers on duty.

Eight pensioners were killed when a bomb recently hit the

(Continued on Page 6.) See LONDON.

British Raiders Bag Nazi Planes

LONDON, April 19. — (AP) — An air ministry communique said Saturday:

"Aircraft of one of our bomber squadrons on their way to Berlin Thursday night, April 17-18, shot down an enemy night fighter and on their way back shot down another.

"It has also been confirmed that on the night of April 16 an enemy bomber was shot down by anti-aircraft gunfire over northern Ireland. Thus a total of nine enemy aircraft was destroyed during that night."

Final BULLETINS

Body Found In Gorge

VICTORIA, April 19.—(CP)— An unidentified body of an elderly man was discovered in Gorge Inlet today by three soldiers, provincial police reported.

F.D.R. Intervenes

HYDE PARK, N.Y., April 19.—(AP) — President Roosevelt intervened personally today to bring about ratifications by west coast shipyard employers and employees of an agreement to fix wage rates.

Italian Ace Dies

ROME, April 19.—(AP)—The death in a "flying accident" of Maj. Oscar Mol'nari, 35, fighter pilot commander who was cited March 23 for having shot down his 50th "enemy" plane, was announced today.

Hold Slaying Suspect

CHICAGO, April 19.—(AP)— Police Lieut. William Drury said today that a 31-year-old man had been taken into custody for questioning in connection with the slaying of John F. Arena, editor of the Italian Language newspaper La Tribuna.

To Deport Stephanie

SAN FRANCISCO, April 19.—(AP)—The government expects to deport Princess Stephanie Hohenlohe to her native Hungary by way of Siberia, says Major Lemuel Schofield, chief of the Federal Immigration Service.

Floods Leave 8 Dead

SPRINGFIELD Mo., April 19.—(AP)—Floods and storms swept the Missouri and Arkansas Ozarks today, leaving eight dead, forcing the evacuation of a town and parts of others and threatening Joplin, Mo., with a water famine.

Porter's Cap Wins

HAVRE DE GRACE, Md., April 19.—(AP)—C. S. Howard's Porter's Cap, won the $15,000 added Chesapeake stakes today. Leading all the way, Mrs. Louise Palladino's Little Beans and E. K. Bryson's Cavalier third.

Labor Crisis Looms

SEATTLE, April 19.—(AP)— A crisis apparently was approaching today in the Congress of Industrial Organization's sudden move to "organize" the big Boeing aircraft factory here following suspension of the factiontorn American Federation of Labor Aeronautical Mechanics' Union.

Savage Nazi Push Halted

(See map of Greek front on Page 19)

(By Associated Press.)

ATHENS, April 19.—Britain's Imperial forces in Greece, declaring their front nowhere had been penetrated, announced today that they had repulsed a heavy Nazi attack by armored formations and masses of infantry with "severe" losses.

"Despite all efforts, our front nowhere has been penetrated," said a communique.

It added that many prisoners had been taken.

The Imperial troops were reported in action along the entire front as waves of German infantry tried vainly to force a way up the mountains guarding the passes in the face of murderous fire.

Observers said the slopes were strewn with dead and wounded Nazis.

The mountainous country and stout resistance had put Nazi mechanized warfare in reverse, observers said.

FIGHT ON FOOT.

Instead of the German panzer columns breaking through to clear the roads for the infantry, Hitler's legions now must fight their way on foot ahead of the tanks, it was said.

As King George II. worked to shape a new government—possibly a military cabinet — in an overnight change necessary by the death of Premier Alexandros Korizis, word from the north indicated fighting had intensified along the entire defense line.

All reports from the front up until noon today indicated the allied lines were unchanged in the past 12 hours, despite relentless Nazi pressure.

"We mow them down by the hundreds as they try to climb the steep mountain sides, but as soon as one wave is thrown back another pushes forward," said a military officer.

"Their losses are tremendous, unequalled, I believe, by anything they have suffered in the European war to date."

This source said the Nazis were bringing up heavy guns to supplement the bombardment by their Stukas, which fly over 20 and 30 at a time.

(London newspapers today almost unanimously cautioned the public editorially to expect more serious reverses and a possible withdrawal from the Balkans because of numerical superiority of the German army and its mechanized power.

(Should the moment come, as unfortunately it may, when forces of the Empire will be compelled to retire from the Greek

(Continued on Page 6.) See BALKANS.

Woman Tackles Boy Poised on Roof For Death Leap

NEW YORK, April 19.—(AP) —For one hour 13-year-old Billy Rosendale stood on the edge of the roof of a four-storey building in Brooklyn today and threatened to jump because, police said, his mother had threatened to punish him.

Hundreds watched him. A priest, a playmate, police and the boy's mother pleaded in vain.

The nets never were used. Talking quietly to Billy, Mrs. Emily Moore, herself mother of three children, got him a few feet from the edge. Then, without warning, she made a flying tackle and caught Billy around the knees. She fainted; others kept hold of Billy.

They took him to hospital, suffering from hysteria.

43

NAZIS DIE BY THOUSANDS IN SEA BATTLE OFF CRETE

THE VANCOUVER DAILY PROVINCE

47th YEAR—NO. 50 VANCOUVER, B.C., FRIDAY, MAY 23, 1941—56 PAGES PRICE 10 CENTS

Pity Poor Ellen . . . .

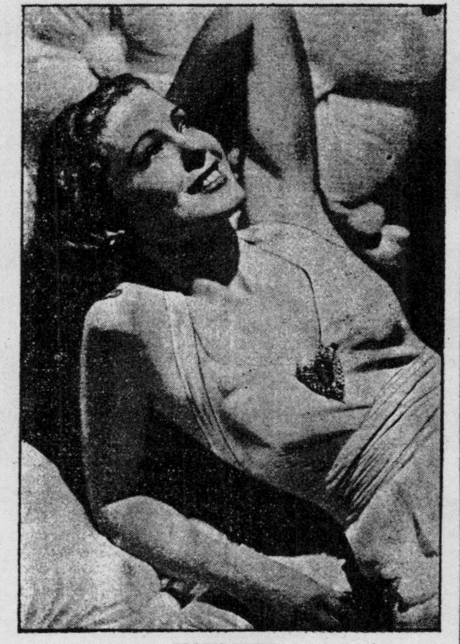

ELLEN DREW.

HOLLYWOOD, May 23.—Ellen Drew has to be spanked by Melvyn Douglas, across his knee, for a scene in "Our Wife." The trouble is that the picture's director is John Stahl—and what Mr. Stahl is especially famous for is taking and retaking a scene indefinitely until he likes it.

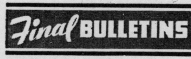

Final BULLETINS

Claim Ships Sunk

BERLIN, May 23.—(AP)—The German high command claimed today its submarines have sunk 110,000 tons of British shipping in the Atlantic in recent operations.

Navy Fuel Depot

WASHINGTON, May 23.—(AP)—The Senate passed today a bill authorizing the United States navy to establish a fuel depot at Middle and Orchard points, Puget Sound, Washington. Cost of the project was estimated at $3,500,000.

Expect Inspiring Talk

ADELAIDE, May 23.—(AP)—Acting Prime Minister Arthur Fadden said today he expected Prime Minister Menzies would bring to Australia an inspiring message when he arrived at Sydney soon after a visit to Egypt, Britain, Canada and the United States.

Iraq Regent Returns

LONDON, May 23.—(AP)—The Press Association said it had learned in London tonight that Emir Abdul Ilah, regent of Iraq deposed in the April coup d'etate, had returned to Iraq soil and was considering formation of a new administration.

Doctors Heroes

MELBOURNE, May 23.—(AP)—Army Minister Spender of Australia said in an interview today that one of the many heroic aspects of the evacuation of British troops from Greece was the spirit of self-sacrifice shown by seven doctors and 150 men of other ranks who remained to care for wounded Australians.

44

Nazis Say Canadolite Captured, Not Sunk

BERLIN, May 23.—(AP)—The Germans claimed today the 11,309-ton Canadian oil tanker Canadolite has been captured by the German navy as a prize.

(London advices yesterday said it was feared the tanker had been sunk off the west coast of Africa.)

The Germans claimed they seized the tanker while it was en route from Freetown, West Africa to Venezuela. No word was available as to the fate of the crew.

Report On Crete

BERLIN, May 23.—(AP)—The German press and radio appeared today to be preparing the German people for an announcement regarding Crete. So far, the people do not know an invasion attempt has been started.

Russ Youth Warned

LONDON, May 23.—(CP)—The conviction that Russia "must hold herself in a state of readiness for war" was expressed today in the Soviet organ of the Communist Youth League in an article quoted by the British Broadcasting Corporation.

Menace Darlan

LONDON, May 23.—(AP)—B. B. C. today quoted reports by the Free French news agency that "violent demonstrations" against Admiral Jean Darlan occurred a few weeks ago when the high Vichy government official went to Bretagne in northern France to confer with German military authorities.

Claim Sinkings

NEW YORK, May 23.—(CP)—The German radio, issuing what appeared to be a further claim of damage against the royal navy today alleged the sinking of three destroyers by air attack, damaging of two, destruction of five speedboats and observation of two cruisers burning.

Windsor Gets Plant

WINDSOR, Ont., May 23.—(CP) — Dinsmore-McIntire Ltd. of Windsor have been awarded the general contract for the construction of the $8,000,000 machine-gun plant to be built here by the Dominion Government and operated by General Motors Corporation of Canada Ltd.

British Cruiser Reports Action

RIO DE JANEIRO, May 23.—(AP) — The British auxiliary Cruiser Asturias arrived at this port today and Lieut. R. W. F. Rule, an aide to Capt. A. H. Ardill, said she had seen action.

He would not tell when, where, or against whom, and to questions whether the German freighter Lech had been sighted or sunk during the Asturias' patrol, in the southern Atlantic. His only answer was "yes and no."

Canada 'Pools' Seamen

RESERVE OF CREWS MADE BY NEW PLAN

OTTAWA, May 23.—(CP)—Establishment of manning pools to provide groups of experienced officers and men to make up deficiencies at short notice in crews of merchant ships sailing from Canadian ports, was announced late today by Transport Minister Cardin.

Under the plan, authorized by order-in-council, a director of merchant seamen will be appointed immediately to head a war-time branch of the transport department which will operate and administer the pools.

Seamen entering the Pools will be provided with board, room and pay "provided they agree in writing to go to sea on any ship of their own nationality or on any ship arranged with the regional director of the Manning Pool."

The Manning Pools will be put into operation "at the earliest possible moment," the announcement added. The first such pool will be established at Halifax, and, when it is in operation, consideration will be given the requirements of other shipping centres.

BASEBALL

AMERICAN LEAGUE.

		R	H	E
Chicago	500 000 200	7	11	0
Detroit	000 000 002	2	11	1

Lyons and Tresh; Bridges and Tebbetts.

2nd game—

		R	H	E
Chicago	000 000 000	0	7	1
Detroit	000 314 01x	9	14	0

Dietrich, Humphries and Tresh, Dicky; Trout and Tebbetts.

		R	H	E
Boston	200 021 022	9	13	2
New York	221 010 120	9	10	1

Game call on account of darkness.

Dobson, Dickman, H. Newsome, Ryba and Peacock; Chandler, Standceau, Breuer, Murphy and Dickey.

NATIONAL LEAGUE.

		R	H	E
Cincinnati	204 001 100	8	10	1
Chicago	003 000 002	4	4	3

Vandermeer, E. Riddle and Lombardi; Passeau, Olson, Erickson and McCullough, George.

Robert Morris Wins Belmont Handicap

NEW YORK, May 23.—(AP)—Robert Morris, flaunting the silks of J. Frederick Byers of Pittsburgh, spread-eabled a field of six other 3-year olds in the $7500 Peter Pan Handicap at Belmont Park today after Whirlaway had been scratched.

Ridden by Alfred Robertson of Toronto, Robert Morris finished the mile and eighth six lengths in front of Lou Taliaferro's Brigh. Gallan. Mrs. H. C. Phipps' King Cole, conqueror of Robert Morris in last Saturday's Withers Mile and the heavily placed favorite, trailed by another five lengths in third place.

Robert Morris, stepping the distance in 1:49, paid $14.30.

May Ration Supplies

LONDON, May 23. — (AP) — Acting Prime Minister Arthur Fadden of Australia "hinted" today at rationing of certain supplies in the Commonwealth and restrictions on imports of non-essential goods, the British Broadcasting Corporation reported.

Hollywood Selections

By TOM GWYNNE,
(Daily Province Race Correspondent)

FIRST RACE—Count Chat, Palacia, Galvalo.

SECOND RACE—Bess Greenock, Valdina Joan, Liberty Bar.

THIRD RACE—Torch Lee, Southern Jane, Jubilo.

FOURTH RACE—Battle Colors, Painted Veil, Verse.

FIFTH RACE—Gold Pomp, Appeasement, Transient.

SIXTH RACE—Dick Naishapur, Iron Bunker, Ecechais.

SEVENTH RACE—Phar, Rong, Pantime, Winter Wind.

EIGHTH RACE—Joharie, Gay Jacket, Chatted.

BEST BET—Torch Lee.

★ ★ ★ ★ ★ FINAL

And This Is Vancouver . . .

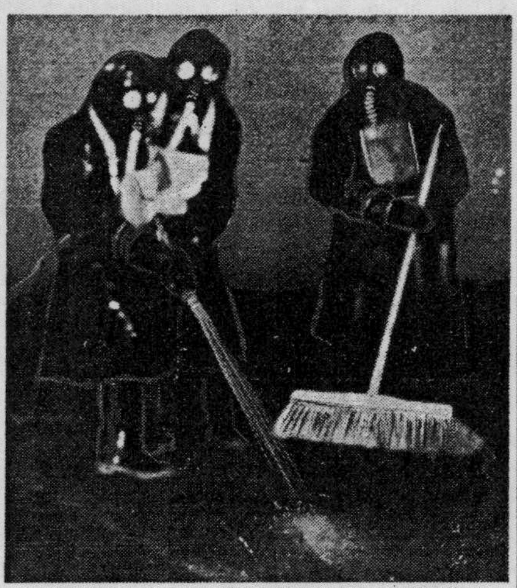

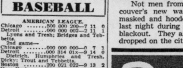

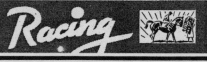

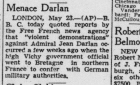

Not men from Mars, but members of one of Vancouver's new wartime protective services are these masked and hooded figures. Their picture was taken last night during one of the "incidents" staged in the blackout. They are mopping up the remains of a flare dropped on the city.

Racing

Suffolk Downs Results

First race—Ask Me (May), $7.40, $4.80, $3.20.
Caboodle (Bodiou), $4.60, $3.40.
Accuse Me (Polk), $4.20.
Time, 1.02.
Scratched—Gala Grip, Bright World

Second race—Saving Grace (Briggs), $5.80, $3, $2.40.
Posterity (Howell), $3.20, $2.60.
Discobolo (McMullen), $3.40.
Time, 1.13.
Scratched—James City, Claro.

Third race—Foxworth (Atkinson), $6.40, $4.20, $2.80.
Hendersonian (Dupps), $5.40, $3.40.
Village Belle (E. Smith), $3.
Time, 1.13 2-5.
Scratched—Sunareve, Gertee Lee, Tea Hour.

Fourth race—Woodville (Dupps), $14, $6.20, $3.20.
Septime (McMullen), $3.80, $2.60.
See See (Hettinger), $2.60.
Time, 1.12 2-5.
Scratched—None.

Fifth race—Zaltoana (Young), $5, $3.40, $2.80.
Eselkay (Taylor), $5.60, $3.60.
Cove Springs (Bodiou), $3.40.
Time, 1.47.
Scratched—None.

Sixth race—White Time (Atkinson), $24.60, $15.20, $10.
Red War (Bodiou), $8.40, $5.40.
Rough News (Young), $6.80.
Scratched—None.

Seventh race—Tedium (Young), $8.60, $4.60, $3.60.
Orcades (Taylor), $5.20, $3.60.
Merry Morn (Vina), $5.80.
Scratched—None.

Eighth race—Bag Grave (Sisto), $8.40, $5.40, $3.60.
Chalcolite (Vina), $6, $3.80.
Yannie Sid (Briggs), $4.
Time, 1.44 4-5.
Scratched—Stable.

Hollywood Park Results

First race—Opening Bid (Neves), $7.20, $3, $3.
Certie (Rodriguez), $3, $2.80.
Old Smokey (Balaski), $5.60.
Scratched—Walter Ca Get Good, Skipper Z, Liberty Lad.
Time, 1.00 1-5.

Second race—Igorette (Balaski), $18.60, $8.40, $5.60.
Bion Gia (Pearson), $4.20, $3.40.
Martin Macaw (Pariso), $10.80.
Time, 1.25.

Third race — Sextus (Westrope), $14.80, $6.00, $3.80.
Praetorian (Neves), $4.60, $3.00.
Peter Takalon (Pariso), $3.80.
Scratched: Duke of War, Mieletta, Bosford, Fervorita.

(Race Entries on Page 2.)

Lincoln Fields Results

First race—Nani Leonie (Wilson), $12.40, $7.20 $4.20.
Memorosa (Borton), $4.20, $3.60.
Grey Ethel (Berger), $11.40.
Time, 1.14 1-5.
Scratched—Takeitfrome, Tiger Teddy, Miss Pittypat, Rio Vista, Inscomira, Burr Hickman.

Second race—*Illinois Tom (Yarberry), $5.20, $5.40, $3.60.
*Falerno (Adams), $5, $5.20, $3.80.
Fly Me (Borton), $3.20.
Time, 1.27.
*—Dead heat for first.
Scratched—High Renown, Farrell.

Third race—Darby Dallas (Berger), $10.40, $6, $4.
Little Hig (LoTurco), $17, $7.80.
Fritz (Marinelli), $3.20.
Time, 1.27.
Scratched—Wacky Jack, Bright and Early, Baby Therese.

Fourth race—Country Miss (Martin), $9.60, $5.20, $3.80.
A One (McCombs), $7, $6.
Valdina Firo (Lemmons), $4.80.
Time, 1.01 4-5.
Scratched—Kee Kee, Genial Guy.

Fifth race—Hover (Adams), $5.20, $3.80, $2.80.
Rose Red (Borton), $5.60, $3.40.
Kilocycle (McCombs), $3.80.
Time, 1.14.
Scratched—Patched Pants, Which Wise, Air Hostess, Missbeville, Mexicana.

Sixth race—Sporting (Brooks), $21, $9.40, $5.40.
Prairie Dog (McCombs), $5, $3.60.
Valdina Dude (Berger), $5.20.
Time, 1.12 4-5.
Scratched—None.

Seventh race—Jim Mike (McCombs), $4.60, $3.40, $2.40.
Water Cure (Haskell), $4.40, $2.80.
Stella Mc. (Cruickshanks), $2.80.
Time, 2.09 2-5.
Scratched — Camaraderie, Hat Check.

Eighth race — Hadaboy (Haskell), $10.0, $5.60, $3.60.
Misecret (Craig), $5.80, $4.40.
Heman (Wilson), $6.20.
Scratched: Gipsy Monarch, Earlinna.

Baer's Big Edge

WASHINGTON, May 23. — (AP)—Buddy Baer had a 35¾-pound weight edge on Joe Louis today as they prepared for their title bout in Griffith Stadium tonight. The challenger tipped the beam at 237½ pounds, while Louis scaled 201¾.

Hitler's E-Boats Prevent Rescue By Naval Ships

ALEXANDRIA, Egypt, May 23.—(AP)—British naval officers related tonight how thousands of Germans have drowned, screaming for rescue, as they clung to lifebelts and boards from transports smashed by the British fleet off Crete. Not a single Nazi, they said, has reached Crete by sea.

British cruisers and destroyers were unable to pick up the survivors of their attack because of the threat of torpedo attacks from German "E-boats," the officers said.

The captain of one British cruiser which took part in the Cretain operations said:

"We sank the German boats with four-inch guns and pompoms (anti-aircraft pieces). Cruisers and destroyers rammed them. The sea was full of thousands of Germans, clinging to the wreckage and shouting for help.

"The havoc we wrought was so great that no Germans managed to land in Crete that night."

Thus, the officers said, was a great German convoy of sailing caiques (Greek boats) and small merchantmen, escorted by a single Italian destroyer, completely destroyed or dispersed.

The might of the fleet met them in pitch darkness on Wednesday night.

"We were steaming eastward," said the cruiser captain, "when suddenly, at about 11 p.m., our destroyer screen opened fire on a darkened ship.

"This was the first intimation that we were in contact with the enemy.

"We altered course and entered the fray.

"Our destroyer fire was very effective. A great bonfire appeared on the ocean, apparently a merchantman burning from end to end.

"The admiral led the squadron, then, through what appeared to be the middle of the convoy.

Large numbers of caiques were sunk by ramming.

"Some of the caiques tried to evade the attack by hiding soldiers they were carrying below decks, and by flying the Greek flag.

"Others retaliated with rifle and machine-gun fire.

"On a subsequent sweep we passed numbers of Germans clinging to the wreckage, shouting for help.

"But the possibility of enemy E-boats catching us at a disadvantage did not permit of our rescuing these survivors."

In the pitch darkness it was impossible to estimate accurately the strength of the convoy, the captain went on, but he thought it amounted to at least 40 caiques carrying about 100 men each, plus a number of small merchantment, each with several hundred troops and stores aboard.

The main action lasted about three hours.

(By Associated Press.)

LONDON, May 23.—The Allied defenders of Crete gained military control tonight of all but one of the German air invasion points on the northern coastal plain of the island and, with 16 Junkers troop-carrying transports already in ruins, turned tanks and field guns in violently renewed assaults on the Nazi-held airdrome of Malemi.

Candia and Retimo, two Nazi footholds, have been recaptured in fierce hand-to-hand fighting, it was announced officially today, and other information indicated that the tide of battle on the Greek island generally was swinging to Britain's advantage.

A large part of this was credited to the Mediterranean fleet which shattered all attempts by the Germans to get sea-borne reinforcements of men and heavy material to their sky shock troops who have been floating down by air on Crete for four days.

At both Heraclean (Candia), the island's largest city, and at Retimo, a Middle East general headquarters communique said, the Germans gained a "temporary lodgment" but "after severe hand-to-hand fighting German detachments were accounted for and the situation in both places is now satisfactory."

Heraclean is about half way along the north coast and Retimo is 30 miles farther west.

Still a bitter battleground is the airport at Malemi, 10 miles southwest of Canea in the Suda Bay area where air-borne Nazi troops are acknowledged still to be arriving. The British forces lost that air base, but it still is dominated by their artillery.

At least 16 Junkers troop transports were shot down by British anti-aircraft gunners in the first three days of the air-borne invasion of Crete.

"In the Malemi area," the war bulletin said, "our counter-attack

(Continued on Page 2.)
See CRETE.

DARLAN DENIES HUNS GET NAVY

(By Associated Press.)

VICHY, May 23.—Vice-Premier Jean Darlan in a broadcast speech today said Hitler had not asked for the French fleet or any colonial concessions during the current negotiations.

Darlan declared "Germany began the war alone and judges herself able to end it alone against any coalition."

"On the result of negotiations in progress," Darlan asserted, "directly depends the future of France. It is necessary for her to choose between life and death. The marshal and government have chosen life."

He said that "in June, 1940, the victor could have refused us an armistice, beaten us and wiped France off the map of the world—but he did not do it."

Now, Darlan said, "in May, 1941, the victor has agreed to negotiate with the French Government."

The vice-premier said he had gone to Berchtesgaden to confer

(Continued on Page 2.)
See DARLAN.

Bad Weather Halts Operations in Air

LONDON, May 23.—(CP)—Bad weather for the second successive night kept the Royal Air Force and the Germans grounded last night.

PRICE OF POP UP ON MONDAY

OTTAWA, May 23.—A general tax of 25 per cent. on the manufacturer's price of all soft drinks, announced last night by Finance Minister Ilsley, is effective today.

An increase of one cent per bottle in the price of soft drinks manufactured by Nelson Bottling Works Ltd., makers of Pepsi-Cola and other brands—will go into effect in Vancouver on Monday, Walter Nelson, manager, announced today.

Whether other local soft drink companies would follow suit and raise their price per bottle to 6 cents remained uncertain at press time. Officials of the Coca Cola Co. of Canada Ltd., and of Orange Crush (B.C.) Ltd., among others, declined to say what action they would take until further consideration has been given the question.

The move follows announcement from Ottawa of a 25-per-cent. tax on manufacturers' sale price of soft drinks, whether carbonated or otheriwse. The new tax replaces the increase in the tax on carbonic acid gas included among recent budget changes.

WAGE GREATEST SEA-AIR FIGHT IN ALL HISTORY

FINAL EDITION

News FOR VICTORY **Herald**

LARGEST MORNING CIRCULATION WEST OF TORONTO

VANCOUVER, B.C., SATURDAY, MAY 24, 1941   3c

Navy Smashes Convoy; German Dead Clog Sea

By RICHARD D. McMILLAN   (British United Press Staff Correspondent)

ALEXANDRIA.—(UP) — The British smashed a German armada trying to land at Crete under cover of darkness, and inflicted such heavy casualties the sea was strewn with German dead and drowning, authoritative sources reported Friday night.

The sea was clogged with German corpses, they said.

The British cruisers and destroyers steamed into the battle zone shortly before midnight on Wednesday, bent on intercepting German forces speeding by sea to the beleaguered island already invaded by German air troops.

Naval guns blasted out of the sea an Italian destroyer escorting the armada, sent a 1,000-ton Nazi transport to the bottom with its 2000 troops, and methodically potted 40 Greek fishing vessels carrying probably 100 men each.

"We turned everything from pompom guns to six-inchers and other heavier stuff on them," said one man who took part in the battle. "The night was filled with screams of terrified Germans as they plunged into the sea."

Throughout the inferno ripping the Axis craft to matchwood the British warships received not so much as a scratch, the informants said.

British naval officers said the warships were forced to cleave through masses of corpses as they hunted out and destroyed the last of the invasion ships.

The captain of one of the British cruisers related:

"It was mass execution."

Sighted Italian Destroyer

"We arrived at the scene shortly before midnight Wednesday, expecting the enemy to try to land troops by sea to aid those who already had reached the island by air.

"The first thing we sighted was a destroyer whose identity it was difficult to establish. But a searchlight beamed through the air from one of our ships at the same time the destroyer fired a torpedo which was easily avoided.

"A curious thing, the enemy seemed slow in seeking to fire. We established the vessel's identity as Italian.

"The destroyer was blown out of the sea immediately. It was escorting a German transport and about 40 Greek fishing vessels filled with about 4,000 men.

"Every one was sent to the bottom."

"It made you realize the ghastliness, the futility, of the Nazi conception of war as their helpless soldiery went down to death.

"After the Italian destroyer went up in a great ball of fire our light forces composed of cruisers with a screen of destroyers steamed on, weaving along the north coast.

"Immediately astern the annihilated Italian vessel we encountered a German transport of about 1,000 tons. Our guns were trained on her, and with a roar like a shipyard working full blast she met the same fate as her Axis ally."

"Then it was the turn of the helpless caiques (small Greek boats).

"Our fire was most deadly. There were an estimated 40 caiques, each carrying perhaps 100 men, while probably 2,000 were aboard the transport. The total thus ran to a rough 6,000 Nazis drowned in the sea action, according to the British.

Other naval attaches returned from the battle agreed that the whole armada was at the mercy of the British guns.

The Weather

Forecast for today: Moderate northwesterly winds, clear skies and warm. Friday's temperatures: High, 65 degrees; Low, 47.

CHILLIWACK SELECTIONS
By WALLACE KELK

1.—Multiscu, Selfish Joss, Blind Fanny.
2.—Sea Pebble, Go Go, Mis Ogden.
3.—Flying Heiress, Silver Fur, Bonnilla.
4.—Mortgage Lifter, Mardido, Billy Easter.
5.—Camp Spur, Sandworth, Love Us.
6.—Tommy Sand, Belle Park, Dunrode.
7.—Arabian Love, Avondale Star, Sugar Cookie.
Best—Camp Spur.

BULLETINS

Forty Poisoned In Salt Lake

SALT LAKE CITY.—(UP)—Salt Lake City Police Emergency Hospital reported Friday night that between 30 and 40 persons had been taken ill as a result of what they said was food they had eaten at a single down-town lunch counter. Eight of them were taken to hospitals for treatment for what hospital authorities said was ptomaine poisoning.

Convicts Give Up Food Strike

FOLSOM PRISON, Calif.—(UP)—A short-lived food strike collapsed Friday night at Folsom Prison when more than 500 convicts ate their dinner without disturbance after refusing to touch a fish dinner at noon.

U.S. Army Must Be Ready Everywhere

WASHINGTON.—(UP)—The U. S. army must be an all-purpose fighting force "prepared to operate in the Arctic or in the tropics, in deserts or in mountains," Chief of Staff George C. Marshall said Friday.

The reason for this, he explained, is "we are in an entirely different position from a European nation which knows its traditional or potential enemies and the terrain over which it will have to fight."

India Independence 'Just Around Corner'

SAN FRANCISCO.—(UP)—Sir Firozkhan Noon, high commissioner of India to London, declared full independence for India is "just around the corner," but emphasized if England loses the battle for Iraq, India is lost.

Australian Veterans In Crete Battle

LONDON.—(BUP)—In addition to British and New Zealand troops, some units of Australian veterans of the Battle of Greece are in the Battle of Crete, it was revealed here.

LONDON, Saturday — (BUP) — German transport planes carrying reinforcements and munitions were reported early today to be landing at the rate of one every five minutes on Crete. Off the island raged what was called the greatest aerial-naval battle of all time."

Britain's Mediterranean fleet was believed to be parrying successfully all Axis attempts to send reinforcements to the beleaguered island by sea.

London newspapers warned the people to be prepared to hear of losses in British warships, though they said German claims undoubtedly were grossly exaggerated.

British sources estimated that the German air force had landed more than 20,000 troops on Crete by parachute, air transport and glider. Latest reports from Cairo indicated that, up to late Friday, the air-borne invasion was continuing.

German planes were believed to be descending at Malemi, airdrome 10 miles southeast of Canea. Cairo advices indicated it was the only airfield still in Nazi hands.

Many others probably were dropping down in open fields since the Germans revealed their ability to land troop carriers in restricted areas during the Greek campaign.

German forces which had occupied Candia and Retimo were said to have been "accounted for" in fierce hand-to-hand fighting and "the situation at both places is now satisfactory."

But around Malemi the British failed to re-take the air and port centre. Fresh masses of German shocktroops were landing by parachute and transports.

45

BRITISH TRAP BISMARCK; HUGE SEA BATTLE RAGES

THE VANCOUVER DAILY PROVINCE

47th YEAR—NO. 51 VANCOUVER, B.C., MONDAY, MAY 26, 1941—28 PAGES PRICE 3 CENTS On trains, boats and in the country, Five Cents

24 Hun Planes Downed

R. A. F. HITS BACK AT HUN CRETE DRIVE

(By Associated Press.)

CAIRO, May 26.—German troops have penetrated British defense lines in an attack west of Canea, but New Zealand forces have counter-attacked and "severe fighting is continuing" in that sector of Crete, Middle East general headquarters said today.

The Germans' strong attack followed the arrival of more airborne reinforcements, the communique said, and came under cover of an intensive air bombardment.

The Germans were said to have suffered heavy casualties.

With the battle raging through its seventh day, British observers saw hopeful signs in reports of a substantial reduction in the number of Nazi parachute and glider reinforcements and the statement of a higher officer that "I think it will be possible to hold Crete."

Reuter's News Agency said today there were signs that the Germans are running short of parachute troops in their aerial invasion.

24 PLANES DOWN.

At least 24 planes were destroyed and others badly damaged in new raids by British fighters and bombers against German forces on the Island of Crete, the Royal Air Force announced tonight.

These raids, staged yesterday and the previous night, as well as scattered air assaults on hostile

(Continued on Page 2.)
See CRETE.

$370,000 B. C. HIGHWAY WORK

VICTORIA, May 26.—Tenders aggregating $370,000 for highway reconstruction and betterment were accepted by the department of public works today. In all cases the contracts have been awarded to the lowest tenderer.

One section of the Malahat Drive work on Vancouver Island will be proceeded with. It is improvement of the road from near the summit to Bamberton, a section that contains many sharp curves on a narrow highway. It is the largest contract awrded, amounting to $148,014. Dawson, Wade & Co. secured the work.

The same firm will undertake the work of road construction from mile 4.58 to mile 7.65 on the Squamish-Britannia road. The amount of the tender was $43,515.

Other contracts awreded were: Hospital road, Pender Harbor, Holmes & Wilson Trucking Co., $10,908; northern Trans-Provincial Highway, Usk-Cedarvale section, approximately four miles of reconstruction, W. C. Arnett & Co., $50,000; Trans-Canada Highway, Silver Creek reconstruction, $20,684; Kootenay-Columbia Highway, south of Golden, General Construction Co. Ltd., $31,898; northern Trans-Provincial Highway, near Feron, Sec. A., Associated Engineering Co. Ltd., $12,533; Sec. B. Sinclair-Mills, Associated Engineering Co. Ltd., $13,075; Trail-Salmo Highway, Cedar Creek section, A.H. Green Co. Ltd., $17,715.

Final BULLETINS

Bakers On Strike

PORTLAND, May 26.—(AP)—Portland housewives dusted off bread recipes today as a bakers' union strike cut off 80 per cent. of Portland's bread supply.

U.S. Men In Army

OTTAWA, May 26.—(CP)—Authorities here today said that at least 8200 United States citizens were members of the Dominion's fighting forces.

Weapon Fund Grows

LONDON, May 26.—(AP)—Lord Kindersley, president of the National Savings Committee, announced today that London's War Weapons Week receipts were £120,041,000 ($534,072,450), an average of £21 for each person in the city.

Torch at Calgary

LETHBRIDGE, May 26.—(CP)—Canada's Victory Torch was taken by automobile from Lethbridge to Calgary today after adverse flying conditions prevented the Royal Canadian Air Force plane from taking off. Heavy skies disrupted flying services over southern Alberta.

Protest Sinking

NEW YORK, May 26.—(AP)—Terming the sinking of the Egyptian steamship Zamzam a 'flagrant violation of international law," William V. C. Ruxton, president of the British-American Ambulance Corps, today sent a letter of protest to State Secretary Hull.

Bomb Wrecks Plane

HALIFAX, May 26.—(CP)—A Royal Canadian Air Force plane was wrecked at nearby station today when it caught fire after a crash landing and a bomb exploded, R.C.A.F. officials announced. The crew of three escaped.

Civil Defense Costs

LONDON, May 26.—(AP)—Civil defense, including air raid shelters, cost Britain £89,000,000 (about $396,000,000) last year.

Report Ship Held

VICHY, May 26.—(AP)—French sources reported today the 3317-ton merchant ship Cap Cantin was being held at Gibraltar after she was escorted there by three British warships.

Churchill Message

LONDON, May 26.—(AP)—Prime Minister Churchill has sent a message of congratulation and good wishes to the people of Newfoundland who today opened a recruiting week, the British Broadcasting Corporation reported today.

Child Is Injured

VICTORIA, May 26.—(CP)—Gordon Hinksman, 8, Nanaimo, received serious head injuries and a possible fracture of the pelvic bone, and Mrs. George Brow of Victoria received slight head injuries when they were knocked down by a car.

Claim Chinese Gains

CHUNGKING, May 26.—(AP)—The Chinese troops were reported gaining the upper hand against the Japanese on several fronts, notably in South Shansi province, where it estimated Japanese casualties at 40,000 in two weeks.

Denies New Millionaires

OTTAWA, May 26.—(CP)—Finance Minister Ilsley told the House of Commons today he did not know how many millionaires there are in Canada but is "morally certain" statements to the effect any number of new millionaires have been created since the start of the war are "purely imaginary."

Racing

Lincoln Fields Results

First race—Chigre (Wilson), $4.40, $2.40, $2.40.
Knights Fors (Farrell), $2.80, $3.20.
Dick Bray (Meloche), $7.20.
Time, 1.48 2-5.

Second race—Sweet Forever (Brooks), $93.80, $54.40, $23.60.
Kiev Singer (Cruikshanks), $10.20, $6.40.
Hills Palm (Borton(, $14.20.
Time 1.48 1-5.
Scratched: Bereit, Honey Roll, Conrad N., Deduce, Belton, Bachelors Bower.

Third race—Pair Zetta (Adams), $7.20, $4.60, $3.00.
Helen Agnes (Boyce), $25.40, $11.60.
Briar Rose (Mills), $3.80.
Time, 1.02 4-5.
Scratched: Woodford Belle, Kee Kee, So Close, Lightsome.

Fourth race—Epiget (Littrell), $13.00, $6.80, $4.40.
Appointee (McCombs), $3.20, $2.80.
Searcy (Mills), $4.60.
Time, 1.26.
Scratched: Bayou Cook.

Fifth race—Bushwacker (Adams), $13.20, $7.60, $6.20.
Court Dance (McCombs), $10.40, $8.20.
Aljack (Cruikshanks), $9.40
Time, 1.13 1-5.
Scratched: Last Call, Weisenheimer, Sun Ginger.

Sixth race—Scrappy W. (Borton), $8.60, $3.40, $3.00.
Cadmium (Farrell), $2.80, $2.40.
Uncle Mose (Littrell), 3.40.
Time, 1.46 1-5.

Seventh race—Some Count (McCombs), $8.00, $4.60, $3.40.
English Harry (Yarberry), $5.40, $3.80.
Margo G. (Johnson), $4.00.
Time, 2.08 3-5.

Eighth race—Shut Eye (Wilson), $8.20, $4.00, $3.20.
Here She Comes (Vandergrift), $6.40, $5.20.
Bonjour (McCombs), $4.60
Time, 1.47.
Scratched: Art of War.

Suffolk Downs Results

First race—Sun Kincsen (Young), $8.40, $4.80, $2.80.
Night Chase (Delucci), $10.20, $4.80.
Nilon (Smith), $2.80.
Time, 1.46.
Scratched: Swing Band, Solar Topi.

Second race—Marjorie S. (Sconza), $13.20, $7.20, $6.00.
Fish Wife (Atkinson), $8.20, $5.40.
Lost Gold (Bodiou), $4.00.
Time, 1.13 4-5.
Scratched: See All, Moo, Differential, Clock Time, Sunareve.

Third race—Tryan Get It (Smith), $28.20, $10.00, $6.00.
All Glee (Young), $3.60, $2.60.
Gala Grip (Briggs), $3.40.
Time, 1.01 3-5.
Scratched: Bright World

Fourth race—Hicomb (Sisto), $12.40, $6.40, $3.60.
Galaway (Atkinson), $10.20, $4.60.
Milk and Honey (May), $2.80.
Time, 1.12 3-5.
Scratched: Mental Giant, Lady Lyonors.

Fifth race—Lone Sentry (Taylor), $3.60, $3.00, $2.40.
Thrift Shop (Young), $3.60, $2.80.
Gold Tower (Briggs), $3.80.
Time, 1.12 2-5.

Sixth race—Cape Cod (Sisto), $7.20, $7.80, out.
Boiled Shirt (May), $2.40, out.
Chance Yen (Atkinson), out.
Time, 1.37.

Seventh race—Light Tack (Atkinson), $4.00, $2.80, $2.40.
March Feet (Packer), $3.40, $2.60.
Levena (Smith), $3.20.
Time, 1.45.

Eighth race—Warring Witch (Hettinger), $20.20, $8.60, $4.40.
Apropos (Wimmer), $8.20, $4.60.
Dead heat: Jack Vennie (Delucci), $2.80; Don Pecos (Smith), $3.60.
Time, 1.47.
Scratched: Ebony Boy.

(Race Entries on Page 6.)

NAZIS DARE U. S. FLEET TO CONVOY

BERLIN, May 26.—(AP)—Defying the United States on the eve of President Roosevelt's speech, expected to touch on the subject, Nazi spokesmen today asserted Admiral Erich Raeder's warning that American convoys would be an "open act of war" which would be met by the guns of the German navy, removed "all possibility of misunderstanding over the significance of convoys and what Germany holds to be an act of war."

The statement of the commander-in-chief of the German navy, made in an interview with Domei, Japanese news agency, and published here yesterday by the German propaganda agency, "puts in precise technical language what has been generally known for some time, especially through the Fuehrer's words," in the opinion of the Wilhelmstrasse.

(By Associated Press)

WASHINGTON, May 26.—(AP)—Secretary of State Cordell Hull accused Germany today of seeking by threats to induce the United States to refrain from any real efforts at self-defense.

Hull made his comment on the statement yesterday of Grand Admiral Erich Raeder, commander of the German navy, that the American patrol system was "aggressive" and that American naval convoys for British ships would "mean shooting."

Stephen Early, presidential secretary, earlier had commented to reporters that he has an idea that Berlin "is trying to do anything it can to becloud" President Roosevelt's fireside chat tomorrow night. Early too was commenting on Raeder's statement.

SEEKS CONTROL FIRST.

Hull told his press conference that Raeder's statement appeared to be some sort of threat to include this country and probably other American nations to refrain from real efforts at self defense until Hitler gets control of the high seas of the world and other continents.

It is a favorite system which Hitler has used in the case of many countries in Europe, Hull said, either by threats of persuasion to include other countries to refrain from any real defense

(Continued on Page 2.)
See F. D. R.

PREMIER KING HINTS JUNE TRIP TO COAST

OTTAWA, May 26.—(CP)—Prime Minister Mackenzie King is considering plans for a trip to the Pacific Coast, probably in June, it was learned today.

Mr. King has made no final decision in the matter, it was said, but well informed circles would not be surprised if he left for the West immediately after the ceremonies in Kingston on June 7 to commemorate the death of Sir John A. Macdonald.

The trip the Prime Minister has in view would require about three weeks so if he could leave around June 7 he could be back in Ottawa before the end of the month.

★ ★ ★ ★ ★ FINAL

Stars Get It, Too

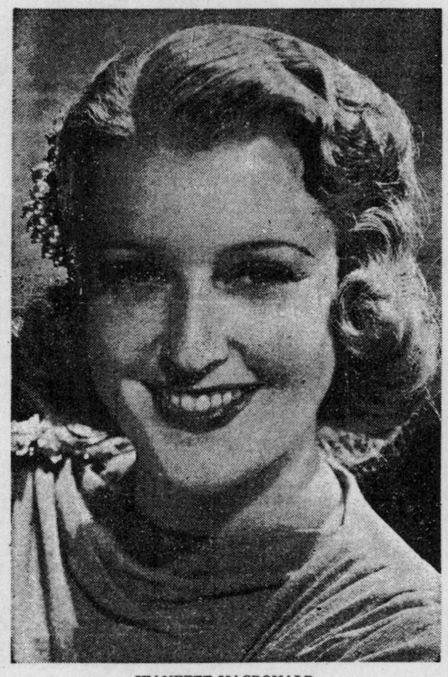

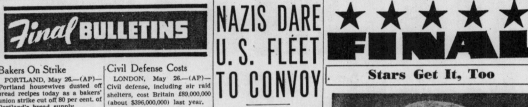

JEANETTE MACDONALD.

HOLLYWOOD, May 26.—Jeanette MacDonald's persistent hay fever is causing a lot of grief to the lighting men on her present film. The movie is in technicolor—and technicolor is cruelly candid about puffy eyes.

BASEBALL

NATIONAL LEAGUE

Philadelphia	002 200 000	4	10	3
Brooklyn	010 040 10x	6	10	1

Blanton, Hoerst, Crouch and Warren; Fitzsimmons, Higby and Phelps, Owen.

AMERICAN LEAGUE

Detroit	100 010 003	5	11	0
Cleveland	000 101 100	3	8	0

Newsom, Thomas and Tebbetts; Smith, Heving and Hemsley.

Roosevelt to Speak On Radio Tuesday

President Roosevelt's "Fireside Chat" will be broadcast to the world on Tuesday evening at 6:30 o'clock. Mr. Roosevelt will speak from the White House in the presence of ambassadors and ministers of Latin-American countries. The broadcast will be heard in Vancouver over local stations CBR, CJOR and CKWX.

Navy Fights To Avenge Hood Loss

NEW YORK, May 26.—(AP)—The German battleship Bismarck and other units of a German squadron now are fighting a superior British naval squadron in the Denmark Strait between Iceland and Greenland, the Oslo radio reported tonight in a broadcast heard here. No detail as to the outcome of the battle was given.

(By Associated Press)

LONDON, May 26.—The British admiralty declared tonight that the fleeing German battleship Bismarck had been hit by an aerial torpedo.

Telling a brief story of the long chase in the North Atlantic of the Bismarck—a 35,000-tonner which destroyed the mighty 42,100-ton British battle-cruiser Hood somewhere off Greenland last Saturday, the admiralty said in a communique:

"The chase of the Bismarck in the Atlantic has been hotly pursued. This evening torpedo bombers of the fleet air arm have scored a hit with a torpedo on the Bismarck.

"The hunt continues."

Most Intensive Hunt In Naval History

(Full story of the sinking of H.M.S. Hood is on Page 3. Her visit here is recalled on Page 13.)

By WILLIAM H. STONEMAN
Special radio to The Daily Province. Copyright, 1941, Chicago Daily News.

LONDON, May 26.—The most intensive hunt in the history of naval warfare was being carried out by the British fleet and air force today in an attempt to locate the triumphant German battleship Bismarck, which sank the British battle-cruiser Hood on Saturday.

While the admiralty kept mum and concentrated on the search, it was generally believed in London that the Bismarck was still somewhere on the high seas searching for a way out of the mighty trap laid for her by the British.

(Continued on Page 2.)
See HOOD.

FEAR 3 B.C. MEN ON HOOD

Two and perhaps three British Columbia naval officers and one Toronto man whose sister resides in Vancouver are believed to have been lost aboard H.M.S. Hood when she went down in battle off Greenland.

They are:

MIDSHIPMAN T. N. K. BEARD, 20, the son of Commander Charles Taschereau Beard, who was in command of H.M.C.S. Prince Robert when she captured the German cargo-liner Weser. Commander and Mrs. Beard reside at Victoria.

MIDSHIPMAN CHRISTOPHER JOHN BIRCHWOOD NORMAN, 19, the son of Mr. and Mrs. Cyril Norman, Victoria.

LIEUT. THOMAS AN-NIS, 45, code decipherer, native of Toronto, whose sister, Mrs. Effie Burnham, is a nurse in Vancouver.

(Continued on Page 2.)
See B.C. MEN.

FEARED DROWNED

Boundary Bay Man Missing

Daily Province Staff Correspondent.

LADNER, May 26.—Robert Gunn, 25, son of Mr. and Mrs. Robert Gunn, pioneer Boundary Bay residents, is missing and fears for his safety are expressed following discovery today of a flat-bottomed punt which he had been operating when last seen.

The punt was found drifting between Birch Bay and Point Roberts by a plane which had been sent to search for it. One oar was found near to Birch Bay.

Gunn had left his home near the beach at Boundary Bay at 8:30 p.m. Saturday to move a gasoline boat out into deep water, in preparation for a picnic outing Sunday morning.

Members of the family saw him anchor the boat about a mile off shore just before dark. He is believed then to have attempted to return in the punt.

At the time of his disappearance a wind had sprung up and he may have been blown some distance off shore.

IN TRAFALGAR SQUARE, UNDER NELSON'S COLUMN

CANADIANS BRING EMPIRE DAY TO LONDON

Britons Do Not Recognize "O Canada," But Right Of Empire Is Instinctive Thing

John Bird, special staff representative of The Vancouver Daily Province and Associated Southam papers in Britain, spoke to the Empire over the B.B.C. newsreel, Saturday night. He described the Empire Day scene around Nelson's monument as crowds listened to a Canadian band.

Below he amplifies that description and emphasizes its significance.

By JOHN BIRD.
Special Staff Correspondent The Daily Province and Associated Southam Newspapers.

LONDON, May 26.—On Empire Day, in the heart of the Empire, I wandered around Trafalgar Square watching music-starved crowds listening intently to a band from Canadian holding units playing a concert by arrangement with the London County Council.

The scene was symbolic. Nelson still stands on his pillar, though one of the lions at its base is slightly shifted by the blitz and has a missing paw concealed with sandbags. The buckle in Big Ben's tower is not visible from this angle, but the spires of Westminster look dreamier than ever encased in scaffolding.

The Union Jack flies proudly atop Canada House, with the red duster of the Canadian merchant marine in front.

Canada House nodded smilingly down on this scene—Canada House where a magnificent job is being done for Dominion and Empire today—for it takes a Canadian band to bring home Empire Day to London citizens so largely unconscious what Empire Day is all about.

Thirty-four out of thirty-nine Londoners interrogated did not know when was Empire Day and a policeman reported many people asked why all the flags were flying.

The band began with O Canada. The crowd shifted uneasily, puzzled by the tune. Was it a hymn? "That's one of your anthems, isn't it?" said an old Cockney woman. They did not recognize it, but men took off their hats reverently, taking their cue from Brigadier F. R. Phelan, who stood at the salute. "Beautiful," said the Cockney woman.

The band swung into "Colonel Bogey." The crowd responded to memories of the last war. It was a typical Empire crowd for Empire Day—bearded, turbanned Sikhs; lots of Scotties; lots of Canadians; aviators from Trinidad; Norwegian tars; Polish airmen and what-have-you? For the Empire today has in a sense fulfilled the words of "Land of

(Continued on Page 2.)
See BIRD.

Admiralty's Own Story—

HOW NAVY'S GUNS SENT BISMARCK TO BOTTOM

The Vancouver Sun

Only Evening Newspaper Owned, Controlled and Operated by Vancouver People

FOUNDED 1886 VOL. LV—No. 202 | VANCOUVER, BRITISH COLUMBIA, TUESDAY, MAY 27, 1941 | Price 3 Cents

★★★★★ FINAL

Wins Contract

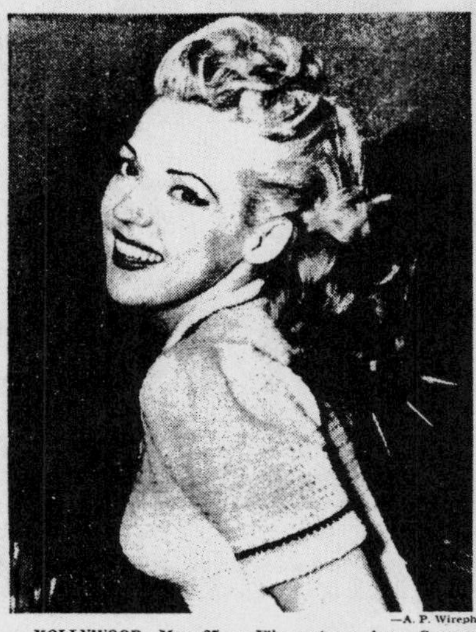

—A. P. Wirephoto

HOLLYWOOD, May 27. — Film actress Anne Gwynne (above) was the possessor today of a new contract from the Universal studio calling for a star's buildup. She got her movie start after graduating from the "little theatres."

Late Bulletins

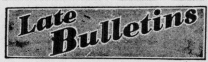

Nuffield Gives $111,000 'Bismarck Thankoffering'

LONDON, May 27.—As a "thank offering" for the sinking of the Bismarck, Lord Nuffield, motorcar manufacturer and philanthropist, tonight gave £25,000 ($111,250) to the Admiralty for the benevolent funds of the navy, the fleet air arm, and merchant seamen.

M.P.'s to Hear Roosevelt

OTTAWA, May 27. — Prime Minister Mackenzie King announced in Commons today the House will adjourn at 10:15 o'clock tonight so members may hear the broadcast address of President Roosevelt.

Powell River Man on Hood

A fifth British Columbian is feared to have been lost in the sinking of HMS Hood between Iceland and Greenland. Petty Officer Leonard Ramsbottom, who comes from Powell River, is believed to have been serving on the battleship at the time it met disaster.

Six Canadian Deaths

OTTAWA, May 27.—Death of six Canadian soldiers overseas was included in a casualty list issued today. None were western men. Lieut. J. D. Cuyler Holland of Esquimalt, B.C., is reported seriously ill. His father is W. G. C. Holland of 355 Armit Road, Esquimalt.

Alberta Boxer Dies After Bout

EDMONTON, May 27.—Inquest into the death of Fred (Cyclone) Taylor, 22-year-old colored boxer of Gibbons, Alta., opened here today. Taylor died from a blow on the head following a bout at Two Hills, Alta., May 24. His opponent was Mike Verekna of St. Paul, Alta.

Ship Known Here Seized

WASHINGTON, May 27.—French sources here said they understood the French ship Winnipeg had been seized by the British and taken to the Barbadoes. The ship is a combination passenger-cargo vessel which prior to the war was in service between French ports and North American west coast ports, such as San Diego, Calif., and Vancouver.

Churchill 'Mum' About Hess

LONDON, May 27.—Still choosing to remain mum about Rudolf Hess, Prime Minister Churchill gave short answers when the No. 3 Nazi and his flight to Scotland were mentioned in the Commons today. When the Communist member, William Gallacher, urged investigation of an assertion that the Duke of Hamilton had met Hess at the Olympic Games in Berlin in 1936, the Speaker said Sir Archibald Sinclair's statement last week to the effect that Hess and the Duke never met "finishes the matter."

WASHINGTON, May 27.—The House Naval Affairs Committee today instructed its aeronautics sub-committee to investigate the use of gliders as military aircraft "in view of the invasion of Crete with gliders."

Radio Talk Tonight to Give 'U.S. Stand'

Roosevelt Asks More Billions for Planes

(See Page Two for New York Times Comment)

WASHINGTON, May 27. — In the midst of preparing a momentous pronouncement on government policy, President Roosevelt asked the United States Congress today for $3,319,000,000 in appropriations for additional airplanes.

Stephen Early, presidential secretary, told reporters that the president will extend his fireside chat tonight an extra 15 minutes and asserted:

"I think you can say that by Wednesday morning there can no longer be any doubt as to what the national policy of this government is. Think I'll just stand on that."

(Mr. Roosevelt's broadcast will begin at 6:30 p.m., Vancouver time. It will be carried in Canada by the full network of the Canadian Broadcasting Corporation.)

HEAVY BOMBERS

Early announced that the request for huge new funds for planes was being sent to Capitol Hill in a letter to Speaker Sam Rayburn.

Of the total, $2,790,000,000 would be for the army and $529,000,000 for the navy.

Early declined to estimate the number of planes to be ordered with the money, but it

Please Turn to Page Twelve
See "Roosevelt"

Leaders Called Into Conference

WASHINGTON, May 27.—President Roosevelt late today called in Congressional leaders of both parties for an 11th hour review of the fireside chat he will deliver to the nation and the world tonight.

The White House indicated Mr. Roosevelt was giving the Congressional leaders a "detailed rehearsal" of his momentous address.

Missing Man's Body Taken From River

The badly decomposed body of a man, identified by Provincial Police in Richmond as Ed. H. Ellwood, missing from his home at 829 Fifth Street, New Westminster, was taken from the North Arm of the Fraser River, about 200 feet below the C.N.R. bridge, near New Westminster, today. Police said the body was found floating in the Canadian White Pine booming grounds by Ray Herrling, boomman.

Churchill Says:

Struggle For Crete In Balance

LONDON, May 27. — The sinking of the Bismarck, pride of Germany's dwindling naval power, brought vociferous cheers from a crowded House of Commons when it was announced today by Prime Minister Churchill.

The Prime Minister previously had recited to a solemn House details of heavy British sea losses in the Battle of Crete where, he said, "the issue of magnificent resistance hangs in the balance."

Mr. Churchill had completed his statement on the war, telling of the pursuit of the Bismarck and promising that the warship soon would be finished off, and the House had passed on to other matters of routine business.

In the midst of these dull proceedings Mr. Churchill asked permission to interrupt. He rose to his feet, poker-faced, while a hush spread over the chamber.

He stood a moment and then

Please Turn to Page Twelve
See "Churchill"

Hunt Speeded for Cruiser Which Left Bismarck Behind

'She Had Been Pursued More Than 1750 Miles'

—The Admiralty

LONDON, May 27. — Following is the Admiralty's detailed story of the Hood-Bismarck naval battle, issued in the form of a communique:

Air reconnaissance by coastal command aircraft revealed that a German battleship and cruiser, which they had previously located in the Norwegian port of Bergen, had sailed.

Certain dispositions were therefore ordered, and as a result HMS. Norfolk (Capt. A. J. L. Phillips, RN), wearing the flag of Rear Admiral W. F. Wake-Walker, CB, OBE, and HMS. Suffolk (Capt. R. M. Ellis, RN), were ordered to take up a position in the Denmark Straits.

On the evening of May 23, Admiral Wake-Walker reported sighting an enemy force of one battleship and one cruiser proceding at high speed to the south.

Visibility in Denmark Strait was bad and extremely variable. The range of the enemy was only six miles when he was first sighted, and storms of snow and sleet and patches of mist at times reduced visibility to one mile.

Despite difficulties of visibility, HMS Norfolk and Suffolk shadowed the enemy successfully throughout the night.

Meanwhile, other units of the Royal Navy were taking up dispositions at high speed with a view to intercepting the enemy and bringing him to action with our heavy forces.

Bismarck Afire At Battle Start

Early in the morning of May 24, HMS Hood (Capt. R. Kerr, C.B.E., R.N.), wearing the flag of Vice-Admiral L. E. Holland, C.B., with HMS Prince of Wales (Capt. J. C. Leach, M.V.O., R.N.) in company, made contact with the enemy. Action was immediately joined.

During the ensuing engagement, the Bismarck received damage and was at one time seen to be on fire.

HMS Hood, as has already been announced, received a hit in the magazine and blew up.

HMS Prince of Wales sustained slight damage.

The chase was continued on a southwesterly course with HMS Norfolk and HMS Suffolk shadowing the enemy and maintaining contact despite all his efforts to shake off pursuit.

It appeared at this time that the enemy's speed had been slightly reduced, and reconnaissance aircraft of the coastal command reported that she was leaving a wake of oil.

On the evening of May 24 HMS Prince of Wales again made contact with the enemy and action was joined for a short time. The German ships at once turned away to the westward and then swung round on to a

Please Turn to Page Twelve
See "Admiralty Text"

Prince Eugen, New Cruiser of Hipper Class, Slipped Away During Battle, Presumably for French Port

By NED RUSSELL
Special to The Vancouver Sun
Copyright, 1941, by British United Press

LONDON, May 27.—British torpedoes and naval shells sank the 35-000-ton pride of the Nazi Navy, Bismarck, today after a 72-hour pack hunt in which at least half of Britain's Battleship force was turned loose, seeking vengeance upon the warship which sank the great HMS Hood.

Details of the three-day sea drama which started in the blizzard-swept Denmark Straits between Greenland and Iceland, last Friday night and ended at 11 a.m. this morning, 400 miles or so off Brest, were made public by the Admiralty and Prime Minister Winston Churchill.

The coup de grace was delivered upon the Bismarck, the Admiralty revealed, by the 9975-ton Cruiser Dorsetshire which was ordered to close in and sink the Nazi battleship with torpedoes after she had been crippled and virtually put out of action by heavy ships of the Royal Navy and devastating aerial torpedo attacks.

Meanwhile the Navy is hunting the new Nazi cruiser Prince Eugen which was escorting the Bismarck but fled during the battle.

The Admiralty revealed that emergency orders had mobilized a huge naval force to run down and kill the Bismarck after word crackled through by wireless that the Hood had

Please Turn to Page Six See "Naval Battle"

Hood Struck At 13 Miles

The shell, probably a 15-inch, which penetrated to the magazine and blew up the Hood on Saturday was fired from 23,000 yards, about 13 miles. Details of the battle are told in today's despatches.

At the Race Tracks

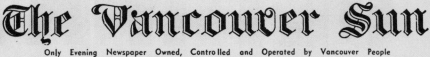

SUFFOLK DOWNS

FIRST RACE—One mile:
Cuckoo (Bodiou) $12.40, $6.40, $3.40.
Allmar (Sisto) $5, $3.60.
Legion (Hettinger) $3.60.
Time, 1:40 1-5. Scratches: Victory March, Dinah Desmond, Powers Gouraud and Sun High.

SECOND RACE—Six furlongs:
Village Belle (Smith) $7.80, $4.60, $3.40.
Balmorhea (Sconza) $13.60, $8.
Moo (Atkinson) $7.
Time, 1:13 3-5. Scratches: Tillie L., Sunareve, See All and Entitle.

THIRD RACE—One mile:
High Finance (Hettinger) $4.40, $3.40, $2.80.
Bissakerry (May) $9.80, $5.20.
Three o' Three (Bates) $3.60.
Time: 1.40 3-5.
Scratches: Chance Maker, Bright News, Double Tough and Sunabell.

FOURTH RACE—Four and one-half furlongs:
Bingo Bridget (Snyder) $20.20, $7.60, $4.20.
West Ho (May) $3.20, $2.60.
Strolling Easy (Smith) $3.20.
Time: .53 3-5.
No scratches.

FIFTH RACE—Six furlongs:
Boredom (Atkinson) $5.40, $3.60, $2.80.
Lady Lyonors (Briggs) $16.60, $7.80.
Hermar (Taylor) $3.40.
Time: 1.12 1-5.
Scratches: Rough Egg and Mill Tower.

SIXTH RACE—One mile:
Multitude (Snyder) $13.40, $6.00, $4.60.
Master Key (Hettinger) $5.00, $3.80.
Old Joe (Smith) $4.40.
Time: 1.38.
Scratch, Sir Elmer.

SEVENTH RACE—Mile and one-sixteenth:
Orcades (Taylor) $7.80, $3.60, $3.40.
Red Breast (May) $3.60, $3.20.
Cangrierron (Snyder) $9.00.
Time: 1:46 4-5. Scratches: Sun Victor and Stable.

EIGHTH RACE—Mile and one-sixteenth:
Fore Isus (Atkinson) $8.60, $4.00, $2.60.
Franco Saxon (Bodiou) $6.00, $3.20.
Essjaytee (Oros) $3.20.
Time: 1:46. Scratched: Saxonian.

HOLLYWOOD PARK

FIRST RACE—Five furlongs:
Anoakia (Rodriguez) $15.40, $6.40, $4.40.
Oso Mae (Gilmore) $10.20, $6.80.
Winsome Lady (Schunk) $20.
Time: 1:01. Scratched: Carmen Ann.

SECOND RACE—Six furlongs:
Clipperd II (Frye) $5.40, $3.60, $2.80
Irrelevant (Deering) $5.40, $4.40.
Tory Tom (Corbett) $5.40.

THIRD RACE—Five furlongs:
Okoole Maluna (Jones) $32.80, $9.40 $3.80.
Lover Lass (Neves) $4.60, $2.80.
Seedoe (Longden) $2.80.

LINCOLN FIELDS

FIRST RACE—Six furlongs:
Paul Lee (Meloche) $12.40, $5.60, $4.80.
Pretty Rose (Wilson) $18.60, $13.20.
Nigrette (Berger) $5.40.
Time, 1:14 2-5.
Scratches—Master Time, Getabout, Baby Therese, Band O Silver, Saxons Pride, Panic Releif and Tiger Teddy.

SECOND RACE—Five furlongs:
Latent (Mills) $4.20, $3.20, $3.00.
Vanman (Garner) $8.00, $6.40.
Cuteye (Litzenberger) $9.00.
Time, 1:02 4-5.
Scratches—Lorraine Reid, Inscogirl, Lady Infinity, Quick Tool, Bolo Whisk and Gean Way.

THIRD RACE—Sir furlongs:
Late Pass (Richards) $9.00, $5.00, $3.80.
Jimmie Tom (Martin) $7.60, $4.80.
Monon Lad (Vanderberg) $7.20.
Time: 1.14 1-5.
Scratches: The Trout, Dinner Horn, Dust Off, Honored Miss, Bargain Hunter and Viragin.

FOURTH RACE—Five furlongs:
Kirkwin (Hartlos) $26.40, $15.20, $9.40.
Alsbyrd (Littrell) $28.40, $13.00.
One Link (Steffen) $6.40.
Time: 1.00 4-5.
Scratches: Zig Zag, Wawfield and Bright Bell.

FIFTH RACE—Six furlongs:
Crumpet (Borton) $27, $10.20, $6.80.
Illinois Tom (Yarberry) $5.40, $4.
Hasty Star (Boyce) $5.40.
Time, 1:13 4-5. Scratches: Dorothy Rock and Donnagina.

SIXTH RACE—Six furlongs:
Prairie Dog (McCombs) $4.20, $2.60, $2.20.
Leading Article (McAndrew) $2.80, $2.40.
Mattie J (Borton) $2.60.
Time, 1:13 3-5. No scratches.

SEVENTH RACE — Mile and one-sixteenth:
Winnamac (Littrell) $15.80, $6.40, $4.20.
Ebon Flag (Brooks) $7.20, $4.40.
Birka Boy (Pool) $6.40.
Time: 1.48 2-5. Scratch: Earliana.

EIGHTH RACE—Mile and one-sixteenth:
Time Flight (Adams) $10.00, $4.40, $4.20.
Buckstans (Vandergrift) $5.60, $3.60.
Colonel Joe (Marinelli) $4.80.
Time: 1.48 1-5. Scratches: Bell Ringer, Lady Federal, Buddie Treacy, Pelter, Alspur, Port O' Call and Manatella.

LONDON, May 27. — United States Ambassador John G. Winant will fly to the United States before the end of the week to discuss the war situation with President Roosevelt, it was learned tonight.

Race Entries on Page 12

Selections

By BLUE LARKSPUR

SUFFOLK DOWNS

1—Howard, Red Raider, Supreme Flag.
2—All Time High, Gleeman, Advancer.
3—Paddy, Count Cotton, Rough Brigade.
4—Bright Camp, Stingaling, Rebbina.
5—Within, Meadow Dew, Molinara.
6—Rough Pass, Votum, Topee.
7—Primadonna, Bonified, Misty Quest.
8—Knights Sox, Sir Time, Maecaro.
Best—All Time High

LINCOLN FIELDS

1—Tiger Teddy, High Landmark, Cantata.
2—Fritz, Our David, Nogalo.
3—Quarterback, Misecret, Dickory Dock.
4—Say No More, Rangle, Grand Appeal.
5—Busy Lutrecia, You Alone Honey Roll.
6—Play Quest, Superose, Valdina Valet.
7—Lady Federal, Jim Mike, Copper Tube.
8—Beau Insco, Bell Ringer, Worpoise.
Best—Lady Federal

HOLLYWOOD PARK

1—Drift Silver, Little Penaio, Liberty Luke.
2—Palacio, Red Cannibal, Tommy Whelan.
3—Islam's Girl, Certie, Hubub.
4—Bon Boots, Uallno, Sentimantalist.
5—Less Time, Flying Bonny, Balmy Spring.
6—Sr Jeffrey, Our Mat, Runaway Bey.
7—Praetorian, Sextus, Albino.
8—Torch Lee, Count Us, Like Greenock.
Best—Islam's Girl

BASEBALL

AMERICAN

		R	H	E
First Game—				
Philadelphia	000 001 010—	2	7	1
Boston	111 020 00x—	5	7	0

Hadley and Hayes; Wagner and Pytlak.

		R	H	E
Second game—				
Philadelphia	001 400 600—	11	12	1
Boston	000 000 100—	1	3	1

Marchildon and Hayes; H. Newsome, Dickman (5), Judd (7) and Peacock.

		R	H	E
St. Louis	003 002 000—	5	11	0
Chicago	010 000 010—	2	6	3

Muncrief and Ferrell; Rigney, Hallett (7), Humphries (9) and Tresh.

		R	H	E
Detroit	111 010 300—	9	12	0
Cleveland	110 002 200—	6	10	1

Rowe, Gorsica (7) and Tebbetts; Milner, Brown (7), Eisenstat (9) and Hemsley.

(Unfinished.)

New York	101 412 01
Washington	001 005 20

Ruffing, Murphy (6), Chandler (7) and Rosar; Chase, Anderson (2), Cartasquel (6), Zuber (7), Masterson (9) and Early.

NATIONAL

		R	H	E
Brooklyn	102 003 000—	6	8	0
Philadelphia	000 000 000—	0	7	1

Casey and Phelps; Podajny, Grisson (6) and Warren, Livingston.

Only games scheduled.

CHILLIWACK, May 27.—Wm. Gaynor, aged 86, who was admitted to the Chilliwack General Hospital suffering from cuts and bruises on Sunday morning following a traffic accident, has remained in a semi-conscious state ever since. His condition is reported as serious.

39 Rescued From Steamer

By Associated Press

WASHINGTON, May 27.—The Coast Guard and Navy reported today that 39 survivors of the British steamship Marconi, 7402 tons, had been rescued by the Coast Guard cutter General Greene, about 270 miles southeast of Greenland.

The navy reported that about 40 more crew members—the Coast Guard said 60—of the Marconi are believed drifting in two lifeboats in heavy fog in the same vicinity. The Coast Guard cutter is searching for them.

Sun Newscast to Follow Roosevelt

This evening from 6:30 to 7:15 o'clock, President Roosevelt's broadcast will be carried over station CKWX.

The Sun's regular 6:30 newscast therefore will follow immediately after Mr. Roosevelt.

Sun Annual Walking Marathon Tomorrow; First Race at 2 p.m.

See Pages 17 and 25 for Details of Entries, Route, etc.

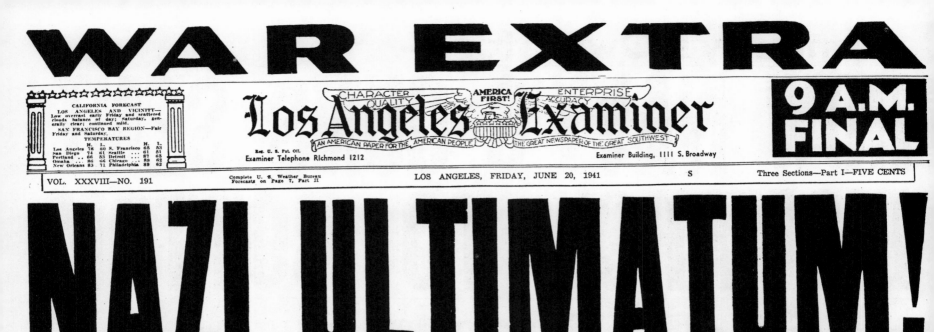

WAR EXTRA

CALIFORNIA FORECAST

LOS ANGELES AND VICINITY—Low overcast early Friday and scattered clouds balance of day; Saturday, generally clear; continued mild.

SAN FRANCISCO BAY REGION—Fair Friday and Saturday.

TEMPERATURES

	H.	L.		H.	L.
Los Angeles	78	60	S. Francisco	65	53
San Diego	74	61	Seattle ...	61	51
Portland ..	66	53	Detroit ...	87	65
Omaha ...	86	66	Chicago ...	89	62
New Orleans	83	71	Philadelphia	89	62

CHARACTER QUALITY — AMERICA FIRST! — ENTERPRISE ACCURACY

Los Angeles Examiner

AN AMERICAN PAPER FOR THE AMERICAN PEOPLE — THE GREAT NEWSPAPER OF THE GREAT SOUTHWEST

Reg. U. S. Pat. Off.

Examiner Telephone Richmond 1212 — Examiner Building, 1111 S. Broadway

9 A.M. FINAL

VOL. XXXVIII—NO. 191 — Complete U. S. Weather Bureau Forecasts on Page 7, Part II — LOS ANGELES, FRIDAY, JUNE 20, 1941 — S — Three Sections—Part I—FIVE CENTS

NAZI ULTIMATUM!

Russians Must Give Up Vital Ukraine, Baku Oil Fields or Face War With Reich

IN THE NEWS

June 5, 1941.

Mr. W. R. Hearst,
Wyntoon,
McCloud, California.
Dear Mr. Hearst,

IF WE are capable of learning from history, we cannot doubt that nothing is permanent in life except change.

Heraclitus, ancient Hellenic philosopher, in recognizing this principle, long ago observed that *"all is flux."*

In the contemporary scene, the rate of change has been accelerated throughout the world. Map makers in Europe, Asia and Africa are busier than ever trying to keep apace of events.

In the face of this spectacle, the plain citizen is more than ever concerned about his own economic security. Catering to this demand, Congress wisely passed the Social Security Act, which brought more than 40,000,000 American breadwinners under the protection of old-age benefits. This development supplements the private efforts of 65,000,000 others to achieve security through life insurance, and of upwards of 44,000,000 saving depositors and more than 12,000,000 owners of shares in American corporations to get along in the world.

Thus, theoretically at least, we Americans have created more nest eggs for the future than were ever provided at any time in the past.

Yet popular uneasiness continues.

Thoughtful persons realize that the value of these stakes in the future is contingent on a healthily functioning national economy.

When the Temporary National Economic Committee undertook two years ago to make an audit of the institution of life insurance, many were hopeful of a candid analysis of the factors needed to make the people's security genuinely secure.

Out of the prolonged inquiry on life insurance has emerged Monograph No. 28, written by two staff members of the SEC.

The report is disappointing. It deals mainly with the alleged foibles and personality defects

(Continued on Page 2, Cols. 5-6)

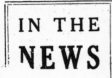

LOW INCOMES FACE DRASTIC NEW SURTAXES

Proposed Rates Will More Than Double Levy on All in U. S. Earning Less Than $10,000

By Cecil B. Dickson
Staff Correspondent International News Service

WASHINGTON, June 19.—Individuals and corporations will pay 71 per cent of the Administration's $3,500,000,000 defense revenue program under new rates approximately doubling income taxes on individuals, drastically increasing excess profits levies and imposing a special 10 per cent anti-war millionaires tax tentatively approved today by the House ways and means committee.

Chairman Doughton (Democrat) of N. C., announced $2,480,900,000 in net revenue would be produced, leaving another billion to be raised from estate, gift and excise levies to complete the program.

The committee voted to impose new surtaxes on individuals beginning with 5 per cent on the first taxable dollar up to $2000, and then graduated up to 75 per cent on incomes over $5,000,000. The existing 4 per cent normal and 10 per cent defense taxes are retained as well as the present personal exemptions of $800 for single persons, $2000 for married and $400 for dependents.

The new rates more than double income taxes for those earning less than $10,000 and then the increases are modified gradually upward. They are expected to reach the great bulk of the nation's earners.

A married person earning $2500 now pays $11 and under the new rates will pay $38.50. A $10,000 married person now pays $528 and will pay $1166 under the new plan, while a $25,000 married man now contributing $3,843.40 will pay $6,505.40. A $50,000 married man will be

(Continued on Page 10, Cols. 4-5)

Dykstra to Quit Mediation Board

WASHINGTON, June 19.—(AP)—The resignation of Dr. Clarence A. Dykstra as chairman of the National Defense Mediation Board, effective July 1, was accepted today by President Roosevelt.

Krick Offers New Weather Theory

Cal-Tech Meteorologist Will Forecast 10 Years Ahead

By Magner White

Of sensational scientific, economic and military significance, a new hypothesis for forecasting weather trends five to 10 years ahead came out of a California Institute of Technology laboratory yesterday.

Developed only a few hours before, it was presented immediately by Dr. Irving P. Krick,

Other stories of Science Association meetings on Page 6.

Caltech meteorologist, to the American Association for the Advancement of Science, and was recognized as a revolutionary challenge to all former forecasting systems.

The new method, which Dr. Krick said came to himself and his associates Wednesday night when they discovered certain patterns in hundreds of records of weather data, is based on conditions set up in the earth's atmosphere by constant bombardment of the sun's rays.

This constant sun-ray bombardment causes huge "cell-like structures" in the atmosphere, he explained. These, sometimes hundreds of miles long and wide, are already familiarly known as "high and low pressure areas."

Floating over the earth, form-

(Continued on Page 11 Col. 1)

'Keep Dockmen Busy,' Plea to Avoid Strike

By L. W. Meredith
Staff Correspondent International News Service

WASHINGTON, June 19.—Joseph Ryan, head of the A. F. of L. Longshoremen's Union, tonight appealed to the National Mediation Board to step in and avert a threatened strike of stevedores on July 1 which would tie up shipping in all Atlantic and Gulf coast ports, including cargoes bound for Britain.

Ryan, who revealed that telegrams also had been sent to the White House asking for President Roosevelt to intervene, said he did not want the strike to be called.

"I am as patriotic as anybody and I do not want to do anything that will hamper the defense program in any way," Ryan declared. "But my men have been thrown out of jobs by the Maritime Commission transferring ships to Great Britain, and the Maritime Commission has done nothing for them. The men are impatient and they want to strike, but I am holding them in until all possible mediation sources are exhausted.

"Our position is this: something must be done for the stevedores and men thrown out of work by transfer of ships to England."

About 700 of the A. F. of L. longshoremen and checkers are on strike in New York against the Morgan lines after the Maritime Commission, Ryan charged, took over 10 of the Morgan Line ships. Ryan said that in event of a strike he would try to keep it confined to the Morgan Lines, which would affect about 5000 men in Atlantic and Gulf ports.

"But the men are threatening a real strike," Ryan said. "If something isn't done for them, 30,000 may go out, and we will tie up all shipping at the Atlantic and Gulf coast ports. We can do it."

(Other labor news on pages 14 & 28.)

House Speeds Bill to Defer Men of 28

WASHINGTON, June 19.—(INS)—The House rules committee today gave legislative right-of-way to a Senate-approved bill deferring men 28 years old and older from the draft.

Chairman May (Democrat), Kentucky, of the military affairs committee said he would seek House passage of the measure next week.

U. S. ORDERS CUT IN RUBBER CONSUMPTION

Manufacturers of Auto Tires Face Percentage Allowance; East Facing Gas Rationing

WASHINGTON, June 19.—(AP)—The effects of the defense program were brought sharply home to consumers today when the Government ordered a cut in the consumption of rubber, spoke of the possibility of gasoline ration cards for Eastern motorists and sought to freeze gasoline prices at existing levels for the present.

Officials of the office of production management said rubber consumption would be cut to a rate of about 600,000 tons annually in the last six months of 1941. At present consumption is proceeding at the rate of 817,000 tons annually.

About 70 per cent of the rubber used in the United States goes into automobile tires. It was made plain that tire manufacturing would be curtailed, but extent of the curtailment was not known.

PERCENTAGE ALLOWANCE

A formula will be worked out under which rubber processors will be allowed a fixed percentage of the rubber they formerly processed.

Much of the rubber used in the United States comes from the Dutch East Indies and British Malaya. There has been considerable concern in some quarters lest the supply be cut off by a Japanese move into that area of the world. The rubber saved by the cut in consumption will go into stock piles for use in the defense program.

It was stated that there was no shortage of rubber now but controls were considered necessary because of shipping uncertainties and the necessity of building up adequate stocks for defense.

The possibility of gasoline ration cards for Eastern motorists arose today as officials considered ways of combating a threatened oil shortage in this area of the country.

Interior Secretary Ickes told his press conference that a ration

(Continued on Page 10, Cols. 7-8)

Soviet Surrounded, Seen Surrendering

U. S. Consuls Ordered Out by Axis

Spies, Say Nazis; Must Leave by July 15

By Hugo Speck
Staff Correspondent International News Service

BERLIN, June 19.—Charging "subversive activities and espionage," the German government tonight requested all United States consular officials and employees of the American Express Company to leave the Reich and all German-occupied zones by July 15.

All consulates and express company offices must be closed by that date, a formal German note said.

(The Italian government acted in concert with Berlin and ordered the United States to close all consular offices in Italy and withdraw consular employees by July 15. However, the order did not close American express offices but reserved the right to take action later.)

ACT OF REPRISAL

Germany acted in speedy reprisal for a similar order issued this week by President Roosevelt, directing German consular officers and employees of three German concerns to quit the United States by July 10.

Nazi authorities accompanied the order with the assertion that "overwhelming evidence" is in

(Continued on Page 8, Cols. 2-3)

BULLETIN

ROME, June 20.—(AP)—The **Italian high command reported today fierce fighting had broke out again in Ethiopia.**

Stalin Said to Be Studying 'Partnership' Proposal

By Alexander Szalai
Staff Correspondent International News Service

BUDAPEST, June 19.—Dictator Josef Stalin was reported tonight in dispatches reaching Budapest from Istanbul to be studying a personal note from Adolf Hitler inviting Soviet Russia to join the Axis and sign a sweeping 40-year economic pact with Germany.

Terms of the pact were said to be so stringent that they would virtually place all of Russia under Nazi economic domination.

Hitler's note reportedly pointed out that the situation in the East now demands immediate and urgent decisions. The Istanbul dispatches said Hitler also proposed that Russia begin conversations on the possibilities of returning Bessarabia to Rumania.

Stalin and his colleagues were understood to be giving close attention to Hitler's note.

Hitler was said to have proposed to Stalin an immediate extension of Germany's network of roads into the rich grain fields of the Ukraine and the Batum oil fields.

Hitler also proposed, according to the Istanbul version, a sort of partnership under which Russia and Germany would, in common, extract all the riches to be gotten from European Russia.

The Riechsfuehrer advocated further, Istanbul said, that German industry be transferred deep within Russia out of the range of British bombers. He offered to give the Soviet the benefit of German workers, machines and capital in developing Soviet natural resources.

In return for Soviet cooperation economically, Hitler was said to have promised Stalin a brotherhood of peace between the two nations, wealth beyond immediate Soviet hopes, and an invitation to join with Germany, Italy and Japan in the Axis pact.

All roads along the Rumanian railways were closed to private traffic, it was learned in Budapest, and an airtight ban was imposed on motor traffic.

MoscowMaking Counteroffer as Nazis Set for Attack

By Robert G. Nixon
Staff Correspondent International News Service

WASHINGTON, Jun 19.—The United State was informed tonight tha Germany has delivered virtual ultimatum to So viet Russia, demandin German military occupa tion of the Ukraine an Baku oil fields.

The Soviet government ha countered, according to thes diplomatic advices, with an off to provide Germany greatly i creased supplies of wheat, mi erals and oil.

Germany, with an estimate 1,500,000 blitz troops poised the Soviet borders from Finla to the Black Sea, is ready march into the Ukraine unle Russia meets its terms, it w stated.

SURRENDER SEEN

Despite Moscow's present ou wardly stubborn front, sufficie information has reached Was ington that the Soviet prob will accede to the German mands.

The White House is watchi the situation with the clos attention, a spokesman said.

While these reports reach Washington, officials were s mindful of the German strateg used on numerous occasions the past, of throwing up a t mendous propaganda smo screen to cloak a full-scale fensive in an entirely differ direction.

Washington has treated second and third-hand rum that have deluged the State D partment for several days w the utmost reserve. Subsequ reports, arriving through Uni States diplomatic channels, ho ever, have brought the conv tion that the German-Soviet sis is founded in fact. Signing the Turko-German nonaggr sion pact, sealing the Germ right flank, furthered this bel

Neither official or Soviet qu ters here, however, have recei any confirmation of reports an actual outbreak of fight between German and Rus

WAR EXTRA

CHARACTER QUALITY — AMERICA FIRST! — ENTERPRISE ACCURACY

Los Angeles Examiner

AN AMERICAN PAPER FOR THE AMERICAN PEOPLE — THE GREAT NEWSPAPER OF THE GREAT SOUTHWEST

Reg. U. S. Pat. Off.
Examiner Telephone RIchmond 1212
Examiner Building, 1111 S. Broadway

9 A.M. FINAL

CALIFORNIA FORECAST
Los Angeles and Vicinity—Clear Monday, scattered high clouds Tuesday; continued warm; gentle westerly winds. San Francisco Bay Region—Partly cloudy, sprinkles Monday, Tuesday fair. Mild temperature. Moderate westerly winds.

TEMPERATURES
H. L.   H. L.
Los Angeles 79 57   New York ... 96 76
San Francisco 72 55 Boston ... 95 71
San Diego ... 72 61 Chicago ... 77 61
Seattle ... 74 55   Detroit ... 93 70
Portland ... 74 58 Philadelphia 93 72

VOL. XXXVIII—NO. 194   Complete Weather Bureau Forecasts on Page 7, Part II   LOS ANGELES, MONDAY, JUNE 23, 1941   S   Two Sections—Part I—FIVE CENTS

REICH ARMY RIPS DEEP INTO RUSSIA

IN THE NEWS

By George Rothwell Brown

THE war between Germany and Russia has obviously been developing for a long time.

In the first place, it is the natural conflict in the whole European situation.

Germany dreads Russia and the possibility of an Asiatic invasion of Europe led by Russia.

Hitler has always opposed Communism.

In fact, both Fascism and Naziism sprang up as political parties to overcome Communistic anarchy.

Opposition to Communism was the link that united Italy and Germany in spite of their former antagonisms.

Germany anticipated war with Russia.

Germany built his armies for two reasons.

First, to insure Germany against aggression from the west.

Second, to create a formidable force for the successful invasion of the Ukraine, Russia's most valuable and useful province.

GERMANY has sufficient reason for invading Russia and appropriating the Ukraine.

One reason was that the black soil belt of the Ukraine is of immense richness and fertility.

The Ukraine is the granary of Russia.

The acquisition of that valuable province would almost insure Europe against Russian invasion.

The separation of the Ukraine from Russia would greatly diminish Russian reserve food supplies, and would make the provisioning of great armies difficult.

While the acquisition of the Ukraine by Germany would make the protection and provisioning of Germany and of Europe easier.

Still another reason why Germany projected the invasion and acquisition of the Ukraine was because a great

(Continued on Page 2, Cols. 5-7)

Senate Fears Sub Tragedy Caused by Giving Away Ships

Navy Shortage May Impel Use of Old Craft; Thorough Probe Sought

By George Rothwell Brown
(Special to the Los Angeles Examiner)

WASHINGTON, June 22. — Congressional concern increased today over the unexplained sinking of the submarine O-9 with total loss of life of all officers and members of the crew.

Demand already is being heard for a thorough investigation either by the Navy Department or by committees on naval affairs of the Senate and House.

Chairman Vinson of the House naval affairs committee, has announced that his committee will promptly be informed of all the facts.

GRAVE APPREHENSION

At the Senate there is grave apprehension that the United States may have transferred so many American naval vessels to Great Britain under the Lend-Lease law that it has become necessary to restore unseaworthy vessels to the active list of the Navy for the use of our own fleet.

It was felt by some at the Capitol today that if our Navy is being so badly stripped of vessels of any type for all-aid-to-England as to require the commissioning of obsolete ships for our own use, Congress should promptly be informed of all the facts.

"There are indications that somebody in the Navy has fallen asleep on the job," said Senator Wiley of Wisconsin, Republican member of the Senate Naval Affairs Committee.

"There must be a thorough investigation of this tragedy. I am not prepared yet to say that it should be made by Congress, but I am willing to wait and see how swiftly and

(Continued on Page 9, Column 1)

Pat Harrison, Noted Senate Leader, Dies

WASHINGTON, June 22.—(AP)—Pat Harrison, the Senate's president pro tempore, chairman of its finance committee and beloved by all his colleagues, died today in Emergency Hospital.

The tall, genial 59-year-old Mississippi Democrat, a colorful and influential figure during 30 years in Congress, had undergone an operation for an intestinal obstruction last Monday. He rallied well after this ordeal, but in midweek took a turn for the worse.

"Senator Harrison died at 6:35 a. m.," said the brief announcement by his personal friend and physician, Dr. Sterling Ruffin. "He had grown steadily weaker during the night and was unable to take any nourishment. He died of exhaustion."

WIFE, SON AT BEDSIDE

At the bedside were his wife, the former Mary Edwina McInnis of Leakesville, Miss., and his son, Pat Jr.

Two other children, Mrs. James W. Cummings of Bethesda, Md., and Mrs. Irvin Miller of Nashville, Tenn., a brother, Burroughs Harrison of Kilmichael, Miss., and a sister, Mrs. C. E. Saunders of Crystal Springs, Miss., also survive.

When word of his death spread, there was an immediate outpouring of expressions of grief from Administration officials and members of Congress.

Colleagues suggested a state funeral in tribute to Harrison's statesmanship and popularity, but the family, knowing his

(Continued on Page 9, Column 7)

U.S. FEELS WAR PROVES WORLD RULE NAZI AIM

By Robert G. Nixon
Staff Correspondent International News Service

WASHINGTON, June 22.—Germany's full-scale onslaught against Soviet Russia was viewed by the American Government tonight as affording final proof that the Reich is bent upon world conquest.

The startling turn of events that sent Hitler's mechanized legions—aided by Finland and Rumania—swarming across Russian borders from the Arctic to the Black Sea rocked Washington like a bomb explosion.

Sober minds in the Government warned against the American people taking too optimistic a view of the new blitzkrieg.

BREAKING SPELL

At the same time, the battle of the two titanic exponents of the opposing philosophies of Nazism and Communism aroused speculation here that they might, in the end, destroy each other.

But, regardless of the outcome, one fact stood out foremost to give encouragement both to Great Britain and the United States. This was the certainty that a breathing spell had been gained for hard-pressed Britain against an immediate invasion attempt by Germany and against mounting pressure in the Eastern Mediterranean. It also gives the United States time to reach a state of greater preparedness and bring its war production to a point where it will be of real aid to England.

The address of Prime Minister Winston Churchill was heard with interest, especially his pledge that Britain will aid the Soviet Union in every possible way and his appeal for other

(Continued on Page 7, Column 1)

Sebastopol Blasted; Reds Report Foe Drive Halted

Churchill Asks U.S. to Aid Russ

(Full text of Churchill address on Page 4)

By George Lait
Staff Correspondent International News Service

LONDON, June 22.—Prime Minister Winston Churchill tonight, in a radio address heard all over the world, pledged Britain's help to Soviet Russia in her conflict with German invaders and called upon the United States and Britain's "friends and allies in every part of the world to take the course and pursue it steadfastly to the end."

The prime minister warned Finland and Rumania, newly allied with Germany in the invasion of Russia, that "any man or state who marches with Hitler is our foe," and declared that all "quislings" would be brought to the bar of Allied justice, like Hitler himself, when victory shall have been won.

INTENSIVE BOMBING

He pledged that Britain will bomb Germany night and day with ever-increasing ferocity, and declared that within six months the weight of American Lease-Lend aid, especially in heavy bombers, will begin to swing the scales toward Britain and her Allies.

Churchill's pledge followed soon after Soviet Ambassador Ivan Maisky held a long conference with Foreign Minister Anthony Eden at the foreign office. A spokesman at the Soviet embassy asserted that the talk was "highly satisfactory."

Denouncing Hitler as a "monster of wickedness," Churchill said Germany's invasion of Russia came as no surprise to him. In fact, he said, he had warned Soviet Dictator Joseph Stalin that Nazi invasion was coming.

The British Prime Minister described the latest German "outrage" as a prelude to an attempted invasion of the British Isles.

"Hitler hopes, no doubt, that all this can be accomplished before winter comes, and if he can overwhelm Great Britain

(Continued on Page 5, Cols. 2-3)

Fear Flames in East Over Russia Fate

By Karl H. von Wiegand
(Veteran war correspondent who has reported 10 wars, now reporting the present conflict from Shanghai—the only remaining uncensored "listening post" and news transmission point in Europe, Africa or Asia.)

SHANGHAI, June 22.—The Far East, from Kamchatka, Vladivostok, Japan and China to Indo-China and Java, was electrified this morning by the dramatic news that Adolf Hitler and Josef Stalin are at last at war.

With the Soviet realm stretching more than 5000 miles from the Baltic to the Pacific, and Japan an Axis partner, invasion of Russia by Nazi Germany is a greater sensation throughout Asia than the outbreak of the Anglo-German conflict.

It completely surprised some 20,000 white and red Russians living in Shanghai. But it also gave joy and hope to some 20-odd thousand Jewish refugees here.

It came as a shock to the Chinese, for it will automatically shut off all Soviet Russian aid to free China, since

(Continued on Page 5, Column 1)

Admit Nazi Advance of 10 Miles; Finns Suffer; Berlin Boasts Destruction by Big Blitz Attacks

BERLIN, June 23 (Monday).—(INS)—German authorities today declared Russian losses are increasing hourly as heavy fighting rages on the eastern front.

They declared the vast Reich army, supported by hundreds of planes which blasted a path, pushed deep into Russia along a 2500-mile front defended by some 2,400,000 Red army troops.

"War-important establishments" were declared to have been heavily bombed in a blistering Luftwaffe raid on Sebastopol yesterday.

By the Associated Press

Germany's dawn-sprung onslaught on a 2000-mile eastern front from the northern Baltic through the Balkans forced the massive Red army back in the first day's fighting, but the Russians declared today (Monday) the gains were small and costly.

The Red army's first communique of the war declared the Nazis were stopped in their tracks with heavy losses during the first half day of attacks, but by nightfall Sunday they had made advances of 10 miles into Soviet territory.

The Russians said Hitler's forces were attacking along the entire front, but the principal Nazi thrust the Russians mentioned apparently were part of a drive northeast from East Prussia into Lithuania, now Soviet guarded, and east into Soviet-occupied eastern Poland.

The Russians said the Germans moved into the villages of Kalvaria, Stoyanuv and Tsekmanovets and were pushing toward Grodno and Kristinopol.

The communique indicated that the Red army—expected to give some ground in order to fight from a firmer defense line deeper in its own territory—still was determined to take a fighting toll of the Nazi advance.

Russia's warplanes were in the fight, too, and the

49

The Weather

Light to moderate easterly winds, cloudy and mild with some light rain in the evening is the weather forecast for today. Temperature Thursday veered between 54 and 72 degrees.

News **FOR VICTORY** Herald

LARGEST MORNING CIRCULATION WEST OF TORONTO

FINAL EDITION

VANCOUVER, B.C., FRIDAY, JULY 4, 1941

3c

REDS CLAIM NAZIS AVOID TANK FIGHTS

MOSCOW, Friday.—(UP)—Russia's armed forces unleashing "crushing blows," are inflicting great losses on the Germans in the fierce battle of the Berezina River, 360 miles west of Moscow where Napoleon's army met disaster 129 years ago, today's Soviet war communique reported.

Huns Say Defense Broken

BERLIN, Friday — (UP) — German, Rumanian and Hungarian forces are advancing steadily against Russian defenders of the Ukraine, despite bad weather and snow storms in that sector, the official DNB news agency said today.

The rarity of high command military reports since Tuesday indicated there will be a period of a few days during which the high command will keep silent again—only giving out information that "operations were proceeding according to plan" until these operations are ripe for publication.

Last night German columns were reported advancing into Russia over vast areas laid in fiery ruin by "Scorched Earth" tactics of the Red armies, which the high command said were in general retreat all along the 1,500-mile battlefront.

The official DNB agency reported "stubborn resistance by Soviet troops" in contrast with an early high command statement that the Red Army's powers of resistance "now seem broken."

A communique from Hitler's headquarters in the field said that the Red Army's powers of resistance "now seem broken" and that "on the entire front backward movements of the enemy's armies are visible."

Informed Nazi quarters said that the high command's report of the breaking of Soviet resistance indicates that great developments may be expected within a few days, perhaps even surpassing the "battle of annihila-

(Continued on Page 17)

Fear Fishboat Skipper Drowned

Mystery shrouded the disappearance Thursday night of Einar "Slim" Hagen, skipper of the fishing vessel "Sea Angel," feared drowned in a plunge over the vessel's side half a mile off White Island about 8:45 p.m.

Hagen disappeared from the wheelhouse of the small vessel while steering enroute to Comox.

He was missed when William Murray, 3850 Parker Street, mate, and Jack Keleng, deckhand, felt the vessel swing sharply while talking in the galley.

BULLETINS

Buenos Aires 'Quake' Kills Three

BUENOS AIRES.—(UP)—Three persons were killed and several injured, one critically, in a series of earth shocks which struck Buenos Aires, Cordoba, La Rioja, San Juan, Mendoza and San Luis.

"Vigilance Is The Watchword"

TOKYO.—(UP)—The Japan Times and Advertiser, supported by the Foreign Office, commenting today on the government's policy concerning Russia and Germany, said that vigilance is the watchword, along with caution and preparation."

Mexico To Compensate Oil Company

WASHINGTON.—(UP)—The Mexican Embassy Thursday night announced that complete agreement had been reached between the government of Mexico and the Penn-Mex Fuel Company, a Sinclair subsidiary, on compensation for its properties seized on March 18, 1938.

Claim High Toll Of British Shipping

BERLIN.—(UP)—Britain lost 768,850 tons of shipping in June and 109 planes in the week ending Wednesday, the high command claimed Thursday.

Ontario To Build Raid Shelters

TORONTO.—(BUP)—Attorney-General Conant said Thursday night that Toronto and other Ontario centres may build air raid shelters soon.

Ontario Faces Milk Shortage

TORONTO.—(BUP)—Ontario faces a serious milk shortage due to dry weather, Roy Lock, secretary of the Ontario Whole Milk Producers' League, declared here Thursday.

RAF Downs 18 Germans

By HOMER JENKS

LONDON, Friday — (UP) — The Royal Air Force, continuing its relentless pounding attack on the Reich, last night bombed objectives in northwestern and western Germany, it was reported authoritatively today.

Yesterday 18 German and British planes, 11 of them Messerschmitts, were shot down in battle over Northern France when the R.A.F. carried out daylight attacks against air bases, invasion ports and railroad targets, the Air Ministry reported.

The daylight attacks followed night assaults on Bremen, Cologne and Duisburg which started big fires in the industrial sections of the three cities, all vital war production centres.

The American Eagle Squadron which took part in a cross-Channel daylight raid Wednesday was said to have lost one man in its first full-scale engagement with the Germans.

William Hall, native of Springfield, Vt., an Eagle Squadron pilot, was reported missing in the Wednesday operations.

communique reported.

The communique, covering Thursday's fighting, told of "violent" clashes on three sectors of the 1800-mile long front —around Dvinsk in the north, where the Germans are pushing toward Leningrad, along the Berezina River, and around Tarnapol in the south at the western frontier of the rich Ukraine.

Thousands

The communique told of "thousands of German dead, burning tanks and wrecked German planes" littering the battlefields as result of "the stubborn defending Red army troops.

"The enemy is unable to withstand the bayonet charges of our troops," the war communique reported.

The Germans, it was said, have recognized after 12 days of war the superiority of the Red army's heavy and medium tanks, and "it has been proved that the enemy tanks avoid battle" with them.

Supremacy

Likewise in the raging war of the air "wherever our fighting planes appear they quickly win supremacy in the air," it was stated.

It was admitted that on the northern Dvinsk sector of the front, along the frontier of Lithuania and Latvia, the Germans had succeeded in storming northward across the Dvina River to the Jacobstadt region after bringing up reserves to battle the stubbornly defending Rer army troops.

"In the direction of Minsk, as result of the stubborn resistance of our troops considerable losses were inflicted on the enemy," it was said.

The communique said that Russian planes had dealt heavy, destructive blows to German "panzer" forces on the Dvina

(Continued on Page 17)

50

U.S. NAVY TAKES OVER ICELAND; DEFIES HITLER

The Vancouver Sun

Only Evening Newspaper Owned, Controlled and Operated by Vancouver People

FOUNDED 1886
VOL. LV.—No. 237

VANCOUVER, BRITISH COLUMBIA, MONDAY, JULY 7, 1941

Price 3 Cents

FINAL

Late Bulletins

Moscow Declares Nazi Troops Are Deserting

By British United Press

MOSCOW, July 7.—A Soviet communique reported today that German troops are surrendering in "daily increasing" numbers in "protest" against the attack on Russia and quoted war prisoners as stating "unanimously" that Adolf Hitler "wants to drown the whole world in blood."

The communique, distributed by the Tass News Agency, reported that a large German unit had come over to the Soviet side in an unidentified sector "lately."

Japanese Stocks Slump

TOKYO, July 7.—Nearly all prices on the Tokyo Stock Exchange declined today, reflecting general uneasiness over Japan's international position.

Canadian Missing in Ethiopia.

REGINA, July 7. — Lieutenant James Charlton Gardner, 20, serving with the Royal Tank Regiment in Ethiopia is reported missing.

U.S. Patrol Plane Missing

WASHINGTON, July 7.—The United States Navy Department announced today that a plane of the northeastern Atlantic coast patrol has been missing since July 3 with 2 officers and 5 enlisted men aboard.

Vancouver Girl Weds Airman

BRANDON, Man., July 7.—Flight Sergeant Michael George O'Brien, formerly of Ottawa, was married today to Ruth Anne Power, daughter of Mr. and Mrs. Charles Edward Power of Vancouver, at the station mass at No. 1 Air Navigational School at Rivers, Man.

Actress Has Wedding Annulled

HOLLYWOOD, July 7.—Actress Lillian Roth today obtained an annulment of her marriage to Eugene Weiner, New York importer who wooed her with a punch on the jaw and then broke up their romance with another beating that landed him in jail.

Jack Dempsey Recruit Booster

OTTAWA, July 7.—Jack Dempsey, one-time world heavyweight boxing champion, will appear tomorrow night at a recruiting rally staged by the Ottawa Citizens' Recruiting Committee. After the rally he will referee a wrestling match.

Myrna Loy at Calgary Stampede

CALGARY, July 7.—Crammed with color, thrills and music, Calgary's 1941 edition of the Stampede parade swept down Seventh Avenue today to the cheers of a crowd of nearly 50,000. Myrna Loy, screen star now holidaying in the Rockies, was a spectator.

Star Athlete; Not for Army

DENVER, July 7.—Byron (Whizzer) White, 1937 All-America football star from Colorado University, Rhodes scholar and professional gridiron hero, has been turned down by the United States marine corps because he can't tell the difference between red and green.

'Common Canada-U.S. Defense'

OTTAWA, July 7.—A common system of civilian defense for Canada and the United States was recommended today by Geoffrey May, assistant co-ordinator for defense in the federal security agency at Washington.

Ignored Census; Fined $20

BRANTFORD, Ont., July 7.—Two Indians who refuse to answer questions by the census enumerator on the grounds that Indians of the Six Nations Reservation were immune to laws of Canada learned differently today when Magistrate R. J. Gillen fined them $20 and costs.

Storm Blanks Yankee Game

TORONTO, July 7.—An exhibition baseball game between New York Yankees and a combined team of Baltimore Orioles and Toronto Maple Leafs had to be postponed today after a storm swept the field at Maple Leaf Stadium. Proceeds were for the Red Cross British War Victims Fund.

Army May Reconsider Louis' Status

CHICAGO, July 7.—Heavyweight Champion Joe Louis faces a reconsideration of his 3-A draft status as a result of financial disclosures in his wife's divorce action. Louis was granted a deferment on a claim of dependents. It was said that Mrs. Barrow's divorce suit revealed the prize-fighter has enough funds available to support his dependents if he should be called into service.

Two Edmonton Fliers Killed

EDMONTON, July 7.—Two Edmonton airmen, Sgt.-Pilot Lowell Vance, 22, and Sgt.-Ob. W. A. Bartleman, 20, have been killed in flying accidents in England, according to word received by their parents here today. Sgt.-Pilot Vance was the son of the late C.N. Vance and Mrs. Vance; Sgt.-Ob. Bartleman was the son of Mr. and Mrs. J. Bartleman

'Heaviest Raid Yet'

RAF Sets Factory Ablaze

LONDON, July 7. — The RAF non-stop air-blitz started 22 days ago has jammed German communications on a deep arc from Brest to Kiel and softened German defenses along a thousand miles of the continental coast.

A reliable authority today credited the repeated attacks with:

1. Hampering German personnel and material movement, this weakening the German drive into Russia.
2. Slowing production of German armaments, oil and other war supplies.
3. Smashing facilities the Germans need to invade Britain.
4. Smoothing the way, if Britain sends an expeditionary force to the Continent.

By SIDNEY WILLIAMS
Special to The Vancouver Sun
Copyright, 1941, by British United Press

LONDON, July 7. — British fighter and bomber squadrons today blasted at German war targets—including a big French airplane factory, which was set afire near Amiens—in the heaviest sustained daylight offensive yet hurled at northern France.

The aerial attacks, which followed heavy night raids on the German Ruhr industrial area, struck along the coast in the Boulogne and Calais sectors and surged far inland to bomb objectives in Nazi-occupied France for hours.

The offensive began in the morning and continued late this afternoon in a cloudless sky

Please Turn to Page Two
See "Air Armada"

Seattle Youth Follows Father's War Example

A young man from Seattle followed in his father's footsteps when he enlisted in the RCAF in Vancouver recently.

He was John C. Stevenson Jr., who left immediately for No. 2A Manning Depot at Penhold, Alberta, to become a pilot.

Stevenson, 22, is the son of a former King County commissioner who flew with the Royal Flying Corps in the last war. He was born a few days after his father was shot down and interned in Holland in 1918.

He received some flying instruction from his father before coming to Canada to join hundreds of his countrymen in His Majesty's uniform.

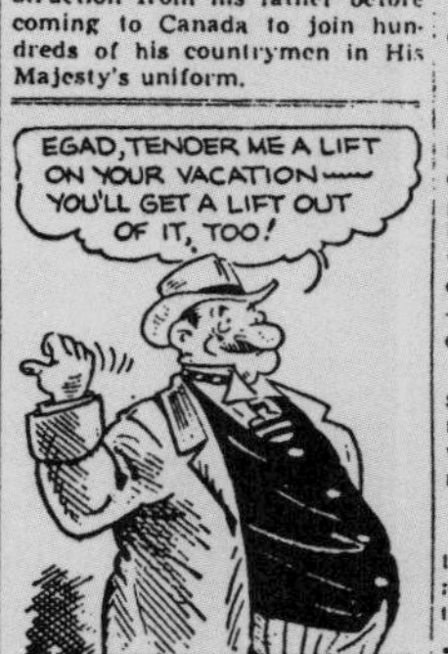

No matter where you go this summer you'll find no one just like Major Hoople. To make sure you see him and all the other comic stars every day, phone our circulation department and have The Vancouver Sun sent to your vacation address. Delivered by carrier at regular city rate.

Late Stocks on Page 2

Roosevelt Makes Armed Move Outside Western Hemisphere

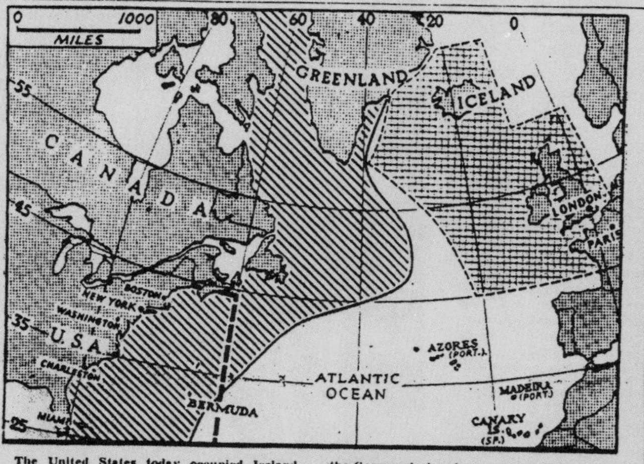

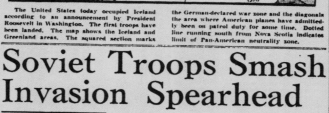

The United States today occupied Iceland according to an announcement by President Roosevelt in Washington. The first troops have been landed. The map shows the Iceland and Greenland areas. The squared section marks the German-declared war zone and the diagonals the area where American planes have admittedly been on patrol duty for some time. Dotted line running south from Nova Scotia indicates limit of Pan-American neutrality zone.

Nazis Had Declared Iceland, 1100 Miles from Norway, To Be 'In the European War Zone'

By LYLE C. WILSON
Special to The Vancouver Sun
Copyright, 1941, by British United Press

WASHINGTON, July 7.—President Roosevelt today announced that American forces have occupied Iceland.

Mr. Roosevelt said he had ordered the naval forces to take "all necessary steps" to insure safety of communications "in the approaches between Iceland and United States, as well as on the seas between United States and all other strategic outposts."

(Hitler has declared Iceland to be within the European "War Zone." Reykjavik, Iceland's capital, is 1100 miles from Nazi-held Norway).

Simultaneously United States closed the Panama Canal to all night sea traffic.

The President announced the move in a special message to Congress, advising the Legislators that American naval forces had arrived there to supplement and replace British troops.

He advised Congress that he had received a communication from the Prime Minister of Iceland and had sent the Prime Minister a reply.

"In accordance with that message, forces of the United States navy today arrived in Iceland to supplement and eventually to replace British forces which have been stationed there," the President said.

FIXED U.S. POLICY

The movement of the naval forces, it was disclosed, culminated today when the first contingent arrived in Iceland.

Mr. Roosevelt said the occupation is in line with the fixed American policy of refusing to "permit the occupation by Germany of strategic outposts in the Atlantic to be used as air or naval bases for eventual attack against the Western Hemisphere.

Again proclaiming that United States has no aspirations for permanent acquisition of these outposts, but is moving solely in self-defense, Mr. Roosevelt told Congress that "the occupation of Iceland by Germany would constitute a serious threat in three dimensions:

1. **Against Greenland and the northern portion of the North American Continent, including the islands which lie off it.**
2. **Against all shipping in the North Atlantic.**
3. **Against the steady flow of munitions to Britain—which is a matter of broad policy clearly approved by the Congress."**

MUST HALT HITLER

Mr. Roosevelt told Congress that the dispatch of naval forces to Iceland follows the same pattern as dispatch of troops to Atlantic bases acquired from Britain and was designed "to forestall any pincers movement undertaken by Germany against the Western Hemisphere."

"It is essential that Germany should not be able successfully to employ such tactics through

Please Turn to Page Two
See "Iceland"

U.S. to Provide Both Land and Sea Forces

LONDON, July 7.—A government spokesman said today that both British and U. S. forces may be in Iceland temporarily but that the British will be withdrawn "by stages."

Asked whether the action meant that Britain also would be relieved of the necessity of patrolling the waters off Iceland, he replied, "I cannot answer that question."

The agreement under which the United States is sending forces to Iceland is strictly between the United States and Iceland, but Britain is in the fullest agreement and support, he added.

He said the matter of Denmark's claims respecting Iceland is one to be settled after the war, "when we have kicked the Germans out of Denmark."

A United States understanding to assure Iceland full supplies of essential commodities and an exchange of diplocatic representatives between those countries is expected soon. Britain has a minister in Iceland, who will remain there.

Although authoritative sources declined comment on the effect the United States occupation would have on patrol of the North Atlantic, as sea-lanes, President Roosevelt's announcement generally was accepted here outside of official quarters as a further step of U.S. co-operation to insure safe delivery of lease-lend supplies to Britain.

It is understood here that the United States is sending land and air forces as well as naval men to Iceland.

Unofficial quarters attached significance to the fact that the United States now is in position to maintain both sea and air patrols over most of the North Atlantic shipping routes from bases of Newfoundland, Greenland and Iceland.

Soviet Troops Smash Invasion Spearhead

London Optimistic Over Red Army's Prowess; Fierce Night Battle of Tanks Ends in German Defeat

LONDON, July 7.—Authoritative sources said today that the Russians are fighting well, that the Germans have failed to gain superiority in the air, that the Russians are harassing the German advance armored forces seriously, and that, in general, there is no immediate cause for pessimism regarding Russian prospects even though the Germans have not been stopped everywhere.

Radio Moscow tonight reported that Soviet tanks have counter-attacked in the Ukrainian sector, destroying 300 Nazi tanks, capturing 12 long-range guns and taking 500 German troops prisoner.

By HENRY SHAPIRO
Special to The Vancouver Sun
Copyright, 1941, by British United Press

MOSCOW, July 7.—A Red Army counter-blitz offensive on the vital central front was reported turning back the German Panzer spearhead pointed at Moscow, today, after inflicting heavy losses on Nazi units in a fierce night battle of tanks.

The Russian war communique said that "heavy defeat" was inflicted on enemy mechanized forces in pitched battles from Ostrov to Polotsk, and that the Red Army, seizing the offensive, still is striking hard at the Germans in the Lepel direction, forcing them on to the defensive.

Although the morning communique did not specifically mention the Berezina river front where the Germans had been reported repulsed with heavy losses in the Borisov and Bobruisk sectors, it said that there was no adverse change in the Russian position anywhere.

On the southern front, it added, the enemy was repulsed in attempts to break through the Novograd-Volynsk sector

Please Turn to Page Two See "War in Russia"

U.S. Moves to Control Canal Ship Movements

By Associated Press

CRISTOBAL, Canal Zone, July 7.—The Commandant of Cristobal Port put into effect today new regulations under which ships will not be permitted to clear or enter Cristobal and Balboa harbors between the hours of sunset and sunrise.

Captain C. E. Coney, U. S. navy, in command here, announced that the regulations, effective immediately, would continue in effect throughout the present emergency.

Cristobal and Balboa are at the Caribbean Sea and Pacific Ocean entrances, respectively, of the Panama Canal.

Precautionary measures were taken last week to control coastwise traffic using the two ports. Small vessels were forbidden to use the east breakwater opening near Fort Randolph, which guards the Atlantic—or Caribbean—entrance to the canal.

Steamship agents are revising schedules to conform to the new regulations, notifying inbound vessels to hasten or delay arrivals.

The word "sheriff" comes from the old English title "shirereeve," meaning custodian of the country's peace.

Race Results At Calgary

FIRST RACE—Six and one-half furlongs:
Tea Club (Duncan) $4.80, $3.70, $2.55.
Ruby Aurelius (Russell) $11.60, $4.50.
Lady Aurelius (Cizik) $2.65.
Time, 1:23 2-5.
Also ran: Bachelor's Flag, Olivia D., Virgilio, Royal Pirate.

KILLED BY AUTO

LOCKPORT, Man., July 7. — Haldor Williams, 63-year-old druggist of nearby Selkirk was killed instantly when struck by an automobile as he walked along a highway.

CHICAGO, July 7.—Henry Struck, 24, of Jackson Heights, N.Y., who builds model airplanes for a wind tunnel test company, has been awarded the championship trophy in the national model airplane competition.

Feller-Wyatt Duel Tomorrow

No games were scheduled in either the American or National Leagues today.

DETROIT, Mich., July 7.—Whitlow Wyatt of Brooklyn and Bob Feller of Cleveland were tentatively named today to oppose each other on the mound tomorrow when the National and American Leagues clash in their ninth annual all-star game.

Bill McKechnie, manager of the Nationals announced his tentative batting order would be: Stan Hack, Chicago, third base. Lonnie Frey, Cincinnati, second base. Pete Reiser, Brooklyn, centrefield. Johnny Mize, St. Louis, first base. Mel Ott, New York, right field. Bob Elliott, Pittsburgh, left field. Eddie Miller, Boston, shortstop. Mickey Owen, Brooklyn, catcher. Whitlow Wyatt, Brooklyn, pitcher.

McKechnie indicated that his own pitching ace, Bucky Walters, probably would be the National League's second hurler.

Del Baker of the Detroit Tigers, manager of the Americans, declined to give out a line-up.

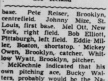

NANAIMO'S CHINATOWN CLOSED TO ARMY

The Vancouver Sun — FINAL

Only Evening Newspaper Owned, Controlled and Operated by Vancouver People

FOUNDED 1886 VOL. LV.—No. 240 — VANCOUVER, BRITISH COLUMBIA, THURSDAY, JULY 10, 1941 — Price 3 Cents

Late Bulletins

Three Unidentified Ships Hit Mines; All Sunk

STOCKHOLM, Sweden, July 10.—Three ships of undisclosed foreign nationality struck mines and sank in the Baltic Sea off the Swedish east coast last night with thunderous explosions heard over a wide seaboard area, it was reported today. Sixteen injured survivors have been landed. A Swedish ship with surgeons and nurses was sent from the port of Kalmar.

France Returns Spanish Trophies

MADRID, July 10.—France will return to Madrid trophies of the Napoleonic wars which she had obtained from Spain, it was learned today.

Two Trawlers Sunk

LONDON, July 10.—The Admiralty announced today that the 600-ton naval trawler Ash, completed shortly after the war began, and the Trawler Akranes, have been sunk.

Ulster Would Give U.S. Port

BELFAST, July 10.—Ulster Prime Minister J. M. Andrews today offered ready agreement to suggestion by Wendell Willkie that the U. S. establish a military base in North Ireland.

Canada Defends Newfoundland

WINNIPEG, July 10.—Canada has made "important commitments" for the defense of Newfoundland and its ports, Prime Minister Mackenzie King announced in a luncheon address here today.

Russia Lists Needs With U.S.

WASHINGTON, July 10.—Constantine Oumansky, Russian ambasador to the U.S., said today after an hour's conference with President Roosevelt that the President has complete lists of Russia's acute war needs.

Canadian Seaman Killed

TORONTO, July 10.—Able Seaman Edgar Benjamin, 26, a native of Regina, serving overseas with the Royal Canadian Navy, was killed Monday by enemy action, said information received by his wife and parents here today.

Men Enlisted; Rugby Club Quits

HAMILTON, July 10.—Hamilton Tigers may withdraw from the International Football Union before the 1941 season opens Sept. 27, it was learned today from a club official who said the executive recently voted unanimously to withdraw.

Accident Deaths Alarm Manitoba

WINNIPEG, July 10.—Following week-end accidents that took a toll of seven lives, the Accident and Prevention Branch of the Manitoba Labor Department today issued a special bulletin appealing to Manitobians to be more careful.

Heavy Crate Kills Radio Worker

PORTLAND, Ore., July 10.—Russell S. Murphy, 17, night attendant at the transmitting station of KGW-KEX, Portland, was fatally injured early today when a packing case, containing 1000 pounds of radio equipment, toppled over on him.

Newspapermen Barred From Iceland

LONDON, July 10.—A group of U. S. newspaper correspondents were all set yesterday to leave for Iceland. But, on instructions of the U. S. State Department in Washington, they were refused permission at the last minute to make the trip.

Fire Engine Hits House; Sets It Afire

OAKLAND, Cal., July 10.—Six men were injured today when a speeding fire engine crashed into a house, setting the building ablaze.

The fire engine and a tractor also were aflame when additional firemen arrived.

Mother Makes Son Give Himself Up

PORTLAND, July 10. — Martin Jensen's mother talked her 28-year-old son into confessing to police that he ran down and killed Fritz Neumiller, 75. He appeared at the courthouse with his mother, and said that the aged man was walking along the edge of the highway and that he did not see him until too late.

'McGinnis Night'; Player Called Up

Paul McGinnis, regular third baseman and field captain of the Vancouver Capilanos, will be playing his last game for the Caps when they meet Spokane at Athletic Park tomorrow night. A special "McGinnis Night" celebration is being staged as a farewell party for him. McGinnis has enlisted in the U.S. Air Force and has special permission to play this one more game for the Caps before joining his unit.

52

'Sitdown Strike' at Longacres Track

SEATTLE, July 10.—Fifty owners and trainers staged a "sit-down" strike today at the Longacres race track, refusing to enter their horses for tomorrow's card because they compained the track was too hard. Entries for the next day's races, which are normally made at 10 a.m., had not been made several hours past the deadline. President Joe Gottstein of the Washington Jockey Club said the track had not cancelled a racing card in its nine-year history and wouldn't postpone tomorrow's program.

Poland to Help Russia If—

OTTAWA, July 10.—Polish conditions for organization of armed forces which would participate in the war against Germany in Russia, were set out at conference in London between Polish and Russian representatives, Victor Podoski, Polish Consul-General in Canada, said he was informed today.

The report said that Gen. W. Sikorski, Polish Prime Minister, told the Russian Ambassador in London that organization of Polish forces to fight in the East would depend on Russian restitution of wrongs done to the Polish population.

Chinese Injured In Row

Military Authorities Act Promptly to Prevent Further Trouble

NANAIMO, July 10. — Nanaimo Chinese community will in future be forbidden territory to all soldiers in Camp Nanaimo, at all times, by order of Brigadier O. M. Martin, officer commanding.

The order follows a recent attack on Lee Yun, Chinese cook from Chemainus, who suffered painful injuries when assaulted in Chinatown.

THREE ARRESTS

Shortly after the Chinese was attacked Saturday night, three soldiers from Ontario, quartered in Camp Nanaimo, were arrested.

They were charged in city police court Monday with robbery with violence, and the case was remanded for eight days.

Lee Yun told police he was robbed of $35. He was treated in Nanaimo Hospital.

APPEALED TO CONSUL

On Wednesday, Nanaimo Chinese held a meeting to inquire into the incident.

From it, they sent a request to the Chinese consulate in Vancouver, asking that consular officials seek a restraining order.

P. C. Yum, acting consul, told The Vancouver Sun this afternoon he had taken up the matter with army authorities, and the closure resulted.

Brigadier Martin did not comment on the order, but confirmed that he had placed Chinatown "strictly out-of-bounds."

King Going to London Soon

By NORMAN MacLEOD
Copyright, 1941, by British United Press
Special to The Vancouver Sun

WINNIPEG, July 10.—In the last public address of his present tour of Canada's war effort from the Pacific Coast to the prairies, Prime Minister King warned here today that "unless Britain survives and the forces that seek to preserve the freedom of the seas triumph in the Battle of the Atlantic, an attempt at invasion of this continent of North America would follow as inevitably as night follows day."

Speaking at a combined gathering of the Board of Trade, and the Canadian and Empire Clubs, the Prime Minister indicated clearly that his present tour is but a prelude to, and preparation for, an early visit to the United Kingdom.

Mr. King discouraged any idea of early conscription for overseas service.

He also revealed for the first time that Canada has accepted important commitments for the protection of Newfoundland territorial waters.

Late Stocks Page 10

Floating Logging Camp Comes to Town

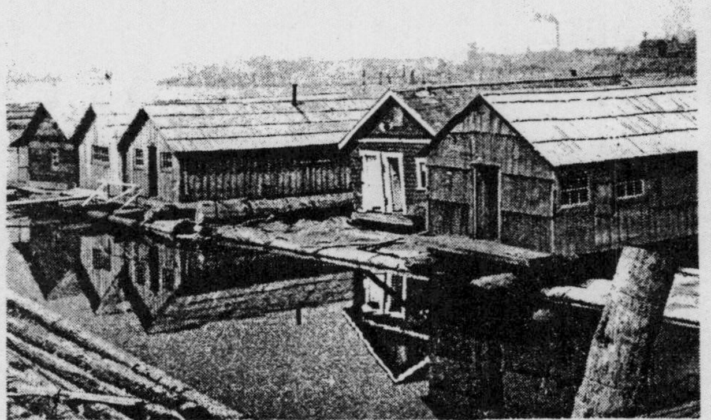

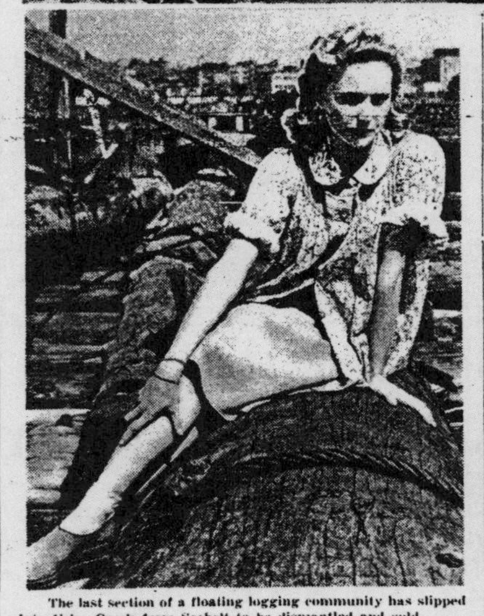

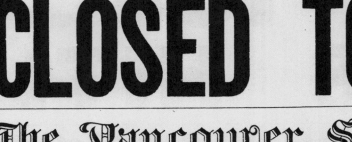

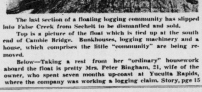

The last section of a floating logging community has slipped into False Creek from Sechelt to be dismantled and sold.

Top is a picture of the float which is tied up at the south end of Cambie Bridge. Bunkhouses, logging machinery and a house, which comprises the little "community" are being removed.

Below—Taking a rest from her "ordinary" housework aboard the float is pretty Mrs. Peter Bingham, 21, wife of the owner, who spent seven months up-coast at Yuculta Rapids, where the company was working a logging claim. Story, pge 15

Western Softball League Launched

MOOSE JAW, July 10. — An ambition cherished for many years by softball officials was realized with the formation of the Western Canada Softball Association at a meeting here last night.

Women's playoffs will be inaugurated next year.

The only province not represented at the meeting was British Columbia and correspondenc indicated that it would affiliate at a later date.

BOY DROWNS

GANGES, July 10.—Frank Hillier, 16, son of Mr. and Mrs. Thomas Hillier, of Beaver Point, was drowned in Weston Lake Wednesday.

Police Seeking CIO Secretary and $2000

SEATTLE, July 10.—Authorities today sought W. J. Holman, 32, on charges of absconding with $2107 in funds of Local 9-26, International Woodworkers of America (CIO), of which he was formerly secretary. He disappeared June 30, union officers said.

BASEBALL

CHICAGO, July 10. — Mrs. Grace R. Comiskey, owner-president of the Chicago White Sox, said today that Manager Jimmy Dykes, indefinitely suspended and publicly "spanked" by American League President Will Harridge, will be "backed to the limit by our office" in the squabble which grew out of his run-in last Saturday with Umpire Steve Basil.

AMERICAN LEAGUE

Boston at Detroit, postponed, rain.

NATIONAL LEAGUE

Chicago	100 000 110—3	8	1
Boston	000 001 000—1	7	1

Olsen and McCullough; Javery and Masi.

Cincinnati	000 100 020 - 3	8	1
Brooklyn	320 300 00x- 8	10	1

Vander Meer, Moore (2), Beggs (3) and Lombardi; Higbe and Owen.

AT THE Race Track

Selections

By RAILBIRD

1—Liverpool, Be Mine, Legato.
2—Vade Retra, Alsantro, Barbralyn.
3—Si Green, Belle Park, Golden Belt.
4—Middie Blouse, Hi Hun, Craiglee.
5—Sahara Chief, Some Turley, Sandworth.
6—Vena Marcus, Avondale Star, Master Beau.
7—Simonette, Dr. Pills, Arabian Love.
SUB.—First Vee, Maridor, Ascot Maid.

ONE BEST—SI GREEN.

By OUR GRACIE

1—Legato, Be Mine, Pandomint.
2—Vade Retra, Sky Dust, Finished Gift.
3—Golden Belt, Si Green, Maymint.
4—Craiglee, Dry Hills, Middie Blouse.
5—Beban Entry, Buck-On, Sandworth.
6—Vena Marcus, Avondale Star, Novito.
7—Ynomis, Simonette, Dr. Pills.
SUB.—Maridore, Silver Fur, Bonnyrigg.

By LUCKY GOLD

1—Legato, Liverpool, Misme.
2—Vade Retra, Alsantro, Finished Gift.
3—Si Green, Golden Belt, Maymint.
4—Ascot Watch, Dry Hills, Middle Blouse.
5—Some Turley, Sahara Chief, Once in a While.
6—Master Beau, Avondale Star, Vena Marcus.
7—Dr. Pills, Simonette, Ynomis.

ONE BEST—DR. PILLS

BRIGHOUSE PARK

FIRST RACE—Six furlongs:
Broderick (Haller) $48.60, $20.70, $20.90.
Lady Giovando (Bassett) $5.50, $4.20.
Vanbank (Christensen) $8.05.
Time, 1:13 1-5.

SECOND RACE—Six furlongs:
Teeworth (Kelly) $7.75, $4.15, $3.00.
Peggy Dot (Haller) $3.60, $2.70.
Liloade (Sporri) $3.05.
Time: 1.13.

DOUBLE—$217.05

CALGARY RESULTS

FIRST RACE—Six and one-half furlongs:
Tea Club (Russell) $4.65, $2.90, $2.70.
Saucy Maid (McTague) $3.40, $2.75.
Man of Iron (Northcott) $4.70.
Time, 1:25 1-5.
Also ran: Dancing Don, Sweep Wine, Moonsan, Florence Bar.

SECOND RACE—Five furlongs:
War Chimes, $3.45, $3.65, $3.05.
Sun Twister, $8.35, $5.45.
Bel Lomond, $3.50.
Time:, 1:02.

U.S. Demands Nazis Free Americans

WASHINGTON, July 10.—The United States has taken action to obtain the immediate repatriation of Americans held prisoners by the Nazis or detained in Germany, Italy ano Nazi-conquered Europe.

Sun Handicap

by ALF COTTRELL

The bracketed figures after the weight indicate the rating for this particular race. If a horse carries more than the weight stipulated in the entries, deduct one point for each pound of overweight carried.

FRIDAY, JULY 11

1st Race—Claiming. 4-year-olds and up. — 6 Furlongs

4153	**PANDOMINT**	116	(101)	Must break faster (1)
4151	**LEGATO**	111	(94)	Lost a tough one (7)
(4142)	**BE MINE**	118	(89)	Class; one to trim (10)
4130	Miss Goldstream	106	(89)	All races excellent (9)
——	Misme	118	(—)	Speed; first out (3)
4135	Liverpool	116	(87)	Really dangerous (12)
——	*Polvo's Pride	118	(—)	Mud preferred here (2)
——	Sis Simony	106	(—)	Went well at 'Peg (6)
4144	Noyo	118	(81)	Fair but spot tough (11)
——	Shasta Plucky	118	(—)	May need a race (4)
4136	Sky Breeze	116	(—)	Speed at longer (5)
4150	Skirock	118	(—)	Showed nothing (8)

2nd Race—Claiming. 3-year-olds and up. — 6 Furlongs

4144	**ALSANTORO**	x113	(92)	Drops wt.; speedy (6)
4144	**VADE RETRA**	111	(84)	About due to score (2)
4118	**SKY DUST**	x113	(81)	Will improve here (1)
——	Lisa Belle	113	(—)	Always fair sort (7)
——	Barbralyn	107	(—)	Southern form okay (9)
4106	Trahison	118	(78)	Will be coming (4)
4144	Queen Irene	111	(78)	May have been short (5)
4135	Bill's Rose	113	(—)	Far back other day (8)
——	Finished Gift	101	(—)	Not bad youngster (3)

3rd Race—Claiming, 3-year-olds and up foaled in Western Canada. — 6 Furlongs

4153	**SI GREEN**	116	(88)	Is long overdue (5)
4140	**GOLDEN BELT**	111	(81)	Ready for best (7)
4145	**BELLE PARK**	111	(76)	Hung on gamely (1)
4145	Maymint	111	(74)	Knocking at door (3)
4156	Cardo Queen	111	(—)	Lacks early speed (2)
——	Zelpha Lad	116	(—)	Prairie form fair (8)
4110	Sunny May	111	(—)	Will need easier (6)
——	Royal Suzy	111	(—)	Seems ordinary sort (4)

4th Race—Claiming. 3-year-olds and up. — 6 Furlongs

(4144)	**DRY HILLS**	114	(91)	Edge in hard race (6)
(4131)	**CRAIGLEE**	109	(93)	Made classy time (7)
(4128)	**MIDDIE BLOUSE**	113	(90)	Ran lovely race (4)
4113	Frisco Boy	118	(87)	Might be the day (2)
——	Hi-Hun	118	(—)	Best; may need mud (1)
4152	Ascot Watch	108	(85)	Prefers route race (5)
4141	Hi-Ginny	108	(75)	Will improve some (3)

5th Race—Allowance. 3-year-olds and up. — 5 1-2 Furlongs

4155	**SOME TURLEY**	108	(102)	Best at weights (5)
4133	**SAHARA CHIEF (a)**	113	(99)	Training better (3)
4152	**KINGSWAY'S AUR.**	106	(94)	Hooking tough ones (2)
——	Sandworth	108	(—)	Prairie form poor (6)
4141	Buck-On	120	(—)	Short in first try (8)
4109	Once in Awhile	110	(—)	Too much speed here (4)
——	Bucket Brigade	115	(—)	Grey; nice sprinter (7)
4133	Truely Flo (a)	108	(—)	Has some early foot (1)

(a)—Beban entry.

6th Race—Claiming. 3-year-olds and up. — 1 Mile 70 Yards

5156	**AVONDALE STAR**	109	(91)	Nice spot for him (7)
4149	**MASTER BEAU**	116	(74)	Hard knocking sort (4)
4156	**DARK HANDS**	99	(74)	In with feather (5)
4131	Vena Marcus	104	(—)	On rail: real threat (1)
4149	Spangle Hen	104	(72)	Been slow improving (8)
4149	Novito	116	(69)	Also below tops (3)
——	Billy Easter	109	(—)	Prairie races good (6)
4140	Super Miss	106	(—)	Strictly longshot (2)

7th Race—Claiming, 3-year-olds and up foaled in Western Candaa. — 1 Mile 70 Yards

(4146)	**YNOMIS**	x104	(81)	At wts. can repeat (7)
4150	**DR. PILLS**	114	(78)	Always in fight (1)
4151	**SIMONETTE**	109	(78)	Be no surprise (2)
——	Arabian Love	109	(—)	Some 'Peg form okay (6)
4156	John B.	112	(77)	Speed and on rail (1)
4130	Piroyal	107	(—)	Charged in sprint (5)
——	Hazel King	107	(—)	May need a race (3)

Substitute Race—Claiming. 3-year-olds and up. — 6 Furlongs

4139	**FIRST VEE**	107	(88)	This is nice spot (1)
4140	**SILVER FUR**	118	(85)	Been sprinting well (5)
4147	**ASCOT MAID**	100	(83)	Youth on her side (10)
4140	Miss Montrose	106	(—)	Likes this track (2)
4124	Maridore	106	(—)	Off works a chance (3)
4151	Bonnyrigg	101	(—)	Needs more racing (8)
4123	Valdina Phara	102	(—)	Can improve here (7)
——	Lullaby Lady	106	(—)	Probably need race (9)
——	Ad Lib II	106	(—)	Fair sort if ready (6)
——	Wild Deer	107	(—)	May do later (11)
4124	Sable Lass	101	(—)	Shown nothing (4)
4124	Broxess	95	(—)	Trailed her field (12)

Weather Clear, Track Fast — **First Post 2:15 p.m**

x Apprentice Allowance Claimed

Turks State French Fleet Has Fled

CAIRO, July 10.—The Anatolia News Agency said tonight that the Vichy French fleet, comprising 16 vessels based on Beirut, had left Syrian waters, anchored in Alexandretta harbor and given themselves up to Turkish custody.

Earlier the Turkish radio announced that French warships fleeing from Syria would be interned if they entered Turkish ports.

The radio said panic had begun in Syria and that French civil servants with their families were arriving in Turkey.

French sources at Ankara said

Burned Man Wanders; Found in Vacant Lot

Ernest H. Bagley, 1030 West Pender Street, was found lying in a vacant lot near that address, suffering from burns on hands and face, about 2:30 p.m. today.

Police were told there was a fire in his room early today, and that after the fire Bagley wandered away and later collapsed.

His condition is not considered serious by General Hospital authorities.

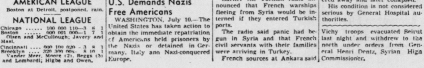

Vichy troops evacuated Beirut last night and withdrew to the north under orders from General Henri Dentz, Syrian High Commissioner.

Free French Losses

LONDON, July 10.—Free French casualties in the Syrian campaign total between 1,200 and 1,300 men to date, headquarters of Gen. Charles de Gaulle reported today.

Street Fighting in Talinn

STOCKHOLM, July 10.—An Estonian news broadcast from Koenigsberg, quoted by the newspaper Aftonbladet, indicated that street-fighting was in progress in Talinn today.

(Complete Russian war developments page 12.)

SABOTAGE WRECKS NAZIS' 2 GREATEST LINERS

Says U.S. Hamburg Consul

★★★★★ FINAL

THE VANCOUVER DAILY PROVINCE

47th YEAR—NO. 108 VANCOUVER, B.C., FRIDAY, AUGUST 1, 1941—34 PAGES PRICE 3 CENTS On trains, boats and in the country, Five Cents

THE PROVINCE HANDICAP

By JOHNNY PARK

FOR SATURDAY RACING (First Post 2:15 p.m.), Vancouver, B. C., Aug. 2. (Star Before Weight Carried Denotes 5 Pounds Apprentice Allowance.)

Lansdowne Park MILE TRACK 2nd MEETING ***1st Day***

1st Race— Claiming 3-year-olds and up **6 Furlongs**

Index No.	Horse	Weight		Post No.
(4182)	LEGATO	115	Rested, fresh, ready.	(2)
(4248)	TOMMY SAND	113	Won from cheaper field.	(9)
4120	SILUMO	*105	Weight makes contender	(6)
(4197)	Bosworth	124	Always have him to beat.	(3)
(4237)	Stolen Color	122	Good weight packer.	(1)
4195	Mint Boy	118	Early flash only out.	(4)
4241	MacLeod Breeze	*110	Needs best for part.	(7)
4182	Sky Dust	*110	Helps force the pace.	(8)
4244	Silver Fur	122	Good race every out.	(5)

2nd Race— Claiming. 3-year-olds up. Foaled in Western Canada **6 Furlongs**

4194	JUNGLE HEN	113	Needs best to get home.	(5)
4248	MAIZIE B	113	Needed last tightener.	(4)
4248	SPARTAN BEAUTY	113	Improving, look out.	(2)
4243	Kaywood	118	Keen speed at Hastings.	(6)
——	Margery Daw	*108	If ready, one to beat.	(10)
4193	Avondale King	118	Has had lots of chances.	(9)
4215	Piroyal	108	Runs only in spots.	(8)
——	Belle Marcus	108	If ready could be close.	(3)
4213	Ascot Maid	102	Uncertain, but has chance.	(12)
4236	Zelpha Lad	*113	Contender in cheap field.	(1)
——	Sunny Monday	118	Been looking for spot.	(11)
4233	Broxa M	112	Not much up to date.	(7)

3rd Race— Claiming 3-year-olds and up **6 Furlongs**

4251	BUCK-ON	114	Rounding to his top form.	(9)
4227	HI-RYTHM	108	Lots of speed, contender.	(7)
4251	JANISY	111	Will battle with leaders.	(5)
(4233)	Bucket Brigade	118	Won easily at Hastings.	(1)
4148	Green Tea	113	Keen mare, on edge.	(6)
4245	Flagboro	104	In light, due to improve.	(4)
4230	Dry Hills	111	Question of getting up.	(2)
——	Bubbling Spray	113	Reported to be fair sort.	(3)
4227	Ascot Jane	106	A long shot, chance.	(8)

4th Race— Lansdowne Handicap 3-year-olds and up **1 Mile and 1-16**

(4252)	FRANWORTH	111	Beat him, take the money.	(10)
4176	COOPERSTOWN	116	Rested, lots of speed.	(3)
(4176)	NANAFFRAN	118	Has beaten them before.	(1)
——	Palmera T	115	A Longacres special.	(7)
4176	Dalkeith	107	Needs her best effort.	(2)
(4229)	Wilkie	112	Tough spot for youngster.	(9)
4252	Contributor	108	Charges through stretch.	(8)
4206	Sunny Park	102	Yet to show best form.	(6)
4252	Fern Creek	104	In light, may be upset.	(4)
4252	Rattle Hocks	107	Field seems trifle tough.	(5)
4252	Some Turley	110	Long overdue.	(11)

5th Race— Hamber Cup. 3-year-olds and up. Bred and owned in B. C. **One Mile**

4252	FRANWORTH	110	May catch leaders tiring.	(7)
4229	KILLARNEY L	120	May lead throughout.	(6)
4176	DALKEITH	108	Distance, weight suits.	(4)
4252	Maid of Broxa	106	Discard her last out.	(2)
4206	Sahara Chief	115	Fast, strong contender.	(3)
4206	Sunny Park	102	On rail, will go well.	(1)
4252	Some Turley	110	At weights could surprise.	(5)

6th Race— Claiming 3-year-olds and up **6 Furlongs**

4226	QUEEN IRENE	113	Last was much improved.	(11)
4180	CISCO KID	108	Good chance with these.	(4)
4189	BELL RAP	110	She's due any time now.	(6)
——	Hasty Day	118	First out, has speed.	(8)
4226	Pipes Pal	115	Yet to reach his peak.	(9)
——	Acero	118	May take it all.	(10)
——	Guaranty	118	Could lose these once.	(2)
——	Goldie's Pride	110	If ready, real threat.	(3)
——	Trivelda	101	First out, look once.	(7)
4230	Once in Awhile	110	Flash for a quarter.	(5)
4219	Patolan	100	Showed a flash only out.	(12)
4197	East Calling	112	Wait for another day.	(1)

7th Race— Claiming 3-year-olds and up **1 Mile and 1-8**

4216	ARKY	106	At weights has edge.	(9)
4246	RUSHING BY (a)	*113	Fast, one to catch.	(3)
4254	BOLD COURTIER	113	Consistent, one of choices.	(6)
4254	Rodney Pan (a)	*113	Part of strong entry.	(4)
4253	Ida S	*108	Route, track suits her.	(8)
(4244)	Masked Revue	116	Has won three this year.	(2)
4247	Thirsk	113	Distance suits better.	(1)
4239	Cardq Queen	101	In light, could win it.	(5)
(4242)	Tangle Tim	109	Nosed out cheaper bunch.	(7)
4208	John B	111	Fast but in tough field.	(10)

(a)—Copenhaver entry.

8th Race — HURDLES 4-year-olds and up **1 Mile and 3-4**

4254	FAVORSOME (a)	160	In lighter today.	(3)
4255	BOY O' MINE (b)	150	The main contender.	(4)
(4255)	MY GENTLEMAN	158	Picks up weight.	(2)
4255	Shawnigan (a)	145	Must not be discarded.	(5)
4255	Vancouver Express	145	Contender in open heat.	(1)
4164	Sweepen	144	Appears outclassed.	(6)
4161	Gold Normanne (b)	144	Not much at best.	(7)

(a)—Hammond entry. (b)—Chiappa entry.

★★★★★—FAVORSOME.

Sub. Race — Claiming 3-year-olds and up **6 Furlongs**

Selections in order: DRIFT ON, MAC PHALARIS, JELSWEEP, The Pagan, Cetoma, Broderick, Polvo's Pride, Liverpool, Frisco Boy, Gordelius, Sweet Lavender, Saucy Maid.

2nd Sub. Race— Claiming 3-year-olds up **6 Furlongs**

Selections in order: BILLY EASTER, ROSE AGAIN, NANNIEWORTH, Victorian Star, Epitome, Undulate, Broadway Star, Chesterton, Zebella, Clear Title, Ad Lib II., Time Ball.

Johnny Mann Selections

FIRST RACE—Bosworth, Tommy Sand, Stolen Color.
SECOND RACE—Maizie B, Spartan Beauty, Kaywood.
THIRD RACE—Green Tea, Janis, Flagboro.
FOURTH RACE—Nanaffran, Dalkeith, Palmera T.
FIFTH RACE—Killarne L., Franworth, Maid of Broxa.
SIXTH RACE—Cisco Kid, Bell Rap, Hasty Day.
SEVENTH RACE—Bold Courtier, Rodney Pan, Thirsk.
EIGHTH RACE—Boy o' Mine, Favorsome, My Gentleman.
1ST SUB RACE—MacPhalaris, Polvo's Pride, Jelsweep.
2ND SUB. RACE—Billy Easter, Rose Again, Zebella.
BEST BET—Nanaffran.

Clocker Selections

FIRST RACE—Silumo, Tommy Sand, Legato.
SECOND RACE—Spartan Beauty, Jungle Hen, Maizie B.
THIRD RACE — Buck-On, Hi Rythm, Dry Hills.
FOURTH RACE — Cooperstown, Franworth, Nanaffran.
FIFTH RACE—Dalkeith, Maid of Broxa, Killarney L.
SIXTH RACE—Guaranty, Cisco Kid, Queen Irene.
SEVENTH RACE—Tangle Tim, Ida S., Bold Courtier.
EIGHTH RACE—Favorsome, Boy o' Mine, My Gentleman.
1ST SUB. RACE—Broderick, Mac Phalaris, Drift On.
2nd SUB. RACE—Billy Easter, Undulate, Broadway Star.
BEST BET—Cooperstown.

BULK OF 3RD DIVISION NOW IS OVERSEAS

By ROSS MUNRO
Canadian Press Staff Writer.

A BRITISH PORT, Aug. 1. Under the command of Major-Gen. C. B. Price, a section of the 3rd Canadian Division arrived safely in Britain after a speedy Atlantic crossing. (In Ottawa today, Defense Minister J. L. Ralston announced the troops arriving in England comprised the bulk of the 3rd Canadian Division.)

The ocean was like a millpond all the way across as Canadian and British warships again proved sea mastery to bring the second large Canadian troop convoy in a month through the Atlantic danger zones without incident.

THOUSANDS ARRIVE.

Thousands of cheering Canadians, keen to be with their brothers in arms of the First Division, Second Division and the Canadian Army Tank Brigade, lined the rails as the gray troopships eased to anchorages.

Canadian High Commissioner Vincent Massey, David Margesson, secretary of state for war; Maj.-Gen. P. J. Montague, chief of Canadian military headquarters, London, and several high-ranking British officers went out to the ships to welcome the troops.

The contingent was led by various third division headquarters units and included infantry regiments from Nova Scotia, New Brunswick, Eastern, Central and Western Ontario, a French-Canadian regiment and certain units

(Continued on Page 8.)
See TROOPS.

SEEK SLAYER OF AGED MAN

Eighty-three-year-old Frank Thom died in General Hospital at 8:30 a.m. today, his head crushed by repeated blows from a hammer wielded by a brutal slayer in his Powell street cabin.

Thom was found sprawled unconscious across his bed in cabin 12, 1100 Powell street, at 5:30 p.m. Thursday. He had been brutally attacked several hours previously but his cries for help had not been heard.

Incentive for the attack is believed to have been robbery. Thom, an old age pensioner, received his pension cheque Thursday morning and no trace of the cheque or cash can be found.

The aged man put up a gallant fight for his life in the cabin, according to evidence in the bedroom. A lamp, which hung on a nail above the bed, was found in three parts on the floor, as though Thom had thrown it at his assailant.

Both his hands were ripped and torn as he tried to ward off the hammer blows. The right side of his head was badly crushed, his left ear torn and his right eye blackened.

Thom's cabin consists of two rooms—a kitchen, without a stove, and a bedroom about 9 feet by 13 feet. The stove, police learned, had been sold two weeks ago.

(Continued on Page 3.)
See MURDER.

NEW PROPAGANDA SHOWS . . .

Nazis Feel First Fear Of Defeat

By EDGAR ANSEL MOWRER.
Special radio to The Daily Province. Copyright, 1941, Chicago Daily News.

WASHINGTON, Aug. 1.—If anything could make officials in this city feel that all is not going well with the German offensive against Russia, it is the reawakening of German propaganda in the last few days.

This propaganda takes the form of a story which runs something this way:

Admittedly, no one can consent to make peace with Hitler and the chief Nazis. The German people are, at a certain point, prepared to meet their adversaries halfway and eliminate Hitler and his unspeakable Nazis. All they will want is to be sure that they will not, at the peace conference, be held responsible for the Nazi crimes.

If punishment is intended, then all Germans are prepared to rally around the Reichswehr and "fight to the death." But if promised complete immunity and the status quo of before the war, the "good Germans" will be quite prepared to throw over their seducers, make peace, and enter into international co-operation in a big way, on a basis of perfect equality.

So runs the thesis—incidentally included in a new set of peace terms that are current in New York and Washington.

"GOOD GERMANS" TOOLS.

Who starts these stories? Who is busy trying to make the ground soft for a defeated Germany to fall upon? None knows exactly but most students of German affairs here are confident that they originate in Berlin.

Nazis are obviously worthless

(Continued on Page 8.)
See MOWRER.

Final BULLETINS

WON'T LIFT OIL BAN

TORONTO, Aug. 1.—(CP)—G. R. Cotterelle, federal oil controller, today turned down the request of the Ontario Hotel Association, and other groups interested in the tourist business, that United States' visitors be permitted to buy gasoline on Sunday, at least until September 15.

Report Windsors to Visit August 21

CALGARY, Aug. 1.—(CP)—The Calgary Herald said today it had learned on good authority the Duke and Duchess of Windsor are planning to visit the Duke's ranch at Pekisko, 60 miles south of Calgary, around August 21, unless something unforeseen happens which would force a change in arrangements.

The Herald said it was reported possible that the couple will spend about six weeks in the Calgary district.

Three Flyers Killed

MONTEREY, Calif., Aug. 1.—(AP)—Three United States army air corps men lost their lives today as two observation planes locked wings in midair. Another man escaped death by parachuting but was injured seriously.

British, Finns Part

LONDON, Aug. 1. — (AP) — Britain and Finland formally completed their severance of diplomatic relations tonight and the British minister in Helsinki was instructed to ask for his passport.

Hockey Player Overseas

AN EAST COAST CANADIAN PORT, Aug. 1.—(CP)—Pte. George Marshall, 35, of Calgary, arrived today in England with the 3rd Canadian Army Division units. Marshall formerly was a hockey defenseman with the New York American.

Malahat to Open

VICTORIA, Aug. 1.—(CP)—Malahat Highway will reopen to traffic at 5 p.m. tomorrow, the department of public works announced today, permitting travel over a reconstructed portion at Mile 22, for the week-end.

Leaves Son Here

VICTORIA, Aug. 1.—(CP) — Mrs. Ethel Morrison, 59, collapsed and died in a Yates street coffee shop this morning. Besides her husband, she is survived by one son in Vancouver.

Heian Maru Sailing Here Is Delayed

SEATTLE, Aug. 1.—(AP)—The Noppon-Yusen-Kaisah today cancelled the 3 p.m. P.S.T. (4 p.m. Vancouver time) sailing of the big MS. Heian Maru and prepared to discharge cargo after the United States marshal had tied her up under service of five libels filed by East Coast importers to whom cargo had been consigned.

Line officers said they had been assured she would be cleared by customs for departure for Vancouver, when the Seattle cargo was unloaded. (See also Page 8).

Passengers for Vancouver, 69 in number, from the Heian Maru, will tranship to this port by coastwise steamer, reaching here at 9 a.m. (daylight saving) Saturday morning, according to an announcement by B. W. Greer & Son Ltd. The ship herself will come to Vancouver later, they state, to discharge her Canadian freights and take on passengers for Japan and China.

She will sail from Vancouver on August 5.

BASEBALL

NATIONAL LEAGUE.

		R.	H.	E.
New York	000 000 012—	3	11	0
Pittsburgh	004 010 10x—	6	11	1

Hubbell, McGee, Adams and Danning; Butcher and Lopez.

AMERICAN LEAGUE.

		R.	H.	E.
St. Louis	000 000 000—	0	5	1
New York	303 012 00x—	9	14	1

Auker, Newlin and Swift; Gomez and Dickey.

Regina Race Results

First race—Chinese Custom (Godley), $10.80, $6.45, $4.15.
Meto Boy (Hamilton), $4.75, $3.70.
Man of Iron (Roy), $4.75.
Time, 1.15 2-5.
Also ran—Marelius, Tillie Queen, Bonouri, Wrackdale.

Second race—Cave Boy (Godley), $6.40, $3.75, $2.70.
Tabs Bid (Roy), $3, $2.45.
Prevaricate (Soloman), $2.70.
Time, 1.12 2-5.
Also ran—Dancing Don, Bob's First, Boniluna.

Third race—Purple Mantle (Northcott), $23.25, $10.60, $5.75.
Diana A. (Russell), $3.50, $3.05.
Sunny City (Godley), $3.60.
Time, 1.41 4-5.
Also ran—Big Joe, Yorkshire Lassie, Lady Fay, Lady Moira, Dutch Lily.

DAILY DOUBLE, $291.65.

'Europa And Bremen Are Burned Out'

By Associated Press

NEW YORK, Aug. 1.—Alfred R. Thomson, ousted United States consul-general in Hamburg, said today he understood that both the Bremen and the Europa, famous German passenger liners, had been "completely burned out inside by saboteurs."

Thomson arrived here today on the U. S. liner West Point from Lisbon, Portugal, with 387 other passengers, mostly consular service employees, amid scenes reminiscent of the first returns of American soldiers from the first Great War.

"While I have no authority for this information," said Thomson, "it is spoken of by everyone along the north German seaboard. The Bremen is understood to be in Bremen. I don't know where the Europa is.'

"There are very few large ships in the Hamburg harbor. I took a tour around the waterfront recently, and all I could see were smaller ships, the neutral ones brilliantly lighted.

"Whatever damage is done to Hamburg harbor is quickly cleared up as it is in Hamburg proper. Within days, even within hours, squads clean up all the debris. And if an entire building is shattered, within a short time there remains only a cleared vacant lot. None of my staff has been injured.

"It is difficult to ascertain the morale of the German people because they are non-vocal."

Approximately 2400 relatives and friends lined the pier as the huge camouflaged West Point was tied up and a tumultuous cheer arose as soon as those on board were allowed on the pier. Embraces mingled with joyful tears reminded observers of early 1919 when returning war veterans received a like greeting.

Among the consular officials returning from Europe was Frederick A. Sterling, minister to Sweden, whose ill health caused him to seek a three-month leave of absence. Sterling said he would report to Washington before beginning a recuperative leave.

See Russian Climax Near

By WILLIAM H. STONEMAN.
Special radio to The Daily Province. Copyright, 1941, Chicago Daily News.

LONDON, Aug. 1.—It is now the studied opinion of British military experts that the "next week or two" will decide the course of the Russo-German war.

This period, it is figured, will be sufficient to determine whether or not the Germans have enough power, equipment and men to exhaust Russian supplies of first-class equipment. If they can, they may press right on to key Russian cities; if not, the war may develop into a standstill, which may ultimately turn into a complete stalemate.

A real stalemate, however, is not expected to materialize as long as either side has enough armored divisions to attack the other.

Of the two principal German drives—one toward Leningrad and the other in the Smolensk area—the former is regarded at present as the more dangerous. Capture of Leningrad, it is pointed out, would deprive the Russian fleet of bases and supplies. The capture of Smolensk, on the other hand, would simply mark another step on the road to Moscow, which is still far away and strongly defended, and it might scramble up Russian communications by cutting the railways.

(Continued on Page 8.)
See MOSCOW.

Jury Says G. N. Crew To Blame

NEW WESTMINSTER, Aug. 1.—Blame for the railway crash which cost the lives of four men and injuries to more than a score of passengers, was placed on the train crew of the Great Northern Railway by coroner's jury at the conclusion of the inquest this afternoon.

The verdict stated in part: "We do find that the accident was due to negligence on the part of the train crew of the Great Northern train, No. 359, for failing to identify a passenger train. We do not believe the negligence to be in the category of manslaughter.

"We recommend to the railway commissioners that an automatic block safety signal system be installed on the single track between New Westminster and Endot."

(Special to The Daily Province.)

NEW WESTMINSTER, Aug. 1. —"We had nothing on an extra Canadian National train," said E. D. Flanders, testifying at the inquest here today into the collision of the Great Northern train on which he was conductor, and a Canadian National train at Burquitlam July 24.

When the Great Northern passed a Canadian National passenger on the double track, Mr. Flanders said he did not personally identify it but assumed his engine crew had done so when they did not stop at Endot. He explained he was busy with tickets and attending to passengers so he did not have the time to check. Before reaching Endot, however, he gave a signal on the whistle cord to call the engineer's attention to the train order to wait for the passing of the Canadian National train.

George Mountain, Seattle, brakeman on the Great Northern Railway, remembered passing the C.N. extra six miles before the collision, but failed to catch signals or its number.

(See page 9 for earlier report.)

No Rationing Of Gasoline For Canada

OTTAWA, Aug. 1.—(CP)—Canadian motorists and tourists entering this country need have no fear of compulsory gasoline rationing, Mr. Justice T. C. Davis, associate deputy minister of national war services, said today.

Death Sentence Commuted

The shadow of the gallows was removed from Teras Krawchuk, Ukrainian section hand from Prince George, at Oakalla jail today, but the good news brought little joy to the condemned man.

When Warden Walter Owen broke the good news to him in the death cell this morning, Krawchuk merely raised his eyes slowly and said "Thank you." Then he relapsed into the brooding which has characterized his behavior since his arrest at Prince George last September 14.

The Ukrainian was under sentence to hang next Wednesday for the murder of his wife, but word was received today from E. H. Coleman, undersecretary of state, that sentence had been commuted to life imprisonment.

News of the commutation brought great relief to his lawyer, T. F. Hurley, who believes firmly in his client's innocence, and has worked unceasingly on his behalf.

Warden Walter Owen of Oakalla was also relieved, for his kindness and understanding had done much to break down

(Continued on Page 8.)
See PRISON.

Wismer Warns

CITY TO HAVE NEW BLACKOUTS

The Vancouver Sun

Only Evening Newspaper Owned, Controlled and Operated by Vancouver People

FOUNDED 1886 VOL. LV.—No. 267 — VANCOUVER, B.C., MONDAY, AUGUST 11, 1941 — On trains, boats and outside Greater Vancouver, 5c — Price 3 Cents

★★★★★ FINAL

Late Bulletins

Strike Threatens Twelve Eastern Gold Mines

KIRKLAND LAKE, Ont., Aug. 11.—R. H. Carlin, secretary of the CIO Kirkland Lake Mine and Mill Workers' Union, said today the membership has instructed the executive to conduct a strike vote on Friday.

Rejecting arbitration proposals made by the Industrial Disputes Commission, the companies offered to pay a wartime cost of living bonus of $2.40 a week to full time workers and a proportionate bonus to part time workers, this bonus to be calculated on the index as of Aug. 1939 to June 1941.

The mines concerned include Lake Shore, Wright Hargreaves, Teck Hughes, Sylvanite, Bidgood, Macassa, Upper Canada, Kirkland Lake Gold, Golden Gate, Brock Mines and Toburn.

Bombers Over Berlin Again

LONDON, Aug. 11.—The Berlin Radio suddenly went off the air at 10:30 o'clock tonight, indicating another bombing of the German capital by either the Russian air force or British air squadrons.

Australia Gets Gasoline

MELBOURNE, Aug. 11.—Senator George McLeay, Minister of Suply, said today the addition of six tankers obtained during the past four weeks will give Australia an additional gasoline supply of 21,500,000 gallons.

Lord Willingdon Seriously Ill

LONDON, Aug. 11. — It was reported today that Canada's former Governor-General, Lord Willingdon, 74, reported to be seriously ill, "did not have a good day at all."

No U.S. 'Offer' to Japan

WASHINGTON, Aug. 11.—There is no basis, Secretary Cordell Hull stated today, for a report that the United States has offered a plan of settlement involving certain concessions to Japan if the Japanese will withdraw from the Axis

Weygand Not at Vichy Parley

VICHY, France, Aug. 11.—Gen. Maxime Weygand, Vichy's North African pro-consul, returned to North Africa from Vichy today without attending a cabinet meeting of the military situation in territories under his jurisdiction.

Jackie Coogan, Bridegroom, AWL

FORT ORD, Cal., Aug. 11.—Private Jackie Coogan, one-time child movie star, now in the army, failed to return on time from his weekend honeymoon today and was listed technically as AWL. He eloped Saturday with Flower Parry, 19, actress.

Plans for 'Longest Pipeline'

WASHINGTON, Aug. 11.—Petroleum Co-ordinator Ickes announced today the oil industry has submitted to him an $80,000,000 plan for the longest single type pipeline system in the world—1820 miles—which would pour 250,000 barrels of crude oil a day from the southwest into the New York area.

'Admits' He Saved Five Lives

SEATTLE, Aug. 11.—Saving two women and three children from drowning in Lake Washington was all in a day's work for Lee Eldridge, 20, who admitted bashfully today he was the unidentified hero. Eldridge, a Boeing Aircraft Company employe, had silently resumed polishing his auto after rescuing the five persons Saturday.

Offers Plant to Navy

KEARNY, N.J., Aug. 11.—The Federal Shipbuilding and Drydock Company today offered its Kearny plant to the U.S. navy "for immediate production and operation." The Kearny shipyards have been closed for four days by a strike of 14,000 members of the CIO Industrial Union of Marine and Shipbuilding Workers.

Chungking Bombed 9 Hours

CHUNGKING, China, Aug. 11.—Japanese planes kept Chungking under alarm for nine and a half consecutive hours today in what it described as the city's worst bombardment.

It is estimated 400 hostile aircraft have dropped more than 3000 bombs in the past four days.

54

Royal City AA Gunner Knocks Down Junkers

LONDON, Aug. 11.—A Canadian anti-aircraft gun crew knocked a Junkers 88 from the sky a few nights ago, it was revealed today by the Ministry of Information.

The gunners, from British Columbia, spotted the big, black plane in a searchlight beam.

Gnr. Alex Watson fired three shots, the plane showered sparks, burst into flames—then plunged into the sea off the coast.

Gnr. Alex Watson is a New Westminster boy, and a former Vancouver Sun carrier and submanager.

He is 20, the son of Mr. and Mrs. James H. Watson, 1418 Seventh Avenue, New Westminster, and one of a family of three boys and four girls.

He enlisted with the 1st Searchlights Regiment here, and transferred to the 16th Light Anti-Aircraft Battery, going overseas early this year.

Bonus for B.C. Civil Service

Periodic Defense Practise

Public Warned Notice to Be Short

Vancouver moved a long step forward in defensive preparation for war when Attorney General Gordon S. Wismer announced today that blackouts would be held periodically here starting in September.

He was unable to give a definite date for the practice blackout next month, but he was definite in his statement that there will be many trials to perfect the ARP organization and get citizens accustomed to such a situation.

The announcement was made at a conference between Mr. Wismer, Dr. W. O. Glidden, Federal ARP officer, and Inspector S. F. M. Moodie, provincial civilian protection officer.

Citizens will not get as much warning before the next blackout as they did in the first trial a few months ago, Mr. Wismer said.

SHORTER NOTICE EACH TIME

"The period of warning will be decreased with each practice blackout," Mr. Wismer said.

"That is the system which was used on the Atlantic Coast, until now there is no warning, and no one knows when the sirens are going to signal a blackout," declared Dr. Gliddon.

Mr. Wismer and Dr. Gliddon both expressed the hope that warning signals, probably sirens, would be installed in all vulnerable districts of the province before the next practice blackout gets under way.

20,000 VOLUNTEERS

Dr. Gliddon expressed satisfaction at the completeness of the ARP setup on the Pacific Coast, after hearing a report of Mr. Wismer and Inspector Moodie that practically the whole province has been organized.

"More than 20,000 volunteers are keyed into the ARP organizations throughout the province, and this number is growing rapidly," said Inspector Moodie.

Mr. Wismer said that while this effort was almost entirely voluntary there were certain expenditures which had been borne by the provincial government.

"Supplies for the training of these people have been satisfactorily arranged for by the federal government," said Mr. Wismer. "We are assured of sufficient supplies for training purposes."

Mr. Wismer also expressed satisfaction with the progress being made to arrange for compensation for ARP workers injured on duty.

"The problem has been before the Justice Department at Ottawa and it is now being considered by the Insurance Department," he said.

Bus Wage Probe

NANAIMO, Aug. 11.—A conciliation board opened hearings here today on a dispute of wages and union recognition between bus drivers of Local No. 1, National Drivers Union of Victoria, and Veterans Sightseeing and Transportation Co. Ltd. of Victoria, which operates busses here.

B.C. Girl Gets Break

Alexis Smith, tall blue-eyed blonde from Penticton, is to be built up similar to Ann Sheridan, Hollywood oomph girl. Here the 20-year-old starlet is seen weighing a summer outfit she usually wears. The whole outfit weighs 15 ounces.

Penticton Starlet Hollywood Oomph Girl

A British Columbia starlet is to become a Hollywood oomph girl.

Tall, blonde, befreckled Alexis Smith, 20, who only a year ago was playing small parts in the films, will be given a build-up similar to that given Ann Sheridan, original oomph girl, by Warner Brothers Studio, according to advices here from Hollywood.

Alexis, born in Penticton, was scouted for the films while in a play at Los Angeles City College and has been under contract since last October with Warner Brothers, playing bit parts.

Recently she played her first lead opposite Errol Flynn and Fred MacMurray.

The studio said the comment on Alexis was encouraging enough for a big-time campaign.

Now all it needs is a slogan.

"No name-change," says Alexis. "I'm named for my daddy, Alexander. As for Smith, it's good enough for me, even if it wasn't for Mary Pickford."

Alexis' career has been phenominal.

At 10, she was accounted an exceptionally good pianist at 11, she had added dancing and singing to her repertoire; at 13, she was dancing in the Hollywood Bowl; at 16, she won a California State declamation contest for doing a scene from "Elizabeth the Queen"; at 17, she was a co-ed at Los Angeles City College, where she majored in drama.

Please Turn to Page Two
See "Starlet"

Ottawa Action Awaited

City Hall May Also Make Cost of Living 'Boost'

By Sun Staff Reporter

VICTORIA, Aug. 11. — Attitude of the provincial government toward granting a cost of living bonus to civil servants will be considered this week, it is expected in sources close to the cabinet.

The B. C. cabinet, it was learned, has been withholding its decision on the question until Ottawa acted.

In view of the federal government's plan to grant the bonuses the way is now clear for provincial action.

When the bonus proposal was first raised some weeks ago it was given consideration here but action was delayed after communication with Ottawa.

The government was not anxious to make wage increases that could be taken as leading an inflationary trend.

The government here has been keeping a close month-to-month tab on the cost of living and the indexes for British Columbia show that costs may be mounting here slightly faster than the national average.

When details of Ottawa's bonus plan are received here the province is expected to follow suit.

Serious consideration is being given by civic authorities to a cost of living bonus for civic employees, **The Vancouver Sun** learned at City Hall today.

Authorities revealed that data is being accumulated on the subject and action can be expected in the very near future.

Mayor Cornett, who was queried on the matter, stated he could make no statement at present, but he agreed that some action is contemplated.

Kenney, Liberal Choice in Skeena

TERRACE, Aug. 11. — E. T. Kenney, M.L.A., was nominated Liberal candidate for Skeena riding at a Skeena District Liberal Association nomination convention here today.

Resolutions, urging that the highway construction be continued east of here and that a landing wharf be constructed at Kalum Lake, were adopted.

J. L. McEwen was elected president and K. Warner, secretary.

BASEBALL

ST. LOUIS, Aug. 11.—Enos Slaughter, St. Louis Cardinal outfielder, has a broken clavicle and will be out for the rest of the season. Slaughter ran into a wall in a game at Pittsburgh yesterday.

AMERICAN

Boston .... 001 600 100—8 15 1
New York .. 000 000 000—0 4 1
Wilson and Peacock; Breuer, Stanceu (4) and Dickey.

St. Louis .... 100 200 501— 9 14 2
Chicago .... 301 002 26x—14 14 1
Auker, Trotter (7), Newlin (8) and Swift; Rigney, Hallett (7), Appleton (9) and Resh.

Cleveland-Detroit, postponed; rain.

NATIONAL

New York .. 000 002 005— 7 7 1
Brooklyn ... 700 116 00x—15 17 2
Carpenter, Bowman (1), Adams (7) and Danning; Higbe and Owen.

Philadelphia .. 040 000 110—6 15 1
Boston .... 000 100 200—3 9 3
Beck and Warren; Lamanna, Hutchings (2), Proedel (8) and Berres, Montgomery.

Tension in Far East Growing

Australia Defies Japanese Early Fear of War With U.S. Holding Back Tokyo

By Canadian Press

LONDON, Aug. 11.—A sudden, critical turn in the Far East situation was reported from Australia today and from informed quarters in London, from Chinese diplomats and Australian and New Zealand sources, it was evident that all eyes are turned on Washington.

Expectation is widespread that Japan intends to disregard last week's warnings by United States Secretary of State Cordell Hull, and Foreign Secretary Anthony Eden, and perhaps embark upon moves north and south in a grandiose joint plan of German and Japanese strategy aimed at seizing all the strategic points dominating the world's oceans.

But Japan is delaying hoping to learn that U.S. will not fight in any contingency.

It is clear that Britain is clinging to a policy of defense of British interests in the Far East with respect to Japan. Informed sources say it is evident that when Britain acts it will be jointly or on parallel lines with United States measures which, it is predicted, will go beyond the present economic blockade of Tokyo.

In Australia, always a sensitive barometer to Far East developments, Prime Minister Robert Menzies described the situation as "grave."

He declared flatly that Australia would fight with all the forces at her command any attempt by Japan to advance upon Singapore.

He suddenly cancelled a tour of the western part of the Dominion and returned to Melbourne for a special full meeting of the Cabinet today.

Please Turn to Page Two See "Japan"

'Developments' Expected

By Associated Press

LONDON, Aug. 11.—Reuters News Agency reported tonight from Tokyo that "important developments" were expected there shortly.

The agency did not say what was expected, but linked the expectation to a return to the city of United States Ambassador Joseph C. Grew and British Ambassador Sir Robert Leslie Craigie.

It was not said where the envoys had been, but it is likely that both had been away from Tokyo for a long week-end.

'Met at Sea,' Says Paris

'Churchill, F.D.R. Decide on Far East'

LONDON, Aug. 11. — Prime Minister Churchill and President Roosevelt have reached a decision regarding Anglo-American action in the Far East crisis after a long conference aboard the Presidential yacht Potomac, the Nazi-controlled Paris radio announced Sunday night.

The decision regarding action against Japan will be announced Monday, the Paris station predicted.

It asserted the conference aboard the Potomac, on the high seas off the American Atlantic Coast, was attended by the chiefs of the American army and navy.

Adding fuel to the speculative fires was today's announcement that the freedom of Portsmouth had been conferred "in absentia" on Mr. Churchill and Harry Hopkins, Mr. Roosevelt's lend-lease administration. Mr. Hopkins is reported to be "in" on the Churchill-Roosevelt conferences, wherever they are being held.

(Columbia Broadcasting System reported in New York Sunday that its London correspondent, Ed. Murrow, stated during his regular broadcast that Americans "would know more Thursday" about Britain getting outside aid.

AIR ARMY TAKES IRAN OIL FIELDS

The Weather
A disturbance giving general light to moderate rains over southern British Columbia, elsewhere it has been partly cloudy and mild.
Temperature at 10 a.m. today: 60.
Temperature during 24 hours ending 4:30 a.m. today: maximum 62, minimum 57.
Forecast: cloudy and mild.
Official weather report on page 22.

The Vancouver Sun
Only Evening Newspaper Owned, Controlled and Operated by Vancouver People

Today's Tides
Vancouver Harbor
Low 3:11 p.m. 4.0 feet High 8:52 p.m. 12.6 feet
English Bay
Low 2:46 p.m. 4.8 feet High 9:09 p.m. 12.9 feet
First Narrows
Low slack .. 3:44 p.m. High slack .. 9:37 p.m.
Tomorrow's tides appear on page 22.

FOUNDED 1886
VOL. LV.—No. 260
VANCOUVER, BRITISH COLUMBIA, TUESDAY, AUGUST 26, 1941
Price 3 Cents
On trains, boats and outside Greater Vancouver, 5c
MArine 1161

FRENCH REBEL PARLIAMENT MEETS

Deputies Organize to Fight Vichy

Today In Britain

War events analyzed by Fleet Street writers, cabled from the London Bureau of The Vancouver Sun.
(Copyright, 1941)

LONDON, Aug. 26.—Attention is called by The London Economist to the notable rise of high-grade securities on this market. The British Government's 2½ per cent consol, for instance, which had brought 68⅜ at the end of 1939 and 76⅞ at the end of 1940, had risen last month to 82½.

The average price of 20 typical fixed-interest securities, which stood at 120½ a year before, last month reached 130.

Considering that, on the average British Commodity prices have advanced one-half since outbreak of the war, this strength in securities whose interest rate remains unchanged was at least contrary to what the familiar traditions of "inflation" might suggest. It is not the less so from the fact that London's average of industrial shares is practically the same as it was at the beginning of the war.

In both London and New York the course of the market has been determined by the very low rate of interest, the wish for safe investment, and by the accumulation of capital.

* * *

London Rolls On

An American visitor finds the war's effect on the British capital very slight. He says: "This is my first trip since the outbreak of war and I am struck by the comparatively small amount of damage done by the German air force in its bombing raids that at times continued for periods of 10 to 11 hours. There are damaged buildings in London. Many of them. But there are many hundreds standing untouched to every one in ruins.

"The changes you notice first are the numbers of men and women in uniform and great

Please Turn to Page Two
See "Britain Today"

Markets on Page 2

Sabotage Wreck Injures 12 in Cherbourg Area

Special to The Vancouver Sun
Copyright, 1941, by United Press

VICHY, France, Aug. 26.—More than 100 Members of Parliament have met here and formed themselves into an opposition to the regime of Marshal Henri Philippe Petain, it was disclosed today.

Disclosure of this new organized opposition to the Vichy regime coincided with revelation that 12 passengers were injured in a new railway accident in occupied France, suspected to have resulted from sabotage.

An autorail and a freight train collided at the Carneville station at Cherbourg.

French Hatred of Boche Increasing

By Canadian Press

LONDON, Aug. 26.—Hatred of the Germans is developing rapidly in Paris where living conditions are becoming "more lamentable," a French journalist, who has arrived in Britian to join the Free French forces, said in an interview.

The journalist, who rejected "alluring" offers from the Nazi-controlled French press, described long queues trying to buy food and incidents which resulted in the Germans opening theatres and restaurants for their own use.

Summing up the conditions in the capital, he said:

"The situation — conditions of life, food and transport, is becoming more difficult and lamentable every day. God knows what it will be like next winter.

"The Nazis are becoming more and more detested. As the enemy's occupation goes on and the Parisians see the Boche installing himself everywhere, taking command of everything, anti-German hatred is developing and disgust growing among the population.

"You should have seen the scenes in cafes whenever the sirens sounded an alert as RAF bombers were approaching airdromes in the Paris region. There were broad smiles on Parisians' faces, followed by explosions of delight: 'Good!' . . . 'Bravo!' . . . 'Capital!' . . . The English are going to give us some entertainment.

Rains Aid Russian Defense

Moscow Admits Novogorod Lost To Invaders

MOSCOW, Aug. 26. — Red Army forces, in a savage counter-offensive on the central front, were reported today o have formed and recaptured street-by-street a large ancient city in White Russia (probably Gomel) that had been in German hands five days.

MOSCOW, Aug. 26.—Total destruction of a Rumanian division and defeat for two others outside the besieged Black Sea port of Odessa was reported in Soviet front dispatches today.

(Meanwhile German emphasis on a new big scale attack of the air force against Russian positions all along the front was taken to indicate today that a combination of bad weather and Russian resistance might have slowed the German drives against Leningrad and the Russian Dnieper River line. Heavy rains are making quagmires of the fighting fronts.)

Reports of the Odessa fighting came as an official communique announced that Marshal Semyon Timoshenko had withdrawn his armies from Novgorod, 100 miles south of Leningrad, a battle for which was growing increasingly furious.

Novgorod, a city north of Lake Ilmen, was given up only after days of desperate Russian resistance, the early morning communique said.

A heavy rain is reported along the front. Dispatches said the downpour had been incessant for the last 24 hours.

If it continues, the rain is expected by the Russians to have a tremendous effect on all or many parts of the front. Roads other than main routes are bogged.

More rain would make the soft soil of the Ukraine and the marshy country around Leningrad impassable for tanks.

Red Army Finds Cure for Blitz

By PRESTON GROVER
Associated Press Staff Writer

ANKARA, Aug. 26.—The Russians have failed to halt the German drive, but they have taken the sting out of Hitler's rapier-like armored thrusts, a military source in direct touch with the Soviet front disclosed today.

He said the Germans started off their invasion by sending tanks and motorized troops far through the Red Army lines, leaving the infantry to trail along afterwards — just as they did in France.

But where it worked well in the West it failed in the East and the Nazis have had to revise quickly their offensive tactics.

The Russians carefully followed every phase of the invasion of France and when the Germans came their way they had a solution.

They would let the tanks through, but then would throw masses of their own infantry at the oncoming Germans, something the French could not do because of the disorganization caused by the Germans behind their lines.

The German tanks which tore the Soviet lines still were too tough to handle by day, but the Russians got them by night, blasting them with guns brought up under cover of darkness in hit-and-run fashion.

War's Newest Battleground

Iran, fabled land of the Medes and Persians, is the newest world war battleground, following its invasion by British and Russian forces, with the avowed intention of driving out German fifth columnists. Above are two types of Iranian soldiers, one in modern uniform and the other representing the old army. Below is a scene near the oilfields, where British air-borne troops represented by the Anglo-Iranian Oil Company have landed today. British financial interests dominate the fields. The troops are said to have been flown in for the protection of British workers and their families.

7 Hun Ships Captured in Bandar Port

Teheran Police Order Ousting Some Germans Hints at Iranian Hopes Of Settlement With Allies

Special to The Vancouver Sun
Copyright, 1941, by British United Press

LONDON, Aug. 26.—British Indian troops, striking in blitzkrieg tempo into western Iran, have captured the port of Bandar Shahpur with seven Axis ships, and the important oil station of Naft-i-Shah, while British air borne troops occupied the oil fields to protect British families, it was announced today.

British troops met resistance at Abadan, near Bandar Shahpur, and in the Naft-I-Shah and Asr-I-Shirin areas, it was admitted authoritatively, and the British forces continue to meet slight resistance everywhere during their advance.

(An indication that the Iranian government might seek an understanding with Britain and Russia came today in the issuance by Teheran police of orders to 16 small, obscure German businessmen to get out of Iran within a fortnight.)

Russian troops, moving down the towering mountains from Armenia in a rapid sweep, are nearing Tabriz., Iran's second city.

Gen. Wavell in Command

There is no immediate intention of effecting a juncture with the Russian forces as the prime object is swift efficient consolidation of positions allotted in advance.

Britain's first communique of the Iran campaign, disclosing a dramatic landing byq British air borne troops in the oil fields where the families of employees of the Anglo-Iranian Oil Co. had been isolated, came from headquarters of Gen. Sir Archibald Wavell, Commander-in-Chief in India and of the British part of the Iran campaign, at Simla.

(At Simla it was reported that British troops had also occupied Abadan, site of one of the world's three biggest oil refineries.)

Pamphlets Advise Iranians

The British used naval ships, airplanes, infantry and motorized troops in addition to air borne troops, moving in from three points.

As they did, British planes flew over Teheran and other Iranian towns, dropping leaflets explaining the reasons for the invasion and emphasizing that Britain had no quarrel with the Iranian people and no designs on their independence or territory, the communique said.

German and Italian reports said British planes had bombed Teheran and other towns. Berlin and Rome reported also a Russian raid on Tabriz.

Though it was admitted that the Iranians were resisting, Gen. Wavell's communique said the British operations had proceeded with such rapidity that only minimum losses had been suffered by Iranian troops.

'I'd Like to See Them In'

Beaverbrook Says U.S. War Work in Full Swing

LONDON, Aug. 26. — Lord Beaverbrook, Minister of Supply, who has just returned from conferences in Washington, declared today that United States is in full swing of production and that there had been no slowdown since Germany invaded Russia.

Asked at a press conference if United States is near to entry into the war, Lord Beaverbrook replied that such a decision is the business of the people of United States.

"What do you think?" reporters persisted.

"I'd like to see them in," he said, lifting his voice.

Then, repeating this statement, he said:

"It's nobody's business other than citizens of United States, but if I am not to be hypocritical I'd like to see them in now."

He commented that there was no need for tank modernization in United States.

"They have fine light tanks in the M-3," he said, adding that U.S. tanks are arriving in Britain "in considerable numbers."

35,000 Tonners for Navy

HMS Duke of York Ready for Service

By Canadian Press

LONDON, Aug. 26.—Britain's latest battleship, HMS Duke of York, launched by the Queen last year, was reported today as ready to take her place with the fleet. Shipyard men working night and day shifts have completed the 35,000-ton battleship, sistership of HMS King George V and HMS Prince of Wales.

Rt. Hon. A. V. Alexander, First Lord of the Admiralty, recently inspected HMS Duke of York.

Naval sources which refused to confirm or deny that the Duke of York is actually ready for action, also would not comment on the present stage of construction of HMS Jellicoe and HMS Beatty, the other battleships of the King George V. class of five ships all laid down in 1937.

There has been no authoritative information of progress of the Lion class of four ships of around 40,000 tons each, which were laid down in 1939 and originally scheduled for completion in 1943.

Today's Scratches At Hastings Park

Weather Cloudy
Track Muddy

First race—Streamline, Broderick, Leba Trebor, Ascot Maid.

Second race—Bubbling Lake, Dark Hands, Pharima, Mathison.

Third race—First Vee, Hill Wind, Miss Hominy, Bill's Rose.

Fourth race — Streakworth, Chief Richie.

Sixth race—Dr. Pook, MacPhalaris.

Seventh race is out.

Firsts Sub becomes the seventh—Cisco Kid, Tangle Tim, Little Gloomy, Arabian Love.

(Sun Handicap and Selections Page 14.)

Australian Crisis

Gov't-Labor Deadlock on Premiership

By Canadian Press

CANBERRA, Aug. 26.—The Menzies cabinet today rejected a Labor Party demand that it resign. An official statement to that effect was issued after Prime Minister R. G. Menzies and his colleagues held a five-hour cabinet meeting.

The cabinet meeting was called shortly after a Labor caucus rejected Mr. Menzies invitation to Labor to join in a national government.

Labor, instead, demanded the way for a Labor government.

The Labor caucus had deliberated only a few minutes, early today, before unanimously rejecting the suggestion of an all-party government with Mr. Menzies at its head.

In a letter to the prime minister, John Curtin, Labor leader, suggested the resignation on the ground that Mr. Menzies was "unable to provide any longer stability of government and effective leadership of the nation."

RAF Daylight Raids Follow Rhine Attack

By Canadian Press

LONDON, Aug. 26.—A Royal Air Force fighter squadron, diving over the white cliffs of Dover to skim at times just above the sea, roared toward the French coast today as a follow-up to overnight raids on Germany.

Principal objectives of the bomber raid overnight were the industrial centres of Mannheim and Karlsruhe in the Rhineland.

The air ministry said that despite unfavorable weather there were clear intervals over the target areas and large fires were observed as the bombers turned home after dropping huge explosives. Six British planes were lost.

(Nazi sources in Berlin admitted fires were started by British planes raiding southwestern Germany during the night.)

Nazi aerial activity over the British Isles continued on a small scale. No casualties were suffered when bombs dropped at two points on the coast of South Wales and at one point in southwest England.

The Admiralty reported today British torpedo-carrying seaplanes have attacked "military objectives north and south of Tempio on the island of Sardinia, starting large fires. One Nazi plane was shot down into the sea.

The date of the attack was not given.

Three RAF Spitfires on a strafing raid caused a violent explosion by spraying a wireless station near Cherbourg with machine-gun and cannon fire last night, the air ministry said.

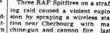

RUDOLF HESS ON HUNGER STRIKE

FINAL

The Vancouver Sun

Only Evening Newspaper Owned, Controlled and Operated by Vancouver People

FOUNDED 1886 VOL. LV.—No. 309 VANCOUVER, B.C., TUESDAY, SEPTEMBER 30, 1941 Price 3 Cents On trains, boats and outside Greater Vancouver, 5c

Insists He's Not Prisoner

Parachute Visitor From Germany Terms Himself 'Special Envoy'; Demands Release to Return to Nazis

By Canadian Press

LONDON, Sept. 30.—Rudolph Hess, Hitler's former deputy who made a sensational flight to Scotland last April, was reported tonight to have started hunger strikes twice in his place of detention in anger because he was being treated as a prisoner of war and not as a "special envoy."

The Star, London evening newspaper, reporting that Hess was being confined "within a very easy distance of London," said he was contending that as an "envoy" he should be allowed to return to Germany at once.

When Hess, then the No. 3 Nazi, flew to Scotland alone early in May in one of the most sensational episodes of the entire war he was reported widely to have brought peace overtures from Hitler.

The Star implied that Hess now is living in comfortable quarters, saying:

"Some of our very senior officers who have been captured by the enemy now occupy decent villas. Has Hess a villa or something better suited to his higher rank?"

Government officials, who have been silent regarding Hess since his spectacular landing nearly five months ago, declined to comment on the Star story.

B.C. Offers To Build 200 Wooden Vessels

2-Year Plan by 15 Firms

Delegates Will Lay Proposals Before Ottawa

By DON MASON

A two-year plan to build 150 to 200 sea-going wooden cargo ships in enlarged existing yards in Burrard Inlet, Coal Harbor, False Creek and on the Fraser River, or in new yards, will be placed before Ottawa next week by two well-known local boat builders.

The two men who will go to Ottawa—Arthur Mercer of the Star Shipyard (Mercers) Ltd., New Westminster, and Gilbert Jukes of Vancouver Shipyard, Coal Harbor—will represent 15 Greater Vancouver and Royal City wooden boat builders who are interested in the scheme.

They will leave for Ottawa at the end of this week, or at the latest next Monday.

Cost of the eastern expedition is to be defrayed by the 15 interested boat builders and by jobbing firms who would construct auxiliary equipment for wooden cargo ships to be built here.

The wooden ships would be an all-B.C. product. Engines and auxiliary parts would be built by British Columbia plants as far as possible.

FIRST JOINT EFFORT

The plan, is to build, in record-breaking time, wooden cargo ships of 3000 deadweight tons, to supplement Canada's already

Please Turn to Page Two
See "B. C. Ships"

Churchill Says Sea Losses Cut

Germans Facing Shortage in Air; Hitler's Plans Mystery But Britons Are Alert

LONDON, Sept. 30. — An authoritative source, discussing Prime Minister Churchill's references today to the possibility of invasion of the Continent, said the Germans were maintaining 26 divisions in France against just such an eventuality and that a land attack now by the British army "would do Russia no good and might result in another Dunkirk."

By FREDERICK KUH
Special to The Vancouver Sun
Copyright, 1941, by British United Press

LONDON, Sept. 30. — Great Britain, fighting "in intimate concert" with America and Russia, has cut losses in the Battle of the Atlantic by two-thirds since July but must face the possibility that Germany will launch an all-out offensive against the Suez Canal, through Spain against North Africa and against the British Isles, Prime Minister Winston Churchill said today. (Text of speech on page 9.)

But, he emphasized, "Hitler is facing a serious shortage in the air" and Britain has seized the initiative in this form of warfare.

Referring to the current heavy air attacks on Italian cities, Mr. Churchill said the RAF would not hesitate to bomb Rome itself if the needs of war so dictate.

Great Britain and United States, Mr. Churchill told the House of Commons, must make the utmost sacrifices and exercise the greatest effort to increase the flow of war aid already started to the Soviet Union.

The question of a British invasion of Europe to relieve the Red Army has been considered but not settled.

"We are in complete ignorance of what Hitler is going to do," the Prime Minister explained in reference to failure of the British invade the Continent at present.

Mr. Churchill, the prime minister, painted the brightest picture that he had been able to give the British people since Dunkirk, but he tempered this with emphasis on the danger of "all out" German blows in new directions in the coming months.

CHIEF POINTS

In the course of his speech, Mr. Churchill said:

1. British shipping losses in the Battle of the Atlantic were reduced in July, August and September to one-third of the total of the previous three months, and Britain (aided by the American patrol system) is confident that the expected intensification of U-boat warfare can be defeated. Axis sea losses have been increased 150 percent in the last three months.
2. Britain will not hesitate to bomb Rome if the needs of war dictate such action.
3. The United States war effort has achieved "majestc momentum" with the upward surge in American shipbuilding to keep supplies flowing to the foes of the Axis and materials already are pouring into Russia to aid in maintaining the "valiant" resistance of the Red Army.
4. Germany's "only shortage is in the air" but it is a very serious shortage although Hitler still clings to the initiative in the war.
5. A new alliance will soon be announced of Britain, Russia and Iran, probably making Iran—key Near East kingdom on the supply route to the Soviet Union—an active ally.

Liberal May Be Out; Papers Filed Late?

(See Also Page Two)

Ezra C. Henniger, former Liberal member of the B. C. Legislature, was 15 minutes late today in filing nominations papers as a candidate in the Grand Forks-Greenwood riding, The **Vancouver Sun** was informed this afternoon by T. A. Love, the Conservative candidate, by long distance telephone from Grand Forks.

Mr. Love, who is president of the B.C. Conservative Association, said according to the elections Act, Mr. Henniger is disqualified.

He added, however, that the returning officer for the riding is consulting P. Walker, the deputy provincial secretary, at Victoria, before rendering a decision.

Disqualification of Mr. Henniger leaves Mr. Love and Alan Clapp, C.C.F. nominee, in a two-party fight.

Only C.C.F. Will Oppose Pattullo

PRINCE RUPERT, B.C., Sept. 30.—G. W. Weaver, C.C.F., will be Premier T. D. Pattullo's only opponent in Prince Rupert Riding in the October 21 provincial general election.

The nomination papers of Edward V. Ling, Independent, Vancouver, were rejected by the returning officer because they were insufficiently signed.

B.C. LADS GRADUATE

MACDONALD, Man., Sept. 3.—Latest group of wireless air gunners and air observers to receive flying badges at No. 3 bombing and gunnery school here were announced Monday. The graduates included Thomas C. Brayshaw, Vernon, B.C., and A. M. Hill, Lynn Creek, B.C.

Medal Sought For MacKay

A proposal to recommend Donald MacKay, M.M., for the King's Police Medal, as well as to re-employ him as chief of the Vancouver Police Department, will be considered by the Police Commission at a special meeting to be called late this week by Mayor Cornett.

It was learned at City Hall today that tentative negotiations have already been conducted with the idea of obtaining Imperial recognition of Mr. MacKay's service to the city over the past 35 years.

Those supporting the proposal point out that the King's Medal may be conferred, among other things, for the following reasons:

1. **"A specially distinguished record and administrative or detective service or other police service of conspicuous merit."**
2. **"Prolonged service, but only when distinguished by exceptional ability or merit."**

Mr. MacKay's career conforms with these qualifications, his associates state.

The medal was awarded in 1923 to former Fire Chief J. H. Carlyle (firemen are also eligible).

The only other local recipient is Constable Donald Maxwell, who received it Sept. 13, 1940, for conspicuous bravery in the disarming and capture of two bandits, who held up a branch of the Canadian Bank of Commerce in 1938.

Jap Parachute Attack Smashed

CHUGNKING, Sept. 30.—The Japanese army landed a small detachment of parachute troops yesterday at Chuchow, important rail junction 30 miles south of bitterly-contested Changsha, but all were either killed or driven away, a Chinese military authority declared today.

Chinese Recapture Tungsten Centre

HONG KONG, Sept. 30.—Chinese field dispatches announced today the recapture of Toishan, tungsten-producing railroad city in Kwangtung province, which the Japanese entered a week ago, and three towns north-west of it. Toishan is 30 miles south-west of Canton and 60 miles by airline west of Hong Kong.

Britain Boosts Allowances to Men in Service

By Canadian Press

LONDON, Sept. 30. — Increased family allowances will be granted British army, air force and navy officers. They will apply Jan. 1, 1942. For army officers the new rates will be the equivalent of 96 cents a day for a wife, $1.54 for a wife and one child and $1.80 for a wife and two children. For each additional child the allowance is 24 cents a day.

Meanwhile family allowances for Britons are sought in a motion supported by 45 members of Parliament.

The motion recommands the establishment of allowances for dependent children as a means of "safeguarding the health and well-being of the rising generation."

Nova Gets Mere $71,765

(See also page 12.)

NEW YORK, Sept. 30.—Joe Louis ran his total ring earnings to over $2,000,000 with the $193,274 he received for knocking out Lou Nova in the sixth round last night at the Polo Grounds in the nineteenth defense of his heavyweight boxing title.

Louis' share was 40 per cent of the gate which grossed $583,821 and netted $499,300, according to the official figures announced today by Promoter Mike Jacobs.

Nova's 17 per cent gave him $71,765 as salve for his wounds.

The attendance was 56,549: the federal tax $55,457 and the state tax $29,312.

Royal City Fiier Wins Air Force Cross

LONDON, Sept. 30.—Flt. Lt. F. E. W. Birchfield of New Westminster, B.C., a Royal Air Force flying instructor, today was awarded the Air Force Cross.

Although this officer's duties are not operational, they are of vital importance in building up the Air Force from strength to strength, the air ministry said in announcing the award.

Late Stocks on Page 2

Race Results at Belmont

NEW YORK

FIRST RACE—Seven furlongs:
b-Betty's Broom (C. Bierman) $30.20, $11.70, $7.50.
Okabbit (McCreary) $8.70, $6.40.
Purling Light (Strickler) $3.90.
Time, 1.26 2-5.

SECOND RACE—Six furlongs:
Rascal (Donoso) $11.90, $6.80, $4.
Bardia (Westrope) $20.90, $7.40.
Fire Warden (Eads) $3.10.
Time, 1.12 1-5.

THIRD RACE—Six furlongs:
Pet (Skelly) $28, $17.70, $8.40.
General Jack (Hildebrand) $9.50, $5.90.
Poppa Deets (Schmidl) $9.70.
Time, 1.12 3-5.

FOURTH RACE—One mile:
Bright Willie (C. Bierman) $3.80, $3, $2.60.
Blue Gino (Eads) $5.20, $3.40.
Liste (Wall) $3.60.
Time, 1.37 2-5.

FIFTH RACE—Six furlongs:
Overdrawn (Coule) $7.50, $3.80, $3.10.
Speed to Spare (Wall) $3.10, $2.60.
Victory Morn (McCreary) $6.30.
Time, 1.11 1-5.

SIXTH RACE—Mile and one-half furlongs:
Up The Hill (McCreary) $5.60, $3.50, $2.70.
Dark Discovery (Madden) $12.20, $5.40.
Pretty Pet (Schmidl) $4.
Time 2:30.

SEVENTH RACE—Mile and one-eighth:
Count Happy (Day) $4.40, $2.70, $2.50.
Darby Du (James) $4.10, $3.40.
Brown Bomb (Wright) $4.50.
Time: 1:52 1-5.

Race Entries on Page 10

Dorothy Thompson Says Today:

". . . we didn't make America by avoiding war. We made it by raising the emblem of the rattlesnake and the cry, 'Don't step on me!'"

Read her stimulating article on page 1 today.

Board Splits On Pardon for Valtin

SAN FRANCISCO, Sept. 30.—Jan Valtin, who wrote the best seller, "Out of the Night," was denied a pardon today by the State Advisory Pardon Board.

Valtin, 36, under his true name of Richard Krebs, acting as a Communist, was convicted in 1926 of assault with a deadly weapon in Los Angeles, and was sentenced to 10 years. He was released in 1929 and deported, but recently re-entered this country illegally.

He attacked Communist and Nazi activities in his book, and told of amazing tortures at the hands of the Nazis.

The Advisory Board voted two-to-two against pardon. Gov. Culbert L. Olson may grant a pardon or refuse one.

LONDON, Sept. 30. — Vast smoke screens extending for many miles were reported Monday night to be in use in Britain to protect industrial centres from air attack.

Sets of smoke-producing apparatus manned by soldiers were said to have been set up all over the country.

Race Results at Hawthorne

ILLINOIS

FIRST RACE—Six furlongs:
Some Ad (Thompson) $21, $7, $6.20.
Lochness (Lowe) $3.80, $2.80.
Gin Call (McAndrews) $5.60.
Time, 1.15 2-5.

SECOND RACE—Mile and one-sixteenth:
Catechism (Wellander) $44.80, $15.80, $6.40.
Chosen Time (Robertson) $5.80, $4.
Chance Kay (Haskell) $3.60.
Time, 1.49 2-5.

THIRD RACE—Six furlongs:
Illinois Tom (Robertson) $11.60, $5.40, $3.20.
Silent Host (Garner) $4.80, $3.20.
Bar Thirteen (Cruickshanks) $3.
Time, 1:14.

FOURTH RACE—Six and one-half furlongs:
De Kals (Phillips) $17.20, $6, $3.20.
Sir Kid (McAndrews) $3.40, $2.40.
Remote Control (Cruickshanks) $2.60.
Time, 1.18 4-5.

FIFTH RACE—Six furlongs:
Black Flame (Cruickshanks) $16.20, $8.60, $4.40.
Camfin (Gellespie) $10.40, $4.80.
Grand Central (Berger) $3.80.
Time, 1.13 4-5.

SIXTH RACE—One mile:
Heartman (Wellander) $4, $2.80, $2.20.
Smacked (Richards) $3, $2.40.
Shaun G. (McAndrews) $2.60.
Time 1:40.

SEVENTH RACE—One mile:
Uncle Walter (Brooks) $6.80, $4.40, $3.00.
Dissension Sir (Cruickshanks) $9.60, $5.20.
Syl's Betty (Berger) $2.80.
Time 1:13 1-5.

EIGHTH RACE—Mile and one-sixteenth:
Radio Wave (Wellander) $10.80, $7.40, $6.20.
Rough Diamond (Cruickshanks) $13.60, $8.20.
Nanita (Berger) $8.00.
Time: 1:48 1-5.

Late Bulletins

Three Axis Ships Hit In RAF Channel Raid

LONDON, Sept. 30.—The Air Ministry reported tonight that three Axis ships were attacked off the French and Norwegian Coasts in British air sweeps today.

More Troops at Singapore

SINGAPORE, Sept. 30.—A large number of British troops direct from the United Kingdom arrived today.

Hurricane Levels Town

MANGUA, Nicaragua, Sept. 30. — Official reports said today that a hurricane has levelled every building in the town of Cape Grace.

Outlaw Strikes Keep 30,000 Idle

DETROIT, Sept. 30. — Unauthorized departmental strikes kept approximately 30,000 auto workers at the Chrysler Corporation's Dodge and Plymouth divisions idle today.

New British Pact With Turkey

ISTANBUL, Sept. 30. — A new British-Turkish agreement under which Britain will purchase about $3,000,000 worth of Turkish food products was announced today.

Turkey Calls Ministers

ANKARA, Sept. 29. — Turkish ministers to four Axis powers—Germany, Italy, Rumania and Bulgaria—either are in the Turkish capital or are on their way here for conferences.

Tail Lights for Horses

DENVER, Sept. 30.—Tail lights for horses were decreed today by the Colorado Department of Revenue. The new regulation applies to all horses on Colorado highways or streets.

More Social Security

WASHINGTON, Sept. 30.—President Roosevelt announced today that he plans to ask Congress soon to extend the social security program to give protection to twice as many workers as now are covered.

3000 More Italians Captured

NAIROBI, East Africa., Sept. 30.—British military headquarters for East Africa today reported continuing activity against remnants of the Italian army in Ethiopia. The Italian Commander at Uolchefit and his 3000 men are now in captivity.

No Talks With Italy

WASHINGTON, Sept. 30.—Secretary of State Cordell Hull said today he knew of no political conversations between the U.S. and Italy. He has been asked about recent reports that Italy might seek U.S. assistance to break away from the Axis.

Books for Soldiers

OTTAWA, Sept. 30.—Postmaster General Mulock announced today that in the interest of soldiers, sailors and airmen stationed in Canada and Newfoundland all Canadian post offices will accept books for soldiers, not stamped or addressed.

Poles Fight for Russians

WASHINGTON, Sept. 30.—Two divisions of Polish troops already fighting for Russia against Germany and the number may soon be increased to 100,000 soldiers, it was revealed today in a letter released by the State Department.

Charge Against Chief

BOWMANVILLE, Ont., Sept. 30.—Crown Attorney Harry Deyman said today he had authorized Provincial Constable W. F. Thompson to lay a charge of dangerous driving against Chief Constable D. C. Draper of Toronto whose auto was involved in a head-on collision Sunday.

War Prisoner Released

LONDON, Sept. 30.—Sir Lancelot Oliphant, former British ambassador to Belgium who was captured when the Germans overran that country in May, 1940, arrived in England from Lisbon today. He was one of several diplomats involved in a recent exchange of British and German prisoners.

Want $10,000 Job?

EDMONTON, Sept. 30.—Owing to war demands for engineers and technically trained men, the Alberta government is having difficulty in filling a $10,000 job, it was disclosed today by Hon. N. E. Tanner, Minister of Lands and Mines. The post is that of chairman of the Provincial Petroleum and Natural Gas Conservation Board.

Passengers Rescued

EDMONTON, Sept. 30.—Two United Air Services Ltd. pilots were winging their way south from Aklavik, N.W.T., today with 27 passengers off S.S. Distributor which, according to reports reaching Edmonton, will be "frozen up" in the far northern point unable to come south due to low water in the Mackenzie river.

Coming in The Sun—

Berlin Diary!

The most talked-of book today.
The book everyone wants to read.
Edwin L. Shirer, famous as commentator from Berlin to the Columbia network, came home to write this amazing expose.
The Vancouver Sun has secured exclusive rights to BERLIN DIARY in this territory.
It will appear daily in this newspaper starting soon.
Watch for further announcements.

DESPERATE SORTIE BY SOVIETS EASES MOSCOW PRESSURE

BLUE STREAK ★★★★★ FINAL

THE VANCOUVER DAILY PROVINCE

47th YEAR—NO. 180 VANCOUVER, B.C., MONDAY, OCTOBER 27, 1941—26 PAGES PRICE 3 CENTS On trains, boats and in the country, Five Cents

F.D.R. DEFIED BY LEWIS ON MINE STRIKE

WASHINGTON, Oct. 27.—(AP) — President Roosevelt made a third appeal late today to John L. Lewis, president of the United Mine Workers' Union, for a resumption of operations at the captive coal mines.

WASHINGTON, Oct. 27. — John L. Lewis rejected today for the second time a request by President Roosevelt to order 53,000 miners back to work in the captive coal mines.

In a letter to the President, replying to Mr. Roosevelt's request that the strikers go back to work in the interests of national defense, Lewis said that defense output in the mines was not impaired and would not be impaired for an indefinite period.

"This fight," said the United Mine Workers' president, "is only between a labor union and a ruthless corporation — the United States Steel Corporation."

FEARS A.E.F. IS NEXT STEP

WASHINGTON, Oct. 27.—(AP)—Senator Arthur Vandenberg denounced the bill to revise the Neutrality Act today as a "disingenuous preface to . . . a two-ocean shooting war."

Vandenberg predicted the first American ship carrying an American crew and an American cargo through a European combat zone would be "shortly followed by the first American transport that takes the second A. E. F. to Europe."

(By Associated Press)

WASHINGTON, Oct. 27.—Saying that United States merchant vessels "are being sunk by the brutal and murderous doctrine of unrestricted submarine warfare," Senator Tom Connally, Texas Democrat, told the Senate today that "as a proud nation, the United States must claim its rights to the seas."

B fore crowded galleries, the chairman of the foreign relations committee opened debate on legislation granting American merchant vessels the right to carry arms and to sail to any port in the world, both now forbidden by the 1939 neutrality law.

Democratic leaders who discussed the neutrality measure with President Roosevelt this morning reported they had told the President that the bill probably would be passed in less than two weeks.

"This resolution is a defense measure, not a war measure," Connally told his colleagues.

(Continued on Page 2.) See U. S. SHIPS.

Clash On Border

LONDON, Oct. 27.—(AP)—Reuters quoted a despatch relayed today from Vladivostok by Tass, official Russian news agency, as saying a force of 20 Japanese soldiers had attacked Soviet frontier guards near the village of Raskino on October 23.

The despatch said there were some wounded on both sides and that the Japanese had left some rifles and ammunition on Soviet territory.

HAPPY DAZE FOR WARSPITE SAILOR—Image in the camera of C. P. Detloff, Vancouver Daily Province staff photographer, was distorted when he snapped the picture reproduced above. But it was just right to register the way Stoker R. Fowler felt after a hectic joyride in the sidecar of a motorcycle piloted by Constable Roy Bell of the New Westminster police. Stoker Fowler was not the only Warspite sailor who felt like he looks above after the enthusiastic receptions given them by Vancouver and New Westminster over the week-end.

RACING RESULTS

Empire City Results

First race—Brave Sir (Eads), $15, $7.70, $4.80.
Cruiser (McCreary), $7.60, $5
Eric Knight (Lindberg), $3.30.
Time, 1.10.
Scratched—None.

Second race—Alca Gal (Lindberg), $25.60, $12.90, $9.50.
Cove Spring (Strickler), $7.40, $4.40.
Daily Dublin (Eads), $10.70
Time, 1.46 2-5.
Scratched—Cortez, Black Bun, Mill Briar, Dewy Dawn.

Third race—Pat N Mike (May), $12.50, $6.60, $3.60.
Count Haste (Stout), $7.10, $3.60.
Beamy (Day), $2.50.
Time, 1.09.
Scratched—None.

Fourth race—Feathery (Robinson), $4.90, $3.50, $2.80.
Jorie Mar (McCreary), $11.40, $6.10.
At Which (Westrope), $3.90.
Time, 1.10.
Scratched—Coppit.

Fifth race—Pump Gun (Robinson), $18.90, $6.90, $5.90.
Vintage Port (Hildbrandt), $7.80, $5.70.
Olympus (Westrope), $7.10.
Time, 1.45 2-5.
Scratched—None.

Sixth race—Cross Question (Westrope), $8.80, $5.30, $3.80.
Maezaca (Eads), $7.30, $4.60.
Keyman (Schmidl), $5.40.
Time, 1.47 1-5.
Scratched—Dunfrese, Wooden Indian, Ballast Reef, Buckboard, Wise Hobby, Mae Cloud, Rufus.

Seventh race—Perfect Rhyme (Strickler), $9, $4.30, $3.10.
Play House (Garza), $4.20, $3.
Drudgery (Eads), $4.10.
Time, 1.52.
Scratched—Hotzea.

Laurel Park Results

First race—Ingerfire (Berg), $60.80, $24.30, $15.70.
Snow Top (Coule), $18.40, $10.70.
Recognize (Page), $25.90.
Time, 1.15 2-5.
Scratched—Tribal Papoose, Cliath, So Fast, Katses.

Second race—Phantom Player (Keiper), $84.30, $14.80, $6.10.
Gay Call (Berg), $4.40, $3.
Smug (Smith), $3.20.
Time, 1.46 4-5.
Scratched—Miss Belfonds.

Third race—Good Conduct (Keiper), $4.20, $3.60, $2.90.
Scout About (Duncan), $26.40, $12.60.
Palkin (Scott), $4.90.
Time, 1.54 3-5.
Scratched—Tanganyika, Officiate, Kate Smith, Bounding Count.

Fourth race—Bally Arnett (Coule), $24.70, $9.10, $6.
Bill's Rita (Smith), $3.70, $2.70.
Pretty Lady (McCombs), $3.10.
Time, 1.45 2-5.
Scratched—None.

Fifth race—Greedan (Keiper), $7.90, $4.90, $2.80.
War Key (McCombs), $14.70, $5.30.
Jacsteal (Remerascheid), $2.50.
Time, 1.46 3-5.
Scratched—One Tip.

Sixth race—Dollar Bay (McCombs), $14.70, $8.20, $3.30.
Rough Time (Dabson), $16.60, $5.60.
Son Altesse (Berg), $2.50.
Time, 1.45 4-5.
Scratched—None.

Seventh race — Ginoca (Remerascheid), $6.50, $4.20, $2.80.
Banker Jim (Smith), $7.50, $4.
Miss Brideaux (Duncan), $2.90.
Time, 1.53 1-5.
Scratched—None.

Eighth race—Janegri (Coule), $8, $3.80, $3.20.
Ballotant (Wagner), $3.20, $2.60.
Sir Broadside (Basile), $4.40.
Time, 2.02.
Scratched—Dupliket, Purport, Triphammer, Cartel.

(Race Entries on Page 2.)

Roosevelt to Speak On Radio Tonight

President Roosevelt's address this evening from the Navy Day dinner in Washington will be heard in Vancouver at 7 o'clock, and it will be carried over the American networks and all local stations.

Fight Gains In Violence; 'No Retreat'

MOSCOW, Oct. 28.—(Tuesday)—(AP)—Giant battles raged on with undiminished intensity throughout yesterday on the fronts before Moscow and in the Donets basin, the Soviet information bureau said early today.

(Compiled from late despatches to the Associated Press.)

MOSCOW, Oct. 27.—The defenders of Moscow were reported today to have eased somewhat the threat on the capital by wresting a village from the Germans in a counter-drive across the Nara River.

As the Battle of Moscow mounted in violence along the southern approaches facing the Russians' left wing, Gen. Gregory K. Zhukov, commanding the central front armies, said in an order to his troops:

"Not a step back! Halt the Fascists! Do not let them reach Moscow! Every man must fight like 10."

Russia's line southwest of Moscow, admittedly shoved back by fierce German onslaughts was said to have withstood Nazi attempts to blast an opening through toward the capital.

In the south, however, the Germans apparently were pushing steadily ahead toward Rostov, Russia's important oil pipeline terminus and rail junction at the gateway to the Caucasus.

With the situation in the south conceded to be desperate for the Russians, British authorities again yesterday renewed heated demands on their government to strike in the west to divert some of the Nazi pressure from the Russians. There were indications British forces might fight side by side with the Russians to protect Soviet oil resources.

Evidence of the growing weight of German blows on the southern front was indicated by Russia's acknowledgment that Stalino, important Donets basin industrial centre, had fallen although the German's cost was said to have

(Continued on Page 2.) See RUSSIA.

Hun Troops Practice Invasion

ISTANBUL, Oct. 27.—(AP)—Travellers from northern Poland reported today that German forces there are being put through intensive training in rehearsal for an attempt to invade Britain.

The Germans have gathered great barges powered with obsolete airplane motors all along the coast of the Baltic Sea and the Gulf of Danzig, the travellers said, and every day German soldiers practice debarking from these craft, swimming in full equipment and protecting themselves from air and sea while on the barges.

Final BULLETINS

143 DIE IN REVOLT

ZAGREB, Croatia, Oct. 27—(AP)—A newspaper despatch from Belgrade tonight said 143 persons described as Communists had been killed and 89 captured in a two-day battle against Serbian troops in Sumadien province of Yugo-Slavia. The Communists were said to have held positions in hills and woods in the area where they had stored a great quantity of military equipment.

Robbery at Trail

TRAIL, Oct. 27.—(CP)—Police today were investigating theft last night of a small safe from the Motor Inn filling station and garage in downtown Trail.

Sees All-winter Fight

BERNE, Switzerland, Oct. 27.—(AP)—The Berlin correspondent of the Tribune De Geneve predicted today that the Russian Moscow front might hold out all winter.

Poles Reach England

LONDON, Oct. 27. — (AP) — First large contingent of Polish volunteer airmen has arrived in Britain from Canada to join the Polish squadrons of the Royal Air Force.

Axis In Turk Plot

ROME, Oct. 27. — (AP)—Virginio Gayda, Fascist editor, hinted today that Foreign Minister Ciano is discussing with Hitler a new diplomatic move which observers thought might involve Turkey's entrance into the Axis program.

Western at Spokane

SPOKANE, Oct. 27. — (AP) — Spokane will be the site of the 1942 United States western amateur golf tournament.

Fight Above Clouds

LONDON, Oct. 27.—(AP)—R.A.F. fighters and a number of German Messerschmitts were believed to have fought a battle above the clouds over the Straits of Dover this afternoon.

Wings for City Men

KINGSTON, Ont., Oct. 27.—(CP)—In the class of pilots who received their wings today at No. 31 Service Flying Training School were H. C. K. Housser, H. Johnson and R. F. Levack, all of Vancouver.

16 Hurt In Crash

MONTREAL, Oct. 27.—(CP)—Sixteen persons were injured, five seriously, today in a rush-hour street car collision in which a tram running downhill crashed into the rear of a stationary street car, forcing it into the back of a third.

ONE IN A THOUSAND—A thousand girls were interviewed by Paramount in search of suitable "Louisiana Belles" for its forthcoming screen version of Broadway's "Louisiana Purchase." Alaine Brandes, above, is one of the 13 who were chosen. A former Chicago model, she will play a model's role in the movie.

Ralph Ingersoll

REPORT On Russia

No series of articles since the war started stirred as much interest as those in The Vancouver Daily Province of Ralph Ingersoll, editor of New York's newspaper PM, on Britain. He was the first to point the peril of near-defeat which faced Britain in the September blitz after Dunkerque—revelations later admitted by leaders in Britain.

Today, on his return to New York from an equally thorough examination of the situation in Russia, Ingersoll commences another important series of articles for his own newspaper and The Vancouver Daily Province.

Like the others, they are realistic, comprehensive, completely independent. They point out the flaws as well as the advantage of the Russian situation.

First of the series is on Moscow, city of contradictions, now facing its greatest menace. He was there when it, too, was blitzed, and saw an answer to Hitler stronger than London's. He saw a drab city with arteries for 20 lines of traffic; a colorful city where proletarians have country houses; a city unlike any in America. The series is copyrighted in all countries by the newspaper PM.

By RALPH INGERSOLL.

I have just come back from six weeks in the Soviet Union, from a trip which took me around the world to visit every fighting front in the war against Fascism.

I am trying to put what I have seen and heard on paper as rapidly as I can.

And as I sit down to write, news comes that the city I have just left is under siege at last—that my friends in the embassy and among the journalists have gone east and that armed citizens are in the suburbs fighting their enemies.

Ralph Ingersoll

I have been through these suburbs, driven 30 miles down the broad, smooth Smolensk road—a distance which must be half way to the front lines now. The ground is gently rolling, woods interspersed with fields. The defenses are not continuous fortifications, lines of trenches or barricades.

They are an almost infinity of strong points. Camouflaged positions are on every rise of ground and on the edge of every woods.

And on the roads through the woods, when I was there, were columns of tanks, parked trucks, supplies. The positions on the hills were dug in the ground and covered with netting on which patches of canvas had been stuck—the canvas patches painted the color of the landscape.

The guns were under them. They were very hard to see from a little way off.

There were no troop movements when I was there. Everything seemed to be in place, ready, waiting. Civilian groups had begun multiplying the strong point system.

You saw them all over the hills, a hundred here and a hundred there, digging. They were mostly women.

In Moscow, the men were in what in England would be called the Home Guard. You saw them drilling in small detachments, marching through the streets, often singing. They did not carry arms then.

The most distinctive military feature of Moscow was its anti-aircraft barrage. That was terrific. It extended in a belt around the whole city, and I have been to batteries over 30 miles from the centre.

When the German planes came over the whole business seemed to let go at once. I had been through the end of the blitz in London last year, and watched anti-aircraft work in China and Egypt. I've seen nothing to compare with the volume and intensity of the barrage around Moscow. Other observers who had been in England agreed with me.

When the Nazi planes came, the Russians just turned it on and left it on, hour after hour until the sky was a continuous rippling sparkle of exploding shells and fragments tinkled continuously in the big squares and struck so many sparks they looked like fields of fireflies.

(Continued on Page 8.)

RALPH INGERSOLL.

Nipponese Declare War On U.S., Britain

★ ★ ★ ★ ★ ★   ★ ★ ★ ★ ★   ★ ★ ★ ★ ★   ★ ★ ★ ★ ★ ★

JAPS BOMB HONOLULU

Single Bomb Kills 350 Americans

NEW YORK.—(UP)—An N.B.C. observer reported Sunday night from Honolulu that 350 men had been killed in a direct bomb hit at Hickam Field there.

NEW YORK.—(UP)—The U.S.S. Oklahoma, a battleship, was set afire in Sunday's air attack on Pearl Harbor, an N.B.C. broadcast from Honolulu reported.

HONOLUL.—(UP)—Japanese bomber squadrons, torpedo planes and parachute troops attacked the United States' great naval and air base at Pearl Harbor Sunday, blasting furiously at warships and war installations but suffering loss of "many" attack craft.

Several persons were believed killed as about 50 Japanese bombers swept over the island posts, dropping explosives.

A group of four-motored bombers bearing the rising sun insignia of the Nipponese air force swung over Honolulu proper, and were met by a terrific barrage of anti-aircraft fire.

A bomb fell within 25 feet of the Honolulu Advertiser building.

The attacking planes bombed Pearl Harbor, Ford Island, Wheeler Field, Honolulu Municipal Airport, Hickam Field and the new navy air repair base at Kaneohe.

Anti-aircraft guns went into action immediately, and soon large clouds of billowing smoke rolled up from the areas under attack.

Witnesses said fires were started, apparently by bombs, on Ford Island.

A Japanese plane crashed and burned behind the courthouse at Wahiawa, a few miles east of Schofield Barracks.

Pearl Harbor and Hickam Field, the big army bomber base, apparently were worst hit.

Witnesses reported three fires raging at Pearl Harbor after
(Continued on Back Page)

WAR Bulletins

"WAR MOVE NEAR"

WASHINGTON. — (UP)—A United States declaration of war on Japan was believed but a matter of hours Sunday night after Japanese air attacks upon American army and navy bases in Hawaii and aMnila. (Formal declaration requires action by Congress.)

CHURCHILL EXAMINES POSITION

LONDON.—(BUP—An authoritative statement Sunday night said Prime Minister Winston Churchill had been advised of the Japanese attacks and was examining the British position.

WHITE HOUSE MEET

WASHINGTON. — (UP) — Legislative leaders said Sunday night after hurried telephone conferences with President Roosevelt that a joint session of Congress Monday, perhaps to hear a war message, is under consideration.

WANTS DECLARATION

WASHINGTON. — (UP — Assistant House Republican Leader Earl C. Michener, R., Mich., Sunday demanded a "clear-cut declaration of war" against Japan.

SIGHT CHUTE TROOPS

HONOLULU. — (UP) — Parachute troops were sighted off Harbor Point Sunday.

Declaration of War Made By Tokyo

LONDON. — (UP) — The Tokyo Radio broadcast a High Command communique Sunday saying "Japanese naval and land forces are now in a state of war with American and British military forces in the West Pacific."

WASHINGTON—(UP)—Secretary of State Cordell Hull angrily told the Japanese "peace or war" envoys Sunday that their government's answer to his recent document on the U.S. position in the Far East is "crowded with infamous falsehoods and distortions".

As Japan declared war on the U. S., the cabinet of President Roosevelt went into an early evening session (8:30 p.m. Eastern Standard Time, 5:30 p.m. Vancouver time) and there were the following other chief developments:

IN BRITAIN—

British action—which the Prime Minister promised would "follow within the hour" if the U. S. became involved in war with Japan—was expected almost immediately.

AT OTTAWA—

Prime Minister Mackenzie King called the Canadian cabinet into session at 7 p.m., E.D.T. (3 p.m., Vancouver Time), thereby suggesting that Canada was preparing to act in concert with Britain.

IN VANCOUVER—

An emergency meeting of the Air Raid Pro-
(Continued on Back Page)

58

U.S. SHIPS RECALLED; WAR TENSION IN CITY

Quiet o n the surface with tension underneath as officials moved quickly to act on new problems, marked the immediate local reaction to outbreak of war on the Pacific.

R.C.M.P. officers reported the situation is well in hand and said a further statement might be forthcoming after consultation with Ottawa.

Police in Vancouver, Richmond, New Westminster and Steveston are on the alert, but no trouble has been reported between Japanese and other citizens.

Japanese residents maintained silence regarding developments in the Pacific.

I. Kawasaki, Japanese consul, was not at his home or office and could not be located for comment.

Meanwhile, U.S. Army men on leave in Vancouver flocked to bus and train terminals and loaded into private cars to rush back to Camp Lewis, just south of Tacoma, Washington, while U.S. naval men, leave cancelled, rushed back to their posts.

Residents of Chinatown remained quiet in face of developments that brought renewed hope for their country, battered by Japanese armies since 1937.

Pender Street showed no unusual activity early this afternoon. Chinese walked impassively up and down but in no greater numbers than on the usual Sunday.

Most wore colored tickets given donors to Chinese war relief funds and a number of Chinese girls were taking donations in the streets.

Few Japanese were noticeable on the streets early in the afternoon.

SIRENS SCREAM IN BUENOS AIRES

BUENOS AIRES.—(UP)—Sirens began screaming in the city Sunday, announcing the Japanese attack on Hawaii, and hundreds of persons rushed into the streets. The Japanese ambassador was reported playing golf.

JAPANESE

PANAMA CITY.—(UP)—The Panamanian Government Sunday ordered the arrest of all Japanese nationals in the country.

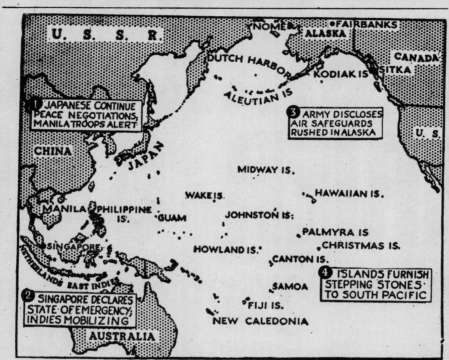

WAR IN THE PACIFIC.—Events leading up to a state of war between Japan and the U. S. and Britain are clearly shown on the map above. Without warning Japanese bombers swept across the once peaceful Pacific to blast U. S. key naval bases at Pearl Harbor, Honolulu, on the Hawaiian Islands and Manila in the Phillippines, centre of U. S. for east war strategy.

BULLETINS

NAZIS "SURPRISED"

BERLIN. — (UP) — Berlin was electrified Sunday night at the news of the Japanese attacks. The story, datelined New York, was carried by the official news agency DNB a few minutes before 10:30. The story was brief and added that "Japanese" reaction to Early's (Hhite House Secretary Stephen Early) announcement is not yet available."

ALL IN UNIFORM

WASHINGTON. —(UP)—The War Department requested the United Press to announce that Secretary Henry L. Stimson had ordered all officers in the United States to ewar uniforms when reporting for duty on Dec. 8.

Bombing Toll Heavy

(Continued from Front Page)

the first attacks, but said that "at least three ships" were hit at Pearl Harbor, but there was no confirmation of this latter report.

Hickam Field was reported unofficially to be "badly damaged."

Troops cleared away debris to prepare for "renewed battle," it was announced.

Go. Joseph B. Poindexter declared a state of emergency.

His first order to the public was to "remain calm" and stay off the streets.

The first attack began at 7:55 a.m. and several more attacks followed.

The planes apparently were based on an aircraft carrier. They came in at great altitude but swooped low in dive attacks.

The dive bombers were accompanied by at least one torpedo carrying plane, which skimmed a mountain peak and loosed its missle in the direction of United States warships in Pearl Harbor.

This correspondent saw one dive bomber swoop down in an attack, the red ball on its wing tip clearly discernible.

It now is possible to reveal that this was no surprise attack. The Hawaiian department had been waiting for it for a week.

Declaration of War!

(Continued from Front Page)

tection committee was called for 4 p.m. today by Mayor J. W. Cornett. Members met in camera at the city hall with Col. C. G. Beeston, officer commanding the Vancouver military district, also attending. It is understood Col. Beeston was to be advised of the progress made by the committee and assured utmost co-operation in civilian protection should Vancouver be attacked.

WASHINGTON.—(UP)—The Whitehouse announced Sunday that Japanese airplanes have attacked Pearl Harbor, principal American base in the Hawaiian Islands, and Manila.

The announcement was made at mid-afternoon by White House Secretary Stephen Early. He said President Roosevelt had given him this statement.

"The Japanese have attacked Pearl Harbor from the air and all naval and military activities on the island of Oahu, principal American base in the Hawaiian Islands.

Subsequently Early revealed that Manila also had been attacked.

"A second air attack is reported. This one has been made on army and naval bases in Manila."

President Roosevelt immediately ordered th army and navy to execute "all previously prepared orders," working to the defense of the United States.

The attacks came, Early said, when both nations were "at peace, within an hour or so of the time the Japanese Ambassador Kichisaburo Nomura and the special envoy, Saburo Kurusu, had handed Secretary of State Cordell Hull Japan's reply to the Secretary's memorandum of November 26."

As Early hastily summoned a special press conference, the President called in Secretary of War Henry L. Stimson and Secretary of the Navy Frank Knox.

Congressional leaders immediately were advised of the crisis.

Attaches of the Japanese Embassy began burning secret documents in the embassy yard.

A group of newspaper reporters and photographers stood by watching and after a few minutes were ordered to leave. The embassy door were closed.

There was no disorder. Embassy officials declined comment. When the gates of the embassy were closed, an official told reporters:

"We do not expect to be molested. We have faith in the fairness of the American people."

As word spread through the capital of the air attacks, large crowds began gathering in front of the embassy.

SAN FRANCISCO. — (UP) — The U.S. Coast Guard Sunday ordered all craft on the Pacific Coast to put into their home ports "pending clarification of the situation arising from the Japanese air attack on Hawaii and the Philippine Islands."

Lt. Com. Paul Clark of the local coast guard station said the order in this region would affect 18,000 motor boats and 1000 fishing boats in district bounded by the Oregon border and the San Luis Obispo County southern line.

WIRE CENSORSHIP

Globe Wireless said Sunday the U.S. Navy had imposed censorship on all messages to and from Manila, scene of a Japanese plane attack.

The Globe gave this information to the United Press here when a message was presented the communications firm for transmission to United Press, Manila.

FORT LEWIS, Wash.—(UP) —The Ninth Army Corps ordered all officers and men back to Fort Lewis immediately Sunday.

SACRAMENTO.—(UP)—The army Air Corps today placed the huge Sacramento army air depot at McClellan Field on a 24-hour wartime basis.

LOS ANGELES. — (UP) — All Deputy sheriffs, police and more than 8000 special reserve officers and trained civilians Sunday were ordered to stand by for emergency duty by Sheriff Eugene Biscailuz and Police Chief C. B. Horrall of Los Angeles City and County.

Flashes

MEXICO CONFERS

MEXICO CITY — (UP) — President Manuel Avila Camacho and Foreign Minister Ezequiel Padilla conferred hurriedly Sunday apparently to orient Mexico's position in face of hostilities in the Pacific.

NAZIS BLAME U.S.

LONDON. — (UP) — The Berlin radio said Sunday night that "as a result of war mongering by the President of the United States the first clashes have occurred in East Asia between Japanese and American forces. Thus, this war monger No. 1 has at last achieved his aim and brought war over his people."

NEWS ELECTRIFIED LONDON

LONDON.—(BUP)—The city was electrified Sunday night by news of the air attack on Hawaii. Official quarters had been alert for signs of the first outbreak in the Far Eastern warfare, but they had not expected it to come from that area.

LONDON. — (UP) — Responsible quarters said tonight as Prime Minister Winston Churchill weighed the British position relative to Japanese attacks in the Pacific that Britain would declare war against Japan "within an hour" if the United States proclaimed a state of war.

BILLINGS, Mont.—(UP)—Senator B. K. Wheeler, leading Isolationist, said Sunday, when informed Japan had attacked U.S. bases at Honolulu and Manila, "That means war, and we'll have to see it through."

59

The Weather
Forecast for today: "Moderate southeast wind, cloudy and mild with rains." Sunday's temperatures: high 47, low 37.

News **FOR VICTORY** Herald

LARGEST MORNING CIRCULATION WEST OF TORONTO

FINAL EDITION

VANCOUVER, B.C., MONDAY, DECEMBER 8, 1941

3c

Canada Declares War On Japan

★ ★

U.S. SINKS JAP CARRIER, 6 SUBS

★ ★

F.D.R. Break With Hitler Impends

NEW YORK.—(UP)—The British radio was heard broadcasting a report that four Japanese aircraft, six submarines and one aircraft carrier have been destroyed in Honolulu "and in the naval battle of Honolulu."

As war flared along a 6000-mile front in the Pacific—with Britain and the United States striking back against surprise attacks by Japan on land, at sea and in the air—there were the following developments:

● 1—Canada declares a state of war exists with Japan. (See Page 2).

● 2—Britain prepares to implement Churchill's pledge of "action within the hour" if U.S. become embroiled in war with Japan. (See Page 2). Cabinet meets at 3 p.m. (6 a.m. Vancouver time).

● 3—Congress, which alone in the U.S. possesses authority to declare war, makes ready for extraordinary joint session of house and senate at 12:30 p.m. (9:30 a.m., Vancouver time) when President Roosevelt is expected to call for formal war declaration to counter "Japan's treacherous attack." (See Page 2).

(The president's momentous address will be broadcast over Stations KOMO and KJR at 9:30 A.M., Vancouver time.)

● 4—Added nations rally to cause of Allies as Netherlands East Indies, Nicaragua and Costa Rica reportedly declare war on Japan. Mexico and other Central and South American countries indicate action near.

These formalities of war followed by almost a half day the realities of war in "Our Ocean,"—the "Pacific." Where the new war rages is shown in a News-Herald map on Page 14.

Results of major engagements to date include:

● 1—Surprise attacks by Nippon took the following heavy toll, chiefly at Hawaii and Guam, before American retaliatory action was initiated:

NAVY—Two and possibly three U.S. battleships lost along with several smaller naval craft.

PLANES—Loss indicated of 100 to 300 planes caught on the ground at Pearl Harbor.

MERCHANT VESSELS—Heavy loss by merchant marine, including several large vessels, feared through "blitz" character of attack.

LIVES—All estimates vague but toll feared to extend far into hundreds through bombing and ship losses.

● 2—Japanese expeditionary force landed in northeastern Malaya and subjected to strong attack by British land and air forces. Nippon directs air attack at Singapore. Ten Japanese ships en route to Thailand, also invaded by Nippon, attacked by British air forces off Bangkok.

● 3—Scattered points in Philippines bombed and U. S. bases on Wake and Midway islands in Pacific believed raided. (Page 22).

The United States probably will enter the second World War today with formal declarations of hostilities not only against Japan but also Tokyo's Axis allies—Germany and Italy.

(Continued on Page 21)

Singapore Attacked

SINGAPORE. — (UP).—Japanese Expeditionary Forces landed on beaches in northeast Malaya and were strongly attacked by British land and air forces, a communique said today shortly after an enemy air raid on the big naval base of Singapore.

Ten Japanese ships also were attacked by British aircraft off Bangkok, where they apparently were attempting an invasion of Thailand.

(The British radio reported without confirmation that Bangkok had been attacked from the air, CBS said.)

Some of the landings in Malaya were repulsed but fighting was still in progress near Kota Bharu, the communique said.

Enemy airplanes raided Singapore shortly before dawn, causing slight damage and some civilian casualties.

Landings made by enemy troops after 1 a.m. were repulsed the communique said.

NEW YORK.—(UP) — The London radio in a broadcast heard by the Columbia Broadcasting system this morning said that Japanese warships have surrounded the U. S. islands of Guam. "The oil reservoir and the hotel have been set on fire," the broadcast said.

TRIES TO BURN JAPANESE HOUSE

First anti-Japanese violence reported in Vancouver came at 9:15 p.m. Sunday when a would-be arsonist hurled a blazing, oil-soaked cloth into the doorway of a Japanese rooming house at 143 Alexander Street.

The blaze was discovered by police patrolling the district when they saw a man enter the house and then run away. Failing to catch the fleeing man, the officers returned to the rooming house and found the blazing rag in the hallway.

Another victim was S. Hayashi, 788 Denman Street. An unidentified man tossed a large stone through his store window at 9 p.m. Police said the window measured six feet by nine.

BULLETINS

Churchill Authorizes War on Japan

LONDON.—(BUP)—Prime Minister Winston Churchill, in the name of King George VI, has instructed the British ambassador at Tokyo to declare to the Japanese government the existence of a state of war between Great Britain and Japan, effective at the moment Japan started hostilities, it was understood today.

Report Two U.S. Battleships Sunk

WASHINGTON.—(UP)—Two battleships—the 29,000-ton Oklahoma with a crew of 1301 and the 32,600-ton West Virginia with a crew of 1923—were reported sunk and a third dreadnaught was believed damaged or lost, along with smaller vessels.

Australia To Declare War Today

NEW YORK.—(UP)—The British radio today broadcast a Melbourne dispatch which said that the war cabinet of Australia is expected to declare war on Japan later today.

Vancouver Moves to Meet War Danger From Pacific

Vancouver stepped into the front line of battle Sunday as Japan went to war on America.

● 1. A few scant hours after Nippon planes blasted at Hawaii, Vancouver's A. R. P. met hurriedly, appointed Col. G. H. Kirkpatrick supreme chief, planned to cut all red tape, promised early blackouts for the city. (See page 4).

● 2. Army, navy, and air force units were ordered back to their posts immediately. (See Page 3.)

● 3. Sergeant J. Barnes, R. C. M. P., secretary of the standing committee on Orientals in the city, gave an assurance that "adequate measures were being taken." (See Page 4).

● 4. In Vancouver's Japanese section, Canadian-born Nipponese were stunned, silent, bewildered. (See Page 3).

● 5. All Japanese fishing boats were ordered to report immediately for routine inspection. (See Page 10).

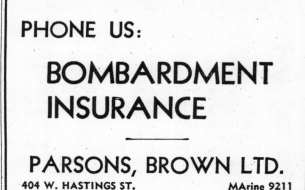
60

BRITISH-U.S. SMASH AT 6000-MILE JAP FRONT

SPORTS STOCKS

The Vancouver Sun

Only Evening Newspaper Owned, Controlled and Operated by Vancouver People

★ ★ ★ ★ ★ FINAL

FOUNDED 1886
VOL. LVI—No. 58 | MArine 1161 | VANCOUVER, BRITISH COLUMBIA, MONDAY, DECEMBER 8, 1941 | Price 3 Cents On trains, boats and outside Greater Vancouver, 5c

'Fiendish' Bomb Raid on Manila

Late Bulletins

RCAF Flying Boat Crashes; 1 Dead, 5 Missing

HALIFAX, Dec. 8.—A flying boat crashed into the sea off Halifax today. One man is known dead, five are injured and five missing.

Lindbergh for War Now

CHICAGO, Dec. 8.—Charles A. Lindbergh, Isolationist spokesman, today said we must meet war with Japan "as united Americans."

'Must Fight,' Says Hoover

POALI, Pa., Dec. 8 — Former President Herbert Hoover took the stand today that the U.S. "Must fight with everything we have."

Higher Taxes for U.S. Now

WASHINGTON, Dec. 8.—Secretary of the Treasury Henry Morgenthau, Jr., today declared that the war with Japan makes the need for higher taxes more pressing than ever.

Butter, Egg Prices Frozen

WASHINGTON, Dec. 8. — The Commodity Exchange Administration today ordered government-supervised exchanges to freeze soy bean, butter, egg and flaxseed prices at today's quotations.

'Our Scrap Iron Is Coming Back'

SEATTLE, Dec. 8.—A contractor with a grim sense of humor (he advertised that "our scrap iron is coming back") today hurriedly offered to erect air raid shelters for Seattle householders fearful of Japanese bombs.

C.C.F. Refuses to Withdraw

EDMONTON, Dec. 8.—M. J. Coldwell, acting leader of the C.C.F. in Commons, today rejected an appeal that the C.C.F. withdraw from opposing Hon. Arthur Meighen in the forthcoming federal by-election in South York.

Seattle Calls for 40,000 Guards

SEATTLE, Dec. 8.—Mayor Earl B. Millikin today called for 40,000 volunteers to help guard the city, joining 8000 persons already organized. Millikin's call was made for air raid wardens, ambulance drivers, auxiliary firemen, police and other units.

Volunteers Swamp Recruiting Offices

PORTLAND, Dec. 8.—Long lines of men stood in front of Army, Navy and Marine recruiting offices today to sign up for the "duration." The navy was getting the biggest rush, but officers in all branches of service reported they were swamped with applicants.

Clipper Wrecked by Bombs

SAN FRANCISCO, Dec. 8. — Pan-American Airways' Hong Kong Clipper has been wrecked by Japanese bombs in Hong Kong harbor, it was reliably reported today. The big seaplane was empty at the time of the attack.

Welders Threaten Strike

WASHINGTON, Dec. 8.—Lloyd Payne, Secretary of the Independent United Brotherhood of Welders, Cutters and Helpers, today telegraphed locals claiming to represent 125,000 workers to "prepare for a sudden and determined walkout." The telegrams revoked a message yesterday calling off the strike scheduled for tomorrow.

Football Players in Peril

SALEM, Ore., Dec. 8.—Grave concern for the safety of the Willamette University football party of 51 persons, now in Honolulu, was expressed by relatives and friends in Salem today. The team played the University of Hawaii Saturday afternoon, just a few hours before bombs rained down within a few miles of the playing field.

Bandit Holds Up Bakery

For the fifth time in a week the Canadian Window Bakeries had one of its branch stores held up today.

An armed bandit, who entered the Davie Street branch of the company at 1245 Davie, ordered Miss Betty Aitchison, 1654 West Ninth Avenue, clerk, to turn over the contents of the till and escaped with $15, after giving the warning:

"Don't look at my face."

'Fire Is Simply Raging'

Manila Broadcaster Describes Fierce Jap Attack

By British United Press

NEW YORK, Dec. 8.—The National Broadcasting Company correspondent at Manila reported today that Japanese planes carried out a heavy attack on Ft. McKinley and Nichols airfield at Manila at 3:09 a.m. Tuesday (11:09 a.m. PST Monday), and started large fires.

The broadcaster said that the attack, which was in progress as he broadcast, was carried out with "fiendish accuracy."

The Japanese bombers, despite a terrific curtain of American anti-aircraft fire, touched off a huge fire, apparently in a gasoline dump.

Broadcasting from a dugout, Bert Silen, NBC correspondent, said that "the fire is simply raging out there"—at the point where U.S. gasoline stores apparently were set afire.

Another objective of the Japanese raid was the big transmitter of the Radio Corporation of America, Manila's chief communications link with the outside world.

The broadcaster said it was reported that an American destroyer was damaged in the raid.

Japanese planes which attacked Clark field this morning were driven off, but 300 casualties were reported at the big army air base. Some 25 American planes were reported destroyed by the Japanese attack.

No Radio

SEATTLE, Dec. 8.—Brig.-Gen. Carlyle Wash, of the 2nd Interceptor Command, said there probably would be a cessation of all radio broadcasting, and a blackout in this area tonight.

SAN SALVADOR, El Salvador, Dec. 8.—El Salvador declared war on Japan today by unanimous vote of Congress.

Race Results

CHARLES TOWN

FIRST RACE—About seven furlongs:
Olympian (LoTurco) $3.20, $2.60, $2.20.
Roils oRugh (Shaffer) $9.20, $4.80.
Chief Teddy (Grant) $3.40.
Time 1:27 2-5.

SECOND RACE—Six and one-half furlongs:
Glitter Gal (Kely) $8, $4.20, $3.40.
Two Ply (Carrillo) $4.20, $3.40
High Rose (W. Kirk) $5.
Time 1:21 2-5.

THIRD RACE—Six and one-half furlongs:
Aldridge (Glidewell) $4.40, $3, $2.40.
Flagetta (Kelly) $4.40, $3.40.
Apprehend (LoTurco) 4.40.
Time 1:22.

FOURTH RACE—Six and one-half furlongs:
Indian Sea (Wright) $12, $6.80, $3.20.
Long Legs (Datillo) $4.60, $2.80.
Ring Up (Kirkpatrick) $2.60.
Time 1:21.

FIFTH RACE—Mile and one-sixteenth:
Persian Queen (Scocca) $9.40, $6, $4.80.
Pitsburg (Palumbo) $12.80, $6.
Feed Patch (Page) $4.20.
Time 1:48 3-5.

SIXTH RACE—About seven furlongs:
Rough Time (Cowley) $8.20, $4.40, $3.20.
Fritz (Datillo) $7.40, $3.
Imperial Impy (LoTurco) $2.20.
Time 1:26 3-5

SEVENTH RACE—Mile and one-sixteenth:
Rough Brigade (Glidewell) $3.60, $2.40, $2.20.
Centreville (C. Wright) $2.40, $2.40.
Speed Ship (Kelly) $3.60.
Time 1:47 4-5.

City Men Called to Arms

Three members of the 2nd Battalion Irish Fusiliers (Reserve Army, rushing down to barracks yesterday afternoon in answer to an emergency call-up. Reservists streamed into unit headquarters all afternoon, were released late in the evening.

(EDITORIAL)

Citizens, Be Calm!

Canada is at war with Japan for the first time in our history, and for the last—because when this conflict is ended, Japan will be put in her proper sphere as an Oriental power, and democratic China will be re-established.

Here in British Columbia we have an entirely domestic problem, and it can be met and solved instantly, if we keep our heads. We have in this province nearly 25,000 Japanese, many of them Canadian-born. These latter, and the overwhelming majority of the former, are intensely loyal to Canada. They have nothing to do with the policies of imperial Japan; they are not in sympathy with those policies, and if our regulations allowed it their young men would be in uniform against the Axis to which Japan belongs.

If there be any among the Japan-born aliens with us who are not in sympathy with Canada rest assured that the Mounted Police and the military officials have them tabbed, and they will be appropriately dealt with.

Let us leave that task to the authorities. We should not subject anyone to indignity nor to harsh condemnation. Be alert! If you have definite suspicions, make them known to the police.

Above all let us KEEP OUR HEADS. This is no time for folly, panic or prejudice.

Death Cheated by Nanaimo Autoist

NANAIMO, Dec. 8. — Thomas B. McArravy, well-known architect, narrowly escaped death or serious injury when his auto crashed through the railing of a bridge and landed on the bank of Millstone River, 15 feet below. McArravy swerved his auto to avoid a collision with another auto in front of his. He escaped uninjured. His auto was only slightly damaged.

Race Entries on Page 10

Dorothy Thompson

". . . . Declare war on the Axis now," or Germany will strike the United States when it suits her." Page 5.

Bruce Hutchison

"United States, now emotionally at war, will break all records in history for war production." Page 10.

Read what these two gifted writers say of the Pacific conflict.

Hong Kong, Malaya Invaded; Siam Quits

U.S. Fleet Challenging Japanese Striking Force Which Rained Havoc on Hawaii; Great Naval Battle Believed Waging East of Pearl Harbor

By British United Press

Britain and United States smashed back at Japan today on a 6000-mile Pacific war front which flamed from Hawaii's coral beaches to the jungle shores of Malay and Thailand.

The American battle fleet was reported challenging the Japanese striking striking force which raided Hawaii with heavy loss of life and naval damage. A great engagement is raging in the waters west of America's Pacific Gibraltar.

Meanwhile in London, Prime Minister Winston Churchill, and President Roosevelt at Washington, each presented to their respective assemblies, and received immediate approval, formal declarations of war against the Japanese Empire. Thus, at last, United States and the British Empire found themselves full military allies in a world at war.

Here is a picture of Pacific war in tabloid:

MANILA: Japanese planes make heavy attack on Ft. McKinley and Nichols airfield at Manila at 3:09 a.m. Tuesday (11:09 a.m. Vancouver Time Monday), and started large fires. Gasoline depot at Nichols field reported destroyed. U.S. army base at Fort Stotsenburg, Davao and the vicinity of Bagiuo, also bombed.

TOKYO: Japanese naval command claims sinking of U.S. battleships Oklahoma and West Virginia; damage to four other battleships; damage to four heavy cruisers; heavy destruction of U.S. planes; sinking of U.S. Aircraft carrier (rumored to be U.S.S. Langley); capture of "many" enemy ships; sinking of U.S. Minesweeper Penguin at Guam.

HAWAII: White House reports 3000 casualties, including 1500 fatalities, in Japanese air attack; loss of "old" American battleship and destroyer.

THAILAND: Gave in to the Japanese with little or no fight; Japanese troops moving into the country under "agreement" reached with Bangkok government, in preparation for drive on Singapore.

SINGAPORE: British battling Japanese landing forces at five points along eastern coast; Royal Air Force heavily engaged.

CHUNGKING: China declares war on Germany and Italy and formalizes the long existing state of war with Japan.

CHINA: Japanese attack Hong Kong twice by air, take

Please Turn to Page Eleven **See "War in Pacific"**

Acclamation For 6 Chief Magistrates

At least six chief magistrates were elected by acclamation today it was indicate das results of nominations in 26 cities and 27 municipalities were received in Vancouver.

Richmond, West Vancouver, Kent, Mission and Chilliwack re-elected their heads by acclamation and Chilliwack City named its mayor in the same manner.

Reeve J. M. Grauer, Reeve J. Edwards Sears, Reeve W. A. Jones, Reeve W. B. Catherwood and Reeve W. T. Richardson were honored thus. Chilliwack City named Theo McCammon to succeed Mayor C. A. Barber.

The Royal City will see a stiff three-cornered fight for the mayoralty.

No acclamations were accorded there, 27 candidates seeking the various 13 vacancies in the mayoralty, city council, school board, park board and police commission.

Nominations received up to press time follow:

NANAIMO

Mayor—Mayor V. B. Harrison; J. G. Hindmarch.

Council (three seats) — Ald. John Kerr; Donald Campbell, Ald. George Addison, W. E. Bray.

Schol Board (four seats) — George Addison, John Barsby, A. W. Bradfield, Harold Thorneycroft.

NEW WESTMINSTER

Mayor—Mayor John Frederick Hume, William Malcolm Mott, James Lewis Sangster.

Council (three seats, two-year term) — John Alexander Courtney, John Charles Bigby, John Greenall, John Leonard Higginbotham, Frederick Herbert Jackson, Edward Charles Mills, Mrs. Marian Russell McDonald, Harry Jos. Suilivan, Christopher Yates; (one seat, one-year term): John Percy Copp, Harry Dyer, Samuel Stanley Hughes, Roderick Angus McDonald, Edward Navey.

School Board (four seats)—

Please Turn to Page Eleven
See "Nominations"

Late Stocks on Page 11

U.S. Declares War on Japan in 33 Minutes

WASHINGTON, Dec. 8.—President Roosevelt this afternoon signed the declaration of war against Japan.

By LYLE WILSON
Special to The Vancouver Sun
Copyright, 1941, by British United Press

WASHINGTON, Dec. 8 — Congress today proclaimed existence of a state of war between the United States and the Japanese Empire 33 minutes after the dramatic moment when President Roosevelt stood before a joint session to pledge that we will triumph—"so help us, God."

Democracy was proving its right to a place in the sun with a split second shiftover from peace to all-out war.

The Senate acted first, adopting the resolution by a unanimous roll call vote of 82 to 0, within 21 minutes after the President had concluded his address to a joint session of both Houses.

The House voted immediately afterward and by 1:13 p.m. a majority of the House had voted "aye."

The final House vote was announced as 388 to 1.

The lone negative vote was cast by Rep. Jeannette Rankin (R., Mont.), who also voted against entry into the First World War.

Please Turn to Page Eleven **See "Washington"**

BLACKOUT Again Tonight

The Weather
Mostly cloudy and mild with scattered showers on the coast, some rain and snow in Cariboo, mostly fair on the coast.
Temperature at 1:30 p.m. today: 46.
Temperature during 24 hours ending 4:30 a.m. today: maximum 49, minimum 40.
Forecast: partly cloudy, mild.
Official weather report on page 22.

The Vancouver Sun

Only Evening Newspaper Owned, Controlled and Operated by Vancouver People

Today's Tides
Vancouver Harbor
Low 4:12 p.m. 8.1 feet High 8:30 p.m. 9.5 feet
English Bay
Low 4:08 p.m. 9.0 feet High 8:03 p.m. 10.1 feet
First Narrows
Low slack (w) 4:48 p.m. High slack (w) 8:43 p.m.
Tomorrow's Tides Appear On Page 22

FOUNDED 1886
VOL. LVI—No. 59 HOME EDITION VANCOUVER, BRITISH COLUMBIA, TUESDAY, DECEMBER 9, 1941 ***C Price 3 Cents On trains, boats and outside Greater Vancouver, 5c MArine 1161

ARP on the Job in Vancouver

Activities of 3300 ARP workers to make last night's blackout effective were recorded at this nerve-centre of Vancouver's civilian defense. It is the control room at ARP Headquarters in City Hall where the full drama of last night's developments was unfolded.

In the picture, R. Smylie, chief warden, has just handed over a report from one of the 23 district posts to the control table, while H. A. Dennison, St. John Ambulance Brigade, marks up its location on the large map. Seated at the table are Constable C. E. Blythe of the Vancouver Police Department (left), Florenz Sweeney of the Canadian Women's Training Corps, Corps Officer John Cartmill of the St. John Ambulance Brigade, and Rose Hart of the CWTC.

Today In Britain

War events analyzed by Fleet Street writers, cabled from the London Bureau of The Vancouver Sun.

(Copyright, 1941)

LONDON, Dec. 9.—President Roosevelt's declaration pledging rapid assistance to Turkey under the lease-lend act has provoked widespread satisfaction in Turkey.

The Turkish General Staff and the army itself are profoundly pleased with Mr. Roosevelt's statement. The Turkish Army leaders appear to welcome the official stamp upon American aid, which has heretofore been routed through British channels.

Referring to "the Turco-American friendship, unshaken in the post-war period," Falih Rifki Atay, in the Ankara journal Ulus, went on to state Turkish foreign policy as outlined by the Republic Day speech of President Ismet Inonu, on October 29, and added:

"Turkish policy is neither a policy of weakness nor one of passive defense. We continue to take military measures coincident with our political steps.

"Geographically," continued Mr. Atay, "we are in a delicate situation. We have, on our honor, assumed certain responsibilities toward our people and toward others. The statement issued from the White House is a further evidence of the faith which

Please Turn to Page Ten
See "Britain Today"

Blackout's Not Play Now—It's for Keeps

When Vancouver's lights winked out last May, it was all a jolly game which most of us didn't take very seriously.

Tonight, when the city hides under a blanket of darkness, we will be playing for keeps—which means for an indefinite period.

Military and civilian protection heads stress two facts which every citizen is urged to accept.

The threat of a Japanese attack on the Pacific Northwest, broadcast by Western Air Command Monday evening, was grimly and utterly authentic.

Blackout restrictions are law, and are supported by the full weight of police and military authority. They will be strictly enforced, with penalties for those who break them.

The "lights out" order was fairly well observed by residents last night, but the city at large was less prepared than it will be in future.

TRAFFIC LIGHTS

Vancouver will begin its second blackout at 5 p.m. today. This order was received by the Greater Vancouver Civilian Protection Committee by telephone today from Major S. F. M. Moodie, civilian protection officer at Victoria, as civic heads and representatives of utilities met with the committee at the city hall to work out arrangements for making the blackout complete.

City street lights will not be turned on this afternoon except for intersection lights, which the city engineer's department is attempting to make invisible from the air by blueing.

Please Turn to Page Ten
See "Blackout"

U.S. Senator Hears 'Large Part of Our Navy Wiped Out'

WASHINGTON, Dec. 9.—Sen. Charles W. Tobey (Republican), New Hampshire, said today it was "reported on the Senate floor that a large part of the Pacific fleet had been wiped out," and demanded that the American people be informed of the true situation.

Tobey spoke on the Senate floor, questioning Chairman David I. Walsh (D., Mass.) of the Senate Naval Affairs Committee about current reports of damage to the fleet at Pearl Harbor.

Walsh had obtained the floor to make a statement on the subject for the Senate's information.

"The pride of the American people in their navy and their confidence in some of their officials has been terribly shaken," Tobey said. "The public is entitled to know the truth."

Liquor Stores to Close at 4:45 p.m.

For the period of the blackout shortened hours are applied to liquor stores in Vancouver and the coastal area. Stores will open at 9 a.m. and close at 4:45 p.m.

Hart Sworn In

New 8-Man B.C. Cabinet Announced

By BRUCE HUTCHISON

VICTORIA, Dec. 9.—John Hart today became premier of British Columbia, and tomorrow will head a coalition government composed of five Liberals and three Conservatives.

The coalition move succeeded finally today when the Conservative caucus in Vancouver accepted a new offer by Mr. Hart.

Where the premier had first proposed a cabinet of six Liberals and four Conservatives he suggested last night as a satisfactory compromise a smaller cabinet of eight, including five Liberals and three Conservatives.

This proposal was approved by the Conservatives this morning and assured British Columbia of a smaller cabinet than that of T. D. Pattullo, who had eight colleagues, making a total of nine.

NEW CABINET PERSONNEL

The new government will be sworn in at Government House tomorrow at 4:30 p.m.

It will include, besides Mr. Hart, G. S. Pearson, Wells Gray, K. C. MacDonald and H. G. Perry, Liberals; R. L. Maitland, K.C., Herbert Anscomb and R. W. Bruhn, Conservatives.

The distribution of portfolios is to be the subject of a personal conference between Mr. Maitland and Mr. Hart this afternoon.

Please Turn to Page Ten
See "Cabinet"

'Do's' and 'Don'ts' for Blackout

In order that every Vancouver resident may play his part in the blackout without confusion or misunderstanding, The Vancouver Sun obtained a detailed list of instructions from Inspector S. F. M. Moodie, civilian protection officer for British Columbia.

Instructions follow:

"1. There will be a continuous blackout until such time as the Royal Canadian Air Force gives instructions which permit lifting the order.

"2. Householders must see that no light shines from their residences into the street. The only way one can be sure is to go into the street and make a careful, complete inspection.

"For blacking out windows, we have found the cheapest and most satisfactory material is black paper (not tar paper) put into a frame and placed over all windows in rooms where a light is desired. Blankets, tar paper or any material impervious to light may be used in an emergency.

"3. Our advice to motorists is to get home as soon as you can, and stay there. If you must travel owing to emergency, headlights must be blinded save for a vertical slit three inches long by ¼ inch wide. Use such materials as are available. Tail-lights must be blinded save for a small disc in the centre.

"4. **Merchants must see that interior lights, those in their show windows, and neon signs are turned off before they quit their stores.**

"5. Street railways will operate under the same instructions that govern motorists. Head and tail lights must be masked. It may be found that blinds pulled down inside the car do not prevent outside glow sufficiently, in which case orders will be issued.

"6. Citizens are urged to use the telephone as little as possible. Remember that an emergency exists, and refrain from social calls.

"7. **In Vancouver, as in all other British Columbia centres, the blackout warning will be given by steam whistles as announced Monday.**

"8. Pedestrians, if they must be abroad after the signal sounds, must keep to the sidewalks. They may not walk along a street which has no sidewalk. No diagonal crossings are to be made."

News Under The Sun
Where to Find It

U.S. Planes Hunt Jap Carrier Near Coast; 2 Alerts in New York

U.S. East Coast Given Dramatic Raid Practise

WASHINGTON, Dec. 9.—War Department officials said today that the air raid alarm in New York city resulted from a "phony" tip that set into motion the planes and equipment which have been ordered held on a constant "alert" basis.

By Associated Press

NEW YORK, Dec. 9.—Public safety officials revealed today that a series of air raid alerts and alarms which electrified the eastern seaboard this afternoon were merely a dress rehearsal and that reports of approaching enemy planes were false.

An "all clear" signal in New York and Boston ended air raid alarms that kept the North Atlantic coast on guard against possible hostile aircraft for more than two hours.

NO EVACUATION

Officials said the order was a general precaution and was not based on any information that enemy bombers were approaching New York City or elsewhere.

The "alert" was ordered by Maj.-Gen. Henry H. Arnold, chief of the U.S. Army Air Forces.

At the same time, officials retracted that personnel was being evacuated from Mitchell Field, N.Y., under the alert program.

There had been reports that enemy planes were within two hours of New York and that Mitchell Field was being evacuated by non-essential personnel.

In spite of these explanations Maj.-Gen. Herbert A. Dargue, commander of the First Air Force, said, "I do not think the series of air raid alarms in the eastern section of the United States was a rehearsal."

ARP ON JOB

Most of the precautionary activity centred in Boston, where civilian defense units were ordered on duty, 12,500 air raid wardens were summoned to 24-hour duty and police were ordered to advise manufacturers to prepare for an air raid.

Explaining that no confirmation of the presence of hostile aircraftoff the coast had been obtained, Lieut.-Gen. Delos Emmons, chief of the Army Air Force Combat Command, announced through the White House in Washington that "we're taking no chances and remain on the alert."

About 280 planes took off from Mitchell army airfield, near New York, for reconnaissance flights.

Fire-fighting apparatus and ambulance details went to emergency posts at Mitchell Field, and rifles, steel helmets and gas masks were issued to the 7500 men at the field.

CHILDREN QUIT SCHOOL

Air raid sirens sounded throughout Nassau County on Long Island and children were sent home from schools and told not to return until further notification. School children in the borough of Brooklyn also were sent home.

The entire day shift of 14,000 men at the Bethlehem Steel Company's Fore River shipyard at Quincy, Mass., was

Please Turn to Page Ten
See "New York"

A WORLD AT WAR

WASHINGTON. — President Roosevelt placed Japanese, Italians and Germans in the United States in the category of "enemy aliens" today and prescribed by proclamations the conduct they must follow.

SAN FRANCISCO — Enemy planes which approached the Golden Gate, but which dropped no bombs, reported again over American west coast waters.

NEW YORK—Two air alarms as hostile planes reported "two hours from Boston." Brooklyn and Long Island schools and Bethlehem steel plants at Quincy, Mass., evacuated; 280 U.S. planes on patrol.

PORTLAND, Ore. — Intercepter planes hunt Jap aircraft carcarriers 600 miles off coast.

HONG KONG — Canadians help defeat of first Jap attack.

SINGAPORE—Fierce fighting all night; 25 Jap transports off coast.

MANILA—Night and day air raids; civilians take to hills; Japs land on small island 80 miles from capital.

GUAM—U.S. admits loss of minesweeper Penguin; Guam under Japan flag.

AUSTRALIA — Australia and New Zealand formalize war against Japan.

PACIFIC AMERICA — Canadian and American coast points ordered to blackout tonight again.

ASSAM—Indian province of Assam, northwest of Burma included in war zone.

BULLETINS

BATAVIA, N.E.I. — British forces have broken up a second Japanese landing party in North Borneo, Netherlands News Agency reported today.

WASHINGTON, Dec. 9.—President Roosevelt today announced an attack had been made on Clark Field in the Phillippines and that there were casualties among the officers and soldiers there.

KUIBYSHEV, Russia. — Russia maintains official silence regarding the U.S.-Japanese war, but diplomatic circles anticipate "important developments" in view of American lend-lease aid and Russia's obvious strategic potentialities in the Oriental war theatre.

NEW YORK, Dec. 9.—Ford Wilkins, CBS correspondent in Manila, reported at 6:12 a.m. P.S.T., today that there had been unverified reports of bombings of the Japanese island of Formosa and the cities of Tokyo and Kobe. (Tokyo officially denied any hostile planes over Japan.)

Radio Curfew at 5:30 Tonight

All radio stations on the Pacific Coast as far east as Chilliwack will be off the air from 5:30 p.m. to 8 a.m.

This announcement was made today by W. Howard, Dominion Government radio inspector, under instructions of the Western Air Command.

It is believed that the stations will remain silent as long as the blackouts and the period of emergency last, as part of the precautions taken against air raids.

"The carrier wave of radio makes an excellent beam which might guide bombers to the centre of the city. For this reason the stations are being silenced," Mr. Howard said.

Yule Leave for Troops Unlikely

OTTAWA, Dec. 9.—War on the Pacific appears to have blacked out the highlights of Christmas festivities for men of the armed forces, particularly on the west coast.

National defense headquarters said cancellation of leaves for various units of the Pacific commands, and retention of forces at full strength, was expected to mean Christmas or New Year leaves would not be possible.

Whether the tense Pacific situation would affect the leaves of units in other commands remained a question.

Fierce Fighting in Malaya; Canadian Troops in Action at Hong Kong; Japs Seize Philippine Foothold

SEATTLE, Dec. 9.—The Times today quoted the 2nd Interceptor Command as saying two or three Japanese aircraft carriers and some submarines had been reported operating off the Pacific coast, but Brig.-Gen. Carlyle H. Wash, head of the Command, refused to confirm or deny the report.

General Wash said the aerial hunt would cover a strip of ocean 600 miles wide and as far north and south as possible. He said planes would go out the full distance, then fly a criss-cross pattern toward shore, at a high altitude.

"Every hour that passes lessens the chance of a surprise attack," he said.

Panama Radio reported a Japanese airplane flew over the coastline but no bombs were dropped.

By DAVID WAITE
Special to The Vancouver Sun
Copyright, 1941, by British United Press

SINGAPORE, Straits Settlement, Dec. 9.—Japan has succeeded in landing additional troops in northern Malaya and savage fighting continued throughout last night for the important Bharu airdrome, a communique of the Malaya Command said today. Bombs were dropped in the city zone outside the naval base early today but no important damage was reported.

Meanwhile Japanese airmen hammered at Manila in daylight raids following an all night 'alert' and aided by fifth columnist fishermen, Japanese naval forces were reported to have landed on Lubang, an island 80 miles from the Philippine capital.

In the third main sector of the far-flung Pacific war, Britain's Crown Colony of Hong Kong successfully withstood the shock of a first Japanese attack. With Canadian forces in action, British batteries repelled the Japanese advance across the frontier.

ABCD Powers Act Together

In official and semi-official reports of the Malaya fighting it was indicated that the Japanese have succeeded in landing additional troops also in the Patani and Singora areas on the east coast of Thailand, above the Malaya border.

A communique, asserting that British reinforcements should reach the battle area today, commented:

"Information has been received from the commanding General of the Philippines, from Australia and from the Netherlands East Indies that pre-arranged reinforcement and reconnaissance plans have been fully implemented.

"The fullest co-operation among the ABCD powers (America, Britain, China and the Netherlands Indies) in the Far East has been manifested in these first two days of the conflict."

New Invasion Fleet Spotted

Japanese planes are believed to be laying mines off the west coast between Malaya and Netherlands Sumatra, dispatches from local officials said.

A British United Press dispatch from Calcutta announced that the Indian state of Assam, adjoining Burma on the northeast, has been put officially in the war zone.

British reconnoitering planes established yesterday that 25 Japanese transports are proceeding down the coast of southern Thailand, apparently with the intention of landing more troops in the Singora and Patani areas and the Kota Bharu region, the communique said.

"Thus all the transports which were located by air reconnaissance Dec. 6 and 7 are now apparently engaged in these landings on the KRA isthmus and northeastern Malaya."

Please Turn to Page Ten
See "Pacific War"

Hitler to State Policy On Japan War Tomorrow

By Associated Press

BERLIN, Dec. 9.—An authorized Nazi spokesman said today he was unable to state whether German - American relations would change within the next 24 hours, but well-informed sources said a "clarifying statement" on the American-Japanese war was expected soon.

(A Stockholm report predicted a declaration of war by Germany against United States "within two hours," but the time went by without any Berlin action.)

There were unconfirmed reports that the Reichstag would meet tomorrow to receive a statement by Hitler.

There was no hint of the form or contents of the "clarifying statement," said the Dienst aus Deutschland commentary, but "in view of the far-reaching importance of this question such a statement will not be long delayed."

Reports that the Reichstag was called coincided with sudden cancellation of an opera performance at the Kroll Opera House, where the Reichstag meets.

U.S. 'Carrier' Safe, Minesweeper Sunk

MANILA, Dec. 9.—U.S. naval sources denied reports today that the Seaplane Tender Langley was bombed during a Japanese attack on Davao yesterday. They said the Carrier was safe and carrying out routine duties.

U.S. Minesweeper Penguin, 840 tons, was sunk when attacked by the Japanese outside Guam Harbor, the Navy announced today

News FOR VICTORY Herald

VANCOUVER, B.C., DECEMBER 10, 1941

FINAL

Prince of Wales, Repulse Lost

JAPS SINK 2 BRITISH WARSHIPS

LONDON.—(BUP)—The British Admiralty today confirmed the loss of H.M.S. Prince of Wales, the Royal Navy's 35,000-ton battleship, and the battle cruiser H.M.S. Repulse, in action against the Japanese fleet off the east coast of Malaya.

An official Admiralty spokesman said: "A report has been received from Singapore that His Majesty's ships Prince of Wales and Repulse were sunk while carrying out operations against the Japanese in attacks on Malaya."

"No details have yet been received, except those contained in an official Japanese communique which claims that both ships were sunk by an air attack."

The Admiralty said that a statement would be issued tomorrow on the general war situation "which, from many viewpoints is both favorable and adverse and has undergone important changes during the last few days."

The Japanese Imperial Headquarters, whose communique was quoted by the Admiralty, said that the British Far East Fleet was sighted at 11:30 a.m. today near the coast of Malaya and that Japanese planes went into ction immediately.

(The Repulse, a battle cruiser, which obtained 32.6 knots on the measured mile trial, was 750 feet long with a displacement of 26,500 tons and carried 4,250 tons of oil fuel. It had six 15-inch guns, seventeen 4-inch guns and an armour belt of six-inch thickness.)

(The battleship Prince of Wales, which attained a speed of 30 knots or better, displaced 35,000 tons and was equipped with ten 14-inch guns.)

The Prince of Wales aided in trapping and sinking the German warship Bismarck in the North Atlantic last May. She was a sister ship of the George V Both these ships were the latest in British battleship design.

The Weather

Forecast for to-day: "Light northerly winds, partly cloudy and mild." Temperature for Tuesday: high: 47, low, 40.

Reich Considers Self At War With U.S.; F.D.R.

WASHINGTON. — (UP) — Warning Germany and Italy also consider themselves at war with the United States, President Roosevelt told the nation Tuesday night that it faces a long, hard war with Japan in which American forces already have suffered a "serious setback" in Hawaii.

Influential senators were quick to interpret the President's warning as an indication there might be a war declaration forthcoming very soon from the Reichstag.

The President, in a nationwide radio address reporting on the first 36 hours of the hostilities with Japan, declared Nippon is now engaged in "actual collaboration" with Germany and Italy

In his first nationwide speech as a war President, he conceded Japanese successes in the Pacific but pledged "we are going to win the war and the peace that follows."

He said he did not have sufficient information to state the ex-

(Continued on Page 13)

War's Progress

Combat between land forces figures largely for the first time today in reports of the struggle in the Western Pacific, with the following chief developments:

• HONG KONG—British forces presumably including Canadian detachments recently landed there, halted the Japanese advance from occupied territory in China's Kwangtun province, although fighting is still believed in progress. Unconfirmed reports said Japanese have occupied Kowloon, the mainland section of Hong Kong, but have in turn, been brought under attack by Chinese guerilla fighters. (Page 2).

• MANILA—U.S. bombers scored direct hits on three of six Japanese transports attacked during landing operations as Nippon gave strong naval and air support to a fierce land assault initiated in the northern section of Luzon island, on which Manila is situated. One of the transports capsized and bombs fell close to the transports which were not hit directly.

Japan is believed attempting to establish preliminary bases from which later attacks may be directed against Manila. Tokyo claimed Gen. MacArthur, U. S. Philippine (Continued on Back Page)

63

Blackout Off Till Further Notice

The Vancouver Sun

Only Evening Newspaper Owned, Controlled and Operated by Vancouver People

The Weather

Note! On no account will any of this information be transmitted by radio.
A disturbance passing over British Columbia gave moderate rains on the coast, light rains and snow in interior, temperatures are normal.
Temperature at 1:30 p.m. today: 44.
Temperature during 24 hours ending 4:30 a.m. today: maximum 44, minimum 38.
Forecast: cloudy and mild.
Official weather report on page 22.

Today's Tides

Vancouver Harbor
Low 4:12 p.m. .. 6.4 ft. High 11:17 p.m.. 8.9 ft.
English Bay
Low 6:04 p.m. .. 7.2 ft. High 11:03 p.m.. 9.2 ft.
First Narrows
Low slack 6:44 p.m. High slack 11:43 p.m.
Tomorrow's Tides Appear On Page 22

FOUNDED 1886
VOL. LVI—No. 61
HOME EDITION

VANCOUVER, BRITISH COLUMBIA, THURSDAY, DECEMBER 11, 1941 ***C

Price 3 Cents
On trains, boats and outside Greater Vancouver, 5c

MArine 1161

Official Warning:

'Get Ready For Further Blackouts'

Order Lifted Today, But May Be Clamped Down Again Any Hour; Use Time to Perfect Your Arrangements'

Here, at a glance, are the instructions concerning the lifting of the blackout:

1.—All night shifts at industrial plants are to report for work tonight.

2.—All citizens must be prepared to blackout their homes, and business places at a moment's notice.

3.—Auto headlights must be kept covered with only a slit of light showing.

4.—Signal for blackout may be by any means of communication.

5.—A skeleton staff of ARP wardens will remain on duty.

6.—Store hours returned to normal.

7.—Street lights will be kept burning.

8.—Speed limit remains at 15 miles per hour until further notice.

9.—Regular B. C. radio schedules resumed.

The lights of Vancouver will shine again tonight.

Shortly after 11 a.m., an order authorizing a temporary lifting of the British Columbia blackout was flashed from a conference of military and civilian protection heads in Victoria.

But—and this is of vital importance to every householder, every motorist, every merchant or industrialist of the coastal area—citizens must hold themselves in readiness for an instant resumption of the blackout between dusk and dawn.

"The war isn't over," said Inspector S. F. M. Moodie, civilian protection officer who released the announcement.

"The blackout has been called off for the time being, but residents must be ready to act instant on receipt of any future warning."

BE . . .. FOR CITIZENS

If such a warning is issued before the regulation sirens ordered from the East arrive, it will be sounded "by any means available," Inspector Moodie said.

Whistles, sirens, radio and telephone will be pressed into service.

Vancouver's first reaction was a sigh of relief. After three darkened nights, the blackout had lost most of its novelty. Next reaction was mild dismay.

"What shall we do with our screens and curtains?" was the question.

AUTO LAMPS STAY BLACK

ARP officials and police are ready with the answer.

"Keep 'em handy," they say. "Don't consider this provision a waste of time and money, because none of us know how soon you'll need them again!"

Car lights will still be permitted to shine only through a vertical slit three inches long by 1/4 inch wide, and ARP wardens will continue to check up motorists whose headlights are not cloaked.

Traffic on Vancouver streets during the night hours will not be speeded up despite the fact that blackouts of the city have been cancelled until further notice.

Inspector Wilfred Lemon told traffic officers today to maintain the speed limit of 15 miles an hour set by City Council Tuesday for the blackout periods.

The ARP will maintain a skeleton staff of 24 in the City

Please Turn to Page Twelve
See "Blackout"

Today In Britain

War events analyzed by Fleet Street writers, cabled from the London Bureau of the Vancouver Sun.

(Copyright, 1941)

LONDON, Dec. 11.—Afternoon newspapers emphasized Mr. Churchill's declaration that Hitler made a colossal mistake in attacking Soviet Russia, and that eventually London writers, was the turning-point in the war and it will eventually mark the downfall of Hitlerism. The Germans are running out of oil and other essentials.

Today the invincible armies that have overrun Europe from Narvik to the Sea of Azov are in full retreat for the first time during the war. The Germans have been forced to turn back at the most important point in their forward march. It is an omen that they have stretched their striking power beyond its limits.

Hitler had arrived at the very gate of the Caucasus and was forced to retreat. This was at a time when they had in their hands the main-line to the oilfields and the key to the backdoor of Persia.

• • •

Axis Fears for Oil

Hitler was fighting for new supplies of oil and found that he couldn't make it in a winter campaign and still have enough oil left to turn a wheel.

He had to accept defeat at Rostov. Reserves of oil were available only for seventy days of fighting, according to careful estimates in London, and the German leaders could not see victory in that time against Russia.

It is expected that the Germans will be forced to try again in the spring to take these areas but today their time schedule is completely ruined.

Already in several sectors of the Russian front the Germans have been forced to limit their

Please Turn to Page Twelve
See "Britain Today"

Ottawa Bans All Tire Sales

OTTAWA, Dec. 11.—The Munitions and Supply Department late today announced a "freezing" order on all rubber tires in Canada.

The order, effective at noon (Vancouver Time) prohibits any sale or purchase of rubber tires in Canada of any new tires on newly purchased cars.

All last night departmental experts worked on the compilation of information on rubber stocks to enable a decision today on the order just announced.

Exempt from the freezing order, in addition to new tires on newly purchased cars, are used tires, tubes and re-treated tires.

Hawaii Avenged

U.S. Sinks 3 Japan Warships

29,000-Ton First Line Battleship Sent Down

WASHINGTON, Dec. 11.—The Navy announced today that the defending marine garrison on Wake island has sunk one Japanese light cruiser and one destroyer by air action.

The garrison has defended the island in the South Pacific against four separate attacks in the last 48 hours by enemy aircraft and one by light naval units.

The Japanese were expected to resume the attack and attempt a landing.

By British United Press

WASHINGTON, Dec. 11.—Secretary of War Henry L. Stimson today confirmed the sinking of the 29,000-ton Japanese Battleship Haruna off the northern coast of Luzon yesterday by U.S. army bombers.

Thus the United States has revenged at least in part the Japanese attack on Pearl Harbor Sunday in which the loss of one old U.S. battleship has been officially announced and other losses reported.

Today's war department communique said that there were continued attempts by strong Japanese forces to establish themselves along the northern coast of Luzon.

Determined resistance has confined this action to the attack in the vicinity of Aparri, at the extreme northern tip of Luzon, where the Japanese attempted to establish a beach head yesterday," the communique said.

"Air activity continues in the vicinity of Manila, with intermittent attacks on air fields at Cavite and Nichols Field throughout the day."

APARRI LOCKED IN

Stimson said Aparri is just a small landing place," which is shut off from the main part of the island by mountains, and if the Japanese attempt to transport an army through the passes, it will "be a slow job."

Mr. Stimson sent a message to Lt. Gen. Douglas MacArthur, commander of the United States Far Eastern forces, congratulating him for the sinking, his defense against "great odds" and the conduct of the U.S. Army and Philippine troops.

He predicted the ultimate triumph of the allied cause over the "autocratic" powers.

There was a "heavy loss" of planes in Hawaii during Sunday's surprise raid, Mr. Stimson said, but added it "can and is being made good at the present moment." Full details of the attack are not yet known, but the principal concern of the war department is getting defenses strengthened everywhere.

"We do not believe in recrimination or placing of the blame on anybody at this time," Stimson said. "That is a sign of immaturity. The investigation can come later. Now we are stressing preparedness."

Stimson told newsmen, "We must expect initial reverses, but

Please Turn to Page Twelve
See "Far East"

Japanese Claim Lexington Sunk

LONDON, Dec. 11.—The Berlin radio today quoted the Japanese as saying the United States Aircraft Carrier Lexington had been sunk off Hawaii. (There was no immediate American comment.)

(The 33,000-ton Lexington, completed in 1927 at a cost of more than $45,000,000 was built to carry a maximum of 90 aircraft and a normal crew of 2,122 including flying personnel.)

News Under The Sun
Where to Find It

U.S. Declares War on Hitler: All Powers on 5 Continents Now Enter Finish Fight

WORLD AT WAR

By JOE ALEX MORRIS
Special to The Vancouver Sun
Copyright, 1941, by British United Press

Today it is a real World War.

The line-up:

Great Britain, America, the Soviet Union, China and the refugee governments of Europe for the Allies.

Germany, Italy, Japan and Axis-dominated governments for the Axis.

Adolf Hitler and Benito Mussolini formally extended the war to five continents by joining Japan in the conflict against the United States, mobilizing the total Axis strength for a finish fight and leaving only South America under an uneasy peace.

'Long, Hard Struggle Ahead'

Even as the dictators spoke at Berlin and Rome, the millions of men who will fight and die before peace comes again were in action on the frozen hills before Moscow, along the dusty escarpment of the Libyan desert, in the steaming jungles of Malaya and along the beaches of the Philippines.

From opposing leaders of the armed forces came almost simultaneous declarations that they are prepared for a long, hard struggle but confident of victory.

In London, Prime Minister Winston Churchill told the British nation that this war is a life or death struggle and that "we will go forward to victory."

In Berlin, Hitler declared that Axis-held Europe is "impregnable" and that Germany would break all opposition.

In Rome, Mussolini shouted: "We shall wage war to conquer."

Only at Moscow, where Josef V. Stalin is a key figure in the war, ... struggle, was there silence on the new phase of host ... throwing ... the red ... marshal in the offensive ... with the great re ... army ... this ... last hopes of vic... America.

Significantly, be..lin, Rome and Tokyo were silent regarding possible Soviet participation in the far eastern war.

The Situation in Brief

A quick glance at the main centres of conflict gives the following brief summary:

WASHINGTON—Congress votes war on Italy and Germany in half an hour after President's message.

MANILA—U.S. airmen bomb and sink 29,000-ton Jap battleship, light cruiser and destroyer; Jap invaders stalled on Luzon Island.

SINGAPORE—2000 survivors from HMS Prince of Wales and Repulse arrive; Australian airmen bomb Jap air base on Pobra, East Indies island.

MALAYA—British forces hold Jap invaders in check; little action reported.

RUSSIA—Red Army makes new gains; great offensive launched to sweep Huns from Donetz Basin; new cracks in Hun line at Leningrad.

BERLIN—Hitler boasts of united Axis but listeners sing "Deutschland Ueber Alles" dolefully.

ROME—Mussolini boasts of victory to come.

LIBYA—British force Germans backwards; destruction of Axis forces appears assured.

LONDON—Churchill expects long hard war but confident of ultimate victory and total destruction of all Axis powers.

CBS Eyewitness Tells of Fight

2300 Men Rescued From Sea Disaster

By British United Press

LONDON, Dec. 11.—The Admiralty reported tonight that approximately 2330 officers and men have been saved from the sunken battleships, Prince of Wales and Repulse.

The Admiralty said about 130 officers and 2,200 seamen were saved from the two warships sunk off Singapore.

Complement of the Wales was 1615. The Repulse had a complement of 1300, making a total complement of 2915 officers and men, indicating loss of between 500 and 600 men in the sinkings.

Cecil Brown, correspondent for Columbia Broadcasting System, was among those rescued from HMS Repulse, Capt. William G. Tennant.

(Admiral Sir Tom Phillips, commander of the Far Eastern Fleet, and Capt. John Leach, commander of the Prince of Wales, are both missing, but Capt. W. G. Tennant of the Repulse and Capt. L. H. Bell, captain of the fleet, are safe, it was announced at Singapore.)

Please Turn to Page Twelve
See "War at Sea"

Election Winners

Following is the list of successful candidates in yesterday's city election:

CITY COUNCIL

Ald. H. L. Corey.
Ald. George Buscombe.
Ald. Charles Jones.
Jack Price.

SCHOOL BOARD

James Blackwood.
Mrs. Ada Crump.
A. Fellowes.
E. Meredith.

PARK BOARD

R. Rowe Holland.
Don Brown.
S. Smith.

(Complete Details on Page 17)

60 Jap Planes Attacked at Once

SINGAPORE, Straits Settlements, Dec. 11.—More than 2000 survivors of the battleship Prince of Wales and the battle cruiser Repulse arriving in Singapore today, told how the great British battle craft had gone down fighting under perhaps the most ferocious airplane attack in naval history. More than 60 Jap planes attacked at one time.

The guns of both ships were

Forward

MR. CHURCHILL
From a Caricature in London Star

Churchill Confident Of Victory

By EDWARD ...
Copyright, 1941, by British United Press

LONDON, Dec. 11. — Prime Minister Winston Churchill, addressing the House of Commons today as Germany and Italy declared war on the United States, said the British Empire, America, Russia and China are fighting for their lives "and will go forward to victory—not over Japan alone but over the Axis and all its works."

"Our foes are bound by their ambitions and their crimes, implacably, to the destruction of the English-speaking world and all it stands for," Mr. Churchill said.

(TEXT OF MR. CHURCHILL'S ADDRESS ON PAGE 15.)

JOINT RESOLVE

"I know I speak for the United States as well as for the British Empire when I say we would all rather perish than be conquered. . . . It would indeed bring shame on our generation if we did not teach the enemy a lesson which will not be forgotten in the records of a thousand years."

In a wide-sweeping review of the war, Mr. Churchill said Hitler in attacking Russia had made one of the outstanding blunders of history, that the German and Italian forces in Eastern Libya face destruction and that in the Battle of the Atlantic shipping losses had decreased.

"We can already see after six months of fighting in Russia that Hitler has made one of the most outstanding blunders of history and the results so far realized constitute events of cardinal importance in the final decision of the war," he said.

LIBYA VICTORY

Starting off one of the major speeches of a war which now extends to all the continents, he told of the Libyan situation:

"On November 18 Gen. Auchinleck set out to destroy the entire armed forces of the Germans and Italians in Cyrenaica (eastern Libya). Now! on December 11, I am bound to say that it seems very probable he will do so . . . The German army in Libya is stubborn and in every way worthy of the tomb prepared for it."

Of the sinking of the battleship Prince of Wales and the battle cruiser Repulse off Malaya, he said HMS Prince of Wales was sunk by repeated attacks of bombing and torpedo-carrying planes and there was no reason to suppose that any new weapons or explosives had been employed.

Congress Rushes Through Formalities In Record Time After Roosevelt's Message; 'America Really United'

By LYLE WILSON
Special to The Vancouver Sun
Copyright, 1941, by British United Press

WASHINGTON, Dec. 11. — President Roosevelt today signed congressional resolutions of war against Germany and Italy, putting the United States all-out in the war against the Tokyo-Rome-Berlin Axis to stop "its course of world conquest."

He signed the German resolution at 3:05 p.m. (12:05 p.m. Vancouver time) and the resolution for war against Italy one minute later.

Congress took only 34 minutes from the time Mr. Roosevelt asked for the resolution to quick-time them through today.

Speeding through the House and Senate in the wake of the war resolutions was legislation to remove restrictions against sending citizen-soldiers outside the Western Hemisphere.

It was a series of unanimous votes on both the recognition of the existence of states of war and on the Bill to send United States men wherever they are needed.

Brief Blunt Message

Both ocean coast lines and the Gulf area were on a war-time alert today for the duration and there were troop, airplane and ship movements ... ... mail war against Italy and Germany in six blunt paragraphs which comprised his message to Congress.

He reported that Germany and Italy had declared war on the United States and asked Congress to recognize the state of hostilities thus thrust upon us.

"Delay invites danger," he said. "The forces endeavoring to enslave the entire world now are moving towards the Western Hemisphere."

Congress agreed, without debate, and as soon sent the resolutions to the White House for signature.

The signing ceremony was simple and quick. Six representatives and six members of the Senate entered the President's office a moment or two after 3 p.m. and gathered around his desk.

Present were Speaker Sam Rayburn, House Majority Leader John McCormack, D. Mass.; Chairman Sol Bloom of the House Foreign Affairs Committee, D., N.Y.; Rep. Charles Eaton, R., N.J.; Rep. Luther Johnson, D., Tex., and House Minority Leader Joseph W. Martin, Jr., R., Mass.

There also were Vice-President Henry A. Wallace; Senate Majority Leader Alben W. Barkley, D., Ky.; Chairman Tom Connally, D., Tex.; of the Senate Foreign Relations Committee; Senate Minority Leader Charles L. McNary, R., Ore.; Sen. Warren R. Austin, R., Vt.; and Sen. Carter Glass, D., Va.

Glass, elderly veteran of the Senate, related how Mr. Roosevelt commented to the legisla-

...tive leaders that some members of the Senate Foreign Relations Committee had wanted to phase the resolutions for proclaiming a state of war against Germany ... ... ians of the ... countries.

"Hell, we not only want to hurt their feelings but we want to kill them," Glass told the President.

Vice President Wallace related a remark of Mr. Roosevelt who said he had heard things always came in threes, offering as an example the two declarations on the desk before him which made a total of three he had signed since Japan attacked the United States. (Significantly U. S. airmen sank three Jap warships today.)

Please Turn to Page Twelve
See 'U.S. at War'

Russians Prepared to Clean Out Donets Basin

By HENRY SHAPIRO
Copyright, 1941, by British United Press

KUIBYSHEV, Russia, Dec. 10. (Delayed)—Smashing Russian counter-drives on the Leningrad and Moscow fronts today cleared the way for an all-out Russian offensive in the southeast aimed at routing the Germans from the entire Donets Basin.

While communiques confirmed Soviet recapture of Yelets on the central front and the railroad city of Tikhvin in the north, official reports from the southeast said a reinforced Red Army has launched "heaviest" attacks on the Donets Basin to recapture German-held Stalino and Makeevka.

In London, Exchange Telegraph reported that the Russians have cleared the Germans from inside Moscow and Tula, 100 miles south of the capital.)

...the southeast will be to recapture the strategic city of Kharkov, 405 miles south of Moscow.

Nineteen thousand Germans were killed and wounded in the Tikhvin and Yelets battles which ended in Nazi routs, the official Russian news agency reported.

An official announcement said Russian troops Tuesday drove German and Fascist forces from Yelets 125 miles east of Orel, after four days of fierce fighting. The Soviets smashed the 45th and 95th Nazi infantry divisions and said the Germans suffered 12,000 casualties.

Charge Suspect In Bakery Holdups

★ ★

HITLER OUSTS ARMY CHIEF

It's RED Again

THIS MUCH—No words are needed to explain the story told by The News-Herald map above. The splotches of red measure the extent of the first general defeat suffered so far by the Nazi forces. They show how far Soviet forces have driven back Hitler's invading hordes. They show that RED is a good color on the map, alike as the marking of nations in the British Commonwealth and to show an Allied victory over civilization's foes. Details of Soviet advances after this map was completed appear on Page Two.

Troops Protect Workers

SAN FRANCISCO.—(UP)—Rear Admiral John W. Greenslade Sunday night summoned marines and troops to escort workers through picket lines of striking United Brotherhood of Welders (Ind.) at the Pacific Bridge Company, Alameda.

Ninety-three soldiers took up stations at the plant. Shortly afterward the welders' picket line dispersed without incident. Employees within the plant said they were "taking orders from the government."

The Welders' Brotherhood had called a walkout at major California shipyards and other defense plants working on more than $1,000,000,000 contracts for the U. S. and Britain.

(See also story Page 2)

BULLETINS

BERLIN.—(From official German broadcasts recorded by U. P. listening posts)—The high command claimed Sunday night that fighting in Russia continues with "unabated fierceness," and that Axis troops are battling "heroically" in Libya.

Belgium Declares War on Japs

LONDON—(UP)—The Belgian free government has declared war on Japan and ordered its ambassador to leave Tokyo it was reported reliably Sunday night.

Japs Bomb Manila Air Field

NEW YORK—(UP)—The Japanese Domei news agency, in a broadcast heard here by the United Press listening post, said that Japanese army planes subjected Manila and surrounding districts to 32 minutes of bombing beginning at 12 a.m. Monday during which Nichols airfield and other military objectives were "heavily damaged."

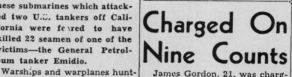

News Herald
FOR VICTORY

LARGEST MORNING CIRCULATION WEST OF TORONTO

VANCOUVER, B.C., MONDAY, DECEMBER 22, 1941   3c

U.S. SMASHES 14 AXIS SUBS

WASHINGTON—(UP)—Secretary of the Navy Frank Knox announced Sunday night that the U.S. navy had sunk or damaged at least 14 enemy submarines in the Atlantic.

He added that American naval vessels already have effectively dealt with several Japanese submarines in the Pacific.

He said probability of these losses in the Atlantic, coupled with the prevalence of bitter North Atlantic weather, "may account for the recent comparative security of the North Atlantic convoy routes."

It was disclosed that Japanese submarines which attacked two U.S. tankers off California were feared to have killed 22 seamen of one of the victims—the General Petroleum tanker Emidio.

Warships and warplanes hunted grimly for the enemy undersea craft.

The crew of the Emidio, which was shelled and torpedoed off Cape Mendocino, 200 miles north of San Francisco, abandoned ship and took to lifeboats, the navy announced in a communique released in Washington, D.C.

"Three lifeboats were destroyed by submarine gunfire," the communique said. "Thirty-two survivors have been rescued. There were 54 in the crew."

Life Boats

The communique indicated that the 22 missing men may have been in the lifeboats shattered by the submarine's guns.

The second attacked tanker, the Richfield Oil Company's Agwiworld, was shelled eight times by a submarine 20 miles off Cypress Point, Monterey, and 80 miles south of San Francisco, but was not hit.

Both attacks were made Saturday afternoon without warning. The Agwiworld was attacked first.

Additionally U. S. and Canadian forces investigated a report a third enemy submarine chased the Union Oil tanker L. P. St. Clair into the Columbia River.

Captain F. B. Goncalves of the Agwiworld reported his attacker fired eight shells but that heavy seas "made the Japs' aim a little too high."

"If we'd had a gun," Captain Goncalves said, "there might have been one less submarine. All we had was two pistols."

The Weather

Today's forecast: "Light variable winds, overcast and mild with rain." Sunday's temperatures: High, 43; low, 37.

Hitler Fires Army Chief; Red Gains Bring Crisis

LONDON—(UP)—Adolf Hitler has fired Field Marshal Walther Von Brauchitsch, commander-in-chief of the German army, and has taken over the command himself, issuing an order of the day to the troops commanding them "to defend our front in the East with fanatical determination," the Berlin radio announced.

It was evident from the tone of the Berlin broadcasts that a crisis has arisen in German war operations, presumably as the result of the smashing Russian offensive on the Moscow front, which has hurled the Germans back 70 miles in two weeks and has destroyed many of the best German divisions.

If the Russian drive continued to gain momentum, Germany itself soon would be in peril of invasion, and the impression gained here from the Berlin broadcasts was that Hitler and his generals had quarreled over the best way to meet the situation.

There also were reports of alarm in Italy.

An Exchange Telegraph dispatch from Zurich relayed the news from Rome that Virginio Gayda, authoritative Fascist editor, has published a sensational dispatch in the newspaper Giornale D'Italia asserting that Italy has thrown all her air, land and sea forces into the battle for Libya, which also was approaching an Axis rout, and that "on their fate depends the fate of Italy."

Continued on Page 19.

Charged On Nine Counts

James Gordon, 21, was charged Sunday with seven armed robberies of city bakeries and two attempted bakery holdups.

He was arrested at 11.30 p.m. Saturday at Robson and Richards streets by Constables Charles Campbell and E. Pinkerton—who reported he carried a fully loaded .32 calibre revolver—and identified in a lineup in police court Sunday by his women victims.

The gun was identified as the one stolen by three men who held up Jaynes Drug Store, 1901 East Hastings Street, about 9 p.m., Dec. 14.

Arrest of Gordon culminated several weeks of intensive police investigation in charge of Superintendent of Detectives W. Gordon Grant in which the entire criminal investigation branch took part.

Detectives have been guarding bakeries for several days,

(Continued on Page 3)

British Raid Thailand

LOS ANGELES—(UP)—British Broadcasting Company in London, quoting official announcements from Rangoon, Burma, said Sunday night British planes have raided enemy airdromes in Eastern Thailand, destroying planes and gasoline dumps.

65

To You All, the Old, Old Wish — A Happy Christmas!

HUNDREDS SEE JAP SUB TORPEDO CALIFORNIA SHIP

The Vancouver Sun

Only Evening Newspaper Owned, Controlled and Operated by Vancouver People

★ ★ ★ ★ ★ FINAL

FOUNDED 1886 VOL. LVI—No. 72 VANCOUVER, B.C., WEDNESDAY, DECEMBER 24, 1941 Price 3 Cents On trains, boats and outside Greater Vancouver, 5c

Late Bulletins

400 U.S. Marines Held Up Japanese 14 Days

WASHINGTON, Dec. 24. — The marine garrison which held out on Wake Island for 14 days against Japanese attacks from the sea and air, and sank four Japanese warships, numbered less than 400 men, the Navy revealed late today.

The Navy earlier in the day announced that the island probably has been captured.

The marines fought off 14 Japanese attacks with equipment consisting of 12 fighter planes, six five-inch guns, 12 three-inch anti-aircraft guns, 18 .50 calibre anti-aircraft machine guns and 30 .30 calibre anti-aircraft machine guns, plus the usual light weapons such as rifles and pistols.

The garrison included 13 marine officers and 365 marines.

A communique issued earlier today revealed that the marines had sunk two enemy destroyers.

Alaskans Brought to Seattle

SEATTLE, Dec. 24.—A naval transport has arrived in Seattle with 724 women and children evacuated from Alaska as a precautionary measure.

Millionth Ton of Food

WASHINGTON, Dec. 24.—Secretary of Agriculture Claude R. Wickard was advised today that the millionth ton of U. S. food shipped to Great Britain under the lease-lend system had arrived safely.

Present for Hitler

SEATTLE, Dec. 24.—Boeing Aircraft Co. workmen built a Christmas tree today out of a piece of steel pipe covered with aluminum shavings. On it was a present for Adolf Hitler—a miniature gallows.

Gen. McNaughton O.K. Again

SOMEWHERE IN ENGLAND, Dec. 24.—Lt.-Gen. A. G. L. McNaughton, commander of the Canadian Corps, has completely recovered from his minor lung infection, his doctors announced today.

Nazis Claim 'Invasion Bases' Ready

NEW YORK, Dec. 24.—The BBC today quoted a German propaganda broadcast as claiming intensive fortification works along the Atlantic Coast of Europe have been completed, furnishing "a complete base and support for offensive operations against Britain.

Buddy Baer Hurt in Auto Crash

LONG BRANCH, N.J., Dec. 24.—Heavyweight challenger Buddy Baer of California suffered face scratches and bruises today in an auto accident just outside of Long Branch. Baer is scheduled for a return bout with Champion Joe Louis at Madison Square Garden, Jan. 9.

U.S. May Put 'Ceiling' on Incomes

WASHINGTON, Dec. 24.—Congressional tax leaders believed today that the war-time need for revenue may make it necessary ultimately to fix an arbitrary individual income ceiling, perhaps $15,000, $20,000 or $25,000. Such a plan, if adopted, would mean that no person could retain income earned in excess of the ceiling.

Von Ribbentrop Cheers Up Germans

BERLIN, Dec. 24.—Axis powers must fight to the end, German Foreign Minister Joachim von Ribbentrop declared today.

Commenting on reports that Germany has sent "peace feelers," he said they are "stupid gossip" and predicted Germany would finish her job on the Eastern Front "definitely next year."

German Guns Shell Dover

FOLKESTONE, England, Dec. 24.—Germany's big cross-Channel guns broke the peace of Christmas Eve tonight by shelling the Kentish coast. Children were singing Christmas carols at some of the towns along the white cliffs of the Dover Strait when the guns across the water at Cap Griz Nez opened up full-throat. Shells thundered across the moonlit Channel during two periods of 15 minutes each. Buildings were shaken but the caroling went on.

66

At the Race Tracks

TROPICAL PARK

FIRST RACE—Six furlongs:
Roman Descent (Lynch) $8.70 $4.60, $3.80.
Hunting Home (May) $9.80, $6.90
Queen Echo (Gonzales) $8.10.
Time: 1.13 1-5.

SECOND RACE—Six furlongs:
Marksman (Berg) $4.30, $3.10, $2.80
Tower Guest (Campbell) $7.50 $6.10.
Bagdad (Bodiou) $9.40.
Time: 1.14.

THIRD RACE—Six furlongs:
Water Cracker (MacMullen) $6.70 $3.70, $2.50.
Range Dust (Durando) $5.20, $3.30.
Lady Infinite (Strickler) $2.60.
Time: 1.13 1-5.

FOURTH RACE—Six furlongs:
Captain Rae (Torres) $12.80, $5.00 $3.10.
Tomochichi (Atkinson) $4.40, $3.10
Eire (Stout) $3.00.
Time: 1:12 1-5.

FIFTH RACE—Six furlongs:
Scotch Trap (Garner) $9.40, $5.40 $5.70.
Miss Goshen (Schmidl) $12.30, $8.50
Equistone (McCreary) $4.80.
Time: 1.12 2-5.

SIXTH RACE—Mile and one sixteenth:
Blue Warrior (Connelly) $9.30 $4.20, $2.60.
Sun Eager (Skelly) $4.20, $2.40.
Homeward Bound (Harrell) $2.50.
Time: 1.47 4-5.

SEVENTH RACE—Mile and 70 yards:
Pomiva, $3.90, $3.00, $2.20.
Inscolad, $7.70, $4.30.
Magic Stream, $2.80.
Time: 1:45.

EIGHTH RACE—Mile and seventy yards:
Psychology, $8.90, $4.40, $2.80.
Port Spin, [illegible] $2.80.
Cove [illegible]

Manila Situation Serious

Japanese Land New Troops in Philippines

By FRANK HEWLETT
Special to The Vancouver Sun
Copyright, 1941, by British United Press

MANILA, Dec. 24. — Gen. Douglas MacArthur, commander of U.S. forces in the Far East, took the field today, assuming personal command of American and Philippines forces combatting an all-out Japanese air and land assault against this capital and bastion of American defenses in the Pacific.

Macarthur sent into the battle raging on the Lingayen Gulf, 135 miles north of Manila and on the eastern Atimonan area, 75 miles distant, the "Forward Echelon" of his general headquarters.

The announcement was taken to indicate that the grand battle of the Philippines had now been joined.

Reports from Batangas, 65 miles due south of Manila, said that American armed forces have repulsed all Japanese attempts to obtain a foothold in that area and have inflicted heavy casualties upon the Japanese.

(Associated Press reported that as the new overland threat to Manila developed, army headquarters announced, military authorities were considering declaring the capital an Open City to spare it from "any possible air or ground attacks." The announcement recalled similar declarations were made with Paris, Brussels, Athens, Rome "and other capital" earlier in the war).

The Japanese, having moved an expeditionary force estimated at 80,000 to 100,000 men, to the Lingayen Gulf, approached the southeast coast with a force possibly half that large and started a concentrated air attack on Manila which gave this capital four air alarms between dawn to dusk.

ODDS FAVOR JAPS

The odds of numbers are on the side of the Japanese. They appear to have sent against the island of Luzon more than 150,000 men. In addition to the major landings at Lingayen and Atimonan are smaller forces landed at Vigan, Legaspi and Aparri.

Authoritative army sources said Japanese claims to the capture of Davao city, in their drive on Mindanao Island, south of Luzon, are untrue, but it was admitted that unreliable communications made it difficult to assess the exact situation.

7 SHIPS SUNK

Refugees from Mindanao reported that seven Japanese troopships had been sunk in Davao Harbor and that the defense forces were giving a good account of themselves in landing fighting.

Forty Japanese troop transports appeared off the Luzon Island coast, 75 miles southeast of Manila, to reinforce a new Japanese landing group in the Atimonan area, when the first enemy planes appeared over the capital.

Within a few minutes, bombs, estimated to weigh as much as 1100 pounds, were dropping in the port area and smoke could be seen rising from fires.

By mid-afternoon the third raid of the day was under way.

Please Turn to Page Nine
See "Philippines"

Hong Kong Troops Win Back One Position

Hong Kong—Christmas, 1941

Forced Back by Jap Onslaught At Another

By British United Press

SINGAPORE, Dec. 24. — Hong Kong's defenders are striking back with renewed fury at Japanese attackers coincident with indications that Chinese onslaughts from the rear are hampering Japanese operations.

A Singapore general headquarters communique said that during the 24 hours which ended at 5 p.m. Tuesday, the Japanese kept up pressure on the British positions at Hong Kong. The Japanees also intensively bombarded the defenders.

"Some ground in the Repulse Bay area has been given up but in the central part of the island a party of Royal Marines recaptured a position which was overrun Monday night," the communique said.

"There are indications that pressure by Chinese troops and guerillas in the new territories (fringing Kowloon on the mainland) already is having some effect on Japanese efforts at Hong Kong."

The Repulse Bay area is across the island from the city and port.

(In London a message was received from Sir Mark Young, Governor of Hong Kong, dated 2:30 p.m. Monday which said there had been no substantial change in positions. He said the Japanese were attacking from both land and air but were suffering heavy casualties due to spirited counter-attacks by Imperial forces).

Chinese Relieve Hong Kong Pressure

CHUNGKING, Dec. 24.—Chinese dispatches reported today that the Japanese had withdrawn 3000 to 4000 of their troops from the assault of Hong Kong to counter-attack Chinese forces threatening their rear near Shumchun on the mainland.

Both sides were said to have suffered considerable casualties in heavy fighting which ensued.

Chinese forces have captured Namling, 50 miles north of Hong Kong on the important Kowloon-Canton railway, the official Chinese news agency said today.

Namling is the next big station north of Shumchun on the Kowloon-Canton railway.

The British embassy, meanwhile, announced it had been in touch with the Hong Kong defenders at mid-day and said they were "still fighting valiantly."

The civilian population in Hong Kong is taking the situation calmly, although about 100 bombs were dropped on the island yesterday, the embassy declared.

A Chinese spokesman declared that all the troops which the Japanese were employing in their offensive against Malaya had been withdrawn from China, but said those attacking the Philippines came from elsewhere.

Hong Kong holds out and members of the American Consulate General staff under Consul General Addison E. Southard are carrying on under shell fire in the Hong Kong-Shanghai Bank Building, a message from Hong Kong said today.

Vancouver Demands Bomb Insurance

Urgent pleas by Vancouver business and labor organizations for immediate establishment of a federal plan of bombing insurance were rebuffed today by Hon. J. L. Ilsley, Minister of Finance.

His refusal to commit the Dominion government angered representatives of the Vancouver Board of Trade, Canadian Manufacturers' Association, Trades and Labor Council, Associated Property Owners and Vancouver Real Estate Exchange who were in conference with Mayor Cornett at City Hall.

On their behalf the mayor promptly began to apply new pressure. He notified Lieut.-Gov. W. C. Woodward of the impasse, sent a telegram to Hon. John Hart and Wired Hon. Ian Mackenzie saying that "the whole community joins me in saying that this definitely is not good enough in view of the risk to which we are exposed here and vast amounts involved in homes and industries through risk of enemy action."

Premier Hart was requested to add his word to the demand from British Columbia for a government insurance plan to fill the gap in business practice left by the withdrawal of private companies from the field.

It is known that Col. Woodward shares the concern expressed in today's exchange of telegrams and phone calls.

GOV'T 'CONSIDERING'

While the meeting waited, the mayor telephoned to Mr. Ilsley at Ottawa.

"I asked him to give assurance that the government would announce a plan at once," His Worship reported after the conversation," but I was unable to get any indication from him as to what the government intends to do or when they might do it."

Mr. Ilsley merely said the government is "considering" the matter and declined to be drawn further.

The subsequent wire to Mr. Mackenzie containing the statement by His Worship that "I must urge you to impress on your colleagues the necessity of immediate action and a prompt statement that any loss incurred through bombing or otherwise will be met, leaving details to be worked out later."

Delay was heavily condemned by J. S. Eckman, vice-president of the C. M. A. He contrasted the government's inaction with swift steps taken by the United States.

Washington set up a $100,000,000 company within 48 hours of the outbreak of war.

No Sun Tomorrow Hear the News Over CKWX

Christmas will be a holiday for the staff of The Vancouver Sun, and no regular editions will be published.

Complete and up-to-the-minute news will be given in Sun newscasts over CKWX at the regular week-day hours, with the exception of 6:30 p.m., which will be moved to 6 p.m. due to the re-broadcast of the King's message at 6:30.

Times for Christmas newscasts will be:

7:30 a.m., 12:05 noon, 6 p.m., 10 p.m.

On Boxing Day all editions of The Sun will be published as usual.

Roosevelt, Churchill Broadcast

WASHINGTON, Dec. 24. — President Roosevelt, in a Christmas message to the nation today, asked all Americans to light their trees and exchange presents to signify their faith in "the dignity and brotherhood of man" which they are fighting to uphold.

Standing on the south portico of the White House with Mr. Roosevelt was Prime Minister Winston Churchill, who spoke after the President to a crowd of thousands assembled on the White House lawn for the traditional ceremony of lighting Washington's No. 1 Christmas tree.

"Our strongest weapon in this war is that conviction of the dignity and brotherhood of man which Christmas Day signifies —more than any other day or any other symbol," the President said in his prepared address which was broadcast internationally.

WE KNOW THE ANSWER

The President said it was natural in times like these that men and women of America would asked themselves how they could light their trees and exchange gifts when the world is caught in an overwhelming conflict.

"Even as we ask these questions, we know the answer," the President said.

"Against enemies who preach the principles of hate and practice them, we set our faith in human love and in God's care for us and all men everywhere."

"RIGHT TO LIVE"

Prime Minister Churchill dedicated Christmas Eve to the children, but pledged that leaders of the democracies would turn tomorrow to the stern tasks of sacrifice and daring which shall give children a right to live in a free and decent world.

Enemy Craft Disabled

Freighter Also Crippled Off Long Beach

SAN FRANCISCO, Dec. 24. —In plain view of hundreds of persons ashore, a Japanese submarine torpedoed and crippled the U.S. freighter Absaroka off a southern California coastal town today in a continuation of enemy activity against shipping in California waters.

Eleventh naval district offices at Long Beach said the Absaroka was left in a "sinking" condition."

A dozen boats surrounded the craft and rescued the 35 members of its crew.

Warplanes and warships searched the area for the attacker which, witnesses said, remained boldly on the water for some time after the torpedoing.

At least one depth charge was dropped.

USED NO GUNS

Witnesses said they first believed the submarine was a fishing boat but that it seemed to be running too smoothly for the heavy sea that prevailed. The submarine used only a torpedo in its attack. There was no deck artillery in action.

The Absaroka did not sink immediately. The navy expressed hope the vessel might be salvaged. It was the eighth ship attacked by enemy submarines off the California coast since last Thursday.

Navy officers investigated a report the submarine had been disabled but said there was no evidence to back it up.

The Absaroka's home port is San Francisco. It is owned by the McCormick Steamship Company.

U.S. Bombers Sink Two Japanese Subs

By LEICESTER WAGNER
Special to The Vancouver Sun
Copyright, 1941, by British United Press

SAN FRANCISCO, Dec. 24.—Long-range Japanese submarines that invaded California coastal waters in an attempt to disrupt shipping by attacking seven American vessels with torpedoes and guns, were pursued today by navy bombers which already are believed to have hunted down and destroyed at least two enemy submersibles.

The best information seems to indicate at least two—and possibly four—undersea craft are operating off the Pacific Coast between the Columbia River and Los Angeles, an 800-mile sector. Repeated appearance of the submarines operating far from known bases indicate they have a range of 16,000 miles which would give them ample time for more than just hit-and-run tactics.

ROSEBANK SAFE

Tuesday they invaded the shipping lines to sink the Union Oil tanker Montebello with a torpedo. The Richfield oil tanker Larry Doheny was shelled, and the Texas Company oil tanker Idaho was driven to the security of a small cove by shell fire from another submarine.

The Canadian freighter Rosebank, feared a submarine victim because it was overdue, ar-

Please Turn to Page Nine
See "Jap Sub"

1942

The Japanese sweep through the Far East continued through 1942 while America—the sleeping giant—awoke to organize the immense productive capacity that would be needed to defeat the Axis powers. Germany continued its headlong dash through southern Russia, although its headway had been halted around Moscow and Leningrad. It was not until the end of the year that Russia's productive capacity had recovered from the moving of thousands of factories to the east of the Ural Mountains out of reach of the Germans. By then, the Red Army had amassed the equipment necessary to mount the offensive that turned the tide of the war and saved Stalingrad. In October, the British had engineered a similar success at the Battle of El Alamein, driving the Axis forces out of Egypt.

MAJOR EVENTS

January-May 1942

JAPANESE SWEEP THE FAR EAST

The Japanese surprise attacks throughout the Far East in December of 1941 achieved instant victories. Wake Island and Guam were taken from the Americans, Hong Kong from the British, and the shocking sinking by aircraft of the mighty British battleships *Prince of Wales* and *Repulse* spread gloom and doom among the Allies. Worse was to come in the new year.

MALAYA AND SINGAPORE. The capture of Singapore was the last act in a brilliant campaign by the Japanese, when they landed 60,000 troops in Northern Malaya and swept down the peninsula to take Singapore, sitting on an island at its southern tip. One of the jewels of the British Empire, its naval base had immense strategic value. Although 130,000 British troops outnumbered the Japanese two to one, their disorganization and inept leadership guaranteed their defeat at the hands of the Japanese.

[See pages 60–64, 71]

DUTCH EAST INDIES. The Dutch Empire fared no better at the hands of the Japanese. Borneo, The Celebes, Timor, Sumatra, Java—the entire Dutch East Indies—fell by March 12th. A cornucopia of oil, rubber, metals, rice and timber became available to bolster Japanese war production. The native population was happy to see the last of their Dutch rulers, and at first welcomed the Japanese and their "co-prosperity sphere." *[See pages 62, 73]*

BURMA. French Indo-China, Thailand and Burma were next to go, but it was Burma that outweighed the others in strategic importance, as the "Gateway to India." No one knew what the Japanese plans were for India, so the British based their battle plans on defending the subcontinent at all costs. In the meantime, the British abandoned Burma to the Japanese and considered themselves lucky to escape across the Indian frontier by May 19th with 17,000 of the 30,000 troops with which they had begun the war. They didn't return to drive the Japanese out until 1944.

THE PHILIPPINES. Unbelievably, the Americans ignored the early warnings of yet another radar installation, this one in The Philippines, when, on December 8th, Japanese bombers flew in and destroyed the entire American complement of 150 warplanes on the ground. That left the sizeable American Asiatic Fleet with no air cover, so the commanding admiral sailed his 16 surface ships away to the Dutch East Indies. Supposedly out of harm's way, the whole fleet was sunk in the Battle of the Java Sea, along with the Dutch navy.

That left General Douglas MacArthur to face the Japanese invaders with only 16,000 American and 12,000 Filipino troops. Against them the Japanese landed an army of two divisions supported by their Third Fleet of five cruisers and 14 destroyers, their Second Fleet of two battleships, three cruisers and four destroyers, plus another force of two aircraft carriers, five cruisers, 13 destroyers and two land-based fleets of aircraft.

Against such overwhelming force, MacArthur withdrew his forces to the Bataan Peninsula and the Island of Corregidor. There the Japanese starved them out. MacArthur escaped by submarine on March 12th, and those left behind surrendered April 8th. The Japanese marched them off to prison camp in the infamous Bataan Death March that killed many of the sickly, starved men.

Those on Corregidor survived, under constant shelling, until May 6th, when they surrendered with their commander, Lieutenant-General Jonathan Wainwright.

[See pages 61–62, 66, 74]

May 5, 1942

MADAGASCAR INVADED

In 1942 Madagascar was as unknown as it is today—a mysterious island in the Indian Ocean off the African coast. Then, however, it was a French colony in the hands of the turncoat Vichy government that might easily fall into the hands of either the Germans or the Japanese. One would be as bad as the other, because they could block Allied shipping around the Cape Horn destined for India and Russia.

Churchill decided to despatch a force of 13,000 Royal Marines under the command of Major-General Robert Sturges to take the island. The capital, Diego-Suarez, one of the world's great ports, was guarded by old but workable guns. The other side of the peninsula was only 21 miles across, so an approach from the rear was decided upon.

Troops hit the beach at 3 AM on May 5th, and everything came off without a hitch while the 8,000-man Vichy force slept soundly through the night. The landing force entered Diego-Suarez at 4:30 PM that afternoon, while another landing force attempted to take the naval base across the bay. They met with some resistance, and it took until the morning of May 7th to break through. The whole garrison surrendered, including the gun batteries, and the British fleet sailed in victoriously to anchor in the bay. *[See pages 74–75]*

June 22, 1942

JAPS SHELL VANCOUVER ISLAND

The war came home directly to British Columbia when a Japanese submarine surfaced out of the Pacific depths and shelled the Estevan Point Lighthouse on Vancouver Island. Only windows were broken, but the stunned public realized how vulnerable the undefended west coast was.

During World War I the British Columbia government had actually bought two submarines of its own to defend the western shores. This time British Columbians had to rely on strategically placed shore battery gun emplacements and the RCAF Coastal Command, with its DeHavilland Stranraer and PBY flying boats and an odd assortment of Hurricanes, Bolingbrokes and Blackburn Shark torpedo planes. The Royal Canadian Navy was almost totally involved in vital convoy duty on the Atlantic, guarding the sea lanes to Britain. *[See pages 76–77]*

August 19, 1942

DIEPPE

As 1942 dawned, things looked blackest for the British on all fronts, with the Japanese seizing outposts of the Empire in the Far East and the Germans threatening Suez. It became necessary to "show the flag" in battle near home, if only for the sake of Home Front morale. A major raid across the Channel was decided upon, and the 2nd Canadian Infantry Division, champing at the bit for action, was picked to supply the majority of the troops.

Regiments from across Canada that saw action included the Royal Hamilton Light Infantry, the Mont-Royal Fuseliers, Toronto's Royal Regiment of Canada, the South Saskatchewan Regiment and the Cameron Highlanders of Canada.

The place picked for battle was Dieppe, a French seaside resort just a few miles across the English Channel. With the resources of the Royal Navy, the Royal Air Force and eight RCAF squadrons backing them up, some 6,000 ground forces were put ashore over a period of several hours. A thousand were British Commandos, 5,000 were Canadians under Major-General J. H. Roberts and 50 were American Rangers in their first battle.

In the dark for maximum surprise, just before sunrise, the Commandos and Rangers were landed successfully east and west of Dieppe in a flanking movement to silence guns menacing the beach. At the same time, three Canadian Regiments landed on the beaches in a frontal attack to secure a beachhead for the tanks and main infantry to follow.

For identification purposes the landing beaches were assigned different colours. Toronto's regiment was put ashore in Blue Beach in the light of German flares fired into the darkness when they heard the motors of the landing craft. As the ramps came down the withering fire of guns from the cliffs and pillboxes and machine guns in the villas overlooking the beach broke upon the hapless troops as they dashed headlong across the beach for the shelter of the sea wall. Their senior officer, Major Scholfield, was killed instantly as he stepped off the landing ramp, and his troops lay dead and wounded every few feet along the beach. Few reached the safety of the wall. Of 544 men, 94 percent became casualties, with only 32 left unwounded to return to England later in the day.

Simultaneously, the South Saskatchewans under Lieutenant-Colonel Cecil Merritt landed on Green Beach. They suffered 66 percent casualties and prisoners, but actually held part of the town for a time. Merritt repeatedly led his troops over a bridge beset by heavy enemy fire, bravery for which he was awarded the Victoria Cross, although he spent the rest of the war in a German prison camp.

For all the Canadian infantry and tank regiments landing, then and later, the situation was the same. The German shore defenses were undisturbed by any shelling from the sea or bombing from the air. Hence the German batteries were not "softened up" in the traditional way—they just sat there, alert and waiting and not even surprised.

It was hell. It was so disastrous, in fact, that early withdrawal was decided upon and 1,000 Canadians waiting at sea were never landed. Of those landed only 1,000 returned to England.

[See page 80]

August-December 1942

STALINGRAD

History was being made Tuesday, August 15th, when *The Province* FINAL edition hit the streets with the small headline "Stalingrad Peril Grave." Other headlines dominated the front page, but that modest heading heralded the beginning of the Battle for Stalingrad, which was to turn into one of the most heroic defenses of a city in the history of warfare.

It was also a contest of wills between Hitler and Stalin, whose interest in the city was obvious—it bore his name. But Hitler had decided he must have Stalingrad for its publicity value as part of a greater plan to take the Caucasus and its oil. His generals advised against it, but nevertheless he ordered the hapless Colonel-General Paulus to take the city. Lieutenant-General Chuikov was the Russian defender, and there was not one inch given or taken without a fearful price being paid.

House-to-house, cellar-to-cellar, room-to-room, the hand-to-hand fighting see-sawed through September and October. There were many tales of magnificent bravery and desperate sacrifice, but there was no winner as yet.

Unbeknownst to the Germans, the Russian factories that had been moved beyond German reach to the Urals had produced, in the last six months alone, 16,000 aircraft and 14,000 tanks. Marshal Zhukov had been secretly amassing these reserves, with the armies to use them, for a winter offensive to relieve Stalingrad.

On November 19th, the Red Army struck. To the north of Stalingrad they overran the Rumanian Third Army and from the south they routed another German-Rumanian force with their overwhelming superiority. Joining up, the two Red Armies surrounded Paulus and the 200,000 Germans fighting at Stalingrad.

Hitler refused to allow them to surrender, instead ordering his troops to fight to the last man. It took until January 31st to subdue the broken, starving Germans, whose ranks by then were reduced to 110,000, including wounded. At the end of the war, only a few thousand returned from captivity in Siberia. [See pages 79, 81]

October-November 1942

THE BATTLE OF EL ALAMEIN

The desert war in North Africa consisted of a number of skirmishes between Italian and British troops until early 1941, when Erwin Rommel arrived from Germany with his Deutsches Afrika Korps. Soon dubbed the "Desert Fox," Rommel employed clever tactics to drive the British back to El Alamein, within 70 miles of Alexandria on the Nile Delta.

Now things got serious. The Germans were within striking distance of the Suez Canal—a shipping lifeline—and the Arabian oil fields beyond. Churchill came out from England to look things over and decided to send in a new team: General Sir Harold Alexander as Middle East commander-in-chief, and Lieutenant-General Bernard Montgomery as commander of the 8th Army at El Alamein.

Montgomery, a great morale booster for his troops, amassed an army of 195,000 men, 1,350 tanks and 1,900 artillery pieces. Ranged against them, the Afrika Korps consisted of 100,000 German and Italian troops, 510 tanks and 1,325 guns.

Surprise was to be a major element in Montgomery's plan, but when he began his attack under a full moon on the night of October 23rd, he was himself surprised when his troops met very stiff resistance from the leaderless Germans. Rommel was on sick leave in Austria and had to rush back for the battle, but he had left his troops well prepared.

The battle dragged on, with attacks and counter-attacks by the evenly matched forces, until November 4th, when the British 7th Armoured Division broke through, surrounded several Italian infantry divisions and took them prisoner. The German divisions were motorized and got away, crossing into Libya on November 7th. Now down to 20 tanks, Rommel realized he would have to abandon North Africa to the Allies as, by then, the Americans had invaded Morocco and Algeria.

El Alamein had turned the tide, and it led Churchill to remark, "Before Alamein we never had a victory; after Alamein we never had a defeat."

[See pages 78, 83–84, 89–93]

HOME EDITION

News FOR VICTORY **Herald**

LARGEST MORNING CIRCULATION WEST OF TORONTO

HOME EDITION

VANCOUVER, B.C., FRIDAY, FEBRUARY 13, 1942

3c

Nazi Warships Blast Way Through English Channel

LONDON.—(BUP)—A German fleet headed by the 26,000 ton battleships Scharnhorst and Gneisenau and covered by a great armada of Nazi fighter planes forced its way through the cloud-shrouded English Channel and the Straits of Dover yesterday in a mighty battle which cost Britain 42 planes, the Germans at least 18, and probably resulted in the damaging of many of the German ships.

Troops Still Hold East Half of Isle

LONDON—(BUP)—British Imperials still hold roughly the eastern half of Singapore island and bitter fighting is raging along a line extending from the northwest suburbs of the city to the naval base on the northern shore, reports reaching London said today.

The Imperial line was reported to extend "around" the reservoirs north of Singapore city, indicating that the determined although apparently doomed defenders were holding their water supply to prolong the hopeless fight as long as possible.

Vichy Report

At the same time radio Vichy reported that several thousand British troops were fighting in Singapore City and that others still were resisting elsewhere on the island.

(A Domei broadcast from Tokyo heard by the United Press in New York said that Japanese observers were "flabbergasted" by the "inhuman sense of duty" of British army leaders in rejecting Japan's "humane proposal" for surrender of Singapore.).

Singapore's doomed but determined defenders yesterday successfully counter - attacked the Japanese left flank, won an air-battle over Malaya.

The cable and wireless company reported at 1 a.m. (7 a.m. Singapore time, 11 p.m. Thursday P.W.T.) that communications with the city were still normal.

The last previous direct news from Singapore had been a radio message from the doomed city at 3 p.m. Thursday (10 a.m. E. W.T.) saying "We Shall Win."

Other Pacific war front reports page. 2.

McGregor McIntosh

B.C. Japs 'Menace'

VICTORIA.—(UP)—The presence of 24,000 Japanese on the Pacific Coast is one of the worst menaces we face and Ottawa must be convinced without delay of the serious danger which threatens, McGregor McIntosh, former Conservative member who was on the recently dissolved committee on Oriental affairs, told British United Press Thursday night.

"Being free from committee duties, I can now pursue public efforts to have the Japanese removed from coastal areas," he said.

Apart from seizure of fishing vessels, little has actually been done, he said. The Japanese still remain in protected areas and possess cameras and radios. Many of them live in localities where they could do serious harm.

"This I know from my investigations with the committee."

McIntosh said "the evacuation plan should include Japanese of all ages since those outside the 18 to 45 group are still potentially dangerous."

He indicated immediate action would be taken to try to get results from Ottawa.

King May Answer Hepburn on Fleet

OTTAWA—(BUP) — Mounting anger was evident in government circles Thursday night over slurs against the U. S. navy made by Premier Mitchell Hepburn of Ontario.

It was understood that Prime Minister Mackenzie King was contemplating a statement in the House of Commons in answer to Hepburn.

On Wednesday, Navy Minister Angus MacDonald rebuked the Ontario leader for his recent statement in the Welland by-election that the United States navy was "in hiding from the Japs."

In Toronto, Thursday, Hepburn refused to modify or apologize and was quoted as saying, "the Japs have a much better navy than the U. S."

(Hepburn told the British United Press Thursday night that what he said in a speech Thursday was that "Japan has naval supremacy in the Pacific" and because of that fact "the United States navy is in hiding.")

(He declared he did not say the Japanese navy was better, but reiterated the Japanese have naval supremacy.)

Dover Straits Battle

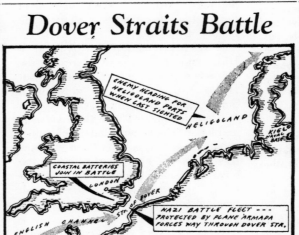

ENEMY HEADING FOR HELIGOLAND PORTS WHEN LAST SIGHTED

HELIGOLAND

KIEL

COASTAL BATTERIES JOIN IN BATTLE

LONDON

DOVER

NAZI BATTLE FLEET --- PROTECTED BY PLANE ARMADA FORCES WAY THROUGH DOVER STR.

ENGLISH CHANNEL

STR. OF DOVER

BREST

NAZI WARSHIPS MOVE FROM BOMBED BREST HARBOR

U.S. Ships Smash 16 Jap Warcraft

WASHINGTON—(UP)—Units of the U.S. Pacific fleet destroyed 16 Japanese warships and auxiliary vessels and smashed enemy planes in the surprise raid on the Marshall and Gilbert islands Jan. 31, the navy disclosed Thursday night.

Five Jap combat vessels — a 17,000-ton aircraft carrier, a light cruiser, a destroyer and two submarines— were included in the toll of vengeance exacted in partial repayment for the sneak Japanese raid on Pearl Harbor, Dec. 7.

The attack also resulted in widespread destruction of Japanese shore installations, including six hangars, several ammunition dumps and other vital establishments.

The daring thrust, carried out by a "well-balanced force of aircraft carriers, cruisers and destroyers," cost the Americans 11 naval bombers. One American cruiser was damaged.

Known Japanese plane losses consisted of 11 scout bombers, 10 other bombers, 15 fighter planes and two large seaplanes.

In addition, three enemy patrol planes were destroyed in an attack on Makin Island in the Gilbert group.

This destruction compared (Continued on Page 19)

Australia To Hold Emergency Session

CANBERA — (UP) — Prime Minister John Curtin today called an emergency session of parliament for Feb. 20 to review the war.

It was the most successful German naval action of the war and removed the two big battleships and the 10,-000-ton German cruiser Prinz Eugen from the harbor at Brest, in Nazi - occupied France, where they had been under almost constant British air attacks for many months.

None Sunk

None of the German ships was sunk, it appeared, although a number of them may have been badly damaged.

The battle still was not regarded as finished,

For the moment, it appeared that the British had come out second best and some experts said that if the Germans got their ships safely to Heligoland bases, it would be a bigger blow to British prestige than the loss of the Prince of Wales and Repulse off Malaya.

(The apparent escape of the German fleet brought closer a showdown over the conduct of the war by the Churchill Coalition Government, which already was threatened with parliamentary revolt because of disasters in the Far East.)

The British losses included six torpedo-carrying Swordfish planes, 20 bombers and 16 fighters. German air losses were 15 fighters shot down by British fighters and three shot down by British bombers.

Visibility at the time the battle started was limited to three to five miles, and at no time was the action visible from the English shore, but coastal batteries on both the English and French sides of the straits joined blindly in the fighting.

The communique, issued jointly by the Air Mnistry and Admiralty, said that one of the torpedo - carrying Swordfish planes scored at least one hit on one of the three big ships.

"One of our motor torpedo boats also claimed a possible hit (Continued on Page 23)

News Herald
FOR VICTORY

LARGEST MORNING CIRCULATION WEST OF TORONTO

VANCOUVER, B. C., MONDAY, FEBRUARY 16, 1942   3c

FOR VICTORY—

One Bright Spot...

The News-Herald's color scheme is changed slightly this morning, to suggest that those of us on the home front can find one bright spot in the dire news of war developments. It lies in the fact that those of us here, unable to enter into combat, may still help our side to triumph through participation in the Victory Loan Campaign opening today.

'U.S. Entry Into War Outweighs All Else'

PRIME MINISTER CHURCHILL
By EDWARD W. BEATTIE

LONDON—(BUP)— Prime Minister Churchill notified the Empire by radio Sunday night that Singapore has fallen and that it was a "heavy, far-reaching military defeat," but, he said, the United States' entry into the war now outweighs everything else in the world.

Going over the head of Parliament to the people, for support in the worst political crisis of his career as Prime Minister, Churchill acknowledged that the Empire was in a serious predicament, but he said the U.S.'s great power and resources will still save the day.

The speech was essentially for Empire consumption, rather than for the united nations.

Furthermore, he said, the

Germans are still retreating in Russia and "three-quarters" of the human race are on Britain's side.

"Are our chances of survival better or worse than in 1941?" he asked. Answering the question in the affirmative, he said:

"First and greatest, the United States is now unitedly and wholeheartedly in the war with us."

"Never in our history, not even after the collapse of

'Marvelous Comeback'

Russia's "marvelous comeback, for which we thank God," is the next most promising factor, he said.

"When I survey and compute the power of the United States, with its vast resources, and feel that now they are in it with us however long it lasts—till death or victory—I cannot believe there are any other facts in the whole world which can compare with that," he said.

Elaborating on the second point, he said that the Russian armies for the first time have broken the Hitler legend.

"The Russian armies have not been beaten, have not been torn to pieces," he said. "The Russian peoples have not been con-

quered or destroyed. Russia's armies in the field are not holding a line in the Urals or a line on the Volga, but they are advancing victoriously, driving the foul invader from that native soil they have guarded so bravely and loved so well."

He also reminded Britons that last Autumn when Russia was in dire peril, with vast numbers of her soldiers dead or captives and one-third of her munitions making capacity was in German hands, the Russians did not fall to bickering among themselves, but they "just stood together, worked and fought all the harder and have not lost their trust in their leaders or tried to break up their government."

(Continued on Page Eight)

Press Tone Tempered By Address

LONDON — (BUP) — Prime Minister Winston Churchill's address yesterday tempered the British Press' criticism of him personally, but Monday morning papers continued to clamor for government changes to avert "disasters worse than Singapore."

"Never in our history, not even after the collapse of France, has there been greater need for cool thinking and dispassionate appraisal of the situation both at home and abroad," said the Daily Mail.

"Once again we urge Churchill most urgently to put it right. If he does not make radical changes in the general direction of our war effort now, the day may come soon when these changes will be forced by the impact of further disasters."

"Some change in the system has now become inevitable," said the Times. "The inquiry, which must precede it should be brief, thorough and conducted without fear or favor."

The Daily Express said "Loyally we must stand under the great leader this land has produced for our trial. There's no other man among us with his qualities, no man approaching him. More than ever, now we must give him the strength and power of all our loyalty."

'SINGAPORE FALL AUSSIE DUNKIRK'

CANBERRA, Australia—(UP) —Premier John Curtin said today that the fall of Singapore marks the opening of the "battle for Australia" upon whose outcome hinges "in large measure the fate of the English-speaking world."

He described the surrender of Singapore as "Australia's Dunkirk."

At Sydney, War Minister Francis M. Forde said that it still was possible to save The Netherlands East Indies and Australia as bases from which the United nations may attack the Japanese.

Fall Of Singapore Ends Heroic Stand

(Compiled from late dispatches of United Press)

Japan claimed and Prime Minister Churchill announced the fall of Singapore Sunday. The end came after a week of bloody fighting and "last ditch" resistance by the outnumbered fortress garrison. Apparently surrender was hastened by capture of the Island's water reservoirs during Friday and Saturday. Terms of the British surrender were reportedly signed late Sunday afternoon

Tokyo announced that under terms of surrender, negotiated by Japanese and British commanders, up to 1,000 British soldiers were left under arms to maintain order until the Japanese army completes the city's occupation. (A late Domei dispatch Sunday night said that some of the defending forces in Singapore, and what it called "hostile elements," were still resisting occupation forces).

Tokyo said that British Commander Lieut. Gen. Arthur E. Percival was attended at the surrender ceremony in the Ford Motor Co. plant outside the city by his staff officers.

The din of battle reportedly ceased at 10 p.m. Lieut. Gen. Toroyuki Yamashita, commander of the Japanese army in Malaya and Lieut. Gen. Percival were said to have signed surrender terms three hours earlier.

Tokyo's announcement said that the defenders sent out in early afternoon a party of four officers, bearing a truce flag. Major C. H. D. Wild who headed the group asked to be taken to Japanese army headquarters.

Japs Claim Java Landing

LONDON — (BUP) — The News Chronicle said today that the German radio had carried a report from Tokyo that Japanese troops have landed on the Dutch island of Java. There were no other details.

(Pacific war front developments reported in late United Press dispatches Sunday night).

● NETHERLANDS INDIES: Jap troops landed on the shores of southern Sumatra were driving inland towards Palembang, important air center within easy range of Batavia, Java. Dutch said they had burned the great Palembang oil refineries, destroyed all other installations which might be of value to the enemy. The Jap vanguard of several hundred parachute troops was wiped out. Direct hits were scored on three of the transports from which the Jap land forces went ashore.

● BURMA: Jungle fighters were believed to be opening a drive towards Thaton, important railway station at the head of the Gulf of Martaban, west and north of Rangoon, after crossing the Salween river. Advance forces were filtering through thinly held British territory.

● PHILIPPINES: Gen. MacArthur reported that fighting was limited to patrol skirmishes

(Story page two).

Aussie Ship Saves Troops

LONDON—(BUP)—An Australian warship was reported Sunday night to have rescued 1300 British troops being evacuated from Singapore after 40 Japanese bombers attacked a transport seven miles off the doomed island and set it on fire with three direct hits.

When the warship was loaded to capacity, 200 more men aboard the transport took to the small boats of the two vessels and headed back for Singapore, the Sydney radio reported in a dispatch cabled from Batavia.

(Japanese Imperial headquarters claimed that from Tuesday to Saturday the Japanese sank, damaged or forced aground 32 enemy warships and transports in Singapore waters. Travelers from the Far East reported recently in New York that the former French luxury liner Il De France, 43,000 tons, had been seen in transport service in that area).

All Saved

Though the dispatch was not entirely clear on the point, it appeared that all 1500 troops and crewmen were saved from the transport, which was described as "one great sheet of flames" at the end of a long and intensive attack.

Even while the rescue operations were in progress, the warship was attacked repeatedly by Japanese planes. Its anti-aircraft gunners warded off the raiders as best they could and shot down three bombers.

How The News-Herald Would Look IF...

Neueste 卐 Nachrichten

~~News~~ 卐 ~~Victory Herald~~

LARGEST MORNING CIRCULATION WEST OF TORONTO

TODAY'S NEWS—
That German phrase above says "Today's News." But turn the page for authentic news, and see editorial "No Joking Matter," Page 12, for explanation of this front page.

VANCOUVER, B. C., THURSDAY, FEBRUARY 26, 1942   3c

'NEW ORDER' FOR B.C.

Streng Verboten

IHRE AUFMERKSAMKEIT!!

It Is Proclaimed and Ordered That:

1. This territory is now a part of the Greater Reich and under the jurisdiction of Col. Erich von Neurenberg, Gauleiter of the Fuehrer.

2. No civilians will be permitted on the streets between 8 p.m. and daybreak.

3. All public places are out of bounds to civilians, and not more than eight persons can gather at one time in any place.

4. Every householder must provide billeting accommodation for five soldiers.

5. All organizations of a military, semi-military or fraternal nature are hereby disbanded and banned. Girl Guide, Boy Scouts and similar youth organizations will remain in existence but under direction and control of the Gauleiter and Storm troops.

6. All owners of motor cars, trucks and buses must register same at Occupation Headquarters where they will be taken over by the Army of Occupation.

7. Each farmer must immediately report all stocks of grain, and livestock, and no farm produce may be sold except through the office of the Kommandant of Supplies in Vancouver. He may not keep any for his own consumption, but must buy it back through the Central Authority in Vancouver.

8. All national emblems excluding the Swastika must be immediately destroyed.

9. Each inhabitant will be furnished with a ration card, and food and clothing may only be purchased on presentation of this card.

10. The following offences will result in death without trial:
    (a) Attempting to organize resistance against the Army of Occupation.
    (b) Entering or leaving the Province without permission.
    (c) Failure to report all goods possessed, when ordered to do so.
    (d) Possession of fire-arms.

NO ONE WILL ACT, SPEAK, OR THINK, CONTRARY TO OUR DECREES

Published and ordered by the Authority of

(Signed)

ERICH VON NEURENBERG,
Gauleiter.

As Fuehrer Marched In ...

These dramatic scenes were enacted in Vancouver as the victorious German army marched into the city. Above, Der Fuehrer is seen graciously accepting the acclaim of thousands of cheering Canadians who lined Granville Street. Below, the former mayor, J. W. Cornett, is seen embracing his wife before leaving on a journey at the invitation of authorities. It was understood that he would be entertained at a camp somewhere in the Rocky Mountains.

Raids Halt Bond Sale

The victorious Nazi Fifth Army columns poured down the Fraser Valley Wednesday after Canadian defenders were blasted from strongholds and sea defences were crippled by heavy fire of German naval units and dive bombers.

Trapped by land and sea forces, all defenders were either killed or captured as General Weiderheim's forces occupied Vancouver and the entire Lower Mainland.

Curfew Set

Major General Putznagel was appointed Gauleiter for Vancouver and has set an arbitrary curfew of 8 p.m., after which civilians seen on the streets will be shot without warning.

The Victory Loan campaign must be stopped immediately. Joachim Von Oderlutz, chief of the Gestapo ordered headquarters in the Rogers and Royal Bank Buildings.

Effective this morning German Reich Victory Bonds will be placed on sale and citizens of Vancouver were advised to come to headquarters and purchase a $500 bond in cash, silver or gold. The city voters list will be checked and failure to call and purchase a bond will result in a heavy fine and forced labor on the roads.

Criminals Shot

Thousands of citizens rounded up by the German troops are already at work repairing damage to roads and railways in the Fraser Valley caused by fleeing Canadian troops who endeavored to halt the victorious German advance by despicable efforts at sabotage.

Many of these criminals were shot on the spot.

Theatres and newspapers have been placed under supervision of agents of Dr. Paul Joseph Goebbels in order to quell the warmongering, reptilian, snake-in-the-grass lies despised by all Germans of the Third Reich,

ALLIES HIT BACK IN JAVA

INVADERS SMASHED FROM AIR

British Troops' Mystery Visit To New York

FINAL

A "mystery brigade" of battle-seasoned British troops, some of whom are shown above being welcomed by American soldiers, arrived in the U.S. for an assignment of undisclosed nature. Although the detachment is small, the number of "Tommies" to arrive is a secret. The visitors are shown being toasted with beer by the American troops at a U.S. Army post, "Somewhere in the New York metropolitan area," where they are billeted.

The Vancouver Sun

Only Evening Newspaper Owned, Controlled and Operated by Vancouver People

FOUNDED 1886
VOL. LVI—No. 128

VANCOUVER, BRITISH COLUMBIA, MONDAY, MARCH 2, 1942

Price 3 Cents

On trains, boats and outside Greater Vancouver, 5c

LATE NEWS BULLETINS

U.S. Tanker Fights Sub Off San Francisco

SAN FRANCISCO, March 2.—The United States Navy announced today that an American tanker and an enemy submarine exchanged shots off the Golden Gate Saturday night.

The tanker William H. Berg was attacked without warning by gunfire but was not hit.

Crews manning the tanker returned the fire but the submarine was invisible in the darkness.

Radio stations in the San Francisco Bay area left the air for half an hour during the encounter.

Society Woman Steals Jewels

NEW YORK, March 2.—Mrs. Margaret Boyle, 48, a Washington society woman, was sentenced to one and a half to three years in prison today for theft of more than $41,000 worth of jewelry.

Wants Winchell Called Up

WASHINGTON, March 2.—Chairman Carl Vinson, of the House Naval Affairs committee said today he had advised the Navy Department either to call Walter Winchell, columnist and radio commentator, to active duty or drop him from the reserve list.

Hong Kong Probe Opens

OTTAWA, March 2.—Hearing of the Royal Commission appointed to inquire into circumstances surrounding dispatch of the Canadian contingent to Hong Kong opened today with Chief Justice Sir Lyman P. Duff presiding.

That Trans-Canada Highway

OTTAWA, March 2.—In Commons today C. E. Johnston N.D., (Bow River,) asked Prime Minister King if he knew when the trans-Canada highway will be completed. Mr. King replied that he did not know and did not think anybody else knew.

U.S. Navy Plans Pacific Offensive

WASHINGTON, March 2.—Admiral Ernest J. King, Commander in Chief of the U. S. fleet, declared today that the Navy is engaged in building up vital air and sea communications preliminary to developing a general offensive against the Axis Powers.

Norwegian Bishops Quit

NEW YORK, March 2.—The British radio today quoted a Stockholm dispatch that said "all the bishops in Norway have resigned in a body."

The broadcast, recorded by the Columbia Broadcasting System said the bishops declared in a joint letter they could not carry on their work "while the Quisling (Premier Maj. Vidkun Quisling, government continues to co-operate with the enemy."

Gas Applications Rejected

OTTAWA, March 2.—Oil Controller G. R. Cottrelle said today many motorists seeking preferred categories may be without gasoline when the rationing system starts April 1 because application forms are being filled out improperly.

"All such improperly completed forms must be sent back at the public expense," Mr. Cottrelle said. "By that time it may be too late to get out the licenses in time for April 1."

Japanese Can Sell Autos

VICTORIA, March 2.—RCMP authorities here said today it will be two or three days before they begin confiscating Japanese autos. Meanwhile some Canadian-born Japanese are trying to arrange a party to leave for the interior.

Police said the Japanese could dispose of their cars in any way they like before they were confiscated.

Police said they have been instructed not to arrest Japanese found on the streets after dark but to take them home. (See also page 13.)

Defense Board Urges:

Alaska Highway 'At Once'

Joint Commission Forwards Finding President Roosevelt

By J. F. SANDERSON
Canadian Press Staff Writer

WASHINGTON, March 2. —The Canadian - American Joint Defense Board at a meeting in New York last week, decided to recommend an immediate start on the construction of the Alaska Highway, it was reported here today.

The recommendation will go to Prime Minister Mackenzie King and President Roosevelt within the next few days and, meanwhile, the United States War Department is completing engineering plans to rish completion on the strategic highway to the northern gateway to the continent.

The Board, it was understood, will make no recommendation on a route but the War Department is understood to favor a line roughly paralleling the chain of airfields constructed last year by the Canadian government north from Edmonton to White Horse in the Yukon.

The Joint Defense Board, it was reported, came to the conclusion the highway is required for the defense of the west coast of the two countries, particularly to rush men and equipment to Alaska irrespective of sea routes and their control.

The present plan is to start work as early as possible, perhaps as early as April 1, on a combined survey job and rough road which it is hoped to complete this season.

The weight of the Statue of Liberty on Beldoe's Island in New York harbor is 225 tons.

How to Cash In On Your Patriotism

Victory Loan provides an amazing anomaly. You can be patriotic—and selfish—at the same time.

Hon. R. W. Bruhn sent a personal letter to his people in the fine fruit-growing district of Salmon Arm and said: "To suggest that the Victory Loan is a sound investment ought to be unnecessary."

It is a safe investment inasmuch—and insofar—as Canada itself remains a solvent country. The best way to ensure that is for everyone to do his part. In this way, the Victory Loan will help greatly to assure the safety of Canada.

As a matter of blunt fact, the government is making available to us a sanctuary for our savings. By using our funds in this way, we can guarantee their continuing value. We are aiding and abetting the cause of victory, it is true—but it is important to note that we are also taking the quite selfish path of looking after our own business interests.

The man who has money which he can save, in any possible way, and who turns away from this chance to buy Victory Bonds, is therefore being much more than untrue to this country. He should not be charged with lack of patriotism only. What he suffers from is—quite plainly—lack of hard-headedness as to his own personal welfare.

There is no question of vital sacrifice. Better to save a proportion of earnings, for investment in this way, than to risk losing everything. It's as straight and as simple as that.

But to think of this matter of sacrifice for a passing moment — it must surely occur to those of us who are pursuing our regular peace-time routine, making money in the process, that we are being saved by the very genuine sacrifices of someone else. The men who are in uniform are risking their lives. Theirs is the sacrifice. What can they save out of army pay to buy bonds to protect themselves in the future?

Money from Victory Loan investors will help to pay for all those goods produced to sustain our fighting forces at war, food, clothing, guns, ships and tanks. Thus the fighting services are assured supplies while farmers and artisans get regular payment for their products and labor.

The least we can do is to make our money available to keep in motion the wheels of industrial warfare on which this dominion, this province and THIS COMMUNITY depend.

To do less is incredible from the standpoint of good business judgment—discreditable from the standpoint of patriotism.

Frightful Slaughter On Beaches

Whole Fleet of Invasion Barges Sunk by United Nations' Air Force; No Immediate Threat to Capital

(Complete map of Island of Java on Page Eleven.)

By WITT HANCOCK
Associated Press Staff Writer

BANDOENG, Java, March 2. — Supported by a smashing aerial assault which has wrought havoc among Japanese on the beaches, a desperately-determined taxicab army has been rushed into a counter-attack and may already have fought a vital engagement against invaders who landed at three points, and who, in two short days, swept to within 30 miles of this military headquarters of the United Nations.

A stream of taxicabs and camouflaged trucks loaded with green-clad Indies and Malayan reserve troops today rumbled down the volcanic slopes toward the northern coastal plains where the invaders established footholds in three places Sunday night, in spite of appalling losses.

(A Reuters dispatch to London fr[illegible]d there was reason to believe that in the counter-[illegible] Allied troops already had cut off the Japanese c[illegible]ch had penetrated 40 miles inland to Subang, w[illegible] miles of Bandoeng.)

Allied counter moves against the invaders' three hard-won beachheads were described in the communique with these words:

"From well-informed circles it is heard that action against the Japanese troops developed satisfactorily. Although in connection with the character of the operations no details can be published, it can be said that the enemy received fair hits."

'Scorched Earth' at Batavia

Aneta, Indies news agency, said the Japanese had attempted no more landings on the island since Saturday night, and a special communique of the High Command pointed to the probability that the terrific hammering of Indies and American planes may have upset the Japanese schedule of reinforcements.

The communique said a smashing attack by Indies fighter planes Sunday, sank nearly every one of the heavily-laden barges engaged in landing men and tanks from 20 transports near Rembang.

Please Turn to Page Eleven See "Java Battle"

Russian Trap Tightens on 96,000 Nazis

By M. S. HANDLER
Special to The Vancouver Sun
Copyright, 1942, by British United Press

MOSCOW, March 2.—Russian forces have captured a key village straddling eight roads near Staraya Russa, 96,000 Germans are trapped, and are pressing forward on the southern front despite spring thaws and heavy rains which have transformed that sector into a quagmire, dispatches from the fronts said today.

The newspaper Izvestia said the Germans are forcing civilians at Staraya Russa and 35 surrounding places to construct for-

Please Turn to Page Eleven See "Russia"

Australia Orders Compulsory Service

MELBOURNE, March 2. — In anticipation of the war's spread to Australia, the government has ordered compulsory service for all civilians, has tightened control over the three branches of the armed service and has abolished for the first time in history five major holidays.

Race Results at Oaklawn Park

ARKANSAS

FIRST RACE—Six furlongs:
Bright and Early (Datillo) $6.50, $3.60, $3.00.
Cloudy Weather (Balaski) $4.70, $2.90.
Pearl Alma (Franklin) $2.60.
Time, 1:16.

SECOND RACE—Six furlongs:
Columbus Day (Craig) $4.40, $3.30, $2.70.
Symmetry (Wallace) $4.60, $3.20.
Max Greenock (Martinez) $4.60.
Time, 1:16 4-5.

THIRD RACE—Six furlongs:
Valdina Bishop (Westrope) $11.70, $4.30, $3.60.
Cinesar (Franklin) $7.20, $4.60.
Chance Sord (Brooks) $8.70.
Time, 1:15.

FOURTH RACE—Six furlongs:
Quiz Kid (Datillo) $3.90, $2.50, $2.30.
Pittistraw (Kelper) $2.80, $2.50.
Henry Greenock (LeBlanc) $2.60.
Time, 1:16 2-5.

FIFTH RACE—Six furlongs:
Marogay (Wallace) $7.10, $2.70, $2.60.
Book Plate (Brooks) $2.30, $2.20.
Time Counts (Westrope) $2.50.
Time 1:16 2-5.

SIXTH RACE—Mile and seventy yards:
Forsooth (Wilson) $8.70, $6.30, $4.80.
Lucia's Son (Franklin) $5.40, $3.70.
Battery (Longdon) $3.40.
Time: 1:49 1-5.

Race Results at Hialeah Park

FLORIDA

FIRST RACE—Three furlongs:
Runebb's Pride Scurlock) $10.20, $4.80, $3.50.
Betty Leon (Meade) $5.80, $3.50.
Credentials (Hanford) $12.70.
Time :34.

SECOND RACE—Seven furlongs:
One Tip (James) $14.70, $6, $4.40.
Victory Bound (Brunnelle) $6.20, $4.20.
Blockader (Harrell) $8.90.
Time 1:26.

THIRD RACE—Six, furlongs:
Billy O (Arcaro) $6.90, $3.30, $3.60.
Stimstone (Woolf) $3.70, $3.60.
Macpal (Atkinson) $7.10.
Time 1:13 3-5.

FOURTH RACE—Six furlongs:
Kansas City (Stricler) $9.50, $3.20, out.
Big Ben (Arcaro) $2.70, out.
Speed To Spare (Eads) out.
Time 1:12 2-5.

FIFTH RACE—Mile and one-eighth:
Trois Pistoles (Day) $5.20, $3, $2.30.
Minnelusa (Pierson) $3.20, $2.40.
Arestino (Weilander) $2.50.
Time 1:59 2-5.

SIXTH RACE — Mile and one-eighth:
Pomaya (James) $10.50, $6.20, $3.80.
Silverstra (Eads) $14.60, $5.80.
Dark Discovery (Arcaro) $3.10.
Time, 1:50 4-5.

SEVENTH RACE—Mile and one-eighth:
All Even (McCreary) $103.90, $29.70, $10.80.
Wayriel (Weilander) $4.40, $3.30.
Here She Comes (Strickler) $4.30.
Time, 1:53 2-5.

EIGHTH RACE—Mile and one-eighth:
Perfect Rhyme (Roberts) $18.60, $9.00, $6.40.
Silver Tower (Young) $6.60, $4.70.
Calexico (Scheihamer) $3.80.
Time: 1:51 2-3.

Race Entries on Page 11

British Lines Still Holding Japs in Burma

By Associated Press

RANGOON, March 2.—The British command indicated tonight that its lines were holding unchanged along the Sittang River, facing a growing number of Japanese apparently preparing for a new assault toward Rangoon and Pegu.

Meanwhile the once-great Oriental seaport of Rangoon—abandoned now by virtually all except weary British troops and looters defying military control—awaited today the final assault from reinforced Japanese invaders.

Scant official reports indicated the enemy is increasing his patrol pressure, presumably searching for a soft spot at which to establishe a bridgehead

Please Turn to Page Eleven See "Burma"

Must Stand Trial

TRAIL, B.C., March 2. — Martha Aileen White, 19, was committed by Magistrate Parker Williams today to stand trial on a charge of manslaughter arising out of the death of her infant son whom a coroner's jury previously found died of malnutrition.

$100,000 Story-

That's what Metro-Goldwyn-Mayer paid Michael Kanin and Ring Lardner Jr. for "Woman of the Year." You'll enjoy every moment of this witty story, which stars Katharine Hepburn and Spencer Tracy on the screen and which The Vancouver Sun presents in three instalments, starting today. Begin it on Page 13.

B.C. Curlers Lose

Final curling scores in the Canadian Bonspiel is Northern Ontario 13, British Columbia 10.

Tailoring Firm Sues Commodore

Pacific Coast Tailors Ltd., of Victoria has started action in Supreme court here against Commodore W. J. R. Beach of Esquimalt for damages for libel allegedly published by him daily since February 5, and for damages for ordering the firm out of bounds and causing the premises to be picketed by naval police.

The firms is asking for an injunction to stop the picketing, and an order compelling Commodore Beach to rescind his order declaring the company out of bounds

JAPS ON CORREGIDOR

SPORTS STOCKS

The Vancouver Sun

Only Evening Newspaper Owned, Controlled and Operated by Vancouver People

★★★★★ FINAL

FOUNDED 1886
VOL. LVI—No. 182

MArine 1161

VANCOUVER, BRITISH COLUMBIA, TUESDAY, MAY 5, 1942

Price 3 Cents — On trains, boats and outside Greater Vancouver, 5c

BRITISH FIGHT FRENCH ON MADAGASCAR

SCENE OF ATTACK

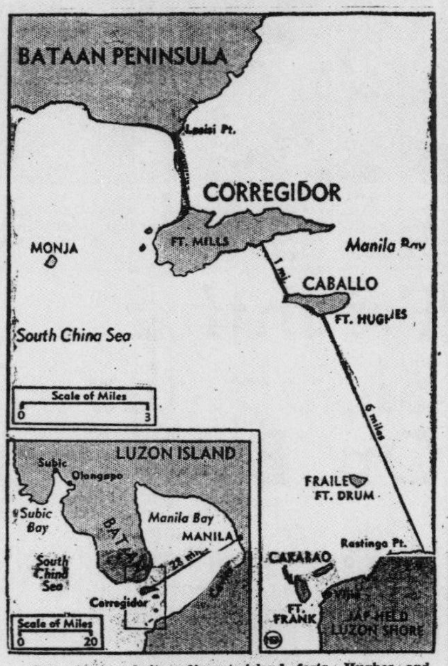

Corregidor and its adjacent island forts, Hughes and The Japanese late today were attempting to storm is a d headquarters of Lieut.-Gen. Jonathan Wainwright, bums United States stronghold in Luzon.

City Sea Captain Rescued

John Park Among Survivors From Torpedoed Ship

COCOA, Fla., May 5. — Captain John Park of Vancouver, B.C., pilot of a medium - sized British freighter torpedoed off the eastern coast of the United States early Sunday, today reached safety with 87 other survivors of two lost vessels.

When the British ship was torpedoed and began to sink Park gave orders for his men to leave the vessel.

"I had given the order," he said, "when the gunner came to me and told me that he thought he could see the sub. He begged me to let him try to hit it. I told him to go ahead, but we were settling all the time."

The gunner, Sid Webber of Beamsville, Ont., said 15 shots were fired and several near-misses were scored on the submarine.

"I don't know that we did any damage," he reported.

TORPEDO HITS LIFEBOAT

Twenty-three men lost their lives in the two sinkings.

Seventeen of them died when a torpedo struck their lifeboat as it was being lowered over the side of a medium-sized United Nations freighter.

Please Turn to Page Two
See "Captain"

Japs Force Landing on Corregidor

Nipponese Assault Corregidor in Force and Collapse Is Imminent After Terrific Bombardment

WASHINGTON, May 5. —The U.S. War Department announced late today that the Japanese had assaulted Corregidor Fortress in Manila Bay and that the landing attack was in progress there at midnight Tuesday, Manila time.

The attack apparently followed concerted air attacks which have been blasting at the island on a thirteen-a-day basis for the past four days.

In addition, enemy batteries based on the shores of Manila Bay have been pouring hundreds of shells into Corregidor and the other island forts—Fort Drum and Fort Hughes—almost incessantly.

The imminence of the collapse of Corregidor was disclosed in a brief report from Lieutenant General Jonathan M. Wainwright that the landing attack had been started across the narrow stretch of water separating the fortified island from Bataan Peninsula.

There was no estimate of the number of troops who have been holding out against almost continuous aerial and artillery bombardment since fighting ceased on Bataan a month ago, but the force on Corregidor and the three other island forts at the entrance of Manila Bay may have totalled 7000 or more.

The communique announcing the landing attack also contained the text of a message sent to Wainwright earlier today by President Roosevelt expressing Mr. Roosevelt's "growing admiration" of the "heroic stand against the intensity of bombardment by enemy planes and heavy siege guns."

Skoda Plant Bombed

RAF Squadrons Soar 700 Miles Over Germany

LONDON, May 5.—The RAF made four offensive sweeps over the Channel today, attacking Zeebrugge in Belgium and points in occupied France. Six British planes were lost

By Canadian Press

LONDON, May 5.—Great new RAF bombers ranging as far as 700 miles over enemy territory, attacked the huge Skoda armamen works at Pilsen last night for the second time in 10 days struck in force at Stuttgart, a major manufacturing city in southwest Germany, and raided the docks of German-occupied Nantes.

Then resuming their day sweeps, RAF fighter squadrons sped over the Straits toward the French coast early this afternoon at great heights.

A squadron of Stirlings, heavy four-motored craft capable of carrying eight tons of explosives each, was sent on the long foray against the Skoda works in old Czecho-Slovakia.

It was the second time the new Stirling bombers had attacked Pilsen, which they bombed on April 25.

Air experts, noting that the raids were carried out in the face of unfavorable weather and enemy oppostiion with the loss of only three bombers, called the night's work "one of

Please Turn to Page Two
See "War in Air"

'Occupation Operations Proceeding'

'Our Casualties Have Been Light'; Commandos, Navy and Parachutists Participate in Landing

LONDON, May 5.—The Admiralty and War Office announced tonight "operations are proceeding steadily (on Madagascar) and our casualties have so far been light."

"It is understood that the Governor-General of Madagascar has declared his intention to resist," the communique added.

Vichy reports state British forces have driven to Andrakka, less than four miles from the great naval base of Diego Suarez and six miles from their landing place on Courrier Bay.

British Commandos, marines and infantry landed on the northern tip of Madagascar today, and a Vichy news agency broadcast that they were attacking the strong French naval base of Diego Suarez from the rear while warships and squadrons of airplanes assaulted the harbor frontally.

British parachute troops also were used in the attack, Vichy broadcast said.

The troops landed at Courier Bay and started pushing 10 miles across the northern isthmus against the base in an attempt to forestall its seizure by the Japanese.

The Vichy broadcast said the British naval forces consisted of two cruisers, four destroyers, two troop transports and probably an aircraft carrier. Two British planes were reported shot down.

JAPS MAY STRIKE

As the occupation force moved in on the Vichy French colony, informed London sources declared there was "a possibility the Japanese may take the boldest course and strike directly at Madagascar."

In view of the swift British action, however, they thought the Japanese, who are believed to have a powerful battle squadron on the move somewhere in the Indian Ocean, would seek first to obtain bases on the British islands of Ceylon or Mauritius. The Allied naval position in those waters remain obscure.

Informed quarters agreed that the United Nations had "won the first trick" in the Indian Ocean by the British landing on Madagascar at dawn, but there was wide speculation on the possibility of Axis attack.

French forces are said to be commanded by a General Gullemet, a former artillery officer. A Reuters dispatch quoting a Vichy news agency said that Marshal Petain and Admiral Darlan, Chief of the Armed Forces, sent him a message urging him "to resist attack and defend the honor of the French flag."

Operations still are in progress and the British forces have cap

Please Turn to Page Two
See "Madagascar"

Roosevelt Tells Vichy Not to Fight

WASHINGTON, May 5. — The U.S. is following a day-to-day policy with regard to French possessions, Secretary of State Cordell Hull said today.

The problem of Martinique, strategically located French possession in the Caribbean, is receiving attention with other phases of the French situation, he told a press conference.

Hull had been asked whether in view of the fact that Madagascar is—or was—under the same government as Martinique, the latter would be seized.

WASHINGTON, May 5.—President Roosevelt today despatched a note to the Laval government of France expressing complete United States approval of the British Commando attack on the island of Madagascar, and warning Vichy that any warlike act by the French would be construed as against all of the United Nations.

Please Turn to Page Two
See "Reaction"

$5 Bonus for Single Civil Servants

VICTORIA, May 5. — Single persons after six months in B.C. Government employ will receive a $5 a month cost-of-living bonus, Premier John Hart said today.

Only those earning under $2100 a year will be eligible.

"Salaries are also being investigated and where there are any real grievances consideration is being given to inequalities," the Premier said.

Some weeks ago it was announced married persons and household persons earning under $2100 a year would receive $10 a month living bonus.

The $5 bonus will be retroactive to April when married persons received their $10 extra.

LATE NEWS BULLETINS

Reserve Army Draft 'Under Consideration'

OTTAWA, May 5.—Consideration is being given to the calling of men of draft age in the reserve army for compulsory military training, it was learned today.

Action has not yet been taken but as a result of a study being made of reserve army conditions it is thought highly probable in official circles that district boards will shortly receive instructions on a new policy dealing with the calling up of reserve army men.

Soldiers' Vote 4 to 1 'Yes'

OTTAWA, May 5.—It was learned tonight that in the Plebiscite vote of the Armed Services 251,118 voted Yes and 60,885 voted No.

Norwegian Ship Torpedoed

WASHINGTON, May 5.—The U.S. Navy announced today that a medium sized Norwegian merchant vessel has been torpedoed and sunk off the Atlantic Coast. Survivors have been landed at an East Coast port.

Four Planes Raid English Town

LONDON, May 5. — Four bomb-carrying German fighter planes raided a southeast coast town briefly tonight, machine-gunning the streets and bombing property. Several casualties resulted in small homes which crumbled.

First Newfoundland Airmail

The first air mail letter to reach Vancouver from Newfoundland arrived today. The letter, posted with the first air mail delivery from the British Crown Colony off Labrador, took only four days to come to Mrs. S. A. Efford, 3537 West Twentieth Avenue.

Why Women Were Not Called

WASHINGTON, May 5.—The projected registration of women was abandoned because too many women felt it would be premature and feared it might presage their immediate drafting into war jobs, Mrs. Franklin D. Roosevelt told a press conference today.

Hanging at Edmonton

EDMONTON, May 5. — The scaffold at the Fort Saskatchewan jail was completed today in preparation for the execution early Wednesday of Chester Warren Johnston, 24, former Edmonton hardware clerk. Johnston is to die for the stabbing last Nov. 15 of 14-year-old Dorothy Maxine Hammond.

Race Results at Pimlico Park

MARYLAND

FIRST RACE—Four and one-half furlongs:
Flying Junior (Haas) $5.20, $3.20, $2.60.
Pretty Is (Malley) $3.50, $3.
Lance Leaf (Campbell) $4.30.
Time, :55 2-5.
Scratched: Light Vale, Go Wes, Chance Oak.

SECOND RACE—Six furlongs:
The Killer (Roberts) $5.10, $3.50, $2.70.
Magnify (Haas) $6.20, $4.80.
Malvois (Cuisiamano) $8.40.
Time, 1:14 1-5.
Scratched: Shepson, Hessytime, Cliath, Happy Gallop.

THIRD RACE—Jumps) two miles:
Glenna Mona (Russell) $150.90, $25.80, $8.60.
Jacket (Owens) $3.70, $2.90.
Dundrillin (Roberts) $3.10.
Time, 3:53 2-5.
Scratched: Meeting House.

FOURTH RACE—Four and one-half furlongs:
Ringe Me Now (Roberts) $2.80, $2.40, $2.20.
Berty Jr. (S. Young) $3, $2.40.
Defense Board (Mower) $3.10.
Time, 54 1-5.
Scratched: Mae James, Hasteville.

FIFTH RACE—Six furlongs:
Pompion (Kelper) $14, $4.30, $3.60.
Third Degree (Arcarro) $2.80, $2.80.
Designator (Schmidl) $5.20.
Time, 1:11 1-5.
Scratched: Miss Goshen, Abrasion.

SIXTH RACE—Mile and one-sixteenth:
Grey Wing (DeCamillias) $6, $2.80, $2.30.
Incoming (Mora) $3.10, $2.20.
Rascal (Madden) $2.70.
Time, 1:46 2-5.
Scratched: Cals Pet.

SEVENTH RACE—Mile and one-half:
Exploration (Campbell) $7, $4.20, $2.50.
High Arch (Roberts) $6, $3.40.
Rahannee (Datillo) $2.90.
Time, 2:35 3-5.

EIGHTH RACE—Mile and one-half:
Connachita (Madden) $45.50, $17.30, $11.40.
Silver Rocket (Schmidl) $7.00, $5.40.
Stand Alone (Berg) $7.00.
Time: 2.35 4-5.
Scratched—Rough Going, Skirmish, Brilliant One.

Vancouver Gunner Presumed Dead

Sgt. Alexander Fernie Dickson, 26, Vancouver air gunner with the RCAF overseas, who was reported as missing in air operations on November last, is listed as "presumed dead for official purposes," in the latest Air Force casualty list released in Ottawa today.

He was a son of Mr. and Mrs. G. Dickson, 1075 Beach Avenue.

BASEBALL

NATIONAL

New York ..	100 000 000 0	—1	5	0
Cincinnati ..	000 010 000 1	—2	5	0

(10 innings).
Schumacher and Danning; Walter and Lamanno.

Boston	021 000 013	—7	16	0
Pittsburgh .. .	000 001 000	—1	6	2

Wallace and Klutz; Dietz, Lanning (4), Hamlin (8) and Lopez.

Philadelphia ..	200 001
Chicago	000 110

Podgainy and Warren; Passeau and McCullough.

(Unfinished)

St. Louis	000 000 0
Brooklyn	000 000 1

AMERICAN

Chicago ...	211 000 000 0	—4	8	1
New York ..	000 103 000 1	—5	8	2

(10 innings).
Rigney and Turner; Lindell, Borowy (3) and W. Dickey.

Detroit	000 000 001	—1	3	1
Philadelphia ..	000 000 02x	—2	7	1

Trout and Tebbetts; Christopher and Wagner.

St. Louis	000 201 000	—3	8	4
Washington ..	000 302 00x	—5	5	0

Harris, Biscan (7) and Swift; Wynn and Early, Evans.

Cleveland ...	100 001 100	—3	12	4
Boston	016 302 10x	—13	18	1

Kennedy, Eisenstat (5), C. Brown (5), Embree (8 and Desautels; Chase and Peacock.

Wooden Trawlers To Be Built in B.C.

OTTAWA, May 5.—Hon. C. D. Howe, munitions minister, said today that plans are under way to build wooden fishing trawlers in British Columbia coast yards.

The minister said he does not know how many of the fishing craft will be built. He added that so far as he knows there is no intention at present to build larger wooden vessels at the coast. (Other details on page 12).

Farm Superintendent Worried; Ends Life

NEW WESTMINSTER, May 5.—Robert Muir, 60, a superintendent of attendants at Colony Farm attached to Provincial Mental Hospital, Essondale, was found dead with a bullet wound in the temple, in his room at the farm. A suicide verdict was returned by the jury at an inquest held today. Police state that Muir left a note stating that he was melancholy and intended to end it all as he had just received notice of superannuation.

Great Britain to Ration Chocolates and Candies

LONDON, May 5.—Food Minister Lord Woolton announced today that chocolates and other candies will be rationed, starting July 27. A new personal ration book will be issued to facilitate distribution.

Race Results at Jamaica Park

NEW YORK

FIRST RACE—Five furlongs:
Bottom Rail (Robertson) $68.10, $16.70, $8.30.
Sugar Ration (Meade) $3, $2.60.
Toss Up (Neves) $11.20.
Time 1:01 1-5.
Scratched: Zac.

SECOND RACE—Six furlongs:
Wise Hobby (Robertson) $22.50, $11.60, $8.
Deicer (Clingman) $27.20, $15.60.
Short Cake (Zufelt) $6.50.
Time 1:14.
Scratched: Aerial Fire, Little Davey, Ladies First, Smoky Snyder, Sun Traid, Day Off.

THIRD RACE—Five furlongs.
Witch Water (Mann) $4.20, $2.60, $2.50.
Now Mandy (Zufelt) $2.90, $2.80.
Esterita (Robertson) $8.90.
Time 1:00 2-5.

FOURTH RACE—Six furlongs:
Phar Rong (Peters) $9, $4.70, $3.40.
Alohort (James) $4.20, $3.10.
Scotland Light (Meade) $3.70.
Time 1:12 3-5.

FIFTH RACE—Mile and one-sixteenth:
Painted Veil (Westrope) $3.50, $2.20, out.
Pomayya (Robertson) $2.30, out.
Love Day (May) out.
Time 1:44 3-5.

SIXTH RACE—Mile and one-sixteenth:
Portable (Meade) $6.50, $3.20, $2.90.
Billy O (Hanford) $3.90, $3.30.
Brave Friar (Robertson) $4.30.
Time 1:44 4-5.

SEVENTH RACE—Mile and one-eighth:
Miss B B (Wall) $5.50, $3.40, $2.90.
Enoch Borland (Stout) $4.10, $3.20.
One Shen (Coule) $4.10.
Time, 1:34 1-5.

Race Entries on Page 20

Say Yanks to Help Garrison Madagascar

FOR VICTORY
VANCOUVER NEWS-HERALD
WESTERN CANADA'S GREATEST MORNING NEWSPAPER
FINAL
VOL 10—NO. 13 | VANCOUVER, B.C., FRIDAY, MAY 8, 1942 | TELEPHONE PAcific 2272 | PRICE 3c Outside City, 5c. By Carrier, 65c Month.

GREAT SEA BATTLE RAGES —U.S. WARSHIPS BLOCK JAP FLEET

TORNADO DRIVES CAR 100 FEET, KILLS FIVE PERSONS—This automobile, owned by farmer Dale Paddock, was tossed under the trees as shown by a freak tornado which swept Oberlin, Kansas, killing five persons and wrecking a number of homes. Paddock's farm home was levelled and the car was blown over 100 feet before being upended, a virtual wreck.

BULLETINS

Locusts Invade South Mexico

MEXICO CITY, May 8.—(UP)—Hordes of locusts are swarming into the southern Mexican state of Chiapas from Guatemala and other Central American Republics, the ministry of agriculture announced Thursday.

Mexico To London For De Gaulle Meet

MEXICO CITY, May 8.—(UP)—Jacques Soustelle, Free French representative in Mexico, left here Thursday by plane en route to a conference called in London by General Charles De Gaulle. Soustelle, it was understood, will travel by clipper from New York to Europe.

No Plans For Canadian Fleet Air Arm

OTTAWA, May 8.—(BUP)—Close co-operation between the navy and the air force has developed in the defence of Canada's coasts, but there are no plans for a fleet air arm in the Royal Canadian Navy, Navy Minister Angus MacDonald told the House of Commons Thursday night.

Urge Installment Payments On Loans

WASHINGTON, May 8.—(UP)—Federally-supervised banks throughout the U.S. Thursday night were urged by government officials to require installment payments on all personal loans in order to speed amortization and "encourage reduction of individual tests."

Japs Occupy Manila Bay Island

TOKYO, May 8.—(Radiocast recorded by UP, New York)—Japanese forces completed occupation of Corregidor and the three other fortified islands at the entrance of Manila Bay, at 8 a.m. Thursday, about 33 hours after the first successful landing on Corregidor Tusday night, an Imperial Headquarters communique asserted Thursday night.

GEN. MACARTHUR'S HEADQUARTERS, Melbourne, May 8.—(UP)—American and Japanese warships and planes were still locked in a great naval and air battle in the southwest Pacific today, it was announced officially after eight Japanese ships were sunk in the initial clash Monday.

The announcement issued at Gen. Douglas MacArthur's headquarters said that in the "initial phases" of the battle, Japanese vessels sunk comprised one light cruiser, two destroyers, four gunboats and one supply vessel—the same losses detailed in the U.S. Navy department communique released in Washington on Thursday describing the Monday engagement.

Badly damaged, according to MacArthur's communique, were a 9000-ton Japanese seaplane tender, a light cruiser and a cargo vessel. The Washington communique said that a troop transport also was badly damaged.

* * *

There was no immediate elaboration as to the present locale of the battle, though Washington said that the clash on Monday occurred in the vicinity of the Solomon Islands northeast of Australia.

(Detailed earlier report, Page Two.)

* * *

(The Navy department in Washington declined to comment on MacArthur's Friday announcement that the battle was continuing.)

COMMUNIQUE

The text of MacArthur's communique:

"A great naval and air action is now taking place in the southwest Pacific area.

"In the initial phases, our forces inflicted damage on the enemy.

"His losses consisted of one light cruiser, two destroyers, four gunboats, and one supply vessel.

"Badly damaged were one 9,000-ton seaplane tender, one light cruiser, and one cargo vessel.

"Our losses were slight."

A hint as to the possible direction of the Japanese thrust was contained in Gen. MacArthur's daily operational communique, issued shortly earlier, revealing that a Japanese fleet—it did not say whether it was the same one attacked near the Solomon Islands—had reached the Luisiade Islands, only 500 miles east of the vital Australian outpost at Port Moresby.

DESTROY TRANSPORT

American and Australian bombers, roaring to the attack on this fleet, already have destroyed a transport, the communique said.

The Louisiade Islands lie off the eastern tip of New Guinea, some 400 miles southwest of Bougainville in the Solomon Islands, the nearest by sea the Japanese previously have been reported to Port Moresby, and approximately 700 miles from the northeastern coast of Australia.

'Will Make Captured Base Impregnable Against Japs'

LONDON, May 8.—(BUP)—The big Diego Suarez naval base in northern Madagascar has fallen to the British in a lightning assault and roundabout reports today said "huge reinforcements" of United States and South African troops soon would make the vital stronghold impregnable against any Japanese thrust across the Indian Ocean.

The French defenders, swamped by a 48-hour assault which cost the British more than 1000 men, surrendered the naval base, dominating stronghold of the entire island, early yesterday.

Soon afterward, all of northernmost Madagascar was in British hands.

Reports that American as well as South African troops would help garrison the naval base were published in the Daily Mail this morning in a Madrid dispatch.

MAKE BASE IMPREGNABLE

"Already, according to reports from Vichy, huge reinforcements of South African troops and American units, with masses of artillery and planes, are pouring into the base to make it impregnable against Japanese attacks and to consolidate it as a British naval bastion," the dispatch said.

The London Daily Star said Thursday that Radio Vichy had broadcast the arrival of an American expeditionary force in Natal, South Africa.

Official circles in London declined to comment on the report that American troops would be based on the island.

Vichy French resistance collapsed like a punctured balloon under the final British land attack during the night on Antsirane, chief town of the great land-locked harbor, after Diego Suarez had fallen Wednesday.

Gov.-Gen. Armand Annet notified Vichy that "all other parts of the island will be defended with the same determination."

FIGHT MUST CONTINUE

Jules Brevie, secretary of colonies, messaged Annet that "the fight must continue in Madagascar despite the loss of Diego Suarez."

The British naval force off Madagascar was cleaning out the mined approach to Diego Suarez bay preparatory to steaming in and putting the final seal on the conquest.

Majunga, on the northwest coast, is considered the only other base of any real naval value.

Free French sources here, commenting on unsubstantiated rumors that Vichy might now turn over the French fleet to the Axis, said it was "absurd" to suggest that Pierre Laval would take any such action, adding that "that is the only thing France has left."

CHURCHILL DEPLORES BLOODSHED

Prime Minister Winston Churchill, announcing the French capitulation in the House of Commons, deplored the "bloodshed that has occurred between troops of our two countries, whose peoples at heart are united against a common foe."

'French To Defend Rest Of Island'

VICHY, May 8.—(UP)—The government announced Thursday night that while Diego Suarez had fallen to "enormous masses" of British forces, all the rest of Madagascar would be defended against any further aggression to the utmost limits of French resources.

Col. Edward Claerecout, commander of the Diego Suarez garrison, and the commander of the French naval forces at the Indian Ocean base, were captured by the British along with their men, a message from Gov. Gen. Armand Annet revealed.

The French forces at Diego Suarez surrendered "only after having fought foot by foot and reoccupied some positions, and thrown aviation into the fight regardless of the sacrifice," Annet said.

French military strength on Madagascar appeared to have been cut to less than 5,000 troops with no naval support and meager air strength.

Minister Hints Sailors' Grant To Equal That Of Soldiers

OTTAWA, May 8.—(BUP)—Navy Minister MacDonald told the House of Commons Thursday he expected to announce today that dependents of men in the navy would have their allowance brought to parity with other services.

MacDonald admitted that last Thursday he thought he had convinced the treasury board on the wisdom of "certain course of action," but on Saturday he found his efforts were less successful than he supposed.

He added he continued his efforts and hoped to announce today that as far as the treasury board was concerned the navy's lower allowances to dependents would be raised.

Conservative Leader R. B. Hanson said the Navy Minister appear to be forcing the treasury board's hand. He warned the board consisted of "hard boiled men."

Several members of Parliament have protested the lowness of navy allowances.

In the eyes of the wives of navy men today there is a glimmer of hope, following the announcement Thursday night that Navy Minister Angus MacDonald held out high hopes of raising navy men's wives pay to equal that of soldiers' wives.

The young mother of a year-old girl, whose husband does convoy duty on the Atlantic Ocean, was jubilant last night just at the thought of a possible raise.

"It is so hard to manage on what we get now," she said. "And none of us see why we should get less than the wife of a soldier or airman."

$15 TO $25

The wife of another convoy man was equally elated at the news.

She has two children, and for them she gets only $15 a month, while the soldier's wife receives $25.

"It costs $15 a month to feed one child alone," she said

"The cost of living has gone up much since the war started, that it is impossible to live properly on the allowance we receive. I think we should at least get as much as the wives of other services."

A young naval wife who is expecting her first child is hopeful that the money will come through in time to help meet hospital expenses, and then later to provide the necessities for her baby.

News-Herald's Efforts Praised

Praise of The News-Herald's efforts to have sailors' dependents' allowances increased, was given Thursday by Lieut.-Col. the Rev. C. C. Owen of the Vancouver Sailors' Home. Lieut.-Col. Owen had fallen in line with the women of Vancouver in their attempts to have the allowance paid to sailors' wives and children equal that paid to the wives and children of soldiers.

Thursday, Lieut.-Col. Owen said: "At the present time sailors are particularly in the "front line," and their heroism and constant sacrifices are in our papers nearly every day. Surely then, this is a very good time that the subject (of allowances) should be taken up, and while we are grateful that the women should lead in this, it is a matter that should be taken up by our government."

He said that the articles published Thursday morning by The News-Herald "will arouse a keen interest in our sailors. May I say that we are distinctly grateful to any newspaper that takes up causes like this one that need to be looked into."

Germans Bomb South England

LONDON, May 8.—(BUP)—Two German planes were shot down Thursday night in raids on points in southeast England during which a few bombs were dropped, a communique of the Air and Home Security Ministries said today.

The German bombs did slight damage to one place but there were no casualties, the communique said.

Air raid sirens sounded in the outer London area today. No planes were heard immediately.

RAF raiders heaved tons of bombs into Stuttgart, south German industrial centre for the third successive day early Thursday and officials here were confident that the water, sewage, electric power and communications systems in the city of 460,000 population have been severely strained if not disrupted.

Crippling of the city was only an incidental objective, however, for bombs were aimed mainly at war plants, including the Daimler-Benz and Bosch establishments which turn out vital parts for planes and U-boats.

Though the latest attack, which the Air Ministry said was carried out in force, probably was the heaviest of the three on Stuttgart, it was believed that the city has on no night taken as much punishment as the Baltic ports of Rostock and Luebeck. Bad weather hampered the Stuttgart raids.

Seven bombers were missing, bringing to 14 the total sacrificed in the three attacks on Stuttgart.

U-BOAT SINKS DOMINICAN SHIP

CIUDAD, Trujillo, May 8.—(UP)—A German submarine has sunk the 1,973-ton Dominican ship San Rafael and 30 crew members are missing, it was announced officially Thursday night. The announcement did not say when or where the vessel was attacked.

'Norse Quit Coast Fear Attack Near'

SAN FRANCISCO, May 8.—(UP)—German authorities have placed 10,000 men at work on coastal fortifications in the Trondheim area of the Norwegian coast, and many residents are "fleeing inland in fear of military action," radio Moscow said Thursday night in a broadcast heard here by CBS.

Work is proceeding "feverishly" on the task of setting up batteries of long-range guns in the surrounding hills, the broadcast said.

PGE, Alaska Link Interests Hart

VICTORIA, B. C., May 8.—(BUP)—Extension of British Columbia's Pacific Great Eastern Railway line through Prince George to Alaska by either the Dominion government or the United States government, appeared a distinct possibility today.

The extension would provide a direct rail link between the U. S. and Alaska which would be a supplement to the Alaska Highway by way of the originally proposed "B" route for the Alaska Highway.

Premier John Hart, intimating the government was greatly interested in the matter, which was understood to be under discussion at Ottawa, admitted an option regarding the P.G.E., which had been forwarded to the provincial government by a private concern had been rejected.

OTHERS SEEK DATA

Mr. Hart also disclosed Attorney-General Maitland had been approached by separate concerns desiring information.

Outlining the government's policy, Mr. Hart said they would continue to refuse to deal with intermediaries, but any bona-fide proposal would receive full government consideration.

'Yes, We Have No Bananas'---Ship Shortage

Yes, we have no bananas—and that's nothing to sing about.

Vancouver hasn't had any bananas for the past week, may not have any for another week or more.

And after that shipment is consumed, Vancouver, British Columbia, all of Alberta, may have to do without bananas indefinitely.

Officials of a leading banana agency here told The News-Herald Thursday night that shortage of ships, particularly on the Atlantic coast, is responsible for the banana "drought."

The market for bananas in British Columbia and Alberta, served by the one distributor, obtains its fruit from Panama and Costa Rica. The bananas are carried in ships from Central America to United States ports, and from there come by rail to Vancouver.

Occasionally the ships bring them right to Vancouver. Normal consumption in B.C. and Alberta is approximately 1000 carloads a year.

J. G. Bowers of Slade & Stewart Ltd., said his firm had a shipment of bananas en route now from Central America but was uncertain as to when it would arrive. There was another shipment due after that, he said, but it would not arrive for several weeks and might be the last one to arrive.

A comparatively small supply of bananas was received from Fiji at one time but shipments from there stopped many months ago.

So Vancouver banana-lovers had better be prepared to do without the fruit for some time to come.

RUGGLES WEDS FORMER WIFE OF BOXER

LAS VEGAS, Nev., May 8.—(UP)—Charles Ruggles, film comedian, and Marion La Barba, former wife of Fidel La Barba, retired featherweight boxing champion, were married here tonight by district Judge George E. Marshall.

The ceremony was witnessed by Director Wesley Ruggles, brother of the bridegroom, and Mrs. Ruggles.

75

FOR VICTORY
VANCOUVER NEWS-HERALD
WESTERN CANADA'S GREATEST MORNING NEWSPAPER
FINAL
VOL. 10—NO. 36 VANCOUVER, B. C., THURSDAY, JUNE 4, 1942 TELEPHONE PAcific 2272 PRICE 3c Outside City, 5c. By Carrier, 65c Month.

2ND JAP RAID ON ALASKA; B C COAST DEFENSES READY

The war came to the Pacific Coast Wednesday on the wings of Jap bombers and fighters which twice during the day raided the United States base at Dutch Harbor.

Even before full outcome of these raids was made known, they brought the following developments:

- All B. C. defence forces were on the alert, ready for any eventuality.
- Precautionary blackout was ordered in Prince Rupert at 10:30 p.m.
- All radio stations in the B. C. coastal area were ordered off the air at 9:45 p.m., followed closely by stations on the coast all the way to Mexico.
- Civilian protection precautions were doubled in Vancouver, Victoria and other coastal centres.

• • •

WASHINGTON, June 4.—(UP)—Japanese planes struck twice Wednesday at U. S. military and naval bases at Dutch Harbor, Alaska.

The attacks occurred six hours apart—one at 9 a.m. (PWT) and the other at 3 p.m. (PWT).

Four bombers and about 15 escorting fighters participated in the first attack which inflicted no serious damage and caused few casualties.

The Navy said a "few warehouses were set on fire" in the initial thrust—the first time in history that North America proper has been attacked by air.

There were no details on the second attack.

In the absence of details on the second foray it was speculated that the first raid was a "feeler" and that the second was an attack in force.

The presence of fighter planes suggested the Jap attackers came from an aircraft carrier since Dutch Harbor is more than 1400 miles from the nearest Japanese islands—far beyond the flying range of fighter planes.

The carrier—if one was involved—conceivably approached within striking range of Dutch Harbor unseen in the fog which frequently shrouds that area.

There was no information whether any of the attacking planes were shot down.

A west coast dispatch quoted a high navy official that the initial attack "was not a surprise" and that the defenders were prepared to meet it.

The fact the Japs struck twice within such a short time at Dutch Harbor—most formidable American bastion on the Aleutian Island chain which stretches 1500 miles across the north Pacific—suggested this might be the prelude to a Nipponese attempt to knock out American bases in Alaska preparatory to a blow against Russian Siberia.

It was pointed out unofficially that such an attempt would be logical inasmuch as the Alaskan bases constitute a vital threat to any Jap move into Siberia. A knockout try would be calculated to remove the danger of a flanking blow should the Japs attempt a thrust into Soviet territory.

The raids also were viewed as reprisals for the April 18 American air attack on Tokyo and other Japanese centers—raids which conceivably would be expanded to reach the United States mainland.

The initial blow against Dutch Harbor was made at the favorite Nipponese attacking hour—dawn. The stab-in-the-back thrust on Pearl Harbor last Dec. 7 also came at dawn.

(Continued on Page 2)

B.C. Defenses Go On Alert

All British Columbia defense forces were on the alert last night as the presence on this coast for the first time in history of enemy bombing and fighter planes put the whole coastal area, from Alaska to Mexico, on a near-emergency footing.

All radio stations were ordered off the air and A.R.P. officials prepared for a possible blackout. The radio silence was ordered at approximately 9:45 p.m. and prevailed all night but no blackout was called.

Major General R. O. Alexander general officer commanding the Pacific Command, told the British United Press that British Columbia defense leaders were "keeping close touch with American authorities" and that the members of the joint defense council for the western military district were "working closely together."

• • •

The radio "blackout" was called because of the presence of suspected enemy aircraft off the Pacific Coast, the stations announced before going off the air.

Similar action was taken in all coast cities and in some instances precautionary blackouts were ordered, the United Press reported.

To all ARP wardens went warnings to be prepared for any emergency and at Provincial Civilian Protection headquarters, under direction of Inspector S. F. M. Moodie, precautions were doubled.

But in one respect, Vancouver was not prepared for a blackout Despite warnings published frequently during recent months, and a final last-minute request from radio stations as they went off the air, many citizens ignored the plea not to use the telephone for any but essential calls.

(Continued on Page 2)

SAN FRANCISCO HAS BLUE ALERT

SAN FRANCISCO, June 4.—(UP)—A nine-minute blue-alert was flashed in the San Francisco bay area Wednesday night when "an unidentified target, later identified" was found in the area, the western defense command and Fourth Army announced.

The blue-alert was flashed at 10:28 p.m. P.W.T. and the all-clear came at 10:38 p.m. P.W.T.

Commandos Raid Northern France

Obtain Valuable Information In Night Thrust

LONDON, June 4.—(BUP)—Black-faced British Commando troops swarmed ashore in the Boulogne-Le Touquet area of northern France before dawn today and obtained "valuable information" in a reconnaissance raid on the German-held coast a special communique announced.

The Commandos were re-embarked by the British navy while squadrons of Hurricane and Spitfire fighter planes provided a protective "umbrella" overhead, the communique said. It described the raid as "minor."

A number of German troops were believed to have been taken prisoner and brought back to Britain.

'SECOND FRONT' MOVES

The surprise assault came as Britain was increasing the tempo of its aerial assault on Germany and occupied territory in what some observers interpreted as an attempt to soften German resistance for an eventual full-scale invasion of Western Europe and the consequent opening of a "second front."

One purpose of today's raid, it was believed, might have been to obtain information as to the strength of German defenses and disposition of forces in the Boulogne-Le Touquet area, which lies directly across Dover Strait from southeastern England.

It was the fourth Commando raid on northern France since last February.

R.A.F. Again Over Germany

LONDON, June 4.—(BUP)—British bombers struck again at Germany early today after strewing death and destruction through the great industrial Rhineland and Ruhr valley in three mammoth pre-dawn raids in four days, two of them by more than 1000 planes.

The night's objective was not disclosed immediately, British authorities saying merely that the Royal Air Force was over Germany during the night.

However, radio Berlin reported that British planes attacked several towns in the northwest Germany coastal area, damaging business and residential quarters. German night fighter planes and anti-aircraft batteries shot down 10 of the raiders, the broadcast said, an indication that the British force may have numbered in the hundreds.)

Early Wednesday 300 bombers dumped their cargoes into factory areas in the Ruhr that had been burning since the previous morning's 1000-plane assault.

In four nights of raiding, beginning with the knockout attack on Paris industrial suburbs Friday night, the R.A.F. had dumped an estimated 7000 tons of bombs into German war production areas at a cost of exactly 100 planes. The losses being seven planes Friday night, 44 at Cologne Saturday, 35 around Essen Monday, and 14 Tuesday.

Jap Subs Attack Three Ships Off Southeast Australia Coast

MELBOURNE, June 4.—(UP)—Japanese submarines have attacked three United Nations ships off thickly-populated southeastern Australia, a United Nations communique reported today.

Two small cargo vessels were attacked 35 miles east of Sydney, and another ship, 225 miles south of Sydney, the communique said. However, it disclosed neither the fate of the ships nor the dates of the attacks.

The attacks were announced less than four days after Allied warships sank three Japanese midget submarines attempting to raid shipping in heavily-defended Sydney harbor. Two of the submarines were sunk inside the harbor and the third, just outside the mile-wide entrance.

One ship was sunk by the Sydney harbor raiders—a naval auxiliary depot ship used as a floating barracks.

The new attacks marked the farthest south the Japanese have yet struck either by sea or air and observers speculated that they might be the first blow in a Nipponese attempt to cut sea communications lines between Australia and New Zealand as well as the life line between Australia and the U. S.

The communique failed to specify whether the Japanese submarines which made the latest attacks were of the same midget type as those sunk off Sydney, but United Nations warships have been engaged in a hunt for the submarine mother ship since Sunday.

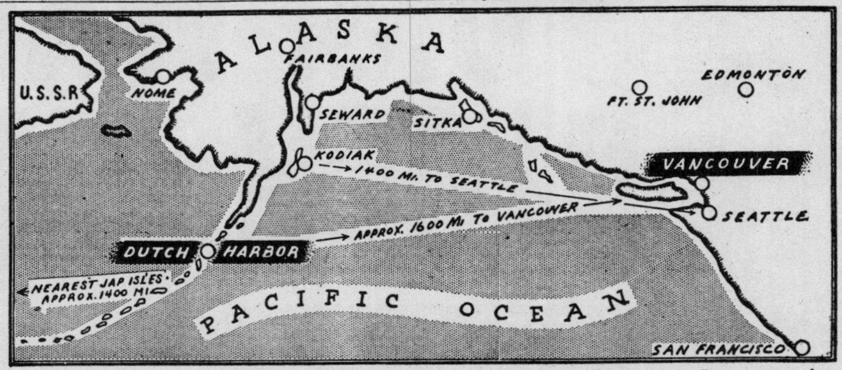

TODAY'S WAR MAP.—Map showing location of Dutch Harbor raided twice Wednesday by Japanese war planes. Note its position in relation to Alaska, Japanese islands, and Pacific coast centers.

Rommel Opens New Offensive

CAIRO, June 4.—(UP)—Col. Gen. Erwin Rommel has partly repaired the terrific damage suffered by his armored army in Libya and has hurled 100 tanks against the Free French and Indian forces holding the left anchor of Imperial defenses at Bir Hacheim, 50 miles southwest of Tobruk, it was revealed Wednesday night.

Rommell apparently was staking all on a bid to lop off Bir Hacheim, where Italian forces took a bad beating in two previous attacks.

If successful, it would minimize British counter-attacks on the northern fringe of the salient he had established in the Libya line, cut off British forces which had swept 40 miles from there to Rotunda Sengali, where they menaced his rear, and permit him to throw in reinforcements for a new drive on Tobruk.

The new attack began at dawn Wednesday, as a violent sandstorm subsided.

They had been organized west of the salient in the Knightsbridge area, 28 miles southwest of Tobruk, where Rommel was still patching up the remnants of his main army.

As the storm lifted, British tanks resumed their fierce counter-attacks on the northern edge of the salient, which Tommies dubbed the "cauldron" because of the burning blasts of windswept sand that caused action to be broken off temporarily Tuesday night.

It was revealed that Rommel had sent the bulk of the Italian forces, including part of the Ariete "Battering Ram" division and motorized forces, to the rear for reorganizatoin

SALICA WINS OVER LINDSAY

Lou Salica, world's bantamweight boxing champion, outpointed Vancouver's Kenny Lindsay in their ten-round fight at Athletic Park last night. (See story Page 10.)

'Few' Nazi Planes Raid South Coast

LONDON, June 4.—(BUP)—German planes raided two towns within a few miles of each other on the southwest coast of England early today, dropping incendiary bombs which were reported to have damaged residential areas.

An authoritative source said that five German planes were brought down during the night, one over Britain and four over German bases in Northern France.

Though it first was feared casualties would be heavy, the Air and Home Security Ministries reported in a communique that only a small number of persons was killed or injured. Only a "small number" of raiders participated in the attack, which caused "some damage," the communique said.

Fires soon were brought under control and fire watchers and air raid wardens were credited with rescuing a number of persons from burning homes.

PASTE, CREAM TUBES NOW GOVT. PROPERTY

OTTAWA, June 4.—(BUP)—Empty tooth paste tubes and shaving cream tubes have been declared government property and it is now an offense and against the law to throw them away or keep them, the Wartime Prices and Trade Board announced Wednesday night.

The order was effective as of June 1. The Board said a government owned company, Wartime Salvage Ltd., was the only organization allowed to acquire used tubes. Collection will be carried out from drug stores, cigar stores, general and departmental stores.

Cancel Leaves In Canal Zone

BALBOA, C. Z., June 4.—(UP)—The United States army announced Wednesday that army and navy forces had been in a state of alert throughout the Canal Zone since noon Tuesday, with all local leaves and passes cancelled.

Sees Raid Prelude To All-Out Attack To Destroy Alaska Base

REAR ADMIRAL YATES STIRLING, JR.
U.S.N. Retired
(United Press Naval Analyst)

The Japanese have staged two air attacks on the U. S. air, sea and land base at Dutch Harbor, Alaska, and it is possible that an all-out Japanese effort to smash the Alaskan bases prior to a Nipponese invasion of the Soviet Far East is impending.

• • •

The first raid came at dawn Wednesday Alaskan time, with about 19 Japanese planes—four bombers and 15 fighters—participating. The second attack followed six hours later, at noon.

The fact that a second attack was carried out—and it may be significant that the number of enemy planes in the second raid was not given—in the first announcement—would indicate that the Japanese mean business and more attacks may be expected if the enemy has the strength to deliver them.

RAID FROM CARRIER

One would guess that the next 48 hours may bring news of the utmost importance from the Alaskan theatre, and possibly from the regions around Vladivostok and Kamchatka in the Soviet Far East.

The raiding planes very likely came from a medium-sized aircraft carrier which, escorted by two cruisers and four destroyers, approached the entrance to Dutch Harbor at high speed during the hours between 6 p.m. Tuesday and 6 a.m. Wednesday, Alaska time.

In such an operation the raiding planes would take off, gather in formation, carry out the raid as quickly as possible, and then return to their ship base.

As soon as the planes left the carrier that vessel and its escort would move quickly to an arranged location to which the planes would return, after the raid, to be taken aboard.

It would seem certain that an aerial battle must have taken place since a raid on Dutch Harbor had been expected ever since the U. S. raid on Tokyo, and other centres in Japan, during mid-April.

And it would be a good guess that some of the attacking planes were destroyed by U. S. airmen.

As soon as the Japanese appeared U. S. planes would take off, engage the enemy, and attempt to chase him back to his ships and sink them if possible.

POLICE HOPE TO GET THIS BIRD

A Vancouver citizen, Wednesday night stumped the ingenuity of the City Police force, in reporting the loss of a rare African canary.

The bird escaped from its cage during the afternoon.

Police officers believe that they could take most assignments in their stride but this particular type of bird is half the size of an ordinary canary and the officers think that this is much too much. Or not enough.

207 Czechs Slain In Hun Reprisals

LONDON, June 4.—(UP)—The Prague radio announced today that the German Gestapo executed 25 more Czechs Wednesday raising to 207 the number slain in reprisal for the attempted assassination of Reinhard Heydrich, whose spleen was removed in an effort to save his life.

Of the new group of victims, 15 were executed in Prague and 10 in Brno, two of the latter on accusation of "harboring parachute agents," the German broadcast from the old Czechoslovak capital said.

The Tuesday toll was given in radio reports from Prague as 21. Among them 14 persons, apparently some of them Jews, charged only with having "approved" the attack on Heydrich. For the first time since the reprisal blood bath started, the Germans were said to have slain indiscriminately a number of Czech Jews.

The German-controlled Prague radio, which announced the new killings, also appealed to the populace not to flood the Gestapo with "misleading and immaterial" information about the possible assassins, indicating that Czech patriots might be using that as a means to slow down the Nazi attempt to solve the crime.

A dispatch to a Stockholm newspaper from Berlin said Heydrich's condition was critical but that there was hope for his recovery because of his strong physique.

The British Broadcasting Co. said Heydrich's spleen had been removed and that he had undergone two more blood transfusions.

(Rome radio said that Nicola Vito, "right hand man" of the district leader at Ljubljana, Croatia, was murdered Tuesday night. It said he was on the streets after the curfew and was "lured" into an ambush in the woods where his body was found today.)

Claim 3-1 Edge in Battle for Air Mastery

Red Shock Troops Slay 5000 On Kalinin Front

MOSCOW, June 4.—(UP)—Russian shock troops attacking suddenly on the Kalinin front have driven a salient into tactically important German lines, and 5730 enemy troops have been killed in brisk clashes all along the front, the Red Army reported Wednesday night.

The army newspaper Red Star said the Soviet air force destroyed 1366 German planes in May and lost 479 in a successful frontwide struggle for mastery of the air against "enormous strength" massed by the Germans at new fields close behind the battle line.

"The contest for command of the skies is going on with growing intensity," the newspaper said, with the Soviet airmen holding the initiative everywhere.

The Germans were said to have constructed two new types of airdromes—fighter bases immediately behind their forward positions, holding 30 to 50 planes charged with fighting off raiders and covering the troops, and bomber bases 15 to 70 miles from the front to attack Soviet formations and communications.

Anticipating the Germans, the Red air force struck a series of surprise blows on the northwestern, central, Bryansk and southwestern fronts, Red Star said, and disabled a substantial number of planes.

• • •

The official Tass news agency said thousands of Russian guerrillas were waging a full scale war against German army, Gestapo and Hungarian forces in the Orel area 200 miles southwest of Moscow. They have slain 4180 invasion troops in a mounting campaign, 3200 in a battle raging from May 10 to 20, and the 200th Hungarian brigade has "practically ceased to exist," the agency reported.

SURPRISE SUCCESS

(The German high command said local attacks on the central Russian front "annihilated" encircled Soviet groups, the Red army losing 1500 killed, 2000 prisoners and 54 guns.)

The most effective operation on the entire front appeared to be the Red army surprise attack in one sector of the Kalinin area. Red Star said a Soviet detachment was ordered to dislodge the Germans from strategic lines and capture their positions, and "the attack was crowned with complete success."

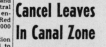

Hundred Thousand Dollars Damage In Lumber Yard Fire Here--Page 3

FINAL EDITION

FOR VICTORY

VANCOUVER NEWS-HERALD

WESTERN CANADA'S GREATEST MORNING NEWSPAPER

VOL. 10, NO. 51 — VANCOUVER, B.C., MONDAY, JUNE 22, 1942 — TELEPHONE PAcific 2272 — PRICE 3c Outside City, 5c. By Carrier, 65c Month.

'CONSTANT ALERT' AFTER SUB SHELLING ON ISLAND

★ ★ ★ ★ ★ ★ ★ ★ ★ ★ ★ ★ ★ ★ ★ ★ ★ ★ ★ ★

Huns Claim 25,000 Prisoners At Tobruk

Expect Egypt Assault

CAIRO, June 22.—(UP)—Tobruk has fallen after the most terrific attacks of the whole Libyan war and its garrison of possibly 25,000 men probably has been captured, along with whatever supplies could not be destroyed by the British, it was reported today.

Bardia, on the coast seven and a half miles from the Egyptian border also is in Axis hands, according to unofficial reports reaching here.

Some units may have broken through the Axis encirclement at Tobruk, and the British there had been doing their utmost to keep the amount of supplies that could fall into enemy hands down to a minimum, but it was evident that the British have suffered a serious blow.

German Col. Gen. Erwin Rommel was now in position to launch an immediate assault on the Egyptian border, and it seemed inevitable that he would do so.

• • •

A British communique said Rommel began a terrific assault on Tobruk early Saturday, only two days after he had cut the coastal road to the east to isolate the fortress. His troops penetrated its outer perimeter defenses. But there has been no official confirmation here of the capture.

Military quarters said that Rommel struck before the Tobruk garrison had time fully to organize a siege defense, while the British Eighth Army was withdrawing from the front lines through Tobruk to the east.

• • •

The passage of the long lines of tanks and supply convoy through the Tobruk defenses necessitated gaps in the mine fields which could not be closed until they had cleared the area. Rommel realized this and apparently delivered his main attack through the gaps.

Nearly all the forces which intended to withdraw got out, however, before Rommel moved in and sped southeast toward Sidi Rezegh, where a tank battle developed. But Rommel had not had time to bring up sufficient anti-tank weapons to cut off the retirement, and the engagement ended with the loss of only a few tanks on each side.

These British forces guessed that Rommel would try to crack Tobruk before the mine fields were closed and sought to delay him with two attacks —one on the Tobruk flank, north of Sidi Rezegh, and another from the south on his right flank.

That portion of Libya turns into nearly trackless desert a few miles back from the coast and is ideal country for British light mobile operations, which it is assumed will be resumed as soon as the Imperials are reorganized along the border.

British officials frankly admitted the defeat is a disaster which might upset the United Nations' whole war strategy in the Middle East.

The British losses of men and

(Continued on Page Two)

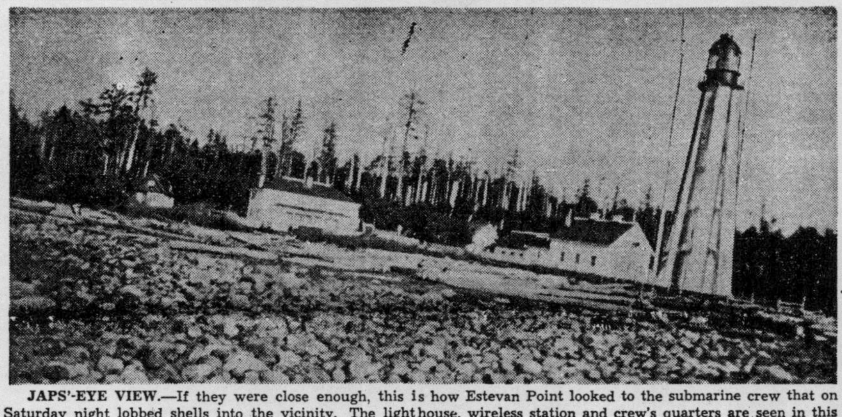

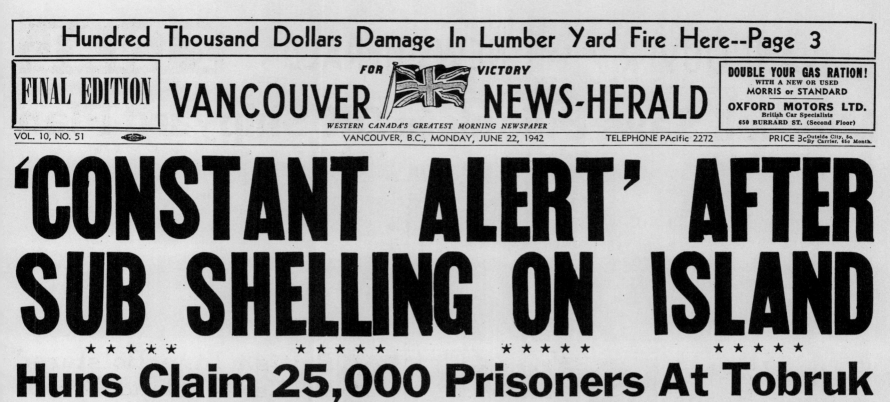

JAPS'-EYE VIEW.—If they were close enough, this is how Estevan Point looked to the submarine crew that on Saturday night lobbed shells into the vicinity. The lighthouse, wireless station and crew's quarters are seen in this picture, taken from the water's edge.

VICTORIA, B.C., June 22.—(BUP)—Lt.-Gen. Kenneth Stuart, Canadian chief of staff and acting general officer commanding the Pacific Command, Sunday night said one missile from the enemy sub which shelled the Estevan Point wireless station "fell near enough to shatter windows."

"The others fell harmlessly on the beach." the General added.

Meanwhile, defense forces remained on constant alert.

The shells which landed at Estevan Point were the first to land on Canadian soil from hostile guns since the War of 1812.

The view that the submarine was a Japanese craft trying to manoeuvre into waters from which it could bombard Vancouver or Victoria was expressed tonight by A. W. Neill, Independent member for Comox-Alberni, in whose riding Estevan is located.

"This attack is certainly bringing things very close home to Canadians," said Neill.

"And it emphasizes the importance," he added, "of what other British Columbia members and I have been endeavoring to emphasize in the way of urgent need for the strengthening of our Pacific Coast defenses."

There are at present no Japanese residents in the immediate vicinity of Estevan Point, Neill said, and he did not believe the attack had been carried out in collusion with any Japanese on the Island.

Neill pointed out that the wireless station itself was an important objective for the sub, because it served shipping along the Vancouver Island West Coast.

OTTAWA, June 22.—(BUP)—For the first time in Canada's history as a Dominion enemy shells have landed on Canadian soil, it was disclosed Sunday in a defense ministry announcement that a submarine had lobbed shells harmlessly at the government telegraph station at Estevan Point, Vancouver Island.

The bold action, announced by Defense Minister J. L. Ralston, occurred at 10:35 p.m., Pacific time, Saturday.

"No damage resulted," the announcement said.

It was presumed that the submarine was Japanese.

• • •

While it was the first time that an enemy submarine had attacked shore installations in Canada, it was the second such incident of this war along the North American Pacific Coast.

On the night of Feb. 23 a Japanese submarine loosed about 25 shells on oil field installations near Santa Barbara, Cal. The shells caused only about $500 worth of damage and no casualties. The Santa Barbara shelling occurred while President Roosevelt was addressing the nation by radio.

• • •

The defense minister did not elaborate his statement and it was not known immediately how many shells were fired or whether Canadian air and shore defenses attacked the sub.

Estevan Point is located on the deeply indented western shore of Vancouver Island, almost at the centre of its 275-mile length.

It is close to vital shipping lanes from the Port of Vancouver northward, including the 1700-mile route to the United States air and naval base at Dutch Harbor, Alaska.

Approximately 75 persons live in the little community, most of them employed in the large lighthouse there and the wireless station which is one of the largest on the west coast.

Ralston's information came from Lieut.-Gen. Kenneth Stuart, chief of the general staff, who at present is in personal command of Pacific coast defenses.

RAF On Raids

LONDON, June 22.—(UP) — Strong R.A.F. formations swept northern France almost ceaselessly today after 300 or more bombers had pounded at Emden, submarine base and maritime port on the northwest German coast, for the second night in a row.

There still was no official explanation for the terrific, sustained gunfire and other heavy explosions heard from the French coast and the English Channel between Dunkirk and Boulogne almost all night and some persons believed that the British had carried out a new Commando raid.

Watchers on the English coast heard the deep drone of small surface craft and saw huge flashes, some of them low on the water and others in the sky. Explosions rocked the coast for more than three hours.

Furious Nazi Attack Cracks Russian Sevastopol Defences

By HENRY SHAPIRO
U. P. Staff Correspondent

MOSCOW, June 22.—(UP)—German troops have driven a wedge into the defenses of Sevastopol in spite of enormous losses — estimated at 100,000 men in 15 days—it was announced officially today as the Russian war blazed into its second year.

On the critical Kharkov front, however, Russian troops blasted their way across a river (presumably the Donets) and recaptured a number of localities in a terrific counter-attack, the Monday morning war communique announced.

The location and extent of the Sevastopol break-through was not revealed. The communique said: "In the Sevastopol sector of the front our troops repelled repeated, furious German attacks. At a cost of enormous losses the enemy succeeded in driving a wedge in our defensive positions."

It had been admitted earlier that the German-Rumanian siege army, bolstered by strong reinforcements, had forced the Russians back from an outer to an intermediate defense line at one point south of Sevastopol.

• • •

On the Kharkov front two German regiments, supported by tanks and airplanes, crossed the river after a terrific battle and forced the Russians back, the communique said.

In the counter-attack, the Russians hurled the Germans back to the river, then crossed to the western bank and swept through a number of nearby localities. The Germans left many dead and wounded on the field, the communique said.

Other sectors were reported

(Continued On Page 14.)

Capture German

MONTREAL, June 22. —(BUP)—An officer of the German air force, who roamed at will for four days, today was in jail following his arrest by United States Border Patrol troops near Rouse's Point.

The report of the capture of the flyer, which was released by R.C.M.P. officials Sunday night, said he claimed to have escaped from an Ontario prison camp last Wednesday, despite the fact that there was no official report of such an escape.

The airman, who is being held while Ottawa authorities attempt to establish his identity, spoke perfect English. He said he was in Montreal Friday night. He said also that after crossing a bridge leading from Montreal he was given a lift towards the south by a tourist.

Jap Aleutian Forces Push To Kiska Under U.S. Fire

WASHINGTON. June 22.—(UP)—Japanese forces, operating under cover of the eternal fogs rolling down from the Arctic circle, have pushed their occupation of the Aleutians to Kiska, the navy announced today, but only under the continuing blows of U. S. bombers which hit another cruiser and sank a transport.

• • •

The hits on the Jap ships brought to nine and possibly 10 the number of vessels in the enemy invasion fleet which have been sunk or damaged by army and navy fliers defending the chain of far-flung islands stretching like a dagger to within 2000 miles of Tokyo.

• • •

Kiska is approximately 100 miles east of Attu Island, which the navy announced on June 12 had been occupied by the Japanese, and some 650 miles west of Dutch Harbor.

• • •

The occupation, however, came as no surprise since in its first announcement the navy said a Jap invasion fleet had been seen in Kiska Harbor, one of the best natural anchorages in the Aleutian chain.

• • •

The navy said "tents and minor temporary structures were observed to have been set up on land."

• • •

A break in the weather within the last few days enabled discovery of the occupation of Kiska, the navy said, adding that "a small force of Japanese ships in the harbor was bombed by army aircraft.

"Hits were reported on one cruiser and a transport has been sunk."

The navy previously had reported damaging three Jap cruisers, one destroyer, one gunboat and a transport in the Aleutian area. Lieut. - Gen. Henry H. Arnold, commander-in-chief of the army air force, had disclosed additionally the sinking of a Jap cruiser and the damaging of an aircraft carrier in these operations.

Ace Correspondent Tells of 'Wait and See' Attitude

Lack Of Aggressive Spirit Was British Weakness In Libya

(Editor's note: The author of the following dispatch has just returned to Cairo from the Libyan front.)

By RICHARD D. McMILLAN
U. P. Staff Correspondent

CAIRO, June 22. — (UP) — How did it happen?

Britain had the best equipped army she ever put into the desert, but today, German Col. Gen. Erwin Rommel is lining up his Africa Corps along the approaches to Egypt.

After watching every phase of this campaign from front line points of vantage, my answer to the foregoing question is: Lack of aggressive spirit.

I don't mean that as a reflection upon the fighting of the troops themselves. No men could have fought more determinedly, courageously or tirelessly. But in the general direction of Britain's fighting machine there seemed a disposition to wait and see rather than act.

I heard, far more often than I liked, around desert headquarters the words: "I wonder where Rommel will strike next?" I seldom heard, "I wonder where we'll hit Rommel now?"

• • •

Throughout the entire campaign the British never counter-attacked on the scale of which they were capable.

The opportunity was lost when we had Rommel on the run through the mine fields two weeks ago. Instead of attacking at that time the British dallied for days, then their effort was not nearly what it should have been.

Another phrase heard in the desert was: "Don't let Rommel become a bogey."

The fact is, Rommel appears to be the biggest bogey to the higher-ups.

The surprise of the campaign certainly has been the extensive use of 88-millimeter anti-tank guns by the enemy. Yet why was that a surprise?

The British knew the Germans had those guns but they contented themselves on relying mainly on their 25-pounder, with a far shorter range.

Rommel's Africa Corps consequently was able to keep British tanks out of range of his tanks while pounding them with his longer range artillery.

Then there was the disastrous sortie by British tanks trying to break through from southwest of Tobruk to get at the southern flank of the Germans. They ran into hidden batteries of these deadly anti-tank guns. It began as a tank-to-tank battle, but the enemy lured the British on toward the 88's in ambush, with the saddest results.

The British forces by no means were eclipsed in numbers. Rommel's forces were no greater than in the last campaign, but the Italians were better trained and had been stiffened by their German masters.

It looks, therefore, as if bold and clever tactics gave the enemy the edge.

If asked to generalize, I would say that the British should shake out the idea that this is a local and frontier war. It is the only front on which the British are fighting the Germans. Why should there not be a concentration on this front as a major battlefield — shipping enough from Britain and America to swamp Rommel and to drive the Axis from Africa for good?

Finally, rest assured that the RAF saved the day, and anyone criticizing it does not know what he is talking about. It has taken a long time to put Spitfires in the Libyan skies, but we need more of them quickly.

FOR VICTORY
VANCOUVER NEWS-HERALD
WESTERN CANADA'S GREATEST MORNING NEWSPAPER
FINAL
VOL. 10, NO. 58 — VANCOUVER, B.C., TUESDAY, JUNE 30, 1942 — TELEPHONE PAcific 2272 — PRICE 3c Outside City, 5c. By Carrier, 65c Month.

Mitchell Says Unionists OK Shipyard Plan

YANKS REINFORCE EGYPT AS ALEXANDRIA PERILLED

"Keep Working" —Union Heads;

OTTAWA, June 30.- (BUP)—Delegates of B. C. shipyard workers declined to comment Monday night on Labor Minister Humphrey Mitchell's 30-day formula to pave the way for industrial peace in Pacific coast shipyards.

"We have nothing to say tonight," said Alex McAuslane, member of the western delegation. He added, however, that before the delegation left tonight for the west by plane they might have a short statement to issue.

He stated that most of what the delegates had to say would be revealed when they returned to B.C.

At the end of a 30-day interval the government will decide whether or not to accept the union's plan for a six-day week.

• • •

The formula was said by Mitchell Monday night to have won the endorsement of the strikers' delegation. The understanding is, he said, that the delegation will recommend acceptance of the forn ıla by the workers.

In connection with the formula, Mitchell expressed the view that B. C. yards, because of their climatic and other advantages, should handle 60 per cent. of the government's cargo boat program. The labor minister emphasized in a letter to the union Monday night that the formula implied no commitment on the government's part to abandon the scheme for seven-day operations.

• • •

Meanwhile in Vancouver all shipyard workers are being exhorted by the All Union Shipyard Conference and union leaders to avoid any action of an individual or group nature while awaiting the report of their delegates.

• • •

The wires received from delegates said nothing of a further 30-day test of the seven-day production plan reported Monday. That from R. Daniels of the Machinists Union stated simply: "Plan under advisement by government. Appeal for no work stoppage until detailed report submitted." The wire received by the Boilermakers' Union commenced the same way exactly, as did that from Chas. Saunders to E. E. Leary of the Dock and Shipyard workers, giving rise to the presumption that all were in agreement to maintain silence until arrival in Vancouver. Mr. Saunders set the date of arrival as Thursday, July 2.

A statement released by Malcolm McLeod for the Publicity Committee of the Conference on Monday night made an earnest appeal to the workers to await quietly the arrival of the delegates.

(Detailed story on Machinists' stand, Page Two).

'RAF Again Blasts Bremen'

LONDON, June 30. — (BUP) — Britain's powerful bomber command was believed to have smashed at Bremen, Germany's second largest port, early today for the third time in five days.

A British announcement said that British planes bombed objectives in Germany during the night and the official German news agency said Bremen and other towns in the coastal area of northwest Germany were attacked.

The size of the raiding force was not disclosed immediately, but the German agency's claim that 10 raiders were shot down indicated that it must have been in the hundreds.

Bremen is the largest submarine-building center in Germany and also is the site of the Focke-Wulf aircraft works, where crack fighter planes and long-range bombers are built. One of the biggest oil refineries in the Reich is in the outskirts.

THE ODD SPOT

HONOLULU, June 30. — (UP)—It's a little confusing, but because the U. S. army bombers crossed the international dateline to bomb Japanese targets on Wake Island they technically returned to their Hawaiian base the day before the raid.

The bombers took off Friday, June 26, reached Wake on Sunday, June 28, (Wake time) and returned here Saturday, June 27.

(Eyewitness story on raid, Page Two).

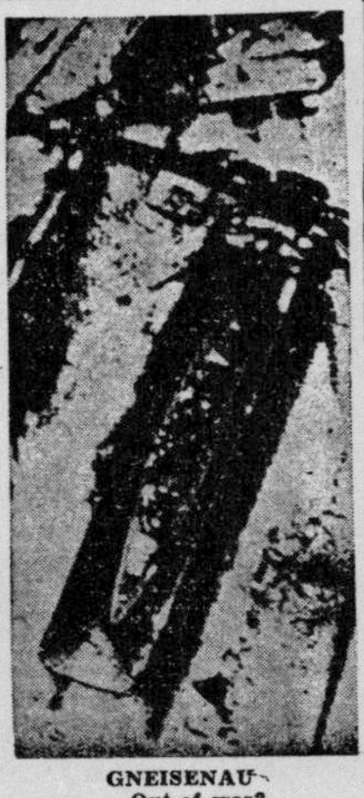

GNEISENAU . . . Out of war?

Photos Hint 'Gneisenau' Out Of War

LONDON, June 30. — (BUP)—The German battleship Gneisenau, her gun turrets dismantled and her decks ripped by bomb hits scored by the R.A.F. at Brest, in the English Channel, and at Kiel, lies at the Polish harbor of Gydnia, so badly crippled she may be left there for the duration of the war, the air ministry announced today.

Photographs taken in daylight by fast R.A.F. reconnaissance planes that made the 1600-mile round trip flight to the Bay of Danzig showed the one-time sleek battleship moored at the dock, part of her wounds hidden by camouflage.

GAS RATION UNIT RAISED IN MARITIMES

OTTAWA, June 30.—(BUP)—The value of the gas rationing unit in New Brunswick, Nova Scotia and Prince Edward Island will be raised from two to three gallons at 7 a.m. local time July 1, Minister of Munitions and Supply C. D. Howe announced Monday night.

He emphasized that the oil supply problem in the Maritimes was still acute. The minister explained that to make the increase possible, reserve stocks at bulk stations elsewhere would be drawn upon.

Sudden Death Of Calgary Visitor

Alfred Lemuel Schurman of Calgary collapsed and died shortly after noon Monday while riding in his son-in-law's car.

The deceased was visiting at the home of S. W. Metcalfe, 6361 Churchill Street, his son-in-law, and decided to accompany him to town. Mr. Metcalfe made a stop on the way down and upon returning to the car found the deceased dead.

Death was attributed to natural causes.

Nazis Deport 8,000 French

VICHY, June 30.—(UP)—German authorities have ordered the deportation of 8,000 persons from Lorraine and 50 French hostages from the industrial area of northwestern France, in an attempt to check a rising tide of anti-Nazi violence, it was announced Monday night.

• • •

Gauleiter Josef Buerckel of Lorraine, border province taken over by the Germans, ordered the mass deportation to Poland for what he described as punishment of parents whose sons fled to avoid obligatory German army or labor service.

• • •

Most of the 8.000 were expected to be sent to the Cracow area, lying along the border of Slovakia.

THREATEN OTHERS

The German military commander of French Flanders issued an order at Lille for the deportation of 50 hostages in reprisal for a series of attacks on communications in the industrial region. The order said that if the perpetrators of the acts were not caught by July 1, another 50 would be deported.

• • •

Meanwhile in London spokesmen for the World Jewish Congress charged that Germans have massacred more than 1,000,000 Jews since the war began in carrying out Hitler's proclaimed policy of exterminating the race.

• • •

They said the Nazis have established a "vast slaughter-house for Jews" in Eastern Europe, and that reliable reports showed that 700,000 Jews already have been murdered in Lithuania and Poland, 125,000 in Rumania, 200,000 in Russia and 100,000 in the rest of Europe.

Thus about one-sixth of the pre-war Jewish population in Europe, estimated at 6,000,000 to 7,000,000 persons, would be wiped out in less than three years.

The Germans were said to have set up reserves to which Eastern European Jews are being systematically deported for slave labor.

A spokesman said 10,232 persons died in the Warsaw Ghetto from hunger, disease and other causes between April and June last year, and that 4,000 children between the ages of 12 and 15 recently were removed from there by the Gestapo to work on farms.

Other spokesmen said the entire male Jewish population in Rumania had been pressed into compulsory labor.

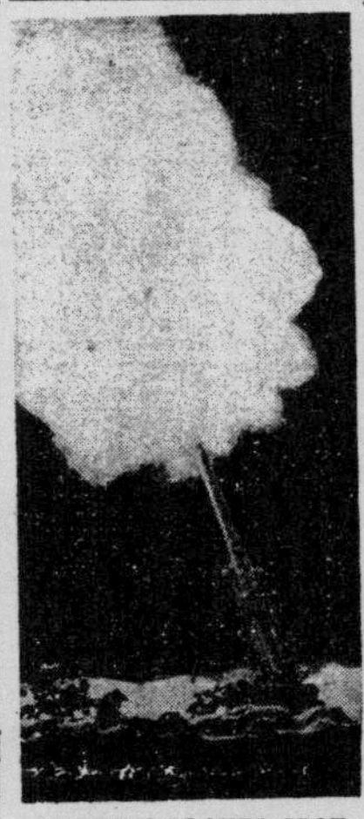

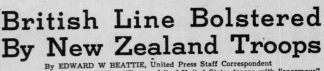

GERMAN PLANES SPOTTED—Night fighting is one of the most important phases in the war, and the sunken anti-aircraft gun you see in action is that of the Russian army. The gun crew has spotted alien planes and are powdering the air with plenty of death. The Germans claim the Russian anti-aircraft defences are excellent.

Cost Plus Plan Hit In Report

OTTAWA, June 30.—(BUP)—Checks and controls on the cost of war contracts exercised by the Department of Munitions "do not operate as well in practice as they appear to in theory," the War Expenditures Committee declared in an interim report Monday.

The report was filed by a sub-committee of the main body appointed to check expenditures made in connection with the war program.

"This committee strongly criticizes the use of the cost plus percentage contract, but realizes that in some instances resort must be had to it,"

The committee added, however, "the munitions contract branch of the department (of munitions) dislike the cost plus percentage contracts and prefer a fixed price contract arrived at after competition

Australia Front Has Quiet Spell

MELBOURNE, June 30. — (UP) — A communique from Gen. Douglas MacArthur's headquarters today reported "only limited air activity in all sectors Monday."

British Line Bolstered By New Zealand Troops

By EDWARD W BEATTIE, United Press Staff Correspondent

LONDON, June 30.—(BUP)—"Thousands" of United States troops with "enormous" quantities of equipment have arrived in Egypt to buttress British forces battling Axis armies that already have broken defence lines at Matruh and now threaten the great Alexandria naval base, 150 miles to the east, Cairo dispatches reported today.

Reinforcements of American airmen and planes also were said to have reached Egypt to join U.S. Army Air Corps units that are pounding German Marshal Erwin Rommel's Africa corps day and night in the desert.

Though there was no confirmation of either report in London, reinforcements of New Zealand troops were known to have been thrown into the battle.

A dispatch filed from Cairo at 8 o'clock Monday night said that Matruh, the last important port on the Egyptian coast west of Alexandria, was abandoned by the British Eighth army without a fight and that a terrific battle was under way on a wide front east of there.

77 MILES OFF

Overwhelmed by Marshal Erwin Rommel's vast army of German tanks and artillery, the British were believed withdrawing toward El Daba, only 77 miles from Alexandria, for another stand—their third in defence of Egypt.

Elements of the second New Zealand Expeditionary force have been thrown in to bolster the British, "which means that reinforcements are already in the field," the Cairo dispatch said.

(Where the New Zealanders came from was not indicated, but it was assumed that they probably came from Syria or other points in the Near East.)

• • •

(There has been speculation on the possibility that Gen. Douglas MacArthur might rush reinforcements to the Middle East from Australia, since his army has easier access to that area than any other Allied force.

The North African crisis was acute now, with Rommel charging headlong for the Alexandria naval base, whence Hitler could rule the Eastern Mediterranean, the rich, mystic valley of the Nile and threaten the whole Middle East.

The latest Cairo communique said British and Axis mobile and armored forces were locked in battles southwest and southeast of Matruh, the second defense line the British had thrown up in Egypt after having been routed from their chain of forts on the Libyan border.

• • •

The strategy of Gen. Sir Claude Auchinleck, British Middle Eastern commander, was to draw Rommel deeper into the Egyptian desert, stretch his communication lines, attempt to wear him down and stall for time in which to mass all available Allied forces in the Middle East.

Alexandria, guardian of the western approach to Suez, already was under air attack. The interior ministry announced that a few bombs fell there this morning, causing slight damage.

British cotton merchants feared that $80,000,000 worth of long staple Egyptian cotton stored in Alexandria warehouses might have to be put to the torch if Rommel got any closer.

The story of Matruh was almost identical with that of Tobruk which fell eight days earlier. The British were outgunned by Rommel's 88-millimeter (3½-inch) self-propelling artillery pieces; they were outmanoeuvred by his superior tank forces in spite of the R.A.F.'s claims of air superiority.

BULLETINS

Mexico Curbs Enemy Alien Travel

MEXICO CITY, June 30.—(UP)—In what was believed the first of a new series of restrictions against enemy aliens, the department of interior Monday night cancelled the traveling privileges of foreign-born agents of Axis firms.

Sears Roebuck President Dies

CHICAGO, June 30.—(UP)—Thomas J. Carney, president of Sears Roebuck& Co., died Monday night at St. Luke's Hospital after an illness of five months. He was 56.

Hitler Hurls Fresh Troops At Sevastopol Defenders

LONDON, June 30—(BUP)—The Vichy radio said Monday night that German forces besieging Sevastopol had reached the inner defences of the Crimean fortress. (The claim was unconfirmed by any Allied sources.)

MOSCOW, June 30.—(UP)—Germany is hurling formidable reinforcements at Sevastopol in a supreme effort to knock out that battered Crimean fortress, the high command announced today, and has loosed a series of attacks west of Moscow possibly presaging a full scale offensive on the central front.

A midnight communique said the Red Army successfully repulsed massive German attacks on the Kursk front, where Marshal Fedor Von Bock had launched a new offensive in an apparent attempt to flank the Russian defenses in the Ukraine and swing southward toward the Caucasus.

"On the central front our troops repulsed several German attacks, killing 1500 enemy troops," the high command said, a hint that Hitler's summer campaign begun in the Crimea and Ukraine might be spreading north.

The reinforced Axis siege army succeeded at heavy cost in advancing slightly on the Sevastopol front, but the battle-grimed defenders fighting in their fourth week with virtually no rest beat back numerous attacks, the Russians reported.

The fighting was described as of a "particularly violent character," even by the standards of ferocity already set in the battle.

"The German command, attempting to break the defenders of Sevastopol, is bringing up large numbers of tanks and planes," the high command said. "The gallant defenders repulsed tank and air attacks and inflicted heavy losses on the enemy."

The latest reports from the southern battlefronts said the defenders of Sevastopol had pledged themselves to fight to their last shell, while east of Kharkov Marshal Semyon Timoshenko had checked the enemy and recaptured some lost territory.

BUDGET DEBATE TO OPEN TODAY

OTTAWA, June 30—(BUP).—The debate of Finance Minister J. L. Ilsley's war budget will begin today with government expectation that it will be over by the week's end, T. A. Crerar told the House of Commons just before it rose Monday night. The debate will be opened by Conservative Leader R. B. Hanson.

REDS SMASH NAZI DRIVE AT KLETSK

The Vancouver Sun

Only Evening Newspaper Owned, Controlled and Operated by Vancouver People

FOUNDED 1886
VOL. LVI—No. 255

VANCOUVER, BRITISH COLUMBIA, FRIDAY, JULY 31, 1942

Price 3 Cents

On trains, boats and outside Greater Vancouver, 5c

Shipyard Guards? They Don't Bother A Determined Man

Sun Reporter Finds It Easy to Get Into Yards

By CHRISTY McDEVITT

Are Vancouver shipyards well guarded?

Is the average person assuming any risk going through those yards?

Are the nearly - completed vessels patrolled to keep strangers from going aboard and descending into the vitals of the ship?

Those three questions can be answered with a loud and definite "no."

Knowing that shipyard police carried guns and believing that strangers were not welcome in a place where it is important that every move be carefully supervised, I had definite qualms about trying to enter the yards for a "look-around."

GUARDS A WORRY

That was my assignment. To go into the yards without benefit of credentials and to see how many points of the industry I could survey before the police or interested workmen discovered my identity.

The armed guards were my greatest worry.

Guarding a vital war industry those men are prepared to shoot first and pick up their information, if necessary, when the smoke clears away.

It was even simpler than I had anticipated.

About nine men were lounging around the outer gate when I approached the guard there. Two of the men were talking with the guard. I waited until there came a break in the conversation. The guard looked my way.

"I want to see Mr. ——," mentioning the manager of the shipyard. I told him, as anyone else could.

The guard swung his gate back. "Go right through," he said, "his office is over there."

I walked right through.

This was only the outer part of the yard. I could have slipped through but, glancing back I saw the man at the gate was watching me so I went on into the office.

ASKS FOR CHIEF

There was a girl at the switchboard.

"I want to see Mr. ——," this time I asked for the chief guard.

She appeared annoyed.

"The guard at the gate could have shown you where his office is," she said rather testily.

I thanked her and left the office. I went through to the main part of the yard. The din was terrific. Men were swarming back and forth and trucks wheeled slowly up and down the

Please Turn to Page Twelve
See "Shipyards"

STRANGERS WELCOME HERE

This picture was taken on the upper deck of a nearly-completed boat being constructed in a West Coast Canadian shipyard. The Vancouver Sun reporter, indicated by arrow, is seen walking toward the temporary gangplank which connects two ships. The workers accept him on there as an everyday occurrence. Many of them were willing to pause and chat for a few moments. From here the reporter went down the hold of the ship.

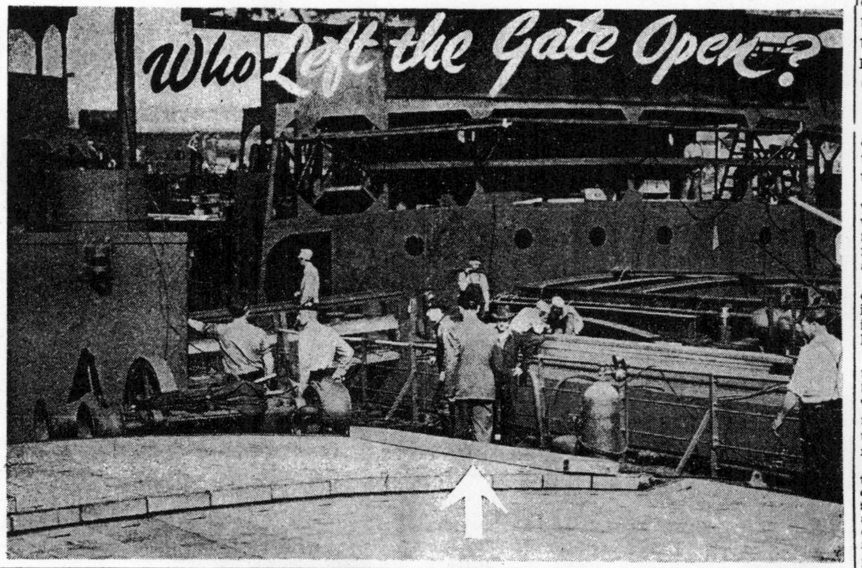

Reinforcements to Turn Tide in Big Stalingrad Battle

Moscow Admits 'Slight Advance' of Invader in Bataisk Sector; Berlin Says Don Crossed on 150-Mile Front

By HENRY SHAPIRO
Special to The Vancouver Sun
Copyright, 1942, by British United Press

MOSCOW, July 31.—A stiffening Russian defense beat off the concentrated might of the German army with increasing success today, and the Soviet noon communique reported the crushing of the greatest Nazi effort to cross the Don in a battle which raged for eight days.

(Meanwhile Associated Press reported that armored trains of the Red Army rolled into the shell-torn steppes of the Don Bend today, bringing up vast, fresh reinforcements for the defenders.)

Todays communique acknowledged only a "slight advance" by the Germans around Bataisk, 12 to 15 miles southwest of Rostov, and stated that enemy losses were enormous. It emphasized, however, that the peril to Russia is not diminished, and the situation might become worse at any hour.

(The German High Command claimed its forces had crossed the lower Don on a 150-mile front and that some of its spearheads were 112 miles south of the river, with the important railway station of Kushchevka captured by a Nazi division.)

It was around Kletsk, 70 miles northwest of Stalingrad, that the big German attack was crushed. The Germans have been pouring reinforcements into their attempts to force the Don there for eight days.

"Last night our troops fought the enemy in the region of Voronezh, as well as Tsimlyanskaya, south and southeast of Bataisk and southwest of Kletsk," the communique said. "There were no changes on other sectors."

PINCER EFFORT

Tsimlyanskaya is half-way between Rostov and Stalingrad. The Germans have been trying to drive across the Don there and at Kletsk, to catch the great bend of the Don and Stalingrad, 50 miles beyond, in a great pincers.

Front-line dispatches report that an "unparalleled battle" continues to rage along the 125-mile front from Tsimlyanskaya to Bataisk, and that Russian resistance is stiffening against continually arriving enemy reinforcements.

The Russians have slowed and steadily pressed back the Germans on the northern end of the Don front at Voronezh. The government organ **Izvestia** said Soviet soldiers had repulsed an Hungarian attack and seized a favorable height on the west bank of the Don.

ACTION NEAR BRYANSK

The noon communique reported "fighting of a local character" around Bryansk, south-west of Moscow. The enemy, having received reinforcements, attacked on one sector, it said. The attack was met by the concentrated fire of Soviet trench mortars, and the Nazis began falling back Soviet soldiers, taking advantage of the confusion, broke into German positions and seized a fortified point.

By Associated Press

MOSCOW, July 31.—Red Star charged today that Red Army uniforms had been used by the Germans for attacks in two sectors, in the Caucasus front, but said the deception was discovered and the attacking forces, totalling three battalions, were wiped out.

White tabs, not worn by the Russians, had been placed on the collars, the army newspaper said.

Britain Bans Pleasure Cars 'For Duration'

LONDON, July 31.—Motorists put their pleasure cars away "for the duration" today because, effective tomorrow, gasoline will be sold to only business and professional automobiles.

400,000 Japs In Manchukuo To Attack Reds

By Canadian Press

LONDON, July 31.—A British military source said today that Japanese forces nearly 400,000 strong are concentrating in Manchukuo opposite the 1000-mile Soviet frontier from Lake Baikal to the Pacific, and "there is little doubt they are planning to attack."

"The Japanese are already in position to attack whenever they choose," said this source who declined to permit identification by name.

Japanese engineers have used large numbers of Chinese prisoners to construct and develop road and rail communications with the present concentration areas, it was declared.

"Like all aggressors," the Japanese can strike wherever they choose along a long frontier," the source said, predicting that they would make at least three drives in the north in an attempt to isolate Vladivostok.

"August and September are the best months for campaigning in that area," he said, "and the Japanese inactivity in all other spheres except the North Pacific indicates that Siberia is their objective for the last half of 1942."

Hun Saboteurs Lose in Court

WASHINGTON, July 31. — The seven alleged Nazi saboteurs lost today in their effort to escape jurisdiction of President Roosevelt's military commission by appeal to the United States Supreme Court. Their Habeas Corpus application was rejected.

Twenty minutes before the decision was handed down the Government had concluded summation of its case against the defendants before the military commission.

Maj.-Gen. Myron C. Cramer, Army Judge Advocate General, delivered the Government's summation arguments and was believed to have asked the death penalty for at least seven of the eight defendants.

Petrillo Stands Pat on Record Ban

NEW YORK, July 31. — James C. Petrillo, president of the American Federation of Musicians, today stood by his order that will stop 140,000 union musicians at midnight from making any more phonograph records or radio transcriptions for commercial use.

He said last night he had not answered Elmer Davis, director of the Office of War Information, who had appealed to him to rescind the order "as a patriotic duty." Petrillo said he would answer Davis when he had a chance.

Earl O'Malley, B.C. Lumberman, Dies

Earl O'Malley, 3594 West Thirty-seventh Avenue, well-known in British Columbia lumbering circles, died today in St. Paul's Hospital.

PENSION SCALE

WASHINGTON, July 31. — President Roosevelt today signed legislation fixing the rate of pensions for widows and other dependents of members of the regular army and navy at 75 percent of World War I pension rates.

Canada Paratroop Units Are to Be Trained in U.S.

OTTAWA, July 31.—Canada's first paratroops will take their training at Fort Benning, Ga., until training facilities have been established in the Dominion, it was learned today.

Defense Minister Hon. J. L. Ralston told Commons last Monday night that a battalion of paratroops had been authorized and that instructors were leaving for the United States to get "immediate instruction" on paratroop training there.

Some little time will elapse—perhaps six months—before arrangements are completed for full training in Canada.

Exact location of the planned Canadian school has not been made public.

Guards Patrol Miami Beaches

MIAMI BEACH, Fla., July 31. —Armed soldiers, Coast Guardsmen and military police patrolled 12 miles of the ocean front today and civilians were ordered to stay away from beaches.

The patrols were put out and the edict issued to bathers last night. Neither army nor navy officials would comment, although it was indicated that some highly important reason had prompted the action.

1500 Crow's Nest Miners Out on Strike

By Canadian Press

BLAIRMORE, Alta., July 31.—More than 1500 mine workers in the Crow's Nest Pass remained idle today as a result of alleged violations by the mining companies of the Pass of the wage scale agreements with the United Mine Workers of America, District 18.

Miners concerned are those employed at the International and McGillivray Creek mines at Coleman and at the Greenhill Mine of West Canadian Collieries here. The West Canadian's Bellevue mine and the Hillcrest-Mohawk mine at Maple Leaf are working. Pickets were on duty this morning at the Greenhill mine.

A mass meeting of pit workers has been called for this afternoon here when the matters in protest will come for discussion.

Cessation of work comes at a time when mines are working full blast. One matter under dispute, it was learned, is the charge that boys are being used for men's jobs, yet they are being paid boy's wages.

LITVINOFF SEES FDR

WASHINGTON, July 31.—Maxim Litvinoff, the Russian ambassador, conferred for nearly a half hour with President Roosevelt Thursday.

Japs Defeated in Darwin Air Battle

By Canadian Press

ALLIED HEADQUARTERS, Australia, July 31.—In the biggest outburst of aerial warfare in the Australian area since the Coral Sea battle, allied airmen destroyed nine of 49 Japanese raiders over Port Darwin yesterday, set an enemy transport aflame off New Guinea, shot up her destroyer escort, and downed one enemy fighter and possibly another in that area. The defenders lost one plane.

Allied fighters tore into the attack force of 27 heavy bombers and 22 escorting Zero fighters over Port Darwin, knocking down seven of the fighters and two bombers at a cost of only one defending plane.

The Japanese formations were completely broken up in this "Allied performance, described by headquarters communique as a piece of "brilliant interception."

The big raid upon the northern port came in the afternoon after a light, ineffective morning attack.

2 OTHER RAIDS

In other thrusts at the Commonwealth, nine high-flying Japanese bombers made the first attack of the war on Port Hedland, small freight port southwest of Broome, in Western Australia, causing slight damage and one casualty, and made a futile, single-plane night attack on Horn Island, in the Torres Strait.

Keeping up their own offensive operations, Allied heavy bombers pounced on the destroyer-escorted Japanese transport, 100 miles off Gona, New Guinea, and scored five direct hits, leaving the vessel spouting flames visible for 30 miles.

Then the destroyer escort was machine-gunned from low-level and her anti-aircraft guns were silenced.

FIFTH SHIP SUNK

The transport, described by today's communique as a medium-sized cargo vessel, was the fifth enemy ship damaged or sunk since the Japanese invaded the Papuan Peninsula, New Guinea, last week.

From all yesterday's operations three Allied planes were missing.

For the first time in several days Allied headquarters said there was no ground activity at Kokoda, inland village midway between Gona and the Allied base at Port Moresby. The latter was attacked by three Japanese night raiders without damage.

Emergencies Too Much for Japanese

SEATTLE, July 31.—Prof. I. J. Fisher, for 17 years on the faculty of the Imperial Japanese Naval College at Tokyo, said today the Nipponese were "great fighters on a long-prepared plan," but were "not disciplined to meet emergencies."

Fisher said that weakness "may prove their undoing."

"If the sudden, unexpected thing happens, they haven't the resources within themselves to cope with it," Prof. Fisher said.

Soviet Bombers Sink Ten Ships

MOSCOW, July 31.—Fliers of the Russian Baltic fleet's air arm have sunk 10 enemy ships and damaged 10 others in attacks during July, the official Tass Agency reported today.

In one recent operation, it was said, fliers led by Maj. I. M. Karassev, "Hero of the Soviet Union," sank or damaged 16 enemy ships.

RAF Fighters Make 2 Raids On Hun Bases

By Canadian Press

LONDON, July 31. — British fighters swept across the Channel in the direction of Boulogne this morning in a resumption of daylight raids on the occupied French coast after a night of scattered German bombing attacks upon Britain.

Nazi planes also were active over the Channel during the forenoon and heavy anti-aircraft fire was audible for several minutes on the outskirts of London, which had two quick alarms during the night —the fifth and sixth of the week.

Eight towns in the Midlands were hit with high explosives and incendiaries by the German night raiders who followed the usual practice of lighting up the target area with flares before unloading their bombs.

CHURCH BOMBED

One Midlands town had its first real raid of the war. In a second, a well-known church was damaged, and in a third low-flying planes machine-gunned the streets.

(Berlin radio said Birmingham was the object of the Midlands attack).

Eight of the raiders were shot down by British defenses and a ninth destroyed over its base in occupied France by an RAF fighter, a communique said.

Bad weather kept the RAF bombing squadrons at home.

Today in Britain

War events analyzed by Fleet Street writers, cabled from the London Bureau of The Vancouver Sun.
Copyright, 1942.

LONDON, July 31.—Debarkation of a new contingent of thousands of Canadian troops and the arrival of Brig.-Gen. Frank O'D. Hunter, commander of American fighting plane units in Britain, stirred anew today the speculation that an Allied invasion of the continent might be in the offing.

Sir Stafford Cripps' guarded statement yesterday in the House of Commons, where he answered questions concerning possible establishment of a second front by saying that the government had certain "intentions," also added fuel to these speculations.

The London press, however, refrained from playing up the situation.

"When even the village idiot could see that an Allied invasion must be in the cards, there can be no harm in making the enemy jumpy about it," the Daily Telegraph said, adding: "In these circumstances silence, even in Parliament, is surely golden."

Please Turn to Page Twelve
See "Britain Today"

War in Tabloid

RUSSIA.—Soviets crush Nazi thrust at Stalingrad after eight-day battle near Kletsh, on the Don River "bulge"; heavy reinforcements reach Timoshenko. Soviets admit "situation grave" south of Rostov.

LONDON.—Capital had two air alarms early today but no bombs. Birmingham and other Midlands towns raided. Nine Germans downed. RAF fighters sweep Northern France last evening and again today.

EGYPT.—Axis bombs Alexandria. Cairo recalls Churchill's pledge to bomb Rome if "Holy" Cairo attacked. Germans bombed Cairo Wednesday. Land fighting still stalled. RAF still battering Rommel lines.

AUSTRALIA.—Japs decisively beaten in biggest air fight over Darwin. Seven Jap Zero fighters and two heavy bombers shot down. Light Jap raids also on Hedland, Australia, and Horn Island off Darwin coast.

WASHINGTON.—U. S. Supreme Court denies habeas corpus writs to Nazi saboteurs now on trial.

'Only Waiting for Green Light'

Nelson Backs Kaiser Cargo Plane Plan

WASHINGTON, July 31.—Henry J. Kaiser, West Coast shipbuilder, today told a Senate military subcommittee that War Production Board Chairman Donald M. Nelson had assured him of "full support" for his plan to build a fleet of 5000 cargo-carrying airplanes as a means of beating the submarine menace.

"I am now free to disclose," Kaiser said, "that I have had, everst nce Donald Nelson came in, a tremendous amount of support from him. I have taken this up with him. He has given me his full assurance of his full support in the construction of these flying boats.

"All I'm waiting for is the green light," Kaiser said. "I'm sure I'll get approval if I can convince them I can do it. We must convince the Martin people and the Douglas people (aircraft companies) that we must all pull together."

BUFFALO, N.Y., July 31.—Bad news for Hitler, Hirohito and Co., was released here today with the announcement that the new Curtiss Commando (C46) military transport plane had passed exhaustive tests and is in quantity production.

The Commando, more than twice as large as any domestic airliner now in operation, can transport troops and scout cars simultaneously.

An idea of its size can be gained by research engineers' claims that 35 of these craft could have transported all of the estimated 30,000 tons of material carried by 7700 trucks over the Burma Road during onemonth—and more quickly.

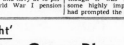

'I Saw Canadian Heroes Die at Dieppe'

By ROSS MUNRO
Canadian Press Staff Writer
(Copyright, 1942, by The Canadian Press)

WITH THE CANADIAN RAIDING FORCE AT DIEPPE, Aug. 19 (Delayed).—For eight raging hours, under intense Nazi fire from dawn into a sweltering afternoon, I watched Canadian troops fight the blazing, bloody Battle of Dieppe.

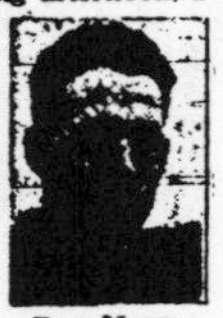
Ross Munro

I saw them go through the biggest of the war's raiding operations in wild scenes that crowded helter skelter one upon another in crazy sequences.

There was a furious attack by German E-boats while the Canadians moved in on Dieppe's beaches, landing by dawn's half-light.

When the Canadian battalions stormed through the flashing inferno of Nazis defenses, belching guns of huge tanks rolled into the fight, I spent the grimmest 20 minutes of my life with one unit when a rain of German machine-gun fire wounded half the men in our boat and only a miracle saved us from annihilation.

A few hours later there was the spine-chilling experience of a dive-bombing attack by seven Stukas, the dreaded Nazi aircraft which spotted out the small assault landing craft waiting off-shore to re-embark the fighting men.

Our boat was thrown about like a toy by their seven screeching bombs that plunged into the water around us and exploded in gigantic cascades.

There was the lashing fire of machine-gunning from other Nazi aircraft and the thunder of anti-aircraft fire that sent them hustling off.

Over our heads in the blue, cloud-flecked French sky were fought the greatest air engagements since the Battle of Britain, dog-fights carried on to the dizzy accompaniment of planes exploding in the air, diving down flaming, some plummeting into the sea from thousands of feet.

Hour after hour guns of the supporting warships growled salvoes at targets ashore, where by now our tanks also were in violent action.

Unearthly noises rumbled up and down the French coast, shrouded for miles in smoke-screens covering the fleet.

There was heroism at sea and in the skies in those hours but the hottest spot was ashore, where the Canadians fought at close quarters with the Nazis. They fought to the end, where they had to, and showed courage and daring.

They attacked the Dieppe arsenal of the coastal defense. They left Dieppe silent and afire, its ruins and its dead under a shroud of smoke.

The operation against Dieppe started from a British port Tuesday evening. I boarded a ship which also carried the Royal Regiment of Toronto. It was 7 o'clock and only then were we told that Dieppe was our destination.

The Royals took it cooly enough. They had been trained with the rest of the force for several months on Combined Operations for just such a job.

Maps, mosaics and photographs of Dieppe were issued and as the boat put to sea with the other ships of the raiding fleet, the troops were briefed in their tasks.

It was a muggy night but the sky was clear. The sea was calm. It was Combined Operations weather.

Below deck the men sat around cleaning weapons, fusing grenades and loading the magazines of Stens, tommy-guns and Brens.

In darkness formed the flotilla, shadowy tank-landing craft that looked like oil tankers, a score of small assault boats, destroyers, gunboats, motor launches and torpedo boats.

A few officers in the raiding party drank beer with the ship's captain, and chatted about everything but the operation. We had a snack of bully beef, bread and butter, and tea, and then went over the side into assault craft.

After leaving the mother ships our flotilla of little craft took positions in line astern. The Royals were to land at a point one mile east of Dieppe and establish themselves in that flanking area.

Just as we were pushing away from the mother ship, an old British tar whispered to us: "Cheerio laddies, the best of luck, give the —— a bellicking."

It was pleasant in the open assault boats. Nobody seemed particularly nervous about the coming business though it was to be the Canadians' first time in action.

I made myself think in terms of manoeuvres exercises in which I had taken part with these men in preparation for his night.

Please Turn to Page Ten
See "Ross Munro"

Only Evening Newspaper Owned, Controlled and Operated By Vancouver People

The Vancouver Sun

Today's Tides
Vancouver Harbor
High 2:31 p.m.; 10.2 feet   Low 7:16 p.m.; 8.2 feet
English Bay
High 2:02 p.m.; 10.4 feet   Low 6:47 p.m.; 8.9 feet
First Narrows
High slack 2:50 p.m.   Low slack 7:35 p.m.

FOUNDED 1886
VOL. LVI—No. 272   HOME EDITION   VANCOUVER, BRITISH COLUMBIA, THURSDAY, AUGUST 20, 1942   ★★★   Price 3 Cents   On trains, boats and outside Greater Vancouver, 5c   MArine 1161

Railway North 'In the Bag,' Thinks Hart

Premier Back From Edmonton Parley With American Military Chiefs; Decision Within 'Month or More'

By JAMES DYER

Construction of a railway northward from Prince George, along the much-discussed "B" route surveyed for the Alaska-B.C.-Yukon highway, seems definitely assured, and its most important future result may be the opening, in post-war years, of a new and great chapter of expansion in the history of Northern British Columbia.

"There is no question but that British Columbia, particularly the North, is going to share in the tremendous forward strides that will come to the Pacific Northwest and Alaska after the war," was the word of British Columbia's premier, Hon. John Hart, when he stepped off a Canadian National train from Edmonton this morning.

MEET U.S. GENERAL

Mr. Hart had gone to Edmonton to take part in discussions, together with public works department and P.G.E. Railway officials, held at the request of Major General Brehon Somervell, chief of supply for the United States Army. The conference was on railway matters.

Mr. Hart was unusually secretive about the matters discussed or conclusions reached. But he said, cryptically:

"The impression I got—the impression that seemed to prevail was that the "B" route, north from Prince George, is regarded as the most feasible."

"However," he added, "I cannot say more at this time. I went there at the request of the United States Army, merely to give information. The man who will undoubtedly make the decision is General Somervell."

Would the P.G.E. fit into the Prince George Railway scheme? Mr. Hart was asked.

Mr. Hart smiled mysteriously.

Please Turn to Page Ten
See "Railway"

Today In Britain

War events analyzed by Fleet Street writers, cabled from the London Bureau of The Vancouver Sun
(Copyright, 1942)

LONDON, Aug. 20.—The raid on Mainz, where 100 are dead and a great cathedral was destroyed, is discussed at length in an editorial in the Frankfurter Zeitung.

British air raids on German cities, it asserts, are primarily designed to terrorize civilians in the hope of driving them to desperation. The newspaper rejects the British justification of their procedure, which allegedly cites the German bombing of Warsaw and Rotterdam as precedents.

Both cities, replies the Frankfurter Zeitung, were in the active fighting zone and the native troops defending them were also engaged in attacking the Germans.

The newspaper then reminds the British that the Germans have not been asleep since 1940 and that bigger bombs are now available. When the hour strikes, it warns, the British will experience something of which they have not even the slightest premonition.

• • •

Victory Acclaimed

The British press today hailed the Allied attack on Dieppe as a "complete success" and all agreed it was a prelude to the establishment of a second front.

The News Chronicle said, "the raid, though obviously planned independently of Moscow decisions, was thus psychologically most opportune. We look on it as an earnest of still bigger things to come."

The Glasgow Herald asserted that the "relatively prolonged nature of the daylight attack and the very extensive provision of air cover" in addition to the use

Please Turn to Page Ten
See "Britain Today"

Success Assured By RCAF

Vancouver Man Led Protection for Dieppe Raid

By ALAN RANDAL
Canadian Press Staff Writer

LONDON, Aug. 20.—Canadian airmen protecting their own troops from enemy air assault for the first time gave the Dominion's attack force in the Battle of Dieppe the greatest aerial cover ever provided, it was indicated today.

Sqdn. Ldr. R. F. Begg of Vancouver, commanding an Army Co-operation squadron, supervised the operations of his crews.

Flying with the RAF, Spitfire and Army Co-operation squadrons of the RCAF formed a big proportion of the trans-channel shuttle service during the operations yesterday.

Some made two and three trips, pausing only long enough at their home base to refuel and reload with ammunition.

While Canadian losses were not announced—it is known Allied losses were 98 planes and the Nazis 91—the Canadian victory score stood at nine German aircraft destroyed and many probably damaged.

But these were just early figures on the Canadians' part in this amazing triumph over the German air force in French skies—amazing from the Canadian and Allied points of view because the losses were so nearly equal, whereas the Germans lost four and five to one in the Battle of Britain.

TALLY INCOMPLETE

It is expected that Canadians' tally will rise as all reports are checked and double-checked. It is likely that planes probably destroyed or damaged will run well beyond a score.

One quarter said "the early figures probably will not do full justice to the Canadians' accomplishments."

At one station, while awaiting their dispersals from the takeoff on the third sweep of the day,

Please Turn to Page Ten
See "Airmen"

U.S. Declares All But Totally Unfit Liable to Serve

WASHINGTON, Aug. 20.—The United States selective service Wednesday abolished its "limited service" Class 1-B, the group with minor physical defects, and ordered all but the totally unfit reclassified as available for military service.

Nearing exhaustion of the pool of A 1-A registrants, the army recently called for induction of men from the 1-B class.

Draft members will either be placed in 4-F, if totally unfit for service, or shifted to 1-A.

The order is effective today but the reclassifying of men in this group will begin Sept. 1, and be completed by New Year's Day.

Marines 'Mop Up' Last Jap Troops In Solomons

WASHINGTON, Aug. 20.—The Navy announced today that U.S. Marines are now mopping up the remaining Japanese troops on the islands they recently seized in the Solomon Archipelago.

The Navy also reported that an enemy destroyer or cruiser had been bombed and set afire by aerial forces.

British Eye-Witness Story

Accidental Discovery Nearly Wrecked Raid

HER SON LED THE COMMANDOS

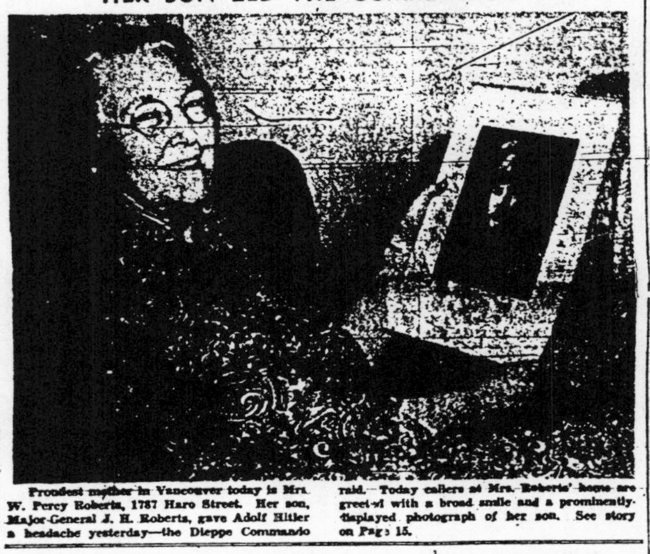

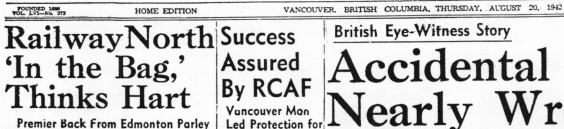

Proudest mother in Vancouver today is Mrs. W. Percy Roberts, 1787 Haro Street. Her son, Major-General J. H. Roberts, gave Adolf Hitler a headache yesterday—the Dieppe Commando raid. Today callers at Mrs. Roberts' home are greeted with a broad smile and a prominently displayed photograph of her son. See story on Page 15.

German E-Boats Poured Deadly Fire Into Canadian Barges; Beaches Stormed

The following eye-witness account of the Allied attack on Dieppe was written by a British correspondent who watched the action from a tank-landing craft off the Dieppe shore.

By ALAN HUMPHRIES
Representative of the British Press

LONDON, Aug. 20—For eight hours I watched our forces battling against the concentrated opposition of the enemy on the beaches at Dieppe. The sky was filled with British aircraft throughout the whole operation.

By a thousand-to-one chance the raiding craft carrying some Commandos were intercepted just before it was due to land.

An enemy patrol was the cause and the result was not only that the Canadian Commando craft was severely damaged by German flak (anti-aircraft), ships and E-boats which held their fire until the landing craft was within 200 yards, but that a much more important warning was given to the Germans coastal batteries, which were the Commandos' objectives.

Then the Commandos did succeed in landing at their assigned place on the beach they walked into a curtain of fire which came from every small arm the enemy could muster.

Vancouver Colonel Proves Hero

LONDON, Aug. 20. — The bravery of a young Colonel from Vancouver was the talk of every man who saw him in action in the Dieppe Commando raid. He fought with every infantry weapon and led his men with cool courage, not giving a thought to his own danger.

Navy's 'Superlative Job'

The defenders even trained their anti-aircraft guns on the beach.

Against this rain of death, the Commandos, who had needed some measure of surprise, spent themselves in vain.

The guns which were the objective of the raid were never silent.

This initial setback was felt throughout the whole operation and was partly responsible for the later difficulties.

A demonstration of complete mastery of the sea and sky was given us by the Navy and RAF.

The navy did a superlative job of getting the large and complicated convoy in the right spots at the right time. This was accomplished without incident.

So Dominant was the navy's supremacy that during the entire raid, while the fleet lay two or three miles off Dieppe, not one attempt was made by the enemy to attack with surface craft.

See "Raid"
Please Turn to Page Ten

French Raid Proves 2nd Front Possible

By EDWARD BEATTIE
Special to The Vancouver Sun
Copyright, 1942, by British United Press

LONDON, Aug. 20.—A conclave of high leaders of the British, American and Canadian fighting forces was summoned less than 24 hours after the successful Dieppe attack, it was learned today, to study application of the Commando tactics to the eventual invasion of Europe.

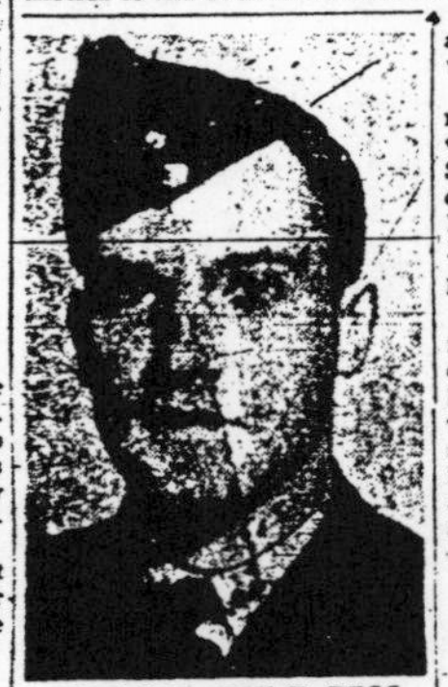

SQDN.-LDR. ROY F. BEGG of Vancouver a son of F. R. Begg, director and general manager of Begg Motor Co. Ltd., commanded an Army Co-operation Squadron during the commando raid on the French coast, Wednesday.

He learned to fly at Vancouver Airport while he was a university student and was presented with his wings by Air Group Capt. Duncan Bell-Irving.

Outstanding in the results of and lessons learned from the raid was this:

The toughest troops of four nations—Canadian shock-troops who will be the spearhead for the Second Front, British Commandos, U.S. Rangers and Fighting French—proved that the Second Front is feasible.

RECORD AIR RAID

The attack on Dieppe was carried out under the greatest mass of airpower ever provided a land force in the west, it was revealed today. For the first time since the Battle of Britain the Nazi Luftwaffe went all out in a vain attempt to beat off the smashing concentration of Allied forces.

German planes — estimated by one correspondent at about 500 — attempted to break through the RAF-RCAF protective cover but were smashed back with such losses that the result was described as a "decisive Allied victory."

Throughout the night the Commandos streamed back across the English Channel and on—through cheering English

Please Turn to Page Ten
See "Beattie"

Seven Canadian Units

Sherwood Lett Of Vancouver In Dieppe Raid

(Picture on Page 10)

By ROSS MUNRO
Canadian Press War Correspondent

LONDON, Aug. 20.—Units of two infantry regiments—the Royal Hamilton Light Infantry and the Essex Scottish of Windsor, Ontario—with the Calgary Tank Regiment carried the main Canadian attack on the Dieppe raid yesterday right into the town itself and battled the Germans in the streets to capture the main portions of the town.

Maj.-Gen. J. H. Roberts, senior ranking officer of the expedition, commanded the Canadians.

Other high Canadian officers who took part in the operation, Brig. Sherwood Lett, Vancouver, and Brig. W. S. Southam, Toronto.

On the flank, units of the South Saskatchewan Regiment and the Cameron Highlanders of Winnipeg landed at Pourville, two miles west of Dieppe, and the Royal Regiment of Toronto went in at Puits, one mile east of the port.

Units of the Fusiliers Mont Royal, a French-Canadian battalion, were floating reserves and finally were sent into Dieppe.

What Allies Learned From Dieppe Raid

LONDON, Aug. 20.—United Nations military authorities said today that the Dieppe Commando raid proved these important things:

1. That a Second Front can be opened in the west at a price which may be calculated in advance.

2. To open it while half-ready would be suicidal.

3. There will have to be more, and even bigger raids before the Second Front comes.

4. The new raids must test the ability of shock forces to consolidate and expand a bridgehead of the kind formed yesterday.

5. Where companies of 300 men engaged the Germans at Dieppe, divisions of 15,000 men will be needed for the Second Front.

6. Allied plane forces dominated the air. On the present scale they probably could not do so if the Second Front were opened in the north, as the relatively thinly held Norwegian coast.

7. The Germans will have to bring fighter planes to the west at once and they may have to reinforce their invasion coast armies.

Secret Radio Stations Seized

Brazil Holds Nazis as Hostages

RIO DE JANEIRO, Aug. 20.—The government today prohibited about 100 Germans, who intended to embark on two Brazilian diplomatic vessels to Lisbon, to leave the country, ordering them held as hostages for 11 Brazilians arrested by the Germans in Compeigne, France.

Meanwhile, reports from Bahia to the newspaper O Globo said that a German submarine had been attacked by a patrol plane today off the coast of Bahia, but the results were not verified. Seven Axis submarines had been attacked earlier this week, and one and possibly two of them were sunk.

Brazil appeared to be making war preparations today and Brazilian, United States and British planes swept the seas in a relentless hunt for German raiders that sank five Brazilian steamers with heavy loss of life Saturday.

Police in various parts of the country seized four clandestine radio transmitters in the past 12 hours.

Minister of War Gen. Eurico G. Dutra ordered all Brazilian officers and privates on leave or doing special training to rejoin their regiments immediately.

Crowds still roamed the streets, clamoring for war against the Axis.

The chief of police tightened curfew regulations, ordering all bars and coffee shops closed by 8 p.m., and theatres by 10 p.m.

SANTIAGO, Chile, Aug. 20.—President Juan Antonio Rios warned Chile last night to "be prepared for any surprise these uncertain days may bring."

He addressed the nation by radio, after the Foreign Office had protested the sinking of five Brazilian ships.

Pleads Not Guilty

WASHINGTON, Aug. 20.—Silver Shirt leader William Dudley Pelley and three other defendants charged with conspiring to impair the morale of the nation's armed forces, entered pleas of not guilty when arraigned today.

King's Speech On Page 22

Sweeping new measures for the utilization of every labor resource in Canada's war effort are detailed on page 22. They were announced by Prime Minister King in his broadcast last night.

Four Axis Planes Downed in Egypt

CAIRO, Aug. 20.—British fighters destroyed at least four enemy planes in a sudden increase of aerial activity over the Egyptian battle front west of El Alamein, British headquarters reported today.

The communique reported no bombing raids, however, and said there was nothing to report concerning land operations yesterday.

PACIFIC BATTLE OUTCOME VEILED

THE VANCOUVER DAILY PROVINCE ★★★★★ FINAL

48th YEAR—NO. 128 VANCOUVER, B.C., TUESDAY, AUGUST 25, 1942 —22 PAGES PRICE 3 CENTS the country. Five Cents On trains, boats and in

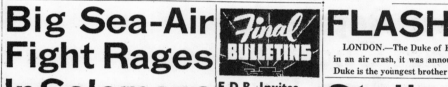

DUKE OF KENT DIES AS BRITISH PLANE CRASHES

FLASH--

LONDON.—The Duke of Kent has been killed in an air crash, it was announced today. The Duke is the youngest brother of the King.

Big Sea-Air Fight Rages In Solomons

(By Associated Press.)

WASHINGTON, Aug. 25. — The United States navy announced today that the Japanese have counter-attacked American forces holding the south-eastern Solomon Islands and that a great sea and air battle had developed in which the enemy had suffered more than half a dozen ships damaged.

The battle began developing on Sunday afternoon and already army and navy carrier-based planes have effectively bombed the following Japanese ships:

Two carriers,
One battleship,
One transport,
One cruiser,
An unspecified number of other cruisers which the navy described only as "several."

The transport and one cruiser were left burning fiercely after an aircraft attack on them north of Guadalcanal Island yesterday.

In addition 21 Japanese planes were shot down in a single engagement Sunday.

Hinging on the outcome of the Japanese counter-attack against hard-won American footholds in the first U. S. land offensive of the war was control of strategic points which cover supply lines to Australia and provide a spring-board for still further offensives against Japan's distended empire.

The main action of the battle, the navy communique indicated, is still in progress and the navy said that it was "a large-scale battle" between American sea and air forces and a strong Japanese striking force which has approached the southeastern group of the Solomon Islands from a northeast direction.

Army and navy units backing up the American marines in the Solomons had expected a violent attempt by the Japanese to recapture their lost bases in the Tulagi area, and so, the navy said, were apparently were fully prepared to meet it.

On this point the navy said succinctly, "this counter-attack has developed and is now being met."

As the navy related the developing battle action it said that preliminary reports "indicate that the enemy striking force has been attacked by United States army flying fortresses and that our carrier-based naval aircraft are in action.

A large Japanese carrier, the name of which was not given, was attacked by army bombers which reported scoring four hits.

Navy carrier-based aircraft

(Continued on Page 2.) See PACIFIC.

RHINELAND IS R.A.F. TARGET

LONDON, Aug. 25.—(AP)—An air raid warning, the first by daylight in exactly a month, sounded in London this afternoon, apparently caused by a lone scouting plane which approached the northern environs. Persons who were leaving work at the time ignored the alarm except for occasional skyward glances.

The all-clear signal sounded shortly after the first alarm. There were no reports immediately of any incidents.

(By Associated Press.)

LONDON, Aug. 25.—A "strong force" of R.A.F. bombers smashed at Frankfurt and Wiesbaden and other objectives in the upper Rhineland last night in the first R.A.F. night attack on Germany in a week, the air ministry said today.

The exact strength of the

(Continued on Page 2.) See R. A. F.

Dieppe Casualties Now Total 584

The eighth and ninth Canadian (Active) Army casualty lists since the battle of Dieppe were issued today, bringing the total unofficial count of casualties since the attack to 584.

Of the total 88 have been reported dead, 372 wounded, and 125 missing. The total number of men reported dead and missing since the start of the war stands at 978.

For the seventh and eighth lists see page 8. For the ninth list see page 18.

Final BULLETINS

F.D.R. Invites Dominion Heads To J.S. Parley

WASHINGTON, Aug. 25. — (AP)—President Roosevelt, coincident with the arrival in this country of Prime Minister Peter Fraser of New Zealand, announced today he also had invited the Prime Ministers of Australia and the Union of South Africa to come to the United States. He hoped they would be here later in the year.

Spy Gets Ten Years

HARTFORD, Conn., Aug. 25.—Rev. Kurt Molzahn, Philadelphia clergyman convicted of peacetime espionage, was sentenced to 10 years imprisonment today in Federal Court.

Plane, 14 Missing

WASHINGTON, Aug. 25. — (AP)—The United States Navy announced today that a large navy plane with 14 officers and enlisted men aboard was missing on a flight from Alaska to Seattle.

Nazis Raid Archangel

BERLIN (from German broadcasts), Aug. 25.—(AP)—The German high command said today that German bombers attacked "important war objectives at Archangel, Northern Russia, yesterday.

Nazis Kill Six

LONDON, Aug. 25. — (CP) — Belgian sources reported today six men had been executed by Germans in Belgium on charges of having killed a German soldier. They said four were French, one a Pole and one Belgian.

Identify Skeleton

A mystery which caused wide interest some five years ago was believed cleared up today with the identification of a skeleton found last week in the bush at Stanley Park as that of Terrence W. Lang, former Vancouver contractor. Lang, who was about 50, disappeared in September, 1937.

Sugar for Apples

OTTAWA, Aug. 25. — (CP) — To encourage greater consumption of the earlier varieties of apples, which are in surplus this year, S. R. Noble, sugar administrator of the Wartime Prices and Trade Board, announced today that "until further notice," domestic consumers may purchase by voucher extra sugar at the rate of one pound per eight pounds of such apples consumed in the household.

BASEBALL

AMERICAN LEAGUE.

First game—

		R.	H.	E.
Cleveland	..002 000 000 01—	3	4	2
Boston	.....000 020 000 02—	4	7	0

Ferrick and Denning, Hegan (9); Chase and Peacock.

Chicago	.......200 100 000—	3	12	2
New York	.....000 000 32x—	5	7	1

Humphries and Turner; Bruer,

Stalingrad Peril Grave; Twin Thrust

BERLIN (from German broadcasts), Aug. 25.—(AP)—German armored columns, driving toward Stalingrad from the southwest, have broken through a 12-kilometer (nearly eight miles) deep belt of bunker defenses, the German radio claimed tonight.

By EDDY GILMORE.
Associated Press Staff Writer.

MOSCOW, Aug. 25.—(AP)—More than 1,000,000 strong, the Nazi army in southern Russia tonight had driven to within less than 40 miles of Stalingrad and 170 miles from the Caspian Sea.

Stalingrad's peril appeared to be growing greater hour by hour as the invaders drove north-eastward from the region of Kotelnikovski, while huge tank forces which had crossed to the eastern bank of the Don River came from the northwest.

Dive-bombers swarmed through the skies and parachutists descended in both the Don and the Caucasus areas with anti-tank guns and motorcycles to menace further the Red army positions.

The German forces were estimated by the Russians as between 80 and 100 divisions, composed of from 9000 to 20,000 men each.

(The Soviet radio broadcast a new warning of "great danger" in the Caucasus last night, hinting that developments might jeopardize second-front chances. The Russian publicist, Yemelyan Yaroslavsky, speaking from Moscow, said the Germans were threatening to cut off the south from the rest of Russia.

("This would have grave consequences for the entire country and for all freedom-loving humanity," he said. "It would mean a new threat to Moscow and Leningrad. Hitler would also become more daring in the west, throwing released forces toward that front.")

A front-line despatch to Comsomol Pravda, paper of the young Communist organization, said the Germans had been able to concentrate large masses of men and machines across the Don.

It said the Nazis brought up

(Continued on Page 2.) See RUSSIA.

"The Japs Are Tough"

CANUCKSATHONGKONG LAUDED BY U.S. ENVOY

By JACK SULLIVAN.
Canadian Press Staff Writer.

JERSEY CITY, N.J., Aug. 25.—High praise for the bravery of Canadian troops who fought in the unsuccessful defense of Hongkong was given today by the chief United States diplomatic officer in Hongkong during the Japanese siege of the base.

Anderson E. Southard, United States consul-general in Hongkong, a passenger aboard the exchange ship Gripsholm which arrived here today with 1451 Canadians, Americans and others from Japan and Japanese-occupied areas in the Orient, said the fighting performance of the Canadians won the admiration of all.

(Continued on Page 2.) See HONGKONG.

LONDON, Aug. 25.—(CP) — Lieut. Sam F. Junkin of Natchez, Miss., is the first American fighter plane pilot to gain a victory over a German plane in combat operation, United States army headquarters in Britain announced today. The action occurred over Dieppe last week.

Moon Eclipse Tonight

TORONTO, Aug. 25.—(CP)—The second total eclipse of the moon this year will take place tonight and will be visible in most of the western hemisphere, observatory officials here said today.

The moon will go into the shade at 7 p.m., P.D.T., and the total eclipse will start at 8:01. Them oon will not leave the shadow completely until 10:35 p.m.

Post-Time SPECIALS By the LITTLE COLONEL

HASTINGS PARK. — Those horsemen who had their fingers crossed early this morning hoping for a sloppy track or even soft mud will have to wait a little longer before they get the racing strip they desire.

Little Saratoga absorbed the early rains without any trouble. The track, however, was starting to get muddy at the tail end of the downpour. It is expected that at post time, 4:45 tonight, it will be classified as good.

Happy Dianh off her best brilliant effort when she jogged to a decisive victory may show the way in the opening heat. **Sable Gift** may outrun her with the edge in weights but the post position, number one, favors **Dinah**. It is possible that **Ronrico** or **Si Green** may come barging through the stretch to pick up the pacemakers.

Ed Trusty appears to have the winner of the second with **Penicuik**, **Slalacum** and **Our Somers** appear the main threats but **Angus Macpherson** may uncover another sleeper with the **Midlothian's Dalmaboy**.

The sprint for two-year-olds is wide open. **Franklin D** gets the call on his consistent past performances. He has the speed to go with the pace. **Witherngower, Duddingston, Opus, Nitrogen** and **Lorelei D** rate close together.

Torey has a glorious chance to cop the fourth but the old mare, **Miss Goldstream** may surprise him. She has been showing excellent form and appears to have the speed to go on top.

Take your choice in the fifth. All contestants figure. **Contributor** and **George Corn**, as an entry, will probably rule the choice but they have a battle on their hands. **Patage** has been going at tops. **Steveston Bill** is fit. **Simtee** is ready for his best again. **Ascot Jane's** record is impressive and **Lace Broom** is getting better each time out..

A cheap field goes in the sixth. **Plucky Jake** may hold a slight edge. **Idamark** and **Miss Selfish** appear the chief contenders.

The seventh draws a limit field and the slow speed in the race gives the stretch runners a chance to get up. **Little Gloomy** should go out in front and may stay there. **Acero** and **Pandomint** should be right with him. **Dodd** may also elect to force the issue. The Little Colonel likes **Acero, Pandomint** and **Little Gloomy.**

THE PROVINCE HANDICAP

By JOHNNY PARK

For Today's Twilight Racing

4:45 P.M. — FIRST POST TIME — 4:45 P.M.

HASTINGS PARK FIFTH MEETING 5-FURLONG TRACK 3RD DAY

VANCOUVER, B.C., TUESDAY, AUGUST 25, 1942.

("X" Before Weight on the Horse Denotes 5-Pound Apprentice Allowance)
(In the flat races, the first eight go. In the hurdles, the first six go.)

First Race— Claiming. 3-year-olds and up. **6½ Furlongs**

Key	Horse	Weight	Comment	Post No.
(4385)	**HAPPY DINAH**	120	**Won galloping only out**	(1)
4393	**SABLE GIFT**	x103	**Just missed last time**	(3)
4386	**LEV'S DUST**	109	**Consistent, could take it**	(2)
4394	Si Green	114	Fresh, keen chance	(6)
4393	Mortgage Lifter	x109	May go better in mud	(5)
4406	Ronrico	121	Been going good	(6)
4385	Lovesick	x115	Will force pace	(7)
4286	Silumo	x104	In a tough spot	(8)

Second Race— Claiming. Maiden 3-year-olds and up foaled in West. Canada **7 Furlongs**

Key	Horse	Weight	Comment	Post No.
4339	**PENICUIK**	107	**Will be out in front**	(3)
4360	**OUR SOMERS**	107	**May upset them**	(2)
4403	**SLALACUM**	118	**This may be the spot**	(6)
—	Easter Park	118	Been waiting for spot	(5)
4402	Dalmahoy	112	Nothing to beat	(4)
4330	Territorial	x113	Never has shown much	(1)
[illegible]0	Hill Wind	118	Getting lots of chances	(7)

Third Race— Claiming 2-year-olds **5 Furlongs**

Key	Horse	Weight	Comment	Post No.
	FRANKLIN D	112	**One to catch and beat**	(4)
	WITHERNGOWER	[illegible]	**Just missed previous**	(2)
	DUDDINGSTON	[illegible]	**Clever B.C. juvenile**	(5)
	Opus	104	**Showed speed fast**	(6)
	Nitrogen	109	**May trim them all**	(7)
[illegible]1	Journeyman	107	Recent trials good	(3)
4368	Eltorada	104	Appears to need racing	(1)
—	Lorelei D	106	Reported to be fast	(8)

Fourth Race— Claiming. 3-year-olds and up. **7 Furlongs**

Key	Horse	Weight	Comment	Post No.
4387	**TOREY**	x113	**Appears to hold edge**	(3)
4365	**MISS GOLDSTREAM**	106	**In light, royal chance**	(4)
4402	**WEXFORD BOY**	111	**Ready for best effort**	(6)
4353	Belle Marcus	101	Yet to show any class	(105)
4403	Jelsweep	115	Figures with leaders	(7)
4389	Miss Montrose	106	Early foot, stops	(8)
4387	Rapid Mortgage	113	Lacked speed recently	(1)
—	Bell Rap	x108	Does better in slop	(2)

Fifth Race— Claiming. 3-year-olds and up. **Mile and 1-16**

Key	Horse	Weight	Comment	Post No.
4383	**LACE BROOM**	104	**Improves every start**	(4)
4406	**GEORGE CORN (a)**	109	**Flies through stretch**	(7)
4406	**PATAGE**	109	**The one to beat**	(5)
4376	Ascot Jane	107	As good as any	(3)
4406	Steveston Bill	109	At tops, wide open race	(1)
(4395)	Simtee	109	Galloped to cheaper	(2)
4405	Contributor (a)	112	Closes very fast	(6)

Sixth Race— Claiming. 3-year-olds and up. **7 Furlongs**

Key	Horse	Weight	Comment	Post No.
4236	**IDAMARK**	107	**Looms as one to beat**	(7)
4381	**PLUCKY JAKE**	111	**Figures in cheap field**	(2)
—	**TRIP OVER**	112	**First out, contender**	(5)
4331	Lora Somers	106	May be close to pace	(4)
4389	Pagan Royal	106	Rates excellent chance	(6)
4365	Miss Selfish	113	Has chance to get call	(3)
4331	Skylounge	105	Been resting too much	(1)
4338	Ann's Worry	107	She has real chance	(8)

Seventh Race— Claiming. 3-year-olds and up. **7 Furlongs**

Key	Horse	Weight	Comment	Post No.
4370	**LITTLE GLOOMY**	116	**Could lead throughout.**	(2)
4372	**ACERO**	116	**Always in the fight.**	(4)
4372	**DODD**	116	**As good as any.**	(6)
4385	Pandomint	x111	Recent efforts excellent.	(7)
4391	Avondale King	109	May get up in stretch.	(5)
4394	Britannia	109	May need easier spot.	(1)
4379	Novito	116	Could find easier bunch.	(3)
(4360)	Shasta King	103	At weights rates high	(8)

★★★ HAPPY DINAH

Tomorrow's Handicap on Page 12

Clocker Selections

FIRST RACE—Happy Dinah, Sable Gift, Si Green.
SECOND RACE—Penicuik, Slalacum, Our Somers.
THIRD RACE—Franklin D., Nitrogen, Duddingston.
FOURTH RACE — Torey, Miss Goldstream, Jelsweep.
FIFTH RACE—The Entry, Ascot Jane, Simtee.
SIXTH RACE—Idamark, Lora Somers, Plucky Jane.
SEVENTH RACE—Little Gloomy, Dodd, Acero.
BEST BET—Idamark.

Johnny Mann

FIRST RACE—Happy Dinah, Sable Gift, Ronrico.
SECOND RACE — Penicuik, Slalacum, Our Somers.
THIRD RACE—Franklin D., Duddingston, Witherngower.
FOURTH RACE—Miss Goldstream, Rapid Mortgage, Torey.
FIFTH RACE—Lace Broom, Patage, Steveston Bill.
SIXTH RACE—Trip Over, Idamark, Plucky Jake.
SEVENTH RACE—Pandomint, Little Gloomy, Acero.
BEST BET—Franklin D.

The Little Colonel

FIRST RACE—Happy Dinah, Sable Gift, Si Green.
SECOND RACE—Penicuik, Slalacum, Our Somers.
THIRD RACE — Witherngower, Franklin D., Duddingston.
FOURTH RACE — Miss Goldstream, Wexford Boy, Torey.
FIFTH RACE—Patage, Simtee, Ascot Jane.
SIXTH RACE—Idamark, Plucky Jake, Miss Selfish.
SEVENTH RACE — Avondale King, Acero, Little Gloomy.
BEST BET—Penicuik.

City Delegate Makes Attack On Mitchel

WINNIPEG, Aug. 25.—(CP)—John W. Bruce of Vancouver, general organizer of the United Association of Plumbers and Steamfitters, told the annual convention of the Trades and Labor Congress of Canada today that "if ever a minister of labor deserved open condemnation of this convention, that man is Humphrey Mitchell."

Mr. Bruce charged the federal labor minister had favored unions affiliated with the Congress of Industrial Organizations as against those affiliated with the American Federation of Labor.

The Vancouver delegate charged that an order-in-council stabilizing wages in shipyards and naval dockyards had raised wages of certain employees in shipyards and had reduced those paid in the naval dockyard. He said C.I.O. unions were organized in the shipyards and his own union in the naval dockyards.

The government's wages policies were "breaking down the morale of shipbuilders and cutting down production."

The convention passed a resolution requesting restoration of dockyard employees' wages to their former rates.

Britain Looks for Explosion

CHURCHILL TRIP BATTLE PRELUDE

(By Associated Press.)

LONDON, Aug. 25.—Prime Minister Churchill conferred with war cabinet members today on the results of his talks with Joseph Stalin and his visits to vital war bases in Egypt and Iran.

The feeling that spectacular developments soon may follow the Prime Minister's return grew among Britons with the disclosure he had visited Iran and Iraq, as well as Egypt, during his three-week flight.

These visits both brought quick, unforeseen consequences—establishment of a separate military command for the Iraq-Iran area and the assignment of Gen. Sir Harold Alexander to succeed Gen. Sir Claude Auchinleck as commander-in-chief in the Middle East.

Some Britons also saw signs of Allied determination for quick action to avert any possible disaster in Russia in the announcement that Mr. Churchill would confer with Field Marshal Sir John Dill, who represents Britain on the combined chiefs of staff group in Washington.

Sir John's return to England at this time appeared to British observers as more than coincidence.

Political sources foresaw no recall of Parliament from its summer recess for a statement by the Prime Minister, who, they said, is too occupied with essential conferences either to prepare a message to the Commons or a broadcast on his talks in the Kremlin.

(Continued on Page 2.) See CHURCHILL.

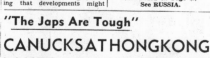

81

Passerboys Quit; Ship Rivetters Idle

CANADA WILL SHACKLE 1300 HUN PRISONERS

The Vancouver Sun

Only Evening Newspaper Owned, Controlled and Operated by Vancouver People

FOUNDED 1886 VOL. LVII—No. 8 | MArine 1161 | VANCOUVER, B.C., FRIDAY, OCTOBER 9, 1942 | Price 3 Cents On trains, boats and outside Greater Vancouver, 5c

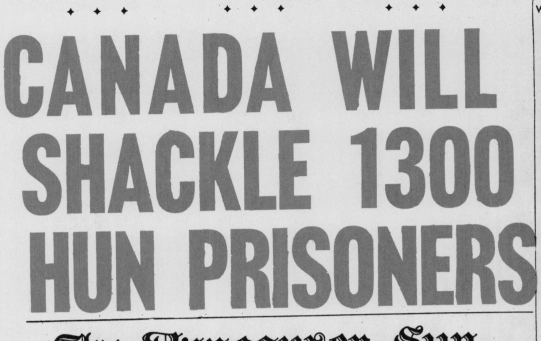

WAR BUT ARMY NURSES MUST HAVE 'BEAUTY PARLOR'

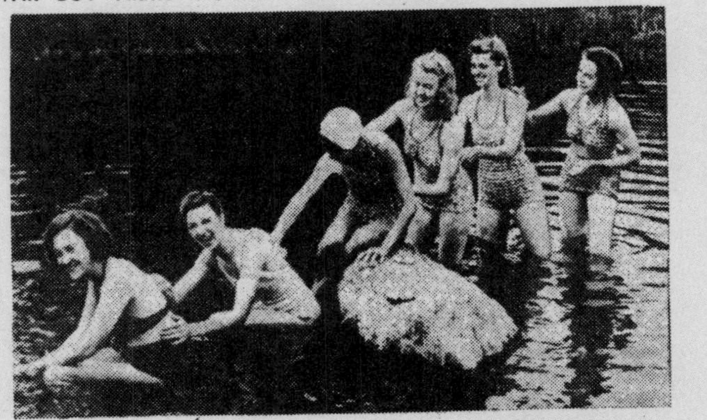

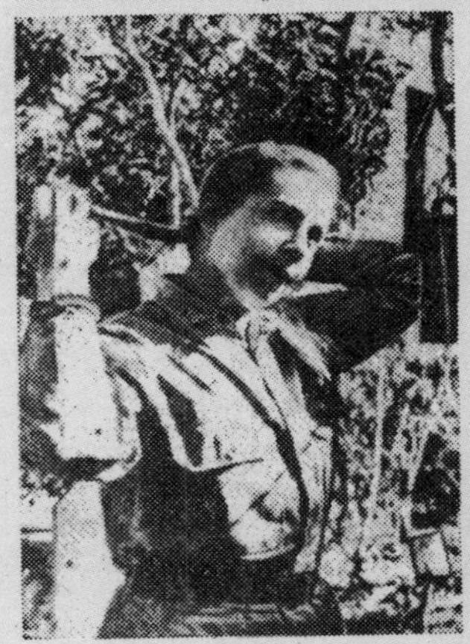

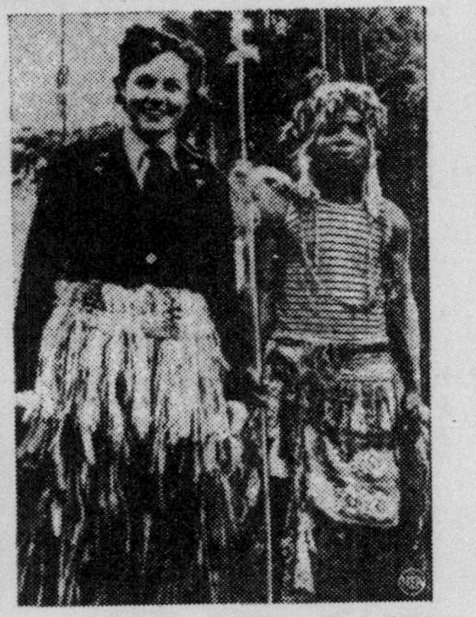

Even in war-straffed New Caledonia Army nurses (U.S.) find time to relax and primp. At top a group is cavorting in an ol' swimmin' hole down under. Lower left, Lieut. Beatrice Bacon makes the best of her bush-country boudoir. Right, Lieut. Wanda Engel poses wearing grass skirt at Kanaka feast. Note native's store smoke.

Ottawa Reprisals For Nazi Chaining Of Canadian Boys

Action Tomorrow If Germans Do Not Remove Fetters From Men Captured at Dieppe

TORONTO, Oct. 9.—The Daily Star says in a newspage story from Ottawa that "plans are being completed here today for the shackling early tomorrow afternoon" in Canada of 107 German officers and 1269 men, prisoners of war in Canada.

"This will be done if the Nazis fail to remove the fetters from Canadian and British prisoners captured in the Dieppe raid before 12 o'clock noon tomorrow," says The Star today.

OTTAWA, Oct. 9.—Senior officials of the External Affairs Department met this afternoon in the east block on Parliament Hill at a meeting which was believed to be in connection with plans for reprisals for German action in manacling Canadian and British prisoners taken at Dieppe.

It was anticipated an official statement outlining Canada's position in regard to reprisal action would be issued some time late today—probably soon after the afternoon External Affairs Department meeting ended.

PORTLAND, Ore., Oct. 9.—Police today sought to identify and capture a smooth-working bandit who held up a card room here late yesterday, escaping with $2380.

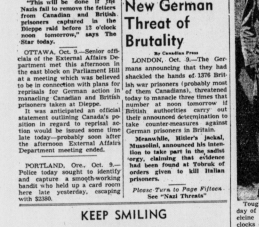

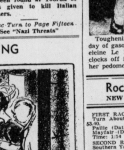

New German Threat of Brutality

By Canadian Press

LONDON, Oct. 9.—The Germans announcing that they had shackled the hands of 1376 British war prisoners (probably most of them Canadians), threatened today to manacle three times that number at noon tomorrow if British authorities carry out their announced determination to take counter-measures against German prisoners in Britain.

Meanwhile, Hitler's jackal, Mussolini, announced his intention to take part in the sadist orgy, claiming that evidence had been found at Tobruk of orders given to kill Italian prisoners.

Please Turn to Page Fifteen
See "Nazi Threats"

KEEP SMILING

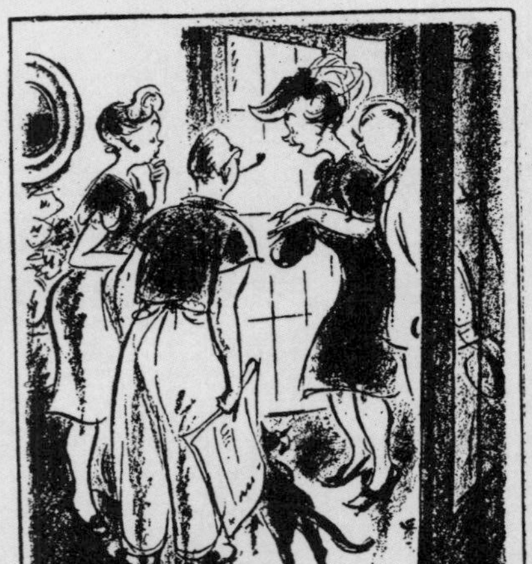

"I know we haven't called on you for ages, but we take a walk every evening instead of driving and George said, 'Let's drop in on the Joneses—my feet are killing me!'"

SOCK CLOCK

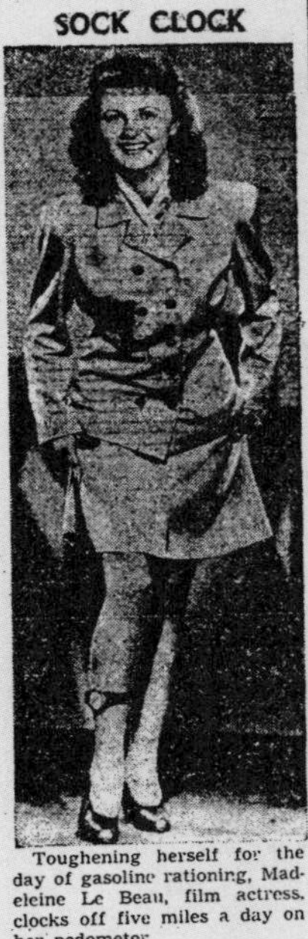

Toughening herself for the day of gasoline rationing, Madeleine Le Beau, film actress, clocks off five miles a day on her pedometer.

Rockingham
NEW HAMPSHIRE

FIRST RACE—Six furlongs:
Turn About (DeLara) $6.60, $3.20, $3.40.
Pallle (Dattilo) $7.40, $4.80.
Mayfair (Durando) $3.40.
Time: 1:14 2-5.

SECOND RACE—Six furlongs:
Southern Yam (Delara) $8.20, $4.40, $3.00.
Betty Leon (Finnegan) $4.40, $340.
Valdina Rip (Williams) $10.20.
Equal Chance (Stevenson) $3.80.
(Dead heat show.) Time: 1:15.

THIRD RACE—Six furlongs:
Equistone (Bates) $8.20, $4.20, $3.
Argos (Moore) $3.60, $2.80.
Circus Wing (Atkinson) $3.60.
Time, 1:13.

FOURTH RACE—Six furlongs:
Castle Ride (DeLara) $25, $14, $7.
Shasta Man (Bates) $5.80, $3.80.
Rosy Brand (Craig) $3.60.
Time, 1:13 2-5.

FIFTH RACE—Six furlongs:
Lost Gold (Turnbull) $21.60, $8.20, $5.40.
Zoic (Craig) $11.40, $5.80.
Sizzling Pan (Atkinson) $10.20.
Time, 1:13.

SIXTH RACE—Six furlongs:
Battery (Chaffin) $23, $7.80, $3.60.
Prairie Dog (Moore) $3.40, $2.20.
Balmy Spring (Delara) $2.60.
Time, 1:12 3-5.

SEVENTH RACE—Mile and one-sixteenth:
Rebbina (Chaffin) $12.80, $6.40, $3.40.
Uvalde (Dattilo) $4.20, $2.80.
Noodles (Brennan) $2.60.
Time 1:48 3-5.

EIGHTH RACE—Mile and one-sixteenth:
In Dutch (Brennan) $35.80, $11.40, $7.80.
Fairmond (Stevenson) $4.60, $4.
Cheetah (DeLara) $9.40.

Shipyard Boys Out On Strike

Absence of 110 Youths Ties Up 50 Crews

The passerboy strike was reported "settled" late this afternoon following a meeting between representatives of the boys, the firm, and the Provincial Department of Labor.

Rivet passerboys at West Coast Shipbuilders' yard today went on strike refusing to work on the 7:20 a.m. shift.

The move was termed "another quickie strike" by a representative of the firm this morning.

There has been growing discontent among the boys, who recently formed a union under the auspices of the Boilermakers' and Iron Shipbuilders' organization, for reclassification of the jobs and an increase in wages from 45 to 60 cents an hour.

Approximately 110 boys are affected, the company states, and an equal number of rivetters are unable to continue work at the same time. About 50 rivetting gangs were tied up this morning.

The Boilermakers' Union declined comment this morning on the move.

It is expected that the passers may return to work tomorrow, or at the evening shift tonight.

Army Call For 24,000 More Men

19-Year-Olds Liable in Next Month's Draft

OTTAWA, Oct. 9.—Within the next month the Department of National War Services will try to call up 24,505 men for service in the army, it was learned at the department today.

This total includes the 22nd requisition for 18,000 men who will be ordered to report between October 19 and November 13, and a supplemental requistion to the 19th requisition of July, under which 6505 men will be sought between October 12 and October 23.

The original July requiistion was for 15,000 men and the fact that a supplementary requisition now is required indicates that the calls issued in that month did not produce the number of men required.

Under the recent extension of the callable age group, 19-year-old single men and aliens of non-enemy nationality will be liable to calls to meet the two new requisitions.

Anscomb Home

VICTORIA, Oct. 9.—Mines Minister Anscomb returned to his office today after a brief business visit to Winnipeg.

Education Minister Perry has returned from Port Alberni.

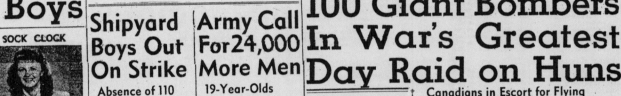

LATE NEWS BULLETINS

New Name for Reserve Army

CALGARY, Oct. 9.—Consideration is being given to changing the name of Canada's Reserve Army to one more fitting the important part it is playing in the defence of Canada, Col. E. R. Knight, officer commanding the 41st Reserve Brigade in M.D. 13, said.

Dieppe Soldiers' Pay Cut 'Outrage'

TORONTO, Oct. 9.—Controller Fred Hamilton today quoted Prime Minister Mackenzie King as saying "it is an outrage that the assigned pay of soldiers was cut off when the men were reported missing at Dieppe."

"Mr. King said he was not aware that such things were going on and promised a full investigation."

STOCKHOLM, Sweden, Oct. 9.—Germany, apparently dissatisfied with Danish apathy toward the Nazi cause, was reported today to have asked King Christian's government to recruit at least 30,000 "volunteers" for service on the eastern front.

100 Giant Bombers In War's Greatest Day Raid on Huns

Canadians in Escort for Flying Fortresses in Big Attack on Industrial Area of Lille

By Canadian Press

LONDON, Oct. 9.—More than 100 United States four-motored bombers — Flying Fortresses and Liberators — bombed the Lille industrial region of northern France today.

Four of the United States bombers were lost but the crew of one was safe in the biggest American bomber and fighter force ever to take the air in the European theatre, United States Army Headquarters announced. Canadian fighter planes formed a part of the 500-Spitfire escort.

The great bombers' fighter protectors, some of whom were Canadians, shot down five of many enemy fighter planes which rose to challenge this extraordinarily heavy daylight assault. The bombers themselves "had many successful combats but the number of enemy fighter destroyed by them is not yet known."

United States Army Air Force Headquarters, promising a more detailed announcement later, issued this terse communique:

"More than 100 U.S. bombers attacked targets in the Lille area this morning.

"Many squadrons of fighters took part in this operation."

A big part of the bombing force, an extraordinary number for a daylight raid, was made up of four-motored Flying Fortresses.

Many squadrons of RAF and other Allied fighters joined in the action.

The Fortress bombers and escorting fighters—many of which were Spitfires and Hurricanes flown by United States pilots—

Please Turn to Page Fifteen
See "Mass Raid"

Hart Summons Auto Delegation

Premier John Hart has signified his intention of granting an interview to a delegation asking lower license fees for automobiles driven in British Columbia.

Frank Bird, secretary of the B.C. Automobile Club, today received a telegram from the premier, stating he would meet the delegation in his office at Victoria Tuesday at 10:30 a.m.

Delegates from all organizations which endorsed the campaign for lower license fees are asked to go to Victoria on the midnight boat Monday.

British Cruiser Coventry Sunk

LONDON, Oct. 9. — The Admiralty reported tonight that the cruiser Coventry, 4290 tons, has been sunk.

The Coventry was an anti-aircraft cruiser. Its complement was 400 men.

Thanksgiving Holiday

There will be no issue of The Vancouver Sun on Monday, October 12.

Advertising copy for Tuesday's issue, October 13, should be received by 9 p.m. Saturday, October 10.

Telephone MArine 1161.

Race Entries at Bay Meadows
CALIFORNIA

FIRST RACE—Six furlongs:
What Fun (Martin) $3.60, $2.60, $2.40.
Justice Court (Woodhouse) $4.40, $3.30.
Narbada (Hanauer) $8.80.
Time 1:12 3-5.

SECOND RACE—Six furlongs:
My Porter (Chojnacki) $6.80, $4, $2.90.
Lucky Pilot (Martin) $3.60, $2.90.
Friarhaired (Dodson) $4.50.
Time 1:12 1-5.

THIRD RACE—Mile and one-sixteenth:
Keep Punchin (L. Jones) $36.10, $13.30, $5.40.
Iron Hills (Neves) $4.80, $3.30.
Soldiers Call (Koyk) $3.
Time, 1:48.

Wood, Fabric Plane Used by Russians

MOSCOW, Oct. 9.—Russian fliers are using a low-speed light bomber made of wood and fabric for accurate night attacks upon Axis positions around Stalingrad, the army newspaper Red Star said today.

Race Entries, Page 9

Big Canadian Troop Convoy Lands Safely

By DOUGLAS AMARON
Canadian Press Staff Writer

A BRITISH PORT, Oct. 9. — Thousands of Canadian soldiers from a score of formations across Canada have arrived in Britain to join the armored division commanded by Maj.-Gen. F. F. Worthington.

There were ordnance, artillery, engineer, army service and medical corps men aboard the ships.

All anxious to have their names taken down so their families would know they had arrived safely.

Easterners were in the majority of this contingent.

Maj. John Proctor of Edmonton was brigade major of one brigade, while another officer of headquarters staff was Maj. H. E. N. Hacking of Vancouver.

Sappers included P. R. Porteous of Vancouver.

RCAF reinforcements included men for ground and air crews, among them was LAC Bob Rose, Vancouver, radio technician.

The cheerful bronzed Canadians sounded their own welcome as the big troopships which carried them across the Atlantic without incident moved slowly to berths.

Most of the arrivals were beretted troopers of the armored divisions, but there were reinforcements for other formations as well, and hundreds of Canadian, British, Australian and New Zealand airmen.

The convoy also brought Canadian nursing sisters, firefighters and a draft of the Royal Canadian Navy.

Japs Land New Troops in Solomons

BRITISH SCORE 'CLEAN BREAK THROUGH' IN EGYPT

All 'Horrible Lie' Says Errol Flynn

The Vancouver Sun

Only Evening Newspaper Owned, Controlled and Operated by Vancouver People

FINAL

FOUNDED 1886
VOL. LVII—No. 28

VANCOUVER, B.C., TUESDAY, NOVEMBER 3, 1942

Price 3 Cents On trains, boats and outside Greater Vancouver, 5c

BLONDE ACCUSER

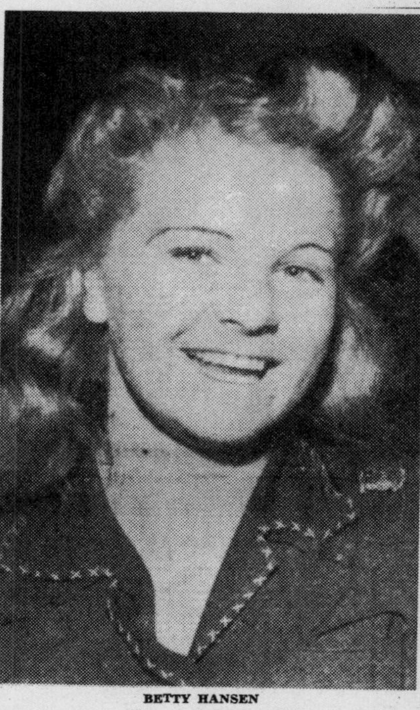

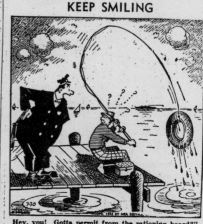

BETTY HANSEN
Sipped a green-colored cocktail

Elections Delay Film Star's Trial

By FREDERICK OTHMAN
Special to The Vancouver Sun
Copyright, 1942, by British United Press

HOLLYWOOD, Nov. 3.—Errol Flynn received a one-day respite for movie heroics today between charges by a pair of 17-year-old beauties that he had intimate relations with them.

Yesterday Flynn listened to blonde Betty Hansen tell of his removing her clothes, all but her shoes, in a Bel Air boudoir. Today he makes movie love to Ann Sheridan. Tomorrow he returns to court to hear Peggy Satterlee, a dark-eyed youngster with her black hair in pigtails and blue ribbons, tell of being intimate twice with him, once on the way to Catalina Island aboard his yacht, and once on the way back.

Flynn's preliminary hearing, at which most of the testimony to date has had to be expurgated from print, was interrupted for a day to give all participants, except the accusers, who were too young, an opportunity to vote. The first session ended with Flynn's lawyer, Jerry Geisler, getting into the record his client's initial reaction to Miss Hansen's story:

"It's all a horrible lie," Flynn

Please Turn to Page Twelve
See "Flynn"

Sailor Hanged As Traitor

Betrayed British Ships to Nazi Agents

By Canadian Press

LONDON Nov. 3 — Duncan Alexander Croall Scott-Ford, a British subject, was executed today in Wandsworth prison for treachery, the Home Office announced.

Scott-Ford was a 21-year-old British merchant seaman who made regular trips between Britain and Lisbon, Portugal.

In Lisbon, the announcement said, he was approached by a German agent and, for payment of $72, supplied secret information concerning the merchant fleet, movements of convoys between Lisbon and Britain, weather conditions and aircraft protection. He also promised additional data, the Home Office said.

"When Scott-Ford returned on a second visit to Lisbon with the information he had collected the Germans threatened they would expose him to British authorities unless he continued to perform further services, to collect more valuable information and to undergo greater risks in their interest," the announcement said.

After his arrest, Scott-Ford admitted associating with German spies and making notes at the request of the German agents, the Home Office said.

He also admitted that he toured public houses, mixing with fellow seamen and members of the services in order to pump them for information in their possession," it was said.

Whirlaway Beaten In Mud by Riverland

BALTIMORE, Nov. 3.—Louisiana Stable's Riverland today pulled his second smashing upset in four days' time when he defeated Calumet Farm's mighty Whirlaway in the 17th running of the $10,000 added Riggs handicap at Pimlico.

'Much Hard Fighting Ahead'-Knox

U.S. War Secretary Warns of Over Optimism Regarding Pacific Situation

WASHINGTON, Nov. 3. — U.S. land forces, aided by dive-bomber and destroyer bombardment of Japanese positions, are continuing their offensive west of Guadalcanal Airport, the Navy announced today.

But the enemy has succeeded in landing reinforcements on the east flank of the American forces.

In a communique bringing action up to Monday night (island time) the Navy disclosed that U.S. destroyers had taken advantage of the recent withdrawal of Japanese naval craft to move inshore and shell enemy positions west of the Matanikau River.

American marines previously had driven across the river, as announced yesterday, and had pushed the Japanese back two miles in one sector.

Announcement of continued ground action followed press conference disclosures by Secretary of Navy Frank Knox that two additional Japanese cruisers and a destroyer have been sunk in naval action the night of Oct. 11-12.

Dive-bombers carried the fight to Japanese land forces on Guadalcanal on the night of Sunday-Monday (island time), the communique said, and U.S. destroyers entered the battle, Monday morning.

The number of enemy troops put ashore was not disclosed.

It was believed the landing was probably in the nature of a diversion. Neither side, it appeared, had a very strong hold on the area involved before the enemy forces moved in.

Secretary Knox had warned earlier that the enemy was still powerful in the Solomons and that "desperately hard fighting" lies ahead.

"There is no warrant for optimism," the Secretary said, adding that "some of the headlines this morning were more optimistic than the situation justified."

Race Results at Empire City

NEW YORK

FIRST RACE—About six furlongs:
Iceland (Thompson) $31.80, $15.50, $8.90.
War Master (Gorman) $19.80, $10.60.
Roseate Dreams (Mehrtens) $4.40.
Scratches: Dr. Johnson, Chief Mate, Mister Billy, Fly Whisk, Spring Tornado, Mugs Game.

SECOND RACE—About six furlongs:
Wise Maiden (Schmidl) $6.20, $4.60, $3.30.
Valdina Joe (Westrope) $8.50, $6.50.
Count Haste (Nodarse) $5.80.
Scratches: Bowling Green, Lady Golden, Late Dawn, Roncat, Javert, W. H. Kelly.

THIRD RACE—Mile and seventy yards:
Mon Flag (Torres) $16.60, $8.70, $4.80.
Reapers Blade (Westrope) $6.80, $4.10.
Rice Cake (Nodarse) $3.90.
Scratched: Grand Adventure.

FOURTH RACE—About six furlongs:
Doublerab (Thompson) $7.20, $4.40, $3.10.
Cassis (Mehrtens) $8.10, $4.10.
Parasang (Stout) $3.
No scratches.

FIFTH RACE—Mile and seventy yards:
Blue Sword (Longden) $3.80, $3.10, $2.50.
Chop Chop (Thompson) $4.60, $3.10.
Bossuet (Stout) $3.70.
No scratches.

Jury Told Gov't Not On Trial

Verdict Awaited in B.C. Police Supply Case

By Sun Staff Correspondent

VICTORIA, Nov. 3. — Mr. Justice Sidney Smith deplored that "so much insinuation has besmirched so many" when he charged the jury today at close of the Assize Court trial of Leonard J. Simmons, former Provincial Police quartermaster, and Joseph A. Walsh, shoe merchant, charged with conspiracy to defraud the government.

"You will appreciate," Mr. Justice Smith told the jury, "that you are not here to hold an inquiry into any government department, police or otherwise. You are only concerned with the two accused charged with these affairs.

The judge said that he liked to think that governments, federal, provincial and municipal, were composed of as good a body of men and women as could be found anywhere.

"We have heard a lot of criticism in this court about public servants. These people

Please Turn to Page Twelve
See "B. C. Police"

Race Results at Rockingham

NEW HAMPSHIRE

FIRST RACE—Six furlongs:
Neddie Jean (Gross) $10.40, $6.20, $4.60.
Burnt Bridges (Bates) $10.80, $8.20.
Tally Ho (Finnegan) $3.40.
Scratches: Buckets, Still Gallent.

SECOND RACE—Six furlongs:
Centuple (Gross) $10.60, $5.80, $4.60.
Jungle Moon (Chaffin) $4, $3.40.
Within (Craig) $5.
Scratches: Catapult, Carnarvon, Jellwell, Bonified, Unimond.

THIRD RACE—Five and one-half furlongs:
Cabanisi (Robart) $21.60, $9.60, $4.20.
Betty Leon (Finnegan) $4.80, $2.80.
Belle Feathers (Moore) $3.
Scratches: Miss Cold, Silver Vane, Love Veuture, Crackers.

FOURTH RACE—Six furlongs:
Wise Decision (Datillo) $7.60, $4, $3.
Old Whitey (Turnbull) $6, $3.80.
Trimmed (Daniels) $5.20.
Scratches: Wise Fox, Canterup, Not Yet, Red Meadow, Belmar Arra, On Location.

FIFTH RACE—Six furlongs:
Water Cracker (Stevenson) $7, $4, $3.20.
La Scala (Datillo) $4.60, $3.20.
Flaming High (McMullen) $4.70.
Scratches: Argos, Bellermine.

SIXTH RACE—Mile and one-sixteenth:
Texalite (Datillo) $6.20, $3.60, $2.60.
Searchlight (Stevenson) $4.40, $2.80.
Poppycock (Chaffin) $3.
No scratches.

SEVENTH RACE—Mile and one-eighth:
Display Style (Daniels) $4.40, $2.80, $2.20.
Veris (Finnegan) $4, $2.20.
Mintack (Wood) $2.20.
Scratched: Gallant Dick.

EIGHTH RACE—Mile and one-sixteenth:
Ranchos Boy (Maschek) $4.20, $3.00, $2.20.
Catomar (Stevenson) $4.20, $2.60.
Noodles (Wood) $2.20.
Scratches: Glyndontown.

Rommel's Defenses Smashed

Tanks Pour Through and Battle on Large Scale Is Developing Near El Alamein

By FRANK L. MARTIN
Associated Press Staff Writer

WITH THE BRITISH EIGHTH ARMY ON THE EL ALAMEIN FRONT, Nov. 3. — Using several of his most powerful armored units and infantry troops last night in an all-night attack, Lt.-Gen. Bernard L. Montgomery's forces made a clean break-through in the enemy's defenses.

The new breach was made in the neighborhood of the previous gap cut through the northern end of the El Alamein line by infantry and artillery

Then at the first light of day the allied tanks moved north to engage the 21st German Armored Division which was approaching from the north.

At the same time British armored cars poured through the gap and turned south where they began chopping up enemy infantry detachments and in fact anything of the enemy's that came in sight.

The 8th Army's armored attack began as darkness fell yesterday over a 4000 yard front and by morning it had slashed through to a point WHERE THERE WERE NO FIXED ENEMY DEFENSES AHEAD.

(Reuters recorded a German radio broadcast today saying that the British have "thrown in some 500 tanks in the greatest tank battle of the whole African campaign.")

Marshal Erwin Rommel, attempting to prevent the Australians from flanking his coastal positions and thus paving the way for a large-scale breakthrough which might unhinge his entire North African campaign, attacked British positions Sunday night, the communique said.

His Africa Korps was thrown back by Lt.-Gen. B. L. Montgomery's Eighth Army Imperials.

"Yesterday," the communique said, "an armored battle of considerable scale developed. Heavy fighting continues."

Please Turn to Page Twelve
See "Egypt"

Garage Bandits Lock Youth in Auto Trunk

Two armed bandits entered the office of the Georgia Garage and U-Drive, 678 Howe, shortly after 9 p.m., Monday, held up Jack Merryfield, 20, UBC student, locked him in the rear compartment of a coupe and escaped with $29 in a stolen U-Drive auto.

Young Merryfield, relieving night attendant at the garage, was a helpless prisoner in the cramped compartment for between 30 and 45 minutes. George Mendels, 1385 West Eleventh, proprietor, heard his cries and released him.

One of the bandits looked into the office, went out, and returned immediately with his partner, the holdup victim told police. Each wore a white handkerchief around the lower part of his face.

The men ordered him to sit down, than told him to lie down on the office floor. They threatened to shoot if he did not tell them "where the money was."

Merryfield told them where the operating cash, $29, was.

After taking the money, the bandits ordered Merryfield to get into the coupe's rear compartment and locked him in with a warning to "keep quiet for 10 minutes."

The men escaped in one of the company's U-Drive cars, and Merryfield started to shout for assistance as soon as they drove away.

Mendels heard him when he returned to the office half an hour later.

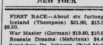

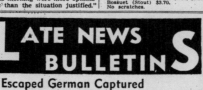

LATE NEWS BULLETINS

Escaped German Captured

RUIDOSO, N.M., Nov. 3.—Four German seamen, escaped prisoners from a federal detention camp at Fort Santon, were trapped today by armed possemen in Gabalon canyon.

RAF Raiding Germany Today

LONDON, Nov. 3.—Britain's four-motored Stirling bombers attacked industrial points in Western Germany by daylight today. Other bombers raided communications in the Low Countries.

KEEP SMILING

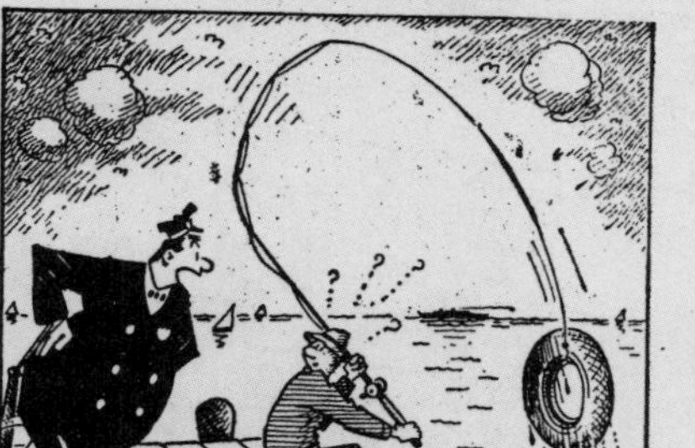

Hey, you! Gotta permit from the rationing board?"

B.C. Quota Now $100 Million—Buy Victory Bonds

REDS OPEN GREAT NEW OFFENSIVE

—Story Page 2

VANCOUVER NEWS-HERALD **FINAL**

VOL. 10, NO. 210 VANCOUVER, B.C., FRIDAY, DECEMBER 25, 1942 TELEPHONE PAcific 2272 PRICE 3c

DARLAN ASSASSINATED

Vichy Leader Who Joined Allies Shot To Death In Govt. Palace; 'Murder In First Degree'--F.D.R.

WASHINGTON, Dec. 25.—(AP)—President Roosevelt Thursday night denounced the assassination of Admiral Jean Darlan as "murder in the first degree."

The text of his statement:

"The cowardly assassination of Admiral Darlan is murder in the first degree.

"All leaders of all the United Nations will agree with that statement.

"Nazism and Fascism and military despotism hold otherwise. I hope that speedy justice will overtake the murderer or murderers of Admiral Darlan.

GIRAUD MAY SUCCEED DARLAN

LONDON, Dec. 25. —(AP)—The assassination of Admiral Darlan may have settled in one stroke the most difficult diplomatic problem which has confronted the Allies since the beginning of the war.

The death of the former collaborationist wrote a bloody new chapter in unfortunate France's participation in the present war.

Elimination of Darlan from the North African political scene came at a moment when Allied leaders in London and Algiers were reliably reported exerting all efforts to obtain unity of all French forces.

It was considered possible in London that Gen. Henri Honore Giraud, who has been serving as military commander under Darlan and who, because of his record of opposition to the Germans is also acceptable to the Fighting French, might become a potential candidate for Darlan's position as high commissioner of North Africa.

On the other hand, the death of Darlan might create a touchy situation for Lieut. Gen. Dwight D. Eisenhower in North Africa, inasmuch as the admiral was believed to be highly popular with French authorities there who might not so readily accept another appointee as high commissioner.

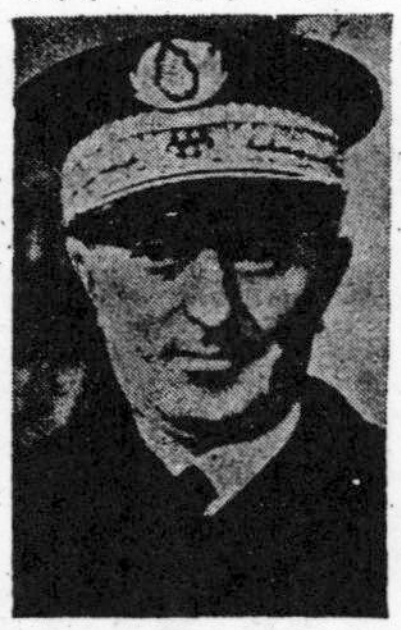

ADMIRAL DARLAN

ALGIERS, Dec. 25.—(AP)—Admiral Jean Darlan, head of French North Africa who has been co-operating with the Allies since the Americans landed in November, was assassinated Thursday afternoon in the French Government palace.

The killer has been captured but his identity had not been learned by this morning.

• • •

(The CBS correspondent in Algiers broadcast that the slayer was a young Frenchman. Other sources speculated on whether the murderer might have been acting for the German or Italian governments or, again, was a Frenchman bitter over the choice of Darlan to head the civilian administration in French Africa.)

Darlan was about to enter his office at 4:30 p.m. when the assassin fired five shots, two of which hit the admiral.

An official announcement by the French government said Darlan died en route to the hospital.

Darlan only Thursday issued a statement to the French press in North Africa appealing for the "union—at once" of all Frenchmen fighting against the Axis and declared it did not matter whether they rallied behind him or someone else.

Long noted for his antipathy and enmity to Britain, Darlan was known in the days of the Vichy government before the Allies moved into North Africa as an arch-collaborationist with Germany as vice-premier of the Vichy government.

He quickly turned to the Allies, however, when he was found by the Americans in Algiers as they took that city and it was his cease-fire order which ended French resistance in the vast Moroccan and Algerian territories.

Darlan's agreement with United States Lt.-Gen. Dwight D. Eisenhower for French-Allied co-operation in French Africa was severely criticized in both Britain and the United States, even provoking debate in the House of Commons.

The British government expressed its agreement with Mr. Roosevelt's statement in reply to critics of the Darlan move.

Santa Takes a Rest
It's All Over Now

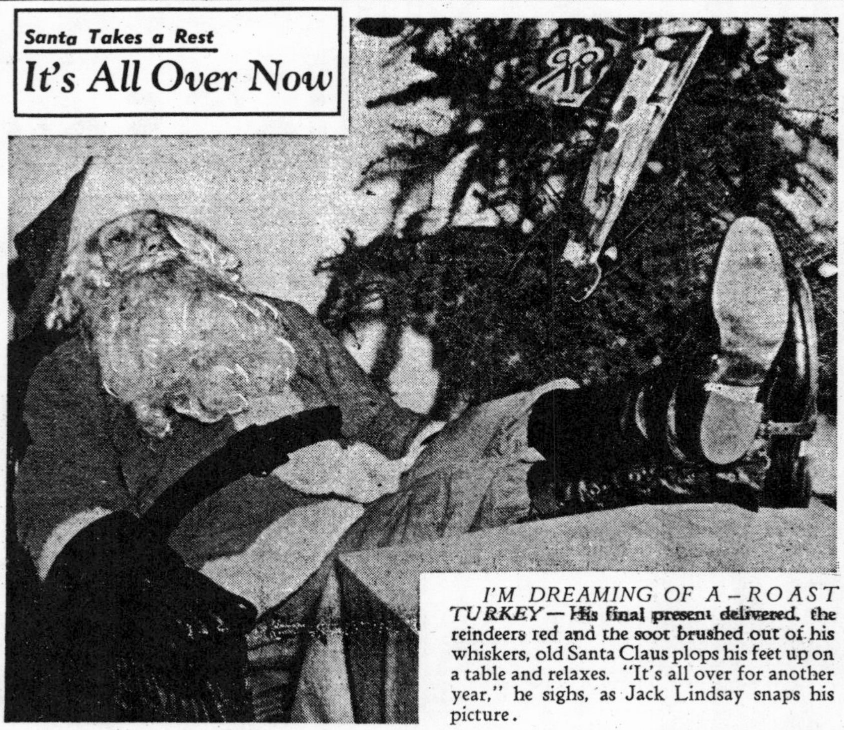

I'M DREAMING OF A—ROAST TURKEY—His final present delivered, the reindeers red and the soot brushed out of his whiskers, old Santa Claus plops his feet up on a table and relaxes. "It's all over for another year," he sighs, as Jack Lindsay snaps his picture.

Allies Take Tunisia Hill From Axis

LONDON, Dec. 25—(CP)—A Fighting French communique broadcast today by the Brazzaville radio said French forces coming up from the Lake Chad region had routed an Axis motorized detachment in the region of Fezzan.

The Fezzan territory is in the middle of the north-central African desert, generally in the vicinity of the corner of Libya, Algeria, and French West Africa.

LONDON, Dec. 25.—(CP)—Allied soldiers fighting in the rain and mud of central Tunisia have thrown the enemy out of a height dominating the important junction point on Medjez-El-Bab, 35 miles southwest of Tunis, Allied Headquarters reported from North Africa Thursday night as the British 8th Army doggedly pursued Field Marshal Rommel westward across Libya.

An Allied Command communique announced the capture of the heights and added that Allied troops held it against counter-attacks by the enemy.

Dispatches from Allied Headquarters in North Africa pointed out that this was the first significant offensive action reported on the central Tunisian battlefront in two weeks.

The Allied Command also said there was patrol activity on the northern sector of the Tunisian front while on the southern sector, west of Kairouan, "French troops repelled enemy attacks."

SMALLPOX HITS U.S. FARM AREA

LEWISTON, Pa., Dec. 25.—(AP)—Medical experts of the State Health Department went on 24-hour duty in the quarantined Kishacoquillas Valley farming section to battle a spreading smallpox outbreak among Amish farm folks.

Heard Plane In Yale Area

Searchers today will check a report received by Canadian Pacific Air Lines officials that two railwaymen at Spuzzum, B.C., had heard a plane which they believed to be the missing transport, between 7:30 and 8 p.m. Sunday. The plane, they reported, was heading southwest, when they heard it. Spuzzum is on the main line of the C.P.R., 17 miles east of Yale, and within the area now being searched.

Their day shortened by a return of bad weather, flyers seeking the missing city airliner and its 13 occupants returned to their bases early Thursday evening with nothing new to report.

• • •

The big airliner has been missing since Sunday evening, when it was only 15 minutes' flying time from Vancouver, en route from Prince George.

• • •

On Thursday, searchers, directed by H. Hollick-Kenyon, supervisor of operations, western lines, Canadian Pacific Air Lines, and Sergt. W. J. Thomson of the Provincial Police, extended the search farther south into the state of Washington.

• • •

Reports from Lynden, Wash., of a sudden, bright fire on a mountain in that vicinity Wednesday night were thoroughly checked, both by ground parties and two aircraft. Nothing was found of the missing ship, however.

NORWICH, England. — (CP)—Rev. Ernest Hardy, Methodist, and Rev. Stanley Baker, Baptist, "factory padres," visit war factories and chat with workers; they sing a hymn duet. Their visits are "booked" far ahead.

Two Killed In Bus Mishap

BALTIMORE, Dec. 25.— (AP)—A special bus carrying between 40 and 60 Glenn L. Martin Company aircraft workers plunged into a 20-foot ravine Thursday night and at least two persons were reported dead and 27 injured. The accident occurred after the vehicle apparently skidded along a narrow, lonely road.

Police Captain William J Forrest said some still were believed trapped in the wooden wreckage lying in the shallow waters of Hering Run. He said the exact number of dead and injured was unknown. The bus was enroute to the aircraft plant.

Ambulances rushed the injured to nearby hospitals.

Houses in the section, including the Children's Home of Baltimore, were darkened as the bus cut down a power line on its careening path.

U.S. REVEALS SECRET MOBILE WEAPON MADE

DETROIT, Dec. 25. —(AP)—Production of a secret mobile weapon was disclosed with United States Army approval Thursday by the Cadillac division of General Motors corporation.

Cadillac engineers and production men have been working with Ordnance Department's Tank-Automotive Centre to design and perfect the weapon.

Nicholas Dreystadt, president of Cadillac, delivered the first production model today to Brig-Gen. A. R. Glancy, Assistant Chief of Ordnance in charge of the Tank-Automotive Centre, and Brig.-Gen. John Christmas, Assistant Chief of the Centre.

Mrs. Roosevelt To Visit Canada

MONTREAL, Dec. 25.—(CP)—The French-language daily newspaper La Patrie said Thursday that Mrs. F. D. Roosevelt, wife of the President of the United States, will come to Montreal January 19 to address an "Aid-to-Russia" meeting at the Montreal Forum.

The newspaper added that Prime Minister Mackenzie King and Premier Adelard Godbout of Quebec would be among the speakers.

NELSON LOOKS FOR GREATEST U.S. PRODUCTION

WASHINGTON, Dec. 25.—(AP)— Chairman Donald M. Nelson of the War Production Board looked ahead to 1943 Thursday for "the greatest co-ordinated production this country has ever seen or envisioned—greater by far than anyone a year ago thought possible."

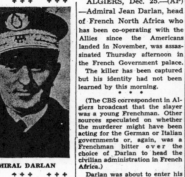

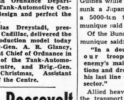

Japs Lose Main Buna Position; Allies Sink Warship, Transport

ALLIED HEADQUARTERS, New Guinea. Dec. 25.—(CP)—Allied troops have overrun the Japanese main defensive positions. in the Buna area of New Guinea while the aerial arm has sunk a Japanese destroyer and a 5000-ton transport, a communique said today.

Of the Buna fighting the communique said:

"In a double envelopment our troops overran the enemy's main defensive positions and drove him back into his last line of defence in this sector."

Allied heavy bombers blasted the transport from the ocean's surface near Gasmata, New Britain, despite the efforts of 15 Zero planes which rose to its protection. Medium bombers scored the knockout on the destroyer off the New Guinea coast near Salamaua.

Allied planes suffered no losses in this action.

The final positions to which the Japanese now have been driven in the Buna area, the communique said, centres on Giropa Point and extends approximately a mile along the coast and is between 500 and 600 yards deep.

• • •

"It is a prepared and fortified citadel of resistance," the communique said, adding:

"We now control practically all of the Buna main airdrome."

U.S. LAUNCHES TWO SUBMARINES IN RECORD TIME

PORTSMOUTH, N.H., Dec. 25.—(AP)—Two submarines, whose construction time broke records, were launched Thursday at the Portsmouth Navy Yard. They were the U.S.S. Cisco, which was on the ways a few hours more than 56 days, and the U.S. Cabrilla. Both craft broke a record of 101 days set last summer on the U.S.S. Steelhead, but the figure for the Cabrilla was not announced.

Accidents Fill Hospital Ward

Emergency Ward of Vancouver General Hospital was called upon to attend a record number of accident cases Thursday night as automobile accidents, fights and strong-arm robberies sent dozens of persons there for attention. None was considered serious.

• • •

Two pedestrians were injured as a result of being struck down by traffice at Thirty-third Ave. and Granville Street. They were Miss Cecilia Walker, 65 Woodstock Avenue, who was struck by a car and Gordon Curtis, 9031 Hudson, who was hit by an army truck. Extent of injuries was not known at press time, but neither case was considered serious.

• • •

William Grant, Hazel Hotel, East Hastings Street, suffered severe head injuries as a result of an attack in which he was robbed by two "strong-arm" men, police said.

• • •

James Finn, visitor from Prince Rupert, suffered undetermined injuries when involved in a fight.

Every bed in the emergency ward was filled with accident victims early in the evening

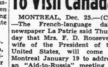

The News-Herald Extends The Season's Greetings To All Its Readers

1943

The Axis forces suffered military reverses right around the globe during 1943, although sometimes at a terrible cost to the Allies. Americans were "island hopping" in the Pacific in a series of pitched batteries over tiny plots of ground. The Red Army went permanently on the offensive and began rolling back the Nazi juggernaut from its soil. The Allies' most definitive success was in Italy, where King Victor Emmanuel fired Mussolini and then unconditionally surrendered after losing Sicily to Allied forces. Yet, the invasion of Italy was still a struggle, as the Germans had effectively seized control of the country and were willing and able to fight for every inch of it.

MAJOR EVENTS

January-December 1943

THE RED ARMY GOES ON THE OFFENSIVE

Although defeated at Stalingrad, in January 1943 Germany retained a vast amount of western Russia. The Red Army, now on the offensive, had to win back every hard-fought zone in brutal air-to-air, hand-to-hand, tank-to-tank combat. There was no other way, and the Russians were prepared.

The Russian factories were turning out war equipment in such vast quantities that the Red Army was the only one with whole artillery divisions armed with thousands upon thousands of guns and rocket launchers, a revolutionary new weapon. Tank divisions were equipped with what were unarguably the best tanks in the world—the T-34 heavy tank, designed by American Walter Christie, that outperformed and outshot the famous German Tiger and Panther tanks. Air divisions were equipped with the YAK-3, one of the four best fighter planes of the war, at least as good as the Spitfire, the Messerschmitt and the Zero.

Besides the massive Russian war production, the Americans were pouring in lend-lease equipment by way of Iran and Murmansk. By 1943, 183,000 trucks alone had arrived along with thousands of Bell Airacobra fighters, much-liked by Russian pilots.

After Stalingrad, it was only a matter of time before other Russian cities started hitting the headlines—Kharkov, Rostov, Mtsensk, Orel, Kiev, Minsk, Kursk, Gomel, Smolensk—as the mighty Red Army rolled westward. The Russian offensives of 1943 saw gigantic, well-equipped armies of millions of men manoeuvring along a front of over a thousand miles.

The *News-Herald* headline of December 25, 1942 announced a great new Red Army offensive. Emanating in the Caucasus on the Don River front south of Stalingrad, its aim was to free Rostov, which it did by February 14, 1943.

Farther north another offensive was aimed at recapturing Kharkov and Kursk, which was also accomplished by mid-February. The Germans, however, were not good losers, especially the brilliant Field Marshal von Manstein, who launched a counter-attack towards Kharkov on February 20th. By March 12th he reached the city, having trapped and destroyed the entire Soviet 3rd Tank Army along the way. This was a temporary victory only, but a shock to the Russians, who once again experienced German fighting qualities at their best.

A similar German counter-attack against the Kursk salient was launched with much more preparation later in July. It did not fare as well, partly because the Russians learned of it well in advance from a spy planted in the German army command. The Russian defenses were well prepared with land mines, thousands of anti-tank guns and more thousands of the famous T-34 heavy tanks. The Kursk engagement developed into one of the decisive battles of the war, and was certainly the greatest tank battle in all of history. On both sides, 13,000 tanks were involved in the fighting, as well as four million troops, 69,000 mortars and artillery pieces and 12,000 aircraft.

The Germans had hoped to pinch off the salient, thus trapping a whole Russian army and taking Kursk at the same time. Instead, the Russians held Kursk and retook Orel and the area above the salient, as well as Kharkov and the area below the salient, thus straightening out the front.

The Russian steamroller continued throughout the year, with Gomel retaken in October and Kiev, the capital of Ukraine, freed in early November. Altogether, 1943 was a banner year for the Red Army, with the tide of war now turned in its favour.

[See pages 84, 88–90, 94–95, 97–99,
101–2, 105–7, 110–12]

July 9, 1943

SICILY INVADED

The Allied invasion of Sicily with eight seaborne and two airborne divisions was led by two famous generals: British General Montgomery of El Alamein fame and U.S. General George Patton.

There were Italian troops in Sicily, but the ones that mattered most were the German Hermann Goering Panzers and the 15th Panzer Grenadiers, who provided stiff resistance to Montgomery's drive on Messina, at the very northern tip of the island.

Further resistance developed for Patton's forces when Hitler sent two more divisions to aid the Italians. The Allied advance became more and more laborious, but victory was achieved on August 17th, when they entered Messina.

The 1st Canadian Infantry Division and the 1st Canadian Army Tank Brigade, under command of Major-General G. G. Simonds, distinguished themselves in their first exposure to hostilities. The progressively bloodier battles in which they became engaged culminated in the taking of Agira on July 28th, after a five-day battle.

[See pages 93, 97, 99–100]

July 25-August 8, 1943

MUSSOLINI ARRESTED; ITALY QUITS

The Italians never had much heart for the war. Even with victory there would be little benefit to them. Mussolini would strut a little bigger on the world stage, but with the Germans as senior partners there would be no joy added to their lives.

So when the Allies looked like they really were going to win, and were sitting in Sicily ready to attack the mainland, Italy's Fascist Grand Council decided it was time for Mussolini to go. On July 25th King Victor Emmanuel ordered his arrest and imprisonment; Nazi paratroopers freed him later in October.

The Italian surrender which followed Mussolini's downfall gave the Germans in Italy a free hand to defend the country as they wished. Italians living in northern Italy were shipped to Germany as slave labour. Germany also benefitted by not having to supply oil and raw material to keep Italy going.

Some German troops were diverted to Italy from other fronts, but it took few divisions to defend mountain passes compared to the hundreds of divisions employed on the Russian Steppes. Italy, very mountainous, became a quagmire for the Allied armies as they laboriously fought their way up the boot.

[See pages 96, 103–6]

CANADIANS IN ITALY

Montgomery's 8th Army, with the Canadian forces from Sicily in the vanguard, invaded Italy September 3rd, while peace negotiations were in progress. They landed at Reggio south of Naples and pushed inland to take Potenza, just east of Salerno, in 17 days.

Advancing to the Adriatic coast, the Canadians fought their way north to Ortona, which the Germans defended savagely through Christmas of 1943. The house-to-house battle lasted seven days, with the Germans finally withdrawing when the Canadians threatened to surround the town.

By the new year there were 75,000 Canadian troops in Italy, with the arrival of the 5th Canadian Armoured Division. They were organized into the 1st Canadian Army Corps, under Lieutenant-General H. D. G. Crerar.

The Canadians saw further action in May of 1944 at Cassino, and the breakthrough of the Hitler Line by tanks of the 5th Armoured Division opened the way to Rome.

In late August of 1944, Canadian troops were thrown into the battle for Rimini in northern Italy. There they battled the stubborn Germans through the rain and mud of an atrocious Italian winter, going nowhere. All Canadian forces were withdrawn from Italy in February 1945 and sent to Holland to rejoin the 1st Canadian Army, from which their detachment had caused considerable controversy. For the rest of the war, the Canadians fought as one.

In 20 months of fighting in Sicily and Italy, the Canadians had acquitted themselves with distinction, at the expense of 25,000 casualties, of whom 6,000 were dead.

[See pages 102–3, 108–9]

SALERNO

The broad beaches at Salerno, south of Naples, were picked for the second landings in Italy, and American General Mark Clark's 5th Army was given the task. It was composed of one untested American division and two veteran British divisions from the desert war.

Unbelievably, the Americans came up with a plan to surprise the enemy by landing on the beaches with no advance bombing and shelling. A year earlier this had been tried at Dieppe, with disastrous results. Now, Vice-Admiral Hewitt, the naval task force commander, argued with Clark about the foolhardiness of his plan, but to no avail.

The British refused Clark's plan and would only land with massive fire support in advance of and during the landings. The first advance salvo came from a thousand rockets blasting the enemy mine fields in the beach landing area. Few Germans survived the five minutes of flaming devastation.

In contrast, the Americans approached the beach in absolute silence, while the Germans waited, undisturbed, with their machine guns, heavy artillery and mortars behind barbed wire and mine fields. As the landing craft touched shore, the Germans opened up by the light of a sky filled with flares. Whole landing craft disintegrated with their cargoes of troops in a hail of fire. Troops who managed to get ashore found the beach alive with exploding mines and gunfire.

The battle was saved by sheer numbers. The Allies poured three divisions ashore while the Germans had only one with which to defend the entire area. The Allies gained the beachhead, but there was nowhere to go as it was ringed with mountains and the passes were filled with German troops. Naples was the Allies' goal, if only they could break out. British troops finally got there October 1st, but only after the Germans had withdrawn to protect Rome.

[See pages 107–9]

Ottawa to Conscript Skilled Workers

KHARKOV FALLS

'Their Mission Fulfilled'

★ ★ ★ ★ ★ FINAL

The Vancouver Sun
The Vancouver Evening Newspaper Owned and Operated By Vancouver People
FOUNDED 1886
VOL. LVII—No. 115
VANCOUVER, BRITISH COLUMBIA, TUESDAY, FEBRUARY 16, 1943
PRICE 5 CENTS BY CARRIER $1.00 per month

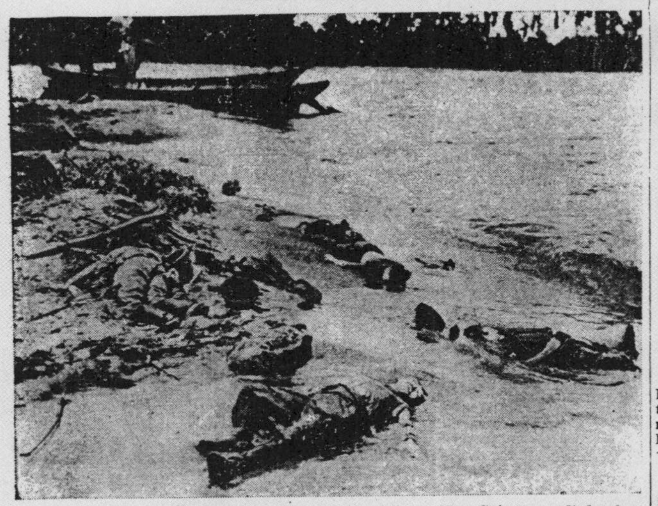

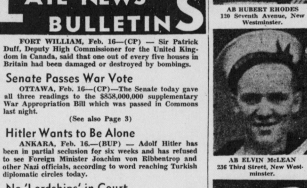

Japanese attempts to land on the western beach of Buna, New Guinea, resulted only in casualties, as shown above. In the background, the landing barge floats, deserted. Tokyo announced that the Japanese forces had been withdrawn from Guadalcanal and Buna "after their mission had been fulfilled."

15 Japanese Warships Sunk; U.S. Loses Two

WASHINGTON, Feb. 16 — (BUP) — American bombers damaged two Japanese destroyers and carried out three new attacks on enemy positions in the New Georgia group in the Central Solomons, the Navy announced late today.

By British United Press

WASHINGTON, Feb. 16.—The heavy cruiser USS Chicago and a U.S. destroyer were lost in a week-long series of air-naval engagements in the Solomons area which cost the Japanese two destroyers sunk and 13 other ships probably sunk or damaged, the Navy dept. announced today.

In addition at least 60 Japanese and 22 American planes were destroyed. Three U.S. motor torpedo boats also were lost.

The actions, resulting from Japanese attempts to evacuate troops from Guadalcanal and to interfere with American reinforcements, covered the period Jan. 29-Feb. 4 (Solomons time) inclusive.

NO SEA BATTLES

It was all air versus ships; no surface ships were engaged with each other.

The encounters, revealed in detail for the first time today,

Please Turn to Page Two
See "Solomons"

LATE NEWS BULLETINS

FORT WILLIAM, Feb. 16—(CP) — Sir Patrick Duff, Deputy High Commissioner for the United Kingdom in Canada, said that one out of every five houses in Britain had been damaged or destroyed by bombings.

Senate Passes War Vote

OTTAWA, Feb. 16—(CP)—The Senate today gave all three readings to the $858,000,000 supplementary War Appropriation Bill which was passed in Commons last night.

(See also Page 3)

Hitler Wants to Be Alone

ANKARA, Feb. 16.—(BUP) — Adolf Hitler has been in partial seclusion for six weeks and has refused to see Foreign Minister Joachim von Ribbentrop and other Nazi officials, according to word reaching Turkish diplomatic circles today.

No 'Lordships' in Court

WINNIPEG, Feb. 16.—Mr. Justice R. M. Dennistoun in the Manitoba Bar News voices objection to the use of certain terms in court. Judges of the court of appeal and King's bench have no legal right to be addressed as "my lord" or "your lordship," in addressing the court, he said. "We are not lordships. In a country where real titles have been discarded, it is inconsistent to perpetuate fictitious ones."

Sgt. Pilot 'Hump' Payne RCAF Dies Overseas

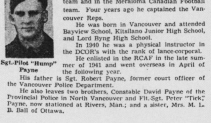

Sgt.-Pilot Humphrey Owen Blake "Hump" Payne, 27, former Meraloma football star, was killed in action overseas on Sunday, according to word received Monday by his parents, Mr. and Mrs. Robert Payne of Galiano Island.

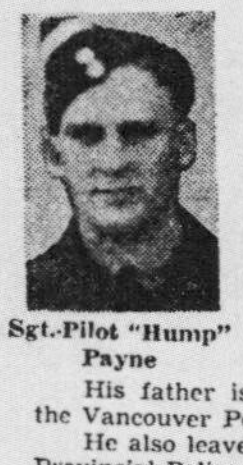

Sgt.-Pilot "Hump" Payne

Sgt.-Pilot Payne was an outstanding player both in the Meraloma English Rugby team and in the Meraloma Canadian Football team. Four years ago he captained the Vancouver Reps.

He was born in Vancouver and attended Bayview School, Kitsilano Junior High School, and Lord Byng High School.

In 1940 he was a physical instructor in the DCOR's with the rank of lance-corporal.

He enlisted in the RCAF in the late summer of 1941 and went overseas in April of the following year.

His father is Sgt. Robert Payne, former court officer of the Vancouver Police Department.

He also leaves two brothers, Constable David Payne of the Provincial Police in North Vancouver and Flt.-Sgt. Peter "Tick" Payne, now stationed at Rivers, Man.; and a sister, Mrs. M. L. B. Ball of Ottawa.

88

Race Results

FIRST RACE—Six furlongs:
Valdina Phao (Zufelt) $3.20, $2.20, $2.20.
Nedco (Garza) $3, $3.20.
Cee Lot (Barney) $8.60.
Scratches: Apptoplay, Furcoat Avec, Hadalass.
Time, 1:13 3-5.

SECOND RACE—Six furlongs:
Scarlet Insco (Skoronski) $9.80, $3, $2.20.
Quatrebelle (Murphy) $2.20, $2.20.
Tides Dream (Clingman) $2.20.
Scratches: Monen Lad, Poppycock, Disinherit, Gummed Up.
Time, 1:13 2-5.

THIRD RACE—Six furlongs:
La Jaconde (Eads) $4.20, $3, $2.60.
Manamaid (Murphy) $4.20, $3.80.
Optimal (Hauer) $3.20.
Scratches: Early Delivery, Challante, Cold Crack, Crepe, New Wrinkle, Good Gosh.
Time, 1:13 2-5.

FOURTH RACE.—Two furlongs.
Sweeping Ahead (Hauer) $18.60, $9.80, $4.20.
Green Belle (McCoy) $6.00, $3.20.
Smart Shiela (Eccard) $3.70.

FIFTH RACE.—Mile and one-sixteenth.
Barnegat (Skelly).
Hattie Belle (Barney).
Mad Bunny (Brooks).

Race Entries on Page 20

Canadian Corvette Torpedoed

38 Die When Dominion War Vessel Goes Down in Mediterranean; One Vancouver Man Missing

(Six B.C. men on lost warship; see page 2)

By JOHN DAUPHINEE
Canadian Press Staff Writer

OTTAWA, Feb. 16.—Sinking of the Canadian corvette Louisburg with loss of 38 lives as a result of enemy air attacks while on convoy duty in the Mediterranean was announced today by Hon. Angus Macdonald, navy minister. Forty-seven of the crew survived.

SURVIVORS

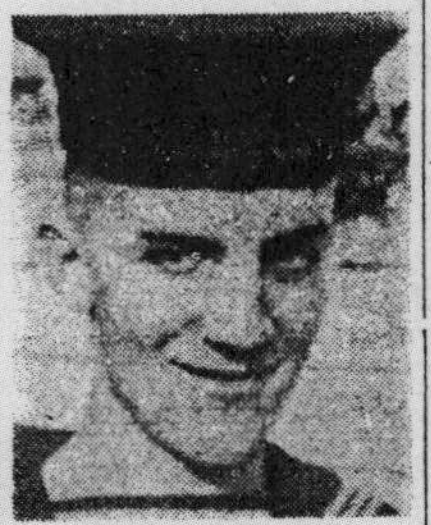

AB HUBERT RHODES
120 Seventh Avenue, New Westminster.

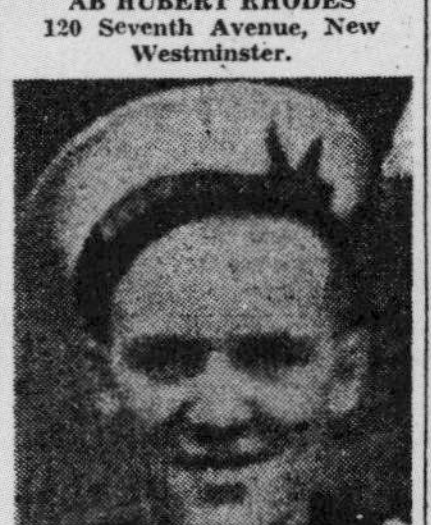

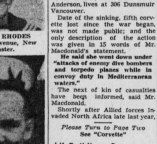

AB ELVIN McLEAN
236 Third Street, New Westminster.

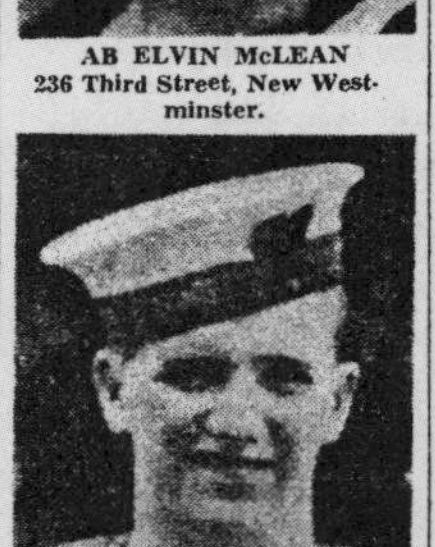

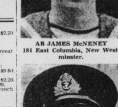

AB JAMES McNENEY
184 East Columbia, New Westminster.

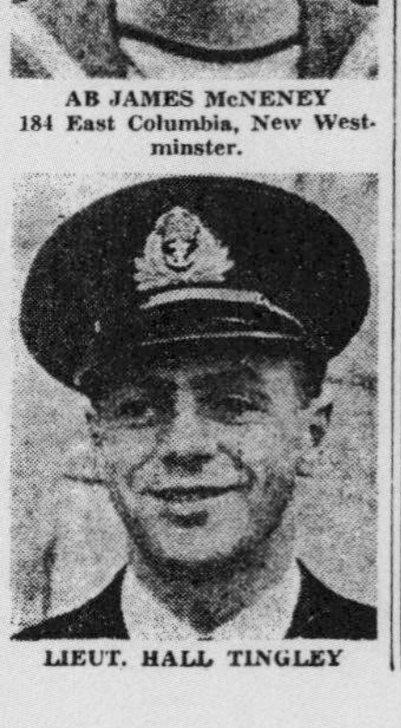

LIEUT. HALL TINGLEY

It was the first time in Canadian naval history that a Canadian ship has been sunk in the Mediterranean — and the first time a Canadian ship has been destroyed by an air attack.

Lt.-Cmdr. William Franklin Campbell, 39, of Saskatoon, is among the two officers, 33 Canadian ratings and three Royal Navy ratings listed by the navy as "missing, presumed killed in action."

Only one British Columbian appeared on the casualty list. He was Stoker (1st Class) Archibald Frederick Anderson, RCNVR, whose mother, Mrs. Catherine E. Anderson, lives at 306 Dunsmuir Vancouver.

Date of the sinking, fifth corvette lost since the war began, was not made public; and the only description of the action was given in 15 words of Mr. Macdonald's statement.

He said she went down under "attacks of enemy dive bombers and torpedo planes while in convoy duty in Mediterranean waters."

The next of kin of casualties have been informed, said Mr. Macdonald.

Shortly after Allied forces invaded North Africa late last year,

Please Turn to Page Two
See "Corvette"

All Buildings Put Under Gov't Ban

Temporary suspension at least of all new building in Vancouver was ordered today, because of an unprecedented shortage of lumber.

Vancouver construction companies understand that the ban will be lifted as soon as lumber supplies increase, but D. D. Rosenberry, regional timber controller, warned that the ban might be for the duration.

Beaver Cove Fire

VICTORIA, Feb. 16—(CP)—A warehouse, bunkhouse and hotel at the northern Vancouver Island town of Beaver Cove were destroyed by fire yesterday afternoon, provincial police headquarters here learned by radio today.

The buildings were owned by the Canadian Forest Products.

Army to Release Artisans

'Rejects' for Military Service Must Take New Jobs

By BRUCE HUTCHISON
Vancouver Sun Ottawa Bureau

OTTAWA, Feb. 16.—Canada will begin immediately to conscript workers for industry and to take men out of the army on a large scale to provide industrial labor.

Under a sweeping policy now unfolding here, young men called for army service but found unfit will be sent directly to essential industries and not back to their old jobs as in the past.

JAPS FOR FARMS

At the same time the government will fine-comb the army for skilled workers and send them into raw-material industries like lumbering and mining.

Finally, the government intends to use many war prisoners in agriculture this year and will move B. C. Japanese out of road-building camps and into farms.

By such methods, unprecedented in the history of the nation, the government hopes to avoid a threatened manpower breakdown in the spring.

The Vancouver Sun learned today that the movement of men from the army into industry is now a definite government policy, forced upon the ministry by the desperate needs of basic industry.

B.C. DESPERATE

British Columbia will feel the results of this new program perhaps more than any other part of the country.

It is in British Columbia that the labor situation is regarded as

Please Turn to Page Two
See "Hutchison"

Dies On Way to Commit Suicide

SAN FRANCISCO, Feb. 16 — (BUP)—On house stationery at the hotel where he was staying, Nels L. Nelson wrote a note: "It is a very lovely day to commit suicide."

He stuffed the note in a coat pocket, packed a pistol in a shoe box and boarded a street car for the beach.

Police found his body half way between the car line and the water.

"Heart failure," said the coroner.

TORONTO, Feb. 16—(CP)—The Ontario Legislature today held one of its shortest sittings in many years as Premier Gordon Conant's illness with a heavy cold held deliberations to just five minutes.

Betty Grable's Legs 'Set in Concrete'

HOLLYWOOD, Feb. 16 — (AP)—Posterity will have a permanent record of Betty Grable's shapely legs. The film actress placed herself in a reclining position in the forecourt of a popular theatre last night while imprints of her legs were made in wet concrete.

Hers are the latest Hollywood symbols to be placed beside such others as the skate marks of Sonja Henie, the John Barrymore profile and Bob Hope's nose.

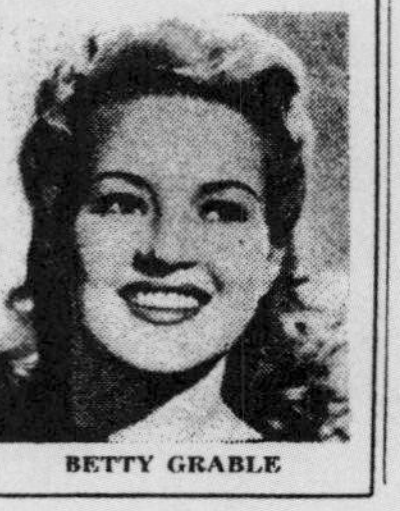

BETTY GRABLE

'Greatest Victory of Campaign'

Capital of Ukraine Captured by Powerful Onslaught and Fierce Street Fighting

By British United Press

LONDON, Feb. 16. — Russian assault forces captured Kharkov today after a powerful onslaught and fierce street fighting, routing a crack German Army corps to score the greatest offensive victory of the Red Army's winter campaign.

A special Soviet communique broadcast from Moscow announced the liberation of Kharkov, industrial capital of the Ukraine and the last great bastion anchoring the German front in South Russia.

Smolensk is next.

Routed in the short-lived battle for Kharkov were two elite German tank divisions, one motorized division and a number of infantry divisions and special units, the Red Army reported.

The loss of Kharkov after Rostov and Kursk, other major German "bolt" positions on the southern front left the Axis without any apparent chance of establishing a new defense line east of the Dnieper.

DRAMATIC ANNOUNCEMENT

In addition to robbing the Germans of a vital base, the Russians by seizing Kharkov reclaimed one of the main centres of Soviet industry and agriculture.

The Moscow Radio announced the Red Army victory in a dramatic manner. Broadcast music hit a crescendo, dead silence followed, then there was played the opening bars of, "There is no other country where the people breathe so freely."

"This is Moscow. We bring you the latest news," a solemn male voice called. "Attention! Moscow calling! Our troops have captured the city of Kharkov. . ."

There were no reports from the battle lines northeast, north

Please Turn to Page Two
See "Russia"

Box Score in Sea Battle

Here is a breakdown of losses by both sides in the scattered Solomon Islands encounters:

JAPANESE—

Sunk—Two destroyers

Probably sunk — Four destroyers

Damaged— Six destroyers, 1 corvette and 2 cargo ships

Planes—Destroyed, 28 or 29 Zeros, 12 torpedo planes and 20 unidentified types

Probably destroyed—7 Zeros

UNITED STATES—

Sunk—Heavy cruiser Chicago; unidentified destroyer; 3 motor torpedo boats

Damaged—Not reported

Planes—Six fighters, 4 torpedo planes, 2 bombers and 10 unidentified types

SEVEN DIE IN FIRE

AUGUSTA, Maine, Feb. 16—(AP)—Death toll in a midnight rooming-house fire rose to seven today with the death of an 18-year-old youth.

KEEP SMILING

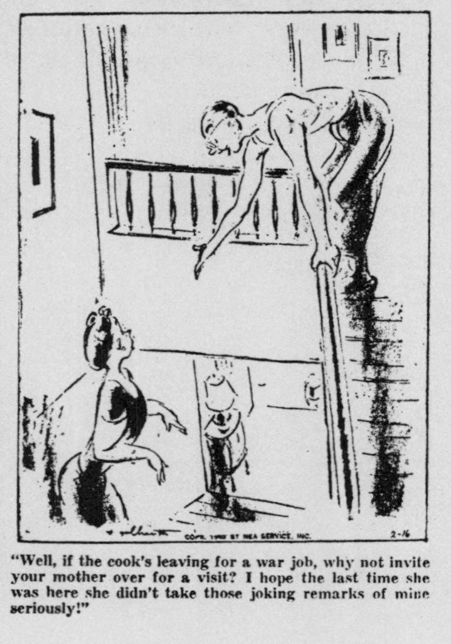

"Well, if the cook's leaving for a war job, why not invite your mother over for a visit? I hope the last time she was here she didn't take those joking remarks of mine seriously!"

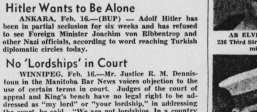

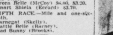

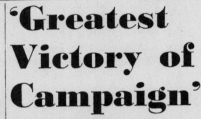

BLACK MARKET EXPOSED

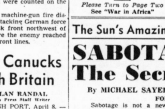

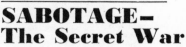

The Vancouver Sun
The Vancouver Evening Newspaper Owned and Operated by Vancouver People
FOUNDED 1886 VOL. LVII—No. 159 | VANCOUVER, B.C., THURSDAY, APRIL 8, 1943 | PRICE 5 CENTS $1.00 per month BY CARRIER

ITALY DECLARES 'STATE OF ALERT'; FEARS INVASION

Sun Man Uncovers Rackets

Auto Tires for $50, Gas at 50 Cents, Butter for $1

The Black Market has established itself in Vancouver.

It has even set up a list of basic prices for the commodities others cannot or will not sell without receiving ration coupons as well as cash in exchange.

The prices are a "bit" higher than those asked in your corner grocery, but they are based on the same principle—so much for tires, for gasoline, butter, tea, coffee, sugar.

Here are the Black Market prices obtained by a Vancouver Sun investigator who wrote them down as they were offered to him:

1. Butter sells for $1 a pound on the Black Market, and there's a heavy demand for it. The legal retail price for it is 41 cents.

2. A new auto tire can be bought on the Black Market for up to $50. If a motorist happens to be in the category which allows him to buy a new tire he'll pay $21 to $25 for it.

3. Re-capped tires sell at a black market price of $25 each, while dealers can sell them to those who can buy for $9.

4. Auto tubes can be had, too, for from $2 to $5.

5. Sugar on the black market costs $10 a hundred pounds. This is only $2 more than the legal retail price.

50-CENT GASOLINE

6. Coffee and tea prices on the black market are the same—about $1 a pound, or nearly double the legal retail price. The Sun investigator was told that the price of these commodities depends on the brand.

7. Black market gasoline sells at 50 cents a gallon, 21 cents per gallon profit. There is plenty of "bootleg" gas and plenty of buyers.

8. There is a traffic in "loose" gasoline ration coupons that has reached amazing proportions, but the most popular method of obtaining extra gas seems to be by buying it direct from a gas bootlegger. There isn't the risk then of having a service station operator refusing to sell to you.

9. Whisky prices have jumped again on the Black Market. Mickeys of rye sell at from $8 to $11, and 26-ounce bottles at $18 "tops." But this business has fallen on evil days, some say. Liquor is too hard to get.

All the commodities listed above were offered to The Sun's investigator by Black Market intermediaries during the course of his probe, and the prices listed are those at which the average citizen can buy "if he is in the know."

NO STRANGERS

Black Market retailers will not sell direct to strangers. They are plenty careful. Police have little chance to nab them red-handed.

"Stool pigeons" might be the answer, but the Black Market operators are suspicious of everyone, and act accordingly.

Commodities sold on the Black Market come from many and varied sources. Much of it, of course, is stolen, but it is hinted strongly that some restaurants are not averse to making a little extra profit out of extra butter, sugar, tea or coffee.

Private auto owners have held

Please Turn to Page Two
See "Black Market"

50-Gallon Still Found on North Shore

NORTH VANCOUVER, April 8.—First evidence that the shortage of liquor in B. C. had caused stills to be set up for the manufacture of illicit alcohol was shown here today with the confiscation of a still and the arrest and sentencing of its operator.

Tom Nolan, 136 West Balmoral, pleaded guilty to operating the still.

He was fined $350 with alternative of serving six months in jail with hard labor.

Nolan was arrested by Provincial and Royal Canadian Mounted Police after the still was discovered in the North Lonsdale district.

The still was made out of a 50-gallon gas drum with a coil inside and a condenser outside.

Four barrels of mash were seized but only one small bottle of "moonshine" could be found.

Wares of the Black Racketeer

Below are some of the goods offered to The Sun investigator in the Vancouver Black Market and the prices asked for them:

Because certain well-known brands of reputable firms are entangled in the accompanying pictures of black market operations, it should be pointed out that the manufacturers are not in any way involved in this nefarious business. In fact, it is obvious that the black-marketeer operates with greatest ease and security when he acquires, by theft or some other underground channel, the goods of established brands and of well-known and decent business houses. (See Editorial Page 4.)

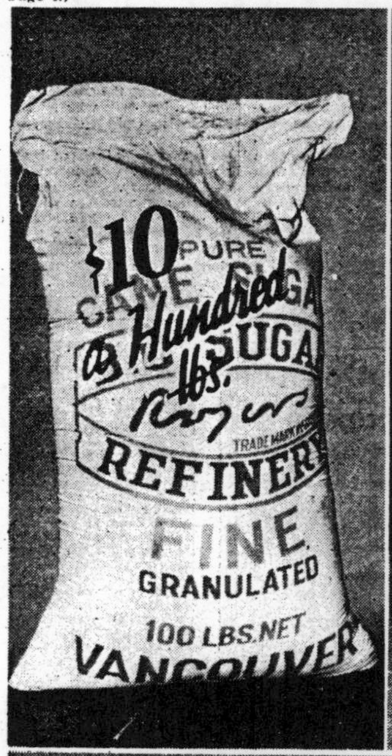

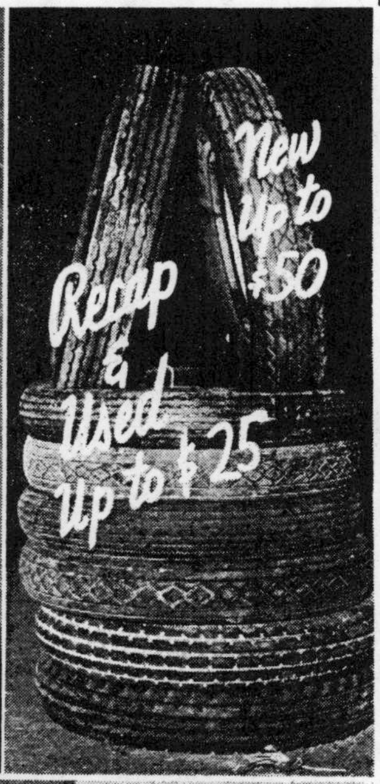

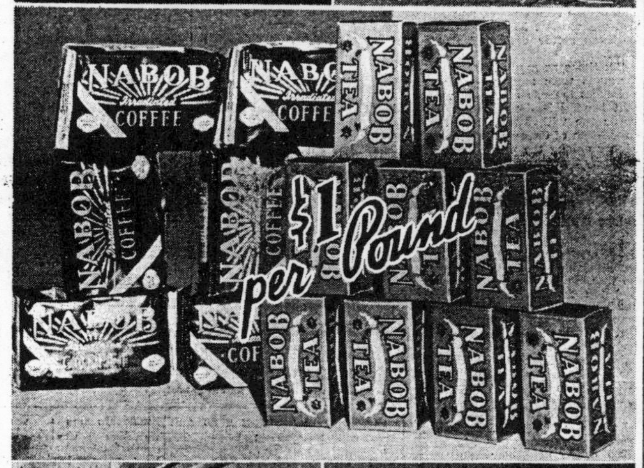

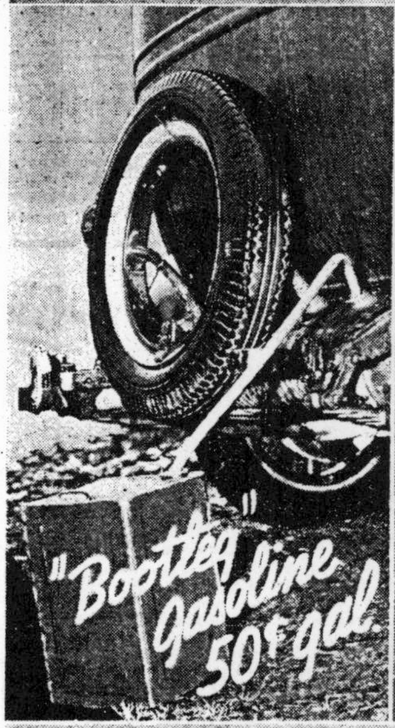

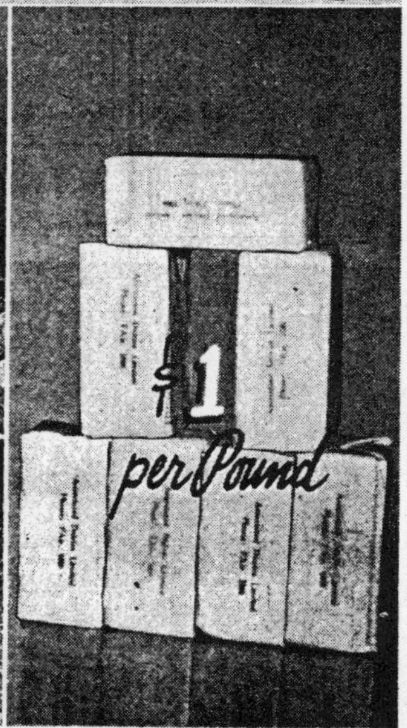

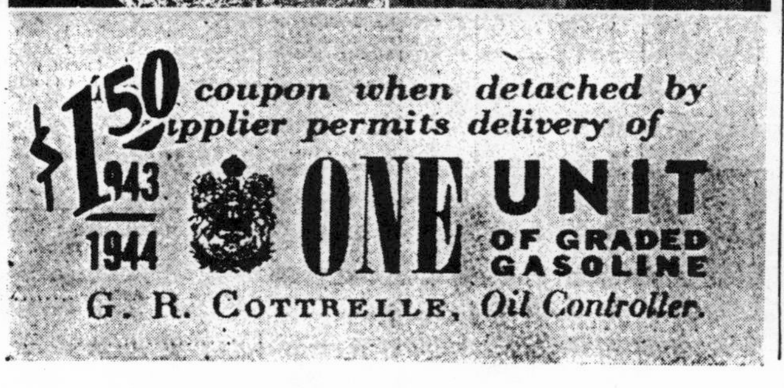

Hitler and Mussolini To Confer

By ROBERT DOWSON
Special to The Vancouver Sun
Copyright, 1943, by British United Press

LONDON, April 8. — Invasion jitters increased in Axis Europe today with Germany beginning extensive troop manoeuvres along the North Sea coast and an Algerian broadcast reporting that the Italian army has been placed in a State of Alert against an Allied landing.

(A British broadcast recorded by the Federal Communications Commission quoted Swiss reports that Adolf Hitler and Premier Benito Mussolini will meet soon in the Brenner Pass to discuss the defense of Europe against Allied landings.)

Axis broadcasts pictured United States and Britain as a graver menace to the "New Order" in Europe than Russia, now that the Soviet winter offensive has ended.

PROTEST "BARBARISM"

They assert that intensified Allied aerial attacks were "terror raids" and said that the two air forces have brought more suffering to France than did the Luftwaffe in the whole campaign of 1940.

"We have never heard tell of even the Bolsheviks sending their air squadrons over open cities to slaughter," the Paris radio said.

"In the west it is a war of barbarism. In the east it is a war of gentlemen."

Informed sources here said German troop manoeuvres under way in Holland and Belgium were designed to prepare for defense against an Allied invasion, which Axis reports have predicted may come next month.

TABLES TURNED

In the summer of 1940, the Germans were practicing in Belgium, Holland and France for an invasion of Britain that never came off.

An Algiers broadcast said that Italy now regards the intensified aerial offensive against Sicily, Sardinia and southern Italy as a prelude to an Allied landing.

(Associated Press despatches from Stockholm and Berne, Switzerland, also tell of Axis moves in fear of invasion.

(Stockholm reported that in Norway the Gestapo has arrested 8000 suspected or known anti-Nazis, while Swiss advices said Nazis are planning a special zone in Eastern France to provide a corridor direct to Germany from Italy and the Mediterranean.)

British Check Burma Drive

NEW DELHI, India, April 8.—British artillery has pounded back a Papanese attempt to advance during the continuing fight in the Indin area of Burma, a British communique said today.

It said the Japanese withdrew after suffering heavy casualties.

There has been no change in the last 24 hours in fighting in the Arakan area.

Allied aircraft hit an enemy airfield at Shwebo, in central Burma, attacked the railway station at Wuntho, and strafed Pinlebu and another enemy village west of Katha yesterday, the war bulletin announced.

Italian General Boss in Tunisia

By Canadian Press

NEW YORK, April 8.—A London broadcast said today that General Giovanni Messe, an Italian, was the new commander-in-chief in Tunisia.

"A Berlin military spokesman says that Rommel and Von Arnim are now both under General Messe's command," it quoted the broadcast as saying.

General Messe was in command of the first Italian expeditionary force sent to the Russian front.

Germans Quit Attempting to Control Donets

By HENRY SHAPIRO
Special to The Vancouver Sun
Copyright, 1943, by British United Press

MOSCOW, April 8.—The Red Army, wresting the initiative from the apparently exhausted Germans south of Izyun, seized several favorable positions today to widen the Soviet bridgehead on the south bank of the Donets river.

At least 200 German troops were killed and four guns, nine machine-guns, one trench mortar and two enemy truckloads of supplies were destroyed in the Russian advance, the Soviet midday communique reported. Four German planes were shot down.

The Germans hurled thousands of troops and scores of tanks against the Soviet bridgehead south of Izyum during the past week in a vain effort to drive the Russians back across the Donets, but the enemy finally abandoned his offensive after suffering heavy losses.

On the Smolensk front, all is quiet except for artillery exchanges following a sudden Soviet thrust yesterday which resulted in the capture of two villages northeast of the Axis bastion,(the first captured in this sector in nearly a week.

Three enemy detachments launched a new attack against a Russian-held height on the Volkhov front southeast of Leningrad, but were thrown back to their initial positions by a Soviet counter-attack. One hundred enemy dead were counted on the battlefield.

Rifle and machine-gun fire dispersed an attacking German force on the Sevsk front northwest of Kursk before the enemy reached the Soviet front lines.

More Canucks Reach Britain

By ALAN RANDAL
Canadian Press Staff Writer

A BRITISH PORT, April 8. — Arrival of reinforcements for the Canadian Army in Britain was announced today.

They included armored corps, artillery, infantry and other service unit reinforcements, but it was indicated it was not a large movement.

The arrival was announced together with the fact that a new draft of men for the overseas RCAF and the largest group of the air force women's division ever to debark in Britain had been dispersed to reception depots and will soon be working at their appointed tasks.

A submarine alert was sounded aboard one of the ships carrying the RCAF personnel. Later it was reported a submarine had been sighted aft of another part of the convoy.

Allied Armies Driving Ahead For Final Test

By Canadian Press

ALLIED HEADQUARTERS in North Africa, April 8.—The British 1st Army in Northern Tunisia has plunged forward in an attack co-ordinated with the successful advance of British and American forces in Southern Tunisia and has gained much ground in the region of Medjez-el-Bab, 36 miles southwest of Tunis, an Allied communique said today.

The pursuit of the enemy from his broken defenses at the Wadi el Akarit, 20 miles north of Gabes, is being pressed relentlessly by the British 8th Army, the communique said, and many more prisoners and much abandoned material have been taken.

The British 1st Army, in its advance in the Medjez-el-Bab area has taken many prisoners.

The almost general advance followed the special announcement last night that the United States Second Army Corps had joined arms 15 miles east of Gafsa with the British 8th Army.

The communique also announced that the French troops had moved forward on the southern flank of the Americans, capturing a number of prisoners and 20 guns.

The French attack was described as a "successful advance." Thus almost the entire Allied military machine in Tunisia is now on the move.

The 1st Army's advance was made between Medjez-el-Bab and Munchar.

Allied aerial assaults continue. In southern Tuniisa light bombers and fighter-bombers carried out "heavy and continuous attacks" on the enemy.

On the northern front, Allied planes attacked enemy transports and started fires among parked vehicles. Nine Junkers-87's were destroyed.

The Sfax-Sousse road was attacked Tuesday night and the same night big bombers attacked the railway yards at Tunis, starting fires. One Allied plane was reported missing.

The communique also disclosed that five additional Axis planes, previously unreported, were shot down Tuesday.

Please Turn to Page Two
See "War in Africa"

How Tommies, Yanks Met In Tunisia

By PHIL AULT
Special to The Vancouver Sun
Copyright, 1943, by British United Press

EL GUETTAR, Tunisia, April 8.—Six American jeeps creeping cautiously along a black macadam road yesterday afternoon met three British Eighth Army armored cars.

The Americans and the British paused for a moment beside a 67-kilometer road marker on the road from Gabes to Gafsa. Then there was a burst of shouts from dust-parched throats and the Allied soldiers who had come from opposite shores of Africa leaped from their vehicles.

Hands scarred by the hard sands of Tripolitania clasped hands grimy with the red dirt of the Tunisian hills. Then they grabbed one another, pounded one another on the back and shouted congratulations.

That was the junction of the British Eighth Army, which fought its way from El Alamein, with the Americans in Tunisia.

The Sun's Amazing New Serial

SABOTAGE— The Secret War

By MICHAEL SAYERS and ALBERT E. KAHN

FOREWORD

Sabotage is not a new device in war. Until recently, however, sabotage was regarded as an auxiliary weapon. But with the Nazis, sabotage became state policy.

It is in the hope of bringing about an understanding of this, and of thus contributing to the war effort, that this book has been written.

INSTALMENT I

It was 9:15 p.m., March 16, 1941. The Cleveland-Pittsburgh Express was thundering across the snow-blanketed Pennsylvania countryside. Rushing alongside the Ohio River, the train neared the littel town of Baden.

Suddenly, the giant engine swayed violently, leaped from the tracks and hurtled down the river bank. The passenger cars were catapulted one after another into the dark icy water, crumpling like toys. . . .

Five persons were killed. One hundred and twenty-one were injured.

Pennsylvania Railroad officials said, "Definitely caused by sabotage!" The Interstate Commerce Commission reported the results of its investigation on May 8: "Malicious tampering with the track" had caused the wreck.

Experts expressed the belief

Please Turn to Page Six
See "Sabotage"

SFAX TAKEN

THE VANCOUVER DAILY PROVINCE

49th YEAR—NO. 14 | DIMOUT TIMES: Tonight 8:25; Sun. 6:01 a.m.; Sun. 8:27 p.m.; Mon. 5:59 a.m. | VANCOUVER, B.C., SATURDAY, APRIL 10, 1943—50 PAGES | PRICE 10 CENTS BY CARRIER $1.00 per month

From The Times:

Today In Europe

News and comment on international events from the London Times of this date and cabled from The Vancouver Daily Province London Bureau, Times Building, Printing House Square.

(Copyright, 1943, by Southam Co.)

LONDON, April 10.—The 8th Army's pursuit of Rommel's retreating forces, says the Times correspondent with General Montgomery's troops, is stretching them to the utmost. Already the German flanks are in danger and the supply of food and ammunition must be becoming a grave problem.

The enemy is showing nervousness and uncertainty and it is believed he is deliberately sacrificing the Italian troops to save his shipping space when evacuating the Africa Corps becomes necessary.

General Alexander is well satisfied with his progress to date, says the Times Algiers correspondent, and full of hope for the future though he recognizes most of the strenuous fighting lies ahead of the British forces.

In the north wet, windy weather has delayed progress of the British 1st Army, but the Royal Air Force has been able to shoot up vehicles as usual, and dislocate transport generally. The Germans are slowly withdrawing near Mateur. It is now disclosed that Rommel was building up a panzer division to drive back the Americans from the Maknassey area when the 8th Army's sudden flank attack upset all his plans.

* * *

Editorially the Times stresses the Axis' admissions of the danger and difficulty of getting supplies and reinforcements into Tunisia against the British naval and Royal Air Force's attacks.

The quickest way of ending the campaign, says the Times, would be a direct British 1st Army drive on Tunis and Bizerte. But the difficulties of transport stand in the way, and the task of driving Rommel into the sea will fall most likely on the 8th Army.

There is the greatest necessity for speed because along the coasts of Western Europe and the Mediterranean today German concrete mixers are piling up defenses and the Nazis are beginning a defense warfare against invasion.

Russia, too, is waiting to see if another Nazi offensive can be launched in the Donets region. The Soviet people are suffering hardships never experienced in Britain.

Final defeat of the Axis in Tunisia will have a big moral effect in Europe. There must be a quarter of a million troops in North Africa, with an immense amount of equipment which still reaches enemy-occupied harbors. But the Nazis' air strength is obviously inadequate and the Royal Air Force has been able to reach a new peak in the intensity of its blitz.

The climax of the long struggle that began in Egypt is now at hand.

* * *

Analyzing the great Russo-German struggle on the Donets, the Times Stockholm correspondent explains that after Stalingrad Russian victories were such that the German high command admitted the battle for the Donets Valley

(Continued on Page 2.)
See TIMES.

Eight Bombers Lost

RUHR MUNITION PLANTS TARGET IN R.A.F. BLITZ

Duisburg Again Picked Out for Wholesale Hammering

(By Associated Press.)

LONDON, April 10.—Duisburg and other industrial points in Germany's Ruhr Valley were the targets for Royal Air Force explosive and incendiary bombs as the R.A.F. continued its day-and-night hammering in another raid last night, an air ministry communique said today.

Eight bombers did not return.

Enemy shipping off the Norwegian coast also was attacked early in the night by coastal command aircraft, which torpedoed one tanker. Two coastal command planes are missing, it was announced.

THE THIRD RAID.

It was the fifty-eight raid on Duisburg, large inland port last blitzed on the night of Mach 26. About 12 miles west of Essen, it has many important war factories, and is one of the biggest railway junctions in the Ruhr.

The new round-the-clock bombing of the continent was resumed Thursday night with a heavy R.A.F.-R.C.A.F. raid on the Ruhr area, but the objectives that night were not announced.

Four Focke-Wulf 190's were shot down and several others severely damaged by Spitfires and Typhoons on offensive pa-

(Continued on Page 2.)
See AIR.

Battle of Burma

CLAIM BRITISH UNIT TRAPPED

(By Associated Press.)

NEW YORK, April 10.—A Japanese imperial headquarters communique broadcast by the Italian radio and recorded by the Associated Press, said today that the 6th Brigade of the India-British forces has been completely encircled at the Burma-India border, on the shores of the Bay of Bengal, that the commander of the brigade had been captured, and that it was being annihilated after continuous attacks.

There was no confirmation of the claim from any Allied source.

R.A.F. Bombers Strafe Jap Shipping, Roads

NEW DELHI, April 10.—(AP)—R. A. F. bombers staged a series of raids yesterday on Japanese shipping and highway traffic among the strong enemy defenses of southern Burma, a British communique said today.

At one river front 60 miles northwest of Taungup, a 60-foot cargo barge was hit and left sinking.

Not far away, on the road between Taungup and Letpadan, seven trucks were attacked and some troops in two of them were killed, the communique said, and on the Taungup-Dalc road 10 or 12 trucks in another highway convoy were destroyed and the other two were damaged.

Queen To Broadcast To Women of Empire

LONDON, April 10.—(AP)—The Queen will broadcast a message to the women of the Empire at 9 p.m. Sunday, London time (noon Vancouver time). It will be her ninth broadcast since she became Queen and her fifth during the war.

The broadcast, which will last about seven minutes, will be carried by the Canadian Broadcasting Corporation's national network.

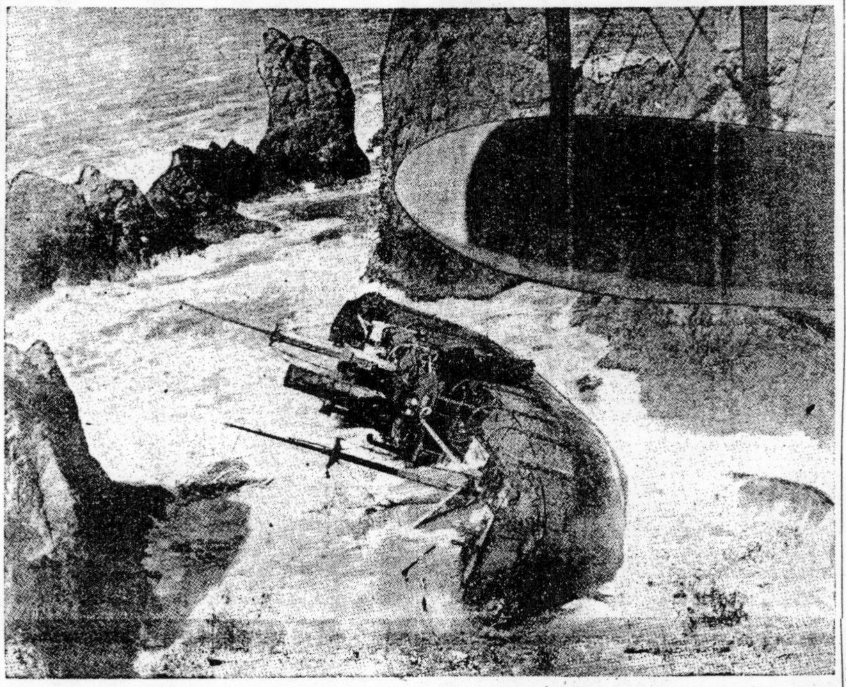

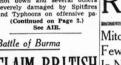

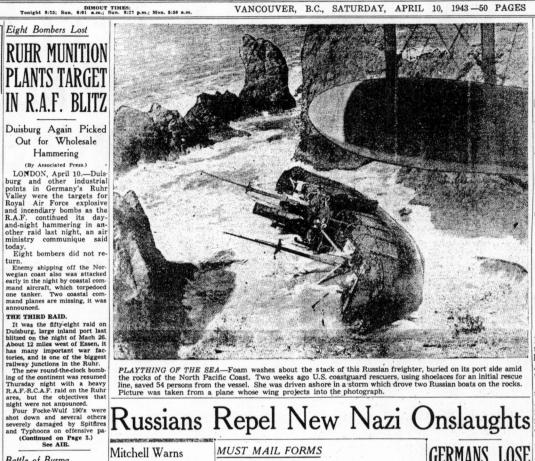

PLAYTHING OF THE SEA—Foam washes about the stack of this Russian freighter, buried on its port side amid the rocks of the North Pacific Coast. Two weeks ago U.S. coastguard rescuers, using shoelaces for an initial rescue line, saved 54 persons from the vessel. She was driven ashore in a storm which drove two Russian boats on the rocks. Picture was taken from a plane whose wing projects into the photograph.

Russians Repel New Nazi Onslaughts

GERMANS LOSE 1200 TROOPS

By EDDY GILMORE.
Associated Press Staff Writer.

MOSCOW, April 10.—Massing new forces, the Germans have tried again to smash the Red Army line south of Balakleya but have lost more than 1200 dead and a number of tanks in the battle for bridgeheads along the Donets River.

In their newest thrust, the Nazis sought to drive through the Russian line to reach an unidentified settlement but were forced back.

FIERCE BATTLES.

The army newspaper Red Star said battles are fierce in this area 27 miles northwest of Izyum but there is no indication the assaults are on the gigantic scale which the Russians turned back on the northern Donets line. Front despatches said the Germans were using fresh forces south of Balakleya. The biggest single attack was with 20 tanks and an infantry regiment thrown against a narrow sector. A hail of artillery, machine-gun and rifle fire met them, and successive enemy charges were smashed.

The noon communique did not mention fighting in the sector south of Izyum but the Red Army presumably still holds its original bridgeheads along the river.

There still were no large-scale fights on the western front but in the sector south of Bely the Russians, advancing toward Smolensk, captured a height of vital importance as more activity was noted.

Mitchell Warns Few to Be Left In Non-essential Jobs

NIAGARA FALLS, April 10.—(CP)—Hon. Humphrey Mitchell, Dominion labor minister, told a gathering of Niagara district manufacturers that within six months there would be "very few" men or women in this country in non-essential jobs.

He said that all single men are being re-examined and reclassified and will be either in the army or essential industry. He added that single men would not be allowed to return to non-essential jobs if they were turned down by the army.

Concientious objectors, Mr. Mitchell said, would be taken from camps and put on farms to help the war effort. Use of prisoner-of-war labor was also under consideration, the minister said.

Taxes Win Out Over Bank Liens

VICTORIA, April 10.—Attorney-General R. L. Maitland has just received notification from Ottawa of a judgment on reference to the Supreme Court of Canada in favor of a contention of the province, in association with Alberta, Saskatchewan and Quebec, that municipal taxes constitute a preferred lien on property above bank and mortgage liens.

The reference was made by the Dominion Government to the Supreme Court on legislation passed in Alberta giving priority over bank and mortgage liens to municipal taxes.

U.S. To Import Feed From Canada

WASHINGTON, April 10.—(AP)—Plans for importation of livestock feed supplies from Canada and Australia were announced today by Chester Davis, United States food administrator, who also announced a new price control and production program, including a five-cents-a-bushel boost in the ceiling price of corn in surplus producing areas.

MUST MAIL FORMS

Start City-wide Compulsory Housing Survey on Thursday

A total of 77,481 householders in Vancouver, North Vancouver and part of Burnaby will be asked to reveal what living accommodation their homes contain with the delivery of forms in Vancouver's compulsory housing survey Thursday and Friday.

Forms to be filled in and returned in five days will be delivered by mail carriers. The deadline for the return of the completed forms will be April 21. No postage is required for their return.

L. S. Davis, executive assistant to the Real Property Administrator in Ottawa, who is here to conduct the survey, emphasizes that there is no question of compulsory billeting; the survey is to determine what housing accommodation is available. It is compulsory, howover, to complete the forms and return them.

SIX QUESTIONS.

The forms ask six simple questions. They will ask:

1. How many rooms in the house?
2. What type of rooms are they? Living-room, bedroom, kitchen, etc.?
3. How many people live in the house?
4. What is their relationship to the householder? Family, boarders, etc.?
5. Would you be willing to offer accommodation in your home?
6. Waht ttype of accommodation can you offer? Complete, self-contained unit? Sleeping room? Kitchen privileges?

Compulsory housing surveys have already been carried out at Windsor, lKngston, St. Catharines, Sarnia and Brandon and a survey is now proceeding at Ottawa.

First Sinking off U.S. Since Summer

WASHINGTON, April 10.—(AP)—The first sinking of a merchant vessel off the United States east coast by an enemy submarine since last summer was announced today by the U. S. navy.

"A medium-sized United States merchant vessel was torpedoed and sunk by an enemy submarine early in April off the east coast of the United States," the navy said. "Survivors have landed at Miami, Fla."

Mussolini Reported Preparing to Move

LONDON, April 10.—(AP)—Reuters reported in a Zurich despatch today that Mussolini was understood to be preparing to evacuate his government from Rome.

The despatch said Mussolini was reported to have appointed secret commissions to make the necessary arrangements. Florence and Bologna have been mentioned as likely places for the new seat of government, it said.

U.S. Bombers Surprise Japs

WITH THE U. S. AIR FORCE IN CHINA, April 9—(Delayed)—(AP)—Japanese-occupied Fort Bayard, its airdrome, radio station and dock area and the nearby Japanese commander's headquarters in the former French-leased territory of Kwangchowan, on the South China coast, were heavily attacked by American P-40s today.

No planes were found on the airdrome and there was no enemy attempt to intercept, although the raiders met anti-aircraft fire which slightly damaged three planes.

"The Japs apparently had no warning of the raid, which was the first in this area and a great surprise," said Major Harry M. F. Partage.

Nearly 10,000 rounds of heavy-calibre machine gun bullets nosed into warehouses and other installations and several pilots reported seeing Japanese soldiers killed.

One flyer observed the dock area in flames from incendiary bullets.

". . . . IF YOU CAN GET IT"

Sawdust Restriction Lifted

Fuel restrictions which limit the amount of sawdust and mill-wood purchased or stored by a consumer have been lifted until further notice, R. M. Brown, regional wood fuel officer, announced today.

Purchase of wood fuel was previously limited to two units of sawdust and two cords of wood if the consumer's bins were empty.

Today's order allows Vancouver home owners all the sawdust and wood they want . . . if they can get it.

City fuel dealers said they believed the order, which comes at a time when milder weather makes the fuel problem less svere, is designed to clear the way for a general stocking up of sawdust and wood in Vancouver basements during the summer months when fuel may be more plentiful.

Eighth Army Sweeps Past Key Axis City

Hint Rommel Is Surrendering All But Pocket Around Tunis

"A FIRST-CLASS DUNKERQUE"

ALLIED HEADQUARTERS, North Africa, April 10.—(AP)—Gen. Sir Bernard Montgomery, in a message thanking his 8th Army for its victories at Mareth and the Gabes Gap, urged his men on to even greater efforts today.

"Let us make the enemy face up to and endure a first-class Dunkerque on the beaches of Tunis," his message said.

(Tunisian war map on Page 7)

By EDWARD KENNEDY.
(Associated Press Staff Writer.)

ALLIED HEADQUARTERS, April 10.—Gen. Sir Bernard L. Montgomery's 8th Army occupied Sfax, third largest Axis-held Tunisian city and port, in a lightning pursuit of Field Marshal Erwin Rommel's Africa Corps today, crushing opposition and continuing its northward chase up the coast.

Rommel, strongly posting his armor in the mountain passes to hold off side-door attacks by British, Americans and French, appeared headed for a surrender of nearly all Tunisia and establishment of a new defense line on a ridge in the Enfidaville area only 40 miles south of Tunis.

The British pursuit was being pressed by four divisions, plus armor.

Heavy Allied bombers worked in close harmony with naval aircraft in pounding the lines of retreating forces, already badly mauled.

(A Morocco radio broadcast, recorded in London, said planes from aircraft carriers were bombing the coastal road.)

GAIN 40 MILES IN DAY

Hurling themselves forward with crushing speed, Montgomery's veterans had gained about 40 miles in 24 hours, occupying Mahares, 50 miles north of Gabes, and sweeping on through Sfax, where they were about 150 miles south of Tunis.

The city was occupied at 8:15 a.m.

At the same time British, Americans and French on Rommel's flank launched successful new attacks in the central and northern sectors.

Today's communique from Allied headquarters said the British 1st Army again had advanced and had marked up a 10-mile gain in the last four days in the Medjez-el-Bab area.

Americans and French combined to capture high ground north and south of Fondouk, occupying Pichon, north of Fondouk, and cleaning out an area 80 miles northwest of Sfax. A new threat to Rommel's rear appeared to be shaping up.

The 1st Army had taken 1000 prisoners since beginning its offensive April 6 and the Americans and French captured 500 more in their advance in the central sector, the communique disclosed.

This brought Axis prisoners to more than 20,000 since the break through the Mareth Line.

SCANT AERIAL OPPOSITION

Hurled back at all points where the Allies' attacked, the Axis was able to put up but scant opposition in the air.

Allied pilots reported the German bomber crews bailed out at the approach of Allied fighters withou even a shot being fired.

ITALIAN GENERAL TAKEN.

Caught in the rush of British and American forces from the south and the side was General Mannerini, commander of an Italian Saharan group, who was taken prisoner at his headquarters when he was cut off by the junction of the United States 2nd Army Corps and the 8th Army.

While Rommel's withdrawal was still too methodical to be called a rout, the speed with which the Axis forces were retreating made it nearly so.

The 8th Army's vehicles were rushing ahead so fast that for the first time, Rommel's sappers had little or no time to plant mines to delay the pursuit.

Today's communique said British advance elements were still fighting the Axis rearguard of infantry and tanks, however.

BEATEN IN TANK BATTLES.

It was disclosed today that Rommel, after being driven back from the Wadi el Agarit line 20 miles north of Gabes, pulled his men back to a bottleneck between the sea and the Sebkret en Noual salt marsh west of La Skhirra and stood in that position 15 miles north of El Akarit until Thursday morning.

Montgomery attacked and a battle was fought southeast of the swampy lake that morning.

The enemy forces withdrew and by late afternoon had formed a screen around Mezzouna to the northwest on the road from Maknassy to Mahares in a desperate attempt to prevent the Americans in the Maknassy area from cutting them off in an attack on their rear.

(Continued on Page 2.)
See TUNISIA.

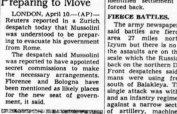

Allies Capture Both Tunis, Bizerte

TRIUMPH IN TUNISIA

Nazi Defeat Turned Into Debacle

The Vancouver Sun

The Vancouver Evening Newspaper Owned and Operated by Vancouver People

FOUNDED 1886 VOL. LVII—No. 182 VANCOUVER, B.C., FRIDAY, MAY 7, 1943 PRICE 5 CENTS $1.00 per month BY CARRIER

FINAL

Axis Ousted From Last Strongholds In North Africa

Official Announcement Bares Overwhelming Success of Two-Day Massed Drive; Enemy Literally Blown From Air and Land Defenses

By Associated Press

ALLIED HEADQUARTERS, NORTH AFRICA, May 7.—The capture of both Tunis and Bizerte was announced officially tonight. The capitulation of the Axis armies in their last two main African bases occurred late in the second day of overwhelming, air-supported drives.

By EDWARD KENNEDY
Associated Press Staff Writer

ALLIED HEADQUARTERS, NORTH AFRICA, May 7.—The doom of Hitler's legions in Northern Africa swept nearer with lightning speed today as the British First Army, aided by the greatest artillery, tank and aerial forces yet seen in this theatre of war, drove across the Tunis plains and smashed through the outer defenses of Tunis before the paralyzed Axis hordes could stem the tide. With few facilities for prolonged defense, capture of the city was held certain within a short period.

(A Morocco Radio broadcast recorded by the Associated Press said:

("Every minute reports pour in which indicate the magnitude of the Allied victories and the defeat of the Axis forces, which now constitutes a total debacle.")

Meanwhile after day and night fighting, the American 2nd Army Corps stormed and captured Ferryville, naval dockyard town on the southern shore of Lake Bizerte, and then drove on into the outskirts of the great naval base itself. First Allied troops to crash the city's outskirts were native French Moroccan Goums, spearheading the rapid drive of a French-U.S. army fighting along the seacoast north of the Lake.

Fierce fighting was reported in progress in both sectors as the British 1st Army and American forces capitalized on deep penetrations through collapsing enemy positions all along the northern Tunisian front.

"Our troops have continued their victorious advance," a special communique said.

Heaviest fighting raged about Tunis, the capital, as the Germans and Italians vainly sought to check the offensive.

The Tunis suburb of Le Bardo, where the treaty which made Tunisia a French protectorate was signed in 1880, was occupied by British forces.

The Bey of Tunis has his main palace in Le Bardo. It was not learned here whether the Bey remained there, moved into Tunis or had fled to Europe by the Axis.

Signs of 'Dunkirk' Under Way

Meanwhile in aerial action Allied aircraft—bombers and fighters—sank a dozen vessels, including a destroyer, and damaged 15 others.

As some of these were heading toward Italy it might be said the Axis had started a partial evacuation, though all indications are that it will not be able even to attempt getting out the bulk of its forces in Tunisia.

(A broadcast by Grant Parr, NBC reporter attached to Allied headquarters, said 25 enemy ships had been "sunk in the Tunisian straits," suggesting another powerful sweep against surface transports which might attempt to withdraw the Axis survivors.

("The spirit of the German troops appears to have been broken," Parr said.)

Allied planes, completely dominating the sky, maintained heavy attacks upon Axis transport columns which clogged the roads of retreat.

"Because of complete air domination," said a statement issued by the RAF and the USAAF, "the tactical

Please Turn to Page Four See "War in Africa"

Russians Split Hun Defenses

Red Army Thrust in Novorossisk Costs Axis 10,000 Men

By EDDY GILMORE
Associated Press Staff Writer

MOSCOW, May 7. — The Red Army, smashing forward in increasingly violent battles which have cost the Germans nearly 10,000 dead, has driven a wedge between the German and Rumanian forces operating north and south of the Kuban river in the Caucasus and is tightening its net about Novorossisk, front line dispatches reported today.

Aided by strong air forces, Soviet troops cut one road after another in the Kuban valley, severing Axis supply lines and avenues of escape.

One dispatch said the Russians cut an important road and captured a height dominating the approaches to a large city, the name of which was not given.

Red Star, army newspaper, said the Germans were pouring

Please Turn to Page Four See "Russia"

B.C. Buys Some More Victory Bonds

VICTORIA, May 7—(CP)—The government of British Columbia bought another $105,000 in Victory Loan Bonds today, making a total of $8,405,000. Today's purchase came from Workmen's Compensation Board funds.

BASEBALL

AMERICAN LEAGUE

Philadelphia ..	000 000 101—2	6	1
New York	004 010 10x—6	10	1

Black, Burrows and Swift; Wagner, Wensloff and Dickey.

NATIONAL LEAGUE

Brooklyn	030 000 211—9	10	2
Boston	103 201 000—7	15	1

Head, Webber (5), Allen (7) and Owen; Javery, Jeffcoat, Tobin (9) and Klutlz.

KEEP SMILING

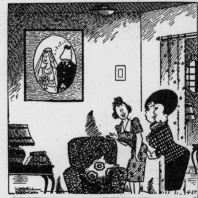

"And this is my husband—he had a rather blank expression on our wedding day!"

Oakalla Fugitive Flees Bullets

Several shots were fired by Oakalla Prison guards as Thomas Kenyon, 18, convicted robber, ran into the bush in a successful bid for freedom about 10:30 a.m. today.

None of the shots hit the fleeing convict.

Prison officials reported that Kenyon was working near bush outside the prison walls.

They said he dropped his tools and ran towards the bush.

Guards immediately spotted him and fired in an effort to halt him.

Search was immediately started of the surrounding bush country but, failing to find traces of the youth, prison officials spread the alarm throughout the Lower Mainland.

Prison officials said that Kenyon had only two months more to serve of a six-month sentence imposed in Chilliwack for theft of groceries.

Prairies Hit By 'Worst' May Blizzard

WINNIPEG, May 7—(CP)—Winter returned to Manitoba Thursday as the worst May blizzard in five years brought a halt to farming operations, delayed air and highway transportation and left a thin blanket of snow over a wide area.

Temperatures dropped quickly and the low for the day at Winnipeg was 27 degrees above zero. Melfort, Sask., was the coldest spot on the prairies during the night with a low of 18 above zero.

Cleaners Protest New 'Callup' Order

VICTORIA, May 7—(CP)—Mayor Andrew McGavin today wired Arthur McNamara, director of Selective Service, endorsing the protest of local dry cleaners against Labor Department ruling requiring employees of the industry in the military call-up categories to report for possible transfer to more essential industries.

Clark Gable in Antwerp Raid

LONDON, May 7—(AP)—**Capt. Clark Gable went on his first raid in the flying fortress attack on May 4 on Antwerp and "enjoyed it and learned a lot," the U.S. Eighth Air Force today quoted him as saying.**

Capt. Gable, former film star, flew as an observer on a fortress which went through the raid without encountering enemy plane and sustained only two small flak holes.

Hitler Finds German War Losses 'Tragic'

NEW YORK, May 7—(AP)—Hitler, speaking at a funeral service today for Viktor Lutze, Storm Troop chief of staff, who was fatally injured May 3 in a motor car accident near Potsdam, said that the National Socialist Party's losses were particularly heavy in a war that had claimed many sacrifices of men, women and even children.

"It is particularly tragic for me to experience how almost every year one or other fighter or co-operator is becoming one of those who, according to the author of the National Socialist revolutionary song, are marching with us in spirit," he said in the speech broadcast to Germany.

"We have achieved what he fought for—a Reich made secure against its enemies by its own strength and upheld by its own people," Hitler said.

Propaganda Minister Goebbels, who also spoke at the services held in the mosaic hall of the Reichschancellery, told the German people that Lutze's 18-year-old daughter also died in the accident.

New U.S. Base in Alaska

Island Close to Kiska Well Fortified

By WILLIAM L. WORDEN
Associated Press Staff Writer

AMCHITKA ISLAND AIRBASE, Feb. 16. — Despite a series of eight Japanese bombing raids, this United States air base only a few minutes flight from Kiska Island went into operation today.

Less than 18 hours after the latest attempt to bomb the operation to a standstill, American fighting planes landed on a new flying field this morning. By the time they landed no trace was left of any damage done by Japanese planes.

This island, only about five miles wide, is the nearest piece of land to Kiska, save for a few minute dots unfit for bases.

A month ago it contained only the barren tundra and the ruins of an Aleut village nestled between the low hills.

Today the village has disappeared except for half a dozen Russian orthodox crosses marking the old cemetery.

These crosses now are grotesque in the midst of anti-aircraft and ground force installations.

The ancient harbor, formerly used only by fishing boats, tiny native craft and occasional survey vessels, is filled now with warships and cargo carriers which have in a few weeks poured in supplies for a formidable army.

That army is so well dug in that the eight Japanese raids have been withstood with negligible casualties and no property damage.

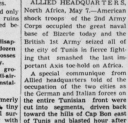

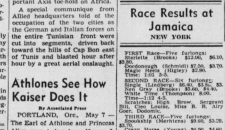

LATE NEWS BULLETINS

Admits Theft of Letter

VICTORIA, May 7—(CP)—Edgar Madden Dunn, postal clerk, pleaded guilty today to charges of stealing a letter and of opening a letter. He was remanded for sentence to Saturday when postal inspectors from Vancouver will be here to give evidence.

F.D.R. Favors Canadian System

WASHINGTON, May 7—(AP)—President Roosevelt was reported today to have approved the principle of subsidizing the cost of living with government money.

(This is the system already in effect in Canada.)

Post-War Business Boom

WINNIPEG, May 7—(CP)—A post-war boom in business produced by the backlog of consumer needs now being built up was forecast today by W. E. Davidson of Winnipeg speaking at a Credit Men's Conference. He said that profits after the war would be very narrow due to increased competition and continuation of taxes.

'We Are Still in Chains'

LONDON, May 7—(CP)—Lieut. Arthur M. Hueston of Sarnia, Ont., officer in the Essex Scottish Regiment who was taken prisoner at Dieppe last summer, wrote in a card received in London today that "we are still in chains."

Terrific Air Bombardment Forced Climax

By VIRGIL PINKLEY
United Press Staff Correspondent

ALLIED HEADQUARTERS, North Africa, May 7.—American shock troops of the 2nd Army Corps occupied the great naval base of Bizerte today and the British 1st Army seized all of the city of Tunis in fierce fighting that smashed the last important Axis toe-hold on Africa.

A special communique from Allied headquarters told of the occupation of the two cities as the German and Italian forces on the entire Tunisian front were cut into segments, driven back toward the hills of Cap Bon east of Tunis and blasted hour after hour by a great aerial onslaught.

Athlones See How Kaiser Does It

By Associated Press

PORTLAND, Ore., May 7 — The Earl of Athlone and Princess Alice saw today how Henry J. Kaiser sets records for ship construction when they visited Kaiser's three yards in Portland and Vancouver, Wash., and participated in the launching of the tanker S.S. Fort Dearborn.

Before leaving Portland Saturday they will inspect war housing projects and visit Vancouver, Wash., barracks.

Two Measles Deaths In Victoria Area

VICTORIA, May 7—(CP)—The Times said today two fatalities from measles had been reported in outlying districts of Victoria as in the city itself 25 more cases were listed in the past two days, bringing the total since the beginning of the year to 635, mainly since the start of April.

Race Results at Jamaica

NEW YORK

FIRST Race—Five furlongs:
Sterlette (Brooks) $12.00, $6.10, $3.80.
Docdonough (Schmidl) $7.50, $3.70.
Magic Heels (Higley) $2.90.
Time: 1:01 3-5.

SECOND RACE—Six furlongs:
Single (Lindberg) $6.40, $3.80, $3.
Nen Gray (Brooks) $5.60, $4.40.
White Time (Thompson) 8.00.
Time—1:12 4-5.
Scratches: High Brow, Sergeant Bill, Cleo Louise, Miss B. B, Airy Goer, Dodomic.

THIRD RACE—Five furlongs:
Spookship (Merhtens) $9.60, $5.20, $3.70.
Crazy Horse (Young) $6.90, $4.60.
Test Flight (Brooks) $4.70.
Time—1:02 1-5.

FOURTH RACE—Six furlongs:
Camptown (McCreary) $4.50, $3.30, $2.90.
Lovely One (Reinzl) $14.70, $8.50.
Golden Fleece (Deering) . $7.70.
Sratches—Sea Loard, Sun Storm, Tricks, Tim o' Shank, Devie, Marmaduke.
Time—1:14 2-5.

FIFTH RACE—Mile and one-sixteenth:
Pomayya (Robertson $7.10, $3.10, $2.70.
Vagrancy (Malley) $3.00, $2.50.
What Not (Murphy) $4.90.
Time—1:13.

SIXTH RACE—Six furlongs:
Ariel Play (Brooks) $13.10, $6.80, $6.00.
Rewarded (Atkinson) $4.70, $4.00.
Head Over Heels (Grohs) $6.60.
Time—1:13.

SEVENTH RACE—Mile and one-eighth:
Cherry T (Reinzl) $6.80, $2.90, $2.60.
Free Speech (Brooks) $2.60, $2.60.
xTop Suit (Skyrm) $4.30.
xSouth Drive (McCreary) $2.60.
xDead heat for third place.
Time—1.53 4-5.

Race Entries on Page 14

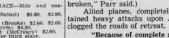

Alexander's Victory Order

By Canadian Press

LONDON, May 7.—Gen. Sir Harold Alexander declared in an order of the day to his Army Group on the eve of the great Tunisian offensive:

"Soldiers of the Allies:

"We have reached the last phase of this campaign. We have grouped our victorious armies and are going to drive the enemy into the sea.

"We have got them just where we want them—with their backs to the wall.

"You have proved yourselves masters of the battlefield and therefore you will win this last great battle which will give us the whole of North Africa.

"The eyes of the world are on you and the hopes of those at home.

"Forward then to victory!"

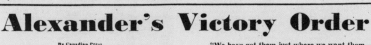

U.S. Subs Sink Ten Japanese Ships

ONTARIO MILLIONAIRE DIES MYSTERIOUSLY

PROBE DEATH

SIR HARRY OAKES, BART.
Multi-millionaire, whose death police are investigating.

The Vancouver Sun
The Vancouver Evening Newspaper Owned and Operated by Vancouver People
FOUNDED 1886
VOL. LVII—No. 231 VANCOUVER, B.C., THURSDAY, JULY 8, PRICE 5 CENTS

5 ★★★ ★★

Fresh Hun Troops in Red Battle

400,000 Germans Storm Soviet Lines In Costly Effort to Isolate Kursk; 30,000 Slain in Three Days

By WILLIAM McGAFFIN
Associated Press Staff Writer.

MOSCOW, July 8.—Fresh Nazi reserves were reported pushing through smoke and dust along paths marked by wrecked machines and the dead today to bolster the Kursk plains offensive which the Red Army, fighting more brilliantly than ever before, has limited to small gains in the Belgorod sector.

Russian forces killed 30,000 Germans, destroyed or damaged 1539 tanks and shot down 649 planes in the first three days of the battle, it was announced officially.

Nazi air squadrons are attached constantly to the armored columns under a new German plan of attack by which Hitler's high command hopes to pinch off the 60-mile deep Soviet salient extending westward from Kursk. The immediate assignment of the Germans obviously is to attempt to push north from Belgorod and south from Orel, 165 miles apart, to a junction somewhere behind the Russian-held rail city.

(A Berlin military spokesman declared in a radio broadcast that tank battles yesterday in the area of Belgorod and south of Orel were "the greatest ever fought on the Eastern Front.").

TANK AGAINST TANK

Soviet dispatches said the Germans were finding their objectives packed with Red Army men determined to fight to the death rather than give an inch. The Red Air Force was declared to be on at least an equal footing with the German.

The Russians for the most part are fighting tanks with stationary artillery, but also are employing tanks against tanks, a throwback to earlier tactics. A Tass correspondent said Soviet medium tanks made in Britain had engaged a group of 60-ton tigers—approximately double their size—and destroyed four.

(A Transocean dispatch broadcast by the Berlin radio said air forces were used by both sides in masses hardly ever witnessed before and that both Germans and Russians "now are employing tanks in unexampled numbers."

(The German high command communique, also broadcast from Berlin, declared army units, artillery, fighter-bombers and tactical air forces destroyed more than 400 Soviet tanks and 193 planes yesterday.)

Veronica Lake Becomes Mother

HOLLYWOOD, July 8—(AP)—Screen actress Veronica Lake gave birth today to a three-pound boy, two months prematurely. The child was placed in an incubator and her physician said both apparently are doing well.

Miss Lake went to the hospital last Thursday after she tripped and fell on a motion picture set.

Her husband, Maj. John Detlie, is in the army in Seattle.

Crete Put Into 'State Of Siege'

By JOHN PARRIS
Special to The Vancouver Sun
Copyright, 1943, by British United Press

LONDON, July 8.—The Axis high command has ordered a state of siege on Crete and two other key Aegean islands, on the Balkan invasion route, an Ankara dispatch said today as Lisbon reported almost daily arrival of convoys in North Africa with huge quantities of war material for Allied armies.

Axis broadcasts estimated the Allies had concentrated 1,000,000 tons of shipping on the coast of North Africa, presumably including the vessels and equipment needed to move against the European coastline.

Siege orders affecting Crete, nearby Scarpanto and Lero Island to the north followed a British Commando-like raid feeling out the Crete defenses, reportedly manned by 180,000 German troops, Ankara said.

Lisbon said the convoys moving past Gibraltar suffered only insignificant losses because of strong air and naval escorts.

In Algiers the French ministry of information announced that the Germans had ordered a number of areas on both the Atlantic and Mediterranean coastlines of France evacuated because they are "urgently threatened."

The order was described as a Nazi attempt to "drain France of her youth and resistant elements before an Allied landing occurs."

The areas affected include Sete (West of Marseilles) on the Mediterranean and Hendaye, Saint Jean de Luz, Baronne and Biarritz on the Bay of Biscay.

Race Entries on Page 22

Late News Bulletins

BOMBS EXPLODE

RED BLUFF, Cal., July 8—(BUP)—Ten tons of fragmentation bombs carried on a truck trailer exploded on the Red Bluff-Mineral highway in a blast felt 18 miles miles away, county authorities reported. No injuries were reported.

CALDER IN HOSPITAL

LONDON, July 8 — (CP Cable)—Flying Officer Jack Calder, RCAF observer, who has been interned in Eire since he was forced to bail out there in October, 1941, has been transferred to a hospital in England for medical attention, it was reliably learned today.

BATTLES FOR LIFE

CHICAGO, July 8 — (BUP)—Fred B. Snite, Jr., who has lived for seven years in an iron lung, waged a new battle for his life today after suffering a heart attack. Snite, 32, an infantile paralysis victim, was stricken by the heart attack a week ago, his family disclosed.

JAPANESE AGENT

NEW YORK, July 8 — (AP)—A federal grand jury today indicted Frederick Heizer Wright, identified as a Daily News copy editor, on charges that for 10 years he had acted as a paid agent of the Japanese government and had not notified the state department of his employment.

GREEKS RESIGN

LONDON, July 8—(CP)—The Algiers Radio reported today the Minister of Public Works and Chief of Police at Athens have resigned as a result of street demonstrations by Greek patriots following upon Allied air raids on landing fields near Athens and Salonika two weeks ago.

APPROVE BILL

WASHINGTON, July 8—(BUP) — The Senate today approved by voice vote and sent to the House a bill to increase the government's allotments to certain dependents of enlisted men in the armed forces. The allotment for the first child of a service man would go from $12 to $16 a month. The allotment for each additional child would be $11 a month instead of $10.

Clapper Writes From Africa

Raymond Clapper, whose articles from Sweden and England won him wide acclaim—one of them being reprinted in Readers' Digest—is now in North Africa. The leading Washington commentator - reporter will do a series of articles that will be carried exclusively in The Vancouver Sun. His first article will be found on Page 4 (Editorial) today.

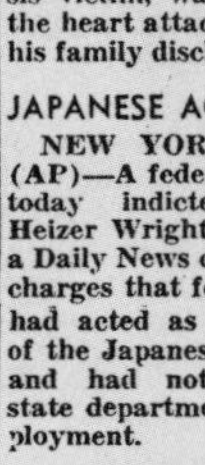

IS IT TRUE WHAT SHE SAYS ABOUT DIXIE?

HOPE DARE DAVIS

The former Broadway show girl, charges cruelty and asked $200 monthly alimony in a Los Angeles divorce suit against "Dixie" Davis, one-time "attorney-general" of the Dutch Shultz rackets. She said that Dixie now has a $250 weekly income from his Burbank ice cream business and his interest in a road show. Hope married Davis about the time he was appearing before New York's racket-busting Thomas Dewey, contributing colorful testimony on the activities of the Shultz racketeers.

Callers at 6:30 a.m.

'Come Back at 8'; Two Bandits Do

Two bold young thugs, one of whom was armed, carried out a daylight robbery in the heart of the downtown district here this morning when they bound and gagged Moses Freeman at his jewelry store, 507 Richards Street, at 8 o'clock and escaped with $250 and $1000 worth of jewelry.

Freeman told police that the same two youths came to his door at 6:30 a.m. and asked him to unlock the door so that they could enter and buy a watch.

Freeman replied that he was not open for business so early in the day, and asked them to return at 8 a.m.

The men returned promptly at 8, shortly after the storekeeper had opened his safe in preparation for the day's business.

"IT'S A HOLDUP"

One of the men brandished a revolver and told Freeman that it was "a holdup."

The other tied Freeman's wrists and legs with telephone wire, gagged him with a towel and dragged him to the rear of the store.

The young men then took $250 and some diamonds from the safe and made their escape at about 8:20.

Fifteen minuts later Mrs. H. Gilfin, 1046 Seymour, was passing the shop when she heard a muffled cry within.

She drew the attention of a truck driver and he summoned aid.

Inspector E. Pettit and Detective Alex Paton, who were summoned to the scene, received "fair" descriptions of the men. Freeman told them that one wore a raincoat.

At 9 a.m. police picked up two young men, one of whom carried a raincoat.

The two men were taken to police station, and Freeman was asked whether they were the same men who held him up.

Freeman replied that he could not definitely identify them.

Detective Superintendent Gordon Grant told The Vancouver Sun that he did not think there would be sufficient grounds to detain the two men, and that they would be released.

"Their faces were uncovered when I let them in, but when they were tying me up they were wearing handkerchiefs over their faces," Freeman told The Vancouver Sun.

Both bandits were of slight build, with a dark complexion and were described by the victim as "good looking." One was wearing a black raincoat, had dark hair and carried the gun. The other was wearing a long khaki coat.

(Picture on Page 2)

Sir Harry Oakes Left Estate of $200,000,000

Fly Miami Police to Nassau to Investigate Death of Famous Canadian Exile

By Associated Press

NASSAU, Bahamas, July 8.—Sir Harry Oakes, Bart., one of the richest men in the world, died at his home here last night. The body was found this morning, and officials immediately launched an investigation.

(At Miami, Fla., the Daily News said Detective Captain James J. Baker and Captain E. W. Melchen of the Miami homicide squad had been summoned to Nassau this morning on a secret mission.)

Oakes, whose fortune was rated at $200 million, was made a baronet in 1938, was born at Sangerville, Me., December 23, 1874.

Sir Harry maintained homes at Niagara Falls, Ont.; London, Eng.; Palm Beach and Nassau.

HEALTH AND TAXES

Oakes, whose income was estimated in 1939 to be about five-and-a-half millions, left Canada because he got tired of paying taxes.

"When a man has money he has to keep two jumps ahead of the people who are trying to take it off him," he told a newspaperman who interviewed him in the Bahamas in June, 1939.

But that wasn't the only reason, he insisted. He said he was near choking to death with bronchial trouble. He was living in Niagara Falls, Ont., which he admitted was a nice little city but had a Canadian climate.

So in 1934, Harry Oakes, verging on 60, with five children, a couple of hundred million dollars and the world like a pack of hounds on his tail, picked up and left Oak Hall, his magnificent Niagara Falls home, and headed for the Bahamas.

$17,500 A DAY

When he was named in the King's birthday honors in 1939 there were loud protests from across the country about a man who had made his fortune in Canada, and then fled to a country where there is no income tax. But the new Sir Harry was untroubled by the criticism.

He claimed he hadn't been able to live in Canada, where he was a naturalized citizen, more than 90 days a year and at the rate of taxes he was paying that meant $17,500 a day for calling the Dominion home. He just didn't think it made sense.

Harry Oakes was born in Maine, prospected for gold in the Yukon in '98, risked his life prospecting for gold in New Zealand, starved and froze all over the world until he drove his stakes into a little plot of earth at Kirkland Lake and called it Lake Shore Mine. Since 1916 Lake Shore Mine has been pouring millions into his pockets.

Four More Jap Ships Damaged

WASHINGTON, July 8—(AP)—The United States Navy announced today that American submarines had sunk 10 enemy non-combatant ships and damaged four others in the Pacific.

A Navy communique said:

"Pacific and Far East:

United States submarines have reported the following results of operations against the enemy in the waters of these areas:

One large transport sunk,

One medium-sized transport sunk,

Two medium-sized cargo vessels sunk,

One large tanker sunk,

One medium-sized tanker sunk,

One large cargo vessel sunk,

One medium-sized passenger cargo vessel sunk,

One small cargo vessel sunk,

One small schooner sun.

Four medium-sized cargo vessels damaged.

These actions have not been announced in any previous Navy communiques."

American submarines have now sunk or damaged a total of 283 enemy ships in he Pacific area, according to Navy communiques. The total includes 200 sunk, 29 probably sunk and 54 damaged.

Airman Falls 20,000 Feet, Lives

NEW DELHI, July 8—(CP)—A record-breaking delayed parachute drop was made by an RAF pilot, Warrant Officer Francis D. C. Brown of Canterbury, New Zealand, who fell 20,000 feet while unconscious and lived to tell about it.

In a half-dazed condition Brown pulled his rip-cord when only 3000 feet from the ground and landed safely. He escaped from his plane after it had been damaged.

Gen. Giraud Will Visit Ottawa

OTTAWA, July 8—(CP)—Prime Minister Mackenzie King today told Commons he expects Gen. Henri Giraud will visit Canada within the next week or 10 days.

The House applauded.

BASEBALL

AMERICAN LEAGUE

Washington	100 001 000—	2	7	2
Cleveland	022 010 00x—	5	5	0

Pyle, Haefner (3) and Early; Reynolds and Rosar.

Boston	001 000 010—	2	7	1
St. Louis	100 020 20x—	3	12	0

Dobson, Lucier (7), Woods (8) and Conroy; Sundra and Hayes.

NATIONAL LEAGUE

Cincinnati	000 001 000—	5	10	0
Philadelphia	301 001 000—	5	10	0

Vandermeer and Mueller; Johnson, Dietz (4), Matheson (7), Fuchs (9) and Livingston.

Atherton Confirmed

WASHINGTON, July 8—(AP)—Ray Atherton of the State Department was confirmed by the Senate yesterday as United States Minister to Canada.

Women To Run BCER Cars

Women will be employed by the British Electric Railway Co. Ltd., on Vancouver street cars to relieve the manpower shortage, aggravated by increasing wartime transportattion demands, as soon as facilities can be provided for them, it was learned today.

First of the feminine conductors and motormen are expected to be taken on within the next month, while no figures are available on the number of women streetcar operators to be hired at first, they will probably total up to 50, with more employed later as the need requires.

UNION APPROVES

The move has the full backing of the Street Railwaymen's Union which recently approved the employment of women to aid the strained personnel of some 1200 men.

"We are getting desperate for men," said Charles Stewart, union president. "We want more help and we hope that women will be taken on as soon as possible. At present the men can't get an extra day off at any time. There just aren't men to take their places."

Seventy men left the car service recently and there is a possibility another 70 may go shortly.

MEN JOIN UP

Increased transportation services required by wartime needs and the inability to get replacements for men leaving the service for other jobs or on superannuation brought employment of women on the streetcar system to the front.

Generally the present male personnel on the cars is not within military draft call, but Stewart pointed out that if the callup age were raised to affect many of the men, the need for women would increase accordingly, possibly up to several hundred.

Clinic Burns Down

WATROUS, Sask., July 8—(CP)—The Manitou Beach health clinic and annex were completely destroyed by fire this morning.

'Killed Every Jap'

By HAROLD GUARD
United Press Staff Correspondent

SOMEWHERE IN NEW GUINEA, July 7 — (BUP)—(Delayed)—Allied bombers dropped 106 tons of bombs and fired thousands of machine-gun bullets on the four square miles of New Guinea jungle, near Mubo, today, probably killing every Japanese soldier in the area with the heaviest co-ordinated aerial blow on a land objective ever made in the Southwest Pacific.

As the fliers cleared out after the 45-minute raid, Australian ground troops pushed through the smoking jungle terrain and captured Observation Hill, a mile north of Mubo.

I rode with the crew of a bomber on this attack. More than 50 Liberators, Mitchells and strafing craft took part, under the heaviest kind of fighter cover. Not since the Bismarck sea battle had a continuous operation assumed such proportions and this one was pinpointed, while that was spread over a wide area.

The crew of our Mitchell agreed after the attack that it would be a miracle if any Japanese soldiers were alive in the area. Thick black smoke shrouded the entire target area as we wheeled for home.

VANCOUVER ✠ NEWS-HERALD

WAR EXTRA

VOL. 11, NO. 65   VANCOUVER, B.C., FRIDAY, JULY 9, 1943.   PRICE 5¢   By Carrier, 85c Month, Outside City, 5c copy.

CANADIANS LAND IN SICILY; INVASION ON

"All Canada Will Be Proud," King

OTTAWA July 10 (CP)—Armed forces of Canada are "in the forefront of an attack which has as its ultimate objective the unconditional surrender of Italy and Germany," Prime Minister Mackenzie King said in a statement confirming that Canadians are in the Allied force which attacked Sicily early this morning, Mediterranean time.

"All Canada will be justifiably proud to know that units of the Canadian Army are a part of the Allied force engaged in this attack," the prime minister said.

"The soldiers of Canada have gone into battle exceptionally well-trained, superbly equipped, keen and full of spirit, ready for offensive warfare."

Mr. King, who had received the news somewhat in advance of the announcement to the public, had prepared his statement for use when the information was released generally.

The prime minister had sat through a day and evening session of the House and had just left for his home when the news was flashed.

When the House adjourned at 11 o'clock at night the prime minister, discussing the subject for consideration when the House resumes Monday, said he could not foretell what would happen in 24 hours but hoped to be able to proceed with his external affairs estimates.

To spectators in the galleries his words seemed to indicate that he expected some important war developments.

Defence Minister Ralston was in the prime minister's office in the Parliament Building with Mr. King's secretary, Walter Turnbull, when the flash came announcing the landing.

The defence minister said he would have no statement to make tonight and would not comment in any way on the latest development.

Mr. Turnbull said the prime minister would go on the air at the time of the first news broadcast Saturday morning—8 a.m., E.D.T.

There was no immediate information as to whether Canadian naval forces were participating in the attack.

R.C.A.F. squadrons seemed likely to have taken part.

Four Years' Work Backs Canuck Blow

OTTAWA, July 10.—(CP)—Nearly four years of hard work, study, accumulation of weapons, training and patient waiting is behind the Canadian Army as it moves into Sicily with British and United States Forces on one of the biggest ventures yet undertaken by the armed forces of the United Nations in the present war.

While the role of the Canadian Army in this venture may not be fully disclosed for some time it is a self-sufficient, heavily mechanized and fully-trained force ready for any type of operation, capable of hitting hard and travelling fast.

While the circumstances of war favored the building of the Canadian Army to its present size and state of efficiency, its creation out of the youth of a practically demilitarized nation has been the full-time job of thousands of the keenest and boldest men of the country for upwards of three years—from the army commander, Lt.-Gen. A. G. L. McNaughton, down.

When war broke out in September, 1939, Canada had a permanent army of 4500 men with a non-permanent militia organized in units across the country and endowed with more willingness than military training or experience.

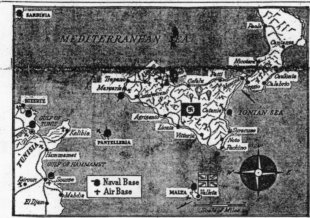

Map above shows position of Sicily, strategic Italian island invaded by Canadian and Allied troops.

Softening up of Island.—This photograph, approved by the British censors, showing the results of a recent Royal Air Force attack on the chemical works at Catanzaro, Sicily. Reports submitted with this picture told of a factory and a train at the railroad station being hit.

Allies Round Out Week's Raids On Battered Sicily

ALLIED HEADQUARTERS IN NORTH AFRICA, July 10.—(AP) — The crushing Allied aerial assault on Sicily, Italy's island defence line, neared the end of a full week Friday without letup and spread from primary targets to secondary objectives deep in the interior of the island.

Allied planes of 11 types from the three b in the Mediterranean th tre — Northwest Africa, Middle East and Malta—roared out in the hundreds Thursday against Sicilian airdromes, ports, communications and war plants, shooting down 21 enemy fighters and destroying a considerable number on the ground.

Catania was particularly hard hit. Heavy bombers from the Cairo command threw 250,000 pounds of bombs down on the city,

The Gerbini network of airdromes was blasted from two directions. British and American heavy bombers in separate raids covered Catania with fire and steel. The long-bombed air centres of Comiso and cca were hat again, as was a less familiar target—Cap Passero.

Canucks, British, American Forces Effect Landing From Allied Bases In North Africa

WASHINGTON, July 10.—(Saturday)—(AP)—The invasion of Sicily by Canadian, British and United States forces under the command of Gen. Dwight D. Eisenhower was announced early today by the United States War Department.

A brief communique from advance headquarters said the landings were preceded by an air attack while naval forces escorted the ground troops and bombarded the coast defences during the landing operations.

The text of the announcement:

"Anglo-American-Canadian forces, under command of Gen. Eisenhower, began landing operations in Sicily early this morning (July 10, North African time). Landings were preceded by an air attack. Naval forces escorted the assault forces and bombarded the coast defences during the assault."

There was no additional information concerning the scale of the landing assault on Sicily, which is separated from Tunisia by only a narrow strait.

The island has been under steady bombardment by the Northwest African Air Force since the Axis forces in Tunisia collapsed and surrendered in May.

Canuck Bomber Units In Africa

LONDON, July 10.—(CP Cable) — Canadian fliers from Vancouver to Halifax will make things increasingly hot for the Axis in North African skies, informed quarters here predicted Friday, following an announcement from Ottawa by Air Marshal L. S. Breadner, Chief of Air Staff, R.C.A.F., that Canadian Wellington bomber squadrons have arrived in the Mediterranean theatre.

Exact number of these Canadian bombers was not specified in Air Marshal Breadner's announcement.

Informed quarters here said the R.C.A.F. squadrons are well-trained in bombing tactics after service with the Canadian group of the bomber command in Britain. They said their arrival in North Africa should add considerable weight to the Allied punching power against the Axis.

Although Canadians have been active in the Mediterranean theatre for some time, the squadrons from the Canadian group in Britain are the first all Canadian bomber squadrons in the Middle East.

The communique supplied the first information that Canadian troops had joined the British and American forces under Eisenhower in North Africa.

In connection with the landings in Sicily, Eisenhower broadcast an announcement to the people of France telling them the invasion of the island off the toe of the Italian boot was "the first stage in the liberation of the European continent," but warning them not to expose themselves to reprisals by premature action based on any assumption that an invasion of France was imminent.

The translation of this broadcast from North Africa, supplied by the War Department, follows

"Announcement to Frenchmen of France:—

"Anglo-American-Canadian armed forces have today launched an offensive against Sicily. It is the first stage in the liberation of the European continent. There will be others.

"I call on the French people to remain calm, not to allow themselves to be deceived by the false rumors which the enemy might circulate. The Allied radio will keep you informed on military developments. I count on your sang-froid and on your sense of discipline. Do not be rash, for the enemy is watching. Keep on listening and never heed rumors. Verify carefully the news you receive.

"By remaining calm and by not exposing yourselves to reprisals through premature action, you will be helping us effectively.

"When the hour of action strikes, we will let you know. Till then, help us by following our instructions. That is to say: Keep calm, conserve your strength. We repeat: When the hour of action strikes, we will let you know."

(At Ottawa, Prime Minister Mackenzie King announced that Canada's armed forces are "in the forefront of an attack which has as its ultimate objective the unconditional surrender of Italy and Germany." He confirmed that Canadians are in the force which has invaded Sicily.)

Canadian, British and American troops comprised the invasion forces.

TRAP THREATENS NAZIS

First Official Pictures of Our Invading Canadians

Canadian troops who took part in the invasion of Sicily are shown on the dock, their equipment piled beside them, as they waited to board troopships.

These Canadian troops who took part in the assault on Sicily are shown aboard a tender as they prepared to embark on troopships for the voyage.

Canadian troops who took part in the invasion of Sicily, are pictured aboard a tender as they embarked for the Mediterranean in this first picture of any phase of the Canadian participation in the action to reach Canada. This, and the other official Canadian Army photographs on this page, were flown to Britain, radioed to eastern Canada and then flown to Vancouver.

One of the Canadian nursing sisters in the contingent which went to Sicily, goes up the gangplank of a troopship carrying her full equipment.

The Vancouver Sun

The Vancouver Evening Newspaper Owned and Operated by Vancouver People

FOUNDED 1886
VOL. LVII—No. 255　　VANCOUVER, B.C., JULY 19, 1943　　PRICE 5 CENTS

Thousands Of Huns Face Death

Russian Drives at German Rear Threaten Encirclement; Hitler Retreat Endangered

MOSCOW, July 19 — (BUP) — Russian armored forces probing deep into the hedgehog defenses of Orel, made scythe-like swipes at the rear of several big German units today, threatening thousands of troops with encirclement and annihilation.

Front reports of slow but steady Soviet advances tightening a steel band against the Orel salient said advance elements were racing on ahead to slice in behind German pockets of resistance and threaten their retreat route.

Field dispatches indicated the three-way drive on Orel had brought one striking force to a point between 12 and 20 miles east of the city. A descent from the north toward the Bryansk-Orel railway registered more progress, threatening to cut the line and slice across the base of the German bulge. The southern group reported steady but undefined progress.

The Soviet press said the bitterness of German resistance was explained by the "mortal fear of another Stalingrad looming"—the trapping and extermination of a Nazi army as that of Marshal von Paulus was exterminated at the Volga city last winter.

The newspaper Pravda said that one river valley after bitter battles the Russians cleared a wide area and established a firm bridgehead from which they were preparing to storm a key objective.

German broadcasts reported that Russian attacks had spread from the Orel area along a front reaching 600 miles to the south.

"Isolated penetrations" of the German lines were admitted in the Kuban area of the northwest Caucasus, along the Mius river near Taganrog and along the Donets river.

Another broadcast said the "greatest tank battle of all time" was being fought near Belgorod, 165 miles south of Orel.

Montgomery In Suburbs Of Catania

By VIRGIL PINKLEY
Special to The Vancouver Sun
Copyright, 1943, by British United Press

ALLIED HEADQUARTERS, North Africa, July 19.—Allied invasion armies advanced along the whole Sicilian front again today, meeting heavy opposition around the east coast city of Catania, seizing the road centre of Caltanissetta on the central front, and fanning out from Agrigento and Port Empedocle on the west.

(A dispatch broadcast from an Army Command post said Allied troops were pushing into the suburbs of Catania as fires lighted the lowlands and heavy artillery shelled the sector from the river Simeto to Catania).

Canadian forces smashed 15 miles northwest from Caltagirone on the Central Front and took the town of Piazza Armerina, and then joined Americans in a pincers drive against the Axis base of Enna, 10 miles from Caltanissetta. The Canadian troops have advanced 50 miles or more from their landing places on ... ly, further than either U.S. or ... itish forces.

GAINS ON EAST

With one-third of Sicily already in Allied hands, the British and Canadians, in the hardest fighting of the campaign, seized vital bridge positions on the Catania plain and pushed to within easy gun range of the burning coastal city, leaving many dead Germans and Italians on the field. A spokesman warned, however, that stiff fighting lies ahead at heavily bombarded Catania.

SPLIT AXIS TROOPS

The Canadian-American operations, thrusting northward at a point about 55 miles west of Catania, appear to be intended

Please Turn to Page Two
See "Catania"

B.C. Man With Legion in Sicily

OTTAWA, July 19—(CP)—Canadian Legion announced today that overseas supervisors of Canadian Legion War Services attached to units of the 1st Canadian Division in Sicily include J. R. Marrs, Victoria.

Kansas City Reform Leader Slain

KANSAS CITY, July 19—(AP)—Louis G. Lower, first member inducted into the Order of De Molay, Masonic organization for young men, and one of the wreckers of Tom Pendergast's Democratic machine, was shot and killed Sunday at the Union Station Plaza.

Pope Visits Ruins Left By Americans

By RELMAN MORIN
Associated Press War Correspondent

ALLIED HEADQUARTERS IN NORTH AFRICA, July 19.—An all-American force of Flying Fortresses, Liberators. Mitchells and Marauders carried out the war's first bombing of Rome, it was disclosed tonight.

The Vatican ra ... said tonight that Pope Pius visited the bombed districts.

The fliers concentrated on military targets in the Eternal City, taking particular care that no damage was done in the vicinity of the Vatican. For more than three hours the railway yards and suburban airdromes were subjected to a terrific bombardment. Cairo reported 700,000 lbs. of TNT dropped in the target area.

Rome radios officially announced that terrific damage had been done, while a Rome report, via Berne, Switzerland, said panic spread through the city, overcrowded with thousands of Italians who had fled there from other centres in the belief that Rome would be spared all aerial attack.

Specially Trained Bomb-Aimers

Flying Fortresses led the way and while they were attacking the San Lorenzo yards, Liberators bombed the Littorio railway freight yards.

Simultaneously hundreds of Marauders and Mitchells, escorted by Lightning fighters, began a lengthy attack on the Campino airdrome.

Please Turn to Page Two　　*See "Rome"*

'Italians Surrender En Masse'

By Associated Press

ALLIED HEADQUARTERS, N. Africa, July 19.—Almost incredible first-hand reports of broken morale among Italians in Sicily poured in to Allied headquarters today.

Italian troops were said to be surrendering in organized units.

Civilians continued to show genuine joy over the arrival of Allied armies.

An Allied officer who read the proclamation of Gen. Sir Harold Alexander announcing the determination of the Allies to smash Fascism was hoisted on the shoulders of a Sicilian crowd and carried about in triumph in one town.

The people shouted: "This is the day of our deliverance."

A British officer, who returned after six days in Sicily, said the people themselves were tearing down the symbols of the Fascist party.

Not Opposed to King for Spain

MADRID, July 19—(AP)—Gen. Francisco Franco said Saturday he does not oppose the possibility of a restoration of the Spanish monarchy but added that the monarchy should never serve as a tool for foreign propaganda.

The Phalange Party and its program, he said, is "the only just and true solution" of Spain's problems.

LATE NEWS BULLETINS

American in 'Amgot'

ALLIED HEADQUARTERS, NORTH AFRICA, July 18—(Delayed) — (BUP) — Lieut. Col. Charles Poletti, former Governor of New York State, has assumed the post of Senior Civil Affairs Officer in "Amgot," the new Allied military government set up in Sicily under Gen. Sir Harold R. L. G. Alexander.

'War's Biggest Defense Battle'

NEW YORK July 19—(BUP)—The Berlin Radio quoted Nazi military sources today as saying a Russian summer offensive now is in full swing and German troops are fighting "the biggest defense battle of the whole war."

'Rome Raid Justified'

PORTLAND, Ore., July 19—(AP)—British Ambassador Lord Halifax advocated a "harsh peace" for Germany today and said the bombing of Rome was justified by military tactics.

Rome Dwellings Burn

ALLIED HEADQUARTERS, North Africa, July 19—(AP)—The Rome Radio said today that many residences were left aflame from the bombing of Rome but made no assertion that any damage had been done to church, cultural or historical structures.

City Man Found Dead

NANAIMO, B.C., July 19—(CP)—Harold Elmer Sward, 60, camp cook, who registered at a downtown hotel Saturday on arrival from Ucuelet, was found dead in bed today. Coroner W. H. Jones is conducting an investigation as a bottle of liquid was found in the room and some contents had apparently been removed from it. His national registration card gave his address as 621 Hamilton Street, Vancouver.

GERMAN BASTION FALLS

The historic blasting given Rome yesterday was carried out by more than 500 Flying Fortresses like the one pictured here. Today Allied headquarters described the raid as an "outstandingly successful operation" and announced that the Americans lost only 5 planes. (See story Page 2.)

6 ★★★★★★ FINAL

The Vancouver Sun

The Vancouver Evening Newspaper Owned and Operated By Vancouver People

FOUNDED 1886
VOL. LVII—No. 240

VANCOUVER, BRITISH COLUMBIA, TUESDAY, JULY 20, 1943

PRICE 5 CENTS

Today's Tides

Vancouver Harbor
Low 2:39 p.m., 0.4 feet. High 10:01 p.m., 14.1 feet.
English Bay
Low 2:22 p.m., 1.0 feet. High, 9:38 p.m., 14.4 feet
First Narrows
Low slack 3:20 p.m. High slack 10:26 p.m.

Reds Drive Across Two Rivers

Russians Gain in Orel and Southern Sectors, Capture Mtsensk; Report Stalin at Front

By ROBERT MUSEL
British United Press Staff Correspondent

LONDON, July 20.—The Red Army has captured the great German defense bastion of Mtsensk, smashing the northeast corner of the Orel salient, and in a double offensive in the south has driven across the Donets and Mius Rivers, a Russian communique announced tonight.

In the fourth of a series of victories unapproached since the historic days of the winter offensive, the Russians have driven back the Germans on the Belgorod Front south of Orel for gains of from 6 1-4 to 7 1-2 miles.

It was believed that Marshal Josef Stalin was at the front personally directing the Orel offensive.

THOUSANDS IN TRAP

Gains of from 3¾ to 6¼ miles were made on the whole perimeter of the Orel salient, where the Red Army was driving the Germans into a narrowing sack which threatened to become a death trap for tens of thousands of them.

Thirty towns and villages were captured in Tuesday's fighting north of Orel, including Mtsensk and nine other fortified German held towns.

The capture of Mtsensk, 27 miles north-east of Orel, on the trunk railway to Moscow, represented the biggest single Russian victory since the winter campaign which rolled the Germans westward from Stalingrad to the approaches of the Dnieper River.

With the corridor closing, the Russians likened the situation to that at Stalingrad last winter, when the Red Army nipped off the pocket jutting into the Volga city and killed or captured 330,000 German troops.

The Army driving in behind Orel from the north advanced within seven miles of the Orel-Bryansk railroad, described as the last rail line left to supply the threatened German garrison.

BIG TOWN RETAKEN

Later dispatches said Russian pressure forced the Germans to retreat all along the line below Orel. Concentrating their onslaught against a tactically important hill and village, Soviet forces captured them and the Germans had to make a general withdrawal from that sector.

McNaughton In Africa

ALLIED FORCE HEADQUARTERS, North Africa, July 21 — (AP)—Lt.-Gen. A. G. L. McNaughton, Commander of the Canadian Overseas Army, is in North Africa on an inspection trip, it was officially announced tonight.

Canuck Advance Slowed

ALLIED HEADQUARTERS, North Africa, July 20 —(BUP)—Slashing halfway across Sicily, American troops by-passed the vital road junction of Enna today and rounded up hundreds of Italians who surrendered in wholesale mutiny against their German officers.

Late reports said the Americans were in the vicinity of Santa Caterina, 13 miles west and slightly north of Enna, and across the last lateral railway on the island, except the vulnerable north coast line, after a seven-mile northward advance from captured Caltanissetta.

DEFENSES CRUMBLE

Another American column was reported considerably closer to Enna on the southwest and Canadian troops were battling their way toward the Sicilian communications hub from Piazza Amerina to the southeast.

Stiffening resistance by units of the restored German 15th Panzer Division slowed the Canadians' advance, an Allied communique said, but along the entire American front the enemy defenses were reported disintegrating.

NAZI REVERSES

A bitter battle was reported continuing on the southern approaches to the east coast port of Catania where the British Eighth Army inflicted heavy casualties on the desperate German defenders.

Long lines of Italians were surrendering without a fight and the communique said there were signs they did so after openly defying the orders of their German commanders to stand at all costs.

(The lone stumbling block in the otherwise rapid conquest of Sicily was Catania where German parachutists, pressed in as infantry, and the crack Hermann Goering Division were battling Gen. Sir B. L. Montgomery's Eighth Army on the plain south of the city.) (See story page 2)

BASEBALL

PACIFIC COAST LEAGUE

San Diego	000 000 000—8	8	2
San Francisco	021 000 10x—4	10	1

C. Johnson and Salkeld; Joyce and Sprinz.

LATE NEWS BULLETINS

WASHINGTON, July 20—(AP)—The government had received no protest from the Vatican against the bombardment of Rome, up to noon today.

Axis Bombs Malta

VALETA, Malta, July 20—(BUP)—Axis planes made a concentrated attack on Malta today for the first time in several months. Bomb damage to private property was revealed.

Berlin Threatens Reprisal

NEW YORK, July 20—(AP)—Dr. Paul Schmidt, German Foreign Office spokesman, was quoted by the Berlin radio today as threatening Axis retaliation for yesterday's bombing of Rome.

1000 Canucks Under Japs

OTTAWA, July 20—(CP)—Prime Minister Mackenzie King said today in the House of Commons that external affairs department information indicates there are 1000 Canadians in Japan and Japan-Occupied China.

FBI Charges Sheriff

WASHINGTON, July 20—(UP)—FBI Director J. Edgar Hoover announced tonight the arrest of Sheriff Rodney F. Chambless, 29, of Madison County, Texas, on charges of aiding in the escape of two Federal prisoners from the county jail in Conros, Tex.

Slay Twenty Italian Workers

LONDON, July 20 — (CP) — A Reuters News Agency dispatch from Stockholm quoted a Swedish dispatch today as reporting that German SS troops (Elite Guards) killed 20 Italian workers who demonstrated at a synthetic rubber factory and demanded to be sent home.

Final Battle For Munda

SOUTH PACIFIC HEADQUARTERS, July 20—(BUP)—The final phase of the American drive on Munda was reported underway tonight as U.S. soldiers and marines, aided by a punishing land and aerial barrage, battled through the last positions of Japanese jungle defenses to reach the outskirts of the strategic air base.

Ex-RAF Flier Indicted

SAN FRANCISCO, July 20—(BUP)—A federal grand jury today indicted Harold Ebury, 45, former Royal Air Force flier, on four counts of illegal use of cable code and violation of American censorship regulations in connection with alleged smuggling of platinum from Columbia to Buenos Aires dealers representing Axis interests.

Questions Rome Raid

LONDON, July 20—(CP)—The bombing of Rome was projected into Parliament for the first time today when Viscount Fitzalan, one of Britain's leading Roman Catholic noblemen, asked whether the bombing had been necessary and whether any damage had been done to cultural or religious buildings.

Henry Fonda Invited To Take Paternity Test

By British United Press

HOLLYWOOD, July 20.—Barbara Jane Thompson, 24-year-old divorcee who claims Henry Fonda is the father of her baby daughter, invited the former film star today to submit to a paternity blood test.

"We are willing to submit the mother and her child to a blood test to determine the father any time Fonda will agree to it," said Julian P. Van Dyke, Miss Thompson's attorney.

Such a test could not prove conclusively that Fonda is the father of the child, but it could prove his innocence.

Fonda, now a quartermaster 3rd class aboard a destroyer stationed at Bremerton, Wash., previously had said he did not know Miss Thompson.

Jap Naval Base Gets Pounding

By British United Press

WASHINGTON, July 20.—American heavy bombers yesterday morning struck at the important North Pacific base of Paramushiru and succeeded in starting fires, the Navy announced today.

A communique said that Japanese ships in the Paramushiru straits were also bombed and a number of near hits on them were observed.

It was the first raid on Paramushiru — the Japanese "Pearl Harbor" of the northwest—to be announced by the navy.

Paramushiru is the northernmost island of the 700-mile Kurile Chain. It is about 1200 miles northeast of Tokyo, and is 765 miles from American-held Attu and 965 miles from the U.S. base at Amchitka in the Aleutians. These were considered likely starting points for the American raid.

Paramushiru is Japan's No. 1 naval base in the North Pacific and in strategic importance is compared by some military commentators with the American base at Pearl Harbor, Hawaii. The base, one of the largest and most powerful of all Japanese naval installations, is surrounded by several airfields.

It is just south of the tip of Russia's Siberian peninsula of Kamchatka.

It is generally believed that Japan's sea-air thrust against the Aleutians in June, 1942, originated from Paramushiru.

Race Results at Saskatoon

FIRST RACE—Five Furlongs:
Cyn Marnock (Jasperson), $3.90, $2.55, $2.15.
Dune's Choice (Sivewright) $2.80, $2.35.
Nellie Goldust (Taves) $4.20.
Time: 1.04 2-5.

SECOND RACE—Five furlongs:
Drop In (Taves) $11.20, $4.90, $4.20.
Star Naught (Young) $5.60, $5.10.
Emir (Godley) $4.50.
Time: 1.04 4-5.

DAILY DOUBLE—$24.80.

THIRD RACE—Five furlongs:
Miss Mobile (Jasperson) $3.80, $2.70, $2.25.
Gibson Gower (Braddish) $3.00, $2.20.
Shaganappy (Russell) $2.20.
Time: 1.06 1-5.

FOURTH RACE—Six and one-half furlongs:
Baron A.A. (Sivewright) $47.20, $19.30, $11.50.
Pagan Queen (Russell) $3.70, $3.70.
Hasty Chap (Taves) $6.80.
Time: 1.25 4-5.

FIFTH RACE—Seven furlongs:
Amsterson (Russell) $8.50, $3.75, $2.40.
Pepper Pot (Young) $4.45, $2.40.
And San (Craigmyle) $2.40.
Time: 1.31 4-5.

SIXTH RACE—Six and one-half furlongs:
Hazelgreen (Braddish) $8.05, $4.15, $3.30.
Yeo Marcus (Russell) $3.75, $2.60.
Buddy Marcus (Taves) $2.65.
Time: 1.24 1-5.

SEVENTH RACE—Mile and one-sixteenth:
Dr. Larry (Craigmyle) $7.60, $4.70, $2.85.
Major S (Godley) $4.00, $2.80.
All Sweep (Russell) $2.55.
Time: 1.56 4-5.

QUINELLA—$25.60.

HAPPY HOOFER

Terpsichorean ability may have helped, but more than likely the face and figure displayed by smiling 21-year-old Jane Hale, former Hollywood dance instructor, had a lot to do with her landing a film contract.

Soldiers Remanded In London Murder

LONDON, July 20 — (CP) — Ptes. George Frederick Brinacombe, 21, of Montreal, and Henry Smith, 20, of Kinistino, Sask., members of the Royal Canadian Army Service Corps, were remanded for three weeks today on charges of murder in connection with the death of William Raven last October. Raven was found dead in bed in his apartment with his skull fractured.

Drowned Naval Rating Identified

VICTORIA, July 20 — (CP) — The name of the naval rating drowned at nearby Thetis Lake Sunday was given by the Navy today as Joseph Paul Poupart, 20, RCNVR, of Montreal, Que.

He was stationed at HMCS Givenchy. The body was recovered Monday and an inquest will be conducted Thursday.

26 Saved From Sea

BUENOS AIRES, July 20—(AP)—The Argentine ship Mejico was reported today to have picked up 26 survivors of a torpedoed merchant vessel about 65 miles off the Brazilian port of Santos.

The identity of the sunken vessel was not immediately disclosed.

Hitler, Duce Met During Raid on Rome

By WILLIAM B. DICKINSON
British United Press Staff Correspondent

LONDON, July 20.—Adolf Hitler and Benito Mussolini were meeting in northern Italy Monday, in an emergency defense conference, when Rome was blasted by American bombs, it was revealed tonight.

"The Axis leaders discussed the military situation created by the desperate onslaught of tremendous Soviet masses against the European front in the east and by the landing attempt carried out by the Anglo-Americans in the Mediterranean area," the German official news agency DNB said in announcing the meeting.

It was indicated that news of the bombing of Rome, received while the meeting was in progress, had considerable effect on the former Austrian paper hanger and the former Italian tub-thumper.

Axis broadcasts recorded here said that Hitler flew with his staff to the meeting place Monday morning and Mussolini was waiting for him. They conferred until afternoon when Hitler left for his headquarters.

HIGH OFFICIALS KILLED

Berlin said that the chiefs of the German high command and other military leaders and experts attended the meeting.

German broadcasts implied plainly that the Axis leaders were frightened and all reports from neutral capitals and the Axis indicated that the history-making American raid on Rome had terrorized those Italians within its range.

Rome broadcasts said that Mario Buzzichini, editor of Mussolini's own newspaper Popolo D'Italia of Milan; General Hazon, supreme chief of the Italian military police, and his chief of general staff Colonel Barnego were among those killed.

Neutral capital dispatches emphasized the sheer panic of the people.

CANCELS MEETINGS

Berne said that thousands ran to mass in St. Peter's square, before the Vatican, confident that the Allies would spare that area.

Panicky Rome sounded a second air raid alarm Monday night, apparently fearing that Allies planes which raided Naples and unspecified targets in other parts of southern Italy were returning to Rome.

Pope Pius suspended public audiences for the rest of the week, fearing the danger of massing many people in public places, Axis radios said.

Year for Theft of 'Death Car'

Jack Dillon was sentenced to one year in Oakalla by Judge Whiteside in County Court this afternoon after he was convicted of theft of an auto, involved in a crash on Hastings-Barnett Road several months ago. Two women were killed in the accident.

Frank Risely, charged with him, was acquitted.

Mrs. Mildred Norris, 24, was fatally injured and Gwendoline Pearce, 21, instantly killed when the auto in which they were riding with Dillon and Risley careened from the road and overturned during a chase by Provincial Police in Burnaby.

The car, owned by James Alfred Pearson, Bellingham, had earlier been stolen from the Old Mill Garage on Commercial Drive, according to evidence at the trial.

Earlier details of the trial on Page 17.

Faces Double Murder Trial

EDMONTON, July 20—(CP)—Samuel Baptiste Desjarlais, 18, half-breed Cree of the Lac La Biche district, today was committed for Supreme Court trial on murder charges in connection with the deaths of Carl Hemmingsen, trapper, and George Pappas, Greek fur buyer. George Desjarlais, 21, a cousin of Samuel's was committed for trial on a charge of murdering Hemmingsen.

BULLETIN

ALLIED HEADQUARTERS, Australia, July 20—(BUP)—Allied bombers sank a Japanese cruiser and two destroyers in the Vella Gulf, a communique announced today.

Another destroyer was probably sunk and one transport and a fourth destroyer were damaged, the communique announced.

The Allied bombers intercepted an eleven-ship enemy convoy at Vella Gulf en route to reinforce the enemy garrison at Vella. The remaining enemy vessels were forced to withdraw without reaching their objective.

Fleeing Italian Troops Left 'Dope' Behind

By PAUL KERN LEE
Associated Press Staff Writer

WITH ALLIED FORCES IN SICILY, July 18—(Delayed)—Today I went ashore at Augusta, Sicily, where I found that the more than 20,000 inhabitants who deserted the ancient city hurriedly, just before the British forces entered, now are clamoring for permission to return and are begging for food.

Only four decrepit automobiles were found in the town, the others apparently having been used for the evacuation.

One strange fact discovered by investigating officers was the quantity of cocaine and heroin found in many personal kits left behind by Italian officers, and the finding of similar stocks in numerous homes. Apparently they were not intended for first aid or hospital use but for personal use.

MUSSOLINI QUITS KING HEADS ARMY IN ITALY CRISIS

Yanks Seize Marsala 110,000 Foe Trapped Sicily Victory Near

ALLIED HEADQUARTERS IN NORTH AFRICA, July 25.—(AP)—Allied troops in 14 breath-taking days have annihilated Axis armies in all of Sicily except the northeast corner—trapping 110,000 enemy soldiers—and are converging in a shattering land, sea and air attack on the last enemy bastion, the Mt. Etna line.

American troops seized Marsala in the lightning mop up of the western part of the island, headquarters announced today, and it was the official estimate that 50,000 more prisoners would be added to the 60,000 already in Allied hands. Americans captured 40,000 of this first 60,000.

Reuters reported Allied troops had entered Trapani, the last major city in Western Sicily, today. The naval base, half way between Marsala and Palermo, had expected to fall at any moment as it was cut off from aid. The deep water harbor will provide excellent facilities to speed unloading of American supplies and cut off the main home base from which Axis submarines have been operating in the Sicilian Strait.

Messina, key Sicily evacuation port across the straits from Italy.

Pope Denies He Sent Protest To Roosevelt Over Rome Raid

LONDON, July 25.—(AP)—The Vatican radio, in a German language broadcast beamed to Germany Saturday night branded as "entirely unfounded" German and Italian news agencies reports that Pope Pius XII had protested to President Roosevelt over Monday's bombing of Rome, and also said that the Pontiff did not believe that American pilots intentionally set out to damage holy places.

The broadcast, which emphasized that the Pontiff is impartial in the war, denied the Axis statements that after the raid the Pope called to the Vatican U.S. Charge D'Affairs Harold H. Tittman, Jr.

A partial text as recorded by the Associated Press:

"Reports put out by DNB (German official news agency) according to which the Pope had made a personal protest to President Roosevelt about the bombing of Rome, as well as a report that United States Charge D'Affaires Mr. Tittman had been called to the Vatican on the evening of the day the bombing took place, are both entirely unfounded."

FIGURES IN TODAY'S SHAKEUP

BENITO MUSSOLINI ... he's out   KING VICTOR EMMANUEL ... Commands Forces   MARSHAL PIETRO BADOGLIO ... he's in

Musssolini---The Agitator Who Turned Fascist

Mussolini, one-time socialist agitator, organizer of the Fascist thugs, ravager of Ethiopia, the man who stabbed France in the back was ousted today, four days before his 60th birthday.

Born July 29, 1883, at Dovia, Italy, Benito Mussolini, "Il Duce," rose from the gutter to rule great countries and to oppress millions of people.

His father, a man of no formal education, was a blacksmith, who had internationalist, revolutionary and anti-religious convictions. His mother was a school teacher; From the former, Benito received his early political ideas; from the latter, he gained a taste for letters and the ambition to rise to great heights.

The organization of the Fascist Party took place under Mussolini's guidance in 1919. In the elections of 1921, it presented a common list of candidates with the Nationalist Party, and, on account of the numerical support of its ally, succeeded in electing 35 deputies, among whom was Benito Mussolini.

Mussolini's dissatisfaction with parliamentary action was soon apparent, and in 1922, after a succession of cabinet changes and an increase in the impotency of the government to conduct the affairs of state, he led his forces, dressed in black shirts to Rome. Mussolini was made prime minister and virtual dictator. In short, he became "Il Duce."

Since that time, Mussolini has directed the affairs of Italy, developed and strengthened Fascism and built the Fascist state. He succeeded in establishing the unquestioned sway of the Fascists between the years 1922 and 1925. He crushed other political parties and organizations by force. Several attempts were made on his life, but he escaped on each occasion.

Badoglio---Italy's Number One Fighting Man

NEW YORK, uly 25.—(CP)—Italy's new Premier—Marshal Pietro Badoglio—also is the country's number one fighting man.

While Mussolini demanded an Italian Empire, Badoglio created it.

Badoglio was a farmer's son, born in Piedmont Province in 1871. He went through Italy's military schools and learned the smell of gunpowder in Ethiopia in 1896 and '97 as a young lieutenant. Thirty-nine years later, he was to head the victorious Italian army that marched into Addis Ababa.

Badoglio underwent his second baptism of fire in the war between Turkey and Italy in 1911 and 1912, rising to the rank of major for the part he played in the capture of Zanzur. During the first world war he rose even faster, gaining six promotions. King Victor Emmanuel named him Marquis of Sabotino and later he became a member of the Rome Senate.

While Mussolini and his Blackshirts rose to power Badoglio remained aloof. In fact, when Il Duce marched on Rome he is said to have offered to disperse the Blackshirts with a single regiment.

In 1924, Mussolini bundled the army chief off to Brazil as ambassador. Two years later, he recalled him as chief of the general staff and had him created a marshal—Italy's highest military rank.

The Italian war chief is just what might be expected of a military leader. He has a stern, impassive expression, close-cropped gray hair and shaggy eyebrows.

(Ever since last November, reports have been spreading that Marshal Badoglio had started a movement in Italy for a separate peace with the Allied nations. Although it was impossible to obtain confirmation of this, it is considered possible he has already offered to King Victor Emmanuel and the Italian people a safe way out of the Axis pact.)

Marshal Badoglio Commander Of New Military Government --Rome Radio Announcement

LONDON, July 25.—(CP)—King Victor Emmanuel accepted the resignation of Fascist Premier Benito Mussolini today and assumed command of all Italian forces for "a stand against those who have wounded the sacred soil of Italy," the Rome radio announced tonight.

Marshal Pietro Badoglio, 71-year-old former Italian chief-of-staff who had been dismissed Dec. 6, 1940 by Mussolini, was appointed Premier by the king.

Badoglio also issued a proclamation saying "on orders of His Majesty the King, I am taking over the military government of the country with full powers."

"The war continues," he added. "Italy, grievously stricken in her invaded provinces and in her ruined towns maintains her faith in her given word, jealous of her ancient traditions."

The king in his proclamation said Italy, "by the valor of its armed forces and the determination of all its citizens, will find again a way of recovery."

These sensational announcements, recorded by the Associated Press, may be the opening peace moves.

They came as Allied troops were sweeping across Sicily off the southern Italian mainland, less than a week after the 500-plane American air attack on the Fascist capital of Rome, and amid reports that widespread peace demonstrations had occurred in Italy's main cities.

An official statement was expected tonight on this startling political and military turn in the war.

"No consideration must stand in our way and no recrimination must be made," said King Victor's proclamation. "We must stand against those who have wounded the sacred soil of Italy."

The "resignation" of the bald, squat, boastful Mussolini ended a career that began with the Fascist march on Rome in 1922. The international and domestic standing of Mussolini, however, has steadily deteriorated since he led his country into war in the summer of 1940.

Mussolini met Hitler last Monday when the huge air attack was delivered on rail and airport installations at Rome.

Mussolini apparently appealed to Hitler for aid in resisting the Allied onslaughts which clearly are aimed at knocking Italy out of the war as quickly as possible.

If that was his plea he undoubtedly failed in his mission. The king's proclamation, which in effect dismissed the originator of Fascism, followed.

Badoglio, long out of favor with the Fascists, had been reported a likely successor to Mussolini once the country decided to sue for peace.

The resignation of Mussolini, whose empire vanished under converging Allied troops, also apparently ended the Fascist party as it had been constituted.

The king's proclamation specifically said that the resignation of Mussolini as premier and "secretary of the Fascist party" had been accepted.

'Beginning Of The End,' Says Prime Minister

OTTAWA. — July 25.—(CP)—Prime Minister Mackenzie King said today that the ousting of Mussolini from power in Italy "appears to be the beginning of the end of the Fascist regime."

The Canadian prime minister added that it is too early to say what effect Mussolini's resignation will have on Italy's withdrawal from the war. But he said that the fall of the Italian dictator is certainly a step in the right direction. Mr. King issued his statement on receiving a bulletin from the Canadian Press on the news of Mussolini's resignation.

U.S. Raid Rips Norway Base

LONDON, July 25.—(AP)—In an unprecedented 7800-mile round trip to the erde of the Arctic Circle, a strong force of American Flying Fortresses pounded Trondheim in Norway early Saturday, leaving that big German U-boat base a raging mass of exploding bombs, flaming oil tanks and black smoke which mushroomed up thousands of feet.

The attack, announced early today in a U.S. Army headquarters communique, was the first American one on Norway, and one Fortress formation also smashed an aluminum plant at Heroya in southern Norway.

96

The Vancouver Evening Newspaper
Owned and Operated
By Vancouver People

The Vancouver Sun

Today's Tides
Vancouver Harbor
High 4:03 p.m., 10.4 feet. Low 8:40 p.m., 8.5 feet.
English Bay
High 3:44 p.m., 10.9 feet. Low 8:24 p.m., 9.2 feet.
First Narrows
High slack 4:32 p.m. Low slack 9:12 p.m.

FOUNDED 1886
VOL. LVII—No. 245 MArine 1161 VANCOUVER, BRITISH COLUMBIA. MONDAY, JULY 26, 1943 PRICE 5 CENTS BY CARRIER $1.00 per month

Fascist Party Ousted

MARTIAL LAW IN ITALY; DUCE REPORTED ARRESTED

Week End Of Record Air Raids

Essen, Hamburg, Cologne, Holland, And Leghorn, Northern Italy, Suffer Devastating Assaults

By Canadian Press

LONDON, July 26.—RAF and RCAF heavy bombers made a concentrated attack on Essen last night, while Mosquito aircraft of both Britain and Canada struck at Hamburg and Cologne, and swept over northwest Germany, the Low Countries and France, it was announced today.

The Air Ministry listed 24 planes as missing in far-flung overnight operations, and of these three were RCAF bombers and one an RCAF fighter.

Five enemy aircraft were shot down, one of them by an RCAF Mosquito pilot.

The raiders encountered good weather over the target area at Essen and preliminary reports indicated the bombing was concentrated and effective.

The great formations of night raiders scarcely had returned to their bases when fresh squadrons of Allied raiders swept out across the English Channel this morning to continue the smashing aerial offensive—the greatest in history—by daylight.

WAR'S BIGGEST RAID

Last night's raids followed a mighty series of round-the-clock blows delivered by the RAF, RCAF and U.S. 8th Army Air Force, British and Canadian bombers striking at battered Hamburg Saturday night in the heaviest raid of the war, and American airmen heaping destruction on the smoking ruins Sunday in their deepest penetration into Germany.

Essen, a vital industiral centre in the Ruhr, was last raided on the night of May 27.

Last night's raid was the 57th on Essen—one of the most heavily bombed cities in the world.

Please Turn to Page Two
See "Air Raids"

Today's Scratches At Hastings Park

FIRST RACE—Bahask, Lady Serajevo, Red Fez, Shasta Sue, Jeff Himself, Selaris.

SECOND RACE—Off; fourth race becomes second.

First sub becomes fourth. Scratch, Tadpole, Broad Royal, Will Hudson, John B.

SIXTH RACE—Born To Run, Shellmond, Just Islam, Valdina Joy, Jockwell, Valdina Bully.

SEVENTH RACE — Hatteras Light, Solomon Somers, Mancy's Beau, Corinthian, Maize B., Scotch Jean.

Race entries and selections on Page?

(Selections and Entries Page 20.)

DEFIED DUCE

KING VICTOR EMMANUEL Of Italy, who, after 21 yeas of submission to Mussolini, refused to adbidcate and save Il Duce's face, and thereby forced the Fascist dictator to resign.

Allies May Be Willing to Talk With Badoglio

By HARRISON SALISBURY
Special to The Vancouver Sun
Copyright, 1943, by British United Press

LONDON, July 26.—An authoritative diplomatic commentator today reported United Nations' readiness to talk peace terms with the new Italian regime.

Signs multiplied that the new government, while seeking to maintain a semblance of Italian resistance in order to strengthen its bargaining position, soon will begin feeling out the Allies regarding peace terms, presumably through Pope Pius XII, Turkey or Sweden.

If the Baloglio government does ask for terms, an authoritative British diplomatic commentator said Britain will be preperad to deal with him "provided that it is evident he exercises full authority in Italy."

The only "terms" acceptable to the Allies, as specified by President Roosevelt and Prime Minister Churchill, will be "unconditional surrender." However, both United States and Britain had refused even to discuss a separate peace for Italy so long as Mussolini remained ate the helm.

The British Cabinet soon will meet to examine the implications of Mussolini's deposal and decide its attitude toward the new government, the commentator said. The government is watching closely to see whether the Badoglio regime will overthrow the Fascist system or merely substitute a new figurehead for Mussolini.

"Meantime," the commentator said, "the war against Italy continues."

HunsWreck Orel Before Moving Out

By HENRY SHAPIRO
Special to The Vancouver Sun
Copyright, 1943, by British United Press

MOSCOW, July 26.—Soviet military advices said today that the Germans were wrecking Orel in apparent preparation for withdrawal and the Red Army was expected to drive into it at any time.

Frontline reports said a Russian column, driving behind Orel from the north, had cut the railroad to Bryansk and advanced to bring under fire the highway roughly paralleling the line about 20 miles to the south.

The plight of the German garrison was described as critical. Its sole route of retreat from Orel, against which Soviet troops are advancing from three directions, is said to be a dirt road angling down to the southwest.

STALIN AT FRONT

(William McGaffin, Associated Press writer says Joseph Stalin has been at the Orel front much of the time, personally directing operations.)

That the Germans realize their peril is indicated by reports that they are engaged in the methodical demolition of Orel, making clear their intentions of giving it up rather than face the growing

Please Turn to Page Two
See "Russia"

Allied Net Tightens In Sicily

Yanks Boost Captive Total to 70,000; Canadians Gain

By VIRGIL PINKLEY
Special to The Vancouver Sun
Copyright, 1943, by British United Press

ALLIED HEADQUARTERS, North Africa, July 26.—Allied troops drove the Axis deeper into its last foothold of northeastern Sicily today as the Americans captured the port of Termini Imerese, 20 miles southeast of Palermo, and boosted their number of prisoners to more than 70,000.

As the final lunge to crush the enemy on Sicily approaches, German and Italian forces have fallen back to a line starting in the foothills of Mt. Etna south of Catania and running north and west to San Stefano on the north coast. The enemy-held coastline already has been reduced to little more than 135 miles.

Sweeping eastward to help jam the Axis farther back on its escape bridgehead on the straits of Messina, the American Seventh Army took 7000 new prisoners, including six Italian generals and an Admiral.

Axis resistance stiffened as the combined British Canadian and U. S. drive under continuous air support drove the enemy back with pressure from all sides.

U. S. forces strengthened their hold on the northern coastal road on which Termini Imerese is a major point. The capture of the new Generals brought the total of Italian Generals now in Allied hands to 10.

Canadian troops pushing forward in the centre drove 10 to 15 miles northeast of Enna in athreat to cut squarely through the middle of the Axis lines.

Strong German forces, still resisting the British 8th Army before Catania on the east, are re-

Please Turn to Page Two
See "Sicily"

Home of Fascism Reported Burned

BERNE, Switzerland, July 26—(AP)—An unconfirmed report reaching Berne from Italy today said that the birthplace of Fascism in Milan had been burned along with the building of the Fascist newspaper **Il Popolo d' Italia**, there.

Italian commissioners of public safety at Chiasso and other frontier cities were reported ordered by military authorities to remove all Fascist insignia. Travellers from Italy also were ordered to take off party buttons.

Victor Emmanuel Names New Premier

MUSSOLINI

First Major Break in Axis Seen as Prelude to Bid for Separate Peace With Allies

LONDON, July 26.—Martial law was proclaimed throughout Italy today in a swift succession to a government shake-up which eliminated Benito Mussolini and his Fascist cabinet and installed the conservative Marshal Pietro Badoglio as Premier.

There was no Axis announcement of what had become of Mussolini but unconfirmed reports from Stockholm said he had been arrested while trying to flee to Germany.

Roundabout Stockholm reports also told of demonstrations in northern Italy with thousands of Italians shouting "Down with Hitler," "Out with the Germans," and "We want peace."

King Victor Emmanuel made the change in the war leadership, first major break on the Axis front and a possible prelude to an Italian bid for peace.

Badoglio ordered the Army to take over the preservation of public order throughout the country, forbade gatherings of moe than three persons, directed the people to remain at work and empowered the troops to fire on any one who violated the instructions.

Hour by hour, developments in the situation which may hasten the end of the struggle into which Mussolini plunged Italy with the attack, as Germany's ally, upon France, June 10, 1940, were broadcast by the Rome radio and recorded by listening posts throughout the world.

New Chief Says: War Continues

Confronted by some of the gravest problems that the commander of beaten and dispirited army ever faced, with the bulk of Sicily overrun by Allied armies, with German troops and German police on Italian soil, and with mainland cities beset by bombings which threaten ever increasing force, Badoglio said "the war continues."

In addition to his instructions to the people, the new Premier issued a special Order of the Day stating that the voluntary Fascist Militia "is an integral part of the armed forces of the nation and with them, as always, cooperates in the common work and intentions for the defense of the Fatherland."

The 250,000 Blackshirts—once Mussolini's private army—are the best-equipped group among Italy's military forces of about 2,000,000 men.

The broadcast did not bring out why Badoglio considered such a special order necessary, but it may have been a tacit warning to the militiamen that they would remain under his control to the end, despite the withdrawal of Mussolini and the Fascist ministers.

Berlin radio said Badolglo had appointed Baron Raffaele Guariglia, 54, Italian ambassador to Turkey for the last six months, as Foreign Minister in Italy's new government. The foreign ministry was among the portfolios held by Mussolini.

One Italian political source in London predicted that Italy would be out of the war against the Allies within a week. Others were not so optimistic.

This source credited the bombing of Rome and related events, particularly the Vatican radio's denial of Axis propaganda concerning the raid, for the an-

Please Turn to Page Two
See "Mussolini"

BADOGLIO

Churchill Speaks At Next Sitting

LONDON, July 26. — Prime Minister Churchill will give the House of Commons a comprehensive picture of the Italian war situation at the next sitting, it was reported today.

BULLETIN

OTTAWA, July 26—(CP)—The Prices Board today froze stocks of canned goods in the hands of canners and wholesalers "to assure supplies of canned fruits and vegetables for civilian and military requirements for next winter."

Lord Wedgwood Dies

LONDON, July 26—(CP)—Lord Wedgewood, 71, staunch advocate of a union of Great Britain and United States, died at his London home today.

Soviet Joyous At Duce's End

MOSCOW, July 26 — (BUP)—Russians were jubilant at the news of Benito Mussolini's resignation. People on their way to work thronged parks and open squares to stand before glass show-cases where Pravda, official Communist party organ, was displayed with brief official reports on the resignation, the appointment of Marshal Pietro Badoglio, the assumption of military leadership by King Victor Emmanuel and a short biography of Badoglio.

Overseas Air Mail

MONTREAL, July 26—(CP)—A large mail from members of the Canadian Armed Forces overseas arrived here Sunday by the new Trans-Canada Air Lines Atlantic service.

Too Much Hot Air Breaks Any Balloon

97

THE VANCOUVER DAILY PROVINCE ★★★★★ FINAL

49th YEAR—NO. 115 VANCOUVER, B.C., TUESDAY, AUGUST 10, 1943 —24 PAGES PRICE 5 CENTS BY CARRIER $1.00 per month.

CHURCHILL IN CANADA

4 o'Clock Specials — By the Little Colonel

ALL RACES WIDE OPEN

HASTINGS PARK.—With a slow track in prospect for the opening this afternoon, and a lightning fast strip before the program is completed, Shed Row was ready for the Little Colonel when he reported for the Four o'Clock Specials at the race track.

The card gave promise of being replete with thrills, as practically all of the races were packed with contention. **Jockwell**, off his previous brilliant effort, was given the call in the opener, and in the balance of the bill the selectors picked **Franklin D, Risky Play, Streamline, Steveston Bill, Persian Boy** and **Simtee.**

The entire field in the opener was figured to extend **Jockwell.**

In the second, the boys gave **Franklin D.** the call even though he breaks from the outside post position in the sprint.

Happy Duster is making her first start here this season and is reported to have recovered from her recent sickness. She may need racing, however, to attain her peak stride. There is lots of speed in this dash and the horse lucky enough to get around the first turn on top may take the money.

The third brings out a cheap field, and while **Risky Play** is favored, **Wise Witch** and **Stretch** are potent contenders.

Take your choice in the fourth. They all figure. **Streamline** won

(Continued on Page 2.)
See COLONEL.

CLOCKER

FIRST RACE—Colonel Bret, Flagboro, Brilliant Help.
SECOND RACE—Peggy Dot, Lady Pagan, Simony's Boy.
THIRD RACE—Dusty Polly, Divulge, Lady Double.
FOURTH RACE—Miss Olivia, Ione Special Arpeggio.
FIFTH RACE—Teeworth, Patage, My Universe.
SIXTH RACE—Kendahar, Valdina Sun, Youville.
SEVENTH RACE — Corinthian, Fair Cloud, Riverworth.
1ST SUB. RACE—Marion Somers, Swift Heels, Solomon Somers.
2ND SUB. RACE—Ship Biscuit, Drift On, Stolen Color.
BEST BET—Colonel Brett.

JOHNNY MANN

FIRST RACE—Sherron Ann, Colonel Bret, Flagboro.
SECOND RACE—Nanaffran, Lee Somers, Peggy Dot.
THIRD RACE—Divulge, Lady Double, Duty Polly.
FOURTH RACE—Tyler Gulch, Flying Chant, Eltorada.
FIFTH RACE — Ronrico, Teeworth, Patage.
SIXTH RACE—Youville, Ynomis, Kendahar.
SEVENTH RACE—Hi-Ginny, Fair Cloud, Cooperstown.
1ST SUB. RACE—Marion Somers, Eunice Broom, Arab Somers.
2ND SUB. RACE—Watch Tick, Ship Biscuit, Valdina Bully.
BEST BET—Nanaffran.

Province Handicap

★ BY JOHNNY PARK —

For Wednesday's Racing

WEST COAST JOCKEY CLUB
Hastings Park — SECOND MEETING ⅝-MILE TRACK — 4th Day
VANCOUVER, B.C., WEDNESDAY, AUGUST 11, 1943
FIRST EIGHT HORSES TO START
TRACK FAST — FIRST POST 3:30 P.M.

1st Race — Claiming. 3-year-olds and up. 7 Furlongs

Index No.	Horse	Weight		Post No.
4416	COLONEL BRET	117	Just missed last out	(3)
4382	SHERRON ANN	112	Will be tough to beat	(8)
4414	FLAGBORO	108	Will force the pace	(7)
4416	Little Ruler	112	Keen speed on rail	(1)
——	Little Argo	120	If ready, dangerous	(2)
4337	Selfish Joss	115	Has some early lick	(4)
——	Shasta Racket	120	First out, old fave	(6)
4378	Brilliant Help	110	Gradually improving	(5)
	Also eligible—			
4414	SI GREEN	110	At weights first chance	(9)
4372	Rapid Mortgage	112	Should be close up	(10)
4405	Goldie's Pride	112	Could surprise them	(11)
4394	Silver Fur	117	Yet to show best	(12)
4418	Dark Devil	117	Will do later on	(13)
4416	Spanish Ball	117	Not in form yet	(14)

2nd Race— Claiming, 3-year-olds and up, foaled in Western Canada. 7 Furlongs

(4368)	NANAFFRAN	115	Closes fast	(1)
(4434)	PEGGY DOT	115	The one to beat	(7)
4448	SIMONY'S BOY	120	Toughest spot yet	(2)
4400	Lady Pagan	113	Will be in fight	(6)
(4455)	Fay Park	115	Won cleverly Monday	(5)
4461	Lee Somers	120	At tops this season	(4)
4455	Bruntsfield	118	Does better in mud	(3)

3rd Race— Allowance. 2-year-olds. 5 Furlongs

(4429)	DUSTY POLLY	110	Has lots of early foot	(2)
(4457)	LADY DOUBLE	110	Showing keen speed	(1)
4429	SOMERS BAND	104	Could improve here	(3)
4429	Divulge	110	Is right on edge.	(5)
4457	Gallant Simon	104	Needs more racing	(7)
4429	Placerville	111	Due to improve	(6)
4408	Will Call	108	Gradually improving	(4)
——	aQueen Dot	108	First out, no line	(8)
	Also eligible—			
——	aDuro Fox	108	First out, no line	(9)
	(a) C. T. Clifford entry.			

4th Race— Allowance. 3-year-olds. 7 Furlongs

4407	BONNIE PARK	113	Stumbled last out	(6)
4430	MISS OLIVIA	113	On rail, early foot	(1)
4407	FLYING CHANT	113	Tired with better field	(2)
(4358)	Miss Gallator	106	Will be in fight	(7)
(4458)	Tyler Gulch	118	Won cleverly Monday	(8)
4407	Ione Special	113	Has royal chance	(3)
4415	Arpeggio	106	Running below 1942 form	(5)
——	Glad Answer	108	May surprise them	(4)
	Also eligible—			
4458	Special Lady	108	Has an outside chance	(9)
4452	Paddygoeasy	111	Closes very fast	(10)
4458	Eltorado	108	Tired other day	(11)
4452	Special Briar	113	Has early speed	(12)
4458	Miss Betty B	108	In trouble last out	(13)

5th Race— LANSDOWNE HANDICAP 3-year-olds and up. Mile and 1/16

(4459)	DALKEITH	118	May repeat here	(6)
(4424)	TEEWORTH	119	At top of form	(4)
4459	PATAGE	116	At tops, one to beat	(1)
4445	Saffworth	108	Will close fast	(3)
4459	My Universe	115	At weights figures	(7)
4438	Singing Heels	112	A real threat	(8)
4459	aRonrico	111	Will improve off last	(5)
4424	Maginot Line	106	Appears outclassed	(2)
	Also eligible—			
4445	Killarney L	112	Route trifle far	(9)
4445	Sahara Chief	111	Dangerous at weights	(10)
4424	Mesmerist	105	In light, look out	(11)
4445	aHi-Rythm	108	Just a long chance	(12)
	aMiss R. Bain entry.			

6th Race— Claiming. 3-year-olds and up. Mile and 3-8

4461	YOUVILLE	111	Will be close up.	(5)
4453	ASCOT MAID	108	Watch out at weights.	(7)
(4423)	MARCO	120	Won last handily.	(1)
4461	East Calling	120	Runs for new owner.	(3)
4461	Valdina Sun	123	Has a royal chance.	(6)
4466	Kandahar	120	Could take it all.	(2)
444	Ynomis	105	Improving (tab.)	(4)

7th Race— Claiming 3-year-olds and up. Mile and 1/16

(4453)	HI-GINNY	113	May be three in row	(2)
(4412)	FAIR CLOUD	115	Right at tops	(8)
4447	CORINTHIAN	113	Consistent, overdue	(7)
4451	Riverworth	111	Rates with pack	(5)
4449	Pinchconard	115	Will be charging	(6)
4440	Vegas Jeanne	115	Figures with leaders	(4)
(4432)	Cooperstown	120	Tougher bunch today	(3)
4452	Journeyman	105	Tough field to whip	(1)

FIRST SUBSTITUTE RACE—Mile and One-Sixteenth—Selections in order — Marion Somers, Swift Heels, Solomon Somers, Arab Somers, Silumo, Eunice Broom, Scotch Jean.

SECOND SUBSTITUTE RACE—Seven Furlongs — Selections in order—Belle Park, Truely Flo, Stolen Color, Valdina Bully, Ship Biscuit, Little Gloomy, Watch Tick, Drift On, Nickajack, Zelpha Lass, Barmetto, Go-Getter, Even Roll, Queen Irene.

★★★ DUSTY POLLY

RUSS AIM AT SMOLENSK

LONDON, Aug. 10.—(AP)—Russian forces captured Khotinets, a district centre and railway station 45 miles east of Bryansk, and 30 other hamlets today, Moscow announced tonight.

In the Kharkov drive the Red Army advanced 5 to 7 miles, capturing more than 70 populated places, including Liptsi, 12 miles northeast of Kharkov.

Moving up on Sumy—an objective in the general drive toward Kiev—the Russians stormed into Bolshoi Doblik, 14 miles southeast of Sumy, a special communique said.

By HENRY C. CASSIDY.
Associated Press Staff Writer.

MOSCOW, Aug. 10. — Kharkov, third largest city in Russia, was reported within range of the Red Army's heavy guns today as the fast-moving Soviet forces stepped up their assaults on the Ukrainian city and also on the big German base of Bryansk, 250 miles to the north.

(Continued on Page 2.)
See RUSSIA.

Ship Worker Killed In Fall

NORTH VANCOUVER, Aug. 10.—Harry Joseph Sugden, Burrard Drydock employee, 344 East Hastings, Vancouver, died Monday night in North Vancouver General Hospital from injuries received when he fell 30 feet from a ladder into the hold of a ship.

Sugden was climbing out of the hold and had a hammer and wrench in one hand and was holding to the ladder with the other. He apparently slipped or missed a rung of the ladder and fell backwards. He struck his head, fracturing the skull and breaking both of his arms.

An inquest will be held Thursday.

FIRST PICTURE OF PLANE WRECK

This tiny ringed blotch on the vertical face of a 7000 foot peak in the Fraser Valley is where 13 passengers and crew of a Canadian Pacific airliner lost their lives on December 20 last year. The picture, with other exclusive photographs on Page 14, was taken three hours after Pilot Don Patry's discovery of the wreckage had ended a personal hunt of months for the missing plane. The pictures were snapped as Patry's plane dodged among jagged peaks to get as close to the scattered debris of the machine as he could. See other pictures on Page 14.

Final BULLETINS

Protest Votes

EDMONTON, Aug. 10.—(CP)—Results in the four federal by-elections Monday, in which Liberal candidates were defeated, "are protest votes against ceilings on wages and farm prices, and the general war-time restrictions," Hon. James A. MacKinnon, federal minister of trade and commerce, said in an interview today.

Prisoner Stabbed

FOLSOM, Cal., Aug. 10.—(AP)—Warden Clyde I. Plummer of Folsom prison, announced today that "Smiling Joe" Chavez, four-time loser who was doing 10 years to life for assault in Santa Barbara, was stabbed to death in the old cell block house today while en route to the mess hall for breakfast.

Faces Murder Charge

REGINA, Aug. 10.—(CP)—Pte. Edward William Stonechild, 25, Regina, appeared in R.C.M.P. Court and was charged with the murder of Evelyn Severight, 16, who died in North Annex, Regina suburb, Sunday morning. He was remanded without plea. The girl was found dead in a bed. Police said that she had apparently been beaten late Saturday night. Pte. Stonechild is a treaty Indian from the Pasqua Reserve.

B. C. Pioneer Buried

REVELSTOKE, Aug. 10.—Funeral services were held here for Samuel D. Crowle, 82, who walked into the present site of Revelstoke in 1885 before the railway, and farmed here since. He was a native of England.

City Men Held

WINNIPEG, Aug. 10.—(CP)—Joseph H. Ireland and James Grant, both of Vancouver, were committed for trial at the next assizes on a charge of attempted shopbreaking today when arraigned for preliminary hearing in Police Court here. They were arrested by Royal Canadian Mounted Police July 31 after they were alleged to have made several attempts to break into a Winnipeg drug store.

Victoria Men Killed In Sicily

VICTORIA, Aug. 10.—(CP)—Lieut. Douglas McIntyre, last week reported wounded in action in Sicily on July 22, died the same day, according to a cable received by his mother, Mrs. D. N. McIntyre. He is the first Victoria officer reported killed in action in Sicily.

Word has been received by Mrs. A. desSeres, of the death of her only son, Pte. Raymond Henry Hunter, 23, who was killed in action in Sicily July 10.

WRECK LIKE RUBBLE PILE

Observers who flew over Peak today for a third look at the wrecked Canadian Pacific Air Lines' transport plane found Monday saw two black bears in the vicinity of the wreckage, Captain Don Patry, chief pilot for the company in the west, reports.

By DON MASON.

Mystery of why a Canadian Pacific Air Lines' plane lost its way 15 minutes out of Vancouver last December 20, and carried 13 people to sudden death on a snow-laden mountain 75 miles southeast of here, may be solved by the last words written in the ship's log.

The plane — battered and smashed until metal parts are scattered all over the mountainside—rests 100 feet from the top of a 5000-foot peak nine miles from Agassiz. It is 7000 feet above sea level.

It was sighted from the air at noon, Monday, by C.P.A.L.'s chief pilot in the west, Captain Don Patry.

"The passengers and crew must have died instantly.

(Continued on Page 2.)
See WRECK.

Came Within 3 Miles of Wreck

A ground search party looking for the lost Canadian Pacific Air Lines' plane last Christmas stood only three miles away from the wreckage but failed to see it because of the heavy blanket of snow.

"We were looking straight at it," George Strevens.

SUB. MARY CHURCHILL
. . . Accompanies father.

ARRIVES FOR WAR PARLEY; TO SEE F.D.R.

(By Canadian Press.)

QUEBEC, Aug. 10. — Prime Minister Churchill has arrived in Canada and before he returns to Britain will confer with President Roosevelt and the combined chiefs of staff of the United States and the United Kingdom.

It was the Prime Minister's fourth visit to the American continent.

His arrival coincided with United Nations victories in the Mediterranean, Russia and the southwest Pacific.

He was accompanied by a top flight array of his military advisers. He will consult with President Roosevelt after a series of conferences with Prime Minister W. L. Mackenzie King.

NO RUSS DELEGATE.

(Shortly after an announcement of Prime Minister Churchill's arrival in Quebec, President Roosevelt told his press conference there would be no Russian participation in the new conferences, although he said this did not mean that he would not be glad to have the Russians present. This was in response to a question whether Russia would be represented.)

Mr. Churchill was greeted on his arrival here by Prime Minister King.

During his stay in Canada he will be a guest of the Canadian Government.

The following is the terse statement issued late this afternoon by Mr. King's temporary office in Quebec:

"The Prime Minister of Great Britain has arrived in Canada accompanied by Lord Leather, the minister of war transport for the United Kingdom, and the British chiefs of staff.

"Mr. Churchill will have discussions with Mr. Mackenzie King and later will attend a conference with President Roosevelt and the combined chiefs of staff of the United States and the United Kingdom."

Mr. Churchill was accompanied by his wife and his daughter, Subaltern Mary Churchill of the British Auxiliary Territorial Services.

MANY NOTABLES.

In his party, according to an official announcement, was Wing Commander G. P. Gibson, D.F.C., who led the air squadron which successfully bombed the Mohne Eder dams.

Others listed in the British Prime Minister's party are Lord

(Continued on Page 2.)
See CHURCHILL.

Youth Dies After Day At Beach

Clifford Robinson, 17, son of Mr. and Mrs. A. Robinson, 111 West Tenth, died suddenly in the General Hospital Monday afternoon.

Police reports say that the youth was in good health on Sunday and spent the day at Kitsilano Beach. He complained of a severe headache early next morning, and was sent to the hospital where he died half an hour after being admitted.

RACING HANDICAPS AND SELECTIONS

NEW FRANCE INVASION FEARS GRIP GERMANS

Clark Gable in Big Raid on Ruhr

The Vancouver Sun
The Vancouver Evening Newspaper Owned and Operated by Vancouver People
FOUNDED 1886 VOL. LVII—No. 260 VANCOUVER, B.C., THURSDAY, AUGUST 12, 1943 PRICE 5c

Flak Hits Film Star's Fortress

LONDON, Aug. 12—(AP)—Capt. Clark Gable, the former movie star, rode in the leading Flying Fortress of the U. S. 8th Air Force group which attacked Gelsenkirchen today and returned to base unhurt although enemy anti-aircraft fire cut 15 holes in his ship.

Gable stood during the entire six-hour flight between the pilot, Maj. Theodore R. Milton of Washington, D.C., and the co-pilot, Lt. John B. Carraway of Raleigh, N.C., shooting movies for a gunnery training film.

By British United Press

LONDON, Aug. 12.—Massive fleets of American Flying Fortresses dealt record-shattering blows at the German Ruhr and Rhineland today, concentrating their great weight of bombs on the tightly packed war targets of Gelsenkirchen, Bonn and Wesseling.

In action for the first time this month, the Fortresses, in very large formations, carried out perhaps the greatest effort of the American air forces in Britain, sweeping by daylight over the most strongly defended region in the world to hammer home their destructive blows.

The Ruhr raiders flew at the greatest altitude the Forts yet have used where the temperature was 45 degrees below zero. They bombed a number of targets, including the vital synthetic oil factories at Gelsenkirchen.

Another huge formation—one crewman reported that "I saw more Forts in the sky than I knew there were"—struck targets at Bonn, famous university town, rail hub and industrial centre 15 miles south of Cologne. Bonn also is the birthplace of the composer Beethoven.

FIGHTERS ON JOB

In diversionary operations, medium bombers attacked without loss the Poix airfield in France.

Please Turn to Page Two
See "Ruhr Raid"

Churchill Thrills One Picanniny

NIAGARA FALLS, N. Y., Aug. 12—(AP)—As Prime Minister Winston Churchill's special train left Niagara Falls today, Freddie Jones, a Negro clerk at the American Railway Express office at the station, trotted beside the rear platform.

"Please, Mr. Churchill," he asked, "give me that cigar you're smoking."

The Prime Minister shook his head negatively, but at the same time reached into his pocket. "Here's another one," he said, dropping a smoke to the Negro who had followed the train for 50 yards.

"Boy," Jones said, "it's a 30-center."

Premier Hart In Golf Final

VICTORIA, Aug. 12—(CP)—Premier John Hart and Dr. J. P. Loudon of Yakima will meet over 18 holes tomorrow morning for the grand championship of the Seniors' Northwest Golf Association.

In today's semi-finals Hart defeated D. R. Munro, Portland, 2 and 1, while Loudon won by a similar margin from R. E. Campbell, Seattle.

LATE NEWS BULLETINS

'Italy Out in Ten Days'

LONDON, Aug. 12—(CP)—Radio France in Algiers said in a broadcast tonight that the secretary of the Italian embassy in Istanbul, Turkey, had declared publicly that Italy in 10 days would no longer be in the war.

Logger Killed on Island

VICTORIA, Aug. 12—(CP)—Albert Hendrickson, 30, a logger, was killed Wednesday night at the Franklin River camp of Bloedel Stewart & Welch Ltd., B.C. Police headquarters here learned today. Hendrickson was struck by a snag.

U-Boat Crews Mutiny

STOCKHOLM, Aug. 12—(BUP)—The newspaper Handels Tidningen, quoting a clandestine radio, reported today that crews of German U-boats had refused to go to sea because Heinrich Himmler, Nazi Gestapo chief, had ordered censors to delete all references to bombings in letters from home.

Marigny Denied Killing

NASSAU, Bahamas, Aug. 12—(AP)—A statement by Alfed De Marigny flatly denying that he killed his millionaire father-in-law, Sir Harry Oakes, was read today at a preliminary hearing for the yachtsman.

MOVIE STAR IN FORTRESS RAID ON RHINE

Living a part far more dramatic than any he ever played on the screen, Capt. Clark Gable rode in the leading plane as U.S. Flying Fortresses raided the German Rhineland today. Gable, an air gunnery instructor, shot movies of the action for a training film.

Americans Bomb Japan Kurile Base

WASHINGTON, Aug. 12—The Navy department announced today that nine United States army bombers attacked enemy installations in the Kurile Islands which guard the northern approaches to the Japanese homeland. Five enemy fighter planes were shot down and two American bombers are missing.

By British United Press

WASHINGTON, Aug. 12.—An American bombing raid on the northern end of the Japanese Kurile Island chain was reported by Tokyo radio today, and nervous enemy propagandists warned their people that it was a forerunner of U.S. attacks on the heart of Japan.

Tokyo broadcasts recorded by the Federal Communications Commission said the attack on the Kuriles was made at 7:20 a.m. today Japanese time (3:20 p.m. Vancouver Time, Wednesday) by five B-24 Liberators and three B-17 Flying Fortresses based in the Aleutians.

It was possible the bombers had hit for the second time at the Paramushiru naval-air base 765 miles west of Attu, westernmost of the Aleutians.

Paramushiru guards the northern approaches to the Japanese home islands.

Churchill in U.S. To Meet Roosevelt

By HAROLD FAIR
Canadian Press Staff Writer

NIAGARA FALLS, Ont., Aug. 12. — Prime Minister Churchill and his daughter Mary today visited this border tourist centre and then motored across the Lower Arch Bridge over the Niagara river to Niagara Falls, N.Y.

Mr. Churchill left Niagara Falls, N.Y., to meet President Roosevelt, it was made known here today. The time and place of the meeting were not disclosed.

The Prime Minister and his daughter, who arrived at Victoria Park station in a six-car special Canadian Pacific railway train, viewed the falls area before motoring across the river. Mrs. Churchill remained in Quebec.

They saw the falls, which Mary pronounced "absolutely wonderful," the whirlpool and the monument to General Sir Isaac Brock, killed in a battle during the war of 1812.

For the British Prime Minister, it was no new sight, but for Mary the tour was one of sheer delight. She bought souvenir postcards at one point.

"My lad, I saw the falls before you were born," Mr. Churchill told a Canadian Press man when asked if he had been here before. "They have been going quite a long time." He had seen them first in 1900, he added.

Mary Churchill told Mrs. Inglis, wife of the Niagara Falls mayor, that she nearly fell out of bed when she heard she was

Please Turn to Page Two
See "Churchill"

Police to Round Up 'Young Loafers'

OTTAWA, Aug. 12—(CP)—Arthur MacNamara, director of National Selective Service, said today that municipal, provincial and Royal Canadian Mounted Police are being used in some parts of Canada to round up "young loafers and vagrant jobless" for compulsory work placement.

MacNamara explained that "chronic" loafers and persons unemployed for more than six months can be sent to a work camp for refusal. So far municipal police forces have had such assignments only at Fort William and Windsor.

167 Britains Killed

LONDON, Aug. 2—(CP)—Civilian air raid casualties in Britain during July were 167 killed and 210 injured, it was announced today.

Bold British Sub Exploit Revealed

STOCKHOLM, Aug. 12.—The Swedish Norwegian Press Bureau reported from Oslo today that new information had disclosed that a British submarine was responsible for the Easter attack on five ships in Oslo harbor.

Three boats were sunk and two were damaged by torpedoes. A Norwegian American Line steamer in the Trondheim Fjord, used by the Germans as a transport ship, also was damaged by a torpedo when attacked off Arendal in the Skagerrak.

The press bureau said a German officer described the exploit as "one of the boldest submarine enterprises of the entire war."

The Germans first believed that saboteurs were responsible and arrested about 12 men.

City Fuel Profiteer Fined $500

The heaviest sentence ever meted out for violation of Wartime Prices and Trade Board ceiling prices on fuel was handed down today by Magistrate Mackenzie Matheson when he sentenced Kartar Singh, wood dealer, of 872 Homer, to three months in jail and a $500 fine or an additional three months.

He was charged with selling mill wood at a higher price than that allowed by the board. He sold a cord and a half of mill wood for $14.50. The ceiling price is $3.90 per cord.

After the Prices Board inspector had suggested that the customer should get a refund, Kartar gave back $8.50.

W. H. Campbell, board counsel, asked for a heavy penalty.

"This has become a racket in this city—one of the worst the prices board has to contend with," he said.

"The dealers have been givn fair prices and in many cases have been given increases. A lot of dealers are giving short measure and the board is seeking the severe penalty as a preventive against offenses of this kind, which are very prevalent in Vancouver."

Youth Warned for Wearing Uniform

For wearing a uniform of His Majesty's land forces without authority, R. L. Shortt, 21, no fixed address, was sentenced to one month at hard labor by Magistrate Matheson today, but the warrant of commitment will be held for 48 hours to give him a chance to leave town.

Detective Len Cuthbert told the magistrate Shortt had worn the unform in order to buy a return ticket, Vancouver to Saskatoon, at half fare.

Shortt said he had been in the army three years and was discharged January last year in Toronto after an accident in which he lost the sight of one eye.

MOOSE JAW, Aug. 12—(CP)—Two members of the Royal Air Force attached to No. 32 SFTS (RAF) were killed Wednesday night when a training plane crashed near the school.

BASEBALL

AMERICAN LEAGUE

First game—		R	H	E
Boston	005 004 002—	10	9	1
Chicago	103 100 100—	6	12	1

Ryba, O'Neil (5), Brown (7) and Conroy; Dietrich, Swift (8) and Tresh.

		R	H	E
Philadelphia ..	000 100 002—	3	10	1
Cleveland ..	100 001 02x—	4	10	3

Arntzen and Wagner; Bagby, Heving (9) and Rosar.

NATIONAL LEAGUE

		R	H	E
St. Louis	101 010 010—	4	9	0
New York	000 010 000—	1	3	2

C. Cooper and W. Cooper; Chase and Lombardi.

		R	H	E
Chicago ..	000 002 000 000—	2	7	1
Boston ..	200 000 000 001—	3	11	1

(12 innings.)

Wyse and McCullough; Javery and Klutz.

Racing Program, Handicap and Selections, Page 2.

Huns Get Jitters As Evacuation of Sicily Under Way

STOCKHOLM, Aug. 12—(BUP)—Svenska Dagbladets' Berne correspondent reported today the Germans taking measures to meet an expected Allied invasion of the French Atlantic coast.

Nazi fears apparently are based on reports from reconnaissance planes of troop movements in Britain.

By NOLAND NORGAARD
Associated Press War Correspondent

WITH THE BRITISH 8TH ARMY IN SICILY, Aug. 12—German evacuation of troops and equipment from Sicily to the Italian mainland was reported to be in full swing today with at least 80 vessels plying night and day across the Messina Strait under a record umbrella of anti-aircraft fire which was growing steadily in intensity.

Strong German rear-guards, well entrenched with mortars, machine-guns and artillery, and extensive road demolitions continued to make progress slow for the Allied armies converging on Messina and the evacuation beaches while the bulk of the German troops were being withdrawn.

Determined to save all possible equipment, the German High Command was reported to have decreed "the passport to Italy is a gun," meaning that troops must bring their weapons along if they want places in the boats at Messina.

British forces advancing along the east coast encountered a skeleton enemy force in a strong line covering the only avenues of approach with heavy mortar fire and a battery of possibly 16 88-millimetre guns.

The narrow, winding mountain roads the Germans are defending made it extremely difficult to dislodge them.

BERLIN ADMISSION

Confirming the evacuation reports, Capt. Ludwig Sertorius, German military commentator, in a Berlin broadcast today said:

"The situation in Sicily is now characterized by a systematic new disengagement movement by German and Italian troops. . . . What matters is to prevent the enemy from extending his operations to objectives on the mainland."

Meanwhile in a second amphibious flank attack on the north coast of Sicily, units of the American 7th Army landed east of Cape Orlando and supporting naval guns beat off serious enemy counter-attacks.

Allied headquarters communique said Cape Orlando was outflanked in the surprise attack Tuesday night.

The Americans' first amphibious flanking attack was made three days ago when sea-borne infantrymen landed at the mouth of the Rishmarino River, three miles east of San Agata, where they were joined by the main forces of the American column after the town's capture.

In the island drive on Randazzo, the American 7th Army column was reported to have advanced half way along the road from Cesaro to that bitterly-defended German stronghold, with the Canadians attacking northward in close co-operation.

The Germans were fighting a strong rear gard action on the east coast, but the 8th Army driving northward toward Messina has captured a village south of Prajola and the village of Zafferana Etna, on the eastern slopes of Mount Etna about five miles from fallen Guardia.

Soviet Troops Cut Vital Railway Near Kharkov

LONDON, Aug. 12—(AP)—Russian troops advanced to within five miles of Kharkov from the northeast today while other columns driving up from the southeast captured Chugeyev, 22 miles away from the Ukrainian manufacturing centre, Moscow said tonight.

By HENRY C. CASSIDY
Associated Press Staff Writer

MOSCOW, Aug. 12. — The Russian stranglehold on Kharkov tightened today as Red Army troops drove within 7½ miles of the big Ukrainian city from the northeast and severed the Poltava-Kharkov railway, main lifeline of the defending Nazis, over a 10-mile stretch west of the nearly encircled bastion.

The big drive against Bryansk rolled ahead through fresh German tank divisions which had been rallied in an effort to halt the advance.

East of Kharkov, where Red Army forces were fighting their way tenaciously into the city's suburban districts, the Germans were reported felling cherry and apple trees to construct pillboxes among the ruins of the villages.

The drive on Bryansk from Orel pressed forward through 70 more villages yesterday and drew steadily closer to the main objective.

Both the Nazi high command and transocean, German Propaganda Agency, said tremendously powerful Russian attacks continued south and southwest of Vyazma on the Smolensk front, an offensive not yet even hinted at in dispatches from Moscow.

★★★★★ RACING HANDICAPS AND SELECTIONS ★★★★★

KEY SICILY TOWN FALLS

PEACE RIOTS IN MILAN

Fourteen direct hits killed this Japanese destroyer, pictured here in its death throes off Cape Gloucester, New Britain. Helpless Jap crew can do nothing but cower before the certain devastation as U.S. Army bombers rock the destroyer with direct hits. One of the bombs can be seen (left) just about to strike the vessel. After stopping the Jap ship dead with accurate bombing, the bombers winged back to home base, returned the next day to send her to the bottom.

The Vancouver Sun

The Vancouver Evening Newspaper Owned and Operated by Vancouver People

VANCOUVER, B.C., FRIDAY, AUGUST, 13, 1943 PRICE 5¢

1000 Tons TNT Blast Italy City

By ERNEST AGNEW
Associated Press Staff Writer

LONDON, Aug. 13—(BUP)—The Swiss radio said tonight that anti-war demonstrations broke out in Milan today a few hours after British planes had dropped more than 1000 tons of bombs on the city, and that troops were patrolling the streets.

By British United Press

LONDON, Aug. 13.—Hammering home Prime Minister Churchill's warning that Italy would be "seared, scarred and blackened from end to end" if she remains in the war, the industrial cities of Milan and Turin in northern Italy were heavily bombed last night during operations which probably put 1000 or more fighters and bombers into the air. At the same time Berlin was raided by a cloud of Mosquito bombers.

Milan was the principal target of the great force of bombers.

The Air Ministry said that a far heavier load of bombs was dropped on Italy last night than in any previous single raid, with more than 1000 long tons showered upon Milan alone.

Big planes from the Canadian Bomber Group participated in the smash at Milan, while other Canadians, notably those serving with the RAF Stirling squadrons, flew on the raid against Turin.

Thirteen bombers were reported missing from the night's operations.

Industries and communications of Milan, Italy's second largest city and chief industrial centre, were the objectives of the heavy raid on that city, the Air Ministry report said, and added that first reports showed that both the Italian attacks were well concentrated.

100

Swiss reports said the hour-long assault on the northern Italian city resulted in explosions that could be heard on the border and that the glow of raging fires could be seen plainly.

British intruder planes struck at the continent last night, attacking Axis shipping and airports in France, and shooting down a German plane over France.

The night raids followed daylight attacks on three German Ruhr and Rhineland cities yesterday by American heavy bombers.

BASEBALL

AMERICAN

Washington	350 003 000	11	11	1
Detroit	000 001 101	3	6	2

Candini and Gulliani; Overmire, Dana (1), Gorsica (2), Orrell (7) and Unser.

Ex-Gov't Official Charged With Theft

VICTORIA, Aug. 13—(CP)—Three charges of theft of securities valued at $1200 were read in city police court today against D'Arcy C. Martin, former deputy inspector of trust companies and deputy assessor of probate and succession duties for the provincial government.

Magistrate M. C. Hall set bail at $5000 for the three charges.

The accused through his counsel, Joseph McKenna, elected higher court trial. He was remanded until next Friday when a day for the preliminary hearing will be set.

Racing Program, Handicap and Selections, Page 3

Quebec Meeting On Japan

By Canadian Press

LONDON, Aug. 13.—Moscow announced officially today that Soviet participation "was not and is not envisaged" in the forthcoming Churchill-Roosevelt conference at Quebec, and first London reaction was that the talks would deal primarily with the war on Japan.

In a broadcast recorded here by the Soviet Monitor, the official Soviet News Agency TASS said it had been authorized to state that foreign reports Russia would attend the conference "are based on a misunderstanding."

"The Soviet government," the statement said, "did not receive an invitation to be present at the meeting, and because of the nature of the conference the participation of any one representative of the Soviet government at the meeting in Quebec was not and is not envisaged."

Some London quarters thought the reference to the "nature" of the conference significant.

Since Russia is not at war with Japan, it is not likely that the Soviet would be invited to any conference concerned chiefly with fighting in the Pacific.

The wording of the Moscow announcement made it seem clear, however, that Premier Stalin had been given advance details of the conference. In this connection, it was recalled that the British and American ambassadors conferred with Stalin this week.

New Red Offensive Launched on Smolensk

LONDON, Aug. 13—(CP)—A new Soviet offensive in the central front airmed at Smolensk, 85 miles to the north-west, began near Spas Demensk a few days ago, a special Russian bulletin announced tonight.

The offensive struck in two directions: From the district north-west of Spas Demensk southwards, and from the region south-east of the town towards the north-west.

The troops moving south cracked the strongly fortified German defense line on a front of 22 miles, the bulletin said.

This column in the north advanced 13 miles, while the column in the south gained 11 miles after breaking through the front in a nine-mile swathe.

The two attacks apparently were aimed at converging on the railway to Smolensk.

MOSCOW, Aug. 13.—Russian vanguards smashed into the northern suburbs of Kharkov today as Red armies began a final assault to capture the city and drive the Axis back to the Dnieper river.

The German garrison, only recently reinforced by fresh troops, rushed directly from the Reich, was reported falling back steadily into a narrowing corridor southwest of the city.

At one point southeast of the city, the German retreat had become a rout with the enemy forces fleeing in disorder, the Soviet High Command said. Prisoners and booty were mounting by the hour.

The capture of Chuguev, defense anchor 22 miles southeast of Kharkov, appeared to have sealed the fate of the big industrial city, the "Pittsburgh of the Ukraine."

'Glider Girl' Is Thriller

When Capt. Jimmy Carr commenced an epochal glider tour over the continent it had been extensively advertised that he would be accompanied in the spectacular flights by his fiancee, Loraine Stuart. But Loraine's rival for Jimmy's love, Bat Friday, went instead, and Loraine was left behind, fuming. Were there ructions? There were!—and how! Read the sensational novel "Glider Girl," which will appear, complete, in tomorrow's magazine section of The Vancouver Sun.

Premier Hart First Triple Golf Champ

VICTORIA, Aug. 13—(CP)—Premier John Hart today became the first triple champion in the history of the Seniors' Northwest Golf Association, defeating Dr. J. P. Loudon, Yakima, 5 and 3, in the 18-hole final at Oak Bay. Hart had previously won the crown in 1935 and 1936.

Brilliant putting and more steadiness off the tees gave Hart a distinct edge over his Washington opponent. Turning point in the match came on the sixth, seventh and eighth holes. With the match all even Hart got a par four at the sixth, and Loudon conceded the hole to go one down.

And Now—Duce Drowns Off Sub

NEW YORK, Aug. 13—(BUP)—The New York Post said today that "according to reports in circles frequently well informed, Benito Mussolini was drowned in a submarine while attempting to escape from Italy.

Mussolini, the newspapers said, was reported to have boarded the submarine "probably at Leghorn, within a short interval after his political downfall." "The submarine was sighted by Allied airmen, who bombed it repeatedly and sent it to the bottom."

Americans Blast Rome Rail Yards

By RELMAN MORIN
Associated Press War Correspondent

ALLIED HEADQUARTERS, North Africa, Aug. 13.—An American air armada of possibly 500 planes swarmed over Rome shortly before noon today, smashing the San Lorenzo and Littorio railroad yards, key hubs of the Axis communications system in Italy.

The first waves of heavy bombers roared over the San Lorenzo yards a little after 11 a.m., while medium bombers were coming in at low level over the Littorio yards, bombing and pouring tracers into the already burning target area.

The number of bombers participating in the mass attack was said to equal those that raided the Italian capital July 19, when 500 heavy American bombers and 200 fighters took part. A total of 1100 tons of explosives were loosed then.

The attacks today brought home to the Italian people recent warnings that the mass attacks were about to be resumed.

The huge fleet was escorted by American fighters.

As far as was known, no statement of explanation was radioed to the Italian people this time as was done before.

The new attack was a warning that the Allied threat to bomb Rome again would be maintained.

While it was not officially stated, it was believed the attacking force probably encountered heavier fighter opposition than in the previous raid when few Axis interceptors and almost negligible anti-aircraft fire were found over the target.

There have been indications that the German air force has had to send new fighter squadrons into southern Italy in an attempt to bolster their shattered strength over Sicily.

Drowns in Columbia

CASTLEGAR, Aug. 13—(CP)—Cyril Plotnikoff, nine, drowned Thursday while swimming in the Columbia River.

Randazzo Captured By Allies

ALLIED HEADQUARTERS, North Africa, Aug. 13—(BUP)—Allied troops have captured Randazzo, strategic Sicilian communications centre on the northern slope of Mount Etna, it was announced today.

Capture of Randazzo, which lies in the pass between Mount Etna and the Caronian mountain range, left the Axis without any good link between the northern and eastern coasts of Sicily.

By REYNOLDS PACKARD
Special to The Vancouver Sun
Copyright, 1943, by British United Press

ALLIED HEADQUARTERS, North Africa, Aug. 13.—American troops plunged ahead eight miles on the north coast of Sicily, capturing Cape d'Orlando and two towns beyond it, in general Allied advances against fierce rear guard action covering a "quickening" German evacuation of the island, it was announced today.

As the campaign went into its final phase with tacit Axis acknowledgement that the Battle for Sicily was lost, the Allied bag of prisoners rose to 130,000, including another Italian general. This one named Fiumara, believed to be the commander of the Naples division. His mount was a donkey.

Capitalizing on the second landing behind the German lines, the United States Second Army drove eastward behind a shattering sea air bombardment.

The landing force and the main army swarmed through the Cape d'Orlando, anchor of the Axis north coast defenses and forward to occupy the towns of Naso and Brolo.

8TH ARMY GAIN

On the east coast, the British Eighth Army moved up four miles to occupy the village of the Archirafi and threaten the neighboring towns of Gaiire and Riposto.

While wings of the Allied push reached within 35 miles of Messina, American and Canadian forces thrusting through the centre at the key junction of Randazzo gained about four miles in the rugged mountain pass west of the town, which already was under light artillery fire.

Dispatches from the Sicilian front say the evacuation of Sicily by the main body of German troops is in full swing.

Prairie Girl Missing

SHELL LAKE, Sask., Aug. 13—(CP)—Police dogs today aided a search party in a hunt for Margaret Wildred, 11, missing from her home here since Sunday.

LATE NEWS BULLETINS

No Peace Bid From Italy

WASHINGTON, Aug. 13—(BUP)—Secretary of State Cordell Hull said today that no tangible armistice feelers had yet come from Italy.

Confesses Killing Twins

CLEVELAND, Aug. 13—(CP)—The slain bodies of Charles and James Collins, 13-year-old twins, missing more than 24 hours, were found today in bushes in Suburban Bay Village. Detectives said a 19-year-old youth, recently released from the psychopathic ward of a hospital, had confessed the shootings.

British Ask Prisoner Probe

LONDON, Aug. 13—(AP)—Switzerland, as the protecting power of British interests in Axis and occupied countries, has been asked by the British government to investigate reports that Italy is transferring British prisoners of war to Germany. The Daily Express in a Berne dispatch reported 2500 prisoners had been moved in one group recently and said, if this were true, it might have an adverse effect on conditions imposed on Italy if she surrenders.

Canadians Role Disputed

By ALAN RANDAL
Canadian Press Staff Writer

LONDON, Aug. 13.—Canadians apparently are no longer fighting in Sicily and it is believed in London they are the subject of Canadian-British discussions now on how they should be used—as a complete Canadian Army or broken up and integrated into British armies in future actions.

From what I have heard, I think it can be said that Canadian authorities are desirous that their troops be used as a complete army.

It is considered here that the mising of this question may have been the reason why Col. J. L. Ralston, Canadian Defense Minister, raced home after only a few days in Britain. When the Minister arrived it was believed he would stay some time and it is understood here his business is still to be cleaned up so he is likely to return shortly.

From Algiers, Louis V. Hunter, Canadian Press war correspondent, has written that the Canadians are believed to be resting.

In the London Bureau the first question our editors asked was, "What is Hunter trying to tell us?" Maybe he was not trying to tell us anything, but it was realized he was writing against censorship and security and was unable to say much, and if the Canadians are not fighting it is obviously factual that they are resting.

But there is a feeling that there is something more to the Canadians' inactivity than the need of rest and perhaps some grounds for conjecture that the Canadians were pulled from the line while discussions took place as to their ultimate disposition in the armed line-up of the United Nations.

Undoubtedly the use of the Canadian Army must be high on the agenda of Mr. Churchill's discussions with Canadian leaders at Quebec.

Canadian war correspondents who move with the troops in Britain say the men want to fight as a whole and feel they will eventually.

Army men are as puzzled as anybody as to why the Canadians are not included in reports of the Sicily clean-up assaults.

They were among the first to notice that Ross Munro, Canadian Press war correspondent who landed with the Canadians in Sicily, now is covering the doings of the British 8th Army.

THE VANCOUVER DAILY PROVINCE

49th YEAR — NO. 125 | VANCOUVER, B.C., SATURDAY, AUGUST 21, 1943—50 PAGES | PRICE 10 CENTS

KISKA TAKEN

★ ★

Canadian-U.S. Troops Land; No Opposition

From The Times:

Today In Europe

News and comment on international events from the London Times of this date and cabled from The Vancouver Daily Province, London Bureau, Times Building, Printing House Square.

(Copyright, 1943, by Southam Co.)

LONDON, Aug. 21.—Arguing for recognition by the Quebec conference of French National Committee for Liberation, the Times, editorially, today stresses the committee's growth in authority, its unification of all French Fighting Forces, its collaboration with both Generals Giraud and De Gaulle and its weeding out of Vichy supporters in North Africa.

It is therefore desirable, says the newspaper, now to establish the committee as a provisional authority before France is liberated so that no party or faction may assign to itself a monopoly of political power in France for the future.

The people of France are bewildered, says the Times, at the Anglo-American failure to recognize the committee.

German propaganda represents the committee as the agent of British-American imperialism.

This preposterous statement might affect some section of the French people and so tend to discredit the greatest unifying force in France today.

What part France will play after the war depends on how the Allies treat her now.

A hostile France or one distrustful of the friendly intentions of the British Government can not be reconciled with an ordered and peaceful Europe.

Arguments for recognition are strengthened by Moscow's approval in advance. All three governments now agree on it.

* * *

The Italian mainland is under heavy attack from sea and air. The British fleet, says the Times Algiers correspondent, has bombarded Calabria and Allied aircraft have pounded airdromes at Foggia .nce more.

A general blitz is maintained over a wide area of southern Italy.

The Lipari Islands, to which victims of Mussolini's hatred were exiled, have surrendered but it is not yet known whether any political prisoners incarcerated there have been found.

A mood of deepest gloom has descended on Italy as the people have discovered Mussolini's overthrow does not mean the end of the war.

Flags and smiles, says the Times diplomatic correspondent, have all disappeared and King Victor in his message to Sicilians gave no ray of hope.

The truth is that Italy is defenseless and everyone knows it.

(Continued on Page 2.) See TIMES.

Japs Quit Air Base In Guinea

Defenses at Salamaua Smashed; Enemy in Full Retreat

LEAVE GUNS

(By Associated Press.)

ALLIED HEADQUARTERS, THE SOUTH PACIFIC, Aug. 21.—The Japanese are in headlong retreat before bomb-battered Salamaua.

Their mountain frontline cracked wide open, they have abandoned heavy guns in precipitous flight toward the last defenses barring the Allies from that highly-prized air base on New Guinea's northeast coast.

The enemy is "in full retreat to his inner citadel of defenses at Salamaua itself," said today's communique from Allied headquarters.

"Machine guns and artillery were abandoned along with more than 350 buried dead. Our troops are mopping up.

PLANES WIPED OUT.

The Japanese crackup was hastened by the virtual wiping out at Wewak, 350 miles up the coast, of an air force of 225 planes, most of them trapped on the ground, by Allied bombers Tuesday and Wednesday.

Yesterday, big bombers with a fighter escort went back to Wewak with 66 tons of bombs and added 24 more planes to the 225 previously destroyed there.

Attacking air reinforcements which the Japanese had moved in hastily, the raiders probably destroyed six more planes and damaged three at a cost of two Allied aircraft.

Salamaua has a fine airdrome. From it in peace time big cargo planes took off for the nearby goldfields.

Decline Comment

Official Plane Search Party Back in City

Three members of a Provincial Police party came down Friday night from the mountain on which lies the wrecked Canadian Pacific Airliner. They are in Vancouver today conferring with police heads.

It is believed the three men—Game Wardens Art Butler and Percy Cliffe and Alpinist William Henderson of Vancouver—reached the wreck scene sometime Friday, and are now reporting their findings.

They were accompanied to Vancouver by Sgt. W. J. Thompson, head of the Provincial Police at Chilliwack, who has been in charge of this party's activities.

Henderson, a member of the B.C. Mounteering Club, said he had been sworn to secrecy by the Provincial Police.

He refused to say whether or not the three men had actually reached the top of the ridge which was climbed by a Vancouver Daily Province party last Sunday.

KISKA: Canadians, Americans take over from Hirohito.

INVASION OF ITALY 'IN FEW DAYS'

Left in Bag

$2400 STOLEN FROM CITY MAN

A club bag containing $2400 in cash and $150 in Victory bonds was stolen from W. K. Mackie, guest at Pennsylvania Hotel, Carrall and Hastings, on Friday night.

Mackie told police that the bag had been left with the day clerk after he had checked out as he planned to take the night boat to Victoria.

The clerk said it was there at 4 p.m. He was unable to find it when Mack was preparing to leave for the boat.

The bag was padlocked, and the cash was in a locked tin box.

Dan Michette, 831 Gore avenue, had his trousers stolen from the bedroom where he and his wife were asleep. The pants held his wallet containing $150.

Mrs. Michette awakened in time to see a tall thin man leaving the room.

Elson to Broadcast From Quebec Sunday

R. T. Elson, Washington correspondent for The Vancouver Daily Province, who is covering the Allied war conference, will broadcast from Quebec from 11:04 to 11:15 a.m., P.R.T., Sunday over the C.B.C.

SOONER THAN MOST EXPECT

Kiska Provides Springboard For Offensive Against Japan

By TORCHY ANDERSON.
(Daily Province Staff Correspondent.)

QUEBEC, Aug. 21.—Significance of the announcement of the reoccupation of Kiska goes far past the cleaning out of the last Japs on North American soil.

It goes past defense and becomes the first step on one of the many roads to Tokyo.

It brings Canadian infantry into another theatre of war and opens wide a range of strategy to the United Nations in the Pacific.

It is the northern horn of a pincers that, however wide the present gap between points, may close more rapidly than any person now expects.

Here in Quebec, where the fast-moving events in Europe have overshadowed the Pacific to some extent, the announcement comes as added emphasis to the fact that long-range plans for the Pacific war have taken a great deal of the time of this great gathering of the Allied world's military and political authorities.

SPRINGBOARD FOR ATTACK.

It has been emphasized many times that the Aleutians are a springboard for attack on the Japanese mainland from the north.

With these islands secure it is anticipated that they will provide a firm, safe base from which aggresive action will follow.

Out of the fog of the Aleutian Islands may emerge the main road to Tokyo.

... When the Leaves Of Autmn Fall—

By DAVID M. NICHOL.
Leased wire to The Daily Province.
Copyright, 1943, Chicago Daily News

MOSCOW, Aug. 21.—Some Russians thought they saw a hopeful omen for the future today. Lime trees in front of the Turkish embassy, in Ulitsa Gertsena, lost their handful of yellow autumnal leaves. They had fluttered down in the street during the night.

ATTACK SOUTH OF NAPLES DUE

LONDON, Aug. 21.—(AP)—Radio France, in a broadcast from Algiers, quoted Swiss reports as saying the Italians expect an invasion of the mainland within the next few days somewhere south of Naples on the west coast of the peninsula.

In the meantime German occupation authorities in France instituted new measures of security amid increasing Axis tension at the prospect of Allied invasion of the continent.

An ultimatum has been issued to Frenchmen to hand over their firearms and the Axis has announced a new law is being prepared to provide a special summary trial which may inflict the death penalty for the destruction of crops.

The announcer, commenting on arson and sabotage in France, said "This wave of sabotage is spreading all over France."

Strolling Piper Sues City Police

John Sutherland, Vancouver's strolling piper, took the offensive in his fued with police today when he issued a writ in Supreme Court against Constables L. C. Mead and Gordon Bell for damages for alleged false arrest and malicious prosecution.

J. A. Grimmett, barrister, acted for Sutherland.

Japanese Flee Under Terrific Sea-Air Blows

Invading Force Discovers Signs of Hasty Evacuation from Last Aleutian Toehold

FIRST NIPPONESE RETREAT

By J. F. SANDERSON
(Canadian Press Staff Writer.)

QUEBEC, Aug. 21.—A joint Canadian-American force has recaptured the Aleutian island of Kiska, the last-known segment of North American soil occupied by the Japanese, Prime Minister Mackenzie King and President Roosevelt announced jointly today.

A communique issued at the same time by the United States Navy indicated the rocky, fog-bound island was taken without fighting after a terrific naval and air bombardment, the Japanese having slipped away before the landings which started August 15.

It was the first officially-reported time in the war that the Japanese have given up a major base without a fight.

Previously on Attu, their other Aleutian stronghold, they had fought almost to the last man against U.S. troops, and in the final organized resistance there some Japanese soldiers had even battled with bayonets tied to the end of sticks before committing suicide with hand grenades.

(Despatches from the southwest Pacific today also noted that the precipitate Japanese flight from defenses before Salamaua in New Guinea was the first of its kind.)

RECENT, HASTY EVACUATION

The Canadian-U.S. landing came 14 months after Tokyo first reported Japanese occupation of islands in the Aleutian chain, which stretches from Alaska westward toward Japan's home islands.

The naval communique reported that when the Canadians and Americans landed "no Japanese were found."

"There were indications of recent, hasty evacuation of the garrison.

"Presumably the heavy bombardments by our ships and planes that have carried on for some time and the danger to their supply lines by the capture of Attu made the enemy positions on Kiska untenable.

"It is not known how the Japanese got away, but it is possible that enemy surface ships were able to reach Kiska under cover of the heavy fog that has been prevalent."

Originally, there were 10,000 Japanese on the island but many of them must have been killed by the air and sea bombardments and it was impossible to estimate how many were evacuated.

(Continued on Page 2.) See KISKA CAPTURED.

CANADIAN FORCES SPECIALLY TRAINED

Announcement that Canadian troops had joined U.S. forces in re-occupying Kiska, last of the Japanese-held Aleutian Islands, was news which had been anxiously awaited at Pacific Command headquarters here for the last two weeks.

For two months it had been known that Canadians would take part in the Kiska "battle." It was known, too, that Home Defense troops, the army's conscripts who are drafted for service in North America, would be included in the units from the Dominion which would land on the rocky, fog-bound island to wrest it back from the Japs.

Under a cloak of secrecy, selected infantry, artillery and specialist battalions were moved to a west coast training centre to prepare for the first Canadian offensive launched in the Dominion itself since the war of 1812.

Thousands of troops from every section of the nation were gathered at the huge military encampment.

Special clothing was issued, clothing designed to combat the wet and cold of the far north, and training on new types of equipment was begun.

Japanese weapons and equipment, seized when the Americans took Attu several months ago, was studied and the men were taught to use it so that they could take advantage of captured equipment in the battle.

There was additional instruction and training in combined operations, landings from invasion barges were practiced

(Continued on Page 2.) See CANADIANS.

Penetrate 'Fortress Europe'

'8TH', CANADIANS INVADE ITALY!

VANCOUVER NEWS-HERALD

VOL 11, NO 112 | VANCOUVER, B.C., FRIDAY, SEPTEMBER 3, 1943 | ★ ★ ★ | PRICE 5c

Reds Cut Huns' Key Railway

By JAMES M. LONG

LONDON, Sept. 3—(AP)—Russia announced Thursday that five Red Armies plunging westward had cut the Bryansk-Kiev Railway, 150 miles from Kiev, smashed German reinforcements in a six-mile gain on Smolensk, and rolled up Axis lines in a new 45-mile wide spurt in the Donets Basin.

Earlier Marshal Stalin in an order of the day said that the Ukraine Citadel of Sumy, 90 [illegible] of Kharkov, had [illegible] to Gen. Nikolai Vatutin's [illegible], and a communique announced the capture of Krolevets and Yampol, two points on the vital Bryansk-Kiev Railway linking the enemy's central and southern fronts.

Lisichansk, Voroshilovsk, Slavyanoserbsk, and other cities were seized in the Donets Basin, while Budenovka, 20 miles from Marupol, was taken in the push along the rim of the Sea of Azov, said the communique recorded by the Soviet monitor.

The swiftness of the Russian advances and the tone of the communique indicated that the Germans were engaged in a large-scale retreat toward the Dnieper River, particularly in the huge Donets Basin. The bulletin, however, emphasized that the Germans were fighting stubbornly all along the 600-mile front.

NEWS-HERALD CONSENSUS OF SELECTORS' CHOICES

	WALLACE KELK (News-Herald)	BARRIE STEVENS (News-Herald)	JOHNNY PARK (Province)	CLOCKER (Province)	ALF COTTRELL (Sun)	RAILBIRD (Sun)	CONSENSUS
1st	Riverworth Shasta Chub Jazzy Fay	Dr. Pook Riverworth Maize B.	Jazzy Fay Riverworth Maizie B.	Riverworth Jazzy Fay Brilliant Help	Riverworth Jazzy Fay Shasta Chub	Jazzy Fay Golden Belt Shasta Chub	Riverworth (13) Jazzy Fay (11) Shasta Chub (4)
2nd	Nalod Stretch Ouimax	Stretch Nalod Wingaway	Wingaway Nalod Stretch	Wingaway Stretch Nalod	Welbeck Nalod Build Up	Wingaway Stretch Welbeck	Stretch (10) Nalod (10) Wingaway (10)
3rd	Somers Band Queen Dot Doc McKeon	Somers Band Doc McKeon Lady Double	Somer's Band Gallant Simon Queen Dot	Somers Band Doc McKeon Queen Dot	Somers Band Gallant Simon Queen Dot	Somers Band Queen Dot Gallant Simon	Somers Band (18) Queen Dot (7) Doc McKeon (5)
4th	Commendable Colonel Bret Streamline	Streamline Broad Royal Commendable	Commendable Flying Bud The Klondiker	Commendable Broad Royal The Klondiker	Streamline Fay Park Bruntsfield	Commendable Broad Royal The Klondiker	Commendable (13) Streamline (7) Broad Royal (6)
5th	Tuxedo Eddy Battleford Ascot Jane	Ascot Jane Corinthian Buck-On	Tuxedo Eddy Buck-On Ascot Jane	Buck-On Ascot Jane Battleford	Battleford Buck-On Ascot Jane	Buck-On Battleford Tuxedo Eddy	Buck-On (11) Ascot Jane (8) Battleford (8)
6th	Killarney L. Ronrico Ebony Latch	Killarney Ebony Ronrico	Killarney Ebony Ronrico	Brig D'Or	Getwise	Brig D'Or	Killarney L. (12) Ebony Latch (9) Ronrico (6)
7th	Naperton Dodd Taken	Lady Giovando Lucky Card Dodd	Lady Giovando Taken Dodd	Naperton Dodd Lady Giovando	Little Dee Lady Giovando Naperton	Naperton Dodd Lady Giovando	Lady Giovando (10) Naperton (10) Dodd (8)
Sub.	Tyler Gulch Slateford Special Briar	Special Briar Timely Ayre Ione Special	Timely Ayre Tyler Gulch Slateford	Slateford Timely Ayre Ione Special	Ione Special Special Lady Special Briar	Special Briar Slateford Tyler Gulch	Special Briar (8) Slateford (8) Timely Ayre (7)
Sub	Train Signal Golden Sable Valdina Joy	Camp Spur Train Signal Valdina Joy	Camp Spur Train Signal My Tom	Golden Sable Train Signal Camp Spur	Train Signal Camp Spur Simonette	Valdina Joy Camp Spur My Tom	Train Signal (12) Camp Spur (11) Valdina Joy (5)
Best	Riverworth		Tuxedo Eddy	Commendable		Killarney L.	Somers Band (18)

Publish Answer To Comment In U. S. Newspapers

Soviet Press Charges Former Fascists On Allied Pay Roll

MOSCOW, Sept. 3.—(AP)—A.M.G. — the Allied Military Government for occupied territories, formerly called AMGOT—was sharply criticised Thursday in the Soviet paper, War and the Working Class.

The magazine said "the administration itself is of a military government based on principles which have nothing in common with the principles of democracy."

The magazine said that the "disrespectful name of 'gauleiter schools'" had been given to places where officers are prepared for posts under A.M.G.

It quoted various dispatches as stating that there is absence of freedom of speech in Sicily and that high standing former Fascists are on the Allied pay list.

SECOND FRONT ISSUE

On the issue of establishment of a land front in western Europe, Maj.-Gen. M. Galaktinov, writing in the magazine, said that "nothwithstanding repeated Soviet offers, the Allies never once expressed a desire to have troops side by side with our armies on the Soviet-German front."

He said that "the second and third fronts," as he described the operations in Sicily and the air offensive over Europe, "not only did not drag away a single German division from our front but they did not even hinder Hitler from greatly increasing the number of German divisions operating on the Soviet-German front."

The general's article was published as an answer to comment in United States newspapers, in particular to statements that the Russians had refused to allow the Allied air forces to operate from Black Sea bases and that the Russians had declined a British offer of assistance when the Germans began to break into the Caucasus.

Ottawa Sanctions Release Of U. S. Imported Synthetic Rubber Tires

OTTAWA, Sept. 3 — (CP)—The Munitions Department announced Thursday night that under tire rationing regulations passenger car tires made of synthetic rubber imported from the United States will be released for sale immediately, and that manufacture of the synthetic tires has already begun in Canada.

The departmental announcement emphasized that existing tire regulations have not been relaxed, and that the synthetic tires will be available only to essential users eligible to buy new tires.

Rubber Controller Alan H. Williamson said tests so far have shown that synthetic rubber is not as tough as natural rubber for tire manufacture, and that the new synthetic tires therefore must be driven "at low speed and with great care."

Cars equipped with the new tires should not be driven at more than 35 miles an hour, and overloading must be avoided, Mr. Williamson said. Inflation pressures should be checked at least once weekly.

The making of reclaimed tires, the announcement said, now will be discontinued. Only limited quantities of synthetic tires will be manufactured and they will be sold by tire ration permit.

Berlin Fires Still Raging

STOCKHOLM, Sept. 3—(AP)—Roundabout reports from Berlin said Thursday night that 450 fires were still burning in the German capital after Tuesday night's R.A.F. and R.C.A.F. raid that killed an estimated 5,000 persons and paralyzed the city's transportation system.

• • •

Swiss dispatches in Swedish newspapers said some of the fires were so large firemen merely tried to isolate them instead of saving the blazing buildings. Fire apparatus was called from five German cities to aid.

Nazis Planning Danish Council

STOCKHOLM, Sept. 3.—(AP)—Faced with a rebellious Danish population, the Nazis sought Thursday to form an 18-man administrative council similar to that set up in Norway in 1940 to enable them to step out of their role as military dictators of Denmark.

• • •

King Christian, however, assured of the absolute loyalty of his people, appeared to hold the key to the situation.

MRS. ROOSEVELT IN AUSTRALIA

CANBERRA, Australia, Sept. 3 — (Friday) — (CP) — Mrs. Franklin D. Roosevelt, wife of President Roosevelt, arrived today by plane.

(The dispatch did not state from where the plane came but she previously had been in New Zealand.)

Plan Helicopter Service Between City, Victoria

VICTORIA, Sept. 3 — (CP)—Harold Husband of Victoria announced today the Vancouver Air Lines Limited has applied to federal authorities at Ottawa and Washington for licenses to provide passenger and freight services by helicopter between Victoria and Vancouver Island points and mainland cities in both the United States and Canada.

Logging Firms Decline To Sign Pact With Union

Prospects of a peaceable settlement between International Woodworkers of America and the Queen Charlotte Islands logging operators appeared very remote Thursday, when R. V. Stuart and Robert Fillberg, company representatives, [illegible] sign a memorandum of [illegible]ment drawn up by George [illegible]rie of the Federal department of labor.

• • •

The memorandum was presented by Mr. Currie to a point meeting called by him of the company representatives and Harold Pritchett and Nigel Morgan, of I.W.A. District Council No. 1, and Ernest Dalskog of I.W.A. Local 1-71, in the department's offices Thursday afternoon.

The union representatives accepted the agreement after reading it, but the company representatives declined to do so, stating they wished to present further proposals.

• • •

It is possible there may be another meeting today, but union officials are pessimistic concerning the outcome.

• • •

"It is the absolute minimum we could agree to," said Harold Pritchett, "and if they do not accept, and we hear no more on Friday from Ottawa concerning a strike vote, I am flying there immediately to see Hon. Humphrey Mitchell."

"The operators have given a written undertaking to Federal conciliator G. W. Currie outlining their collective bargaining proposals," said R. V. Stuart.

"Union recognition, wages, hours of work, and other details are not an issue," he said.

"The companies feel that their submission fulfills their legal obligations, and provides a sound basis for future collective bargaining," he concluded.

A statement from the union, released Thursday, expressed the men's willingness "to accept the proposals submitted by Mr. Currie as a basis for fair settlement, and to urge their adoption by the Queen Charlotte Island loggers."

(Continued on Page Nine)

Warships, Planes Aid Allied Thrust Across Straits Of Messina

ALLIED HEADQUARTERS, NORTH AFRICA, Sept. 3.—(CP)—Allied forces, crack Canadian units among them, moved across the narrow strait of Messina early today to land in Southern Italy and launch the long-heralded invasion of the European continent.

The brief announcement from Allied Headquarters disclosing the attack, said the invasion force was spearheaded by the veteran British 8th Army and that Canadian forces were [illegible]ded.

The Canadian 1st Division has been [illegible] to the 8th Army under Gen. Sir Bernard Mont[illegible]ce the [illegible] of Sicily July [illegible] Maj.-Gen [illegible] of Kingston, Ont. command the [illegible]

It was recalled that Canadian troops had been withdrawn from the Sicilian fighting 10 days before it ended. At that time, it was generally understood the Canadians were preparing to help spearhead some new attack.

• • •

Invasion of the continent came quickly on the heels of the clean-up of the Sicilian campaign and brought to a victorious conclusion 38 days later with all Axis troops either killed, routed or prisoners.

A special communique, announcing the mainland landings, said the forces of "General Eisenhower continued their advance. British and Canadian troops of the 8th army, supported by Allied sea and air power attacked across the Straits of Messina early today and landed on the mainland of Italy."

• • •

The landing had been presaged for several days by ever increasing aerial blows at all of southern Italy.

British and American warships also had participated in the mighty pre-invasion bombardment of the Italian mainland.

• • •

It was the first time Allied troops had set foot on European soil since the Canadian-led Dieppe raid of August, 1942.

The new blow was struck about dawn today.

As in the Sicilian landings, powerful air and sea fleets gave protection to the landing troops.

By moving across the Straits of Messina from the eastern shore of Sicily, the Allied forces had only a few miles of water to cross. The strait at its narrowest point at the extreme northeastern corner of Sicily is only a little more than two [illegible] wide and can be crossed by [illegible] boat in about 20 minutes.

• • •

A Mutual Broadcasting Company commentator said in Algiers the landing took place at 4:30 a.m.

A CBS commentator said the landings were made opposite the city of Messina.

COMMANDO RAIDS PRECEDED ITALY LANDING

LONDON, Sept. 3—(CP)—In a broadcast this morning from Algiers, John Daly, CBS correspondent, reported the invasion of South Italy was preceded by a number of successful commando and reconnaissance missions in the last few nights.

Daly said these missions were successful in helping to knock out enemy coastal defences.

"Snappiest Girl in School"

is the girl who wears these
MAN TAILORED SHIRTS by Tooke
Always so fresh; so easily washed: they iron so crisp and new.
You're sure to want several at from 2.00 to 5.00
WILLARDS
681 GRANVILLE

Your Chesterfield
Suite Relined and
Recovered
3 PIECES—Special TODAY 59.50
Including Material . . . Guaranteed Workmanship
Convenient Terms
See Samples in Your Home
No Obligation
Phone MAr. 4959 or MAr. 2740

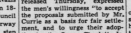

JULIUS SHORE
Mail Order House Ltd. 1275 Granville St.

Your Old Friend
MILTON
• Excellent Food
• Courteous Service
• Modern Surroundings
Plus Dancing While You Dine . . . Every Night!
All at Popular Prices!
Empire Cafe Ltd.
Remember—GOOD EATS CAFE is the best place to eat . . . at Granville St. . . . next to Vogue Theatre.

SURE YOU CAN FINISH IT!
or make those contemplated alterations to the interior of your building with
ACE•TEX INSULATING FIBRE BOARD
Attractive appearance and insulation against heat, cold and sound.
At your ACE•TEX dealer's.
Canada Roof Products LTD.
makers of
—The ACE•TEX Line—

150 Killed, 90 Hurt In U.S. Train Wreck

★★★★★   ★★★★★   ★★★★★   ★★★★★

ITALIANS ASK PEACE TERMS

Two lithe young women show the effects of superb training in the Pro-Rec display Monday at Brockton Point. Hours of practice result in the smoothly co-ordinated muscles necessary for this graceful but arduous work.

A rivetting gang at work in the war industries display at Brockton Point shows the timing and precision with which Vancouver-made ships are built. The heater throws a white hot rivet to the passer boy who, in turn, passes it to the rivetter, boss of the gang.

Interpreting The War News

By HAMILTON W. FARON
Associated Press War Analyst

Strong support for a belief that the Italian government may soon seek a separate peace has come from Berlin itself in a broadcast announcing the evacuation of at least part of the foot of the Italian boot.

By withdrawing northward and maintaining their record of no serious opposition to the Allied invasion of the Italian mainland, the Italians may be hoping to secure a better peace than if they took a stand.

The withdrawal of German and Italian troops—and civilians — from lower Calabria was announced by D.N.B., official German news agency, remains unconfirmed in Allied capitals, as this was written. However, in Washington, it was generally accepted as true in view of the astonishing lack of resistance of any kind encountered by the invading armies.

Also significant was the plaintive plea by the Rome radio that Britain and the United States pledge themselves to guarantee Italy's 1919 frontiers. This shows the change that has come over the Italian leadership since the days, not so long ago, when Mussolini was making his pretensions to vast empire.

However, it is unlikely that a suggestion for anything except "unconditional surrender" would be acceptable to the Allied leaders.

Despite all the indications pointing toward peace proposals, however, there could be a movement to new defence lines where German troops could put up stiffer opposition to the ultimate conquest of Italy by Allied armies.

8000 At Rally

City Unionists Mark Labor Day

Ideal weather, an enthusiastic crowd, and a well-handled program of sports and musical entertainment all combined to make the Labor Day rally at Brockton Point Oval an outstanding success Monday afternoon.

Approximately 8,000 unionists, of all affiliations, crowded the stand and the grounds, without one mishap of any kind marring the enjoyment of the day.

"Vancouver labor has taken a proud place in war production," Mayor J. W. Cornett told the crowd in opening the rally.

"The city's record of shipbuilding has challenged the attention of the world, and it has been accomplished with few labor troubles and with credit to all concerned."

"Canada realizes that time lost in production is time gained for Hitler," the mayor stated, amidst applause.

E. E. Leary, president of Vancouver Labor Council, reminded the workers of the necessity for unity.

"The trade union movement is stronger than ever in the history of Canada, and the unity of all three union centres is essential," he declared.

"We want the trade unions, irrespective of affiliation, to unite on the common ground of the issues affecting them all," said Mr. Leary.

"We want to be in a position to win the peace after winning the war, for we don't desire to go back to the years of 1930-1939, with the workers walking the streets looking for a job," he stated.

BOARD OF TRADE PARTY AT HOPE AFTER TREK

HOPE, B. C., Sept. 7.— Representing 12 Coast and Interior Boards of Trade, a party of 100 persons, including six women, arrived here at 5:45 p.m. Monday following a trip from Princeton to Hope and an inspection of the Japanese evacuation camp at Tashme. The Boards of Trade delegation made the trip from Princeton to here by truck—walking the seven mile incomplete section of the roadway.

Monday evening they were dinner guests of the Pacific Coast Militia Rangers.

RUSSIANS SMASH TOWARD STALINO

LONDON, Sept. 7.—(AP)— The Red army smashed to the outskirts of burning Stalino in the Donets basin Monday and also captured the northern Ukraine citadel of Konotop in a direct plunge toward Kiev, 125 miles beyond, Moscow disclosed officially Monday night.

U. S. To Bear Equal Responsibility In Peace As In War, Says Churchill

CAMBRIDGE, Mass., Sept. 7. (AP)—Prime Minister Winston Churchill declared Monday that the United States, which could not escape responsibility in this time of global conflict, would have an equal responsibility in the peace that follows.

"The price of greatness is responsibility," he told a special convocation of Harvard University faculty and overseers, called together to award him an honorary degree of Doctor of Laws.

Mr. Churchill, in a bright red gown over dark suit coat and gray trousers, was cheered and applauded for a full two minutes as he accepted the honor from President James Bryant Conant of Harvard. The accompanying citation said:

"Winston Leonard Spencer Churchill—an historian who has written a glorious page of British history; a statesman and warrior whose tenacity and courage turned back the tide of tyranny in freedom's darkest hour."

The "gift of a common tongue," Mr. Churchill told his Sanders Theatre audience at Harvard, most of whom were in uniform, is a "priceless inheritance" to the British and American peoples, which has "enabled us to wage war together with an intimacy and harmony never before achieved among Allies."

"It may well become the foundation of a common citizenship," he added.

One Killed

Stalled Car Hit By Train

One person was killed and two others injured when a C.P.R. transcontinental train, Vancouver-bound struck their car at the Barnett Crossing near Kapoor Mills shortly before 9:00 a.m. Sunday.

Dead, David Nagy, aged 40, driver of the car; injured, Agnes Nagy, sister-in-law of the dead man, suffering from shock and lacerations and Mrs. Nagy's fourteen-months-old baby, internal injuries. Authorities at the Royal Columbian Hospital, New Westminster state the condition of Mrs. Nagy and the baby as good.

According to the Provincial Police at Barnett, Nagy, accompanied by his sister-in-law and the baby were driving toward the city and when crossing the C.P.R. tracks were struck by the flyer.

The impact hurled the car about 50 feet along the right-of-way, the occupants being thrown clear. Kingsway Ambulance from Vancouver rushed all three to the Royal Columbian Hospital.

Mystery Shrouds Derailment Of Fastest Limited

PHILADELPHIA, Sept. 7.—(AP)—One hundred and fifty persons were reported killed and more than 90 injured in the wreck of the Congressional Limited, fastest train of the Pennsylvania Railroad in northeast Philadelphia Monday night.

The estimate was made two hours after the accident by Matthew A. Ross, chief deputy coroner.

A priest who entered one of the cars to administer last rites to the dying said there were 75 persons in the car and he believed at least half of them were dead.

Many were still trapped in the cars and acetylene torches were being used in an effort to cut an opening through to them.

Every available ambulance was rushed to the scene at the request of railroad officials, and police were dispatched to nearby hospitals to straighten out "traffic congestions" in the emergency wards.

Northeast Hospital reported it had six dead—three soldiers and three women.

Railroad officials said six cars were derailed — two coaches, a twin diner unit and two pullmans. They still had no explanation of the derailment at 7:45.

Frankford Hospital reported shortly after the accident that it was "full of injured" and could take no more. Many others were taken to Northeast and Episcopalian hospitals.

The train left Washington at 4 p.m. E.D.T. and was due in New York at 7:35. It makes no stops between the capital and the metropolis.

Four wrecking trains were sent to the scene. The six wrecked cars were tossed crosswise on the four tracks, closing the railroad's main line. Trains were detoured over the Reading lines.

Missing Man Found Drowned

The body of a man believed by police to be George Pratt was found floating in the water near the Gulf of Georgia Towing Company wharf early Monday.

The discovery was first made by two airforce men who were patrolling the area in an airforce launch. From the condition of the body it had not been in the water for any great length of time.

In one of the pockets of the clothing worn by the deceased man police found a NRC card in the name of George Pratt, giving an East End hotel address.

A check made with the management of the hotel disclosed that the drowned man was last seen Sunday about noon time and appeared to be in excellent health. The body is at the city morgue.

"We Do Not Want To Haggle" Says Rome Broadcast

LONDON, Sept. 7.—(CP)—The Rome radio, in a home and overseas broadcast recorded by the Ministry of Information, asked Britain and the United States Monday night whether they were prepared to guarantee Italy's 1919 frontiers.

In words reflecting Italy's thoughts of peace, the broadcast stated:

"We do not want to haggle over words. We are prepared to face stark reality.

"We, therefore, ask you Britain and America—do you intend to respect the independence and unity of our unfortunate country?

"If you do, why don't you say so?"

"Do the war and peace aims of the Anglo-Saxons guarantee Italy's 1919 frontiers, or do they mean further amputation?"

The broadcast asserted that the insistence of unconditional surrender proved that Britain and the United States were unwilling to give Italy such an understanding and had caused Count Carlo Sforza to abandon the position he had assumed in the Italian anti-Fascist movement abroad.

Somaliland, Eritrea and Libya were Italian possessions in 1919. The frontiers did not officially embrace Fiume, which was Yugoslavian until 1924. Although a raiding party led by Gabriele D'Annunzio remained for a time as "commandant." Italy in 1919 did not have Albania which was independent, the Dodecanese Islands or Ethiopia.

Ten Towns Fall To Eighth Army

By NOLAND NORGAARD

ALLIED HEADQUARTERS, North Africa, Sept. 7.—(AP)—British and Canadian troops drove 10 miles inland from their 40-mile beachhead on the Italian toe through extensive demolitions and stood Monday night on the forbidding slopes of Aspromonte, a 6000-foot mountain nearly halfway across the Calabrian peninsula.

A Berlin radio account quoting DNB news agency said the Axis had evacuated southern Calabria, the Italian province cradled in the toe.

Ten more towns fell. Prisoners swelled to 3000. Columns invading the European mainland were nearing Palmi in their drive north. Others curling around the south tip of the Italian toe extended their holdings beyond Melito on the Ionian Sea.

Resistance continued feeble, though some tanks were encountered. The Straits of Messina were opened for Allied navigation as the invaders compelled the Axis troops to withdraw their coastal cannon from range.

LEONARD RETAINS ALBERTA TITLE

EDMONTON, Sept. 7.—(CP)—Stan Leonard, the Vancouver pro shotmaker, Monday successfully defended his Alberta open golf championship against a strong field of contestants to win the 72-hole medal play 293.

Henry Martel, of Edmonton, an amateur, was second, and at one time during the play in the last round drew close to Leonard but fell behind shortly after and wound up with a total of 295 for the 72 holes, two behind the champion.

EXTRA

ITALY QUITS

UNC'DITIONAL SURRENDER

Rationed Foods

Preserves—Coupon D-1 now valid.
Meat—Pair of coupons, No. 16, valid tomorrow.
Sugar—Coupons up to No. 14, now valid.
Canning Sugar—All coupons invalid on September 30.
Tea or Coffee—Pair of coupons, No. 14 and 15, now valid.
Butter—Pair of coupons, No. 26 and 27, now valid.

The Vancouver Sun

The Vancouver Evening Newspaper Owned and Operated By Vancouver People

Today's Tides

Vancouver Harbor
Low 7:26 p.m., 8.6 ft. High 0:29 a.m., 11.1 ft.
English Bay
Low 7:08 p.m., 9.4 ft. High 0:07 a.m., 11.7 ft.
First Narrows
Low slack 7:56 p.m. High slack 0:55 p.m.

FOUNDED 1886
VOL. LVII—No. 282 MArine 1161 VANCOUVER, BRITISH COLUMBIA, WEDNESDAY, SEPTEMBER 8, 1943 PRICE 5 CENTS BY CARRIER $1.00 per month

Eisenhower Reports Military Armistice Granted Badoglio

ALLIED HEADQUARTERS, NORTH AFRICA, Sept. 8.— Gen. Dwight D. Eisenhower today announced the unconditional surrender of the Italianarmed forces.

Eisenhower announced that the Italians had been granted a military armistice.

Thus the minor member of the Berlin-Tokyo-Rome Axis met the stipulation that has been insisted upon by Prime Minister Churchill and Presiden t Roosevelt—unconditional surrender and nothing less.

The announcement came as dispirited Italian troops by the hundreds surrendered to British and Canadian troops advancing up the Calabrian peninsula, where the Allies landed last Friday on the heels of a 38-day Sicilian victory which sent the Germans fleeing to the Italian mainland.

Berlin Reports New Landings

LONDON, Sept. 8.—A German communiue said today that Allied forces had landed at the Gulf of Eufemia, in Italy, about 40 miles north of the point at which British and Canadian forces hae been fighting.

An Allied communiue, issued earlier at headquarters in North Africa, made no mention of any landing on the instep of the Italian Boot.

The German radio reported that there are "indications" that the U.S. 7th army stationed in the Mediterranean area has gone to sea.

"News of the beginning of landing operations is not yet available," sai da broadcast recorded by the Associated Press.

The 7th Army participated din the conquest of Sicily.

Ottawa Hails 'Milestone'

OTTAWA, Sept. 8—(CP)—Singing of the Italian armistice was hailed with satisfaction as one of the greatest milestones of the war in official circles here today.

Prime Minister Mackenzie King summoned correspondents to a press conference at 9:20 a.m. (Vancouver time). Subject of the conference was not disclosed, but it is presumed he will make a formal announcement of the Italian surrender.

Vancouver Man's Death Probed

CALGARY, Sept. 8—(CP)—George Dingle, 56, Vancouver, a civilian employee who lost his life in a dormitory at No. 31 EFTS, RAF, Dewinton, on Saturday, "died as a result of a fire of unknown cause," according to a verdict reached by a coroner's jury empanelled here Tuesday.

Dingle came to Calgary from Vancouver. There are no known relatives in Canada, but he is believed to have a sister residing in England.

Soldier Goes On Trial for Murder

SASKATOON, Sept. 8—(CP)—The trial of TR James William Angus Clark, 20, of Hamilton, Ont., charged with the murder of TR. Arthur Ernest Clifford, 19, of Toronto, at Dundurn training centre July 7, opened before Mr. Justice P. M. Anderson here Tuesday.

Evidence was given by two officers, Lt. L. S. Walker, camp engineer and Lieut. J. H. MacDonald, camp adjutant, and by three soldiers.

Canine Delinquency Jumps

Even Mayor's Dog Stepping Out

S. S. Gordon, 65, who planted a big victory garden on a city-owned lot only to have his good crop destroyed by dogs, suggested in a letter to civic licenses committee, Tuesday afternoon, that dog owners be required to keep their pets on their own property between April 1 and Sept. 30.

Aldermen sympathized with him but admitted they are pretty much stumped about the dog problem here.

"This is not a question of unlicensed dogs but of uncontrolled dogs," commented Chairman Ald. Charles Jones. Ald. Jones said there are around 24,000 licensed dogs in the city and every year the same complaints come to City Council.

"It's surprising there aren't more with the number of dogs there are," said Ald. John Bennett. "A lot of people must look after their dogs."

Mayor J. W. Cornett, who admitted he'd had a lot of complaints on the subject, declared there are more dogs licensed in the city now than ever before.

"We've already a bylaw providing for what is asked, but the trouble is it is not enforced, isn't that right?" queried Ald. H. L. Corey.

The mayor said he doubted whether a person could be made to pay a license if his animal wasn't allowed off his property. He added that he couldn't keep his own dog at home.

License Inspector H. A. Urquhart was asked to take what steps he could to abate the nuisance, but aldermen agreed they couldn't do anything about Mr. Gordon's second request. He asked Victory gardeners be given time to harvest their crops in the event of a lot being sold.

Ald. Jones explained all the produce on city-owned lots on which gardening is allowed go to the gardener at no cost, but with provision for purchase.

KEY FIGURES IN ITALY PEACE

GENERAL DWIGHT D. EISENHOWER

KING VICTOR EMANUEL

MARSHAL BADOGLIO

Gen. Eisenhower, United Nations commander-in-chief in the Mediterranean theatre of war, announced today the unconditional surrender of Italian armed forces under Marshal Badoglio and King Victor Emanuel.

Only One Winner; He Was With Show

AJAX, Ont., Sept. 8—(CP)—Magistrate F. S. Sims on Tuesday fined Joseph Smith of Vancouver $275 and costs and confiscated a wheel-of-fortune and $109 in cash seized by police officers at a carnival near here last week.

The fine was levied after officers told a court they found only one winner at a horse-racing wheel which paid off at 5-1, and the one winner, the officers said, worked for the carnival.

CRASH INJURES THIRTY

TORONTO, Sept. 8 — (CP) — Thirty persons were injured Tuesday when two street cars collided at the intersection of Danforth and Broadview avenues.

Sleeper Had Money to Burn

RICHMOND, Va. Sept, 8—(AP) — John W. Burrell, 67, handyman, regretted today that he looked at his alarm clock yesterday morning. Burrell struck a match to see the clock, then went back to sleep, and awoke later to find the match which he believed extinguished had ignited his trousers. The trousers cantained $1058.

Athlone Visits Canadian Air Base in Alaska

PRINCE RUPERT, B.C., Sept. 8—(CP)—The governor general paid his first visit to Alaska yesterday when he personally piloted part of the way northward from Prince Rupert a large amphibian bomber of the Royal Canalian Air Force.

The Earl of Athlone and his party visited an air base outpost in southeastern Alaska. His Excellency expressed himself as being keenly delighted with the aerial expedition, which started in the morning and concluded with his return to Prince Rupert by early evening.

At the air base His Excellency saw a striking example of international co-operation between the United States and Canada in the defense of the Pacific Coast.

He inspected and lunched at a Canadian-manned air base on Alaskan soil and for his benefit there was a demonstration of anti-aircraft fire by a battery directed by Capt. S. F. Maunsell of Vancouver.

The United States Army garrison and service camp establishment operated in connection with the air base also was visited and particular interest was taken in a United Statas military hospital where a staff of six doctors and six nurses are operating a 100-bed establishment.

Immediatel yon alighting from the plane which carried him to the base His Excellency inspected guards of honor of the United States and the Royal Canadian Air Force and reviewed a mach past in eacvh case.

The governor general visited the naval station here today and spent the rest of the day with the United States Army.

Two Fined for Whisky Theft

E. Tweedle, 38, of 177 West Pender and Harold G. Ackerman, a member of the Canadian Navy, were each fined $15 or 10 days in jail by Magistrate H. S. Wood Tuesday when they were convicted of having stolen a bottle of whisky from Pte. R. Johnson, stationed in Vancouver.

Tweedle and Ackerman were arrested by Constables W. J. Walker, J. B. Finnie and George E. Boyd after they were chased along Water Street from Carrall tto Abbott Monday evening.

Police followed the two men when they heard calls for help by Johnson.

Alderman Adamant

Civic Building Bylaw Snag in Housing Plan

Aldermen decided again Tuesday afternoon that they are not prepared to make any change in the civic Building Bylaw that will allow a different type wiring in houses altered under the government conversion plan.

A few weeks ago a civic housing committee refused the request of jocelyn Davidson, Regional Housing Administrator, in this regard. Tuesday a similar request came through Mrs. Gordon Selman, chairman of the Vancouver Housing Committee

"Mr. Davidson tells me that he is afraid the whole plan will collapse because of the high cost per unit, one reason for which is the cost of electrical wiring," Mrs. Selman wrote, in asking a temporary relaxation of regulations to permit cheaper conduits being used.

'CAN'T ALTER BYLAW'

Ald. W. D. Greyell, chairman of the civic utilities committee, before which Mr. Davidson appeared, protested:

"Mr. Davidson told us they couldn't get the material. Now it seems to be a question of cost."

Ald. G. C. Miller recalled the Regional Housing Director saying it was not a question of cost.

"We can't alter the bylaw to make exceptions for any one group," Ald. Miller declared.

1601 HOUSES NEEDED

Mrs. Selman's letter told tne committee that the conversion plan "is our only hope at present."

She said her office had reached hte limit of its resources and the only three courses open are to press for more wartime housing, to urge more people to share their homes, and to facilitate in every way the government's plan for converting buildings into suites.

"At the end of July we had 1601 applicants for family dwelling units waiting on our files for accommodation. War workers and their families are coming here in greater numbers than ever before and some are living under terrible conditions."

ZONING COMES FIRST

Meanwhile an amendment to the city building bylaw which will prevent erection or alteration of any building that will contravene the zoning bylaw, was approved by civic building committee.

Under this the "building inspector may require of any such applicant a sworn statement as to the purpose to which the housing accommodation is to be ut should the alteration in question be made."

The amendment was drawn up following protests from the Town Planning Commission that the zoning plan for the city is being broken down in all districts.

Howe, Mitchell 'Slave Drivers'

WINNIPEG, Sept. 8—(CP) — Winnipeg Trades and Labor Council unanimously approved an open letter Tuesday which will be sent to Prime Minister MacKenzie ing demanding "an early, clear and unequivocal declaration of post-war policy."

"The actions of some of your ministers, particularly of the Minister of Munitions and Supply, and the Minister of Labor, lead us to believe that just as soon as the sharp emergency of war is over, the slight consideration which has been shown to labor during the war will be replaced by the whip of the slave driver."

Welfare Drives Seek $5,000,000

OTTAFA, Sept. 8—(CP)—Canada's social workers, employing a combined operations technique, soon will ask the public for 5,033,412 so 425 welfare agencies can continue their work for another year.

The fall campaigns of Canadian community chests will run through late September to October 1, and the Canadian Welfare Council of Ottawa, named in 1939 as national centre of chest activity, has adopted the slogan "Worth Fight For—Worth Giving For" to the spur drives.

Three Years for Bigamy

KINGSTON, Ont., Sept. 8 — (CP)—William Stanley Martin of Vancouver and Kingston today was sentenced to three years in Kingston penitentiary when he was found guilty on a charge of Bigamy.

Noted Artists to Appear With Symphony

The Vancouver Symphony Orchestra program during the forthcoming season will include concerts directed by several internationally famous conductors, and will also feature a number of celebrated concert artists as soloists.

First concert, to be held October 3, will be conducted by Sir Thomas Beecham.

Other noted directors and soloists who will appear with the symphony during the season include William Steinberg, Fabien Sevitsky, Howard Barlow, Sir Ernest MacMillan, Gertrude Huntley and Jan Cherniavsky.

Concerts will be held in the Orpheum theatre, and tickets may be obtained at the J. W. Kelly Company, 632 Seymour.

Statement of Victory--- In the following statement, Gen. Dwight Eisenhower, commander-in chief of the Anglo-American forces in the Mediterranean, today announced the victorious end of the Battle of Italy.

"The Italian Government has surrendered its armed forces unconditionally. As Allied commader-in-chief, I have granted a military armistice, the terms of which have been approved by the governments of the United Kingdom, the United States and the Union of the Soviet Socialist Republics. Thus I am acting in the interests of the United Nations.

"The Italian Government has bound itself to abide by these terms without reservation. The armistice was signed by my representative and the representative of Marshal Badoglio, and it becomes effective this instant," (9:30 a.m. P.D.T.)

"Hostilities between the armed forces of the United Nations and those of Italy terminate at once. All Italians who now act to help eject the German aggressors from Italian soil will have the assistance and support of the United Nations."

Statement of Defeat--- The text of Badoglio's proclamation of surrender: "The Italian Government, recognizing the impossibility of continuing the unequal struggle against the overwhelming power of the enemy, with the object of avoiding further and more grievous harm to the nation, requested an armistice from Gen. Eisenhower, commander-in-chief of the Anglo-American Allied forces. This request has been granted. The Italian forces will therefore, cease all acts of hostility against the Anglo-American forces wherever they may be met. They will, however, oppose attacks from any other quarter."

THE VANCOUVER DAILY PROVINCE

49th YEAR—NO. 139 VANCOUVER, B.C., WEDNESDAY, SEPTEMBER 8, 1943—32 PAGES ★ ★ ★ PRICE 5 CENTS BY CARRIER $1.00 per month.

Military Armistice Signed

ITALIAN FORCES QUIT WAR

BERLIN ADMITS LOSS

Fleeing Germans Abandon Stalino; Donets Retaken

From The Times:

Today In Europe

Compiled from the news and editorial comment of the London Times, and cabled from The Vancouver Daily Province London Bureau, Times Building, Printing House Square.

(Copyright, 1943, by Southam Co.)

LONDON, Sept. 8.—Allied air forces operating in great strength have made prolonged attacks on the Naples area, smashing airfields and cutting railways.

British, Canadian and United States pilots bombed steadily for 36 hours—an awe-inspiring demonstration of aerial might, says the Times Algiers correspondent, that can not have been without its effect on the Italian mind. In many places no enemy aircraft appeared. British tanks have been landed at points along the Calabrian coast and good progress by the 8th Army into the interior of the country continues.

The German retreat from the Donets industrial area proceeds, despite desperate bids to prevent the Red Army from outflanking them. A big battle has been raging south and west of Kharkov where the Nazi high command is attempting to save its rearguards. Soviet troops advancing into the northern Ukraine are only 10 miles from Bakhmach, strategically important railway junction on the enemy's front.

The Red Army is also threatening Mariupol on the Sea of Azov, says the Times Stockholm correspondent. Unless the Nazis leave Mariupol quickly they are likely to be cut off, as at Taganrog. On this southern battlefront the Germans have made no strong stand. There is a marked threat to their forces around Izyum, where, unless they retreat in time, they may experience another disaster.

* * *

More than 30,000 Soviet citizens died in the German concentration camp at Orel, according to evidence collected by the Atrocities Commission, which names German officers responsible for these inhuman deeds.

Graves containing thousands of bodies were found in the forests outside Orel. Bodies of children who had been buried alive were found in ditches. Some inmates of the camp were poisoned and others executed in batches almost every morning. Mass abduc-

(Continued on Page 8.) See TIMES.

Capture of Key Base Announced By Stalin.

TRAP LOOMS

NEW YORK, Sept. 8.—(AP) — Marshal Stalin triumphantly announced in a special order of the day today that the Donets Basin is cleared of the Germans."

The announcement, broadcast by the Moscow radio, added, "Our troops captured a number of cities, including the city of Stalino."

The action came, the Soviet Premier continued, "as a result of skilled manoeuvres and a determined offensive in the last six days."

By LEWIS HAWKINS.
Associated Press Staff Writer.

LONDON, Sept. 8. — Capture of fiercely - defended Stalino by the Russians was acknowledged by the Germans today, restoring the last of the great industrial cities of the Donets Basin to the Red Army which already has won back two-thirds of the Ukraine's rich grain lands.

The Red Army advance also crossed the rail line to Mariupol, 65 miles southwest of Stalino on the Sea of Azov, making it almost certain that Nazi forces which have been fighting east of that town must withdraw to escape entrapment by the southward turning move.

SEVER RAIL LINK.

The Red Army newspaper Red Star reported that other units had severed the main railroad from the Donets Basin to Dnieperopetrovks, 115 miles west of Stalino.

The German communique, recorded by the Associated Press, said Stalino, Russia's 12th largest city, had been evacuated "to shorten the front" after all military installations had been destroyed.

Russian despatches indicated Stalino fell in flanking moves rather than by direct assault.

This new victory followed

(Continued on Page 8.) See RUSSIA.

TO EXCHANGE PRISONERS

By CHARLES BISHOP.
From Daily Province Ottawa Bureau.
(Copyright, 1943, by Southam Co.)

OTTAWA, Sept. 8. — Authorities here today, while stating that the terms of the armistice might be a factor, expressed the view that "there will undoubtedly be an exchange of prisoners," resulting from the surrender of Italy. Italian prisoners of war in Canada, it is said, will be released, along with Canadian prisoners of war taken by Italy wherever they may be.

This, however, will be done according to certain definite conditions prescribed by the usage.

The surrender of Italy also will involve in time a release of Italians in Canada from whatever inhibitions they are subject to.

HITLER LOSES 27 DIVISIONS

By WILLIAM SMITH WHITE.
Associated Press Staff Writer.

LONDON, Sept. 8. — The war for the Western World entered its final and decisive phase tonight with the fall of Italy, bloody and prolonged though that phase may be.

It was a collapse that laid the whole German position in the south open to attack over the full course of the Mediterranean, along whose shores immense Allied forces were marshalled and ready for campaigns of destiny now ahead.

It was the first great payment on Hitler's bill of defeat: the loss to him of what was by far the strongest of his European allies. The loss was perhaps as punishing and fateful as was the Kaiser's loss in 1918 of his southern flank when Bulgaria, and then Turkey, and then Austria-Hungary collapsed. Then came catastrophe.

The capitulation was the greatest turn of the war since the Russians demonstrated their ability to hurl back the Germans.

It had the immediate effect of stripping Hitler's Balkan defenses of an estimated 27 Italian divisions and putting him in imminent peril in such vital areas as Rumania, where he is believed to have been getting a fourth of his entire oil supplies.

The longer range effects of Italy's surrender were even more staggering to the Nazis, for the final defeat of the first home of Fascism and Germany's ally put in grave question Hitler's ability to hold on militarily anywhere in southeastern Europe.

ONLY MILITARY TRUCE

Armistice Not Political

(By Associated Press.)

LONDON, Sept. 8.—A statement from 10 Downing street—official residence of Prime Minister Churchill, who now is in Washington—said today that the Italian armistice is purely a military instrument and that political, financial and economic terms would be imposed later.

The text of the statement:

"Gen. Eisenhower has announced from Algiers this afternoon unconditional surrender by the Italian Government. The United Nations will recognize in this event a further signal weakening of the Axis forces.

"The armistice is strictly a military instrument signed by military authorities and does not include political, financial and economc terms which will be imposed later. Furthermore it is evident that the present position does not permit of public announcement of the content of a military document signed in these circumstances.

"It is not therefore at present proposed to alter the date of the meeting of Parliament but the Prime Minister expects to be in a position to make a full statement to Parliament on its reassembly."

Attempt To Conquer World Ends With Unconditional Surrender

Armistice Arranged Last Friday, at Moment Canadians Launched Invasion of Italy

(By Associated Press.)

ALLIED HEADQUARTERS IN NORTH AFRICA, Sept. 8.—Gen. Dwight D. Eisenhower today announced unconditional surrender for Italy in the greatest knockout victory for Allied arms in four years of war.

Simultaneously, the Italian Government ordered its troops to drop the fight against Allied forces, but to "oppose attacks from any other quarter."

Russia as well as Britain and the United States approved the granting of the armistice. Eisenhower announced.

It was signed in Sicily last Friday—on the very day that Italy was invaded—and Italy, accepting all the terms, agreed that it would become effective "at a moment most favorable for the Allies."

HITLER "FORTRESS" IS CRACKED

That moment has now arrived," an official statement declared.

Italy will be obliged to "comply with political, economic and financial conditions" which the Allies will impose later.

Simultaneous announcement by the Allies and the Italian Government was agreed upon in view of "the possibility of a German move to forestall publication of the armistice" by the Italians, headquarters said.

Hitler's European fortress was cracked, the way was opened for new offensives, the course of the second Great War immeasurably shortened.

Eisenhower called on the Italians to join the Allies in helping to eject the Germans from their country, and promised that all who do so will have the "assistance and support of the United Nations."

Marshal Pietro Badoglio's proclamation for the Italian armed forces to cease fighting but oppose attacks "from any other quarter" was closely related to this.

Surrender of Italian armed forces "unconditionally" was made by the government of Marshal Pietro Badoglio, successor of Benito Mussolini, the architect of Fascism.

Thus the Casablanca "unconditional surrender" ultimatum received its first application.

PAMPHLETS DROPPED.

Events may continue to move swiftly in the coming hours and days.

Italy's main contribution to Germany in the war was her geographical position, and this now is lost to the Germans except insofar as they may be able to hold on to part of northern Italy themselves.

As soon as the announcement was made, Allied planes roared over Italy—not to bomb, but to bring the Italians the news that the Allies no longer are fighting them.

The planes dropped pamphlets telling the Italians that the opportunity has come to take "vengeance on the German oppressors."

VENGEANCE ON GERMANY.

The pamphlets declared:

Italians! Backed by the might of the Allies, Italy now has the opportunity of taking vengeance on the German oppressors and aiding in the expulsion of the eternal enemy from Italian soil"

The headquarters announcement on surrender was as follows:

"Some weeks ago the Italian Government made an approach to the British and American governments with a view to concluding an armistice. A meeting was arranged and took place in neutral territory. It was at once explained to the representatives of the Italian Government that they must surrender unconditionally.

MEETINGS IN SICILY.

"On this understanding representatives of the Allied commander in chief were empowered to communicate to them the military conditions which they would have to fulfill.

"One clause in these military terms binds the Italian Government to comply with the political, economic and financial conditions of the Allies which will be imposed later.

"Further meetings were arranged and took place in Sicily.

"The armistice was signed at Allied advance headquarters there on September 3, but it was agreed with the representatives of the Italian Government that the armistice should come into force at a moment most favorable for the Allies, and be simultaneously announced by both sides. That moment has now arrived.

"The possibility of a German move to forestall publication of the armistice by the Italian Government was discussed during the negotiations. To meet this eventuality, it was agreed that one of the senior Italian military representatives should not return to Rome. He now is in Sicily.

"Further, Marshal Badoglio arranged to send the text of his proclamation to Allied headquarters."

WHERE WILL NAZIS STAND AND FIGHT? — Just where Hitler's legions will choose to make a stand against the Allies in Italy is engaging the attention of military analysts. Some believe the Nazis will withdraw from Italy entirely because a defeated army would be decimated by aerial bombardment in the narrow confines of the Brenner Pass. Others anticipate a determined Nazi stand along one of the three defensive lines indicated in map above.

SURRENDER BRINGS GOOD CHEER

VANCOUVER UNITES IN REJOICING

Italian Colony, Business Men, Workers Celebrate Surrender

From every walk of life in Vancouver today, from people of every trade, class and nationality — including native-born Italians—came words of rejoicing in response to the news of Italy's surrender.

Even rival political factions were united in a common bond of thanksgiving. Labor leaders, business heads, churchmen, lawyers, ex-servicemen, Liberals, Conservatives and Socialists all had a word of thankfulness and praise for the victorious Allies.

WILL BLESS DAY.

By far the larger majority expressed kindly intentions toward the Italian people. They felt the Italians had been liberated from slavery and would live to bless the day they surrendered.

"This will be a happy day in the lives of the Italian people," commented Angelo E. Branca, Vancouver barrister and solicitor, when told of Italy's surrender this morning.

"They are better off now than they have been for many years past."

Archbishop W. M. Duke said: "We rejoice to learn that Italy has taken this step. It means the saving of numberless lives and the shortening of the incredible sufferings of the people of every-day life.

"It is in accord with the wishes of the Holy Father that peace should return as soon as possible to the world. His recent words on September 1 were: 'Nothing is lost by peace. All can be lost by war.'

"The sacrifice of the Empire and the Allies in the colossal task they have set before them of ridding civilization of state dictators is beginning to reap its just reward.

"It is our prayer and firm conviction they will, before long, bring to suffering humanity the blessings of a just and lasting universal peace."

"This is the turning point in the war," said Mayor J. W. Cornett. "Now that Italy has gone, Germany will have less spirit for the war and her people will begin to realize they are fighting a losing fight.

"The Italians have done the best thing possible for their own future and for the future of civilization."

PBY'S WILL HELP.

"That's fine," said Tom Price, business agent for Aeronautical Mechanics' Lodge No. 756. "That's great news. The aircraft workers will rejoice. They have been turning out planes to help defeat the Axis. Now the next thing is to concentrate on the heart of Germany, and then go after the Japs. The PBY's made in Boeing plants will help dislodge the Japs."

E. E. Leary, president of the Vancouver Labor Council, said: "It's a good thing. It ensures a quicker victory, with the Italians knocked out. They never should have been in the war in the first place.

"It gives the Allies a great chance to start their second front. It will give the French a chance to reorganize. That will be some help to the Allies."

(Continued on Page 8.) See CITY.

"Don't Shout Too Soon," Mayor's Warning

"Don't shout too soon!" said Mayor Cornett today when asked if the city would hold a special celebration to commemorate the fall of Italy.

"The war has still to be won. We have a big Victory Loan campaign coming on soon. Ships have to be built and munitions placed at the disposal of the Allies.

"While we rejoice at this signal victory which may well be the turning point of the war, we can not afford to relax our efforts until victory is finally achieved."

River Barrel At Rosedale

ROSEDALE, Sept. 8. — The New Westminster Rotary Club's Fraser River Sweepstake Barrel passed here, 25 miles east of Chilliwack, at 8 a.m. today. This was 12 hours ahead of last year's time.

The barrel had spent the previous 41 hours bobbing through the rapids of the Fraser. It was not delayed to any extent by whirlpools or back-eddies, which held it up last year. The barrel was launched at Lytton at 3 p.m. Monday. Level of the river, unusually low this year, is rising, officials say.

Celebrations Cancelled

OTTAWA, Sept. 8.—(CP) — The Navy, Army and Air Force late today cancelled celebrations planned for 5 o'clock, local time, across Canada to mark the Italian capitulation.

FINAL ★★★★★ LATE WAR NEWS ★★★★★ FINAL

Germans May Make Stand in North

Italians Will Fight Nazis, Says Badoglio

ITALIAN NAVY ORDERED TO MAKE ALLIED PORTS

The Vancouver Sun

The Vancouver Evening Newspaper Owned and Operated by Vancouver People

FOUNDED 1886 VOL. LVII—No. 282 VANCOUVER, B.C., WEDNESDAY, SEPT. 8 PRICE 5 CENTS

Germans May Rush Reserves To Italy

By British United Press

ALLIED HEADQUARTERS, North Africa, Sept. 8.—The signing of an armistice with the government of Marshal Pietro Badoglio does not mean that the fighting in Italy is over.

Almost certainly the Germans will begin at once to draw upon their reserves elsewhere and pour them through Brenner Pass, if necessary battering their way in against Italian resistance.

The Allied task was to forestall the Nazis as much as possible, but little likelihood was seen that the line of the Po in Northern Italy would be reached without stiff resistance.

Hun Bastion Captured by Red Army

By HENRY SHAPIRO
Special to The Vancouver Sun
Copyright, 1943, by British United Press

MOSCOW, Sept. 8. — The Red Army has captured Stalino, industrial capital and railway hub of the Donets basin, Premier Josef Stalin revealed today.

(Berlin radio said the Germans evacuated Stalino "according to plan in the course of elastic disengaging operations after the complete destruction of war important installations"—Nazi verbiage for losing the city.)

The Russians also captured Krasnoarmeiskoye, key railroad junction northwest of Stalino, through which pass two of the four railroads out of the Donets basin, Stalin announced.

Capture of Stalino, which had a prewar population of nearly 300,000 and is the control point

Please Turn to Page Eight
See "Russia"

BULLETIN

CAIRO, Sept. 8 — (BUP) — Gen. Sir Henry Maitland Wilson, British Middle East commander, declared in a broadcast tonight that "Italian troops in the Balkans must not obey German orders; they must obey my orders."

Badoglio, King Did Not Tell Berlin of Move

LONDON, Sept. 8 — (CP) — The German Radio tonight took cognizance of Italy's surrender — hours after it had been announced by the Badoglio Government and Allied headquarters in North Africa.

A Berlin broadcast said well-informed "foreign office circles" in Berlin understood that the German government was not informed of the step taken by King Victor Emmanuel and Badoglio.

"These circles state that Germany has taken precautionary measures for the security of the Reich and its allies for the prosecution of the war to final victory," added the broadcast.

Prisoner Exchange Expected

LONDON, Sept. 8 — (BUP)—Under the Geneva Convention the conclusion of an armistice normally provides for the repatriation of war prisoners. There are an uncertain number of Canadians, British and Americans in Italian hands, taken in Africa and Sicily.

The assumption here was that the exchange of prisoners between Italy and the Allies would be carried out speedily.

Fight Promoters To Stand Trial

VICTORIA, Sept. 8.—Sidney E. Beech and John Price, promoters of the boxing bout staged at the Royal Athletic Park here last July 6, will stand trial before Magistrate H. C. Hall in city police court here next Monday.

The two promoters have been charged with making collections for a war charity without authorization in writing of an officer duly designated under the War Charity Act.

BASEBALL

NATIONAL

Pittsburgh	100 000 000—1	7	0
St. Louis	120 110 00x—5	9	3
Philadelphia ..	200 000 100—3	9	1
New York	001 001 000—2	9	1
Boston	000 000 000—0	1	2
Brooklyn	000 010 11x—3	7	0

LATE NEWS BULLETINS

The Shipyard Union Conference today called a meeting for Friday to draft a letter to local shipyard operators asking a definite clarification on the seven-day week continuous production program which the unions claim is threatened through the recently announced slowdown in launchings. Decision to draft the letter was made at a union conference today.

Japs Threaten to Seize Island

CHUNGKING, Sept. 8—(BUP)—The Chinese Central News Agency said today the Japanese are threatening to seize Portuguese Macau on the South China Coast because of Portugal's refusal to accept Japanese advisers in the colony's government.

Allied Raiders Over Europe

LONDON, Sept. 8—(BUP)—Allied bombers and fighters were over Europe in great strength early this evening. Wave after wave of twin-motored bombers with formidable Spitfire escort, as well as American Thunderbolt fighters, crossed the southeast coast.

Three Months for Threat Letters

REGINA, Sept. 8—(CP)—Charged with sending threatening letters to his wife, William Carl McDonald, 31, was sentenced today to three months in jail. Judge Maclean said he was unable to give McDonald suspended sentence because of a previous conviction of nine months for theft while at Vancouver.

Eden, Maisky, Winant Meet

LONDON, Sept. 8—(CP)—The first actual Anglo-Soviet-American meeting since a tri-partite parley was proposed at the recent Quebec conference took place here today when Foreign Secretary Anthony Eden had luncheon with Ivan Maisky, Soviet Vice-Commissar for Foreign Affairs, and U.S. Ambassador John G. Winant.

Ship Commanders Told To Elude Hun Capture —Reds Okay Armistice

ALLIED HEADQUARTERS, North Africa, Sept. 8—(AP)—It was learned today that the Italian Navy has abandoned Taranto, on the inner heel of the Italian boot, as a naval base.

Warships recently steamed out of the much-bombed port and proceeded to Pola, apparently for safekeeping. Pola is on the western coast of the Adriatic south of Trieste and is about the farthest Italian port from present areas of war activity.

LONDON, Sept. 8. — Admiral Andrew Browne Cunningham appealed to the Italian fleet by radio today to prevent the Germans from seizing its ships.

He urged the Italian fleet to make for Allied ports.

Cunningham was heard on radio Algiers by the United Press listening post here.

Cunningham, commander-in-chief of the Allied Mediterranean fleet, urged all Italian ships to head for Gibraltar, Tripoli, Malta, Haifa, Aleppo or Sicilian ports. Italian ships in the Black Sea were urged to make for Russian ports.

Merchant vessels unable to make port safe were told:

"Do not let your ships fall into their (German) hands. In the last resort scuttle them or sabotage them rather than let them fall into the hands of the Germans to be used against Italy."

(CBS heard the Allied headquarters radio in Algiers broadcasting a message to the Italian fleet.

It admonished commanders of Italian warships to "take heed that you do not scuttle your ships or allow them to be captured."

The Italian navy consists of seven battleships, three aircraft carriers building, two heavy cruisers, nine lighter cruisers, 25 destroyers, and 60 submarines.

Besides completing the Allied control of the Mediterranean, the new acquisition of the Allies curtails German U-boat operations there.

With the use of Spezia, Pola, Taranto and Genoa naval bases, the Allies will be able to command and blackade the French coast, as well as the Adriatic including the Jugoslavian, Albanian and Greek coasts.

Italian shipping resources remaining in the Mediterranean are estimated at 300 vessels totalling 1,500,000 tons. Italy had 2,000,000 tons of shipping in the Mediterranean when she entered the war.

An official announcement credited the Italians with still having possession of the Rex and Conte di Savoia, two luxury liners, despite a Washington announcement that one of the class was sunk off Bagnara last August.

Berlin Calls It 'Treachery'

LONDON, Sept. 8—(CP)—The Berlin Radio broadcast an official statement tonight saying that since July 25 "The German Government was prepared for such open treachery (as Italy's surrender), and therefore took all military measures required."

The broadcast, recorded by the Associated Press, declared that "this criminal plot . . . will fail, just as all similar actions."

Carillion Plays 'Internationale'

Special to The Vancouver Sun

OTTAWA, Sept. 8.—The first bells to ring out in Canada for the victory of Italy were the bells of the carillon of the Peace Tower and Victory on Parliament Hill. Immediately after General Eisenhower's broadcast the bells pealed out the national anthem, followed by "O Canada," the "Star Spangled Banner" and the Russian "Internationale." During the noon hour the city broke out in a rash of flags.

Churchill, FDR Wait Stalin Word

WASHINGTON, Sept. 8 — (BUP) — President Roosevelt kept silent today on the capitulation of Italy, feeling, the White House said, that "it is Gen. Eisenhower's story — let him tell it."

By MERRIMAN SMITH
Special to The Vancouver Sun
Copyright, 1943, by British United Press

WASHINGTON, Sept. 8.—President Roosevelt and Prime Minister Winston Churchill, partners in the planning of Anglo-American military strategy, received today the news they had been expecting and waiting for — the news that the Axis had been split asunder with the capitulation of Italian armed forces.

The news, tersely flashed to world from Gen. Dwight D. Eisenhower's North African headquarters, represented the culmination of brilliant military operations conceived, in consultation with their staffs, by Mr. Roosevelt and Prime Minister Churchill in conferences begun here in December, 1941, and climaxed—so far as the Mediterranean theatre was concerned—in the historic meeting at Casablanca—early this year.

That Italian "unconditional surrender was imminent had been surmised here because of Churchill's prolonged stay in this country after conclusion of the Quebec conferences last month.

Canadiar Gun Salute Off

Arrangements for a 21-gun salute and military parade to mark the surrender of Italy were abandoned by Pacific Command authorities at 2 p.m. following receipt of instructions from defense headquarters at Ottawa.

A Canadian Press bulletin from the capital stated that celebrations by army, navy and air force, set for 5 o'clock local time across the Dominion had been cancelled.

No reason was given for the cancellation.

On authority of Ottawa, high officials here had planned the cannon salute, and a parade from Larwell Park to the Art Gallery by 800 troops from units in the area.

Associated Press Staff Writer
By EDWARD KENNEDY

ALLIED HEADQUARTERS, NORTH AFRICA, Sept. 8.—Gen. Dwight D. Eisenhower today announced unconditional surrender for Italy in the greatest knockout victory for Allied arms in four years of war.

Simultaneously, the Italian government ordered its troops to drop the fight against Allied forces, but to "oppose attacks from any other quarter."

(This order, given by Marshal Badoglio, was a clear indication that Italian troops will join forces with the Allies in expelling German troops.)

Russia as well as Britain and the United States approved the granting of the armistice, Eisenhower announced.

It was signed in Sicily last Friday—on the very day that Italy was invaded—and Italy, accepting all the terms, agreed that it would become effective "at a moment most favorable for the Allies."

"That moment has now arrived," an official statement declared.

Italy will be obliged to "comply with political, economic and financial conditions" which the Allies will impose later.

Simultaneous announcement by the Allies and the Italian government was agreed upon in view of "the possibility of a German move to forestall publication of the armistice" by the Italians, headquarters said.

"To meet this eventuality, it was agreed that one of the senior Italian military representatives should not return to Rome. He is now in Sicily.

"Further, Marshal Badoglio arranged to send the text of his proclamation to Allied headquarters."

Hitler's 'Fortress' Cracked

Hitler's European Fortress thus was cracked, the way was opened for new offensives, the course of the second great war immeasurably shortened.

Eisenhower called on the Italians to join the Allies in helping to eject the Germans from their country, and promised that all who do so will have the "assistance and support of the United Nations."

See Page 15 for a brief history of Italy's inglorious part in the war.

Marshal Pietro Badoglio in a proclamation to the Italian armed forces ordered them to cease fighting but oppose attacks "from any other quarter."

The text of Badoglio's proclamation:

Please Turn to Page Eight See "Italy Surrenders"

Italian People Told Chance for Vengeance On Nazi Oppressors

ALLIED HEADQUARTERS IN NORTH AFRICA, Sept. 8—(AP)—The Italian people are being informed by radio and leaflets of the surrender of their government to the Allies.

The leaflets telling the news of the armistice also carried the following instructions to the Italian people:

"Italians! Backed by the might of the Allies, Italy now has the opportunity of taking vengeance on the German oppressor and of aiding in the expulsion of the eternal enemy from Italian soil.

"Italians! Here are your battle orders for this phase of the war for the liberation of Europe:

"1. In all territories occupied by the Allied armies give them all your assistance and obey precisely the orders of the commander in the field.

"2. In all areas where the German armies operate do nothing whatsoever to assist the Germans. Show your natural unity and your will to resist them by disciplined, unanimous refusal to become the accomplices of the German pirate.

Workers! The war in Italy is your battle of transport. He who wins the battle of transport wins the war.

"In this battle the Italian people and in particular the Italian transport workers, railway workers, dock workers and road workers can and will play a decisive role.

"Railway workers! See that no single train carrying German material is permitted to pass.

"Dock workers! See that no single ship carrying German troops or materials is permitted to move in the area where you work.

"Italians! Make a supreme heroic effort now. In the next crucial week, by your disciplined resistance against the Germans, you can paralyze their communication lines and so help to win the Italian war of liberation."

Gunman Robs City Bank

Staff Locked In Vault

Strolling into the Bank of Nova Scotia branch at 2804 Granville St., a few minutes before closing time Wednesday afternoon, a short, white-faced, khaki-shirted gunman herded nine employees and a customer into the vault and escaped with an estimated $7,614 from the teller's drawer.

Just before 3 p.m. the man approached Accountant G. M. Smail, said he was a lumberman and wanted some money transferred here from a Toronto bank.

While waiting for some customers to leave he calmly wrote a cheque. Suddenly he pulled a long black revolver from his pocket and jabbed it into Mr. Smail's stomach.

"This is a hold-up," the pint-sized gunman barked, shoving the startled accountant into the office of Bank Manager C. M. Chisholm, who was talking to a woman client.

Impatiently, the bandit forced the staff of six girls and three men and the customer into the vault at the back of the bank, slamming and bolting the heavy door behind them.

"Luckily he left the light on," Mr. Chisholm told The News-Herald. "We had a candle in there, but there is little enough oxygen in those vaults. With ten people in there the oxygen would have been used up pretty quickly while we tried to force the door in the dark."

With a screw driver and a hammer, which he broke while hammering at the lock, Mr. Chisholm removed the tumblers holding back the bolts and forced the vault door open.

"But it took a full 15 minutes," the manager related. "I had them lock me in the vault a few weeks ago just to see how long it would take to get out and it was quite easy. But he must have slid the bolts further than usual, I guess."

Mr. Chisholm was full of admiration for his feminine staff. "I was expecting some of them to faint or get hysterical," he said, "but they were real bricks." They just waited calmly until we got the door open."

While the bank staff was locked in the vault, the gunman scooped the $7,600 from the teller's drawer and walked out—leaving the front door open.

Convict Escapes Oakalla Prison

Tommy Skin, inmate of the Oakalla Prison Farm, made a bold and successful escape shortly before 5 p.m. Wednesday. At a late hour Wednesday night Provincial Police and prison guards were scouring the surrounding bush for him.

According to prison authorities, Skin had been working during the day around the barns. Prior to quitting time he was seen to run around to the rear of the barns and climb the fence. By the time the alarm was sounded Skin had disappeared.

FRASER BARREL MAY END TRIP BY NOON TODAY

If tides are favorable, the Fraser river sweepstake barrel should be in New Westminster by noon today, according to officials who conveyed it for 18 hours Tuesday in a rowboat.

The barrel, sponsored by New Westminster Rotary Club, passed Stave River at 6:30 p.m. Wednesday, 24 hours ahead of last year's time. Stave River is 2 1-2 miles east of Whonnock which is 25 miles from New Westminster.

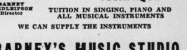

VANCOUVER NEWS-HERALD

VOL. 11, NO. 116   VANCOUVER, B.C., THURSDAY, SEPTEMBER 9, 1943   PRICE 5c

ALLIES INVADE HEART OF ITALY

Hun Lines Crumbling In Soviet

LONDON, Sept. 9.—(AP)—The Soviet army smashed in Wednesday to capture Stalino, steel making centre, wiped out the entire German salient in the important Donets Basin and flung its might against the retreating German army along a 600-mile front north to Smolensk, Moscow announced Wednesday night.

The Germans, now menaced by the capitulation of Italy, the sagging of the Balkans and threat of an Allied invasion from the west, appeared to be falling back to their last ditch line in Russia, abandoning gains in more than two bitter years of war.

* * *

Even as 224 Moscow guns thundered their salute for Stalino, tank spearheads were stabbing 40 miles northwest of the city—named for Marshal Joseph Stalin—so swiftly they captured German planes still parked on an airfield and seized trainloads of supplies.

In the Donets basin the Soviet army was reported to be 100 miles from Dniepopetrovsk, on the Dnieper river line to which the Germans appeared to be 'retreating. Far to the north, near Konotop, the Red Army slashed to Borzna, 100 miles from Kiev, key city on the Dnieper.

Capture of the Donets basin returned to Russia an area rich in mines and factories and straightened the line south from Kharkov to the Sea of Azov.

Miners To Take Vote On Strike

CALGARY, Sept. 9—(CP)—The executive board of district 18, United Mine Workers of America, announced Wednesday a strike ballot would be held on Sept. 21 in connection with demands of the membership for higher wages and holidays with pay.

A statement issued by the board said the Western Canada Coal Operators' Association refused to meet the mine workers to discuss the situation, and a meeting Sept. 1 with a committee representing Drumheller and Lethbridge coal operators achieved no progress.

The demands, formulated at a recent district convention, are:

1. Increase of $2 for all employees, and time and a half rate for the sixth day of the week.

2. Two weeks' holidays with pay for employees who have served one year with the coal company concerned.

There are about 9,000 coal miners in District 18, which covers Alberta and British Columbia.

John Bond, secretary of Cumberland Local, U.M.W.A., told The News-Herald Wednesday he had no information on the move as yet.

"John H. Cameron, president of our local is representing all Vancouver Island min-

Nervous and frightened after being imprisoned in a stuffy vault by a lone gunman, Wednesday afternoon, nine Bank of Nova Scotia employees, at Twelfth and Granville, escaped to find their "jailer" had walked away with an estimated $7,600 from the teller's drawer. Above are the "escaped" employees, from left to right, C. D. Grieve, Mrs. C. Randall, Mrs. I. Miller, Mrs. M. Kerr, Shirley Tran, D. Schofield, Dorothy Stewart, G. M. Smail, who was first accosted by the small bandit, and Mr. Chisholm.

Vancouver Vice Control Charge

Police Chief Stoutly Denies Statement By Lt.-Col. Williams

The charges made Wednesday by Lt.-Col. D. M. Williams, of Ottawa, in charge of venereal disease control for the Department of Pensions and National Health, that white slavery of a vicious type is in progress "within a stone's throw of the Vancouver Police Station," brought a swift and absolute denial from Chief Constable Donald MacKay.

In commenting on the statement the Chief Constable said, "Read the article and then carry on your own investigations and you will find that statements contained therein are not in accordance with the facts."

"Why the doctor would make a statement of this nature in Vancouver and when speaking across the line in the U.S.A. praise Vancouver as being one of the cleanest cities on the North American continent is quite beyond human understanding."

According to police officials, one man and one man alone was responsible for breaking the Celona case and sending that individual to penitentiary, Inspector Andrew Rae, present head of the morality squad. Police authorities were unstinted in their praise of this officer's work in connection with this case.

Crediting the R.C.M.P. in connection with this case, they said is rather far-fetched as the record discloses the closest they came to the case was when an ex-member of that force was hired to guard certain women witnesses pending the assize hearing.

As to the disposition of these cases after an arrest has been made that is a matter entirely up to the magistrates hearing the case. One veteran officer said, "The good doctor is mixing his medicine with the Criminal code of Canada."

In two instances mentioned by Lt.-Col. Williams in his charge that some of the would-be madams, own their own homes and have lived in them for a period of years. This type of operator is extremely hard to convict, the officials said, as they may run open house for a couple of days and then close for the rest of the month.

Powerful British, American and Canadian Armies Move To Trap Retreating Germans

LONDON, Sept. 9.—(CP)—The Swiss radio reported today that large forces of the American 7th Army had landed on the Tyrrhenian Coast of Southwest Italy and also to the north at Leghorn.

The broadcast, recorded by Reuters, added that "hundreds of Allied planes are about to land on Italian airfields."

ALLIED HEADQUARTERS, NORTH AFRICA, Sept. 9.—(Thursday)—(AP)—Allied troops landed early today in the Naples area, a third of the way up the Italian boot, a few hours after the surrender of Italy was announced.

Occupation of the bomb-battered area presumably places Allied forces behind at least some of the German troops retreating from Southern Italy.

The Allied announcement said merely that "further operations have started on the Italian mainland in the vicinity of Naples."

(This dispatch did not indicate the makeup of the landing parties. A Tunis radio broadcast last night in New York, however, said powerful British, Canadian and American armies participated.

Naples, in peace time a city of almost 1,000,000 population, is a vital link in Italy's north-south railway communications and a major supply port.

The one-sentence announcement of the new operations came just 12 hours after that of the Italian surrender. No details were immediately available.

(Multiple Allied landings upon the west coast of the peninsula were reported by two Swedish newspapers and an Italian language broadcast from the Allied-controlled Tunis radio, as President Roosevelt told the American people "we must drive the Germans out of Italy."

(The Swedish papers reported Allied landings at Naples, Genoa, Gaeta and Civitavecchio as well as on the island of Sardinia. The Stockholm Dagens Nyheter said there were rumors that parachute troops had dropped at the Calabrian town of Pizzo on the instep of the Italian boot.

Nazi Radio Propagandists Kept Busy

Germany 'Betrayed' By Former Axis Partner, Berlin Wails

LONDON, Sept. 9 — (AP)—The German radio screamed "betrayal" in giving the German people news of Italy's unconditional surrender Wednesday night.

Just after July 25, when Mussolini fell, Berlin said Fascism in Italy had proved sterile and was quite properly ousted. Then the Germans obviously hoped to keep Italy in the war through the Badoglio government.

"Since the criminal plot against Il Duce of July 25 and the coup d'etat prepared in co-operation with the British and Americans for removal of the Fascist regime, which was loyal to the alliance, German authorities were prepared for such open treachery and they therefore took all the measures required by the situation," said the broadcast.

All telephone communication between Berlin and Italy has been severed, Berlin announced tonight, declaring that the Germans had refused to accept urgent calls by way of Hungary or Switzerland.

scribed as loyal to Berlin.

Just after July 25, when Mussolini fell, Berlin said Fascism in Italy had proved sterile and was quite properly ousted. Then the Germans obviously hoped to keep Italy in the war through the Badoglio government.

This Is A Rationed Paper

Under terms of the new order of the Newsprint Administrator, The News-Herald's consumption has been cut from 71 tons in August to 62 in September. Corresponding reductions have been ordered in the case of many other Canadian newspapers.

To comply with this order The News-Herald must reduce either the number of its pages or the number of its readers. If further newsprint restrictions are ordered it may be necessary for us to do both. This was the case in Britain, where many newspapers not only reduced their size, but also cut thousands of their circulations.

It may not be possible to supply all the people who wish to buy the paper at the corner boxes or from the newsboys on the street. But we hope to continue to serve all the present home readers of the paper. We are going to do that by means of condensing and a closer editing of news. We are aiming to give you a complete newspaper in a smaller size.

We regret the step we have been compelled to take. But the wartime shortage of manpower in the pulp industry gives us no alternative.

THE NEWS-HERALD MANAGEMENT.

VICTORIA HALTS VICTORY PARADE

VICTORIA, Sept. 9—(CP)—Complete arrangements for a large victory parade here Wednesday were completed before word from the National Defence Department forced postponement.

ers at the meeting where the decision was made," he said. "We will not have a full report until he returns."

He stated that the strike vote decision would undoubtedly affect B. C., but to what extent he could not as yet determine.

107

TIDE OF COMBAT SWAYS IN ITALY

VANCOUVER NEWS-HERALD

This Is A Rationed Newspaper
SAVE IT FOR
WAR SALVAGE
Tie up in 50 lbs. Phone FAirmont 7000

VOL. 11, NO. 121 VANCOUVER, B.C., WEDNESDAY, SEPTEMBER 15, 1943 PRICE 5c

Double Holdup In The West End

3 Men Sought By Police

At an early hour this morning police were searching the West End for three men believed to have committed two holdups within the space of one hour.

Fred George Whitworth, 75, 1017 Nelson St., an old age pensioner, was robbed by three thugs at 11.10 p.m. while reurning to his home.

The men struck their victim over the head with a pipe wrench and robbed him of a billfold containing his national registration card and a wrist watch. Police found a wrench lying on an adjacent lawn.

Police called to the scene took the man to St. Paul's Hospital, where he was treated for scalp lacerations.

Whitworth told Detectives Walter Mulligan and Lawrence McCulloch that three men approached him just as he was about to enter his home.

At 11:50 p.m. the officers were called to the rear of the Queen Anne Apartments, 1235 Nelson St., where a few minutes previously Dick Halhed, chief announcer for C.B.R., was robbed of 75c in cash and a valuable stop watch belonging to Roy Dunlop of C.B.C.

Halhed told the officers that he was taking a shortcut home when the three men approached and with hands in their pockets, as though holding revolvers, forced him to hand over the money and the watch. They then fled down the lane.

THE ODD SPOT

DYERSBURG, Tenn., Sept. 15.—(AP)—And now comes the gentleman who caters to those plagued by the shortage of washwomen. Homer Pressler has installed washing machines and other equipment in his furniture store here. Patrons do their own wash, then take it home for ironing.

JAPAN EASES PEACE TERMS FOR CHINESE

WASHINGTON, Sept. 15.—(AP)—China is constantly receiving peace proposals from Japan and the terms become more liberal as the Japanese become more hard pressed, T. V. Soong, Chinese Foreign Minister, said Tuesday.

Soong said the Japanese are ready to get out of China (except for Manchuria and Formosa) if China will leave the United Nations and join Japan in a racial war against the white man.

IWA Suspension Plea Withdrawn

MONTREAL, Sept. 15.—(CP)—The Canadian Congress of Labor convention here will not have to hear an appeal by the British Columbia District Council No. 1 International Woodworkers of America, against suspension of its charter by the executive council of the congress, President A. R. Mosher told delegates Tuesday.

The appeal had been withdrawn, Mr. Mosher announced, and the Woodworkers now purposed making an application to the executive council of the congress for reaffiliation.

• • •

(The charters of the Woodworkers' District Council and of Local No. 1, Boilermakers' and Iron Shipbuilders' Union of Canada, Vancouver, were suspended last January.)

At the morning session Tuesday, the congress president had said the Woodworkers' appeal would be heard in the afternoon, although there was some question as to whether it could be considered officially filed. He said, however, that he was inclined to overlook any "irregularity" in the filing of the appeal and to allow it to come before the convention.

"I do not want any charge of dictatorship bandied about the country," he added, "that anyone coming under the ban of the executive council has no chance to state his case."

This camp of tents in a district of Stalingrad houses the men who are rebuilding the Soviet city following its recapture by advancing Russian forces. Latest big Soviet city to fall before the westward advance was Bryansk.

Bad Feeling Between Countries Flares

Turkish Paper Charges Russia Responsible For War In Europe

ANKARA, Sept. 15.—(AP)—Misunderstanding and bad feelings between Soviet Russia and neutral Turkey flared openly Tuesday as the newspaper Aksam attacked a Soviet magazine article which had declared Turkey's neutrality favored Germany.

• • •

The Russian magazine, "War and the Working Class," had complained that, "If Ankara would depart from the neutrality which is favoring Germany the inevitable catastrophe for Germany would be accelerated."

• • •

The Aksam editorial retorted sharply:

"Turkey is proud of the political road she has chosen. She has gained the admiration of the entire world, except perhaps Russia."

• • •

The editorial set forth that the accord which Turkey, allied to France and Britain, should have signed with Russia would have completed dispositions for the security of Europe and would have prevented the war. It declared that Russia had made the war in Europe possible, that she had preferred to come to an understanding with Germany.

"Even more," the editorial went on," Molotov, violently criticizing the Anglo-Turkish alliance, declared openly in a speech that Turkey would repent for having concluded that alliance . . . It is necessary to remember that when Turkey signed an accord with Germany, the Germans were in the Balkans and Crete.

• • •

England was alone in the face of a dangerous situation and that Russia was at the moment in full collaboration with Germany in her partition of Poland and the Baltic countries."

The best information is that the foreign office held talks with the Russian ambassador, Serguei Vinogradov, after the journalistic exchange, and the result likely may be a revival of cordiality between the national neighbors.

INCREASED LIQUOR RATION DOUBTFUL SAYS KENNEDY

By News-Herald Staff Writer

VICTORIA, B.C., Sept. 15. — The drinking public who have high hopes that there may be some loosening up in October of restrictions that limit them to 13 ounces of hard liquor monthly, or two dozen pints of beer, or certain quantities of wine, are probably barking up the wrong tree.

• • •

According to W. F. Kennedy, head man of the liquor situation, it is "doubtful if there will be any change," from the existing setup.

• • •

On Tuesday Mr. Kennedy said it was too early in the month to make any decision of the possible October allowance, but he declined to raise any false hopes. "We have to wait until near the end of this month in order to start to figure out the next one," he said.

BULLETINS

Report 9th Army Sailed From Near East

STOCKHOLM, Sept. 15.—(AP)—The British 9th Army long stationed in the Near East, has embarked for an "unknown destination," the Budapest correspondent of the newspaper Svenska Dagbladet said Tuesday, quoting reports from Ankara.

Severe 'Quake Reported in South Japan

SANTA CLARA, Calif., Sept. 15.—(AP)—A two hour earthquake registered on University of Santa Clara seismograph Tuesday centred in the southern islands of Japan and was "twice as severe as the destructive quake of last Friday, which Japanese sources said caused many casualties and much property damage."

Miners Strike; Protest Sentence

LONDON, Sept. 15.—(CP)—A strike in the Nottinghamshire coal field spread Tuesday night with nine pits employing 10,000 men idle in protest over the sentencing of a surface worker to one month in jail for refusing to work underground.

Nazi Paratroopers Guard Vatican City

NEW YORK, Sept. 15.—(AP)—The German radio was quoted by the BBC Tuesday night as saying in a Rome dispatch that German parachute troops armed with anti-tank guns had mounted guard in St. Peter's square "to prevent by force any one penetrating into Vatican City." The BBC broadcast was recorded by CBS.

Anglo-American Forces Battle To Hold Hard-Won Bridgehead; Concede Germans Gain Ground

LONDON, Sept. 15.—(AP)—Lt.-Gen. Mark W. Clark's 5th Army of American and British troops was locked in a bitter battle at Salerno Tuesday night, but the British-Canadian 8th Army was lashing up from the southwest and the decision was yet to fall as to whether this was to be the first great Allied defeat in Italy or whether it was likely to be the enemy's last spasm of effective resistance in the lower half of the peninsula.

The Allies have suffered a serious setback, and it appeared that even the Salerno bridgehead, so hard won, now was in danger. Gen. Dwight D. Eisenhower's headquarters conceded that ground had been lost before savage Nazi counter-attacks.

All the details were not clear as to what had happened at Salerno, but this much seemed plain:

1. The Allied forces were so far advanced from fighter airfields as to be under rather thin air cover.
2. The terrain favored the enemy, for he occupied hilly positions and the Allied troops were out in the open flats.
3. The Germans had anticipated the area of the landing and were in greater strength than had been thought. Moreover, the Germans had received reinforcements.

ALLIED HEADQUARTERS, North Africa, Sept. 15.—(AP)—British and American troops fought hand to hand Tuesday night with elements of three crack German divisions on the Salerno bridgehead as Field Marshal Albert Kesselring made a supreme effort to drive the 5th Army into the sea.

One officer at headquarters summed up the crucial fighting at Salerno in these words:

"The fighting is extremely heavy and it certainly is the bitterest land fighting encountered by an Allied landing force in this war."

CANADIANS IN ACTION

During the day and into the night Allied warships poured out everything from machine-gun bullets to shell fire to help protect the narrow beachhead extending 24 miles south of Salerno and the entire 5th Army was engaged in a grim battle.

The German overseas news agency broadcast Tuesday night a report that Canadians "with many tanks and motorized infantry" are taking part in the bloody fighting on the Salerno bridgehead.

A Berlin radio broadcast recorded in New York by CBS declared, without elaboration that Salerno was "now in German hands," and that the British and American landing forces were everywhere on the defensive.

The Allied-controlled Tunis radio said in a post-midnight broadcast that: "German tanks and infantry are pouring against the Allied lines, but our positions are being firmly held against all these assaults."

(Continued on Back Page)
See BATTLE

MOSCOW IGNORES BRYANSK VICTORY

LONDON, Sept. 15.—(AP)—The Russians announced Tuesday night that Red Army forces had swept 15 miles nearer Dniepropetrovsk and gained in other sectors, but ignored a German statement that Nazi forces had abandoned Bryansk.

More than 4,300 Germans were killed and 1,000 captured in the fighting Tuesday, said a communique broadcast from Moscow and recorded by the Soviet monitor.

Boilermakers' Demand For Inquiry Refused; Act Said Ultra Vires

That Section 7 (1) of the Industrial Conciliation and Arbitration Act "appears to be ultra vires," is one of the reasons given by Hon. G. S. Pearson, minister of labor, to the Boilermakers' and Iron Shipbuilders' Union, Local No. 1, for his refusal to prosecute Electro-Weld Metal Products Ltd. for alleged infractions of the act.

The minister's decision followed legal opinion to this effect given him by the attorney-general's department in a statement which also protested that not enough evidence had been produced to justify prosecution.

"The union is demanding a public inquiry into the activities of a group fostering company unionism, and using it to defeat the purpose of the I.C.A. Act," stated Tom MacKenzie, secretary of the union, on receipt of the minister's communication.

Mr. MacKenzie said the union would not itself institute prosecution proceedings "in the face of the minister's failure to do so."

• • •

On Aug. 26 the union, through John Stanton, attorney, presented a brief to the minister, charging the company had fostered company unionism and discrimination against Boilermakers' union members.

The minister, in reply, stated the matter had been referred to the legal department, and later to the attorney-general's department, and his decision was received Tuesday.

In a letter enclosing a copy of the legal opinion, the minister states:

"In view of this I cannot agree to entering a charge against this company, but this does not preclude you or anyone else from entering such a charge if you feel that it can be substantiated in court."

Section 7 (1) of the act deals with intimidation of employees to prevent them joining a union. As this matter has been dealt with by subsequent legislation of the dominion passed in 1939 as Section 502-A of the Criminal Code, and the courts have laid down that where the legislative field within the jurisdiction of the dominion has been occupied by the dominion, provincial legislation on the same subject becomes invalid."

(Continued on Back Page)
SEE I.C.A. ACT

More Tanks Rushed Ashore

8TH ARMY HELP NEAR AS ALLIED POSITION GRAVE

The Vancouver Sun

The Vancouver Evening Newspaper Owned and Operated By Vancouver People

FOUNDED 1886
VOL. LVII—No. 288 | VANCOUVER, B.C., WEDNESDAY, SEPTEMBER 15, 1943 | PRICE 5 CENTS

STUDIO PIN-UP PARTY

Like most of the other soldiers who were invited by Metro-Goldwyn Mayor to take "pin-up" pictures of some of the studio's cuties, this soldier gravitates toward the model—Gloria Anderson. Thirty-four pretty actresses obligingly posed and found themselves besieged with invitations to sit on a soldier's lap "for just one picture," or were asked for dates, autographs, or kisses.

A Day Inside Italy

Reporter Spy's Bold Exploit

EDITOR'S NOTE—Here is one of the notable journalistic "firsts" of the present war. It was obtained at great personal risk by Aldo Forte, manager of the Bern, Switzerland, bureau of the United Press. Carrying no credentials except an out-of-date Italian newspaper card (Forte was formerly on the U.P. staff in Rome), he crossed into German-held Northern Italy disguised as a mountain climber and spent 13 hours talking with soldiers and civilians.

By ALDO FORTE
British United Press Staff Correspondent

CHIASSO, Swiss-Italian Frontier, Sept. 15 — Italians in Northern Italy have a burning hatred for the Germans who are occuping their soil, and men, women and children in some parts of the area I have just visited are digging trenches and preparing to resist Adolf Hitler's troops.

They are woefully short of weapons, and some men with whom I talked during my 13-hour tour asked why the Allies did not parachute arms and ammunition to them.

Pouring out questions on how soon the Allies could be expected in Northern Italy, the people told me that the whole upper part of the country was willing and eager to fight to the last man against the Nazis, but lacked the arms to do it.

These descendants of men who fought the Germans down through the generations left no doubt of their bitter antipathy for the Nazis. They told tales of German plundering and killing, and of Germans stripping men and women of jewelry and their money in the streets.

Through the Border Wires

German youths in khaki shorts, bare to the waist, were reported patroling roads radiating from Milan, arresting all men between 18 and 50 for concentration at the central Milan station—which was patrolled by Tiger tanks—later to be shipped in sealed box cars to unknown destinations.

Como, the centre of the area through which I traveled, was flaming with the war spirit. I saw women and children helping their menfolk dig trenches in the various sections of the city itself and especially along the sector facing in the direction of Milan.

The rail station "Norte Milano" was patrolled by Bersaglieri who looked surprisingly gay in their plumed helmets. Carabinieri in swallow-tailed Napoleonic coats marched in the nearby streets. They allowed me to pass undisturbed — even saluted occasionally.

Please Turn to Page Two — See "Reporter Spy"

Sun Handicap

by ALF COTTRELL

The bracketed figures after the weight indicate the rating of the horse for that particular race. If a horse carries more than the weight stipulated in the entries, deduct one point for each pound of verweight carried. Bracketed figures at end of line indicate post position.
Jockeys, post positions, subject to late changes.

THURSDAY, SEPTEMBER 16

1st Race—Claiming; three-year-olds and up: **6 Furlongs 30 Yds.**

SPECIAL BRIAR	112	(93)	Class of this party	(10)
GALLAMAR	102	(90)	Game and in light	(6)
ARPEGGIO	105	(89)	Had no zip other day	(7)
Eltorada	109	(88)	Rail gives nice chance	(1)
Ouimax	114	(87)	Is improving rapidly	(9)
Eno Heather	109	(86)	Last was brilliant race	(4)
Lord Broxa	105	(86)	Meeting rough society	(8)
Groves	105	(83)	Might be real comer	(5)
Ann's Worry	114	(75)	Probably need easier	(3)
Happy Duster	105	(73)	Had a bad season	(2)

2nd Race—Claiming, four-year-olds and up foaled in Western Canada. **Mile and 70 Yds.**

STREAMLINE	116	(108)	With best could click	(3)
MERCHISTON	116	(102)	Improves every race	(5)
SIMONY'S BOY	116	(101)	Last not his best	(10)
Nalod	118	(100)	Beat a similar field	(6)
Avondale Star	116	(100)	Always in the battle	(1)
Broderick	116	(95)	Chance; race wide open	(7)
Wild Deer	113	(95)	Needs luck to score	(8)
Beauty Warm	113	(95)	Last wasn't too bad	(4)
Marion Somers	113	(94)	Stumbled in last try	(2)
Plucky Jake	116	(91)	Has smart old trainer	(9)

3rd Race—Claiming; three-year-olds and up: foaled in Western Canada: **5½ Furlongs**

FRANKLIN D	109	(97)	Should have no trouble	(3)
FLAGBORO	x104	(83)	Old mare well rested	(4)
GOLDENWORTH	106	(80)	Check Wednesday try	(5)
Lasswade	114	(73)	If right is a threat	(7)
Zelpha Lad	112	(72)	Done nothing to date	(6)
Wavelength	112	(70)	Speedy and on rail	(1)
Zebella	109	(68)	Also has early foot	(2)
Wingaway	109	(66)	Post position no help	(8)

4th Race—Claiming: three-year-olds and up: **1 Mile**

LORNE SABLE	x106	(107)	Shut off against better	(4)
MAIZIE B	108	(101)	Most speed; big threat	(8)
ASCOT MAID	108	(93)	Route seems trifle short	(6)
Crackade	x110	(91)	Been showing new life	(7)
Tadpole	118	(90)	Erratic sort of runner	(2)
Marco	x113	(86)	May get up for part	(5)
Mosca	115	(85)	Not much at best	(1)
Lucky Card	118	(85)	Young; stable winning	(3)

5th Race—Claiming; three-year-olds and up: **1 Mile**

CRAIGLOCHART	105	(94)	Just missed other day	(1)
GOLDEN SABLE	x105	(87)	Ready for a victory	(3)
BOOTER BILLY	x112	(87)	Last was promising	(12)
Chief Lon	106	(87)	Could be the upset	(9)
Dodd	117	(82)	Much luck; all bad	(4)
Delano C	x112	(80)	Long overdue to score	(2)
Ynomis	107	(80)	Been devoid of life	(11)
Selfish Joss	114	(78)	Has improved slightly	(8)
Blore Heath	110	(77)	Had speed some races	(7)
Black Chick	107	(77)	Fast; fair longshot	(6)
Our Haven	114	(76)	Had terrible season	(10)
Glad Answer	108	(—)	Shown nothing to date	(5)

6th Race—OAKS HANDICAP, F and M., three-year-olds and up: **6 Furlongs 30 Yds.**

WEE BIDDY	109	(116)	Speed and should stick	(5)
MESMERIST	105	(115)	Might come with rush	(6)
MAID OF BROXA	109	(106)	Keen; could upset them	(4)
Witch's Taxi	111	(104)	Had no speed in last	(1)
Bonnie Park	108	(98)	Young but spot tough	(2)
Some Turley	111	(98)	Failed in last try	(3)

7th Race—Claiming; four-year-olds and up: **Mile and 1-16**

CETOMA	108	(112)	Likes this racetrack	(10)
RUBY PAGAN	103	(109)	Chance to steal race	(7)
BROAD ROYAL	113	(102)	Off best is danger	(8)
Watch Tick	110	(100)	Going nicely of late	(2)
Little Gloomy	118	(99)	Good; packs big load	(5)
Valdina Sun	118	(97)	Beat easier in drive	(6)
Simtee	111	(91)	Not breaking records	(4)
Pipe Down	113	(87)	Fair; may need easier	(1)
New Car	118	(83)	Seems in-and-outer	(3)
Lloyd Pan	118	(82)	Might need longer	(9)
Barsac	118	(81)	Hasn't beaten these	(11)

Substitute—Claiming; three-year-olds and up: **Mile and 1-16**

NICKAJACK	x111	(106)	Last below best notch	(6)
GOLDEN BELT	x101	(102)	Speed and feather up	(8)
PAPER HEELS	109	(100)	Should be close up	(7)
Ancient Rites	109	(94)	Been a constant threat	(3)
Bob Jack	x104	(93)	Also packs light load	(11)
Little Dee	106	(91)	Beat easier by a neck	(1)
Iron Judge	x111	(89)	Closed well at shorter	(10)
Sean Ghall	116	(87)	Chance on some form	(2)
Pandomint	116	(84)	Nice third to Stockton	(5)
Shasta Sue	x108	(81)	Seems to prefer slop	(4)
Bahask	113	(78)	Stamina is doubtful	(9)

Track fast — **First post at 2:50 p.m.**

x—Apprentice Allowance Claimed

Marauding Bear Shot in Burnaby

A fourteen-day-old hunt came to an end at noon today when Victor Davies, 3149 Norfolk Street, Burnaby, shot and killed a half-tamed black bear in the bush at the rear of his house.

Women and children have been frightened by the bear who was seen in the vicinity of Burnaby Lake two weeks ago and again last Saturday around Burris Street, Burnaby.

The one-year-old bear has been stealing fruit and vegetables and chickens. Reg. King, game warden for Burnaby district, has been hunting the animal and was present when he was shot today.

Famine in N. Italy

BERNE, Sept. 15—(AP)—The spectre of famine hangs over Rome and the Nazi-occupied cities of northern Italy.

Sun Selections By Railbird

1—Eno Heather, Gallamar, Eltorado.
2—Streamline, Avondale Star, Nalod.
3—Franklin D., Zabella, Wavelength.
4—Tadpole, Ascot Maid, Lorne Sable.
5—Golden Sable, Dodd, Delano C.
6—Wee Biddy, Bonnie Park, Some Turley.
7—Valdina Sun, Ruby Pagan, Watch Tick.
Sub—Pandomint, Nickajack, Little Dee.
One best: FRANKLIN D.

Ottawa Post

OTTAWA, Sept. 15—(CP)—Norman Wilks of Victoria has been appointed a special assistant to the financial advisor of the Munitions Department, it was announced today.

'IKE' DECORATES 'MONTY'

This photo, radioed across the Atlantic, was taken before the Allied invasion of Italy. It shows General Dwight D. (Ike) Eisenhower (left), Allied Commander-in-Chief in the North African Theatre, as he decorates Gen. Sir Bernard L. Montgomery, Commander of the British 8th Army, with the Order of Commander of the Legion of Honor—the highest award that the U.S. can bestow on other nationals. The ceremony took place at Gen. Montgomery's Sicilian headquarters.

Balkan Invasion Looms As 9th Army on Move

By Canadian Press

LONDON, Sept. 15.—Unconfirmed reports reaching London from Stockholm via Ankara today said that Britain's 9th Army—a force which the Germans assert has been designated for an Allied drive into the Balkans—was on the move today from its Middle East bases facing the island pathway into Greece.

British military officials had no comment to make on the Ankara reports, published in the Stockholm **Svenska Dagbladet**, which said that the army commanded by Lt.-Gen. W. H. Holmes had embarked for an "unknown destination."

The dispatch coincided here, however, with authentic accounts of ferment in the Balkans, of sweeping new successes by Jugo-Slav guerrillas, and reports of fierce fighting between German and Italian troops in the Dodecanese islands off the Turkish mainland.

Algiers radio today again forecast that "important new military developments are imminent," and it was pointed out that the surrender of the Italian navy has cleared the Mediterranean for any assault against German positions in southeastern Europe.

Bases of the 9th Army in Syria and Transjordania are only 400 miles from the island of Rhodes and less than 600 miles from Crete, Axis outposts in the Mediterranean.

Six Liberals, Two Tories Lead in P.E.I.

CHARLOTTETOWN, Sept. 15—(CP)—Scattered first returns from today's balloting in the Prince Edward Island general election showed six Liberals and two Conservatives in the lead in four ridings.

At this preliminary stage of the count, an hour after the closing of the polls, none of the CCF or Independent Liberal candidates was in front. The returns were only fractional and by no means indicative of a trend.

Opposition leader W. J. P. MacMillan, running in the 5th Queen's District, was leading a Liberal and a CCF candidate in the race for councillor. T. W. L. Prowse, Liberal, was ahead in the fight for the Assemblyman's seat.

Bulletin

LONDON, Sept. 15—(BUP)—Air alarm sirens sounded in London shortly before 9:50 o'clock tonight. Heavy gunfire was heard in the London area.

BASEBALL

NATIONAL LEAGUE

Morning game:

		R.	H.	E.
New York	000 000 000—	0	4	0
Philadelphia	000 010 00x—	1	5	0

Mungo, Adams (8), Wittig (8) and Lombardi; Kraus and Seminick.

Second game:

		R.	H.	E.
New York	301 200 000—	6	11	1
Philadelphia	000 001 200—	3	8	1

East, Wittig (7) and Mancuso; Lee, Karl (6), Kimball (8) and Culp, Seminich (3).

AMERICAN LEAGUE

		R.	H.	E.
Philadelphia	000 000 030—	3	6	1
New York	310 021 00x—	7	10	0

Arntzen, Scheib (2), Ciola (8) and Swift; Borowy and Dickey.

Expected At Salerno By Friday

By NOLAND NORGAARD
Associated Press War Correspondent

ALLIED HEADQUARTERS, NORTH AFRICA, Sept. 15.—Allied troops have beaten off fierce German counter-attacks against the Salerno bridgehead in Italy but were forced last night to yield some ground gained earlier, in order to straighten their lines.

(An NBC broadcast from Allied headquarters tonight said that the situation on the Salerno bridgehead had not deteriorated today although it still remained grave.)

The NBC broadcast also reported that the British Eighth Army was speeding from the south of Italy to attack the German rear in the bloody Salerno battle. It estimated that Montgomery's men might reach Agropoli, at the southern end of the Allied bridgehead by Friday to relieve the Americans.

Germans reported last night without confirmation that Canadians "with many tanks and motorized infantry" are engaged in the Salerno fighting. London had earlier reported, also without confirmation, that units of the Canadian 1st Army Tank Brigade were in the vicinity.

(Men returning from Salerno said German artillery fire prevented sufficient American tanks getting ashore in the early stage of fighting but that more landing craft had put tank reinforcements ashore and "they are now in action" against about five Nazi divisions, which normally would be some 50,000 to 75,000 men.

(The railroad junction of Battipaglia, just southeast of Salerno, changed hands several times in bloody fighting and may now be held by the Germans. NBC broadcaster estimated that the British 8th Army, moving from south Italy, might reach Agropoli, at the southern end of the Allied bridgehead by Friday.)

Germans Regain Two Towns

New support came to Lt.-Gen. Mark W. Clark's forces—the strongest air attacks of the Mediterranean war and the thunder of naval guns offshore.

Today's Allied communique disclosed that savage, close-quarter combat is raging along the whole front from Salerno to Agropoli, 27 miles south, with both sides throwing heavy reinforcements of troops and armor into battle.

(A United Press bulletin reported that Allied invasion forces at one time penetrated 10 miles inland from the

Please Turn to Page Two — See "Fierce Fight" Pages

LATE NEWS BULLETINS

Anyone who goes out in a blackout just out of curiosity should take extra care, Mr. Justice Sidney Smith said today as he dismissed the city's first blackout damage suit. He added that Daniel George Gordon Lang, 67-year-old veteran of the Frist Great War, did not do this and was the author "of his own misfortune." **(See also page 9.)**

108 Killed, Missing in Raids

LONDON, Sept. 15—(CP Cable)—Civilian air raid casualties in Britain in August totalled 108 killed or missing, believed killed, and 164 injured and detained in hospital.

Asia Campaign Hinted

NEW YORK, Sept. 15—(CP) — The BBC today quoted Air Chief Marshal Sir Richard Pierse, commander-in-chief of the RAF in India, as saying that the campaign season "is just about to begin." The broadcast quoted him as telling RAF detachments: "Today we stand in battle array, not only ready to meet the enemy but waiting to go out and find him."

Yanks Top-Heavy Favorites

ST. LOUIS, Sept. 15—(AP)—Betting Commissioner James J. Carroll today made the New York Yankees top-heavy favorites in the 1943 World Series, quoting 13-20 odds on the American League club and 13-10 on the St. Louis Cardinals. He listed the same odds on the opening game.

146 Lose Lives

One Survivor

CANADIAN NAVY DESTROYER SUNK

VANCOUVER NEWS-HERALD

VOL. 11, NO. 135 | VANCOUVER, B.C., FRIDAY, OCTOBER 1, 1943 | PRICE 5c

Russian Guns Open Battle For Kiev

By JAMES M. LONG

LONDON, Oct. 1.—(AP)—Soviet troops fought to clean up the eastern bulge of White Russia Thursday in new advances that overwhelmed Krichev, 57 miles east of the Dnieper River crossing at Mogilev, while to the south a crescendo of guns and bombs announced the beginning of the battle for Kiev, Moscow said Thursday night.

The capture of Krichev was said to have given the Russians an "important strongpoint and railway junction." To take the town where railroads to Mogilev and Orsha cross, the Soviets forced the Sozh river.

But it was only one move in a widespread battle on a 50-mile front to clear the area between the Besyad and Sozh rivers. The Soviet midnight bulletin, broadcast from Moscow and recorded by the Soviet monitor, said Red Army mobile detachments were ferreting out the German emplacements, taking "a considerable number of prisoners."

Much war material was captured and 2,200 Germans were reported killed in this area alone.

SUBURBS HELD

At Kiev Soviet forces, installed in the cross-river eastern districts of the city, were less than 100 yards across a narrow part of the Dnieper from the cliffs of the ancient city. Here German guns answer the attack from emplacements in the ancient cells of monks.

While the fight for the greatest prize since Kharkov was shaping, the Soviet daily communique, recorded by the Soviet monitor told of the capture of Krichev and more than 170 other populated places in advances up to 12 miles while Soviet forces marched on toward Gomel and Vitebsk in the battle for White Russia.

The taking of Kiev would mean crossing the Dnieper at the heart of that vital German defence line.

Red Army guns shelled the Germans on the high cliffs from their newly won eastern emplacements. The Russians held both railway and highway bridges on the eastern side of the villages outside the city.

Await Report From Brewers

Vancouver citizens will receive the good news of an increased beer ration for October this morning, if brewers report a hoped-for surplus.

W. F. Kennedy of the Liquor Control Board told The News-Herald Thursday evening that breweries throughout the province were working all night in an endeavor to have figures ready in regard to beer surpluses.

"I hope to know by 10 a.m. Friday, so that I can phone the stores in town, if there is to be a change," said Mr. Kennedy.

Stores of beer are reckoned on a yearly basis, Mr. Kennedy explained, and figures are being tallied up as the end of the year draws closer. At the beginning of the year, he said, 160 per cent of stocks were being sold, whereas only 90 per cent was the allotment, and that difference has had to be made up in the past few months.

There is no hope of the hard liquor ration being upped, according to Mr. Kennedy, who said he had given up hoping. He held out very little hope for extra rations for the Christmas season, but said it all depended on the stores on hand.

"I haven't done my Christmas shopping yet," he remarked.

REPORT QUEEN HELD PRISONER

NEW YORK, Oct. 1.—(AP)—Queen Mother Ioanna of Bulgaria, widow of King Boris, "is reported to be held a prisoner in Sofia by the regency government," the BBC said Thursday

H.M.C.S. Hamilton, sister ship to the St. Croix is pictured above. These two ships, along with five others, were turned over to the Canadian Navy after the 50-destroyer exchange for naval bases between Britain and the U. S. In the U. S. navy, the St. Croix was called the McCook. Following transfer to Canada, she was renamed for a river and, to commemorate her origin after a river common to the United States and Canada. The other four-stackers were named, the Annapolis, Columbia, Niagara, St. Francis and St. Clair.

SERVICES' JOINT PLAN

OTTAWA, Oct. 1.—(CP) —A co-operative recruiting program for Canada's three armed services, placing top emphasis on air crew, was announced Thursday night in a joint statement by the defence ministers, Defence Minister Ralston for the Army, Air Minister Power and Navy Minister Macdonald.

Details of the navy's participation are still incomplete, but main points of the plan disclosed Thursday night are:

1. All men fit for aircrew will have an opportunity to enlist in that capacity.

2. Those fit for overseas army service but without specialist qualifications for aircrew will be enlisted in the army.

3. Men fit for army overseas service or possessing specialist qualifications for aircrew will not be allowed to enlist for air force ground crew.

4. An "equitable exchange" of men will be made between the army and air force at recruiting centres.

5. Men discharged from the army in the recently announced reorganization of home forces will be given opportunity to join the air force.

6. Transfers on a controlled and voluntary basis will be made between the army and air force overseas.

(Continued on Back Page)
See RECRUITING

'ALLIES DESERVE SHARE IN RED ARMY SUCCESSES'

LONDON, Oct. 1.—(CP)—Air Chief Marshal Sir Philip Joubert said Thursday night that only one-fourth of Germany's fighter planes, one-half of her bombers—including dive-bombers— and about two-thirds of her divisions are fighting the Russians.

Sir Philip declared in a broadcast that credit for the 1943 Soviet Army successes went first to Russia, but that the Allies deserve a share for their contributions of materials, weapons and food, and for diverting Nazi military power to other fronts.

Assure Equality Coal Deliveries

OTTAWA, Oct. 1.—(CP)—The Munitions Department announced Thursday night that to assure the most equitable distribution of available coal supplies dealers now must give to consumers who have less than one-quarter of their annual fuel requirements on hand priority on deliveries up to that one-quarter.

The new order, issued by Coal Controller E. J. Brunning, applies only to consumers who use less than 50 tons of coal a year. It provides that customers who agree to accept 25 per cent of their requirements in Class "B" fuel in order to obtain 75 per cent in Class "A" must take delivery of the former within 30 days of delivery of the Class "A" fuel.

Class "A" fuel includes all anthracite coal larger than buckwheat; low volatile bituminous coal, briquettes and coke. Class "B" refers to all other types of coal fuel.

NAZIS FLEE TO NORTH

ALLIED HEADQUARTERS, North Africa, Oct. 1. — (AP) — Beaten German forces streamed north out of burning Naples Thursday night toward their next defence line in the hills just short of Rome, 135 miles away, as Allied tanks clanked into the outskirts of the great port from the south after skirting Mt. Vesuvius.

(A Berlin dispatch to Stockholm said the Germans had evacuated Naples, and the Nazi-controlled Italian radio said a British fleet was shelling the ravaged city.)

At last report, Allied armored columns had fought their way past the ruins of ancient Pompeii to reach Torre Annunziati, arms and iron centre nine miles south of Naples and within clear view of their goal.

The frontal and flanking approaches to Naples were mined and demolished extensively. These familiar German retreat tactics were particularly annoying to the British and American troops of the army beating upon Naples along the narrow coastal bottleneck between Vesuvius and the sea. But already the army was well ensconced on the Naples plains and exerting ever-increasing pressure with strong armored forces—tanks, armored cars, mobile artillery and the like.

(Continued on Back Page)
See NAPLES

City and B.C. Men Missing

Following is the Royal Canadian Navy's official list of 15 B. C. men reported missing with official numbers and next-of-kin.

OFFICERS

DeFreitas, Percival Francis Mayow, Lt.-Cmdr., R.C.N.R., Mrs. Olive Isabel DeFreitas (wife) 2626 Windsor Rd., Oak Bay, Victoria.

Porter, Robert Noel Timothy, lieut., R.C.N., Noel E. Porter (father) 1255 Broughton St., Vancouver.

RATING

Armstrong, William Morrison, mechanician (2nd class) 21375, R.C.N., Mrs. Thelma Armstrong (wife) Box 163, Kamloops, B.C.

Barwis, William Donald, AB., V30612, R.C.N.V.R., C. W. A. Barwis (father) care of British Columbia Police, Nelson, B. C.

Brookman, Stanley Bertram, OS., W45202, R.C.N.V.R., Mrs. Louisa M. Brookman (mother) 3312 Rumble St., Burnaby, B.C.

Butterfield, Thomas William James, E.R.A. (4th class), V47,-041, R.C.N.V.R., Mrs. Pera I. Butterfield (wife) 515 Salsbury Drive, Vancouver.

Coates, Daryl Leslie, leading stoker, 21789, R.C.N., Mrs. Elizabeth Coates (mother), 1046 Sutlej St., Victoria.

Deeks, William Richard, OS., V47243, R.C.N.V.R., Mrs. Freda Deeks (mother), Box 517, Vernon, B.C.

Des Brisay, Gordon Montgomery, ordinary sigmn., V39948, R.C.N.R.V., Mrs. Naomi Des Brisay (mother) 4988 Granville St., Vancouver.

Hutton, Jack, leading sigmn., 2199, R.C.N., Mrs. Lily Isobel Hutton (wife), 1579 Second Ave. E., Vancouver.

Kidson, Weldon Alexander, leading stoker, A1797, R.C.N.R., Mrs. Phyllis F. Kidson (wife), 451 Davida St., Victoria.

Mitchell, William Wallace, AB., 3266, R.C.N., William J. Mitchell (father), 2524 Georgia St. E., Vancouver.

McNeney, James Robert, yeoman of signals, 3036, R.C.N., Mrs. Mary J. E. McNeney (mother), 184 Columbia St. E., New Westminster, B.C.

Pastorek, John, OS., V46082, R.C.N.V.R., Mrs. Violet Elaine Pastor (wife), Hammond, B.C.

Thicke, Charles Frederick, AB., 4386, R.C.N., Mrs. Elizabeth Thicke (mother), R.R. No. 1, Wellington, B.C.

15 B.C. Men Listed As Missing Aboard H.M.C.S. St. Croix

OTTAWA, Oct. 1.—(CP)—Loss of the Canadian destroyer St. Croix with 146 men was announced today by Navy Minister Macdonald —second proof in a week that German submarines are back in the North Atlantic preying on trans-ocean convoys.

The ship, one of seven United States destroyers turned over to the Canadian navy after the 50-destroyer exchange for naval bases between Britain and America in pre-Pearl Harbor days, was hit by torpedoes from a submarine and all but one of her complement of 147 are missing.

The sole survivor was Stoker W. A. Fisher, of Black Diamond, Alta.

The Navy gave no details of the engagement in which the St. Croix was lost, except to say the destroyer was "on convoy duty." But probably the action was the one that in which five R.C.A.F. long-range Liberator bombers engaged six submarines in two days recently. Probably, too, it was the one mentioned by Prime Minister Churchill in a recent speech to the British House of Commons and which formed the basis for a German claim that 12 destroyers and nine merchant vessels had been sunk from a west-bound convoy.

(There has been no confirmation of this German claim from Allied sources.)

As additional reports are received and security considerations permit it is probable the St. Croix loss will appear in its full setting as part of a major naval engagement marking the return of the U-boats to the seas, better equipped for fighting off destroyers, corvettes and aircraft assigned to their destruction.

The St. Croix is the 13th Canadian naval vessel lost in the Second Great War which has seen Canadian ships sailing and fighting in the Atlantic, the Pacific and the Mediterranean. She is the fourth destroyer lost, but first of the former U. S. "four-stackers" received by Canada to go down. Besides the destroyers the navy has lost five corvettes, two patrol vessels and a minesweeper, either by mishap at sea or enemy action.

The toll of life in the St. Croix sinking — 146 reported missing — is the navy's largest single loss in men, just topping the loss of 142 when the destroyer Margaree was sunk in the North Atlantic, cut in two by a large steamship while manoeuvring in defence of a convoy against a night submarine attack.

* * *

Lt.-Cmdr. Andrew H. Dobson, 42, of Halifax, was in command of St. Croix and is listed among the missing.

So is Lt.-Cmdr. D. F. M. DeFreitas of Victoria, recently cited for fine work in command of one of the Canadian ships which assisted the United States navy in operations against the Aleutians in the Pacific.

Among the missing also was Surgeon Lt. William Lyon Mackenzie King, nephew and namesake of the Prime Minister of Canada. Lieut. King was born in Ottawa. His mother now lives at Bedford, N.S.

Men from all provinces, many with long records at sea in the ceaseless struggle waged by the Canadian Navy against submarines, are missing. The casualty list shows 50 whose next-of-kin live in Ontario, 22 in Quebec, 15 in British Columbia, 14 in Nova Scotia, nine in Manitoba, eight in Saskatchewan, seven in Alberta, six in New Brunswick, and two in Prince Edward Island.

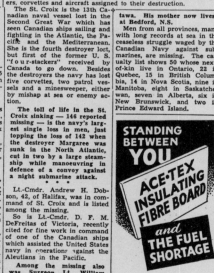

Yankees Win Series Four To One

VANCOUVER NEWS-HERALD

VOL 11, NO. 143 — VANCOUVER, B.C., TUESDAY, OCTOBER 12, 1943 — ★ — PRICE 5c

RUSSIAN FORCES IN SUBURB OF GOMEL

BILL DICKEY'S BIG WALLOP DEFEATS CARDS

SPORTSMAN'S PARK, St. Louis, Oct. 12.—(AP)—New York Yankees re-established their supremacy in baseball Monday by conquering the desperately struggling St. Louis Cardinals 2-0 before 33,872 fans for their fourth victory in five games of the 1943 World Series.

* * *

It was the 10th world championship for the Bombers from the Bronx and the clincher was delivered by two of the veterans who have shared in the spoils of many of those previous triumphs—Pitcher Spud Chandler and Catcher Bill Dickey.

* * *

The 36-year-old Dickey, one of the greatest backstops in the history of the game, decided the final skirmish in the sixth inning with a two-run homer that landed on the roof of the right field pavilion, 325 feet from the plate.

It was a mighty blow to climax the lustrous career of Dickey, who has been on nine Yankee squads in the World series, starting as a rookie in 1928, and it helped Chandler, 34-year-old dean of New York's mound staff, to his second success of the series.

* * *

Without this hefty run the last contest of the classic might easily have gone either way in spite of the shutout pitching of the Georgia right-hander, for Chandler was pelted for 10 hits and was kept in almost constant trouble by the Cardinals.

(Turn to Page Ten)

TWO AIRMEN KILLED IN PLANE CRASH

VICTORIA, Oct. 12.—(CP) — Two airmen were killed and two others are missing after their light bomber crashed into the sea near Sidney Island off Vancouver Island Saturday afternoon.

The bomber, an R.A.F. machine, was on a flight from a nearby base. Next-of-kin have been notified and names will be issued shortly.

Hundreds of passengers aboard the Princess Alice en route to Victoria from Vancouver saw the crash as the plane swept over the vessel and plunged into the water. Two of the airmen floated clear of the wreckage and were taken aboard the boat. One died later.

Using table serviettes to silence the blast of their explosives, yeggs wrecked the Cave Cabaret safe early Monday morning and escaped with $2,000 in cash. The door, blown completely off its hinges is inset in the picture of the wrecked safe above.

$2,644 Taken During Week-end

Yeggs Blow Cabaret Safe, Escape With Cash; Petty Thieves Active

Safe crackers, hold-up men, burglars and petty thieves, taking advantage of the long Thanksgiving weekend, staged a series of crimes from which they obtained booty consisting of $2644 in cash, a revolver, clothing, furs, jewellry, ration books, gas coupons, auto accessories, tools, meal tickets; bedding and linen, groceries, cigarettes, tobacco and a dinghy.

* * *

Most serious of the major crimes reported was the blowing of the safe at the Cave Cabaret, Hornby St., where the yeggs escaped with $2000 in cash.

James Masson, manager of the night club, told detectives that the safe had been locked at 2:30 a.m. Sunday morning. When he returned to the premises at 9:00 a.m. Monday he found the office door had been forced open and the safe blown.

The yeggs secured entrance to the cabaret by forcing a trap door on the roof and made their exit by way of the fire escape door.

The safe had been moved away from the wall prior to the blowing. The dial knocked off and several charges of explosives used to force the door.

Police found portions of two bars of soap at the scene believed to have been left behind by the cracksmen.

Inspector J. J. Morrison, and Detectives Rex Mackie, MacKay and Lamont are conducting the investigation.

* * *

Wong Bing Won, 1091 Davie St., was held up by armed bandits in the 500 block Carrall St., at 9:30 p.m. Sunday and robbed of $81 in cash besides personal papers. One man covered Wong with a small black revolver while the other searched his pockets. After taking his money they fled east across the Gyro playgrounds on the east side of Carrall St.

* * *

Two teen aged youths are in custody of police following their arrest in a stolen car late Sunday night. The two held have been charged with the theft of an auto. A third youth is being sought.

Police say the pair admitted stealing 10 cars during the past six weeks in the Kerrisdale district

REPORT GERMANS WILL EVACUATE BALTIC STATES

STOCKHOLM, Oct. 12.—AP) — Unconfirmed reports reaching Sweden Saturday night said the Germans intend to evacuate the Baltic States by Oct. 31 as the invasion-jittery Nazis acknowledged that British and American air armadas control the skies over much of Germany and Europe and that naval supremacy in the Mediterranean permits the Allies to strike anywhere in the Balkans.

German heavy guns and troops already are being withdrawn east of Leningrad, and some evacuation of troops from the Peterhof district began last week, Finnish infor-

NEW BRITISH MIDGET SUBS HIT TIRPITZ

Penetrate Nazi Hideout, Cripple Mighty Warship

LONDON, Oct. 12.—(CP)—British midget submarines, penetrating the heavily-guarded Norwegian hideout of the German fleet, have crippled the mighty battleship Tirpitz, and left her apparently immobilized.

Three of the small subs—a hitherto undisclosee British weapon—are missing. A group of the submersibles, 1,000 miles from home, threaded their way some 50 miles into narrow Alten Fjord, through mine fields and heavy patrols, to attack the Tirpitz, Sept. 22, an admiralty announcement disclosed Monday. They attacked the Tirpitz beneath her waterline.

The size of the raiding force was not disclosed but the announcement said three submarines had failed to return and there was a possibility some of their crews had been captured by the Germans.

The admiralty said it was impossible to assay the damage at the time of the attack, but reconnaissance photographs taken three weeks later showed the 35,000-ton pride of the Nazi fleet had not moved from her anchorage and oil spouting from her great tanks had spread for two miles.

Details on the size and complement of the little craft were not announced. Jane's authoritative "Fighting Ships" shows British Class "H" training submarines of 410 to 500 tons with a complement of 22, but presumably the midgets are much smaller.

RUMOR PORTUGAL WILL CEDE BASES

BERNE, Swtzerland, Oct. 12.—(AP)—Allied warships are policing the waters off the Azores, Portuguese Islands in the Atlantic, a reliable source said Monday night and there were unconfirmed rumors that Portugal would cede naval bases to the Allies.

A dispatch from Madrid, where interest has been manifest as to Portugal's recent strengthening of her military establishment, said the report of the ceding of bases was heard there, but was not verified.

RACING NEWS

ROCKINGHAM ENTRIES

FIRST RACE—Mile Sixteenth

Moja, 110	Snow Moon, 112
Frelan, 115	Free Trader, 113
Ack Ack, 115	Josies Pal, 107
Ladys Count, 115	Yannie Sid, 110
Good Conduct, 113	Keene Advice, 105
Michigan Sun, 110	Enoch Borland, 110
Molasses Bill, 118	

SECOND RACE—Mile Sixteenth

Border Battle, 112	One Dollar, 109
Still Pond, 110	Jopler, 109
Precious Years, 109	Calvert, 112
Cabanisi, 107	Five A.M., 109
Glory Land, 112	Omaha Mike, 107
Seaward Bound, 112	Spanish Sun, 109

THIRD RACE—Six Furlongs

Master Spirit, 111	Oaking, 112
Emerson, 111	Cab Sir, 115
Renraw, 111	Tufano, 117
Open Fire, 117	Gornil, 108

FOURTH RACE—Six Furlongs

Ladies First, 107	Top Transit, 115
Chance Sord, 107	La Reinette, 109
Roman Descent, 114	Kleig Light, 105
Gatineau, 110	Sun Ginger, 107
Terry May, 112	Guile, 112

FIFTH RACE—Six Furlongs

Morocco Sir, 112	Hillsun, 107
Collect Call, 110	Blue Steel, 111
Visiting Nurse, 109	War Result, 109
Easy Blend, 112	Airy Goer, 109
Polymelior, 107	Strolling Easy, 108
Buildinger, 111	Page 11, 112

SIXTH RACE—Mile Sixteenth

K. Dorko, 108	Skipper Z, 102
Arthur Murray, 108	White Hope, 116
Goober Lad, 111	Believe, 105
Wise Moss, 110	

SEVENTH RACE—Mile Sixteenth

Landslide, 109	Star Boarder, 118
Study Period, 104	Rest Awhile, 115
Alca Gal, 109	Just Tourist, 107
Fettacairn, 118	Squadron, 110
Valdina Joe, 112	Pollenator, 104
Dingmans, 115	

EIGHTH RACE—Mile Sixteenth

Mitza, 110	Manamaid, 110
Silver Beam, 113	Seafoam, 107
Sparrow Chirp, 108	Majorette, 108
Magic Lady, 107	Jelwell, 113
Infant Queen, 111	Mattie J, 102
Mary Mick, 108	Tangelo, 103
Tea Clipper, 100	Hattie Belle, 110
At Bat, 107	Pamphlet, 100

ROCKINGHAM RESULTS

FIRST RACE—Six Furlongs
Puro Oro (Williams) $6.40, $3.60, $2.60.
Centuple (Gross) $6.60, $3.40.
Flaming High (Trent) $4.20.
Scratched: Dark Mischief, Cruiser, Alsbyrd, Rough Command.

SECOND RACE—Six Furlongs
Ho Hum (Hettinger) $63, $20.20, $8.40.
Ned's Queen (Seabo) $6, $4.
Gorse Hill (Leblanc) $3.80.
Scratched: Pariferda, Ilefetchit, War Gleam.

THIRD RACE—Six Furlongs
Pipeliner (Koyk) $13.80, $6.60, $4.60.
Ellen Mist (Seabo) $4.80, $3.80.
Record March (Martin) $6.40.

FOURTH RACE—Mile Sixteenth
Mine Cap (Balzoreti)) $9.60, $6.20, $4.40
Plane Spotter (Hettinger) $33.60, $13.20.
In Balance (Stevenson) $4.80.

FIFTH RACE—Mile Sixteenth
Boot and Spur (Turnbull) $6.60, $3, $2.60.
Star Whiz (Lynch) $3, $2.60.
Bonheur (Gross) $3.60.

SIXTH RACE—Mile Sixteenth
Gallant Dick (Trent) $15, $5.20, $2.80.
Cairngorm (Turnbull) $3.20, $2.40.
Blockader (Williams) $2.60.

SEVENTH RACE—Mile Eighth
Boris N (Stevenson) $8.80, $4, $3.40.
Fly Whisk (Durando) $4.60, $4.20.
Consomme (Daniels) $5.20.
Scratched: Tony Porter.

EIGHTH RACE—Mile Sixteenth
Grand Day (Datillo) $7, $4.40, $4.20.
Davitt (Williams) $17.20, $10.80.
New Life (Scawthorn) $28.20.
Scratched: Enoch Borland, White Hot, Batik, Wanna Hygro.

WALLACE KELK'S SELECTIONS

1—Ack Ack, Frelan, Ladys Count.
2—Precious Years, Border Battle, Seaward Bound.
3—Open Fire, Cab Sir, Tufano.
4—Ladies First, Top Transit, Kleig Light.
5—Visiting Nurse, Morocco Sir, War Result.
6—Arthur Murray, D. Dorko, White Hope.
7—Fettacairn, Alca Girl, Pollenator.
8—Infant Queen, Sea Foam, Tea Clipper
BEST—Infant Queen.

ALLIED DRIVE MENACES NAZI DEFENCE LINE

British-Canadians Fight Way Forward; Opposition Stiffens

ALLIED HEADQUARTERS, ALGIERS, Oct. 12.—(AP)—Fighting their way northwestward from Benevento through sticky Italian mud, Lt.-Gen. Mark W. Clark's American and British forces have captured Pontelandolfo and thrown into jeopardy the entire Nazi defence position along the flood-swept Volturno River north of Naples.

Seizure of Pontelandolfo, 12 miles beyond Benevento, placed the Allies astride a main highway which winds westward to the Mediterranean coast north of the Volturno. The Nazis either must meet this new threat successfully or soon resume their full-scale withdrawal toward Rome.

Pontelandolfo, on the eastern flank of the Volturno where it turns northward, is in the mountainous country between that stream and the Tammaro River and about six miles north of one bend of the Calore River.

CANADIANS LEAD

On the Adriatic end of the Italian fighting line Gen. Sir Bernard Montgomery's British and Canadians of the 8th Army were reported slugging their way slowly forward against intense opposition, averaging gains Sunday of between two and three miles along the Biferno River.

William Stewart, Canadian Press war correspondent, in a despatch datelined with the 8th Army in Italy, reported that Canadian troops pushed across a valley west of a town while there were signs of a German withdrawal to a new line. He said French-Canadian troops formed the vanguard of the drive.

Troops from a Western Canadian formation gained an important cross road objective without encountering opposition. This was in contrast to an earlier action for a crossroads drive in which western Canadian troops had a sharp battle before driving the enemy back from well-defended points.

Push Threatens Hun Flank On 200-Mile White Russia Front

By JUDSON O'QUINN

LONDON, Oct. 12.—(AP)—The Red Army crashed into the vital rail suburbs of Gomel Monday, threatening to flank the entire 200-mile German line in White Russia and snap its link with the Middle Dnieper River, where Soviet forces spilled on westward through three widening holes established on the west bank, Moscow announced Monday night.

(Russian troops "already have penetrated the outer defence of Kiev," Ukraine capital on the Dnieper, the BBC said in a broadcast recorded in New York by CBS. It also quoted Berlin as reporting heavy Russian attacks in the Nogaisk steppes, on the northern approaches to the Crimea.)

A communique broadcast by the Moscow radio announced the Red Army's seizure of Novo-Belitsa, a rail junction suburb of Gomel on the east bank of the Sozh River just across from the main prize, whose railways radiate to Warsaw, Minsk and Mogilev.

Other localities were seized in the Gomel sector as the Russians steadily hurled back the Germans on the northern edge of the Pripet Marshes.

Two-hundred miles to the north other Soviet troops converging on Vitebsk, the upper anchor of the Axis White Russian defence line, raced through 40 more villages.

Dispatches reaching here said there was a possibility the Germans already we pulling out of Kiev as successful Russian crossings north and south of the Ukrainian capital imperilled the city, which already is under fire from Soviet big guns mounted on the eastern bank just across the Dnieper.

"Our divisions have penetrated far beyond the river," said a front correspondent of Moscow's Pravda, "and have captured the defence zone of the Germans along the river and dozens of settlements on the western bank."

The smash into Novo-Belitsa made Gomel's fall an imminent possibility. Such a development would dissolve Germany's southern defence anchor in White Russia and open the way for a drive on the capital at Minsk.

It also would leave the Germans only a circuitous route across the Pripet Marshes connecting their sagging northern and southern fronts. That route is the Zhlobin-Mozyr-Korosten railway 45 miles west of Gomel, the last lateral Axis-held line short of the Olish border.

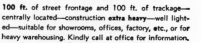

REDS TAKE KIEV

The Vancouver Sun
The Vancouver Evening Newspaper Owned and Operated by Vancouver People

FOUNDED 1886   VANCOUVER, B.C., SATURDAY, NOVEMBER 6, 1943   PRICE 10 CENTS
VOL. LVIII—No. 31

Fall of Third City Opens Way to Poland

Ukraine Capital Taken in 48 Hours After Sudden New Soviet Assault; Stalin Announces Triumph

By Associated Press

LONDON, Nov. 6.—Kiev has fallen to the victorious Russian Army, Premier Joseph Stalin announced today in a special order of the day.

The recapture of Russia's third city—largest ever taken by the Germans—came on the 26th anniversary of the Red revolution. Its fall now opens the way for a Russian drive to the old Polish frontier, 120 miles distant.

The key Dnieper river bastion and ancient capital of the Russians fell to Soviet columns which had been poised above and below the city for weeks after the Soviet offensive carried to the river barrier.

Suddenly the Russian columns swung into action two days ago, blasting holes through the Nazi positions and closing in on the city.

The German high command had announced a few hours previously that the great fortress had been evacuated, with German troops pulling out under the threat of encirclement.

The German announcement, broadcast from Berlin, said also that other Soviet columns had renewed their attacks on both sides of the Kerch Straits in the eastern Crimea and against the Perkop Isthmus, the northern entry to that peninsula.

Stalin's announcement termed the assault which drove the Nazis from the ancient fortress "a gallant outflanking manouvre" which at daybreak "captured by storm the capital of the Soviet Ukraine, the town of Kiev, vital industrial centre and most important strategic centre of German resistance on the right flank of the Dnieper."

324-GUN SALUTE

It also termed the capture of the "greatest importance in driving the Germans from the western Ukraine."

Indicating the significance Stalin attached to the Kiev victory, he ordered 324 cannon to boom out 24 salvoes in Moscow this evening in the greatest victory salute of the Russian offensive.

Stalin also gave some indication of the great weight of men and material thrown into the push to take Kiev when he singled out 11 infantry divisions, nine air divisions, four mortar and artillery divisions, an anti-aircraft division, three tank corps and numerous battalions and brigades for special honors in reward for their part in the battle.

The 1st independent Czechoslovak brigade also was singled out by the premier-marshal to be rewarded for its part in the fight.

German withdrawal from the great cathedral city came barely 48 hours after the Russians launched a surprise attack against the northern and western suburbs from their bridgehead base on the west bank of the Dnieper River, 16 miles to the north.

Breaching two German defense lines guarding the city, the Russians outflanked the enemy's positions on the west and north, leaving only a single escape route to the southwest open.

It was this route which the Germans evidently used to complete the evacuation of the city.

WAY OPEN TO POLAND

Announcement of the capture of this third largest city of the Soviet Union and capital of the Ukraine, which was captured by the Germans exactly three months after the Nazi armies crossed the Russian borders, came on the eve of the twenty-sixth anniversary of the Soviet Revolution and climaxed the victorious Red Army's gigantic autumn onslaught.

Moscow dispatches said it was believed there were 14 German divisions in and around the city when the final assault was launched Thursday.

The Germans now have no important natural defense line between Kiev and the former Polish frontier, just 120 miles to the west.

The fall of Kiev vastly enhances the possibility that the Red Army will be able to cut in two the remnants of the German armies still in southern Russia.

Kiev, with four main railway lines converging on it, was the transportation centre for the entire Crimea.

Big Sea-Air Fight Rages In Pacific

Japs Claim Two U.S. Air Carriers Sunk by Torpedo Planes; Battle May Surpass Midway Clash

By SANDOR KLEIN
Special to The Vancouver Sun
Copyright, 1943, by British United Press

WASHINGTON, Nov. 6.—An air-sea battle which may be the biggest since Midway was believed in progress today between American and Japanese forces in the southwest Pacific.

Military and naval experts, who believe that the opposing forces already have joined battle, said there appeared no doubt that the Japanese were making an all-out effort to halt the Allied drive aimed at Rabaul, key enemy stronghold on New Britain Island.

JAP CLAIMS

They said it was possible that the various Japanese naval elements spotted en route from the enemy naval base at Truk may be the forward or screening forces for a bigger battle force.

Meanwhile, there was no comment in the navy department on Japanese claims that two American torpedo planes sank two American carriers and four other warships Friday night in the vicinity of Bougainville Island in the northwestern Solomons. The Japanese frequently put out such reports in order to "fish" for information.

Both sides have land bases from which aircraft can be operated, although the enemy's bases are closer to the scene of action.

The reported presence of a whaling ship in one of the Japanese forces moving toward Rabaul aroused the curiosity of naval experts. One suggestion was that it was being used to transport midget submarines to aid in the defense of Rabaul.

VITAL BASES

That the Japanese would make a determined effort to hold Rabaul has been expected, because it is the mainstay of the enemy's south-west Pacific defense line. If they lost Rabaul the Japanese would be forced to pull completely out of New Guinea, New Britain, New Ireland and other islands in the vicinity, and expose one of the flanks of the naval base at Truk.

RAF Mosquitos Swarm Over Germany Again

By COLLIE SMALL
Special to The Vancouver Sun
Copyright, 1943, by British United Press

LONDON, Nov. 6.—Swarms of British Mosquito bombers pounded western Germany last night to add to the devastation wrought by 3500 to 4000 Anglo-American planes across Axis Europe with 6000 tons of explosives during the previous 60 hours in the heaviest air assault in history.

Specific targets were not announced. The twin-engined Mosquitos returned to their bases without the loss of a single plane, but a coastal command Beaufighter was lost during a night patrol over the North Sea.

The night raids followed the heaviest American daylight assault of the war on inland Germany. More than 400 flying fortresses and Liberators, with an escort of perhaps 600 Thunderbolt and Lightning fighters, hit synthetic oil plants at Gelsenkirchen and railway yards at Munster yesterday.

Only 24 hours earlier, other formations of American heavy bombers and fighters — also 1000 strong — had smashed at the big naval base at Wilhelmshaven in northwest Germany. British four-engined bombers followed through Wednesday night with a 2000-ton raid on Dusseldorf and a diversionary attack on Cologne.

Other British and American planes by day and night scattered fire and demolition bombs over a wide area of western Germany, France, Holland and Belgium.

Thousands of Jews Coming to Canada

Special to The Vancouver Sun

OTTAWA, Nov. 6.—As an indication of the government's hostility to any race prejudice, it has been revealed here that some thousands of Jewish refugees from Europe are to be admitted immediately to Canada, despite a good deal of anti-Semitism in the large cities of the East.

Women Injured In Traffic Mishaps

Mrs. Williamina Syme, R.R.1, Pitt River Road, suffered an ankle injury Friday when the auto in which she was a passenger, crashed into the rear of a parked auto in the 3100 block Turner.

Mrs. S. C. Irvine, 1376 West Fifth, suffered a head laceration when she was struck by a street car in the 1900 block West Fourth.

REPORTS SUCCESS

GRAHAM F. TOWERS

As chairman of the National War Finance Committee, Graham F. Towers, governor of the 4 Bank of Canada, was able Friday night to announce the complete success of Canada's Fifth Victory Loan with the objective of $1,200,000,000 already exceeded by nine million. The B.C.-Yukon area contributed to this success, going well past quota of $120 million early Friday.

Canada Goes Over Top in Victory Loan

By Canadian Press

OTTAWA, Nov. 6.—Canada's $1,200,000,000 Fifth Victory Loan passed its objective at close of business Friday night with sales at that time totalling $1,08,708,200, national loan headquarters announced today.

The official statement said that today—last day of the three-week drive—loan salesmen are out for a "rousing over-subscription," because "all we can get" is their real goal.

Late returns boosted last spring's $1,100,000,000 Fourth Victory Loan to $1,309,317,300 when the books finally were closed some time after the actual campaign ended. It seemed likely the present loan will exceed that figure ultimately and thus become the greatest borrowing drive in Canadian history.

The $1,200,000,000 minimum objective calls for subscriptions averaging about $100 for every man, woman and child in the Dominion.

The grand total of subscribers in the Fifth Victory Loan up to Friday night was 2,127,113, compared with 1,825,496 for the same period of the last loan.

City Flier Dies In Nazi Prison

WO 1 Keith Oliver Perry, son of Mr. and Mrs. R. A. Perry, 1343 William, is reported to have died while a prisoner of war. It was announced from air force headquarters at Ottawa today.

According to information received by his parents from the International Red Cross at Geneva, he died August 23, and was buried in East Prussia.

WO Perry attended Britannia High School and enlisted in the RCAF while in his second year at the University of B.C., in January, 1941. He went overseas a year later.

A Tokyo broadcast today claimed that torpedo planes sank "one large aircraft carrier, one medium aircraft carrier and two heavy cruisers."

Two other Allied ships, identified as either cruisers or heavy destroyers, were also destroyed. Three torpedo planes were admitted lost in the attack of Bougainville last night.

German Night Losses Exceed British

RAF's Power Increased 12-Fold

LONDON, Nov. 6—(CP)—Britons learned last night from Sir Archibald Sinclair, secretary of state for air, that there had been a twelve-fold increase in the RAF Bomber Command's striking power to "open the road to Berlin."

Sir Archibald told an audience at Cheltenham that there was, at the start of the war the RAF home force was about one-fourth as strong as the German air force, the strength of the Metropolitan air force, including bomber, reconnaissance and coastal commands, now is about four times what it was in the critical summer of 1940.

He gave the first official description of the new "secret weapon" plane which the Germans have used in recent night stabs at London.

Sir Archibald said the Messerschmitt-410 was a twin-engined fighter-bomber, developed from the ME-210, which has been rocket-shelling heavy bombers in daylight. He described the new Nazi plane as "something comparable" to his Mosquito bomber in performance.

Since October 6 per cent of the German night aircraft operating against Britain have been shot down, and Sir Archibald said this rate was substantially more than the losses of British heavy bombers making the devastating attacks against Germany.

German Defenses Smashed

Vasto, Venafro Fall To Allies in Italy

By EDWARD KENNEDY
Associated Press War Correspondent

ALGIERS, Nov. 6.—Allied forces in Italy smashed away the last remnants of the German's powerful Massico Ridge-Trigno line in taking the key points of Vasto on the Adriatic and Venafro in the upper Volturno Valley, Allied headquarters announced today.

Forging ahead in the western sector, British patrols of the 5th Army crossed the Garigliano River to probe the new line which the enemy has formed north of these.

FRESH TROOPS

Americans of the 5th Army right wing drove ahead into the mountains after occupying Venafro in a fierce fight in the upper reaches of the Volturno.

The Germans attached such importance to this mountain fastness that they threw a new division—the 305th Infantry—into the fight in a last minute effort to save it, but even these fresh Nazi fighters from the north were routed.

In the air war, medium bombers knocked out a large portion of the German air forces operating from Albania with a raid yesterday on Berat Kucov airfield in the centre of the country. The field was one of the bases from which the Germans were operating against patriot forces in the Balkans.

There now are five German divisions in battle on the 5th Army front, it was disclosed, and three opposing the 8th Army.

PUSH TO NEW LINES

In addition to a five-mile surge up the Adriatic coast to take Vasto, 8th Army troops also made gains of more than one and one-half miles in the region some 25 miles inland, capturing Pietracupa, Sessano and Duronia. These towns were taken by the left, Canadian, wing of the 8th Army pushing north ward fro mthe captured Isernia-Carpinone region.

In striking to Vasto, British troops of the 8th Army swept through San Salvo where the Germans had held out more than a week, and on the basis of reports from the front today British troops are within 15 miles of the Sangro River, where the Germans undoubtedly will attempt another stand.

The Nazis still are resisting at some places along the north bank of the Trigno River, but their forces are threatened on both sides by Gen. Sir Bernard Montgomery's troops and they are not likely to stay much longer.

The crossing of the Garigliano by British patrols was made near the Tyrrhenian coast where the enemy flooded fields near the river.

The area north of Venafro, into which the Americans now are pushing, is rough terrain. The U.S. troops have as their probable objective the highway town of Cassino, on a main highway to Rome.

Heavy bombers hit the railway bridge at Falconara-Marittima just north of Ancona on the east coast line in Italy, impeding movement of German reinforcements of troops and supplies.

One plane was lost in all operations.

Frost Forecast for Washington Tonight

SEATTLE, Nov. 6—(BUP)—Frost was forecast for Washington tonight in the U.S. Weather Bureau forecast for the 36 hours ending at 10 a.m. Sunday. The forecast for Washington says: "Fair today and tonight, but locally heavy frosts in exposed places and valleys west of Cascades tonight. Increasing cloudiness Sunday, with rain probable along coast by Sunday night."

MOSCOW, Nov. 6.—This is the Russian front as defined today in an official war map published by Moscow newspapers. Shaded area is German-held. Right-hand border of shaded area is battlefront, as it appeared on Russian map.

Coal Strike Settlement Now Rests With Cabinet

By Canadian Press

OTTAWA, Nov. 6.—Approval of a proposal which may end the strike of 8500 western coal miners, now in its sixth day, rested today with the cabinet.

A special meeting was set for this morning, with Labor Minister Hon. Humphrey Mitchell scheduled to meet a delegation representing District 18, United Mine Workers of America, following the Cabinet session.

A meeting of the Minister and miners had been planned for last night but was postponed when Mr. Mitchell reported the Cabinet had not completed its discussion of the coast strike, in which Alberta and British Columbia miners seek an increase of $2 a day, time and one-half for overtime and two weeks' vacation with pay.

Robert Livett, district 1 president, had said earlier that he expected to be able to make "an important statement" after the meeting with the Minister—the fourth since the delegation arrived in Otawa Tuesday.

REVERTED TO RANKS

The alternative was to resign their commissions in Canada. In almost every case the officers agreed to go overseas under these conditions rather than run the stigma of resigning altogether and leaving the impression they would not fight except as officers.

On arrival in England they were given tests and the best selected to retain their commissions, the others reverting to the rank of sergeant or corporal. Many of those who reverted later won their commissions in the field.

The situation in the present war is complicated by the fact that the surplus is in officers on duty in Canada. Regional survey boards are now combing through the roster of officers and National Defense Headquarters are studying the situation to decide what is to be done with the surplus.

PUT ON SPOT

The officers themselves are on the spot, for many of the veterans of 1914-18 took on another war job because an officer's pay and allowance permitted them to do so without undue reduction in the family standard of living.

They may now be faced with the prospect of reverting to the ranks or dropping out of the Army, the latter being a humiliation for them.

Defense headquarters are very reticent to discuss the matter.

Army Stumped, Has Surplus Of Officers

Special to The Vancouver Sun

OTTAWA, Nov. 6.—The disbandment and rearrangement of army forces in Canada is bringing to the surface a plethora of officers and National Defense hardly knows what to do with them.

In the Great War more than enough officers had been trained in Canada by 1917 than the army overseas required and as reinforcement drafts went overseas the officers were warned that they might have to revert to junior ranks or to the rank and file.

Shipyard Report Not Yet at Ottawa

OTTAWA, Nov. 6—(CP)—Labor department officials said late Friday they have not yet received the report of a conciliation board investigating the request of eight unions in West Coast shipyards and Hamilton Bridge (Western) Ltd., for a closed shop.

Reports from Vancouver said a majority report of the commission had turned down the request. A departmental spokesman said it was understood that the report had been mailed but it had not yet reached Ottawa.

'Bombsight Bertha' Dead

LONDON, Nov. 6 — (CP) — "Bombsight Bertha," 23, English girl expert on RAF bomb sights, was killed recently on a test flight. Her real name was Dorothy Robson.

Guerrilla General

MADRID, Nov. 6—(AP)—One of the most powerful guerrilla forces operating in France is led by Maj.-Gen. De Lattre de Tassigny, who attempted a military revolt when the Allies invaded North Africa, a Paris dispatch said.

Fall Kills Chinese

Jung Suey Wing, 68, was killed on Friday when he fell 16 feet down a flight of stairs at 3½ Canton Alley. He died before reaching the General Hospital.

Incendiary Army Camp Fire Costs 'Millions'

CAMP BORDEN, Nov. 6—(CP)—Damage "in the millions" was caused in the three-hour early-morning fire today which destroyed two Royal Canadian Ordnance Corps' workshops as well as a number of tanks, military vehicles and other ordnance equipment at Camp Borden, the Canadian Army's largest training centre.

Col. J. D. Conover, acting adjutant quartermaster general in the camp issued a statement saying the fact the fire started in both wings of the ordnance workshop "was a clear indication that the blaze was of incendiary origin."

A court of inquiry will investigate.

The blaze, which raged uncontrolled for two hours and burned for another hour before being extinguished, was held to be a small section near the northern entrance of the 29-square-mile camp.

The barracks were not threatened and no person was injured.

There was no official estimate of the amount of the damage although it was believed to be large.

Col. Conover's statement said that due to prompt action of the Camp Borden fire department the boiler room and all adjoining buildings were saved although some tanks and trucks were destroyed.

The fire is believed to have broken out "simultaneously in both wings of the workshop" and a court of inquiry will be held, Defense Headquarters announced.

There was no elaboration of the reference to the outbreak at one time in two places.

Nazi Radio Charges Allies Bomb Vatican

LONDON, Nov. 6—(CP)—The German-controlled Rome radio, in a special broadcast early today, claimed Vatican City was bombed Friday night, and that "considerable damage" was caused by four bombs which well among the historic buildings.

There was no confirmation of this report from Allied sources.

The Allies warned last July of the possibility of bombs being dropped on Vatican City in the event of bombing of Rome by the Axis powers who likely would claim Allied aircraft made the attack.

As far back as April, 1941, an official statement from 10 Downing Street announced it had come to the knowledge of the government that an Axis squadron was being held ready in Rome to drop captured British bombs if the Vatican should a British raid be made on Rome.

Invasion Expected

LONDON, Nov. 6—(CP)—The zero hour for the Allied invasion of France may strike at any moment, Jean Paquis, Paris radio military commentator, said tonight.

CABINET NOT AGREED

Postponement of last night's meeting, however, was regarded as evidence that the Cabinet is less ready to give its final approval to a proposal which apparently offers concessions to the miners.

There were two schools of thought on the nature of the government's strike settlement plan —one that it was a straight wage increase made effective by order-in-council; the other that means would be provided for an application for wage increases to be made without reference to the National War Labor Board, possibly by extending the powers of a Royal Commission already established to investigate wage rates in western coal mines.

comments available from official sources.

No details of any British or American air activity over Italy Friday night were available in London early today nor were any

OFFICIAL REPORT ON HISTORIC ALLIED PARLEY IN EGYPT

WAR EXTRA

BIG THREE PLEDGES

WAR EXTRA

STRIP JAPANESE OF ALL CONQUESTS

The Vancouver Sun

The Vancouver Evening Newspaper Owned and Operated by Vancouver People

FOUNDED 1886 VOL. LVIII—No. 51 VANCOUVER, B.C., DECEMBER 1, 1943 PRICE 5c

Tojo's Empire to Be Reduced to Home Islands

Reds Threaten German Gomel 'Escape Line'

LONDON, Dec. 1 — (CP) — Red Army troops captured Narovi, on the west bank of the Pripet River, 14 miles east of Yelsk, and overcame counter-attacks to continue their drive today northwest of Gomel, where they already have come within artillery range of Zhlobin, the German-held stronghold guarding the 17-mile-wide Gomel escape gap, Moscow announced tonight.

By HENRY SHAPIRO
Special to The Vancouver Sun
Copyright, 1943, by British United Press

MOSCOW, Dec. 1. — Soviet front reports said today that "dozens" of German infantry and armored divisions were attacking ceaselessly in the Korosten sector of the northwest Ukraine in an all-out attempt to break through the rim of the Kiev bulge.

After evacuating Korosten the Russians fell back eastward beyond the Korosten-Zhitomir highway a short distance beyond the town military dispatches reported.

(Berlin radio reported tonight that the Russians had attacked in force in both sides of the Smolensk-Orsha road and forced wedges into the German lines at two places. Pressure on the Gomel front forced the Germans to withdraw to shortened lines, the broadcast said.)

LINES INTACT

The dispatch contained no numerical estimate of the German attacking strength but the use of the term "dozens" suggested it would run into some hundreds of thousand men.

The Red Army was reported rushing reinforcements into the Korosten front in an effort to stop the Germans.

How Will We Regain Jap Loot?

What have the Japanese stolen—and how are the Allies going to get it back? A comprehensive map and story on Page 14 list the loot of the Nippon warlords while another story on the same page tells of all five routes to Tokyo the Allies may take to conquer Japan and regain the territories she has stolen.

Japs Shipped City Prisoner On Horse Boat

JERSEY CITY, N.J., Dec. 1—(AP)—Cecil Copley of Vancouver, a repatriate aboard the Gripsholm from the Far East, spent many months as a Japanese prisoner in two widely separated camps—Manila and Shanghai. He was first interned in Santo Tomas camp, Manila, to which city he had moved the Rockefeller Foundation Far East office in 1940. He was the office manager.

In September, 1942, Copley and many other Santo Tomas internees accepted a Japanese offer to go to Shanghai. They made the trip in 10 days aboard a horse boat. They slept between decks immediately above the horses. They were served Japanese food, mainly rice and seaweed. The boat made one stop, at a port in Formosa.

Glass Boring Thief Gets $437 Jewelry

An ingenious thief who cut or punched a hole in the show window of the Pagoda Shop, 558 Granville, Tuesday night, just large enough to admit his arm, stole jade jewelry valued at $437.

Leg Fractured

Boy Chin, 65, of 332 Keefer, suffered a fractured leg on Tuesday when he was struck by an auto at Main and Hastings. He was taken to the Vancouver General Hospital.

Two Skaters Drowned

EDMONTON, Dec. 1—(CP)—RCMP headquarters here said the bodies of Harvey Larsen, 19, and Ralph Melin, 15, of the Calmar district, drowned while skating on Conjuring Lakes Sunday afternoon, have been recovered.

Flier Safe

SAINT JOHN, N.B., Dec. 1—(CP)—The wife of Sqdn. Ldr. Albert Lambert, DFC, missing since his plane was shot down July 15, received official word yesterday of his arrival at a British port.

Late News Bulletins

'QUAKES HIT CHILE

PASEDENA, Calif., Dec. 1 — (AP) — Strong earthquakes in Chile and New Guinea were recorded at the California Institute of Technology, seismologists announced today.

HIT HUN CONVOY

LONDON, Dec. 1—(CP Cable)—Beaufighters of the RCAF squadron of coastal command scored hits on two merchant vessels in attacking an enemy convoy off the Norwegian coast yesterday, the Air Ministry announced today. In the attack was WO. L. F. Page of Nanaimo.

EXTEND SUBSIDIES

OTTAWA, Dec. 1—(CP)—Extension of the termination date of the subsidy on commercial wood fuel was announced today in an order-in-council published in Canadian war orders and regulations. The time within which wood may be contracted for, cut, delivered or held to a dealer's account now is extended to March 31, 1944.

DENIES CCF CHARGE

TORONTO, Dec. 1—(CP)—Gladstone Murray of Toronto, public relations counsel, today denied the statement made by E. B. Jolliffe, Ontario CCF leader, in a speech at Hamilton last night, that Maj. Murray has been hired by the Progressive Conservative party as an adviser on the "mind of the masses and how to frighten them against the CCF."

U.S. Won't Observe 'Pearl Harbor Day'

WASHINGTON, Dec. 1—(BUP)—The White House announced today that President Roosevelt has vetoed a joint resolution setting aside December 7, 1943, as Armed Services Honor Day, on the grounds that commemoration of the "day of infamy" on which the Japanese attacked Pearl Harbor is "singularly inappropriate."

Britain Raps Spain

LONDON, Dec. 1—(CP)—The British government has demanded an official apology from Spain on a charge that uniformed Falangists in November forced their way into the British Vice-Consulate at Saragossa and insulted the vice-consul and members of his family.

The Foreign Office, it was learned, has taken a serious view of the incident and is demanding an assurance from Spain that the guilty persons will be punished.

The Foreign Office issued an official statement on the incident which said:

"Parties of Spanish Falangists in uniform November 19 and 20 forced their way into the British vice-consulate at Saragossa and made insulting remarks to the Vice-Consul and members of his family.

"A serious vie wis taken of this occurrence and the Spanish government is being asked by the British government for an official apology and for an assurance that the guilty persons will be properly punished."

Marshall's Attendance Hints Early Naming As Allied Chief

By LEWIS HAWKINS
Associated Press Staff Writer

LONDON, Dec. 1.—The Cairo conference declaration of determination to smash Japan was seen in London as a heartening sign of Allied solidarity, but the first reaction was that the war in Europe retains top priority and that still bigger news in that sphere may be expected soon.

The presence of President Chiang Kai-Shek at the conference table with Prime Minister Churchill and President Roosevelt for the first time was welcomed as reassurance to those fearful that Britain might slacken her efforts after Hitler is eliminated. This unique meeting also raised hopes that Joseph Stalin might soon join in conference with British and American leaders.

The presence of Gen. George C. Marshall, who is widely expected to become commander-in-chief of an invasion of western Europe, is particularly interesting to this island, which is gaining strength daily as a base for such a climactic blow against Hitler.

There was speculation that the American's appointment to that post might be announced perhaps as a climax to any meeting of Mr. Churchill, Mr. Roosevelt and Mr. Stalin.

Stilwell at Talks

Admiral Lord Louis Mountbatten, Southeast Asia commander, and Lt.-Gen. Joseph Stilwell, chief of staff of Allied forces in China, attended the conference.

This might indicate that operations against Japan still are at diplomatic and strategic levels not requiring the presence of men directing the field forces.

The communique issued after the five-day meeting naturally left much unanswered, including some questions of great interest to Britain. The announcement said all territories obtained by Japan in a half-century of expansion would be taken from her, but it was not specific about what would be done with them.

COUNCIL FOR ASIA, TOO

The implication seemed to be that they would be returned to the previous owners, but it was recalled that Germany owned the Pacific islands which were mandated to Japan as a result of the First Great War.

The implication seemed clearer that the Indies would be restored to the Netherlands, British territory to Britain, and the Philippines and other American island to the United States, with any subsequent granting of independence—as in the case of Korea—to be worked out later.

All such questions might be considered in the scope of some international organization for Asia along the lines of the European Advisory Commission created at the recent Moscow conference of foreign secretaries.

Race Results on Page 12

GEN. GEORGE C. MARSHALL

50 Men Search for Lost Island Hunter

VICTORIA, Dec. 1 — (CP) — More than 50 determined searchers, including some of the most experienced bushmen of Vancouver Island, at dawn today made their way into the thickly-wooded area between Shawnigan Lake and the Koksilah Ridge, to comb the 44 square miles for Kenneth Duncan, 21-year-old Victoria hunter, missing since Saturday.

A group of soldiers stationed at Duncan also took part in the search.

Four Leaders Are Reported in Teheran

LONDON, Dec. 1.—Dispatches received in Lisbon from the Middle East today said Prime Minister Churchill, President Roosevelt and Premier Joseph Stalin have opened a momentous conference in Teheran, Iran, and that Generalissimo and Mme. Chiang Kai-Shek also were in the Iranian capital.

The Lisbon Daily Oseculo published a dispatch quoting the inter-information agency of Ankara that the "big three" leaders were meeting in Teheran where they had been joined by Laurence Steinhardt, U.S. ambassador to Turkey.

It gave no indication as to whether Chiang would participate. American and other Allied short-wave radio transmitters in broadcasts to the world said the Chinese leader had conferred with Roosevelt and Churchill in Cairo recently and suggested that he also would meet Stalin.

Axis broadcasts and copies of German and neutral European newspapers reaching Lisbon indicated that reports of the meeting had created a sensation throughout the Nazi-occupied continent.

Both Axis and neutral accounts agreed on the importance of the reported conference, particularly in that Stalin was said to be participating.

They indicated that Berlin had been taken by surprise. German propaganda for months has hammered at the idea that Stalin could not be brought into agreement with his allies.

Radio Tokyo followed the line that Chiang had been included to "appease" the Chinese for their non-participation in the recent Moscow conference of foreign ministers.

U.S. Allows More Meat in December

WASHINGTON, Dec. 1 — (BUP)—The office of price administration today announced reductions in meat point values to give consumers approximately 30 percent more in December than they had in November, but left the ration point value of butter unchanged and increased the value of cheese and most canned fish.

Nazis Round Up Italian Jews

BERNE, Dec. 1—(BUP)—Italian frontier advices, quoting official sources, said today that all Jews in German-occupied Italy were being taken to concentration camps for shipment to labor camps in Poland.

Churchill, Roosevelt And Chiang Kai-Shek Meet in Africa

By JOHN CHESTER
Associated Press Staff Writer

CAIRO, Dec. 1.—President Roosevelt, Prime Minister Churchill and President Chiang Kai-Shek, flanked by their full general staffs in an extraordinary five-day session, have agreed on plans for smashing Japan as a military power, stripping her of all territory acquired since 1894 and freeing Korea.

The communique summing of the decisions of the three Allied leaders said:

"The several military missions have agreed upon future military operations against Japan. The three great Allies expressed their resolve to bring unrelenting pressure against their brutal enemies by sea, land and air. This pressure is already rising.

"The three great Allies are fighting this war to restrain and punish the aggression of Japan.

"They covet no gain for themselves and have no thought of territorial expansion.

"It is their purpose that Japan shall be stripped of all the islands in the Pacific, which she has seized or occupied since the beginning of the First World War in 1914, and that all the territories Japan has stolen from the Chinese, such as Manchuria, Formosa, and the Pescadores, shall be restored to the Republic of China. Japan also will be expelled from all other territories which she has taken by violence and greed.

"The aforesaid three great powers, mindful of the enslavement of the people of Korea, are determined that in due course Korea shall become free and independent.

"With these objects in view the three Allies, in harmony with those of the United Nations at war with Japan, will continue to persevere in the serious and prolonged operations necessary to procure the unconditional surrender of Japan."

Unannounced Destinations

All the principal conference figures left the heavily armed and guarded North African area where the meetings were held for unannounced destinations at least three days before the news was made public.

(A Washington dispatch said it was assumed that further conferences to discuss the European phases of the war would be held with Premier Marshal Stalin of Russia present. Since Russia is not at war with Japan, the conference in North Africa was not attended by Stalin.)

The North African conference, the most unusual of the war to date, opened November 22 and closed November 26, and it was obvious from activities surrounding it that it was not devoted entirely to the Japanese conflict. It was the first time the British and American leaders had conferred since the Quebec meeting last August.

The Chinese were noticeably absent from the biggest military meeting of the entire session, held November 26 with Gen. Dwight D. Eisenhower, Allied commander-in-chief in the Mediterranean campaign and second with grand European strategy.

It was reported reliably that the British and American general staffs engaged in long argument and discussion on details of a second front.

Mountbatten Plans Heard

A sense of immediacy was given the decisions against Japan by the fact that Admiral Lord Louis Mountbatten, Allied commander in southeastern Asia, and his subordinates had considerable time to formulate plans for a smash against Japan before the conference met.

Mr. Churchill, President Roosevelt, Gen. Chiang and Mrs. Chiang conferred frequently with the three-power general staffs and met separately on non-military matters with diplomats, including Foreign Secretary Eden; Sir Archibald Clark Kerr, British Ambassador to Russia; Harry Hopkins, adviser to Mr. Roosevelt; W. Averill Harriman, United States Ambassador to Russia; John G. Winant, United States Ambassador to

Please Turn to Page Twelve See "Conference"

BIG THREE MEET STALIN, PLOT HUN ANNIHILATION

★ ★ ★ ★ ★ FINAL

The Vancouver Sun

The Vancouver Evening Newspaper Owned and Operated by Vancouver People

FOUNDED 1886 VOL. LVIII—No. 51 VANCOUVER, B.C., WEDNESDAY, DECEMBER 1, 1943 PRICE 5c $1.00 per month BY CARRIER

DEATH—AND THE MARINES—TAKE TARAWA 'IN HAND'

Jap dead lie sprawled amid the shattered debris of a pillbox on shell and bomb smashed Tarawa Island after United States Marines landed on the enemy stronghold in the Gilbert Islands November 20 and captured it in the bitterest fighting experienced by U.S. forces in this war. Japanese bodies are seen strewn over the defense position, while other Japs were buried alive in the fortification on the once peaceful Pacific atoll.

Momentous Conference Under Way

By British United Press

LONDON, Dec. 1—Dispatches received in Lisbon from the Middle East today said Prime Minister Churchill, President Roosevelt and Premier Joseph Stalin have opened a momentous conference in Teheran, Iran, and that Generalissimo and Mme. Chiang Kai-Shek also were in the Iranian capital.

The Lisbon Daily Oseculo published a dispatch quoting the inter-information agency of Ankara that the "big three" leaders were meeting in Teheran where they had been joined by Laurence Steinhardt, U.S. ambassador to Turkey.

It gave no indication as to whether Chiang would participate. American and other Allied short-wave radio transmitters in broadcasts to the world said the Chinese leader had conferred with Roosevelt and Churchill in Cairo recently and suggested that he also would meet Stalin.

It was also reported that the conference was drafting final plans for complete annihilation of German arms with a co-ordinated Anglo-American-Soviet drive.

Axis broadcasts and copies of German and neutral European newspapers reaching Lisbon indicated that reports of the meeting had created a sensation throughout the Nazi-occupied continent.

BERLIN SURPRISED

Both Axis and neutral accounts agreed on the importance of the reported conference, particularly in that Stalin was said to be participating.

They indicated that Berlin had been taken by surprise. German propaganda for months has hammered at the idea that Stalin could not be brought into agreement with his allies.

Radio Tokyo followed the line that Chiang had been included to "appease" the Chinese for their non-participation in the recent Moscow conference of foreign Ministers.

COMMUNICATIONS CUT

Most broadcasts agreed that a communique covering at least the Roosevelt-Churchill-Chiang meeting would be issued sometime this week.

Almost all the broadcasts reported the meetings without qualification and said they were "announced" in a dispatch carried by the British news agency, Reuters, from Lisbon.

An American broadcast to France, typical of all the Allied broadcasts, said that all communications between Cairo and the outside world were cut during the lengthy conference among Mr. Roosevelt, Churchill

Please Turn to Page Twelve
See "Conference"

How Will We Regain Jap Loot?

What have the Japanese stolen—and how are the Allies going to get it back? A comprehensive map and story on Page 14 list the loot of the Nippon warlords while another story on the same page tells of all five routes to Tokyo the Allies may take to conquer Japan and regain the territories she has stolen.

Japs Shipped City Prisoner On Horse Boat

JERSEY CITY, N. J., Dec. 1—(AP)—Cecil Copley of Vancouver, a repatriate aboard the Gripsholm from the Far East, spent many months as a Japanese prisoner in two widely separated camps—Manila and Shanghai. He was first interned in Santo Tomas camp, Manila, to which city he had moved the Rockefeller Foundation Far East office in 1940. He was the office manager.

In September, 1942, Copley and many other Santo Tomas internees accepted a Japanese offer to go to Shanghai. They made the trip in 10 days aboard a horse boat. They slept between decks immediately above the horses. They were served Japanese food, mainly rice and seaweed. The boat made one stop, at a port in Formosa.

Late News Bulletins

'QUAKES HIT CHILE

PASEDENA, Calif., Dec. 1 — (AP) — Strong earthquakes in Chile and New Guinea were recorded at the California Institute of Technology, seismologists announced today.

HIT HUN CONVOY

LONDON, Dec. 1—(CP Cable)—Beaufighters of the RCAF squadron of coastal command scored hits on two merchant vessels in attacking an enemy convoy off the Norwegian coast yesterday, the Air Ministry announced today. In the attack was WO. L. F. Page of Nanaimo.

EXTEND SUBSIDIES

OTTAWA, Dec. 1—(CP)—Extension of the termination date of the subsidy on commercial wood fuel was announced today in an order-in-council published in Canadian war orders and regulations. The time within which wood may be contracted for, cut, delivered or held to a dealer's account now is extended to March 31, 1944.

DENIES CCF CHARGE

TORONTO, Dec. 1—(CP)—Gladstone Murray of Toronto, public relations counsel, today denied the statement made by E. B. Jolliffe, Ontario CCF leader, in a speech at Hamilton last night, that Maj. Murray has been hired by the Progressive Conservative party as an adviser on the "mind of the masses and how to frighten them against the CCF."

No Raise in Dec. Liquor Ration

The December liquor ration is exactly the same as that for November, it is announced by the Liquor Control Board.

This is one reputed quart of spirits, OR three dozen pints of beer or ale, OR one gallon Canadian wine, OR two bottles imported wine.

Chairman Kennedy expressed disappointment that it has proved impossible to give any beer in addition to a bottle of spirits for December, as he at one time hoped to be able to do.

PROVEN IMPOSSIBLE

"The experiment of giving an extra case of beer to all permit holders who asked for it during the last 10 days showed that this was utterly out of the quetsion.

Facsimiles of the liquor invoices for next year are on Page 19

"It proved that everybody who bought spirits also wanted the beer. There is not enough beer to supply the stores and not enough bottles to put it in. It just could not be done," he said.

Issue of new permits and coupons at the liquor stores has been stopped to lessen congestion. Permit clerks were sent to the Georgia Street coupon depot

Please Turn to Page Twelve
See "Liquor"

Germany to Be Battleground

LONDON, Dec. 1 — (AP) — The Moscow radio in a broadcast Tuesday night warned the German people that they could expect Germany to become a battleground.

Russian spokesmen — including Stalin—always before have confined their statements of military aims to driving the invaders out of the Soviet Union.

During last night's broadcast the Moscow announcer asserted the heavy Allied air "raids are military preparation for what is to come."

Glass Boring Thief Gets $437 Jewelry

An ingenious thief who cut or punched a hole in the show window of the Pagoda Shop, 558 Granville, Tuesday night, just large enough to admit his arm, stole jade jewelry valued at $437.

German Drive Endangers Red 'Kiev Bulge'

LONDON, Dec. 1 — (CP) — Red Army troops captured Narovl, on the west bank of the Pripet River, 14 miles east of Yelsk, and overcame counter-attacks to continue their drive today northwest of Gomel, where they already have come within artillery range of Zhlobin, the German-held stronghold guarding the 17-mile-wide Gomel escape gap, Moscow announced tonight.

By HENRY SHAPIRO
Special to The Vancouver Sun
Copyright, 1943, by British United Press

MOSCOW, Dec. 1. — Soviet front reports said today that "dozens" of German infantry and armored divisions were attacking ceaselessly in the Korosten sector of the northwest Ukraine in an all-out attempt to break through the rim of the Kiev bulge.

After evacuating Korosten the Russians fell back eastward beyond the Korosten-Zhitomir highway a short distance beyond the town military dispatches reported.

(Berlin radio reported tonight that the Russians had attacked in force in both sides of the Smolensk-Orsha road and forced wedges into the German lines at

Please Turn to Page Twelve
See "Russia"

Canadians Back From Jap Camps

By FRANK LOWE
Canadian Press Staff Writer

JERSEY [illegible], Dec. 1.—An enthusiastic group of 217 Canadians repatriated from Japanese interment arrived in New York harbor today on the liner Gripsholm, expressing joy at their return to this continent and determination to "hasten in every possible way" the liberation of those interned in the Orient.

The Canadians were to have been the first to leave the exchange ship after it made its way through the fog-dimmed harbor to its berth on the Hudson River.

But several hours after the ship docked the Canadians were at lunch aboard and it was learned they would be taken on trains this afternoon for the trip to Montreal.

Canadian Army public relations officers had first announced the Canadians had left the ship.

NOT ALLOWED TO TALK

No friends or relatives were on hand to greet the Canadians who, under a joint Canadian-United States government agreement, will not be permitted to talk, except to government representatives, while here.

One of the youngest passengers aboard was two-year-old Michael Sullivan, whose parents come from Winnipeg. Michael was born in Shanghai and has spent 22 of his 24 months in an internment camp.

Please Turn to Page Twelve
See "Gripsholm"

Race Results

(FAIR GROUNDS)

FIRST RACE—Six furlongs:
Lost Gold (Kirkland) $26.80, $10.60, $4.60.
Brown Flowers (Wegryzn) $20.40, $6.20.
Juanita M (Phelps) $2.60.
Time 1:16.

SECOND RACE—Six furlongs:
Vener (Scurlock) $136, $26.60, $6.40.
Top Note (McCaddan) $5.40, $3.40.
Michigan Blue (Castanova) $2.80.
Time 1:15 3-5.

THIRD RACE—Mile and one-sixteenth:
Rex (Jomas) $9.20, $3.80, out.
War Master (Given) $3, out.
Boom On (Pena) out.
Time 1:48 4-5.

FOURTH RACE — Mile and 70 yards:
Olivia L (Brinson) $14.40, $6.40, $6.00.
Ticco (Whiting) $11.20, $5.60.
Spring Glory (Scurlock) $6.20.
Time, 1:50.

FIFTH RACE—Mile and 70 yards:
Blue Serge (Strange), $8.60, $3.80, out.
Bushwhacker (G. Burns), $3.00, out.
Choppy Sea (Basham), out.
Time: 1:46 3-5.

BAY MEADOWS

FIRST RACE—Six furlongs:
Keaton Light (Chojnacki) $8.90, $4.70, $5.30.
Fourth Alarm (Slocum) $6.90, $6.20.
Valdina Vita (Johnson) $8.40.
Time 1:13.

SECOND RACE—Six furlongs:
Seekonk (Lasswell) $30.30, $13.50, $7.30.
Archives (Woodhouse) $26.70, $18.10.
Shasta Hills (Slocum) $23.30.
Time, 1:12 4-5.

THIRD RACE—Mile and one-sixteenth:
Tuxedo Eddy (Hart) $8.60, $4.30, $2.40.
Go Getter (Lasswell) $3.30, $2.30.
Detained (Woodhouse) $2.20.
Time, 1:46.

Race Entries on Page 11

Britain Raps Spain

LONDON, Dec. 1—(CP)—The British government has demanded an official apology from Spain on a charge that uniformed Falangists in November forced their way into the British Vice-Consulate at Saragossa and insulted the vice-consul and members of his family.

The Foreign Office, it was learned, has taken a serious view of the incident and is demanding an assurance from Spain that the guilty persons will be punished.

The Foreign Office issued an official statement on the incident which said:

"Parties of Spanish Falangists in uniform November 19 and 20 forced their way into the British vice-consulate at Saragossa and made insulting remarks to the Vice-Consul and members of his family.

"A serious vie wis taken of this occurrence and the Spanish government is being asked by the British government for an official apology and for an assurance that the guilty persons will be properly punished."

U.S. Won't Observe 'Pearl Harbor Day'

WASHINGTON, Dec. 1—(BUP)—The White House announced today that President Roosevelt has vetoed a joint resolution setting aside December 7, 1943, as Armed Services Honor Day, on the grounds that commemoration of the "day of infamy" on which the Japanese attacked Pearl Harbor is "singularly inappropriate."

Nazis Round Up Italian Jews

BERNE, Dec. 1—(BUP)—Italian frontier advices, quoting official sources, said today that all Jews in German-occupied Italy were being taken to concentration camps for shipment to labor camps in Poland.

Two Skaters Drowned

EDMONTON, Dec. 1—(CP)—RCMP headquarters here said the bodies of Harvey Larsen, 19, and Ralph Melin, 15, of the Calmar district, drowned while skating on Conjuring Lakes Sunday afternoon, have been recovered.

KEEP SMILING

"In case I get shipwrecked I'll have something to look at!"

3-Way Blows to Crush Germany

Rationed Foods
Preserves—Coupons D6 and D7, now valid.
Sugar—Coupons Nos. 19 and 20, now valid.
Meat—Coupons 22 to 25 expired; 28 now valid.
Canning Sugar—All Coupons valid until further notice
Tea or Coffee—Nos. 22 and 23, now valid.
Butter—Coupons Nos. 38 and 39, now valid; 34 to 37 to expire.

The Vancouver Sun

The Vancouver Evening Newspaper Owned and Operated by Vancouver People

Today's Tides
Vancouver Harbor
High 2:30 p.m., 13.1 feet Low 9:31 p.m., 3.9 feet
English Bay
High 2:08 p.m., 13.7 feet Low 9:13 p.m., 4.9 feet
First Narrows
High slack 2:48 p.m. Low slack 10:05 p.m.

FOUNDED 1886 VOL. LVIII—No. 55 MArine 1161 HOME EDITION VANCOUVER, BRITISH COLUMBIA, MONDAY, DECEMBER 6, 1943 *** PRICE 5 CENTS $1.00 per month BY CARRIER

EXCLUSIVE—FIRST PICTURE OF HISTORIC TEHRAN CONFERENCE

TEHRAN, Iran, Dec. 6.—This is the first picture of an event the whole Allied world has been anxiously waiting for two years. Here are seen Marshal Joseph Stalin (left), Russian Premier, President Franklin D. Roosevelt of the United States and Prime Minister Winston Churchill (right) of Great Britain on the porch of the Russian Embassy during their historic four-day conference here. During this epochal parley the three Allied leaders drew plans to concentrate the military might of Russia, the United States and Britain on a "relentlessly increasing" basis guaranteeing victory over Germany. The picture was taken by U.S. Army 12th Air Force photographers.

Program Drawn at Tehran

Big Three Map Peace 'For Generations' At Parley

By OSKAR GUTH
Special to The Vancouver Sun
Copyright, 1943, by British United Press

TEHRAN, Iran, Dec. 6. — President Roosevelt, Prime Minister Churchill and Premier Stalin have agreed on a master plan to crush Germany by powerful offensives on three fronts — including invasions of Western Europe and possibly the Balkans — and have mapped a peace that should endure for "many generations."

The "Big Three" of the Allied nations announced their decisions in broad terms in a declaration issued today after 100 hours of unparalleled conferences that embraced military, diplomatic and political questions both of the war and the peace to follow.

After concluding their four-day sessions last Wednesday, Premier Stalin returned to Moscow and Roosevelt and Churchill to Cairo to translate speedily into action the decisions that their joint declaration said guaranteed "victory will be ours."

With the Tehran conference, the Allies completed the blueprint for the war in the months to come in both the Atlantic and Pacific. The previous week, Roosevelt and Churchill conferred with Generalissimo Chiang Kai-Shek and laid down the broad strategy calculated to bring Japan to her knees.

DECLARATION HIGHLIGHTS

Specifically, the three heads of states proclaimed in their joint declaration:

1. "We have reached complete understanding as to the scope and timing of operations which will be undertaken from the east, west and south."

2. No power on earth can prevent our destroying the German armies by land, their U-boats by sea, and their war plants from the air. Our attacks will be relentless and increasing.

3. "We recognize fully the responsibility resting upon us and all the United Nations to make a peace which will command good will from the overwhelming masses of the peoples of the world and banish the scourge and terrors of war for many generations."

4. "We will welcome . . . as they may choose to come into the world family of democratic nations . . . all nations, large and small, whose peoples in heart and in mind are dedicated, as are our own peoples, to the elimination of tyranny and slavery, oppression and intolerance.

5. "We came here with hope and determination. We leave here friends in fact, in spirit and in purpose."

Contrary to expectations in many quarters, the declaration contained no ultimatum to the German people to throw out their Nazi leaders and surrender unconditionally to avoid complete devastation of their homeland.

It was believed that the "Big Three" may have decided to delay any such ultimatum until a moment when success was assured. Most Allied authorities agreed that German morale has "not yet reached the breaking point."

Mr. Roosevelt, Churchill and Stalin in a subsidiary statement on Iran's part of the war said they counted upon the participation of all "peace-loving nations, in the establishment of international peace, security and prosperity after the war, in accordance with the principles of the Atlantic Charter, to which all

Please Turn to Page Two
See "Allied Invasion"

Allies Take More Heights in Italy

ALGIERS, Dec. 6—(AP) — The Anglo-American 5th Army, bypassing German strongpoints, has captured new heights commanding the road to Rome west of Mignano, while the British 8th Army's drive has carried to the Moro river, 10 miles north of the Sangro, Allied headquarters announced today.

The Nazis launched strong counter-attacks against British and American infantry storming the heights in bitter hand-to-hand battles, and threw in new reinforcements including mechanized grenadiers against the 8th Army in a desperate attempt to halt the Allied drives. A flame-throwing tank was captured by British troops.

Lt.-Gen. Mark Clark's headquarters announced that the enemy, who is fighting stubbornly for every inch of ground, had been driven from three commanding elevations by Americans who are smashing into Nazi fortifications in the area of the rugged slopes of Mount Aggiore. British infantry of the 5th Army are rooting out Nazi defenders in the equally-rough area of Mount Camino.

From their newly-won positions the Allied troops could gaze out across the valley to Cassino, and beyond it to the valley which leads northwest into Rome.

British warships were disclosed to have supported the 8th Army's drive up the Adriatic coast in recent days with bombardments oi German supply routes, bases and shipping.

U.S. Bombers Hit Marshalls

By British United Press

WASHINGTON, Dec. 6. — American bombers spread ruin through Japan's island network of defenses in the central Pacific, a communique disclosed today, as Gen. Douglas MacArthur's southwest Pacific raiders hammered relentlessly at the approaches to the great enemy naval and air base at Rabaul, New Britain.

Ranging far to the north and west of the conquered Gilbert Islands, U.S. Army Liberators dropped 50 tons of bombs on Mili atoll in the Marshall Islands Saturday and pounded Japanese phosphate mining installations on Naurur Island.

Japanese planes struck back in small force at Tarawa and Makin islands in the Gilberts, while another enemy formation gave Calcutta its first raid since January 19, causing slight damage.

Nazis Rush Troops to Turk Border

By J. EDWARD MURRAY
Special to The Vancouver Sun
Copyright, 1943, by British United Press

LONDON, Dec. 6. — German troops are massing in Bulgaria near the Turkish frontier, a Stockholm dispatch said today as speculation mounted that the Roosevelt-Churchill-Stalin conference may bring a Balkan invasion and draw Turkey into the war.

The German movement toward the Turkish border began during the weekend and continued at a rapid rate, Hungarian circles in Stockholm said a large troop concentration was reported at Khaskovo in southeastern Bulgaria, while a Nazi motorized detachment and two cars of officers continued on to Svilengrad, only six miles west of the border, yesterday.

Allied and neutral sources have speculated ever since the Tri-Power conference at Moscow a month ago that the Allies might prevail upon Turkey at least to provide bases under the terms of her mutual aid pact with Great Britain for an Allied offensive in the Balkans, even if not actively entering the war.

Troops Give 'Winnie' Gift

TEHRAN, Iran, Dec. 1—(Delayed)—(AP)—Prime Minister Churchill in an informal speech to British troops who guarded the compound of the British legation where he stayed during the British-American-Russian conference declared he hoped the decisions the three powers were taking in Tehran would shorten the war.

The troops, members of PIFORS — the Persian-Iraq Forces — gathered around the Prime Minister at his invitation after they presented him with a birthday gift.

City to Light Up Yule Trees

Vancouver's Christmas tree dimout dating from Pearl Harbor was lifter today with an announcement that seven or eight large outdoor evergreens will be illuminated by the city in the next few days, depending on how far its strings of colored globes can be stretched.

Ald. W. D. Greyell, chairman of Civic Utilities Committee, disclosed a tentative program calling for the decoration of one tree each at Victory Square, the Georgia Street entrance to Stanley Park, Thornton Park in front of the CNR station, and English Bay, and two trees each on grounds at the court house and city hall.

Strings of colored lights across downtown streets have worn out and cannot be renewed, he said. The customary flood lighting of the city hall tower will not be resumed because the spot lights have been dismantled.

New Labor Code

Cost-of-Living Bonus to Be Added to Basic Wage

OTTAWA, Dec. 6 — (CP) — Existing cost of living bonuses will be added to basic wage rates, and there will be no occasion for further bonuses, Prime Minister King announced Saturday night in a spech over the CBC national network.

Mr. King said a revised wage control order will be made public at the beginning of this week. He also made the following other announcements:

1. The government is prepared to accept the main proposals on which majority and minority reports of the National War Labor Board agree, as a "basis for a revised labor policy."

2. A new labor code providing for compulsory collective bargaining will be established.

3. The government believes it can hold the cost of living at its present level, but if the cost rises more than 3 percent and remains at that level for two consecutive months the government will review the whole program of price and wage control and take "appropriate action."

4. Legislation will be proposed at the coming session of parliament to provide a floor for farm prices after the war.

5. Plans for "a national minimum of human welfare" for all the people after the war will be outlined on another occasion. They should embrace useful employment for all willing to work, standards of nutrition and housing, social insurance against unemployment, accident, death of the breadwinner, ill-health and old age.

Mr. King appealed to farmers and labor especially to hold the line in the battle of inflation.

He said if the price ceilings are not held the war effort will suffer and solutions of post-war problems will be more difficult.

Feeling that the war is nearly over has become "far too

Please Turn to Page Two
See "King Speech"

Col. Ralston Visits Canadians in Italy

WITH CANADIAN FORCES IN ITALY, Dec. 6 — (CP Cable) —Col. J. L. Ralston, Canadian Minister of National Defense, who has been visiting Canadian troops in Italy spent some time at the front where some of the Dominion's most famous regiments and other 8th Army troops have been administering to the Germans the "colossal crack" Gen. Sir Bernard Montgomery promised them.

Col. Ralston was accompanied by Lt.-Gen. Kenneth Stuart, chief of the Canadian general staff. They flew from Britain and before coming to Italy visited Canadian troops in Africa.

Cherkasy Encircled in Soviet Drive

By HENRY SHAPIRO
Special to The Vancouver Sun
Copyright, 1943, by British United Press

MOSCOW, Dec. 6. — The Russians have encircled Cherkasy, biggest German-held stronghold on the west bank of the Dnieper between Kiev and Dnepropetrovsk, and are fighting in the streets of the burning city, front reports said today.

Fierce German counterattacks designed to break through the Soviet ring from both within and without were being repulsed all around the western rim of the city and its approaches were littered with the bodies of Germans and the wreckage of German tanks and armored cars.

The liquidation of the sizeable garrison at Cherkast would enable the Russians to push southeastward along the west bank of the Dnieper and contact other Red Army troops below Kremenchug, 65 miles down the river, and establish a continuous bridgehead of nearly 200 miles.

The Russians also posed a new threat to the Germans in the Dnieper bend by beating off an enemy landing on the Kindurinskaya peninsula on the south side of Dnieprovsky Bay at the mouth of the Dnieper and Bug rivers and massing strength there for a possible thrust to the opposite shore.

In White Russia, the Russians captured three more towns and villages on the approaches to the railway junction of Zhlobin, tightening the siege arc on three sides of the city.

Premier King In Washington

WASHINGTON, Dec. 6—(CP) —Prime Minister Mackenzie King arrived in Washington by train today, after an overnight trip from Ottawa, and said in an interview the Tehran and Cairo declarations "mark the dawn of a new world." This afternoon he saw Leighton McCarthy, Canadian ambassador-designate to the United States, and tonight he was to dine with State Secretary Cordell Hull.

Mr. King planned to remain in Washington overnight and then go south.

The Changing Times

SALT LAKE CITY, Dec. 6—(AP)—County sheriff's deputies answered a call at a night club. They ordered two women to leave the place. A soldier said the women were annoying him.

Commandos Smash Factory, Swiss Say

LONDON, Dec. 6—(CP)—The Swiss radio quoted advices from Sweden today as saying that an Allied landing party had blown up a foundry at Arendal in southern Norway in a daring raid the night of November 20. The broadcast was recorded by Reuters news agency.

B.C. Women Share $343,778 Estate

SARNIA, Ont., Dec. 6—(CP)—Arthur Cameron Johnston, municipal engineer who died last Sept. 10, left an estate valued at $343,778, it was shown in his will, filed for probate.

Principal beneficiaries are a son, Lieut. A. C. of the United States Army, and three sisters, Mrs. Jessie M. Clegg of Vancouver, Mrs. Mildred Jones of New Westminster, B.C., and Mrs. Marjorie Hull of New York.

Ciano Reported Shot For Treason to Duce

LONDON, Dec. 6—(CP)—A Reuters news agency dispatch from the Swiss-Italian frontier said today that Count Galeazzo Ciano, former Fascist foreign minister of Italy and Benito Mussolini's son-in-law, was shot this morning by a firing squad, according to reports reaching the frontier.

Mussolini's son-in-law turned against him in the Grand Council meeting last July which ousted the discredited Duce as Italy's dictator.

The reports, which were not confirmed, said Ciano was shot in the back after being accused of high treason and "sentenced to death by a special court of Mussolini's "republican Fascist" government, a German puppet organization. The execution was said to have taken place somewhere in northern Italy.

Plane Workers to Vote on Strike

OS ANGELES, Dec. 6—(BUP) —The threat of a strike ahose today at the ockheer Aircraft Company's sprawling Burbank, Cal., warplane plant.

Employees, who belong to the International Association of Machinists (AFL), voted almost unanimously yesterday to demand that a strike vote be taken under the Smith-Connally Act.

Three Die in Crash

WINNIPEG, Dec. 6—(CP)— An instructor and three students from No. 33 Service Flying Training School, RAF, at Carberry, Man., were killed at midnight Friday when their training plane crashed near Sidney, Man.

Churchill's Birthday Tehran Highlight

'Joe' Walks for 34 Toasts

By Associated Press

TEHRAN, Iran, Nov. 30.—(Delayed.) — Prime Minister Churchill, President Roosevelt and Premier Stalin matched eloquence tonight in a demonstration of mutual admiration as the British Prime Minister, atan enthusiastic birthday dinner he gave himself, eased into his seventy year amid the exhilirating applause of his two fellow statesmen. There were 34 toasts.

Stalin, who set the key to the evenings' atmosphere, breezed into the British Legation talking freely through an interpreter to the assembled guests, removing his greatcoat and lifted a glass to Mr. Churchill.

The dinner - jacketed Mr. Churchill shepherded his guests into dinner in the Victorian setting of the legation dining room. Mr. Roosevelt sat on Mr. Churchill's right and Premier Stalin on Mr. Churchill's left.

Mr. Churchill's WAAF daughter, Mrs. Sarah Oliver, the only woman present, served as hostess.

Capt. Randolph Churchill was also present.

The menu consisted of Persian soup, boiled salmon and trout from the Caspian Sea, Turkey ice called "Persian lantern" and cheese souffle. This was followed by a small birthday cake on which there were 69 cadnles crowded over the "V" sign marked in the white icing.

Mr. Churchill toasted Mr. Roosevelt twice—once as Roosevelt the President and once as Roosevelt the man. Then he toasted "Stalin the Great."

Stalin replied with toasts to "my fighting friend Churchill," and to "my fighting friend Roosevelt." Mr. Roosevelt replied to both with apprpriate words.

Please Turn to Page Two
See "34 Toasts"

'Monty' to Command British Forces

YANKS' EISENHOWER TO LEAD EUROPE INVASION

The Vancouver Sun
The Vancouver Evening Newspaper Owned and Operated by Vancouver People
FOUNDED 1886 VOL. LVIII—No. 71 VANCOUVER, B.C., FRIDAY, DECEMBER 24, 1943 PRICE 10c

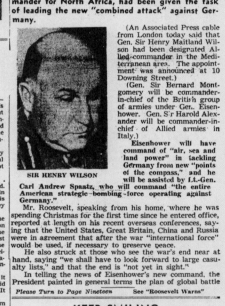

★★★★★ FINAL

Berlin and Hun Rocket Bases Hit

By GLADWIN HILL
Associated Press Staff Writer

LONDON, Dec. 24.—A great fleet of American Flying Fortresses and heavy bombers, guarded by soaring swarms of fighters, joined in possibly the Allies' heaviest daylight assault of the war today for a Christmas Eve attack on the Pas De Calais "rocket-gun coast," hard on the heels of the seventh smashing night blow by the RAF and RCAF at Berlin.

An unending all-day procession of heavy, medium and light bombers, fighter-bombers and fighters roared across the Channel for the fifth successive day of hammering at mystery objectives on the French coast, popularly thought to be installations for shelling England.

This thunderous aerial parade began a few hours after the RAF-RCAF night fleet returned from battering the Nazi capital with another 120 tons of explosives in an attack which proved so deceptive that Berlin's weary fighter plane defenses were utterly foiled.

This seventh major bombardment of Berlin in five weeks, likely rounding out the destruction of three-fourths of the city, and other operations, cost the RAF but 17 bombers. No planes were lost from the RCAF squadrons of Lancaster bombers and Pathfinders. RCAF inIntruders also flew night patrols without loss.

SPOUTING VOLCANO

The daylight caravans of medium bombers, as well as other light and heavy aircraft, made late Christmas shoppers in south England stop in their tracks and stare skyward.

Because the targets were in a concentrated area close to the coast the Pas de Calais operation took on the appearance of an invasion rehearsal — the greatest since last September

Please Turn to Page Nineteen
See "Berlin"

$950 Wrapped Up in Roast

Somebody on Thursday got $950 tucked in with today's roast of beef.

How it all happened was told to police by W. J. Matthews, proprietor of Bill's Meat Market, 2492 East Hastings.

He said he put $950 in cash and cheques in a paper bag preparatory to taking it to the bank.

He served a customer and when he went to get the deposit found it was missing.

Matthews thinks he inadvertently wrapped up the bank deposit with a customer's meat order.

Victorian Wounded

VICTORIA, Dec. 24—(CP)—Capt. P. D. Crofton, 29, who fought through the Sicilian campaign, was wounded in action Dec. 10 in Italy, his mother, Mrs. Fred Crofton, Harbor Hotel, Ganges, learned today from Defense Headquarters, Ottawa.

Russians Launch Great Offensive

By ROBERT MUSEL
Special to The Vancouver Sun
Copyright, 1943, by British United Press

LONDON, Dec. 24.—The German high command reported today that the Red Army had launched a new offensive with several divisions in lower White Russia and had regained the initiative in the Kiev salient, where the biggest Nazi counter-attack of the campaign had fizzled out.

An official Berlin broadcast said the Russians attacked in force along the upper Dnieper northeast of Zhlobin, key rail junction of southern White Russia. It added that "heavy fighting" is going on, significantly giving no hint of the trend.

Premier Marshal Joseph Stalin, in an order of the day broadcast by Moscow radio, announced that the 1st Baltic army stormed and captured the German stronghold of Gorodok, 19 miles north of Vitebsk on the Vitebsk-Nevel railroad line.

German attacks southeast of Korosten and east of Zhitomir had collapsed. It was in the region of those towns west of Kiev that the Nazis apparently had expended their supreme effort to reverse the sweeping gains of the Red Army's summer and early winter offensive.

The reported Russian offensive near Zhlobin apparently was synchronized with the Nevel drive bearing down into White Russia from the north and threatening the keystone bases of Vitebsk and Polotsk.

A British United Press dispatch from Moscow said Gen. Ian Bagramian's army was developing

Please Turn to Page Nineteen
See "Russia"

Bayonet Clash In Ortona

By WES GALLAGHER
Associated Press War Correspondent

ALGIERS, Dec. 24. — Fighting in snow and rain, the 8th Army has driven northward ana captured the village of Vezzani thiee mlies southwest of Ortona and the Canadian 1st Division is digging the last Germans out of Ortona with bayonets, it was announced today.

The whole Italian front was blanketed by wet, wintry weather which handicapped operations both aground and in the air.

A military commentator said the enemy still held one corner of Ortona—eastern anchor of a crumbling defense line—and that many of the Germans were sticking to the death rather than retreat. This had turned the Canadians' struggle for the city into a house-to-house campaign with bayonets and small arms.

Other units of Gen. Sir Bernard Montgomery's 8th Army were pressing relentlessly northward despite the weather.

Vezzani, the village which British troops captured yesterday, is about a mile north of the

Please Turn to Page Nineteen
See "Italy"

Race Results

TROPICAL PARK

FIRST RACE.—Six furlongs.
Air Beauty (Skoronski) $13.70, $5.50, $4.60.
Son Islam (Acaro) $4.50, $3.30.
Balmy Spring (ettinger) $4.90.
Time 1:12 1-5.

SECOND ACE.—One mile and seventy yards.
Miss Reward (Skoronski) $15.90, $7.30, $4.70.
Whippet (Gorlock) $16.60, $8.80.
General War (Snider) $8.00.
Time 1:46 2-5.

THIRD RACE—Mile and one-sixteenth:
Precision (Layton) $16.40, $9, $6.80.
Neddie Lass (Permane) $6, $5.
Valdina Joe (Martin) $10.90.
Time, 1:46 2 -5.
Scratched: Cosine, Illinois Star.

FOURTH RACE—Six furlongs:
Reztips (Haskell) $3.10, $2.90, $2.40.
Hillsun (Brennan) $6.70, $3.20.
Star Bien (Roberts) $3.20.
Time 1:12.
Scratched—None.

FIFTH RACE—Six furlongs:
Robins Crown, (Haskell) $30.20, $11.90, $6.50.
Night Bomber (Bierman) $4.60, $3.30.
Class Book (McMullen) $6.50.
Time: 1.13 4-5.

SIXTH RACE—Six furlongs:
Dream Parade (Atkinson) $9.40, $4.20, 3.20.
Free Air (Permaine), $3.50, $3.40.
Blue Pom (Snider) $4.60.
Time 1.11 3-5.

SEVENTH RACE — Mile-one-sixteenth:
Toy Quay (Atkinson) $18.00, $6.80, $4.10.
Marmeduke (Arcaro) $5.60, $3.50.
Displayer (Claggett) $4.00.
Time: 1.45 4-5.

EIGHTH RACE—Mile and one-sixteenth:
Tony Steel (Breen) $9.60, $4.70, $3.10.
Beamy (Skoronsky) $4.90, $2.90.
Santa Domingo (Atkinson) $3.
Time 1.47.

FAIR GROUNDS

FIRST RACE—Six furlongs:
Linn Creek (Givens) $9, $5, $4.
Kelspride (Thornburg) $3.40, $2.60.
Joey B (Alphonso) $2.80.
Time: 1:15 4-5.
No scratches.

SECOND RACE—Six furlongs:
Diego Red (Bailey) $4.40, $2.80, $2.20.
Count Chat (Butcher) $3.60, $2.40.
Venci (Scurlock) $2.20.
Time: 1:15.
Scratched: Flash Town, Black Flame, Celesti F., Annie Alone.

THIRD RACE—Six furlongs:
Rover (Jemas) $3.80, $3.20, $2.40.
Late Issue (Scurlock) $17.40, $5.20.
Mere Markette (Bailey) $3.00.
Time: 1:15 1-5.

FOURTH RACE—Six furlongs:
Granny Reigh (Jemas) $9.40, $4.60, $2.80.
Valdina Czar (Hooper) $6.00, $5.00.
Napoo (Swain) $3.00.
Time: 1:15 3-5.

FIFTH RACE—Six furlongs:
Zig Zag (Bailey) $4.00, $2.40, $2.20.
Regimental (Cook) $3.40, $2.80.
Kirwin (Wegryzn) $2.80.
Time 1.14 2-5.

WILL DIRECT ASSAULT

GEN. DWIGHT D. EISENHOWER
Four-star General is leader of assault on Europe

'Sitdown' Yule For Canadian Troops in Italy

By WILLIAM STEWART
Canadian Press War Correspondent

WITH THE CANADIANS IN ITALY, Dec. 24.—Canadian soldiers living in slit trenches, alongside guns and tanks and trucks, in mud-stained tents and in the bowels of shell-torn houses are planning to make the best of their first Christmas in action.

Many will spend the day right up at the front among the exploding German shells and mortar bombs while many more will be spread back through the Canadian area where they perform the jobs that contribute to the advances by the frontline fighters.

RATIONS PLENTIFUL

The Canadian commander has issued orders that wherever possible his troops will have "sitdown" Christmas dinners with their officers and non-commissioned officers waiting on them in the old army tradition.

Rations will be plentiful and include such extras as nuts, oranges and apples. Thousands of mince pies are being cooked all over the Canadian area.

Uniformed padres who have been with the troops in the worst moments of battle will hold Christmas services where they can and say prayers for the soldiers who have given their lives and for a victorious peace which the men who have been spared hope may bring them home by next Christmas.

The wounded in field hospitals will have tasty meals as well as band concerts or other special entertainment that day. The Canadian commander will cali at their bedsides and the winners of awards for bravery will be presented with their ribbons.

ROAST CALF

Every man will get extra Christmas cigarettes and chocolates.

The postal service has concentrated on delivery of parcels for he last few days so that as many as possible will have had something from home.

Western infantrymen had their eye on roast calf for a

Please Turn to Page Nineteen
See "Canadians"

LATE NEWS BULLETINS

LONDON, Dec. 24—(CP)—The Red Army stormed its way into Gorodok, 20 miles northwest of Vitebsk, today and captured more than 60 other large populated places, Moscow announced.

NEW YORK, Dec. 24—(AP)—Fourteen persons died and at least 10 others were injured today when a fire mushroomed through a "Bowery type" lodging house known as the Standard Hotel, a five-story structure on 42nd Street between Ninth and Tenth Avenues.

BEIRUT, Lebanon, Dec. 23—(Delayed)—(AP)—Premier Raid El Solh told an extraordinary session of the Lebanese Chamber of Deputies today that France had agreed during the recent Damsacus negotiations to transfer to Lebanon and Syria all powers exercised over them. The agreement becomes effective Jan. 1.

LONDON, Dec. 24—(CP)—More than 1300 aircraft of the 8th U.S. Air Force were in the task force which attacked special military installations in the Pas de Calais area of France today, U.S. Army headquarters announced tonight. This included the largest number of heavy bombers ever dispatched by the 8th Air Force on a single mission.

General Wilson Takes Over in Mediterranean

FDR Announces American Supreme Allied Chief In European Theatre; Montgomery to Lead British Armies in Assault on Continent

By British United Press

HYDE PARK, N.Y., Dec. 24.—President Roosevelt today announced the appointment of Gen. Dwight D. Eisenhower as commander of the forthcoming Allied invasion of Europe.

In a Christmas Eve radio address, Mr. Roosevelt said as a result of the international conferences at Cairo and Tehran, Eisenhower, now Allied commander for North Africa, had been given the task of leading the new "combined attack" against Germany.

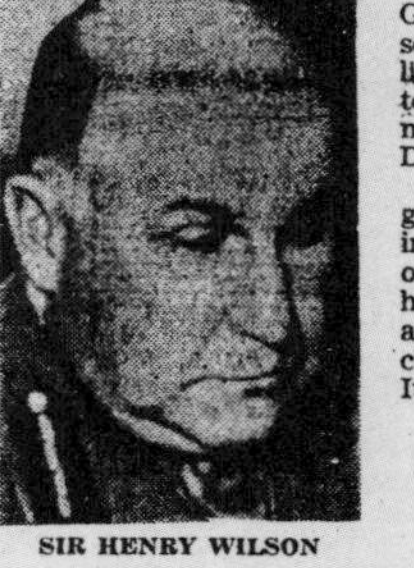

SIR HENRY WILSON

(An Associated Press cable from London today said that Gen. Sir Henry Maitland Wilson had been designated Allied commander in the Mediterranean area. The appointment was announced at 10 Downing Street.)

(Gen. Sir Bernard Montgomery will be commander-in-chief of the British group of armies under Gen. Eisenhower. Gen. Sir Harold Alexander will be commander-in-chief of Allied armies in Italy.)

Eisenhower will have command of "air, sea and land power" in tackling Germany from new "points of the compass," and he will be assisted by Lt.-Gen. Carl Andrew Spaatz, who will command "the entire American strategic bombing force operating against Germany."

Mr. Roosevelt, speaking from his home, where he was spending Christmas for the first time since he entered office, reported at length on his recent overseas conferences, saying that the United States, Great Britain, China and Russia were in agreement that after the war "international force" would be used, if necessary to preserve peace.

He also struck at those who see the war's end near at hand, saying "we shall have to look forward to large casualty lists," and that the end is "not yet in sight."

In telling the news of Eisenhower's new command, the President painted in general terms the plan of global battle

Please Turn to Page Nineteen See "Roosevelt Warns"

Mrs. 'Ike' Is Silent But 'Very Proud'

WASHINGTON, Dec. 24.—Mrs. Dwight D. Eisenhower's first reaction to President Roosevelt's Christmas Eve announcement that her husband had been chosen to lead the Anglo-American invasion of Europe was tongue-tied silence.

When she found words, they were about what the general must be thinking, and not about her own feelings.

"I think . . . he must . . . must be very proud," she said. "From the first he has been in there to finish the job. This is the greatest reward they could give him."

Mrs. Eisenhower heard the news with her 21-year-old son John, who graduates from the military academy at West Point this year. He is home on a four-day furlough. Neither had any advance preparation for the President's announcement.

"I'm still trying to take it in," Mrs. Eisenhower said when asked for comment. "It caught me by surprise."

She laughed and added: "I'm always the last person to know anything about my husband."

"I'm very proud," she said. "Any wife would be."

No Refreshments, No Reception

VICTORIA, Dec. 24—(CP)—There will be no reception at Government House on New Year's Day.

It has been found impossible to make satisfactory provision for supplying refreshments and His Honor the Lieut-Governor has been regretfully forced to cancel the function, which has always been regarded as the highlight of New Year's Day here.

No Sun On Christmas Day

In order that members of the staff of The Vancouver Sun may observe Christmas Day, no regular editions will be published on Saturday. Regular editions, however, will be published on Monday, Boxing Day.

Subscribers may be kept up to the minute on the latest news developments by listening to regular Sun newscasts over radio station CKWX at 12:05 noon and 10 p.m. on Christmas Day and 10 p.m. on Sunday.

KEEP SMILING

"Yes, those same stars shine over Italy, and Dad's probably looking at them and thinking about next year's Christmas just like us!"

The Sun Wishes All Its Readers a Merry Christmas

1944

D-Day was the major event of 1994, but it was merely the beginning of the unbridled success of Allied arms in the west. In the east the Red Army swept victoriously into Poland and headed for the heart of Germany after gigantic battles involving thousands of tanks and millions of men. The Germans stood stubbornly in Italy, however, causing the Allies no end of trouble in dislodging them. The Japanese were equally stubborn in giving ground and could only be rooted out of their island bunkers with flame throwers. They were gradually being rolled back towards their home islands, but at great cost.

MAJOR EVENTS

June 6, 1944

D-DAY: THE SECOND FRONT

D-Day. At last! The biggest news of the war since Pearl Harbor. We were attacking Germany where it counted—near the heart. Defeating the Germans in the desert, in North Africa, in Sicily, in Italy, was good for our morale but didn't seem to count for much. What had we won compared to being so ignominiously thrown out of Europe in 1940? We knew in our heart of hearts that we had to go back the way we left—through France.

And ever since 1941, after Hitler attacked Russia, there was talk of a Second Front in the west. Stalin wanted it immediately as the Red Army reeled backwards, deeper and deeper into the heartland, until the Germans had conquered most of European Russia. The Greater German Reich now encompassed the whole of Europe.

It had been hard enough to leave France through Dunkirk; it was going to be a lot harder to get back in. The whole coast was fortified, from Denmark to Spain—the "Westwall" it was called.

The Americans had talked of a Second Front since joining the war, but the British wouldn't move until a vast armada had been assembled that would assure victory. No more Dieppes for them. It took the productive capacity of the Allies until 1944 to build up the necessary forces:

39 infantry and tank divisions
  (20 U.S., 14 British, three Canadian, one Free French, one Polish)
2,300 transport planes,
2,600 gliders,
7,000 warships and landing craft,
11,000 aircraft, including 5,000 fighters

Manning the Westwall, the Germans had 62 divisions (46 infantry, two airborne, 10 Panzer, four kriegsmarine), but only 160 aircraft, composed of 70 fighters and 90 bombers. This disparity in airpower gave the Allies complete mastery of the skies, thus ensuring a minimum of casualties.

Since it was impossible to hide their vast array of military hardware from the Germans, the Allies tried to keep them guessing as to the exact time and place of the coming invasion. So clever was this trickery that, even after the initial landings in Normandy, Hitler still believed the main force would land at Calais, across the Channel from Dover.

Battle plans divided up the Normandy beaches by names: Utah, Omaha, Gold, Juno, Sword. The Americans landed their 1st Army on Utah and Omaha, with two airborne divisions landing west of Utah to protect their right flank. Many of these troops were captured, however, and some drowned in fields flooded with water by the Germans.

Meanwhile, the Americans were having a bad time on Omaha Beach. The German fire was intense and accurate, and within an hour the beach was littered with 2,500 casualties and wrecked equipment. General Omar Bradley, the commander, even considered withdrawing, but finally more troops came ashore with tanks, and a manageable beachhead was established at last.

The British 2nd Army landed on Gold and Sword beaches with the help of special tanks devised for the occasion, and had limited casualties.

The 3rd Canadian Division and 2nd Canadian Armoured Brigade landed 14,000 troops on Juno Beach the first day. They suffered over 1,000 casualties, including 375 dead. After overcoming fierce opposition, they joined up with the British and drove nine miles inland by nightfall. The 1st Canadian Parachute Battalion functioned as part of the British 6th Airborne Division, which provided flank protection.

With the Royal Navy guarding the Channel from marauding German PT boats, and the Allied air forces in complete control over the beaches, an immense load was taken off the armies on the ground. They could concentrate on enlarging their beachheads, an increasingly difficult task as German resistance stiffened from the second day on. The British and Canadians expected to take Caen the first day, for example, but did not manage it until a month later, on July 9th. The Americans managed to capture the port of Cherbourg by June 18th, which became immediately useful for landing the vast quantities of supplies and equipment a modern army consumes. The worst storms in 80 years had blown up in the Channel and made the floating docks brought from England difficult to use. Fuel was pumped over from England in a special pipeline laid on the sea floor.

Out of 150,000 troops landed on June 6th, there were only 6,000 American and 3,500 British and Canadians dead and wounded. The harsh lessons learned at Dieppe had paid off.

[See pages 119–25, 127–28]

July 3, 1944

MINSK FALLS

A simple two-word headline— MINSK FALLS—in the final edition of *The Vancouver Sun* for July 3, 1944 belied the massive life-and-death struggle on the Russian front that was begun on June 22nd with the Red Army summer offensive. Stalin planned it to coincide exactly with the date three years earlier on which Germany attacked Russia.

By 1944 the Red Army consisted of 19 million men, 133,000 guns, 11,800 tanks and 22,000 aircraft. For the offensive in Belorussia alone, the Red Army committed 166 divisions consisting of 2,400,000 front line troops, 30,000 guns, 5,200 tanks and 6,000 aircraft. In reserve were an additional 645,000 troops, 9,500 guns, 1,800 tanks and 2,900 aircraft. This strength gave the Red Army a four to one advantage over the Germans in artillery, tanks and aircraft, and a two-to-one advantage in troops. A whole army corps of cavalry was also thrown into the battle, just to complicate things.

The aim was to destroy the German Army Group Centre by attacking along a 300-mile front on a line from Smolensk to Minsk. In a pincer movement aimed at closing beyond Minsk, the Germans would be surrounded.

The Red Army had become a well-oiled fighting machine, but it was helped immeasurably by thousands of partisans fighting guerilla war behind the German lines. Many Wehrmacht divisions were kept busy just coping with them, similar to the situation in Yugoslavia, where Marshal Tito was operating so successfully.

The Germans were surprised to find the offensive continuing in full swing even after Minsk was in Russian hands. By July 15th, 25 German divisions were trapped, surrounded and destroyed. At least 300,000 troops were killed, wounded or taken prisoner, and 31 of 47 Corps and division commanders were captured. The battle was declared officially over when 57,000 German prisoners were marched through the streets of Moscow on July 17th, on their way to Siberia.

Minsk was a major battle and a major victory for the Red Army, but an additional 320,000 Germans became casualties elsewhere on the Russian front during that same period. Vast numbers, vast spaces, titanic battles—this is where the real war was fought that spelled the doom of Nazi Germany.

[See page 126]

FRANCE

A GREAT TANK BATTLE. After D-Day, German resistance was dogged, making Allied headway painfully slow. Hitler conceived a plan for a gigantic tank battle, to begin on August 7th, that would encircle the Allies and throw them back onto the beaches. It was a grandiose scheme, but it did result in the greatest tank battle on the western front.

Ten German tank divisions armed with 2,000 Tiger, Panther and Mark IV tanks faced the U.S. Shermans and British Churchills of 10 Allied divisions near Falaise, 25 miles inland from the Normandy beaches.

Tank battles are fluid in nature, involving mobile forces that require dynamic, on-the-spot generalship. The Wehrmacht excelled in these tactics, but on occasion Hitler would take personal control of a major battle and issue all kinds of crazy orders from his headquarters, where he was out of touch with immediate developments as they unfolded. Such was the situation at Falaise, where his inviolable orders led the field commander, Field Marshal von Kluge, to send 300,000 troops making up two Panzer armies straight into an Allied encircling movement that quickly became a gigantic trap.

But by August 29th, thousands of Germans made good their escape, leaving behind 50,000 dead, 200,000 prisoners and 1,300 wrecked tanks.

[See pages 130–31]

PARIS LIBERATED. With the Falaise disaster coming on the heels of the monstrous defeat at Minsk, Hitler, still recuperating from a recent attempt on his life, decreed vindictively that Paris be turned into another Stalingrad, defended block-by-block, house-by-house, room-by-room. The civilized world rejoices that Paris was not destroyed as Hitler intended. There was great relief when General Leclerc fought his way into Paris August 23rd with his Free French 2nd Armoured Division. There was spirited, last-ditch German resistance, but nothing like Hitler had ordered. In fact, the next day, commander of the Free French Forces General Charles de Gaulle himself was able to enter the city to cheering crowds.

Credit for the ease with which the city was surrendered goes both to the German commander, General von Cholitz, and to the citizens of Paris. The Parisiens effectively mounted such a demonstration of civil and military resistance—even seizing some buildings—that von Cholitz realized the futility of attempting to fight the advancing Allied army while coping at the same time with a guerilla uprising within the city.   *[See page 132]*

FRENCH RIVIERA INVADED. Operation Anvil was the long-planned Allied invasion of Europe through its "soft underbelly"—Churchill's famous phrase—meaning the Mediterranean side of Europe. On August 15th, the Allies finally mounted a third front by invading France's Riviera from Marseilles to Nice. Churchill's phrase was extremely apt, as there was almost no German resistance to the 7th Army of three American and five Free French divisions. Another whole division of paratroopers was dropped behind the German 19th Army defenses, which were quickly overcome. Such weak resistance allowed the Allied forces to race up the Rhone Valley on a direct line for Paris. This fast-approaching army may have been a factor in the early surrender of that city.

[See pages 130–31]

Canadians In Van Of Montgomery Army

WAR EXTRA

ALLIED FORCES LAND IN FRANCE

The Vancouver News-Herald

VOL. 12, NO. 37 VANCOUVER, B.C., TUESDAY, JUNE 6, 1944 ★ ★ ★ ★ PRICE 5c

General Eisenhower Officially Announces Historic Drive's Start

NEW YORK, June 6.—(AP)—The Office of War Information reported today this statement by Gen. Eisenhower was broadcast by Allied radios in London:

"People of western Europe! A landing was made this morning on the coast of France by troops of the Allied Expeditionary Force. This landing is part of the concerted United Nations plan for the liberation of Europe, made in conjunction with your great Russian allies.

"Although the initial assault may not have been made in your own country, the hour of your liberation is approaching." • •

By Associated Press

SUPREME HEADQUARTERS, ALLIED EXPEDITIONARY FORCE, June 6.—Gen. Dwight D. Eisenhower's headquarters announced today that Allied troops began landing on the northern coast of France this morning strongly supported by naval and air forces.

Text of the communique:

"Under the command of Gen. Eisenhower Allied naval forces supported by strong air forces began landing armies this morning on the northern coast of France."

Canadian forces were in the attack, headquarters said.

The Germans had said the landings extended between Le Havre and Cherbourg along the south side of the Bay of the Seine and along the northern Normandy coast.

A second announcement by SHAEF (Supreme Headquarters Allied Expeditionary Forces) said that "it is announced that Gen. B. L. Montgomery is in command of the army group carrying out the assault. This army group includes British, Canadian, and U.S. forces."

The Allied bulletin did not say exactly where the invasion was taking place, but Berlin earlier gave these details:

Allied naval forces, including heavy warships, are shelling Le Havre. "It is a terrific bombardment," Berlin said.

Allied parachute troops floating down along the Normandy coast were landing and being engaged by German shock troops.

Other Allied units were streaming ashore into Normandy from landing barges.

Berlin first announced the landings in a series of flashes that began about 6:30 a.m. (9:30 p.m. P.D.T.).

The Allied comunique was read over a trans-Atlantic hookup direct from General Eisenhower's headquarters at 12:32 P.D.T., designated "Communique No. 1."

(The News-Herald brought first word of the Allied attack in an "extra" street sale edition Monday evening.)

The official Allied announcement followed a welter of German reports.

Dunkerque and Calais, just across the channel coast from Britain, were under attack by strong formations of bombers, D.N.B. said.

In a special order of the day issued to all soldiers, sailors and airmen under his command, Gen. Eisenhower said:

"We will accept nothing except full victory."

Eisenhower told his men they were "embarking on a great crusade toward which we have striven these many months," and warned them that they were facing a tough, well-prepared enemy.

Berlin said the "centre of gravity" of the fierce fighting was at Caen, 30 miles southwest of Le Havre and 65 miles southeast of Cherbourg.

Caen is 10 miles inland from the sea, at the base of the 75-mile-wide Normandy peninsula.

Heavy fighting also was reported between Caen and Trouville.

One of Berlin's first claims was that the first British parachute division was badly mauled.

General Montgomery, hero of the African desert, was leading the assault of the Allied liberation army.

The German D.N.B. agency said Le Havre was being "violently bombarded at the present moment" (7 a.m. German time, or 10 p.m. P.D.T.).

"German naval forces are engaged in fighting with enemy landing craft off the coast."

Calais and Dunkerque, which Berlin said were under heavy air attack, are also important French ports along the invasion coast 150 miles northeast of Le Havre.

(Continued on Page Two)
SEE LANDINGS

B.B.C. Warns Dutch

NEW YORK, June 6.—(AP)—The B.B.C., in a Dutch language broadcast recorded by N.B.C., warned European underground workers today to report to their leaders with all speed and to "be prepared for anything."

"Keep away from military installations," the broadcast said. "Underground members report to your trusted leaders. Act with speed. Be prepared for anything.

"There is bombardment in the port of Le Havre," the B.B.C. quoted Berlin as saying.

LONDON, June 6.—A spokesman for Gen. Eisenhower, in a London broadcast, told the people living on Europe's invasion coast today that "A new phase of the Allied air offensive has started" and warned them to move inland to a depth of 35 kilometres (about 22 miles).

In a special broadcast over the B.B.C., directed to France and other coastal countries, the spokesman said:

"A new phase of the air offensive has started. It will affect the entire coastal zone situated not less than 35 kilometres inland from the French coast. People will be advised by special announcements dropped from Allied planes."

'U. S. TROOPS LAND ON WEST COAST OF AFRICA'

LONDON, June 6.—(AP)—The Paris radio says an important contingent of American troops has arrived in Angola, Portuguese West Africa."

The broadcast was unsubstantiated by any other source.

Angola is on Africa's west coast. To the north is French equatorial Africa and to the south is the Union of South Africa.

French Radio Off Air

LONDON, June 6. — (CP-Reuter) — The whole French radio network including the Paris, Bordeaux and Normandy transmitters went off the air at 7:25 a.m. B.S.T. (12:25 a.m. C.D.T.) today in the middle of a physical training broadcast.

Allied Armies Chase Germans Battered And Fleeing In Italy

By Associated Press

ROME, June 6. — Allied armor and motorized infantry have roared through the Eternal City, crossed the Tiber and are proceeding with the grim task of destroying two battered German armies fleeing to the north.

The British 8th Army, meanwhile, was advancing from the east and meeting stubborn German opposition, particularly northeast of Valmontone.

The enemy was bewildered by the slashing character of the Allied assault, which in 25 days had inflicted a major catastrophe on German forces in Italy and liberated Rome almost without damage to the historic city.

Five hundred heavy bombers blasted railyards at five points in northern Italy along which the Germans might attempt to move reinforcements to bolster Marshal Kesselring's beaten armies.

Pope Pius, addressing an enormous crowd including many Fifth Army soldiers in St. Peter's Square, expressed thanks to God that Rome had not been destroyed by war.

(In Naples, it was announced that King Victor Emmanuel had signed a retirement decree conferring his powers upon his son, Crown Prince Humbert, whom he named lieutenant-general of the realm. The monarch retained the title as head of the House of Savoy, thus remaining a king without power.)

The inhabitants' reception to the troops approached hysteria as the day wore on, and homemade confetti soon littered the streets. (Detailed story Page 11.)

Allied warplanes swept down highways leading northward. Twelve hundred Nazi transport vehicles were destroyed from dawn to dark Sunday and hundreds more yesterday.

City Girl Masquerading As A Boy, Forty-five Year Old Chinese Held

A strange case of a 15-year-old white girl masquerading as a boy to elude capture and allegedly living with a 45-year-old Chinese as his common-law wife was brought to light Monday by city police.

The Chinese, Chu Yung, 45, 223 E. Georgia St., was arrested by police and lodged in city jail on a charge of contributing to juvenile delinquency.

The girl is being held in juvenile home.

The girl's disguise was discovered by Constable D. W. Scotland at 2:45 Monday morning when he stopped what he thought to be a young man beside the Royal Theatre in the 100 block E. Hastings St. "The young man" gave his name as Thomas Jackson, 17, of Room 18, 223 E. Georgia St.

Constable Scotland, suspicious of the "youth's" mannerisms, took his captive to police headquarters, where she confessed to being a girl sought by police since April 5, when reported missing from her home in the city.

Constable Scotland and Constables D. I. MacGregor and J. K. Pinchin went to Room 18, 223 E. Georgia, where they found Chu.

The Chinese attempted to escape through the bedroom window, according to police. He was taken to city jail, where he was charged.

On his person police say they found notes pertaining to the girl.

The proprietor of the rooming house and his daughter both are said to have told police that the Chinese and the girl had been living together since registering in the rooming house on April 16.

GENERAL MONTGOMERY
In Command of Landing Forces

Ilsley For Federal Pensions Program

OTTAWA, June 6.—(CP) — Finance Minister Ilsley has told Commons that a contributory old age pension plan may not be instituted in Canada until the provinces agree to transfer their jurisdiction in the pension field to the Dominion government.

Mr. Ilsley said the present system of old age pensions was unsatisfactory because of the division of responsibility among the Dominion and the provinces, but he hoped it would soon be possible to have the system under one jurisdiction.

"I have never disguised the fact that I consider the present system unsatisfactory," Mr. Ilsley said during resumed debate on a $16,000,000 item in his war appropriations estimates providing a supplement for pensions to the aged and the blind.

"I have been saying for the past year or two now that I hoped we would soon have a satisfactory system under one jurisdiction where the pensions would be more generous and where they will be payable at an earlier age."

He said he felt a contributory pensions scheme entirely under Dominion administration would provide the solution to present problems.

(Continued on Page 2)
SEE PENSIONS.

Mackenzie Backs B. C. Jap Ouster

Complete repatriation of the Japanese after the war was urged by Hon. Ian Mackenzie, minister of pensions and national health, when he addressed the Monday afternoon session of the 10th convention of the Canadian Legion's Dominion Command in Hotel Vancouver.

The minister, backing a resolution of the B.C. Command of the Legion, adopted at its 15th convention here last week, declared that B.C. was not intended for the Japanese after the war.

"If I am then in public life I shall not remain 24 hours in any government or party which allows the Japanese on B.C. shores," he said.

Mr. Mackenzie asserted that the fruit lands, mines and fish resources of this province are for the "men from Ortona, Atlantic storms and air battles."

The resolution he endorsed was passed at the Friday session of the B.C. Command and stated that "with the termination of hostilities the Japanese and their children shall be shipped to Japan, and be forbidden ever again to re-enter Canada."

Discussing the rehabilitation plans of the government, Mr. Mackenzie said that "we shall make Canada as a whole a land worthy of the blood that has been shed, a worthy homeland for those who shall have saved it."

(Continued on Page Two)
See MACKENZIE

Germans Laconic

LONDON, June 6.—(CP) — The German agency D.N.B. commentator, Capt. Ludwig Sertorius, declared in a broadcast early today that the "great contest between the Reich and the Anglo-Americans has begun."

"The Allied landing in the west today has put the German armed forces in the mood which they express with a laconic 'they are coming'," he said.

Nazis Leave Starvation, Disease In Italy

'One Up And Two To Go'--FDR On Rome's Liberation

WASHINGTON, June 6. — (AP)—President Roosevelt last night hailed the fall of Rome as the first Axis capital to be liberated by the Allies but cautioned that the ultimate victory over Germany "still lies some distance ahead."

"That distance will be covered in due time—have no fear of that," the President said in a radio broadcast. "But it will be tough and it will be costly."

The President welcomed the fall of the Eternal City at the opening of his address with these words "one up and two to go!"

He continued, however, that Germany has not yet been driven to surrender and observed:

"Germany has not yet been driven to the point where she will be unable to recommence world conquest a generation hence."

The President extended to Italy the invitation to help in establishing a lasting peace and said, "all the other nations opposed to Fascism and Nazism should help give Italy a chance.

"The Germans, after years of domination in Rome, left the people in the Eternal City on the verge of starvation. We and the British will do everything we can to bring them relief. . . We have already begun to save the lives of the men, women and children of Rome."

The Italian people "are capable of self-government," Mr. Roosevelt continued. "We do not lose sight of their virtues as a peace-loving nation."

Speaking of the military operations still to come in Europe, the President said:

"We shall have to push through a long period of greater effort and fiercer fighting before we get into Germany itself. The Germans have retreated thousands of miles, all the way from the gates of Cairo, through Libya and Tunisia and Sicily and southern Italy.

"They have suffered heavy losses, but not great enough yet to cause collapse."

In Italy, the President said, the people had lived so long "under the corrupt rule of Mussolini that, in spite of the tinsel at the top, their economic condition had grown steadily worse.

"Our troops have found starvation, malnutrition, disease, a deteriorating education and lowered public health — all by-products of the Fascist misrule."

(Continued on Page 11)

INVASION SIDELIGHTS

NEW YORK, June 6.—(N.Y. Times)—Broadway received the flash from German sources that the invasion had begun with skepticism and indifference.

Washington Aroused

WASHINGTON, June 6.—The capital was aroused to excitement in the early morning hours by dramatic radio bulletins that German broadcasters had announced the invasion of Europe.

Director Elmer Davis of the office of war information rushed to his headquarters immediately after his aides advised him of the enemy broadcasts.

"We have no more information than you have," he told reporters. "I'll stay here until I find out whether the story is true or not."

Cover Entire Area

LONDON, June 6.—(CP) — The Berlin radio said today that "combined British-American landing operations against the western coast of Europe from the sea and air are stretching over the entire area between Cherbourg and Le Havre."

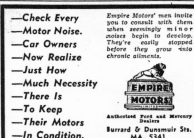

Eisenhower Announces:

INVASION!

11,000 Planes, 4000 Ships Strike

ALLIES WIN BEACHHEAD IN FRANCE

Churchill Hints at Surprise

SUPREME HEADQUARTERS, ALLIED EXPEDITIONARY FORCE, June 6.—Allied troops have secured a beachhead and dug in, military circles here heard early this afternoon. It is not known at present how deep the penetrations are.

Although the initial phase of the invasion apparently was confined to the Normandy coast of France, an Allied headquarters spokesman hinted that operations soon may be extended to Holland and possibly to other countries in Western Europe.

From AP and BUP Dispatches

SUPREME HEADQUARTERS, Allied Expeditionary Force, London, June 6.—Allied armies today stormed northern France with history's greatest invasion armada—11,000 planes, 4000 ships and thousands of smaller craft—and in the first few hours seized beachheads that threatened to isolate the Normandy Peninsula and win a railroad pointed straight at Paris.

Some six hours after the first waves of American, British and Canadian assault forces landed by sea and air on the Normandy peninsula, Prime Minister Churchill told Commons that the invasion was proceeding "according to plan."

"Obstacles which were constructed in the sea have not proved so difficult as was apprehended," Churchill said.

"The fire of shore batteries has been largely quelled.

"Massed air-borne landings have been successfully effected behind enemy lines and landings on the beaches are proceeding at various points at the present time."

Churchill declared that "there already are hopes that tactical surprise has been achieved."

Obviously enjoying his resumption of the role of the great war reporter, Churchill added:

"I cannot, of course, commit myself to any particular details as reports are coming in at rapid succession. So far, the commanders who are engaged have reported that everything is proceeding according to plan—and what a plan!"

'Monty' Leads Troops

The invasion was announced by Gen. Dwight Eisenhower, Supreme Allied Commander at 9:32 a.m. (12:32 a.m. Vancouver time), in a message to his troops.

Commander of the army group now storming France was revealed to be Gen. Sir Bernard L. Montgomery, "Monty of El Alamein," who led the famed British 8th Army all the way from the approaches to Alexandria, Egypt, to southern Italy.

His command included American, British and Canadian troops.

German news agencies said Allied shock forces and paratroops landed along the north coast of the Normandy Pen-

Please Turn to Page Two

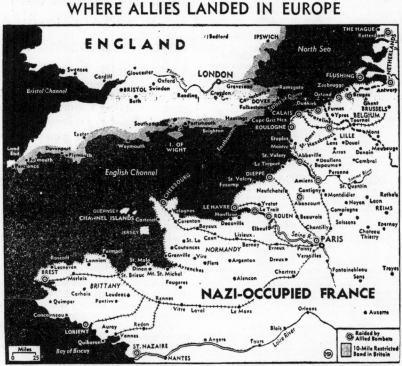

WHERE ALLIES LANDED IN EUROPE

NAZI-OCCUPIED FRANCE

Allied forces landed in German-occupied northern France today, crossing the English Channel from Britain. There have been no details from Allied headquarters as to the exact places where the landings were made, but the German radio has reported fighting around Caen, in the neighborhood of the big French port of Le Havre, and many paratroop landings throughout Normandy.

insula—which juts out from France some 90 to 110 miles below the English south coast—all the way from the Cherbourg area at the northern tip to Le Havre at the mouth of the Seine, 110 miles northwest of Paris.

The Germans said the heaviest fighting developed in the area of Caen, on the main Cherbourg-Paris railway some nine miles inland from the mouth of Orne River.

Air-borne troops were landing deep inland on the peninsula, the official Nazi DNB agency said, in an effort to seize a number of strategic airfields, cut off the Normandy Peninsula, and capture Cherbourg, one of the two main ports for Paris.

Nothing Less Than Victory

Ringing in their ears, the British, American and Canadian forces who made the landings had these words from their Supreme Commander, Gen. Dwight D. Eisenhower:

"You are about to embark on a great crusade. The eyes of the world are upon you and the hopes and prayers of all liberty-loving peoples go with you. . . .

"We will accept nothing less than full victory."

Eisenhower himself wished Godspeed to the parachutists who were the first to land on the enemy-held soil of France.

For three hours previous to the Allied announcement the German radio had been pouring forth a series of flashes reporting that the Allies were landing between Le Havre and Cherbourg along the south side of the Bay of the Seine and along the north coast of Normandy.

This would be across the Channel and almost due south of such British ports as Hastings, Brighton, Ports-

See "Canadians Join"

Crerar to Canadians

Germans Fear Our Fighting Qualities

By ROSS MUNRO
Canadian Press War Correspondent
Copyright, 1944, by the Canadian Press

WITH THE CANADIAN ARMY IN FRANCE, June 6—Lt.-Gen. H. D. G. Crerar, CB, DSO, the Canadian army commander, sent this personal message to Canadian assault forces on the eve of embarkation for the invasion of Continental Europe:

It is impossible for me to speak to each one of you, but, by means of this personal message, I want all ranks of the Canadian army to know what is in my mind, as the hour approaches when we go forward into battle.

I have complete confidence in our ability to meet the tests which lie ahead. We are excellently trained and equipped. The quality of both the senior and junior leadership is of the highest. As Canadians, we inherit military characteristics which were feared by the enemy in the last great war. They will be still more feared before this war terminates.

This would be across the channel and almost due phase of the war with full faith in our cause, with calm confidence in our abilities and with grim determination to finish quickly and unmistakably this job we came overseas to do.

As in 1918, in Italy and in northwest Europe, we will hit the enemy again and again until, at some not distant time, converging Allied armies link together and we will be rejoined, in victory, with our comrades of the First Canadian Corps.

Premier to Speak

OTTAWA, June 6 (CP)—Prime Minister Mackenzie King will make a brief broadcast on the Allied invasion of Europe over the CBC national network.

We enter into this decisive

BULLETINS

NEW YORK, June 6—(AP)—The BBC, in a broadcast recorded by the federal communications commission, said that King George would deliver a special broadcast tonight at 9 p.m. London time (12 noon Vancouver time).

* * *

LONDON, June 6—(BUP)—The weather over the Straits of Dover on invasion day:

The sun broke out after a daybreak shower. Broken clouds swept up from the northwest. The wind blew fairly hard during the night but lost some of its strength after dawn. A moderate sea was running.

Visibility was good and improving. Temperature was around the 60's. The barometer had fallen slightly in the last 12 hours. High tides at Dover and Calais today, 12:50 a.m. and 12:48 p.m.

* * *

LONDON, June 6—(CP)—The German radio reported today that four British parachute divisions had landed between Le Havre and Cherbourg in France.

This was four times the size of the Nazi parachute forces dropped on Crete in the Mediterranean.

* * *

LONDON, June 6—(UP)—The German Transocean news agency said today that Allied paratroops were landing on the islands of Jersey and Guernsey, west of the Norman Peninsula.

* * *

NEW YORK, June 6—(AP)—The Berlin radio broadcast a DNB dispatch today claiming that one Allied cruiser and a large landing vessel carrying troops had been sunk in the area of St. Vaast La Hougue, 15 miles southeast of Cherbourg.

* * *

NEW YORK, June 6—(AP)—King Haakon of Norway in an invasion broadcast today to his homeland warned his people against premature uprisings, said a broadcast from supreme headquarters, Allied Expeditionary Force, heard by NBC.

The King broadcast special orders to both organized and unorganized resistance groups in Norway.

* * *

LONDON, June 6—(AP) — The German agency DNB said in a broadcast shortly before 10 a.m. (1 a.m. Vancouver Time), that Anglo-American troops had been reinforced at dawn at the mouth of the Seine River in the Le Havre area.

* * *

LONDON, June 6—(CP)—The Berlin radio said today that "combined British-American landing operations against the western coast of Europe from the sea and air are stretching over the entire area between Cherbourg and Le Havre."

* * *

SUPREME HEADQUARTERS, ALLIED EXPEDITIONARY FORCE, LONDON, June 6—(BUP)—The invasion will be a rough show but it will succeed.

That's the word of the man who today commanded the Allied army group attacking the shores of Hitler-held Europe—Gen. Sir Bernard L. Montgomery.

Canada Proud, Says Premier

OTTAWA, June 6—(CP)—In a statement on the invasion issued early today Prime Minister Mackenzie King declared:

"We have received official word that the invasion of Europe has begun and that Canadian troops are among the Allied forces landing this morning in France. Canada will be proud to learn that her troops are being supported by units from the Royal Canadian Navy and of the Royal Canadian Air Force.

"Great liberating operations from the west may prove to be the decisive phase of the war against Nazi Germany.

"The fighting is certain to be bitter and costly. We must not expect early results. We should be prepared for local reverses as well as successes.

"No one can say how long this phase of the war may last, but we have every reason for confidence in the ultimate outcome.

"The hearts of all in Canada will be filled with silent prayer for the success of our own and Allied forces and for the speedy liberation of Europe."

Canadians In Van

ALLIES SMASH INTO CONTINENT

Churchill Tells Cheering House

4000 Allied Ships Carry Big Armies

LONDON, June 6. — (CP) — Prime Minister Churchill told the House of Commons today that an immense Allied armada of 4000 ships with several thousand smaller craft had carried Allied forces across the Channel for the invasion of Europe.

Mr. Churchill also said that massed air-borne landings had been successfully effected behind the Germans' lines.

"The landings on the beaches are proceeding at various points at the present time," Mr. Churchill said.

"The fire of shore batteries has been largely quelled."

He said that "obstacles which were constructed in the sea have not proved so difficult as was apprehended."

The Prime Minister said the Allied forces are sustained by about 11,000 first-line aircraft, which can be drawn upon as needed.

"So far," he said, "the commanders who are engaged report that everything is proceeding according to plan."

"And what a plan!" he declared.

Mr. Churchill said the vast operation was "undoubtedly the most complicated and difficult which has ever occurred."

To cheers of members, Mr. Churchill took "formal cognizance of the liberation of Rome," and added:

"American and other forces of the 5th Army broke through the enemy's last lines and entered Rome, where Allied troops have been received with joy by the population.

"This entry and liberation of Rome means that we shall have power to defend it from hostile air attacks and deliver it from the famine with which it was threatened."

"Britain's war leader paid high tribute both to Gen. Sir Harold Alexander and Lt.-Gen. Mark W. Clark in Italy and said: "Complete unity prevails throughout the Allied armies. . . There is complete confidence in the supreme commander, Gen. Eisenhower, and his lieutenants, and Expeditionary Force Commander Montgomery."

Invasion Time-table

Invasion fleet comprised 4000 ships.

Eleven thousand first line aircraft flew with Allies

First landings reported at Le Havre, Cherbourg.

Four parachute divisions landed behind enemy lines.

Landings made from 9 p.m., Monday, to 11:25 p.m. Vancouver time.

First official announcement was made at 12:32 Vancouver time (Tuesday).

First German invasion bulletins 9 p.m., Monday, Vancouver time.

Final BULLETINS

FOUR PARACHUTE DIVISIONS

LONDON, June 6.—(AP)—The German radio reported today that four British parachute divisions had landed between Le Havre and Cherbourg in France. This was four times the size of the Nazi parachute forces dropped on Crete in the Mediterranean.

DIEPPE AREA ATTACKED

LONDON, June 6.—(AP)—The Berlin radio, in a broadcast recorded by NBC, said this morning that strong Allied air attacks have been launched on the Dieppe area.

ALLIES REINFORCED

LONDON, June 6.—(AP)—The German agency D.N.B. said in a broadcast shortly before 10 a.m. (3 a.m., C.D.T.) that Anglo-American troops had been reinforced at dawn at the mouth of the Seine River in the Le Havre area.

GREATEST CANADIAN ARMADA

LONDON, June 6. — (CP Cable) — The greatest force of Canadian bombers ever put in the air today roared across the English Channel to attack three targets in France.

ALLIED PLANES OVER REICH

LONDON, June 6.—(AP)—The Luxembourg radio announces today that Allied planes were over southwestern Germany.

CLAIM CRUISER SUNK

NEW YORK, June 6.—(AP)—The Berlin radio broadcast a D.N.B. despatch today claiming that one Allied cruiser and a large landing vessel carrying troops had been sunk in the area of St. Vaast la Hougue, 15 miles southeast of Cherbourg.

KING TO BROADCAST

NEW YORK, June 6.—(AP)—The BBC, in a broadcast recorded by the Federal Communications Commission, said that King George would deliver a special broadcast tonight at 9 o'clock London time (noon Vancouver time).

LAND ON CHANNEL ISLANDS

LONDON, June 6.—(CP)—Allied troops have landed on the Channel Islands of Guernsey and Jersey, the German agency Transocean News said.

NAVAL BATTLES RAGE

SUPREME HEADQUARTERS, ALLIED EXPEDITIONARY FORCE, June 6.—(AP)—German destroyers and E-boats are rushing into the operational area off the northern coast of France. German broadcasts said a furious battle between Nazi E-boats and Allied warships was raging off Le Havre.

H-Hour for the invasion ranged from 6 to 8 a.m. (9 p.m. to 11 p.m., Monday (Vancouver time).

GERMAN RAIL CENTRE HIT

LONDON, June 6.—(AP)—R.A.F. bombers last night blasted the northwest German railway centre of Osnabruck, the Air Ministry announced today. All planes returned safely.

Invasion Forces Slash Inland From Beaches Along Normandy Coast

(By Associated Press.)

An 8th U.S.A.A.F. Photo Reconnaissance Base, June 6.—(AP)—Allied Landing Forces have established beachheads on the coast of Northern France and are slashing their way inland, the first Photo Reconnaissance pilots back from the scene of the initial thrust said today.

Supreme Headquarters, Allied Expeditionary Force, June 6.—Allied forces including Canadians under Lieut.-Gen. H. G. Crerar, landed in Northern France early today in history's greatest overseas operation, designed to destroy the power of Hitler's Germany and wrest enslaved Europe from the Nazis.

The German radio said the landings were made from Le Havre to Cherbourg, along the north coast of Normandy and the south side of the bay of the Seine.

Allied headquarters did not specify the locations, but left no doubt whatever that the landings were on a gigantic scale.

Ringing in their ears, the British, American and Canadian forces who made the landings had these words from their supreme commander, General Dwight D. Eisenhower:

"You are about to embark on a great crusade. The eyes of the world are upon you, and the hopes and prayers of all liberty-loving peoples go with you . . .

"We will accept nothing less than full victory."

Roughly three hours after the invasion started, Canadian fighter pilots reporting back to their station said: "Things seemed well organized on the beach," though there was "lots of shooting going on at the beachhead."

One pilot said: "I've never seen so many ships in all my life."

The German radio filled the air with invasion flashes for three hours before the formal Allied announcement came at 7:32 a.m. G.M.T. (12:32 Vancouver time).

It acknowledged deep penetrations of the Cherbourg Peninsula by Allied parachute and glider troops in great strength.

The assault was supported by gigantic bombardments from Allied warships and planes, which the Germans admitted set the coastal areas ablaze. The fleet included several British and United States battleships.

A senior officer at Supreme Headquarters said rough water caused "awful anxiety" for the seaborne troops, but that the landings were made successfully, although some soldiers were undoubtedly seasick.

The sun broke through heavy clouds periodically this morning after a daybreak shower. The wind had blown fairly hard during the night but moderated somewhat with the dawn. The weather outlook remained somewhat unsettled.

Supreme Headquarters' first communique was this single sentence:

"Under the command of General Eisenhower, Allied naval forces, supported by strong air forces, began landing Allied armies this morning on the northern coast of France."

It was announced moments later that Britain's General Sir Bernard L. Montgomery, hero of the 8th Army victories in North Africa, Sicily and Italy, was in charge of the assault, and the announcement added: "This army group includes British, Canadian and United States forces."

(Continued on Page 2)
See INVASION.

INVASION COAST

THE VANCOUVER DAILY PROVINCE

50th YEAR—NO. 60 | OFFICIAL FORECAST: FAIR AND MILD. | VANCOUVER, B.C., TUESDAY, JUNE 6, 1944—26 PAGES | ★ ★ ★ | PRICE 5 CENTS | BY CARRIER $1.00 per month

CANADIANS UNDER MAJ.-GEN. G. H. CRERAR ACHIEVE INITIAL OBJECTIVE

Amphibious Allied Invasion Armies Plunge Into France, Advance On Broad Front Against "Weak Opposition"

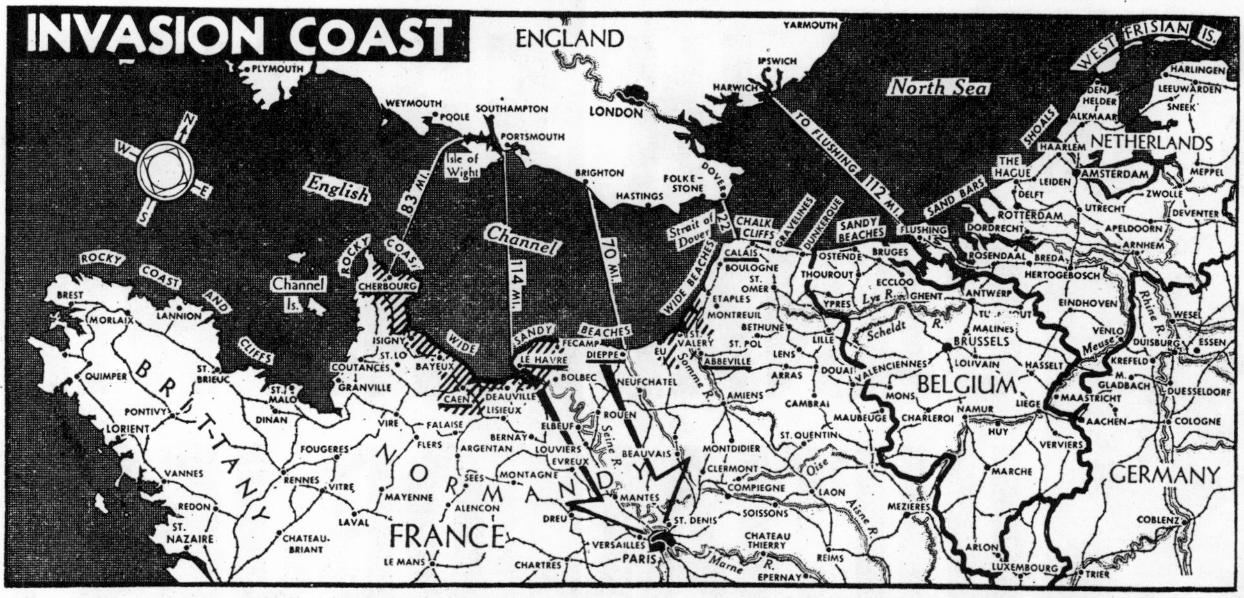

Shaded area of French coast indicates regions where Allied invasion armies are reported to have established beachheads and where airborne troops have landed.

11,000 Planes, 4000 Ships Take Part in Big Push

CHURCHILL PLEASED

OTTAWA, June 6.—(CP)—Amid an uproar in the Commons today, Prime Minister King said that Canadian invasion forces had gained their initial objective and were making good progress.

By WES GALLAGHER.
(Associated Press War Correspondent.)

SUPREME HEADQUARTERS, ALLIED EXPEDITIONARY FORCE, June 6.—Allied forces, including Canadians under Maj.-Gen. Crerar, landed in the Normandy area of northwest France today and have thrust several miles inland against unexpectedly slight German opposition, with losses "much smaller than had been anticipated."

The grand assault—scheduled for Monday but postponed until today because of bad weather—found the highly-vaunted German defenses much less formidable in every department than had been feared.

Airborne troops who led the assault before daylight on a huge scale suffered "extremely small" losses in the air, even though the great plane fleets extended across 200 miles of sky and used navigation lights to keep formation.

Naval losses for the seaborne forces were described at headquarters as "very, very small." 4000 ships and several thousand smaller craft participated in taking the British, Canadian and American troops to France.

Coastal batteries were almost silenced by the guns of the British and Allied fleets, including battleships, and the beachheads were speedily consolidated.

The German radio said the scene of the landings was a 100-mile stretch of coast from Cherbourg to Le Havre, around the bay of the Seine and the northeast shore of the Normandy peninsula.

Prime Minister Churchill, in announcing the successful invasion to the House of Commons at noon—six hours after the first seaborne troops landed—said the landings were "the first of a series."

LOSSES LIGHT.

"Many dangers and difficulties which this time last night appeared extremely formidable are behind us," the Prime Minister added. "The passage of the sea has been made with far less loss than we apprehended.

"The resistance of the batteries has been greatly weakened by the bombing by the air force and superior bombardment of our ships quickly reduced their fire to dimensions which did not affect the problem."

"The outstanding feature has been the landings of airborne troops on a scale far larger than anything ever seen before," he said. "These landings took place with extremely little loss and with great accuracy. The airborne troops are well established and the landings and followups are all proceeding with very much less loss than we expected.

CAPTURE BRIDGES.

"There is fighting proceeding at various points and we have captured various bridges which are of importance and which were not blown up. There is even fighting proceeding in the town of Caen inland."

Mr. Churchill disclosed that 11,000 Allied planes were available as needed for the battle. The Allied bombers, climaxing 96 hours of steady pounding, lashed German coastal defenses this morning with 10,000 tons of explosives.

Fighters who went out to guard the beaches had little to do, however, as the German air force up till noon had flown only 50 sorties against the invading forces.

The Germans were known to have probably 1750 fighters and

(Continued on Page 2.)
See INVASION.

"IT HAS COME"

Today in Europe

Special cables from the London Times and A. C. Cummings, London Bureau of The Vancouver Daily Province

By A.C. CUMMINGS

LONDON, June 6. — Wave of profound relief, eager hope and keen expectation swept over Britain today when officials gave out news the greatest air, sea and land invasion in history had been launched.

"At last it has come," said everybody, who month by month, week by week, day by day ever since February last, had been expecting every week-end to bring them the fateful news that hundreds of thousands of their husbands, fathers and sons would be hurled in battle against the fortress of Europe, reputed to be the most deadly defended ever known.

Now that historic "D" Day has come, the nation looks back upon the preparations for it, extending over two and a half years since the second front was first publicly agitated for, and believes its work and sacrifices during that long laborious time well worth while.

Will Test Work

Today and for many months to come that work will be tested in the fire of battle. It has involved production of machinery for warfare in unparalleled scale. All Britain has been a vast factory for four years.

It has turned out secret new weapons in large numbers, provided warships, aircraft guns and equipment at a rate undreamed of five years ago, trained splendid young men for the mechanized army, keen as a razor for action and provided it with leadership, tried and tested by modern warfare.

In recent weeks I have watched pouring along quiet English country lanes long convoys of trucks, guns and vehicles bound for the invasion bases and all bearing the white star that marks them as for use in continental battles.

Canadians Keen

Once I came upon Canadian troops hidden in the woods around one of "stately homes of England." Men were almost riotously eager to know "When do we get cracking? It can't be long now."

They were cheerful and confident and ready.

And out upon the southern downlands I have watched hour after hour mighty air fleets hurtle in thunder across the summer skies to disappear in the English Channel's blue haze.

They too were part of Britain's pre-invasion preparations.

What went into building up these air fleets can only be told after the end of the war lifts the censorship on information useful to the enemy.

Hardly for an hour during the last 14 weeks have sirens ceased to shriek warning in German, French, Belgian and Dutch cities. Each 24 hours has brought its story of havoc, wrought to the enemy communications, and the Germans have taken to shipping to carry supplies. Aerial torpedoes and rocket projectiles have littered the narrow seas from Heligoland to the Bay of Biscay with wrecks. There is no question but that the Huns' invasion defenses have been crippled in some places by the might of the Allied air assault.

Their communications have been interrupted to such an extent that military commentators here agree that the enemy has been deprived of "essential supplies" just when he most needs them.

Moreover, the once all-power-

(Continued on Page 2.)
See CUMMINGS.

Give Day's Pay To Red Cross To Mark Invasion

CHEMAINUS, June 6.—Between 300 and 400 workers at Chemainus Lumber Co. here are planning to give a day's pay to the Red Cross to mark Invasion Day.

"We feel that now the invasion is started the Red Cross will need all the help it can get and more," a union spokesman said today.

West Vancouver Services Tonight

WEST VANCOUVER, June 6.—A special invasion service will be held tonight at 8 o'clock at Ambleside Park, to which all citizens of the municipality are invited. The clergy of all denominations will have charge of the service. The Boys' Band will play.

Cut Off In Coast Area

NAZIS TRAPPED BELOW ROME

By SID FEDER
Associated Press War Correspondent

NAPLES, June 6.—Allied 5th Army forces drove steadily beyond liberated Rome today, some units plunging as much as five miles out from the Tiber River against what was officially termed "only weak resistance."

"The battle to destroy the enemy continues without pause," said a communique.

Lt.-Gen. Clark's troops have crossed or reached the Tiber all the way from Rome to the sea and enemy divisions still in the flatlands south of the city are in desperate straits.

ESCAPE CUT OFF.

In the coastal area alone well over 2000 Nazis apparently will be unable to scramble out of the Allied net because all Tiber bridges from Rome to the sea have been blown up or captured.

In Rome, however, where 11 crossings remained intact, 5th Army formations poured across in a constant stream to chase the Germans fleeing northward.

(French troops have captured Tivoli on the Rome-Avezzano highway, 18 miles east of the capital, the B.B.C. announced.

Canadian corps troops are believed out of action, resting after their drive up the Sacco Valley.

In the area immediately north of Rome Monday more than 375 German vehicles were destroyed or damaged by fighter-bombers. Heavy bombers meanwhile pounded northern Italy rail lines, particularly in the Po Valley.

Fined for Setting Fire

KAMLOOPS, June 6.—(CP)—John Ross was fined $50 and costs, or two months, when he was convicted on a charge of starting a fire during the closed season.

BULLETINS

COASTAL GUNS WRECKED

NEW YORK. June 6. —(AP)— An N.B.C. reporter who flew over 20 miles of the invasion coast this morning said "not a single German coastal gun was firing in the entire invasion zone," and N.B.C. said this indicated "we have completely knocked out initial line of defenses of the much-vaunted Atlantic Wall."

1000 BOMBERS HIT FRANCE

SUPREME HEADQUARTERS, Allied Expeditionary Force, June 6. — (AP) — More than 1000 heavy bombers continued attacks on French coastal defenses by daylight today.

NEW ITALIAN CABINET

NAPLES, June 6.—(AP)—Premier Marshal Pietro Badoglio dissolved his Italian Government today and was charged by Crown Prince Humbert with forming a new government to include political leaders in liberated Rome.

REPORT ALLIED VICTORY

BARCELONA, Spain, June 6.—(AP)—German reports received here today said Allied forces were in full possession of Honfleur at the month of the Seine. Honfleur is across the river from Le Havre.

NAZIS CLAIM SUCCESS

LONDON, June 6.—(AP)—German forces launching a counter-attack knocked out 35 heavy Allied tanks at Asnelles in the Seine Bay area by noon, a D.N.B. report from Berlin said today.

640 NAVAL GUNS

SUPREME HEADQUARTERS, ALLIED EXPEDITIONARY FORCE, June 6.—(AP,—More than 640 naval guns ranging from four to 16 inches in size are bombarding the beaches and enemy strongpoints in support of landing forces, it was announced today.

FIERCE FIGHT AT CAEN

SOMEWHERE IN ENGLAND, June 6.—(AP)—Canadian fighter pilots, returning from their third sortie of the day over the invasion beachhead, reported a few hours before dusk tonight that Allied land troops were penetrating inland from their beachhead, particularly around Caen.

"It looks as if fierce fighting is going on around there," one flyer said.

LONDON, June 6.—(AP)—The Paris radio today broadcast an appeal by Marshal Petain to Frenchmen to refrain from actions "which would call down upon you tragic reprisals."

"Time for Prayer"

CITY ACCEPTS NEWS QUIETLY

Citizens have taken the awesome news of all-out Allied assault on France in their stride, with calm confidence and grim determination.

Thousands are praying to Almighty God to "see our boys through their ordeal by fire."

Church doors are opened wide.

Evidence of the prevailing spirit was the fact that The Vancouver Daily Province telephone exchange was congested throughout the latter part of the day with enquiries as to where church services were to be held.

Except for crowds on downtown streets, the darkened city seemed to sleep through the early stages of invasion.

Comparatively few heard the first German claims of Allied landings. Official confirmation did not come through from General Eisenhower until 12:30 a.m. today.

ANTI-CLIMAX.

Radio news programs were on the air all night, but Vancouver slept on.

The "real" invasion was almost an anti-climax after months of anxious waiting and after Saturday's erroneous radio report that electrified the continent.

The first German report flashed to the world about 9:30 p.m.

In a few minutes Vancouver theatre audiences, notified that The Vancouver Daily Province special invasion service had re-

(Continued on Page 2.)
See CITY.

Grain Exchange Halts Trading For Prayer

WINNIPEG, June 6.—(CP)—Traders on the Winnipeg Grain Exchange today observed a two-minute prayer period, a tribute to Canadian and Allied forces in the invasion of Europe.

Announcement of the invasion brought a wave of buying in the rye market. Prices advanced as much as 4½ cents a bushel, but values dropped quickly when selling orders developed. At the high point, the July future was quoted at $1.11, but it later dropped to $1.08⅛.

Strawberry Strike Planned by Growers

HANEY, June 6.—Plans for "a strawberry strike" were made at a meeting Monday by berry growers of this district.

If other growers of the lower mainland and Fraser Valley give support, delivery of all crated strawberries will likely be halted for the season.

Suggestion is that growers pack their entire crop in preservatives.

INVASION BREVITIES

LONDON, June 6.—(AP)—Reuters)—Prime Minister Churchill and the King late today visited supreme headquarters Allied Expeditionary Force and headquarters of the Allied Expeditionary Air Force.

WASHINGTON, June 6. —(AP)—Closeted in his bedroom, President Roosevelt spent the early morning hours of the invasion writing a prayer for victory for the Allied forces of liberation.

Mr. Roosevelt will broadcast at 7 o'clock P.D.T. tonight, with the hope that the United States will join him in the prayer he wrote.

MONTREAL, June 6.—(CP)—The Montreal Stock Exchange and curb market observed a two-minute period of silence today in tribute to fighting men participating in the Allied invasion of the European continent.

WITH THE CANADIAN INVASION FORCES, June 6. —(CP)—The Canadian ensign—popularly known as the "Canadian Flag"—went into battle today with Canadian forces for the first time in this war. Up to now, the Union Jack has been flown.

Shipyard Workers Pray for Victory In Mass Service

More than 4000 workers at West Coast Shipbuilders bowed their heads and silently prayed for the success of the Allied invasion, at a service in the yards today.

The shipyard workers gathered during their lunch period to listen to a service conducted by Rev. T. W. Scott, and a lesson read by W. D. McLaren, general manager.

At the close of the ceremony the huge chorus sang "Eternal Father, Strong to Save,' and "Nearer My God to Thee."

Chronology of D-Day

9:37 p.m. Vancouver time—German Agency Transocean broadcasts that Allied invasion has begun.

10:00 p.m.—German D.N.B. Agency broadcasts Le Havre being bombarded violently and German naval craft fighting Allied landing craft off coast.

10:56 p.m.—Calais radio says: "This is D-day."

11:31 p.m.—Spokesman from Gen. Eisenhower in broadcast from London warns people of European coast that "a new phase of the Allied air offensive has begun" and orders them to move 22 miles inland.

12:29 a.m.—Berlin radio says: "First centre of gravity is Caen," big city at base of Normandy peninsula.

12:32 a.m.—Supreme Headquarters, Allied Expeditionary Force, announces that Allied armies began landing on northern coast of France.

12:40 a.m.—Allies announce Gen. Sir Bernard L. Montgomery is in command of assault army, comprising Britons, Americans and Canadians.

12:42 a.m.—Berlin says heavy Allied warships are shelling Le Havre and parachute troops are floating down on Normandy.

1:07 a.m.—Germans say Allies reinforced at dawn at mouth of Seine near Le Havre.

1:47 a.m.—French patriots warned to evacuate areas 22 miles coasts to escape aerial bombardment.

2:35 a.m.—Berlin claims cruiser and landing boat sunk off Cherbourg.

2:49 a.m.—Enemy says four British parachute divisions landed between Le Havre and Cherbourg.

2:24 a.m.—Prime Minister Churchill says 4000 ships and several thousand lesser craft formed probably world's greatest invasion armada; "Everything is proceeding according to plan."

4:03 a.m.—German destroyers and E-boats rushing into operational area and "no doubt are being dealt with," headquarters says. H-hour announced as between 6 and 8 a.m. British summer time (9 p.m. Monday and 11 p.m. Monday, Vancouver time.)

4:08 a.m.—Allied landing forces establishes beachheads and are advancing inland, aerial pictures show.

4:24 a.m.—Swedish reporters in Berlin report dozen landings with main attack toward Caen.

4:32 a.m.—Supreme headquarters announces beachhead secured and dug in.

5:01 a.m.—Germans announce Allied landings on Channel Islands of Guernsey and Jersey; say Allied tanks land at Arromanches midway between Cherbourg and Le Havre; Allies incessantly employing assault boats off Oystreham.

5:10 a.m.—Paris radio says battle in Normandy "seems to be gaining depth."

5:34 a.m.—Berlin reports "fierce fighting going on everywhere" with Nazi counterthrusts in progress.

6:20 a.m.—Marshal Petain broadcasts to Frenchmen to avoid reprisals.

LANDS NEAR R.C.A.F. PLANE WRECK

U.S. Rescue Blimp Crashes

Caught in a downdraft near Mount Whymper, Vancouver Island, while aiding in a search for missing R.C.A.F. flyers, a United States Navy blimp crashed Monday afternoon.

All aboard escaped injury.

The crew consisted of nine U. S. officers and men; and two R.C.A.F. liaison officers.

They are making their way slowly through heavy forest to the base camp of searchers for the crew of the R.C.A.F. bomber which hit the side of the mountain on May 26.

Members of the blimp crew, forced down near the scene of the bomber crash, saw no sign of the missing R.C.A.F. flyers. One body was found by searchers on Monday. A burial service will be held at the scene.

Extent of damage to the blimp is not known. It is believed to have been deflated when it ripped into tree tops.

Ground parties are combing the rough terrain for the other four men who were aboard the R.C.A.F. bomber. There is some hope that they may have parachuted before the crash and may be located alive in the bush.

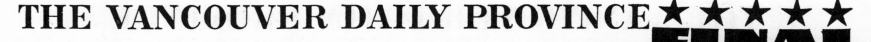

THE VANCOUVER DAILY PROVINCE ★★★★★ FINAL

50th YEAR—NO. 60 | VANCOUVER, B.C., TUESDAY, JUNE 6, 1944—26 PAGES | PRICE 5 CENTS | BY CARRIER $1.00 per month

By GAULT MacGOWAN.
Copyright, 1944, by Daily Province. From North ... Newspaper Alliance.

AN AIR BASE IN BRITAIN, June 6. — Daybreak came to this British base accompanied by the incessant roar of thousands of planes and it reached the French invasion coast in a thunderous assault of bombs which blasted at miles of Nazi fortifications.

This is the second front.

I saw it open from the air in a Marauder bomber to be picked up by a terrific naval bombardment as the first of our troops were nosing into the shore from their landing craft under a protective screen of screaming steel. Through a great sea of clouds, 5000 feet thick in places, the great Allied Air Force arm threw 11,000 aircraft into the most stupendous assault man has made upon man since history has been recorded.

Through it all the vaunted Luftwaffe did not put in an appearance.

NO VAST RESISTANCE.

Before returning to this base to write an eye-witness account of our break-through of the Hitler fortress, I flew for miles inland. Patches of flack dotted the sky, but there were no German pilots to contest our way and peering down on the French roads and fields I saw no German armored divisions on the move. But the fields were dotted with parachutes where airborne Allied forces had landed early and were already attempting to consolidate their positions.

Riding high above the earth, I could see the first signs of the battle below through a naval smoke screen and we could hear and feel the detonations of warships shelling the coast.

GREAT ARMADA

Contrary to expectations, the Channel wasn't jammed with shipping. On every hand, however, there were forces of ships pounding at the coast with their guns or bringing up troops to pour through the gaps ripped in the German lines by bombs and shells.

The world has never seen, nor can the mind readily conceive of the air umbrella which the Allies raised to cover the men and tanks. No outfit seemed to be without its protective shield in the sky and the force was far in excess of that raised at Dieppe, which assault I saw and reported from a ship.

POUND COAST

There were so many of us in the air today that we had to get up there by co-ordinated degrees to avoid crossing each other's paths. From a 'vantage point in the air I could see the invasion armada, troopships filled with men who were to write a great and immortal page of history; and the attendant warships shepherding them across the Channel. This first thrust in great strength was carried out with superb organization and tactical skill.

(Continued on Page 2.)
See BOMBER.

ALLIES GAIN IN FRANCE, CANADIANS WIN INITIAL OBJECT

"... AND FOR THOSE IN FRANCE ... TODAY ..."

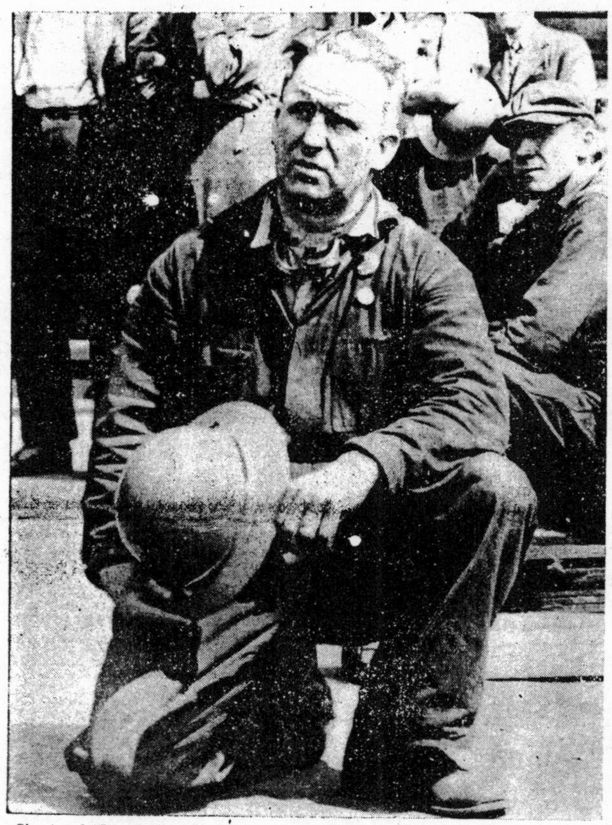

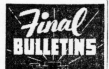

Shouts of "Invasion" and whispers of prayer mingled everywhere around the world today. And not only in the churches were prayers heard. At a special ceremony at West Coast Shipyards Ltd., a workman kneels in supplication. The rites were held during lunch hour so that there would be no loss of time in ship production program.

INVASION BULLETINS

Initial Phase Pleases "Monty"

ALLIED ARMIES' HEADQUARTERS, June 6.——(CP)—Gen. Montgomery, commander of the group of armies invading France, said he was pleased with the initial phase of the landing operations.

The general told of a five-point recipe for victory he had given his officers shortly before the invasion signal. He listed the five points as : 1—Allied solidarity; 2—Offensive eagerness; 3—Enthusiasm; 4—Confidence, and 5—All out effort.

French-Canadians Land In France

A BRITISH PORT, June 6.—(CP)—French-speaking Canadian troops were among the soldiers who crossed the English Channel today for the Allied invasion of France.

Invasion "Up to Schedule"

WASHINGTON, June 6.—(AP)—President Roosevelt said today the invasion of Europe is up to schedule."

Coastal Guns Wrecked

NEW YORK, June 6.—(AP)—An N.B.C. reporter who flew over 20 miles of the invasion coast this morning said "not a single German coastal gun was firing in the entire invasion zone," and N.B.C. said this indicated "we have completely knocked out the initial line of defenses of the much-vaunted Atlantic Wall."

1000 Bombers Hit France

SUPREME HEADQUARTERS, Allied Expeditionary Force, June 6. — (AP) — More than 1000 heavy bombers continued attacks on French coastal defenses by daylight today.

640 Naval Guns

SUPREME HEADQUARTERS, ALLIED EXPEDITIONARY FORCE, June 6.—(AP,—More than 640 naval guns ranging from four to 16 inches in size are bombarding the beaches and enemy strongpoints in support of landing forces, it was announced today.

Fierce Fight at Caen

SOMEWHERE IN ENGLAND, June 6.—(AP)—Canadian fighter pilots, returning from their third sortie of the day over the invasion beachhead, reported a few hours before dusk tonight that Allied land troops were penetrating inland from their beachhead, particularly around Caen.

"It looks as if fierce fighting is going on around there," one flyer said.

Nazis Claim Success

LONDON, June 6.—(AP)—German forces launching a counter-attack knocked out 35 heavy Allied tanks at Asnelles in the Seine Bay area by noon, a D.N.B. report from Berlin said today.

Report Allied Victory

BARCELONA, Spain, June 6.—(AP)—German reports received here today said Allied forces were in full possession of Honfleur at the month of the Seine. Honfleur is across the river from Le Havre.

15-MILE FRONT

LONDON, June 6. — (AP) — Transocean News Agency in a Berlin broadcast today said the Allies had established a 15-mile front from a mile to half a mile deep between Villers-Sur-Mer and Trouville.

This area is about seven miles south of the big port of Le Havre where transatlantic liners docked in pre-war days and takes in the beach resort area of Beauville.

Petain Warns France

LONDON, June 6.—(AP)—The Paris radio today broadcast an appeal by Marshal Petain to Frenchmen to refrain from actions "which would call down upon you tragic reprisals."

Invasion Armies Plunge Forward From Beachheads

OTTAWA, June 6—(CP)—Amid an uproar in the Commons today, Prime Minister King said that Canadian invasion forces had gained their initial objective and were making good progress.

By WES GALLAGHER.
(Associated Press War Correspondent.)

SUPREME HEADQUARTERS, ALLIED EXPEDITIONARY FORCE, June 6.—Allied forces, including Canadians under Maj.-Gen. Crerar, landed in the Normandy area of northwest France today and have thrust several miles inland against unexpectedly slight German opposition, with losses "much smaller than had been anticipated."

The grand assault—scheduled for Monday but postponed until today because of bad weather—found the highly-vaunted German defenses much less formidable in every department than had been feared.

Airborne troops who led the assault before daylight on a huge scale suffered "extremely small" losses in the air, even though the great plane fleets extended across 200 miles of sky and used navigation lights to keep formation.

Naval losses for the seaborne forces were described at headquarters as "very, very small." 4000 ships and several thousand smaller craft participated in taking the British, Canadian and American troops to France.

Coastal batteries were almost silenced by the guns of the British and Allied fleets, including battleships, and the beachheads were speedily consolidated.

The German radio said the scene of the landings was a 100-mile stretch of coast from Cherbourg to Le Havre, around the bay of the Seine and the north-east shore of the Normandy peninsula.

Prime Minister Churchill, in announcing the successful invasion to the House of Commons at noon—six hours after the first seaborne troops landed—said the landings were "the first of a series."

LOSSES LIGHT.

"Many dangers and difficulties which this time last night appeared extremely formidable are behind us," the Prime Minister added. "The passage of the sea has been made with far less loss than we apprehended.

(Continued on Page 2.)
See INVASION.

Canadian Ships Aid Invasion

LONDON, June 6.—(CP)—Proportion of warships in the Allied invasion naval armada was three British to one American and the overall proportion, including landing craft, was three British to two American, a British naval commentator discloses. "There was a big Canadian contribution as well as many Norwegian, Polish, Netherlands, French and Greek ships," he said.

Allied Fleet In Channel

LONDON, June 6. — (CP) — Late tonight 15 cruisers and 50 to 60 destroyers were operating west of Le Havre, according to a German military spokesman quoted by the German D.N.B. agency.

The military spokesman said that north of the mouth of the Orne River and north of Baueaux, 22 miles further west, large numbers of enemy landing craft of varying tonnage has been observed.

"German air reconnaissance leads to the conclusion that the heavy Allied navy group west of Le Havre is meant to screen the bringing up of more forces to the bridgehead north of Caen," said the spokesman.

King Urges House Speed Business

OTTAWA, June 6.—(CP)—Prime Minister King urged in the Commons that the House "get on with its business" as expeditiously as possible and added that if progress continued at its present rate "I don't see how we can complete the business on the order paper by the end of the year."

Gordon Graydon, Progressive Conservative House leader, said that Mr. King would find a responsive echo for the "speed up" suggestion.

VANCOUVER CALM, GRIM

Citizens have taken the awesome news of all-out Allied assault on France in their stride, with calm confidence and grim determination.

Thousands are praying to Almighty God to "see our boys through their ordeal by fire."

Church doors are opened wide.

Evidence of the prevailing spirit was the fact that The Vancouver Daily Province telephone exchange was congested throughout the latter part of the day with enquiries as to where church services were to be held.

Except for crowds on downtown streets, the darkened city seemed to sleep through the early stages of invasion.

Comparatively few heard the first German claims of Allied landings. Official confirmation did not come through from General Eisenhower until 12:30 a.m. today.

Radio news programs were on the air all night, but Vancouver slept on.

The "real" invasion was almost an anti-climax after months of anxious waiting and after Saturday's erroneous radio report that electrified the continent.

(Continued on Page 2.)
See CITY.

New Italian Cabinet

NAPLES, June 6.—(AP)—Premier Marshal Pietro Badoglio dissolved his Italian Government today and was charged by Crown Prince Humbert with forming a new government to include political leaders in liberated Rome.

Final BULLETINS

Fierce Air Fights

LONDON, June 6.—(CP) The Berlin radio reported big air battles developed over Romania today between Nazi fighters and bombers of the Allied Mediterranean Air Force.

Heavy Loss In Crash

SAN DIEGO, Cal., June 6.—(AP)—A Liberator bomber crashed on Kearny Mesa with apparently heavy loss of life. Two buildings on the auxiliary airfield were destroyed and others damaged. The navy said the plane exploded and burned after hitting the ground.

Invite Garbo to Island

VICTORIA, June 6.—(CP)—Greta Garbo, reportedly interested in production of a film story based on the exploits of the Norwegian merchant marine, has been invited by the provincial department of mines and industry to make her picture on Vancouver Island. E. G. Rowbottom, deputy minister, said.

Aircraft Workers Pray

TORONTO, June 6.—(CP) — Aircraft plants across the Dominion halted production momentarily to engage in prayer for the success of the invasion, it was announced by the Aircraft Industry Relations Committee. Plants at Prince Albert, Sask., and Fort Erie and London in Ontario arranged to hold special services in addition to the two-minute devotional period.

Allies Trap Nazi Troops In Italy

By SID FEDER.
(Associated Press War Correspondent.)

NAPLES, June 6.—Allied 5th Army forces drove steadily beyond liberated Rome today, some units plunging as much as five miles out from the Tiber River against what was officially termed "only weak resistance."

"The battle to destroy the enemy continues without pause," said a communique.

Lt.-Gen. Clark's troops have crossed or reached the Tiber all the way from Rome to the sea and enemy divisions still in the flatlands south of the city are in desperate straits.

ESCAPE CUT OFF.

In the coastal area alone well over 2000 Nazis apparently will be unable to scramble out of the Allied net because all Tiber bridges from Rome to the sea have been blown up or captured.

In Rome, however, where 11 crossings remained intact, 5th Army formations poured across in a constant stream to chase the Germans fleeing northward.

(French troops have captured Tivoli on the Rome-Avezzano highway, 18 miles east of the capital, the B.B.C. announced.

Canadian corps troops are believed out of action, resting after their drive up the Sacco Valley.

In the area immediately north of Rome Monday more than 375 German vehicles were destroyed or damaged by fighter-bombers. Heavy bombers meanwhile pounded northern Italy rail lines, particularly in the Po Valley.

Russ Repulse Nazis

LONDON, June 6. — (AP) — Russian troops have repulsed new German attacks in the area north and northwest of Iasi in Romania, the Soviet communique reports.

Wilby Freed, Arrested

VICTORIA, June 6.—(CP)—Ralph M. Wilby, former chief accountaint for the William T. Knott Company Inc., New York, operators of a chain of department stores, who has been held in custody here since March 12 at request of New York authorities to face 17 charges of grand larcency totalling $275,984, was granted his application for a writ of habeas corpus by Mr. Justice A. D. Macfarlane in Supreme Court chambers this afternoon.

Wilby was immediately taken into custody again by city detectives acting under the order of extradition by County Court Judge H. H. Shandley issued April 11.

Prayer at Nanaimo

NANAIMO, June 6. — Prayer for speedy victory, to which all citizens are invited, will be held in St. Andrew's Presbyterian Church tonight under the auspices of Nanaimo Ministerial Association. Rev. George Knox and Rev. A. Wilson will be in the pulpit. Representatives of all Protestant churches will be present.

Canadians Achieve First Objective

ALLIES 'IN' 9 MILES

Battle Rages for Caen

RUSSIANS MASSING FORCES

The Vancouver Sun
FOUNDED 1886 VOL LVIII—No. 258 VANCOUVER, B.C., JUNE 6, 1944 PRICE 5c

Late Invasion Flashes

FRENCH-CANADIANS IN INVASION

A BRITISH PORT, June 6—(CP)—French-speaking Canadian troops were among the soldiers who crossed the English Channel today for the Allied invasion of France.

AIR BATTLE OVER RUMANIA

LONDON, June 6—(CP)—The Berlin Radio reported tonight that big air battles developed over Rumania today between Nazi fighters and bombers of the Allied Mediterranean air force.

NAZI COMMANDERS 'ON SPOT'

LONDON, June 6—(BUP) — The German DNB News Agency reported tonight that Marshal Karl von Runstedt and Marshal Erwin Rommel, Nazi commanders in western Europe, "are on the spot of the developments."

ALLIES LAND WEST OF LE HAVRE?

LONDON, June 6—(BUP)—The Berlin radio said tonight that about 15 Allied cruisers and 50 to 60 destroyers were standing ready west of Le Havre, and late in the day a great number of landing craft were seen in the same area, apparently awaiting orders to hit the coast.

BOULOGNE-CALAIS LANDINGS

LONDON, June 6—(BUP)—Radio France at Algiers quoted a purported German broadcast to Spain tonight as saying Allied troops had landed and gained a foothold in the Boulogne-Calais area of northern France. The report lacked confirmation in any responsible source. It also said Allied paratroopers captured an airdrome in the same region.

U.S. NAVAL LOSSES LIGHT

WASHINGTON, June 6 — (BUP) — President Roosevelt reported late today that the invasion of Europe is running "up to schedule."

He said that up to noon American naval losses in the operation comprised two destroyers and one landing ship.

He told a news conference that air losses were relatively light, amounting to about one percent.

RAF REPORTS BEACHNEADS SECURE

LONDON, June 6—(BUP)—A dispatch for the combined Allied press from an advanced fighter base this evening quoted RAF pilots returning from low-level flights over the beachheads in France as saying the troops were moving inland and there is no longer any opposition on the beaches.

"We could easily tell the beaches were secure—we could see our soldiers standing up," one airman was quoted.

LA MARSEILLAISE SUNG IN COMMONS

OTTAWA, June 6.—The Canadian Commons sang today with the stirring strains of La Marsellaise, joining Maurice Lalonde, a French-Canadian member who hailed coming liberation of France and wound up his speech with the old song of liberty. It was followed by God Save the King.

The Prime Minister had made reference to the invasion, cited Churchill's speech and appealed to the House to intensify its work and eliminate non-essentials. The House agreed.

WHERE ALLIES INVADED FRANCE

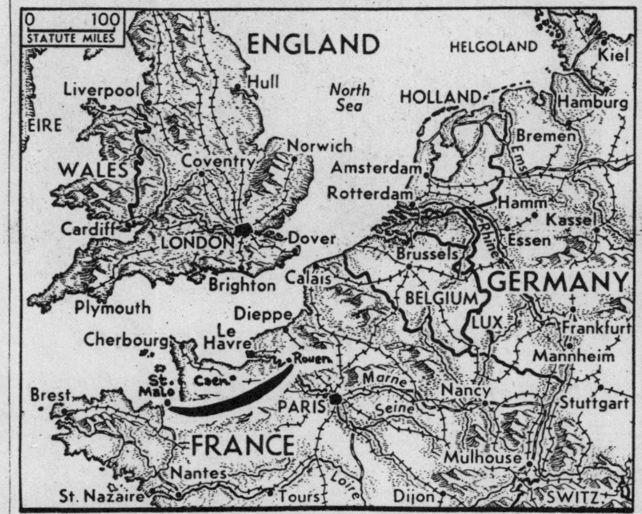

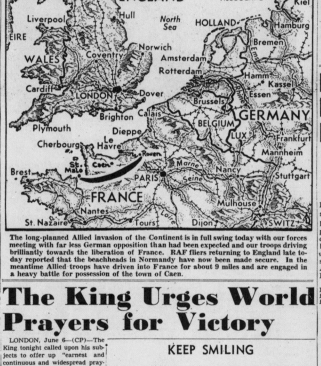

The long-planned Allied invasion of the Continent is in full swing today with our forces meeting with far less German opposition than had been expected and our troops driving brilliantly towards the liberation of France. RAF fliers returning to England late today reported that the beachheads in Normandy have now been made secure. In the meantime Allied troops have driven into France for about 9 miles and are engaged in a heavy battle for possession of the town of Caen.

Steady Progress Reported by All Invasion Units

FINAL

Masses of Allied Planes Reported Bombing Dunkerque and Calais; Liberation Army 'Over First Hurdles'

OTTAWA, June 6—(CP)—Amid an uproar of desk-thumping in the Commons today, Prime Minister Mackenzie King said that Canadian invasion forces had gained their initial objective and were making good progress.

"The fact that an Allied landing has taken place on the continent is of itself a great feat," said Mr. King.

Both local and general counter-attacks are to be expected, however, and it is important not to over-rate minor successes, he said.

"It is not to be supposed that the offensive launched today will not be followed by other offensives in other parts of Europe," he said.

LONDON, June 6 — (CP) — The German-controlled Vichy radio asserted tonight masses of Allied planes were bombing the Calais and Dunkerque regions.

From AP and BUP Dispatches

SUPREME HEADQUARTERS, ALLIED EXPEDITIONARY FORCE, LONDON, June 6.—American, British and Canadian invasion forces landed in northwestern France today, established beachheads in Normandy, and by evening had "gotten over the first five or six hurdles" in the greatest amphibious assault of all time.

Prime Minister Winston Churchill revealed that Allied troops were fighting inside Caen, 9½ miles inside northwest France, that the invasion penetrations had reached several miles in depth in some cases, and that footholds had been established on a broad front as the operation proceeded "in a thoroughly satisfactory manner."

Gen. Dwight D. Eisenhower's supreme headquarters revealed that the Allied armies, carried and supported by 4000 ships and 11,000 planes, encountered considerably less re-

Please Turn to Page Two See "Allies Attempt"

Red Army Prepares For Drive

Hitler Soon to Find Himself Facing Real Two-Front War

By HENRY N. CASSIDY
Associated Press Staff Writer

MOSCOW, June 6—(AP)—Russian armies were understood today to be massing and preparing to perform their part of the joint Allied task of crushing Germany with a blow from the East, combined with Gen. Eisenhower's invasion from the West and Gen. Alexander's thrust up the Italian Peninsula.

The invasion of northwest France was the "second front" for which the Russians had called for three anxious years.

Fresh forces of Nazi infantry attacking in the week-long German offensive in the Iasi section in Rumania were repulsed yesterday, while Red airmen hammered the Bessarabian railway junction of Chisinai, 70 miles east and a little south of Iasi, Moscow reported today.

In yesterday's fighting near Iasi the Nazis lost 41 tanks and 33 planes, Moscow said.

Much enemy transport and equipment were destroyed at Chisinau, and military objectives in the town also were hit, the communique added.

'Going as Planned'

'Greatest Fleet Ever'-Churchill

LONDON, June 6—(CP)—Allied invasion forces have penetrated in some cases several miles inland after an effective landing on a broad front, Prime Minister Churchill informed the House of Commons tonight.

The Prime Minister said in his second invasion report of the day that "the landings along the whole front have been effective and the troops have penetrated in some cases several miles inland.

Mr. Churchill, after visiting Gen. Eisenhower's headquarters with the King, told the House he could state that "this operation is proceeding in a thoroughly satisfactory manner.

"Many dangers and difficulties which this time last night appeared extremely formidable are behind us," the Prime Minister added.

"The passage of the sea has been made with far less loss than we apprehended.

"The resistance of the batteries has been greatly weakened by the bombing by the air force and superior bombardment of our ships quickly reduced their fire to dimensions which did not affect the problem."

"The outstanding feature has been the landings of airborne troops on a scale far larger than anything ever seen before," he said.

"These landings took place with extremely little loss and with great accuracy. The airborne troops are well established and the landings and followups are all proceeding with very much less loss than we expected.

"There is fighting proceeding at various points and we have captured various bridges which are of importance and which were not blown up. There is even fighting proceeding in the town of Caen inland.

Please Turn to Page Two
See "Churchill"

The King Urges World Prayers for Victory

LONDON, June 6—(CP)—The King tonight called upon his subjects to offer up "earnest and continuous and widespread prayer throughout the present crisis of the liberation of Europe."

Prayer, he said, would fortify the "determination of our sailors and airmen who go forth to set captives free."

"At this historic moment surely not one of us is too busy, too young or too old to play their part in the nationwide, perchance worldwide, vigil of prayer as the great crusade sets forth," the King said in a BBC broadcast.

"After nearly five years of toil and suffering we must renew that crusading impulse on which we entered the war and met its darkest hour.

"We and our Allies are sure that our fight is against evil and for a world in which goodness and honor may be the foundation of life of men in every land.

"That we may be worthily matched with this new summons of destiny, I desire solemnly to call my people to prayer and dedication.

"We are not unmindful of our shortcomings of the past and present.

"We shall not ask that God may do our will, but that we may be enabled to do the will of God; and we dare to believe that God has used our nation and Empire as an instrument for fulfilling His high purpose."

KEEP SMILING

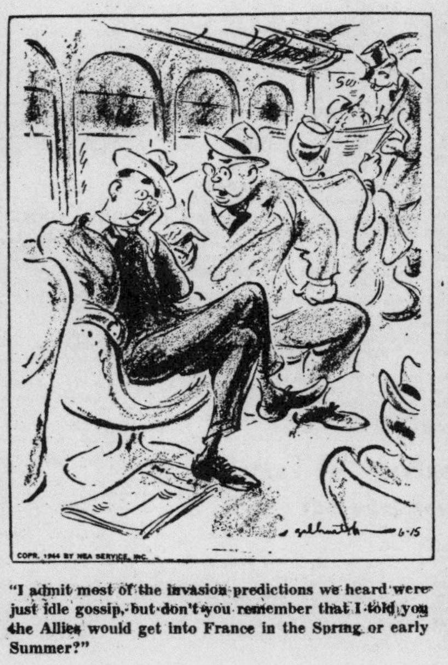

"I admit most of the invasion predictions we heard were just idle gossip, but don't you remember that I told you the Allies would get into France in the Spring or early Summer?"

All Races Off; It's D-Day

WINNIPEG, June 6.—(CP)—R. James Speers, managing director of the Manitoba Jockey Club, announced today that because of the invasion today's card of races at Polo Park here has been postponed. The complete card has been scheduled for tomorrow when the meet resumes.

Races were also cancelled at Belmont and Suffolk Downs.

Nelson S. Lougheed Funeral Friday

Funeral services for the late Nelson S. Lougheed, former provincial cabinet minister who died early today, will be held in the Center & Hanna Vancouver chapel Friday at 2 p.m., Rev. Dr. A. M. Sanford and Rev. G. Bruce Ridland of New Westminster, a brother-in-law, officiating. Interment will be in the family plot in Mountain View Cemetery. The funeral will be under direction of the Canadian Legion, Mr. Lougheed having been a veteran of the Boer War.

Evader Jailed

Special to The Vancouver Sun

PARKSVILLE, June 6.—For failing to report for military duty, William P. Strange of Parksville was sentenced to 30 days in Oakalla jail by Magistrate R. C. Weld.

Troops Behind Barbed Wire

By ROBERT C. MILLER
British United Press War Correspondent

INVASION PORT, England, June 6 — (BUP) — Thousands upon thousands of U.S. invasion troops were told exactly where they were going and what they would do on D-Day, it now can be disclosed, and then were placed under a quarantine so rigid their food was prepared in an outside area and passed to them through barbed wire.

So far as is known only two men escaped from the quarantined area and both were captured immediately.

Guards inside and out were under orders to "shoot to kill" anyone attempting to leave the area.

Precautions to guard the security of the attack were supervised by the office of counter-intelligence and it was one of the greatest feats of the war.

RENO GAMBLERS CLOSE

RENO, Nev., June 6—(BUP)—All of Reno's gambling clubs closed their doors this morning out of respect to the invasion of Europe.

Canada's Fighters On Own Vessels

WITH THE CANADIAN FORCES IN FRANCE—June 6—(CP) — Two landing-craft flotillas of the Royal Canadian Navy carried a portion of the Canadian assault troops to France and put them down on the beaches in the first wave of attack.

By ALAN RANDAL
Canadian Press Staff Writer

LONDON, June 6. — In pre-dawn darkness today, while London and southeast England reverberated with the thunder of aerial armadas, Canadian troops landed with British and American units on the coast of northern France.

Three hours later, Louis Hunter of the Canadian Press reported from an RCAF airfield that returning fliers said operations on the beach seemed "well organized."

CANADIAN SHOW

Unconfirmed by the Allies, the Germans placed the landings on the north coast of Normandy.

Part of the mammoth assault was all Canadian.

Ships of the Royal Canadian Navy carried the troops from the Dominion who landed in the first assault waves, and their reinforcements, and then began a ferry service to the beachheads.

Planning of the great operation included making during the last two years more original maps of France than the country itself made since the days of Julius Caesar.

STRATEGIC DRICE

Caen, around which the Germans almost immediately reported heavy fighting, is the most important road junction in the southeastern part of the Cherbourg Peninsula.

On the River Orne, 10 miles from the sea and 180 miles northeast of Paris, Caen offers direct access to Rouen, Le Havre and Cherbourg.

Please Turn to Page Two
See "Canadians"

'Five-and-Ten Heiress Fighting for Son Here

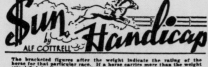

★ ★ ★ ★ ★ FINAL

MINSK FALLS!

Sun Handicap
by ALF COTTRELL

The bracketed figures after the weight indicate the rating of the horse for that particular race. If a horse carries more than the weight stipulated in the entries, deduct one point for each pound of overweight carried. Bracketed figures at end of line indicate post position. Jockeys, post positions, subject to late changes.

TUESDAY, JULY 4

1st Race—Claiming. 3-year-olds and up. — 6 Furlongs

—	SIMONETTE (Sporri) ..	112	(92)	Should trim this field (9)
4404	GUSTA'S GAL (Bassett)	117	(88)	Debut wasn't too bad (2)
—	CRAIGLOCHART R. J'n)	x12b	(87)	Maybe due for revival (11)
—	Wise Witch (Haller)	117	(76)	Speed: might hang on (3)
—	Ascot Gal (Siveright) ...	107	(72)	Youth is on her side (1)
—	Parlan (Dye)	107	(67)	Been no world-beater (6)
—	Pala Hills	112	(—)	Would need to improve (5)
—	Royal Suzy (Bailey)	112	(—)	Once had some speed (7)
4403	Brown Band (Clode) ...	112	(—)	Jazz Bands all threats (12)
—	The Mouse	117	(—)	Had plenty of rest (4)
4403	Brown Earth (Couture)	x107	(—)	Just possible long shot (10)
4401	Lea Treor	x112	(—)	First try ust ordinary (8)

2nd Race—Claiming. 4-year-olds and up. foaled in Western Canada. — 6 Furlongs

(4401)	SIMONY'S BOY Hrushk)	118	(106)	Could come right back (4)
4402	WINGAWAY (E. Neal)	110	(99)	Speed; could surprise (3)
—	ASCOT MAID (Bassett)	110	(95)	May Cobe with rush (7)
—	Eagle Crest (Bailey)	115	(93)	Also comes at finish (5)
—	Lady Macduff (Sivew't	112	(—)	Fit; route maybe short (2)
—	Act Three Couture	x105	(75)	Never was much yet (6)
—	Lilloade	110	(—)	Runs odd good one (1)

3rd Race—Allowance. maiden 2-year-olds. — 4 Furlongs

—	MALINKA (Haller)	112	(—)	Best off her trials (4)
—	GOLD HEIR (Hrushak)	115	(—)	Can put up a fight (6)
—	MELINDA	118	(—)	Said to be good one (1)
—	Ascot Bell (Bassett) ...	112	(—)	Speed; may get part (2)
—	Lahadion (Slocum)	115	(—)	Grand-looking colt (5)
—	Bandra (Hrushak)	115	(—)	One o fthe Jazzy Bands (3)

4th Race—Claiming. 3-year-olds and up. — 6 Furlongs

4401	Si Green (Sporri)	117	(104)	Narrow margin in here (1)
4402	BRUNTSFIELD Couture)	x112	(104)	Due to win one soon (7)
4401	GORDELIUS (Dye) ...	112	(102)	Might lead and upset (8)
—	Kaywood (Haller)	117	(100)	Pretty handy plater (3)
—	Peggy's Girl	x107	(—)	On some form is threat (6)
4404	Maizie B(a) (Bassett)—	112	(98)	In softer spot here (2)
4404	Be Mine (Dennis) ...	112	(93)	Well back other day (5)
—	Golden Belt(a)	112	(93)	Runs well at all times (4)
4403	Bashak (R. Johnston)..	x112	(92)	Debut was nice effort (9)

(a) Joe Brazeau entry.

5th Race—THE INDEPENDENCE DAY HANDICAP. 3-year-olds and up. — 6 Furlongs

—	STEVESTON BILL (B't)	108	(132)	Can whip this company (7)
—	WINNAMUCCA (Si'rhgt)	108	(122)	Been good on prairies (6)
—	RONRICO (Krushak) ..	118	(120)	Rail and one to beat (1)
—	Water Tower (Neal) ...	118	(—)	Some form excellent (3)
—	Pilot Biscuit (Bailey)	103	(—)	Been a nice runner (8)
4405	Eno-Heather (R.Jo'ston)	100	(116)	May need easier sort (2)
—	Nalod (Slocum)	105	(113)	Never better than now (4)
—	Plucky Jake (Sporri) ..	110	(110)	Never beat this kind (5)

6th Race—Allowance, 3-year-old maidens. — 6 Furlongs

—	WILL CALL (Sporri)....	113	(85)	Game little racemare (5)
4403	RIO ROSE (Neal)......	113	(83)	Debut was nice effort (7)
—	ASCOT PEGGY	106	(82)	Much promise off works (4)
4403	Nancesworth (Bailey) ..	111	(80)	Bi colt will charge (11)
—	aPonda Pete	111	(77)	Look for improvement (3)
—	True Act (Haller)	106	(—)	Has worked very well (9)
4403	Hardtocatch (Hrushak).	113	(65)	Went fairly steady (2)
—	Tick Over	113	(—)	Fair speed; might do (1)
—	Island Gold (Dye)	106	(—)	Definitely will improve (10)
—	aSandrock Girl (Johnsn)	106	(—)	Can sizzle for a half (8)
—	Lilloot Boy	111	(—)	May be trifle green (6)
—	My Rivalry	111	(—)	Fair sort from south (12)

a—Mrs. G. Appleby entry.

7th Race—Claiming. 3-year-olds and up. — 1 Mile 70 Yds.

—	MY FENG	x112	(121)	Class should turn trick (4)
4402	MAID OF BROXA(Spor)	110	(121)	Ready for great effort (8)
4406	TREASURE ISLE (Hair)	120	(107)	Finished well at shorter (3)
—	Jest Once (Couture) ...	x110	(—)	Bay Meadows form OK (1)
—	Ascot Jane (Sivright)..	107	(104)	Be running at wire (7)
4406	Maestro Sascha (Dye)..	120	(91)	First try below tops (2)
—	Daddy (Bailey)	117	(—)	Not much line on him (5)
—	Tellus	115	(—)	Seems in tough spot (6)

Substitute Race—Claiming. 3-year-olds and up. — 6 Furlongs

4401	RED FEZ (Wilbourne)	112	(103)	Off first is tops here (1)
4404	SHOWUM (Siveright) ..	117	(98)	Should be right there (7)
—	BRITTANIA	x112	(90)	May need longer race (8)
4403	Craig an Ariff (Haller)	112	(86)	Can improve on last (10)
—	Sun Box (Bailey)	112	(—)	Fair kind across line (4)
4409	Your It	107	(—)	Youth may help some (2)
—	Silumo (R. Johnston) ..	x107	(78)	Old gal looking spry (5)
—	Jock on Top (Couture)	x112	(—)	Should rate chance (2)
—	Happy Eva	104	(—)	In with a leather (3)
—	Black Mist	112	(—)	Look this one over
—	Somer Holiday (Hrushk)	112	(—)	Seems ordinary sort (11)

Weather clear. Track fast. First post 3 p.m.
x—Apprentice allowance claimed.

RAF Bombs Bucharest Oil Plants

By WALTER CRONKITE
Special to The Vancouver Sun

LONDON, July 3—(BUP)—RAF heavy bombers struck across the Alps from Italy at the Prahova oil refinery in Bucharest last night and today strong formations of American heavy bombers attacked oil refineries and storage and transport facilities in Rumania, Hungary and Yugoslavia.

Enemy accounts said more than 500 Italy-based American planes attacked Budapest today, for the second time in 24 hours.

Bad weather again restricted aerial operations from Britain today, but the German radio said Allied planes were over northwestern Germany.

Blimp on Island Will Be Salvaged

NANAIMO, July 3.—A United States Army blimp, which crashed early last month, while attempting to get to the scene of the wreck of an RCAF plane 25 miles east of here is to be salvaged.

A USAAF crew, assisted by local game wardens and loggers, reached the blimp on Sunday. The blimp, worth $500,000, was not badly damaged, they reported.

Nazis Reported in Aland Islands

STOCKHOLM, July 3—(AP)—Reports without official confirmation circulated in Stockholm that German troops had begun to occupy the Aland Islands, strategic stepping stones across the mouth of the Gulf of Bothnia between Finland and Sweden.

This report, coming close upon Finland's accord with Germany for full military collaboration, was received simultaneously with the broadcast of a speech by Finnish Premier Edwin Linkomies in which he virtually ruled out a separate peace.

NOTED TENOR REPORTED DEAD

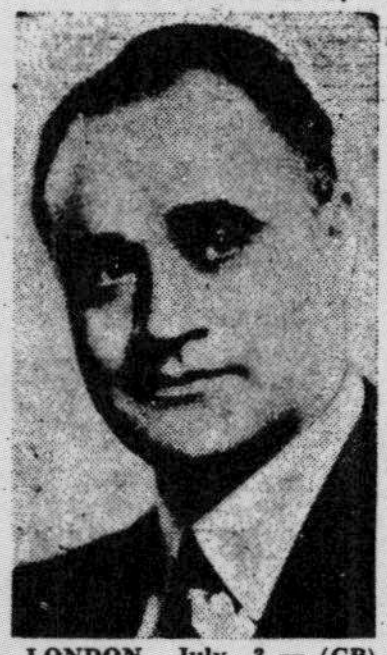

LONDON, July 3 — (CP) —Naomi Jacobs, novelist, said today she had received a message by secret means saying Beniamino Gigli (above), former Metropolitan Opera tenor, had died in Italy.

Miss Jacobs said: "I do not think he died a natural death. I think it is something else."

There was no confirmation of the report. June 22 Gigli was barred from singing in an army concert in Rome.

Robots Kill 2 Noted Men

LONDON, July 3—(BUP)—The Germans intensified the robot bomb blitz of southern England today, sending over man-flown planes to observe the results, while it was announced that Sir Percy Alden, former member of Parliament, and Major-Gen. Sir Arthur Scott, retired, were killed in recent attacks by the mechanical aerial weapon.

Lady Scott, novelist and playwright, was injured in the same incident that resulted in the death of the two prominent Britishers, it was announced. Gen. Scott was commander of the 12th (eastern) division from 1915 to 1918.

An unidentified number of American soldiers were among the victims when a pilotless plane struck one building and damaged others in southern England today, it was announced.

'Babs' May Come Here For Lance

Vancouver has become the scene of an impending legal battle between Barbara Hutton Grant, dime store heiress, and her former husband, Count Haugwitz-Reventlow, one-time Danish count.

This time the issue between the ex-count and "Babs," whose marriage ended after a hectic court interlude in London several years ago, is the custody of their nine-year-old son Lance.

IN WEST VANCOUVER

Today Lance and his father were in seclusion in the waterfront home in West Vancouver of D. N. Hossie, KC, Vancouver lawyer.

Visit of the handsome former count and his son from California to Vancouver will more than likely be followed by legal action on the part of the boy's mother, who is now the wife of movie star Cary Grant.

Under an agreement reached in England at the time of their seperation, Lance was to live alternately for six months with each parent. The boy was to be turned over to Mrs. Grant last Saturday, her attorneys in Los Angeles said.

Haugwitz-Reventlow's appearance in Vancouver was preceded by a series of court manoeuvres, charges reminiscent of the days when Babs' domestic troubles were the source of almost daily headlines.

MAY SEEK FULL CUSTODY

Thursday in California the ex-count's counsel filed a dismissal of an action in which Haugwitz-Reventlow had sought to enjoin Mrs. Grant from assertedly influencing the boy against him and from using "coarse and vulgar language" in the son's presence.

He had asked that he be allowed to supervise Lance's rearing and education.

Mrs. Grant's attorney said she had planned to file an action in Los Angeles shortly seeking complete custody of the boy and that she still plans to do so.

In Los Angeles on Saturday, the ex-count's attorney asserted that Mrs. Grant had planned to take Lance to Spain before his father whisked him away to Vancouver.

This charge was flatly denied by Babs' counsel, who said the report was "absolutely without foundation."

'SITTING TIGHT'

Haugwitz-Reventlow's Los Angeles attorney also got off a press statement in which he said that the separation agreement did not require that Lance be kept in California or near his mother.

Mrs. Grant was "very much upset and distressed" when informed that her son had been taken to Canada, her attorneys said.

Here in Vancouver, the ex-count, who is now an American citizen, was apparently sitting tight waiting for the boy's mother to make the next move.

"If Mrs. Grant thinks she has a right to the child, she knows

Please Turn to Page Two
See "Heiress"

Railbird

1—Pala Hills, Simonette, Wise Witch.
2—Simony's Boy, Ascot Maid, Act Three.
3—Malinka, Gold Heir, Melinda.
4—Bruntsfield, Si Green, Golden Belt.
5—Ronrica, Steveston Bill, Winnamuca.
6—Nancesworth, Rio Rose, Island Gold.
7—My Feng Maid of Broxa, Treasure Isle.
Sub.—Showrun, Red Fez, Sun Box.
One Best—MALINKA.

The Vancouver Sun
FOUNDED 1886
VOL. LVIII—No. 280
VANCOUVER, B.C., JULY 3, 1944
PRICE 5c

HUN PRISONER APES HIS FUEHRER

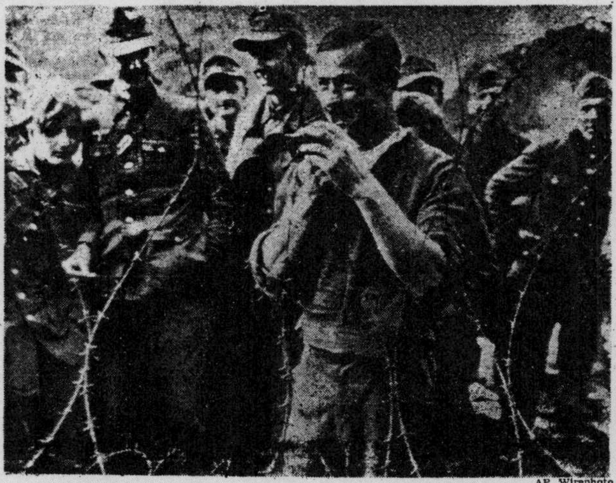

AP Wirephoto

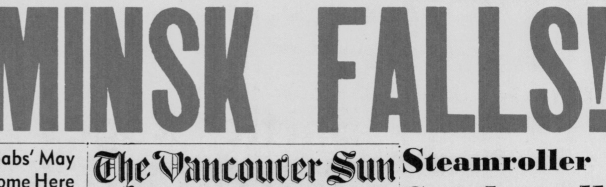

A German prisoner of war fixes his moustache and hair to look like Hitler as his fellow prisoners look on at an interment camp at Cherbourg, France.

Essential Housing to Get Priority in Vancouver Area

Building contractors throughout the Greater Vancouver area today approved the Ottawa announcement that henceforth priority in securing building materials was to be given on houses for immediate occupancy by "bona fide" home owners rather than on houses built for speculation.

The move came as a direct result of a survey conducted recently by Major-General J. P. Mackenzie, newly-appointed associate construction controller. He used the information gathered to formulate a construction permit policy within the limits of the availability of construction materials.

Prior to the time the first ration order was announced in Ottawa about one month ago, The Vancouver Sun had drawn attention to the dire need for such action and had pressed for the institution of some system that would meet the more pressing needs of the greatest number of genuine home builders in this city.

It is understood that some time before the present survey was begun the local office of the federal construction control had been advised to cut down severely the number of permits being accepted and forwarded to Ottawa for approval.

QUOTA TO BE CUT

Although no specific number was given in General Mackenzie's statement, which followed an announcement of Federal policy made Friday by Munitions Minister Howe, it is believed here the action may cut in half the original 400 per month quota on construction permits issued from the Vancouver office.

General Mackenzie reported that to May 31, 1944, about 2000 housing units in Greater Vancouver were licensed by the construction controller compared with only approximately 1500 in the first five months of 1943. At present more than 600 applications for the building of dwellings in the Vancouver area are under consideration.

"Plans for housing construction should be deferred, wherever possible, until the period of material scarcity is over," said Gen. Mackenzie.

MUST BALANCE MATERIAL

"In the Vancouver area we intend to permit the construction of all the essentially needed houses conforming to present regulations for which materials can be provided without hurting the war effort."

Hitler Seeks Jap Refuge Says Rumor

LONDON, July 3—(CP)—The following dispatch from the Cairo office of Reuter was received today, together with a note from that news agency calling attention to the fact that the report is without confirmation:

"The Egyptian newspaper, Al Ahram, today published an unconfirmed report from a special correspondent in Istanbul saying that, according to information received in German quarters there, Hitler, Goering, Goebbels and Mussolini were preparing to flee to Japan in a special plane via eastern China.

LISBON, July 3—(BUP)—German cargo planes, carrying an undisclosed number of cases of gold bars, arrived here over the week-end, it was reported today.

Jap Troops Cut China Rail Line

CHUNGKING, July 3—(AP)—Japanese troops which by-passed the encircled rail junction of Hengyang have thrust a spearhead 46 miles south of the city in their drive to capture the entire Canton-Hankow railway route, the Chinese high command indicated tonight.

Earlier a communique had reported that the Japs had cut the railway at Leiyang, 34 airline miles southeast of Hengyang.

Japanese troops making a "suicidal attempt" to penetrate the Allied-held main airport at Myitkyina in northern Burma, have been wiped out by American forces, another Chinese communique announced.

Cyclone Hits Saskatchewan

REGINA, July 3—(CP)—One man was killed, at least six persons were injured and severe crop damage was done Saturday night when a cyclonic storm whipped across the southwest corner of Saskatchewan.

Big, jagged hailstones accounted for crop damage ranging from 10 to 100 percent in some areas, especially in the Ravenscrag and Scotsguard districts, and killed pigs, chickens and wild game.

At Wynyard, Town Constable Harry C. Smith was electrocuted when he came in contact with fallen power wires he had been guarding.

At Moose Jaw five persons were taken to hospital for treatment for bruises and shock after three cabins were overturned at the Moose Jaw tourist camp.

A farmer named Snowden, near Ravenscrag, was injured when his horses, stung into fury by hail, ran away. He was taken to hospital.

Coldwell Preaching Revolution—Hanson

OTTAWA, July 3—(CP)—Hon. R. B. Hanson (PC—York-Sunbury) said today in Commons that M. J. Coldwell, CCF national leader, was "encouraging those in this country who openly preach revolution, and he and those around him have started forces which he cannot control.

He said that "Communist and Socialist" elements were knocking at the door of the CCF and "they will soon be in charge."

Longacres Selections

1—Teton Pass, Count Arturo, Busy Ellen.
2—Jockwell, Brig O'Bay, Whistling Boy.
3—Flying Banshee, Nickajack, Jubilo.
4—Spare Parts, Musical Jack, Seekonk.
5—Dedlock, Pio Pico, Darby Doc.
3—Overland Trail, Marada, Matadora.
7—Lavengro, Sir Jeffrey, Okana.
8—Fighting Words, Friendly Paul, Clover Leaf.

RCAF Leader Wins Sixth Decoration

LONDON, July 3—(CP)—Acting Wing Cmdr. James Edgar (Johnny) Johnson, foremost Allied fighter ace in the European theatre, and leader of the RCAF fighter wing in Normandy, has received a second bar to his DSO in awards announced today.

Johnson, with 33 victories to his credit, now has six decorations.

Here is a log of his awards: Sept. 29, 1941, DFC; June 26, 1942, bar to DFC; June 3, 1943, DSO; Sept. 24, 1943, bar to DSO; Jan. 18, 1944, American DFC; July 3, 1944, second bar to DSO.

Steamroller Crushes all Resistance

Victory Opens Gates to Red Army Surge Towards Polish Capital

LONDON, July 3—(AP)—Minsk, the capital of Soviet White Russia and last major German stronghold in the pre-war Soviet union, fell today to two great Red Army groups who have thus capped their 1944 summer offensive with its greatest triumph.

The city, whose population is believed to have approached 300,000 before the war and enemy occupation left it a battered ruin, fell to the storm troops who rode down all resistance in another incredible burst of speed.

The fall of the city came almost to the day of the third anniversary of its occupation by enemy troops—the Germans announced its capture on July 1, 1941, only a few days after the beginning of their invasion of the Soviet Union.

The victory opened the gates to a Red Army surge down the main railways to Warsaw, Polish capital, 300 miles to the east, to Wilno and Riga in Lithuania and Latvia to the northwest.

The great base on the dividing high ground between the Baltic and the Pripyat marshes to the south fell to an accelerating Soviet steamroller only 11 days after Stalin launched his central front offensive. That offensive now has carried the Russian armies forward more than 150 miles over a battlefield 300 miles broad.

Minsk is but 15 miles east of the pre-war frontier of Poland and Russia and its many-sided pivotal communications afford first rate routes into the Baltic countries and south and central Poland.

Stalin said troops of the Third and First White Russian fronts captured the city by encircling manoeuvre and assault.

Dope Thieves Secure Haul

Drugs were stolen when Fraser Drug Co. store, Forty-ninth and Fraser, was broken into about 3:30 a.m. today.

The drugs, including cocaine, morphine and codeine, were a new supply just received, J. Buckshon, proprietor, told detectives.

Police were called to the drug store when tenants of adjoining premises heard noises.

Lucky Gold

1—Craiglochart, Pala Hills, Royal Suzy.
2—Ascot Maid. Simony's Boy, Lady Macduff.
3—Melinda, Malinka B, Kaywood.
4—Si Green, Maizie B, Kaywood.
5—Winnamucca, Steveston Bill, Ronrico.
6—Rio Rose, Nancesworth, Will Call.
7—Ascot Jane, Maid of Broxa, Treasure Isle.
Sub—Britannia, Silumo, Craig An Ariff.
One best—RIO ROSE

Sunstar

1—Simonette, Wise Witch, Craiglochart.
2—Simony's Boy, Ascot Maid, Eagle Crest.
3—No line on the two-year-olds.
4—Si Green, Kaywood, Maizie B.
5—Steveston Bill, Water Tower, Eno Heather.
6—Rio Rose, Nancesworth, Island Gold.
7—Treasure Isle, Ascot Jane, Maid Of Broxa.
Sub—Silumo, Britannia, Red Fez.
One best—SI GREEN.

British Raiders Reach Ukhrul

KANDY, Ceylon, July 3—(BUP)—A British raiding party has reached the village of Ukhrul, key Japanese supply point in India, 35 miles northeast of Imphal, a communique announced today.

Late News Flashes

SUPREME HEADQUARTERS Allied Expeditionary Force, July 3—(AP) — Allied forces have gained ground to the south in the Cherbourg peninsula, and patrols have penetrated deep into enemy positions in the Caen sector to the east, Gen. Dwight B. Eisenhower's headquarters announced tonight.

SPEAKER'S WIFE DIES

VICTORIA, July 3—(CP)—Mrs. Janette Whittaker, 77, mother of Hon. N. W. Whittaker, speaker of the British Columbia legislative assembly, died Sunday. Born in Allan Park, Ont., Mrs. Whittaker came here 55 years ago. A daughter, Miss Rita Whittaker, also survives.

WILL VISIT B.C.

ALGIERS, July 3—(BUP)—Pierre Mendes-France, Finance Minister in Gen. Charles de Gaulle's self-styled French provisional government, announced today that he will leave soon for Washington.

FRUIT PULP ALLOCATION

OTTAWA, July 3—(CP)—Allocation of raspberry and strawberry pulp in British Columbia will be made "soon after the pack becomes available," the Prices Board said today in a return tabled in the Commons for George Cruickshank (L. Fraser Valley). Financing will be done by the packer.

DE GAULLE TO VISIT

ALGIERS, July 3—(AP)—The French Committee of National Liberation today approved arrangements for its leaders, Gen. De Gaulle, to visit Washington within a few days. He is expected to visit Canada.

POSTWAR EXPANSION

WASHINGTON, July 3—(BUP)—The nation's airlines have formulated a post-war program designed to utilize virtually all government-owned transport planes, stimulate new plane production, and provide quicker airlines expansion, a spokesman revealed today.

FDR TO VISIT EUROPE?

BERLIN, July 3—(BUP).—Radio Berlin speculated today over the possibility of an imminent visit to Europe by President Roosevelt, asserting that rumors are circulating "in American diplomatic circles in Lisbon" that the President will leave Washington in the next few days, making his first stop at newly-captured Cherbourg.

Harry Warren Dies

NANAIMO, July 3.—Harry Warren, 69, retired farmer, resident here two years and formerly of Alberta, died in Nanaimo Hospital.

He leaves two sons, George, Nanaimo; John T., Alberta; one daughter, Mrs. May Hepburn in Washington State. Jenkins' chapel Ltd. have charge of funeral arrangements.

HITLER WOUNDED BY ASSASSIN'S BLAST

Official Weather Forecast

Vancouver and vicinity—Generally cloudy and mild today, with light rain or rain showers, cloudiness decreasing tonight. Friday, cloudy and mild with occasional rain showers. Winds moderate. Wednesday's temperature: High 76, low 57.

The Vancouver Sun

Rationed Foods

Canning Sugar—Coupons F1 to F10 now valid.
Sugar—Coupons 36, 37 now valid.
Butter—Coupons 70, 71 valid today.
Preserves—Coupons 23, 24 now valid.
Tea or Coffee—Coupon T36 now valid.

FOUNDED 1886 VOL. LVIII—No. 295 MArine 1161 VANCOUVER, BRITISH COLUMBIA, THURSDAY, JULY 20, 1944 PRICE 5 CENTS $1.00 per month BY CARRIER

British Now Seven Miles Past Caen

Nazi Defenses on Orne Breached Along 10-Mile Front as Rommel's Armor Falls Back Towards Paris

ALLIED SUPREME HEADQUARTERS, July 20 —(CP)—The British 2nd Army has pushed armored spearheads seven miles south and east of Caen and breached Nazi defenses on the Orne River along a 10-mile front, driving battered remnants of 5½ crack SS. and Panzer divisions back towards Paris and the Seine.

Caen and its southern suburb of Fauborg de Vaucelles have been left behind by advancing British and Canadian columns rolling into the plain southeast of the city and overrunning village after village fortified by the Germans to stem General Montgomery's advance.

Field Marshall Rommel was on the run again and it was not clear whether he intended to risk a major battle in the Caen plain or stage a fighting withdrawal towards Paris.

Near VINONT

He has lost heavily already in me nand material in the new British-Canadian thrust.

Strong British and Canadian armored formations have captured 12 towns and now are approaching Vimont, eight miles southeast of Caen on the road to Paris, headquarters announced.

Just short of Vimont the armored drive led by Lt.-Gen. Sir Richard Nugent (Rory) O'Connor—who was captured in the African desert in 1941, but escaped from an Italian prison camp—jabbed into battered German positions after carving out a four-mile-wide spearhead south from the vicinity of Troarn, east of Caen.

Comparative quiet was registered on the American front except for local advances between St. Lo and Periers which took three villages, headquarters announced.

In addition to the great armored push in the plain east and south of Caen, General Montgomery's troops, turning south from cleaned-up Faubourg de Vaucelles, immediately below Caen, drove south for two and

Please Turn to Page Two
See "Normandy"

Canadians Take Vital Hill Base

By ROSS MUNRO
Canadian Press War Correspondent

WITH THE CANADIANS ON THE CAEN FRONT, FRANCE—July 20.—Canadian troops have captured Hill 76, three miles south of Vaucelles, after taking the town of Fleury on the east bank of the Orne River.

Infantry carried out the attack on this dominating hill with tanks supporting them and a heavy Canadian artillery barrage preceding the assault.

Earlier, other Canadian infantry cleaned up Cormelles, a mile southeast of Vaucelles, and Canadians also occupied the village of Ifs between Fleury and Cormelles.

TEAMWORK

While the Canadians slug their way forward on the right flank of this salient, British troops are fighting in the outskirts of Troarn and have cleaned up the Cagny area on the Vaucelles-Vimont road. There also is fighting in the Bourgeous area.

A British staff officer at 2nd Army headquarters said the big achievement of the current battle was the capture of the Caen-Vaucelles area.

It was Canadian troops which carried out the assault here but

Please Turn to Page Two
See "Canadians"

VICE-PRESIDENT IN FIGHTING MOOD

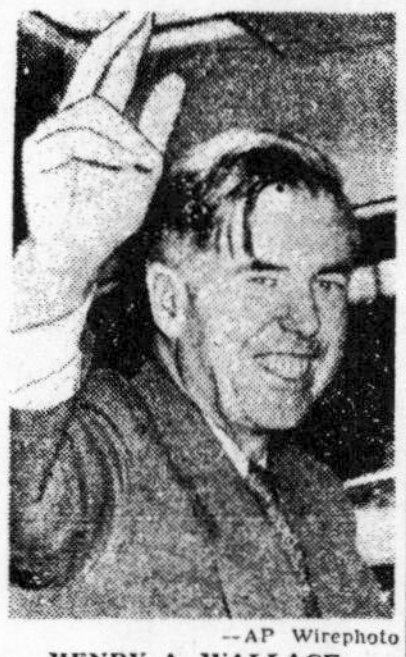

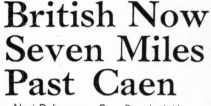

—AP Wirephoto

HENRY A. WALLACE

Arriving in Chicago to battle for renomination as President's running mate.

Supporters Of Wallace Hold Rally

CONVENTION HEADQUARTERS, July 20 — (BUP) — Western states supporters of Vice-President Henry A. Wallace today pushed a campaign for his renomination after hearing his personal assurance that he intended "to fight in every way I can."

Arriving unexpectedly at a midnight mass meeting of western delegates, Wallace spoke extemporaneously and thanked his friends for riding his fight for Liberalism and renomination.

Wallace said he was making his fight "in a joyous manner, without concern as to who my opponents may be." Then turning to a supporter of his liberal principles, Wallace said:

"The American people really are on the march and will not stop, the vital position taken by labor, such as the political action committee (CIO), is only one of manay signs, an index of the temperament of the people. There is a fresh wind blowing through the United States, which will rise ever stronger until we are using all our power and skills for a higher standard of living.'

Mrs. Helen Gahagan Douglas, Hollywood actress and retiring California committeewoman who organized the Wallace Testimonial meeting, led the ovation Wallace received.

Underground in Belgium Revolts

ALLIED SUPREME HEADQUARTERS, July 20—(AP)—An underground revolt in Belgium was reported tonight in a special communique from Allied Headquarters.

Victoria Man Wounded

VICTORIA, July 20—(CP)—Spr. Robert Marshall, formerly with the Provincial Police here, was wounded in France two weeks ago, his wife was advised Wednesday.

Reds at Prussian Border

Berlin Reports Heavy Fighting 8 Miles From Frontier

By JOSEPH GRIGG
Special to The Vancouver Sun

LONDON, July 20—(BUP)—The Red Army hammered at the gates of East Prussia today. Berlin indicated in reporting heavy fighting only eight miles from the frontier, and far to the south the Russians drove within sight of the great fortress city of Lwow in lower Poland.

Nazi broadcasts reported that Soviet assault forces had pushed to Augustow, 38 miles northwest of Grodno and on the border of the Suwalki triangle eight miles from the soil of Germany proper.

UNDER FIRE

"Our troops see Lwow," the Russian government newspaper **Izvestia** was quoted. "Now our tanks have started forward to attack the city."

Lwow, the biggest German base on the southern route to Berlin, already was under fire from Soviet artillery, and Red Army shock troops were closing in for the final assault on the nine-way rail hub.

North of Lwow the right wing of Marshal Ivan S. Konev's 1st Army of the Ukraine already was swarming across the Bug River into the part of Poland from which Adolf Hitler launched the invasion of Russia.

Moscow and Berlin reports agreed that Soviet armies were driving forward in all key sectors of the battlefront from the upper Baltics to lower Poland, and threatening half a dozen key bases vital to the Nazi defenses.

CLOSE ON CITIES

The Nazi report of violent fighting at Augustow, directly before lower East Prussia, was the first sign of a Soviet drive to the immediate environs of the German province.

Midway between Lithuania and Lwow, other Russian forces were closing on Brest-Litovsk from positions less than eight miles away, and the early storming of Bialystok from a springboard less than 25 miles distant was in prospect.

Churchill to Speak Aug. 2

LONDON, July 20—(CP)—Prime Minister Churchill will deliver a statement to the House of Commons on the war situation August 2, Foreign Secretary Eden told the House today.

Mr. Eden announced that the House of Commons probably would adjourn August 3 until September 26, but said that if necessary its members would be recalled.

Fuehrer Burned by Bomb Blast; Generals Injured

TOO BAD THEY MISSED

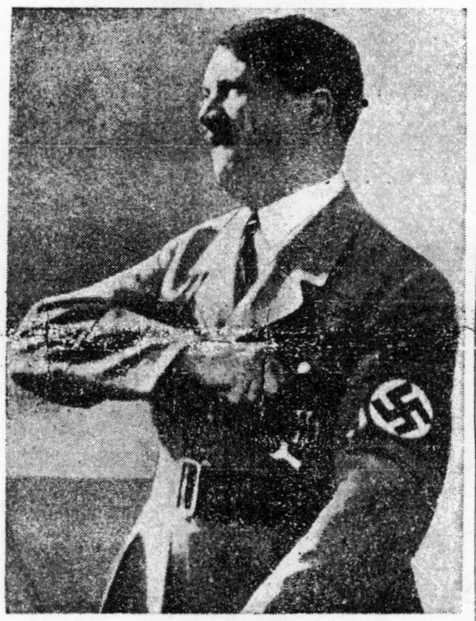

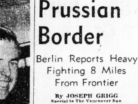

ADOLF HITLER

Suffers Slight Concussion in Explosion Just Before Meeting Mussolini; 'Inside Job' Hinted

LONDON, July 20—(BUP)—Adolf Hitler was slightly burned and bruised and received a "light brain concussion" and a number of his high-ranking army and navy officers were injured, four of them seriously, today in what the German DNB news agency said was "a bomb attempt on the life of the fuehrer."

DNB said that shortly after the attempt, Reichsmarshal Hermann Goering—who Hitler designed as the heir to Nazi leadership at the beginning of the war—"joined the fuehrer."

This indicated that Goering was not present when the explosives went off.

DNB added that after the explosion, Hitler "resumed his work" and received former Italian premier Bénito Mussolini, "as intended."

Officers Shield Hitler

Officers clustered around Hitler apparently received the full strength of the blast, shielding Hitler himself. Those listed as seriously injured were:

Lieutenant General Schmundt.
Colonel Brandt.
Lieutenant Colonel Borgmann.
Borgmann's aide, Berger.

The following were listed as receiving minor injuries:

Gen. Alfred Jodl, Chief of Hitler's personal staff.
Maj. Gen. Guenther Korten, chief of staff of the luftwaffe.
General Buhlke.
Gen. Karl Bodenschatz, liaison officer between Hitler and the air marshal's office.
General Heusinger.
Gen Scherff.
Admiral von Puttkamer.
Admiral Voss.

DNB did not spcify whether the explosion was caused by a bomb planted inside the room in which Hitler and his commanders were conferring or whether the explosion might have been from a bomb launched from an Allied plane and pin-pointed as in recent attacks on German headquarters in Holland and France.

The fact that the attempt evidently occurred inside Hitler's personal headquarters—as difficult to penetrate as the White House or No. 10 Downing Street—raised speculation in London that it might have been an "inside job" by Germans disgruntled with the conduct of the war and hopeful for a negotiated peace if the leader of Nazism were removed.

May Be More Serious

This is the first assassination attempt, so far as is known, in which Hitler was injured. The only previous publicized attempt was on November 8 1939, when a bomb exploded in a Munich beer hall shortly after the Fuehrer appeared at a Nazi party meeting there.

This was regarded at the time as a Gestapo trick to strengthen the German home front.

It was considered possible that Hitler's injuries were more serious than was broadcast to the world by DNB and that the agency's careful statement that the Fuehrer resumed his work and received Mussolini and Goering was a coverup.

Observers believed the attempt on Hitler's life was in some way connected with a 14-hour interruption of communications between Germany and neutral countries yesterday and today.

Two Jap Premiers To Succeed Tojo

'Moderates' to Take Over Control; Peace Offensive Expected

WASHINGTON, July 20—(BUP)—Emperor Hirohito today commissioned Gen. Kuniaki Koiso and former Premier Admiral Mitsumasa Yonai, both known to be friendly toward the United States before Pearl Harbor, to form a new Japanese cabinet in successio nto that of Gen. Hideki Tojo, which resigned en bloc after confessing it could not win the war.

Announcement by the official Japanese Domei news agency that two political "moderates" had been entrusted with the organization of a new government confirmed that the extremist military clique which put Tojo in power and engineered the sneak attack on Pearl Harbor had lost control of Japan.

PEACE MOVE

The move was regarded as the first step toward an ultimate Japanese attempt to win a negotiated peace, though no immediate peace bid was aticipated.

Sources familiar with the Japanese political situation suggested the new cabinet would attempt to intensify the Japanese war effort, then give way to another governmnet within the next few months as American successes in the Pacific mount.

Only when a wholly civilian government comes into power, these sources believed, will Japan make a real effort to withdraw from the war

Domei broadcasts heard by FCC monitors said that Koiso,

Please Turn to Page Two
See "Japan"

Robots Launched Well Inside France

LONDON, July 20—(CP)—Belief that the Germans now are launching their flying bombs from bases inside France which thus far have largely escaped Allied air assaults, was expressed here today as the robots continued to rain upon London and southern England.

Last night's robot assaults were somewhat less violent than those of yesterday when the barrage reached a record.

Minister of Health Henry U. Willink told the House of Commons more than 170,000 women and children had been evacuated from London since July 2.

Six Dead, Eight Injured

Transport Crash Kills Four Vancouver Fliers

Western Air Command announced today that four Vancouver men were among the six persons killed when an RCAF transport crashed while taking off from a west coast station at noon Tuesday. Eight other persons were injured in the crash, four of them seriously.

The dead are:

Lt.-Col. O. W. Steele, Western Command Dental Officer, whose wife resides at 3779 West Fourth.

FO. William J. Curtis, second pilot of the plane, whose wife and year-old daughter reside at 227 West Seventeenth.

WO-1 L. C. Rideout, radio operator, whose wife resides at 2181 West Tenth.

Sgt. C. D. Kippan, whose mother, Mrs. Jessie Kippan, lives at 4098 West Sixteenth.

Flt.-Lt. T. E. Daniels, pilot of the plane, son of Louis H. Daniels, Gardenia, California.

Flt.-Lt. Wallace B. Stroud, whose wife lives at 31 Keppela, Toronto.

EIGHT INJURED

Injured are:

Cpl. O. N. Perry (WD), whose father, H. R. Perry, resides in East Kelowna, B. C., seriously injured; Skipper J. M. Olsen, RCNVR, 2880 West Twenty-fourth, seriously injured; Sgt. E. J. Hillard, 81 Dynedor Road, Toronto, serioulsy injured; LAW. G. E. Dalton, daughter of W. H. White, Edmonton, seriously injured; Flt.-Sgt. James H. Pigden, Eburne, B.C., slightly injured; C. H. Wallace, Caledon East, Ont., slightly injured; LAW. B. M. Hartley, Edmonton, slightly injured; Flt.-Sgt. S. Jurmain, Prince Rupert, slightly injured.

The big plane, named "The Northern Witch," crashed while taking off and burst into flames when it struck the ground. It was almost completely destroyed.

TOP-NOTCH PILOT

Other pilots of the Air Transport Command described Flt.-Lt. Daniels, pilot of the plane, as "one of the best, if not the best, pilot we have." It was his first accident in more than 15 years of flying. He had 1500 hours of transport flying alone to his credit.

Pilots of this Transport Command fly a nine-hour round trip

Please Turn to Page Two
See "Plane Crash"

Pincers Air Blow Hits Munich, Central Reich

LONDON, July 20—(BUP)—Two great American fleets totaling some 3000 planes smashed at a dozen Nazi war plants and airdromes today in a two-way onslaught from Italy and Britain which scattered destructive bomb loads through Munich, Leipzig, Friedrichshafen, and other cities.

More than 1200 Fortresses and Liberators of the 8th Air Force with a formidable fighter escort swept from Britain deep in central Germany to hit at least eight prime targets, while the 15th Air Force heavyweights hopped over the Alps from Italy and plastered five or more objectives around Munich and Friedrichshafen.

The pincers assault from west and south covered key centres in most of central, western and southern Germany.

The 8th Air Force bombers and fighters flew over scattered cloud formations and found good hunting among aircraft, ball bearing and synthetic oil plants strung through Germany from the Rhineland to Leipzig, 90 miles south of Berlin.

Today's Scratches At Hastings Park

FIRST RACE—Dolly Somers Be Mine, Irish Punch, Simtee.
SECOND RACE—The Chimera, Happy Eva.
THIRD RACE—Si Green.
SEVENTH RACE—Tettie B. Special Lady, Liloade, Royal Suzy.

For entries, Sun Selections and Handicap, see page 19.

Four-Year-Old Discovers New Physical Principle

Robot Repeller Credited to Child

NEW YORK, July 20—(AP)—A 4½-year-old boy was credited by the president of a precision instrument company today with discovering a new physics principle that might lead to the repelling of Nazi robot bombs now being directed at England.

The boy, Frederick Andrus Gautesen of Plainfield, N. J., sat silently at a press conference given by Mrs. H. M. McNab, president of McNab Inc., of Bridgeport, Conn., manufacurers of precision instruments.

Mrs. McNab said a device intended as a counter-agent of the robots had been developed on the basis of the child's chance conversation with a mechanic concerning the similarity of movement between a garter snake and an elastic wrist watch band.

J. Scott Williams, a member of the board of directors of the company, said the principle questioned Newton's third law of motion, that "every action has an equal and opposite reaction."

Mrs. McNab declined to elaborate on the device or the principle, but said:

"Scientists believe it is sound and that it is a step in the direction of repelling the Nazi robot bombs and another weapon that may come from Germany and Japan.

"The army and navy have both been advised, and officials of the company and other scientists who have been working on the project will go to Washington, D.C., tomorrow."

The child's mother, widow of Alf O. Gautesen, a marine engineer killed in an automobile accident two years ago, said the boy was unusually observant.

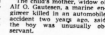

ATTEMPT TO KILL HITLER 'INSIDE JOB'

The Vancouver Sun

FOUNDED 1886
VOL. LVIII—No. 295 VANCOUVER, B.C., JULY 20, 1944 PRICE 5c

Montgomery Drives on Five Miles

Rommel's Armored Forces Falling Back Towards Paris; Caen Left Behind

ALLIED SUPREME HEADQUARTERS, July 20 —(AP)—British tanks and infantry have pushed four or five miles deep on a wide front into the plain country south of Caen, headquarters announced tonight.

The advance of British and Canadians of the British 2nd Army carried into the streets of Bourgeubus, south of Caen, and expanded both east and west of the towns.

More heavy fighting swirled around the outskirts of Troarn, east of Caen.

NEAR VIMONT

The supreme command said there was "no stabilization of the front" and that armored columns were pushing forward in all directions.

Field Marshal Rommel was on the run again and it was not clear whether he intended to risk a major battle in the Caen plain or stage a fighting withdrawal towards Paris.

Strong British and Canadian armored formations have captured 12 towns and now are approaching Vimont, eight miles southeast of Caen on the road to Paris, headquarters announced.

Just short of Vimont the armored drive led by Lt.-Gen. Sir Richard Nugent (Rory) O'Connor—who was captured in the African desert in 1941, but escaped from an Italian prison camp—jabbed into battered German positions after carving out a four-mile-wide spearhead south from the vicinity of Troarn, east of Caen.

REGINA, July 20 — (CP) — Hon. George H. Williams, minister of agriculture, confined to hospital suffering from a heart attack, is reported to be "improving slightly."

Late News Flashes

NON-STOP FLIGHT

WASHINGTON, July 20—(AP)—First non-stop flight from London to Washington, D.C., was made this week by an army air transport command crew in a C-54, four-engined Douglas transport plane, the war department disclosed today.

The flight covered 3800 miles and was made in exactly 18 hours elapsed time.

BONIN ISLANDS HIT

WASHINGTON, July 20 —(AP)—Big navy bombers, presumably flying north from Saipan, attacked the Bonin Islands only 632 miles from Tokyo Tuesday, Admiral Chester W. Nimitz, Pacific commander in chief, reported today.

The attack was the first by land-based bombers on the Bonin group, which is well within the inner defenses of Japan.

INJUNCTION SOUGHT

DETROIT, July 20—(AP)—Henry J. Kaiser, West Coast shipbuilder who has been credited with plans to enter the automobile industry after the war, filed a petition in federal court here Wednesday for a temporary injunction restraining two Detroit consulting engineers from disclosing details of three inventions adaptable to automobiles.

FIREMEN BOMB VICTIMS

OTTAWA, July 20—(CP)—Listing three recent Canadian firemen casualties overseas, War Service Minister LaFleche said today in the Commons that a Canadian detachment has been organized for service in Europe.

He listed the casualties as:

Dead: Senior Fireman John Stewart Coull, Winnipeg.

Injured: Leading Fireman John Robert, Cook Leguee, Winnipeg; Senior Fireman Joseph Antoine Willie Cassidy, Campbellton, N.B.

He said the casualties were the result of "enemy bombs somewhere in England."

BASEBALL

AMERICAN LEAGUE

At Detroit— R. H. E.
Washington .. 203 000 002— 6 11 0
Detroit ...... 230 011 00x— 7 11 4
Cardini, Wolff (2), Lefebvre (8) and Ferrell; Beck, Gentry (3), Newhouser (9) and Richards.

NATIONAL LEAGUE

R. H. E.
Pittsburgh .. 002 200 000— 4 11 1
Philadelphia . 001 000 000— 1 10 0
Starr and Davis; Lee, Karl (8) and Peacock.
Second game— R. H. E.
Pittsburgh 000 000 020 00— 2 9 1
Philadelphia 100 100 000 01— 3 11 0
Sewell, Roe (8), Rescigno (10), Strincevich (11) and Lopez; Barrett, Schanz and Finely.
Cincinnati .... 003 100 200— 6 7 1
Brooklyn ..... 000 000 000— 0 8 0
Gumbert and Mueller; McLish, King (7), Branc (8) and Owen.
(14 Innings)
Chicago 000 300 001 000 00—4 8 0
Boston 110 011 000 000 01—5 17 5
Wyse, Derringer, Holm (7), Williams (9) and Kreitner; Tobin and Masi.
St. Louis ... 205 000 201—10 12 0
New York ... 011 000 000— 2 9 2
M. Cooper and W. Cooper; Brewer, Pyle (3), Heusser (8) and Mancuso.

VOT HIT ME, HERMANN?

According to news dispatches, Reichsmarshal Hermann Goering joined Hitler soon after he was victim of a bomb attempt on his life. "Too bad they weren't more successful" was the general comment in Vancouver today.

Wallace in Surprise Comeback

CHICAGO STADIUM, July 20.—Henry A. Wallace, regarded by many as all but counted out only 24 hours ago, hit the comeback trail in his fight for renomination today as a convention which is overwhelmingly for a fourth term for the President was split wide open in a major row over second place.

Kansas, its 16 convention votes previously unpledged, caucused and balloted unanimously in favor of the tousled-haired Iowan —possibly indicating a new trend among some of the previously uncommitted delegations.

Man in Hospital From Gun Wound

John Fillmore Warne, 35, was taken to General Hospital shortly before noon today suffering from a gunshot wound in the head. Hospital authorities said later he was "doing fairly well."

The shooting took place at 1235 Hornby where the injured man had rooms. Police found a .38 calibre revolver.

Yank Casualties In Italy 73,000

WASHINGTON, July 20—(BUP)—Acting Secretary of War Robert P. Patterson reported today that Fifth Army casualties in Italy from the initial landings through June 12 totalled 73,166—an increase of 2767 above the June 3 total.

RCMP Probes Speeches at Quebec Rally

OTTAWA, July 20 — (CP) — Justice Minister St. Laurent said today in Commons that the RCMP are investigating the accuracy of a report which quoted Jacques Sauriol, Montreal newspaperman, as having criticized English soldiers at a political rally.

Gordon Graydon, Progressive Conservative house leader, said that Mr. St. Laurent might also have the mounties investigate a CCF meeting at Lethbridge, Alta," where they seem to have taken the law into their own hands."

He was referring to an interruption of a speech by M. J. Coldwell, CCF leader, in which the interrupter failed to apologize and was bodily removed from the hall.

Mr. St. Laurent replied that he hoped the leader of the opposition did not expect his department "to investigate every little brawl that occurs."

Churchill to Speak Aug. 2

LONDON, July 20—(CP)—Prime Minister Churchill will deliver a statement to the House of Commons on the war situation August 2, Foreign Secretary Eden told the House today.

Mr. Eden announced that the House of Commons probably would adjourn August 3 until September 26, but said that if necessary its members would be recalled.

Railbird

1—Ever Lazy, True Act, Little Pine.
2—Black Mist, Chief Lon, Red Fez.
3—Maid of Broxa, Valdina Jill, Maestro Sascha.
4—Showum, Naperton, The Mouse.
5—Sun Madras, Perfect Prince, Timely Ayre.
6—Black Memory, Pass Forward, Ebony Lad.
7—Daisy Boy, Lady Giovando, Brilliant Help.
ONE BEST—Daisy Boy

4 City Fliers Die In Crash

Death Toll of Six In Transport Crash; Eight Injured

Western Air Command announced today that four Vancouver men were among the six persons killed when an RCAF transport crashed while taking off from a west coast station at noon Tuesday. Eight other persons were injured in the crash, four of them seriously.

The dead are:

Lt.-Col. C. W. Steele, Western Command Dental Officer, whose wife resides at 3779 West Fourth.

FO. William J. Curtis, second pilot of the plane, whose wife

Please Turn to Page Two
See "City Fliers"

Cholera in India Takes Heavy Toll

PAINA, India, July 20 — (CP) A severe cholera epidemic has taken a toll of 34,850 lives in North Bihar since its outbreak three months ago, according to official figures disclosed Wednesday. The largest mortality is in the districts of Muzzafarpur and Champaran.

Canadians Take Vital Hill Base

By ROSS MUNRO
Canadian Press War Correspondent

WITH THE CANADIANS ON THE CAEN FRONT, FRANCE—July 20.—Canadian troops have captured Hill 67, three miles south of Vaucelles, after taking the town of Fleury on the east bank of the Orne River.

Infantry carried out the attack on this dominating hill with tanks supporting them and a heavy

Please Turn to Page Two
See "Canadians"

Sun Handicap

by ALF COTTRELL

The bracketed figures after the weight indicate the rating of the horse for that particular race. If a horse carries more than the weight stipulated in the entries, deduct one point for each pound of overweight carried. Bracketed figures at end of line indicate post position. Jockeys, post positions, subject to late changes.

FRIDAY, JULY 21

1st Race—Allowance, 3-year-olds and up. **7 Furlongs**

4412	**EVER LAZY (Neal)** ..	113	(79)	**Rail gives narrow margin**	(1)
4479	**PENNDID (a)**	112	(78)	**Speed but bad post spot**	(10)
4477	**HAPPY EVA (a) (Cl'm)**	102	(78)	**Seems fairly shifty sort**	(7)
(4459)	True Act (Haller)	107	(77)	Last strictly sensational	(2)
4468	Sword Dance (Bassett)..	118	(74)	Was bet on and missed	(5)
4458	Little Pine (Hruschak).	108	(68)	Last race was only fair	(4)
4472	Sonny Rock (Allen) ...	108	(67)	Closed world of ground	(9)
4459	Hardtocatch (Jasperson)	102	(64)	True Act beat him easily	(6)
——	McGregor (Young) ...	107	(—)	Been green but can run	(3)
4422	The Chimera	113	(—)	Hasn't shown ability yet	(8)

(a)—L. Luce entry.

2nd Race—Claiming, three-year-olds and up. **7 Furlongs**

4450	**BLACK MIST (Slocum)**	113	(97)	**Bad post but very sharp**	(8)
4471	**BELLE GLORY (Siv'ght)**	103	(86)	**Speed gives royal chance**	(11)
(4438)	**RED FEZ (Young)** ...	113	(84)	**Improved and dead fit**	(3)
(4466)	Chief Lon (Bailey)	118	(78)	Won in Jog; is improved	(7)
4457	Goldenworth (Bassett)..	108	(75)	Might catch them fading	(4)
4470	Act Three	108	(75)	May help with the pace	(9)
4425	Sa[illegible]worth (Haller) ...	113	(—)	Mud might turn scales	(5)
4458	Your It (R. Johnston) ..	103	(—)	Probably needs racing	(6)
4457	Brown Band	108	(68)	Seems overmatched here	(10)
4457	Jeff Himself (Arnold)..	108	(—)	May need maiden race	(12)
——	Proud Baby	108	(—)	First start; may do later	(1)
4466	Pala Hills (Hruschak)	108	(—)	Would need improvement	(2)

3rd Race—Claiming, three-year-olds and up. **1 Mile and 1-16**

(4464)	**HI-MEADOWS (R. John.)**	x103	(93)	**Could upset at weights**	(2)
(4462)	**MAID OF BROXA (B'l'y)**	108	(92)	**Beat the same bunch**	(4)
4468	**WELBECK (Clode)**	x113	(88)	**Trainer surprised them**	(7)
4462	Maestro Sascha (Sloc'm)	118	(86)	Only lost in last strides	(5)
4462	Valdina Jill (Bassett) ..	109	(83)	Doesn't win many races	(1)
——	Blue Countess (Sive'ght)	108	(—)	Fair sort from prairies	(3)
——	Nell Strome	108	(—)	Another handy race mare	(6)

4th Race—Claiming, three-year-olds and up. **7 Furlongs**

4417	**SHOWUM (Sivewright).**	110	(88)	**Should get the nod here**	(2)
4470	**SILUMO (Slocum)**	105	(80)	**Old gal going well now**	(1)
4463	**LADY SERAJEVO (Jo'n)**	x105	(79)	**Bit better than thought**	(10)
4432	Naperton (Bailey)	115	(78)	Fresh and rates as threat	(3)
4470	The Mouse (Haller) ...	110	(77)	In traffic jam last try	(4)
——	Gatlin. (Clode)	x110	(—)	Fair router at Caliente	(6)
4457	Build Up	105	(73)	This one could close fast	(13)
4420	Will Call	102	(—)	Went well as 2-year-old	(11)
4466	Somer Holiday (Bassett)	108	(67)	Is gradually improving	(5)
4458	Liloade (Neal)	105	(—)	Occasionally gets close	(8)
4466	Glad Answer	110	(—)	Had speed; may surprise	(15)
4432	Taken	115	(—)	Bad-legged; mud may aid	(16)
4465	Bridge City	113	(—)	Never shown any class	(14)
4453	Half Moon Bay (Jasp'n)	115	(—)	Drops down with easier	(7)
——	Better News	108	(—)	Stranger to these parts	(12)
4466	Parlan (Hruschak) ...	103	(—)	Been failure to date	(9)

(First eight to start, balance to be used as substitute, if necessary.)

5th Race—Allowance, three-year-olds and up **7 Furlongs**

4460	**LITTLE GLOOMY (K'ly)**	118	(89)	**Tough spot but real sharp**	(2)
4475	**PLUCKY JAKE (R. J'n)**	118	(89)	**Threat with these horses**	(11)
4440	**SUN MADRAS (Wilb'ne)**	118	(88)	**Favorite and one to trim**	(6)
——	Perfect Prince (Siv'ght)	113	(—)	Speed; tough one to catch	(1)
4467	Watch Tick	113	(81)	Debut tightened this one	(9)
4474	Timely Ayre (Bailey) ..	113	(78)	Should cop a dash soon	(3)
4468	Nalod (Haller)	113	(75)	May be awaiting a spot	(4)
4474	Jazzy Fay (Slocum) ..	108	(73)	This one might awaken	(7)
4469	Eno-Heather (Arnold)..	113	(75)	Probably needs cheaper	(10)
4427	Band O'Gold (Bassett)..	108	(—)	Speed; is a possibility	(5)
4422	Bonnie Park (Duncan)	113	(—)	May need more racing	(8)

6th Race—Claiming, 3-year-olds and up. **1 Mile and 1-16**

4455	**PASS FORWARD (D'c'n)**	118	(95)	**Should have margin here**	(6)
4468	**MARION SOMERS (W'n)**	107	(89)	**Fit and has light packafe**	(5)
4464	**EBONY LAD (Haller)** ..	118	(85)	**Good router mud or dry**	(1)
(4456)	Wild Deer (Slocum)	108	(85)	Meeting tougher gang here	(3)
4455	Lady Macduff (Siv'ght)	106	(84)	Stamina and is danger	(2)
4462	Black Memory (Bassett)	109	(83)	Tired but with classier	(4)

7th Race—Claiming, three-year-olds and up. **7 Furlongs**

(4460)	**BRILLIANT HELP (H'r)**	113	(95)	**Chance to win another**	(3)
(4467)	**LADY GIOVANDO (H'k)**	108	(91)	**Never better; one to beat**	(5)
4450	**SI GREEN (a) (Kelly)**	113	(88)	**Always rates a thought**	(1)
(4436)	Daisy Boy (Slocum) ..	118	(88)	Beat top one at Lansdowne	(6)
4464	Trip Over (Bailey) ...	118	(81)	Can run when in mood	(2)
4480	Little Ruler (b) (Sl'm)	111	(—)	Check Thursday race	(4)
4481	Spanish Ball (Bassett)	118	(78)	Also went on Thursday	(7)
4443	Bob-Jack (b)	111	(77)	Mud moves him up some	(8)
4444	Simonette (a)	108	(76)	Been gallant race mare	(9)

(b)—Lochead entry. (a)—J. A. H. Stable entry.

One Best—SHOWUM.

Weather drizzling. Track slow. First post 3:30 p.m.
x—Apprentice allowance claimed.

'Assassins Being Pursued'—Berlin

LONDON, July 20 — (BUP) — Belief grew here tonight that today's attempt to assassinate Adolf Hitler with a bomb was an "inside job."

The official German news agency DNB announced that Adolf Hitler and 13 of his top military and naval collaborators were injured in an attempt on the fuehrer's life when a bomb exploded during a conference at the fuehrer's headquarters.

DNB listed Hitler's injuries as slight burns, bruises, and BBC listeners quoted the agency as saying that Hitler also had a slight concussion of the brain.

The weight of the blast fell upon a cluster of gold-braided Nazis around him. They included seven generals and two admirals. Three were wounded seriously and 10 others, among them Gen. Alfred Jodl, chief of Hitler's personal military staff and an ardent Nazi, escaped with minor injuries.

Radio Berlin subsequently charged the Allies with the attempt on Hitler's life, asserting:

"Fate protected the fuehrer from an attempt by the enemy, who has so often worked with murderous methods and who once again tried to achieve with murder what he couldn't achieve by fair methods."

(The NBC in New York reported that the Berlin radio announced that the assassins had escaped "but police are on their trail.)

Mussolini Escapes

Benito Mussolini, "premier of the Republican Fascist state in northern Italy, appeared to have escaped the bombing by a few minutes.

DNB said Hitler was about to confer with Mussolini when the explosion occurred and tha tafter the debris had been cleared and the wounded cared for, the fuehrer "resumed his work and conferred with Mussolini as intended.

The Nazi propagandists also recorded that Reichsmarshal Hermann Goering—whom Hitler had picked at the outset of the war as the heir to his leadership—arrived shortly and conferred with Hitler. Propaganda Minister Paul Joseph Goebbels also arrived after the explosion.

One of the four seriously injured was Lt. Gen. Schmundt, chief adjutant of the Wehrmacht since 1938 and described by the German Transocean News Agency as "belonging to the closest following of Hitler."

The DNB dispatch indicated that Goering was not present when the blast occurred.

Officers Shield Hitler

Officers clustered around Hitler apparently received the full strength of the blast, shielding Hitler himself. Those listed as seriously injured were:

Lt. General Schmundt.
Col. Brandt.
Collaborator Berger.

The following were listed as receiving minor injuries.

Gen. Alfred Jodl, chief of Hitler's personal staff.
Maj. Gen. Guenther Korten, chief of staff of the Luftwaffe.
Gen. Buhlke.
Gen. Karl Bodenschatz, liaison officer between Hitler and the air marshal's office.
Gen. Heusinger.
Gen. Scherff.
Rear Admiral Hans Erick Voss, member of Hitler's personal staff.
Rear Admiral Karl-Jesco Puttkammer, naval aide de camp to Hitler.
Lt. Col. Borgmann.
Naval Capt. Assman.

GEN. JODL.

DNB did not specify whether the explosion was caused by a bomb planted inside the room in which Hitler and his commanders were conferring or whether the explosion might have been from a bomb launched from an Allied plane and pin-pointed as in recent attacks on German headquarters in Holland and France.

The fact that the attempt evidently occurred inside Hitler's personal headquarters—as difficult to penetrate as the

Please Turn to Page Two See "Hitler Blast"

Lucky Gold

1—Happy Eva, Sword Dance, Ever Lazy.
2—Chief Lon, Black Mist, Red Fez.
3—Hi Meadows, Maid of Broxa, Valdina Jill.
4—The Mouse, Naperton, Silumo.
5—Sun Madras, Little Gloomy, Jazzy Fay.
6—Pass Forward, Black Memory, Wild Deer.
7—Daisy Boy, Trip Over, Lady Giovando.
One best—THE MOUSE.

Sunstar

1—Ever Lazy, Happy Eva, The Chimera.
2—Chief Lon, Red Fez, Black Mist.
3—Maid of Broxa, Hi Meadows, Valdina Jill.
4—The Mouse, Naperton, Silumo.
5—Little Gloomy, Nalod, Sun Madras.
6—Black Memory, Wild Deer, Pass Forward.
7—Lady Giovando, Si Green, Daisy Boy.
One best—CHIEF LON.

Few Attacks on Hitler

LONDON, July 20—(AP)—For a dictator, Hitler's life has been singularly free of recorded attempts to assassinate him.

The most notable episode developing from internal opposition to Hitler was in June, 1934, shortly after he had taken power in Germany, when he led the ruthless "blood purge" of Capt. Ernst Roehm and his associates.

Roehm's movement was described as a "rebellious riot" in the Reichstag session which Hitler summoned to hear his accounting.

Helmuth Hirsch, 21, a Jew, was arrested December 20, 1936, however, on what informed persons in Berlin at the time said were charges of carrying explosives for the purpose of making an attempt on the life of a high German personage. Berlin dispatches at the time said his intended victim may have been Hitler.

Hirsch was executed despite intercession on his behalf by the United States Government. Hirsch was a naturalized U. S. citizen, who was arrested at Berlin upon his arrival from Prague, Czechoslovakia.

In the Munich beer hall bombing in 1939, Hitler left the hall just nine minutes before a time bomb exploded in a pillar of the wall near the rostrum where he had spoken to his party followers. Six persons were killed and more than 60 injured in the blast.

An arrest was made for the bombing, but Berlin authorities never announced the outcome of their investigation. At the time the Gestapo attempted to pin responsibility on British agents.

THE KING IN ITALY

★★★★★ FINAL

THE VANCOUVER DAILY PROVINCE

50th YEAR—NO. 100 VANCOUVER, B.C., MONDAY, JULY 24, 1944—20 PAGES PRICE 5 CENTS BY CARRIER $1.00 per month

Russ Smash 50 Divisions; Nazis Flee From Poland

Red Armies Score Big Advances

LONDON, July 24.—(CP)—Russian troops have reached the River San in Southern Poland on a front of 50 miles in another big westward advance, the Russian communique announced tonight.

LONDON. July 24. — (AP) — Premier Stalin announced tonight the capture of the rail centre of Lublin in southeastern Poland.

By DANIEL DE LUCE.
(Associated Press War Correspondent.)

MOSCOW, July 24.—The German Army fled in disorder through central Poland today as the Russians advanced within 70 miles of Warsaw and fought through the streets of Lublin only 25 miles from the Wisla (Vistula) River line, which Hitler must hold to stave off a direct assault on the Reich.

In Stalin's juggenaut offensive, entering it's second month with increasing momentum, the Red Army has captured 23 German generals and knocked out possibly 50 of the Germans' 250 divisions in the East—perhaps 500,000 or more men.

The battle of Poland, already assuming catastrophic consequences for Hitler's eastern front, was shaping into a struggle for Prussia itself.

PASS BREST LITOVSK.

The Red Army moved deeply into the Baltic republics and in the south struck close to the Carpathian defenses of Hungary and Czechoslovakia, but it was over the wide, rolling Polish plains that Stalin's war of movement hourly gained new decisions.

Brest Litovsk was by-passed in a pocket 40 miles deep. Soviet troops mounted a front attack which battered into that Bug River city's suburbs.

Red Army columns spearing from rail lines northeast and southeast advanced as close as 20 miles from Siedlice, 50 miles east of Warsaw.

Seventy miles to the south, despairing and trapped Germans were driven street by street from Lublin.

GERMAN BLEAT.

The German radio asserted today that Russian troops had advanced within 50 miles of Warsaw and had broken into Lwow and Lublin, great Polish rail centres.

Marshal Rokossovsky's vanguard of cavalry and tanks was within 25 miles of the Upper Wisla (Vistula) River on a steadily widening front. Red Army engineers rushed bridging materials and prepared to span this river line as swiftly as the Bug was crossed last week.

Once the Wisla (Vistula) defense zone is turned, the way

(Continued on Page 2.)
See RUSSIA.

Fingerprint Jails Murder Suspect After 19 Years

WINNIPEG, July 24.—(CP)—Sought by police for 19 years, Alexander Danilhik, 55, wanted in Detroit for murder and armed robbery, was arrested by Royal Canadian Mounted Police here at the week-end.

He is charged with being a principal in the murder of Andrew Kaczarek in Detroit November 1, 1925. Police said three other men were implicated in the crime.

Kacznarek was robbed of a bankbook, and then killed. His body, weighted with cement, was thrown in the Rouge River at Detroit. With the bank book and a forged order, the men obtained $11,577 from Kacznarek's account in the People's State Bank.

A routine fingerprint check at the plant of the Dominion Industries Ltd. in Transcona, near here, led to his arrest.

Vancouver Men

Wounded Veterans In Canada

Between 15 and 20 veterans of overseas service, from Vancouver or vicinity, some of them veterans of the bloody fighting in Italy and Normandy have arrived in Canada aboard the hospital ship Lady Nelson.

They are expected to arrive here within the next few days.

Pte. H. E. Fretz, whose wife and two children, Alchea and Meryl, live at 1415 Rupert, was wounded in Normandy on June 14, but came back because of lung trouble.

Pte. Fretz, with the Engineers, was engaged in financial business here before his enlistment early in the war. He has been away for four years, three of them overseas.

He was born in Ontario but has lived in Vancouver for a number of years. A brother, Vernon Fretz, lives near Penticton.

(Continued on Page 2.)
See WOUNDED.

FUN IN OTTAWA RIVER FOR R.C.A.F. GIRLS

Kicking up their heels in the Ottawa River at Britannia Bay are these R.C.A.F. women personnel. Left to right, in the water: LAW. Rita Doig, Winnipeg; LAW. Joan Guertin, North Bay; Cpl. Dawn Bliss, Toronto; Cpl. Pat Lloyd, Toronto; LAW. Betty Bellhouse, Vancouver; LAW. M. Asseltine, Edmonton. On the rocks are Sgt. Mary Ditta of Toronto, lying down, and Sgt. M. MacIntosh, New Glasgow, N.S.

Firing Squads Work Overtime

BERN, July 24.—(AP)—Journal de Geneve in a despatch from Germany said today "there have been mass executions of officers of all grades" to quell the rebellion against Hitler.

Firing squads worked overtime in interior Germany and also at the front, the despatch said, with hundreds of officers put to death on three days ended July 21.

"At Langericht and Grause Haus," (two notorious Vienna prisons), the article asserted, "executions of military persons for the past four weeks occurred regularly, twice a week. At Grause Haus two cells were dovoted to this bloody and regular work.

$1000 Stolen From City Cafe

Burglars broke into the living quarters at the rear of the Allied Cafe, 1553 Powell, over the week-end, and stole $1000 in bills, 1500 pennies, $3 in American money, a child's bank, three children's bracelets, and a $5 cheque.

A neighbor told police she saw two men hanging around the premises about 10:30 p.m. Sunday.

Returns from Normandy

Signs Of Weakness Seen By Churchill

(By Associated Press.)

LONDON, July 24.—Prime Minister Churchill, back in Britain after a three-day tour of the Normandy front, gave the first official Allied word on the crisis in Germany.

While visiting an R.A.F. flying field in France yesterday, Churchill declared there were "grave signs of weakness" in Germany. He predicted the war "might come to an end earlier than we have a right to say."

Declaring the Germans were not happy on the fighting front, Mr. Churchill remarked:

"And now, suddenly boiling up in their stomachs, has come a deadly quarrel at home. It is not a nice thing for a man to hear of a revolution going on in his own country when he is being attacked."

"Think how you would feel if there was a revolution at home and they were shooting at cabinet ministers."

Of the attempt on Hitler's life, Churchill said with a grin: "They missed the old bounder (rough approximation) — but there's time yet."

The Prime Minister told the airmen: "We seek nothing that is not our own."

FOR THE COMMONWEALTH.

"But what is our own is the Commonwealth—that we don't want any other people to express an opinion about. That we will firmly retain."

"Over the ocean, over the seas and over the fields of France lies the victory that will send you back to your great country. It is a long way from Canada but it 's in the right direction."

"I have no hesitation in saying that the British Commonwealth, with Canada in the van with our Old Country, saved the world and has given other countries time to rearm or time to recognize where their place was in the struggle.

(Continued on Page 2.)
See CHURCHILL.

German Soldiers Must Now Give The Nazi Salute

LONDON, July 24.—(AP)—The "Hitler salute" has been introduced in the German armed forces, the German radio said today.

The regular German Army hitherto had been compelled to give the ordinary army salute. However, Elite Nazi and S.S. forces gave the Hitler salute.

THE HITLER RUMOR POT

Admits Civil War

Marcel Deat, arch-collaborationist and minister of labor in the Vichy cabinet, admitted in a broadcast that there is "civil war" in France and said French forces of the interior are wrecking transport and disorganizing the food supply.

Wilhelmshaven Clash

LONDON. — The German underground radio (Deutsche Volksender) reported that clashes had occurred in Wilhelmshaven between marines and SS. troops. The radio said more officers are being arrested and shot by Himmler's SS. men in garrison towns.

Endorse Judgment

NEW YORK.—The B.B.C. broadcast the following statement to Europe:

"The attitude of the Allies is simple and clear. We endorse the judgment of the generals if not their motives. We would welcome a mass movement in Germany to end the war by capitulation and would accept capitulations from whomever is in a position to offer it and is prepared to carry it out."

Koenigsberg Under Siege

LONDON. — The Moscow radio quoting the Stockholm newspaper Aftontidningen as saying that a "kind of state of siege" had been proclaimed in Konigsberg after East Prussian troops had mutinied. The broadcast said that SS. (Elite Guard) troops had been rushed into Konigsberg, capital of East Prussia, and that street fighting was going on.

Couriers Caught By SS.

MADRID, July 24. — Bordeaux reports said two German military couriers were caught by SS. men en route to Spain, presumably on a contact mission for the anti-Hitler clique.

Hitler Expresses Thanks

LONDON.—Adolf Hitler today thanked the "so many" who had thought of him following the attempt on his life, and said he had received "numerous congratulations and demonstrations . . . particularly from the party and the armed forces."

Say 200 Houses Vacant in City

Claims that there are 200 vacant houses in Vancouver despite a housing shortage were made to Mayor Cornett by a committee of Grandview residents.

The group also protested against pending eviction of George Allan, his wife, and three children from a house at 1416 Odlum drive.

M.P.'s Work Six Days

OTTAWA, July 24. — (CP) — The House of Commons today decided to work six days a week for the rest of the session. It will sit on Saturday, morning, afternoon and evening.

100,000 Watch Bombers Crash

SPOKANE, July 24.—(AP)—A crowd of 100,000, too stunned to make outcry, watched yesterday as two attack bombers collided in diving into a natural amphitheatre and fell in flames during a war show, killed four men.

The ships were part of a parade of various types.

Three of the ships peeled off in formation to dive on the bowl. They banked away from the crowd toward the centre of the amphitheatre.

Stacked up in turning, one of the ships slid into another. Wreckage showered out from them and they fell the few hundred feet to the bottom of the bowl.

Aboard Steam Yacht

TAKE WILBY FOR TRIAL IN NEW YORK

VICTORIA, July 24. — The steam launch Nancy Lee on which Ralph M. Wilby and his police escort left Sunday afternoon for Fort Angeles, was unable to make headway against strong winds and tides and was taken off its course, docking at Friday Harbor, San Juan Islands.

The party's present whereabouts are unknown, but it is presumed they have reached or are heading for Port Angeles, for which the customs papers are made out.

The fireworks which have colored Ralph M. Wilby's four-month battle against extradition to New York fizzled out like spent Roman candles Sunday as United States detectives started him on his way to trial on 17 charges of grand larceny.

Wilby was rushed from Victoria to Port Angeles, Wash., aboard a 40-foot, privately-owned steam yacht, escorted by Sgt. Fred Hains and George Salayka, New York detectives, and Louis Callan, Victoria officer.

Hains and Salayka are the men Wilby's counsel, Gordon S. Wismer, K.C., of Vancouver, threatened to charge with kidnapping after the most spectacular event on the Wilby calendar of exciting occurrences.

CASE CLOSED.

In Vancouver today Mr. Wismer said the case is closed, as far as he is concerned.

"There is nothing I can do now," he said.

"Apparently the minister of justice decided to act at once after Wilby's application for appeal to the Privy Council in London, Eng., was turned down at Victoria Friday.

"The case is out of reach of the Canadian courts now."

Mr. Wismer and W. H. S. Haldane, Victoria, put up a spectacular battle in Vancouver and Victoria courts.

Police Chief J. A. McLellan, Victoria; Claude L. Harrison, city prosecutor and counsel for New York State, and George L. Hunter, assistant district attorney, New York City, refused comment at Victoria, but it was learned that a new "order of surrender" was received Saturday from Ottawa.

The New York detectives acted immediately.

WILBY DISAPPEARED.

Wilby, former chief accountant for William T. Knott Co. Inc., operators of a chain of U.S. department stores, is wanted on grand larceny charges involving $275,000.

He was arrested at Victoria on March 12.

Since then the case has been in court continually.

Fireworks really began on March 4, when Wilby disappeared

(Continued on Page 2.)
See WILBY.

Brigadier Lett Wounded Again

Brig. Sherwood Lett, D.S.O., M.C., seriously wounded at Dieppe, has again been hit in Normandy.

Word to his family here did not indicate how seriously he had been hurt. It was understood he was commanding a Canadian infantry brigade.

Brigadier Lett, well-known lawyer here, was a Rhodes scholar from the University of B.C. in 1920. He has also served on both the senate and board of governors at U.B.C.

Britain's Monarch In Naples

(By Canadian Press.)

NAPLES, July 24. — King George of Great Britain arrived here last night.

His Majesty, on his first visit to Italy since the outbreak of war, was met at the airfield by Gen. Sir Henry Maitland Wilson, Mediterranean commander-in-chief, and Admiral of the Fleet Sir Andrew Browne Cunningham, Britain's first sea lord and chief of naval staff.

Final BULLETINS

Need 2000 Workers

EDMONTON, July 24.—(CP)—Two thousand harvesters from eastern Canada will be needed this year to aid in Alberta's harvest.

To Close Schools

REGINA, July 24.—(CP)—A number of schools with an enrolment of less than 15 pupils will be closed in Saskatchewan in a move designed to ease the acute shortage of teachers in this province, Education Minister Woodrow Lyoyd said today.

EDMONTON, July 24. — (CP) —Body of Mrs. Elsie Alyan, 52, with the throat cut, was discovered on the floor of her bedroom by her husband, Patrick Olyan, Sunday, police said today.

Mrs. Olyan had been in illhelth for some time.

Establish Public's Council

MOSCOW, July 24.—(AP)—The Polish Council of Liberation announces a "people's national council" has been given temporary executive power for "safeguarding the independence and re-establishing the Polish state."

Douglas In Ottawa

OTTAWA, July 24.—(CP)—Premier T. C. Douglas of Saskatchewan, paying his first visit to Ottawa since his party was elected, planned to confer with Finance Minister Ilsley in an effort to make arrangements for paying off feed grain advances owed to the Dominion. Dating back to 1938, they amount to $14,000,000 in principal, and $3,000,000 in interest.

Quebec Member Quits

OTTAWA, July 24. — (CP) — Speaker J. A. Glen announced today that he had received the resignation of Louis Philippe Lizotte, Liberal member for Kamouraska, in Quebec. (It was announced a few weeks ago that Mr. Lizotte planned to give up his federal seat and contest his home constituency in the Quebec elections, August 8.)

Eats Gopher Poison

EDMONTON, July 24.—(CP)—Royal Canadian Mounted Police said today Mrs. Ella Margaret Nighswonder, 20, Botha district, mother of a three-weeks-old baby, committed suicide on Saturday by eating gopher poison at Botha, 110 miles southeast of Edmonton.

Missing Lad Dead

TRAIL, July 24.—(CP) – A search party including police and fire departmants ended its hunt today for seven-year-old Barry Christiano when they found the lad's body in the Columbis River near Salmon Island. Son of Mr. and Mrs. Christiano, the youngster had beenmissing since yesterday.

Heiress Gave Mate $3,000,000

LOS ANGELES, July 24. — (AP)—Barbara Hutton Grant heiress to dime store millions, today sued her ex-husband, the former Danish nobleman Court Haugwitz-Reventlow, for sole custody of their nine-year-old son, Lance. She alleged that his purpose in removing the child to Vancouver, B.C., last month was to harass her in the hope of obtaining large sums of money for the boy's return.

Mrs. Grant, wife of Film Star Cary Grant, asserted Reventlow is not a fit custodian for the boy; "that the desire for money and accumulation of wealth without work . . . is paramount" with him "to the exclusion of other ideas or sentiments."

Mrs. Grant alleged that Reventlow was given to violent fits of temper, disregarded the boy's welfare, and that he is of German birth and ancestry "and indoctrinated with the idea" of his own superiority.

After their marirage, she said she transferred to his bank account $1,477,697. As a price for his consent to a divorce, she said she established for him a trust fund for the same amount.

Under a separation agreement, Mrs. Grant and Reventlow were to share Lance's custody for alternate six-month periods. Mrs. Grant was to obtain possession of the boy July 1, but on June 30 Reventlow's attorneys announced he had taken Lance to Canada.

Mrs. Grant's complaint alleged that on July 12 she phoned Reventlow in Vancouver, B.C., demanding Lance's return. Reventlow, she said, told her negotiations must be carried on with his lawyers. The boy is staying with his father in West Vancouver.

No Canadians Among Killed Prisoners

OTTAWA, July 24.—(CP)—Prime Minister Mackenzie King said today in Commons that no Canadians were included in the latest list of Allied war prisoners shot by their German captors. He recalled that six of the original 50 prisoners shot in Germany were Canadians.

BASEBALL

NATIONAL LEAGUE.

St. Louis	001 041 010—7	11	0
Boston	000 000 100—1	5	2

Wilks and W. Cooper; Tobin, Klopp (6); Hickey (9); and Masi.

AMERICAN LEAGUE

Washington ..	000 001 000— 1	4	1
Cleveland	025 000 30x—10	15	0

Wynn and Ferrell; Klimen and Rosar.

City Moves to Beaches

Week-End Temperature 84

With the thermometer registering a humid 84 degrees, sweltering Vancouverites crowded city beaches and parks and nearby summer resorts Sunday.

During the night the temperature dropped to a minimum of 62 degrees and today, with cloudy skies, the weather remained cooler.

The forecast for Tuesday is "partly cloudy and warm."

The weather menu for Victoria is "very warm today and Tuesday," for the Cariboo, "partly cloudy and warm," and for Okanagan and Kootenay "partly cloudy and warm, becoming cloudy during the afternoon with a few showers over the ridges today and Tuesday."

THE VANCOUVER DAILY PROVINCE

50th YEAR—NO. 119 | OFFICIAL FORECAST: FAIR AND WARM WEDNESDAY. | VANCOUVER, B.C., TUESDAY, AUGUST 15, 1944 —20 PAGES ★ ★ ★ | PRICE 5 CENTS | BY CARRIER $1.00 per month

Allies Drive Deep Into South France

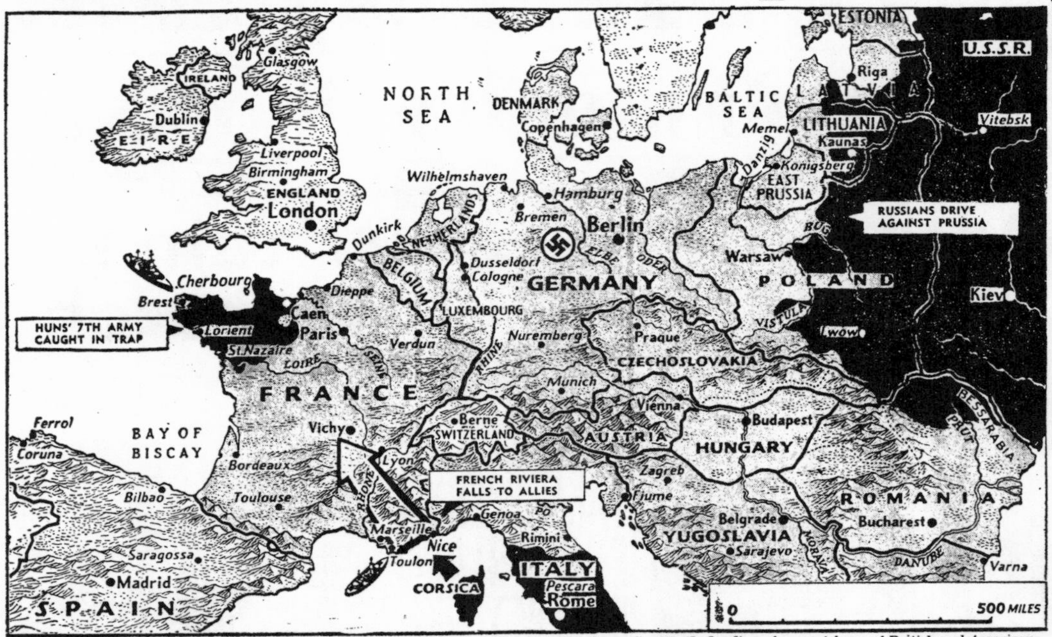

The Allies tore open another breach in the walls of Hitler's so-called "Fortress Europe" with the landing of a great force of British and American troops on the French Riviera. Hitler's weakening armies are thus confronted with a fourth and major front as the Allies in Normandy draw ever closer the noose about von Kluege's 7th Army south of Caen, as the Russians hammer at the gates of Warsaw and East Prussia, and as Sir Harold Alexander's forces bring liberation to the people of Italy. Blacked-in areas in map are those hold by the Allies.

Gen. Maitland Wilson's Invasion Armies Batter Past Weak Resistance

Spanish Radio Reports Canadians in Van of New Assault of Festung Europa

MOST OF RIVIERA CAPTURED

ROME, Aug. 15.—Allied armies clamping a giant vise upon France, broke through the southern wall near the great French naval base of Toulon today in successful landings against weak enemy resistance.

A few hours after Gen. Sir Maitland Wilson's army of the Mediterranean had set foot on the beaches of Southern France, the Allied invasion troops, composed of the army of France and a great force of British and American forces, were several miles inland, well into Southern France.

A report, circulated by the Spanish radio (Radio National) said that one of the first Allied landing craft to arrive on a beach was "loaded with Canadian and French soldiers.

Few details were available on the actual progress of the invasion armies but Herbert Matthews, New York Times correspondent, representing the combined American press said in a report at 4 o'clock p.m:

"A flabbergasted American army numbering many, many, thousands, is well into southern France this afternoon and going fast.

"It has been done so virtually without opposition and with amazingly small casualties.

"What few Germans were waiting for us have been scattered or captured.

"Men, tanks, artillery and material of all kinds have been pouring into three separate beaches since H-hour at 8 o'clock this morning, and by now we have built up such strength that it seems almost certain we have come not only to stay but also to push on.

"This ought to be the decisive blow for France, and everybody is astounded that it went off so easily."

FEW LIVES LOST.

Eric Sevareid of the C.B.S., broadcast that the Allied armies were several miles inland this afternoon.

Sevareid gave this location as "a pine-covered hill several miles inland from the French south coast."

"Only a few lives were lost" ni the landings, Sevareid said.

"It is now very quiet here." Where the Germans are now, the bulk of them, I can not tell you, but you may find out very suddenly.

"They've done very little harm to this famous holiday coast."

Spain's national radio said 15,000 Allied troops had landed in southern France by 1 p.m., five hours after the first assault. Two thousand men landed from seven invasion ships between 8 a.m. and 10 a.m., said the Spanish account.

BEACHES SEIZED.

A special communique a few hours after the blow was struck, said beaches along a considerable length of the Riviera had been seized by mid-morning, according to schedule, with scarcely any ground opposition and no air opposition.

An Allied spotter plane flew 60 miles inland without sighting a single enemy troop concentration.

One of the greatest airborne combat forces ever assembled paved the way for the assault and likewise carried out operations successfully far inland. Most of the airborne troops were believed to be British.

BRITISH MENTIONED.

A communique from Gen. Maitland Wilson, Mediterranean commander, mentioned British troops as part of the invasion force while a naval communique mentioned only that French and American forces were being landed. It was presumed, therefore, that the British forces were part of the airborne units.

Striking after sunrise, seven waves of infantry splashed ashore in the first two hours and seized their initial objectives with

(Continued on Page 2.)
See INVASION.

BULLETINS

FRENCH TROOPS PREDOMINATE

NEW YORK, Aug. 15.—(CP)—The B.B.C. said today that "it is officially stated that the French troops predominate" in the landings in Southern France.

PARATROOPS DESCEND ON MARSEILLES

NEW YORK, Aug. 15.—(CP)—The German radio announced that Allied parachute troops have been dropped in Marseilles.

SUPREME HOUR HAS STRUCK

LONDON, Aug. 15.—(AP)—"The supreme hour has struck," the German radio said tonight. "It is the hour when we must throw into battle the last little ounce of strength."

Four Powerful Allied Armies Crush Battered 7th Army in Falaise Pocket

From The Times:

Today In Europe

Compiled from the news and editorial comment of the London Times, and cabled from The Vancouver Daily Province London Bureau, Times Building, Printing House Square.

(Copyright, 1944, by Southam Co.)

LONDON, Aug. 15.—Aim of Allied strategy in Normandy, states the Times in a review of the military situation there, is to strike so decisive a blow to German forces that they will never again be able to meet the British and United States armies on equal terms.

It is hoped, indeed, that the present retreat may leave only a remnant of enemy troops, incapable of reinforcing the next line on which a stand might be made. What the German high command has now to do is to keep the Falaise gap open long enough to pass its armored units through to the rear.

Hitherto, Canadians have been held back from Falaise by use of this arbor, but now General Crerar's men are well on the move. They are supported by the Royal Air Force medium bombers, which are battering the last remains of the Caen "hinge." Inside the "Normandy cauldron" there are still many more Nazi armored divisions than those which got away.

Phase by phase, General Montgomery's master plan unfolds, and day by day the weather at last helps the Allies.

Beat to Punch

Responding to General Crerar's battle cry, "Hit him first, hit him hard, and keep on hitting him," Canadians again sprang at the hill above Falaise.

130

Royal Air Force smothered the guns against which the Canadian attack a week ago first broke. Infantry in armored carriers, protected by smoke screens, crossed the Laison River easily and are now within 7000 yards of Falaise. Armored chassis of 105-millimetre, self-propelled guns were converted into highly successful carriers.

The German escape rout from Falaise is now under artillery fire, and once Canadian and United States troops meet in this region, the gap will be closed. Already from wheat fields round about, Allied troops can look down upon key Argentan on the road to Paris less than 20 miles from Falaise.

The Red Army has captured the last big German fortress on the East Prussian border, namely Osowiec, only 18 miles from

(Continued on Page 2.)
See TIMES.

Canadians Within One Mile of Vital Escape Junction for Von Kluege

WITH THE CANADIAN 1ST ARMY IN FRANCE, Aug. 15.—(AP)—Canadian troops advanced to within a mile of Falaise today.

This advance closed the German escape gap to nine miles. Fighting in the Canadian salient changed from a slugging match to highly fluid character.

(By Associated Press.)

SUPREME HEADQUARTERS, Aug. 15.—The roof of the German escape corridor at Falaise appeared to be collapsing today under Allied hammer blows as an avalanche of tanks and troops cut up the dying 7th Army in the tightening Normandy trap.

The Americans now control German escape roads to the south with the capture of La Ferte Mace between Domfront and Ranes.

Four separate British, American and Canadian armies crushed in upon Field Marshal von Kluege's wrecked 7th army. His Falaise escape neck was reduced to 10 miles.

HUNDREDS CAPTURED.

Hundreds upon hundreds of Germans were captured.

The trap upon von Kluge was nearly snapped shut. Again this morning the Germans tried to break out eastward, but the route south of Canadian-dominated Falaise was blocked by a wall of bombs and shells.

On all sides the Allies pressed in. The pocket was slimmed to half its size. Thousands of Germans were still believed caught.

A British staff officer said von Kluege was throwing in reinforcements, but they were apparently 80 per cent. "slave troops," tossed in as sacrifice rearguards while von Kluege sought to save his armor and his best men.

UNPRECEDENTED BATTLE.

(Berlin broadcasts said "a furious battle unprecedented in living memory is being fought" for this narrow gap.)

The German bastion of Conde was thrown into immediate jeopardy as British infantry captured St. Denis de Mere.

Other swift-striking columns of General Dempsey's British 2nd Army advanced eastward along the Vire-Vassy road to within three miles of Vassy.

The German Transocean Agency said Allied troops were attacking fiercely on all sides of the Normandy entrapment ring, but asserted Field Marshal Gen. Guenther von Kluege's "regrouped and reinforced" forces in the inner circle had made local counter-attacks.

Stray R.A.F. Bombs Fall on Canadians In Falaise Assault

By ROBERT C. WILSON.
Associated Press War Correspondent.

WITH THE 1ST CANADIAN ARMY IN FRANCE, Aug. 15.—R. A. F. heavy bombers dropped a number of explosives behind the Canadian lines in yesterday's assault causing (four words censored) casualties (23 words censored).

The explosives fell as far back as Cinthaux and one result was the halting of some flights of bombers which were sent back with their loads undropped, but a senior Canadian officer said that 80 per cent. of the bombs fell in the target area.

The error occurred a short time after United States heavy bombers were involved in a similar mistake on this front (eight words censored).

U.S. Bombers Blast Formosa, Jap Ships

NEW YORK, Aug. 15.—(AP)—Formosa, anchor on Japan's inner water routes and only 200 miles north of the Philippines, has been attacked by U.S. heavy bombers based on China, Gen. Joseph Stilwell's headquarters announced today.

The raid, directed at one of the island's main ports, complemented heavy aerial blows which have virtually neutralized Halmahera Island at the southern and opposite end of the Philippines. Docks at Takao were hit and three freighters were sunk in the narrow waterway between Formosa and the China coast.

Land-based heavy bombers stabbed again at Iwo Jima in the Volcano Islands some 600 miles from Japan, said Radio Tokyo.

Tito Takes Five Towns In Smashing New Attack

LONDON, Aug. 15.—(CP)—Marshal Tito's Yugoslav Army has smashed out in a new attack 35 miles west of the Italian border in Slovenia and captured five towns, a communique broadcast by Tito's headquarters announced. Among the towns captured were Gornjograd, 20 miles northeast, and Smartno, 15 miles east of the rail junction of Ljubljana.

14,000 Paratroops Dropped in Greatest Airborne Assault

ROME, Aug. 15.—(AP)—The record Allied airborne force which descended on southern France early today consisted of more than 14,000 air combat men.

In no Allied operation before had so many men been dropped as this airborne force sent down behind the German coastal defenses.

Shipyard Workers

$50 Fines For Four Ferry Dice Players

NORTH VANCOUVER, Aug. 15.—Convicted of participating in a dice game, S. Teesdale, M. J. Gardner, E. F. Mayo, and Melvin Alcock, shipyard workers, all of Vancouver, were each fined $50 by Magistrate R. A. Sargent in Police Court.

The charges were laid when provincial police conducted a surprise raid aboard the ferry MS. Crosline en route to Vancouver last Tuesday afternoon.

They broke up five dice games and issued 10 summonses to adults and five to juveniles. Five other men pleaded guilty last Wednesday and each was fined $35.

The five juveniles were convicted and each was fined $10.

Edmonton Bans B.C. Japanese

EDMONTON, Aug. 15.—(CP)—Two applications from Japanese for permission to take up residence in Edmonton were rejected by City Council last night.

One application from Tsukishima of Stirling, Alta., Canadian-born Japanese, was for six weeks' temporary residence to enable him to complete a course in automotive engineering. Council felt that in making any allowances for temporary residence, a precedent would be set which would make it difficult to refuse other applications.

The other request came from Sampel Sugiura, who has been residing in Edmonton for the last two years. He asked permission to bring to the city his wife and six children, who are at present at Kaslo, B.C.

Man and wife were both born in Japan but the children are Canadian-born.

Russians Hammer At Prussia

By DANIEL DE LUCE.
Associated Press Staff Writer.

MOSCOW, Aug. 15.—Russian forces started attacking freshly-dug German entrenchments today in front of Grajewo, two miles south of the East Prussian border, after cracking the steel and concrete forts around Osowiec and winning a bridgehead across the Biebrza River.

Gen. G. F. Zakharov threw the full offensive might of his 2nd White Russian Army group against the Germans' attempts to reorganize their frontier line just below the Masurian Lakes.

A thundering air bombardment supported the Red Army attack.

"DARK WITH BLOOD."

"The waters of the Biebrza ran dark with enemy blood today," a front despatch to Izvestia said. Zakharov smothered a series of tank counter-attacks with his high-powered drive and struck directly in the rear of large enemy forces tied up in the Suwalki triangle (which East Prussia annexed in 1939), by Gen. Ivan Cherniakovsky's divisions.

Not only Grajeko but Lyck in East Prussia, 12 miles to the north, was menaced by the two Russian Army groups. Should these communication centres fall, a German withdrawal from the northeastern corner of East Prussia would be imperative.

The crossing of the Biebrza came while Moscow's victory guns were marking the fall of

(Continued on Page 2.)
See RUSSIA.

Barilla, Logan Execution Dates To Be Fixed Anew

Because the days on which they have been sentenced to hang, October 15 and October 29, are Sundays, Chief Justice Farris in Supreme Court Friday will fix new dates for the execution of Albert F. Barilla, 25, and Robert Harold Logan, 42.

The Court of Appeal at September sittings in Victoria will hear appeals of the two condemned men.

Barilla was convicted of the murder of Wellington Bruce Wallace at Greycourt Hotel on April 3. Logan was found guilty of stabbing his wife to death at 66 West Seventeenth on December 4, 1943.

LIGHTEN LIQUOR BOARD STOCK

Burglars Chisel Brick Walls To Collect Grog Worth $1628

Liquor Board "boss" W. F. Kennedy lost 660 bottles of rationed Scotch and rye from his hoarded store Mondayj night when burglars definitely not interested in the chairman's distribution problems broke through a brick wall into the board's warehouse at 857 Beatty.

The 55 cases of liquor, transported from the scene in a stolen truck, are worth $1628 when sold by Mr. Kennedy, and about $6600 when bootlegged.

Mr. Kennedy, who arrived on the scene about mid-morning, was too busy to talk to reporters. A check-up on the loss took considerable time.

Mr. Kennedy refused to allow pictures to be taken.

The burglars first broke into McNeely's, 835 Beatty, according to police, who were more generous with information and cooperation.

ENTRANCE VIA BOX-CAR.

They climbed to the top of a "spotted" box-car at the rear and forced a small window.

Inside the warehouse, the thieves went to work with a crowbar, two screwdrivers, a cold chisel and a hammer, which the police later found.

They cut through five layers of red brick. The hole is about 10 feet above the floor of McNeely's warehouse.

The liquor was placed in a McNeely truck, which the thieves first emptied of groceries and other goods.

The hole they cut is 22 by 21 inches.

First alarm was given at 7:55 a.m., by R. C. Murray of McNeely's Ltd.

U.S., Hun Patrols Clash In Italy

ROME, Aug. 15.—(AP)—Patrols of the American 5th Army engaged the enemy in a sharp fight three miles southeast of Pontedara but otherwise the Italian front remained comparatively quiet yesterday except for artillery fire, Allied headquarters announced today.

Speaks Here Tonight

Busy Schedule Faces Bracken During Visit

National Leader John Bracken was welcomed by Vancouver officials of the Progressive Conservative party this morning as he arrived at Canadian Pacific depot.

Today and Wednesday Mr. Bracken will visit war industries in the lower mainland and address meetings in Hotel Vancouver and at Queens Park in New Westminster.

Tonight at eight he will meet party supporters at a reception in Hotel Vancouver, sponsored by the Bracken Club.

The Progressive Conservative leader, accompanied by Howard Green, M.P., T. G. Applegath, campaign manager, and Mel Jack, his secretary, visited the Boeing aircraft plant at Sea Island and Burrard's shipyard.

He will speak at the Progressive Conservative rally and picnic in Queens Park at 4 p.m. Wednesday.

On hand to greet him this morning were Mr. Green, who arrived from the east on an earlier train, Mr. Applegath, Reg. McDougall, Ralph Plant, president of the Bracken Club, and R. T. McDonald, the club secretary; M. J. O'Brien, T. E. Wilson, Mrs. A. E. Dennis, J. Eades, Mrs. H. R. Bray, president of the Primrose Club; Mrs. Hilda Swindell, and Mrs. A. McLean.

GREAT TOULON NAVAL BASE, PRIZE OF NEW ALLIED INVASION IN SOUTH FRANCE

'Our Supreme Hour Struck'—Berlin

LONDON, Aug. 15---(AP)---"Our supreme hour has struck," the German radio said tonight. "It is the hour when we must throw into battle the last little ounce of strength."

GERMANS FLEEING BEFORE INVASION

The Vancouver Sun

FOUNDED 1886
VOL. LIX—No. 13

VANCOUVER, B.C., AUGUST 15, 1944   PRICE 5c

Opposition So Weak Allies Flabbergasted

Nazis Die Like Rats In Trap

Falaise Attempt to Break-Through

By VIRGIL PINKLEY
Special to The Vancouver Sun

ALLIED SUPREME HEADQUARTERS, Aug. 15— (BUP) — The German 7th Army lashed out in a desperate attempt to break the Allied trap in Normandy today but was turned back by a heavy crossfire of Allied bombs and shells after a number of tank and infantry units succeeded in escaping to the east.

49,000 LEFT

British United Press war correspondent Richard McMillan reported tonight that the massed guns of the American and Cana-

Please Turn to Page Two
See "Normandy"

Late News Flashes

HUN PRISONERS HUNTED

LETHBRIDGE, Alta., Aug. 15 —(CP)— Police and soldiers continued intensive hunt today for two German prisoners of war who escaped from a hostel near Barnwell early Sunday.

HOLIDAY AT RUPERT

PRINCE RUPERT, Aug. 15 —(CP)—A civic holiday in Prince Rupert this Thursday has been proclaimed by Mayor R. M. Daggett, in honor of the visit of Ray C. Atherton, United States ambassador to Canada.

AIRMEN ACQUITTED

VICTORIA, Aug. 15—(CP) —Charges of theft of RCAF property, laid against seven Canadian airmen, were dismissed by Justice of the Peace F. A. Baker at the conclusion of preliminary hearings in Sidney Police Court today.

STILL FEARS JAPS

SEATTLE, Aug. 15—(BUP)— Possibility of Japanese sneak raid at the West Coast of the United States cannot be discounted, despite continuing Allied successes in the Pacific, Col. Augustine S. Janeway, chief of the protective service of the office of civilian defense, stated here today.

MADRID, Aug. 15—(BUP)— Sporadic street fighting has broken out in Paris, reports from the border indicated tonight.

NEW YORK, Aug. 15—(CP) —The Spanish Radio (Radio Nacional) said today that one of the first Allied landing craft to arrive on a beach in southern France "was jammed with Canadians and French soldiers." There was no Allied confirmation of the report.

WEST FRONT DRIVE SPELL NAZI DOOM
(Arrows indicate position of Allied forces.)

14,000 Parachute Troops Floated Down on Nazis

ROME, Aug. 15—(CP-Reuter)—The record Allied airborne force which descended on Southern France early today consisted of more than 14,000 air combat men.

In no Allied operation before had so many men been dropped as this airborne force sent down behind the German coastal defenses.

NEW YORK, Aug. 15—(AP)—Allied troops invading southern France were several miles inland this afternoon, a broadcast from the invasion beachhead said.

The broadcast was made by Eric Sevareid of CBC, representing all American networks. Sevareid gave his location as "a pine-covered hill several miles inland from the French south coast."

"Only a few lives were lost" in the landings, Sevareid said.

"It is now very quiet here," he related.

"Where the Germans are now, the bulk of them, I cannot tell you, but you may find out very suddenly.

"They've done very little harm to this famous holiday coast."

Spain's national radio said 13,000 Allied troops had landed in Southern France by 1 p.m. five hours after the first assault.

Railbird

1—Shellmond, Zebella, Plucky Boss.

2—Honeypagan, Newsy Lady, Arab Somers.

3—Valdina Joy, Gordelius, Beauty Warm.

4—My Tom, Ample Glory, Maratimer.

5—Ball and Chain, Sunny Park, Storm Orphan.

6—Peniculk, Abydos, Patolan.

7—Shasta King, Watch Tick, New Car.

ONE BEST—SHASTA KING.

BASEBALL

AMERICAN

Chicago	100 000 000—1	3	1
New York	100 000 000—1	8	2
Haynes and Tresh; Zuber and Hemsley.			
St. Louis	000 015 000—6	8	0
Boston	140 000 000—5	7	1
Jakucki, Shirley (2), Coster (7) and Mancuso; Terry, Barrett (5), Ryba (7) and Wagner.			

Sunstar

1—Marion Somers, Si Green, Scotch Jean.

2—Arab Somers, Lady Do, Newsy Lady.

3—Avondale Star, Gordelius, Pandomint.

4—Ample Glory, Lucky Card, Maritimer.

5—Ball and Chain, Sunny Park, Blue Countess.

6—Little Gloomy, Peniculk, Patolan.

7—Shasta King, New Car, Watch Tick.

One Best—LITTLE GLOOMY.

Lucky Gold

1—Si Green, Diamond, Shellmond.

2—Newsy Lady, Sir Broxa, Sariworth.

3—Gordelius, Pandomint, Avondale Star.

4—Lucky Card, My Tom, Gatlin.

5—Air Surf, Nafworth, Ball and Chain.

6—Peniculk, Ulri Thots, Edjay, Patolan.

7—Shasta King, Watch Tick, New Car.

One Best—SHASTA KING.

Armada of 800 Ships Lands Force Which Establishes Bridgehead Between Marseille and Nice

BUP and AP Dispatches

ROME—force struck into southern France from sea and sky today and within a matter of hours overran the Germans' feeble shore defenses and established firm beachheads along a 100-mile strip of the Mediterranean coast between Nice and Marseille.

Herbert Matthews, representing the combined American press, reported from southern France this afternoon that a "flabbergasted Allied army numbering many thousands is well into southern France this afternoon and going fast. It has been done virtually without opposition and with amazingly small casualties."

A miles-long sky train of gliders and transport planes swept in over the coast before dawn to shower thousands of American and British paratroopers across the rolling hills behind the Nazi coastal defenses, and the main assault force splashed ashore from landing craft at 8 a.m.

Between the two forces, the stunned Germans were rendered almost helpless and their once-formidable fortifications were breached almost without a struggle.

"By mid-morning all the landings were proceeding suc-

Please Turn to Page Two   *See "ALLIES SPEED"*

Welders Go Back to Work

Striking welders at Burrard South shipyards returned to work shortly after 1 p.m., a company official reports.

The official said that the strike was illegal and that the men had agreed to resume their duties when peaceful negotiations between bargaining agents, the company and government labor officials.

The men downed tools in protest at demotion of eight charge hands. Their contention was that layoffs and demotions should be conducted on a straight seniority basis.

Ottawa Turns Down Essondale Building

VICTORIA, Aug. 15—(CP)— Ottawa has ruled an occupational therapy building at Essondale is not necessary at present and can wait until after the war.

The Department of Public Works a few weeks ago opened tenders for the building and then applied to Ottawa for a permit to build.

This has been refused.

The building was to have cost about $40,000.

Tenders will be called this week for a 100-bed addition to the home for the aged at Essondale.

672 Bottles of Whisky Stolen

Burglars who cut a large hole through a brick wall into the Beatty Street liquor store escaped early today with 672 bottles of Scotch and rye, which they took away in a stolen truck which they had first unloaded. On the black market the loot would have a value of more than $8000.

Police were called to the liquor store at 8 a.m. by R. C. Murray of McNeely's, 835 Beatty, whose premises adjoin those of the liquor warehouse.

Police found that the burglars had climbed on top of a railway box car spotted at the rear of McNeely's and then pried open a rear window to get in.

H. C. Crumplin, manager of the liquor store, said the premises were closed at 5 p.m. Monday. Each floor is locked separately and the burglars confined their activities to one floor.

Detectives Alec Paton and Cecil McIntosh took from the premises a crowbar, two screw drivers, a cold chisel and a hammer which the robbers used.

The thieves' loot consisted of 26 cases of Scotch, valued at $63 a case on the retail market and 30 cases of rye valued at $40 a

dressing and other groceries.

The thieves cut a hole through the north brick wall into the liquor warehouse at 871 Beatty. They got into the warehouse on the first floor, up from the street, through the hole, a distance twenty-one inches by twenty-two.

Police cleared to the liquor store, said the premises were closed at 5 p.m. Monday.

Then they unloaded one of McNeely's trucks which was fully loaded with cases of salad

THE VANCOUVER DAILY PROVINCE

50th YEAR—NO. 126 | OFFICIAL FORECAST: PARTLY CLOUDY, COOLER. | VANCOUVER, B.C., WEDNESDAY, AUGUST 23, 1944—24 PAGES | PRICE 5 CENTS | BY CARRIER $1.00 per month

PARIS LIBERATED

French Say City Freed

PATRIOTS FREE PARIS AS ALLIES ADVANCE

French patriots liberated Paris as the Allied armies swept forward in northern and in southern France. Open arrows indicate possible Allied sweeps from Seine bridgeheads to outflank the German defenses in northern France and force the Germans to fight with their backs to the sea in the Dieppe-Dunkerque "rocket coast" area.

In southern France, the Allies encircled Toulon and virtually isolated Marseilles while one column thrust far north to Grenoble. Early official reports failed to confirm rumors of an Allied landing near Bordeaux (arrow). Blacked-in area is Allied-held.

Tragedy In England

PLANE STRIKES LANCS SCHOOL; FIFTY KILLED

Thirty-four Children Perish In Church Building

By Associated Press.

MANCHESTER, Eng., Aug. 23.—A plane crashed on the infants' department of a church school in Freckleton, Lancashire, today, killing 50 persons, 34 of them children.

The plane plunged almost in the centre of the village, setting afire the whole area. Several other buildings were wrecked or burned.

Forty-one children of the school's enrolment of 180 were known to have been in the building at the time and a few hours after the crash the bodies of 31 had been recovered. It was feared the death list would mount.

The Press Association said the plane was a Liberator and that at least three of its crew were killed.

VILLAGE IN FLAMES.

American troops joined in rescue work in the flaming wreckage of one of England's worst sky-ground tragedies.

An eyewitness said the whole centre of the tiny village of 1438 inhabitants became a "sea of flames," and added:

"I looked out from a shop window. There was a flash in the air and the plane, which was flying low, caught fire. It turned over on its back and struck the top of the school and then flashed across the road on to the snack bar."

Some of the dead children were evacuees from London, tiny fugitives from Hitler's robot bombs.

A soldier who was near when the plane crashed said "the whole scene is like a battlefield. Windows over a large part of the village are broken. The fire is still burning but under control."

Churchill, FDR May Lead Parade in Paris

By Associated Press.

LONDON, Aug. 23.—The Daily Herald said today that plans were being made for Prime Minister Churchill and President Roosevelt to be present at the triumphal Allied march into Paris "if that is practical."

The march into the city will wait until the "campaign of destruction of the German armies goes a stage further," the paper said, but added that "special newsreel operators who will make a picture record of the march already have been detailed for duty and military bands which will play in the march are now in France practicing."

French troops will head the parade of all Allied troops under the Arc de Triomphe, with Gen. de Gaulle probably having the place of honor, it was said.

3000 Affected

B.C.E.R. Men Get 4½ Cent Wage Boost

A blanket wage increase of 4½ cents per hour for approximately 3000 Vancouver, New Westminster and Victoria street railway and bus operators and repairmen and maintenance crews was ordered today by the Regional War Labor Board for B. C.

The board also directed B.C. Electric Railway Co. to increase the monthly guarantee to extra men from $100 to $108, including the cost-of-living bonus.

While denying the organized street railwaymen's application for an increase in certain wage rates and adjustment of certain working conditions, the board ruled the wage increase and raised guarantee "would be fair and reasonable and consistent with the intent of Wartime Wages Control Order, 1943, P.C. 9384.

LED LIBERATORS

Lt.-Gen. Pierre Koenig, hero of Bir Hacheim, commander of the French forces of interior, this morning announced liberation of Paris by French patriots.

80-Mile Advance

ALLIES STORM INTO GRENOBLE

By NOLAND NORGAARD.
Associated Press Staff Writer.

ROME, Aug. 23.—American troops of the 7th Army, in a spectacular surprise thrust deep into southern France through German defenses, have entered the large industrial city of Grenoble, 140 airline miles north of the Mediterranean coast.

A swift-moving armored and motorized infantry column plunged into the city, long a hotbed of the French patriot movement, with "French forces of the interior playing an effective support role," Allied headquarters said.

EARLY FRUITION.

This quick advance put Maj.-Gen. Alexander M. Patch's forward elements within less than 240 airline miles from the most southerly points officially announced as reached by American troops south of Paris, and it appeared that the two Allied French fronts would be joined much sooner than originally thought possible.

Grenoble, 58 miles southeast of Lyon and situated on a river leading directly to the Rhone Valley, 30 miles to the west, is 80 miles or more beyond the last reported Allied positions in southern France.

Lying in the French Alps, the city has a population of approximately 100,000, and is a rail centre on the Paris-Lyon-Marseilles route.

Towns taken by the Americans en route to Grenoble include Digne, Sisteron, Aspres, Gap, St. Bonnet and l'Argentiere, the latter 35 miles from the Italian border.

11 MILES FROM ITALY.

A broadcast by radio France said Allied forces were less than 11 miles from the Italian frontier but there was no confirmation.

At Grenoble Allied forces were roughly only 70 airline miles from the Swiss frontier and for all practical purposes already had sealed off the Nazi forces in southern France from communication with the enemy in northwestern Italy.

Patriots Rout Nazi Troops From Capital

Once-gay Paris Shakes Loose Shackles Of Four Years of Enemy Bondage

ALL FRANCE STIRRED

By JAMES M. LONG.
(Associated Press Staff Writer.)

LONDON, Aug. 23.—Paris shook the shackles of four years of enemy bondage today and stood free once more, liberated by armed and unarmed tens of thousands of Frenchmen who swept the Nazis from the city's streets, while Allied armed might drew up around the capital.

A special communique from Gen. de Gaulle's headquarters in London announced the liberation after four days of street fighting that recalled scenes of Bastille Day when the mobs of Paris once before struck an historic blow for liberty.

This time, the communique said, the fight was led by 50,000 organized French forces of the interior, bolstered by hundreds of thousands more who joined in with whatever weapons they could find.

The announcement touched off broadcasts to Frenchmen everywhere as the triumphant strains of "La Marseillaise" sounded again to the news of a French victory.

There was no word immediately that Allied troops had entered the city.

TAKE ALL PUBLIC BUILDINGS

The French said they had seized all public buildings, won complete control of the situation, and captured all the Vichy representatives who had not fled.

Paris, the city of light, thus was back in French hands just four years and 74 days from the time Adolf Hitler's troops marched in. German troops, then at the flood tide of conquest, entered June 14, 1940.

Up to 5:35 p.m. (10:25 a.m. CDT), the supreme command public relations office said it lacked news confirming liberation of Paris.

There was no indication in the French communique what casualties had been inflicted on the German forces or how many had been captured. Allied airmen for two days have been reporting the Nazis pulling out of the city to the east over every road.

The thousands of Frenchmen and women who struck down the invaders who had brought misery and despair to their homes rose from the underground of the Montmartre and Montparnasse. They struck from the east and from the west.

French colonies were quick to begin celebrating liberation of their homeland capital. An Algiers broadcast announced Gen. Georges Catroux had ordered the display of the tri-color throughout Algeria and the ringing of all church bells.

The liberation will be celebrated in Algiers at 6 p.m. by salvoes of all the city's batteries and the blowing of sirens on all the city's buildings.

DECLARED AN OPEN CITY

Paris had been declared an open city several days before the Germans had reached it in the black days of 1940. German armor clanked into the stunned capital, rolled past the Arc de Triomphe and down the famed Champs Elysees to the Palace de la Concorde, and saw silent, deserted streets.

Those citizens who remained in the city stayed indoors rather than look upon the degradation.

Confused, disorganized France, its vaunted military machine broken by the lightning German attack across the Maginot Line, and its faith in its generals and leaders broken, had no chance to fight for the capital.

(Continued on Page 2.) See PARIS.

FROM THE TIMES:

Today in Europe

Compiled from the news and editorial comment of the London Times, and cabled from The Vancouver Daily Province London Bureau, Times Building, Printing House Square.

(Copyright, 1944, by Southam Co.)

LONDON, Aug. 23.—The fresh envelopment of the Germans beyond the Seine now depends more on Allied power to bring up necessary supplies than on the Nazis' fighting capacity. The pick of enemy units have been destroyed, and those that are left are only second rate.

According to the Times special correspondent at Allied headquarters in Italy the German retreat up the Rhone valley has also been hastened.

The Royal Air Force has landed from Corsica and is operating Spitfires from new airfields on French soil. The Luftwaffe has made no appearance except to launch a small raid on shipping off the coast at dusk.

132

Powerful Push

Another powerful double-pronged Red Army offensive has been launched in Romania. A violent battle rages at the approaches of Warsaw, says the Times Moscow correspondent. The Russians have made notable gains to the northwest of the Polish capital, despite terrific German efforts to check them.

Tanks in large units are returning to attack ten times daily, supported by regiments of infantry.

The Red Army is holding itself in readiness for a fresh assault when the enemy has exhausted himself.

In the Baltic the Nazis are hurling their heaviest armor against General Bagramyan's positions around Mitau. He is returning blow for blow.

Discover Mistake

The Bulgarian Government has discovered that the declaration of war against Britain and the United States was a mistake. Now the Premier wants to get peace terms from both countries and is taking steps to find out what they are.

Agreement between rival parties in Yugoslavia has been reached and a pact has been signed by Premier Ivan Subasitch and Marshal Tito, leaving aside until after the war such questions as that of monarchy or republic and what form of federal union shall be established.

The government denounces all those who have collaborated with the German invaders, but makes no mention of General Mihailovitch. Marshal Tito, however, makes it clear he still regards Mihailovitch as a traitor.

Sign New Pact

The French provisional government and that of Czechoslovakia have signed an agreement repudiating the Munich pact and all others arising from French appeasement policies. A future alliance is envisaged.

The Germans are planning to evacuate southern Greece, according to the latest reports by the Times Ankara correspondent. There is no indication, however, that they are leaving the Aegean Islands. The problem for the high command now is how far it can retire northward in Greece without endangering its hold on Romania and Hungary.

Employees Lose Bonds

SAFE-BLOWERS TAKE $1500

Between $1000 and $1500 disappeared when thugs blew the safe of Orange Crush (B.C.) Ltd., 3675 West Fourth, Tuesday night.

At least $600 of the money belonged to employees of the company, who had put bonds in the safe overnight.

Reconstructing the crime, C. A. Drummond, regional manager of Orange Crush for western Canada, said thieves must have entered the building through an 18-inch washroom window on the second floor.

ABANDON SAFE.

They blew off the combination lock of one safe, containing petty cash and papers and abandoned it. They then wheeled the safe containing Tuesday's receipts and the bonds to the warehouse part of the building.

There they blew it open, and took away its contents except for one envelope containing $100 in cash.

About 6 a.m. police noticed that the shutter of a window on the second storey at the back of the building above the garage was left open about two inches. They climbed up, went down to the office and discovered the robbery.

The contents of the safe were covered by insurance.

EMPLOYEES LOSE BONDS.

One woman member of the staff lost $200 in registered bonds and $35 in War Savings stamps. The office manager lost another $200 unregistered bond and $200 in registered bonds which were part of the funds of an organization of which he is a member.

F. Detsworth and William Legg both claimed that the shuttered window was barred and bolted.

Two Perish In Valley Crash

(Special to The Daily Province.)

MISSION, Aug. 23.—Two Indians were killed and a third seriously injured when the car in which they were travelling leaped from the Lougheed Highway and crashed into a deep ditch approximately a mile east of Silverdale last night.

The car is believed to have been travelling at high speed toward Mission, when it swerved from the highway. Cause of the accident is unknown. The car was badly damaged.

Sound of the crash attracted the attention of nearby ranchers, who called Dr. E. J. Eacrett of Mission. The injured man was taken to Mission Hospital.

Women of Warsaw Appeal to Pope

LONDON, Aug. 23.—(AP)—Declaring that the world is ignoring their plight, Polish women of Warsaw have appealed to Pope Pius XII. to bless patriot forces battling in the city "for church and liberty," according to the Polish telegraphic agency.

The appeal deplored the fact that "Russian armies which have been standing at the gates of Warsaw for three weeks do not move a step forward," the agency said. Help sent by Britain in the form of supplies dropped by plane was described as insufficient.

Woman Thug Beats Screaming Nick To Punch

Enemies of "Screaming Nick" Kokinas, whose piercing voice has routed bandits from his grocery at 819 Pacific on 15 separate occasions, beat him to the punch on Tuesday.

He was beaten about the head by a heavy-set woman who gave him no chance to scream for help.

Kokinas told police the woman entered his store and ordered cookies. When he bent over the cooky jar to get them she struck him over the head with a heavy object and fled, apparently without loot.

Kokinas was removed to St. Paul's Hospital for treatment.

Cruickshank Renominated

(Special to The Daily Province.)

MISSION, Aug. 23. — George Cruickshank, M.P. for Fraser Valley, was unanimously renominated to contest the riding in the next federal election by Fraser Valley Federal Riding Liberal Association last night.

Officers elected by the association were: R. C. Cox, president, Mission City; Arthur Rundle, first vice-president, Chilliwack, and Elmer Cummings, of Harrison Mills, second vice-president. Executive council remains unchanged until further names are submitted.

The meeting endorsed the Federal Government's agriculture policy, and petitioned the government to insert an insurance clause in the Soldier' Settlement Land Act which free dependents of all liabilities under the contract in event of a soldier's death.

Buenos Aires Bars Paris Freedom Fete

BUENOS AIRES, Aug. 23.—(CDN)—The France-Amerique Committee has been refused permission by the Buenos Aires police to organize a public celebration when and if Paris is liberated by Allied armies.

The police informed organizers that no such festivities could be permitted in view of Argentine's "neutrality."

U. S. COLUMNS 160 MILES FROM REICH

German Flight Across Seine Turns Into Complete Rout

By WES GALLAGHER.
(Associated Press War Correspondent.)

ALLIED SUPREME HEADQUARTERS, Aug. 23.—Allied airmen described the flight of the battered German 7th Army across the Seine as having the appearance of a "rout."

On the left of the Allied line British and Canadian armies raced ahead 10 to 15 miles, pushing the Germans tighter against the Seine and into the fire of American flanking forces moving toward the sea along the left bank.

Meanwhile an American armored column drove more than half way across France and plunged beyond the ancient town of Sens, only 160 miles from the German border to the northeast near the Saar town of Neunkirchen.

ONE OF MANY BLOWS.

The lightning thrust was but one of many bewildering blows hitting the Germans, among which was a dramatic eastward push by the 1st Canadian Army, which carried elements into Deauville, only eight miles across the Seine estuary from Le Havre, and Lisieux, 16 miles southeast of Deauville.

Nowhere along the entire front from the Channel to Sens did the Germans appear able to check the Allies, whose pauses

(Continued on Page 2.) See FRANCE.

ALLIES IN BELGIUM

The Sunday Sun
VOL. XIV—No. 85 FOUNDED 1886 · VANCOUVER, B.C., SEPTEMBER 2, 1944 · PRICE 10c

British Advance In Italy

Eighth Army Smashes Gothic Line In Heavy Fighting

CHIASSO, on the Italo-Swiss frontier, Sept. 2—(BUP)—The German exacuation of Italy is in full swing tonight and heavy guns and equipment are pouring through the Brenner Pass into Germany.

By GEORGE TUCKER
Associated Press War Correspondent

ROME, Sept. 2. — British 8th Army troops have broken the Nazis' vaunted Gothic Line in Italy along a 20-mile front, opening the gates to the Po Valley, Allied headquarters announced today, and a spokesman declared it was only a matter of time before complete destruction of all German forces in Italy will be accomplished.

British, Canadian, Indian and Polish infantry are taking part in the advance which has penetrated to a depth of from three to four miles, a communique said.

It was the first disclosure that Canadian infantry was in action following their exploits in aiding the Allied break through the Gus-

Please Turn to Page Two
See "British"

Late News Flashes

CIVILIANS EVACUATED

LONDON, Sept. 2—(BUP)—The German Transocean News Agency said tonight that all civilians are being evacuated from villages in the Maginot Line in Lorraine.

PARIS ROBOMBED

PARIS, Sept. 2 — (BUP)—German flying bombs fell for the first time last night in the Paris area. First reports said some damage was done but no announcement was made as to where the bombs fell.

BLAST NAZI SHIPS

LONDON, Sept. 2—(BUP)—British and Dutch naval units sank three and damaged several other German vessels which tried to break out of French channel ports threatened by the advancing Allies last night.

HUN AIRSTRIPS TAKEN

LONDON, Sept. 2—(AP)—The U.S. strategic air force in England announced today that more than 65 German airfields in Northern France had been captured, and about 25 others in Southern France "either have been captured or made untenable because Allied troops are too near."

POISONED SISTER

DETROIT, Sept. 2—(AP)—Police said today that William J. Mackay, 19, had confessed to placing poison in foods in the family refrigerator from which his sister, Isabelle, 14, obtained a lunch shortly before her death yesterday. "I wanted to get my father," the boy was quoted as explaining. "He was always after me to get a job."

E-BOATS ROUTED

LONDON, Sept. 2—(CP)——Canadian motor torpedo boats obtained numerous hits when they fired on a number of Nazi E-boats in the vicinity of Boulogne just before midnight last night, an Admiralty communique said.

GEN. GIRAUD WOUNDED

NEW YORK, Sept. 2—(BUP)—The American Broadcasting Station in Europe broadcast an Allies report today that Gen. Henri Honore Giraud, former French commander-in chief, had been wounded slightly when a Senegalese soldier accidentally shot him in the face. The broadcast, heard by FCC monitors in New York, gave no details.

BANNED FROM U.S.

OTTAWA, Sept. 2—(CP)—The Defense Department announced today that due to an increase of infantile paralysis in the northern United States all leave or passes to military personnel to the United States have been prohibited.

Similar steps were taken yesterday by the RCAF.

(See also Page 3)

5★★★★

Sun Handicap

by ALF COTTRELL

The bracketed figures after the weight indicate the rating of the horse for that particular race. If a horse carries more than the weight stipulated in the entries, deduct one point for each pound of overweight carried. Bracketed figures at end of line indicate post position. Jockeys, post positions, subject to late change.

MONDAY, SEPTEMBER 4

1st Race—Claiming, three-year-olds and up. 1 Mile and 1-16

4678	**TRIP OVER (Wilbourn)**	116	(102)	**Takes plenty to beat him**	(6)
4678	**AMPLE GLORY**	111	(100)	**Been close; drops weight**	(7)
(4560)	**CRAIGLOCHART (T'v's)**	114	(98)	**Has hit winning streak**	(5)
4680	Goldie's Pride	111	(94)	Could set all the pace	(9)
4682	Seabread	119	(—)	Check Saturday display	(10)
4673	Pinchconard (a)	113	(92)	Just missed in previous	(12)
4667	Eagle Crest (Sporri) ..	114	(90)	Rail may not help him	(1)
4669	Lady Serajevo (Hrus'k)	111	(89)	Showed an improvement	(3)
4659	Valdina Sun (Braddish)	119	(87)	Stopped as though short	(8)
4622	Jest Once (a) (Haller)	116	(74)	Question of her condition	(4)
4682	Nancy's Sue	113	(—)	Also went on Saturday	(11)
——	Polly Gower (Sive'ght)	102	(—)	Not much line on her	(2)

(a)—Black & Cunningham-McDonald entry.

2nd Race—Claiming, three-year-olds and up. 1 Mile and 1-16

4674	**SUNNY MONDAY**	108	(94)	**May catch them tiring**	(3)
4678	**MAIZIE B (R. Johnston)**	108	(93)	**Rail; seems one to beat**	(1)
4675	**SHASTA SUE**	113	(92)	**Off best is fair threat**	(8)
4656	Fala Hills	109	(90)	Recent races much better	(5)
4661	Ascot Maid (Sporri) ...	108	(89)	Fresh and might surprise	(6)
4660	Blue Suit (Haller)	113	(88)	May take the biscuits	(7)
4674	Lucky Card (Hruschak)	112	(88)	Is hard-knocking horse	(4)
4683	Lady Moira (H. John.)	108	(88)	May like our climate	(2)

3rd Race—Claiming, three-year-olds and up. 7 Furlongs

(4658)	**DRY HILLS Haller)** ...	114	(113)	**Never better; look out**	(4)
(4670)	**COMMENDABLE (W'b'n)**	117	(112)	**Looked very impressive**	(5)
4670	**LADY LEV (Braddish)**	111	(111)	**Rail gives royal chance**	(1)
4658	Witch's Taxi (Taves) .	108	(107)	Beaten by same kind	(2)
(4615)	Pilgrim's Pride (Sporri)	119	(106)	Will come with a whoop	(6)
4685	Sahara Chief (a)	109	(103)	Drops down; seems jaded	(3)
4594	Storm Orphan (Sive'ght)	119	(97)	Has beaten better horses	(8)
(4676)	Little Pine (a) (Hrus'k)	113	(97)	Beat easier in a romp	(7)

(a)—Mrs. F. Beban entry.

4th Race—Claiming, three-year-olds and up, foaled in Western Canada. 1 Mile and 1-16

(4678)	**WILLIE MARC'S (T'v's)**	118	(97)	**Could score right back**	(4)
4688	**TOY BROOM (Sporri)** ..	116	(93)	**Would seem threat here**	(3)
4687	**STREAMLINE (Neal)** ...	116	(92)	**Danger if breaks on top**	(2)
4688	Gallosea (Sivewright) ...	116	(91)	Usually in the struggle	(7)
4662	Shasta King (Hruschak)	118	(87)	Last try sharpened him	(8)
(4675)	Cetoma (Wilbourn) ...	116	(87)	Might make the pace	(5)
4666	Simonette (Braddish) ..	115	(86)	Just possible surprise	(1)
4620	Merchiston (Haller) ...	116	(83)	Mud is his best dish	(6)

5th Race—THE PRESIDENT'S HANDICAP, three-year-olds and up. 1 Mile and 1-8

4672	**DALKEITH (Taves)** ...	115	(118)	**Chance to lead and last**	(5)
4644	**KINSAIL (Haller)**	110	(117)	**Menace off one display**	(8)
4685	**PATAGE (a)**	109	(117)	**Get a poor post position**	(9)
4672	Franworth (Sporri)	123	(115)	Still tough one to beat	(2)
4685	Nafworth (a)	106	(113)	May prefer heavy track	(1)
4685	Maid of Broxa (Brad'sh)	108	(113)	Check Saturday chart	(3)
4685	Hi-Rythm (Hruschak)..	107	(113)	Seems trifle below tops	(7)
4685	Winnamucca (Sive'ght)	107	(112)	Also on Saturday card	(4)
4663	Nalod (Wilbourn) ...	105	(110)	Appears overmatched	(6)

(a)—Lochead-Pepper entry.

6th Race—Claiming, three-year-olds and up. 2 Miles and 1-16

4667	**WILD DEER (Wlbourn)**	107	(109)	**Went well; in light**	(1)
4679	**LITTLE GLOOMY (Sp'i)**	112	(108)	**May have edge in class**	(2)
4646	**WELBECK (Taves)** ...	107	(103)	**Tired; might stick here**	(6)
4673	Thirsk (Haller)	112	(100)	Seems long-winded sort	(7)
4687	Scotch Jean (Hruschak)	104	(93)	Light load; no surprise	(3)
——	Some Do (Braddish) ..	111	(—)	Some form makes menace	(4)
4641	Frisco Boy (R. John.)..	109	(89)	Been trying everything	(8)
4675	Galamond (a)	107	(85)	Hard sort to figure	(9)
4674	Brittania (a)	107	(81)	Been poor this summer	(5)

(a)—A. Smithers entry.

7th Race—Claiming, three-year-olds and up foaled in Western Canada. 1 Mile and 1-16

(4680)	**GALLANT KING (H. J.)**	x111	(99)	**Slim margin in this one**	(1)
4666	**BRILLIANT HELP (Sp'l)**	116	(98)	**Knocking at the door**	(2)
(4679)	**PLUCKY JAKE (Hru'k)**	114	(97)	**Drops down; be favorite**	(9)
4654	Zebella (R. Johnston)..	x106	(97)	Could go with the pace	(3)
4662	Peggy Dot (Sivewright)	113	(96)	Fair chances with these	(5)
4683	Ebony Ship	110	(93)	Check Saturday display	(10)
(4681)	Coon Dog (Haller)	118	(92)	Won last one narrowly	(8)
4671	George Somers (Neal) ..	114	(88)	He surprises at times	(4)
4681	Bet Lomond (Wilbourn)	113	(81)	Form hardly makes threat	(6)
4650	Dalmahoy (Taves)	118	(80)	Distance seems too brief	(7)
4659	Friarworth	112	(78)	Had fair speed last try	(11)

Substitute Race—Allowance, three-year-olds and up. 7 Furlongs

4665	**ROYAL MEMORY (T'v's)**	113	(104)	**Could catch 'em at wire**	(8)
4663	**NALOD (Haller)**	113	(102)	**Been right there of late**	(1)
4685	**WINNAMUCCA (a) (S't)**	118	(102)	**Will come with a rush**	(5)
4663	Riverworth (a)	113	(102)	Never overlook this one	(7)
4663	Band O'Gold (Sporri) ..	110	(92)	Speed gives nice chance	(6)
4676	Arpeggio (Hruschak) ..	108	(92)	Might need softer track	(4)
——	Sweet Olive (Braddish)	113	(—)	Is really shifty mare	(3)
4663	Goldenworth (Wilbourn)	110	(88)	Tired with same company	(2)

(a)—K. R. Darbyshire entry.

Substitute Race—Claiming, three-year-olds and up. 7 Furlongs

4675	**SIR BROXA (Haller)** ..	110	(95)	**Last gives him the duke**	(5)
4661	**GATLIN**	x116	(93)	**Be a threat if gets in**	(11)
4660	**SPECIAL LADY (Wilb'n)**	112	(92)	**Is a slightly easier spot**	(8)
4675	Daddy (Sporri)	115	(90)	Might need soft track	(6)
4669	Eno-Heather (Arnold)..	112	(89)	Faded badly other day	(2)
4671	Ann's Worry (Hruschak)	110	(87)	Last was improvement	(4)
4671	Maratimer	108	(87)	Seems devoid of speed	(9)
4671	Peggy's Girl (R. John.)	110	(84)	Seems rough spot for her	(3)
4457	Double Tide (R. John.)	x108	(—)	Been on shelf; outsider	(1)
4661	Liloade (Taves)	107	(84)	This one could surprise	(7)
4674	Zelpha Lass	107	(82)	Failed to show much	(10)
4683	Rusty Beau	108	(—)	Hasn't been close yet	(12)

One Best—WILLIE MARCUS.

Weather cloudy. Track fast. First post 3:30 p.m.

X—Apprentice allowance claimed.

Railbird

1—Craiglochart, Trip Over, Jest Once.
2—Maizie B, Blue Suit, Lucky Card.
3—Storm Orphan, Dry Hills, Commendable.
4—Willie Marcus, Streamline, Cetoma.
5—Franworth, Dalkeith, Patage.
6—Welbeck, Wild Deer, Scotch Jean.
7—Gallant King, Brilliant Help, Coon Dog.
SUB.—Sir Broxa, Daddy, Special Lady.
One Best—WILLIE MARCUS.

Lucky Gold

1—Valdina Sun, Eagle Crest, Craiglochart.
2—Lucky Card, Pala Hills, Ascot Maid.
3—Commendable, Storm Orphan, Pilgrim's Pride.
4—Merchiston, Shasta King, Streamline.
5—Franworth, Winnamucca, Nalod.
6—Wild Deer, Little Gloomy, Galamond.
7—Brilliant Help, Coon Dog, Gallant King.
1st Sub—Nalod, Royal Memory, Band o'Gold.
2nd Sub—Special Lady, Daddy, Eno Heather.
One best—FRANWORTH

Charlton Honored By Retail Group

TORONTO, Sept. 2—(CP)—Hon. Henri R. Renault of Beauceville, Que., former trade and commerce minister of the province of Quebec, as re-elected Dominion president of the Retail Merchants' Association of Canada at its forty-eighth annual meeting which closed here Thursday.

Other directors include W. S. Charlton, Vancouver.

Victoria Shipyards Laying Off Women

VICTORIA, Sept. 2 (CP)—Women workers are being let out of the shipyards but it is not because of the increasing belief that the war is nearing an end.

Yarrows Ltd. admitted this morning that some women were being laid off but it was claimed that it was but a temporary measure.

VALIANT ENGLAND CARRIES ON

With lifting of pre-D-Day ban against civilian use of southern English beaches, and despite Hitler's robot bombs, hundreds of holidaying Britons flocked to the shore to enjoy what's left of the summer sun. There's nothing in the photo above, showing one of the crowded resorts to indicate that the war is rushing to a climax just a few miles across the Channel.

British-U.S. In Berlin First?

Advance Only Secured After Savage Nazi Resistance

By LEWIS HAWKINS
Associated Press Staff Writer

LONDON, Sept. 2—(AP)—It is possible that Anglo-American troops may stride into Germany as invaders before Russians, but if they do it will not automatically prove an old and favorite theme of amateur tacticians—that once the German leaders have accepted defeat as inevitable, they would "let the British and Americans in because they are afraid of the Russians."

The Western Allies' current spectacular sweep through Northern France, combined with the German army's stubborn stand before East Prussia and Warsaw, may seem to give fresh support to this theory, but any suggestion that the Nazis are "letting" the Allied armies in is a poor tribute to the men whose brain and brawn and bravery broke through to liberate France.

FOUGHT SAVAGELY

The truth is that the Germans fought savagely, and for a while effectively, to battle the Allies within the narrow Normandy bridgehead.

How far they will run is anyone's guess. That they will be able to stop for long much short of their own border is doubtful.

Please Turn to Page Two
See "Berlin"

Hitler Admits Invasion Near

LONDON, Sept. 2—(BUP)—Adolf Hitler's own Berlin newspaper, Volkischer Beobachter, conceded by implication today that the German army would be unable to stop the onrushing Allied armies short of the Reich's borders and perhaps not until they were deep inside Germany.

"The establishment of a new front had to be prepared farther to the rear, even very far to the rear, since the rapidity of modern tank formations otherwise would threaten the new front during its construction," Volkischer Beobachter said in explaining why the Germans were making no stand in France.

Accidents Kill Two Men at Englewood

ENGLEWOOD, Sept. 2.—Two loggers were killed in accidents Friday afternoon at Canadian Forest Products Ltd. camp here.

They are Alan H. Dickinson, 780 Fourteenth Street, West Vancouver, and Walter Baer.

Dickinson died four hours after he was struck in the chest by a choker hook and Baer was instantly killed when struck by a falling snag.

MANUSCRIPTS BURN

STOCKHOLM, Sept. 2—(AP)—All the manuscripts of composer Jean Sibelius were destroyed in a bombing of Leipzig, the Dagaens Nyheter reported from Helsinki Friday.

British Set Pace Equal To Russians

By RICHARD McMILLAN

ON THE ROAD TO MONS, Sept. 2—(BUP) — Crashing on along the high road to Germany and Berlin, the British have advanced to near the Belgian frontier and are exacting their revenge for the dark days of Dunkerque.

Progress is so rapid that even the Russians never have exceeded it. Today columns which pushed ahead to form a 10-mile-wide screen beyond the mining centre of Lens, covered 60 miles in 24 hours.

COLUMNS SLASHED

The high road presents a terrific scene for it is a road of flowers, smiles, tears and blood.

Our tanks crash through miles of rose-strewn fields and lanes amid Flanders poppies and are greeted by people so joyous that they laugh and cry in the same breath.

At every crossroad you see the gory, tangled mess that was once a German convoy before it got caught in the greatest retreat in modern warfare.

Entire columns of German horse-driven trucks were slashed to ribbons by the Allied air force attacks and there they lie — a mass of carnage.

A vivid picture of the scene preceding our arrival was told by an old peasant woman.

TERROR-STRICKEN

"They literally galloped off in their attempt to get away," she said.

"They seized any kind of horse and transport, jumped in and be-

Please Turn to Page Two
See "McMillan"

Vimy Ridge, Scene of Canadian Triumph, Captured by British

CANADIAN MEMORIAL AT VIMY RIDGE

By ROSS MUNRO
Canadian Press War Correspondent

WITH ALLIED FORCES IN FRANCE, Sept. 2.—Vimy Ridge, near Arras, has been captured by the British 2nd Army in new great advances through Flanders.

Capture of the scene of the great Canadian triumph of April 9, 1917, was disclosed in a message from Lt.-Gen. Dempsey, British 2nd Commander, to Lt.-Gen. Crerar, 1st Canadian Army Commander.

Crerar had congratulated Dempsey on the British push to Amiens earlier this week, and Dempsey replied yesterday:

"Many thanks for your message. Today you captored Dieppe and we captured Vimy Ridge — a great day for Canada in which the 2nd Army is glad to have played its part."

No word was avalable immediately as to the condition of the Vimy Memorial. (See Page 2 for an account of the historic Vimy battle.)

U.S. Tanks Roll Over Border

Second Allied Column Reported To Be Within Eleven Miles Of German Boundary

By DON WHITEHEAD
Associated Press War Correspondent

WITH AMERICAN FORCES IN EUROPE, Sept. 2.—I crossed the Belgian border with two Associated Press photographers at noon today.

The American 1st Army drove twin spearheads into Belgium.

The American troops crossed the French-Belgium border at 11 a.m.

They had captured Maubege, France, five miles from the border.

To the west an armored column seized Tornai, about 45 miles from Brussels.

(Seloignes is in the Belgium province of Hainaut, of which Mons is the largest city. Maubege is on the road to Mons). Laughing, cheering and weeping natives decked American tanks, trucks and jeeps with garlands of flowers.

The swift push of the American columns has completely disorganized the enemy.

The German Transocean News Agency said one U.S. 3rd Army column reached Longwy, two miles south of Luxembourg, while another was in the Thionville area, inside the part of Alsace-Lorraine seized by the Germans in the French armistice of 1940, and about 11 miles from Germany proper.

At the same time, British and Canadian troops cut a wide swath across the robot bomb coast to the north, eliminating most of the German robot bases in France and advancing to within 15 miles of Belgium.

"The Germans were falling back at top speed all across the front from the Channel coast to the Lorraine basin, offering only the weakest rearguard resistance to the advancing Allies.

"It is evident that the enemy is withdrawing in fair disorder right back to Germany," a British military spokesman said.

Unofficial front reports and German admissions, which headquarters observers saw no reason to doubt, said units of the American 1st Army were moving through the Forest of Ardennes above Sedan and may already have entered Belgium.

BREACH LINE

To the south, Lt. Gen. George S. Patton's 3rd Army columns

Please Turn to Page Two
See "France"

BULLETINS

LISBON, Sept. 2—(AP)—Adolf Hitler will broadcast a "sensational speech" sometime tomorrow, German diplomats said today.

ALLIED SUPREME HEADQUARTERS, Sept. 2—(BUP)—The Germans began evacuating civilians from their Rhineland border tonight and unofficial reports said American armies had invaded Germany and Belgium and were storming in on the Nazis' Siegfried Line.

NEW YORK, Sept. 2—(BUP)—Radio Atlantic said that Allied forces have crossed the Luxembourg frontier and have reached the city of Siegenhofen. The broadcast was heard by NBC.

Girl Plunges 3 Floors to Death

TORONTO, Sept. 2—(CP)—Six hours after the body of a girl was found in an alley at the back of a small hotel near the City Hall, it was identified this afternoon as that of Mrs. Jean Wells, whose husband was said to be serving with the Canadian forces overseas.

The girl apparently had plunged from a window on the third or fourth floor of the hotel.

The girl was well dressed and the body bore no marks of violence.

BASEBALL

NATIONAL

Chicago	000 001 000—1	7	2
Cincinnati	000 000 33x—6	8	0

Derringer, Lyon (8), Stewart (8) and Williams; Shoun and Mueller.

New York	000 301 000—4	14	2
Brooklyn	112 310 00x—8	11	0

Voiselle, Brewer (3), Adams (4), Fischer (6), Hansen (9) and Lombardi; Davis and Owen.

Boston	000 000 001 000 1—2	9	0
Philadel.	001 000 000 000 0—1	8	1

Hutchings, Hutchinson (8) and Kluttz; Lee and Peacock.

AMERICAN

Washington....	000 001 000—1	9	1
New York....	201 000 00x—3	9	1

Lefebvre and Ferrell; Bonham and Garbark.

Philadelphia..	001 110 110—5	10	1
Boston	300 000 001—6	10	1

Christopher and Hayes, Garbark; Woods, Riba (8) and Partee.

Empire Casualties 925,000

LONDON, Sept. 2—(CP)—Casualties of all ranks of the British Empire forces during the first five years of the war total at least 925,963, it was announced officially tonight. They cover the period up to July 31 but some are up to mid-August.

242,900 DEAD

The total includes: Killed, including died of wounds or injures, 242,995; missing, 90,603; wounded, 311,500; prisoners of war and internees, 290,865.

This compared with a total of 1,989,919 Empire deaths and 2,400,988 wounded in the four year and three months of the First Great War.

Canadian casualties in this war up to June 30 totalled 46,394, compared with total First Great War casualties of 190,092.

Canadian casualties in this war include: Dead, 18,821; missing, 5311; prisoners, 5365; wounded, 16,897.

132,000 CIVILIANS

In addition civilian air raid casualties total 132,092 (56,195 killed or missing, believed killed, and 75,897 injured and detained in hospital) and merchant seamen casualties total 33,573 (dead, including deaths presumed in missing ships, 29,381; internees, 4192.)

Hospital Building Gets Labor Priority

OTTAWA, Sept. 2—(CP)—Construction of veterans' hospitals has been given top labor priority in building activities, Arthur MacNamara, director of National Selective Service, announced today.

In areas where labor shortages exist workmen may be shifted from other construction work to veterans' hospital by compulsory order if necessary. The new priority rating applies to bricklayers, carpenters and other construction labor.

CREDIT MEETING IN 'PEG

WINNIPEG, Sept. 2—(CP)—Annual meeting of the Canadian Credit Trust Association Limited will be held here September 11-14.

No Editions Of Sun Monday

Monday being Labor Day, no regular editions of The Vancouver Sun will be published. Latest developments in the war and other news of interest will, however, be brought to Sun readers in the regular newscasts over radio station CKWX at 12:05 noon and 10 p.m.

133

Allies Make New Schelde Landing

THE VANCOUVER DAILY PROVINCE ★★★★★ FINAL

50th YEAR—NO. 189 VANCOUVER, B.C., TUESDAY, NOVEMBER 7, 1944—22 PAGES PRICE 5 CENTS BY CARRIER $1.00 per month

50,000,000 U.S. ELECTORS CAST RECORD BALLOT

WALCHEREN MOPPED UP BY BRITISH

LONDON, Nov. 7.—(AP)—The German garrison at Dunkerque has smashed "strong" Allied attacks against the eastern sector of the fortress, today's German high command communique reported.

Monday the Germans were granted a two-hour armistice so that they might bury their dead.

By ROSS MUNRO.
Canadian Press War Correspondent.

WITH THE 1ST CANADIAN ARMY, Nov. 7.—Mopping up Walcheren Island, British troops of the 1st Canadian Army today took 2000 prisoners in the towns of Middelburg, in the central part of the inundated island in the Schelde estuary. Veere on the northeast coast also was captured, with 500 prisoners taken there.

Among the prisoners taken in Middelburg was Lt.-Gen. Daser, 60-year-old commander of the German 70th Division.

All organized resistance has ended in Middelburg, but several

(Continued on Page 2.)
See HOLLAND.

ELECTION BULLETINS

(See election map on Page 7)

Electoral Landslide?

NEW YORK, Nov. 7.—(CP)—Elmo Roper, William Lydgate and Archibald Crossley, representing respectively the Fortune survey, the Gallup Poll and the Crossley Poll, at a meeting predicted a probable Electoral College landslide for President Roosevelt.

Predict F.D.R. Victory

LONDON, Nov. 7.—(CP)—Most London newspapers today predicted President Roosevelt's victory over Governor Thomas E. Dewey.

Servicemen Vote

FLEMINGTON, N.J., Nov. 7.—(AP)—The first 250 servicemen's absentee ballots counted for Hunterdon county gave Roosevelt 130 votes to 120 for Dewey. In 1940 the county's total vote was 10,293 for Wendell Willkie against 7886 for Roosevelt.

21-0 for F.D.R.

HENDERSON, N.C., Nov. 7.—(AP)—The 21 registered voters of Nutbush precinct, in the northern part of Vance County, today kept their time-honored reputation of being the first precinct in North Carolina to report its vote.

Leads In Kentucky

LOUISVILLE, Ky., Nov. 7. (AP)—The first 17 of 4304 Kentucky precincts reporting in today's election gave President Roosevelt 4404 votes to Governor Dewey's 2876.

Dewey Has Indecisive Early Lead

(By Associated Press.)

NEW YORK, Nov. 7.—Governor Thomas E. Dewey took leads in early and inconclusive counting in Kansas and New Mexico today as election officials dug into a probable 50,000,000 record vote total.

The returns in those two states, as well as scattered countts in half a dozen others, were too fragmentary, however, to establish a trend.

The first reports on service votes, gave a lead to President Roosevelt in a New Jersey county which went Republican in 1940. Dewey led 1237 to 1029 in initial New Mexico returns.

Cuttyhunk, Massachusetts, which Roosevelt carried in 1940 by 13 votes, gave Dewey 23 to 14 for the President.

Small Massachusetts towns reported about the same proportionate margin that Wendell L. Willkie held in those communities in 1940 when President Roosevelt carried the Bay State.

SAME PROPORTION.

Mashpee, on Cape Cod, gave a count of 89 for Dewey and 81 for Roosevelt. Four years ago the final total was Willkie 97, Roosevelt 89. In the Berkshire Hills, Mount Washington reported a complete vote of Dewey 29, Roosevelt 8. In 1940, it was Willkie 32, Roosevelt 10.

But New Ashford gave Dewey 22 and Roosevelt 21. In 1940, the vote was Willkie 33, Roosevelt 13.

Incomplete unofficial returns from 83 of the 2750 precincts in Kansas give, for President: Dewey 4453, Roosevelt 3031.

LARGER TOWNS.

The returns are from the city precincts in the state where watchers for candidates may announce the vote totals as they are counted. Kansas is usually heavily Republican.

The candidates themselves added their personal ballots to the mounting figures while many hours yet remained before officials generally began to tally the electorate's decision.

ROOSEVELT VOTES.

President Roosevelt voted before noon at Hyde Park's old town hall. As he did four years ago, he gave his occupation as "tree grower." He raises Christmas trees on his Hudson Valley estate.

At about the same time, Governor Dewey put in his ballot at an automobile tourist bureau serving as a polling place in New York City.

Six persons were arrested in New York on charges of illegal registration. They were among 400 indicted last week on that charge.

Serious Choice

Americans Go Quietly To Polls

By W. L. MACTAVISH
Editor of The Vancouver Daily Province.

CHICAGO, Nov. 7.—The American people went quietly and sedately to the polls today to mark their ballots in a presidential election.

There will probably be, as there always are, some reports of hoodlums moving in on polling places, and minor rows.

Nevertheless, it is generally true to say, on the testimony of experienced observers, that it is the quietest and most serious of all American elections in recent years.

(Continued on Page 2.)
See MACTAVISH.

Defends Voluntary Recruiting

McNAUGHTON FACES BOOS, CHEERS AT LEGION MEETING

By TORCHY ANDERSON.
(From Daily Province Ottawa Bureau. Copyright, 1944, by Southam Co.)

OTTAWA, Nov. 7.—Confronted by men with whom he had served in two wars, General A. G. L. McNaughton, minister of national defense since last Thursday, on Monday night faced the first blast of the rising storm against his policy of continuing voluntary reinforcement to reinforce Canadians fighting battalions overseas.

To some 700 members of the Ottawa branch, Canadian Legion, General McNaughton reiterated his firm faith in voluntary service, defending it in the face of indignant questions, hoots and interruptions.

Into the tense, dramatic atmosphere of a meeting that has just given an unanimous endorsement of a demand by Legion national officers for total conscription, stepped civilian-clad "Andy" McNaughton.

He came there at their invitation because they wanted to hear him and gave him a membership token that confirmed the life membership they voted him in May, 1943.

While they alternately cheered, hooted, interrupted and questioned, the new minister met the storm like a veteran of the hustings and stuck to his guns. When they gave him a final cheer it was evident that, even if he had not converted them to his voluntary recruiting policy, they admired "Old Andy's guts."

While they taunted him with having a one-province policy, General McNaughton plodded

(Continued on Page 2.)
See TROOPS.

$2,250,000 City Order

FIRM GIVEN LARGE ORDER

Contracts worth $2,250,000—for 300 Lodormobiles to be delivered to Russia and Great Britain within a year—have been awarded to Canadian Mixermobile Co. Ltd., 263 East Seventh.

Fifty will go to the Soviet, 250 to Britain, announces W. B. Steele, managing director.

440 CRANEMOBILES.

Of 440 Cranemobiles ordered, 250 have been delivered. Ninety more will go to Russia, 100 to the United Kingdom.

Production of the Lodormobiles—rubber-tired, hydraulic-lift machines, used for moving coal, gravel and cement—will start in January.

Completion of this order will take up most of 1945.

About 1000 men are employed in the firm's main and auxiliary plants.

Sues for Reward

MONTREAL, Nov. 7.—(CP)—Roger Lepine, who killed a hold-up man with three shots while working as a bank teller in 1942 here, has sued the Canadian Bankers' Association for $10,000 which he claimed was due him as a reward.

N. Shore Shipyard Strike

"SIT DOWN" ON JOB

About 300 workers at North Van. Ship Repairs Ltd. staged a one-hour "sit-down strike" this morning following dispute between two A.F.L. unions as to who would install evaporator equipment in cargo ships.

The Plumbers and Steamfitters' Union declared it was their work. The International Association of Machinists argued they should do the job.

Machinists claimed that the company gave the work to the plumbers, who went ahead with the job. The machinists sat down for an hour. The management then agreed to hold up installation of the evaporators until a conciliator from the provincial department of labor goes into the matter with the unions. The machinists have been given other jobs in their category in the meantime.

Evaporators are machinery, and so the machinists claim the right to install them. The evaporators also have certain pipe connections, and the plumbers claim that is their job.

Final BULLETINS

Tribute to Canada

BALTIMORE, Nov. 7.—(CP)—The Baltimore Sun paid editorial tribute to the fighting men from Canada, noting that the important news from the western front in the last few days has been made by Canadian and British armies in Holland.

Poison to Japs

LONDON, Nov. 7.—(AP)—Air Chief Marshal Sir Philip Joubert, deputy chief of staff to Lord Mountbatten in the Southeast Asia command, states that British and Indian forces in Burma had to date inflicted a greater number of casualties on the Japanese than any other force in the Pacific theatre.

Strike Ends

DETROIT, Nov. 7.—(AP)—Eight thousand workers resumed production at Continental Motors Corporation and the Freuhauf Trailer Co. today after votes of their United Automobile Workers (C.I.O.) locals to end strikes. At Continental 7000 had been idle several days because of a strike over an incentive pay system.

Robot Raid Possible

WASHINGTON, Nov. 7.—(AP)—The war and navy departments said today that robot bomb attacks by Germany on the United States are "entirely possible."

King to Meet Legion

OTTAWA, Nov. 7.—(CP)—Canadian Legion officials said today Prime Minister Mackenzie King has agreed to meet the Dominion executive council of the Legion to discuss the reinforcement of Canadian forces overseas. The interview is expected to take place late today or tomorrow.

Deny Allegations

BERNE, Nov. 7.—(AP)—Switzerland's federal council denied Soviet assertions that this country had shown a hostile attitude toward Russia. This was the basis of the Soviet's refusal to resume diplomatic relations with Switzerland. The council indicated it would continue to seek such relations.

Climax Near At Leyte

GENERAL MACARTHUR'S HEADQUARTERS, Philippines, Nov. 7.—(AP)—American veteran troops, already four miles south of Carigara Bay, continued an unchecked advance through Japanese mountain defenses on the twisting highway toward Ormoc—16 miles distant—and the finale of the Leyte Island campaign.

Well-equipped Japanese reinforcements were somewhere along the shell-raked highway through Ormoc Valley, waiting perhaps to launch a final attack which is expected to produce some of the campaign's fiercest battling.

Premier Broadcasts On Army Policy Wednesday Night

OTTAWA, Nov. 7.—(CP)—Prime Minister Mackenzie King will give a half-hour address tomorrow night on the subject "Support for the Canadian Army Overseas."

The address will be carried on all Canadian Broadcasting Corporation networks — the Trans-Canada, Dominion and French, from 6:30 to 7 p.m., Vancouver time.

Tires Go Begging

MONTREAL, Nov. 7.—(CP)—Tire-seeking motorists could hardly believe it, when police officials here announced 280 out of 500 stolen tires recovered during the last three months had not yet been returned to their owners—because there were no claimants.

Canadian Index

Industrial Wage Rates Show Gain

(By Canadian Press)

OTTAWA, Nov. 7.—The general index number for wage rates in the 12 chief lines of industrial employment in Canada rose 9.9 points to 139.5 during 1943 from 129.6 in 1942, the labor department announced today.

The 1943 figure showed an increase of 33.8 points over the 105.7 mark set in 1939. The index is calculated on the basis that 100 represents the average wage level for the 1935-1939 period.

Figures for the war years were given as follows: 1939, 105.7; 1940, 109.4; 1941, 120.3; 1942, 128.6, and 1943, 139.5.

Increase in wage rates from 1939 to 1943 in the various lines of employment were as follows:

Occupational Group—	1939	1943
Building trades	103.3	128.8
Metal trades	104.7	132.8
Printing trades	101.9	116.0
Electrical railways	102.7	133.5
Steam railways	105.0	131.5
Coal mining	102.9	128.5
Common factory labor	105.9	149.0
Miscellaneous factory trades	106.0	142.4
Logging and sawmilling	110.5	152.9
Metal mining	102.8	125.3
Steamships	110.0	147.0
Laundries	101.7	131.2
Telephones	103.1	127.3
General average (weighted)	105.7	139.5

Declare Season Open on Doe Deer

(Special to The Daily Province)

VICTORIA, Nov. 7.—An open season for doe deer has been declared by order-in-council in an area extending approximately from one mile north of Cowichan River to the Solarium road at Milbay, and taking in parts of Quamichan, Helmcken, Shawnigan and Cowichan districts. The season will extend from December 1 to 15, and a hunter is permitted to kill one doe during that time.

Deer have been doing extensive damage to crops in the district, and have become so numerous that they are a menace along the island highway at night.

Province Demands Relief Payments

VICTORIA, Nov. 7.—(CP)—Immediate attention will be given a demand letter from the provincial deputy finance minister to the city of Victoria for payment of $300,000 in unemployment relief loans advanced to Victoria in 1935 and 1936, Mayor Andrew McGavin said today.

City May Soon Know Name of Next President

Even before the polls close on the Pacific Coast at 8 p.m. some idea may be gained here of who United States wants for President. With the completion of the vote in some heavy eastern constituencies by 3 p.m. Vancouver time, the trend may be known here within an hour or so of that time.

New York polls do not close until 6 p.m., Vancouver time, but results from Illinois, Michigan and other heavily populated states will be known here considerably before that.

If the early vote swings heavily to Roosevelt or to Dewey, the definite result wi.. be known early. If it is close, the victor may not be known for weeks—until the 3,369,000 soldier vote is counted.

CALL PACIFIC 4211 FOR ELECTION RETURNS, OR LISTEN TO MR. GOOD EVENING OVER CKWX (980 kc.) AT 8:15 P.M.

Miners Fined $50 For Absenteeism

(Special to The Daily Province)

NELSON, Nov. 7.—Four miners charged with absenteeism were each fined $50 by Stipendiary Magistrate John Cartmel.

They were John Ritchie of Silverton, Percy Morrison of Retallack, Almer S. Danielson of Retallack and Denis Delaney of Silverton, all of the Whitewater Mine, Slocan.

Arthur Latham Dies

VICTORIA, Nov. 7.—(CP)—Arthur Latham, 75, who operated a hardware store in Moose Jaw for 25 years before retiring and coming here in 1937, died today. Born in Wales, he came to Canada when a young man and engaged in mining at Trail before going to Moose Jaw. His widow and one son survive.

10 Hours Across Atlantic

MONTREAL, Nov. 7.—(CP)—A transatlantic record of 10 hours and 13 minutes—one hour and one minute less than the previous one set last January—was chalked up by a Trans-Canada Airlines Lancaster flying non-stop from here to Britain.

RACING

Rockingham Race Results

FIRST RACE—Six furlongs.
Mervyn Leroy (Daniels), $11, $7, $4.60; Tee Midge (Martin), $11.80, $6.60; Wilton (Hettinger), $3.
Time, 1.16. Scratched: Briarchal, Detroit Bull, Manchester, Bright and Early.

SECOND RACE—Six furlongs.
Heel Up (Luft), $30.60, $14.60, $8.60; Donedna (Barber), $32.40, $15; Islam King (Hettinger), $4.
Time, 1.16. Scratched: Early Delivery.

THIRD RACE—Six furlongs.
Tinys Choice (Martin), $21.20, $8.80, $5.60; Heat Wave (Pollard), $5.40, $3.60; Over The Dam (Hettinger) $5.60.
Time, 1.16. Scratched: Phaon, Miss Me Now.

FOURTH RACE—Six furlongs.
Darby Duncan (Torres) $15.80, $7.20, $4.60; Sangone (Cross), $4.40, $4; Expediting (Summers), $5.20.
Time, 1.17. Scratched: Light Count, Matlock.

FIFTH RACE—Six furlongs.
Westfleet (Madden), $57.80, $12.60, $6.80; Countess Wise (Seabo), $4.20, $3; In Vogue (Lynch), $4.40.
Time, 1.15⅘. Scratched: Harpsichord, Free Transit, Bold Pat.

SIXTH RACE—Mile, sixteenth.
Ben Gray (Gross), $3.60, $3, $2.40; Budded (Murphy), $5.40, $3.20; Veris (Chaffin), $3.80.
Time, 1.52⅖. Scratched, none.

SEVENTH RACE—Mile, eighth.
Bus V. Z., Pollard), $20.20, $7.40, $5; War Glenn (Chaffin), $5, $3.80; Torch Lee (Lynch), $3.20.
Time, 1.58⅖. Scratched, none.

EIGHTH RACE—Mile, eighth.
Good Ante (Seabo), $7.80, $3.60, $2.80; Penomp (Cavens), $3.40, $2.40; Felt Hat (McMullen), $2.40.
Time, 2.00⅗. Scratched, none.

Hollywood Race Results

FIRST RACE—Five an dhalf furl.
Herodite (Westrope), $18.10, $7.80, $4.40; School Row (Corbett), $5.50, $3.40; Aroc (Zufelt), $2.70.
Time, 1.08⅕. Scratched: Timmy.

SECOND RACE—Six furlongs.
Sea Skipper (Jones), $4.40, $3.50, $2.70; Monfalon (Zufelt), $5.10, $3.80; Cousin Mamie (Campbell), $3.70.
Time, 1.13⅕. Scratched, none.

(Race Entries on Page 2.)

Dope Thefts Threat

WINNIPEG, Nov. 7.—(CP)—Dr. Harvey Agnew of Toronto, secretary of the Canadian Hospital Council, stated here that narcotic robberies from hospitals and doctor's offices in Canada are reaching alarming proportions. One grain of a drug sold on the streets brought the thieves from $20 to $25.

He said: "We are dealing not only with drug addicts, but with some of the most brilliant and unscrupulous men in Canada."

1945

The year when Good finally triumphed over Evil and the whole free world found joyous relief in celebrating, first, V-E Day in May and then V-J Day in August. The Allied armies met in Germany and divided it up, the communists on one side and the democracies on the other. Disposing of the Japanese was going to be bloody, however, until the atomic bomb was perfected by a team of British and American physicists. The obliteration of two Japanese cities with only a single bomb each convinced Emperor Hirohito to surrender. It had truly been a world war of epic proportions.

MAJOR EVENTS

January-April 1945

GERMANY CRUMBLES

IN THE EAST. The war in Russia in early 1945 was so vast, with so many men under arms, that the Red Army organized itself into seven different groups, called "Fronts," of three-quarters of a million to one million men each, with accompanying equipment of every description. Opposing them were three dispirited German army groups, one of which had been virtually annihilated in the battle for Minsk the previous year. German losses in four months of 1944 alone had amounted to 840,000. Such attrition could not be made up any longer, although war production was at an all-time high, thanks to the organizational genius of Albert Speer.

By January 1945, Romania and Bulgaria had made separate truces with Russia. Some 150,000 Bulgarian troops, who had never fought the Russians, joined the 3rd Ukrainian Front and Tito's partisans in besieging and taking Belgrade.

Hungary held out against the Russians, however, because Hitler had taken a personal interest in saving Budapest. He sent in an extra Panzer division in a great effort to defend the city, but by January two Russian fronts had swallowed up Hungary and were striking towards Vienna and Czechoslovakia.

Farther north, the Germans had hoped to make a stand at the Vistula River in Poland with troops under the command of Heinrich Himmler, the Gestapo chief. No military expert himself, Himmler's new army had little to recommend it either. It was made up of rejects who were too young or too old for the regular army.

Needless to say, the invincible Red Army stormed across the Vistula with little opposition. Its momentum carried it through western Poland and East Prussia straight into Germany itself. By February 20th Russian divisions were 50 miles from Berlin, the ultimate prize. All roads going west were clogged with German refugees desperate to escape the Russian troops, who were rampaging their way right across Germany. The Germans had met an adversary capable of waging war on their own level of bestiality, and they were terrified.

IN THE WEST. *Crossing the Rhine*—these magic words, to the Allied mind, marked the beginning of the end of Nazi Germany. Once that river had been crossed, the hinterland of Germany opened up to the Allied armies.

The first crossing was on March 8th at Remagen, where the U.S. 1st Army seized the intact bridge—an exploit made famous in a movie. German resistance was fierce, however, and it was not until March 26th that the bridgehead was expanded and the 1st Army was able to advance 22 miles east to Limburg.

The same day, Patton's 3rd Army advanced 80 miles from the Rhine into Bavaria and entered Frankfurt-on-Main, by then a bombed rubble.

There was fighting all along the Rhine during March before significant breakthroughs were achieved. Field Marshal Montgomery's 21st Army Group, composed of the Canadian 1st, the British 2nd and the U.S. 9th armies, battled across Germany in the north on a line for Berlin. In the centre, the U.S. 1st had taken Remagen, and in the south the U.S. 3rd and 7th armies were headed across southern Germany into Bavaria and Austria.

Such was Allied rejoicing at their successful Rhine crossings and expanding bridgeheads that General Eisenhower was moved to declare on March 27th, as quoted on the front page of *The Vancouver Sun*, that "Germany's Armies Are Whipped." He was correct, but the Germans didn't know that. They did not give up so easily. Exhorted on by their Fuehrer from his Berlin bunker, they continued their determined resistance right through April.

It was not until April 30th that the Red Army and the U.S. 9th Army joined forces at the Elbe River northwest of Berlin, effectively cutting Germany in half. Earlier, the U.S. 1st Army had joined up with the Russians farther south at Breslau, in a scene of great rejoicing, but it was not until May that the Nazi armies started surrendering in significant numbers.

[See pages 127–28, 133–34, 138–43, 144–46, 150]

April-May 1945

THE RACE FOR BERLIN

Churchill saw the political ramifications, as did Stalin, for the side that first took Berlin, where Hitler was ensconced in his command bunker. The Americans, however, couldn't see that Berlin mattered. Eisenhower thought strategically and not politically, and Roosevelt was too ill to think at all. Since the Americans were by now the senior partners in the Western Alliance, there was nothing Churchill could do but sit and watch the Red Army juggernaut roll on past the surrounded Nazi capital all the way west to the Elbe River.

No matter how one looks at it, it was only fair that Berlin should fall to the Red Army, which had taken the lion's share in defeating the Wehrmacht.

On April 16th, when the Russian offensive against Berlin began, Marshal Zhukov's First Belorussian Front had been regrouping on the Oder River 50 miles from Berlin. Its 10,000 guns opened up on the German lines. The German commander who was replacing Himmler was a professional soldier—Colonel-General Heinrici—and he managed to mount a serious defense that bogged down Zhukov's armies. It took 750,000 troops comprising four field armies and two tank armies until May 2nd to raise the Red flag over the gutted Reichstag, which had been defended room-by-room. By the time it was all over the Allies were probably relieved that they had left Berlin to the Russians, who had suffered 150,000 casualties during the ferocious fighting.

[See pages 146, 149–50, 154–55]

April 30, 1945

DEATH OF HITLER

A banner headline on *The Vancouver Sun* EXTRA for May 1, 1945 announced Adolf Hitler's death. It showed as well a photograph of Mussolini and his mistress hanging by their heels in a Milan town square—a much better ending, for all to see in its finality, than Hitler's, where we had to take someone's word that he was dead.

He took cyanide, some said. Shot himself, said others. Some claimed he did both. Faithful servants then took the bodies of Hitler and his new wife, Eva Braun, to the Reich Chancellery garden, poured gasoline on them, burned them, and buried them there. The Russians learned what had happened, dug up the bodies, and took them away to Russia. That is what we know, and it seems plausible, but there is always room for doubt.

Hitler had been holed up in his bunker under the Chancellery in the heart of Berlin since January 16th. Henchmen came and went, with new orders to carry out; generals ventured forth with new battle plans for non-existent divisions. A whole fantasy played itself out in that bunker as the Third Reich disintegrated around it.

And yet the Germans still obeyed. Up above in Berlin's devastated streets remnants of armies still fought for their Fuehrer amid the chaos. Everyone seemed intent on delaying peace as long as possible. Only with news of Hitler's death did his hypnotic spell dissipate and peace became possible

[See pages 152–54]

May 8, 1945

V-E DAY

Peace was official between the Allies and the Germans on May 8th, when the surrender document was signed in Berlin on behalf of Admiral Karl Doenitz, the new head of state after Hitler's death.

Before that, there had been a stream of battlefield surrenders, so that on the Home Front everyone was ready and waiting to celebrate the final surrender when news came. The headlines from May 2nd onward tell the story of whole armies laying down their arms, one-by-one. But on May 7th the nightmare finally ended, and Vancouver, Toronto, London and every other Allied city went wild with joy. *The Daily Province* final edition on May 7th described that thrilling day perfectly. *[See pages 151–65]*

April-June 1945

OKINAWA

If the Allies had continued waging the war by conventional means, without the atom bomb, they would have had to seize Japan's home islands. The invasion of Okinawa on April 1, 1945 gave them a foretaste of the kind of casualties they could expect from fighting the Japanese on their home soil.

On Okinawa, 110,000 Japanese soldiers had fought to the death, with only 7,400 surviving to be taken prisoner. The Americans had averaged 35 percent casualties, including their commanding general, Simon Bolivar Buckner. The navy had committed 1,300 ships to the landings—a massive number that included 18 battleships, 40 carriers and 200 destroyers.

Adding up the figures made horrendous reading for the Allied Chiefs of Staff, and the successful testing of the atom bomb in New Mexico on July 16th relieved them immensely. The proposed 1946 invasion of Japan could now be reconsidered. Okinawa was definitely influential in ushering in the atomic age. *[See page 167]*

August 6-9, 1945

THE ATOMIC BOMB

A joint development of British and American scientists, the atomic bomb eventually entailed the employment of thousands of people working in the New Mexican desert in complete secrecy—quite a feat in itself.

There was evidence that the Germans were also working on a bomb, and serious efforts were made to deter them. Heavy water plants in Norway were sabotaged repeatedly, and laboratories in Germany were bombed.

Fortunately, the Allied efforts were successful, and led to the destruction of Hiroshima on August 6th with one atomic bomb equal to 20,000 tons of TNT. Reconnaissance photos showed that 60 percent of the city was totally obliterated by the searing blast.

A second bomb was dropped on Nagasaki on August 9th with equally devastating results, causing the Japanese Emperor to sue for peace on August 10th. *[See pages 165–67]*

August 15, 1945

V-J DAY

The scenario for the Japanese surrender really began when the first atom bomb was dropped on Hiroshima. President Truman, who with Churchill had to make the terrible decision to use the bomb, told the Japanese "Give up or be wiped out....We are now prepared to obliterate...every productive enterprise the Japanese have above ground." Strong words, and he meant every one of them, but fanatical elements in the Japanese government were dead set against any form of surrender. Anyone who talked of it was arrested. Emperor Hirohito broke the deadlock in favour of peace, announcing his decision to the Japanese people in his first-ever radio broadcast on August 15th, the historic day the war ended.

[See pages 168–74]

CANUCKS RIP THROUGH MAIN SIEGFRIED LINE

The Vancouver Sun

FOUNDED 1886
VOL. LIX—No. 163

MArine 1161

VANCOUVER, BRITISH COLUMBIA, SATURDAY, FEBRUARY 10, 1945

PRICE 10 CENTS $1.00 per month BY CARRIER

RATIONED FOODS

Sugar—Coupons 50, 51 now valid.
Butter—Coupon 95 now valid.
Preserves—Coupons 37, 38 now valid.
All valid coupons in Book 5 good until further notice.

—AP Wirephoto

THE ADVANCE BEGINS—This striking panoramic picture shows troops of the 1st Canadian Army, under Lt. Gen. H. D. G. Crerar, beginning the attack on the Nijmegen front Thursday morning. Substantial gains have already been reported as will be seen by the dispatch in adjoining columns. The men are advancing with and behind tanks. The two soldiers in the right foreground are evidently setting up some sort of automatic weapon. Note the deep gouges in the earth (left foreground) made by the tracks of the mechanized armor.

Crerar's Men Hit Secondary Forts

From AP and BUP Dispatches

PARIS, Feb. 10.—First Canadian Army troops, bursting through the main concrete belt of the Siegfried Line in the Reichswald, struck today to within three miles of Kleve, while the Germans flooded the Roer River on the United States 9th Army front through gushing spillways of the Schwammenauel Dam.

Canadians and British forces, gaining two more miles, were assaulting earthworks of the Siegfried's secondary defense in a power drive rolling toward the outskirts of Kleve, northern anchor of the original west wall.

Other units battled in the Rhine town of Millingen, six miles northwest of Kleve, in the army's swift-developing threat to slice behind the Rhine and the Reich Ruhr industrial area.

Waters of the lower Roer River, along which the American 9th Army is arrayed, rose a foot and a half in an hour at some points as the Germans were reported to have blown up the power station, gate house and bridge of the Schwammenauel dam, which impounds 170,000,000 tons of water.

CAPTURE NEAR

The threat of such a flood had prevented the 9th and 1st Armies from attempting to cross the Roer since they reached it east of Aachen last November.

Field dispatches said the Roer was rising rapidly but the main Schwammenauel dam had not yet been blown up. The dam itself is under direct fire from artillery of the U.S. 1st Army. Infantry were reported preparing to cross the Roer and clinch capture of the dam.

Pent-up power of the 1080-foot long dam, if released all at once, might send an 18-foot tide storming down the Roer Valley.

Still farther south, United States 3rd Army troops fought within three-quarters of a mile of the Siegfried prize of Pruem, and scored advances today of up to a mile northeast and southwest of the road hub. Germans resisted desperately.

As far as could be told immediately the Canadian thrust was a complete breach of the main pillbox line guarding Kleve, which the Germans had made the original northern anchor of the whole Siegfried chain.

10-MILE FRONT

Nuetterden, on the main Nijmegen-Kleve road about three miles west of Kleve, fell to the Canadian onrush in a two-mile drive beyond Kranenberg. The Allied troops were well beyond the town on the last few thousand yards to the outskirts of Kleve this morning.

The Canadian and British troops gained almost five miles and broadened their front to nearly 10 miles yesterday on the second day of their new offensive. The total number of towns captured mounted to 14.

Mayor Says ARP to Wind Up March 31

Vancouver's Civilian Defense organization, which at its peak had a personnel of 19,000, will be disbanded March 31, according to Mayor J. W. Cornett.

The mayor made the announcement at a meeting of the Board of Police Commissioners on Friday, when he told representatives of the Auxiliary Police he hoped when the organization is wound up to see a formal meeting held, at which all branches of the service will be thanked.

CIO Would Wipe Out All Naziism

LONDON, Feb. 10—(CP)—Complete economic subjugation of Germany for years to come was endorsed by the Congress of Industrial Organization today before the world trade union conference.

J. B. Carey, secretary-treasurer of the CIO, said the organization favors internationalization of a part of Germany's industrial areas and believes German labor should be required to rebuild war-wrecked Europe.

He told conference delegates that the CIO supports measures which would completely destroy "every vestige of Nazism and Fascism."

SUBS SINK 7 SHIPS; B.C. MEN AMONG 73 DROWNED

BUP and Special Dispatches

HALIFAX, Feb. 10.—Long-range German submarines, boldly attacking in daylight within sight of the Nova Scotia shore, have sunk seven Allied ships off that northern coast, six of them within one 22-day period, it was announced today.

One of them was the Canadian minesweeper Clayoquot, whose sinking was announced on Jan. 31.

Another was a Canadian merchantman,

GOES DOWN WITH SHIP

Capt. E. H. "Bob" Robinson of Halifax and formerly of Vancouver, went down on the bridge of his freighter as he directed abandon ship operations, survivors said.

The 37-year-old master was making his second voyage aboard the first ship he had commanded.

Seventy-three lives were lost in the sinkings, it was said.

Eight were naval personnel of the Clayoquot.

More than 200 survivors, many of them requiring hospital treatment for wounds and exposure, have been landed at Atlantic ports.

McNAUGHTON'S WARNING

Censors did not identify the 22-day period, but it is presumed to have been recent.

The Clayoquot was believed sunk in January.

It was recalled that Defense Minister General A. G. L. McNaughton said in a Grey North election speech several weeks ago, that the North Atlantic was "alive with German submarines" and "we are having ships sunk day by day."

Survivors said the U-boats operated without their usual caution.

Not content with picking up stragglers, they attacked armed escort vessels, then turned their torpedoes on the unprotected merchantmen.

AFTER TROOPSHIPS

For weeks before the Nazi subs struck in their latest campaign, the undersea raiders had prowled around the North Atlantic seaboard.

They were spotted at different points close to the Nova Scotia coast from Cape Breton to Yarmouth.

Their movements and actions were mysterious.

They did not attack.

There were suspicions that they were "getting their bearings" on convoy lanes or possibly picking out targets for V weapon bombardments.

Then just before Christmas the mine sweeper Clayoquot, which had seen four years of convoy duty in the North Atlan-

Please Turn to Page Three
See "Subs"

ROOSEVELT DOG KEEPING MUM

WASHINGTON, Feb. 10—(BUP)—That dog is here again.

No, not Fala. Blaze.

Sen. Styles Bridges, R., N.H., is firmly convinced that a full dress Senate investigation into the whole question of travel priorities is definitely in order today.

Bridges' conviction stems from a hearing held yesterday by a Senate military affairs subcommittee appointed to inquire into such priority questions as how Blaze, Brig. Gen. Elliott Roosevelt's bull mastiff, got an "A" priority that let him ride in a plane while three service-men had to get off.

The White House has termed Blaze's "A" priority a "mistake," but names of officials responsible for granting it have never been revealed.

If dogs could only talk.

Fierce Fight For Manila

By FRANCIS McCARTHY
Special to The Vancouver Sun

MANILA, Feb. 10—(BUP)—Japanese resistance in Southern Manila flared wtih renewed violence today as the cornered enemy fell back slowly toward the waterfront for a death stand inside the old walled city.

Fighting through a choking pall of smoke that covered virtually all South Manila, elements of two American divisions hit the Japanese front and rear in the Pandacan and Paco districts below the Pasig River.

The converging attack was squeezing several thousand Japanese slowly westward toward the burned-out port area.

After yielding the aPsig River crossing opposite the Malacanan Palace to the U.S. 37th Division almost without a struggle, the Japanese lashed back suddenly at their pursuers with artillery, mortars and rifle fire.

Flying Rights Guaranteed

'TWO FREEDOMS' PACT TO BE SIGNED BY CANADA

By C. R. BLACKBURN

WASHINGTON, Feb. 10—(CP)—L. B. Pearson, Canadian Ambassador to Washington, at the State Department today will sign the so-called "Two Freedoms" air agreement and announce that his signature constitutes acceptance of the agreement by Canada.

The "Two Freedoms" grant to aircraft of the signing countries freedom to fly over the signatories' territory, and to land for service or technical purposes, but not for traffic.

The United States, Canada, Norway and the Netherlands now have done all they can short of legislative sanction to validate the transit agreement.

Twenty-eight others have signed but have not yet backed their signatures by governmental declarations of adherence.

SEEN 'FUEHRER' IN VANCOUVER?

If you meet a man who says he is working for "Der Fuehrer" and keeps clicking his heels together, notify city police.

He is a patient of an Ontario Mental Hospital who escaped January 20, and who is believed to have been seen in Vancouver.

He is a 33-year-old Canadian. When last seen he is reported to have been wearing dark coveralls and engineer's cap.

Tokyo Hit By 'Quake And B-29's

WASHINGTON, Feb. 10—(BUP)—An earthquake and hundreds of tons of American bombs rocked the Tokyo-Yokohama area of central Japan in quick succession today.

The earthquake shook northern as well as central Japan at 1:50 p.m. Tokyo time, a Japanese Domei dispatch said. Neither the intensity of the shock nor the extent of damage was indicated.

LARGE FORCE

At 2:30 p.m. a Japanese Supreme headquarters communique said, 90 superfortresses began an hour-long raid on the Tokyo-Yokohama area. "Some damage" was caused to ground installations, the communique said.

A dispatch from British United Press War correspondent Lloyd Tupling at 21st Bomber Command headquarters, Guam, said the superforts comprised one of the largest forces ever to hit Japan.

The B-29s hit targets in the Tokyo area with "good to excellent results," a spokesman said.

WIDESPREAD QUAKE

The earthquake a little more more than a half hour earlier was felt from Hokkaido, northernmost of the Japanese home islands, down through Honshu, Domei said.

All eastern and central Honshu, including the Tokyo-Yokohama area, were shaken, Domei said.

Reds Take Elbing, East Prussia Port

LONDON, Feb. 10—(AP)—Red Army troops have captured Elbing, East Prussian Baltic port, Marshal Stalin announced today. Earlier, the Berlin radio had reported that German naval units, led by the 10,000-ton pocket battleship Admiral Scheer, were taking part in the Elbing fighting.

From AP and BUP Dispatches

LONDON, Feb. 10.—Soviet tanks driving a wedge between Berlin and the Silesian industrial capital of Breslau have smashed deep into the main German defenses more than 25 miles beyond the Oder River, the Nazis conceded today.

North of Berlin, other Russian forces pushed to within 25 miles or less of the Baltic port of Stettin in a drive to seal off tens of thousands of enemy troops in northeast Germany, the Polish Corridor and Danzig.

CUT COMMUNICATIONS

The Soviet high command threw a cloak of secrecy over the Berlin front itself, but the Germans reported the Russians had crossed the middle Oder 35 miles due east of Berlin and slashed north-south communications between Kuestrin, Frankfurt and Fuerstenberg, key cities in the Berlin defense forefield.

Russian field dispatches told of fierce fighting in Kuestrin and in the suburbs of Frankfurt and Fuerstenberg.

The German communique reported that Mrashal Gregory Zhukov was "pressed back further to the Oder" from bridgeheads between Fuerstenberg and Kuestrin.

BROADEN WEDGE

Ernst von Hammer, military commentator for the official German DNB agency, disclosed that Russian armored spearheads 120 miles southeast of Berlin had

Please Turn to Page Three
See "Russians"

Week-End Cloudy But Minus Rain

No mention of rain is made in the weatherman's forecast for week-end weather.

Hikers and others who enjoy the outdoors will find the skies "partly cloudy," but no rain is due to fall.

Expectations are that temperatures will be slightly higher than Friday. High in the 24-hour period ending at 9 a.m. today was 45 and low was 42.

Jap Cabinet Shaken Up

SAN FRANCISCO, Feb. 10—(BUP)—Premier General Kuniaki Koiso shook up his war cabinet today installing welfare minister Hisatada Hirose to the dual post of chief secretary of the cabinet and state minister of portfolio and ousting Takco Tanaka, former Cabinet secretary, Radio Tokyo said today.

Tokyo called the re-organization a "partial shake-up" and said the new appointees were installed tonight at the Imperial palace.

Hirose also replaced Count Hideo Kodama, former military advisor to the Japanese forces in southern Asia, as state minister without portfolio.

Bombers Hit Fuel Depot

LONDON, Feb. 10—(CP)—United States heavy bombers attacked a German motor fuel depot at Duelmen, southwest of Muenster, today and submarine pens at Ijmuiden on the Netherlands coast. Only 150 heavy bombers and approximately 130 fighters participated in both operations.

Road and rail convoys in the Netherlands and western Germany were attacked last night by continent-based tactical air force light bombers.

Sixty-eight enemy planes, including five jet-powered Messerschmitt-262's were destroyed in daylight yesterday and Allied losses were 26 planes.

Canadian Officer In War One Dies

LONDON, Feb. 10—(CP)—Lt. Gen. Sir Henry Burstall, 74, who commanded the 2nd Canadian Division from 1916-1918, has just died at Meadbourne Warthy, Hampshire, it was announced Friday night.

Cloudy Skies

Cloudy with moderate winds and occasional light showers. Forecast maximum temperature 53. Sunday, fair to partly cloudy, except cloudy in early morning, moderate winds, not much change in temperature. Forecast temperatures, maximum 50, minimum 40.

BODIES BROUGHT BACK TO NETHERLANDS

Canuck Troops Refuse to Bury Dead in German Soil

By DOUGLAS AMARON

WITH THE 1ST CANADIAN ARMY, Feb. 10—(CP)—Battle highlights of the 1st Canadian Army offensive:

Canadian soldiers who died in the capture of the German frontier village of Wyler, about six miles southeast of Nijmegen, Holland, will be buried on Netherlands soil.

The commanding officer of the Western Canada Highland battalion which captured the village gave orders for bodies of soldiers killed to be brought back across the border.

"I don't want to bury any of my men in Germany until necessary," he explained.

The Canadians were elated over this first conquest in Germany.

Wyler, which stretches for about a mile along either side of the road leading from Nijmegen to Kleve, now is well behind the fighting line. It was one of the main enemy defense positions on this front and the base from which outposts guarded the line facing the Canadians on high ground.

Units commanded by Maj. Deb. Kearns of Medicine Hat, Alta., and Captains Nobby Clarke of Turner Valley, Alta. and Alex Keller, MM, of Winnipeg, played a major role.

They fought around the town until the early hours of Friday, especially among log-reinforced dugouts on the northwestern outskirts. Keller's men cleared the enemy from these last positions.

The Germans lost between 200 and 300 prisoners to this battalion and another 130 were captured by French-speaking Canadians who cleared three strongpoints on the Highlanders' right flank. The French-Canadians lost two killed but the westerners' casualties were considerably higher.

Fighting has been stiffer in British sectors but nowhere have 1st Canadian army casualties been heavy.

EXTRA THE VANCOUVER DAILY PROVINCE EXTRA

50th YEAR—NO. 288 | VANCOUVER, B.C., TUESDAY, MARCH 6, 1945—20 PAGES | PRICE 5 CENTS BY CARRIER $1.00 per month.

MUNITION SHIP EXPLODES

Downtown Vancouver Rocked By Blast Of Park Steamship

Heavy Casualty Toll Feared; Windows Shattered Over Wide Area Around Marine Building

Downtown Vancouver was rocked at noon today when tre 10.000-ton Greenhill Park, operated by Canada Shipping, exploded with its cargo of ammunition at Pier B in city harbor.

Entire buildings in the district trembled under the impact of a succession of blasts.

Glass was blown out of store and office windows in all the area around Hastings, Richards, Seymour and Hornby streets and as far south as Robson.

All the glass was blown from the Birks store.

Most of the windows on the harbor side of the Marine Block were blown out.

Police immediately threw a cordon around the area and refused to allow anyone to go nearer to the fire than the C.P.R. Station.

Broken debris and burning fragments rose hundreds of feet into the air and floated over the downtown district.

Early reports did not mention casualties aboard the ship or in the vicinity of the tremendous blasts. Many persons were cut by flying glass.

Clouds of smoke sprouted into the sky. Explosives burst brilliantly high above the waterfront. There were six or seven blasts. The large plate glass windows at The Vancouver Daily Province office bulged inward on each explosion.

Hundreds of windows were shattered in the financial section. The Marine building suffered most damage. Hundreds of panes of glass showered the streets.

The entire downtown region of Vancouver soon was covered by a pall of smoke.

Some loss of life is feared but extent of it is not known. A man was seen jumping from the stricken vessel, it is not known whether he was saved.

The freighter is thought to have carried a personnel of about 53. The crew was 43 and in addition there would be 0 gunners. Few of these were believed to be on board.

Two barges in the harbor caught fire and are burning furiously. There is no fire on the pier. One ship right behind the stricken vessel was not set afire.

DOWN COMES HITLER
hamlet in Germany has its Adolf-Hitler-Strasse (street), and Adolf-Hitler-Platz (square). The Nazi party made sure of that. As the Allies occupy more and more of the Reich these comparatively newly baptized streets revert to their old names. Here a U.S. soldier removes from a building in Duren, Germany, the name-plate of Adolf-Hitler-Strasse. (AP Wirephoto.)

FROM THE TIMES:

Today in Europe

Compiled from the news and editorial comment of the London Times, and cabled from The Vancouver Daily Province London Bureau, Times Building, Printing House Square.

LONDON, March 6. — The Times military correspondent says it is likely that a bridgehead soon will be secured on the last side of the Rhine, but breaking out from it may be troublesome business. On the west bank only two dwindling enemy bridgeheads remain.

There is every prospect that within a few days the United Kingdom, Canadian and U. S. armies will hold the river from Emmuich to Bonn or even Coblenz. This success generally was expected to require a month after crossing of the Roer River.

Von Rundstedt has been able to extricate a good deal of his heavy equipment, says the Times Paris correspondent, but loss of 60,000 prisoners, to say nothing of killed and wounded, is an undeniable measure of the defeat he has suffered.

Security Vote

Dealing with voting procedure in the proposed security council, to be debated at the San Francisco conference, the Times editorially explains that the formula agreed on at the Crimean conference means that each great power is deprived of the right of veto on discussion by the security council of any dispute to which it itself is a party or on any decision to refer such a dispute to one of the regional security bodies contemplated under the Dumbarton Oaks plan.

But the formula maintains the right of veto on any proposal to impose sanctions, so that sanctions against a great power are in fact ruled out by it. It must be confessed, says the Times, that the formula wears a certain air of artificiality.

Means Downfall

If the unity of the great powers was lost on any vote which divided them on any issue of major concern to any one of them, it would inevitably mean the downfall of the security organization. The more clearly and frankly this fact is faced, the less danger there is of such a catastrophe.

Reviewing the work of the British Commonwealth relations conference, the Times says the prevailing view is that the Commonwealth will play its part most effectively in world security after the war by preserving and extending the present habit of intimate consultations without formal commitments.

The true foundation on which the Commonwealth rests today is

(Continued on Page 2.)
See TIMES.

Underwriter Dies

MONTREAL, March 6.—(CP)—C. M. Ormston, chairman of the Canadian Board of Marine Underwriters, died here today. He also was secretary of the Canadian lake hull committee and an authority on marine law.

Lansdowne May Not Operate

Hastings Park's half-mile racetrack, owned by the Vancouver Exhibition Association, may be the only track to operate in B.C. this year.

Monday the private bills committee of the B. C. Legislature approved an amendment to the Municipal Act which, if passed by the House, will permit B. C. municipalities to assess racetracks a daily operational fee of $500.

If this becomes law, then Lansdowne, which did operate for one week last year, may be closed down. Brighouse, adjoining Lansdowne, and also located in the Municipality of Richmond, was not operated last year and presumably there was no intention of reopening this season.

One other track may not be opened this year, The Willows of Victoria, being in the Municipality of Oak Bay. The Willows property has been leased to the racing association by the City of Victoria, which makes it uncertain what action may be taken there.

Allies Plunge Deep Into City

German Opposition Surprisingly Light in Inner Metropolis

By JAMES M. LONG.
(Associated Press Staff Writer.)

PARIS, March 6.—U.S. 1st Army troops driving into Cologne today reached the Ringstrasse rimming the ancient heart of the wrecked Rhineland city against surprisingly light opposition.

Fall of Germany's fourth city was expected hourly as U.S. tanks and infantry rolled through industrial sections in its northwest area and shelled its marshalling yards, among the biggest in Germany.

The Germans this afternoon officially admitted fighting in the western suburbs of Cologne.

Meantime some 50 miles to the north the enemy bridgehead on the west bank of the Rhine was compressed to a scant 11 miles in length as 1st Canadian Army troops moved to the outskirts of staunchly-defended Xanten, key to the enemy's only remaining Rhine crossing-points in that area, and U.S. 9th Army men crashed into Rheinberg, three miles to the southeast.

Perhaps 50,000 Germans were hemmed in by the 1st and 9th against the Rhine bank, but it was believed the enemy retreat still was orderly.

Gen. Crerar's men have raised the total of prisoners taken since they jumped off February 8 to 19,500.

The Allies held the whole west bank of the Rhine from Cologne all the way north to Rheinberg, five miles south of Wesel, except for a tiny pocket in the river bend two miles north of Homberg, and a six-mile stretch from two to three miles deep from south of Neuss to Worringen.

NEAR EMPTY.

Even these were believed squeezed almost empty.

Pilots who flew over Cologne described it as a "dead city."

Nazi parachute troopers wavered and fell back under sledgehammer blows by the U.S. 9th Army, while British vanguards of the 1st Canadian Army pushing through the Bonninghardt Forest only eight miles from Wesel were meeting bitter resistance by Nazi suicide squads.

BLOCK BRIDGE.

R.A.F. pilots said two bridges at Wesel were damaged seriously Monday by 347,000 pounds of bombs. One span of a railway bridge was destroyed and the west end of a road bridge was blocked.

A 9th Army armored division which seized Orsoy, just south of Rheinberg in a 3½-mile thrust yesterday, wiped out the last of two fixed ferry routes across the

(Continued on Page 2.)
See COLOGNE.

Harrison Granted New Murder Trial

Daniel Harrison, 28-year-old machinist and ex-soldier under sentence to hang March 15 for the Mayli Rooms murder of Clifford-Lennox on May 1, 1944, was granted a new trial today when the Court of Appeal allowed his appeal from conviction.

Harrison had been sentenced to hang January 17 for the murder of Clifford Lennox last May 7 in a rooming-house on East Hastings.

He was granted a reprieve until March 15 when he appealed the conviction.

The death sentence had been passed on October 16, 1944, by Mr. Justice Coady, after an Assize Court jury of 12 men, had brought in a verdict of guilty. The jury made a strong recommendation for mercy.

Blind Writer Dies

NEW YORK, March 6.—(AP)—Merle E. Tracy, 66, Scripps-Howard newspaper columnist from 1924 to 1934 and former publisher of Current History Magazine, died here. Mr. Tracy, engaged in writing his autobiography at the time of his death, had been blind almost from birth.

PEARKES SAYS CHARGE FALSE

Replying to the charges made against him by Hon. J. G. Gardiner, minister of agriculture, Major-Gen. George R. Pearkes, V.C., who recently retired as G.O.C.-in-C. Pacific Command, today gave the following statement to the press:

"On February 19 reports appeared in the press of statements allegedly made by Hon. J. G. Gardiner accusing me and other officers of the Pacific Command of disloyalty; these charges he reiterated in a letter published over his own signature in the Winnipeg Tribune of February 27.

"The statements are false and slanderous, but since they referred to my official activities I could not refute them without disclosing information relating to military matters, which I had obtained in the course of my official duties.

SOUGHT STATEMENT.

"I therefore requested the minister of national defense to make a statement protecting the good name of the officers of his department. He is in possession of full details as to the effort that had been made last summer and of the results achieved to obtain volunteers for overseas service from among the N.R.M.A. soldiers in the Pacific Command, and he also has complete information as to the steps recommended and those taken to prevent absenteeism of the men ordered to the assembly camps in Eastern Canada preparatory to their despatch overseas when the order-in-council which authorized sending 16,000 N.R.M.A. soldiers was published.

(Continued on Page 2.)
See PEARKES.

British Dash Across Burma Threatens Whole Jap Position

(By Associated Press.)

WASHINGTON, March 6.—A dashing 85-mile advance by British armored and airborne troops endangered the entire Japanese position in Burma today.

The manoeuvre slashed every communication line between Mandalay and Rangoon. Eight airdromes were seized or captured and 1600 Japanese killed.

On blood-covered Iwo Island Navy Secretary James Forrestal disclosed 2050 Marines have been killed—one for every six Japs known to have been slain. He made no estimate of the American wounded. The last complete U.S. casualty report on Iwo listed seven wounded for each Marine slain.

For the second successive day Admiral Chester W. Nimitz reported battle lines were unchanged. The three Marine divi-

(Continued on Page 2.)
See PACIFIC.

HUNS ORGANIZE EASTERN RHINE

By ROSS MUNRO.
Canadian Press War Correspondent.

WITH THE 1ST CANADIAN ARMY ON THE RHINE, March 6.—The Germans are organizing their defenses on the east bank of the Rhine and are getting more guns into position for the battle of the river, a natural backstop for the shattered Siegfried Line positions in the Rhine-Maas corridor.

Enemy shelling along the river line was increasing today. Under protection of mist and low clouds the enemy pumped 200 shells into the Kleve area during the last 24 hours and tried to shoot up roads in the Canadian Army sector.

Once the artillery now supporting Gen. Crerar's troops in the last phase of the fighting in the Oermans Xanten-Wesel bulge can be turned east again counter-battery work will certainly reduce this enemy fire.

Elimination of the enemy bulge on the west side of the Rhine is continuing slowly and methodically. This bulge is approximately 15 miles wide, extending from a point just north of Xanten to Orsoy, due east of Rheinberg, and varies in depth with its maximum about 11 miles.

Elements of five German divisions are fighting a rearguard action, but Canadian Army troops now are into Sonsbeck, five miles southwest of Xanten, which is one of the anchor points for the final defense.

(Continued on Page 2.)
See CANADIAN.

4 MEN MISSING, 17 HURT IN SHIP BLAST

PATTON SCORES
BREAK THROUGH
—Page 8

The Vancouver Sun

★★★★
FINAL
EDITION

FOUNDED 1886
VOL. LIX—No. 153

VANCOUVER, BRITISH COLUMBIA, TUESDAY, MARCH 6, 1945

PRICE 5c

MUNITIONS SHIP ABLAZE AT DOCK — This picture shows the Greenhill Park, 10,000-ton freighter, burning fiercely at Pier BC after a shattering explosion of chemicals and ammunition which rocked the city at noon today. The freighter was later towed through the narrows and beached near Siwash Rock.

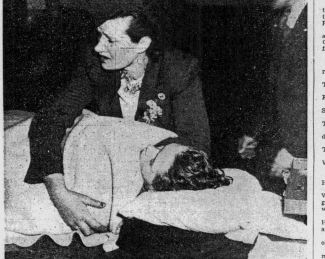

ONE OF THE VICTIMS—Tragedy is etched on the face of this local woman worker who rushed to the scene of the blast at Pier BC today. She is pictured bending over one of the victims. Other pictures on pages two and nine.

Chemical Boat Blows Up at CPR Pier B-C

The Greenhill Park was in English Bay beyond Lions Gate Bridge at 2:30 p.m. Smoke was still pouring from her shattered hull.

The ship's plates were still too hot for anyone to go aboard to ascertain if any men were trapped below decks.

Reports persisted at press time that four or five men were trapped.

At one time Fire Chief Erratt was about to request that the Navy sink the ship for fear that she might explode again, but it appeared that this idea had been abandoned.

The ship was beached at one time, on the shoals at the northern end of Lions Gate Bridge.

Firemen were ordered to fight the fire from the shore while the fireboat J. H. Carlisle joined the battle from the sea.

However, the tide caught the ship by the stern, whisked her out in the channel again.

Shortly after the ship was moved from Pier B-C, which was also heavily damaged by the fire, Fire Chief Errat was assured by a Park Steamships official and a Canadian government cargo inspector that there was no danger of further explosions.

They said there were no munitions on the ship. These had been removed at Esquimalt they said.

There were 500 barrels of sodium chlorate aboard and it is believed this is what caused the explosion.

Fire Chief Erratt told these officials that he wanted the ship sunk. "I won't risk the lives of my men by sending them on board or near it if there is a danger of another explosion, he said.

However, he was assured there was no danger of a further blast.

Flames and smoke shot 100 feet into the air as the explosions of the chemicals set off some of the ship's ammunition and also sent ship flares soaring into the sky in an awesome display of grim fireworks.

Four blasts from the ship caused the waterfront to shudder under the impact and citizens by the thousands who were enjoying their lunch hour were shocked almost into panic.

Newspaper offices were deluged by phone calls as some wondered if there had been an air-raid.

The Greenhill Park was being loaded with lumber at Pier B-C and the scow alongside, loaded with airplane lumber, was also set afire.

It was being loaded with cargo for Australia.

The ship was towed into English Bay shortly after 1 p.m. and the Fireboat Carlisle was brought into action, playing water on the still burning vessel.

There were approximately 100 men, longshoremen, crew and shipyard workers, working on the Greenhill Park.

Some of the men dived over the side to safety.

Others went down ropes and some were even blasted to safety.

First aid organizations all swept into action to aid city authorities.

Most of the injured men from the ship are longshoremen. It is believed, who were working on the big 10,000-ton freighter when she blew up, spraying flaming ammunition over the heart of downtown Vancouver.

The ill-fated vessel was the victim of a series of four detonating explosions, which smashed windows a mile away.

The first explosion came in hold No. 3. A few seconds later, the second blew out No. 2 hold.

The second blast blew the cook from his galley out through a hatch on the No. 2 hold.

His name has not been obtained. He is suffering groin and abdominal injuries.

The third explosion smashed through the two hatches, but stopped short of No. 1 hatch forward.

Windows Blasted From City Blocks

Some Persons Hurt by Flying Bits of Glass; Few Signs of Panic

Broken glass strewing the streets from the 400 block on West Pender as far as Thurlow and from the waterfront up to Dunsmuir, whole office blocks with scarcely a pane of glass left intact, was the picture today after the first confusion caused by the ship blasts at Pier B-C had subsided.

Several persons in the offices of the Vancouver Merchants' Exchange, Marine Building, suffered slight cuts from broken glass as the large plate-glass windows were blown "almost across the whole offices" in the first explosion.

NONE BADLY INJURED

None was injured sufficiently to require medical attention from outside, and were "patched up" by fellow-workers with the office first-aid kits.

No records were lost or destroyed in the Income Tax department's offices at 739 West Hastings, although all windows were blown out. No one was injured, according to officials.

POST OFFICE CARRIES ON

The Post Office reported only one large lobby window and several smaller ones broken. There was no disruption of service after the first shock.

Workers in the Wartime Prices and Trade Board offices, Marine Building, said the explosion sounded as though "every door in Vancouver was being slammed at once."

Glass flew everywhere, they said, but no one was hurt, except for superficial cuts. A few stenographers were blown out of their chairs by the blast.

Several large windows on the north side of the CPR Station were broken, it is reported.

About a dozen windows in the Immigration Building are reported broken.

Window damage also extended as far east as Seymour, according to early reports.

Many of the north windows of Spencer's store were smashed and several of the sales staff suffered from cuts.

While most shoppers kept their heads, a few showed signs of panic and some of the customers who were having an early lunch in the marine view dining room, without waiting to collect hats or coats, in their rush to get to the main floor and outdoors. Some buildings on Hastings lost their southern exposure windows.

Find Blast Debris

Debris from the Greenhill Park landed as far away from the scene as Lumberman's Arch in Stanley Park where strollers found several pairs of sun glasses that had been in the ship's cargo.

Rivets Shoot Out of Ship's Steel Plates

Vancouver waterfront in the vicinity of the CPR docks today looked like nothing more or less than a scene from war-torn Europe.

As the Greenhill Park, her hull ripped wide open on both sides, lay at Pier BC, burning, she presented a picture not unlike a newsreel shot of the harbor at Naples.

The dock and the network of roads around the Pier were littered with everything from rivet heads which were shot out of the ship's steel plates by the explosion to smashed bottles of pickles that were sent flying out of her No. 3 hold.

LIST OF INJURED

Following is the lists of those injured as a result of the blasts from the Greenhill Park:

Eleven from aboard ship and one street victim are in General Hospital. Those from aboard ship are:

Donald Deiley, 717 Powell.
Frank Simms, Naval Barracks, Lapointe Pier.
James Barton, 3566 West Twentieth.
Frederick Lester, 1505 East Fifteenth.
Arden Wangenstein, 8073 St. George.
Sandy McLean, 1772 East Twenty-second.
Joseph Klimek, 389 Blundell Road, Lulu Island.
Stanley Harris, 372 East Thirteenth.
Edward Sickerish, 2556 West Third.
John Adank, 2024 Arbutus.
Mike Stoocknoff, 249 East Hastings.
Mrs. Louise Koven, 2990 West Twelfth, was struck by glass from a Cordova Street window.

Three are in St. Paul's Hospital from the ship. They are:

Jules Lantchier, chief cook of the Greenhill Park;
Don Smith, 250 Commercial; shock;
Alfred Combes, 2846 Trinity, shock and bruises.

Injured on the street and in St. Paul's Hospital are:

Clara Wagner, 1536 East Twelfth;
Thomas Adams, 4474 Quebec Street;
Eva Lutz, 3234 Cambridge.

Treated for injuries in Spencer's store first aid station after the Cordova Street windows smashed from the impact of the blast:

Mrs. H. MacMillan, about 65, 3846 Willingdon, severe shock and cuts on head.
Mrs. D. McLean, 2774 East Sixth, employed in the store.
Mrs. D. Naughton, employed in store.
Donald Douglas, 3, of 6967 Victoria Drive, cuts.

Mexico City Race Results

Canadian Army Under Heavy Shelling

NAZIS ORGANIZE FOR STAND ACROSS RHINE

By ROSS MUNRO

WITH THE 1ST CANADIAN ARMY ON THE RHINE, March 6—(CP)—The Germans are organizing their defenses on the east bank of the Rhine and are getting more guns into position for the battle of the river, a natural backstop for the shattered Siegfried Line positions in the Rhine-Maas corridor.

Elimination of the enemy bulge on the west side of the Rhine is continuing slowly and methodically.

This bulge is approximately 15 miles wide, extending from a point just north of Xanten to Orsoy, due east of Rheinberg, and varies in depth with its maximum about 12 miles.

dern is about 13 miles southwest of Xanten and Wesel eight miles due east.

Enemy shelling along the river line was increasing today.

Under protection of mist and low clouds the enemy pumped 200 shells into the Kleve area during the last 24 hours and tried to shoot up roads in the Canadian Army sector.

Once the artillery now supporting Gen. Crerar's troops in the last phase of the fighting in the Germans' Xanten-Wesel bulge can be turned east again, counter-battery work will certainly reduce this enemy fire.

Elements of five German divisions are fighting a rearguard action but Canadian Army troops now are into Sonsbeck, five miles southwest of Xanten, which is one of the anchor points for the final defense.

They have invested Xanten and have gained several miles along the Geldern-Wesel highway. Gel-

Please Turn to Page Two   See "17 Injured"

140

1ST ARMY CROSSES RHINE; HOLDS FIRM BRIDGEHEAD

★★★★★ FINAL

THE VANCOUVER DAILY PROVINCE

50th YEAR—NO. 290 VANCOUVER, B.C., THURSDAY, MARCH 8, 1945—24 PAGES PRICE 5 CENTS

Take Three More Bodies From Blast-Torn Vessel

'Great Victory Shaping Up'

By HOWARD COWAN.
(Associated Press War Correspondent.)

ACROSS THE RHINE, March 8.—Elements of the United States 1st Army are firmly entrenched on the east bank of the Rhine tonight.

One of the greatest Allied victories of the war is shaping up.

(Compiled from Late Despatches to The Vancouver Daily Province.)

PARIS, March 8.—Lt. Gen. Courtney H. Hodges U.S. 1st Army has crossed the Rhine at Remagen, halfway between Bonn and Coblenz and has established a firm bridgehead on the east bank.

The sensational news was released at 6 p.m. tonight (10 a.m. Vancouver time) after 24 hours of security news blackout—used while events of great importance are shaping.

The crossing started at 4:30 p.m. yesterday. In the hours since then, a steady stream of men and materiel have been pouring onto the eastern bank and moving forward in a drive to get the bridgehead out of range of enemy artillery.

The news blackout on the U.S. 3rd Army was not lifted and there is speculation that the 4th Armored Division of this army has forced yet another cro: ing.

Two-pronged Canadian Attack

Third Army censors passed this message:

"Nothing was reported officially on the 4th Armored Division which reached the Rhine yesterday (Wednesday) but tanks are not yet across."

At the same time British and Canadian units of the 1st Canadian Army launched a two-pronged attack against the enemy bulge at Wesel where rearguards of 20,000 Germans are resisting fanatically in defense of the last important German bridgehead between fallen Cologne and the Netherlands border.

First and 3rd Army units hourly are expected to close a ring on 2500 square miles of German territory, trapping five or six Nazi divisions (upward of 50,000 men) in the Eifel Mountains.

Huns Retreat in Confusion

During the first 24 hours, there was little artillery or mortar fire on the Rhine bridgehead, indicating the enemy was in confusion when he fled back across the river from the ashes of Cologne before Hodges' hard-driving divisions.

First Army's infantrymen spanned the quarter-mile wide river before the startled Germans could grasp what had happened, Associated Press Correspondent Wes Gallagher said.

Other units of the 1st Army captured half of the Rhine university city of Bonn (101,000) and half of nearby Bad Godesberg.

The Germans said the 1st Army was within 17 miles of forming with the 3rd Army near Coblenz a trap of perhaps 50,000 Germans caught west of the middle Rhine.

Gen. Eisenhower had six other armies standing on the west bank of the Rhine and its grey-green waters.

The crossing of the Rhine—one of the great achievements of the entire war—came just two days after the capture of the great Rhineland capital of Cologne—which was cleared today.

Bad Godesberg is three miles up the river from Beethoven's birthplace of Bonn, and is the village where Neville Chamberlain, umbrella in hand, pleaded with Hitler before Munich for "peace in our times." It is 21 miles from 3rd Army positions on the Rhine near Coblenz.

Drizzles soaked the whole front all day.

Shortens War in Europe

Gen. Eisenhower was known from the start of the current campaign to want a bridgehead across the Rhine as quickly as possible, because he felt that a crossing would shorten the war in Europe by weeks.

The swift crossing gave the Germans no time to reorganize ranks or improve defenses east of the Rhine, far beyond the shattered debris of the Siegfried Line. It constituted Field Marshal von Rundsted's greatest defeat since the landings in Normandy.

Strangely, the Germans who customarily have announced transcendent military developments before either the western or eastern Allies, still were silent about the Rhine crossing.

The Rhine crossing was the first by any army fighting its way eastward since the days of Napoleon.

The surge from the Roer River which started February 23 had developed such momentum that the Germans along a 2000-mile front from Holland to the Moselle either were routed, in confusion, or fighting for their very lives.

For the first time, the Americans were meeting some resistance from civilians. The battle of Bonn was much more bitter than that for Cologne.

Although thousands of German civilians still were in Bonn, the enemy was pouring rockets and artillery fire into the town. Many Germans were being killed by their own shells.

Final BULLETINS

Bataan Men Home

SAN FRANCISCO, March 8.—(AP)—A band of the heroes of Bataan came home today after three years of imprisonment under Japanese guards at the dreaded prison camp of Cabanatuan. The party numbered more than 250 officers and men.

Mine Tied Up

DRUMHELLER, Alta, March 8.—(CP)—A complete tie-up of the Newcastle mine is in progress and 130 men are idle. The miners went on strike Wednesday when they said a driver had been unfairly dismissed. Mine Manager Allan Hamilton said the driver had violated mine rules when he did not bring his pony to the stable and left another man to do it.

Officer to Stand

EDMONTON, March 8.—(CP)—Brig. Robert A. Wyman, C.B.E., D.S.O., veteran of the Normandy invasion, will seek nomination as a Progressive Conservative to contest Edmonton East constituency in the next federal general election. A nominating convention will be held March 21.

Fight to Finish

WASHINGTON, March 8.—(AP)—Fleet Admiral Chester W. Nimitz said here that he expects Japanese resistance on Iwo Jima to continue until "the last Jap is killed, wounded or captured." Admiral Nimitz' presence in Washington was made known when he appeared at a news conference.

Liquor Permit Fine

Convicted of possession of a registration card and liquor permit other than his own, Edward Wothe, 1012 Main, was fined $50 or three months on the registration charge and $50 or two months for possession of the permit.

RACING

Mexico Race Results

FIRST RACE—Two furlongs. One Card (Bovine), $21.60, $10.20, $2.60; Red Train (F. Fernandez), $4, $2.20; Bay Sky (Loop), $2.20.

SECOND RACE—Mile, sixteenth. Hobbys First (Weldaman), $29.80, $7.40, $8.80; Royal Cynic (Jones), $5.80, $3.60; Shelia Rhea (Filter), $5.40.

THIRD RACE—Five furlongs. Colleen (M. Sylvia), $13.80, $6.80, $3.60; Tursco (Gomez), $6.40, $2.40; Bellarmine (Neves), $3.

RUSS TANKS SPEED DRIVE ON BERLIN

(Compiled from late despatches to The Vancouver Daily Province.)

LONDON, March 8.—The Germans reported today that the Russians are 25 miles from Berlin in an all-out offensive along a 125-mile front.

Moscow despatches partially confirmed that the grand offensive is under way.

Enemy broadcasts said Marshal Gregory Zhukov's powerful tank spearheads have reached Seelow, 25 miles directly east of the Reich capital, and 12 miles west of the Oder.

Seelow is on the main railway which connects Stettin and Frankfurt. According to the enemy reports, Kuestrin, Oder River fort, was bypassed by the Red Army.

Berlin declared Marshal Zhukov's massive new offensive, timed with the Allied drive to the Rhine, 321 miles to the west, also has reached a point 29 miles from Berlin northwest of Kuestrin. Berlin, a city of nearly 5,000,000, stretches about 20 miles from east to west.

Transocean said Seelow was reached from the Russian bridgehead at Goerlitz, between Kuestrin and Frankfurt, and said terrific fighting was taking place in the area, with many places changing hands.

To the northeast, the Germans said, the Russians have invaded the old Danzig free state and smashed to within 19 miles of Danzig.

Tram Passengers Have Close Call

Passengers of a No. 3 street car narrowly escaped injury when a north-bound Kerrisdale street car trailer ran loose on the wrong track at the Granville and Hastings intersection this afternoon.

Turning on to Hastings street, the back trucks of the No. 7 street car split the automatic switch, causing the trailer to angle across and ride down the other set of tracks.

The slight grade on Granville was enough to carry the trailer into the rear of the Davie car going south. Both street cars were badly damaged.

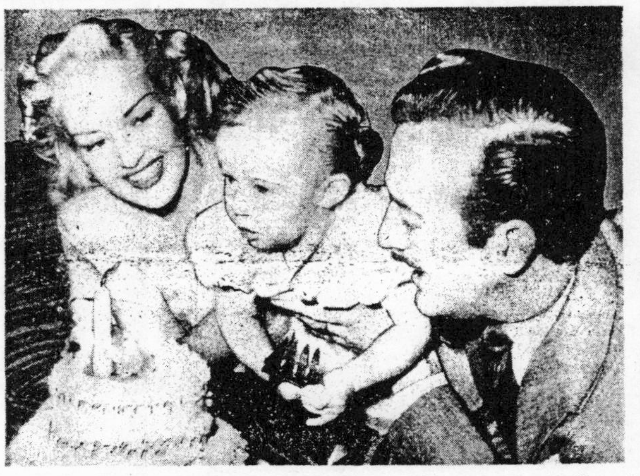

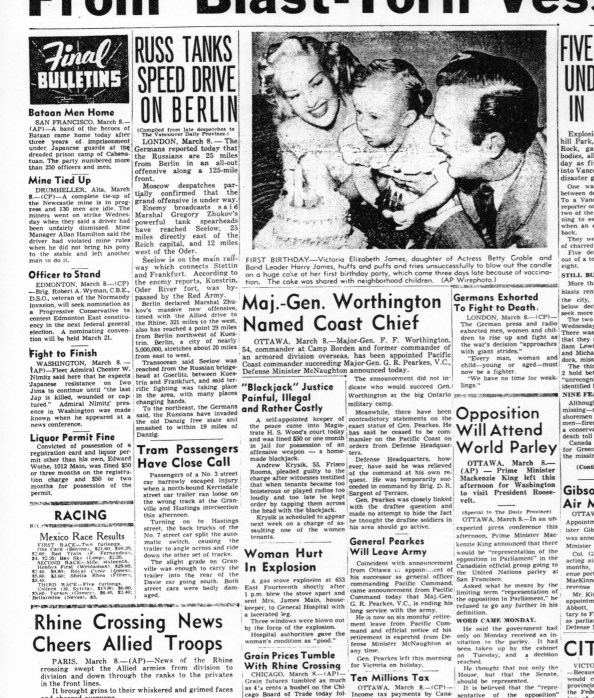

FIRST BIRTHDAY—Victoria Elizabeth James, daughter of Actress Betty Grable and Band Leader Harry James, huffs and puffs and tries unsuccessfully to blow out the candle on a huge cake at her first birthday party, which came three days late because of vaccination. The cake was shared with neighborhood children. (AP Wirephoto.)

Maj.-Gen. Worthington Named Coast Chief

OTTAWA, March 8.—Major-Gen. F. F. Worthington, 54, commander at Camp Borden and former commander of an armored division overseas, has been appointed Pacific Coast commander succeeding Major-Gen. G. R. Pearkes, V.C., Defense Minister McNaughton announced today.

The announcement did not indicate who would succeed Gen. Worthington at the big Ontario military camp.

Meanwhile, there have been contradictory statements on the exact status of Gen. Pearkes. He has said he ceased to be commander on the Pacific Coast on orders from Defense Headquarters.

Defense Headquarters, however, have said he was relieved of the command at his own request. He was temporarily succeeded in command by Brig. D. R. Sargent of Terrace.

Gen. Pearkes was closely linked with the draftee question and made no attempt to hide the fact he thought the draftee soldiers in his area should go active.

"Blackjack" Justice Painful, Illegal and Rather Costly

A self-appointed keeper of the peace came into Magistrate H. S. Wood's court today and was fined $50 or one month in jail for possession of an offensive weapon — a home-made blackjack.

Andrew Krysik, 53, Frisco Rooms, pleaded guilty to the charge after witnesses testified that when tenants became too boisterous or played radios too loudly and too late he kept order by tapping them across the head with the blackjack.

Krysik is scheduled to appear next week on a charge of assaulting one of the women tenants.

Woman Hurt In Explosion

A gas stove explosion at 653 East Fourteenth shortly after 1 p.m. blew the stove apart and sent Mrs. James Main, housekeeper, to General Hospital with a lacerated leg.

Three windows were blown out by the force of the explosion.

Hospital authorities gave the woman's condition as "good."

Grain Prices Tumble With Rhine Crossing

CHICAGO, March 8.—(AP)—Grain futures tumbled as much as 4½ cents a bushel on the Chicago Board of Trade today following announcement that the American 1st Army had crossed the Rhine. The report caused general liquidation in all markets.

General Pearkes Will Leave Army

Coincident with announcement from Ottawa o. appoint...ent of his successor as general officer commanding Pacific Command, came announcement from Pacific Command today that Maj.-Gen. G. R. Pearkes, V.C., is ending his long service with the army.

He is now on six months' retirement leave from Pacific Command and official notice of his retirement is expected from Defense Minister McNaughton at any time.

Gen. Pearkes left this morning for Victoria on holiday.

Ten Millions Tax

OTTAWA, March 8.—(CP)—Income tax payments by Canadian farmers for 1944 are expected to exceed $10,000,000, the revenue department said today in a statement. For 1943 income, 24,153 farmers paid $7,245,900.

Germans Exhorted To Fight to Death

LONDON, March 8.—(CP)—The German press and radio exhorted men, women and children to rise up and fight as the war's decision "approaches with giant strides."

"Every man, woman and child—young or aged—must now be a fighter.

"We have no time for weaklings."

Opposition Will Attend World Parley

OTTAWA, March 8.—(AP) — Prime Minister Mackenzie King left this afternoon for Washington to visit President Roosevelt.

(Special to The Daily Province)

OTTAWA, March 8.—In an unexpected press conference this afternoon, Prime Minister Mackenzie King announced that there would be "representation of the opposition in Parliament" in the Canadiain official group going to the United Nations parley at San Francisco.

Asked what he meant by the limiting term "representation of the opposition in Parliament," he refused to go any further in his definition.

WORD CAME MONDAY.

He said the government had only on Monday received an invitation to the parley. It had been taken up by the cabinet on Tuesday, and a decision reached.

He thought that not only the House, but that the Senate, should be represented.

It is believed that the "representative of the opposition" would be Hon. Gordon Graydon, parliamentary leader of the Pro-

(Continued on Page 2.)
See KING.

FIVE PROBES UNDER WAY IN TRAGEDY

Explosion-torn SS. Greenhill Park, beached at Siwash Rock, gave up three more bodies, all unrecognizable, today as five official enquiries into Vancouver's worst harbor disaster got under way.

One was found at 10 a.m. between decks, and two at noon. To a Vancouver Daily Province reporter on the scene it appeared two of the victims had been running to escape from No. 2 hold when an explosion hurled them back.

They were found under a pile of charred lumber.

Five dead are accounted for out of a total tentatively fixed at eight.

STILL BURNING.

More than 50 hours after four blasts rent the ship and rocked the city, fire is still burning below decks and salvage crews seek more bodies.

The two taken from No. 2 hold Wednesday are "unrecognizable." There was unofficial speculation that they might be those of William Lewis, 3652 West Second, and Michael McGrath, 1714 Pandora, missing longshoremen.

The third body, found in No. 2 hold between decks, was also "unrecognizable," but may be identified by teeth.

NINE FEARED DEAD.

Although eight are officially missing—six Vancouver longshoremen and two merchant seamen—firemen Wednesday said a conservative estimate sets the death toll at nine.

Canada Shipping Co., agents for Greenhill Park, said today the missing seamen are: Donald

(Continued on Page 2.)
See SHIP.

Gibson Named Air Minister

OTTAWA, March 8.—(CP)—Appointment of Revenue Minister Gibson as air minister was announced today by Prime Minister Mackenzie King.

Col. Gibson, who has been acting air minister for several months, relinquishes the revenue portfolio. Trades Minister MacKinnon will serve as acting revenue minister.

Mr. King also announced the appointment of Douglas Abbott, parliamentary secretary to Finance Minister Ilsley, as parliamentary assistant to Defense Minister McNaughton.

Rhine Crossing News Cheers Allied Troops

PARIS, March 8.—(AP)—News of the Rhine crossing swept the Allied armies from division to division and down through the ranks to the privates in the front lines.

It brought grins to their whiskered and grimed faces and cheered everyone.

"If we can hold that bridgehead, it means the war is months nearer an end," said Lt.-Col. Robert Evans of Davenport, Ia.

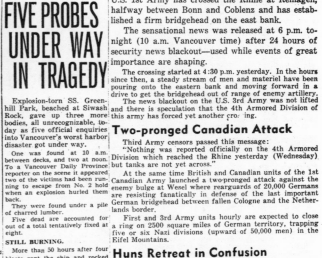

CITY SEEKS SPORT SEAT TAX

VICTORIA, March 8.—(CP)—Because such an assessment would conflict with wartime provincial arrangements with the Federal Government, taxing of sports events by the proposed Vancouver Athletic Commission will be on a seat basis rather than a percentage of take basis, according to a new clause submitted by D. E. McTaggart, Vancouver corporation counsel, to the legislative private bills committee today.

The new clause calls for a maximum tax of 2 cents per seat. The original bill provided for a percentage of the gross receipts being paid over to the commission. Mr. McTaggart said that the Vancouver Council, through enactment of a by-law, would set the rate, perhaps 1 cent per seat.

The committee, in camera, will deal with limiting the powers of the commission to certain sports.

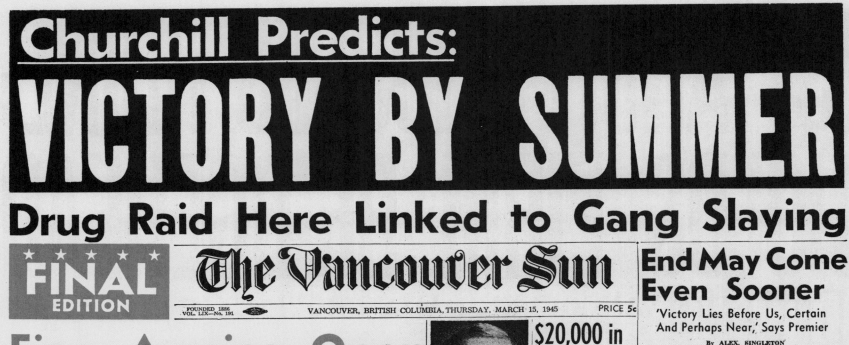

Churchill Predicts:

VICTORY BY SUMMER

Drug Raid Here Linked to Gang Slaying

★★★★★ FINAL EDITION

The Vancouver Sun

FOUNDED 1886 VOL. LIX—No. 191 VANCOUVER, BRITISH COLUMBIA, THURSDAY, MARCH 15, 1945 PRICE 5c

Five Armies Open Great Rhine Push

All-Out Offensive On 200-Mile Front

By BRUCE MUNN
Special to The Vancouver Sun

PARIS, March 15—(BUP)—Five American armies were reported storming the Rhine and Saar Basin defenses of Germany today in a co-ordinated offensive along a 200-mile front from Duisburg to the Karlsruhe corner of Alsace.

A flood of German reports and Allied front dispatches indicated that a general offensive to crush the Nazi armies in the west was in full swing along the entire southern half of the Western Front. (See map on page 2.)

Officially it was disclosed that the U.S. 3rd and 7th Armies were driving with armored and infantry divisions into the northern and southern corners of the Saar Basin.

To the north, the United States 1st Army struck eastward from its Rhine bridgehead in a power drive that may already have cut the Rhine-Ruhr-Berlin superhighway and split the German front east of the Rhine.

Please Turn to Page Five
See "West Front"

RECORD BULL PRICE IN B.C.

Special to The Vancouver Sun

KAMLOOPS, March 15.—Highest price ever paid for a bull in Canada was set here today when Austin C. Taylor bought the champion Hereford bull for $3500 at the annual provincial bull sale here. Mr. Taylor bought the Bull, Circle J. Domino II, for his Eldorado ranch from Bulman Bros., Westwold.

1300-Plane Yank Fleet Raids Berlin

London, March 15—(Reuters)—RAF Lancaster bombers this afternoon dropped 11-ton Volcano bombs on a railway viaduct at Arnsburg, Germany, the air ministry announced tonight. The Arnsburg span, 27 miles southeast of Dortmund, was hit with six-ton "earthquake" bombs yesterday.

LONDON, March 15—(CP)—A fleet of 1350 American bombers attacked the outskirts of Berlin, including the hugh freight yards at Oranienburg, today following the first use by the RAF of a new 11-ton volcano bomb.

Oranienburg, seven miles north of Berlin, is virtually a suburb of the battered capital which has been bombed on 23 successive nights by RAF Mosquitos.

Meantime U.S. heavy bombers based in Italy made a shattering attack on what headquarters called "the most important target in Europe," the gigantic Ruhland oil refinery 65 miles southeast of Berlin.

RAF bombers and fighters this afternoon attacked benzol plants near Essen and Castrop-Rauxel in the Ruhr.

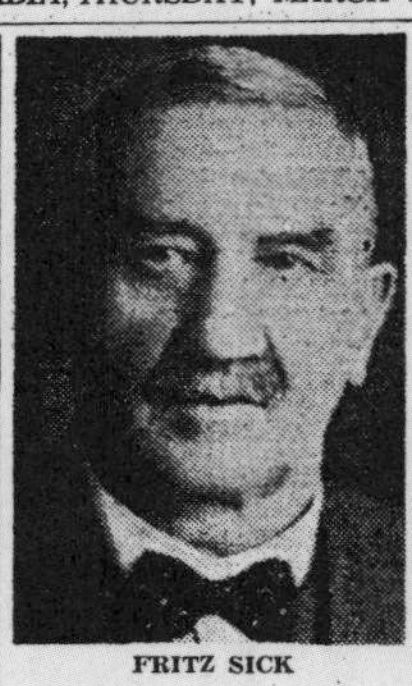

FRITZ SICK

Fritz Sick, Brewer, Dies

Fritz Sick, 85, who landed in New York in 1883 with a $5 bill and a ticket to Cincinnati in his pocket and became head of one of the largest brewing industries on the American continent, died today in Vancouver General Hospital.

He was honorary chairman of Sick's Breweries Ltd.

Mr. Sick came to Vancouver in 1930 with the intention of retiring, but in 1934 organized the Capilano Brewery.

At the same time family interests and associates acquired six plants in the United States, including breweries at Great Falls, Missoula, Spokane, Salem and two in Seattle.

A few years ago Mr. Sick relinquished active management and turned over to his son, Emil, and his associates, more breweries, under one management, than controlled by any other brewing firm on the Pacific Coast.

Mr. Sick spent three and a half years in Cincinnati, then went to California, and later to Tacoma, where he was married.

Mr. Sick leaves three sons: Emil of Seattle, Fred in Courtenay and Leo in Vancouver, and a daughter, Mrs. J. A. Blair, Vancouver. His wife predeceased him in 1941.

Funeral services will be conducted Saturday at 3:30 p.m. in Center & Hanna's chapel, followed by cremation.

$20,000 in Dope Seized In Vancouver

Tipoff to Cops 'Motive' in Toronto Death

Toronto police today linked the death in January of Louis Wernick, Ontario liquor and drug runner, with the seizure by RCMP officers in Vancouver of $20,000 worth of "high-power" Mexican narcotics.

Wernick's bullet-riddled body was found on a suburban Toronto road January 26.

RCMP officials here today tended to discount the theory.

The Toronto announcement came with disclosure that an inquest into Wernick's death on March 26 may reveal evidence supporting the theory that his death followed a tipoff that resulted in the Vancouver seizure.

Toronto police said they learned that Wernick tipped

Please Turn to Page Five
See "Drugs"

End May Come Even Sooner

'Victory Lies Before Us, Certain And Perhaps Near,' Says Premier

By ALEX. SINGLETON

LONDON, March 15—(AP)—Prime Minister Churchill said today that victory over Germany might come "before summer ends or even sooner," and promised Britain its first general election since 1935 as soon as possible after Hitler is beaten.

He served notice that he intended to guide Britain in the trials of peace and pledged the Conservative Party to promotion of free enterprise in the post-war period.

"Victory lies before us, certain and perhaps near," he told the Conservative Party conference.

The 2000 delegates gave their leader a tumultuous ovation as he concluded his 45-minute address.

He cautioned the Conservative party against "humbug and blandishment" and against bidding for votes and party popularity "by promising what we cannot perform."

RAPS SOCIALISTS

His temper obviously taut after recent sharp exchanges with left wing critics in the House of Commons, the Prime Minister struck out at "our Socialist friends" and their program "for nationalizing all the means of production, distribution and exchange."

He asserted that would imply "not only the destruction of the life of the whole of our existing system of society and life and labor, but the creation and en-

Please Turn to Page Five
See "Churchill Calls"

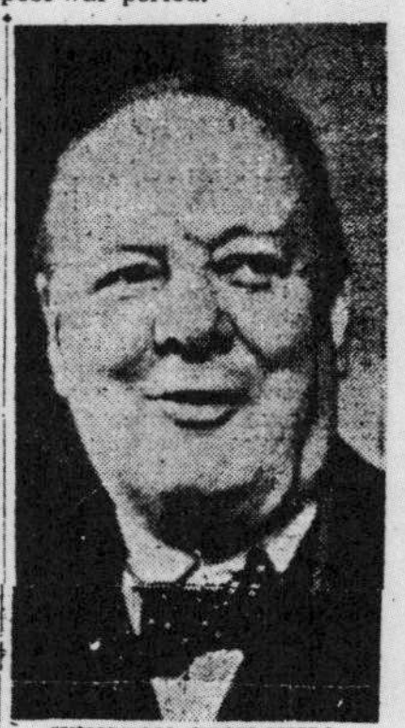

WINSTON CHURCHILL
Victory Soon

LATE FLASHES—

700 Planes Hit Hun Top Headquarters

LONDON, March 15—(BUP)—Almost 700 U.S. heavy bombers attacked German Supreme Headquarters at Zossen, 15 miles south of Berlin, today.

(The Associated Press said in a London dispatch that the German army's general staff headquarters at Zossen were knocked out in the raid.)

26,000 Nazis Flee by Sea

STOCKHOLM, March 15—(AP)—Three steamships, jammed with 26,000 German refugees from Gdynia, now under Red Army siege, arrived in Copenhagen early this week, the Free Danish Press Service said today. Thousands more were expected on foot at the Danish border.

Reds Chop East Prussia

LONDON, March 15—(CP)—The Red Army has smashed its way to the coast along the Baltic, cutting the German grouping on the East Prussian coast in two, the Soviet communique announced tonight.

Sixteen Killed in Crash

WASHINGTON, March 15—(AP)—Sixteen persons, including seven entertainers for the United Services Organization, perished in the crash of an army transport plane in Europe March 3, the United States War Department announced today. The plane was flying from England to Paris.

30 Witnesses at Ship Inquest

Coroner Dr. J. D. Whitbread disclosed this afternoon that 30 witnesses will be called at the inquest in connection with the Greenhill Park disaster Friday. This is one of the longest witness lists in the history of Vancouver's coroner's court. (See earlier story page 11.)

Planes Carry 6000 Troops

LONDON, March 15—(CP)—Approximately 6000 troops, needed recently in Belgium on short notice, were flown from Britain in five days, the Air Ministry disclosed today. The soldiers were transported in transport planes of the RAF and the United States Army air force transport command.

UBC Labs to Aid Industry

Research work in minerals and metals will be undertaken by the B.C. research council with a staff of metallurgists in laboratories provided by the UBC, Hon. E. C. Carson, chairman of the council, announced today.

This work was formerly done by the War Metals Research Board.

The B.C. research council, according to Mr. Carson, plans to lay emphasis on the importance of the scientific extension service where industry may obtain information and assistance on technical problems. J. S. Cummings, assistant to the director, has visited plants in the province to ascertain what assistance can best be given.

Victory, Sure Peace McNaughton Aims

WINNIPEG, March 15—(CP)—Defense Minister McNaughton said today he had two objectives in the task he has undertaken: "I've got to get the victory and I've got to see it confirmed." He was en route to Grenfell, Sask., where he said he "hoped" to accept the nomination as Liberal federal candidate in Qu'Appelle constituency.

It's Happened—Ruth Mat Referee

NEW YORK, March 15—(AP)—Babe Ruth, the home run king, is turning wrestling referee.

Ruth, his wife said today, will inaugurate his mat career April 4 at Boston and if the venture proves successful the former slugger may make a national tour.

Japs Admit Loss Of Life in Raids

SAN FRANCISCO, March 15—(AP)—First indications from Japan of heavy loss of life from American Superfortress incendiary raids on Tokyo, Nagoya and Osaka came today in a broadcast from Tokyo.

The broadcast quoted a Tokyo newspaper as declaring the number of people killed "could never be called small" or "dismissed lightly."

Hart Urges Session to Take Over B.C. Electric

By JAMES DYER, Vancouver Sun Staff Correspondent

VICTORIA, March 15.—Premier Hart proposed this afternoon in the B.C. Legislature to call a special session to pass necessary legislation to permit Vancouver and Victoria to take over B.C. Electric services within their boundaries—provided the people approve, by plebiscite, the cities' entry into that field.

Mr. Hart made the declaration when he addressed the House on second reading of the government's $10,000,000 hydro bill, under which it is proposed to put the province into the power production and distribution business.

This is the bill which the CCF, through Opposition Leader Harold Winch, proposes to refer to a select committee of the House

Please Turn to Page Five
See "Hart Plans"

$600 Fines for Short Weight

Russell Moore, 2036 East First, was convicted on one charge and pleaded guilty to five charges of violating the weights and measures bylaw.

He was fined $100 on each charge.

Moore was charged with delivering manure in lesser quantities than originally called for.

Magistrate W. W. B. McInnes said: "This is the meanest kind of racket. You were convicted several months ago on a similar offence but still you carried on. In future I would suggest to the prosecutor that these charges be laid under the federal code."

Man Admits He Crucified Self

CHICAGO, March 15—(BUP)—Fred Walcher, the 44-year-old tavern porter who police believe planned his own crucifixion, admitted it today.

When Walcher appeared in court, the judge asked why he submitted to the ordeal.

"So many of the boys were dying overseas that I thought I would do something for my country," he replied. He gestured with bandaged hands, now healing from the holes made by the nails with which he was hung to a cross.

British Reject Nazi Peace Bid

STOCKHOLM, March 15—(AP)—An unofficial British statement today confirmed reports that a German approach to Allied representatives was attempted here a few days ago with a view to a possible armistice, but said it was immediately rejected.

"An approach was attempted a few days ago through a third party to a junior member of the Legation staff," the unofficial British statement said.

"The third party was at once told that the British Legation was not in the least interested in any such approach."

The American Legation denied that any feeler had been attempted there.

The third party mentioned in the unofficial announcement apparently was a Swedish business man who, other informants said, was approached by a minor Nazi official in the hope of using him as a medium for talking to the Allies.

Responsible Allied officials regarded the incident as a German propaganda manoeuvre in an effort to split the Allies.

Please Turn to Page Five
See "German Peace"

Seven Killed in Crash

SAN FRANCISCO, March 15—(BUP)—Seven persons were killed and 16 were injured when a twin-engined naval transport plane crashed on a ridge near San Carlos Cal., last night.

Liquor Permit Battle Looms

By Sun Staff Reporter

VICTORIA, March 15.—Opposition is developing in the coalition caucus to Attorney-General Maitland's liquor permit bill.

Several country members expressed the view today that the plan will make "criminals" out of people unwittingly.

The bill specifies penalties from $50 to $300 for people who have possession of a permit not their own" without lawful reason or excuse."

It is aimed at catching bootleggers in Vancouver who accumulate permits to get rationed liquor for resale.

Boy Crushed by Ton of Split Peas

WINNIPEG, March 15—(CP)—Body of Paul Kuzak, 12-year-old son of Mr. and Mrs. Paul Kuzak of Winnipeg, was found under a ton of split peas in a Winnipeg grain yard today after he had been missing since last night. Police believe he met his death when the peas fell on him while playing.

Americans Suffer 425,000 Casualties

WASHINGTON, March 15—(AP)—Casualties of the United States army ground force on the Western Front from D-Day last June to March 1 total 425,007, War Secretary Stimson reported today.

Aggregate casualties since the United States entered the war are 839,589.

SLAIN LEFT AS WARNING

STOCKHOLM, March 15—(AP)—Nazi "flying courts martial" are operating over a wide area of the German eastern front and executed men are left under warning placards where they fall, the Berlin correspondent for the Stockholms-Tidningen reported today after a conducted tour of the front.

B.C. FLIER WATCHES 'TOWN BUSTERS' DROP

'Fountain of Debris' as 11-Ton Bomb Hits Germany

"A terrific flash, followed by a gigantic pall of black smoke and a fountain of debris gushing hundreds of feet into the air."

That's a B.C. airman's description of a direct hit by one of the new 11-ton "town buster" bombs which RAF Lancasters dropped on Germany for the first time, Wednesday.

The flier is FO H. R. Short, flight engineer from Abbotsford, one of scores of Canadians who took part in the history-making attack on a rail viaduct at Bielfeld, according to a Canadian Press report.

Short said that the six-ton "earthquake" bombs also dropped by the raiders "seemed like babies in comparison."

The new 22,000-pound bomb, a 10-tonner by British long-ton measurement, combines great power of penetration with a high explosive force.

Prior to its use, the largest previously dropped on the Germans was the six-ton "earthquake" which sank the German battleship Tirpitz and penetrated 15-foot-thick concrete roofs of U-boat pens.

The air ministry disclosed it takes a six-man crew a half-hour to load the bomb on a Lancaster. It is 25 feet, 5 inches long and has a diameter of three feet, 10 inches.

Designed by B. N. Wallis of Vickers-Armstrong, it was developed by Group Capt. W. Wynter-Morgan and Sqdn.

Leader Davies of the Ministry of Aircraft Production whose "back room boys" have played a formidable role in devising bigger and better projectiles to smash the enemy.

Primary role of the bomb, which carries a high explosive charge of great weight, is for attacks on underground structures.

Air correspondents said the new bomb could be expected to have devastating effect over a radius of "literally hundreds of yards."

It should do 100 times more damage than a one-ton bomb because the extent of damage multiplies more rapidly than the increase in tonnage, they said.

Son Discharged So Father Kills Him

SOUTH BEND, Ind., March 15—(AP)—Detective G. C. Shritron said today Ferdinand J. Sygler, 43, had admitted slaying his 17-year-old son, John, because the boy's discharge from the Merchant Marine had placed "a black mark on the family name."

Edward Hawkins, 53, of 48½ Cordova Street, was seriously hurt today when he fell about eight feet from a pile of lumber onto a platform at the Viaduct Dry Kiln, 633 Taylor. He was rushed to hospital for emergency treatment.

Mexico City Race Results

FIRST RACE.—Two furlongs.
aBay Sky (Weidaman) $15, $5.40, $2.80.
bArmy Flash (Jones) $4.80, $2.60.
Okoee (Neves) $2.60.
Time :22 2-5. Scratches: Lady Itobian, d-Woven Web, d-River Trade, c-Episode, b-Don Galapas, a-Bay Frances.

SECOND RACE—Seven and one-half furlongs:
aLiberante (Neves) $2.80, $2.20, $2.20.
Shelia Rhea (Fernandez) $4.40, $2.80.
At War (Nunez) $4.60.
Time: 1.33 1-3. Scratches: Silent Time.

THIRD RACE—Five and one-half furlongs:
Johns Tip (Gomez) $41.20, $18.60, $8.00.
Miss Belton (Molbert) $8.00, $6.20.
Shasta Rap (Deering) $5.60.
Time: 1.08. Scratches: None.

And Inside—

"This Is It," Say Troops Over Rhine

By DON WHITEHEAD.
(Associated Press War Correspondent.)

ACROSS THE RHINE, March 24--Powerful Allied assaults on the western front have wiped out the Rhine River defenses and Gen. Eisenhower's armies now stand on the threshold of complete victory over Germany.

This is the feeling along this army front tonight.

Not in two and a half years of war has such optimism prevailed among troops and officers as that which is cheering soldiers hearing news of new crossings on the Rhine against light enemy resistance.

There is a growing feeling that "this is it."

Everywhere there is that sense of an impending finish to a long conflict--that this time the Germans can not muster enough strength to stop the powerhouse drives of the Allies.

THE VANCOUVER DAILY PROVINCE ★★★★★ FINAL

50th YEAR—NO. 304 VANCOUVER, B.C., SATURDAY, MARCH 24, 1945—48 PAGES PRICE 10 CENTS

MONTY ON BERLIN ROAD

Final BULLETINS

Big Jap Engine Plant Blasted

GUAM, March 25.—(AP)—(Sunday)—One of Japan's biggest aircraft engine plants on the outskirts of Nagoya was the target of the greatest Superfortress demolition raid against the enemy homeland an hour after midnight this morning. A force of B-29's, estimated to total at least 225, swept in over the sprawling Mitsubishi plant at unprecedently low level for a high explosive raid.

Nazi Captured

PORT ARTHUR, March 24.—(CP)—Gunther Hantzen, German prisoner of war who escaped from a pulpwood supply company timber camp near Long Lac, Ont., was captured at Redditt, Ont. No other details were disclosed.

Tokyo Raid

SAN FRANCISCO, March 24. (AP)—Radio Tokyo reported today that a "new" carrier task force was pushing home a second day's attack upon the nearby Ryukyu Islands.

The broadcast said a carrier plane force with "two or three aircraft carriers as its nucleus" attacked Okinawa Island Friday with 230 planes and returned today to raid both Okinawa and Miyako.

Sarah, Vic Near Break

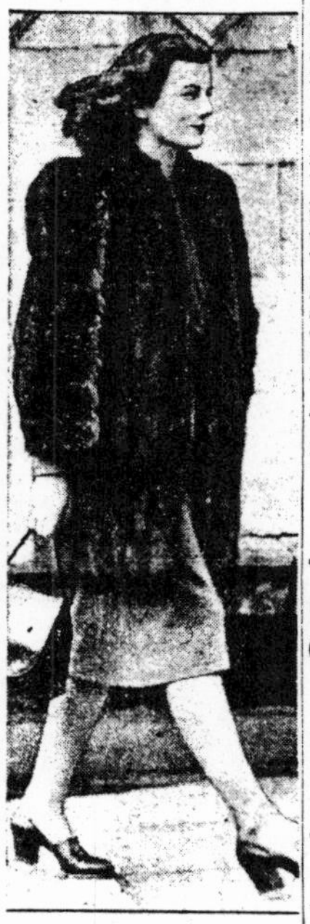

SARAH CHURCHILL.

LONDON, March 24.—(AP)—The marriage of comedian Vic Oliver and Sarah Churchill, the Prime Minister's auburn-haired daughter, which began with a Christmas Eve elopement in 1936 in New York may end Monday.

The 47-year-old Oliver is seeking a divorce from his wife, who once was billed with him on Broadway as "the runaway dancing debutante."

Four years ago Mrs. Oliver joined the Women's Auxiliary Air Force, in which she now is a photographic interpreter officer.

RUSS OPEN NEW DRIVE IN HUNGARY

LONDON, March 24.—(AP)—Marshal Stalin announced a new Russian offensive in Hungary tonight and said Soviet forces had advanced 44 miles on a front of more than 63 miles and captured numerous communications points.

By DWIGHT L. PITKIN.
Associated Press War Correspondent.

LONDON, March 24.—The Germans said today that Marshal Gregory Zhukov had attacked "with strongest forces" from his Oder bridgeheads as part of a decisive drive on Berlin.

With perhaps 1,200,000 men massed along the Oder and ready to join in a multiple east-west Allied assault to crush the last breath out of the Reich, Zhukov threw six infantry divisions, waves of tanks and a tremendous artillery barrage into the new attack on both sides of Kuestrin and succeeded in reaching a point only 31 miles from the German capital, German broadcasts reported.

The German High Command said Zhukov was attacking from bridgeheads on both sides of Kuestrin and that the stubborn German defense had taken a

(Continued on Page 2.)
See RUSSIA.

Two Flyers Die In Heavy Seas Off Charlottes

Two R.C.A.F. officers, one the father of five children, drowned Friday when a small dinghy carrying five men, overturned in heavy seas in the Queen Charlotte Islands area. The three other airmen swam ashore.

Dead are:

Flt.-Lt. A. Newman, Lacombe, Alta., and

PO. H. Leece, Jarvis, Ont.

Newman's body was recovered 15 minutes after the accident, but attempts to revive him failed. Leece's body has not yet been recovered.

The two officers had flown from Prince Rupert to an R.C.A.F. base in the Queen Charlottes. There they boarded the R.C.A.F. motor vessel Stewart, to visit a smaller island.

The Stewart anchored outside a small cove and three airmen came out in a dinghy to take Newman and Leece to shore.

On the way, the dinghy overturned. A heavy sea was running.

Flt.-Lt. Newman had five children.

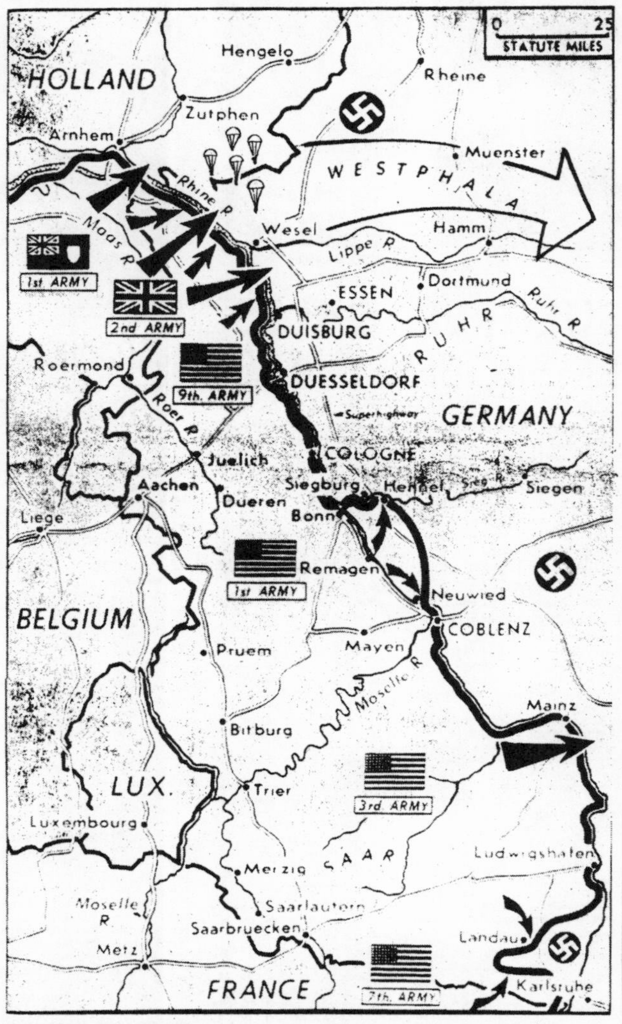

Field Marshal Montgomery's 21st Army group has smashed four miles beyond the Rhine in a 25-mile sector north of Wesel and the Ruhr Valley. The 1st Allied Airborne Army dropped into the Westphalian plains, direct path to Berlin, has linked up with the invasion armies. The U.S. 1st Army is enlarging its Remagen bridgehead. Farther south yet, the U.S. 3rd Army is speedily driving into the waist of Germany from a bridgehead below Mainz.

Doubled License Fee Proposed By Cornett

Doubling of Vancouver business and trade license fees this year will be proposed to the City Council by Mayor Cornett on Monday to provide $500,000 extra revenue for desperately needed expansion of civic services.

The special levy would be for this year only until the city obtains relief from its crushing share of education and social service costs.

The mayor points out doubled license fees would be a "painless extraction" from the majority of city merchants, who otherwise would be obliged to pay the extra charge in federal profits tax.

No attempt would be made to apply the extra impost on small "corner-store" businesses or traders with less than a specified yearly "turnover."

Holders of dog and bicycle licenses also would be exempt.

A large percentage of 1945 business licenses have already

(Continued on Page 2.)
See MAYOR.

RACING

Mexico Results

FIRST RACE—3½ furlongs: Lucero (McCown), $7.20, $4.40, $3.40; Blue Chance (Fernandez), $7.20, $3.60; Gergar (Weidaman), $3.60.
Time, 42 sceonds. No scratches.

SECOND RACE—5½ furlongs: Lovable Spy (D. Meade), $16, $5.80, $4; Expeditious (A. Craig), $3.60, $3; Nancy Carroll (F. Fernandez), $2.80.
Time, 1:07 4-5.

(Race entries on Page 2.)

Here's Lineup On Rhine Front

PARIS, March 24.—Following are the positions of the Allied lower Rhine armies as given late today:

BRITISH 2ND — In Wesel and Rees.

U.S. 9TH—Two miles south of Wesel.

CANADIAN 1ST — Not given.

1ST AIRBORNE — Northeast of Xanten.

U.S. 1ST — In Remagen bridgehead.

U.S. 3RD — Over Rhine below Mainz.

U.S. 7TH — Mopping up Palatinate.

1ST FRENCH — Reported across Rhine below Karlsruhe.

U.S. 15TH—Not given.

Canadian Air Troops Land Across Rhine

WITH THE CANADIANS ON THE RHINE, March 24.—(CP)—A Canadian paratroop battalion was among the Allied airborne units which dropped east of the Rhine in today's great trans-Rhine attack.

This is the battalion's second "D-Day" show. It landed in Normandy on the morning of last June 6, east of the Orne River and northeast of Caen and fought for 11 days in a savage action on the flank of the British 2nd Army. Later it shared in the advance to the Seine River and later fought in the Ardenne forest as infantry.

Now it is in the thick of the fighting again.

(Compiled from Late Despatches to The Vancouver Daily Province.)

PARIS, March 24.—Four great Allied armies—the British 2nd, the U.S. 9th, the Canadian 1st and the Allied 1st Airborne—today won a 25-mile stretch across the lower Rhine and north of the wrecked Ruhr Valley. They drove four miles beyond the river in a mighty land and airborne offensive bidding for final victory this spring.

The final battle for Germany from the west was joined on the broad Westphalian plains on the road to Berlin.

Field Marshal Montgomery told his 21st Army group but a few hours after the first assault troops went across the Rhine and found only slight German resistance, "The last round is going well."

Ten thousand Allied planes struck Germany the greatest co-ordinated aerial blows in history.

Air fleets laid a protecting wall of fire, rockets and bombs around the charging Allied troops.

The British 2nd Army, commanded by Lt. Gen. Sir Miles C. Dempsey, was in the van of the fresh attacks and on all its front the advance was going "according to plan," AP Correspondent Pugh Moore reported.

Tanks already are across the river.

The first British units across the Rhine were from the British 50th Royal Tank Regiment.

The lower Rhine operation was the greatest amphibious attack since the Normandy invasion.

British, American, Canadian and Scottish troops poured across the lower Rhine at perhaps seven places and were "making good progress."

Even as Gen. Montgomery's forces crossed the lower Rhine, the American 1st and 3rd armies were expanding swiftly their previously won fronts east of the great barrier river on its middle and upper courses.

The Allied 1st Airborne Army landed northeast of Xanten in the largest sky invasion in history, gliding and parachuting to earth from an enormous sky train more than 500 miles long. Up to 30,000 sky troops landed after 10 a.m.

260 MILES FROM BERLIN.

The troops of Lt.-Gen. Courtney H. Hodges and Lt.-Gen. Patton are 260-odd miles from Berlin, while those of Field Marshal Montgomery crossed the river 290 to 295 miles from the capital. Gen. Patton's crossings, between Worms and Mainz, are within 302 miles of the Russian armies on the Oder.

Wesel and Rees on the east bank of the lower Rhine were entered. Bislich was captured.

(Continued on Page 2.)
See INVASION.

WAR BULLETINS

LONDON, March 24.—(Reuters)—Scottish troops who crossed the Rhine last night linked up today with airborne forces dropped this morning within range of Allied guns, Chester Willmott, CBC correspondent, reported.

Eisenhower Issues Warning

LONDON, March 24.—(Reuters)—Gen. Eisenhower today issued a proclamation to the German Army and Waffen S.S., broadcast by Luxembourg radio, threatening severe punishment to any German soldiers taking part in the execution of Allied airborne soldiers.

Patton Sends Tanks Across Rhine

U.S. 3RD ARMY ACROSS THE RHINE, March 24.—(AP)—Lt.-Gen. George S. Patton's 3rd Army put tanks across the upper Rhine tonight over a bridgehead at least eight miles long and four deep. Efelden, Astheim, Gersheim and Lesshein, between Mainz and Ludwigshafen, were captured.

Weather Favors Allies

LONDON, March 24.—(CP)—The weather finally turned against Hitler in one of the Allies' big offensives.

Brilliant sunshine favored the Allies as they struck across the Rhine into the plain north of the Ruhr.

'Decisive Victory In Europe at Hand, Churchill Tells Montgomery's Men

LONDON, March 24.—The "decisive victory in Europe will be near" once the Rhine River Line is pierced and the crust of German resistance broken, Prime Minister Churchill today told Field Marshal Montgomery's armies.

Mr. Churchill's message said:

"I rejoice to be with the chief of the imperial general staff, (Field Marshal Sir Alan Brooke) at Field Marshal Montgomery's headquarters of the 21st Army Group during this memorable battle of forcing the Rhine.

"British soldiers, it will long be told how, with our Canadian brothers and valiant United States Allies, this superb task was accomplished. Once the river line is pierced and the crust of German resistance is broken the decisive victory in Europe will be near.

"May God prosper our arms in this noble adventure after our long struggle for King and country, for dear life and for the freedom of mankind."

Gen. Montgomery addressed this message to all 21st Army Group troops:

"1. On the 7th of February I told you we were going into the ring for the final and last round; there would be no time limit. We would continue fighting until our opponent was knocked out. The last round is going very well on both sides of the Rhine—and overhead.

"2. In the west the enemyl has lost the Rhineland, and with it the flower of at least four armies—the Parachute Army, 5th Panzer Army, 15th Army and 7th Army. The 1st Army, farther to the south, is now being added to the list.

"In the Rhineland battles the enemy has lost about 150,000 prisoners, and there are many more to come. His total casualties amount to about 250,000 since the 8th of February.

(Continued on Page 2.) See CHURCHILL.

Officials Feared Greenhill Cargo

NEW PATTON SPEARHEAD RACING TO MEET REDS

FINAL EDITION

★ ★ ★

The Vancouver Sun

FOUNDED 1886 · VOL. LIX—No. 200 · VANCOUVER, BRITISH COLUMBIA, MONDAY MARCH 26, 1945 · PRICE 5c

2 Major Allied Breakthroughs

From AP and BUP Dispatches

PARIS, March 26. — Germany's Western Front cracked wide open today, and Lt. Gen. George S. Patton's U.S. 3rd Army, in the most sensational advance of the day, was reported to have plunged 80 miles from the Rhine to the Bavarian stronghold of Wuerzburg, in an apparent move to split northern and southern Germany and link up with Russian forces driving up to Austria from Czechoslovakia and Western Hungary.

These were the highlights as the tempo of the German break-up increased:

1. U.S. 3rd Army entered Frankfurt-on-Main, Germany's ninth largest city, were reported at Wuerzburg, 60 miles from Frankfurt.

2. The U.S. 1st Army scored a 22-mile gain eastward from its Remagen bridgehead and entered Limburg.

3. A report from the British 2nd Army front said the whole German Rhine defense system appeared to be breaking up. U.S. 9th Army forces on the lower Rhine broke through German defenses on the Lippe River east of Dorsten, 17 miles east of the Rhine and were reported entering the suburbs of Duisburg.

4. At the top of the front the 1st Canadian, 2nd British and 1st Allied Airborne armies were riddling through Nazi defenses east of the Rhine.

Please Turn to Page Two   See "German Defenses"

Officials Knew Cargo Dangerous

CPR, Fearing Chemical, Shipped Load to Coquitlam for Safety

J. P. McNab, inspector of the Bureau of Explosives of the association of American Railroads, told a formal inquiry into the Greenhill Park disaster this afternoon that he had found Board of Transport regulations violated with the omission of yellow caution labels on drums of sodium chlorate stored in Pier B on Feb. 8.

This was a month before the chemical was loaded on the vessel. Mr. McNab said that the labels under the regulations should have been attached by the shipper of the chemical (an Eastern firm).

Three carloads of sodium chlorate—bound for Australia from Quebec—were unloaded at Pier B exactly one month before the freighter Greenhill Park, carrying the chemical, blew up on March 6, but were classed as dangerous by CPR and Dominion explosives officials and were removed to Coquitlam four days later.

This was evidence given before the formal inquiry into the freighter blast, which opened at the Court House this morning, by Capt. Arthur T. Willoughby of 1151 Barclay, CPR wharf freight agent.

MEN WARNED

He said the CPR had made an effort to ship the chemical on another freighter which sailed before the Greenhill Park but shipping space was not available.

Capt. Willoughby told the court, presided over by Mr. Justice Sidney Smith, while under examination by Crown counsel Dugald Donaghy, KC, that he had warned four longshoremen unloading the boxcars on March 5 that the chemical was dangerous.

He said one of them told him they knew, as "it is marked plainly on the drums."

Please Turn to Page Twenty   See "Inquiry"

LATE FLASHES—

U.S. Senate Eyes On Canadian Meat

WASHINGTON, March 26—(CP)—Members of the Senate sub-committee on agriculture today launched an inquiry into food shortages with their thoughts fixed on Canada's reputed abundance of meats and the reasons why Americans cannot get some of it.

Senator Burton K. Wheeler (Dem., Mont.) asked that one of the matters to be investigated be the obstacles in the way of Canadian meat entering the United States.

Probe Veterans' Hospitals

WASHINGTON, March 26—(BUP)—The House prepared to take action today on a resolution to investigate charges of "intolerable" conditions at veterans administration hospitals.

Canucks Hit German HQ.

LONDON, March 26—(CP Cable)—The RCAF told today of an attack Sunday on a suspected German headquarters at Halten, 25 miles east of Wesel, during which Canadian Spitfires scored direct hits and near misses with cannon and machine-gun fire. During the attack a German staff car was seen to drive into a barn. Flt. Lt. W. N. Douglas of New Westminster, B.C., set the barn afire with cannon fire.

No Pension for McNaughton

OTTAWA, March 26—(CP)—Defense Minister McNaughton was not granted a pension after his retirement from the Canadian army during the present war, it was reported today in a reply tabled in the Commons today for D. G. Ross (PC, Souris).

Too Realistic for Vet

'NAZI' KNOCKOUT ON NANAIMO FRONT, TOO

NANAIMO, March 26—(CP)—There was too much stark realism here Saturday for a First Great War veteran from Gabriola Island.

In aid of the present Red Cross campaign a German prison camp scene was re-enacted on Nanaimo's main street. Dressed in the uniform of the German guard two burly soldiers, stationed at Camp Nanaimo, armed with tommy guns, stalked around a barbed wire compound inside of which were six high school students impersonating Canadian prisoners-of-war.

The First Great War veteran who had been a prisoner in the last war apparently misinterpreted the scene. He managed to knock out one of the pseudo German guards before eyewitnesses prevented him from doing further damage.

The veteran apologized later.

Lloyd George Dies at 82; Wife at Side

Empire's First Great War Leader Passes

LONDON, March 26—(BUP)—David Lloyd George, First World War Prime Minister of Great Britain, died today at 81 after a lengthy illness.

Attending physicians said he died in his sleep.

Lloyd George's condition took a turn for the worse in the last 24 hours and his physicians gave up hope.

He died at 8:35 p.m., it was announced.

His condition had been grave for more than a month. He had not been in good health for several years, but had continued to make occasional appearances in the House of Commons until recent months.

(See Page 19 for a picture of Earl Lloyd George and an account of his distinguished career.)

Bruening Hitler 'Heir'—Pravda

MOSCOW, March 26—(AP)—Ilya Ehrenburg, writing in Pravda, asserted Sunday, that Dr. Heinrich Bruening, Hitler's predecessor as Chancellor of Germany, has put forth "his candidacy as the heir of Hitler."

"The salvation of German Imperialism has been turned over to the Catholic Centre," says Ehrenburg.

(Bruening now is professor of government at Harvard University. He held the German chancellorship from March, 1930, until May, 1932. A staunch Catholic, he was a foe of Hitler's policies.)

Outlook Good for Balmy Weather

Only the presence of a wayward storm over Southern Alaska appeared as a vague threat to the delightful spring weather which greeted Vancouver today.

The storm is a weak one, the weatherman pointed out hopefully, and is not even moving in this direction at the moment. Still, repeated disappointments have made the weatherman extremely cautious.

Canada to Stop Making Carriers

OTTAWA, March 26—(BUP)—Canada will stop manufacturing universal carriers on April 30, the Department of Munitions and Supply announced today.

Four thousand of the machines are being produced in Canada.

RCAF Loses 16 Planes in Week

OTTAWA, March 26—(CP)—Planes of the Canadian bomber group and of Canadian fighter squadrons based in the United Kingdom and on the continent ranged widely over Germany during the week, blasting communications and industrial centres, laying mines in enemy waters and supporting ground troops. Thirteen heavy bombers and three fighters are missing from the week's operations.

During the week RCAF squadrons based on the continent flew more than 1650 sorties.

SKYTROOPS IN ACTION

'Two Hours of Real Killing' for Canucks

By DOUGLAS AMARON

WITH THE CANADIANS IN GERMANY, March 26—(CP)—The 1st Canadian Parachute Battalion dropped into battle east of the Rhine Saturday, seized all its objectives within two hours and captured a considerable number of Germans with comparatively light casualties.

These Canadians, mostly veterans of the Normandy invasion last June, were at rest Sunday in a holding position in and around the woods northwest of Wesel.

In a candle-lit cellar on a rise at a busy crossroads beyond which Scottish troops of the British 2nd Army had advanced, Maj. Fraser Eadie of Winnipeg,

Maj. Dick Hilborn of Preston, Ont., and Capt. Jack Simpson of Toronto, combined to tell a story of the landing.

They spoke proudly, for Canada's only parachute battalion again had made a name for itself.

"We met no opposition till we were right over the dropping zone," Eadie said.

The parachutists landed in a field and were in action almost immediately.

"It really was flat-out fighting until about noon," Hilborn said, and Eadie described it as "two hours of real killing."

Please Turn to Page Two   See "Sky Troops"

HOW RHINE WAS CROSSED

See Page 11 for a series of four radioed pictures showing how Allied armies crossed the Rhine.

FUEHRER CALLS EMERGENCY MEET

Special to The Vancouver Sun

LONDON, March 26—(BUP)—A Zurich dispatch said today that Adolf Hitler has called an emergency meeting of his ministers and Gauleiters (district leaders) for tonight at Berchtesgaden.

Subject-matter of the conference was not disclosed, the dispatch said, but it quoted a German war office spokesman as saying that Germany "must be prepared for unfortunate news."

BERLIN JITTERY

The dispatch, distributed by the Exchange Telegraph Agency, said the plans for the meeting were disclosed by an "unquestionable source." Ministers and Gauleiters will be transported to Hitler's Bavarian retreat by plane, it said.

Reports reaching Sweden from Berlin said the Nazi capital was more jittery and tense than at any time since the invasion of Normandy.

Travellers arriving at Malmoe from Germany said the nightly RAF air raids were driving Berliners "to dementia."

Germans expect further surprise airborne landings still deeper behind the German lines, Swedish dispatches said.

Arthur Axmann, Nazi youth leader, called on German girls as well as boys to throw themselves into Germany's last battles.

Please Turn to Page Two   See "Germany"

3 Youths Held in $5000 Loot Case

Three youths were charged by police this afternoon in connection with $5000 worth of allegedly stolen goods found in a Hornby Street house on Saturday. A fourth man is being held for investigation.

Eight charges of retaining allegedly stolen goods and three charges of possession of allegedly stolen goods were laid against Oliver Martens, 21, 619, Gresham Rooms; Des Renwick, 19, Gresham Rooms, and Wesley W. Hyshka, 1032 Hornby.

(See also Page 11.)

THE WAR ON OTHER FRONTS

RUSSIA. — Driving on Vienna, the Russians today were 72 miles from that capital, 32 from the Austrian border. See Page 2.

ITALY. — German patrolling became more aggressive along the Allied 5th Army front today and there were a number of sharp clashes, particularly in the area southwest of Bologna.

BURMA. — British 20th Division armored troops, rushing ten miles northward along a railway from Kume, have captured Myittha, an important rail and road junction in Central Burma.

CHINA. — Chinese First troops have made a junction with the 50th Division 10 miles east of Hsipaw, completing the clearance of the Burma Road from Ledo through Hsipaw.

UNITS NAMED

Canadians Win Bienen

WITH THE CANADIANS IN THE LOWER RHINE BRIDGEHEAD, March 26—(CP)—The North Nova Scotia Highlanders have captured Bienen, four miles northwest of Rees, and advanced a quarter of a mile beyond the town.

The regiment is astride the Rees-Emmerich highway beyond Bienen and also on a road leading northwest of Bienen to Millingen, 1½ miles away.

The Cameron Highlanders of Ottawa provided machine-gunners to support the North Novas in the attack on Bienen, which became the second town to fall to the Canadians in the present operation.

(The Camerons—not to be confused with the Queens' Own Cameron Highlanders, a Winnipeg unit—are the fifth Canadian unit disclosed in action east of the Rhine. As of February they were a 3rd Division regiment.)

The Stormont, Dundas and Glengarry Highlands of Cornwall, Ont., are meeting strong resistance between Bienen and the Rhine Bend.

The British-Canadian bridgehead is being gradually expanded, however, particularly along the perimeter north of Xanten and Wesel where airborne units were dropped Saturday.

The opposition facing the Canadians, back in their accustomed fighting role in Allied advances—on the left bank—is as stiff as at any along the bridgehead perimeter.

The going is inevitably slow over the dead, flat country.

Delivery of POW Parcels Disrupted

OTTAWA, March 26—(CP)—Elaborating on a previous statement on the prisoner of war situation in Germany, Prime Minister Mackenzie King said today in the Commons that parcels, individually addressed to Canadian prisoners, had little hope of reaching the addressees in certain of the German camps which had recently been moved.

He added it was important for Red Cross parcels to continue to reach the prisoners, and promised a new statement on the Canadian forces would be made as soon as possible.

PUSH IN SOUTH MAY UPSET 'LAST STAND'

By LOUIS KEEMLE
British United Press War Editor

NEW YORK, March 26.—It looks more and more as if the crust of German resistance, of which Prime Minister Churchill spoke, is being broken. When that happens, Churchill said, "decisive victory in Europe will be near."

For final victory over Germany, the status of the eastern front must be considered in relation to what is happening in the west.

The Red Army's delay in smashing through to Berlin does not mean that the Russians are behind schedule in the concerted two-way blow planned at Yalta. Berlin is not much more than a political objective now. Its military value has been destroyed from the air.

The Russians are engaged in a major offensive of great significance at the southern end of their long front. The drive through western Hungary and Czechoslovakia north and south of the Danube is really rolling.

The British-Canadian bridgehead is being gradually expanded, however. The Russian objective is evidently to batter through the Dan—

Please Turn to Page Two   See "Keemle"

800 Killed in RAF Mistake

LONDON, March 26—(BUP)—More than 800 persons were killed and 1000 injured in a mistaken bombing of The Hague, Dutch capital, by RAF planes March 3, it was revealed today.

The RAF planes were attempting to attack rocket-launching sites, but their bombs fell wide of the mark and hit the heavily-populated civilian area.

King Sees Early German Collapse

OTTAWA, March 26—(CP)—Announcing the 3rd Canadian Division was participating in the new Rhine offensive with the British 2nd Army, Prime Minister Mackenzie King today declared in the Commons that German resistance west of the Rhine had "practically collapsed" and he had reason to hope that the collapse of Germany "may not long be delayed."

Statement Promised on Italy Canadian Troops

OTTAWA, March 26—(CP)—Hon. R. B. Hanson (PC, York Sunbury) in the Commons today asked if the Department of National Defense was prepared to make a statement on the Canadian forces in Italy.

Douglas Abbott, parliamentary assistant to Defense Minister McNaughton, said an announcement on the Canadian forces would be made as soon as possible.

Time Lost in Strikes Takes 38 Percent Drop

OTTAWA, March 26—(CP)—Time lost through strikes and lockouts during the first two months of this year was 38.7 percent less than for the corresponding period of 1944, the labor department announced to-day.

DISTANCES TO BERLIN

PARIS, March 26—(BUP)—Six Allied armies were closing in on Berlin from the west today.

Here is each army's position and the miles to Berlin.

First Canadian—305 miles (Rees).

British 2nd—270 (near Dorsten).

U.S. 9th—270 (near Dorsten).

U.S. 1st—261 (Dembach).

U.S. Third—235 (Hanau).

U.S. 7th—310 (west of Karlsruhe).

Fliers Blast War Plants

LONDON, March 26—(CP)—Two oil plants, a gun factory and an armored car works in Southeastern Germany were attacked today by 300 escorted American bombers as the airmen switched back to strategic targets after a week-long bombing prelude for the Rhine offensive.

The small force of heavy bombers split into two task forces over Leipzig. One went for a synthetic oil plant and a natural oil refinery at Zeitz, 20 miles south of Leipzig, while the other flew to Plauen, 10 miles from the Czecho-Slovak border, and blasted the twin war factories.

Last night Mosquitos attacked Berlin for the 34th consecutive night and American night-prowling planes joined in hammering German targets.

And Inside—

GERMANY'S ARMIES WHIPPED—EISENHOWER

'Rhine Victory Complete, Crushing'

The Vancouver Sun

FOUNDED 1886
VOL. LIX—No. 201

VANCOUVER, BRITISH COLUMBIA, TUESDAY, MARCH 27, 1945

PRICE 5c

★ ★ ★ ★ ★ FINAL EDITION

Reds 20 Miles From Austria

Soviet Vanguards 65 Miles South Of Vienna in Great New Offensive

By ROBERT MUSEL
Special to The Vancouver Sun

LONDON, March 27—(BUP)—Red Army vanguards today swept to within a scant 20 miles of the Austrian border, some 65 miles southeast of Vienna, aided by precision bombing of the 15th American Air Force which attacked German concentration points in the path of the Russians.

German reports acknowledged that the Soviet pressure on the irregular 170-mile front had increased, and that Red Army spearheads had flanked the important communications centres of Komarom and Gyor in a drive to the Marcal Canal and the lower Raab River.

The Marcal Canal runs about seven miles west of Papa, captured by the Russians yesterday, and joins the Raab northwest of Papa.

The Raab in this area is only about 20 miles from the Austrian

Please Turn to ?age Two
See "Russia"

LATE FLASHES—

Berlin Bombers Stretch 75 Miles

LONDON, March 27—(BUP)—Radio Berlin tonight reported that a "75-mile" stream of fast bombers was over the Reich capital, extending as far as Stettin.

Snowslide Kills Ski Expert

BANFF, Alta., March 27—(CP)—Herman Gȧdner, ski instructor from St. Jovite, Que., and head examiner of the Canadian Ski School, lost his life Monday in a snowslide near Hidden Lake, some twelve miles from Lake Louise.

Auto Dealer Fined $5000

EDMONTON, March 27—(CP)—Erwood (Dutch) Lyons, second-hand automobile dealer, was fined $5000 in police court today by Magistrate H. L. Hawe on an indictment of 70 counts of infractions of prices board regulations.

Red Cross Masks Hun Gun

AT A FORWARD RCAF AIRFIELD IN THE NETHERLANDS, March 27—(CP)—PO. F. B. Gillis, a Spitfire pilot from Pense, Sask., returned to his base yesterday to report he had been shot down from a German post marked by a red cross.

Russia Gets British Warship

MOSCOW, March 27—(CP) — Delivery by Great Britain to Russia of the 29,150-ton First Great War battleship Royal Sovereign was disclosed today by the Red Navy. The United States delivered to Russia the cruiser Milwaukee.

Survivor Credits Royal Navy

ARNPRIOR, Ont., March 27—(CP)—Leading Seaman Weldon Runtz, 21, a survivor of the sinking of the Canadian corvette Trentonian said today the enemy's torpedo attack occurred in mid-afternoon, with the ship in sight of land.

Of the corvette's crew all but six were reported saved, and Runtz credited the low casualty list to the speed with which two Royal Naval motor launches reached the scene in response to the first message of distress.

ALL OVER BUT THE . . .

LOS ANGELES, March 27—(BUP)—Members of the Los Angeles City Council rose and solemnly recited the oath of allegiance today when President Robert Burns announced that Germany had surrendered.

But before the cheers had died down, Burns stood up and announced the report was incorrect.

A wave of groans swept through the chamber.

B.C. Flier Bombs German Ship

LONDON, March 27 — (Reuters) — A Halifax, captained by FO. K. J. Thompson of Vancouver, was one of the RAF coastal command planes which attacked fast-moving enemy convoys believed to be carrying troops and equipment from Norway, in the Skaggerak Sunday night. Thick grey smoke was seen pouring from an escort vessel after it had been straddled with bombs by the Halifax.

Police Find Still, Lay Charge

NEW WESTMINSTER, March 27.—Paul Chykoski, 67, of 453 Rousheau Street, was charged in police court today with being in possession of a still. The dismantled still was discovered Monday night by Detective-Sergeant C. A. Mackie and four RCMP officers. The case was adjourned until Wednesday for lack of an interpreter.

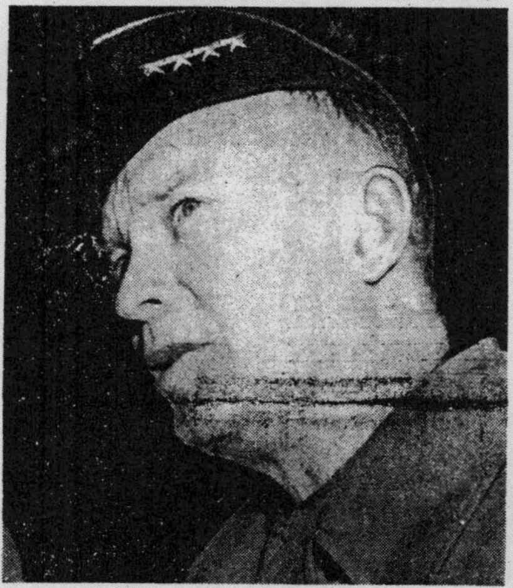

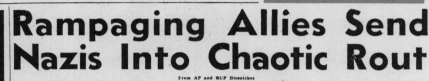

GEN. DWIGHT EISENHOWER
The Germans "are a whipped army."

GOV'T BACKS SUN RAIL RATE FIGHT

By JAMES DYER
Vancouver Sun Staff Reporter

VICTORIA, March 27. — The government of British Columbia has taken the lead in the fight inaugurated by **The Vancouver Sun** to end discrimination against this province in the railway freight rates structure.

Late Monday night, after a short but intensive debate begun by Opposition Leader Harold Winch with his resolution demanding that the government seek redress from the Board of Transport Commissioners and the Dominion, Attorney-General Hon. R. L. Maitland moved an amendment which had almost exactly the same effect.

ADOPTED UNANIMOUSLY

The House adopted the Maitland amendment unanimously.

Only five speakers—Mr. Winch, W. W. Lefeaux (CCF, Vancouver Centre), seconder of the Winch motion; Education Minister Hon. R. H. Perry, Mr. Maitland and Lands Minister E. T. Kenney, who secondeo the amendment—spoke in the debate.

Mr Winch had the highest praise for the public spirit of **The Vancouver Sun** and all speakers agreed with one voice

Please Turn to Page Three
See "Gov't Backs Sun"

'PEACE' HALTS MURDER TRIAL

CHICAGO, March 27 — (Bup)—False peace rumors flooded Chicago today.

The rumors swept through the Loop, the Stock Exchange and the city's courts.

In felony court Judge John Prystalski temporarily recessed a murder trial and sent the jurors to their chambers, expecting a formal peace announcement. Courtroom attaches and spectators were jubilant. Some women were so happy they cried.

Three-Year Term For Forgeries

NEW WESTMINSTER, March 27.—Mike Menouk, Fernie, B.C., has been sentenced to three years in the B.C. Penitentiary by Judge David Whiteside in county court today.

Menouk was found guilty on five charges of forgery of cheques on the Bank of Montreal at New Westminster and Calgary.

Both Menouk and Fred Oneski, a former inmate of Oakalla, were found not guilty of a alleged conspiracy to defraud the Bank of Montreal.

U.S. Adopts Canada Manpower System

WASHINGTON, March 27 — (BUP)—The House voted 167 to 160 today to apply stiff penalties to workers who leave essential jobs and to employers who violate fixed manpower ceilings.

It approved, a compromise manpower bill worked out after long debate by House and Senate conferees.

Rampaging Allies Send Nazis Into Chaotic Rout

From AP and BUP Dispatches

PARIS, March 27.—Gen. Dwight D. Eisenhower declared today the German armies in the west were whipped, as the German retreat from the Rhine broke into a chaotic rout along a 250-mile front from Karlsruhe to the Dutch border.

Marshal Montgomery's 21st Army group broke through into the Westphalian plain from its Rhine bridgehead, and the U.S. 1st and 3rd Armies drove 58 and 90 miles beyond the Rhine as Eisenhower proclaimed the Rhine victory as complete and crushing.

Eisenhower warned that the Nazis might turn and fight again, but said that as a military force on the Western Front they "are a whipped army."

Here is a brief picture of the Western Front today:

1. The U.S. 1st Army crashed 58 miles beyond the Rhine in a plunge to within two miles of Wetzlar, just west of the River Dill.

2. Lt. Gen. George S. Patton's U.S. 3rd Army, officially unreported for nearly 24 hours, was reported to be closing in on the Hessian city of Fulda, 90 miles beyond the Rhine and halfway across the Reich, and in the south to be 25 miles beyond Wuerzburg and only 35 miles from Nuernburg.

3. The British 2nd Army was pounding through the Ruhr screen toward the open plains before Berlin and was within three miles of Essen. Correspondents said its rate of advance was dictated only by the speed with which supplies could be brought up.

4. The U.S. 9th Army drove across the Neue Emscher Canal and broke into the Ruhr city of Duisburg.

5. The U.S. 7th Army was across the Rhine on a 19-mile bridgehead north of Mannheim and moved at least four miles to the east against spotty opposition.

1st and 3rd Joined

The U.S. 1st Army was rolling freely deep into Germany.

Four armored spearheads were pushing ahead and the one two miles west of Wetzlar was only 20 miles from the Frankfurt-Berlin superhighway at a point 254 miles from Berlin.

Fulda, toward which Patton was reported driving, is only 195 miles southwest of Berlin.

The 1st and 3rd Armies had formed a juncture near Lauhnstein, just south of Coblenz.

The 1st had three spearheads at the Dill River at points just west and northwest of Wetzlar and a fourth five miles northeast of Weisbaden which is just north of the Rhine directly across the river from Mainz.

Monty Breaks Through

Gen. Patton's racing 3rd Army tank columns already were reported sweeping half-way across Germany and closing swiftly on the Hessian citadel of Fulda, 90 miles beyond the Rhine and 195 miles southwest of Berlin.

At the "top" of the Western Front, Field Marshal Montgomery's four Allied field armies burst into the Ruhr basin

Please Turn to Page Two
See "German Armies"

Nazi Army Reported Near Revolt

By W. R. HIGGINBOTHAM
Special to The Vancouver Sun

LONDON, March 27—(BUP)—Increasing signs of the military breakdown of Germany were noted today in a series of Nazi broadcasts calling on all German troops to report at once to their units or to local authorities.

The broadcast summons coincided with Stockholm rumors of a possible military revolt in Germany because of the war crisis.

The broadcasts ordered all troops to report to stations and to local authorities. They ex-

Please Turn to Page Two
See "Revolt"

BULLETINS

LONDON, March 27—(BUP) — The German DNB news agency reported tonight that the ancient University of Heidelberg, 12 miles southeast of Mannheim, is under artillery fire from the west bank of the Rhine.

LONDON, March 27—(BUP) — The German high command said today American 3rd Army forces have captured Offenbach, on the south bank of the Main River three miles east of Frankfurt.

WITH U.S. 6TH ARMORED DIVISION, FRANKFURT, March 27—(BUP)—German troops were putting up a stubborn fight today for Frankfurt, laying down a heavy artillery fire.

WITH U.S. FIRST ARMY, March 27—(BUP)—Two German major-generals were taken prisoner by the 9th Armored Division last night.

Nazis Shoot Girl Who Helped Yanks

By HAL BOYLE

BEYOND THE RHINE, March 27 — (AP)—Trudi, a 20-year-old German girl, was in an American field hospital today after risking her life to give first aid to wounded American soldiers.

Vengeful Germans shot her and burned her home, and she was found near the blazing farm house, lying on the ground and writhing in pain.

Her hospital bed is surrounded by gifts of fruit, candy and cookies from grateful Americans for whom she bared the shellfire of her own countrymen.

'CAN'T STOP US'

'End of Hun Resistance'

By CHARLES LYNCH

WITH THE BRITISH 2ND ARMY, March 27—(Reuter's)—This looks like the end of organized German resistance in the west.

The whole of the German defense beyond Wesel is collapsing and folding open for Allied troops to motor into Germany.

Only on one small sector of the West Front — beyond the newly captured stronghold of Rees, on Field Marshal Montgomery's left flank — are Germans maintaining a co-ordinated defense.

(Troops of the 3rd Canadian Division are in action on this flank).

NAZIS 'WHIPPED,' HAVEN'T 'QUIT'

Radio Floods City With Peace Rumors

A peace rumor spread like wildfire throughout Vancouver today because of misinterpretation of statements of Gen. Eisenhower, a false United States radio broadcast and an erroneous report of a news service. All were broadcast by radio stations.

The misinterpretation occurred when the Allied commander announced the main German defense line on the Ruhr had been broken and a crushing defeat had been given the German Army. In later broadcast reports, he warned there is still tough fighting ahead.

The news announcer of a United States station was just starting his newscast at 10 a.m.

"Here's a bulletin," he said. "Eisenhower announces the Germans have quit."

He then went on with his broadcast, and, after reciting about half a dozen items, he broke in to "correct that first bulletin."

"It should have read," he

Please Turn to Page Two
See "Rumors"

Fire Destroys 'Baby Austin'

Fire today completely demolished the baby Austin belonging to Mrs. V. M. Wells, 4037 West Twentieth.

Cause of the fire that took place in the auto in the 3000 block Point Grey Road at noon today was attributed to "just a little bump" by the driver, son of Mrs. Wells.

The vehicle burned so fast and furiously that within 45 seconds the Fire Department had five different calls informing them of the blaze.

Argentina Now at War With Axis

BUENOS AIRES, March 27—(BUP)—The Argentine government has declared war on the Axis, it was announced officially today.

'Long-Time, No Peace'

TOKYO, March 27—(BUP)—Eight influential Japanese have formed a "20-year-war society" to advocate a 20-year-war against the United States and Britain, Radio Tokyo said today.

And Inside—

ALLIES GIVE HUNS SURRENDER PLAN

The Sunday Sun

FOUNDED 1886
VOL. LIX—No. 204

VANCOUVER, BRITISH COLUMBIA, SATURDAY, MARCH 31, 1945

PRICE 10c

★★★★★ FINAL EDITION

'We've Lost War'—*Hitler*

Nazis, Army Leaders Split On Armistice

By W. R. HIGGINBOTHAM
Special to The Vancouver Sun

LONDON, March 31—(BUP)—European reports said Adolf Hitler had finally conceded that Germany had lost the war, and had agreed with the German high command, at a dramatic all-night meeting ending early today, that Germany should seek an armistice.

Action was apparently delayed, however, when the Nazis refused to give up control of the German government immediately.

The High Command informed Hitler that it was prepared to negotiate for an armistice if the Nazi government would quit, a Stockholm Tidningen dispatch quoted by the Exchange Telegraph agency said.

The staff officers were said to have contended that continuation of the war was impossible in view of the Allied break-through in the west and the Soviet threat in the east.

Hitler countered with a proposal to abandon his position as

Please Turn to Page Eight
See "Hitler"

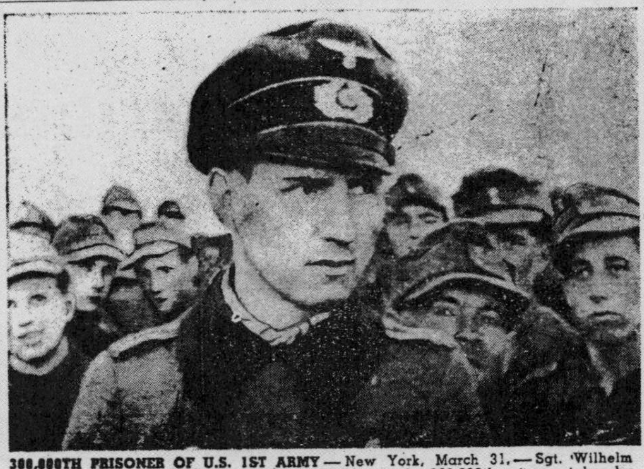

300,000TH PRISONER OF U.S. 1ST ARMY—New York, March 31.—Sgt. Wilhelm Zachmann said, "It's impossible," when told he was the 300,000th prisoner taken by the U.S. 1st Army. Here he is inside a POW cage, and worse still for Wilhelm, it's inside Germany.

Eisenhower Tells Nazis How to Quit

LONDON, March 31—(CP)—Gen. Eisenhower issued a message to the German army tonight calling for surrender.

The broadcast measure was addressed to individual soldiers.

Calling attention to the deep drives of Allied forces "into the very heart of Germany," the Eisenhower message declared the German government "has ceased to exercise effective control over wide areas," and that "the German High Command had lost effective control over many units, large and small."

The message then gave detailed instructions to German soldiers on how to proceed. Troop units were to send emissaries under white flags and to yield "in an orderly manner and with observance of military discipline."

Scattered units and individuals were told to report along the main highways to Allied units and to observe "the customary signs of surrender" by appearing "unarmed and without helmet or web equipment."

It's Almost Here

V-Day could be declared within a week, almost certainly sometime within the next month.—CHARLES LYNCH, REUTERS, at the front.

"An announcement of the greatest importance" will be made at 9 a.m. Sunday.—AKBAR EL YOM, CAIRO NEWSPAPER.

The Allies may have to create a new German government to accept a surrender demand if Hitler flees to the mountains.—U.S. ARMY AND NAVY JOURNAL.

High Command has advised Hitler that continuation of the war is impossible and suggests that his government resign.—STOCKHOLM TIDNINGEN.

An official fresh from the European front expects the "decisive point" to be reached in 10 days.—CANADIAN PRESS STAFF WRITER C. R. BLACKBURN, IN WASHINGTON.

3000 Tanks Drive To Seal Off Ruhr

From AP and BUP Dispatches

PARIS, March 31.—Eight Allied armies, paced by 3000 tanks, the greatest armored host in history, have overrun the western quarter of Germany and today had driven into position for an advance upon Berlin from the Weser River line, 165 miles from the capital.

Field dispatches said all organized German resistance on the northern half of the front at least, had fallen apart, opening the way for a knockout drive on the enemy capital.

Ronald Clark, British United Press correspondent, reported that half the Nazi combat forces in the west already had been killed, wounded or captured, and that the remnants were so badly disorganized that they were no longer able to function as a coherent army.

Here are the highlights of today's action:

1. Field Marshal Montgomery's 21st Army Group scored a fresh advance of at least 16 miles today, but the location of its forward spearheads, driving to a junction with the U.S. 1st Army to cut off the Ruhr from Central Germany, was not revealed.

2. The U.S. 1st Army drove beyond Paderborn in its race to join Montgomery's men, and unconfirmed reports said the armies had already met.

3. The U.S. 3rd Army was approaching Kassel, kingpin of the Weser River Line, 165 miles from Berlin, where the Germans had planned their next stand behind the Rhine. One force was within 10 miles of Kassel.

4. The U.S. 7th Army crossed the Tauber River and captured Werbach, 65 miles due west of Nuernberg.

5. The U.S. 15th Army went into action with the 12th Army Group, including the U.S. 1st and 3rd Armies.

6. The French 1st Army crossed the Rhine.

"This is the Wehrmacht's final hour," London newspapers declared flatly.

British United Press war correspondent Ronald Clark reported that the remnants of five crack German divisions, perhaps 30,000 to 40,000 men, were in headlong flight to escape the closing jaws of the Allied trap.

ABSIE, the American broadcasting station in Europe, report-

Please Turn to Page Eight
See "Bitter Fighting"

Man Killed in Worst Gale

Strongest winds in Vancouver's history lashed the city with near-hurricane force during the night, causing one death, blowing down telephone and electric light poles and threatening harbor shipping.

Sea Island weather officials clocked the wind at 71 miles an hour at 1:15 a.m., strongest blast ever recorded in the district.

Michel Krupp, 25, 1940 Manitoba, was electrocuted when he seized a high tension wire dangling from a broken B.C. Electric line in front of his home early this morning.

Efforts of the inhalator crew to revive him proved in vain and he was pronounced dead on admission to General Hospital.

His wife told police Krupp got out of bed to investigate flashes outside the house and apparently took hold of the live wire.

His hands were badly burned.

It is believed he grabbed the wire to prevent it setting fire to his home.

Krupp, a discharged serviceman, had just returned from overseas.

Please Turn to Page Eight
See "Gale"

U.S. Soldier Killed in Action Has Mother Here

Cpl. Winfred A. Tillotson, whose mother, Mrs. F. E. Simpson, lives at 2515 Franklin, has been killed in action in the Pacific Theatre, the United States War Department in Washington announces.

Mexico City Race Results

FIRST RACE—Two and one-half furlongs:
Mon Teak (F. Fernandez) $10.40, $6.80, $6.60.
Scarface (eJnkins) $11.40, $6.60.
Hass V. Frances (Diaz) $10.60.
Time: 27 2-5 seconds.

SECOND RACE—Six furlongs:
Easy Scot (Andrade) $38.80, $14, $8.40.
Shasta Rap (Hall) $5.60, $3.60.
aNany Carroll (F. Fernandez) $4.
Time: 1:17.

Race Entries on Page 8

LATE FLASHES—

Canucks Threaten V-2 Rocket Bases

WITH THE 2ND BRITISH ARMY, MARCH 31—(Reuters)—Canadian troops fighting on the Dutch German frontier north of Emmerich, today had made advances which, if continued, should cut off the V-2 launching sites in Northwest Holland and probably free Britain from this form of attack.

This would be in the nature of a repeat performance for the Canadians, who last September swept up the French coast to capture the V-1 launching sites and Calais guns, thus relieving the aerial pressure from southern England.

Poland Gets Freed Danzig

LONDON, March 31—Reuters)—The former Free City of Danzig, a Warsaw Provincial Government decree quoted by Lublin radio said tonight, has been incorporated within the territory of Poland.

Reds Storm Across River

LONDON, March 31—(AP)—Marshal Rodio Y. Malinovsky's 2nd Ukraine Army has crossed the Van River in Southern Slovakia and captured Galanta, 28 miles east of Bratislava, Premier Stalin announced tonight.

Royals Whip St. Mikes, 3-1

TORONTO, March 31—(CP)—Montreal Royals scored one of the major upsets of the junior hockey season today by defeating Toronto St. Michael's 3-1 in the first game of the best-of-seven eastern Memorial Cup final.

IF WAR SUDDENLY ENDS

Job Officials Told to Be Ready for All Emergencies

National Selective Service officials in Vancouver today received authorization from Ottawa to implement special "emergency" measures planned for the early post-war period.

The authorization came in a telegram to D. J. Stephenson, assistant regional superintendent of NSS.

It is regarded here as a sign that Ottawa expects the end of the European war any day now.

The NSS plan for B.C., Mr. Stephenson said, sets up machinery for the quick transfer of staff to local offices throughout the region "where any heavy load develops."

He said extra staff might have to be taken on.

Mr. Stephenson said he did not expect any large readjustment in employment in B.C. at present, as activities for the Japanese war will probably keep industrial production at a peak for some time to come.

ReserveArmy 'Calling Up' Own Recruits

WINDSOR, Ont., March 31—(CP)—Men who have received military rejections in Military District No. 1 today were receiving notices from the commanding officer of the Second Battalion (Reserve Army) Essex Scottish Regiment advising them they are eligible for enlistment with the Reserve Army and are instructed to report to headquarters.

The Windsor Star said protests are being made against such notices, as military call-ups are not liable to service with the Reserve Army.

Whether they choose to join Reserve Army units is their own matter.

Ottawa officials told the Windsor Star, however, that Ottawa headquarters would like to assist Reserve units getting recruits and when a man is rejected, the officer interviewing him would "recommend" that he join the Reserve Army.

Protests arose here over a letter in which Lt.-Col. J. E. McCorkell, commander of the Second (Reserve) Battalion of the Essex Scottish, is quoted as writing to rejected men:

"We are in receipt of advice from headquarters, Military District No. 1, that yau have been rejected for active service on medical grounds. Your medical category is such that you are eligible for enlistment with the Reserve Army and you are hereby instructed to report to this headquarters."

Hoarders Blamed in Stocking Shortage

Enough women's stockings are being manufactured to take care of normal needs but too many are disappearing as a result of hoarding and "professional shopping." This statement was made today by Mrs. Mary Hurrell, honorary secretary of the Prices Board's women's regional advisory committee here, on her return from Ottawa, where she attended a national conference of women's committees.

Rationing of stockings, Mrs. Hurrell said, was "out of the question" because of possible complications in technique.

BULLETINS

WITH U.S. FIRST ARMY, MARCH 31—(BUP)—U.S. 1st and 3rd Army forces linked up today at Warburg, 23 miles southeast of Paderborn, and 175 miles southwest of Paderborn, and 175 miles southwest of Berlin.

WITH U.S. 3RD. ARMY, March 31—(BUP)—A U.S. 3rd Army spearhead today drove within five miles of Kassel, 165 miles southwest of Berlin.

WITH THE U.S. FIRST ARMY, March 31—(AP)—Lt.-Gen. Courtney H. Hodges third armored division battled in Paderborn today against enemy troops stubbornly trying to block the U.S. First Army's path to the north.

There was bitter fighting at the southern outskirts of the city—the first real resistance encountered by the First Army since it broke out of the Remagen bridgehead six days ago.

Worker Arrested In Fire Tragedy

WINNIPEG, March 31—(CP)—Police Chief George Smith announces that Peter Mider is being held on a charge of stealing 300 empty sugar bags from the Robinson and Webber warehouse, destroyed here by fire a week ago.

Two firemen were killed when trapped in the building.

NAZI RADIO GOES SILENT

LONDON, March 31—(CP)—All three German news broadcasting channels were blacked out for 15 minutes tonight without explanation, possibly indicating a move from Berlin to new locations farther from the onrushing Allied Armies.

Upon returning to the air the announcers reported that an Allied bombing fleet which had been over southwest Germany had departed. The stations were the DNB home and European channels and Transocean's foreign service.

Russian Tanks Racing Down Road to Vienna

By ROBERT MUSEL
Special to The Vancouver Sun

LONDON, March 31—(BUP)—The German fronts in Western Hungary and Southern Silesia tonight were cracking rapidly and the Red Army was closing upon Vienna, Wiener Neustadt and the South Austrian centre of Graz. (See map, page 8.)

Marshal Stalin announced that troops of Marshal Feodor I. Tolbukhin's 3rd Ukrainian Army swept into the southwest Hungarian border towns of Vasvar, Szentgottard and Kormend, within 38 miles of Graz.

To the north, Soviet forces were across the Austrian border and less than 40 miles from Vienna.

In southern Silesia, Ratibor, 18 miles north of Moravska Ostrava and Bieskau, 13 miles west of Ratibor, were captured.

One report placed some Soviet forces a little more than 20 miles from the industrial centre of

Please Turn to Page Eight
See "Russians"

Meatless Day Instead of Ration Looms

A hint of meat curtailment possibly taking the form of a meatless day or days, is seen in a prices board statement from Ottawa Friday freezing 50 per cent of present stocks of certain grades of chickens in cold storage warehouses in Canada.

The order requires cold storage warehouses to set aside 50 per cent of present stocks of chickens falling in the "A," "B," and "B, milk fed" grades and weighing four pounds and over. No indication as to the disposition of these stocks is made.

The order does not affect stocks of chickens falling within these grades and weights now in retailers' hands. Turkeys, ducks or other fowl are not included in the order.

The "freeze" order, according to the prices board statement, is to assure supplies for the armed forces and other essential needs.

11 Brigadiers Freed in Push

21ST ARMY GROUP HEADQUARTERS, March 31—(AP)—The Allies overran an officers' prison camp Thursday and liberated 11 British brigadiers and three war correspondents, including Godfrey Anderson of the Associated Press, who was captured by the Germans in Africa.

Two Injured in Auto Collision

Two persons were injured when their autos collided at Twelfth and Kingsway Friday afternoon.

Injured were Miss E. Vail, 1637 Nelson, and J. Hamilton, 2260 East Broadway.

Miss Vail suffered shock and abrasions and Mr. Hamilton, shock and badly-bruised knees.

Conveyed to hospital by Kingsway Ambulance, their condition today is reported "fairly good."

And Inside—

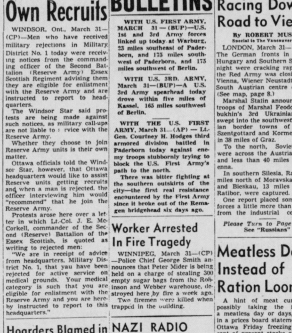

ROOSEVELT DEAD

THE VANCOUVER DAILY PROVINCE

51st YEAR—NO. 15 VANCOUVER, B.C., THURSDAY, APRIL 12, 1945—24 PAGES PRICE 5 CENTS

Succumbs To Stroke

By JACK BELL.

WASHINGTON, April 12. -- (AP) -- The White House announced late today that President Roosevelt had died of cerebral hemo rhage

The death oc[illegible] this afternoon at Warm Springs, Ga., a White House statement said

"The four Roosevelt boys in the service have been sent a message by their mother, which said that the President slept away this afternoon. He did his job to the end, as he would want to do.

"Bless you all and all our love, added Mrs. Roosevelt. She signed the message, 'Mother.'

"Funeral services will be held Saturdya afternoon in the east room of the White House. Interment will be at Hyde Park Sunday afternoon.

On Last Lap To Berlin

WASHINGTON, April 12. --- (AP) --- High army officials told senators toaday the end of organized fighting in Germany probably will come within a few days.

WEIMAR, Germany, April 12.— (AP)— War correspondents rolling eastward through hills topped by ruins of ancient castles in southern Germany with the 3rd Army have not heard a rifle shot in the last 24 hours.

Except for a fight at Erfurt, there was no sign of war. Jeeps, trucks and tanks sped along the broad six-lane autobahns.

(Compiled from Late Despatches to The Vancouver Daily Province.)

PARIS, April 12.—United States 9th Army tanks stormed across the Elbe River today and started to roll along a six-lane superhighway on the last 57 miles toward Berlin.

It was the first crossing of the great German river by a foe of Germany since Napoleon.

Associated Press correspondent Robert Eunson reported from near Magdeburg, where the crossing was made: "The 2nd Armored Division can be at the Brandenburg Gate in Berlin by tomorrow night or Saturday morning, unless the Germans swiftly shift forces from the Russian front."

One report said the Germans are shifting their battered 6th Panzer Army from the eastern front.

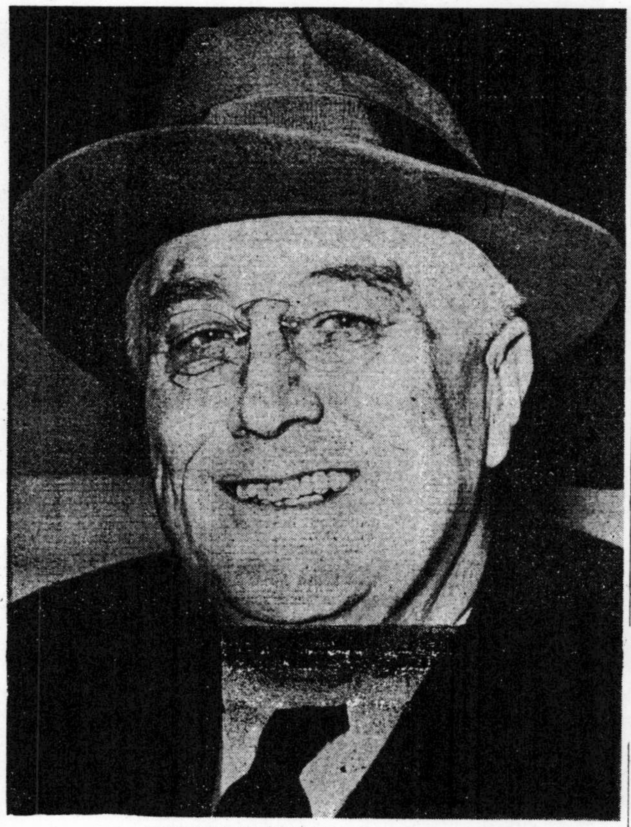

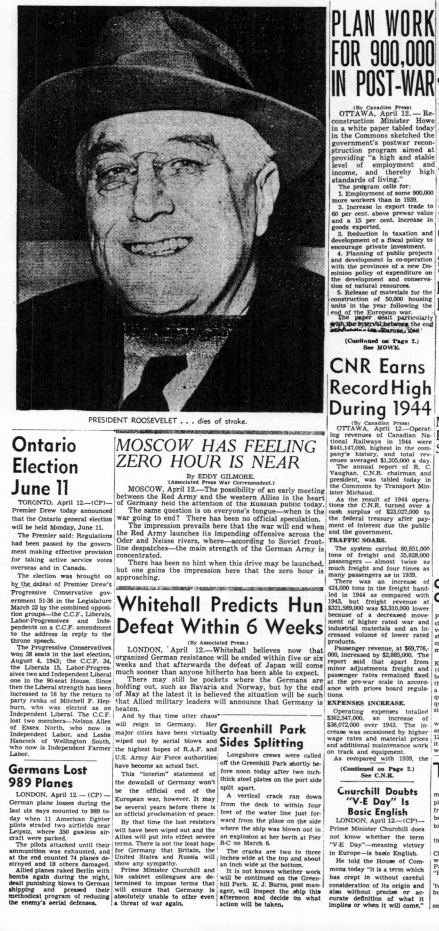

PRESIDENT ROOSEVELT . . . dies of stroke.

PLAN WORK FOR 900,000 IN POST-WAR

(By Canadian Press)

OTTAWA, April 12.—Reconstruction Minister Howe in a white paper tabled today in the Commons sketched the government's postwar reconstruction program aimed at providing "a high and stable level of employment and income, and thereby high standards of living."

The program calls for:

1. Employment of some 900,000 more workers than in 1939.
2. Increase in export trade to 60 per cent. above prewar value and a 15 per cent. increase in goods exported.
3. Reduction in taxation and development of a fiscal policy to encourage private investment.
4. Planning of public projects and development in co-operation with the provinces of a new Dominion policy of expenditure on the development and conservation of natural resources.
5. Release of materials for the construction of 50,000 housing units in the year following the end of the European war.

The paper dealt particularly with the interval between the end [illegible]

(Continued on Page 2.)
See HOWE.

Final BULLETINS

Clash "Unthinkable"

OTTAWA, April 12. — (CP) — Any attempt to pit blocs of discharged veterans against organized labor would be "unthinkable," Group Capt. S. N. F. Chant, veterans' department director-general of rehabilitation, said here today on his return from Montebello, Que., where he had addressed Canadian industrialists.

Charge Denied

LOS ANGELES, April 12. — (AP)—Charles Chaplin from the witness stand today reiterated his denial that he is the father of Carol Ann Berry, 18-months-old daughter of Joan Berry, his former screen protege.

U.S. Sub Lost

WASHINGTON, April 12. — (AP)—The submarine Scamp and a large support landing craft have been lost in the Pacific, the navy announced today.

Hundreds Die In Italian Blast

ROME, April 12.—(AP) Hundreds of Italian civil[illegible] British [illegible] men w[illegible] harbor [illegible] by the explosion [illegible] American Liberty [illegible] with munitions.

A government spokesman placed the toll of Italian dead at 267 and the injured at about 1600.

Goebbels Admits War Near End

(By Associated Press)

LONDON, April 12.—(AP)—Nazi Propaganda Minister Goebbels declared today that "the war can not last much longer in my opinion." The statement was made in a German broadcast.

In an article in his weekly Das Reich, Goebbels said: "We have sunk very low."

Although conceding that Germany's enormous "losses of territory in the east, west and south" had brought the nation to a crisis, the propagandist still tried to hold out hope over salvaging something from the Reich's military collapse.

SEES ALLIED SPLIT.

"On the other hand," he said, "our enemies must finish this war quickly or they will stand no chance of winning this to-be-or-not-to-be struggle at all."

Harping his familiar theme that the Allied coalition was tottering, Goebbels said, "The alliance can only be kept up because the peoples know that the war will come to its conclusion very soon.

"To gain time in this phase of the war means to gain everything," he said, exhorting the people to "leave no stone unturned" in their defense against the Allies.

"National resistance is not something for the Wehrmacht only," he wrote. "It is something for the entire German people. We all must swear rather to die than live under a foreign yoke. We must rather risk the most hazardous enterprise than to resign."

Merchants Seek Regulations to Slow Sale of Extracts

Regulations to control the mounting sale of lemon and other extracts and hair tonics, which is being used for alcoholic drinking, are foreshadowed by representations made in Ottawa by George R. Matthews, B.C. provincial secretary of the Retail Merchants' Association of Canada.

A conference is being arranged by Major-Gen. R. Brock Chisholm, deputy minister of national health, with representatives of the health and welfare departments of the provinces.

Fine Days, Cold Nights Scheduled Today, Friday

Frost painted Vancouver with a white coat during the night and greased the streets with ice, but sunshine melted it all away by midmorning.

Fine clear weather is scheduled for both today and Friday, although the temperature is expected to drop to 34 degrees during the night.

CNR Earns Record High During 1944

(By Canadian Press)

OTTAWA, April 12.—Operating revenues of Canadian National Railways in 1944 were $441,147,000, highest in the company's history, and total revenues averaged $1,205,000 a day.

The annual report of R. C. Vaughan, C.N.R. chairman and president, was tabled today in the Commons by Transport Minister Michaud.

As the result of 1944 operations the C.N.R. turned over a cash surplus of $23,027,000 to the federal treasury after payment of interest due the public and the government.

TRAFFIC SOARS.

The system carried 80,851,000 tons of freight and 35,928,000 passengers — almost twice as much freight and four times as many passengers as in 1939.

There was an increase of 424,000 tons in the freight handled in 1944 as compared with 1943, but freight revenue at $321,589,000 was $3,310,000 lower because of a decreased movement of higher rated war and industrial materials and an increased volume of lower rated products.

Passenger revenue, at $69,776,000, increased by $2,885,000. The report said that apart from minor adjustments freight and passenger rates remained fixed at the pre-war scale in accordance with prices board regulations.

EXPENSES INCREASE.

Operating expenses totalled $362,547,000, an increase of $38,072,000 over 1943. The increase was occasioned by higher wage rates and material prices and additional maintenance work on track and equipment.

As compared with 1939, the

(Continued on Page 2.)
See C.N.R.

Commons Hears Old Strike Echo

OTTAWA, April 12.—(CP) — Pension rights of Canadian Pacific Railway employees involved in the Winnipeg general strike of 1919 were the subject of a question today in the Commons.

Prime Minister Mackenzie King told Stanley Knowles (C.C.F.-Winnipeg North Centre) he could not say offhand whether the railway unions had asked for a Royal Commission on the question, but said if such a request was made it would be considered.

He said he recalled dealing with a similar problem in 1910 as minister of labor and it took 12 years to get justice done, but it was done. He was sure justice would be done in this case

Post-mortem Fails To Explain Death

Dr. Stewart Murray, city health officer, said today that a post-mortem failed to reveal cause of death of 11-year-old Robert Thompson, 3355 West Thirty-second, who collapsed in class at Lord Kitchener School Tuesday and died without regaining consciousness.

Army Train Due Here Saturday

An army train bringing 21 officers, three nursing sisters and 39 other ranks is expected to arrive in Vancouver over C.P.R. lines at 9:20 a.m. Saturday.

Ontario Election June 11

TORONTO, April 12.—(CP)—Premier Drew today announced that the Ontario general election will be held Monday, June 11.

The Premier said: Regulations had been passed by the government making effective provision for taking active service votes overseas and in Canada.

The election was brought on by the defeat of Premier Drew's Progressive Conservative government 51-36 in the Legislature March 22 by the combined opposition groups—the C.C.F., Liberals, Labor-Progressives and Independents on a C.C.F. amendment to the address in reply to the throne speech.

The Progressive Conservatives won 38 seats in the last election, August 4, 1943; the C.C.F. 34, the Liberals 15, Labor-Progressives two and Independent Liberal one in the 90-seat House. Since then the Liberal strength has been increased to 16 by the return to party ranks of Mitchell F. Hepburn, who was elected as an Independent Liberal. The C.C.F. lost two members—Nelson Alles of Essex North, who now is Independent Labor, and Leslie Hancock of Wellington South, who now is Independent Farmer Labor.

Germans Lost 989 Planes

LONDON, April 12. — (CP) — German plane losses during the last six days mounted to 989 today when 11 American fighter pilots strafed two airfields near Leipsiz, where 350 gas-less aircraft were parked.

The pilots attacked until their ammunition was exhausted, and at the end counted 74 planes destroyed and 18 others damaged.

Allied planes raked Berlin with bombs again during the night, dealt punishing blows to German shipping and pressed their methodical program of reducing the enemy's aerial defenses.

MOSCOW HAS FEELING ZERO HOUR IS NEAR

By EDDY GILMORE.
(Associated Press War Correspondent.)

MOSCOW, April 12.—The possibility of an early meeting between the Red Army and the western Allies in the heart of Germany held the attention of the Russian public today.

The same question is on everyone's tongue—when is the war going to end? There has been no official speculation.

The impression prevails here that the war will end when the Red Army launches its impending offensive across the Oder and Neisse rivers, where—according to Soviet front-line despatches—the main strength of the German Army is concentrated.

There has been no hint when this drive may be launched, but one gains the impression here that the zero hour is approaching.

Whitehall Predicts Hun Defeat Within 6 Weeks

(By Associated Press.)

LONDON, April 12.—Whitehall believes now that organized German resistance will be ended within five or six weeks and that afterwards the defeat of Japan will come much sooner than anyone hitherto has been able to expect.

There may still be pockets where the Germans are holding out, such as Bavaria and Norway, but by the end of May at the latest it is believed the situation will be such that Allied military leaders will announce that Germany is beaten.

And by that time utter chaos will reign in Germany. Her major cities have been virtually wiped out by aerial blows and the highest hopes of R.A.F. and U.S. Army Air Force authorities have become an actual fact.

This "interim" statement of the downfall of Germany won't be the official end of the European war, however. It may be several years before there is an official proclamation of peace.

By that time the last resisters will have been wiped out and the Allies will put into effect severe terms. There is not the least hope for Germany that Britain, the United States and Russia will show any sympathy.

Prime Minister Churchill and his cabinet colleagues are determined to impose terms that will ensure that Germany is absolutely unable to offer even a threat of war again.

Greenhill Park Sides Splitting

Longshore crews were called off the Greenhill Park shortly before noon today after two inch-thick steel plates on the port side split apart.

A vertical crack ran down from the deck to within four feet of the water line just forward from the place on the side where the ship was blown out in an explosion at her berth at Pier B-C on March 6.

The cracks are two to three inches wide at the top and about an inch wide at the bottom.

It is not known whether work will be continued on the Greenhill Park. K. J. Burns, post manager, will inspect the ship this afternoon and decide on what action will be taken.

Churchill Doubts "V-E Day" Is Basic English

LONDON, April 12.—(CP)—Prime Minister Churchill does not know whether the term "V-E Day"—meaning victory in Europe—is basic English.

He told the House of Commons today "it is a term which has crept in without careful consideration of its origin and also without precise or accurate definition of what it implies or when it will come."

Threw "Bombs" Into Sea

Two forgotten pieces of munitions cargo for the Philippines, found deep in the hold of freighter SS. Windermere Park, berthed at Pier B-C, caused a brief sabotage scare.

R.C.M.P. investigation cleared the matter up in short order.

Tuesday morning, Kenneth Chandler, shipyard electrician working aboard Windermere Park, found two tins (marked "Hand Grenade").

They were in No. 1 hold, 'tween-deck, wedged against the bulkhead.

Chandler took them to a guard on deck and on his advice threw the tins into the harbor.

R.C.M.P. officials heard about it at noon today and sent two men to investigate.

They found that, on her last trip, Windermere Park carried munitions to the Philippines, sailing out of Seattle. Part of the cargo consisted of grenades, packed two or three to a canister.

The tins found by Chandler, and described by him to the R.C.M.P., correspond to the grenade canisters.

They had been forgotten during unloading operations, or cached away by someone who wanted a souvenir.

147

TRUMAN NOW PRESIDENT —PLEDGES SAME POLICY

Vancouver News-Herald

VOL. 12, NO. 298 VANCOUVER, B.C., FRIDAY, APRIL 13, 1945 PRICE 5c

FDR'S DEATH SHOCKS WORLD

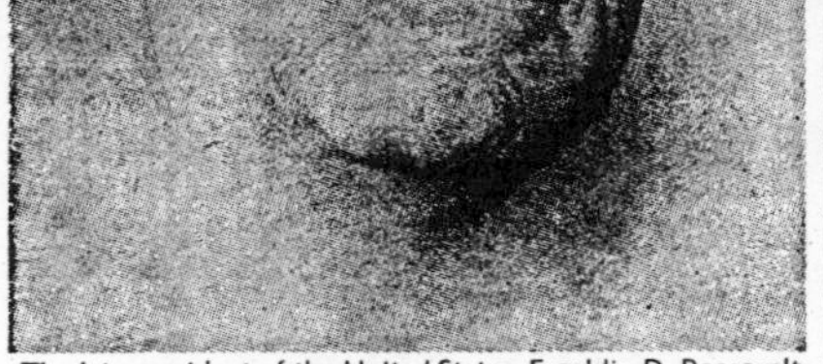

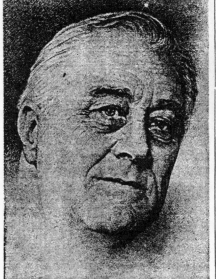

The late president of the United States, Franklin D. Roosevelt

'I Have A Headache' --FDR's Last Words

WARM SPRINGS, Ga., April 13.—(AP)—President Franklin D. Roosevelt, 63, died unexpectedly Thursday at 1:35 p.m. (P.D.T.) of a cerebral hemorrhage.

The funeral will be in the White House east room in Washington on Saturday.

Burial will be at the Roosevelt ancestral home at Hyde Park, N.Y., Sunday. The body will not lie in state.

Mr. Roosevelt was sitting in front of a fireplace in the little White House here atop Pine Mountain when the attack struck him.

His last words, spoken to Cmdr. Harold Bruenn, naval physician, were: "I have a terrific headache."

Mr. Bruenn described its as a massive cerebral hemorrhage.

The president's Negro valet and a Filipino messboy carried him to his bedroom.

He was unconscious at the end.

It came without pain.

CAME TO REST

Mr. Roosevelt, in the third month of his fourth term as president, came here three weeks ago to rest.

The death removed from world councils one of the Big Three—Roosevelt, Churchill and Stalin—who worked together to win the war and laid joint plans for keeping the peace.

Dr. Bruenn said he saw the president Thursday morning and he was in excellent spirits.

"At 11 o'clock," Dr. Bruenn added, "he was sitting in a chair while sketches were being made of him by an architect. He suddenly complained of a very severe occipital headache (back of the head).

"Within a very few minutes he lost consciousness. He was seen by me at 11.30, 15 minutes after the episode had started.

"He did not regain consciousness and he died at 1:35 p.m."

Only others present in the cottage were Cmdr. George Fox, White House pharmacist and long an attendant on the President; White House Secretary William D. Hassett, Miss Grace Vully, confidential secretary; and two cousins, Miss Laura Delano and Miss Margaret Suckley.

Bruenn said he called Vice-Admiral Ross T. McIntyre, Navy surgeon general and White House physician, in Washington and that Admiral McIntyre in turn called Dr. James E. Paullin, of Atlanta, an internal medicine practitioner and honorary consultant to the Navy surgeon general.

Dr. Paullin was present when Cmdr. Bruenn gave the statement of the cause of death to reporters of the three national news services.

Mr. Hassett gave newspapermen the first announcement.

BULLETINS

TORNADOES KILL 22 IN OKLAHOMA

OKLAHOMA CITY, April 13.—(AP)—A series of tornadoes ripped through Oklahoma Thursday, killing at least 22 persons, injuring hundreds of others and causing heavy damage in the cities of Muskogee and Antlers.

Reds Cut Lifeline

LONDON, April 13.—(AP)—Russian armored forces cut the last lifeline to the north of Vienna and left only a seven-mile escape corridor for German troops in the Austrian capital.

5,000 prisoners were taken by the Russians in house-to-house fighting in Vienna. Berlin issued a report that German troops were withdrawing from the Danube Valley toward Hitler's Bavarian mountain fortress at Berchtesgaden. This report was not confirmed by Moscow.

Tank Fight Rages

LONDON, April 13.—British tanks locked in a heavy battle with German Tiger tanks along the Santerno River as the 8th Army surged westward from three bridgeheads.

New amphibious landings were reported north of the new bridgehead with the landing forces linking with other units astride the Reno river.

Won't Delay 'Frisco Parley

WASHINGTON, April 13.—(AP)—President Truman announced Thursday night that the United Nations conference called for April 25 will go on as scheduled.

A White House secretary, Jonathan Daniels, said President Truman, sworn in late Thursday, had authorized State Secretary Stettinius to make a statement that the United Nations meeting will be held as planned.

Several delegations already have arrived in the U.S. President Roosevelt had planned to address the meeting.

It was not known immediately whether President Truman will travel to San Francisco to speak.

The immediate indications were, however, that if the conference goes on as scheduled, Mr. Truman will be there as president to follow the lead taken by his predecessor.

BACKED BY POLICY

Consistently throughout the last campaign, Mr. Truman endorsed wholeheartedly the Roosevelt foreign policies, particularly as they pertained to the organization of a world league to preserve the peace.

Friends said Mr. Truman may be expected to carry out fully the pledges that President Roosevelt made at the big-three conference at Yalta.

These included an agreement with Prime Minister Churchill and Premier Stalin on voting procedure of the proposed world security council.

Truman has supported without reservation the President's plans for the international organization.

As a stunned capital sought to weigh the implications of Mr. Roosevelt's passing, Mr. Truman issued this one-sentence statement:

"The world may be sure that we will prosecute the war on both fronts, east and west, with all the vigor we possess, to a successful conclusion."

A short time earlier Mr. Truman had announced that the United Nations conference would open as scheduled on April 25 to draft a plan for a world organization.

Thus Mr. Truman acted immediately to carry out the twin objectives of winning the war and seeking a lasting peace.

Crowds stood silently outside the White House. Flags on embassies and other public buildings dipped to half staff.

The 60-year-old former Missouri county judge took the oath amid epochal world events—at a time when Germany is tottering and the Allies are getting ready to throw their full strength at Japan.

Mackenzie King To Attend Funeral

OTTAWA, April 13.—(CP)—It is expected Prime Minister Mackenzie King will go to Washington for President Roosevelt's funeral on Saturday, but arrangements have not yet been completed.

Mr. King was a lifelong personal friend of the President as well as a close associate in the business of the two countries during the time both were in office.

Allies Can Enter Berlin Whenever Command Given

PARIS, April 13.—(AP)—U.S. 9th Army tanks smashed across the Elbe River on a six-mile front just 57 miles from Berlin Thursday and U. S. 1st and 3rd Armies in sweeps of nearly 50 miles thundered at the gates of the great city of Leipzig, 75 miles southwest of the capital.

A field dispatch said only orders from the Army's commander were needed to send the 2nd armored division smashing on into Berlin, which could possibbly be reached tomorrow. Wholly unconfirmed French reports said Allied parachute trops had been dropped at Brandenburg, barely 20 miles from Greater Berlin.

Greenhill Park Suddenly Cracks

Battered hulk of the S.S. Greenhill Park was towed across the Inlet from its berth at Ballantyne Pier, about 6:45 p.m. Thursday and beached near North Van. Ship Repairs, just west of the salvage dock.

Official secrecy clamped down on S.S. Greenhill Park Thursday as two large cracks in the port side of the vessel reportedly drove longshoremen ashore at noon.

"As far as we are concerned, our work is finished there," said an official of Empire Stevedoring Company. "We came ashore for the dinner hour."

B.C., City Leaders Mourn Roosevelt

Deep regrets at the death of President Roosevelt, coupled with tributes as to his abilities as a statesman and a leader, were expressed by Premier John Hart and Mayor J. W. Cornett, Thursday.

Said the premier:

"This is one of the greatest tragedies of our time; the world has lost a great man."

"There are few men who have made such an outstanding contribution to the welfare of mankind. His passing must be listed among the casualties of this war."

"He joins the noble dead who paid the supreme sacrifice that liberty, democracy and peace might be preserved and handed on as a priceless heritage to future generations."

"During his tenure of office, a period of more than 12 years, he made history for the United States such as the nation has never known before."

"His unstinting energies most assuredly sapped his strength. It it indeed sad that it was not given to him to witness a world at peace, for that would have been the fulfilment of his work."

"It was my privilege to meet the president when he visited British Columbia some years ago. I found him to be of gracious disposition, deeply imbued with the spirit of public service and a man inspired with a great vision of a world of nations living at peace, one with the other."

"I join with all freedom-loving citizens throughout the world in mourning his loss."

Mayor Cornett said:

"Words fail to express the personal loss every citizen of Vancouver feels at the death of President Roosevelt."

"While he was president of the United States, Canadians regarded him as affectionately as the most loyal supporter of his own country."

"He was Great Britain's friend and a staunch friend of Canada. We revered him for his leadership in the war and for his great humanitarian work in general."

"I am firmly convinced that President Roosevelt will be sincerely mourned in Canada as he will be in his own country."

"He will take his place in history alongside Lincoln as one of the great presidents of the United States and one of the world's foremost leaders."

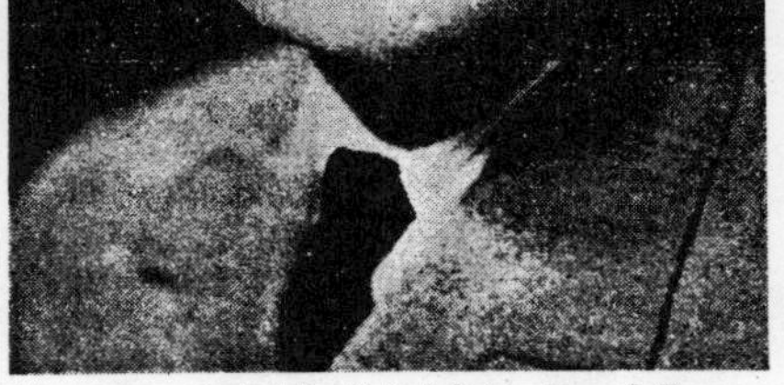

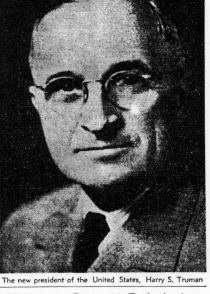

The new president of the United States, Harry S. Truman

What Sort Of Man Is New President?

By ERNEST B. VACARRO

(Member of The Associated Press Senate staff, who travelled with President Truman during Truman's campaign for the vice-presidency last fall.)

WASHINGTON, April 13.—(AP)—Harry S. Truman entered the White House last night in one of the most critical periods in his country's history with humble confidence that he is big enough to meet the burdens of a wartime presidency.

Those of us who travelled with him on a trans-continental speech-making tour for the vice-presidency last fall and who were in daily conference with him before and after his election, think of him as a man:

1. Whose courage has been demonstrated time and again as a campaigner and as chairman of the Senate war investigating committee who never hesitated to criticize those high in administration favor.
2. Whose knowledge of his own limitations is such that he never hesitates to call on others whose qualifications on matters of high importance he may consider superior to his own.
3. Whose ability to "pick the brains" of others raised the Truman committee to a status rarely enjoyed by a congressional committee.
4. Whose friendliness and modesty is the same as it was when he entered the vice presidency and as it probably was when he was a farm boy down in Missouri.

ASSAILED ISOLATIONISTS

During the campaign, Mr. Truman called repeatedly for the defeat of eight Republican candidates for senator whom he termed "isolationists."

Once a reporter asked Mr. Truman whether, in the tragic event of Mr. Roosevelt's death, the 60-year-old Missourian thought himself capable of stepping into his shoes.

Never a question dodger, Mr. Truman promptly came back with that assertion that many newspapers had said he had a knowledge of the war program second only to that of Mr. Roosevelt himself.

Sarah E. Spencer Passes Suddenly

Sarah Ellen Spencer, 2150 W. 49th, wife of Mr. Chris Spencer, president of David Spencer Ltd., died suddenly at her home, Thursday.

An active member of the Ryerson United Church, Mrs. Spencer was born in Yale and came to Vancouver in 1912, following her marriage in Victoria 53 years ago.

Besides her husband, she is survived by a son, Christopher Lloyd, living in Australia; two daughters, Mrs. Fred McGregor, 1525 W. 49th and Mrs. William Armstrong, 6468 E. Boulevard and seven grandchildren.

Funeral services will be held Saturday at 2 p.m. in Ryerson United Church, Rev. E. D. Braden, D.D., officiating. Burial will follow in Mountain View cemetery, in the family plot.

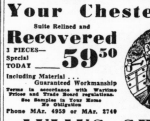

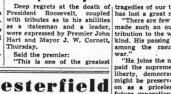

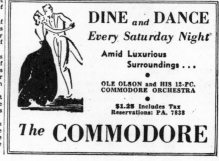

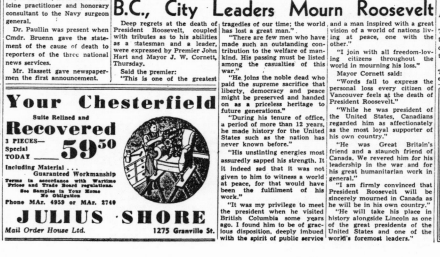

THE VANCOUVER DAILY PROVINCE ★★★★★ FINAL

51st YEAR—NO. 23 VANCOUVER, B.C., SATURDAY, APRIL 21, 1945—48 PAGES PRICE 10 CENTS

RUSS IN BERLIN

★ ★

Soviets 3 Miles Inside

Final BULLETINS

NEW YORK, April 21.—(AP)—A $3 weekly wage increase and a revison of the wage progression schedule were announced as the main points of an agreement which has ended the threat of a strike among 18,000 New York City telephone operators.

General Shot

WITH U.S. 1ST ARMY, in Germany, April 21.—(AP)—American tankmen shot a high ranking German general to death in the Ruhr pocket when he and his men from a house and killed a U.S. soldier with a machine pistol.

Strike Still On

TORONTO, April 21.—(CP)—Hopes of settling a strike of 2500 workers at the new Toronto plant of the Goodyear Tire and Rubber Co., were shattered today after a mass meeting of the striking employees voted to continue the strike until the company agrees to re-establish refreshment concessions to women workers at the plant.

Bigamy Charges

WOODSTOCK, Ont., April 21.—(CP)—Pte. William C. Harington, 31, was brought to Woodstock to face trial on a charge of bigamy. He is alleged to have gone through a bigamous marriage at Tillsonburg, Ont., in 1939 and to have subsequently entered into two marriage contracts in the west.

Churches Hit

VATICAN CITY, April 21.—(AP)—The Vatican press service reported today that the air bombing of Tokyo and Japanese-occupied areas of China has caused "grave damage" to church properties.

Find Hun Gas Dump

PARIS, April 21. — (CP) — American troops have overrun one of the greatest ammunition and gas dumps discovered since the Allied invasion of Europe. It was near Altenhane, Germany, and contained 90 huge bunkers filled with toxic gas and 27,000 poison gas shells.

"Twice-dead" City Man Revived Again

Twice in 10 days—according to Kingsway Ambulance officials and an inhalator crew—R. E. Tuttle, 53, of 116 West Hastings, "has been brought back from the dead."

He is a last war veteran.

Early today a Kingsway Ambulance was called to a downtown cafe to pick up a man who was ill. It was Mr. Tuttle.

On the way to Shaughnessy Military Hospital, according to Don Howell and his partner on the ambulance, Jack Leggatt, the patient stopped breathing. They could not feel his pulse.

"His eyes went glassy," Leggatt said. "Don immediately started artificial respiration, and kept it up for five minutes, until we reached the hospital.

"We got him breathing again, and he came around when a heart stimulant was administered at the hospital.

Ten days ago, Mr. Tuttle collapsed at the Cave Cabaret.

A fire department inhalator crew found that he had stopped breathing.

They worked over him for an hour and a half before he revived.

Today, hospital authorities say Mr. Tuttle's condition is "good."

PARIS SAYS LINKUP MADE AT DRESDEN

LONDON, April 21.—(CP) — The Paris radio said tonight, without any qualification, American and Russian forces have joined in the Dresden district. The Brussels radio said the Red Army has entered Dresden.

(Compiled from late despatches to The Vancouver Daily Province)

PARIS, April 21. — "The muffled thunder of Russian guns" was heard by troops of the U.S. 9th Army in their Elbe bridgehead today.

The dramatic linkup between the armies of the western Allies and the Soviet Union in the very heart of Germany is imminent.

Moscow despatches placed the two forces only 25 miles apart. Unconfirmed messages reported patrols of the two armies already have made contact.

MEETING PLANNED.

Allied Supreme Headquarters said the hookup between the eastern and western Allies will be the result of co-ordinated planning with the juncture carefully planned to prevent confusion in the meshing of forces.

The prisoner bag in the west

(Continued on Page 2.) See LINKUP.

City Planning Great Reception For Dieppe Hero

Mayor Cornett will discuss with City Council Monday plans for a reception for Lieut.-Col. Cecil Merritt, Canada's first Victoria Cross winner, whose return to Vancouver from a German prison camp is expected in the near future.

A large semi-public committee headed by City Council representatives, veterans' organizations and service club delegates, is favored at City Hall to welcome Col. Merritt.

Vancouver-Burrard Progressive Conservative Association, whose candidate Col. Merritt is for the coming federal election, sent the hero a telegram. It read:

"All delighted over your release, inspiring us to greater efforts on behalf of yourself and the future of Canada."

Weatherman Sights Fair Sunday—If It Doesn't Rain

Scattered showers today will give way to partly cloudy skies on Sunday—maybe.

The weatherman is reluctant to predict any sunshine for Sunday, however, because of the unsettled condition of the air. Moist clouds hanging over the city are likely to spill their cargoes on the city at any time.

Early today, fog shrouded the North Shore mountains but the snow is good for skiing.

Highest temperature expected today is 53 degrees, the lowest tonight, 42 degrees, and the highest Sunday, 57 degrees.

Sunday's forecast is: Partly cloudy, becoming cloudy towards evening, slightly warmer, winds moderate.

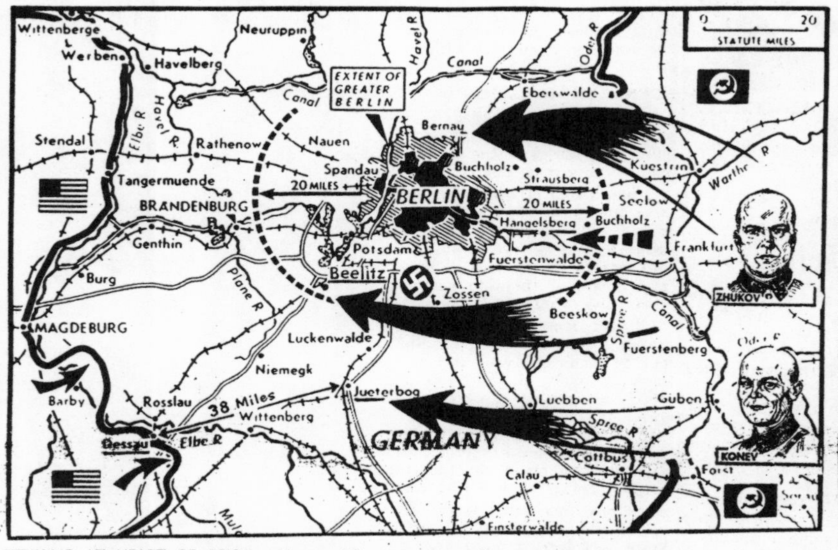

STRIKING AT HEART OF REICH — Masses of Russian tanks and men are smashing into Berlin proper, according to the German radio. The northwestern prong of the Soviet assault (designated by uppermost arrow), has penetrated three miles into the city. The other two prongs have entered suburbs directly east and south of the capital. Marshal Konev has outflanked the city's defenses with a breakthrough drive to Jueterbog.

WAR LOAN ARMY READY

An army of 18,000 salesmen will ask 11,000,000 Canadians to invest $1,350,000,000 "in the best"—Canada's Eighth Victory Loan—when the campaign officially opens Monday.

The over-all objective is an all-time high mark, $50,000,000 above the quota set in the Seventh Victory Loan.

Of this, a minimum objective of $675,000,000 is set for individual subscriptions, an increase of $75,000,000 over the quota in the last campaign.

Each of the 600 loan units throughout Canada has been carrying on extensive organizational work with a view to topping the total of 3,300,000 applications in last fall's drive.

British Columbia has been given a healthy slice of the record objective, with a quota of $135,000,000. Of this $60,000,000 will be from general canvass and payroll deductions.

200,000 CALLS.

More than 300 salesmen will make 200,000 calls in Vancouver to sell the city's quota of $25,300,000 worth of Victory Bonds, an increase of $2,300,000 over the seventh Victory Loan, when 107,294 persons invested an average of $264.

In 205 payroll plants in the city volunteer salesmen will canvass fellow-employees.

Although Vancouver's bond sales campaign will not officially get under way until Monday morning, when J. L. Trumbull,

(Continued on Page 2.) See VICTORY.

Soviet Ship, Laden With Delicacies, Sent to Parley

SAN FRANCISCO, April 21.—(AP)—Russia has sent to San Francisco an entertainment ship well loaded with a cargo of caviar, vodka and other makings of many gay Soviet parties during the United Nations Conference, apparently planning to set the entertainment pace for the parley, which opens Wednesday.

"We're Beginning To Live Again"

—Lieut.-Col. Merritt, V.C.

By FRANK LOW.
(Canadian Press Staff Writer.)

A CANADIAN RECEPTION CENTRE, Southern England, April 21.—Headed by Lt.-Col. Cecil Merritt, V.C., of Vancouver, a half-hundred men for whom the war has been eight hours of blazing battle and nearly three years of prison-camp rigors, returned today from Germany to England.

Men from all the Canadian regiments engaged in the great "Reconnaissance in Force" at Dieppe August 19, 1942, were among the group of freed prisoners. There were men from the Essex Scottish of Windsor, Ont.; The South Saskatchewan Regiment, Weyburn, Sask.; The Royal Regiment of Canada, Toronto; Les Fusiliers Mont-Royal, Montreal—but outstanding among them was the tall, muscular figure of Col. Merritt.

Sunshine After Prison Shadows

This shy, young-looking soldier who won the Empire's highest award for valor—first given a Canadian Army man in this war—for fearless leadership on Dieppe's fire-swept beaches, summed up the feelings of his men when he looked at the sunny English countryside around this camp and said: "We're all beginning to live again."

Then, standing in the shade of a flowering lilac bush, the man who only six days ago was behind barbed wire told what had happened to him since a German bullet pierced his shoulder and led to his capture that day at Dieppe.

German treatment in the prison camp, which was located near Leipzig, was "mean and shabby," he said, "although the officers lived fairly well."

Col. Merritt himself appeared to have stood the privation of prison life remarkably well, looking tanned and fit.

Just before the camp was liberated this week an order came through to march the prisoners deeper into Germany.

(Continued on Page 2.) See MERRITT.

BOLOGNA CAPTURED

ROME, April 21. — Bologna, first major objective of the all-out Allied offensive in northern Italy, fell today to troops of the 5th and 8th Armies.

Polish troops of the British 8th Army, under Maj.-Gen. Bohuszszyska, and the United States 91st and 34th Divisions all entered the historic Italian fortress city on the southern edge of the Po Valley at the foot of the Apennines.

With Bologna captured the major German defense position south of the Po River was eliminated and the enemy once again moved northward.

Gen. Mark W. Clark, Allied ground commander, said his 15th Army group now stands "inside the gateway to the Po plain poised to destroy the Germans who continue to enslave and exploit northern Italy.

The fall of the city of 270,000, which had blocked Allied troops for months, came quickly after 5th Army troops had severed the important Bologna-Modena highway northwest of the city yesterday.

WASHINGTON, April 21.—(AP)—The United States war department announced today that 12 members of Congress will be flown to Germany within the next few days to view evidence of Nazi atrocities.

SMUTS SEES HOPE IN PARLEY

By J. W. DAVIS.
Associated Press Staff Correspondent

SAN FRANCISCO, April 21.—Russian delegates to the United Nations Conference have already achieved one success—they were permitted to buy American-made shoes. Ration Board No. 17 issued the Russians 18 special shoe stamps.

• • •

Twelve military bands set out to learn the national anthems of all the participating countries. They did—except for Saudi Arabia and Syria, which have no national hymn. For Saudi Arabia, a military march will be played; for Syria, an old folk song.

• • •

Jan Christian Smuts, South African Prime Minister and the first major delegate to arrive, said he had "very good expectations of the work we will accomplish."

"I believe this is possibly the most hopeful step we have taken," he told newsmen, "and I feel we must succeed here."

Smuts, the only delegate who played a leading part in Versailles, when the old League of Nations was set up, flew across the country in a Royal Air Force plane.

Foreign Minister Eden declared in Washington: "We are in complete agreement on all points" after a conference with State Secretary Stettinius.

The two presumably discussed the attitude they will take on the ticklish Polish problem at their meeting with the Soviet foreign commissar, V. M. Molotov, who was expected to arrive here tonight or tomorrow.

President Truman will broadcast from the White House Wednesday on a half-hour program between 4:30 and 5 p.m. (Vancouver time), opening the conference.

Nazis Use Boy Troops

LONDON, April 21. — (AP) — "The battle for Berlin has started," the German radio proclaimed at 9:15 p.m. (12:15 Vancouver time.) It said Hitler Youth units as well as the Volksturm, or home army, have been thrown into the fight.

(Boys from the age of 7 to 15 are enrolled in the Hitler Youth.)

(By Associated Press.)

LONDON, April 21.—Russian tanks have slashed three miles inside the Berlin city limits from the northeast, the German radio said tonight.

The Soviet entry was in the Wissensee-Pankow district.

The Red Army's big guns are hurling salvoes of shells into the city.

Berlin's defenders had set fire to forests outside the city in an effort to stall the Russians.

Three hours earlier German broadcasts declared 1,500,000 Russian troops had battered into five Berlin suburbs and flanked the capital on the southwest in a sweep within 32 miles of Amercan lines.

"The enemy has reached Berlin proper," said tonight's broadcast. "Massed enemy forces have reached the outer defense ring of Berlin and the capital proper is now the fighting zone."

"Russian tank speadheads have reached the outer defense ring of Berlin and the capital proper is now in the fighting zone.

Soviet forces, by enemy account, also have fought their way into Berlin suburbs at five places—Bernau, Strausberg, Fuerstenwalde, Koenigs-Wusterhausen and Zossen.

In a swift penetration of German defenses south of the capital, other Russian forces advanced to positions southwest of the capital.

Russian forces in a 35-mile breakthrough also reached the important rail junction town of Jueterbog, 10 miles southeast of Treuenbrietzen and 27 miles south of Berlin.

With this sweep the Russians severed virtually all the southward avenues of retreat out of Berlin.

BLOW UP DAM.

Moscow despatches said the desperate defenders had fired forests and blown up a power dam, unleashing torrents of water on Soviet infantrymen who grabbed at trees, bushes and barns.

A German broadcast said 16 armies, including four tank armies, were pounding at Berlin's gates in a battle "never surpassed in ferocity." Moscow reported the Germans were making suicide charges with fixed bayonets.

The Berlin radio said that Propaganda Minister Goebbels, in his capacity as gauleiter and defense commissioner for Berlin, would address the residents of the besieged city later today.

ANOTHER LINKUP.

Marshal Ivan S. Konev's 1st Ukrainian Army is engaged in the drive south of Berlin.

Farther south in Saxony where Konev's men also were driving toward another linkup with the Americans the Russians reached Kamenz, 19 miles north-

(Continued on Page 2.) See BERLIN.

Power Will Run On Liberal Ticket

QUEBEC, April 21.—(CP) — Maj. C. G. Power, former air minister who resigned from the cabinet over the sending of N.R.M.A. troops overseas last fall, reiterated in a statement today he will run again in Quebec South at the June 11 general federal election, adding that he remained "faithful to my Liberal political principles."

Favors World Organization Open to All

By ALEX SINGLETON.
Associated Press Staff Writer.

BRISTOL, England, April 21—Prime Minister Churchill declared today "a world organization which we must build and shall build will be free and open to all the nations of the world."

Speaking only a few days before the opening of the World Security Conference at San Francisco, Britain's wartime leader asserted that "Nations must live in peace and justice with one another," thus envisaging the ultimate inclusion of even present enemy powers in a world peace organization.

He added significantly: "There must be always the necessary force to restrain aggression."

LONG JOURNEY.

Mr. Churchill said that as far as Europe is concerned "We are coming to the end of the long journey," but added that the defeat of Japan will require "A new leap forward—a new lifting of soul and body."

His views were expressed under a new roof in the great fire-blackened hall of the University of Bristol, to which he came to present honors to two members of his war cabinet, H. V. Alexander, first lord of the admiralty, and Labor Minister Bevin, who received doctor of law degrees.

(Continued on Page 2.) See CHURCHILL.

'Dead Everywhere, the Living Like Corpses'

NAZI CAMP HORROR MAKES NEWSMEN WEEP

By WILLIAM FRYE

BELSEN, Germany, April 21—(AP)—The dead are getting a burial today at this fearsome concentration camp—each nameless dead getting a ghastly burial.

No coffins or flowers at this funeral. No tears or wellbred sympathy. No music.

These naked corpses were hauled in trucks and dumped into a pit. Their pall bearers were German S.S. (Elite Guard) men and women, now Allied prisoners.

Their litany was the hoarse shouts of British soldiers, sick with disgust and fury, ordering these marked members of Hitler's chosen legions about their horrible task.

SKIN COVERING BONES

I saw Belsen—its piles of lifeless dead and its aimless swarms of living dead. Their great eyes were just animal lights in skin-covered skulls of famine.

Some were dying of typhus, some of typhoid, some of tuberculosis, but most were just dying of starvation.

Starvation—the flesh on their bodies had fed on itself until there was no flesh left, just skin covering bones and the end of all hope, and nothing left to feed on.

30,000 PERISHED

Countless thousands—some say 30,000, some say more—died horrible deaths before the British 2nd Army reached this camp on the Aller River southeast of Bremen Sunday.

I saw these dead—hunndreds and thousands — lying in ditches and against walls of huts and piled in heaps.

Some were clothed, but most were naked.

I saw the living beside these dead.

Living—they still walked and talked and stared curiously, unemotionally at visitors and swiped cigarette butts tossed from a passing army car, went to the cookhouse for food and knelt around fires.

REALIZE NOTHING

There were supposed to be 29,-000 of them alive when the British arrived.

Living—but hardly men and women now, their spirits so broken and degraded that the nameless horror around them was without meaning or significance.

I saw there was no sex, no shame, no modesty, no self-respect among these people—driven in a few months backward a million years toward primeval scum.

FACES LIKE MUMMIES

Some habits remained. Women stood naked cleaning themselves with cans of water, unconscious of their flat, empty nakedness.

Men, equally naked, also remembered the habit of bathing. Clothing to these people meant warmth, nothing else.

I saw children walking about in this hell. Children—the first I saw I'll never rub out of my mind. A boy, perhaps 7, and his sister, maybe 5.

The knobs of their joints bulging through their thin clothes, faces like mummies, timorously sneaking up with small pails towards a water truck, their great fierce eyes intent on a chance to rush in and steal pailfuls of water.

HE SAW IT ALL—This is William Frye, Associated Press war correspondent, who today describes the horrors of Belsen.

UNABLE TO RISE

Obviously they were unable to comprehend something being freely given.

I saw SS men and women, once the torturing, brutal guards of this purgatory beyond imagination, put to labor loading the bodies of the people they had killed into trucks.

I saw them at the pits unloading these human carcasses, dragging them through the sand and dumping them into a great hole half-filled with dead.

I saw the living and dead lying beside each other in filthy huts —long, barracks-like buildings— the living no more able to rise than the dead.

EAT BESIDE DEAD

I saw men eating food just brought from the cook-house, eating within a yard of corpses dead for days, unconcerned by the death beside them or by the stench from slow-burning heaps of rags impregnated with filth.

Outside one of these huts within a barbed-wire compound I saw a smouldering heap of rags, and under it the half-burned body of a man, dragged out with the rags and undiscovered until the gradually consumed waste disclosed this one-time human among the ashes.

Inside this hut I saw and heard something else.

Inside this hut I choked and cried.

What once were men lay on the floor clothed in rags.

COULDN'T BE FED

Already they lay in the same gruesome macabre attitudes of the corpses on the heaps a few yards away.

An officer who took me there, Major J. P. Fox of Dublin, Eire, commander of a field hygenic unit, told me "nothing can help these poor wretches. We can't even feed them. They are too far gone to retain any food. They are dying and there is nothing we can do about it."

We could see the light of deliverance flash in those dying eyes. One or two feeble, wasted arms came slowly up and waved a "V" sign.

The officer took me to the cook-house and introduced me to a Polish woman who for several years had been in German prison and concentration camps. She had been in Belsen seven months.

BURNED ALIVE

This is what I heard:

Josef Kramer, SS. Commander of Belsen now under arrest, previously commanded Auschwitz, in Poland, where children were taken from their mothers and burned alive, where a gas chamber killed thousands, where Kramer kept his own orchestra to entertain him with Strauss waltzes while abominations were practiced under his command outside his windows.

At Belsen Kramer's predecessor, also of the S.S. was considerate—prisoners had enough to eat and proper medical care. The vileness began with Kramer's arrival five months ago.

EVEN CANNIBALISM

He instituted starvation as punishment, kept it up as a habit. He enjoyed the shuddering filthiness that Belsen became.

I heard that occasionally men starving in Belsen watched the dying with hunger, and as soon as they were dead, cut out hearts, livers and kidneys and devoured them to sustain their own vanishing lives.

I heard from Madame's lips that one man seized in cannibalism by the S.S. was forced to kneel publicly, holding in his teeth the ear of a corpse, the entire day.

I heard that S.S. men tied one living and one dead together, and burned both on a smouldering heap of scrap leather and worn out shoes and boots, while linking hands in hideous bestial danse macabre around this incredible pyre.

I heard that their sadistic joy in watching the slow distintegration of humans into something less than beasts was not always enough to satisfy Kramer's devils and witches—beatings, chopping off fingers and other glittering savageries gave occasional zest to their jaded appetites.

I heard more—but I cannot go on. Once the woman faltered in her conversation.

Once she broke entirely. Tears streamed down her face. That was when we left. She clung to Major Fox's hand for a moment and said: "We will never forget. We still cannot believe people can be as kind as you have been to us."

What I saw and heard at Belsen is something never seen or heard of in the world before the Nazis created concentration camps of their own bestial, incomprehensible kind.

Robbery, murder, rape—these twisted, warped, unhappy instincts any man who paused to examine himself can find buried in his own nature.

Normally there is a balance and the explosion never occurs.

But here in Belsen there was a deliberate, calculated effort, in most cases successful, to force mankind down the ladder up which he climbed painfully through the ages.

Nazis Made to Dig Up Bodies With Bare Hands

By ROBERT VERMILLION
Special to The Vancouver Sun

GARDELEGEN, Germany, April 21—(BUP)—American soldiers stood guard today while healthy Nazis dug up with their bare hands the hastily-buried bodies of 500 of their former prisoners.

These were the bodies of anti-Nazi Frenchmen, Belgians, Russians, Poles, and Dutchmen who were burned to death and shot a few hours before the Americans took this town. Then they were dumped hurriedly into make-shift graves, some of the corpses still smoldering.

A majority of the townspeople are Nazi Party members. The town looks like any other German town—clean streets, clean homes, clean people with rosy, plump cheeks.

Arrival of the Americans prevented burial of all the victims.

Gardelegan today is filled with hate.

Civilian efforts to be friendly are rejected coldly by the Americans.

They demand an immediate correct and respectful answer questions—and they get it.

Some of them were without shovels, and these an American captain ordered to dig with their bare hands.

They began the job under eyes of the soldiers.

At first some protested, the cold-eyed American capt simply pointed to the grave a said between clenched teeth: "Dig, you son of a ——."

REDS INSIDE BERLIN

'CORPSES EVERYWHERE'
NEWSMAN WEEPS AT NAZI CAMP HORROR
–See Page Two

The Sunday Sun

FOUNDED 1886
VOL. LIX—No. 222 VANCOUVER, BRITISH COLUMBIA, SATURDAY, APRIL 21, 1945 PRICE 10c

★★★★★ FINAL EDITION

Merritt Fooled Nazis; Made Keys

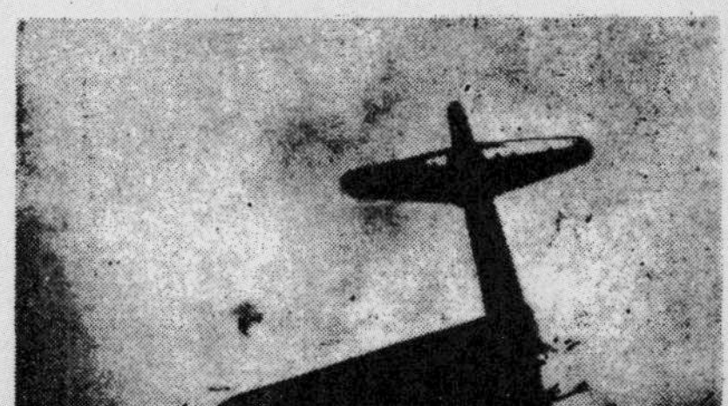

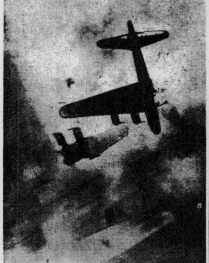

B-17 SHOT APART—A B-17 Flying Fortress of the U.S. 8th Air Force falls in two pieces, after cannon fire from an enemy Messerschmitt chopped off a wing during a raid on airdromes and an ordnance depot at Oranienburg, 18 miles north of Berlin. (AP Wirephoto.)

Shackles Joke To Vancouver VC

By FRANK LOW

A CANADIAN RECEPTION CENTRE, Southern England, April 21—(CP)—Headed by Lt.-Col. Cecil Merritt, VC, of Vancouver, a half-hundred men for whom the war has been eight hours of blazing battle and nearly three years of prison-camp rigors, returned today from Germany to England.

Col. Merritt revealed that though the Nazis shackled him for nine months, he never was chained long. Unknown to the guards, he had managed to contrive a key!

Men from all the Canadian regiments engaged in the great "reconnaissance in force" at Dieppe, August 19, 1942, were among the group of freed prisoners — but outstanding among them all was the tall, muscular figure of Col. Merritt.

This shy, young-looking soldier who won the Empire's highest award for valor—first given a Canadian Army man in this war — for fearless leadership on Dieppe's fire-swept beaches, summed up the feelings of his men when he looked at the sunny English countryside around this camp and said:

"We're all beginning to live again."

Then, standing in the shade of a flowering lilac bush, the man

Please Turn to Page Five
See "Merritt"

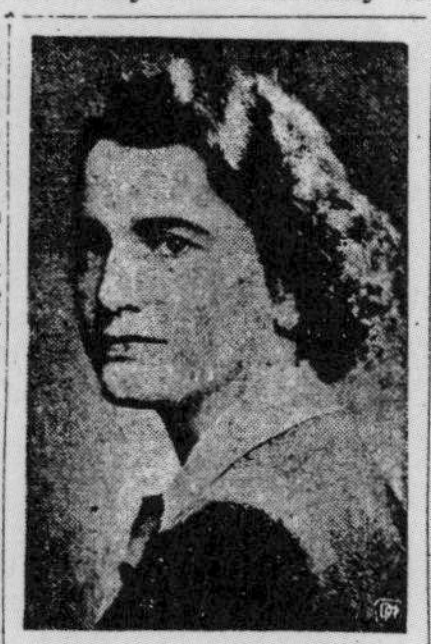

UBC STAR WEDS — The marriage of Mrs. Phyllis Turner of Vancouver, formerly a brilliant student at the UBC, to Frank Ross of Montreal took place quietly in Ottawa today at St. Joseph's Rectory.

Mrs. Ross, who has been Prices Board Administrator of Oils and Fats, resigned that post this week. Mr. Ross, a leading Canadian industrialist, has been liaison officer for the British Admiralty with the munitions department.

Yanks Near Junction With Reds

U.S. 9th Storms Elbe Northwest Of Hun Capital

WITH U.S. 9TH ARMY, Germany, April 21.—The U.S. 9th Army has been put on the alert for a junction with Russian spearhead near the Elbe River, it was revealed tonight. Meanwhile the Paris radio said, without any qualification, that the forces of the two powers had joined in the Dresden district. The Brussels radio said the Red Army had entered Dresden.

PARIS, April 21—(BUP)—American troops were reported storming the Elbe River line at a new point northwest of Berlin today in a major bid to break through and join the Red Army in the final assault on the German capital.

Meanwhile United States and Soviet troops drove toward a junction to split the German front, and the dramatic junction appeared to be only a matter of hours. Patrols may already have met along the Elbe some 75 miles south of Soviet-besieged Berlin.

Word of the new crossing attempt on the U.S. 9th Army front before Berlin was flashed

Please Turn to Page Five
See "West Front"

TANKS INVADE NAZI CAPITAL

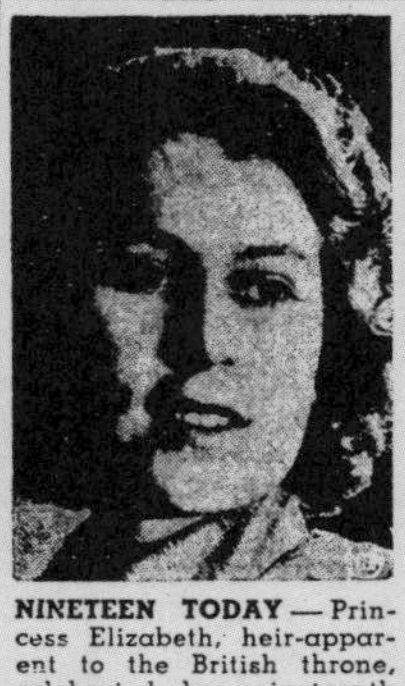

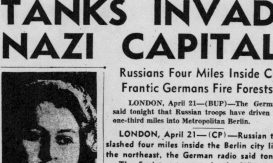

NINETEEN TODAY — Princess Elizabeth, heir-apparent to the British throne, celebrated her nineteenth birthday today.

Russians Four Miles Inside City; Frantic Germans Fire Forests

LONDON, April 21—(BUP)—The German radio said tonight that Russian troops have driven four and one-third miles into Metropolitan Berlin.

LONDON, April 21—(CP)—Russian tanks have slashed four miles inside the Berlin city limits from the northeast, the German radio said tonight.

The Soviet entry was in the Wissensee-Pankow district, the German radio said.

The Red Army's big guns were hurling salvos of shells into the city.

Berlin's defenders had set fire to forests outside the city in an effort to stall the Russians.

Three hours earlier German broadcasts declared 1,500,000 Russian troops had battered into five Berlin suburbs and flanked the capital on the southwest in a sweep within 32 miles of American lines.

"The enemy has reached Berlin proper," said tonight's broadcast. "Massed enemy forces have reached the outer defense ring of Berlin and the capital proper is now the fighting zone.

"Russian tank spearheads have reached the outer defense ring of Berlin and the capital proper is now in the fighting zone.

Weissensee and Pankow are large working-class districts.

The Soviet forces which drove into them stormed ten miles down the road from the northeastern suburb of Bernau.

Both Weissensee and Pankow had large left wing elements before the war, and Weissensee included the biggest Jewish cemetery in Berlin.

Nazi Suicide Charges

Moscow dispatches said the desperate defenders had blown up a power dam, unleashing torrents of water on Soviet infantrymen, who grabbed at trees, bushes and barns.

A German broadcast said 16 armies, including four tank armies, were pounding at Berlin's gates in a battle "never surpassed in ferocity." Moscow reported the Germans were making suicide charges with fixed bayonets.

Massive Russian forces were enveloping Berlin through suburbs on the east, north and southwest after a lightning thrust of more than 50 miles had outflanked the city completely on the south.

This Russian dash reached Jueterbrog, only 35 miles from American positions.

The German High Command claimed the Russians were only three miles from Berlin proper, at Berneau.

A Reuters dispatch said German broadcasts indicated Soviet forces driving from the Proetzel forest were approaching the ring Autobahn, at a point two miles from the Berlin city boundary. There was no confirmation.

But Marshal Gregory K. Zhukov's powerful 1st White Russian Army was reported at "the very gates" of the city, where peace riots were said to have broken out.

Zhukov's men and Marshal Ivan S. Konev's 1st Ukraine Army seized at least eight major strongholds along a 100-mile front from Berlin to Dresden, and were menacing a dozen other fortified towns in the defense ring.

Please Turn to Page Five **See "Great Air Battles"**

Churchill Hints He May Retire

BRISTOL, Eng., April 21 —(BUP)—Prime Minister Churchill hinted today that he might retire—or be retired—after the defeat of Germany.

In a speech accepting the freedom of the city, he said that he "or whoever stands in my place" would have to ask war-weary Britain "for a new leap forward, for a new lifting of the soul and body," to defeat Japan.

Churchill said that in the event that there is a new Prime Minister he would support him, whoever it may be, but did not elaborate further. However, a general election will be held after V-E Day.

"We have the Japanese to finish," Churchill said, "and we

Please Turn to Page Five
See "Churchill"

LATE FLASHES—

Britain, U.S. 'In Full Agreement'

WASHINGTON, April 21—(AP)—Foreign Minister Eden today declared "We are in complete agreement on all points," after a conference with State Secretary Stettinius.

They presumably discussed the attitude they will take on the Polish problem.

PARIS, April 21—(CP)—American troops have overrun one of the greatest ammunition and gas dumps discovered yet. It had 27,000 poison gas shells.

Ike and Monty Confer

PARIS, April 21—(BUP)—Gen. Eisenhower and Field Marshal Sir Bernard L. Montgomery conferred for nearly an hour yesterday on a captured German airfield a few miles from the front.

Halibut Fleet Ready

First section of the B.C. halibut fleet may sail anytime after midnight next Friday, and the second section may sail five days later, George Miller, president of United Fishermen and Allied Workers' Union, announced today.

German General Shot

WITH THE U.S. FIRST ARMY IN GERMANY, April 21—(AP)—American tankmen shot a high-ranking German general to death yesterday in the Ruhr pocket when he and his men ran from a house and killed a U.S. soldier with a machine pistol.

U.S. to Probe Horrors

WASHINGTON, April 21—(AP)—The United States War Department announced today that 12 members of Congress will be flown to Germany within the next few days to view the evidence of Nazi atrocities.
(See Also Page Five).

LONDON PICTURES

Troops Make Public See Atrocities

LONDON, April 21—(CP)—The **Daily Mirror** reported today that moviegoers, unable to stomach atrocity newsreels, tried to leave a Leicester Square theatre but were turned back by Allied soldiers, who told them to return and see what other people had to endure.

"People walked out from cinemas all over the country," the **Mirror** said, "and in many places there were soldiers to tell them to go back and face it."

"It's the only way to break the namby-pamby attitude toward Germans," the paper quoted a soldier as saying. "Many people don't believe such things could be. These films are proof. It is everybody's duty to know."

The **Daily Express** announced that it will display atrocity pictures in its reading rooms throughout Britain.

900,000 Captives

PARIS, April 21—(BUP)—The Allied western armies captured 913,237 German prisoners in the first 20 days of April, headquarters announced today.

U.S. 3rd Army officers in Germany said that German prisoners taken on the Western Front included one admiral, a full general, eleven lieutenant-generals and seven brigadier-generals.

BASEBALL

AMERICAN

St. Louis at Chicago, postponed, cold.

		R	H	E
Philadelphia	003 010 400	8	9	2
Boston	010 000 010	2	10	2

Newsom and Hayes; Hausman, Woods (7), Wilson (9) and Walters.

		R	H	E
New York	001 000 000	1	4	1
Washington	200 000 00x	2	4	1

Bonham and Drescher; Wolff and Ferrell.

		R	H	E
Cleveland	001 000 010 00	2	5	1
Detroit	001 000 100 01	3	9	2

Embree and Ruszkowski; Newhouser and Richards.

NATIONAL

Boston at Philadelphia, postponed, rain.

		R	H	E
Chicago	100 200 100	4	13	0
Pittsburgh	201 000 000	3	13	3

Derringer and Livingston; Roe, Strincevich (6) and Salkeld.

Mexico City Race Results

FIRST RACE—Two and one-half furlongs:
Strange Music (Espejel) $9, $6.40, $4.20.
Lady Itobian (Thornburg) $5.60, $4.
Okee (Craig) $3.40.
Time :29 3-5. Scratched: aChata.

SECOND RACE—Five and one-half furlongs.
Safety Lite (Fliter) $4.00, $2.80, $2.40.
Elma Kerry (Molbert) $6.40, $3.20.
Colleen (Sylvia) $2.80.
Time 1:09 2-5.

THIRD RACE—Five and one-half furlongs:
Tripped (Klinder).
Peemar (Neves).
Anno Vision (Sylvia).

12 Wounded Canucks Free

WITH THE 1ST CANADIAN ARMY, April 21—(CP)—Twelve Canadians were among 44 wounded Allied prionsers liberated the night of April 13-14 when Canadian troops in Holland were approaching Apeldoorn, on the west side of the Ijssel river.

Polish-Red Treaty

LONDON, April 21—(Reuters)—The Lublin radio reported tonight that Poland and the Soviet Union had signed a treaty of friendship.

Race Results At Tijuana

FIRST RACE—Six furlongs:
Otay Comex (Pierson), $33.20, $27.20, $12.60.
Chipwys Wings (Haritos), $5.20, $4.20.
Cadskill (Debelloy), $8.40.
Time: 1:13 2-5.

Race Entries on Page 3.

St. Michael's Wins

TORONTO, April 21—(CP)—St. Michael's Majors jumped into a 3-1 lead in the Memorial Cup finals when they edged out Moose Jaw Canucks 4-3 this afternoon.

And Inside—

These Writers Will Represent The Sun at the San Francisco World Security Meet

PICTURED HERE are seven of the eight special writers who will represent The Vancouver Sun at the United Nations Security Conference opening in San Francisco next Wednesday. The eighth is Marquis Childs. Five of the seven are members of The Sun's own staff. The other two are noted Washington correspondents. See page 14 for today's dispatch from San Francisco.

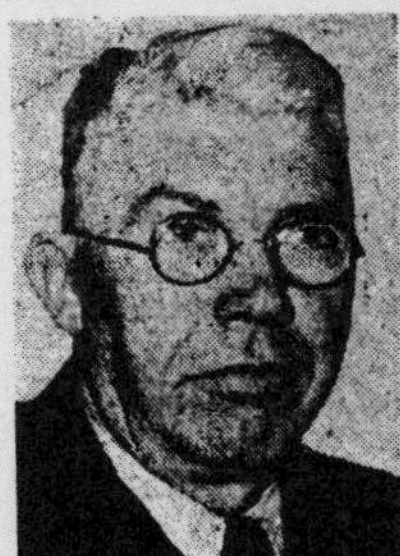

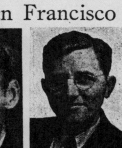

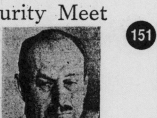

ROY W. BROWN
Editorial Director

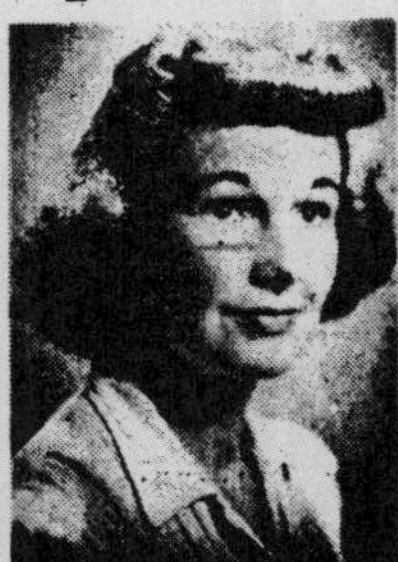

MAMIE MOLONEY
Featured Woman Columnist

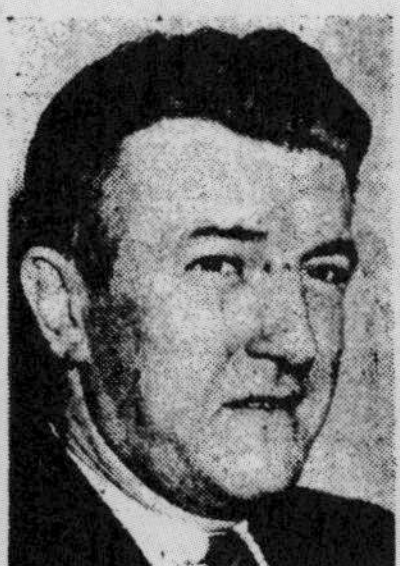

DEL FINLAY
Foreign News Editor

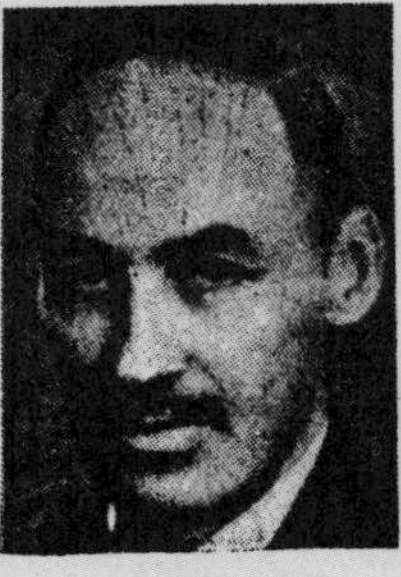

ELMORE PHILPOTT
Columnist

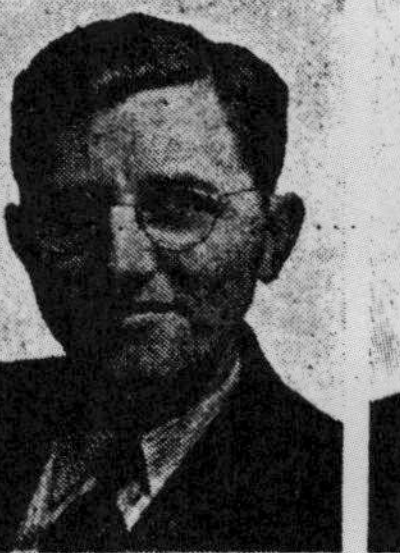

BRUCE HUTCHISON
Columnist

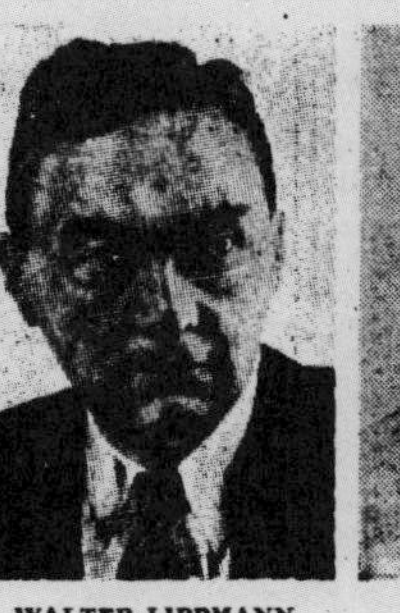

WALTER LIPPMANN
Economist and Author

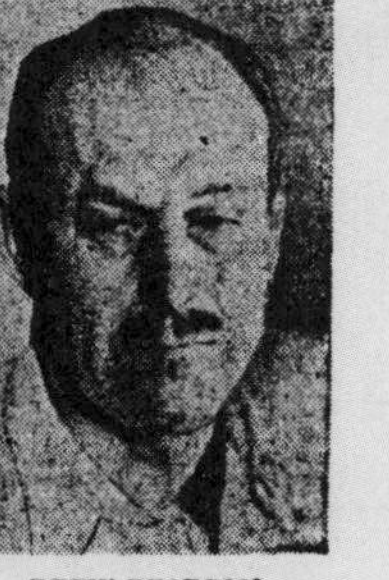

DREW PEARSON
Washington Merry-Go-Round

151

NAZI SURRENDER EXPECTED HOURLY

★ ★ ★ ★ ★ FINAL EDITION

The Vancouver Sun

FOUNDED 1886
VOL. LIX—No. 229 VANCOUVER, BRITISH COLUMBIA, MONDAY, APRIL 30, 1945 PRICE 5 CENTS

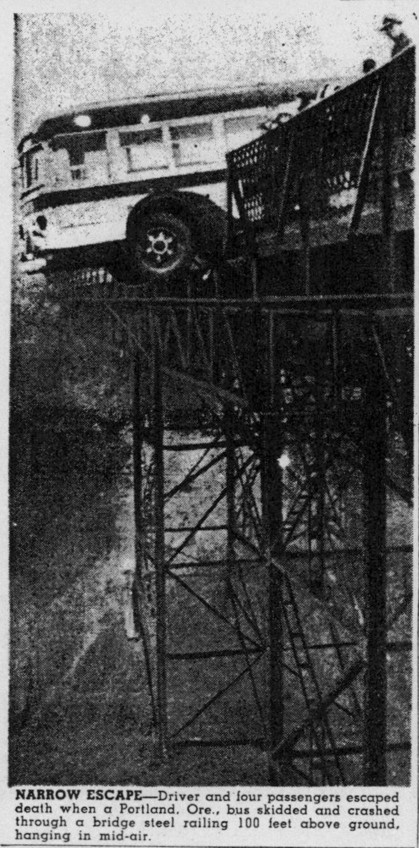

NARROW ESCAPE—Driver and four passengers escaped death when a Portland, Ore., bus skidded and crashed through a bridge steel railing 100 feet above ground, hanging in mid-air.

LATE FLASHES—

Court Quashes Move To Get Out of Army

MONTREAL, April 30—(CP)—Five petitions for writs of habeas corpus on behalf of soldiers seeking release fro mthe Army were refused by Mr. Justice Fabre, Surveyor in Supreme Court, here today.

No More Germany to Bomb

LONDON, April 30—(Reuters) — The bomber offensive in the form that ravaged Germany for so many years, now has drawn to a close, an RAF commentator said today. "The targets have been overrun," he added.

German Marines Mutined

NEW YORK, April 30—(CP) — The Stockholm Dagens Nyheter today said whole companies of German marines mutinied at Kiel last night after authorities ordered them to entrain for infantry duty at the fighting front in the Hamburg sector.

Argentina Gets Parley Seat

SAN FRANCISCO, April 30—(BUP)—The steering committee of the United Nations Security Conference voted today to invite Argentina into its sessions by a vote of 24 to 5. The steering committee also approved invitations to the Ukraine and White Russia. (See also page 19.)

Airman's Election Upheld

EDMONTON, April 30—(CP) — Election of Wing Cmdr. F. C. Colborne, as Air Force member-at-large in the Alberta Legislature was confirmed in recount proceedings completed today by Judge Lucien Dubus. Recount of the votes was asked for by WO1 Roy J. Burton of Edmonton who trailed by eight votes.

Mob Beats Duce's Body Into Pulp

Corpse Hanged Head Down in Public Square

By JAMES E. ROPER
Special to The Vancouver Sun

MILAN, April 30 — (BUP) —The broken body of Benito Mussolini lay unclaimed beside his slain mistress in the Milan morgue today, dishonored in death by the people he led to empire and ruin.

The fallen Duce died badly in the sight of the partisan executioners who killed him and his paramour, Clara Petacci, in their hideout on Lake Como last Saturday.

And the people he ruled for two decades paid him their last tribute by hanging his remains head down from the rafters of a gasoline station in Milan's Loreto Square.

There, for a night and day they spat upon their fallen leader, shot his body in the back and kicked his face into a toothless, pulpy mass.

LAY ON GROUND

For hours after the body of the executed dictator was brought to Milan with that of his mistress and 16 other slain Fascist leaders, Mussolini lay in a filthy pile of dirt in the centre of the square.. Then the mob tied wire about the ankles of Il Duce and Clara Petaci and suspended them upside down from the roof of the gasoline station.

Hysterical men and women closed in screaming about the dangling corpses and beat and

Please Turn to Page Twenty
See "Mussolini"

Burglars Fail In Raids on Three Safes

Thieves failed to secure any loot when they raided three safes in Vancouver and New Westminster over the week-end.

Police recoverd a safe early this morning that had been stolen from John Doe Store No. 1, 1945 Cornwall, about one hour previously. It was found in a vacant lot at Forty-ninth and Carleton. The contents were intact.

Constables J. D. McGillivary and George A. Kerr were summoned to the store at 4.15 by the ringing of the burglar alarm.

Constables O. M. MacLean and R. M. Baldwin reported seeing a car without lights pull away from a vacant lot at Forty-ninth shortly before. Upon investigation they located the small safe hidden in the bushes.

Safecrackers failed to get into the safe at the Market Basket, 4889 McKenzie, after smashing off the dial and trying to punch it open. Nothing is missing from the store.

A charge of nitro-glycerine placed by yeggs on the safe of the School Board office in New Westminster was not sufficient to blast the strong box open, police reports indicate.

There was no money in the safe, anyway, school board officials said.

Race Entries, Page 2

German Admits 21,000 Murders

Nazi Doctors Inject Death Drug Into 110,000 in Kiev Annihilation Plant

By JACK FLEISCHER
Special to The Vancouver Sun

U.S. 12TH ARMY GROUP HEADQUARTERS, April 24 —(Delayed)—(BUP)—Dr. Gustav Wilhelm Schuebbe said today the Nazi annihilation institute at Kiev killed from 110,000 to 140,000 persons "unworthy to live" during the nine months he worked there.

Schuebbe, a crippled drug addict captured by 1st Army troops recently, admitted he had murdered about 21,000 persons.

He told his story voluntarily and showed no feeling of guilt, but occasionally became evasive when he appeared to sense that his actions might be viewed as crimes.

The annihilation institute was established after the Germans captured Kiev in 1941. Schuebbe was there about five months before he became head of it.

He remained at the institute until March, 1942.

The persons "unworthy to live" included epileptics, schizophrenics, Jews, members of foreign races and gypsies, he said.

Each doctor at the institute "processed" about 100 persons per day, but Schuebbe said they worked only about two or three days a week.

Victims were killed by injections of morphine tartrate preparations, Schuebbe said.

The doctors were aided by Nazi secret service men who were dressed in the uniform of medical aid men and whose job it was to hold the patient.

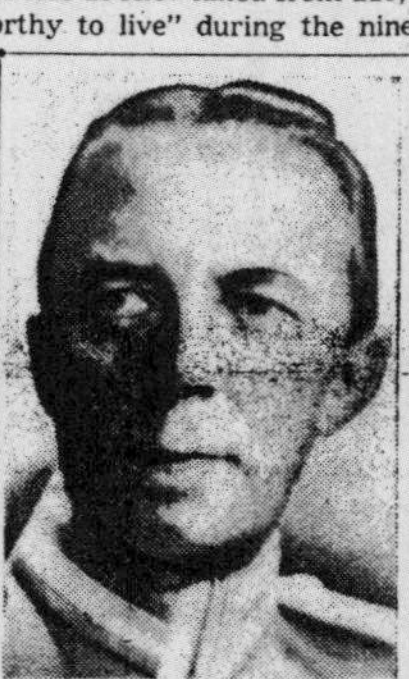

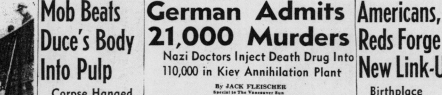

GO-BETWEEN — Count Folke Bernadotte (above), vice-chairman of the Swedish Red Cross, is assertedly the man Heinrich Himmler has selected as his emissary in attempts to surrender Germany.

Ottawa Will Announce End Of Hostilities

OTTAWA, April 30—(CP)—Hon. J. L. Ilsley, as acting prime minister, said in a statement late today that an official announcement will be made on behalf of the Canadian government when hostilities in Europe have ended.

Mr. Ilsley sai dit was intended to follow the announcement with two proclamations—the first declaring the following Sunday to be a day of solemn thanksgiving and remembrance, and the second declaring the day following the announcement to be a public holiday.

"It is, of course, understood that these latter arrangements are tentative only and may have to be altered in the ilght of circumstances."

Berlin in Last Throes Of Death

LONDON, April 30 — (BUP) — Red Armies hammered the last fanatic defenders of Berlin into a flaming, shell-torn eight-square-mile death pocket around the Tiergarten and Unter den Linden today.

Moscow dispatches said the Russians already had driven across the Landwehr Canal into the heavily-fortified Tiergarten—Berlin's central park—from the southwest.

German broadcasts admitted Soviet shock troops also had broken through to the Lustgarten courtyard fronting the old royal palace, the Berlin Cathed-

Please Turn to Page Two
See "Berlin"

Americans, Reds Forge New Link-Up

Birthplace Of Naziism, Munich, Falls

PARIS, April 30 — (BUP) — American 7th Army forces today captured Munich, birthplace of Naziism, Germany's third city, and the most formidable outpost of the Nazis "national redoubt" in the Alps.

From AP and BUP Dispatches

PARIS, April 30. — American and Russian troops effected a second juncture on the Elbe River below Berlin today, broadening to 80 miles the Allied wedge between Germany's collapsing northern and southern fronts.

The new link on the Elbe came as the Nazis' vaunted Bavarian redoubt in the south broke wide open under converging blows by five and perhaps six Allied armies storming in on the mountain stronghold from all sides.

American 9th Army doughboys joined the Russians on the Elbe bend near Winterberg, 40 miles southwest of Berlin, after a fighting, 20-mile advance along the northeast bank of the river from Zerbst.

First accounts indicated that U.S. 1st Army troops might also have linked up with the Soviets around Wittenberg. The 1st Army already has joined the Russians farther south at Torgau and Riesa.

SURRENDER BULLETINS

WASHINGTON, April 30—(AP)—The White House said today that President Truman will report on any end of European hostilities "whenever anything can be released officially and with proper authority."

Press Secretary Jonathan Daniels said, "Meanwhile, there will be all sorts of reports out of all sorts of places."

STOCKHOLM, April 30—(Reuters)—Usually reliable sources said tonight that Gestapo Chief Henrich Himmler is believed to have given to Count Bernadotte, vice-president of the Swedish Red Cross, a capitulation offer addressed to Russia, Britain and the United States.

New Offer 'On Its Way'

From AP and BUP Dispatches

LONDON, April 30—(Reuters)—The Cabinet is standing by for the news that may end the war at any moment—probably in the form of a fresh message from Count Folke Bernadotte, the Swedish Red Cross leader.

A new surrender offer from Heinrich Himmler, presumably to all three major powers, was understood to be "on its way" today.

Meanwhile authoritative circles in London reaffirm the four major points that are the Great Powers' conditions as a preliminary to granting Germany an armistice:

1. Unconditional surrender.
2. The offer to be made equally to Britain, the United States and Russia.
3. No disclosure to Germany by the Great Powers as to the terms of peace they intend to impose.
4. No favor of any kind for Himmler or any other representative in consideration of their part in precipitating the capitulation of Germany.

Prime Minister Churchill is expected to make a statement to parliament this week setting out the facts of the situation, but there is a belief in many quarters that events themselves may anticipate Mr. Churchill.

Himmler, believed to be making his approaches with the authority of the German General staff behind him, does so with full realization that the Great Powers' acceptance of any offer from him merely hastens the day of his indictment as one of the major war criminals.

It is doubtful, however, whether this consideration will be permitted to weigh with him if, it is widely believed, his approaches to the Allies have been made as a result of pressure by the High Command.

With Hitler, dead or alive, clearly out of the picture and Himmler apparently in undisputed administrative authority in Germany, the latter may be considered as having status to approach the Allies.

A V-E Day announcement was expected in London at any hour. Cabinet ministers were ordered to stand by as swiftly-moving developments pointed to Germany's collapse.

Free Danish press reports said Count Folke Bernadotte, vice-chairman of the Swedish Red Cross, and reputed peace intermediary, had conferred with Himmler today at AAbenraa on the German-Danish border.

The Swedish newspaper **Aftonbladet** printed a rumor, however, that Himmler was in Stockholm for direct contact with Allied representatives. There was no confirmation from any source.

Prime Minister Churchill and his colleagues were closeted in a regular meeting of the cabinet, and the authoritative British Press Association said the "peace position was fully discussed." Military leaders attended the meeting as usual.

Many responsible sources believed that if a new Nazi capitulation offer were being forwarded, it would be Himmler's agreement to unconditional surrender since weekend developments evidently made it manifest that the Allies were interested in nothing less.

Working Out Details

There were indications that only details of Germany's surrender remained to be worked out. These may concern whether Himmler or any other ranking Nazi leader could give solid evidence that German pockets on the Atlantic coast and in Norway would lay down their arms.

It was possible that uncertainty over the temper of commanders such as Col.-Gen. Georg Lindemann in Denmark was holding up an agreement on details.

The Press Association said "there is no longer any doubt that armistice moves are in progress and moving swiftly."

Speculation centred around the possibility that May Day might be chosen for a victory announcement.

It was felt here, however, that before this comes Premier Stalin may announce the capture of Berlin—that the Russians are determined to claim this prize before the Nazis will be allowed to give up.

Please Turn to Page Two See "Peace"

Conference Excitement Short-Lived

PARLEY PRESS BOYS HAIL PEACE ANYWAY

By DEL FINLAY, Foreign News Editor, The Sun

SAN FRANCISCO, April 30. — Peace, the blessed Damozel, was with us for a few minutes Saturday night.

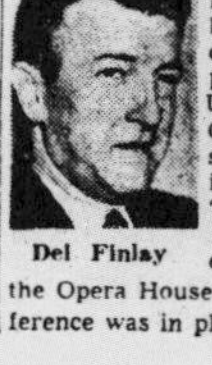

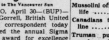

Del Finlay

The fun began when the **Call-Bulletin** on the basis of an Associated Press dispatch from the United Nations Conference here screamed in six-inch type, "Nazis Quit."

Inevitably the extra reached the Opera House where the Conference was in plenary session.

Mr. Molotov was presiding as chairman, dowsing over speeches in tongues he didn't understand, when somebody shoved one of the papers in front of him.

Now Mr. Molotov officially no spikka da English so just what was accomplished by that particular gesture eludes us.

So Molotov's interpreters interpreted it to him.

Mr. Molotov smiled wanly and went on perspiring with the rest of us.

Down at the Palace Hotel the United Nations Conference Committee of San Francisco was throwing a reception for the boys and girls of the press.

The boys and girls of the press were more excited about the free champagne and caviar and pate de foi gras than any peace.

And if it were peace this was as good a place as any to celebrate. It was a reception such as only San Francisco could stage.

See "Parley"
Please Turn to Page Two

Sun Writers Win Reporting Awards

Special to The Vancouver Sun

CHICAGO, April 30—(BUP)—Henry T. Gorrell, British United Press war correspondent today was granted the annual Sigma Delta Chi award for excellence in "spot news" was correspondence.

Gorrell was one of eight newspapermen cited for outstanding work in their posfession during 1944 by the professional journalism profession.

And Inside—

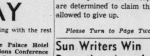

ADOLF HITLER DEAD

Weather Forecast — Partly cloudy, slightly warmer. Tuesday, partly cloudy to cloudy with rain overnight. Sunday's temperatures: high 52, low 47.

The Vancouver Sun EXTRA

FOUNDED 1886 VOL. LIX—No. 230 | MArine 1161 | HOME EDITION | VANCOUVER, BRITISH COLUMBIA, TUESDAY, MAY 1, 1945 | ★★★ | PRICE 5 CENTS | BY CARRIER $1.00 per month

—AP Wirephoto

MUSSOLINI'S BODY HANGS BY HEELS — In Milan's Plaza Loretto the bodies of Benito Mussolini (left) once dictator of Italy, and his woman friend, Clara Petacci (centre), hang by their heels as they are put on public display. At right of the woman's body, Partisans hoist the remains of Lt-Gen. Achille Starace, former secretary of the Fascist Party. The three, with other Fascist leaders, were shot after a summary trial last Saturday, following their capture at Lake Como. This picture was obtained by the New York Times and sent to New York Monday by radio from Bern, Switzerland. Il Duce was buried in an unmarked grave. (Story on Page 2).

Hun Surrender May Come Any Moment—Churchill

From AP and BUP Dispatches

STOCKHOLM, May 1.—Reports still flooded this neutral today that Heinrich Himmler was negotiating with the Allies to effect Germany's unconditional surrender — and one Stockholm paper insisted a new Himmler capitulation offer had already been delivered to the Big Three.

Count Folke Bernadotte, assertedly Himmler's go-between in the surrender negotiations, flew back to Stockholm from German-held Sto k olm today and confirmed he had conferred with Himmler ten days ago.

IN ALLIED HANDS

The Stockholm newspaper Dagens Nyheter said Himmler's reply to an Allied demand that Germany surrender to Russia as well as Britain and the United States was delivered to Allied diplomats here yesterday by a member of the Swedish foreign office.

The emissary in this case was said to be Foreign Minister Christian E. Guenther.

DECISION IN 48 HOURS

Dagens Nyheter said a final Allied decision on the German note was not expected for another 24 to 48 hours because of the "complicated nature of the negotiations."

Nevertheless, it said, the general trend of the negotiations was "favorable."

BULLETIN

LONDON, May 1—(BUP)—The German radio at Hamburg tonight broadcast an announcement that Adolf Hitler is dead.

There was no immediate confirmation from any Allied source.

Prime Minister Hints News May Break Any Time Before Saturday

From AP and BUP Dispatches

LONDON, May 1. — Prime Minister Churchill hinted today that announcement of peace in Europe might come at any moment before Saturday, but told a packed House of Commons he had no statement at this time.

The implication that peace might come before the House rises for the week on Friday evening was the nearest to a prediction that Mr. Churchill permitted himself.

He said he would make the announcement in Commons during its sitting today—if any pertinent information was available.

Confers With King

Churchill conferred with King George in Buckingham Palace and then appeared before a tense House of Commons to deliver a guarded and deliberately vague statement. He did not deny that German surrender negotiations were in progress.

Throughout his brief appearance in Commons he spoke as if Germany's unconditional surrender now were a foregone conclusion and that the armies in Europe might be engaged in occupying their various postwar administrative zones.

Replying to a member's question, Mr. Churchill declared "I have no special statement to make on the war position in Europe except that it is definitely more satisfactory than it was at this time five years ago."

Mr. Churchill said that if information of exceptional importance "reaches the government during the sittings of the House this week—as it might do," he would make a brief announcement.

"With regard to the condition and requisition which would occur if an announcement on decisive consequence justifying celebration were to be made this week or at any time in the future, and V-E Day was announced, a number of arrangements have been prepared, and will be issued tonight in a home office circular," he said.

"Of course," he said, "I shall make no statement here that is not in accord with the statement which will be made by our allies," explaining such announcements

Please Turn to Page Two See "Peace"

Australian Troops Land On Borneo

MANILA, May 1—(BUP)—An Allied invasion of Borneo, Japan's biggest and richest island conquest in the Pacific, was announced by Australian government officials in Canberro today.

A Canberra dispatch relayed to the British United Press in Manila said Australian Treasurer J. B. Chifley announced the invasion of Borneo to the Commonwealth Legislature today.

YANKS, TOO

Chiefley said Australian troops participated in the landing, indicating that American invasion forces were involved.

There was no immediate confirmation at Gen. Douglas MacArthur's headquarters, but an earlier Tokyo broadcast said Allied troops were pouring ashore on the east coast of the immensely rich oil and rubber-producing island in the Dutch East Indies.

The Japanese broadcast said the troops went ashore last night under cover of a naval bombardment in the Tarakan area, 175 miles southwest of American bases at the southern end of the Sulu Archipelago.

LARGE OIL CENTRE

The Tarakan area is one of the largest oil centres in the East Indies. Tarakan itself, however, is a comparatively small island in the Celebes Sea several miles off the east coast of Borneo.

Tokyo said the invasion forces landed late at night and were engaged in "fierce combat" by the Japanese garrison. Although the reported invasion site was not given, it presumably was in the wide delta area on the eastern shore opposite Tarakan.

Monday Warmest Day This Year

The weatherman pulled a fast one Monday afternoon and the result was that Vancouver had its warmest day of the year.

Although official weather forecasts bore no hint of an impending "heat wave," the mercury soared to 66 degrees during the afternoon. Previous high was 61 on April 25.

It was just a teaser though. The city settled back again today to a diet of clouds and showers.

Laval, Henchmen At Swiss Border

ZURICH, May 1—(BUP)—Pierre Laval, Marcel Deat and Jean Luchaire, leading collaborationists during the Nazi occupation of France, arrived at Hoechst on the Swiss border today.

(The dispatch did not clarify immediately whether they were admitted to Switzerland.)

Firm To Build On Part of 'Civic Centre'

Civic authorities received a jolt today when they learned a private business firm was all set to start building on a portion of the proposed "Central School" civic centre site.

Gough & Co. Ltd., electrical equipment dealers of 27 West Pender, have applied to the city building department for a permit to erect a $39,000 warehouse on the west side of Beatty between Pender and Dunsmuir.

This location is in part of what was proposed for the Civic Centre.

Mayor Cornett, Ald. H. L. Corey, civic building chairman, and several of the civic officials conferred today with H. J. Gough, manager of the company, in the mayor's office.

His Worship told **The Vancouver Sun** later that the situation was explained to Mr. Gough who seemed determined to go ahead with his own plans.

"It is a difficult situatjon," said the Mayor. "I don't know what we can do. Mr. Gough owns the property. eH has a federal government license to build and is all set to start tomorrow if he can get his city building permit. I don't see how we can refuse him."

Mr. Gough said, "a civic centre shouldnt be built there in the first place, and in the second place, it's still a pipe dream, ten years off.'

Capture of Berlin Expected Tonight

LONDON, May 1—(BUP)—A Moscow broadcast said today the Russians expected the Red Army to announce tonight the capture of Berlin, where the hammer and sickle already flew triumphant over the Reichstag and a dozen other administrative buildings.

Russian and German reports alike indicated an imminent decision amidst the blood-soaked rubble of Berlin, where the Red Army was hewing out its greatest symbolic victory of the war.

The German High Command joined the chorus of Nazi claims that Adolf Hitler was in Berlin. Its communique said that "in the heart of Berlin the gallant garrison, gathered closely around the Fuehrer, is defending itself against superior Soviet forces." If Hitler were there, he appeared doomed to certain death or capture by the Russians.

REICHSTAG TAKEN

All Moscow broadcasts and dispatches reflected confident expectation that Marshal Stalin would cap Moscow's first glittering May Day celebration of the war with an announcement that Berlin had fallen.

Robert Magidoff, broadcasting over the Moscow radio for NBC, said the Russian people expected the announcement of Berlin's fall tonight.

DROP FOOD

Reports lagging well behind the course of the struggle in the heart of Berlin said the Russians had battled onto Unter Den Linden against faltering resistance. The Russian flag had been hoisted over the Reichstag, the main post office and the interior ministry.

The battle raged within a stone's throw of Adolf's Hitler's one-time ornate Reichschancellery, and in the Tiergarten, where the Nazis were reported to have established a fort for a last-ditch stand.

The German air force made a last-gasp attempt to parachute supplies to the besieged defenders today.

RELIEF STOPPED

The Hamburg radio said that efforts of the German 9th Army to relieve Berlin had been abandoned because of strong Russian attacks, and that the German 4th Army west of Berlin "also has had to endure strong Soviet flank attacks."

Marshal Stalin in a special order of the day said last night the Russian people were celebrating May Day "under conditions of the victorious termination of the great patriotic war."

His triumphant announcement, declaring that Soviet troops had "hoisted the banner of victory over Berlin," said the Germans had lost 1,000,000 men killed and 800,000 captured on the eastern front in the last three or four months. He said the enemy also lost 6000 planes, 12,000 tanks and 23,000 cannons.

These latest figures raised German casualties announced by Moscow in less than four years of war to a total of 11,340,000.

Call-ups To End On V-E Day

Canada's military call-up system—which has files of more than 1,000,000 men still not in uniform—will be shelved on V-E-Day.

This was disclosed officially in Ottawa today by Arthur MacNamara, deputy minister of labor, who told **The Vancouver Sun** that draft calls will stop the day Germany is defeated.

AFFECTS 1,800,000

Current figures released by Ottawa today indicated that about 1,809,000 Canadian men are subject to draft calls.

Of these, 741,000 have enlisted or been enrolled in the armed forces, leaving more than a million still out of uniform.

Of the latter, 270,000 hold military deferments in war industries, and another 593,000 have been declared unfit for military service.

48,000 YOUTHS

End of the call-up will affect some 48,000 youths of the 1926 class, who have their eighteenth birthdays in 1944. They are being called six months after reaching their birthdays. To date, calls have gone to all such youths who were 18 before October, 1944. Completion of call-ups in this class would come in July if the draft system continued.

B.C. mobilization officials declined to give coast figures.

Weather Forecast — Cloudy, light rain tonight. Wednesday, cloudy with showers. Monday's temperatures—high 66, low 44.

'Don't Remember What Was Said'

Merritt, VC, Meets King; Jittery for First Time!

By ALAN NICKLESON

LONDON, May 1—(CP)—Lt.-Col. Cecil Merritt, of Vancouver, whose cool heroism in the bloody Dieppe reconnaissance in force of 1942 won him the Victoria Cross, chatted today with the King for nearly a minute as he received the Empire's highest decoration for valor.

He admitted later he was so excited and "jittery" on meeting his sovereign he couldn't remember one weowrord that was said.

Col. Merritt has just been liberated from prison camp in Germany.

Back from nearly three years in enemy hands, Canada's first VC of the war stood stiff as a ramrod on the royal dais at Buckingham Palace while the Lord Chamberlain read his citation to the King and to an audience which packed the long hall just inside one of the main doors of the Palace.

Col. Merritt bowed after the King penned the medal on his breast, then the two engaged in quiet conversation.

They shook hands as Merritt again bowed and walked away.

Mystery Man Ties Up Oak St. Car

Police are investigating a report concerning a man who early this morning hurled rocks at two other men.

E. Sturgeon, motorman on the Oak Street car line, told police he was slowing down for a switch at Fifty-Seventh and Oak at 3:40 a.m. when a man dashed out and pulled the trolley off the car.

Sturgeon went out to replace it and the man threw a rock at him.

Sturgeon with the aid of FO. J. Little, RCAF, 1436 East Tenth, chased the man for a short distance.

Little said the man had thrown a rock at him too.

Lt.-Gov. Woodward Meets Son Overseas

WITH THE 1ST CANADIAN ARMY, May 1—(CP)—Col. W. C. Woodward, Lieutenant-Governor of British Columbia, arrived in the Canadian Army area April 27. His son, Tr. Charles Woodward, serving with a Manitoba unit, met him at Brussels and spent two days with him on leave there.

Col. Woodward visited the Seaforth Highlanders of Vancouver.

Vatican Marks May Day

ROME, May 1—(BUP)—The Vatican observed May Day for the first time in history today and Italy celebrated it for the first time since eBnito Mussolini was in power.

Flats May Be Used for Park

Hints that there might be early action on improvement of False Creek flats, for which the Park Board has a plan, were given today by Hon. Ian Mackenzie, Minister of Veterans' Affairs, after a tour of new projects with P. B. Stroyan, parks superintendent, and ex-Alderman Harry DeGraves.

"It would take very little to make an attractive park on the flats and we may be able to do something about it," the Minister said.

R. Rowe Holland, board chairman, recalled that Mr. Mackenzie had succeeded in 1939 in securing $50,000 of unexpended unemployment money to fill and level the False Creek site.

Mr. Mackenzie was taken through the alleys adjacent to the Central School site proposed for a civic centre, and he expressed the opinion that demolition of several blocks of Vancouver's oldest houses for a civic centre plan would be a great improvement.

Tomorrow the Minister will address a luncheon meeting of the civic centre committee in Stanley Park pavilion.

Japs Abandoning Burma Capital

BEFORE PEGU, Burma, May 1—(BUP)—British armor and infantry virtually surrounded Pegu today and fall of the city, 50 miles above Rangoon, was expected momentarily, ending what was believed would be the last major battle for Burma.

Anglo-American prisoners of war who escaped to British lines said today that Japanese forces were abandoning Rangoon, the Burmese capital.

Prisoner Gets Away From Cop

One of two prisoners being brought here from outside points to Oakalla Prison Farm escaped from custody of a provincial police officer at the Canadian National Railway station shortly before 9:30 a.m. today.

The escaped prisoner walked

Police said his name was Robert Fagan and he was being brought from Vernon to serve a term at Oakalla.

away from the officer, as the policeman concentrated his attention on his other ward, a Chinese. Neither was handcuffed.

The escapee is described as being 30 years of age, of slim build, weighing 140 pounds and being 5 feet 10 inches tall. He is of sallow complexion. He was wearing a brown pinstriped suit and grey fedora hat when he disappeared.

Fascist Army Surrenders

ROME, May 1—(BUP)—Marshal Rodolfo Graziani unconditionally surrendered the German-controlled Italian Ligurian Army to the Allies today, while New Zealand troops of the 15th Army Group made contact with Marshal Tito's Yugoslavian forces 16 miles northwest of Venice.

Graziani told German and Italian troops of the Ligurian Army that "further resistance would be useless" and ordered his troops to lay down their arms.

The 2nd New Zealand Division crossed the Isonzo River in northeastern Italy and made contact with Tito's forces in the Monfalcone area.

The Fascist Ligurian Army had been fighting alongside the Germans in Northern Italy under the command of Graziani, who reportedly was a prisoner of the Allies.

Allies Suspend Two War Writers

PARIS, May 1—(AP)—Allied Supreme Headquarters announced today that two war correspondents accredited to it had been suspended, but refused to permit other correspondents to disclose their identity or tell the reason for its action.

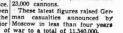

HITLER IS DEAD

THE VANCOUVER DAILY PROVINCE ★★★★★ FINAL

51st YEAR — NO. 31 VANCOUVER, B.C., TUESDAY, MAY 1, 1945 —20 PAGES PRICE 5 CENTS BY CARRIER $1.00 per month.

'Germans To Fight On'

DEAD

City Reacts Quietly, Tensely To News

Vancouver reacted quietly but intensely when Daily Province editions hit the streets seconds after announcement that Adolf Hitler had been killed.

And the papers were snapped up so quickly from news stands that pedestrians stood around in groups peering over shoulders to read the news.

Traffic regulations went unheeded at two principal newsstand corners — Hastings and Cambie, and Granville and Georgia.

At the former, where every paper was sold 30 seconds after the news truck made its delivery, pedestrians ignored traffic signals and swept across the street at the shout of the news vendor, "Hitler Dead."

The vendor's papers were gone in seconds, many people handing across dimes and saying "never mind the change."

"Wonderful if it's true," said a girl with a soldier.

"Ah. I don't believe it," muttered a sailor.

'MAYBE IT'S TRUE."

"Yes, but maybe it's true, and wouldn't that be wonderful," murmured his feminine companion.

A civilian remarked "it wasn't exactly what he wanted but it's a good start," while an airman grinned at the diminishing pile of papers and cracked: "He's doing a hell of a business. I wish I had it."

Hitler's sudden death brought no sorrow to men and women in the labor movement in Vancouver. Some expressed satisfaction, even joy, while others shrugged him off with the hope that his passing might speed the winding up of the slaughter in Europe.

TRAFFIC STOPS.

At Granville and Georgia people crowded around newsvendor, who rubbed out his "Mussolini Gones" sign, dropped his foot on a bundle of Daily Provinces, and shouted extra.

Car drivers slowed to a crawl or stopped halfway across the intersection as they craned out for a brief glance at the headlines. Street car conductors stopped their machines, dashed down to scan the headlines, then raced back to their waiting cars.

H. W. Fleshr, international representative of the Union of Operating Engineers (A.F.L.) simply remarked: "The way of the dictator is hard."

TERSE COMMENTS.

In fact, most of the comments were terse; as if the workers had no time or inclination to bother with post-mortems on one who they felt was the arch enemy of freedom

"Happy day," said Harold Pritchett, district president, International Woodworkers of America. "His death is a devastating blow against those who made him possible. His passing augurs well for freedom."

GOOD RIDDANCE.

Lawrence Anderson, general organizer, B.C. Shipyard General Workers' Federation: "Good riddance. . . . All his followers in Fascism must be obliterated with him."

John Turner, secretary, Vancouver Labor Council (CCL): "It doesn't matter how he died . . . the main thing is that he is dead. . . . An evil source has been removed fro mthe world. . . . The manner in which he met his death is not important."

James (Scotty) Wilson, Amalgamated Building Workers of Canada: "Hardly worth commenting upon."

Navy Chief Takes Over

(By Associated Press.)

LONDON, May 1.—The Nazi radio at Hamburg announced tonight that Adolf Hitler died this afternoon at his command post in Berlin.

The broadcast implied, but did not directly state, that Hitler was slain in battle with the Russians.

(The BBC reported that Hitler actually died of a stroke.)

Admiral Karl Doenitz, commandant of the German Navy, immediately announced over the Hamburg radio that he had succeeded Hitler, having been appointed by the Nazi dictator yesterday.

"At the Fuehrer's headquarters it is reported that our Fuehrer Adolf Hitler has fallen this afternoon in his command post at the Reich Chancellery, fighting up to his last breath against Bolshevism," said the announcement.

The radio broadcast a statement from Doenitz in which he said:

Germany to Fight On

"My first task will be to save Germany from the advancing Bolsheviks. Only for this do we continue the fight."

"Give me your confidence," Doenitz appealed to the German people. "Keep calm and be disciplined. Only in that way will we be able to stave off defeat."

The announcement said Hitler had appointed Doenitz on April 30 (yesterday) as his successor.

No mention was made of Heinrich Himmler, Gestapo chief who had been dickering in an attempt to surrender what remained of Germany to Britain and the United States but was turned down because he did not include Russia in his offer.

Announcement of the death of the fuehrer followed a preparatory warning to the German people over the Hamburg radio. It announced: "The German radio will shortly broadcast a grave and important announcement for the German people."

Lord Haw Haw On Air

The announcer, "Lord Haw Haw," asked listeners to keep tuned in for the announcement.

The statement of Hitler's death followed.

"German men and women, soldiers of the German army, our fuehrer Adolf Hitler has fallen," Doenitz announced dramatically.

"With deepest sorrow and reverence the German people bow.

"He had recognized the horrible danger of Bolshevism very early and consecrated his existence to the fight against it. At the end of this, his struggle, and of his straight and unerring road he dies a hero's death in the capital of the German Reich.

Doenitz Eulogizes Fuehrer

"His life was entirely given to the service of Germany. His struggle against the Bolshevist storm floods was, furthermore, not only for Europe, but for the entire civilized world. The Fuehrer has appointed me to be his successor. Fully conscious of the responsibility, I take over the leadership of the German people in the fateful hour.

"My first task will be to save the German people from

(Continued on Page 7.) See HITLER.

KARL DOENITZ.

New Reich Chief Hates British

Admiral Karl Doenitz, who took over the reins of the dying Nazi regime today, is the thin-lipped man the Germans call the greatest submarine genius of history.

He devised the U-boats' "wolf-pack" tactics, and in 1943 he sent them to sea in multiple, menacing "echelons of packs."

Said he, when he took command of the submarine warfare in February, 1943.

RUTHLESS LEADER.

"I will put the entire concentrated strength of the navy into the submarine war. . . . The entire German navy will henceforth be put into the service of inexorable U-boat warfare. The Germany navy will fight to the finish."

Today he called again for a fight to the finish as he took over from his slain Fuehrer.

He is a ruthless 52-year-old man.

When he took over U-boat warfare, the British knew they could expect intensified assault by U-boats—and they got what they expected until the Allied navies took toll of the undersea raiders.

Doenitz' rise was swift in Adolf Hitler's wartime regime.

He was only a commodore when the war began.

In early 1943, the German radio announced that he had made a 19-day voyage—undoubtedly by submarine—to visit the then Japanese Admiral Nagano.

HATES BRITISH.

Doenitz has a deep hatred of Britain and the British.

He has spent half his professional life studying how to make the submarine a deadlier weapon for use against Britain.

It is said that a year or two before the war he came over secretly in a Nazi U-boat to the United Kingdom naval base at Portland to find out what he could about the set of the currents there.

But a British destroyer discovered him and dropped a few charges around his craft.

The commander surfaced and apologized.

Down in the torpedo room, cursing, was Doenitz—balked of the information he wanted.

Doenitz was born in Berlin and belongs to a middle-class family long interested in shipping. He entered the German Navy in 1910, but saw little chance of advancement.

So, during the last war, after he had escaped to Constantinople in the light cruiser Breslau, he tried to become a naval pilot.

He was not a success, so he joined the submarine service in 1917.

BASEBALL

American League.

		R.	H.	E.
Washington	100 001 020	4	4	0
Boston	120 002 00x	5	10	1

Niggeling, Piretti (8), and Guerra; O'Neill, Woods (8), and Garbark, Holm (8).

		R.	H.	E.
Chicago	000 400 010	5	6	0
Detroit	000 000 000	0	1	0

Haynes and Tresh; Wilson, Mueller (6) and Swift.

World May Never Know How He Died, If He Died

(By Associated Press.)

Whether Hitler actually died at his command post in Berlin today (Tuesday), as the German radio said, the world may not know with assurance for some time—perhaps never.

He may have been dead for days or weeks; he may still be living and this announcement only a ruse to help his escape plans.

However, the Hamburg radio announcement could mean that this is the official end of Hitler, as far as what authority remains in Germany is concerned.

Whether he is living or dead, it could mean that the Nazi hierarchy has decided that the myth of Hitler dead now suits its purposes better than the myth of Hitler living and leading the last forlorn hope in Berlin.

A legend of Hitler dying in a Goetterdaemmerung finale to the terrible tragedy he precipitated may also fit in with Nazi propaganda plans for the years or generations ahead.

The possibility remains that Hitler actually may have died as described.

Molotov Bows Gracefully To Defeat at Conference

By W. L. MacTAVISH.
Editor Vancouver Daily Province.

SAN FRANCISCO, May 1. — Russia gained in stature and prestige at UNCIO yesterday, even though suffering a conference defeat on an issue on which the Soviet foreign commissar forced a public vote.

Russia gained, in my opinion, because the day's proceedings demonstrated the Russian desire to work with other nations for peace, and willingness to accept democratic control of the course to be followed.

Russia was the first of the big powers to put an issue squarely up to the conference to settle; to state her case clearly and directly and ask the conference to rule.

The issue was the invitation to Argentina to join the international organization for security. It was first before the executive council of 14. Then it was before the steering committee, consisting of the heads of all delegations.

AMERICAS LINED UP.

Russia, asking for delay for a few days until the question of Argentina's present status could be studied, was outvoted in both committees.

From a vote point of view the position was hopeless. The Mexico City conference of North and South American republics had set forth certain terms on which they considered Argentina could be readmitted to the comity of nations.

The United States and all the South American countries were anxious, with good reason, to bring Argentina back into the fold after her excursion into a form of Fascism.

They believed her acceptance into the United Nations organization would strengthen the hands of Argentine democratic elements and they believed Argentina had accepted and lived up to the conditions set forth at Mexico City.

Therefore they felt in honor bound to issue the invitation. And they represented almost half the voting strength of the conference.

Mr. Molotov knew that the vote was a foregone conclusion. He knew it still more definitely after the voting in the steering com-

(Continued on Page 20.) See MACTAVISH.

Churchill Hints News By Friday

(By Associated Press)

LONDON, May 1.—Prime Minister Churchill hinted today that announcement of peace in Europe might come before Saturday, but declared: "I have no special statement to make on the war position in Europe except that it is definitely more satisfactory than it was at this time five years ago."

Mr. Churchill said that if information of exceptional importance "reaches the government during the sittings of the House this week—as it might do," he would make a brief announcement.

"With regard to the condition and requisition which would occur if an announcement of decisive consequence justifying celebration were to be made this week or at anytime in the future, and V-E Day was announced, a number of arrangements have been prepared, and will be issued tonight in a home office circular."

NEAREST PREDICTION.

The implication that peace might come before the House rises for the week on Friday evening was the nearest to a prediction that Mr. Churchill permitted himself.

"Of course," he said, "I shall make no statement here that is not in accord with the statement which will be made by our allies," explaining such announcements would be made only after consulting military commanders in different theatres.

NOT WITHHELD.

The Prime Minister said he did not consider that the information in "a major message" reaching the government should be withheld "until the exact occupation of all the particular zones was achieved. The movement of troops and the surrender of enemy troops may both take an appreciable period of time."

"Good news will not be delayed," he said in answer to Lady Astor's question whether, if peace news came while the House was adjourned he would hold it until Commons again sat, or

(Continued on Page 2.) See CHURCHILL.

3RD DRIVES ON HIDEOUT

By AUSTIN BEALMEAR.
Associated Press War Correspondent.

PARIS, May 1.—The United States 3rd Army crashed southward to within 58 miles of Berchtesgaden today as the United States 7th Army advanced south from captured Munich against Innsbruck and the Brenner Pass.

Latest reports placed 7th Army infantry at Scharnitz, 10 miles northwest of Innsbruck and 15 north of the Brenner.

Meanwhile the 3rd Army's 13th Armored Division drove 25 miles out of its Isar bridgehead and reached the Inn River near Braunau, Hitler's birthplace on the Austrian-Bavarian border.

Earlier 3rd Army troops had entered Griesbach in their approach to Hitler's roost in the Alpine redoubt. The town near the Austrian border is 16 miles northeast of Braunau and 47 north of Salzburg, eastern rampart of the final Nazi hideaway.

The 11th Armored Division of the 3rd Army crossed the Austrian border in force at Oberkappel, 27 miles northwest of Linz—which the Germans said was being approached by Russians from west of Vienna.

WOULD FORM TRAP.

A meeting would hem in Czechoslovakia and trap all the Germans in Bohemia and Moravia.

Bernadotte Explodes Peace Report

11:10 P.M. SWEDISH TIME

STOCKHOLM, May 1.—(AP)—Count Folke Bernadotte, Swedish Red Cross negotiator, said at a press conference today:

"I have not seen Himmler during my last visit to Germany and Denmark. I have not forwarded any messages from Himmler or other authoritive German to the Allies."

This sensational development denied previous reports that the Swedish count, chairman of the Swedish Red Cross, was engaged in carrying German peace overtures to the Allies. Bernadotte returned from Copenhagen this morning and it had been reported that he had arranged for German evacuation of Denmark and Norway. After his return he conferred with Swedish foreign office officials. The office issued a statement making clear that it had not received any messages from German authorities.

ALLIES TAKE HORTHY, HUNGARIAN EX-REGENT

ADMIRAL HORTHY.

WITH THE U.S. 7TH ARMY, May 1.—(AP)—Admiral Nicholas Horthy, former regent of Hungary, and his family were taken into protective custody today by 36th Division troops who found them in a castle at Weilheim, south of the Amer See.

The 77-year-old former ruler was reported to be in good health.

Two German field marshals, Wilhelm List and Wilhelm Ritter von Leeb, also were captured by 7th Army troops.

List said he was relieved in 1942 for refusal to make an attack at Stalingrad. Both marshals took major parts in the Polish, French and Russian campaigns. Five German generals also were taken.

BERLIN CAPTURED

ALL GERMANS LAY DOWN ARMS IN ITALY, AUSTRIA

★ ★ ★ ★ ★ **FINAL EDITION**

The Vancouver Sun

FOUNDED 1886 VOL. LIX—No. 231 VANCOUVER, BRITISH COLUMBIA, WEDNESDAY, MAY 2, 1945 PRICE 5 CENTS

Million Nazi Soldiers Quit

LONDON, May 2—(BUP) — The Red Army captured Berlin today.

Marshal Stalin announced the capture. The Red Army's greatest victory of the war, in a triumphant order of the day broadcast from Moscow.

Berlin fell to the Russians after 12 days of siege. Two Russian armies smashed into the city from the east and south and slugged through its historic streets in what Nazis and Soviets alike described as one of the bloodiest struggles in history.

From AP and BUP Dispatches

ROME, May 2.—Col.-Gen. Heinrich von Vietingenhoff today unconditionally surrendered all German land, sea and air forces in Italy and southern and western Austria.

Under the terms hostilities ceased at 12 noon GMT (5 a.m. Vancouver time).

Field Marshal Alexander announced the surrender was signed at Allied Force Headquarters at Caserta Sunday afternoon.

The following terms were imposed in the surrender ending 2½ years of the battle of Italy:

1. Unconditional surrender by Von Vietingenhoff's command of all land, sea and air forces to Marshal Alexander.
2. Cessation of all hostilities on land, sea, and in the air by enemy forces at 12 noon London time (5 a.m. Vancouver time).
3. Immediate immobilization and disarmament of enemy forces.
4. Obligation on the part of the German commander-in-chief to carry out any further orders issued by Field Marshal Alexander.
5. Disobedience of the orders or failure to comply with them to be dealt with in accordance with accepted laws and usages of war.

Von Vietingenhoff's command includes all Northern Italy to the Isonzo River in the northeast, and the Austrian provinces of Vonarlberg, Tyrol, Salzburg, and portions of Corinthia and Styria.

"The enemy's total forces including combat and rear echelon troops surrendered to the Allies are estimated to number nearly 1,000,000 men," Marshal Alexander announced.

Headquarters earlier had announced that Gen. Jahn, commander of the Lombardy corps of the Ligurian Army, had surrendered with 2000 Germans and many Italian Fascist troops.

Opens Southern Gates

The surrender opened the southern gates of the Nazis' southern redoubt in Bavaria and the Austrian panhandle. A junction of the Allied Armies in Italy with three of Gen. Eisenhower's armies in South Germany and in Austria might be expected soon.

The surrender affects nearly a million men commanded by Col. Gen. von Vietingenhoff and Gen. Karl Wolff, chief of police and security for Northern Italy and Western Austria.

Lieut. Gen. W. D. Morgan, of the British Army, who negotiated in behalf of Field Marshal Sir Harold R. L. G. Alexander, supreme commander in the Mediterranean theatre, said the terms "in effect are complete and unconditional surrender."

The documents were signed in the Royal Palace in Rome on Sunday by Morgan and two German officers, one of whom represented Von Vietingenhoff and the other Wolff.

"Fighting troops include remnants of 22 German and six Italian Fascist divisions," Field Marshal Alexander said in today's announcement.

Girl Slain at English Bay

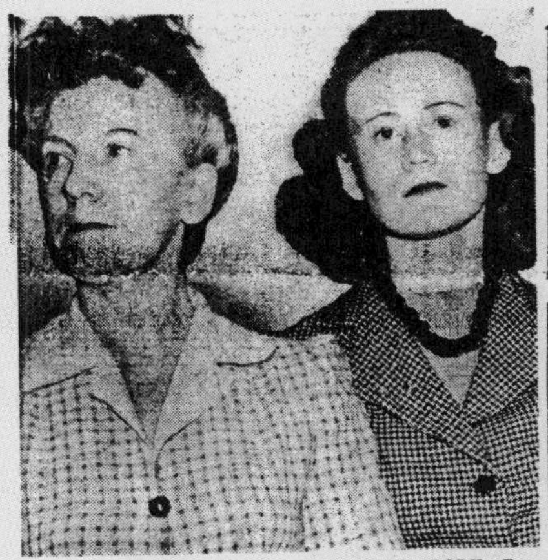

THEY FOUND BODY—Two Calgary women visiting Vancouver, Mrs. Sam Robinson (left) and her daughter, Hazel, were the first persons to reach the scene of the brutal English Bay murder today. They heard a woman's screams and ran from their apartment to meet a Canadian soldier hurrying away from the beach. Miss Robinson later found the body of the murdered woman floating in the water. Police have as evidence these two blood-stained clubs found on the scene.

Battered Body Found in Surf

Police this afternoon identified the battered body of a young woman who was slain early today on an English Bay beach as that of Olga Hawryluk, 22-year-old Vancouver waitress, who was bludgeoned to death and dragged into the surf at 4:30 a.m.

A 29-year-old soldier, arrested at Drake and Granville shortly after West End citizens found the body and notified police, is being held for investigation. No charge has been laid.

A Victoria man whose wallet was found in a sealed envelope near the murder scene, came to the Empire Cafe at 2 p.m. today, saying he had lost the wallet the night before in the cafe and inquired if it had been found. The envelope also contained $40 in cash, five keys, and a bottle of perfume.

He was taken to the police station for questioning.

Identification of the waitress followed finding by police of the girl's purse near Crystal Pool, and footprints, believed to be those of the killer, leading to it from the scene of the crime.

Milton Litras, manager of the Empire Cafe, 160 West Hastings, identified the girl. He said she had been in his employ three months. She came from Harmon Valley in the Peace River country.

Her landlady, Mrs. E. Hague, of 1537 Nelson, had been unable to identify the body in the city morgue earlier because it had been beaten so terribly.

Olga Hawryluk was last seen alive at 3 a.m. in the Empire Cafe, Mr. Litras told The Vancouver Sun, talking to a soldier.

"It all happened," Mr. Litras said, "because she was an innocent girl."

When arrested the soldier's right hand was covered with blood, police said. There were several "red spots" on the right side of his tunic and his right trouser leg.

Police reports said his shoes showed signs of having been in water recently, and sand was found clinging to his boots and trouser cuffs.

His right hand had several cuts

Please Turn to Page Two
See "Murder"

Himmler Bid Verified by U.S. Officials

Nazis Planned To Still Fight Red Armies

WASHINGTON, May 2 — (AP)—The United States acting secretary of state, Joseph C. Grew, today verified reports that Heinrich Himmler had offered a German surrender.

Grew made it clear that Himmler's surrender offer did not extend to Russia, and hence was not accepted by the United States and Britain.

In fact Himmler said, Grew declared, that he hoped to be able to continue to fight on the eastern front. He, Himmler, stipulated that his offer was for the Western Allies only.

He said Hitler was so ill he might already be dead and could not live more than two days, and that he, Himmler, was therefore in full authority. Himmler wanted to meet General Eisenhower to surrender the whole western front.

The first overture by the Nazi Gestapo chief was made the night of April 24 through Swedish Foreign Minister Gunther.

Count Folke Bernadotte, head of the Swedish Red Cross, acted as intermediary.

No Answer

LONDON, May 2 — (BUP) — Radio Hamburg, which announced Hitler's death Tuesday, closed down this morning with its usual "Heil Hitler."

Hydro Import OK if New Plant Rushed

Premier Hart today advised the B.C. Electric the provincial government would approve "temporary arrangement" to import power from Bonneville hydro, "provided satisfactory proof is submitted to the Public Utilities Commission that development of necessary power (within the province) will be proceeded with without delay."

Those last two words, "without delay," promise to be the crux of the whole deal.

W. G. Murrin, BCER president, told the press today the company had already complied with Premier Hart's proviso when it notified the Public Utilities Commission on April 6 it would commence its Bridge River project "as soon as the relevant factors indicate that such action is reasonable and in the public interest."

"It is inconceivable," Mr. Murrin told reporters, "that a $17,000,000 project such as we propose at Bridge River could be started without assurance that it would not disrupt the labor situation."

Truman Says Adolf Hitler Really Dead

'Best Possible Authority' for His Belief

From AP and BUP Dispatches

WASHINGTON, May 2. — President Truman said today he had it on the best authority that Adolf Hitler is dead.

Mr. Truman, in a philosophic remark to his news conference, said it was now a fact—speaking of the death of Hitler and Benito Mussolini—that the two principal war criminals would not have to come to trial.

"Does than mean official confirmation that Hitler is dead?" he was asked.

The President said yes, explaining his confirmation was based on the best possible authority obtainable at this time.

Asked to give his source for this information, the President declined.

Discussing, under questioning, the peace situation in general, Mr. Truman said nothing had been heard from the Nazi peace agent, Himmler, since this country and Britain rejected his offer to surrender to them alone. Himmler was told that Russia had to be included in the offer.

Mr. Truman's revelation came

Please Turn to Page Two
See "Truman"

LATE FLASHES—

U.S. Seizure of Mines Expected

WASHINGTON, May 2 — (BUP) — Government seizure of the nation's anthracite coal mines was expected today unless United Mine Workers President John L. Lewis accepts an extension of the contract which expired at midnight Monday.

The War Labor Board was w iting to 'ear from Lewis on its demand that the 72,000 hard coal miners continue to work under retroactive contract extension until all differences are settled.

King Congratulates Alexander

SAN FRANCISCO, May 2—(BUP) — Canadian Prime Minister Mackenzie King today congratulated Field Marshal Sir Harold Alexander on the final defeat of German forces in Italy.

Hun POW's Doubt Hitler Dead

LETHBRIDGE, Alta., May 2—(CP)—Early reaction of German captives detained at the large prisoner-of-war camp here to the report that Hitler was dead was one of branding the news as "Allied propaganda."

Nazis Hold Four Capitals

NEW YORK, May 2.—With the fall of Berlin to the Russians today, Germans still held four European capitals. They were: The Hague, Holland; Prague, Czechoslovakia; Copenhagen, Denmark and Oslo, Norway.

Policeman Kills Runaway Steer

Detective Rex Moore of Vancouver city police shot and killed a steer near Fifty-sixth and Main today.

The steer escaped from a packing house at Fraser and Marine about 8 a.m., and was chased throughout the bushlands of the district by packing house employees.

Finally an appeal was made to police to aid in the search.

Moore and Detective Harry Whelan finished the round-up. Only one shot was required to kill the animal.

Spain Holds Pierre Laval

MADRID, May 2—(AP)—Pierre Laval, Marcel Deat and the Vichy Education Minister Abel Bonnard arrived at Barcelona by plane today and refused to comply with a personal order from Generalissimo Francisco Franco to leave Spain immediately.

They will be interned at nearby Mountjuich Fortress pending the Spanish government's decision.

Citizens, eager for news of the end of the war, mistook radio reports this morning of the unconditional surrender of German forces in Italy, as meaning the surrender of Germany.

Former West Front Commander Captive

'FIGHTING SENSELESS NOW'—VON RUNDSTEDT

WITH THE 7TH ARMY IN GERMANY, May 2—(BUP)—An American tank crew surprised Field Marshal Karl von Rundstedt at his dinner table and captured the man who had battled the Allies from Normandy to the Rhine, it was announced today.

Von Rundstedt declared today it was senseless for Germany to fight any longer.

Van Rundstedt, twice commander of the German Armies in the West since the Allied invasion, was taken last night at Bad Tolz, a resort town south of Munich.

He was having dinner with his wife and son, Hans Gerd, when an American tank rumbled into the hospital grounds at Bad Tolz. Von Rundstedt, who was taking a health treatment, was living in a house attached to the hospital.

Von Rundstedt said he had not expected the Americans until the next morning. He

FIELD MARSHAL VON RUNDSTEDT

told his captors he last saw Adolf Hitler on March 12.

An American private, who drove Von Rundstedt and his family to the prisoner of war cage, said, "He seemed ready to surrender."

BASEBALL

		R	H	E
St. Louis	100 103 000—	4	13	1
Pittsburgh	100 000 001—	2	7	0

Brecheen and O'Dea; Sewell, Gerheauser (9) and Lopez; losing pitcher—Sewell.

		R	H	E
Boston	200 000 010—	3	6	2
Brooklyn	100 000 000—	1	7	1

Andrews and Kluttz; Lombardi, King (9) and Owen.

Cincinnati at Chicago, postponed: rain.

		R.	H.	E.
Philadelphia	100 000 030—	4	6	1
New York	31C 200 00x—	6	9	3

Christopher, Gassaway (5), Scheib (8) and Hayes; Gettel and Garbark.

		R	H	E
Washington	000 000 000—	0	4	2
Boston	000 000 04x—	4	7	0

Ahefner and Guerra; Wilson and Walters.

		R	H	E
Chicago	001 000 000—	1	4	0
Detroit	200 000 00x—	2	5	4

Grove and Tresh; Benton and Swift.

And Inside—

Race Entries On Page 10

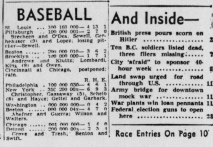

THE VANCOUVER DAILY PROVINCE

51st YEAR — NO. 33 | VANCOUVER, B.C., THURSDAY, MAY 3, 1945—24 PAGES ★ ★ ★ | PRICE 5 CENTS | BY CARRIER $1.00 per month.

Hamburg Surrenders Without a Fight

From The Times:

Today In Europe

Compiled from the news and editorial comment of the London Times and cabled from The Vancouver Daily Province London Bureau, Times Building, Printing House Square.

(Copyright, 1945, by Southam Co.)

LONDON, May 3.—By their surrender in Italy to Field Marshal Alexander, says the Times editorially today, the Germans yield up vast territories, and the best Nazi army left in Europe has now disappeared altogether as a fighting force. This has been accomplished by inferior numbers of Allied troops after one of the most arduous campaigns ever fought.

The victory has been overwhelming, and Field Marshal Alexander's masterly achievement has received its just tribute from Premier Churchill. The Allied Mediterranean forces' mighty blows helped greatly in smashing the formidable German front.

It is altogether remarkable, adds the Times, that an army group which had been relegated to a secondary role in the defeat of Germany should have ended with so colossal a victory and the complete liberation of Italy and the greater part of Austria.

Strategy Justified

Thus British strategy undertaking the Mediterranean campaign has been justified to the uttermost. That the Germans realized it from the first was shown by the despatch of Rommel's expeditionary force to North Africa.

The campaign in Italy, though long and arduous, provided a splendid training ground for troops. Most of the commanders who have proved successful in the west have served in Italy, and General Crerar himself was sent expressly to serve there to acquire experience of the latest conditions of warfare before the Normandy invasion.

Britain's traditional Mediterranean policy has justified itself to the hilt, concludes the Times, and if there had been need to invade the Bavarian redoubt, then the 15th Army Group in Italy was available for the task.

Nazi Party Split

The political chaos in Germany, says the Times diplomatic correspondent, now matches the military chaos. Clearly the Nazi party is split over surrender and Grand Admiral Doenitz is apparently trying to carry on the war with uncertain authority and small resources.

Apart from the news of the dismissal of Ribbentrop, the German radio no longer gives out information, and it is not even known whether Doenitz received his authority as the new Fuehrer from Hitler before his death, or simply took it.

Boermann, who should have succeeded Hitler, because he was deputy Fuehrer in succession to Hess, has disappeared, and such military leaders as Keitel are silent.

Editorially, the Times says of Hitler's career that he was the most pitiless and malignant being that has appeared in human history for centuries. Many leaders before him had broken faith, but none had lied with such effrontery or cared so little for exposure. He was the world's worst and most dangerous malefactor.

De Valera Sorry

President de Valera has personally called on the German minister in Dublin to convey to him Eire's sorrow on the occasion of Hitler's death.

Berlin is almost obliterated. Denmark and Schleswig-Holstein have been completely cut off from Germany. Town after town is surrendering to Field Marshal Montgomery's troops, and so little is seen of the German Army in many places that troops are vainly asking where it is.

The Swedes are still trying to induce the Germans in Norway to surrender, and it is believed that enemy control of Denmark is slowly collapsing.

Ottawa Issues Voting Rules For Servicemen

Service personnel on leave in the Vancouver district, if they are over 21 years of age and on the voters' list, may vote at the civilian polls in the June 11 federal election, or at their barracks whether overseas or in Canada.

This interpretation of the election proclamation so far as it concerns members of the armed forces was given today by Robert Edgar, chief returning officer for Vancouver Centre. He has no information as yet on dates for soldier voting.

Those eligible to vote in the federal election include all service personnel, irrespective of age, who are British subjects and resident in Canada prior to joining the service.

THE WINNERS—Field Marshal Sir Harold Alexander, Allied commander-in-chief in the Mediterranean area, and General Mark Clark, commander of the Allied armies in Italy, were the victors when German armies in Italy and Southern Austria unconditionally surrendered. (AP Wirephoto.)

HUSH OF DEATH OVER BERLIN

V-E Day All Set, But It's a Big Secret

LONDON, May 3.—(AP)—Workmen began erecting a grandstand in front of Buckingham Palace today in preparation for V.-E. Day ceremonies.

A ministry of works official explained that "it must be done by a definite date. But that date is a big secret."

SOLDIER FACES MURDER TRIAL

Stocky, ruddy-complexioned William J. Hainen, Vancouver soldier charged with the English Bay slaying of cafe cashier Olga Hawryluk, appeared in Police Court today and was remanded for one week.

Hugh A. Redpath, Victoria, whose wallet was found with other articles on the sand 30 feet from the victim's body, was ordered held as a material witness.

Magistrate H. S. Wood suggested that Redpath post a $500 bond. When Redpath said he would try to raise the money, the magistrate ordered him held pending its deposit.

Detective William Smith testified that Redpath could give helpful testimony. Police said he was a "victim of circumstances."

ACCUSED CALM.

Hainen was in the box only two minutes.

The dark-haired soldier was unmoved, expressionless.

When a constable asked him if the week's remand was all right, he said his only words:

"All right."

It came in a voice almost inaudible to spectators in the court.

Prosecutor Gordon Scott outlined the case briefly before Hainen was put on the stand.

Olga Hawryluk's body was found at 5 a.m. Wednesday, face down in water two feet from shore, at the foot of Bidwell. Her face was unrecognizable as a result of repeated blows.

BODY DISCOVERED.

A few minutes before that, Mrs. Sam Robinson and her daughter Hazel, Calgary, staying at 1306 Bidwell, heard screams, ran to the beach and saw and spoke to a soldier who "got up from behind some logs."

Some time later, Hainen was arrested at Drake and Granville. He was not charged with murder until 12 hours later, after police

(Continued on Page 2.)
See MURDER.

City Brigadier Takes High Post

OTTAWA, May 3.—(CP)—Defense headquarters announced today the appointment of Brig. W. G. H. Roaf, 36, of Vancouver, as a deputy adjutant-general at headquarters.

Brig. Roaf, a Vancouver sales executive before the war, went overseas in 1939 and was appointed a deputy assistant quartermaster-general of a Canadian division in 1941, later becoming assistant adjutant and quartermaster-general of Canadian reinforcement units.

Unkempt Nazis Shuffle Through Victory Gate

By EDDY GILMORE.
(Associated Press War Correspondent.)

MOSCOW, May 3.—Thousands of dirty and unshaven Germans shuffled through the Brandenburg Gate under the pillars of victory in fallen Berlin today to lay down their arms where goose-stepping Prussians formerly paraded in triumph.

The hush of death lay over the smoking, broken capital, broken only by occasional explosions in the ruins.

The fall of Berlin came as other Soviet armies to the south were swinging westward through Czechoslovakia towards Prague and the western Allies in a drive to shred another developing pocket of Nazi resistance.

North of Berlin, only a twisting, virtually indefensible strip of the Mecklenburg plain remained to the Germans.

There was no further information on the fate of Hitler or Goebbels, who were said by Goebbels' deputy to have committed suicide. The Russians are checking the story.

One well known Soviet commentator, Nikolai Tikhonov, declared in Pravda that "Hitler is not in Berlin."

"Whether he fled to his devils' nest, to the other world or to the embraces of some Fascist

(Continued on Page 2.)
See BERLIN.

V-E Day Due 'In 48 Hours'

Unofficial word came from the United Nations World Security Conference at San Francisco today that V-E Day in Europe will be proclaimed "within the next 48 hours."

An unidentified member of the Canadian delegation to the conference was given as the source of the report. This report coincided with a despatch from C.B.S. correspondent with the 21st Army Group in Germany that "big news" was expected within the next 48 hours.

Canadians reportedly have this information:

If official declaration of VE-Day — presumably to be announced simultaneously in London, Washington and Moscow—does not come before 9 p.m. D.B.S.T. (12 noon, Vancouver time) on any day, the announcement will be withheld until the following day.

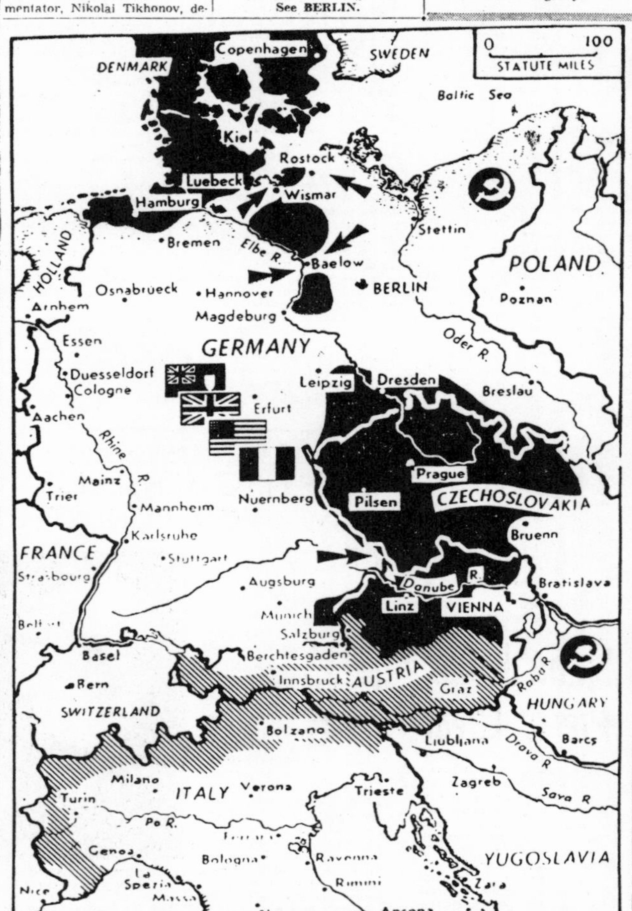

Only 538 square miles of Germany proper—an area of 181,466 square miles—today are in German hands. The great cities of Hamburg and Berlin have fallen. Black areas designate territory in the Reich proper and occupied countries still under Nazi control. (AP Wirephoto.)

Nazi Resistance Collapses In Entire Baltic Pocket

NEW YORK, May 3.—(AP)—The Swedish radio says British forces are expected to enter Denmark "this evening" and reported that a heavy battle between German Army and S.S. troops had broken out near the Danish city of Aarhus. British forces found the bridge across the Kiel Canal intact.

(Associated Press War Correspondent.)

PARIS, May 3.—Hamburg surrendered to the British Army today and Marshal Stalin announced from Moscow the collapse of German resistance in the entire northern German pocket east of Kiel.

Marshal Stalin's order of the day said a link with the British 2nd Army had been established along a 60-mile front from the Baltic to Wittenberge on the Elbe after the overwhelming of the last German resistance on the Mecklenburg Plain.

Denmark and Norway were isolated by the British-Russian junction and Prague was declared a "hospital city" by the Germans.

Hamburg, Europe's largest port and Germany's second city (1,682,220), had been outflanked and besieged for several weeks. It was largely in ruins.

"Hamburg is an open city," the radio there—one of the last in German hands—proclaimed.

"British occupation troops are now entering the city."

Armistice rumors circulated in Paris again. Unconfirmed reports said both Heinrich Himmler and Grand Admiral Karl Doenitz had approached the Allies anew, this time addressing themselves to the Russians as well as to British and United States authorities.

The Luxembourg radio said many German commanders in Zeeland and Jutland are surrendering to Danish Mayors, and that German rule in Denmark seemed to be nearing its end.

Enemy defensive positions in northwestern Germany are tottering as 2nd Canadian Division troops captured Oldenburg, key to the line guarding Emden and Wilhelmshaven.

HOLDINGS SPLIT.

The northern German holdings were split into several untenable pockets and the southern section was shrunk by the surrender in Italy of nearly 1,000,000 German combat and service troops.

The Alpine "redoubt" was virtually wiped out under terms of the surrender. The Germans still hold Bohemia and Moravia, eastern Austria and the mountainous region of northwest Yugoslavia.

Even this southern section is about to be split by a junction of the U.S. 3rd Army and the Russians around the Austrian city of Linz.

LINK WITH RUSS.

Troops of the British 6th Airborne Division, meanwhile, linked with tanks of the 2nd White Russian Army in the area of Wismar, 29 miles southwest of Rostock, Baltic port captured by the Soviet forces. The 1st Canadian Parachute Battalion is part of the British division.

With the loss of Berlin, Hamburg, Luebeck and Rostock, the only large German cities remaining under the Swastika were Breslau, Dresden, Chemnitz and Kiel. At Luebeck, British troops were 38 miles from Kiel and 85 from the Danish frontier. Schwerin (45,000), Wismar and Wittenberge (both 25,000) toppled in the north.

The Danubian fortress of Passau (25,000), guardian city to

(Continued on Page 2.)
See HAMBURG.

Surrender Bulletins

LONDON, May 3.—(Reuters)—Reich Minister Albert Speer, speaking over the Danish radio to the people of Germany tonight, said: "Germany is defeated."

LONDON, May 3.—(CP Cable)—The end of all fighting in northern Germany appeared tonight to be a matter of hours and signs multiplied from every battle area that the cessation of hostilities in Europe was imminent.

A new wave of German surrender reports swept Allied capitals today.

This is the picture:

1. Talk of unconditional surrender is circulating in Moscow. This is significant because Moscow is the only United Nations capital which has never previously indulged in such speculations.
2. Prime Minister Churchill was absent from Commons this morning, reportedly because of "cabinet work."
3. A responsible Swedish diplomat said in Stockholm German surrender in Norway and Denmark "might occur today."
4. **The B.B.C. relayed a broadcast from the German-controlled Danish radio saying that the big naval base of Kiel would not be defended.**
5. Paris reports both Admiral Doenitz and Gestapo Chief Heinrich Himmler negotiating for unconditional surrender.
6. Nazi capitulation in Holland is reported "imminent" by Luxembourg radio.

Maze of Detail Ahead, But Objectives Clear

By W. L. MacTAVISH.
(Editor of The Vancouver Daily Province.)

SAN FRANCISCO, May 3.—So much has been happening here and elsewhere in the world in the past few days that it is a little difficult to realize this conference of the United Nations is just swinging into its second week. But it is, and it has now all sails set to move toward an objective clearly discernible though several weeks' journey away.

Questions that arose over the seating of Argentine, Ukrainian, White Russian and Polish delegates have dominated public discussion, but behind this the work of the conference has been going forward steadily.

The Big Four, the sponsoring nations, have been conferring daily and nightly. The executive committee meets every morning and passes on the results of its work to the steering committee.

Now the entire organization has been completed with four commissions divided into 10 committees, which again, as they get under way, will be divided into numerous sub-committees.

The plenary sessions constitute a sort of parliament, but the work of the conference is done in the commissions and committees. They have the Dumbarton Oaks proposals as the framework of the organization they are to plan and shape.

900 AMENDMENTS.

Already the conference has before it more than 900 proposed amendments to the Dumbarton plan, and suggestions are still coming from every side.

There are thorny problems and many of them still to be tackled—such vitally important questions as the veto power of the permanent members of the security council, the trusteeship of conquered enemy territories,

(Continued on Page 2.)
See PARLEY.

Vancouver Dons Swim Trunks; Ice Man Happy

Vancouver went swimming Wednesday.

As temperatures skyrocketed to a 1945 high of 74 degrees, men, women and children poured onto the beaches, relaxed on the sands in swimming trunks and sun suits through the hot afternoon and into the evening. A few plunged into waters little cooler than average summer temperatures.

It wasn't a record heat wave, but its suddenness caught citizens in wilting winter clothes. E. B. Shearman, Dominion weather bureau, recalled the city hit the seventies long before this time last year.

ICE MAN STIRS.

The ice companies looked at the weather and began looking for more labor. Horace Keetch, National Selective Service, said University students probably would be asked to help.

The warmth will be with us a few more days, probably, the airport forecast station reports. They warn, however, that it may vanish like it came, with thunderstorms now over Oregon bumping it out of the way.

Seattle perspired under blazing sun that shot the mercury up to 86 degrees, an all-time high for May 2.

Victoria temperatures were 81 and 51.

Raid Killed 300,000

NEAR DRESDEN, May 3.—(AP)—British prisoners of war returning through the American lines said Dresden police told them 300,000 persons were killed in the historic 14-hour Allied air raid which wiped out Dresden February 13 and 14.

Lt.-Col. Merritt Visits France

WITH THE 1ST CANADIAN ARMY, May 3.—(CP Cable)—Lt.-Col. C. C. I. Merritt of Vancouver and Belleville, Ont., who received the Victoria Cross he won at Dieppe in a ceremony at Buckingham Palace two days ago, arrived from Britain today to spend a few days with the Canadian Army in the field and to visit the unit he led in the Dieppe raid of 1942—the South Saskatchewan Regiment of Estevan and Regina.

Total Bond Sales Are $667,592,150

Total Eighth Victory Loan bond sales throughout Canada Wednesday amounted to $90,551,000, boosting the total at the half-way mark of the three-week campaign to $667,592,150.

Nine-day total for the previous drive was $661,097,750, while the total for the corresponding day of the Seventh Victory Loan was $85,284,250.

Fighting Peters Out in Italy

ROME, May 3.—(AP)—The British 8th Army has occupied the Italian city of Trieste today as all fighting in northern Italy and western Austria ceased under an unconditional surrender agreement signed by German Gen. Heinrich von Vietinghoff-Scheel.

More than 230,000 prisoners were taken prior to capitulation, and hostilities had ended in the area of von Vietinghoff's command west of the Isonzo River.

The surrender of the German garrison at Trieste was accepted by Lt.-Gen. Sir Bernard C. Freyberg, commander-in-chief of the New Zealand 2nd Corps.

Gen. von Vietinghoff was scheduled to meet Field Marshal Alexander, Allied commander, or Gen. Clark, 15th Army group commander, to give up formally with his staff today.

THE VANCOUVER DAILY PROVINCE

51st YEAR—NO. 34 VANCOUVER, B.C., FRIDAY, MAY 4, 1945 —28 PAGES ★ ★ ★ PRICE 5 CENTS BY CARRIER $1.00 per month.

Huns in Holland, Denmark, Northwest Germany Surrender

WAR IN EUROPE ENDS FOR CANADIAN TROOPS

The war in Europe is apparently ended for the Canadian Army.

General Eisenhower's brief announcement that Holland, Denmark, and northwestern Germany have surrendered brought a sudden end to the task assigned to the First Canadian Army.

It is now probable that the troops from the Dominion will move in to occupy Nazi-held Dutch cities and handle the surrender details in Holland.

For the Royal Canadian Navy, too, the surrender announcement is of vital importance. Germany now has only ports in Norway from which to operate her submarine fleet and it is hardly possible that Norway can hold out for long.

R.A.F. Smashes Flight By Sea

Huns Try Escape To Norway

By HENRY B. JAMESON.
Associated Press Staff Correspondent

LONDON, May 4.—Allied air forces struck continually today at German shipping fleeing toward Denmark and Norway after sinking at least 53 vessels and damaging scores of others in assaults yesterday and last night.

Pilots on dawn patrols around the North Sea and Baltic coasts reported Germans still were trying frantically to escape the mainland in anything that would float.

Many of the larger craft bristled with ack-ack guns and the air ministry reported 12 R.A.F. planes lost.

Three veteran R.A.F. flyers described the scene as more chaotic than Dunkerque, adding that ships could be seen burning in every direction and Nazi soldiers by the hundreds were swimming or rowing lifeboats back to shore where British troops were waiting to take them prisoner.

From The Times: Today In Europe

Compiled from the news and editorial comment of the London Times and cabled from The Vancouver Daily Province London Bureau, Times Building, Printing House Square.

(Copyright, 1945, by Southam Co.)

LONDON, May 4. — Whether or not there is a political struggle between Admiral Doenitz and Himmler for the leadership in Germany does not matter, says the Times editorially, because the prize for which they contend is dissolving into thin air.

National Socialism is collapsing under Allied hammerblows into a chaos, and military resistance is in its last phase. Today the control of Germany does not rest either with Doenitz or Himmler, but with the Allied military command in the Elbe region, where British, Americans and Russians have met.

The remaining history of this war concerns only the suppression of the enemy in areas where fragments of the Schutzstaffel still hold out against inevitable defeat.

Control All East

The Red Army, by capture of Berlin, now controls all eastern Germany. British troops, by the capture of a million Germans, give the Allies control of all northern Italy and western Austria.

Doenitz's declaration that Prague is an open city shows Bohemia will not be defended. Whether the Nazis will make a stand in Denmark or Norway, and whether they will long hold out in western Holland, remains to be seen.

The enemy can have no hope of holding Rotterdam, Amsterdam and The Hague. If the Germans in Norway refuse to intern themselves in Sweden, it can only be because Doenitz desires to maintain U-boat warfare against Allied shipping to the bitter end.

Doenitz is credited with the perverse idea that the honor of the German Navy can in some way be redeemed by keeping up this barbarous form of warfare after all else has been lost. He was lately in Kiel.

Norwegian Haven

Though sinkings of Allied ships have been small recently, and destruction of U-boats satisfactory, he may still have from 100 to 200 operating from the Norwegian coasts. Not much is known of their supplies, which have hitherto depended on north German ports, now in Field Marshal Montgomery's hands.

It is possible Doenitz might be able to operate for a few months longer, provided land forces can protect their bases.

The brilliant success of the Burma campaign comes to its climax with the capture of Rangoon from the Japanese. This gives Lord Louis Mountbatten a sea base of enormous importance and opens up new routes to China.

The Burmese people, having had enough of enemy occupation, now are willingly co-operating with the British despite the fact that Burmese Nationalists never regarded British rule as anything but a passing phase in their country's history. The large measure of self government given Burma before the war and so-called independence granted by the Japanese during their occupation, as well as the existence of a Burmese Army now fighting with the British, says the Times, has created a new political situation of which British policy must take account.

Dominion Status

Dominion status for Burma is already pledged and must be carried through as soon as possible.

The Munich revolt, which took place before U. S. troops entered the city, was a small-scale affair, says the Times correspondent, who has been there. Only three companies of German troops revolted, and they were quickly shot down by Himmler's men. Two hundred army officers were willing to help, but were unable to do much.

FOUR FLEE FIRE IN NIGHT ATTIRE

After four persons fled in night attire from fire at 930 East Sixteenth Thursday night, neighbors pitched in to help move furniture and personal belongings in danger of destruction.

The downstairs living-room and hall of the house were badly damaged.

R. E. Peterson, owner; his daughter and son-in-law, Mr. and Mrs. W. R. Brown, and their two-year-old daughter, were asleep upstairs.

Mrs. Brown wakened about 10:30 p.m. She thought she heard a noise in the furnace and called her father.

They smelled smoke and found that fire had started in a partition above the gas fireplace in the living-room. Mrs. Brown took the baby to a neighbor's.

Little Damage From Heavy Wind; Planes Grounded

Winds sweeping down from the Queen Charlotte Islands in gusts up to 38 miles an hour struck Vancouver Thursday night and early today.

Waves in English Bay were churned into big whitecaps and trees swayed but no serious damage was reported.

A few of the tiny rowboats anchored off homes along West Vancouver shoreline were thrown on the beach.

Trans-Canada flights last night and early today were grounded after the 9:55 p.m. plane climbed to 19,000 feet over the mountains and then was forced to turn back.

Decreasing winds are forecast for today and tonight. Saturday will be moderately windy.

Today's temperature did not exceed 57, and Saturday is expected to reach a high of 60.

Gets Jail Term, Fine On Dope Count

NORTH VANCOUVER, May 4. — Lyle McDiarmid, Taylor street, Vancouver, was sentenced to two years in penitentiary and fined $200 when he pleaded guilty to a charge of possessing opium.

Regent St.—FDR St.

LONDON, May 4.—(CP) — The Daily Telegraph suggested today that Regent street—one of London's main west end thoroughfares—be renamed Roosevelt street in memory of President Roosevelt, "a truly great man."

Bedraggled Nazis at Berlin's Victory Gate

German soldiers, bedraggled, unshaven are shown shuffling through the famed Brandenburg Victory Gate in Berlin toward Russian prison camps. (The picture was transmitted by AP Wirephoto via radio from Moscow.)

NAZIS' ONCE-PROUD WEHRMACHT DYING SHAMEFUL DEATH ON ELBE

By WES GALLAGHER.
Associated Press Staff Writer.

ON THE ELBE RIVER IN GERMANY, May 4. — Germany's once-proud Wehrmacht is dying a shameful death on the banks of the Elbe.

S.S. Panzer troops — once Germany's elite—paddle across the river in makeshift rafts. Sometimes they swim, leaving their medal-bedecked tunics behind.

Their coming has created a grave problem for American military commanders. The American 9th Army does not want them, but they come anyway, and military men are afraid the Russians may feel the western allies are giving shelter to the enemy.

Every effort has been made to discourage surrenders.

The Germans come up to the river under white flags, row across, and say they are going to surrender, and the troops can't do anything but accept them.

Enemy generals come up to regimental command posts to await their turn and nothing is accepted but unconditional surrender.

Anyone standing on the Elbe couldn't help but feel the war is over, V-E declaration or no.

That enemy generals are standing in line is no figure of speech.

At one regimental command post there were two generals, one a Panzer army commander, and a half dozen colonels, all trying to surrender their units. The two generals weren't speaking to one another. All sat with hard Prussian stares while the interpreter for the Panzer general made it clear that the other general "had no rating at all," that he had no authority, and that, besides, the Panzer general was there first.

LONDON, May 4.—(AP)—German soldiers, surrendering to British and United States forces by the thousands in a panicky effort to avoid falling into the hands of the Russians, have created a serious problem for Allied authorities charged with keeping them caged and fed.

The Daily Express says that more than 3,000,000 Germans have been taken prisoner since D-Day, and that under the original agreement Britain must look after half of them, regardless of whether they were captured by British or American troops.

The British Government repeatedly has asked the United States to take a larger proportion of the captured Germans, because all British prison camps are full and the food problem is acute.

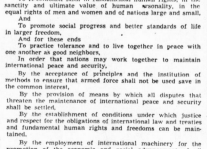

At the maximum only about 650,000 men of the once-mighty Wehrmacht are left today to put up any kind of resistance. Of these from 150,000 to 300,000 are in Norway, where Naziism may make its final stand. Another 350,000 are in Austria-Czechoslovakia, surrender or collapse of which is expected hourly. Black areas designate the two remaining pockets in Europe. Germany is completely occupied. Today's surrender in Denmark, northwest Germany and Holland involves around 500,000 men.

Lone Flyer Captured Rangoon

CALCUTTA, India, May 4.—(AP)—Decisive defeat of Japanese forces in Burma was climaxed today in the capture of the capital of Rangoon, with its big port intact.

Prome, another key city on the lower Irrawaddy, 160 miles northwest of Rangoon, was captured.

Rangoon was found abandoned by the enemy, but an amphibious force which had landed just south of the city to participate in the capture went through with the operation as a practice for bigger things to come—perhaps an attack on Singapore.

The initial British entry into Rangoon, which Allied troops have been fighting to regain since 1942, was effected by a single British airman on foot.

Wing Cmdr. A. E. Saunders of the R.A.F. made a one-man capture of Mingladon airdrome and entered Rangoon by himself Wednesday.

Saunders was flying over the area when he noted the lack of any kind of activity aground and decided to land on Mingladon airdrome. He learned no Japanese had been on the field for days.

He camouflaged his plane there and made his way 30 miles to Rangoon, where he was told that all but a few Japanese stragglers had fled the city April 25.

The airman then seized a sampan and sailed down the Rangoon River to advise amphibious forces making their way northward after landing at the river mouth.

WEEKDAY AFTER V-E DAY TO BE NATIONAL HOLIDAY

OTTAWA, May 4.—(CP)—Hon. J. L. Ilsley, acting prime minister, announced today that the weekday following the day of the official declaration of the end of hostilities in Europe will be proclaimed a holiday and will be observed by government and crown company employees, who will be paid for the day.

Smuts Writes World Charter Of Freedom From Fear, Want

By W. L. MacTAVISH.
(Editor of The Vancouver Daily Province.)

SAN FRANCISCO, May 4.—Jan Christiaan Smuts may be credited in years to come with having written the charter of the world's guarantee of freedom from fear and want. At any rate he has produced a draft of the preamble of the charter of the United Nations which expresses about as well as words could the purposes for which the nations are here convened.

As it stands it is worth quoting in full, and it follows:

The high contracting parties:

Determined

To prevent a recurrence of the fratricidal strife which twice in our generation has brought untold sorrow and loss upon mankind,

And

To re-establish faith in fundamental human rights, in the sanctity and ultimate value of human personality, in the equal rights of men and women and of nations large and small,

And

To promote social progress and better standards of life in larger freedom,

And for these ends

To practice tolerance and to live together in peace with one another as good neighbors,

In order that nations may work together to maintain international peace and security,

By the acceptance of principles and the institution of methods to ensure that armed force shall not be used save in the common interest,

By the provision of means by which all disputes that threaten the maintenance of international peace and security shall be settled,

By the establishment of conditions under which justice and respect for the obligations of international law and treaties and fundamental human rights and freedoms can be maintained,

By the employment of international machinery for the promotion of the economic and social advancement of all peoples,

Agree to this charter of the United Nations.

(Continued on Page 2. See MacTAVISH.)

Wolves Terrorize B.C. Island

(Special to The Daily Province)

PRINCE RUPERT, May 4.—A starving wolf pack is terrorizing Digby Island, three miles from here. Fourteen dogs have been killed and residents fear for the lives of their children.

Only adults are allowed to enter the woods.

The wolves are known to have killed 14 dogs, but others are missing.

Rifle-packing settlers have shot two grey wolves and one black one since the marauders became bold enough to enter the Dodge Cove community.

Single wolves have been seen in vicinity of the Cove in daytime.

The pack roams the uninhabited side of the island.

As many as 17 wolves are running in one pack.

Times Square V-E Barricades Erected

NEW YORK, May 4.—(AP) — Times Square has decided victory is near. The first wooden barricades have been put into place to protect store windows from V-E Day revelry.

Eisenhower Announces Hostilities Will End There at 11 Tonight

WITH THE U.S. SEVENTH ARMY, May 4. — (AP) — It was officially announced tonight that the city of Berchtesgaden had had been captured and cleared.

Practically all organized resistance in the southwestern sector of the Seventh Army front has collapsed along a front of 70 miles. Remnants of the German 9th and 12th Armies southwest of Berlin have surrendered.

(By Associated Press.)

PARIS, May 4. — The Allies liberated all Holland and Denmark and won northwestern Germany today, with Gen. Eisenhower announcing that German troops there had surrendered to Field Marshal Montgomery's 21st Army group. The enemy agreed to lay down their arms at 8 a.m. tomorrow (11 p.m. today Vancouver time).

This wholesale surrender came two days after the surrender of the German forces in Italy and part of Austria, and left only Norway and minor pockets in Germany, France and Czechoslovakia to be swept up before the great war machine that Adolf Hitler built has been brought to a complete halt.

Thus the 1st Canadian Army is spared the difficult task of conquering western Holland, which the Germans had defended by inundating lowlands with water from the Zuider Zee, and also the task of capturing Emden and Wilhelmshaven in northwest Germany.

It was not immediately known how many troops were involved in the latest surrender.

Earlier Allied headquarters announced that the British drive toward Denmark had halted just south of the Kiel Canal in Germany.

Queen Wilhelmina already has returned to the previously liberated portion of the Netherlands awaiting return to the Dutch capital.

1st Canadian Army truck convoys and Allied planes have been penetrating German lines for several days to take food to the famished population.

READY TO TAKE OVER.

In Denmark King Christian is reported ready to resume his prerogatives with most of the members of Parliament already on hand to take over their duties.

Denmark had been under the German heel since the morning of April 9, 1940, when German troops arrived in Copenhagen in the surprise stroke that swept over both that country and Norway.

Holland was invaded a month later, May 10, and the Germans virtually completed their occupation of that country four days later when the Dutch commander surrendered his forces.

The German-controlled Oslo radio had broadcast conflicting reports of a surrender in Holland, and Stockholm reports had insisted that negotiations for a surrender in Denmark and perhaps Norway were in progress.

Gen. Eisenhower's announcement ended uncertainty of several hours in which various reports had told of capitulation negotiations on the Danish frontier and the cessation of hostilities in Holland.

Gen. Eisenhower's announcement said nothing concerning Norway, however.

LAST STAND.

There have been indications that what is left of the Nazi regime might be fleeing to Norway. The latest of these indications was the blasting of German convoys fleeing toward that country.

The United States 7th Army

(Continued on Page 2.) See ALLIES.

Nazis Beaten! —Eisenhower

PARIS, May 4. — (AP)—Gen. Eisenhower said today the Germans were beaten in the land sea and air.

RETURN

QUEEN WILHELMINA.

KING CHRISTIAN.

Surrender Bulletins

SAN FRANCISCO, May 4. — (Reuters)— The final surrender of Germany appears to be only a matter of hours.

Certain moves are reported in progress to bring about surrender on terms as unconditional as those accepted by the Germans in Italy and western Austria.

No V-E Day—Yet

General Eisenhower's announcement of the new capitulation in northwest Germany, Holland and Denmark does not mean this (Friday) is V-E Day.

While less than 5 per cent. of Germany remains to be won by the Allies, Eisenhower has made it clear there there will be no V-E Day until the last German pockets have been cleared.

Getting Set in Ottawa

OTTAWA, May 4.—Workmen today started erecting loudspeakers on Parliament Hill in readiness for V-E Day. Ottawa's formal victory celebration will be held on the Parliament Building grounds on the afternoon of V-E Day.

THE VANCOUVER DAILY PROVINCE

51st YEAR—NO. 35 | VANCOUVER, B.C., SATURDAY, MAY 5, 1945—48 PAGES ★ ★ ★ | PRICE 10 CENTS

Two More Wehrmacht Armies Surrender

From The Times:

Today In Europe

Compiled from the news and editorial comment of the London Times and cabled from The Van-Bureau, Times Building, Print-couver Daily Province London ing House Square.

(Copyright, 1945, by Southam Co.)

LONDON, May 5.—The surrender of 1,000,000 Germans in Holland, Denmark and northwestern Germany to Field Marshal Montgomery, says the Times, is a magnificent climax to the war.

Another great chapter of liberation has been wriitten. First emotion everywhere will be one of deepest relief that the two countries now set free in the last hours have escaped the loss, life and desruction an armed attack on their conquerors would have entailed.

The Dutch rescued at the eleventh hour have been systematically starved. Valor, pride and endurance of the Danes deserves every praise. Once again the Allies may take just and profound contentment from a great revolution of the wheel of fate. Five years of persistent sacrifice have been required. A battlefield surrender was the only form which leaves no loophole for German propagandists hereafter to deny the totality of the Allies' victory.

Committed Suicide

The Times diplomatic correspondent stresses how Nazi Germany has virtually committed suicide, how there is no government, no administration, no one to take charge of anything anywhere. The Allies have a far more difficult task than in 1918, when both the government and administration existed and were prepared to carry on.

The Allied commission must exercise control from Berlin, where either Field Marshal Montgomery or Field Marshal Alexander will act as Britain's representative. This commission will be the real ruler of Germany, and it will rule over an utterly broken nation.

Because of the appalling Nazi mentality which concentration camp horrors have revealed, the commission will also have to reeducate Germany into civilized ideas and behavior—a task of extraordinary complexity.

The Yugoslav Army claims it liberated Trieste and Gorizia and not the New Zealanders, who are also there. The Germans left both cities, the Yugoslavs say, as far back as April 30. On the other hand, General Freyberg's New Zealand command accepted German surrender of Trieste, the Germans having refused to give in to the Yugoslavs.

His Last Hours

Cardinal Schuster, Archbishop of Milan, has given the Times correspondent a striking account of his final interview with Mussolini while the cardinal was trying to bring about a German surrender to save northern Italy further bloodshed.

158

The cardinal pleaded with the fallen Duce to be reasonable and accept surrender to the Allies in the same fashion as Napoleon had done. Mussolini promised to disband all Italian armies, but insisted he himself would retire with 3000 of his Black Shirts to mountains near Como.

"That means continuing resistance," said Cardinal Schuster. "Only for two or three days," replied Mussolini. "Do you imagine you would get 3000 or even 300?" asked the cardinal. Mussolini replied sadly, "Perhaps less than 300."

The cardinal then urged Mussolini to repent all his past sins and face the sad days that were in store for him. He presented Mussolini with a copy of the "Life of Saint Benedict." But with little result. "Ah, no," said the cardinal, "he was still far from any religious belief.

"Surrender, Or The War Will Go On!"

. . . Field Marshal Montgomery

(By Canadian Press.)

LONDON, May 5.—"If you do not agree to surrender, then I will go on with the war and I will be delighted to do so. "All your soldiers and civilians may be killed."

This was Field Marshal Sir Bernard Montgomery's ultimatum to German military leaders who came to negotiate the mass surrender of more than 1,000,000 fighting men in Holland, northwest Germany and Denmark.

Britain and the world heard via a transcribed broadcast the field marshal dictating the terms of surrender in a small tent.

An announcer said the surrender terms were signed "in an ordinary camouflaged army tent" at which Field Marshal Montgomery and the German officers gathered around a table.

Bill Downs, Columbia broadcasting system correspondent, broadcasting from Hamburg tonight, described the surrender.

MISSION SIGNS.

"A German surrender mission, headed by Admiral von Friedeberg, commander-in-Chief of the German Navy, signed articles of unconditional surrender for the German land, sea and air forces, facing the 1st Canadian Army and the British 2nd Army, at 6:25 o'clock this Friday evening.

"Field Marshal Montgomery signed in behalf of the Allied Supreme Commander-in-Chief, General Eisenhower.

"The signing occurred in a tent set up especially for the ceremony in front of Marshal Montgomery's headquarters on the Lunenberg Heath just south of Hamburg.

FOUGHT RUSSIANS.

"What happened was that this drive to the Baltic carried the 2nd Army thrust directly behind the line of retreat of the German Army group, the Nazi armies retreating before the drive in the north by Marshal Rokossovsky's forces advancing westward.

"That explains the large number of staff officers who fell into British hands during these fateful days. We were capturing the generals before encountering their fighting troops.

(Continued on Page 2.)
See MONTY.

Russ Arrest Pole Leaders; Allies Protest

SAN FRANCISCO, May 5.—(AP)—British officials said today the arrest by Russia of a group of Polish Democrat leaders who were seeking to broaden the Soviet-sponsored Warsaw government had disrupted further discussion on the Polish issue at the World Security Conference.

Moscow announced today the Polish leaders, 16 men, had been arrested "for security reasons."

An official British statement said Foreign Secretary Eden had taken the position there could be no further discussions of the Polish question with Soviet Commissar Molotov until the situation was straightened out.

DEMAND EXPLANATION.

A short time later State Secretary Stettinius announced he had asked Russia for a "full explanation" of the arrest of the Polish leaders. He said further discussion of the whole Polish question "must await a reply."

British officials termed the Russian action "a most serious development."

The Moscow announcement of the arrests named the leader of the group as "the well-known Polish General Abulicki."

British Chase Fleeing Japs

CALCUTTA, May 5.—(CP)—British 14th Army troops, after clearing Pegu, are pursuing fleeing Japanese forces eastward toward Moulmein, port city across the Gulf of Martaban from captured Rangoon.

The enemy was presumably retreating along the rail line that runs from Pegu, 50 miles north of Rangoon, to Moulmein.

Allied headquarters said Japanese armies in Burma have been "decisively defeated," leaving 97,000 dead on the field of battle.

Good Weather Promised Sunday

Good weather is predicted for Vancouver this week-end, with moderate winds, clear skies and higher temperatures today and Sunday.

Temperature will hit 66 degrees Sunday, with a minimum of 50.

Skiers can look for sunshine on Grouse and Hollyburn, where average temperature has been 54 degrees.

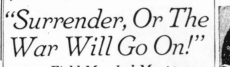

IN FLIGHT—William Joyce, the British traitor who broadcast for the Germans and was named "Lord Haw Haw" by Britons, left for Denmark by car Wednesday night. The chief censor at Hamburg radio station reported Joyce's flight today.

TO USE 25,000 CANADIAN MEN

By ROSS MUNRO.
Canadian Press War Correspondent.

WITH THE 1ST CANADIAN ARMY, May 5. — The war was over on the Canadian Army front at 8 a.m. today, when the cease-fire order became effective, and 80,000 to 100,000 Germans in fortress Holland and possibly 30,000 in the northwest German pocket surrendered to the Canadians.

Canada's occupation force in beaten Germany likely will be 25,000 men.

The Canadians are expected to control the area through which they fought—along the North Sea coast from Holland to the Weser River, with possible extension to the Elbe.

The great ports of Bremen and Hamburg, captured by the British 2nd Army, may be included and it is understood the occupation force will be composed of men with the shortest overseas service.

Either the 1st or 2nd Corps headquarters will administer the occupation force at first and later a special occupation headquarters may be formed.

WILL TAKE TIME.

It was learned it will take considerable time, possibly several months, for Canadian forces in Germany to be shaken down to operational strength, but this can be achieved by return to Canada of men for demobilization or for volunteer service in the Pacific.

The points system for rotation leave to Canada will be continued

(Continued on Page 2.)
See CANADIANS.

Stores to Close Monday, If V-E Day Announced Sunday

Here's the schedule for the closing of stores, liquor vendors and beer parlors should the V-E Day announcement come at the week-end:

If it comes today or Sunday, closing will be effective immediately with reopening set for Tuesday morning.

This schedule is in line with a Federal Government decision to proclaim as a holiday the first week-day following the announcement of the end of European hostilities.

Canada Offers World Basis For Real Peace

By TORCHY ANDERSON.
Special Staff Correspondent of The Vancouver Daily Province and Associated Southam Newspapers.

SAN FRANCISCO, May 5.—Canada made her most ambitious gesture toward suggesting a pattern of permanent peace and a means of eliminating the cause of war, when she offered a rewritten whole chapter of the Dumbarton Oaks proposals on which the United Nations Conference is building a new organization.

International social and economic co-operation, a phase of the work here that is commanding a daily, almost hourly, increase in importance, was the phase on which Canada, herself trail-blazing in several social and economic lines, undertook to suggest changes.

NEED ADJUSTMENT.

Social and economic adjustments on an international scale have been hailed by some of the strongest men at this conference.

Canada has refrained from offering amendments on several matters which she considers have been covered by the amendments of other states already made public. She has refrained from pursuing perfectionist ideals which she considered unworkable or unacceptable to the Big Five powers that will have the main burden of keeping peace.

Canada, for example, will probably give strong support to General Smuts of South Africa

(Continued on Page 2.)
See TORCHY.

Harass Nazis

ROME, May 5.—(AP)—Flyers of the Allied Balkan Air Command continued to harass battered Nazi columns fleeing northern Yugoslavia. Otherwise there were no reports of any hostilities in the Mediterranean theatre.

One Army Holds Out; Norway Surrender Near

Virtually All Nazi Resistance Facing General Eisenhower Now Ended

LONDON, May 5.—(Reuters) — Dr. Hubert Ripka, member of the Czechoslovak Government in London, announced in a broadcast tonight that the Czechoslovak resistance council had taken on the administration of Bohemia and Moravia, and Prague had again become the Czech capital and after nearly seven years Czech flags weer again flying there.

(By Associated Press.)

PARIS, May 5.—Virtually all resistance to Gen. Eisenhower's forces ended today.

The U.S. 3rd Army smashed into Czechoslovakia in a knockout offensive against the last German troops still fighting the western Allies in the south.

Gen. Patton struck out, capturing Linz in Austria, after the 1st and 19th German armies surrendered unconditionally to Gen. Jacob L. Devers' 6th Army group.

The 11th Panzer Division, Germany's last full-rate armored force in the west, was among those quitting the battle.

Supreme headquarters said all resistance to Gen. Eisenhower on active fronts in which his forces were engaged had ended, save for a single German army, the 7th, in Gen. Patton's territory.

MARSHAL KESSELRING
. . . gives up to Eisenhower.

By the best available estimate, 10 per cent. or less of the German army's peak total of around 8,000,000 men remained under arms today.

Norway and small pockets in France remain to be cleared and the status of Norway is in immediate doubt.

QUISLING ASKS "OBEDIENCE"

Norwegian and Russian troops have entered the northern section of Norway, and the German-controlled Scandinavian telegraph bureau predicted the Germans' capitulation there today.

However the Swedish foreign office said it regarded this report as premature and puppet Premier Vidkun Quisling called on his countrymen for obedience.

"All attacks from the outside will be resisted," said the Nazi puppet Premier. "The only task of the Norwegian armed forces in Norway is to maintain peace and order."

Gen. Patton's drive northeastward into Czechoslovakia at points along a 110-mile front sped forward against slight resistance.

Meantime, the U.S. 11th Armored Division and elements of the 26th Infantry Division entered Linz, Austria's third city, without opposition after capturing intact a Danube bridge between Linz and the twin city of Urfahr, which also fell without a fight.

The German 7th Army has been holding the front ahead of the American 3rd and part of the American 1st armies on a line running roughly from Chemnitz, Germany, to Linz, Austria.

"WAR HAS BECOME SENSELESS"

The German high command broadcast: "The war against the western powers has become senseless."

A proclamation by Admiral Doenitz called upon the Germans to continue resistance against the Russian Army.

Supreme headquarters made this announcement:

"Gen. Devers reported to Gen. Eisenhower this afternoon that Army Group G, commanded by Gen. Schulz, surrendered to the 6th Army Group.

"The capitulation takes official effect tomorrow, May 6, at noon, but on both sides radio broadcasts now are announcing the end of hostilities on their front so that there may be no further loss of life.

"This was a battlefield surrender."

A few pockets facing the Allies in France remained to be cleared out, but supreme headquarters apparently did not consider them in the category of organized resistance.

Five-year Bonus Granted Seamen In Jap Fight

Veterans' Affairs Minister Hon. Ian Mackenzie announced here that Canadian merchant seamen who sign up for duration of the Japanese war will receive a 10 per cent. wage bonus retroactive to September 10, 1939.

They will receive the retroactive bonus after the war.

A year ago, the government agreed to give merchant seamen a bonus of 10 per cent. of pay for time spent in enemy waters.

The bonus will be on pay earned aboard Canadian ships.

They will receive the 10 per cent. bonus until the end of the Jap war.

Air Defense End "Symbol of Nazi Defeat:" Eisenhower

LONDON, May 5.—(CP)—Gen. Eisenhower, in a special message to Prime Minister Churchill, referred today to the abolition of Britain's defenses against air raids as one of the brightest symbols of Nazi defeat.

"One of the highlights of the history of this conflict will be the stamina, courage and determination displayed by the British population in the perforance of its indispensable duties under the constant threat of the most terrifying weapons the enemy could devise," the supreme Allied commander said. He added:

"I want you to know how truly happy this whole force is for any part we had in lifting this burden from the people of Great Britain."

Nova Scotian Fires Last Canadian Shot; Germans Shoot Off Flares,. Sing "Lili"

By DICK SANBURN.
(Special War Correspondent of The Vancouver Daily Province and Associated Southam Newspapers)

ON THE LAST CANADIAN FRONT LINE IN EUROPE, May 5.—The war came to a crazy end here in western Holland at 8 a.m. today.

The last Canadian to enjoy the doubtful honor of being shot at by hostile Germans was Private G. S. Warrel of Port Wallec, Nova Scotia, of the West Nova Scotia Regiment.

Private Warrel was the unhappy target of a German two-man patrol which penetrated the Canadian lines near the Zuider Zee at 5:23 a.m., two and one-half hours before the end of the war here.

Probably the last spoken enemy word on the Canadian front in this war was one agonized "Oh," muttered by a German who reeled off into pre-dawn darkness after Private Warrel had sprayed a burst from a Bren gun at the marauding figures. This verbose German unfortunately escaped in the darkness, leaving behind him a battered Canadian Sten gun.

GERMANS ALL CRAZY.

The honor of being the last Canadian battalion to be in action against the Germans goes to the West Nova Scotia Regiment of the First Division's Third Brigade. Commander of the battalion is greying, amiable Lieutenant-Colonel Aird Nesbitt of Montreal.

This eerie patrol which came into our lines just at dawn today was the climax of as crazy a period as ever was witnessed by Canadians at war. Last night, after the radio announcement that the war in Holland would end at 8 a.m. today, German paratroopers facing the West Novas, went slightly mad.

Starting at 10 p.m., they began to fire off all remaining Very signal flares. The Canadians, crouched wonderingly in front-line pits, watched this rather silly display of fireworks, but silently gave credit to the Jerry soldiers for their firing of Very pistols.

At one time, these Germans, about to become prisoners for whom everything was lost, traced on the jet black midnight sky a huge Nazi Swastika in red Very lights, a feat of timing and marksmanship worthy of a better cause and less drunken marksmen.

The night before the Canadians had lain silent in their slit trenches listening to the Germans 300 yards away harmonizing in Wagnerian melancholy the war's all-time favorite song, "Lilli Mariene," which has a last verse beginning, "Time has come for roll call, time for us to part—"

DISTRUSTS GERMANS.

Major W. W. Mair, of North Battleford, commander of the front-line company, was enjoying a fried egg breakfast at 8 a.m. and made no bones about the fact he still distrusted the Boche and the war was still on until Germans proved differently.

"The Germans shelled us for a full 24 hours after the truce was declared a week ago," he said. "We assume they had not received word of that truce. This time, we assume that perhaps they have not heard that the war is over here, so we are taking no chances."

City's Potato Bins Bare

Vancouver is in the midst of a potato shortage which may be acutely felt by householders within the next week.

Heavy sales, inability to secure emergency supplies from Alberta owing to difficulties of loading, and a short crop in B.C.'s interior, have suddenly left many wholesale warehouses bare, and some retailers either out of spuds or down to their last sack.

Relief is expected from outlying Alberta farm areas—mainly the north—where potatoes are plentiful but hard to get to market owing to impassable, late-spring road conditions.

Wartime Food Corporation is understood to be arranging for special freight subsidies on Alberta spuds so that they can be sold under the ceiling here.

New potatoes will not be ready for Vancouver until June 10 or 15.

May Wear Uniform

OTTAWA, May 5.—(CP)—Defense Headquarters announced today permission has been granted for ex-service personnel to wear uniforms in V-Day parades.

WAR ENDS IN EUROPE

Start of German aggression and the move toward conquest began with the bloodless march into Austria in 1938. Then, nation after nation, as indicated on the map, was quickly overrun by the Nazi armies and held fast in the shackles of the German war machine.

At the peak of her power, Germany covered thousands of square miles of territory on the continent and in Africa (black area on map above). Her leaders shouted that the day of the "decadent democracies" was over.' But their world plans were somewhat premature.

The tide turned and the Nazi armies were battered back on all fronts. Mammoth invasions, counterattacks, and huge offensives squeezed the German empire smaller and smaller and finally pushed Hitler's weakened armies right back to the "sacred soil of the Fatherland."

Victory! The conqueror is conquered—and the German militarists are no more. On quiet battlefields, hundreds of thousands of men lie buried, victims of the desires of a few who possessed grandiose dreams of power and conquest and ruthlessly tried to make them realities.

EXTRA   Vancouver News-Herald   EXTRA

VANCOUVER, B.C,. MAY 7 1945   PRICE 5¢

ALLIED LEADERS ANNOUNCE VICTORY

Canadian Army Played Big Part

Through the hot, blistering sun of Sicily and Italy . . . the rain, the cold and the mud of France, Belgium and Holland . . . final VICTORY . . . is the saga of the Canadian Army Overseas.

1939

August 26: N.P.A.M. units called out on Home Service; September 1; Germans attack Poland. Canadian 1st and 2nd Divisions authorized as Canadian Active Service Force. December 17; First contingent of Canadian 1st Division arrives in Britain.

1940

July 5: Hon. J. L. Ralston appointed Minister of National Defence.

June 27—Formation of the Canadian Women's Army Corps.

1941

February 3: Lt.-General McNaughton returns to Canada. August 19: Canadians in raid on Dieppe. First CWAC party arrives in United Kingdom. December 30: First Canadians to Eighth Army in North Africa.

1942

1943

July 10: Canadian 1st Division and 1st Canadian Tank Army lands in Sicily. August 6: Canadians prepare to invade Italy.

1944

May 23: Canadians assault and break Adolf Hitler line. June 6: D-Day.

1945

War in Europe virtually ended for the Canadian Army May 4 with surrender of the enemy in Holland, Denmark and northwestern Germany.

GERMANY

REG MANNING

Official Declaration Marks Foe Collapse

FLASH---LONDON.---Allied leaders announce the end of German resistance in Europe and proclaim victory for the cause of the United Nations.

The announcement followed day-to-day capitulations of German forces in north-west, north, central and southern Europe and in Norway.

Freed Yanks Would Put Reich's Fate Up To Reds

By JULIUS OCHS ADLER
New York Times Copyright

PARIS.—There would be no easy terms for Germany and no distinction made among the Germans as to their responsibility for Germany's crimes if the American prisoners of war I interviewed today had their way. They were men of the "recovered Allied military personnel returning prisoners of war—assembled at a camp on their way home. I visited them in the company of other members of the editors and publishers group touring the front and France on the invitation of Supreme Allied Headquarters.

The men I talked with included more than a score of noncoms and more than 150 privates, mostly from New York, but some were from New Jersey, Pennsylvania, Delaware and other states.

The first question I put to them was this: If they had President Truman's job and could decide the fate of Germany, what would they decide? Spontaneously and overwhelmingly they said: "We would turn it over to the Russians." When I asked why, they said, first, that the Americans did not understand the German problem while the Russians did because of their war experience; second, that the Americans would consequently make too soft a peace.

Did they hold all Germans generally responsible or only some Germans? The answer to this was equally overwhelming, indeed unanimous. They said the Germans all were responsible. They told of having been marched along German streets as prisoners, of women having spit at them, of men having jeered at them, of boys having thrown stones at them.

In the prison camps they were stripped of watches, rings, fountain pens, money and all other personal property. The medical prisoners were stripped of medical supplies. Many noncoms were deprived of their identity papers so that they were classed with privates in violation of the Geneva convention, they said.

War Cost Millions Of Lives, Trillion Of Treasure

By CARL C. CRANMER
Associated Press Staff Writer

Germany's dream of world conquest has come to a shattering end with the collapse of the Reich which Adolf Hitler said would endure a thousand years.

Ended is the European phase of the second Great War of the century, a war which is estimated to have cost close to $1,000,000,000,000—one trillion dollars in money, and the lives of more than 6,000,000 men.

The collapse of Germany was foreshadowed last July 20 when an attempt was made to kill Hitler and seize power by what the dictator said was a small clique of "foolish, criminally stupid" German officers.

This revolt among Hitler's entourage, coming almost exactly a year after Benito Mussolini had been broken in Italy; the rapid advances of Russian armies in the east, the drive of Allied armies in Italy, and the

success of the most difficult amphibious invasion in history, the invasion of Normandy, all suggested that the German army was approaching a debacle.

SNATCHED VICTORY

At the start, the war looked to the world, grossly underrating German preparations, like the throw of a mad adventurer.

It turned out that the Allies snatched victory only after hair-breadth escape from defeat.

Hitler opened it with a razzledazzle of propaganda, secret weapons, armored spearheads, bombing armadas, parachute troops, fifth columns and political sleight-of-hand which established him as a sinister Barnum of war.

Before it ended, merged with the war in Asia and the Pacific by the Japanese attack on Pearl Harbor, it had been fought on

all the oceans and continents.

"In this war there will be no victors and losers, but merely survivors and annihilated," Hitler threatened.

TOTAL WAR!

The conflict became:

A war of secret battles—long silent struggles to smash his invasion fleet on the French coast, to master the submarine which imperilled the United States as never before, to crush robot bomb launching sites in France.

A war of secret weapons—in which the Allies with radar, a brand new conception of massed fleets of invasion barges, the technique of mass bombing through clouds, and a host of inventions, outdid Hitler.

War in the air—in which whole armies of millions engaged. For the first time the capitals of great nations and scores of

other cities were marked for methodical destruction.

A war of cities—Stalingrad, Leningrad, Odessa, Sevastopol, Cassino, Cherbourg — whose streets and houses were turned into trenches and forts. A new technique of battle in the rubble of cities developed. London was blitzed, and Berlin shattered by bombs and finally, by the Red army.

This war saw the advent of the flying bomb and many different rocket weapons, the blockbuster, rapid-firing guns which made artillery barrages more intensive than ever, mass mobility of tanks and vehicles, the airborne army, the flying battleship, amphibious invasion on a grander scale than ever.

All this was started about 3 o'clock on Friday morning, Sept. 1, 1939, when Germany invaded Poland.

EXTRA

GERMANY SURRENDERS

The Vancouver Sun

VANCOUVER, B. C., MAY 7 1945   PRICE 5c

THANK GOD!

Victory in Europe Declared Official

LONDON.—It was announced officially today that Germany has surrendered unconditionally to Britain, the United States and Russia.

The defeat of Germany is now complete. The surrender includes all German land, sea and air forces.

This official announcement bringing the war in Europe to a triumphant conclusion came as the world still reverberated from the impact of great events in Europe which foreshadowed the final collapse of Germany.

It came after Germany had been stripped of most of her territories, her armies and her leader—Adolf Hitler.

First Bid Rejected

The forging of an American-Russian link-up in the heart of Germany, April 26, while the Red Army already was fighting in the German's once mighty capital of Berlin, sent the Third Reich into its death throes.

Then came the first German bid to make peace. The notorious Heinrich Himmler, trying one last desperate Fascist trick, attempted to make separate peace with Britain and the United States, excluding Russia.

But the Allies, standing steadfastly by their gallant Russian allies flatly rejected Himmler's futile bid for Anglo-American favor by promising to continue the Nazis' "holy war" against Bolshevism.

Criminals 'Escape' Allies

Himmler's attempts to make peace, then, led to a premature report of German surrender on April 28 when Senator Tom Connally, vice-chairman of the American delegation to the San Francisco security conference, said Germany had quit. That report was finally scotched by President Truman, but only after victory celebrations had been set off throughout the Allied world.

NOW, HOWEVER, THE ANNOUNCEMENT OF VICTORY OVER THE GERMANS IS OFFICIAL. THIS IS V-E DAY—VICTORY IN EUROPE DAY.

After the rejoicing over the Connally-created peace flurry had subsided the civilians of the Allied world again looked to Germany where their armies were pulverizing the last remnants of Nazi resistance.

The death rattle began in earnest. . . .

The war's two most notorious criminals came to the end of the road, cheating the Allies out of the opportunity of punishing them.

Benito Mussolini, who stabbed France in the back and leaped on the Hitler victory bandwagon, came to an ignoble death in Milan where Italian patriots shot him, then spat on his body and kicked his face into a bloody pulp. The once powerful Il Duce, who had brought Italy pomp and splendor and blood and ruin, was buried in an unmarked grave.

Hitler was next. The Hamburg radio announced dramatically May 1 that the Fuehrer was dead. The Nazis, perhaps seeking to create a new legend for the future generations of Germans, said he died a hero's death at a command post in Berlin the previous day.

The Allies accepted the Nazis' word that Hitler was dead but none believed he had actually gone down "fighting to the last breath" as the Germans claimed.

Admiral Karl Doenitz became Hitler's successor and pledged he would fight on—but his lips had scarcely formed this empty boast when the German commander in Italy and most of Austria surrendered all his land, sea and air forces to the Allies.

Mass Surrender

The same day — May 2 — Marshal Stalin announced triumphantly in Moscow that Berlin had been captured. The Germans were without a capital, without their Fuehrer, and almost without an army.

Hitler's house of cards began to topple down about Admiral Doenitz, the "new Fuehrer."

The day after Berlin fell, the Nazis declared Hamburg an open city and the British 2nd Army marched into the Reich's greatest port without a fight.

German radios in Denmark began to scream the "final hour has arrived . . . Germany is defeated."

German troops threw away their guns and fled to the safety of British lines . . . a half million Huns called it quits in a day.

The chaos on the British front finally subsided on May 4 when Gen. Eisenhower announced that all German land, sea and air forces in Northern Germany, Denmark and Holland had surrendered unconditionally to Field Marshal Sir Bernard L. Montgomery, commander of the Allied 21st Army Group.

The war as the world had known it for almost six years was then virtually over. But the mop-up went on. And Allied troops died wiping out the last of the cornered Nazi beasts.

NOW THEY ARE FINISHED. THE WAR IN EUROPE IS OFFICIALLY OVER.

Big Job Ahead—Truman

WASHINGTON. — President Truman has announced he hopes there will be no celebration over the end of hostilities in Europe "but a national understanding of the importance of the job which remains."

London is proclaiming a two-day public holiday to mark the downfall of Germany. The Home Office reminded that "there should be no relaxation of the national effort until the Pacific war has been won."

2 War Dead Memorials to Be Erected

End of the war in Europe will speed plans already under way for at least two structural memorials to British Columbia's heroes who won't be coming back.

They are a veterans' rehabilitation centre, planned by the Citizens' Rehabilitation Committee

LONDON — (BUP) — Britain's civil defense duties ended May 1 after five and one-half years of service.

under Major Oscar Erickson and a federal administration building to house all local offices dealing with Veteran's Affairs.

4th Extra THE VANCOUVER DAILY PROVINCE

51st YEAR— VANCOUVER, B.C., MONDAY, MAY 7, 1945 PRICE 5 CENTS

WAR ENDS

Reich Surrenders Unconditionally

By EDWARD KENNEDY.

REIMS, France, May 7--(AP) --Germany surrendered unconditionally to the Western Allies and Russia at 2:41 a.m. French time today.

(This was at 7:41 p.m. C.D.T. Sunday).

The surrender took place at a school house which is the headquarters of Gen Eisenhower.

The surrender which brought the war in Europe to a formal end after five years, eight months and six days of bloodshed and destruction was signed for Germany by Col.-Gen. Gustav Jodl is the new chief of staff of the German Army.

It was signed for the Allied Supreme Command by Lt.-Gen. Walter Bedell Smith, chief of staff for Gen. Eisenhower.

Joy at the news was tempered only by the realization that the war against Japan remains to be resolved, with many casualties still ahead.

The end of the European warfare, greatest, bloodiest and costliest war in human history — it has claimed at least 40,000,000 casualties on both sides in killed, wounded and captured—came after five years eight months and six days of strife that overspread the globe.

Began September 1, 1939

Arrogant German armies invaded Poland September 1, 1939, beginning the agony that convulsed the world for 2319 days.

General Eisenhower was not present at the signing, but immediately afterward Jodl and his fellow delegate, General Admiral Hans Georg Friedeberg, were received by the supreme commander.

They were asked if they understood the surrender terms imposed upon Germany and if they would be carried out by Germany.

They answered yes.

It was also signed by General Ivan Susloparoff for Russia and by General Francois Sevez for France.

After signing the full surrender, Jodl said he wanted to speak and was given leave to do so.

"With this signature," he said quietly in German, "the German people and armed forces are for better or worse delivered into the victors' hands."

A discordant note came from the German-controlled radio at Prague. A broadcast monitored by the Czechoslovak Government offices in London said the German commander in Czechoslovakia did not recognize the surrender of Admiral Doenitz and would fight on until his forces "have secured free passage for German troops out of the country."

But the Prague radio earlier announced the capitulation of Breslau, long besieged by Russian forces.

The B.B.C. said telephone conversations were going on between London, Washington and Moscow in order to fix the exact hour of the V-E Day announcement by Prime Minister Churchill, President Truman and Premier Stalin.

The excitement over Denmark's liberation had not entirely subsided. A small detachment of Americans entering Coenhagen yesterday was fired uon by roof-to sniers, resumed to be Danish Nazis.

JERR AT NAZZIS.

Thousands of Danes thronged the square earlier to jeer and spit at more than 400 danish Nazi sympathizers, loaded into trucks and paraded before them.

Occupation of Holland by the 1st Canadian Army was scheduled today. The formal surrender of all German troops in Holland took place yesterday at Wagningen, where Field Marshal Johannes Blaskowitz and his staff officers signed the necessary documents at the direction of Lieut.-Gen. Charles Foulkes of London, Ont., 1st Canadian Corps commander.

LT.-GEN. BEDELL SMITH . . . signed the historic document.

Cease-Fire Order Goes To U-Boats

(Compiled From Late Despatches to The Vancouver Daily Province.)

LONDON, May 7.—First indication that today was to be the day of final Allied victory in Europe came when Grand Admiral Karl Doenitz, who succeeded Adolf Hitler, ordered his U-boat commanders to cease hostilities.

The order was broadcast over the German-controlled Flensburg radio shortly after midnight Vancouver time.

"My U-boat men, six years of U-boat warfare lies behind us. You have fought like lions. Crushing superiority has compressed us into a very narrow area. Continuation of the struggle is impossible from the bases that remain.

"U-boat men, unbroken in your warlike courage, you are laying down your arms after a heroic fight that knows no equal. In reverent memory we think of our comrades who have sealed their loyalty to the Fuehrer and the Fatherland with their death.

"Comrades, maintain in the future your U-boat spirit with which you have fought at sea bravely and unflinchingly during long years for the welfare of the Fatherland. Long Live Germany."

Earlier the Nazi Fuehrer had directed crews of all German warships and merchantmen not to scuttle their ships.

London morning papers in big black type said the end of the European war was only hours away.

"It may be today," said the Daily Mail's front-page bannerline.

"All over in Europe at any hour," said the Daily Herald.

"Germany's final surrender imminent," said the Daily Telegraph.

"The last hour," declared the Daily Express.

"Germans ready to surrender to Russians," said the News-Chronicle, with a sub-head, "V-Day may be announced at teatime."

Perhaps inadvertently contributing to the flood of rumors, Red Army officers were noticed strolling near the Soviet Embassy, with linked arms and singing lustily, in contrast to their usual reserve.

Huns Find Terms Harsh

London, May 7.—(CP)—German Foreign Minister Lutz Schwerin von Krosigk announced to the German people over the wavelength of the Flensburg station that "after almost six years struggle we have succumbed."

He said: "Nobody must deceive himself over the harshness of the conditions. We had to accept them."

Count von Krosigk succeeded Joachim Ribbentrop as German Foreign Minister last week.

Von Krosogk said:

"German men and women: The High Command of the armed forces has today, at the order of Grand Admiral Doenitz, declared the unconditional surrender of all fighting German troops."

"Our sympathy firstly goes out to our soldiers. Nobody must deceive himself on the harshness of the terms which our enemies have imposed on the German people.

"Nobody must have any doubt that enemy sacrifices will be demanded from us in all spheres of life.

"We must take them upon us and stand loyally to our obligations."

"On the other hand," the broadcast continued, "we must not despair. From the collapse in the past we must keep in mind one thing: The idea of our unity, the idea of front comradship, the idea of assistance to each other.

The von Krosigk broadcast said that "as leading minister of the Reich Government," Doenitz had appointed him for the purpose of "winding up all military tasks."

The "Flensburg radio" has been used for several days for the issuance of German communiques and official German orders. Flensburg is just south of the German-Danish border in an area surrendered last week to Field Marshal Montgomery. London authorities said it seemed unlikely that Montgomery had permitted the Germans to continue broadcasting from there, but there was no official explanation.

VICTORY PROGRAM

All schools open.
Stores will close.
Liquor stores, beer parlors and veterans' clubs will close.
Civic offices will be closed today.
Theatres will be open.
All churches open.
Dominion holiday Tuesday.
Memorial service at Ambleside Park, West Vancouver, Tuesday at 7:30 p.m.
Mass religious service next Sunday at Brockton Point Oval, 3 p.m.
Burnaby schools closed.
War plants will work today and close Tuesday.

Mayor Urges Reason

Mayor Cornett appeals, in a statement prepared for release with the news of victory for a celebration within the bounds of decency and good sense."

"My first feeling, now that the war with Germany is over, is one of thanksgiving.

"The horrible tragedies wrought by the Huns have been brought to an end. The democracies of the world remain free to guide the progress and welfare of mankind.

"But in our enthusiasm we must remember that there is little joy today in thousands of Vancouver homes, homes where an only son, or several sons, or a father have laid down their lives and made possible our celebration today.

CHURCHES OPEN.

"Of course I expect each one of us will celebrate the end of the war with Germany in his own way. That is only human nature.

"City churches will be open during the day and I suggest it would be quite appropriate for all of us to give thanks to Divine Providence that the conflict is ended.

"Those untouched by war have much for which to be thankful. To those whose lives have been saddened by the conflict, for what comfort it may be, I say our sympathies are with them.

"I rejoice with all of you in the victory of our fighting men. But while we celebrate, let us do so in a reasonable way, remembering those who can not join so enthusiastically with us and remembering how much thanksgiving we should have in our hearts."

Victory after six long years.

BULLETINS

WASHINGTON, May 7.—(AP)—President Truman was conferring with aides in the executive offices today as news was flashed to the world from Reims of the unconditional surrender of German arms.

Locate Goebbels' Remains

MOSCOW, May 7—(Reuters)—Unconfirmed reports today said that the bodies of Joseph Goebbels and his family had been found in an air raid shelter near the Reichstag in Berlin.

Von Bock's Body Found

WITH THE BRITISH 2ND ARMY, May 7.—(AP) —The riddled body of Fedor von Bock, who as a field marshal commanded the central army group in the invasion of Russia in June, 1941, was found north of Hamburg by British troops. He had been dead about a week, and may have been caught in a strafing raid.

Von Bock was relieved as army commander after German failures to take both Moscow and Stalingrad.

Tokyo Protests Surrender

(By Associated Press.)

NEW YORK, May 7. — (AP) — The Tokyo radio, heard by the FCC, today quoted Japanese Foreign Minister Shigenori Togo as saying that Heinrich Himmler's reported "unconditional surrender offers" violated the terms of the German-Japanese-Italian tri-partite pact.

Japs Flee for Thailand

CALCUTTA, May 7.—(AP)—British armies swung eastward toward Thailand today, pursuing the Japanese retreating from their decisive defeat in the battle of Burma.

British Shell Jap Islands

GUAM, May 7. — (AP) — British battleships and cruisers in their first bombarding operation in the Pacific shelled the southern Ryukyus Saturday and Sunday. The force shelled airdrome targets in the Sakishima group, just northeast of Formosa, despite strong enemy air activity.

CITY TAKES IT CALMLY --AT FIRST

By DON MASON.

V-E Day came quietly to Vancouver.

There were no cheers, there seemed no excitement.

The man and woman on the street—on the way to work when the sirens began to mlow—smiled. It was a slow smile, hard getting started, as though there was start fear this might not be the real thing.

Then, as the sirens continued to wail the glad news; halted and began to wail again, the smile broadened, became a universal grin, a grin of pure happiness.

Yes, peace in Europe came quietly to Vancouver.

It caught half the city asleep, and it came as an anti-climax after last week's day-by-day reports of more and more Germans surrendering.

First news hit Vancouver, via press wires and radio, a few seconds after 6:36 a.m.

"HERE AT LAST."

People who were awake were on their way to work in street cars, in private cars, in buses—or they were still in their homes, finishing breakfast, finishing dressing, washing sleep out of their eyes.

For many it meant a holiday, if they worked in stores and other establishments which remained closed.

On the street cars, passengers cocked an ear to the sirens and then to the "Extra" cry of newsboys.

They turned to the stranger beside them, chuckled, and said:

"Well, guess it's here at last."

But there was no wild excitement.

Heads popped out of windows along the streets.

People wanted to be sure about this thing.

QUIET . . . AT FIRST.

There was no doubting the happiness that spread through Vancouver.

But . . . it was a quiet happiness . . . at first.

What may come later in the day in the form of wild celebration may be another story.

Men and women caught on street corners when the siren first wailed, loked around, smiled and some lifted their hands in the victory sign.

But the theme was quiet.

LINES JAMMED.

Of course there was excitement.

It just didn't show on the surface, that's all.

But ask the girls who handle switchboards for B.C. Telephone Company.

The company had pleaded with people not to rush to telephones when V-E Day came.

They might as well have saved their breath.

Lines were jammed in minutes.

The news was just too good.

People had to talk about it — talk to anyone.

PARIS, May 7.—Lord Lascelles, nephew of King George of Britain, was among a number of Allied notables freed from German prison camps over the week-end.

Gen. Crerar Tells 1st Canadian Army Nazi Wehrmacht "Horror of Past"

By ROSS MUNRO.
Canadian Press War Correspondent.

WITH THE 1ST CANADIAN ARMY, May 7.—Gen. Crerar said today in a V-E message his 1st Canadian Army is about to dissolve and that he believed the future of Canada rests in the hands of Canadian overseas soldiers who will be returning home.

Text of his message:

"V-E Day at long last has arrived. The business we Canadians came over here to do is virtually finished. There will yet be quite a lot of tidying up to complete—but the military might of Hitler's Germany is a horror of the past.

"The world definitely has been delivered from domination by Hitler and his pack of gangsters. And in this prolonged and bitter struggle, now crowned with victory, the army of Canada has played a stirring part. Canadians everywhere are entitled to be very proud of their soldiers.

"I am certainly proud beyond words to count myself one of them. It has been a great inspiration and a great challenge to one's capacities to be a commander of such men.

"I have never met a Canadian commanding officer who has regarded his responsibilities otherwise. The very best one has been able to give them has never been as complete as one would have wished.

"Yet the compelling urge to be fully worthy of these responsibilities has shown itself during all our operations in the outstanding conduct of the Canadian commanders—senior and junior, brigadier and lieutenant-colonel, sergeant and corporal.

"They have led their men in battle. They have never spared themselves. Also they have paid the full price—knowing beforehand that whatever it might be it would the payment.

"We have reached the time when the great and gallant company which has formed the 1st Canadian Army is about to dissolve. By group and by units, with anticipation and joy in their hearts tempered by memories of friends they have lost, the Canadians who survived will be returning home to Canada.

"I believe the future of Canada rests in their hands. It will be a grand future should they be given the opportunity in peace to prove and practice the admiral characteristics they have demonstrated in war.

"What makes a fighting unit, fighting division or magnificent army? I will tell you in a few words. First of all, a cause worth fighting for and, if necessary, dying for. Secondly, good, intelligent, strong men. Thirdly, capacity of its individuals for teamwork, which means willingness to subordinate self for benefit of the side. Fourthly, determination to win through. Finally, knowing or being taught how to fight effectively. We have had these advantages inherited or obtained in the 1st Canadian Army."

Defeated Germans Plead for Mercy

SECOND EXTRA

HUNS SURRENDER UNCONDITIONALLY

The Vancouver Sun

FOUNDED 1886
VOL. LIX—No. 235

VANCOUVER, B.C., MONDAY, MAY 7, 1945

PRICE 5¢

War in Europe Officially Over as Nazis Capitulate

LONDON, May 7—(CP)—The greatest war in history ended today with the unconditional surrender of Germany

Germany surrendered unconditionally to the Western Allies and Russia at 2:41 a.m. French time today.

(This was at 5:41 p.m. Vancouver time Sunday.)

The surrender took place at a schoolhouse which is the headquarters of General Eisenhower.

The surrender, which brought the war in Europe to a formal end after years eight months and six days of bloodshed and destruction, was signed Germany by Col.-Gen. Gustav Jodl, who is the new chief of staff of the German army.

Last Steps in Hun Collapse

The defeat of Germany is now complete. The surrender includes all German land, sea and air forces.

This official announcement bringing the war in Europe to a triumphant conclusion came as the world still reverberated from the impact of great events in Europe which foreshadowed the final collapse of Germany.

It came after Germany had been stripped of most of her territories, her armies and her leader—Adolf Hitler.

First Bid Rejected

The forging of an American-Russian link-up in the heart of Germany, April 26, while the Red Army already was fighting in the German's once mighty capital of Berlin, sent the Third Reich into its death throes.

Then came the first German bid to make peace. The notorious Heinrich Himmler, trying one last desperate Fascist trick, attempted to make separate peace with Britain and the United States, excluding Russia.

But the Allies, standing steadfastly by their gallant Russian allies flatly rejected Himmler's futile bid for Anglo-American favor by promising to continue the Nazis' "holy war" against Bolshevism.

Criminals 'Escape' Allies

Himmler's attempts to make peace, then, led to a premature report of German surrender on April 28 when Senator Tom Connally, vice-chairman of the American delegation to the San Francisco security conference, said Germany had quit. That report was finally scotched by President Truman, but only after victory celebrations had been set off throughout the Allied world.

NOW, HOWEVER, THE ANNOUNCEMENT OF VICTORY OVER THE GERMANS IS OFFICIAL. THIS IS V-E DAY—VICTORY IN EUROPE DAY.

After the rejoicing over the Connally-created peace flurry had subsided the civilians of the Allied world again looked to Germany where their armies were pul-

Please Turn to Page Two   See "Last Days"

LED EMPIRE THROUGH—Their Majesties The King and Queen who led the British Empire safely through six years of the most terrible war the world has ever seen. The King will broadcast to the Empire at 12 noon today Vancouver time.

TOMORROW TO BE V-E DAY HOLIDAY

Tuesday, will be the official holiday to mark the end of the war in Europe, Hon. J. L. Ilsley, acting prime minister of Canada, announced today.

"By all means go to work today," he said. "The end of the war will be officially observed the day after V-E Day."

At the same time as Mr. Ilsley gave his announcement Mayor Cornett proclaimed today a civic holiday for Vancouver. This does not affect business.

However, the retail merchants had previously announced that stores would close when V-E Day is announced.

Schools remained open today as did shipyards and factories.

Jew Baiters All 'End in Oblivion'

There was "deep significance" in the fact that nations that have systematically persecuted or attacked the Jewish people have disappeared into oblivion, Dr. A. O. MacRae told the Burrard Lions Club Friday.

Pleading for tolerance on behalf of the Jewish people, Dr. MacRae declared that much of the dislike for Jews was caused by the world's materialistic outlook and the present emphasis placed on money, fame and power.

Wolf Hunt Planned by Digby Island Parents

Special to The Vancouver Sun

PRINCE RUPERT, May 5.—Wolves are becoming so numerous and so daring that the people of Digby Island are actually nervous about leaving their young children outside without being carefully watched.

Several dogs have disappeared, supposedly the victims of the powerful beasts which come up to the very doorsteps.

Residents of Dodge Cove plan a campaign to rid the island of the danger.

Allied Victories That Beat Germans

By VIRGIL PINKLEY, British United Press War Correspondent

PARIS—(UP)—It took three years of Allied victories to beat Germany to her knees.

The knockout blow carried the accumulative effect of all these mighty land, sea and air efforts.

Once Hitler and the Luftwaffe failed to win the Battle for Britain the war was lost for Germany because only the capture and occupation of Britain could have given the Reich complete mastery of Europe and the ability to establish the so-called new order.

The RAF and the courage of England's little man, especially from the East End of London, thwarted and then stymied Germany's plan to conquer and rule Europe and later most of the other parts of the world, especially Africa, Russia and the Middle and Near East.

The United Kingdom was to be cleaned up fast after the fall of France and the Low Countries. Then all efforts weer to be turned to the east and Russia.

HITLER'S AD GUESS

Hitler believed after Dunkerque that Britain would sue for peace or, failing this, that a blockade by U-boats would force the British to request a negotiated peace, or that the Luftwaffe could bomb the island inot submission.

Without Britain as a fortress and base it would have been virtually impossible to prepare, mount and launch the Anglo-American campaigns in North Africa, Sicily, Italy and France. Without England there would not have been air bascs to enable the RAF bomber command and the ever-rowing powerful American 8th and 9th airforces to bomb, blast and slash the vitals from Germany's war machine and pull much of the Luftwaffe's power off the east front, where Russia needed such relief.

So the first big British and Allied victory was the Battle for Britain.

TWO VITAL LOSSES

Shortly thereafter, two vitally important defeats were inflicted on Hitler's legions in the rubble strewn streets of Stalingrad and and the burning, sandy beaches of El Alamein. Preceding these victories the Russians halted the German drives at th geates of Leningrad and the approaches to Moscow.

The blocking of the German march eastward for oil and the envisaged link with the Japanese brought abruptly to a close the idea of a joined Axis global warfare.

Please Turn to Page Two
See "Victories"

Last Nazi Secret Weapon Uncovered

WITH THE U.S. 9TH ARMY IN GERMANY, May 7—(AP)—One of Hitler's last secret weapons—a piloted flying bomb—has been uncovered by the 9th Army advance.

The new V-weapon was just like the V-1 except that. 12 feet from the tip of the warhead, there was a small cockpit enclosed in glass. It was cramped and had a simple flying instrument panel, elevator controls and a light parachute.

The pilot could drop out in a hurry.

The theory was expressed that the pilot would aim the bomb and then parachute.

New Westminster Girl Winner of $300 Coat

Miss P. Shande, New Westminster, won a $300 coat, second prize offered in a draw by the Democratic Committee to Aid Poland and the Polish Mutual Benefit Association. First prize. a house, went to J. S. Murray, Brantford. where the draw was conducted.

It was signed for the Allied supreme command by Lt.-Gen. Walter Bedell Smith, chief of staff for Gen. Eisenhower.

It was also signed by General Ivan Susloparoff for Russia and by General Francois Sevez for France.

General Eisenhower was not present at the signing, but immediately afterward Jodl and his fellow delegate, General Admiral Hans Georg Friedeburg, were received by the supreme commander.

They were asked if they understood the surrender terms imposed upon Germany and if they would be carried out by Germany.

They answered yes.

Germany, which began the war with a ruthless attack upon Poland followed by successive aggressions and brutality in internment camps, surrendered with an appeal to the victors for mercy toward the German people and armed forces.

After signing the full surrender, Jodl said he wanted to speak and was given leave to do so.

"With this signature," he said quietly in German, "the German people and armed forces are for better or worse delivered into the victors' hands."

This was announced officially after German broadcasts told the German people that Grand Admiral Karl Doenitz had ordered the capitulation of all fighting forces, and called off the U-boat war.

Joy at the news was tempered only by the realization that the war against Japan remains to be resolved, with many casualties still ahead.

The end of the European warfare, greatest, bloodiest and costliest war in human history—it has claimed at least 40,000,000 casualties on both sides in killed, wounded and captured—came after five years, eight months and six days of strife that overspread the globe.

Arrogant German armies invaded Poland Sept. 1, 1939, beginning the agony that convulsed the world for 2319 days.

Unconditional surrender of the beaten remnants of Hitler's legions first was announced by the Germans.

The historic news began breaking with a Danish broadcast that Norway had been surrendered unconditionally by its conquerors.

The new German foreign minister, Ludwig Schwerin von Krosick, announced to the German people, shortly after 2 p.m. (5 a.m. Vancouver time) that "after almost six years struggle we have succumbed."

Von Krosick announced Grand Admiral Karl Doenitz had "ordered the unconditional surrender of all fighting German troops."

The world waited tensely.

Then at 6:35 a.m., Vancouver time, came the Associated

Please Turn to Page Two   See "Surrender"

Tuesday Named V-E Day Holiday

THE VANCOUVER DAILY PROVINCE ★★★★★ FINAL

51st YEAR—NO. 36 VANCOUVER, B.C., MONDAY, MAY 7, 1945—28 PAGES PRICE 5 CENTS BY CARRIER $1.00 per month.

VANCOUVER GOES WILD AS GERMANS SURRENDER

All Enemy Forces Quit In Europe

(Compiled from Late Despatches to The Vancouver Daily Province.)

LONDON, May 7.—The war against Germany, the greatest conflict in history, ended today with the unconditional surrender of all German armed forces.

The end for Nazi Germany came after five years, eight months and six days of bloodshed and destruction.

The Canadian and British Governments have announced tomorrow will be celebrated as V-E Day, a national holiday.

The surrender to the Allies—Great Britain, the United States and Russia — was made at Gen. Dwgiht Eisenhower's headquarters by the German High Command.

The documents of surrender were signed at 2:41 a.m French time (5:41 p.m. Sunday, Vancouver time) by Lt.-Gen. Walter Bedell Smith, chief of staff of Eisenhower's command, for the Big Three, and Col.-Gen. Gustav Jodl, new chief of Wehrmacht staff, for Germany in the name of Karl Doenitz, Fuehrer of the Reich in succession to Adolf Hitler.

(The first Associated Press flash of the surrender reached Vancouver at 6:36 a.m.)

Von Krosigk Gives News to Reich

Previously, however, the Flensburg radio carried a speech by German Foreign Minister Schwerin von Krosigk in which he gave the fateful news to the Reich.

The surrender negotiations took place in a school house which is the headquarters of Gen. Eisenhower.

In signing the documents Lt.-Gen. Smith achieved a unique distinction because it was he who affixed his signature to the papers designating Italy's surrender in 1943.

Prime Minister Churchill will broadcast at 3 p.m. tomorrow (6 a.m. Vancouver time) and the King at 9 p.m. tomorrow (12 noon Vancouver time).

In the hour before the news from Reims, German broadcasts told the German people that Grand Admiral Karl Doenitz had called off U-boat warfare.

The British Press Association attributed "the surprising delay in announcing V-E Day, in spite of the complete capitulation by the Germans," to the importance "attached to synchronizing the news in London, Washington and Moscow."

There were telephone calls all day between London, Washington and Moscow. The Press Association said there apparently were differing views on when the public should be informed, "but finally tomorrow was decided upon."

The Press Association said Gen. Eisenhower and Field Marshals Montgomery and Alexander are expected to speak tomorrow after the addresses by Mr. Churchill and the King.

Germans to March Into Sweden

(In Washington, President Truman said he had agreed with the London and Moscow governments that he would make no announcement on the surrender "until a simultaneous announcement can be made by the three governments." Until then, he declared, "there is nothing I can or will say to you.")

Meanwhile the newspaper Expressens in Stockholm said in a despatch from the Norwegian frontier today a German march across the Swedish border into internment would begin this afternoon under capitulation terms.

Wednesday will also be regarded as a holiday in Britain.

Joy at the news was tempered only by the realization that the war against Japan remains to be resolved, with many casualties still ahead.

The end of the European warfare, greatest, bloodiest and costliest war in human history—it has claimed at least 40,000,000 casualties on both sides in killed, wounded and captured—came after five years eight months and six days of strife that overspread the globe.

Arrogant German armies invaded Poland September 1, 1939, beginning the agony that convulsed the world for 2319 days.

Eisenhower Receives Nazi Leaders

General Eisenhower was not present at the signing, but immediately afterward Jodl and his fellow delegate, General Admiral Hans Georg Friedeberg, were received by the supreme commander.

They were asked if they understood the surrender terms imposed upon Germany and if they would be carried out by Germany.

They answered yes.

It was also signed by General Ivan Susloparoff for Russia and by General Francois Sevez for France.

After signing the full surrender, Jodl said he wanted to speak and was given leave to do so.

"With this signature," he said quietly in German, "the German people and armed forces are for better or worse delivered into the victors' hands."

A discordant note came from the German-controlled radio at Prague. A broadcast monitored by the Czechoslovak Government offices in London said the German commander in Czechoslovakia did not recognize the surrender of Admiral Doenitz and would fight on until his forces "have secured free passage for German troops out of the country."

Marshal Stalin tonight announced the fall of Breslau.

VICTORY COMES TO VANCOUVER

Photo by C. P. Dettloff.

Officially V-E Day is tomorrow. But today Vancouverites learned that the war was over. They celebrated it today. This picture shows what happened in downtown Vancouver. Traffic was jammed as thousands gathered to cheer and sing. Through the vista along Hastings from Seymour towards the Marine Building, office workers left their desks and precipitated a snowstorm of papers from the windows of their tall blocks halted traffic on the streets.

CITY STORES CLOSE UNTIL WEDNESDAY

VICTORIA, May 7.—(CP)—The British Columbia Government has proclaimed Tuesday a public holiday. The declaration will close all schools, stores and factories which come under provincial jurisdiction. Liquor stores, beer parlors and veterans' clubs throughout the province will be closed.

Downtown stores closed today and Tuesday but will be open Wednesday morning as Vancouver celebrates war's end in Europe.

Store officials met after Mayor Cornett's proclamation of a civic holiday closed stores and downtown offices, and Finance Minister Ilsley's office named Tuesday as a national holiday to observe V-E Day.

"Although all stores closed today, Monday, as result of the mayor's proclamation of a civic holiday," an official announcement said, "the Downtown Merchants' Association announces the decision of the three department stores, Hudson's Bay Co., David Spencer Ltd., Wood-

(Continued on Page 2.) See STORES.

OTTAWA, May 7. — Hon. J. L. Ilsley, acting Prime Minister, told the people of Canada in a broadcast address today "there is every reason to believe that official word will be received by the early hours of tomorrow morning that Germany has surrendered unconditionally."

Mr. Ilsley announced the issuance of proclamations making tomorrow, May 8, a public holiday in Canada and authorizing the observance of next Sunday, May 13, as a "day of prayer and solemn thanksgiving."

At the end of his statement, Mr. Ilsley read over the air the two proclamations.

Mr. Ilsley said:

"Fellow Canadians:

"There is every reason to believe that official word will be received by the early hours of tomorrow morning that Germany has surrendered unconditionally. After five years and eight months of war, Germany,

(Continued on Page 2.) See ILSLEY.

Thanksgiving Service

Special thanksgiving services at most city churches at 8 o'clock tonight.

Final BULLETINS

LONDON, May 7.—(AP)—Gen. Boehme, German commander-in-chief in Norway, broadcast an order of the day over the Oslo radio tonight commanding his troops to lay down their arms in obedience to Foreign Minister "Von Krosigk's announcement of unconditional surrender of all German fighting troops."

Allies Demand Russ Evidence

SAN FRANCISCO, May 7.—(AP)—The United States and Britain were reported by United Nations conference officials today to have demanded of Russia that she supply her evidence against the 16 arrested leaders of the Polish underground.

Rusian Foreign Commissar Molotov is slated to quit San Francisco for Moscow around mid-week. So long as he is here speculation continues that Russia may give the conference a sensation by making known her future plans toward Japan.

Canadian Callup Stops Today

OTTAWA, May 7.—(CP)—Labor Minister Mitchell announced today that call-ups for military service under the National Resources Mobilization Act have been suspended as from this date.

He also explained that arrangements have been made for the enrolment for volunteers for the war in the Pacific.

Prime Minister King to Speak

OTTAWA, May 7.—(CP)—Prime Minister Mackenzie King is scheduled to speak over a Canadian Broadcasting Corporation network from San Francisco at 12:20 p.m. (Vancouver time) tomorrow. Mr. King's address will follow that to be delivered by King George. Justice Minister St. Laurent is scheduled to speak after Mr. King.

Celebration Gains Pace During Day

By DON MASON.

Vancouver went sensibly mad today.

War's end came quietly to a city half asleep, but it was the quiet before the storm.

And what a storm.

Excitement mounted slowly until Mr. and Mrs. and Young Vancouver in thousands began to appear downtown.

Before noon there was bedlam.

The first siren wail came at 7:04 a.m.

The man and woman on the street—bound for work when the news came—smiled. It was a slow smile, hard to get started, as though there was still fear this might not be the real thing.

Then as the siren stopped; and wailed again, the smile broadened, became a grin, a grin of pure happiness.

But at first it was quiet, reverent happiness.

Yes, peace in Europe came quietly to Vancouver.

It caught the city half asleep.

People on the streets, in restaurants, on street cars, reacted slowly.

Perhaps they were stunned.

They were happy about victory, but quiet about it. There were "V" signs, there was talking to strangers on either side, but there were no cheers; there was no riotous mood.

"Guess this is it," passersby said quietly.

On all sides two words were said, and said again and again.

"Thank God!"

"NOW HE'LL COME HOME."

A woman said it . . . a woman in once-white coveralls. The tired look left her dirt-smudged face.

"He'll come home now."

Hers was Vancouver's smile, hers the city's first reaction of quiet happiness.

The happiness was to last, the quiet was only a first phase.

Even as the sirens wailed in the early morning, there were isolated incidents which forecast the celebration to come.

In Coal Harbor, where small boats harbor a colony of people, the siren wail brought stunned silence—for a minute.

Then a boat horn blew raucously, and in seconds the harbor was a bedlam of horns, whistles and sirens.

In some apartment houses, people rushed out in night attire, kissing and hugging their neighbors in gay abandon.

But mostly it was quiet.

People continued to run for street cars.

They bought out newsboys' stocks of "War End" extras, but took them to restaurants or street cars to read.

CHURCHES THRONGED.

The calm continued until after 8 o'clock. In Holy Rosary Cathedral and all Anglican churches in the city Victory services proceeded, well attended.

Then first flag-draped autos began to appear. Continued cries of newsboys began to sink into the man on the street.

By 9 a.m. the celebration was under way and promised to be a good one.

First, long streamers fluttered down from the Marine Building.

Auto horns blared continuously. Pedestrians had come prepared. They carried their own noisemakers, and used them.

Every window in the towering Royal Bank Building was open,

(Continued on Page 2.) See CITY.

War End Brings Drastic Cut In Sugar Rations

OTTAWA, May 7.—(CP)—The individual sugar ration was today cut from 14 to 9 pounds for the period June 1 to December 31.

The reduction will be made by allowing consumers one pound a month instead of the present two pounds for June, July, August, October and December. The Prices Board said the September and November rations will remain at two pounds to allow as much home canning as possible.

CANNING QUOTA STAYS.

The home canning allotment of 20 preserves coupons will be left intact and the two regular preserves coupons will continue to become valid each month.

In addition to affecting householders, the reduction will apply to the armed forces, jam and wine manufacturers, bakers, biscuit and breakfast cereal plants, soft drink manufacturers and quota users, such as restaurants and hotels.

Decision to make the cut followed a recent conference in Washington at which it was reported that United Nations requirements are 1,254,000 tons more than available supplies.

Weatherman Plans To Co-operate With City Celebrants

The weatherman promises continued fine weather for the V-E Day holidays today and Tuesday.

Thousands of workers are expected to spend the day in the parks and beaches.

A maximum of 71 degrees is expected today and 72 degrees on Tuesday. Minimum during the night will be about 45 degrees.

Suburbs Turn On Radio, Dance In Street

Small celebrations took place all through Vancouver's suburbs today.

Residents in various localities danced in the streets and held impromptu parties.

Daily Province To Publish Tuesday

All regular editions of The Vancouver Daily Province will be issued tomorrow, V-E Day.

Weather Forecast — Fair today and Wednesday, becoming cloudy Wednesday evening. Monday's temperatures: high 67, low 42.

FINE

The Vancouver Sun

RATIONED FOODS
Sugar—Coupons 56, 57 now valid.
Butter—Coupons 105 now valid.
Preserves—Coupons 45, 46 now valid.
All valid coupons in Book 5 good until further notice.

FOUNDED 1886
VOL. LIX—No. 236 | MArine 1161 | HOME EDITION | VANCOUVER, BRITISH COLUMBIA, TUESDAY, MAY 8, 1945 | ★★★ | PRICE 5 CENTS | BY CARRIER $1.00 per month

FINAL SURRENDER TO BE SIGNED IN BERLIN TODAY

EDITORIAL

WE'RE STILL AT WAR

Downtown streets are carpeted today with torn paper. Bright sunshine bathes the flags and the bunting draped from empty offices. The horns and the shouts are silent. A stillness has settled upon Vancouver in the aftermath of celebration.

"Long live the cause of freedom," said the well-loved voice over the radio at 6 o'clock this morning.

Thanksgiving for the cease-fire in Europe welled in the hearts of men and women. For some it came too late to save their sons, husbands, fathers and brothers. But they rejoiced for their more fortunate friends. Prayers were said for the safety of those emerging from that frightful carnage.

"My boy may not get home before the end of the year," a man on a streetcar said to his neighbor.

Out at Sea Island the work went forward on the production of bomb-bays for B-29's. It is "war as usual" in the Pacific. There was no holiday in the hospital wards. Late casualty lists chattered on newspaper teletypes. Some people went to church. Others meditated in their gardens.

"They hope to see established a peace which will afford . . . . assurance that all the men in all the lands may live out their lives in freedom from fear and want," said the sixth point of the Atlantic charter.

This was a time for remembrance that 35,000 Canadians laid down their lives to stem the tide of savagery; that 50,000 Canadians suffered the agonies of wounds; that hundreds of thousands of men and women had endured privation and sorrow. This was a time of trial for the makers of a planned peace. This was a time of turning from the defeat of one enemy in Europe to the defeat of another, no less barbaric, in Asia and the islands of the Pacific.

This was a time of rededication to the final extinction of bestial nationalism in all its forms. This was a time to pause at a milestone along that road; a time of deliverance from one foe before the onslaught on a companion menace.

This was V-E Day in Vancouver.

One Dead, 7 Injured In V-E Day Traffic

Police Looking for Two Drivers Alleged to Have Fled Scene

Unprecedented Victory Day traffic claimed the life of one man, jumping the city's traffic deaths this year to 13, and police are seeking two alleged hit-and-run drivers.

One of the drivers struck and killed Gerald Bruin, 2144 Dundas, in the 400 block East Hastings, at 12:20 a.m. today, police reported.

KNOCKED OFF BICYCLE

Another knocked Mrs. Charles Lintott, 40, of 2516 East Sixth, off her bicycle in the 600 black Terminal at 10:55 p.m.

She was admitted to General Hospital suffering from head injuries.

Philip Zelenok, 45, 1352 West Seventh, was taken to General Hospital with minor injuries suffered when struck by an auto in the 600 block East Hastings.

S. J. Hatchett, 32, and his wife, aged 35, of 7183 Cypress, were both taken to General Hospital following a collision between their car and another vehicle at Sixteenth and Cypress.

Hatchett has head and back injuries, while his wife suffered shock.

Marg Siemens, 20, Port Hammond, was taken to hospital with mouth lacerations and jaw injuries resulting from an auto collision at Cariboo and Hastings.

FALLS OUT OF CAR

Edwin T. Orr, 2390 Cambie, was taken to hospital with back injuries suffered when he slid out of a rumble seat at Cornwall and Balsam.

James Sim, New World Hotel, received head injuries when struck by a car in the 600 block Pacific.

Halifax Tars Ruin Street

HALIFAX, May 8—(CP)—Rioting broke out anew here this afternoon after a parade in the centre of the downtown district as a mob of approximately 500 people, mostly sailors, marched along Granville Street and literally smashed every window on the west side.

Led by two sailors wielding pieces of wood about six feet long, the mob did damage of thousands of dollars. At least 25 plate glass windows were broken in the space of two blocks.

Naval shore patrol men finally marched into the crowd and partially succeeded in dispersing them.

The major part of the downtown section looks as if a cyclone had swept through, with shattered glass and empty, broken liquor bottles strewing the streets—aftermath of rioting that broke out late last night and ended only after three liquor stores had been looted and a police patrol wagon and a streetcar wrecked.

After nearly six years of war and the inconveniences of a crowded city filled with twice its normal population, servicemen and civilians broke all the bounds of restraint, and went on one mad binge that was like half a dozen New Year's eve parties rolled together. (Earlier details on Page 6.)

10,000 Isolated Nazis Give Up

CAIRO, May 8—(AP)—One of the Germans' most far-flung points of isolated resistance disappeared today when Gen. Gagener, commander of 10,000 troops in the Dodecanese islands, surrendered to a British brigadier. This leaves Crete as the only German outpost in the Mediterranean.

Crown Jewels Captured

U.S. 7th ARMY, May 8—(AP)—The Hungarian crown jewels have been captured by the United States 7th Army, which also seized Count Ference Szalasi, puppet premier of the last German-dominated Hungarian government.

Two More B.C. Men Freed in Germany

OTTAWA, May 8 — ((CP) — Release of FO. George Garnet Farrell of Vancouver and PO. Gordon John Woods of Trail from German prison camps was announced today. Farrell's home is at 759 East Forty-Seventh, Vancouver, with his father, T. P. Farrell.

Still Mourn FDR

WASHINGTON, May 8—(BUP)—The month's period of mourning proclaimed by President Truman for Franklin D. Roosevelt will run its full length—until next Monday—despite the victory in Europe.

Pope to Speak

ROME, May 8—(BUP)—The Pope plans to broadcast a message to the world on the end of the war in Europe at 3 a.m. Vancouver time tomorrow.

'Yet to Crush Japan' Say The King and Churchill

His Majesty Asks People To Give Thanks to God

LONDON, May 8 — (AP) — The King called upon his peoples in a special V-E Day broadcast from Buckingham Palace today to "give thanks to God for a great deliverance."

The sovereign of the world's greatest empire praised Britons for their courage, sacrifices and endurances through nearly six years of war, and urged them to remember that total victory has not yet been won.

"UTMOST RESOLVE"

"Germany, who drove all Europe into war, has been finally overcome," he said. "In the Far East we have yet to deal with the Japanese, a determined and cruel foe.

"To this we shall turn with the utmost resolve and with all our resources."

Following is the text of the King's message:

"Today we give thanks to God for a great deliverance.

"Speaking from our Empire's oldest capital city—war-battered but never for one moment daunted or dismayed—speaking from London, I ask you to join with me in that act of thanksgiving.

"Germany, who drove all Europe into war, has been finally overcome. In the Far East we have yet to deal with the Japanese, a determined and cruel foe. To this we shall turn with the utmost resolve and with all our resources.

"But at this hour when the dreadful shadow of war has passed far from our hearths and homes in these islands, we may at last make one pause for thanksgiving, and then we must turn our thoughts to the tasks all over the world which peace in Europe brings with it.

REMEMBER THE FALLEN

"First let us remember those who will not come back: Their constancy and courage in battle, their sacrifice and endurance in the face of a merciless enemy; let us remember the men in all the services, the women in all the services, who have laid down their lives.

Please Turn to Page Two
See "The King"

Prime Minister Warns Huns Not to Resist Reds

From AP and BUP Dispatches

LONDON, May 8. — Prime Minister Churchill today proclaimed the end of the war in Europe and pledged that Britain now would concentrate all her forces against Japan.

Despite the capitulation, he said, the Germans in some places still were resisting the Red Army.

'NOT SURPRISING'

"Should they continue to do so after midnight tonight," he said, "they will of course deprive themselves of the protection of the laws of war and will be attacked from all quarters by Allied troops.

"It is not surprising that on such long fronts and in the existing disorder of the enemy, the commands of the German high command should not in every case be obeyed immediately."

Britain may allow herself a "brief moment of enjoyment," he told his countrymen in a brief radio speech, but added:

"Japan with all her treachery and greed remains unsubdued. Her despicable cruelties call for justice and retribution. We must now concentrate all forces for the task ahead.

GREAT OVATION

Churchill broadcast from the cabinet room at his official residence, 10 Downing Street, at 6 a.m., Vancouver time.

A few minutes after his broadcast, Mr. Churchill went to a wildly-cheering House of Commons to repeat his epoch-making declaration.

He was smiling broadly as he arose to deliver his V-E Day speech.

As he appeared from behind the Speaker's chair the whole house rose. Members cheered and waved their order papers while those in the side galleries and the strangers' gallery joined in the applause.

There was another great roar

Please Turn to Page Two
See "Churchill"

'Monty' and 'Ike' Thank Their Troops

PARIS, May 8 — Field Marshal Sir Bernard L. Montgomery, in a V-E Day message to the men in his command, asked them to remember their comrades who had given their lives in battle.

Gen. Dwight D. Eisenhower also issued a V-E Day order of the day, thanking the men and women of the Allied Expeditionary Forces. He said they had "taken in stride the military tasks so difficult as to be classed by many doubters as impossible."

"WELL DONE"

Field Marshal Montgomery said in part:

"What I have to say is very simple and quite short. I would ask you all to remember those of our comrades who fell in the struggle. They gave their lives that others might have freedom, and no man can do more than that. I believe that He would say to each one of them, 'Well done, thou good and faithful servant.'

"We who remain have seen the thing through to the end. We all have a feeling of great joy and thankfulness that we have been preserved this day. This is the Lord's work, and it is marvellous in our eyes.

"And so, let us embark on what lies ahead, ful of joy and optimism. We have won the German war. Let us now win the peace. Good luck to you all, wherever you may be."

DEEP APPRECIATION

Gen. Eisenhower said: "To every subordinate that has been in this command of almost 5,000,000 Allies I owe a gratitude that can never be repaid. The only repayment that can be made to them is the deep appreciation and lasting gratitude of all free citizens of all United Nations."

5000 Yet On Casualty Lists

OTTAWA, May. 8—(CP)—The end of the war in Europe Monday caught the Army with a back-log of 4000 to 5000 names of battle casualties in its casualty branch and Army officials said last night they were working on plans to release these names for publication as soon as possible.

Next-of-kin of these casualties have been notified and the big back-log awaiting publication results from the security rule that a casualty must not be made public until 30 days after the action in which the soldier was involved.

With the war in Europe over, this security rule no longer applies.

Defense headquarters said that beginning tomorrow it proposed to lengthen daily lists of casualties from 150 names each to 800 to 1000, and that these would be issued as rapidly as possible.

Jap War May Go On For Another Year

GUAM, May 8—(BUP)—Allied fighting forces in the Pacific pressed unremitting warfare against the Japanese today with no time out for celebrating the end of the war in Europe.

Military authorities predicted that, even with reinforcements from European theatre, it would require another year to beat the Japanese on the mainland. They conceded, however, that Japan might surrender on the mainland.

The "war as usual" brought new Allied blows in the land campaigns on Okinawa, the Philippines and Tarakan and another B-29 assault on Kyushu's suicide plane bases.

Dresden Falls To Red Army

LONDON, May 8—(BUP)—Dresden and the Czechoslovak stronghold of Olmutz fell to the Red Army in a day of bloody fighting today as dichard Nazi units continued the war in isolated European pockets in defiance of their leaders' unconditional surrender proclamation.

Premier Stalin announced that Dresden, the capital of German Saxony and one of the most stubborn enemy resistance centres left on the continent, was captured by Marshal Ivan S. Konev's 1st Ukrainian Army after two days of violent street fighting.

Other pocketed enemy forces were still resisting the Allies in Czechoslovakia, Yugoslavia, The Netherlands and on the Baltic island of Bornholm.

A Czech radio broadcast said the commander of the German forces in Czechoslovakia had again ordered the recalcitrant Nazi troops in Prague to cease firing and surrender to the Allies.

Caterpillars Coming

VICTORIA, May 8—(CP)—An outbreak of tent caterpillars—possibly as bad as the widespread epidemic of 1918—faces British Columbia this year, Department of Agriculture officials here said yesterday.

Belgian Monarch May Abdicate

FREED KING LEOPOLD FACES MIXED WELCOME

LONDON, May 8—(CP)—Liberated after five years of Nazis imprisonment, King Leopold II of Belgium today faced a future beset with uncertainty.

The 43-year-old monarch and his queen—a commoner whom he married while a prisoner—were rescued by U.S. 7th Army men who overpowered German elite guard troops guarding the royal party at Strobl, eight miles east of Salzburg in Austria.

With the king and queen were 18 members of their staff and their four children, three of the latter by his first wife, Queen Astrid, who died in 1935.

Reports from Belgium have indicated the king's homecoming would be received with mingled feelings by his countrymen.

Reported gaining ground was the suggestion that the king abdicate in favor of his heir, 14-year-old Prince Baudouin, with Prince Charles continuing as regent.

Canadians Arrest Nazi Seyss-Inquart

WITH THE 1ST CANADIAN ARMY, Holland, May 8—(CP)—Arthur Seyss-Inquart, German commissioner for the Netherlands, was placed under arrest today by the 1st Canadian Army. He faces war crimes charges.

Details of how Seyss-Inquart was taken into custody are not yet known but he arrived at an airfield near Canadian Army headquarters under military escort.

Seyss-Inquart, wearing a Nazi uniform, was moved by staff car from the airfield to a tent in a barbed wire enclosure at Canadian Army Headquarters.

EXTRA COPIES OF PEACE EDITION

We have had many inquiries for extra copies of Monday's momentous "Peace Edition" from readers who wish to send them to the boys and girls in the services and to friends out of town as souvenirs. The Sun has printed a limited number which may be secured at the regular price of 5 cents a copy from your newsboy, news dealer, delivery boy or by phoning MArine 1161.

AIR CHIEF MARSHAL SIR ARTHUR TEDDER
Britain and U.S.

MARSHAL GREGORY K. ZHUKOV
Soviet Union

GEN. JEAN DE LATTRE DE TASSIGNY
France

FIELD MARSHAL WILHELM KEITEL
Germany

FINAL SURRENDER—These are the three Allied leaders and the German commander who are scheduled to sign the final German surrender documents in Berlin today.

Burglars Don't Lay Off for V-E Day

Burglars took time out from peace celebrations Monday to rob the Grandview Grocery, 1752 Commercial Drive.

Kenneth Chan, proprietor, told police that $250 in bills and change was stolen from several hiding places in the store. Four cartons of cigarettes and two commercial gas ration books are also missing.

Miss E. Thompson, 4189 Quesnelle Drive, reported the theft of a large electric refrigerator, a tri-light and five new electric fixtures from the basement of her home over the week-end.

A small radio was stolen from the home of G. Simpson, 1873 Nelson, sometime Monday.

Hostilities Cease This Afternoon

From AP and BUP Dispatches

PARIS, May 8.—The bloodiest war in European history comes to its official end at 3:01 today, Vancouver time, with the formal end of hostilities on a continent desolated by more than five years of conflict.

The agreement formalizing the unconditional surrender will be ratified in Berlin today, with Field Marshal Wilhelm Keitel, chief of the German High Command, officially acknowledging that Germany is beaten.

Sitting around the table with Keitel in Berlin will be:

For the Western Allies: Air Chief Marshal Sir Arthur W. Tedder, Deputy Supreme Commander.

For Russia: Marshal Gregory K. Zhukov, commander of the 1st White Russian Army.

For France: Gen. Jean de Lattre de Tassigny, commander of the French 1st Army.

Fighting Still Rages

Guns are still blazing and men are still dying in some parts of Europe, but the cease-fire order has gone down from the high command of the Western Allies.

The end of the war was proclaimed by President Truman, Prime Minister Churchill and Gen. Charles DeGaulle of France.

Premier Stalin waited—presumably until Marshal Gregory K. Zhukov, conqueror of Berlin, sits down in the Reich capital and exacts assurance from German leaders that their troops will quit fighting the Red Army.

Such fighting still was going on briskly in Central Europe.

Gen. George S. Patton's U.S. 3rd Army, the last American force fighting in Europe, was brought to a standstill by a cease fire order at 6 a.m. Front reports indicated the army's last shot was fired in the Austrian mountains southwest of Linz.

The German "peace" government of Grand Admiral Karl Doenitz, successor of Adolf Hitler, was carrying on a semblance of official functions at Flensburg on the Danish frontier.

Reichsmarshal Hermann Goering, ousted in the last days of organized resistance from the command of the German air force, was believed to be with the Doenitz government. So was Heinrich Himmler, Gestapo chief and interior minister.

Meanwhile Allied Supreme Headquarters announced the Germans agreed to:

Order all resistance halted.

Yield all ships and aircraft unscuttled and undamaged.

Ensure compliance with all further orders from the Allied Supreme Commander and the Soviet High Command.

The surrender document specified that nothing it contained limited or restricted any terms which might later be imposed on the Reich.

"In the event of the German High Command or any of the forces under their control failing to act in accordance with this act of surrender," it warned, "the supreme commander . . . . and the Soviet High Command will take such punitive or other action as they deem appropriate.

Days of Thanksgiving

The Allied proclamation of victory in Europe was made simultaneously in London, Washington and Paris. No word came immediately from Moscow. It appeared that the Russians might be waiting until Zhukov has signed the surrender document in Berlin later today.

Gen. Charles De Gaulle told the French people by radio that "the war has been won! Victory is here! The victory of the United Nations and the victory of France!" The Germans have capitulated, and the French high command was a party to the act of capitulation, De Gaulle said.

He said it was possible that because of the collapse of central power in Germany, certain enemy units might hold out in isolated resistance.

President Truman in Washington soberly told his radio audience that victory "is only half won," and the job would be done only when unconditional surrender has been forced on the Japanese.

President Truman set next Sunday as a day of thanksgiving for the United States.

Next Sunday will be a day of prayer in Britain and in Canada will be observed as a day of thanksgiving.

Supreme headquarters dispatches made it clear the surrender was to all the Allies, but the Moscow radio was silent even after Mr. Truman and Mr. Churchill had spoken. There had been general expectation that Premier Stalin would speak simultaneously.

OFFICIAL TEXT OF SURRENDER TERMS

PARIS, May 8—(BUP)—The text of the German surrender document signed at Reims:

1. We the undersigned, acting on the authority of the German High Command, hereby surrender unconditionally to the Supreme Commander of the Allied Expeditionary Force and simultaneously to the Soviet High Command all forces on land, sea and in the air who are at this date under German control.

2. The German High Command will at once issue orders to all German military, naval and air authorities and to all forces under German control to cease active operation at 2301 hours central European time on May 8 and to remain in positions occupied at that time. No ship, vessel or aircraft to be scuttled or any damage done to their hull, machinery or equipment.

3. The German High Command will at once issue to the appropriate commanders and insure the carrying out of any further orders issued by the Supreme Commander of the Allied Expeditionary Force and by the Soviet High Command.

4. This act of military surrender is without prejudice to and will be superseded by any general instrument of surrender imposed by or on behalf of the United Nations and applicable to Germany and the German armed forces as a whole.

5. In event of the German High Command or any of the forces under their control failing to act in accordance with this act of surrender, the Supreme Commander of the Allied Expeditionary Force and the Soviet High Command will take such punitive or other action as they deem appropriate.

Signed at Reims, France, at 0241 hours, seventh day of May, 1945.

On behalf of the German High Command: Jodl.

In the presence of or on behalf of the Supreme Commander, Allied Expeditionary Force: W. B. Smith.

On behalf of the Soviet High Command: Ivan Susllaprov.

On behalf of the French High Command: F. Sevez.

(See Page 26 for an eye-witness account of the signing of the Reim's surrender.)

First Official Story of Atom Bomb

WEATHER FORECAST

WASHINGTON — Partly cloudy with a few afternoon and evening showers in the Cascades. Cooler in eastern portion; moderate westerly wind off coast.

AMERICA FIRST
Seattle Post-Intelligencer

Post-Intelligencer Telephone, Main 2000

Post-Intelligencer Office, 600 Pine St.

WAR EXTRA

VOL. CXXVIII, NO. 158   Entered as Second Class Matter at Seattle, Wash.   SEATTLE, TUESDAY, AUGUST 7, 1945   TWENTY PAGES   HH   5c PER COPY

Truman Tells Japs:

'GIVE UP OR BE WIPED OUT BY ATOMIC BOMB'

1st Official Story Of Atomic Bomb

Army Reveals Details of Actual Demonstrations in New Mexico

(Following is the war department's official dramatic account of the test which resulted in the first man-made atomic explosion, releasing a power which President Truman has said could destroy civilization.)

Mankind's successful transition to the Atomic Age, was ushered in July 16, 1945, before the eyes of a tense group of renowned scientists and military men gathered in the heartlands of New Mexico to witness the first end results of their billion-dollar effort.

Here in a remote section of the Alamogordo Air Base 120 miles southeast of Albuquerque the first man-made atomic explosion, the astounding achievement of nuclear science, was set off with an impact which signalized man's entrance into a new physical world. Its success was greater than the most ambitious estimates. A small amount of matter, the product of a chain of huge especially constructed industrial plants, was made to

(Continued on Page 6, Column 2)

U-235 Secret 5 Years Old

By Anne Stewart

An interview granted to The Post-Intelligencer five years ago yesterday lifted the veil of secrecy shrouding U-235—the chemical substance which has loosed the atomic power of the universe for war and for peace.

In a long distance telephone conversation, Dr Arthur H. Compton, Nobel Prize winning physicist and one of the four American scientists who served as governmental advisers

(Continued on Page 6, Column 1)

Punch of Hanford Atomic Bomb Equals 2,000 of These 11-Ton British Bombs

MULTIPLY BY 2,000—Most deadly weapon ever devised, the automatic bomb whose production at the Hanford Project was revealed for the first time yesterday by President Truman, equals the explosive force of 2,000 of the British 11-ton "grand slam" bombs shown above. Note how small a man is by the side of a "grand slam" bomb whose destructive power is dwarfed by the discovery of the automatic bomb.
—(Associated Press Wirephoto.)

Douglass Welch Reports
Drive Over Alaska Link Hair-Raising Ordeal

Douglass Welch, widely known author and Post-Intelligencer staff reporter, is making an automobile trip over the road from Vancouver to Prince George, B. C.—the road which is expected to form an integral part of the projected highway to Alaska. He will report daily to Post-Intelligencer readers on his experiences.

By Douglass Welch
Post-Intelligencer Staff Correspondent

SISKA LODGE, B. C., Aug. 6.—It is exactly 161.3 miles from the Hotel Vancouver to this little mountain auto camp situated on a bench high above the river in the Fraser canyon, seven miles west of the town of Lytton.

Somehow it seems like 400. It has been the most exhausting, nervewracking single day's drive we ever made. It was extremely hot and the heat may have contributed to it. But the road itself reminds one of southern Oregon, on the Siskiyou mountains, on the stretch between Yreka and Redding, California, in the days of 1920.

Do you remember the first road over Snoqualmie Pass? Comparatively it was a speedway and as safe as a padded cell.

By Canadian standards the Fraser Canyon road is good, that is to say it is hard surfaced. By Washington standards it is poor. It is narrow, twisting and climbs and drops unceasingly most of the time without much reason.

There was little attempt on the original location to smooth out any particular grade, just get there, brother, that's all we ask. In fairness to Canadians who speak patronizingly of Canadian roads, we are probably spoiled. Canadians say.

Three of them told us tonight (rather emphatically, too) that the Fraser Canyon road is good, that is

(Continued on Page 4, Column 2)

Atom Bomb Could Have Saved Nazis

By Robert G. Nixon

ABOARD THE CRUISER AUGUSTA WITH PRESIDENT TRUMAN, Aug. 6.—(I.N.S.)—President Truman declared today that if Nazi scientists had succeeded in perfecting the atomic bomb the United States and her allies would have lost the war.

Mr. Truman made his statement to correspondents after announcing that an atomic bomb had blasted Japan with power greater than that of 20,000 tons of TNT.

The chief executive said that scientists in the Reich had been trying throughout the war to perfect the same sort of explosive that ripped Hiroshima yesterday.

He disclosed that 1,300 pounds of uranium were found in German possession at the time the Reich capitulated.

Instead of winning the war, the President said, America and Great Britain now have a weapon that can be used for absolute control of world peace.

He made it clear that only the Washington and London governments know the secret of the bomb.

This secret, he said, will not be revealed until after the peace of the world has been absolutely secured.

dam, personally informed officers of the cruiser of the new bomb.

The President walked unannounced into the Augusta's ward room, where the officers were at lunch. They began to rise from their seats.

"Keep your seats, gentlemen," Mr. Truman said. "I have an announcement to make.

"We have just dropped a bomb on Japan that has more power than 20,000 tons of TNT.

"It was an overwhelming success."

Mr. Truman's words brought thunderous applause from the officers.

The President thus wrote another chapter in history by himself informing the men with whom he sailed of the invention which appears destined to change the whole shape of warfare.

But the officers had not been the first to hear the announcement. A few moments before Mr. Truman told the news to members of the crew with whom he was having lunch.

When he had finished, a you

(Continued on Page 2, Column 5)

Jap City Tastes Super-Explosive

U. S., British Scientists Team To Harness Mightiest Force

Full page of pictures on Hanford atomic bomb project—Page 20.

By Associated Press
President Truman in his statement today on the new atomic bomb said:

"We are now prepared to obliterate more rapidly and completely every productive enterprise the Japanese have above ground in any city. We shall destroy their docks, their factories and their communications. Let there be no mistake we shall completely destroy Japan's power to make war . . . If they do not now accept our terms they may expect a rain of ruin from the air."

By Felix Cotten
WASHINGTON, Aug. 6.—(I.N.S.)— President Truman revealed to an astonished world today that an atomic bomb, more than two thousand times as powerful as the

Creation of Atomic Bomb Threat to Civilization

WASHINGTON, Aug. 6.—(AP)—President Truman has clearly indicated that the scientists who made the atomic bomb have done two things:

1—They have created a monster which could wipe out civilization.

2—Some protection against the monster must be found before its secret is given to the world.

The terrible implications of the destructive force of the bomb are contained in these sentences from the President's statement:

"Normally, everything about the work with atomic energy would be made public.

"But under present circumstances it is not intended to divulge the technical processes of production or all the military applications, pending further examination of possible methods of protecting us and the rest of the world from the danger of sudden destruction."

11-ton "Grand Slam" blockbuster, had shattered Hiroshima, Japan.

He announced that this most terrible of secret weapons, capable of turning steel structures into vapor, had been dropped on the important Japanese air base some time Sunday.

His announcement revealed that American and British scientists, working as a team, had won the old-age race to split the atom and release atomic energy, launching humankind into a new scientific

165

6 A.M. FINAL

AMERICA FIRST

Seattle Post-Intelligencer

Post-Intelligencer Telephone, Main 2000

Post-Intelligencer Office, 600 Pine St.

WAR EXTRA

VOL. CXXVIII, NO. 159 Entered as Second Class Matter at Seattle, Wash. SEATTLE, WEDNESDAY, AUGUST 8, 1945 TWENTY PAGES F 5c PER COPY

DETAILS OF ATOM RAID!

60% of City Wiped Out by Single Bomb

Countless Japs Burn to Death in Inferno

Five Big Industries Devastated; All Life Destroyed in Blast Area

Terrible Effect of Bomb Bared In Tokyo Broadcast

SAN FRANCISCO, Aug. 8 (Wednesday).—(AP)—Practically all living things—human and animal—"were literally seared to death" by the new atomic bomb loosed against the industrial and military center of Hiroshima, radio Tokyo admitted today.

The force of the bomb was so great that "those outdoors burned to death, while those indoors were killed by indescribable pressure and heat," said the enemy broadcast monitored by the Federal Communications Commission.

The terrible effect of the bomb was revealed in the statement that relief workers were unable to even distinguish the dead from the injured much less identify either.

The city was left in "disastrous ruin" with houses and buildings crushed, Tokyo reported. It added that authorities could not establish the extent of civilian casualties and had "their hands full giving every available relief possible under the circumstances."

Destruction was so heavy that even emergency medical facilities were burned out and relief squads were rushed from surrounding districts, the broadcast disclosed.

Text of the Tokyo English-language broadcast, beamed

(Continued on Page 2, Column 6)

Eyewitnesses Tell of Raid

By John Henry

GUAM, Aug. 7.—(INS)—When the Superfortress Enola Gay roared into nocturnal blackness to deliver an earthquaking atomic bomb upon Hiroshima, only three of 11 men aboard knew they were en route to make history with the most devastating weapon yet devised.

Col. Paul W. Tibbets Jr., in a graphic description of the epochal mission, said today that his co-pilot, Capt.. Robert A. Lewis, was unaware exactly what frightful cargo they were carrying.

Capt. Lewis, Ridgefield Park, N. J., calmly was writing a letter home to his mother, Mrs. George Lewis, as the Enola Gay nosed toward Hiroshima.

With the target town in sight, Lewis wrote a casual line then put down his pen. He had told "mom" he would resume his letter momentarily, as soon as bombs were away.

Capt. Lewis found it difficult to describe the thunder-

(Continued on Page 2, Column 4)

Flyers Shocked 10 Miles Away Smoke Billows 40,000 Feet

GUAM, Aug. 8 (Wednesday)—(AP)—Four and one-tenth square miles "or 60 per cent" of Hiroshima were wiped out by the devastating atomic bomb dropped Wednesday by a B-29, the U. S. army strategic air force headquarters reported today.

Five major industrial targets were wiped out in the city of six and nine-tenths square miles.

"Additional damage was shown outside the completely destroyed area," said a communique based on reconnaissance photographs made over the city of 343,000 on the morning of the day the bomb was dropped by a Superfort which felt the concussion while 10 miles away.

The photographs showed clearly that the heart of Hiroshima was wiped out with such awful thoroughness as if some giant bulldozer had swept across the buildings and houses.

The effect of the bomb was so terrific that several man-made firebreaks and seven streams failed to stop the fires.

One of the spanned firebreaks was three city blocks wide and a photograph evaluator said it was one of the best seen on Japan. If ever a firebreak should have stopped flames, it should have done it in this case.

Photographs, taken a few minutes after the atomic bomb blasted Hiroshima, showed a spectacular formation of white smoke rising like a long-necked mushroom over the city. Only several do

VETERAN SUES EX-WIFE FOR HIS 'CIVIE' JOB

By Fergus Hoffman

With the full might of the United States of America behind him, a Seattle war veteran yesterday started court action to force his former wife to reinstate him in his civilian job.

Filed in federal court on behalf of the veteran, Frank J. Van Hoeter, 900 16th Ave., was a petition asking that the Olympic Pie Company be forced to comply with the Selective Service Act by reinstating Van Hoeter as production manager of the firm.

Present owner of the pie company is Mrs. Lemma Wagner, the former Mrs. Van Hoeter.

IN ARMY, DIVORCED

"She divorced me in 1943 after I went in the army, but I still want my old job back," Van Hoeter said last night. "I've asked her to reinstate me, but she won't do it."

Mrs. Wagner, whose present husband, George F. Wagner, is route manager of her company, said she didn't want to talk about the controversy.

The petition, scheduled to be heard August 23, was filed by John E. Belcher, assistant United States district attorney. It alleges that Van Hoeter, 23 years an employe and part-owner of the pie company, was earning $125 a week in salary when he entered the army in 1942.

DIDN'T FORFEIT JOB

"I probably could get another job, but not at any $125 a week to start," Van Hoeter said. "I sold my shares in the company when I entered the service, but I didn't forfeit my job, too."

Van Hoeter, who was an army staff sergeant, assigned as a baker at the Presidio, San Francisco. was discharged last May 15. On May 26, the petition stated, he applied for reinstatement at the pie company, but his application was not acted upon.

Besides reinstatement, the petition asks that Van Hoeter be paid his weekly salary since the day he applied for reinstatement.

—Report From Scandinavia—

Editor Happy Over Norway's Liberation

By Berne Jacobsen
Post-Intelligencer Staff Correspondent

OSLO, Norway—With sandals on his feet, his shirt collar open and his sleeves rolled up, Martin Tranmaez, editor of Arbeiderbladet, second largest newspaper in Norway, leans back in his desk chair and smiles.

After five years of exile, Tranmaez is back at his desk listening to the presses rumble six stories below.

"It's wonderful to be free again in Free Norway," he says and throws back his powerful shoulders as an expression of a burden tossed aside.

Back in 1904, a young man roving about the world, Editor Tranmaez visited in Seattle.

"There was a great city," he says, "There was plenty doing in Seattle then. I remember it as a lively place. I remember the mountains and the forests."

When the Germans invaded Norway they left Arbeiderbladet alone for awhile—except for imposing regulations as to what could be printed. The regulations weren't obeyed too well and in October of 1940 the Germans ordered the paper shut down and arrested certain members of the staff.

"I had gone at the time to a meeting in Sweden," Editor Tranmaez says, "and received word that the Germans had me booked for a concentration camp. So I didn't come back."

The Germans took over the paper's facilities for a "culture center" and for publication of an organ of their own called Free Folk.

The day after the Germans capitulated Editor Tranmaez was back in his office and on May 9 Arbeiderbladet hit the street with its first edition—the first free paper that Norway had read in five years.

"What a mess the Germans left," Tranmaez says. "My office was the office of the editor of Free Folk. There were papers and boxes and trash and empty bottles every place. They got out in such a hurry they even left a lot of their documents behind."

"What is your impression of Oslo?" he asks.

I told him I thought the capital of Norway looks shabby but the people look good.

"Yes, that was my first impression, too," he said slowly, "but after being back a little while I don't see the drabness. It's the spirit of the people that counts."

During the five years of German occupation, Oslo was not permitted to keep its face clean. There was no paint, no material to maintain things. Naturally the city became a bit run down. In the parks unsightly bomb shelters have been built. The German mind ran to destruction and many senseless things occurred like the cutting down of fine old trees.

It will take, in Tranmaez' opinion, two years before Norway is back in a semi-normal condition. There is a great deal of work to be done and at the moment the main task is feeding the people and preparing for the coming winter.

But the Norwegians are free and for a people with hundreds of years of freedom as a tradition, that is the big thing.

• • •

Spent a pleasant evening with relatives of Mr. and Mrs. O. C. Rossoe, 16012 Beach Drive N. E.

At the home of Mrs. Rossoe's sister and brother-in-law, Mr. and Mrs. Johan Orvin, there is happiness at the capitulation of the Germans and comforts long denied.

Mr Orvin tells me he lost 50 pounds in weight during the occupation but in last two months has gained back considerable.

Present also was Mrs. Rossoe's sister, Mrs. Ingvald Johannessen. Another sister is visiting in the country. All three of the children are away from home. The son is now in Germany where he is seeking to locate Norwegians who had been taken to Germany as prisoners and have not returned. A daughter went to the country early in the war to work on a farm and thus escape German recruitment for labor on the continent. She is

(Continued on Page 4, Column 2)

(Advertisement)

Celia Lee's CENTENNIAL TREAT

Pancake-Flour Muffins . . .

★ HERE'S a quickie you'll bake more than once! Easy on shortening and sugar . . . and the prepared flour cuts mixing time down to a minimum.

2 tablespoons shortening
2 tablespoons sugar
1 egg
1 cup milk
2 cups Centennial Pancake and Waffle Flour
½ cup raisins, if desired

Cream together shortening and sugar. Beat in the egg and add milk, flour and raisins alternately. Stir until well mixed. Bake in greased muffin tins at 425°F. about 25 minutes. Serve piping hot with jelly, jam or honey. Delicious!

★ Today, more than ever . . . *The Swing is to Centennial* PANCAKE and WAFFLE FLOUR!

© 1945, Centennial Flouring Mills Co.

First of Doolittle B-29s at Okinawa

OKINAWA, Aug. 8 (Wednesday).—(AP)—The first B-29s of Gen. James Doolittle's Eight Air Force arrived on Okinawa today, swinging spectacularly out of the clouds onto the newly completed coral airstrip.

"It is great to have these boys with us to take their share in the knockout of Japan," said Doolittle, who was among the crowd for the initial welcoming of the Superfortresses to this potent airbase on Japan's doorstep.

Look to LITTLER for the NEW in Men's and Women's SPORTS APPAREL—417 Union & Olympic Hotel Shop.—(Adv.)

Atomic Expert Reveals

Death Rays Lurk In Bombed City

(In the following dramatic, exclusive article, Dr. Harold Jacobson, who worked for two years on the Manhattan Project—the atomic bomb—reveals that areas struck by the bomb remain saturated with death for years. Secondary radiation will kill anyone entering the area. Dr. Jacobson, a physicist who is a graduate of the University of Chicago, worked on the atomic bomb project in the Oak Ridge, Tenn., plant and at Columbia University. He is now associated with Philip E. Wilcox, Inc., New York research engineers.)

By Dr. Harold Jacobson
Written Exclusively for International News Service

NEW YORK, Aug. 7—(I.N.S.)—Any Japanese who try to ascertain the extent of damage caused by the atomic bomb in Hiroshima are committing suicide.

The terrific force of the explosion irradiates every piece of matter in the area. Investigators will become infected with secondary radiation which breaks up the red corpuscles in the blood. This prevents the body from assimilating oxygen which means that those so exposed will die in the same way victims of leukemia die.

Actually, tests have shown that the radiation in an area exposed to the force of an atomic bomb will not be dissipated for approximately 70 years.' Hence, Hiroshima will be a devastated area not unlike our conception of the moon for nearly three-quarters of a century.

Furthermore, rain falling on the area will pick up the lethal rays and will carry them down to the rivers and the sea. And animal life in these waters will die.

I cite these facts to illustrate the awesome force contained in the atomic bomb. It defies the imagination. Flash Gordon looks like a piker compared to it. Yet the physical principle involved has been known for years. Such scientists as Einstein and the Italian, Fermi, were on the threshold of

(Continued on Page 4, Column 1)

FRYE & COMPANY, 2203 Airport Way, needs butchers and boners. New plant. Highest wages. Permanent. Phone MAin 4100, Authorized Referral Required.

WEATHER FORECAST

Seattle and vicinity—Partly cloudy today, cloudy tomorrow morning but turning fair tomorrow afternoon. Cooler tomorrow. Highest temperature today 68; lowest tomorrow 56; highest tomorrow 74. Gentle, variable winds.

WATCH FOR IT! PLATTER CHATTER.—(Adv.).

Atom Bomber

DROPPED BOMB — Maj. Thomas W. Ferebee of Mocksville, N. C., was the bombardier of the Superfortress Enola Gay which dropped the first atomic bomb on the Japanese city of Hiroshima on August 6. He was one of three crew members who knew what the plane was carrying. —(Associated Press Wirephoto.)

AUTO LOANS—6%—No red tape, no delay. Why pay more? Over 30,000 cars financed. S. L. SAVIDGE CO., EAst 8400.—(Adv.)

Hanford Workers Take Atomic News in Stride

By R. B. Bermann
Post-Intelligencer Staff Correspondent

RICHLAND, Aug. 7.—All the rest of the world may be badly excited about the atomic energy bomb with which the United States is seeking to bring the war with Japan to a sudden end. But the men who are making the product which gives the missiles their fabulous explosive force are taking the news in their stride.

They are pleased to know that they have produced something which is really worth while. But they aren't in ectasy like the army officers who have been guarding the secret for the last 2½ years. The army officers feel as if they had been sitting on a volcano all this time and now they are free to get up and walk around.

But the actual workers who, until now, didn't have the faintest idea of what they were making, are going about their business as if nothing whatever had happened.

There wasn't anything even resembling a celebration over the disclosure of the secret. The town's single tavern reported it did no more business last night than any ordinary Monday night. And the Du Pont Company police had no more work on their hands than usual, which is very little, as this is something of a model community.

The quiet elation expressed by R. C. Sievers, 29, who has been employed in the maintenance department since March, 1944, was fairly typical.

"It is nice to know that all the hard work we've done has resulted in something really valuable," he said. "Sometimes it has been a little disheartening, and I got to wondering whether I should be overseas instead of being here, especially since my younger brother came home after being nine months in a German prison camp. But now I'm convinced that everything is all right.

"It wasn't any time for a celebration, though—that can wa

(Continued on Page 3, Column

Genuine PIGSKIN GLOVES for men. We are fortunate in being able to offer you these gloves; all sizes. TALL'S TRAVEL SHOP, 1406 3rd Ave.—(Adv.).

TWO-SUITER CASES for men. complete selection in Seattle. $21.50 up, plus tax. TALL'S TRAVEL SH 1406 3rd Ave.—(Adv.)

SECOND ATOM BOMBING
Nagasaki Hit in New Attack

AMERICA FIRST
Seattle Post - Intelligencer
6 A.M. FINAL

Post-Intelligencer Telephone, Main 2000   20 PAGES   Post-Intelligencer Office, 600 Pine St.

VOL. CXXVIII, NO. 160   SEATTLE, THURSDAY, AUGUST 9, 1945   Entered as Second Class Matter at Seattle, Wash.   F   5c PER COPY

'Results Good' Say Superfort Crews

Crowded Jap Port Devastated; Tokyo Cries for Mercy

By Kenneth McCaleb

GUAM, Aug. 9 (Thursday).—(I.N.S.)—An atomic bomb was dropped for the second time on Japan today devastating the key port and shipbuilding center of Nagasaki, three days after the weapon was first used against Hiroshima.

With 150,000 Japanese estimated to have perished at Hiroshima, the new atomic bomb attack was announced by Gen. Carl A. Spaatz at Guam in a terse communique stating:

"The second use of the atomic bomb occurred at noon of 9 August at Nagasaki.

"Crew members reported good results.

"No further details will be available until the mission returns."

Nagasaki One of Japan's Most Important Ship Centers

The communique did not specify the number of Superforts used in the Nagasaki mission. But—as at Hiroshima, where the Japs said "practically all" life had been obliterated—it was believed only one B-29 carried out the Nagasaki blow.

Nagasaki, lying on the west side of Japan's southernmost island of Kyushu, had a normal population of 253,000 and covered an area of 12 square miles.

The city, which now must have been reduced to a desolate wasteland of flaming destruction, lies south of the major Japanese naval base of Sasebo, fronting the Tsushima Strait, which flows between Nippon and Korea.

Jap Morale Seen Cracking in Tokyo Radio Appeal to Neutrals

A strong indication that Japanese morale is cracking was given by Tokyo radio in a broadcast appealing to neutrals to halt the use of the atomic bomb.

Describing the destruction of Hiroshima, the enemy broadcast reported:

"The impact of the bomb was so terrific that practically all living things, human and animals, were literally seared to death by the tremendous heat and pressure engendered by the blast.

"All of the dead and injured were burned beyond recognition.

"With houses and buildings crushed, including the emergency medical facilities, the authorities are having their hands full in giving every available relief possible

(Continued on Page 4, Column 4)

REDS BATTLE JAPS: INVADE MANCHURIA

7 Scattered Plants At Hanford Project

Honshu Hit by Fleet Planes

GUAM, Aug. 9 (Thursday).—(AP)—Admiral Halsey opened up a new carrier assault on Japan today with his United States Third Fleet and cooperating British carrier planes, achieving what an Associated Press dispatch direct from the fleet called "complete tactical surprise."

Great waves of rocketing and bombing raiders swept over air bases of Northern Honshu Island and would strike soon.

Al Dopking, Associated Press war correspondent with the fleet, said only two Japanese planes showed up and both were shot down "long before they had a chance to get a glimpse of this navy powerhouse." Dopkins said over 1,200 carrier planes participated in the raids.

The fleet attacks are continuing, Admiral Nimitz said.

WAKE HIT AGAIN

Elsewhere, aircraft under Nimitz' command ranged from the Kuriles to Yap and the Palaus.

Only yesterday, an official navy department spokesman in Washington warned the Japanese that Halsey's gigantic force was off Honshu and would strike soon.

On Monday, carrier planes again attacked Wake, tiny Pacific island for which U. S. marines fought desperately against overwhelming Japanese air, sea and land forces early in the war.

They destroyed two ammunition dumps and various buildings, Nimitz said. Only eight days earlier, on August 1 another battleship and lesser fleet units had bombarded Wake, in an attack coordinated with a carrier plane strike.

3 Jap Ships Sunk Off Korean Coast

OKINAWA, Thursday, Aug. 9.—(AP)—Privateers of Fleet Air Wing One yesterday sank three Japanese ships in the Tsushima Straits and off the west coast of Korea.

WEATHER FORECAST

SEATTLE AND VICINITY—Partly cloudy today, increasing tomorrow, with occasional light rain tomorrow afternoon. Little change in temperature both days. Highest temperature both days, 76 degrees; lowest tomorrow morning, 56. Gentle, southwesterly wind.

Berne Jacobsen's

"Report From Scandinavia" will be found today on Page 20.

Desert Miracle Described

(Pictures on Page 3.)

By R. B. Bermann
Post-Intelligencer Staff Correspondent

RICHLAND, Aug. 8.—The curtain was partially lifted on the war's most closely guarded secret today.

And it was revealed that not one but seven widely scattered plants are operating in the desertland where science has turned the atom into history's deadliest weapon.

It marked the first time civilians, not employed at the Richland plants, have been allowed within the secret area that was the birthplace of the atomic bomb.

But even though the tight security regulations were relaxed enough to permit the tour, we were not allowed within several hundred yards of any of the buildings.

None the less, it was a fascinating experience because we were exploring an area which is unlike anything else that the world has ever seen.

The seven different plants are set down in the middle of the desert. In each case, they are separated from each other by several miles—presumably for the benefit of localizing the damage if any of the fantastically destructive material should get out of control.

In one plant, raw materials are processed. There are three other

(Continued on Page 6, Column 1)

U. COED GIVES AID IN STUDENT MURDER CASE

By Lucille Cohen

Three sensational developments last night shed light on the mystery slaying of Walter Bernard Foley Jr., 22, University of Washington sophomore, whose bullet-riddled body was found on a lonely country road in the early morning. They were:

1—Sheriff Harlan S. Callahan disclosed his office had been visited by a University coed who said she had been with Foley until 10 p. m. on the night of his murder—Lois Hanson, of 5264 19th Ave. N. E. Miss Hanson told county detectives she knew nothing of Foley's movements after 10 p. m. when she left him. This was several hours before the murder which the coroner's office said occurred at 6:30 a. m.

2—Miss Hanson asserted that several nights before the killing a mutual male acquaintance had attempted to run Foley's car into a ditch, Sheriff Callahan said.

3—The bullet-riddled car which Foley occupied was found by several miles before the murder. Foley, an honorably discharged veteran of World War II, met death by a neighbors said it had been standing since early morning.

Meanwhile, Sheriff Callahan

(Continued on Page 11, Column 1)

Irreplaceable Loss

THE DEATH of Maj. Richard I. Bong, whose 40 individual victories in the air over Japanese flyers made him America's outstanding ace, is a lamentable loss to the nation he served so brilliantly.

It is also a loss that should make the high command of our air forces revise some of the arbitrary methods by which they assign irreplaceable personnel.

Major Bong was a boy in years. A modest, unassuming boy who in demeanor and aspect could well serve as a model for the ideal American lad.

But in the performance of his duty, in his ability to assume and carry out tasks beyond the call of that duty, he was as poised, mature and gallant as that renowned mirror of knighthood of whom it was said he was the perfect warrior, "without fear and without reproach."

Thus he represented to his country, to this and future generations, the ideal of patriotic valor and personal worthiness that inspires and fortifies American youth.

He had won the honor and borne the burden that entitled him to rest upon the laurels no other had achieved.

He should never have been assigned to the hazardous duty in which he met his death.

He should have been discharged, or placed in a place of safety, not because he might have wanted that, which he did not, but because the country needs living heroes, their example and also their immediate posterity.

But it seems to be a habit or tradition among the high command for certain officers to regard others as expendable, regardless of greater considerations. So it comes that lives of infinite value to the country are put on the delicate balance of fate time after time when there is neither reason nor need for such procedure.

The untimely loss of Major Bong should serve to awaken public inquiry and protest against this practice.

Soviet Planes Hit Nip-Held Korea

Fight in 'Self-Defense,' Says Enemy H. Q.

By the Associated Press

Red army troops slashed across the eastern and western frontiers of Japan's stolen Manchuria early this morning shortly after the Russian declaration of war became effective.

Sharp fighting now is in progress in all invaded areas, the Tokyo radio announced today.

A broadcast Domei dispatch said Russian forces had battered across the eastern frontier of Manchuria at "several points" along a 300-mile line extending southward from Hutou to Hunchun. Hutou, just across the Soviet-Manchuria border, is 350 miles east of Harbin, and Hunchun is about 240 miles southeast of that key industrial and communications center, regarded as a prime Russian objective.

The attack from the west, Tokyo said, was launched in the vicinity of Lupin (Manchouli), in the northwestern elbow of the winding Manchurian

(Continued on Page 6, Column 4)

Declaration of War Elates Moscow

MOSCOW, Aug. 8.—(AP)—Long columns of singing Red army men tramped through the heart of Moscow tonight, 45 minutes after the Soviet radio announced to the people of Russia that the nation would be at war with Japan at one second after midnight.

People piled out of buildings and apartments to cheer the marching soldiers of the Red army, whose force was being turned against the Japanese, the Soviet government said, at the request of the Allies to speed "universal peace."

Foreign Commissar Vyacheslav Molotov disclosed that Emperor Hirohito had asked the Soviet Union to mediate "about mid-July" in the war in the Pacific, but added that Tokyo's rejection of the Potsdam unconditional surrender ultimatum caused the proposals to "lose all significance."

Molotov said the emperor's request was transmitted through a special Japanese mission in the Soviet capital.

The foreign commissar said Presi-

Russia's Action Pleases Wallgren

OLYMPIA, Aug. 8.—(AP)—Gov. Mon C. Wallgren welcomed the news of Russia's entry into the war against Japan as bringing hope for an early end to the war.

"As a true ally of ours I think Russia should take this action and I hope it will mean the saving of many American lives," he said.

Red Embassy Calm About War Entry

WASHINGTON, Aug. 8.—(AP)—The ornate Russian embassy was as stolid as usual on the day Moscow declared war on Japan.

An attendant with a thick accent showed the only evidence of interest in the event. He wanted to know whether the papers were out yet with "thees news." He moved quickly—but with dignity—through the door to hunt a copy.

Soviet Shipmates Jubilant

(Pictures on Page 3.)

By Fergus Hoffman

Jubilantly a pretty little Russian waitress aboard a Soviet ship berthed in Seattle yesterday summed up her reaction to her country's declaration of war on Japan.

"Victor-eee!" she screamed, virtually exhausting her English vocabulary. "Victor-eee!"

And from pert Nina Jaldacova to the ship's master, young Vitaliy Kalinin, 30, one opinion permeated the ship:

"It will be over in six weeks," Captain Kalinin said, nodding his head emphatically. "Six weeks, no more . . ."

Excited Nina, who with her shipmates had hurriedly changed into shoreside clothes for the benefit of a Post-Intelligencer photographer, expressed her happiness more thoroughly to a coast guardsman, Chief Specialist William A. Haffert.

ALL IN THE FAMILY

"Tovarich!" she laughed, "you are my brother!"

"That's right," Haffert grinned. "War make you my elder."

Captain Kalinin, a master merchant mariner since he was 17, scoffed at a proposal to paint out the huge "U. S. S. R." and Soviet

women waitresses lined the starboard rail to make the "V" sign. Some of them held up three fingers.

"Russia, America, England!" Nina explained.

Uptown, in the offices of the Soviet Purchasing Commission, Cmdr. N. J. Bezroukov, head of-the commission here, spoke regretfully of his shore duty, although his post here is of vital importance.

"I wish I would be in Russia now," he said. "Three years I am in Leningrad, through the blockade, and now I rest and now another war. I would like to fight again."

ROUTE PONDERED

Although it was officially announced by George Powell, assistant Pacific Coast director of the War Shipping Administration, that there will be no interruption in loading of lend-lease cargo by Russian ships, there was speculation as to what route the ships will follow from Seattle and other coast ports.

More than 100,000 tons a month has been moved across the North Pacific by the Russians for the past three years. Now, however, safe passage formerly granted by Jap patrol craft will not prevail.

Truman to Report Tonight by Radio

President Truman's report to the nation on the Potsdam conference will be carried over KIRO, KJR, KOL and KOMO from 7 to 7:30 p. m. Seattle time today.

THE VANCOUVER DAILY PROVINCE

51st YEAR—NO. 116 | VANCOUVER, B.C., FRIDAY, AUGUST 10, 1945 —28 PAGES | PRICE 5 CENTS | BY CARRIER $1.00 per month

War Goes On! . . . . White House

JAPAN ASKS FOR PEACE; ACCEPTS POTSDAM TERMS

Peace Bid Finds City Unprepared

Council's VJ-Day Committee Calls Special Meeting

The Jap surrender bid caught Vancouver by surprise . . .

And Vancouver was not alone.

The entire Allied world was surprised at the sudden capitulation, in spite of the atomic bomb and Russia's declaration of war.

But Vancouver recovered quickly.

Ald. Jack Price, chairman of the civic committee on V-J Day celebration, said:

"With the Japanese surrender right on top of us, the committee will meet at once."

He indicated that plans for Vancouver's official day of celebration will be ready by the time official Allied announcement of V-J Day is made.

Mayor Cornett, Lieutenant-Governor Hon. W. C. Woodward and Acting Premier Hon. Dr. K. C. MacDonald expressed jubilation at the news.

The man on the street was jubilant, too, but he wants to know: "What happens now?"

[illegible] be the toughest job of all—the long trek back to peace-time conditions in industry and business.

W. F. Kennedy, chairman of the Liquor Control Board, will not act to close liquor stores or beer parlors on V-J Day.

Beer parlors will remain open if they wish. Closing will be voluntary.

When the war in Europe ended, liquor stores and beer parlors both closed for two days — surrender day and V-E Day.

This time, liquor stores will close only if Ottawa declares a holiday.

ARMY READY.

The army was ready—only organization to be ready.

There is to be no confinement to barracks. The announcement will be read out to the troops in Pacific Command army establishments.

Observances in each camp will be decided upon by the officer commanding.

There will be army field kitchens for service personnel and their friends.

There will be no patrols on the street.

There was no trouble with service personnel in Vancouver on VE-Day, and none is expected on VJ-Day.

All army personnel were to be prepared for a short thanksgiving service.

Wet canteens will be open. Dry canteens will have soft

(Continued on Page 2.) See CITY.

From The Times:

Today In Europe

Compiled from the news and editorial comment of the London Times, and cabled from The Vancouver Daily Province London Bureau, Times Building, Printing House Square.

(Copyright, 1945, by Southam Co.)

LONDON, Aug. 10.—The acrimonious interchanges between King Peter of Yugoslavia and Marshal Tito, who wants to abolish the monarchy, says the Times editorially, must depend on political divisions already afflicting that country.

What Yugoslavia requires, like all the Balkans, is to find a foundation for a peaceful and orderly reconstruction. Though Marshal Tito has proclaimed a political amnesty and proposes to broaden the basis of political life, King Peter says every trace of law has been wiped out, and the proposed plebiscite on the return of the monarchy will take place "by forceful means and under terror."

Yugoslavia is emerging from a condition of chaos due to the German occupation. Before the war there was no democracy, only a police dictatorship, with a "managed" election. A free parliamentary system can not all at once spring forth from such conditions.

Inflicts Harm

And King Peter's immoderate vituperation can not conceivably do anything but harm. It can not be said the Yugoslav monarchists are primarily concerned with creating a full-fledged democracy. On the other side, free elections are not possible where candidates are chosen from a single list largely nominated from a single party.

Scientists and others are writing in the Times today stressing the tremendous peril to future world security if the atomic bomb's secret should be discovered by the Germans, the Japanese or any other aggressive nation in the next few years.

They advocate that the Security Council of the United Nations should create an armaments development department, staffed by international scientists and others, to keep abreast of new results flowing from the basic research.

Technical Advances

The council should also have the power to call on any nation to disclose its technical advances in war weapons. As civil police forces are now equipped with the latest scientific devices to prevent crime, so the International Security Council should be in an analogous position.

The future design of airplanes for war purposes will be revolutionized by the atomic bomb, says the Times aeronautical correspondent. Since 1939 bombing aircraft have had to be continually increased in size to carry bigger and bigger bombs.

RUSS ARMIES SLASH DEEPLY IN MANCHURIA

Sakhalin, Korea Are Invaded

(Compiled from late despatches to The Daily Province)

MOSCOW, Aug. 10. — The Red Army's tanks, infantry and massed cavalry rolled through numerous gates in Manchuria's defenses with sensational advances today.

(Tokyo announced the broadening of the Soviet attacks to Korea and Sakhalin Island.)

(The invasion of southern Sakhalin, known to the Japanese as Karafuto, carried the Soviets into the last oil source still available to the enemy.)

Soviet correspondents said units of the Soviet Pacific fleet had gone into action

Outer Mongolia, a protectorate of Russia's adjoining Manchuria, and Inner Mongolia, on the west, had declared war on Japan.

THREE MAIN ROUTES.

Moving into Manchuria along three main routes of invasion, the former Chinese Eastern Railway from Lupin (Manchouli) in the northwest, the Mongolian Caravan Trail from Lake Bor in the west and the Sungari River Valley from Kharbarovsk in the northeast, the Russians had opened up "numerous gates" in the enemy's carefully-prepared defenses and apparently were bent on a non-stop offensive.

Gains of up to 33 miles yesterday were being enlarged sensationally today.

The first Soviet blow was so well prepared that the Japanese were unable to hold a single defensive line along the frontier, one despatch reported.

The western and northwestern vanguards were driving hard for the city of Hulun (Hailar), Japanese forward base on the Chinese Eastern Railway, 90 miles east.

In the northeastern sector, where the Russians struck from the maritime provinces to protect their important naval and air base of Vladivostok, they also were making steady progress from Khabarovsk and captured Fu Yuan toward Harbin, rail heart of Manchuria 400 miles distant.

Japan Protests Atomic Bombing

SAN FRANCISCO, Aug. 10. —(AP)—Tokyo radio said today Japan had filed an official protest to the United States Government today against the atomic bomb attack on Hiroshima last Monday (Japanese time).

The protest was lodged through the Swiss Government, which is the protecting power for Japanese interests.

Cloudy A.M., Sunny P.M., Saturday Setup

Saturday's weather forecast offers a partly cloudy morning and fair afternoon, with moderate winds.

Maximum temperature at Vancouver airport will be 76 degrees, minimum 58.

Light winds and local fog patches in the early morning are expected in the Fraser Valley area.

THE TERMS

Here, in brief, is what Japanese acceptance of the Potsdam ultimatum implies:

Unconditional surrender;

Disarmament;

Giving up of all conquered areas;

Return of Manchuria and Formosa to China;

Preparation of independence for Korea;

Withdrawal from Malaya, the Netherlands East Indies and China.

Can Strikers Delay Return To Work

Striking American Can. Co. employees declined to return to work today under Controller Gordon Bell until they have obtained information as to their contract, the order-in-council dealing with the matter and the [illegible] of the War Measures Act at the termination of the war

The men's action came after the Federal Government stepped in Thursday and took over control of the plant.

ORDERED TO RETURN.

Gordon Bell, senior partner in the Vancouver real estate insurance firm of Bell & Mitchell was appointed controller and the men ordered to return to work pending arbitration of the dispute.

Mr. Justice S. E. Richards of Winnipeg, veteran arbitrator, was ordered to Vancouver to open arbitration hearings between the men and the company.

They went into conference with Mr. Bell at 10 a.m. today.

SEVEN POINTS PRESENTED.

They placed seven points before him. They are:

1. Status of the union's agreement with American Can Company, expiring August 26.

2. As negotiations had begun on a renewal agreement, the union now wants to know who will be carrying on such negotiations and with whom the agreement will be signed, the company or the government.

3. Whether the union grievance committee will now deal directly with Controller Bell, and how the various steps of grievance procedure will be carried out.

4. Copy of the order-in-council passed with its full details and limitatons.

5. If there will be any discrimination against the strikers, and wehther workers will all be placed on their usual jobs.

6. Whether the company or the goevrnment will derive the profits from the plant's operations while the controllership is in effect.

7. How long the controllership will be in effect, and the status of the War Measures Act at the termination of the war with Japan.

Battle 34 Blazes

(Special to The Daily Province)

NELSON, Aug. 10.—Hard-hitting fire-fighting crews are busy on 34 small fires in the Nelson forest district.

First Canadian Ship To Fire Shot At Jap, Reaches Nanaimo

(Special to The Daily Province)

ESQUIMALT, Aug. 10.—H.M.C.S. Uganda, first cruiser in Canada's navy and first Canadian ship to fire at the now surrendering Japanese, slid quietly into port at Esquimalt shortly after 9 a.m. today.

Whistles screamed; flags were flying and the band of H.M.C.S. Naden was playing as the ship entered the "gates" at 9:25.

The big cruiser came into the harbor escorted by eight Fairmiles. In the outer harbor two frigates, the Matane and the La Salle, saluted the Uganda by dipping their flags and blowing their whistles. The frigates were in the outer harbor on gunnery practice.

The 900 men aboard were to come off ship sometime during the morning. About 200 of them were due to leave for Vancouver on the afternoon boat. For those who remained, Victoria plans a big welcome tonight.

Auxiliary organizations have arranged a series of parties and dances.

The Uganda entered the harbor with Capt. R. E. Mainguy of Duncan and Victoria on the bridge.

The ship came in after more than 115 continuous days at sea. It came to release members of the crew who had not volunteered for Pacific duty.

MONTREAL.—Four C. P. R. troop specials will be on hand at Wolfe's Cove, Quebec, on Saturday to meet the SS. Pasteur and transport the 2100 veterans westward.

A total of 66 cars will make up the trains.

Broadcast Offer Asks Only That Emperor Retain Power

Russian Ambassador in Tokyo Officially Receives Capitulation Bid; Washington and London Anxiously Await Formal Word

WASHINGTON, Aug. 10.—The Japanese Domei Agency announced today that Japan was ready to accept the terms of the Potsdam declaration calling for Tokyo's unconditional surrender, so long as Emperor Hirohito was permitted to retain his prerogatives.

Although the peace offer, which Tokyo said was on its way to all the Allied capitals through neutral sources, had not yet been received officially either here or in London, Moscow radio said Shigenori Togo, Japanese foreign minister, had informed Soviet Ambassador Jacob Malik of Japan's readiness to surrender.

The offer received by Russia seemed to be identical with that broadcast by Domei.

Japan's communication to the Soviet ambassador was reported in a message from Tokyo to the Soviet Tass Agency, whose communications with Japan have apparently not yet been cut off despite Russia's declaration of war yesterday.

Tass said a similar communication would be given to Britain, the United States and China through Sweden.

It appeared that Russia had been the first of the Allied powers to receive the surrender offer formally because the Soviet ambassador has not yet left Tokyo, where the other Allies have no representation except through neutral channels.

The White House made it clear that the offer had not been received officially here and that the war was going on.

The offer was transmitted by the Domei Agency at 4:30 a.m. P.D.T. and picked up in the United States by the Associated Press and government monitors. But it had not come through official diplomatic channels and the White House said at 7:40 a.m. P.D.T. that the United States was continuing to fight.

Despite this, wild celebrations had been set off at Okinawa and at other points throughout the Allied world.

At Behest of Emperor

Domei said the Japanese Government acted in obedience to Hirohito who, it said, "desires earnestly to bring about an early termination of hostilities."

The Domei broadcast was recorded by the Associated Press from an English-language wireless transmission to the United States. The broadcast came shortly after Domei announced that Japan was protesting through diplomatic channels the United States' use of atomic bombs and coincided with new Tokyo reports of Russian advances in Manchuria, Korea and on Sakhalin Island.

The Japanese wireless transmitter went off the air in the middle of a sentence after transmitting 200 words of the announcement of the "desire" to bring about an end to hostilities.

F.C.C. monitors said the transmission ended:

"The Japanese Government hope sincerely that this . . ."

Domei waited a moment, F.C.C. monitors said, and then said "stand by."

Through Swiss, Swedes

Domei said Japan was informing the Allies of her acceptance through the Swiss and Swedish governments—neutral intermediaries.

A later Domei broadcast at 6:30 p.m. P.D.T. retransmitted the statement and gave its ending as follows:

"The Japanese Government hope sincerely that this understanding is warranted and desire keenly that an explicit indication to that effect will be speedily forthcoming."

Once the offer is transmitted through official channels, Japan's condition that Hirohito remain in power—may prove a stumbling block to immediate acceptance by all the Potsdam signatories—the United States, Britain and China.

The Potsdam declaration itself did not mention the Emperor's status, but broadcasts of the United States Office of War Information have refrained from attacking Hirohito.

If the Domei report is borne out by official communications to the United States and Allied governments, it means that the third member of the Tokyo-Berlin-Rome axis has surrendered three months and one day after the capitulation of Hitler's Germany.

It would mean the end of hostilities that started Sep-

(Continued on Page 2.) See JAPAN.

OTTAWA WAITS WORD TO CHANGE PLANS

By TORCHY ANDERSON.

(From Daily Province Ottawa Bureau, Copyright, 1945, by Southam Co.)

OTTAWA, Aug. 10.—If and when Ottawa gets official news that the Japanese war is over, staffs of naval, air and army forces will go into action to modify plans now being carried out for Canadian participation.

While the whole plan must move forward without any delay until the official word of surrender is received, it is known that staffs are considering action that may be necessary within the next few hours.

This morning Ottawa did not appear to have much more information than was available from the news services.

London Cabinet Meets; Awaits Official Word

(By Reuters.)

LONDON, Aug. 10.—A meeting of the cabinet was called this afternoon soon after word was received in London of the reported Japanese surrender offer.

No. 10 Downing Street said Britain was consulting with the United States, Russia and China about the Tokyo broadcast.

No official communication from the Japanese Government had yet been received by Britain regarding the broadcast offer to surrender if Emperor Hirohito is allowed to keep his place.

Mr. Attlee has received unofficial news of the Japanese offer to surrender, the press secretary at 10 Downing street announced earlier.

NOT IN SWEDEN YET.

Herchel Johnson, American minister in the Swedis hcapital of Stockholm, also said no Japanese peace proposal had yet been transmitted to him by the Swedish Government.

The Japanese had said the offer was being sent through the Swedish and Swiss governments.

The Swedish foreign office had not commented, but it was the impression that any offer given to Sweden would have been delivered immediately.

The secretary of the Japanese minister to Stockholm, Suemasa Okamota, said nothing was known at his office of the Domei announcement.

DEPENDS ON EMPEROR.

Most diplomats in London agreed that the whole question of the acceptance by Britain, the United tates, China and Russia of the reported surrender petition revolved around the status of Emperior Hirohito.

Emperor Not Mentioned At Potsdam

WASHINGTON, Aug. 10.—(AP)—As official confirmation of Japan's surrender offer was awaited here, speculation centred around the reported Japanese proposal that the Emperor be permitted to retain his sovereignty.

There was no mention of the Emperor in the Potsdam ultimatum of July 26 which called for immediate surrender.

Thus, there conceivably could be considerable delay among the Allies before they would give a reply to the conditioned Japanese proposal.

The Potsdam ultimatum merely held forth establishment in the future of "a peacefully-inclined and responsible government."

Contrary to the Japanese condition that the Emperor's sovereignty not be compromised, the Potsdam declaration said:

"We will not deviate from our terms. There are no alternatives. We shall brook no delay."

Tokyo Grooming New Boy Emperor

Official Weather Forecast: Today and Sunday, moderate northwest winds, fair and warm. Friday's temperatures: High 71, low 54.

The Vancouver Sun

RATIONED FOODS
Sugar—Coupon 61 now valid.
Butter—Coupon 117 now valid.
Preserves — Coupons P2 to P13 inclusive (canning sugar) now valid.
All valid coupons in Book 5 good until further notice.

FOUNDED 1886 VOL. LX—NO. 10 | MArine 1161 | VANCOUVER, BRITISH COLUMBIA, SATURDAY, AUGUST 11, 1945 | PRICE 10 CENTS $1.00 per month BY CARRIER

ALLIES ACCEPT JAP BID BUT MIKADO TO BE PUPPET

KING-PIN IN PEACE OVERTURES—Focal point of the Jap surrender offer, Emperor Hirohito will be allowed to keep his throne, the Big four have decided, but his administration will be under strict Allied control. In their acceptance of the Potsdam offer, the Japs made only one stipulation: That the Emperor retain his prerogatives. Here, the Son of Heaven is seen in three types of regalia. It is not known if he owns a suit of sackcloth.

Next Move in Peace Offer Up to Nippon

Radio Hints Prince May Be Mikado

SAN FRANCISCO, Aug. 11—(AP)—Japan let the world know today that its boy Crown Prince, Emperor Hirohito's only son, was being publicized at home — thus suggesting that he might be being groomed for an early successor to the throne.

A Domei agency wireless dispatch, directed to North America, said Tokyo's Saturday morning papers carried pictures of the Crown Prince and reports on his activities.

The reported fanfare followed by 24 hours the creation of a special household staff for the young prince, whose birth on December 23, 1933, was the cause of great rejoicing throughout the empire. Hirohito's other three children are all girls.

The broadcast, calling attention of the world to the young prince, said he was living on rationed food at the Peers' School and was greatly concerned over the suffering of his people from air raids.

The broadcast added: "Wearing the same white cap and blue serge uniform with classmates of the peers' school, his imperial highness is robust and the picture of perfect health."

Another effort to picture the heir to the throne as democratic was made in the Domei declaration that:

"From 7 a.m. to 4 p.m., the daily routine of his imperial highness covering study, exercise and discipline is exactly the same as his classmates. His imperial highness even joins in cleaning the classroom."

Tokyo newspapers unanimously admitted "the extreme gravity of the current war situation" and urged the Japanese to maintain "calmness in any contingency," the Domei reported.

Editorials quoted by Domei in an English language broadcast failed to mention yesterday's surrender offer.

Significantly, perhaps, Domei quoted **Ashai Shimbun** as having "pointed out the mission resting on the shoulders of the elder statesmen" and added that "the paper declared that they should firmly maintain tehir own views without being influenced by changes in the situation.

Dim Future For Emperor

WASHINGTON, Aug. 11—(AP)—This is what the reply of the Big Four pawers—to the Japanese offer to surrender—means in effect so far as the royal house is concerned:

1—Because the emperor is the key figure in Japan, the Allies will use him in ruling Japan.

2—But this doesn't mean the emperor can keep his job indefinitely. He can keep it until some future time when the Japanese people can decide whether they want to have an emperor at all.

They'll be given a chance to vote on it.

The Japanese people haven't had any choice like this. They've had an emperor, generation after generation, and thus until now have acicpted the idea of having one.

Can Men At Work Again

Carrying large banners and singing loudly striking American Can Company workers marched back to work this morning—"under protest."

The big plant, idle since 11 a.m. July 27, hummed with activity at 7:30 a.m.

A few minutes later from the main plant and storage warehouses in various parts of the city, and Ballantyne Pier cans were rolling out to an almost strangled canning industry.

Decision to return to work was made at a packed membership meeting last night where members heard a report from C. H. Millard, national director of United Stteelworkers of America, strongly recommending they obey the government's order to go back on the job.

FOOD WASTE

Announcement that the settlement was forthcoming was published exclusively in **The Vancouver Sun** Friday.

The steel local here, 2821, struck when the company refused demands for a union shop.

Please Turn to Page Two
See "Can Men"

Hirohito To Rule As Victors Dictate

WASHINGTON, Aug. 11—(AP)—The big-four Allied powers today made a conditional acceptance of Japan's offer to quit the war—based on retention of the emperor's sovereignty.

The two principal conditions of acceptance:

The Emperor must subject himself to the orders of a Supreme Allied Command.

That a government in Japan be ultimately established ... ordance with "the freely expressed will of ... ese people."

...nguage apparently did not offer any assurance of a permanent continuation of Sun-God throne—somethnig on which the Japanese people will themselves have the last say.

There is at this time no designated Allied Supreme Cocmander—mentioned in the reply to Tokyo—but the White House announced today that an American would be appointed, and it is generally expected that General of the Army Douglas MacArthur will get the post.

Next Move up to Tokyo

The Allied reply put the next move up to the Tokyo Government. The terms acceptable to the Big Four will be transmitted to Switzerland, where it will be handed the Japanese minister for relay to his government.

Since transmission is handled by wireless, the surrender conditions deemed acceptable in Washington, London, Moscow and Chungking could be officially before the Japanese Government by nightfall, central daylight time.

It was considered doubtful whether a reply—and a possible end of the war—would be forthcoming before late Sunday or Monday.

Five Conditions

Replying to Japan through the Swiss Government, State Secretary Byrnes said the United States would accept the enemy's proposal—if the Emperor is made subject to the supreme commanders' orders—and added that his statement also represented the veiwpoints of the United Kingdom, the Union of Soviet Socialist Republics and China.

Mr. Byrnes' message was delivered through the Swiss embassy here at 7:30 a.m. (Vancouver time).

Mr. Byrnes laid out the following five conditions in his message to the Japanese:

"From the moment of the surrender the authority of the Emperor and the Japanese government to rule the State shall be subject to the supreme commander of the Allieed powers, who will take such steps as he deems proper to effectuate the surrender terms.

"The Emperor will be required to aauthorize and ensure the signature of the goveernment of Japan and the Japanese Imperial general headquarters of the surrender terms necessary to carry out the provisions of the Potsdam declarations and shall issue his commands to all the Japanese military, naval and air authorities and to all the forces under their control, wherever loocated, to cease active operations and to surrender their arms and to issue such other orders as the supreme commander may require to give effect to the surrender terms.

"Immediately upon the surrender the Japanese government shall transport prisoners of war and civilian internees to places of safety as directed, where they can quickly be placed aboard Allied transports.

The ultimate form of government of Japan shall, in accordance with the Potsdam declaration, be established by the freely expressed will of the Japanese people.

"The armed forces of the Allied powers will remain in Japan until the purposes set forth in the Potsdam declaration are achieved."

The Allied position was made known after a 24-hour period of conferences among the four capitals on Japan's offer to surrender if she could retain her emperor.

As the British cabinet stood by in London, President Truman held an early morning discussion with Secretary Byrnes. Mr. Byrnes then went to the State Department and talked with chairman Tom Connally of the Senate foreign relations committee.

PRINCIPAL BOARD

The Allied offer would permit the Japanese to "save face" by retaining their emperor as nominal head of the government, as well as spiritual leader.

The Japanese had said in a communication through the Swiss that their surrender offer was submitted "with the understanding that the said (Potsdam) declaration does not comprise any demand which prejudices the prerogatives of his majesty as a sovereign ruler."

The question of retaining an emperor on the throne had been the principal point at issue in

Please Turn to Page Two
See "Japan"

'More Potent, Easier to Manufacture'

SECOND ATOMIC BOMB MAKES FIRST OBSOLETE

GUAM, Aug. 11—(AP)—The world's second atomic bomb, which Thursday was dropped on Nagasaki, was so explosive that it immediately relegated to the obsolete the first bomb, dropped two days earlier on Hiroshima, Brig.-Gen. Thomas F. Farrell, head of the atomic bomb project in the Pacific, said today.

Atomic bomb No. 2 not only was far more potent, but was easier to make, Gen. Farrell said. He watched both bombings and said the blast from the second was far greater.

Thirty percent of Nagasaki, including some of Japan's greatest wartime plants, was oblieerated by Thursday's bombing, the army strategic air forces announced today.

GREAT CRATER

At least 13 important factories were wiped out or badly damaged and almost all of the Kyushu seaport's industrial district was destroyed, but the demolition still was considerably less than that in the first atomic bomb attack which razed 60 percent of Hiroshima on Monday.

The results were announced by Gen. pSaatz after experts studied photographs taken over Nagasaki yesterday, 24 hours or more following the bombing.

The pictures showed a great crater where the bomb struck. Pictures of Hiroshima showed no crater. The Japanese said that both bombs were dropped by parachute, but that the one at Hiroshima exploded in the air. This might account for the greater damage done at Hiroshima.

Another possibility, suggested by Gen. Spaatz, was the geography of Nagasaki, where the 253,000 population live in irregularly-shaped districts reaching up low valleys from the sea and along the Urakami River.

Today's Scratches At Hastings Park

FIRST RACE—Slalacum, Sir Broza, Maratimer.

ECOND RACE—Ascot Bells.

THIRD RACE—Assayer, Yorkton.

FOURTH RACE — Timely Ayre, Si Green, Wingaway, Simtee, Special Lady, Groves, Boss Marcus, Lady Bargello, Be Mine, Black Memory.

FIFTH RACEMSpangle Cock, Goldstreworth, Dalkeith.

SIXTH RACE — Miss Olivia, Duddingston, Malayan, Truely Flo.

SEVENTH RACE — My Tom, Mosca, Galpen, Lady Double.

For Sun program handicap, jockeys, selections, etc., See Page 28.

Missing Persons

Detectives Frank White and John Stevenson, missing persons bureau, police headquarters, are seeking information: Eva Fertuch, Axel Helga, Stanley B. Bone, Ambroiise Moisant and David H. Snow.

Japs Kept in Dark

SAN FRANCISCO, Aug. 11—(AP)—The Federal Communications Commission reported Friday night that none of Japan's domestic broadcasts or Japanese-language foreign broadcasts had yet mentioned Japan's surrender offer.

SIRENS' WAIL SPELLS PEACE

Air-raid sirens will notify the public the moment the war with Japan is officially over, Civilian Defense Headquarters here announced today.

One minute of steady tone will be followed by a 15-second interval, then a minute of the wailing note followed by another 15-second interval and a second minute of steady tone.

Sirens sounded on V-E Day here but at that time the second phase of the signal . . . the wailing note was not given.

Stores Close When Peace Proclaimed

Announcement today by Ottawa that there will be no national holiday on V-J Day does not affect the proposed Vancouver civic holiday or store closing arrangements.

Retail Merchants' Association will carry out the same plan on V-E Day, Secretary George R. Matthews said.

If the big news comes through before noon the stores will ilose for the day, and if afternoon they will close for the balance of the day and on the civic holiday.

Shipyards will not close down except on the civic holiday, spokesmen said.

If the men down tools, W. F. Wardle, Burrard North manager said, they will "probably do so at their own expense."

Dies Cutting Lawn

Mathias Clark, 70, of 2153 West Fifth, collapsed and died while cutting a lawn at 4205 West Eleventh at 1 p.m. Friday.

WAR CURBS TO EASE SLOWLY

More Gas and Liquor Soon After Jap War Terminates

By H. L. JONES

OTTAWA, Aug. 11—(CP)—The surrender of Japan—when it comes— will bring not only the complete peace Canadians have awaited for almost six long year, but will mean the beginning of the end for most of the economic restrictions which geared the Dominion for war.

Government officials in the Capital were quick to point out, however, that while there would be a further easing and possibly a revoking of some restrictions, there would be no immediate wholesale lifting of wartime controls.

Continuing shortages in certain lines, the need for food overseas, committments for UNRRA and requirements of Canada's occupation troops in Europe were considerations in the economic picture.

Here is the way the immediate post-war picture lined up:

1—Canada will still have meat rationing early next month.

2—An immediate easing or perhaps even lifting of gasoline restrictions expected.

3—Probable increased supplies of certain liquors and wines.

4—No immediate change in the rent, wage or foreign exchange control regulations.

Canada already has meatless Tuesdays and Fridays in public eating plaies and the Prices Board has announced that these meatless days will now start at 4 a.m. on each Tuesday and Friday and continue for the 24-hour period following, instead of starting at 2 midnight as at present.

This will allow restaurants to plan menus through a full 24 hour period, including the late midnight meal period.

Nice Weather For Week-End

You can plan your week-end without worrying about the possibility of rain.

The weatherman is promising that it will be "fair and warm" both today and Sunday. There will be moderate north-west winds.

The weatherman also predicts that the mercury will rise today to 74 and Sunday to 75.

U.S. Congress To be Called

WASHINGTON, Aug. 11—(BUP)—Senate Democratic leader Alben W. Barkley, Ky., announced today that Congress probably will be called back into session on September 4.

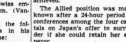

Tokyo Radio Reports

JAPAN ACCEPTS TERMS OF ALLIES

The Vancouver News-Herald

VOL. 13, NO. 95 — VANCOUVER, B.C., TUESDAY, AUGUST 14, 1945 — ★★★★★ PRICE 5c By Carrier 85c Month

Board Rejects Milk Price Raise As Strike Nears

PENTICTON, Aug. 14.—(CP) — The Southern Okanagan Dairymen's Association demand for milk price increases to meet rising production costs was rejected Monday by the Wartime Prices Board.

The milk producers had voted to call a milk strike starting Aug. 17 if their demands were not met by them.

A letter received Monday from K. W. Taylor, co-ordinator Foods Administration, Wartime Prices Board, said, "the board cannot accede to the demands of the Dairymen." The letter was addressed to H. D. Morley, Board of Trade secretary.

HIT 5 CENTRES

A strike would mean that sale of milk by dairymen in Penticton, Summerland, Naramata, Oliver, and Osoyoos would cease except to those who could produce a physician's certificate.

"With milk now available to about half of the population of this town, we have no intention of allowing the matter to drop," Mr. Morley said. "We cannot stop here. Milk can be produced here and should be produced."

Notice of the Dairymen's Association intention to strike was served on the Prices Board last week. Many storekeepers have indicated they will not sell outside milk if a strike is called.

Bonds Loot

Nearly $1,000 worth of Victory bonds formed the haul of thieves who broke into the West Produce Co., 2912 W. Fourth Ave., early Monday, Chow Poy, proprietor, told city police.

Japanese Clique Planned To Quit Early In June

By SPENCER MOOSA

CHUNGKING, Aug. 14. — (AP)—The Chinese Army newspaper Sao Tang Po says Japan was ready to offer up her war leaders as hara kiri victims and retreat to her 1931 boundaries as conditions of peace, even before the first atomic bomb fell and Russia entered the Pacific war.

Quoting Hsieh Nan Kuang, described as a leader of the Formosan Revolutionary League, the newspaper pictures the growth of a surrender clique in Tokyo as fire bombs and explosives fell on Japan's cities, and Allied carrier planes struck her fleet.

It describes the Empress Nagako as a peace pl izer.

Here is the newspaper's account of Hsieh's report:

The first step toward peace was taken June 3 by the imperial household minister, Tsuneo Matsudaira, business manager for the imperial family and its fortune, which has been estimated at four per cent of all the wealth in Japan.

Matsudaira resigned with the aim of organizing a pro-Allied surrender cabinet. The plan failed because of the Army's opposition.

Japan's situation was getting worse daily, however, and on June 28 Premier Admiral Kantaro Suzuki called a meeting of all the elder statesmen, including all former premiers, at which he reported indications that Russia would join the war.

The meeting decided to instruct ambassador Naotake Sato in Moscow to pay special attention to Russia's attitude. Meantime, the government prepared peace proposals for submission through Moscow to the Big Three at Potsdam. These finally were forwarded to Premier Stalin, in Emperor Hirohito's name.

SPLIT ON ISSUE

Japanese army leaders, meantime, split on whether to surrender, but both sides wanted the emperor to take the reins of government. This desire became a demand after Japan's fleet was wiped out as a fighting force on July 18.

The Empress Negako was sent to seek advice of the dowager empress and on her return, it was decided to form a commission to decide definitely on the question of continuing the war or surrendering.

The commission consisted of 21 persons, including the imperial Princess Chichibu and Takamatsu and leading army and navy officers.

Victoria Stages Wild Celebration

VICTORIA, Aug. 14.—(CP)—News that the Japanese government had accepted the Allied governments' surrender terms was the signal for a wild victory celebration in Victoria last night.

Dockyard workers, sailors and residents of Esquimalt, huge west coast naval base, four miles outside the city started the riotous celebration cheering and milling in the streets.

The celebration was picked up quickly in downtown Victoria and the streets rang with cheers and honking of automobile horns. Servicemen mingled arm in arm with civilians for more than an hour and paraded through the streets.

The celebration apparently was based on early radio reports of the acceptance of Allied terms, although the official signal of siren blasts was not heard.

Police had trouble keeping the traffic moving at intersections in the main part of the city.

Shortly after midnight the din subsided and most of the celebrators were making their way home.

The Weather

Vancouver and vicinity and lower Fraser Valley: light winds, cloudy in morning, fair after noon; not much change in temperatures. Monday's: 72, 54.

Advancing Reds 26 Mi. Off Japan --Tokyo Reports

LONDON, Aug. 14.—(AP)—Russian armored columns crashed up to 28 miles through Japanese defences in Manchuria Monday in a five-pronged drive toward Harbin, while Tokyo claimed a Soviet invasion of Japanese territory lying only 26 miles from the enemy home land.

Tank-led Soviet thrusts threatened to disrupt the entire Japanese communication system in Manchuria, playing havoc with the enemy's supply and leaving pockets of enemy troops open to encirclement and annihilation.

Japanese broadcasts said Russian marines had swarmed ashore on strategic Karafuto, Japanese-owned southern half of Sakhalin Island north of Japan proper, but there was no immediate confirmation from the Soviet high command.

Moscow's communique said the Russian armies, advancing into the heart of Manchuria, had seized at least 22 Japanese strongpoints as they swept toward the arsenal city of Harbin from the west, northwest, north, northeast and east.

CROSS MOUNTAINS

On the west, Moscow revealed, Marshal Rodion Y. Malinovsky's Trans-Baikal army crossed the great Kmangan mountain range and captured Solun and Wangyehmiao, 268 and 215 miles west of Harbin. Other forces swept along the Chinese Eastern Railroad and burst into Mientuho, 350 miles northwest of Harbin.

The 2nd Far Eastern Army gained nine to 25 miles northeast of Harbin in a drive between the Sungari and Ussuri Rivers, and while Soviet bombers plastered Manchurian rail junctions, Russian forces on the east captured Linkow, 177 miles east of Harbin.

WIN BEACHHEAD

Tokyo said that Russian invasion forces, going ashore under the guns of the Soviet Pacific fleet, had established two beachheads on the west coast of Sakhalin island in a swift follow-up to the seaborne invasion of Korea.

SURRENDER TO BE SIGNED ON BATTLESHIP MISSOURI

New York Times Copyright

WASHINGTON, Aug. 14.—Although the Navy stated Monday that it had no official information to give out on the subject, it was authoritatively established that present plans call for the Japanese surrender to be signed aboard the mighty battleship Missouri, named after President Turman's home state.

A responsible source said that this decision is "80 per cent certain."

General Douglas MacArthur and Admiral Chester W. Nimitz undoubtedly would sign for the United States. Although Emperor Hirohito's signature probably will be required on the surrender terms, it is likely that he will be permitted to send representative rather than come aboard the Missour w. sign in person

Veteran Plunges Off City Bridge

A 51-year-old veteran of this war plunged 100 feet to the ground from the north end of Burrard Bridge Monday night but was still alive at the Vancouver General Hospital early this morning.

He was semi-conscious and able to talk incoherently shortly after he landed with an impact that embedded his feet eight inches into the ground.

He suffered a broken back, doctors at the hospital told prowl squad officers Bob MacWilliam and Barney Duhamel who attended at the scene.

John Peterson, Boathouse No. 9, beneath Burrard Bridge, told the officers he observed the man standing on the concrete rail, 100 feet above and that he plunged off shortly after.

George Nickels, 1131 Beach Ave., said he saw the man strike the ground feet first then fall over on his side.

A scream followed by a thudding sound brought Frank Hampton, 1731 E. Third, Colin McKinnon and Warren Sorenson, who lives on a float house nearby, running to the spot where they found the injured and groaning man. They ran to the nearby Radio Confectionery store, 1030 Beach, from where the proprietor, C. Attewell, called police and the Kingsway Ambulance.

According to Duhamel and MacWilliam, the plunging man hurtled into a small pile of grass and leaves which slightly broke his fall.

PEACE INQUIRY CALLS SWAMP PHONE COMPANY

News reports that Japan had surrendered led to city telephone service being swamped with calls late Monday and early today, as excited citizens sought confirmation of the report.

News-Herald offices were deluged with calls.

A request to refrain from making unnecessary telephone calls were issued by the B. C. Telephone Co.

Yanks Rewriting Occupation Order

New York Times Copyright

WASHINGTON, Aug. 14. — Miiltary authorities are working at top speed, rewriting previously prepared documents for the occupation of Japan so as to bring Emperor Hirohito's name into the surrender proclamations, a high war department source disclosed here.

Two significant facts were indicated by this disclosure:

First, that the war department regards the Japanese surrender offer as genuine.

Second, that the United States actually intends to use the emperor as an instrument of restoring peace throughout the far-flung corners of the Pacific where Japanese occupation or resistance is in force.

City Bridge Worker Killed In Okanagan

H. Macdonald, 55, of Vancouver, died in hospital at Penticton Monday, from injuries suffered in a 100-foot fall from a bridge.

He was employed by T. H. Bell Construction Co., on a project at Lorna, 36 miles east of Penticton, when he lost his balance. Macdonald was rushed to Penticton aboard a C.P.R. train but failed to regain consciousness and died shortly after arrival.

CHUNGKING, Aug. 14. — (AP) — Front dispatches asserted last night that, following Tokyo's surrender offer, some Japanese troop units in Chekiang province south of Shanghai had ceased fighting and were negotiating their capitulation.

On China's vast battlefronts, however, Gen. Chiang Kai-shek's troops kept up their attacks against Japan's Asiatic forces.

Government Endorses Peace Formula: Domei

NEW YORK, Aug. 14. — (CP) — Domei Agency said the Japanese government has accepted the Allied surrender formula, the Federal Communications Commission reported today. The Japanese broadcast was recorded in New York.

The report also was heard in London by Reuters news agency.

There was no official Allied comment on the Domei Agency statement. Big Four capitals were silent, awaiting the Japanese government's note.

The Allied surrender formula — by terms of which the Mikado would be retained as nominal head of Japan, taking orders from an Allied commander-in-chief — was transmitted to Japan Saturday through Switzerland, a neutral intermediary.

The boadcast followed closely another Japanese broadcast saying an Imperial message accepting Allied surrender terms was expected shortly.

Previously Domei had said the Japanese cabinet was meeting and probably would make a reply accepting Allied surrender terms as soon as "legal procedures" were completed.

The broadcast was preceded by a "flash" warning.

The statement was repeated a few moments later.

The Domei broadcast from Tokyo, directed toward the United States and recorded by the Federal Communications Commission and the American Broadcasting Company, said the cabinet had gone into session Monday as soon as it received the Allied reply to the Japanese surrender offer.

DENIED BY SWISS

The Japanese contended that this reply was not received until Monday morning, although the Swiss, who transmitted it, said it was delivered earlier.

In Washington, all was quiet at the White House. Only newspapermen, and President Truman's naval aide, Commodore James K. Vardaman, were around.

Vardaman arrived at 11:30 p.m. (PDT) and went into the White House. But there was no indication that Mr. Truman was awakened.

Earlier Allied patience appeared to be wearing thin as the Japanese were believed stalling on their reply to the ultimatum.

American Superfortresses took up their offensive against Japan for the first time since the broadcast Japanese surrender offer, attacking Southern Honshu.

U.S. Army strategic air force headquarters at Guam said the raids "will continue." Guam dispatches said they are apparently intended as a prod to hasten the enemy's surrender.

President Truman went to bed at 10:30 p.m. last night and White House press secretary Charles G. Ross said at that time, "there is no news."

At midnight the word was that there would be no information forthcoming from the White House until this morning, if then.

Sailors Cheer News Broadcast

GUAM, Aug. 14 (Tuesday)—(AP) — The communications room of U. S. Pacific Fleet headquarters flashed word over the Guam radio today that the Tokyo radio had reported Japan has accepted the Potsdam ultimatum to surrender. There was no announcement where the broadcast was picked up.

Waves of cheering were heard as the Guam radio broke into a regular broadcast to make the announcement at 3.58 p.m. Guam time (10.58 p.m., P. D. T.)

There were no details—only the brief word that Japan had decided to accept the terms of the Potsdam ultimatum to surrender.

The news came as United States and British fleets were patrolling just off Japan. It was believed that the fleets would head for Japanese ports shortly.

Victory To End U. S. Censorship

WASHINGTON, Aug. 14.—(AP)—Censorship of outgoing news from the United States will end one hour after President Truman announces victory over Japan, the Office of Censorship said Monday.

"We will go out of business after that," said Byron Price, Director of censorship.

Since the beginning of the war all news going to foreign countries from the United States was subject to censorship by the government.

OFFICIAL
PEACE

Around the Clock With Tokyo

Drama of Dying Japan

By Canadian Press

London, 4:30 a.m.—Swiss radio, without quoting source, says Japan has accepted Allied terms.

Zurich, 5:15 a.m. — Swiss foreign office reported still awaiting Japanese answer.

Washington, 6:50 a.m.—White House said Japanese reply in hands of the Swiss.

New York, 7:29 a.m.—Domei says "on Aug. 14, 1945, the imperial decision was granted"; doesn't say what emperor's decision was.

New York, 7:30 a.m.—Domei says transmission "of unprecedented importance" will be made at noon tomorrow (10 p.m., CDT Tuesday).

Bern, 7:40 a.m.—Swiss foreign office says no Japanese note yet received.

New York, 9:01 a.m.—Tokyo radio says "Japanese government's reply to four powers is now on its way to Japanese minister at Bern."

Washington, 9:24 a.m.—Swiss legation memorandum to White House says coded cables received earlier in Bern don't contain Japan's answer.

Bern, 11:05 a.m. — Japanese reply delivered to Swiss Foreign Office.

Bern, 11:25 a.m.—Swiss deliver Jap reply to U.S. minister.

Bern, 12:05 p.m.—Swiss cable reply to Swiss legation in Washington; U.S. minister telephones reply to U.S. State department in Washington.

(all times in Vancouver time)

Guam GI's Cheer Victory

GUAM, Tuesday, Aug. 14—(BUP)—Wild cheering rolled across Guam from thousands of soldiers, sailors and marines today when Tokyo radio broadcast that the emperor would issue a statement accepting the Potsdam surrender ultimatum.

JAPANESE GET EXCITED, TOO

SEATTLE, (BUP) — Dr. Frank G. Williston, acting executive officer of the far eastern department of the University of Washington, has expressed belief that the use of the atomic bomb on Japan was unnecessary.

"The country was already beginning to crack," Williston said.

"It was stuff and nonsense to say that the Japanese would never break without the atomic bombing," he said. "Contrary to popular American belief, the Japanese are not a phlegmatic people who can take endless bombing. They are extremely excitable."

BIG FOUR VICTORS

PRIME MINISTER ATTLEE   **PRESIDENT TRUMAN**

MARSHAL STALIN   **GENERALISSIMO CHIANG**

Surrender May Be On Okinawa

LONDON, Aug. 14, (BUP).—Informed quarters here said today that the formal Japanese surrender would probably be made at Okinawa, or aboard an American battleship (Reports have been circulating in the U. S. for some time that the surrender would be signed aboard the USS Missouri, named after President Truman's home state.)

2000 Specially-Trained Officers Ready

PLAN TO OCCUPY JAPAN DRAWN UP BY STATES

By GWEN MORGAN

WASHINGTON, Aug. 14 — (BUP)—The United States has completed a directive outlying a stern policy to govern the immediate military occupation of Japan, it was learned today.

Informed sources said the order was now being circulated for final approval among the various government agencies involved and would be ready when U.S. troops move into beaten Japan.

Some 2000 specially trained army officers are set to take over administration of the enemy homeland.

In event the four powers occupy Japan jointly, the United single coordinated control policy for the entire country as she did in the case of Germany.

Tremendous long-range problems confront Allied occupation forces these are a few:

1. Breaking the stranglehold of the Zaibatsu, the clique that holds virtually all the wealth and power. This group controls all industry and is tied up with the military and the Imperial family. For years, it has used the position of the emperor as a cloak for aggression.

2. Revising Japan's economy to concentrate on goods needed for a peaceful way of life—production of foods instead of raises only 75 percent of her food supply.

3. Moving the hundreds of thousands of Japanese who have colonized Japan's huge stolen empire back to the home islands. This was said to be a definite U.S. objective.

Jap Government Accepts Our Terms

WASHINGTON, Aug. 14.—The Japanese government has accepted the Allied surrender terms.

This is official.

Peace has definitely come to a world at war since 1939.

The surrender is to all members of the Big Four — Britain, the United States, China and the Soviet Union.

Japan's official news agency flashed to the world at 10:49 p.m. (Vancouver time, Monday) a statement that the Imperial Government would accept the stern and unconditional surrender demands of the Potsdam ultimatum.

The Domei agency's eight word flash touched off a celebration which was becoming worldwide today. It roared up first from American servicemen in the Pacific islands—Hawaii, Guam and the Philippines.

The Domei message said:

"Flash—flash—Tokyo—14-8—Learned Imperial message accepting Potsdam declaration forthcoming soon."

Long Code Messages

The agency interrupted a routine broadcast on the cure for chilblains to send the flash message twice.

Federal communications commission monitors reported long code messages moving from Tokyo radio to the station in Geneva, Switzerland.

A dispatch from Bern, Switzerland, report that the Japanese legation had advised the Swiss Government that Minister Tamao Sakamoto probably would ask for an appointment with the Swiss foreign minister, Dr. Walter Stucki, at 2 p.m., (5 a.m. Vancouver time today).

This capital awakened slowly to the great news. But by 3:30 a.m., there were 200 or more persons gathered in Lafayette Park across the street from the White House.

V-J Day Must Wait

The telephone was flashing the news to sleeping newsmen and photographers. The White House press room began to fill at 4 a.m

This will not be V-J Day. But that occasion probably is just around the corner.

Procedure will be for the Allies to designate the military officers who will meet the Japanese surrender signatories. A place of meeting must be named and an Allied supreme commander must be selected.

General of the army Douglas MacArthur is widely reported to have been chosen.

The White House announced that President Truman would not proclaim V-J Day until the surrender articles actually have been signed.

Mr. Truman went to bed at 10:30 last night and the White House shut down at midnight with announcement that there would be no further word from there on surrender developments before 9 a.m.

But the Domei flash had a rousing effect. Capt. James Vardaman, the president's naval aide, appeared at the White House executive offices at 2:10 a.m. EWT.

As of today the United States and Japan had been at war three years, eight months and seven days. The Japs hit Pearl Harbor at 7:30 a.m., or thereabouts, Hawaiian time, Dec. 7, 1941—"That day of infamy."

The Chinese Times
Entered at Vancouver Post Office at Second
Class Matter

Tuesday, August 14 1945

The Chinese Times

Vol. 7 No 88

THE CHINESE TIMES, PUBLISHERS
1 PENDER STREET EAST
P. O. Box 339　Phone MArine 8941
VANCOUVER, B. C.

大漢公報號外

日本投降

世界回復和平

孔子二千四百九十六年
夏曆歲次乙酉年七月初七日

大漢公報

華盛頓十四日電・日本接納聯軍條件向中美英俄四強投降・其事經部交與美大使夏利民・夏氏即用電話報告華盛頓・美京於今晨三點半已接到・當時有二百餘人在白宮對面之公園候聽・白宮新聞廳於四時即擠擁不堪・美總統杜魯門欲待日本降約簽字乃公佈・杜氏昨夜候至十點半見無消息而就寢・以爲至少到朝早九時內乃有報告・不料日本杜美報社已發出美日三年八個月又七日之戰爭已結束之訊・

倫敦電・今朝四點牛瑞士播音・日本接納聯軍條件投降・

蘇黎支電・今朝五點十五分・瑞士外交部尚謂聽候日本答覆・

華盛頓電・今晨六點牛・白宮謂日本之覆文已在瑞士。

世界回復和平
於昨晚十點四十九分鐘在東京發表・其長電轉致瑞士日內瓦・外交部…

藥氏樂房（王藥行）

極補志在馳名大減價
大補丸補身之功

THE ROYAL BANK OF CANADA
Head Office -- Montreal, Canada

司理極表歡迎
本行顧客・本行
一元・君如願爲
貯蓄限額・僅爲
少而逐未開始貯
故前勿以存欵過
蓄・本行最低之
之前途穩定矣・
欵既貯・則君
[一] 請貯蓄盈餘

賓路銀行

活生藥行啓

好消息

WAT SANG CO.
87 E. Pender Street
Vancouver, B.C.

歡迎僑胞索閱
活生藥行行情表出版

電話 PA. 3766
Optimistic Library
126A Pender Street, Vancouver, B.C.

樂觀圖書館

龔貞信花舖

Jirrell Dee Florist
2396. 4 Ave. W.
Vancouver, B.C.

優待光顧　僑胞惠顧

HEN SANG TONG
天生堂
313 MAIN STREET
Vancouver, B.C. Canada.

長期抗戰

HHD撚花戀情素

撚花戀戰露

Chong Hou Tong, 515 Cormorant St. Victoria, B.C.

172

普天同慶

蔣主席介石

蔣主席介石・是國民黨歷任總裁・富權謀・以黃埔軍校訓練新軍・得俄國餉械之助・北敗軍閥・定都金陵・敗中共於江西・迫夫倭寇入侵中夏・與中共諒解・領導全國抗戰・八載辛勤・支持抗戰至倭寇稱降・提高國家民族地位・受人民及國際之尊敬・果能本眞誠以公開國是・使國家上眞正民主之坦途・救內戰之萌・亟謀國家之善後・則其名垂青史必矣・

美故總統羅斯福

美故總統羅斯福・見國家之危・先國後黨・以美國為民主國家之兵工廠・統制軸心・使財物力足以敗亡軸心・賑濟淪亡・拾己救人・不愧為世界之福星・

英相亞特李

英相亞特李・是工黨領袖・時任副相・力勤邱氏救國・國化工業政策得選以為相・濸三港市世安會及茒斯丹三強會・參訂日本投降條件・富平民化思想・

英相邱卓爾

英相邱卓爾・是英保守黨領袖・能使英國轉危為安・對軸心敗亡・有相當之勞績・在今日總勝利慶祝中・值得景仰・

173

The Vancouver News-Herald

VOL. 13, NO. 96   VANCOUVER, B.C., WEDNESDAY, AUGUST 15, 1945   ★ PRICE 5c By Carrier 81c Month

CITY GOES WILD AS WAR ENDS

Thousands Celebrate In Vancouver Streets

"AT LAST!"

Not everyone said it out loud, thousands simply said that to themselves as they heard Vancouver's air raid sirens sound their finest note — the declaration of war's end — a few minutes after 4 p.m. Tuesday, a date that will live in history for 1,000 years.

The city was prepared for it. Some cautious merchants had even cleared their windows of all merchandise. The Chinese community had been on the verge of celebration for three long-drawn-out days.

Stores and offices hurriedly closed their doors, thousands of workers rushed on to the streets. Cars and trucks moving along the main streets were leapt upon by would-be celebrants.

Flags — British, American, Russian, Chinese — appeared from nowhere into the hands of shouting, merry men, women and children.

RUSH LIQUOR STORES

Government liquor stores suddenly became the most popular places in town. Police officers herded increasing crowds through their doors as the city sought liquid stimulant for the most heart-warming toasts victorious nations have ever known.

Within a few moments of the air raid sirens' signal that the war was over, Vancouver was celebrating from one end to the other.

But it was in the thickly congested business districts that the celebration was most vol-uminous, noisiest, gayest.

JAM PACK STREETS

Thousands upon thousands jammed Main, Hastings, Granville and Pender streets in the Chinese section.

From tall office buildings tons of paper fluttered down upon the crowds and the streets below.

With horns blaring and passengers shouting and waving flags, big trucks rolled through city streets, their springs sagging under the loads of humanity.

It was a repetition of Vancouver's pre-V-E Day celebration, but it was even noisier, more widespread.

'PEACE' COMES AT CITY'S BUSIEST CORNER': All that was normal at Granville and Hastings a few minutes after the sirens sounded at 4:09 p.m., was the traffic light, which jubilant pedestrians and motorists still obeyed. Carpet of torn paper was growing on the pavement from surrounding office windows. In this view of the intersection, crossing with the light, office workers and shoppers jam the corners.

Full Surrender By Japs -MacArthur Taking Over

WASHINGTON, Aug. 15. — (CP) — A new date was blazed on the historic calendar of the world Tuesday — Aug. 14, 1945 — as Japan accepted Allied surrender terms and brought to an end the Second Great War.

President Truman made the announcement at a 4 p.m. P.D.T. press conference in the White House even as Prime Minister Attlee broadcast a similar message over the BBC from London. Moscow radio also carried the news for which the world had waited breathlessly for days.

Orders went out immediately to silence the guns in the far flung Pacific theatre.

Washington, like every city in the Allied world, went wild with the news.

In a brief press conference which sent reporters racing to spread the gladdest tidings they will ever make known, the President read a historic document in the form of a message from the Tokyo government, which was transmitted to him through Swiss government agencies.

President Truman said he regarded the surrender as "unconditional."

The Japanese note, however, directly followed one from State Secretary Byrnes in which the Allies agreed that the Japanese would be permitted to keep

PRESIDENT TRUMAN'S MESSAGE

President Truman made this liest possible moment.

statement:

"I have received this afternoon a message from the Japanese government in reply to the message forwarded to that government by the Secretary of State on Aug. 11.

"I deem this reply a full acceptance of the Potsdam declaration which specifies the unconditional surrender of Japan.

"In this reply there is no qualification.

"Arrangements are now being made for the formal signing of surrender terms at the ear-

"Gen. Douglas MacArthur has been appointed the supreme Allied commander to receive the Japanese surrender.

"Great Britain, Russia and China will be represented by high ranking officers.

"Meantime, the Allied armed forces have been ordered to suspend offensive action.

"The proclamation of (U.S.) V-J Day must wait upon the formal signing of the surrender.

The White House made public the Japanese government's message of acceptance.

TEXT OF JAPAN'S MESSAGE

Communication of the Japanese government of August 14, 1945, addressed to the governments of the United States, Great Britain, The Soviet Union and China:

"With reference to the Japanese government's note of Aug. 10 regarding their acceptance of the provisions of the Potsdam declaration and the reply of the governments of the United States, Great Britain, the Soviet Union and China sent by American Secretary of State Byrnes under the date of Aug. 11, the Japanese government have the honor to communicate to the governments of the four powers as follows:

1. His majesty the Emperor has issued an imperial rescript

regarding Japan's acceptance of the provisions of the Potsdam declaration.

2. His majesty the emperor is prepared to authorize and insure the signature by his government and the imperial general headquarters of necessary terms for carrying out the provisions of the Potsdam declaration. His majesty is also prepared to issue his commands to all the military, naval, and air authorities of Japan and all the forces under their control wherever located to cease active operations, to surrender arms, and to issue such other orders as may be required by the supreme commander of the Allied forces for the execution of the above mentioned terms."

Court Declares Petain Guilty

PARIS, Aug. 15. — (AP) — Marshal Petain was convicted and sentenced to death early today by three judges and a 24-man jury who deliberated almost seven hours.

The high court of justice added it "hoped the sentence would not be executed."

(This recommendation for clemency presumably will be considered by Gen. de Gaulle, president of the French provisional government).

JAPS MAY HAVE QUIT TOO LATE -BIG RAID ON

SAN FRANCISCO, Aug. 15.—(AP)—Robert Shaplen, Newsweek war correspondent in a broadcast Tuesday from Okinawa—closest Allied ground base to Japan—said one of the biggest operations of the war against Nippon by the Far East air forces was planned for Wednesday (Okinawa time).

Shaplen said some fighters already were aloft and it was possible they could not be recalled in time.

Stores, Offices, Plants Closing To Mark Peace

Wednesday will be V-J Day in Vancouver, Mayor J. W. Cornett announced Tuesday afternoon. All stores, offices and industries will be closed to celebrate the civic holiday.

"I hope that everyone in Vancouver will celebrate the Allied victory to his heart's content," the mayor said, but he added that the hope that citizens would set "an example to other cities which have, in their premature celebrations, gone off the deep end."

With the weatherman promising co-operation, Vancouver is expected to celebrate V-J Day in the open air. Usual summer-time haunts, beaches, parks and camps are expected to attract thousands; and at night Ald. Jack Price declares he and his committee are prepared to continue entertainment in the open air.

STREET DANCING

As soon as the sirens announced victory, Ald. Price declared "You will see the whole city celebrate tomorrow as never before." Then he added, "I ex-pect the street dancing will begin tonight."

Downtown entertainment will be the top of Hastings St. where under the shadow of the Marine Building, the Firemen's Band will lead dancers.

SERVICES 'FREE'

No restrictions were placed on army and navy personnel. The army Tuesday night was holding a celebration dance in Vancouver barracks and the navy a dance at H.M.C.S. Discovery.

No army provost are on the streets.

"Everybody's out," an army official said. "We expect not the slightest trouble."

King Declares National Holiday

OTTAWA, Aug. 15.—(CP)—Prime Minister Mackenzie King announced early Tuesday night that Wednesday will be V-J Day in Canada and that next Sunday will be a day of prayer and solemn thanksgiving for the victory over Japan and the ending of the war.

INDEX

SELECT BIBLIOGRAPHY

Anon. *Nazi Europe.* London, 1984.
Anon. *Operation Victory: Winning the Pacific War.* New York, 1968.
Barker, Ralph. *The RAF at War.* Alexandria, VA, 1981.
Bauer, Lt.-Col. Eddy. *World War II Encyclopedia.* New York, 1978.
Blanco, Richard L. *Rommel the Desert Warrior.* New York, 1982.
Chappell, Mike. *The Canadian Army at War.* London, 1985.
Churchill, Winston S. *The Second World War: The Grand Alliance.* Boston, 1950.
Keegan, John. *The Second World War.* New York, 1989.
Macdonald, John. *Great Battles of World War II.* New York, 1986.
Miller, Russell. *The Soviet Air Force at War.* Alexandria, VA, 1983.
Morris, Eric. *Salerno, A Military Fiasco.* New York, 1983.
Pitt, Barrie, ed. *History of the Second World War.* London, 1975.
Ramsey, Winston G., ed. *After the Battle: Dieppe 1942.* London, 1974.
Richards, Denis. *Battle of Britain.* London, 1972.
Robertson, Terrence. *Dieppe: The Shame and the Glory.* Boston, Toronto, 1962.
Rigge, Simon. *War in the Outposts.* Alexandria, VA, 1980.
Russell, Francis. *The Secret War.* Alexandria, VA, 1981.
Shirer, William L. *The Rise and Fall of the Third Reich.* New York, 1960.
Sommerville, Donald. *World War II Day by Day.* Greenwich, 1989.
Willmott, H.P. *June 1944.* Poole, Dorset, 1984.
Young, Brigadier Peter. *Great Battles of the World.* New York, 1978.

ACKNOWLEDGMENTS

I wish to thank the following for contributions that have added immeasurably to the substance of this book:
Terry Berger, my partner, for much-needed editorial advice and general assistance
Marian Reid, my sister and a resident of Vancouver, who served overseas with the Red Cross in wartime London, for special assistance of all kinds
David Mayhew, my neighbour and Yale Professor of Political Science, for consultation on specific aspects of the book
John Soterakos, also my New Haven neighbour and war veteran, for allowing extensive use of his World War II Library
Finally, I wish to record my thanks to the late *Alexander Ross*—Sandy to his friends—for his keen interest in this project and for his generous assistance along the way until his untimely death in Toronto.

R.R.R.